First
Edition

THE STRATEGY OF MANAGING INNOVATION AND TECHNOLOGY

Murray R. Millson, Ph.D.

School of Business
California State University, Monterey Bay

David Wilemon, Ph.D.

Snyder Professor of Innovation Management
Whitman School of Management
Syracuse University

PEARSON
Prentice
Hall

PRENTICE HALL,
UPPER SADDLE RIVER, NJ 07458

Library of Congress Cataloging-in-Publication Data

Millson, Murray R.
  The strategy of managing innovation and technology / Murray R. Millson,
  David Wilemon.--1st ed.
      p. cm.
  Includes bibliographical references and index.
  ISBN-13: 978-0-13-230383-5
  ISBN-10: 0-13-230383-3
    1. Technological innovations--Management. 2. Industrial management.
  3. Technological innovations--Economic aspects. I. Wilemon, David L. II. Title.

  HD45.M52 2007
  658.5'14--dc22   2007002335

Editor in Chief: David Parker
Acquisitions Editor: Mike Ablassmeir
Product Development Manager: Ashley Santora
Project Manager: Keri Molinari
Editorial Assistant: Kristen Varina
Marketing Manager: Anne Howard
Marketing Assistant: Laura Cirigliano
Associate Director, Production Editorial: Judy Leale
Managing Editor: Renata Butera
Permissions Coordinator: Charles Morris
Associate Director, Manufacturing: Vinnie Scelta
Manufacturing Buyer: Michelle Klein
Creative Director: Maria Lange

Design/Composition Manager: Christy Mahon
Composition Liaison: Suzanne Duda
Cover Designer: Bruce Kenselaar
Cover Illustration: Getty Images. Inc.
Director, Image Resource Center: Melinda Patelli
Manager, Rights and Permissions: Zina Arabia
Manager, Visual Research: Beth Brenzel
Manager, Cover Visual Research & Permissions: Karen Sanatar
Composition: ICC Macmillan Inc.
Full-Service Project Management: Jill Traut
Printer/Binder: R.R. Donnelly Willard
Typeface: 10/12 TimesTen Roman

Credits and acknowledgments borrowed from other sources and reproduced, with permission, in this textbook appear on appropriate page within the text.

Pearson Education LTD.
Pearson Education Singapore, Pte. Ltd
Pearson Education, Canada, Ltd
Pearson Education–Japan

Pearson Education Australia PTY, Limited
Pearson Education North Asia Ltd
Pearson Educación de Mexico, S.A. de C.V.
Pearson Education Malaysia, Pte. Ltd.

10 9 8 7 6 5 4 3 2 1
ISBN 10-digit: 0-13-230383-3
ISBN 13-digit: 978-0-13-230383-5

Dedication

This book is dedicated with all my love to my parents,
Constance B. Millson and Edwin L. Millson, whose
unvarying encouragement and memory have
sustained all of my accomplishments; my son,
Murray E. Millson, who is a constant reminder
of the drive needed to excel; and Joan L. Sattler,
who has been an inspiration over the duration
of this book's development.

Murray R. Millson

I am pleased to dedicate this book to my loving
wife Jane, my daughter Elizabeth, and my son
Michael. I also thank all the thousands of
students who have taken innovation management
courses at Syracuse University's Whitman
School of Management. They've had a special
influence on my thinking about this great
field of scholarship and practice.

David Wilemon

Contents

Preface

THE STRATEGY OF MANAGING INNOVATION AND TECHNOLOGY

The innovation process and its management have been examined by scholars and practitioners for many years from the perspectives of a wide variety of disciplines. This edited work is intended to provide a compilation of research such that the reader can obtain an in-depth view of many areas that influence and are influenced by the innovation process. In addition, the concepts that are developed in the included works represent an important part of the progress in the study of innovation and the technological progress that has occurred over the past 100 years. This book brings together a vast array of concepts related to innovation. We believe that our selection of research provides the reader with an excellent appreciation of and a perspective for conceptualizing the innovation process. Two major purposes that drove the development of this book are: (1) it provides the reader, a student of innovation, with the concepts needed to construct a model of innovation that can be employed in many practical business and non-business settings, and (2) it provides a sense of how to implement such a model in the business world. This book also offers a section solely related to service businesses and innovations, which sets this compilation of research apart from others currently available.

This book has three primary audiences. First, it has a high degree of applicability to graduate students particularly in masters-level courses in schools of management and business as well as courses in engineering and technology management programs. For these courses, this book offers a special combination of the works of many of the recognized scholars of innovation and, therefore, represents a variety of articles that are both conceptually and methodologically rigorous. In this vein, this book is also beneficial to doctoral students studying in these areas. Second, this research collection can be used at the undergraduate level to introduce students to the field of innovation. At this level a judicious selection of articles and a brief introduction to many of the methodological procedures that have yet to be studied by such students is suggested.

Third, it has high applicability for practitioners who desire an understanding of innovation concepts and their relationships. The articles in each section vary in their content and approach to the advancement of innovation management. Therefore, this book has a tertiary target, represented by a variety of practitioners who are responsible for organizational change and technological innovation; are looking for ways to modernize their firms, departments, and product lines; and will find information in the following sections that is directly applicable to many of their concerns.

This edited work is applicable to many courses and programs of independent study as a text, a reader, or a reference. A few of the curriculum areas for which this book may be applicable have titles such as: Innovation Management, Entrepreneurship, Management of Technology, Engineering Management, New Product Development, Development of New Services, Product Marketing, Service Marketing, Social and Cultural Implications of Innovation and Technology, and Technology and Public Policy. In addition to this large selection of courses for which this work is applicable as a textbook, it also may be used in conjunction with a number of books that might be employed as textbooks, such as *Winning through Innovation* by Michael L. Tushman and Charles A. O'Reilly III; *Innovation Management* by Allan Afuah; *Innovation Explosion* by James

Brian Quinn, Jordan J. Baruch, and Karen Anne Zien; *Innovation and the General Manager* by Clayton M. Christensen; and *Strategic Management of Technology and Innovation* by Robert A. Burgelman, Clayton M. Christensen, and Steven C. Wheelwright.

This book is divided into 10 sections that include published articles, book chapters, and commentary in the following areas: reasons for innovation; the progression of innovation over time; a historical perspective of invention, innovation, and product technology; product innovation; process innovation; developing and managing service innovation; organizational innovation; managerial practices and innovation strategy; accelerating the innovation process; and the future of innovation and its management. Each section offers a combination of at least four articles or book chapters that relate to a particular thesis. All 10 sections may be used together as a depiction of the history and progress of innovation from most of the twentieth century and the first few years of the twenty-first century, or they may be used individually or in groups to focus on particular innovation topics. Although the chapters and articles that comprise these 10 sections are not sequenced in chronological order, this book does offer insight into the advancement of the body of knowledge concerning innovation over approximately the past 100 years.

Foreword

It is difficult to imagine a more exciting and promising period for innovation and technological advancement than the present. With the arrival of the new millennium, the world is poised on the brink of changes and breakthroughs in many arenas such as those influenced by industrial, political, social, and cultural forces. And, the innovations of the early twenty-first century, like those advancements of the past century, will certainly surprise us, as most of these innovative ideas were not thought possible a few short years prior to their commercialization.

We are part of an electronically interconnected global community. We now have immediate access to information about most anything that occurs anywhere in the world within a matter of seconds. Businesses and other types of organizations all operate in a world of hyper-competitiveness and speed. It is not only that change is occurring at a rapid rate, but also that many changes are occurring as this collection is being prepared, which will significantly alter the way many of us live in the future. Some of these changes will include major breakthroughs in the areas of health care, transportation, education, public policy, and social and cultural processes and structures.

Most important areas of life are affected by innovative processes. In the area of health care, there is an increasing focus on both the physical innovations that assist saving lives and the innovative processes by which these physical innovations can be socially, culturally, and economically integrated into life-giving and sustaining processes. In the area of social change, we speak of "locations" such as silicon alleys and digital districts, which refer to the amalgamation or confluence of work, leisure, and one's place of residence in a post-industrial setting. In the political domain, we discuss the furtherance of individualism and civil rights for all people regardless of what area of the globe they inhabit. Also, new thoughts and concepts are expressed, such as urban culturescapes, which can be represented by the visualization of approximately three billion people globally living in urban centers with well over half of them living in third world countries. Education forms one more area in which enormous innovative strides are taking place. These developments include projects such as the creation and implementation of innovative course materials, curricula, textbooks, software tools, computer-based courseware, and methods of delivering these new educational artifacts. Finally, there are the physical innovations that represent the technological domain of change. Some say that we are at the dawn of computer empowerment, an engine of change, that will power us well into the twenty-first century. Primary foci of these physical advancements come from fields including genetics, health care, telecommunications, computation, power generation and transmissions, and space investigation.

It is difficult to imagine a world different from that in which we live at the moment. But, our world has changed and will continue to do so at an accelerating pace. With this situation in mind, this book has evolved. It has been developed to portray a path from which we can understand the processes of innovation and change, the elements related to change, and the interrelationships among many of the factors associated with innovation, including those embedded in technological, social, cultural, and political environments. By viewing innovation with a very wide angle lens and from many different perspectives, it is hoped that the reader will come away from this work with a sense that the research brought together here has been instrumental in illuminating the concepts necessary to model the innovative process and to shed light on a path to understand how to use such a model to implement innovation in each reader's particular environment.

Introduction

This book has been produced to offer students and practitioners a comprehensive body of research that describes the trajectory and progress of innovation thought from early in the twentieth century to the present. This work provides both the stimulus and grounding for introductory forays into the realm of innovation, in-depth study into various specialized areas of innovation research, and a well-rounded portrayal of the current state of innovation theory and practice. Although the research we have selected is arranged by topic and not compiled relative to the chronological creation of the selected works, our intent is to point out both the progress in this discipline over time and the salient areas of historical and current research. In this introduction, first, we expound upon our historical perspective of the progress of the innovation discipline and, second, we provide a description of the structure of our material.

Historical Perspective

To accomplish our objectives, we assembled a variety of innovation works dating back to 1929, in which Abbott Payson Usher presents his thoughts in *A History of Mechanical Invention.* The salient portions of Usher's thesis lie in his description of technology's place in economic history and his reflections regarding the process of mechanical invention. By providing these early perspectives involving mechanical invention, we construct a foundation to build upon that is based on the development of tangible products that support the subsequent investigations included in this research compilation. Interestingly, many of Usher's early thoughts about the process of invention and innovation have not been altered by others' research since his writing.

We move from the early days of discourse relative to mechanical inventions to a greater elaboration of thought concerning the economic implications of such inventions espoused by Joseph A. Schumpeter in both 1949 and later in 1965. We offer these works not only to demonstrate the changes in thought regarding innovation over time, but also to portray the changing thought processes of individual researchers and practitioners as they come to discover the intricacies of the innovative process and its application. We also offer excerpts from other researchers of the time (mid-twentieth century) including John Jewkes, David Sawers, and Richard Stillerman, and Jacob Schmookler. These authors' works are presented to illuminate the sources of inventive thought and motivation, especially from Jewkes and associates' point of view. Additionally, these authors present the origins and descriptions of a vast number of inventions, such as xerography, the transistor, the helicopter, and insulin, that are most often taken for granted in today's society. Schmookler, on the other hand, offers a somewhat different perspective of the interface between invention and its economic potential in his work Invention and Economic Growth. We have selected Schmookler's chapter, "The Setting of the Problem," to highlight Schmookler's thoughts regarding the causes of invention and his pointed definitions of technology-related terms. We also selected his chapter entitled "Summary and Conclusions" which provides us with the process by which Schmookler gathered data, the stimuli that drives invention, and his explanation of the relationship between capital goods inventions and capital goods sales. His thoughts concerning the nexus of invention, innovation, business, and marketing differ markedly even from Schumpeter's later works. This divergence in thinking provides food for thought relative to where the genuine stimulus for economic growth emanates. Is it the market or is it R&D laboratories?

The research contained in our book relative to innovation thought proceeds from those early days of the twentieth century to the mid-point of the century, in which the rate of advance in the innovation discipline was significantly escalating. During this period of time, from the late 1960s to the late 1980s, many major research streams were being pursued. A few of the research questions being investigated during this time period might be summarized as follows:

- What is the relationship between marketing and R&D and what should it be?
- What are the contributing factors associated with new product success?
- What is the impact of product innovativeness on new product success?
- What are the relationships among concepts such as organizational innovation, product innovation, and process innovation?
- Are successful domestic and global innovation processes similar?

The condition of the innovation discipline during the mid-1980s prompted George W. Downs and Lawrence B. Mohr to ask if "we" have found anything in innovation that is generalizeable. In their article, they point out some conceptually problematic issues with innovation research and offer insights into what they see as the problems' solutions. These and many other questions forged the building blocks of the innovation discipline during this important time. We have compiled many of the major research studies regarding these problems.

We conclude our research anthology with some thoughts about the future of innovation and innovation research. David Wilemon and Murray R. Millson present a new paradigm of new product development in which many of the constructs developed during the past century are combined into a model that offers future developers and innovators potential paths to take for further research, product development, and innovation. Edward Roberts takes a look back at the past research and progress in the innovation discipline and asks, "What have we learned about managing both invention and innovation in an attempt to summarize our current state of beliefs, knowledge, and activity?" We wrap up our adventure in innovation with a peek at the frontier of the study of innovation through the eyes and thoughts of Henry Chesbrough, who provides us with a depiction of *open innovation* and the management of intellectual property.

Content Structure

In the next few paragraphs, we will briefly describe the structure and content of our book. Each of the ten paragraphs that follow represents one of the sections of our book and provides a glimpse of the works of innovation research that are contained in each particular section. We state our reasons for including each article in each section and what the major themes of each section are.

In Section I, which we entitle "Reasons for Innovation," we offer five articles and a book chapter that focus on why innovation is essential to all businesses and organizations. These works present perspectives of firms that range from entrepreneurial to transitional and from domestic to global, and provide a sense of the importance of innovation associated with factors both internal and external to organizations. We have included this section because we feel that it is important to recognize that, first and foremost, innovation has a primary influence on the world's economy, our society, and the lives of many, if not all, inhabitants of the world. David H. Holt (1992) offers insight into much of the language that is crucial for understanding how entrepreneurship and innovation are interrelated and their association with other important concepts such as creativity, the corridor principle, and windows of opportunity. Andrew H. Van de Ven (1986) appeals to researchers to perform longitudinal innovation studies such that a better understanding of the four questions that he poses can be obtained, which will eventually offer insight into why certain innovations obtain good currency and others do not. Arnold C. Cooper and Clayton G. Smith (1992) afford us an analysis of major pitfalls associated with strategic responses to new innovations that attack existing businesses. C. K. Prahalad (1993) provides the reader with a framework with which to understand the role of core corporate competencies and the concept of "a new competitive space." Kiyonori Sakakibara and D. Eleanor Westney (1992) help us understand the Japanese approach to developing new products and why Japanese researchers are under so much pressure to move more of their technological effort off-shore. In the final article of this first section, Christopher A. Bartlett and Sumantra Ghoshal (1990) help us understand the new product development processes employed by multinational firms.

In Section II, "Progression of Innovation over Time," we selected a few authors' perspectives that portray how the innovation process, and specific innovations and firms progress over time. In the first article, George W. Downs, Jr. and Lawrence B. Mohr (1976) take issue with the progress of innovation knowledge development and the methodological processes employed in the innovation discipline. They explain their position and offer suggestions for new research approaches. Thomas S. Robertson (1967) provides the reader with a connection between innovation and consumer behavior. Moreover, he attempts to illuminate the importance of communication in innovation processes. We offer three chapters from James M. Utterback's (1994) *Mastering the Dynamics of Innovation,* in which Utterback describes concepts such as dominant design and warns managers of existing businesses, who are often born and grow in nonthreatening industries, against attacking innovators from outside their industries. William L. Moore and Michael L. Tushman (1982) review the association between the product life cycle concept and technological processes that typically occur in innovating firms. The authors depict what often happens to such firms over time and strategies to employ to sustain an innovative perspective. To conclude this section, we borrow a chapter from Everett M. Rogers' (1995) *Diffusion of Innovations,* in which he details the processes of innovation adoption and diffusion. Rogers explains how the adoption process relates to the diffusion process and the impact that these processes have on the success of innovations.

The next section, "Historical Perspective of Invention, Innovation, and Product Technology," presents a number of the more historical, classical works in the innovation and invention literature. The first author presented in this section is Abbott Payson Usher (1929). Two chapters are included from Usher's *A History of Mechanical Inventions* that provide the reader with a historical perspective of innovative thought from the early twentieth century. In the next work in this section we offer one of the most recognized early innovation and entrepreneurial researchers, Joseph A. Schumpeter (1949). In this book chapter, Schumpeter describes his theory of "development" and its relationship to innovation and entrepreneurial effort. He also makes frequent comparisons between entrepreneurial effort and his concept of the "circular flow." John Jewkes, David Sawers, and Richard Stillerman (1958) provide insights into the sources of invention. They do this with specific reference to many major inventions of the twentieth century. We employ the work of Joseph A. Schumpeter (1965) again in this section. In this article, Schumpeter describes phenomena such as entrepreneurial profits, the concept of creative destruction, and an entrepreneur as a temporary title for an individual performing the entrepreneurial function, not a career path title. Jacob Schmookler (1966), in the final selections in this section, presents another perspective of innovation and economic growth. Schmookler offers interesting definitions of often taken-for-granted terms such as technology and technical progress in addition to his points of view concerning reasons for invention, the measurement of invention through patents, and some perceptions that differ rather markedly from those of Usher and Schumpeter.

We begin Section IV, "Product Innovation," with an article by Donald F. Heany (1983) that describes a typology of new product categories. He presents an assessment of the risks and developmental effort involved with each new product category. F. Axel Johne and Patricia A. Snelson (1988) investigate new products and the processes associated with their development from a program as opposed to a project perspective. They employ the McKinsey 7 Ss framework to execute their analyses. Billie Jo Zirger and Modesto A. Maidique (1990) develop a model for new product development and offer empirical findings and conclusions from their tests of that model. They pose and test eight hypotheses. Michael A. Cusumano, Yiorgos Mylonadis, and Richard S. Rosenbloom (1992) delve into data associated with the videocassette industry to understand the creation, development, and acceptance of a dominant product design. We conclude this section with an article by Robert G. Cooper and Elko J. Kleinschmidt (1993) in which they describe nine lessons derived from earlier research associated with the NewProd Studies involving 203 industrial product projects and over 20 years of research. Additionally, they demonstrate how the Stage Gate NPD system is related to the implementation of prior lessons learned which are associated with the NPD process and new product success.

Section V, "Process Innovation," encompasses five articles. The first article was written by Robert B. Dewar and Jane E. Dutton (1986) and describes their study of the shoe industry in an effort to better understand the adoption of both radical and incremental innovations. Next, Kornelius Kraft (1990) proposes a model and tests the relationship between product innovation and process innovation. He found that product innovation affects process innovation, but not the reverse. Wickham Skinner (1992) writes about process innovation in both process and non-process industries and provides an assessment of its implementation in both industry categories. E. Celse Etienne (1981) presents an article that investigates the area of process innovation and its association with the product life cycle. He proposes a three-stage approach that examines manufacturing processes associated with the development of new products. Nile W. Hatch and David C. Mowery (1998) provide an empirical study that investigates the relationship between process innovation and "learning by doing." Their data was gathered from a large dataset describing the performance of individual manufacturing plants managed by U.S. and foreign firms operating both in the United States as well as other countries. A major finding of this study is that organizational learning is now thought to be under the control of management as opposed to being an exogenous result of output expansion espoused by the learning curve philosophy.

"Developing and Managing Service Innovation" is the topic of Section VI. The first article in this section is by Christian Grönroos (1998). Grönroos offers solutions and implications for service marketing from the perspective of a service consumer. Richard Barras (1986) develops an encompassing theory of innovation in services. His thesis is founded in a reverse innovation cycle that progresses contrary to a capital goods innovation cycle. Christopher Lovelock (1984) investigates the new product development process as it relates to services. His discussion is based primarily on the influence of the "goods" development process with support from Donald Heany's new product typology. Michael R. Bowers (1987) also examines the steps associated with the new service development (NSD) process. His research points out that many new service developers do not perform certain new product development steps during their development of new services. G. Lynn Shostack and Jane Kingman-Brundage (1991) describe a procedure for developing a service. They focus on what is now known as a service "blueprint" to portray their new service development procedure. In the final article, Eric Stevens and Sergios Dimitriadis (2004) provide a depiction of two new service development processes from the retailing and banking industries.

Section VII is entitled "Organizational Innovation." The first article is by Thomas A. Stewart (1992). He develops a picture of what he calls the post-hierarchical organization: a flat, highly productive, networked organization. William Souder (1983) develops four models of organizations that can be implemented based on an organization's innovativeness and the stability of its external environment. He concludes that his Type IV organization is fit for dynamic environments and high levels of innovation that today's firms require. Richard L. Daft (1978) offers a model and insight into the sources of innovation adoption in organizations. He depicts two primary innovation sources and provides evidence for their existence. Danny Miller and Peter H. Friesen (1982) suggest the existence of both entrepreneurial and conservative firms and that each firm type can create momentum along its particular developmental trajectory. They demonstrate that these two types of firms are very different in the factors associated with their development and operation. From the findings of a longitudinal study of the microelectronics industry, Kim Clark and Steven Wheelwright (1992) provide a perspective of the "heavyweight" new product development team. They offer a detailed description of such a team, provide three other team design options that can be employed for developing new products, propose some advantages and disadvantages of each type of team, and indicate the behaviors that firms must exhibit to be effective in the implementation of the "heavyweight" team approach.

The title of Section VIII is "Accelerating Innovation." Its initial article, by Murray R. Millson, S. P. Raj, and David Wilemon (1992), describes five approaches that can be used alone or in concert to accelerate the development of new products. The authors suggest benefits as well as drawbacks associated with each approach, in addition to a prioritization of the NPD acceleration approaches. Christopher Meyer and Ronald E. Purser (1993) offer six steps to shorter new product development cycle times. They define fast cycle times and then describe how each of their six techniques can assist in cycle time reduction. In conclusion, they note that fast cycle times, like most other worthwhile objectives, do not come easily. They also point out that a firm that combines fast cycle times with world-class quality will have a significant competitive edge. Preston G. Smith and Donald G. Reinerstein (1992) present 10 techniques that R&D managers can use to accelerate their new product development processes. These authors encourage R&D managers to use as many of their suggestions as possible because these techniques tend to reinforce one another and provide synergistic effects on cycle time reduction. C. Merle Crawford (1992) warns readers of five important situations that can increase the cost of accelerating new product development processes. These five potential occurrences can be the direct result of well-intentioned and focused new product development strategies. Crawford encourages potential users of accelerated new product development techniques to consider "all" of the costs before proceeding.

Section IX encompasses a series of 12 articles that offer insight into the area of "Managerial Practices and Innovation Strategies." The inclusion of these articles is intended to bring many of the practical aspects of innovation into focus. In this section, the reader will find an integration of product, process, and organizational innovation in a way that provides the innovation practitioner tools to create innovation strategies in organizations as well as the means to scan environments to ascertain future organizational viability. The major focus of the articles found in this section includes the necessary assimilation within organizations of innovation knowledge to develop integrated organizational innovation strategies, the power and opportunities associated with disruptive technologies, the identification and nurturing of champions of innovation, and a process for forecasting innovation profitability. The first article in this series is presented by Lori A. Fidler and J. David Johnson (1984), who describe how issues such as power bases, communication channels, and innovation complexity relate to the successful adoption of innovations. A major point these authors make is that innovation adoption becomes easier when uncertainty is reduced. Richard Cawood (1984) employs a military model to illuminate important factors related to the management of innovation in business settings. He develops military scenarios that provide backdrops for the examination of major innovation-related concepts. In an effort to describe the difference between innovation in high and low innovation firms, Andre L. Delbecq and Peter K. Mills (1986) offer a four-step process of innovation and describe how each step is manifest in high and low innovation environments. Murray R. Millson, S. P. Raj, and David Wilemon (1996) employ a model of relationship creation to explain an alternative method for the development of new products. These authors describe the steps in their partnership maturation process in addition to offering insights into areas such as types of partner firms to consider and problem areas to avoid. In the fifth article in this section, David J. Teece (1987) presents a framework used to evaluate the profits derived from innovation. In the next article, Robert A. Burgelman and Yves Doz (2001) suggest the concept of strategic integration, which is supported by an organization's ability to define a maximum–strategic opportunity set. For business leaders to be able to create integrated strategies in multibusiness corporations, the authors present a two-dimensional framework and five strategically integrative paths for organizations to pursue. The authors warn against the implementation of four of them and suggest that complex strategic integration (CSI) can lead to a firm's discovery of its maximum strategic opportunities. The article by Joseph L. Bower and Clayton M. Christiansen (1995) provides us with a warning by reminding us that *all* industries and technologies have finite life spans. They also note that it is significantly important to distinguish between sustaining and disruptive technologies because these technologies need to be treated differently with regard to their management and commercialization. The eighth article investigates the identification and development of champions of innovation. Jane M. Howell (2005) offers case examples of effective as well as ineffective innovation champions. In doing so, she elaborates on several characteristics and personal actions that differentiate those innovation champions that are more successful than others. She concludes by noting that organizational innovativeness and the champions who move innovations to market are key to the survival of the organizations they serve. In article nine, Jan Inge Jenssen and Geir Jørgensen (2004) address a question that illuminates the human and social capital that innovation champions need as well as the resource acquisition strategies that such champions require to make their innovations successful. These authors pursue their investigation of innovation champions from a resource-based perspective because it is their belief that innovation champions do not initially own or directly control resources. It is the authors' observation that the innovation championing process is inherently a process of acquiring resources. Our next article, by Robert A. Burgelman and Liisa Välikangas (2005), focuses on internal corporate venturing (ICV) cycles during which innovations are developed in major corporations. They suggest four scenarios that often result from the interaction between an organization's mainstream business viability and the availability of uncommitted resources. They conclude with implications for strategic management or internal corporate venturing as well as the potential to build capabilities to manage internal corporate venturing cycles. In the eleventh article, Clayton M. Christensen, Matt Verlinden, and George Westerman (2002) propose a deductively constructed model that managers can use to make in-house versus outsource, or vertical integration versus disintegration, decisions relative to supply chain structure to attain the greatest competitive advantage in a firm's immediate market environment. They review a number of industries, including the computer, automobile, software, photonics, financial services, and microprocessor industries, to explore the implications of their model. Their review of these industries provides early evidence for their theory of the *disintegration* of organizations as technology and market conditions evolve. The final article by Linton (2003) investigates the demand, supply, and pricing in emerging markets associated with disruptive process technologies. In his study, Linton discusses several approaches to forecasting, including microeconomics, "S" curve methodologies, and Delphi and scenario approaches in addition to linear methods. The author constructed a forecasting model using bootstrapping or Monte Carlo simulation techniques and employed microelectromechanical systems (MEMS) to illustrate his procedure.

Our final section is "The Future of Innovation and Its Management." David Wilemon and Murray Millson (1994) present a book chapter in which the focus is a futuristic model of new product development. The authors suggest that this new model attempts to solve many of the problems associated with the traditional NPD model, such as its linearity and its lack of consideration of continuous innovation. The primary focus of the article by Michael A. Mische and Warren Bennis (1996) is to point out the importance of the process of reinventing firms through reengineering. These authors note that, although reengineering is typically difficult and occasionally risky, the results are often recognized as quantum improvements. It is important in such a process to question all managerial assumptions and paradigms to achieve the greatest degree of success. Shona L. Brown and Kathleen M. Eisenhardt (1995) develop an integrative model of new product development based on their review of three major streams of new product literature. Even though their model has not yet been tested, the authors believe that it can become a tool for the investigation of many new product development arenas. Cornelius Herstatt and Eric von Hippel (1992) present a case study based on the "lead user" method of industrial market research. They examine the four steps in this market research process and describe in their case study how each step is implemented. They conclude by noting that the firm that was the focus of their case study developed a product concept twice as quickly as in the past and at half the cost of previous market research processes. Edward Roberts (1988) in the fifth article of this section presents a summary of the knowledge the innovation field has gained during the years 1921 to 1988. He does this with the use of a model of technology management. In his summary, he offers a number of axioms related to the successful management of technology. In the sixth selection, Luke Pittaway and associates (2004) study the relationship between an organization's capacity to innovate and its networking behavior. Their work represents a review of the extant empirical research surrounding the factors and participants associated with innovation through organizational networking. They conclude their presentation with implications regarding the failure of networks and network limitations relative to organizational innovativeness. Next, we present an article by Rajesh Chandy and associates (2003) who take a multifaceted approach to investigating whether managers of dominant organizations are or desire to be radically innovative. Contrary to earlier research in this area, these authors view organizational dominance from a multidimensional perspective and suggest that the concept of *managerial expectations* plays a significant role in the relationship between organizational dominance and innovativeness. In this research, the association between organizational dominance and radical innovativeness is tested, as is the association between organizational dominance and radical innovativeness, moderated by both existing product obsolescence and product enhancement. In the final article in Section X, Henry Chesbrough (2003), provides a discussion of *open innovation* and the management of intellectual property. Chesbrough guides us through a discussion of topics that include the source, valuation, control, and marketing of this important organizational asset.

About the Authors

MURRAY R. MILLSON, Ph.D. Dr. Murray R. Millson is currently an associate professor of marketing at California State University, Monterey Bay. His most recent previous position was the program director (marketing) in the M.B.A. program and an associate professor in the Graduate School of Management and Technology at the University of Maryland University College (UMUC).

He earned a B.S. in electrical engineering and an M.S. in industrial management from Clarkson University (New York) and an M.B.A. and a Ph.D. from Syracuse University (New York). His research has been published in the *Journal of Product Innovation Management, Industrial Marketing Management, International Journal of Innovation Management, Research—Technology Management, Journal of Social Behavior and Personality, International Journal of Healthcare Technology and Management, Technovation,* and *IEEE Engineering Management Society International Engineering Management Conference Proceedings.* He also has co-authored a chapter in *Managing New Technology Development.*

He has taught marketing and management courses at Syracuse, Santa Clara, San Jose State, and Golden Gate Universities; the Helsinki School of Economics and Business Administration, Helsinki, Finland; Bond University (Gold Coast, Australia); and the University of Western Australia (Perth, Australia).

His business career includes 20 years with the General Electric Company in various engineering and management assignments. He is a registered professional engineer in quality engineering in the state of California, United States.

DAVID WILEMON, Ph.D. Dr. David Wilemon is Snyder Professor of Innovation Management in the Whitman School of Management at Syracuse University. At Syracuse University, he co-founded the Snyder Innovation Management Research Center and the Entrepreneurship and Emerging Enterprises Program. He also is a co-founder of the international organization, the Product Development and Management Association (PDMA). He is an active researcher in the areas of corporate ventures, product development, project management, and high-performing teamwork.

He was selected as the Syracuse University Scholar/Teacher of the Year award and also received the Outstanding Teacher/Researcher award within the Whitman School of Management. He was recently named as one of the most prolific researchers in the management of innovation and technology management field in a study published in the *R&D Management Journal.*

His research has appeared in the *Academy of Management Journal, Journal of Marketing, California Management Review, Sloan Management Review, Columbia Journal of World Business, Transactions on Engineering Management, Journal of Management Studies, Journal of Product Innovation Management, Technology & Engineering Management,* and *R&D Management.* He has consulted on innovation management, project management, and new product development with organizations such as AT&T, Lucent, Apple, Corning, Anaren, General Electric, IBM, 3M, the U.S. Air Force, the U.S. Navy, Bechtel, EG&G, the European Space Agency, Management Centre Europe, Bank of Brazil, and Upjohn.

SECTION

I | REASONS FOR INNOVATION

Introduction

This section presents compelling rationale for innovation in all sectors of business and industry. The perspectives offered here are inspired by the thought that change is omnipresent. To be able to "lead the pack," one must be a master of change and able to make change occur faster and convey higher quality than the remainder of the field. These works present perspectives of innovation that encompass changes ranging from the entrepreneurial to the transitional, from domestic to global. Each of these works provides a view of the importance of innovation as it is associated with factors both internal and external to organizations.

The first selection in this section is a chapter from a book entitled *Entrepreneurship* by David H. Holt. This chapter is included because it provides us with concise definitions that students of innovation should know. Most importantly, Holt suggests that an entrepreneur and an innovator are one and the same. This poignant portrayal of one who innovates provides us with our first definition of the concept of innovator. Additional terminology includes the success of entrepreneurs as innovators who take advantage of "windows of opportunity" that are defined by the market timing of new product offerings. Moreover, another concept to consider is the "corridor principle" which describes the association between an entrepreneur's background and progress in a particular area of entrepreneurial endeavor. Holt also provides an approach for obtaining a greater understanding of the steps in the creative process that is often associated with *the heart of innovation.*

Andrew H. Van de Ven, in the second selection of this section, defines the process of innovation as the development and implementation of new ideas. He notes that there is a compelling need to develop a perspective of innovation in a very broad sense from the point of view of a general business manager. He suggests that there are four basic factors that both facilitate as well as hinder the development of innovations. These four factors are associated with four central problems that confront general managers of innovation. Van de Ven's four factors include new ideas, people, transactions, and institutional concepts. The primary problems related to these factors comprise the problem of managing attention, a process problem in transforming new ideas into useable forms, a structural problem related to the management of part–whole associations, and a strategic problem associated with leadership in innovative institutions. The first problem arises from the basic motivation of organizations to protect existing products and processes. The second problem stems from the social and political issues that must be addressed to muster the energy and commitment necessary to become a successful innovator. Because the development of a sophisticated innovation typically necessitates the cooperation of many disparate organizational functions, a third problem arises, related to the leadership needed to coordinate these functions. Finally, successful innovations require accommodating infrastructures that embody the contexts in which innovations are brought to fruition. Van de Ven concludes his discussion of the central problems associated with innovation by noting that inventions and creative ideas do not become innovations until they are implemented or institutionalized. Therefore, he postulates that longitudinal studies of innovations, including their implementations, are needed in order for the basic question, "Why do some new ideas gain good currency while the majority do not?" to be addressed.

The next article, by Arnold C. Cooper and Clayton G. Smith, investigates the decisions that confront managers of firms and industries when new innovations and technologies threaten the status quo. Their primary focus is on problems and pitfalls related to strategic responses to threatening innovations and potential reasons for the occurrence of such problems. In addition, as a corollary to this approach, these authors probe the alternative of entering emerging, innovative industries. Major issues are the assessment of the technological threat, problems associated with the timing of industry entry, the magnitude of commitment required, the degree of separation necessary between the new and old technology within an organization, and what strategy should be created for competing in a new industry. Cooper and Smith conclude by noting that the competition should be watched carefully, as these competitors are typically not interested in attaining the status quo and are often competing with different resources and skill sets.

In the fourth article, C. K. Prahalad explores the role of core competencies. A conceptual framework is created to delve into the reasons for the loss of intellectual and market leadership by United States corporations during the period from 1950 to 1980. He also offers a perspective for what he describes as "a new competitive space." The major avenues for growth for both U.S. and foreign firms are investigated as a basis to rethink the path to competitive success. The framework developed encompasses three major factors: strategic intent, which is the fostering of an obsession for winning throughout corporate structures; a design for leveraging corporate resources that embodies the evolution of an industry and the development of core competencies; and, finally, creating new competitive spaces, which involves the creation of a mindset that embraces challenging price–performance assumptions, understanding how to "lead" customers, and escaping the "served market" orientation.

The fifth piece offered in this section was written by Kiyonori Sakakibara and D. Eleanor Westney. They researched the process by which Japanese firms developed new products over the past few years and pose the question, "Will this approach be successful in the future, especially when basic research is becoming more important?" They point out that the traditional Japanese approach for developing new products and commercializing them is focused on the laboratories that the Japanese have in their home country, and the rapid incremental innovation and commercialization of existing products. They note that, increasingly, Japanese research managers have been under extreme pressure to move more of their technological effort off-shore and increase their basic research activities. These pressures are being caused by the desire to become "true" international organizations and an increasing shortage of scientists and engineers. They conclude their description of these current strategic issues as they relate to innovation in Japan by noting that the challenge for research managers and firms in Japan is immense due to the conflict between the "locus of responsibility for the career paths of technical employees" and the Japanese firms' new international technological strategies. These authors point out that the major decisions to be made relative to this conflict will be played out over the next decade and have the potential to create extraordinary changes in the way Japanese firms approach innovation.

In the final article in this section, Christopher A. Bartlett and Sumantra Ghoshal investigate innovation in multinational firms. They point out that multinational firms have typically adopted one or both of two classic innovation processes: (1) sensing an opportunity by a multinational firm in a domestic market, fulfilling it there by applying centralized resources, and then exploiting the innovation worldwide, and (2) subsidiaries of multinational firms using their local resources to fulfill the needs in their immediate environments. The fact that these two processes are often conflicting in nature at least from a resource perspective has led to the development of two categories of innovation processes. The authors denote these two categories of innovation as "locally leveraged," in which a national subsidiary creates innovations for other markets in addition to its domestic one, and "globally linked," in which the resources of many different multinational organizational components are pooled to jointly develop an innovation for a global market. From their analysis of these innovation processes, the authors conclude that managers in most multinational firms and, perhaps, innovation managers in general, view innovating as a specialized function operating in isolation. This suggests that the primary function of top management is to allocate resources. The trend noted here describes emerging transnational firms that are not solely concentrating on increasing R&D budgets and developing more efficient allocations of innovation funds, but are enhancing and leveraging all of a firm's existing assets and competencies. These firms are not creating one specialized and isolated innovation process, but managing and integrating multiple innovation processes. It appears that such a trend can be synthesized well with the environmental issues and organizational conditions of many mature organizations.

References

Bartlett, Christopher A. and Sumantra Ghoshal. 1990. Managing innovation in the transnational corporation. In *Managing the Global Firm*. Ed. C. Bartlett, Y. Doz, and G. Hedlund. London: Routledge.

Cooper, Arnold C. and Clayton G. Smith. 1992. How established firms respond to threatening technologies. *The Academy of Management Executive* 6(2): 55–70.

Holt, David, H. 1992. *Entrepreneurship*. Englewood Cliffs, NJ: Prentice Hall, Inc.

Prahalad, C. K. 1993. The role of core competencies in the corporation. *Research–Technology Management* (November–December): 40–47.

Sakakibara, Kiyonori and D. Eleanor Westney. 1992. Japan's management of global innovation: Technology management crossing borders. In *Technology and the Wealth of Nations*. Ed. by N. Rosenberg, R. Landau, and D. Mowery. Stanford University Press.

Van de Ven, Andrew H. 1986. Central problems in the management of innovation. *Management Science* 32(5 May): 590–607.

1

ENTREPRENEURSHIP AND INNOVATION

David H. Holt

Objectives

1. Explain the process of creativity.

2. Describe how innovation is important as a dimension of entrepreneurship.

3. Identify major changes that create opportunities for entrepreneurs.

4. Explain the concepts of "windows" and "corridors" for new ventures.

5. Discuss popular myths of entrepreneurship and why they are more fantasy than fact.

6. Describe the main factors that lead to success for new ventures.

Chapter 1 provided a general overview of entrepreneurship and included examples of entrepreneurs who exemplify free enterprise. We also introduced a working definition of entrepreneurship in terms of contemporary high-growth new ventures. An essential part of that working definition is that entrepreneurs instigate change thereby shifting economic resources away from established endeavors into areas of greater yield and higher productivity. This is the process of *wealth creation* rather than *wealth accumulation*. A crucial dimension of wealth creation and every new venture is *innovation*.

In Chapter 2, we explore innovation and the creative endeavor that leads to entrepreneurship. We also discuss how entrepreneurs develop new ideas and, from their ideas, establish new enterprises that *add value* to society. Peter Drucker gives us the following framework for study:

> Admittedly, all new small businesses have many factors in common. But to be entrepreneurial, an enterprise has to have special characteristics over and above being new and small. Indeed, entrepreneurs are a minority among new businesses. They create something new, something different; they change or transmute values.[1]

Building on Drucker's viewpoint, we will explore how entrepreneurs create wealth by creating something new or different and how the opportunities arise. We begin with the topic of innovation. Then we shall see how opportunities arise as "source changes" to inspire new ventures. We will also examine characteristics of new ventures and

Holt, David H. 1992. Entrepreneurship. Englewood Cliffs, NJ: Prentice Hall, Inc., pp. 31–61.

FIGURE 1-1 The Creative Process

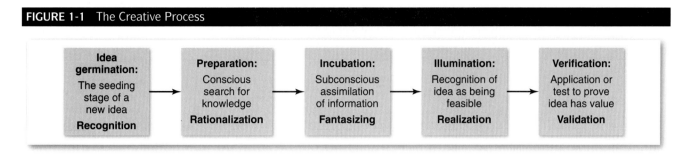

"myths" about entrepreneurship. We conclude the chapter by describing prerequisites for succeeding in new ventures.

CREATIVITY AS A PREREQUISITE TO INNOVATION

The terms *creativity* and *innovation* are often used to mean the same thing, but each has a unique connotation. **Creativity** is "the ability to bring something new into existence."[2] This definition emphasizes the "ability," not the "activity," of bringing something new into existence. A person may therefore conceive of something new and envision how it will be useful, but not necessarily take the necessary action to make it a reality. **Innovation** is the process of doing new things. This distinction is important. Ideas have little value until they are converted into new products, services, or processes. Innovation, therefore, is the transformation of creative ideas into useful applications, but creativity is a prerequisite to innovation.[3]

The Creative Process

Clearly, action by itself has no meaning; it is of little value to simply "do things" without having inspiration and direction. Entrepreneurs need ideas to pursue, and ideas seldom materialize accidentally. Isaac Newton may have been hit on the head by a falling apple, but he discovered gravity through a lifetime of scientific investigation. Ideas usually evolve through a *creative process* whereby imaginative people germinate ideas, nurture them, and develop them successfully. A model of the creative process is shown in Figure 1-1.

Various labels have been applied to stages in the creative process, but most social scientists agree on five stages that we label as *idea germination, preparation, incubation, illumination,* and *verification.* In each stage, a creative individual behaves differently to move an idea from the seed stage of germination to verification, and as we will discuss, behavior varies greatly among individuals and their ideas.[4]

Idea Germination

The germination stage is a *seeding process.* It is not like planting seed as a farmer does to grow corn, but more like the natural seeding that occurs when pollinated flower seeds, scattered by the wind, find fertile ground to take root. Exactly how an idea is germinated is a mystery; it is not something that can be examined under a microscope. However, most creative ideas can be traced to an individual's *interest in* or *curiosity about* a specific problem or area of study.

For example, Alexander Graham Bell had been fascinated with the physics of sound since childhood. He was influenced to study human hearing systems by his mother, who had a serious hearing problem. As a young adult, Bell taught at a school for the deaf and hearing-impaired, and he set up a laboratory for testing new hearing devices. Many of these devices were awkward mechanical "horns" that amplified sound waves. Bell realized the possibilities of altering sound waves in various types of materials such as steel wire during the 1870s, and he experimented for several years with magnetic devices in an effort to produce a hearing aid. In 1875, his lab assistant, Thomas A. Watson, accidentally clamped a magnetized steel reed too tightly to a magnet, and when he plucked at it, the reed came loose with a "twang" that echoed, sending a signal along a wire to Bell's magnet receiver. Bell heard the twang and recognized that an electrical signal had replicated the vibration caused by Watson's steel reed. At that instant, the harmonic hearing aid became a feasible idea, but exactly when Bell conceived of a harmonic telegraph (telephone) is unknown. It was several years before he turned his attention to commercial communications.[5]

Bell's "idea" for a hearing aid was evidently seeded years before he invented the telephone, and it evolved through his interest in helping others. He had already spent years studying the physics of sound and experimenting with sound-transmitting materials so that his mind was "fertile" and open to the opportunities for harmonic telegraphy. For most entrepreneurs, ideas begin with *interest* in a subject or *curiosity* about finding a solution to a particular problem. More recently, Nolan Bushnell founded Atari and the video game industry by trying to create a way to use micro-electronic circuitry to convert home television sets into interactive media.[6]

Preparation

Once a seed of curiosity has taken form as a focused idea, creative people embark on a conscious search for answers. If it is a problem they are trying to solve—such as Bell's determination to help those with impaired hearing—then they begin an intellectual journey, seeking information about the problem and how others have tried to resolve it. If it is an idea for a new product or service, the business equivalent is market research. Inventors will set up laboratory experiments, designers will begin engineering new product ideas, and marketers will study consumer buying habits. Any individual with an idea will consequently think about it, concentrating his or her energies on rational extensions of the idea and how it might become a reality. In rare instances, the preparation stage will produce results. More often, conscious deliberation will only overload the mind, but the effort is important in order to gather information and knowledge vital to an eventual solution.

Incubation

Individuals sometimes concentrate intensely on an idea, but, more often, they simply allow ideas time to grow without intentional effort. We all have heard about the brilliant, sudden "flashes" of genius—or more precisely, we have developed fables about them—but few great ideas come from thunderbolts of insight. Most evolve in the minds of creative people while they go about other activities. The idea, once seeded and given substance through preparation, is put on a back burner; the subconscious mind is allowed time to assimilate information.

In Alexander Graham Bell's example, research on harmonic sound transmission occupied a small percentage of his time during a two-decade period. Perhaps the incubation period for the telephone could be expressed as a three-decade, on-again-off-again fascination with human hearing problems. Art Fry, the 3M engineer who invented Post-it Notes, first thought of semi-sticky paper six years earlier when, as a church choir

---

PROFILE

Nolan Bushnell

In 1972, Nolan Bushnell, an electronics engineer with a passion for mind-teasing games, launched a $20 billion industry with Atari Corporation. His first video game was a version of Ping-Pong, but it was Pac Man that institutionalized video games and created a world market for new games, T-shirts, toys, pop songs, and, later, movies based on video war games. By 1982 more than 400,000 Pac Man machines on three continents had generated 7 billion coin-operated plays. The company

that Bushnell started using toy parts and scrapped electronics in his daughter's bedroom was sold to Warner Communications in 1976 for $28 million. Although Atari has had a roller-coaster history, Bushnell has gone on to found new enterprises, including Pizza Time Theater, a restaurant chain; Catalyst Technologies, a company designed to help other entrepreneurs start business ventures; and Axlon Corporation, a research company engaged in robotics.

Source: An unpublished profile of Nolan Bushnell at the founding meeting of the Hong Kong Venture Capitalist's Association, 1988.

director, he wanted to have page markers for hymn books that would neither damage the books nor slip out easily. He worked on the idea during his spare time at 3M without success, forgot about it for nearly a year, then tried making a new adhesive for the paper, once again forgot about the project for some time, and eventually envisioned a pad of small hymn notes with tear-off edges impregnated with a nonpermanent gum.[7]

Incubation is a stage of "mulling it over" while the subconscious intellect assumes control of the creative process. This is a crucial aspect of creativity because when we consciously focus on a problem, we behave rationally to attempt to find systematic resolutions. When we rely on subconscious processes, our minds are untrammeled by the limitations of human logic. The subconscious mind is allowed to wander and to pursue fantasies, and it is therefore open to unusual information and knowledge that we cannot assimilate in a conscious state. This subconscious process has been called the art of *synectics,* a word coined by W.J.J. Gordon in 1961.[8] **Synectics,** derived from Greek, means a joining together of different and often unrelated ideas. Therefore, when a person has consciously worked to resolve a problem without success, allowing it to incubate in the subconscious will often lead to a resolution.

Illumination

The fourth stage, illumination, occurs when the idea resurfaces as a realistic creation. There will be a moment in time when the individual can say, "Oh, I see!" Bell heard the twang of the steel reed, Fleming watched his penicillin attack infectious bacteria under a microscope, and Art Fry envisioned his gum-lined note pads in use. The fable of the thunderbolt is captured in this moment of illumination—even though the often long and frustrating years of preparation and incubation have been forgotten.

Illumination may be triggered by an opportune incident, as Bell discovered harmonic telegraphy in the accidental twang created by Watson. But there is little doubt that Bell would have had his moment of illumination, triggered perhaps by another incident or simply manifested through hard work. The point, of course, is that he was prepared and the idea was incubated. Bell was ready for an opportune incident and able to recognize its importance when it occurred.

The important point is that most creative people go through many cycles of preparation and incubation, searching for that incident as a catalyst to give their idea full meaning. When a cycle of creative behavior does not result in a catalytic event, the cycle is repeated until the idea blossoms or dies. This stage is critical for entrepreneurs because ideas, by themselves, have little meaning. Reaching the illumination stage separates daydreamers and tinkerers from creative people who find a way to transmute value.

Verification

An idea once illuminated in the mind of an individual still has little meaning until verified as realistic and useful. Bell understood what the twanging steel reed meant, yet he still had years of work ahead to translate this knowledge into a commercial telephone system.

Entrepreneurial effort is essential to translate an illuminated idea into a verified, realistic, and useful application. **Verification** is the development stage of refining knowledge into application. This is often tedious and requires perseverance by an individual committed to finding a way to "harvest" the practical results of his or her creation. During this stage, many ideas fall by the wayside as they prove to be impossible or to have little value. More often, a good idea has already been developed, or the aspiring entrepreneur finds that competitors already exist. Inventors quite often come to this harsh conclusion when they seek to patent their products only to discover similar inventions registered.

CHECKPOINT

Define creativity and distinguish it from innovation.

Identify the five stages of creativity and explain why each is important to the creativity process.

INNOVATION AND ENTREPRENEURSHIP

If creativity is the seed that inspires entrepreneurship, innovation is the process of entrepreneurship. This was Schumpeter's conclusion when he wrote about the economic foundations of free enterprise and entrepreneurship, points that we discussed in Chapter 1. Drucker agrees and elaborates: "Innovation . . . is the means by which the entrepreneur either creates new wealth-producing resources or endows existing resources with enhanced potential for creating wealth."[9]

Earlier, we defined innovation as the process of doing new things. It is important to recognize that innovation implies *action*, not just conceiving new ideas. When people have passed through the illumination and verification stages of creativity, they may have become inventors, but they are not yet innovators. The difference between invention and innovation is shown in Figure 1-2.

Inventors are not limited to those who create new products. They include those who identify new technological processes, new forms of plant life, and new designs. Each of these, incidentally, can lead to new patents, as we shall discuss in a later chapter. Inventors usually are stereotyped as people who deal with "things," such as new products, but most inventions have dealt with new processes or new technical knowledge. Our examples of Bell's harmonic sound transmission and Edison's electric power system illustrate the point, and many new products (and entire industries) were founded on their ideas.

Nevertheless, for an idea to have value, it must be proven useful or be marketable, and to achieve either status, the idea must be developed. Innovation is the development process, as shown in Figure 1-3. It is the translation of an idea into an application. It requires persistence in analytically working out the details of product design or service, to develop marketing, obtain finances, and plan operations. If the entrepreneur is going to manufacture a product, the process includes obtaining materials and technical manufacturing capabilities, staffing operations, and establishing an organization.

FIGURE 1-2 Invention versus Innovation

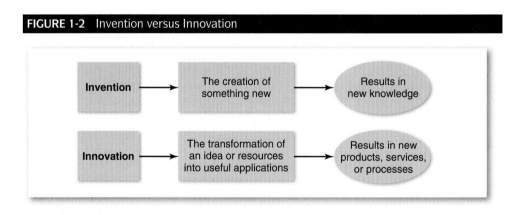

FIGURE 1-3 Elements in the Innovation Process

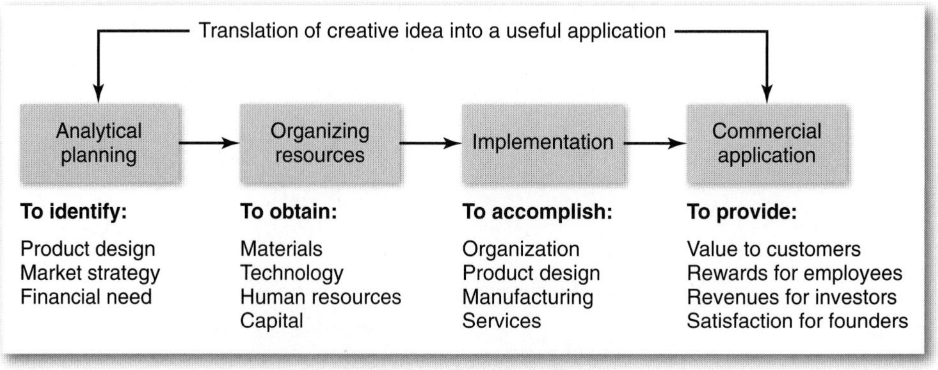

FIGURE 1-4 Left-Brain, Right-Brain Attributes

Left Hemisphere	*Right Hemisphere*
Conscious—Aware and focused on specific problem	Unconscious—Unaware and unfocused on specific issues
Rational—Conscious modeling of issues; linearity	Nonrational—Spacial imagining without direction
Analytical—Use of knowledge in descrete applications to evaluate issues	Intuitive—Total experiences and emotions allowed to influence one's ideas
Logical—Deductive reasoning to establish relationships	Synthesizing—Illogical reasoning and fantasizing to create analogies

Source: Left-Brain, Right Brain Attributes (pp. 60–61) from WHOLE BRAIN THINKING by Jacquelyn Wonder and Priscilla Donovan. Copyright © 1984 by Jacquelyn Wonder and Pricilla Donovan. Reprinted by permission of Harper Collins Publishers.

Using Left-Brain Skills to Harvest Right-Brain Ideas

Creativity was partially explained as a nonrational process of incubating ideas, allowing the subconscious mind to wander and to pursue fantasies. More precisely, half the subconscious mind is working to wander intuitively through nonrational territory. Substantial research has shown that the human brain has two distinct hemispheres. One, the *right hemisphere,* is the creative side where spatial relationships are developed, intuition prevails, and nonverbal imagining influences one's behavior. The other, the *left hemisphere,* is the analytical side where abstract thoughts and concepts may be formulated, but only through logical and rational processes.[10]

Figure 1-4 lists attributes of both hemispheres together with types of managerial activities often associated with skills in each area. Psychologists suggest that most people tend to have a dominant orientation, either to the left side (prone to rational, analytic behavior) or to the right side (prone to creative, intuitive behavior). Indeed, many cultures encourage skills and values that bias human development toward one of these hemispheres. Japan, for example, has been singled out as more left-brain orientated than the United States. The implication is that Japanese youngsters are taught to sharpen their analytical skills and subsequently are rewarded for their technical expertise, but they are not necessarily encouraged to become adept at creative, abstract thinking. In contrast, American youngsters are rewarded for independent thought and abstract, nonrational synthesizing of information. There is, however, no consensus that people can, or should, be taught left- or right-brain skills.[11]

From an entrepreneurial perspective, the right-brain skills are crucial for the vision necessary to be creative, but innovation does not occur until left-brain rationalization takes place. Integrating predispositions from both hemispheres is the critical behavior needed to be a successful innovator, to use left-brain rationality to "harvest" right-brain creativity. Unfortunately, many individuals are only gifted at one or the other. They may be logical and practical, and in the process, be efficient managers, but without some degree of inspired fantasizing, they may be paralyzed by their own analytical behavior. On the other hand, the "inspired tinkerer" may bask in the purity of artistic oblivion without the necessary ability to convert dreams into reality. This dichotomous behavior has been called Janusian thinking. (Janus was a mythological god with two faces looking simultaneously into the future and the past.) To be innovative, the entrepreneur must resolve this dilemma.[12]

Technological Innovation

The battle between rational, left-brain behavior, and creative, right-brain behavior, is a common problem for technological innovation. Because innovation is often explained in technical terms—tangible products or processes that result from technological development—there has been a preoccupation with rational, analytical innovation models. A general model of technological innovation is shown in Figure 1-3. However,

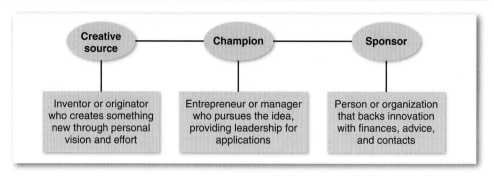

FIGURE 1-5 Key People in Technological Innovation

a number of industrial studies reveal that for a technological innovation to succeed, there are three important people involved and seven important conditions to satisfy. The combination of these people and conditions satisfies the need for creativity and implementation. The three key people are the creative source, the champion, and the sponsor. Their roles are identified in Figure 1-5 and explained as follows:[13]

> *Creative source:* The inventor or originator of the idea that led to the knowledge or vision of something new; the artist of creative endeavor.
>
> *Champion:* The entrepreneur or manager who pursues the idea, planning its application, acquiring resources, and establishing its markets through persistence, planning, organizing, and leadership.
>
> *Sponsor:* The person or organization that makes possible the champion's activities and the inventor's dreams through support, including finances, contacts, and advice.

The creative source is an individual; organizations do not create ideas or incubate fantasies. The champion is also an individual—perhaps the creative source, or an entrepreneur who joins with the inventor, or a corporate manager who has the insight to help pursue a creative idea. The sponsor may be an investor (such as a venture capitalist, described in Chapter 13), or an organization, such as 3M, where corporate resources are allocated to innovative projects and their champions.

The seven conditions required for success in technological innovation are related partially to the success of the three key people involved and partially to the environment in which innovation takes place. Although these conditions were derived from corporate studies in research and development, they apply equally to new entrepreneurial ventures, and they include the following: [14]

1. An outstanding person in an executive leadership position to support strategic decisions that encourage creativity and innovation development.
2. An operational leader to carry out the essential tasks of converting knowledge into a commercial application.
3. A clear need for the application by sufficient potential consumers to warrant the commitment of resources to the innovation.
4. The realization of the product, process, or service as a useful innovation providing value to society.
5. Good cooperation among the crucial players and among diversified functions in an organization, all of whom, together, must bring the idea to fruition.
6. Availability of resources and the supporting technology to succeed in the endeavor.
7. Cooperation and support from external sources who can influence the success of an innovation, including government agencies, investors, vendors, suppliers, and creditors.

These seven conditions and the three major players are illustrated in an extraordinary new development in quantum mechanics. Research is being conducted at Spectra

Diode Laboratories in California to develop the manufacturing process and applications for a semiconductor laser no larger than a child's thumb.[15] This tiny laser is a thousand times more powerful than anything commercially available in semiconductors. The "creative genius" of quantum physics (the science that made possible innovations in atomic energy and semiconductor electronics) was Albert Einstein.

A number of "champions" in several industries have taken Einstein's creative genius to practical applications, but at Spectra Diode Labs, it is CEO Donald Scifres, who is leading the way into semiconductor lasers. The "sponsor" is Xerox Corporation, a joint-venture underwriter of the laser project that provides financial resources and technological knowledge of semiconductor applications markets.

The seven conditions are partially accounted for by the leadership of Scifres, the sponsorship of Xerox, and the collective assimilation of knowledge during the past half century in quantum physics, semiconductor electronics, and computer applications. Still, the tiny laser is no more than a laboratory model because, to date, several conditions for successful innovation remain unsolved. First, the manufacturing technology (process methodology) to produce the lasers does not exist. The lasers require microscopic parts, called quantum wells, that are so small that a million of them would fit onto a pinhead. Second, the lasers must be proved in applications such as replacements for computer chips. In working models, this step has been accomplished—and one laser only $\frac{1}{100}$ the size of a conventional computer chip would quadruple chip performance at one-quarter the power required now. Unfortunately, without cost-effective mass-production technology, the laser is not yet applicable, and consequently, there is no immediate market for it.

Beyond the world of high-tech innovation, entrepreneurs take up the creative challenge of new ideas daily. Many of those innovations we take for granted as we enter the 1990s, but half of all our existing technological applications did not exist two decades ago. This applies equally to products, such as microcomputers; process technologies, such as synthetic fabrics; and services, such as bank credit cards.[16]

In each instance of innovation, there has been an entrepreneurial champion who persisted in developing a creative idea into a marketable application. In each instance, the entrepreneur has been able to recognize *change,* envision the *opportunities,* and harvest right-brain inspiration through left-brain hard work.

CHECKPOINT

Explain "innovation" and distinguish it from invention.
 Describe the concept of right- and left-brain processes.
 Identify and describe the three key roles and seven conditions important for technological innovation.

OPPORTUNITIES THROUGH CHANGE

Entrepreneurs tend to be "strategic thinkers" who recognize changes and see opportunities where others do not. By creating new ventures based on these strategic changes, entrepreneurs make a contribution and are rewarded in terms of wealth and personal satisfaction. Entrepreneurship is therefore the result of inspired strategy to exploit change, but first "change" has to be recognized. In the next few passages, major sources of change are examined together with examples of how entrepreneurs turned these changes into opportunities.

Scientific Knowledge

The history of the Nobel Prize is replete with examples of new scientific knowledge, and our concept of entrepreneurship is stereotyped as a process of commercializing new inventions. Without a doubt, "scientific knowledge" has been at the heart of many new enterprises, and we can see how important it is by tracing the development of computers.

Charles Babbage created a mechanical calculating machine more than a century ago; it was the forerunner of mechanized adding machines. Babbage is mentioned historically as contributing to the concept of a computer because he helped revolutionize numerical manipulation. Herman Hollerith used the binary system to create the first punch card in 1890, but this was to be significant only a half century later. Howard Aiken of Harvard University teamed up with IBM and the U.S. War Department in 1944 to create the first "automatic calculator," and although it was only an electromechanical switching system, his work led to an electronic computer developed at the University of Pennsylvania by J. Presper Eckert and John W. Mauchly. It was not until 1951, however, that a commercial electronic computer was sold to the U.S. Census Bureau by Eckert and Mauchly as the *UNIVAC I*.[17] This early progression of events is shown in Figure 1-6.

That brief history of computers is interesting because the only scientists to exploit their inventions were Eckert and Mauchly of Univac. Meanwhile, hundreds of companies evolved from these pioneer efforts. Burroughs, NCR, and IBM emerged through efforts by their founders, who recognized the commercial value of scientific changes and developed products around early technological advances. The contemporary history of computing includes literally thousands of scientific innovations, each one making computers better, faster, more accurate, easier to use, and less expensive.

William Shockley won his Nobel Prize while at Bell Labs for creating solid-state electronics and the transistor. Shockley left Bell Labs with a group of young engineers to form his own electronics company, but it was Robert N. Noyce, one of those young engineers, who set the pace as the archetypal modern entrepreneur. Noyce left Shockley,

FIGURE 1-6   Evolution of the Electronic Computer

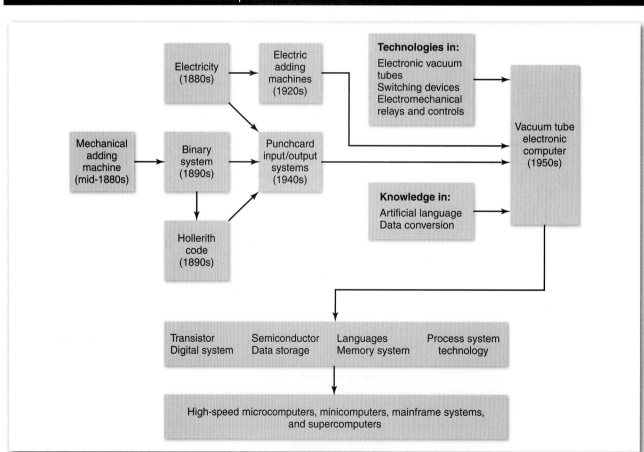

cofounded Fairchild Semiconductor, then moved on to found Intel Corporation. Noyce transformed scientific knowledge of the "silicon" technology into an industry and became known as the "Moses of Silicon Valley," where he established Fairchild and Intel, and he is credited with being the father of integrated circuitry. Noyce provided the inspiration to exploit knowledge. He was the change master who gave *strategic* direction to the microelectronics industry.[18]

Process Innovations

Closely associated with new scientific knowledge is the implementation processes, techniques, and methods essential to make knowledge useful. As noted in Chapter 1, Edison's light bulb was only a curiosity until he developed an electric system for supplying power to consumers. Early computers had little value until operating systems and data storage techniques were developed. In fact, computers had only limited value until symbolic languages were created to encode, manipulate, and store data. Because it developed and controlled the *processes* needed to make computers useful, IBM came to dominate a hardware computer industry. During the late 1950s, when virtually every major company making electrical apparatus and communication equipment was also making computer hardware, IBM was relatively unknown, but IBM technicians created symbolic languages in FORTRAN and COBOL, subsequently setting the industry standards.[19]

This pattern of entrepreneurial activity has been repeated often. Steven Jobs and Stephen Wozniak were largely successful establishing Apple Computer because of their proprietary *software processes*. William Gates III founded Microsoft Corporation and set industry standards in MS-DOS operating systems to coincide with the introduction of the IBM PC in 1981. Gates had been out of high school only five years when he and a companion launched their trend-setting venture.

There are literally thousands of examples of entrepreneurs who have recognized opportunities and transformed knowledge into commercial value. For example, typesetting had not changed since Gutenberg's time when, in 1885, Ottmar Mergenthaler developed the linotype machine. The linotype was an inspiration based on growth in publishing and a demand for timely news. The process of typesetting was archaic prior to the linotype, but with its development, there was the technical *method* needed to establish a nationwide industry of daily newspapers.[20] Today, word processors coupled with desk-top publishing systems enable even small businesses to create professional-quality documents. Each of these innovations has precipitated hundreds of new ventures that provide, for example, desk-top software, data storage systems, and publishing supplies.

Industrial Changes

There is little doubt that eventually power sources will be based on solar devices. Safe nuclear systems are also on the horizon. Meanwhile, energy is based on fossil fuels with some alternatives such as hydroelectric and geothermal power, but *someone, someday* will instigate the transition, and the switch will be turned off on fossil fuels. Petroleum replaced whale oil as an important fuel a century ago when Rockefeller built a refining and distribution system capable of making crude oil usable. An energy revolution happened again with Edison's electric generating system. It may happen again with solar power, and many entrepreneurs will be involved. Figure 1-7 illustrates this transition.

Industrial change can occur through natural events, such as the discovery of oil, or as a result of human events. For example, the recent deregulation of the airline industry forced dozens of major airlines to compete with regional "upstarts" and commuter airlines. Competitors introduced innovations in flights, new fares, travel plans, and new services. People Express, Presidential Airlines, New York Air, USAir, and many others jolted the industry during the 1980s with low-priced fares, no-frills service, and innovations in ticketing, baggage handling, and convenient routing. Some of these have not survived, but others such as Texas International have grown rapidly to be among industry leaders.[21]

A similar pattern of change occurred in postal services that provided unexpected opportunities for UPS, Federal Express, and dozens of regional courier services to establish growth ventures in parcel delivery systems. The breakup of AT&T is yet another incident that created opportunities for competition in long-distance telephone services exploited by MCI and US Sprint. New telephone systems have evolved in dozens of regions, and there have been hundreds of new businesses sprouting from the fringes of the AT&T change. New telephone repair services, PBX systems, telecommunications firms, phone leasing companies, and pay phone franchises are among the many examples.

These opportunities occur often because every industry is fragile and subject to sudden change. New laws, the dissolution of old laws, economic influences, social changes, and new technologies are all threats to industrial stability, providing in their wake ample opportunities for entrepreneurs.

Market Changes

Closely associated with industrial changes are those that take place in markets. Historically, we look at the success of Henry Ford when he developed an inexpensive automobile. Until his Model T, most automobiles were luxuries. He recognized the demand and decided that a car built on simple principles would revolutionize the automobile industry. Domino's Pizza was built on the single, important observation that a lot of people ordered pizza to take out. John H. Johnson, the founder of *Ebony* magazine,

FIGURE 1-7   Major Shifts in Industrial Energy

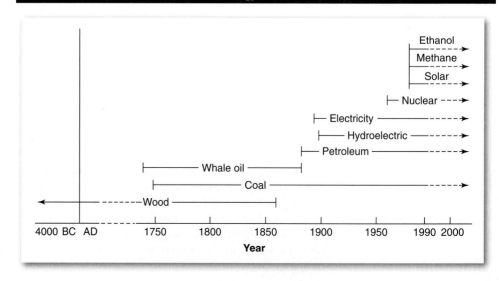

recognized a neglected segment of American readership, the black American. During World War II, Johnson launched *Negro Digest,* and today he heads a publishing empire with subsidiaries in cosmetics, fashions, perfumes, and entertainment that is the largest black-owned corporation in the United States.

An extraordinary change is taking place now as government services are being *privatized.*[22] The government has long been a major market, particularly for federal programs such as defense, and on state and local levels, government agencies dole out hundreds of millions of dollars to private contractors for everything from cleaning services to construction projects. An important trend emerged during the late 1980s as government agencies began to rapidly endorse privatization. This is the process of turning over to private contractors activities once controlled through government agencies. Government has become a more active consumer and a less active employer. Governmental agencies in Washington are contracting lawn services rather than employing maintenance personnel to do these jobs. Trash collection, rapid transit systems, government document printing, road repair services, security systems, training services, and public utilities are "going private" at an accelerated pace.

Market changes have also had a tremendous effect on education. For the 200-year period prior to World War II, the university system was a market reserved for the upper-class consumer. During a brief but active period just prior to World War II, the government sponsored a nationwide movement to expand land-grant colleges. These also served the upper class through a number of limited and specialized programs, but after World War II the American university system became a middle-class market with diversified programs. Metropolitan universities and private institutions grew at a tremendous rate, including such entrants as Pace University, the New York Institute of Technology, Northeastern, and Santa Clara. State systems modified their missions and actively sought the middle-class student. University systems in Wisconsin, New York, and California joined this trend, and with extensive tuition-aid programs, education is now attempting to reach everyone. Entrepreneurs have been an integral part of this change, creating new educational tools, textbook publishing empires, and innovative student services. They have cultivated sporting events and sports-related enterprises, and today entrepreneurs help students compete for limited university spots through programs such as SAT preparation courses, home study courses, and data base search systems that identify scholarship opportunities.

Demographic Changes

Demographic data are concerned with population trends, age, sex, and ethnic characteristics, educational status, and income of a nation's population. As a nation's demographics change, new opportunities to serve human needs arise. By tracking these changes, entrepreneurs can identify opportunities and react to them. Population statistics are well documented by the U.S. Census Bureau, by state and local authorities, and by an enormous number of sociological studies. The composition of human resources is closely tracked to document career behavior, family structures, emigration and immigration, life expectancies, birth rates, and on and on. The data are widely distributed through government publications at all levels, through Chambers of Commerce, and virtually every public library in the United States. An example is illustrated in Figure 1-8.

This information can be exceptionally useful. For example, assume a shrinking family size with, on average, about two children per household born to women with careers who wait several years to bear children. This pattern suggests a trend toward smaller housing units, better access to child care for dual-career families, and eating patterns that imply convenience-type foods. Much more can be read into that scenario.

At the other end of the life spectrum, more older people exist and are living longer. They are also retiring earlier, spending more of their improved retirement incomes, demanding more recreational opportunities, and traveling more. We tend to stereotype "the elderly" as retired persons who settle into retirement homes, but this view is fallacious. The retirement years span nearly two decades of life, from the early 60s to the late 70s; lumping the "elderly" together under one umbrella would be like

FIGURE 1-8   Projected Distribution of U.S. Population in 2000

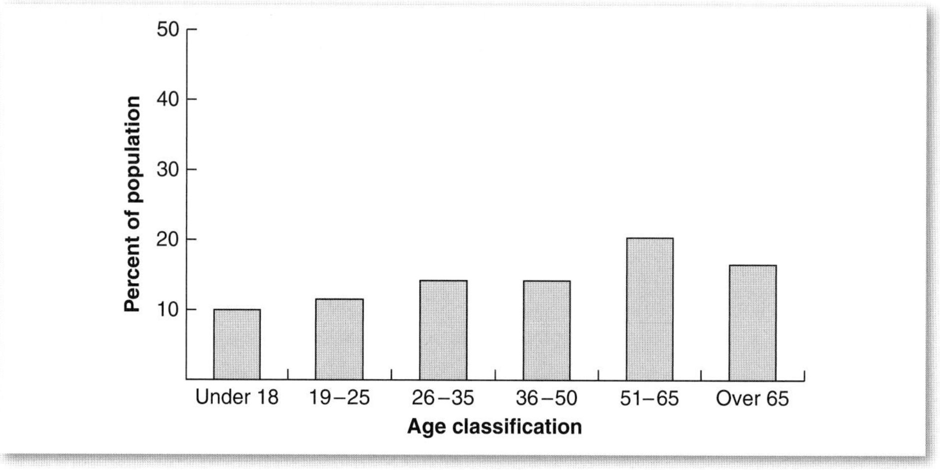

calling all individuals under the age of 21 "children." There are many subtle changes in demand for products and services among more refined stages of retirement. For example, as individuals near retirement, they are at the pinnacle of their careers, and planning for retirement opens opportunities for preretirement counseling, benefit planning, and estate management. Many retirees also seek alternative work, and a question comes to mind: Who provides employment search services for these persons?

Abrupt changes also take place in the composition of populations, such as the periodic thrusts of immigration that have brought significant numbers of Europeans and Asians to the United States. During the 1800s, potato famines brought waves of Irish, and the Chinese arrived in shiploads as the West Coast developed. During the early 1900s, large numbers of Russians and Germans arrived. After World War II, many European Jews came to America. Southeast Asians came in the wake of the Vietnam war. Today, more and more Mexican workers are finding their way into the Southwest. Latin American nations have experienced chronic poverty and periodic revolutions, landing Cubans in Florida, Haitians on the Gulf Coast, and Puerto Ricans in New York. In each instance, sudden bursts of new needs exist for language instruction, specialty foods, bilingual schools, entertainment, exchange banks, housing, and many other services.

The eminent financier J. P. Morgan had a gift of being able to recognize social and cultural shifts, and at the turn of the century he took advantage of these changes to build an extraordinary financial empire.[23] When Morgan was still in his 20s, the House of Rothschild was the dominant banking empire in Europe. The Rothschilds were financiers for the world powers, but it was J. P. Morgan who recognized the transatlantic migration and the tremendous need to provide financial services to these individuals and to underwrite industries that would employ them. Unlike the Rothschilds and most other financiers who served only the wealthy, Morgan served the blue-collar worker who transformed the United States into an industrial nation. He financed Alexander Graham Bell's telephone and helped create the first telephone company in the United States, underwrote Andrew Carnegie (and eventually bought Carnegie's steel mills, renaming the company U.S. Steel), conceived of, and pushed to implement, the Federal Reserve System, financed transcontinental railroads, and set up several immigrant banks.

Aside from these dazzling changes, shifts in population and the structure and composition of that population are continuous and easy to identify. For example, the demand for kindergarten facilities next year (or in four years) is established. The children who will be ready for kindergarten next year were born four years ago; they exist and can be counted accurately. Entering college freshmen candidates for next year are known; they are high school seniors with qualifying grades. We can forecast with accuracy the number of people who will become doctors in the next few years, attain law degrees, start families, retire, and die. We know a lot about a lot of people.

Entrepreneurial opportunities occur whenever a gap exists in services or products for groups of individuals moving into new stages of life cycles, for groups coming into American society, for changes in families, careers, and incomes, and for "systems of needs" that arise from demographic shifts such as those addressed by J. P. Morgan. These opportunities may be on a grand scale, such as new banking systems, or localized, such as new housing construction.

Social and Cultural Changes

Social changes occurred at a snail's pace until the late 18th century. The pace quickened a bit during the 19th century, but as we look back over the 20th century, social changes reached an unprecedented quick pace. There is no evidence of a slowdown as we ready ourselves for the 21st century.

Think of the great historic eras. The Egyptian social order changed little during the 2,000 years preceding the Roman Empire. Rome revolutionized the known world with written language, transportation systems, administration processes, and legal systems. It remained dominant as a military and ruling power for about 500 years. Then the western world entered a thousand-year lull, the medieval era, a time when hundreds of small principalities, city-states, and feudal kingdoms slowly evolved into nations. Very few societies advanced beyond the Roman foundations that preceded them; few innovations occurred in any fashion. The Renaissance was a blossoming of youth, the beginning of modern nations, architecture, mercantilism, education, arts, and the recognition of common "cultures" among peoples with similar ethnic, regional, or religious characteristics.

The industrial revolution stimulated changes in how people lived, worked, spent their money, recreated, and worshiped. Men began working for wages rather than as farmers or in government service. Sailors became merchantmen. Craftsmen moved out of their shops and into factories. Adventurers put aside swords for plows and settled new worlds. These social changes brought new demands that inspired a faster rate of change in innovation. For example, while roads had been made of sand and stone for several thousand years, "industrial city traffic" (although limited to carts, wagons, and buggies) required sturdier materials. Macadam (a material fashioned from coal slag and oil that we know as blacktop) was developed in Scotland. The bicycle, also Scottish in origin, became a useful mode of transportation rather than a curiosity. "Systems" that we take entirely for granted now were major changes made to accommodate growing cities and industrial towns. Sewers, water systems, waste collection, police services, fire brigades, and schools began to evolve during the 19th century. Nevertheless, these thousands of years of innovation are more than matched by innovations that have occurred during the past 20 years. Nearly 70 percent of all scientists and engineers who ever lived were alive in 1980, and about 92 percent of all known technology was discovered or invented during the 20th century; half of that figure and a majority of the living scientists emerged after World War II.[24]

This recent onslaught of innovation could not have happened without commensurate demand for products and services, and this demand has often resulted from social and cultural changes. The demand for timely and accurate information still outraces scientific efforts to provide telecommunications and computer applications. Mass transit systems are at best cumbersome alternatives to fender-bending traffic jams, and we have not yet devised a solution to crowded highways.

In practical terms, many entrepreneurs have found opportunities in such social changes as the increased numbers of dual-career families and working professional women. These changes opened doors for entrepreneurs to create new fashions, to develop educational seminars for career women, and to establish counseling centers for working wives, but entrepreneurs never seem to keep pace with change. Future problems yet unknown will certainly surface to propel the challenge.

CHECKPOINT

Describe technological changes that lead to new products and those that lead to new processes.

Explain how economic and legal changes can occur to create new opportunities for industry.

Describe opportunities that arise from social, cultural, and demographic changes.

WINDOWS AND CORRIDORS

A **window** is a time horizon during which opportunities exist before something else happens to eliminate them. A unique opportunity, once shown to produce wealth, will attract competitors, and if the business is easy to enter, the industry will become rapidly saturated. Bicycles did not become viable commercial products until people needed them as transportation. When that need occurred, hundreds of bicycle manufacturers rushed to take advantage of the "window of opportunity." Literally every successful product and service has had an optimal period of time for commercialization. Those introduced too early have usually failed, and those introduced too late suffered from crowded markets.

A brief period of opportunity opened for electronic spreadsheets when microcomputers hit the fast growth curve. Several entrepreneurs entered the market with good spreadsheet products. The first, VisiCalc, was designed for the Apple PC. VisiCalc was quite successful, and later versions for MS-DOS systems were even more successful. But Lotus 1-2-3 and Microsoft's Multiplan and Excel programs forged into industry markets. By 1986, Lotus had set the industry standard, and today a handful of firms offering spreadsheets virtually control the market. Entrepreneurs, therefore, must not only recognize opportunities, but also take advantage of them while windows exist to be successful.

Another aspect of many successful ventures is called the *corridor principle*.[25] The corridor principle suggests that opportunities evolve from entrepreneurs being positioned in similar work or having had experience with related ventures so that when a window opens it is easy for them to move quickly into a new venture. A corollary is that as a venture becomes expert in one activity, related opportunities evolve, and many of them are more rewarding than the initial activity.

William Gates of Microsoft, for example, was first approached by IBM in 1980 to program an operating system for the PC; Gates turned down the offer. He had a fledgling software company and was "hacking" with minor programs he hoped to sell; the idea of a major software effort was inconceivable. However, he and several friends realized the opportunity and began working independently to create the MS-DOS system. His early efforts probably would have kept Gates in an obscure part of the software industry, but the brief opportunity to create the new operating system led to enormous success. Howard Head, the founder of Head Ski, leveraged his "sports manufacturing" experience to create Prince Manufacturing and a revolutionary new line of tennis rackets.

The corridor principle is well known to scientists. For example, Wilson Greatbatch, the inventor of the Pacemaker for heart patients, was an electrical engineer and 41 years of age before the idea evolved from hundreds of other electrical ideas and gadgets concocted in his garage workshop. Probably a thorough résumé of most inventions and the entrepreneurs who commercialized them would reveal a series of closely related experiences that preceded success.

This does not mean that entrepreneurs must first work aimlessly and wait for a twist of fate to create opportunities. It means that entrepreneurs who are active and watching for changes are more likely to recognize opportunities when they occur. Few new ventures arise through "luck," which is one of the popular and inaccurate myths about entrepreneurial success we address next.

```
┌─────────────────────────────────────────────────────────┐
│                      CHECKPOINT                         │
│                      ══════════                         │
│   Discuss why a window of opportunity is critical for success. │
│   Explain how a corridor influences the evolution of an innovation. │
└─────────────────────────────────────────────────────────┘
```

MYTHS—FANTASIES NOT FACTS

Folk heroes like Steven Jobs and Mitchell Kapor are beset by myths that they "stumbled into success" and got their ideas by accident. Not so. Several references have been made earlier to each of these popular individuals, but what may not be clear is that they spent several years striving for a foothold in their particular fields. Both men *made* success by creating their own brand of luck. There are other myths to be explored, but let's begin by expanding the notion of "luck."

Luck Is for Gamblers

Clearly, there are individuals who seem to have an uncanny ability to be able to spot and to exploit opportunities, and luck (both good and bad) plays a role in the outcome of many ventures. More often, successful individuals have been nourishing a concept for some time or working on closely related projects when a breakthrough occurs.

As noted earlier, Art Fry of 3M created the Post-it note as a result of trying to make nonslip hymn book markers. He spent several years working on the idea, and he also had to fight an uphill battle convincing 3M executives to manufacture his product. Compressing the story of the Post-it pads into a paragraph makes it seem as if Fry stumbled onto the idea, but the product's development, manufacture, and marketing required extraordinary work and commitment.

For John H. Johnson, the founder of *Ebony* magazine, success was the result of four decades of systematic development from a neighborhood newsletter to the publishing empire that exists today. Along the way, Johnson ran into more bad luck than good as an entrepreneur with little money facing a society not yet ready to endorse black business interests. Persistence and determination played greater roles in Johnson's success than luck.

Make or Break on the First Venture

Another popular myth is that entrepreneurs strike it rich with the first great "flash of genius," or, conversely, they fail miserably with the first venture. Entrepreneurship is not a "boom or bust" process, even though many new firms succeed brilliantly and others do not survive for long. The point is that too much distortion exists on both issues. Bankruptcy statistics suggest that of those who have gone bankrupt, 80 percent were in business for less than five years. That figure sounds terrible, but the qualifying point is that statistics are compiled on those firms who *do* go bankrupt. How many continue in business? How many are sold profitably, merged, or incorporated into larger organizations? How many evolve into new businesses through a corridor of innovation? Bankruptcy represents about 1 percent of the total number of new ventures established, whereas most other outcomes, successes and failures, are only vaguely studied.[26] Statistics can be misleading, and many new ventures evolve and change, generally going unnoticed on the grand scale of economic development. Several of these possibilities are shown in Figure 1-9.

Entrepreneurs Are Mavericks and Misfits

Evidence suggests that many entrepreneurs march to the proverbial different drummer. They are not always among the best students, and they tend to be restless in structured jobs. Consequently, they are likely to be unsettled wanderers. It is true that entrepreneurs prefer independence and can be rather rebellious, and both conditions can affect

FIGURE 1-9 Possible Changes in New Venture Status

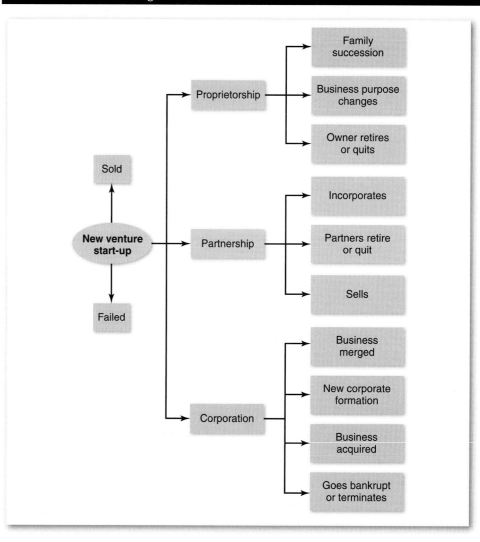

their performance in school and at work. Most successful entrepreneurs, however, are from the ranks of above average students, and they are relatively unlikely to have drug or alcohol problems or to run afoul of the law.[27] Entrepreneurs are *mavericks* in the sense that they instigate change and challenge the status quo, but they are not "misfits."

Are Entrepreneurs Born or Made?

A persistent notion is that most entrepreneurs are "born" with innate characteristics that prepare them for the often topsy-turvy life of new venture creation. Clearly, entrepreneurs have personal characteristics that lead to a more venturesome destiny. As noted in Chapter 1, successful entrepreneurs tend to be optimistic, have a keen sense of determination, are energetic, and often have an entrepreneurial parent. However, there is substantial evidence that entrepreneurial characteristics may be environmentally based. Firstborn children, for example, are often expected to take over parental businesses as heirs to established enterprises. One's childhood background often forges an entrepreneurial spirit as individuals from less-fortunate economic conditions have to find routes to success other than through traditional jobs.

Those who believe entrepreneurs are born conclude that entrepreneurship cannot be taught. This corollary myth would suggest that studying how new ventures are formed or how innovation takes place is of little value. If the environmental theme has credence, then learning as much as possible about the entrepreneurial process will better prepare students to succeed in business.

Other Myths and Misconceptions

Historic examples of inventors are used to illustrate success stories, and although these provide valuable insights, inventors are not necessarily entrepreneurs. Recall that we discussed earlier how entrepreneurs are less often inventors than astute businesspersons who can create an organization to bring new ideas to market.

A related misconception is that entrepreneurship must address whatever is called "high tech" at the time. Currently, information technology and biogenetic engineering are high-tech stereotypes. Twenty years ago it was communications, specifically color television and satellite transmission. Twenty years before that, just after World War II, it was the introduction of jet propulsion and new materials such as plastics. A hundred years earlier it was the telephone, petroleum fuel, and electricity. Entrepreneurship has always been associated with technological advances, but low- and no-tech enterprises remain very important.

For example, during the California Gold Rush period (1849 to 1860), everyone's attention was on gold mining; the "rush" to information technology and Silicon Valley has been compared to that era. However, lumber production in Minnesota produced nearly 40 times more revenue than gold did on the West Coast in the 1950s, and more money was made in lumber for homes, buildings, and ships than from the total gold-mining industry. The rush to information systems development today, although vitally important, is still eclipsed by basic food services and the housing industry.[28]

An unfortunate myth that often accompanies failure is "all you need is money" to be successful. Even those with sufficient money to launch an enterprise find that entrepreneurship requires skills in marketing, manufacturing, planning, and managing human resources, to name a few. Money does not assure success, and in some instances it may be a problem because with excess capital entrepreneurs may encumber themselves with unnecessary assets and inefficient organizations.[29] Too little capital is, of course, a more serious problem to overcome.

CHECKPOINT

Discuss the arguments for and against *luck, boom-or-bust,* and *all-you-need-is-money* perspectives of entrepreneurship.

Contrast the labels *maverick* and *misfit* often ascribed to entrepreneurs.

SUCCESS FACTORS FOR ENTREPRENEURS

Several success factors are apparent from research on innovation and entrepreneurship. We now have fairly solid evidence of what it takes to succeed in a new venture, and although there will always be exceptions, most new ventures succeed because their founders are capable individuals.

The Entrepreneurial Team

At the top of the success factor list is the "entrepreneurial team." The term *team* is used because, more often than not, entrepreneurs do not start businesses by themselves; they have teams, partners, close associates, or extensive networks of advisers. In major studies of entrepreneurs in the United States, Canada, and Europe, between 60 and 70 percent of all technology-based ventures were started by founders with at least one partner or cofounder.[30] Those in nontechnical enterprises (e.g., personal services or merchandising) were less likely to have partners or cofounders, yet they were well networked with associates or expert advisers.

An entrepreneurial team is usually headed by an individual who provides the critical profile of success. This focal entrepreneur typically has an above-average education, with about 35 percent of technical entrepreneurs holding graduate degrees. Most entrepreneurs started their businesses when they were in their 30s, and they had solid job experience. Also, nearly two-thirds of those studied in the United States had attempted a new venture before, and slightly fewer Canadians had made an earlier attempt. Of some interest, far less than half of those from Europe had previously tried to start a business.

Most technical entrepreneurs tend to start businesses closely related to what they did in previous career positions. Those in nontechnical areas often leverage their experience in marketing, merchandising, or a professional service area such as insurance or finance. We can infer that success is closely tied to a solid *knowledge base* and *substantial experience* in related fields of endeavor. They will also have well-developed social and business relationships, and therefore have a strong foundation for building a team or support network. This finding was reinforced in studies of Silicon Valley firms where researchers found entrepreneurs to have good relationships with vendors, potential customers, financiers, bankers, attorneys, and their competitors.[31]

Venture Products or Services

Nearly all successful ventures start small and grow incrementally; few "gear up" with substantial organizations for a big-bang start. Incremental expansion of products and services also tends to stay within the bounds of positive cash flow. Products tend to have strong profit potential with high initial margins rather than small margins that require a substantial volume of sales to meet profit objectives. Service businesses retain good margins by effective cost controls and well-monitored overheads.[32]

In each instance, products and services tend to display a *distinctive competency* in their industries. This is important because very few entrepreneurs start businesses in already competitive situations. This observation relates to an earlier point that we emphasized: Entrepreneurs must assure themselves of a *niche for their services.* A corollary to this rule is that successful entrepreneurs should "stick to their knitting" by concentrating initially on one distinct product or service, making it successful before diversifying.

From an investor's viewpoint, the product or service idea is secondary to the entrepreneur. A popular expression among investors is that they would rather "back a first-rate entrepreneur with a second-rate product than the other way around." This guideline does not mean the business concept can be weak, but it does suggest that investors must have considerable confidence in the entrepreneurial team before buying into the venture.

Markets and Timing

Successful entrepreneurs tend to have a clear vision of both existing and potential customers. A crucial aspect of planning is to have a well-documented forecast of sales based on sensible projections at each stage of incremental growth. A charismatic entrepreneur loaded with talent and a great idea will not convince investors that a venture is viable without valid market research. There are no shortcuts; innovation requires market demand, not simply a good idea.

Markets evolve, and as noted earlier, there are windows of opportunity that can lead to exceptional success. Misjudging those windows can result in dismal failure. Market potential is critically influenced by *timing* of new products or services. Timing pertains to when products or services are introduced, how they are priced, how they are distributed, and how they are promoted. We will pursue these points carefully in Chapters 8 and 9.

Business Ideology

From an entrepreneur's perspective, every venture has an *ideology,* a philosophy or rationale for existing. Although the ideology may be extremely difficult to quantify, it is nevertheless important. A business ideology is defined as a *system of beliefs* about how one conducts an enterprise. These beliefs include a commitment to providing customers with value, the ability to take calculated risks, the determination to grow and to control the fate of the business, the propensity to elicit cooperation among team members, and the perspective of creating wealth realistically. A business ideology may not be entirely defined by these notions, but failure is often blamed on one of them. For example, rarely do we hear that a business failed because the product was flawed, but more often because the firm lost track of its commitment to customers.

CHECKPOINT

Describe the four primary factors associated with new venture success, and relate each to an example from the chapter.

AN ERA OF TRANSFORMATION

Given the perspective of how opportunities emerge, it is important to recognize that we are now in an era of transformation. Only a few years ago, *entrepreneurship* was a vague term occasionally used to explain bursts of economic activity. Today, the popular term *entrepreneur* occurs in television commercials, corporate annual reports, and political speeches. This transformation has had serious implications for business education and the way in which success is defined in the minds of young adults.

Before World War II, young people defined success in terms of a decent job with reasonable wages. After the war, they defined success as having corporate careers. During the past few years, more youthful graduates have been intrigued with independent business ventures. The average age of entrepreneurs who start new ventures is dropping, with more people in their 20s taking the entrepreneurial plunge. This trend is strongly evidenced by the extraordinary growth of the Association of Collegiate Entrepreneurs (ACE), founded in 1984 by a group of university students in a Boston pizza parlor. By 1991, ACE had attracted nearly 4,000 college students and more than 600 successful entrepreneurs still in their early 20s. The association has also established an honor roll called the ACE 100, representing millionaire members who, in order to qualify, must have at least $2 million in annual sales and still be under 30 years of age; those at the top, however, have extraordinary sales.[33]

As we move toward the 21st century, it will be younger people who provide inspiration and innovative leadership. They are the entrepreneurs who will transform society. Just as in centuries past, in the 21st century it will be young entrepreneurs who determine the cadence for change.

CHECKPOINT

Reflecting on information earlier in the chapter, discuss why this is an era of transformation. Are changes taking place today more than 20 years ago? If so, why? Why are younger entrepreneurs starting new ventures? What opportunities do you see for the future?

SYNOPSIS FOR LEARNING

1. *Explain the process of creativity.* Creativity is defined as conceiving of something new. The process of creativity has five stages: idea germination, preparation, incubation, illumination, and verification. Germination is when the seed of an idea is implanted, arising from one's curiosity or interest in a problem or area of study. During preparation, a person embarks on research and a conscious search

for bringing the idea to life. Although this search seldom produces results, a creative person becomes "prepared" by gathering information and knowledge related to the problem. During the incubation stage, a person "sleeps on the problem," often for years of periodic subconscious reflection on the idea or the problem to be solved. Illumination occurs when the idea surfaces through incubation, often seeming to have been a sudden flash of genius when, in fact, it was the culmination of conscious preparation and subconscious incubation. Once the idea becomes clear, a person will seek to verify it. Verification is the process of determining whether the idea has merit—whether it is useful and realistic.

2. *Describe how innovation is important as a dimension of entrepreneurship.* Innovation is defined as the process of doing new things. Therefore, it is often the active translation of a creative idea into a new product, service, or technology. *Innovation* is different from *invention.* Invention is the verified result of a creative idea; innovation is the conversion of something new into useful goods or services. With that distinction in mind, innovation is perhaps the heart of entrepreneurship. Entrepreneurs may also be inventors, but they take the action necessary to redirect resources and convert creations into reality. They build organizations and systems needed to champion ideas and to exploit opportunities.

3. *Identify major changes that create opportunities for entrepreneurs.* Entrepreneurs are often thought to be "inspired" people, and perhaps they are, but more important, they often recognize changes and opportunities that can result from a dynamic world. Scientific knowledge, one source of change, has been rapidly advancing, and the combination of new knowledge often leads to exciting new innovations. This was the case for computers as a century of periodic changes led to artificial languages, mechanics, electronics, and combinations of technology to fashion new industries in semiconductors, computers, and software. Also important are rapid changes taking place in process innovations. "Processes" are the ways we accomplish tasks, and of course, computers have revolutionized office, manufacturing, and organizational systems, but processes such as the assembly line and petroleum refining resulted in far more pervasive changes in industrialized nations. Industrial changes occur for many reasons, including new knowledge and new processes, but also when there is new legislation or changes in society—for example, when airlines were deregulated or when AT&T was broken up. It occurs daily as new laws are passed to encourage trade, provide loans to businesses, and improve minority hiring. Market changes occur as new competitors enter industries, as social and economic shifts occur, and as cultural norms evolve. Markets also change as the demographic structure of a community or nation changes.

4. *Explain the concepts of "windows" and "corridors" for new ventures.* A window is a time horizon during which opportunities exist. This can occur, for example, when a new change in technology takes place so that intrepid innovators rush to become early industry leaders. As opportunities for success become known, however, more competitors enter the industry, and the window rapidly closes with market saturation. A corridor is a route or an aisle down which a person travels, often beginning with one idea that leads to revisions and further innovations. It is not uncommon for a person to pursue a weak idea but, in the process, discover some new opportunity or new product that may not have come to light except through fruitless work on the original idea. Corridors also arise from the proximity of a person who is conducting similar work and is therefore positioned to recognize change more rapidly than others.

5. *Discuss popular myths of entrepreneurship and why they are more fantasy than fact.* Perhaps the most prominent myth is that entrepreneurs are "lucky"; they were just in the right place at the right time. Perhaps in a few cases that assumption is true, but most entrepreneurs make their luck by working hard. They rarely stumble into new million-dollar enterprises but develop the

marketing, manufacturing, and organizing skills needed to bring innovations to fruition. A similar myth is that entrepreneurs are "make or break" people; on the contrary, most ventures start slow and make incremental changes. Entrepreneurs are not misfits, as myth suggests, but they do "disrupt" the status quo. They alter the fundamental course of commerce, and in so doing, are clearly out of step with the rest of the parade. More accurately, they are leading the parade in a new direction. Whether entrepreneurs are "born" or "made" is an unresolved issue, but on balance, evidence suggests that most entrepreneurs are influenced to start new ventures through environmental factors and events encompassing their background, education, family, and careers. Finally, the myth that "all you need is money" to succeed has no credibility because few wealthy people have pursued (or have needed to pursue) new ventures, whereas most successful companies have been founded by people with little money and few resources.

6. *Describe the main factors that lead to success for new ventures.* Perhaps the most important factor is having a good entrepreneurial team. People transform ideas into useful innovations, and few new ventures grow beyond a preliminary start-up stage without a solid team of committed people. Financial backers rarely underwrite an individual but look for a strong team with the diversity of skills and the persistence to succeed. A second success factor is to have a well-planned enterprise that pursues incremental change and growth. It is essential to start with one distinct competency, one product or service, and firmly establish it. To succeed, therefore, a firm must maintain positive cash flow through controlled growth. A third factor is good timing. The most successful firms have timed the introduction of products or services to coincide with windows of opportunity. They did not take shortcuts or enter markets that were already highly competitive. Fourth, successful entrepreneurs have instilled in their companies a sense of purpose. They have created a business ideology to serve their customers, not to exploit them.

Endnotes

1. Peter F. Drucker, *Innovation and Entrepreneurship* (New York: Harper & Row, 1985), p. 22.
2. *Webster's Third New International Dictionary* (Springfield, MA: G&C Merriam, 1976).
3. Thomas J. Peters and Robert H. Waterman, Jr., *In Search of Excellence: Lessons from America's Best-Run Companies* (New York: Harper & Row, 1982), p. 206.
4. Frank Baron. "The Psychology of Imagination," *Scientific American,* Vol. 199 (1958), pp. 151–166. Also see John J. Kao, *Entrepreneurship, Creativity, and Organization* (Englewood Cliffs, NJ: Prentice-Hall, 1989), pp. 15–19.
5. "The Mad Idea," in *Communicating and the Telephone,* a biographical monograph by American Telephone and Telegraph Company, July 1979, pp. 4–5.
6. Kao, *Entrepreneurship, Creativity, and Organization,* pp. 55–56.
7. Hollister B. Sykes, "Lessons from a New Venture Program," *Harvard Business Review,* Vol. 86, No. 3 (May–June 1986), pp. 69–74.
8. W.J.J. Gordon, *Synectics* (New York: Harper & Row, 1961), pp. 3–4, 47–48.
9. Drucker, *Innovation and Entrepreneurship,* p. 20.
10. Henry Mintzberg, "Planning on the Left Side and Managing on the Right," *Harvard Business Review,* July–August 1976. Also Jacquelyn Wonder and Priscilla Donovan, *Whole-Brain Thinking* (New York: Morrow, 1984), pp. 4–6, 24.
11. Wonder and Donovan, *Whole-Brain Thinking,* pp. 60–61. Also see Terence Hines, "Left Brain/Right Brain Mythology and Implications for Management and Training," *Academy of Management Review,* Vol. 12, No. 4 (1987), pp. 600–606.
12. Kao, *Entrepreneurship, Creativity, and Organization,* p. 16.
13. Modesto A. Maidique, "Entrepreneurs, Champions, and Technological Innovation," *Sloan Management Review,* Winter 1980, pp. 59–61.
14. Brian Twiss, *Managing Technological Innovation,* 3rd ed. (New York: Longman, 1986), pp. 15–17.
15. Gene Bylinsky, "A Quantum Leap in Electronics," *Fortune,* January 30, 1989, pp. 113–118.
16. D. Bruce Merrifield, "The Measurement of Productivity and the Use of R&D Limited Partnerships," *U.S. Department of Commerce Papers,* Office of Productivity, Technology, and Innovation, April 1984, pp. 1–2.
17. Steven L. Mandell, *Computers and Data Processing: Concepts and Applications in BASIC,* 2nd ed. (New York: West, 1982), pp. 26–29.
18. John W. Wilson, "Noyce: Silicon Valley's Roving Ambassador," *Business Week,* January 21, 1985, pp. 64–65.
19. "Akers Looks Ahead to IBM's Future Strategies, Principles," *Computer Reseller News,* April 3, 1989, pp. 44–46.
20. Drucker, *Innovation and Entrepreneurship,* p. 70.

21. "Tailspin," *Enterprise II. A Series,* (Boston: WGBH-TV, 1983). Also see Alfie Kohn, *No Contest: The Case against Competition* (Boston: Houghton Mifflin, 1986), pp. 75–78.

22. Jay Finegan, "Star Wars, Inc.," *Inc.,* August 1987, pp. 68–76. Also see John Case, "The Invisible Powerhouse," *Inc.,* September 1989, pp. 25–26.

23. Drucker, *Entrepreneurship and Innovation,* p. 90.

24. D. Bruce Merrifield, "Industrial Survival via Management Technology," *Journal of Business Venturing,* Vol. 3, No. 3 (1988), pp. 171–185.

25. David Kopcso, Robert Ronstadt, and William Rybolt, "The Corridor Principle: Independent Entrepreneurs versus Corporate Entrepreneurs," *Frontiers of Entrepreneurship Research, 1987,* pp. 259–271.

26. Robert C. Ronstadt, *Entrepreneurship: Text, Cases, and Notes* (Dover, MA: Lord, 1984), pp. 36–37. Also see David L. Birch, "Live Fast, Die Young," *Inc.,* August 1988, pp. 23–24.

27. Ronstadt, *Entrepreneurship: Text, Case, and Notes,* p. 33.

28. *The Entrepreneurship: An American Adventure.* Film Series, Vol. 2 and Academic Supplement (Boston: Enterprise Media, 1987), pp. 4–6.

29. Albert V. Bruno and Joel K. Leidecker, "Causes of New Venture Failure: 1960s vs. 1980s," *Business Horizons,* Vol. 31, No. 6 (1988), pp. 51–56. Also see Dawit Kibre, "Myths of Small Business Failure," *The CPA Journal,* September 1983, pp. 73–74.

30. A. B. Ibrahim and J. R. Goodwin, "Perceived Causes of Success in Small Business," *American Journal of Small Business,* Vol. 11, No. 3 (1986), pp. 41–50. Also see Karl A. Egge, "Expectations vs. Reality Among Founders of Recent Start-ups," *Frontiers of Entrepreneurship Research,* 1987, pp. 322–336.

31. Howard Aldrich and Catherine Zimmer, "Entrepreneurship through Social Networks," in Donald L. Sexton and Raymond W. Smilor, eds., *The Art and Science of Entrepreneurship* (Cambridge, MA: Ballinger, 1986), pp. 3–23.

32. Richard B. Robinson, Jr., Moragla Y. Salem, John E. Logan, and John A. Pearce II, "Planning Activities Related to Independent Retail Firms' Performance," *American Journal of Small Business,* Vol. 11, No. 1 (1986), pp. 19–26.

33. "The ACE 100." *ACE Conference News,* February 1991, p. 1.

2 | CENTRAL PROBLEMS IN THE MANAGEMENT OF INNOVATION

Andrew H. Van de Ven

School of Management, The University of Minnesota, Minneapolis, Minnesota 55455

Innovation is defined as the development and implementation of new ideas by people who over time engage in transactions with others within an institutional order. This definition focuses on four basic factors (new ideas, people, transactions, and institutional context). An understanding of how these factors are related leads to four basic problems confronting most general managers: (1) a human problem of managing attention, (2) a process problem in managing new ideas into good currency, (3) a structural problem of managing part-whole relationships, and (4) a strategic problem of institutional leadership. This paper discusses these four basic problems and concludes by suggesting how they fit together into an overall framework to guide longitudinal study of the management of innovation.
(ORGANIZATIONAL EFFECTIVENESS; INNOVATION)

INTRODUCTION

Few issues are characterized by as much agreement as the role of innovation and entrepreneurship for social and economic development. Schumpeter's (1942) emphasis on the importance of innovation for the business firm and society as a whole is seldom disputed. In the wake of a decline in American productivity and obsolescence of its infrastructure has come the fundamental claim that America is losing its innovativeness. The need for understanding and managing innovation appears to be widespread. Witness, for example, the common call for stimulating innovation in popular books by Ouchi (1981), Pascale and Athos (1981), Peters and Waterman (1982), Kanter (1983), and Lawrence and Dyer (1983).

Of all the issues surfacing in meetings with over 30 chief executive officers of public and private firms during the past few years, the management of innovation was reported as their most central concern in managing their enterprises in the 1980's (Van de Ven 1982). This concern is reflected in a variety of questions the CEOs often raised.

1. How can a large organization develop and maintain a culture of innovation and entrepreneurship?
2. What are the critical factors in successfully launching new organizations, joint ventures with other firms, or innovative projects within large organizations over time?

Van de Ven, Andrew H. 1986. Central problems in the management of innovation. Management Science 32(5 May): 590–607. Courtesy of The Institute of Operations Research and the Management Sciences (INFORMS), 7240 Parkway Drive, Suite 310, Hanover, MD 21076 USA.

3. How can a manager achieve balance between inexorable pressures for specialization and proliferation of tasks, and escalating costs of achieving coordination, cooperation, and resolving conflicts?

Given the scope of these questions raised by CEOs, it is surprising to find that research and scholarship on organizational innovation has been narrowly defined on the one hand, and technically oriented on the other. Most of it has focused on only one kind of organizational mode for innovation—such as internal organizational innovation (Normann 1979), or new business startups (e.g., Cooper 1979)—or one stage of the innovation process—such as the diffusion stage (Rogers, 1981)—or one type of innovation—such as technological innovation (Utterback 1974). While such research has provided many insights into specific aspects of innovation, the encompassing problems confronting general managers in managing innovation have been largely overlooked.

As their questions suggest, general managers deal with a set of problems that are different from and less well understood than functional managers. We concur with Lewin and Minton's (1985) call for a general management perspective on innovation—one that begins with key problems confronting general managers, and then examines the effects of how these problems are addressed on innovation effectiveness. The purpose of this paper is to present such a perspective on the management of innovation. Appreciating these problems and their consequences provides a first step in developing a research program on the management of innovation.

The process of innovation is defined as the development and implementation of new ideas by people who over time engage in transactions with others within an institutional context. This definition is sufficiently general to apply to a wide variety of technical, product, process, and administrative kinds of innovations. From a managerial viewpoint, to understand the process of innovation is to understand the factors that facilitate and inhibit the development of innovations. These factors include ideas, people, transactions, and context over time. Associated with each of these four factors are four central problems in the management of innovation which will be discussed in this paper.

First, there is *the human problem of managing attention* because people and their organizations are largely designed to focus on, harvest, and protect existing practices rather than pay attention to developing new ideas. The more successful an organization is the more difficult it is to trigger people's action thresholds to pay attention to new ideas, needs, and opportunities.

Second, *the process problem is managing ideas into good currency* so that innovative ideas are implemented and institutionalized. While the invention or conception of innovative ideas may be an individual activity, innovation (inventing and implementing new ideas) is a collective achievement of pushing and riding those ideas into good currency. The social and political dynamics of innovation become paramount as one addresses the energy and commitment that are needed among coalitions of interest groups to develop an innovation.

Third, there is *the structural problem of managing part-whole relationships,* which emerges from the proliferation of ideas, people and transactions as an innovation develops over time. A common characteristic of the innovation process is that multiple functions, resources, and disciplines are needed to transform an innovative idea into a concrete reality—so much so that individuals involved in individual transactions lose sight of the whole innovation effort. How does one put the whole into the parts?

Finally, the context of an innovation points to *the strategic problem of institutional leadership.* Innovations not only adapt to existing organizational and industrial arrangments, but they also transform the structure and practices of these environments. The strategic problem is one of creating an infrastructure that is conducive to innovation.

After clarifying our definition of innovation, this paper will elaborate on these four central problems in the management of innovation. We will conclude by suggesting how these four problems emerge over time and provide an overall framework to guide longitudinal study of innovation processes.

INNOVATIVE IDEAS

An Innovation is a new *idea,* which may be a recombination of old ideas, a scheme that challenges the present order, a formula, or a unique approach which is perceived as new by the individuals involved (Zaltman, Duncan, and Holbek 1973; Rogers 1982). As long as the idea is perceived as new to the people involved, it is an "innovation," even though it may appear to others to be an "imitation" of something that exists elsewhere.

Included in this definition are both technical innovations (new technologies, products, and services) and administrative innovations (new procedures, policies, and organizational forms). Daft and Becker (1979) and others have emphasized keeping technical and administrative innovations distinct. We believe that making such a distinction often results in a fragmented classification of the innovation process. Most innovations involve new technical and administrative components (Leavitt 1965). For example Ruttan and Hayami (1984) have shown that many technological innovations in agriculture and elsewhere could not have occurred without innovations in institutional and organizational arrangements. So also, the likely success of developments in decision support systems by management scientists largely hinges on an appreciation of the interdependence between technological hardware and software innovations on the one hand, and new theories of administrative choice behavior on the other. Learning to understand the close connection between technical and administrative dimensions of innovations is a key part of understanding the management of innovation.

Kimberly (1981) rightly points out that a positive bias pervades the study of innovation. Innovation is often viewed as a good thing because the new idea must be useful—profitable, constructive, or solve a problem. New ideas that are not perceived as useful are not normally called innovations; they are usually called mistakes. Objectively, of course, the usefulness of an idea can only be determined after the innovation process is completed and implemented. Moreover, while many new ideas are proposed in organizations, only a very few receive serious consideration and developmental effort (Wilson 1966; Maitland 1982). Since it is not possible to determine at the outset which new ideas are "innovations" or "mistakes," and since we assume that people prefer to invest their energies and careers on the former and not the latter, there is a need to explain (1) how and why certain innovative ideas gain good currency (i.e., are implemented), and (2) how and why people pay attention to only certain new ideas and ignore the rest. These two questions direct our focus to problems of managing ideas into good currency and the management of attention.

THE MANAGEMENT OF IDEAS

It is often said that an innovative idea without a champion gets nowhere. *People* develop, carry, react to, and modify ideas. People apply different skills, energy levels and frames of reference (interpretive schemas) to ideas as a result of their backgrounds, experiences, and activities that occupy their attention. *People become attached to ideas over time through a social-political process of pushing and riding their ideas into good currency,* much like Donald Schon (1971) describes for the emergence of public policies. Figure 2-1 illustrates the process.

Schon states that what characteristically precipitates change in public policy is a disruptive event which threatens the social system. Invention is an act of appreciation, which is a complex perceptual process that melds together judgments of reality and judgments of value. A new appreciation is made as a problem, or opportunity is recognized. Once appreciated, ideas gestating in peripheral areas begin to surface to the mainstream as a result of the efforts of people who supply the energy necessary to raise the ideas over the threshold of public consciousness: As these ideas surface networks of individuals and interest groups gravitate to and galvanize around the new ideas. They, in turn, exert their own influence on the ideas by further developing them and providing them with a catchy slogan that provides emotional meaning and energy to the idea.

FIGURE 2-1 Managing Life Cycle of Ideas in Good Currency

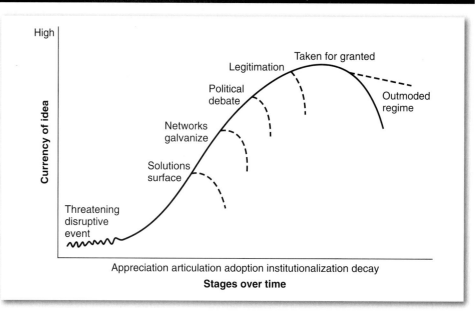

However, Schon indicates that ideas are not potent to change policy unless they become an issue for political debate and unless they are used to gain influence and resources. The debate turns not only on the merits of the ideas, but also on who is using the ideas as vehicles to gain power. As the ideas are taken up by people who are or have become powerful, the ideas gain legitimacy and power to change institutions. After this, the ideas that win out are implemented and become institutionalized—they become part of the conceptual structure of the social system and appear obvious, in retrospect. However, the idea remains institutionalized for only as long as it continues to address critical problems and as long as the regime remains in power.

Schon's description of the stages by which ideas come into good currency is instructive in its focus on the social-political dynamics of the innovation process. The description emphasizes the *centrality of ideas as the rallying point around which collective action mobilizes*—organizational structures emerge and are modified by these ideas. Moreover, it is the central focus on *ideas* that provides the vehicle for otherwise isolated, disconnected, or competitive individuals and stakeholders to come together and contribute their unique frames of reference to the innovation process. Schon (1971, p. 141) states that these stages characteristically describe the process features in the emergence of public policies "regardless of their content or conditions from which they spring." Analogous descriptions of this social-political process have been provided by Quinn (1980, especially p. 104) for the development of corporate strategies, and by March and Olsen (1976) for decision making in educational institutions.

However, there are also some basic limitations to the process that lead to inertia and premature abandonment of some ideas. First, there tends to be a short-term problem orientation in individuals and organizations, and a facade of demonstrating progress. This has the effect of inducing premature abandonment of ideas because even if problems are not being solved, the appearance of progress requires moving on to the next batch of problems. Thus, "old questions are not answered—they only go out of fashion" (Schon 1971, p. 142). Furthermore, given the inability to escape the interdependence of problems, old problems are relabeled as new problems. As a result, and as observed by Cohen, March and Olsen (1972), decision makers have the feeling they are always working on the same problems in somewhat different contexts, but mostly without results.

Except for its use in legislative bodies, the idea of formally managing the socio-political process of pushing and riding ideas into good currency is novel. However, as

Huber (1984, p. 938) points out, the decision process is similar to project management and program planning situations. Thus, Huber proposes the adoption of proven project management and program planning technologies (e.g., PERT, CPM and PPM) for managing the production of ideas into good currency. For example, based upon a test of the Program Planning Model, Van de Ven (1980a, b) concluded that the PPM avoids problems of decision flight and falling into a rut that are present in March and Olsen's (1976) garbage can model of anarchical decision making. This is accomplished by the PPM's three-way matching of phased tasks with different decision processes and with different participants over time in a program planning effort.

A second limitation of the process is that the inventory of ideas is seldom adequate for the situation. This may be because environmental scanning relevant to an issue does not uncover the values and partisan views held by all the relevant stakeholders. Gilbert and Freeman (1984) point out that with the general concept of environmental scanning, current models of strategic decision making gloss over the need to identify specific stakeholders to an issue and to examine their underlying values which provide reasons for their actions. Viewing the process from a game theoretic framework, they state that "effective strategy will be formulated and implemented if and only if each player successfully puts himself or herself in the place of other players and engages in trying to see the situation from the others' viewpoints" (Gilbert and Freeman 1984, p. 4).

A third, and even more basic problem is the management of attention—how do individuals become attached to and invest effort in the development of innovative ideas? Human beings and their organizations are mostly designed to focus on, harvest, and protect existing practices rather than to pave new directions. This is because people have basic physiological limitations of not being able to handle complexity, of unconsciously adapting to gradually changing conditions, of conforming to group and organizational norms, and of focusing on repetitive activities (Van de Ven and Hudson 1985). One of the key questions in the management of innovation then becomes how to trigger the action thresholds of individuals to appreciate and pay attention to new ideas, needs and opportunities.

THE MANAGEMENT OF ATTENTION

Much of the folklore and applied literature on the management of innovation has ignored the research by cognitive psychologists and social-psychologists about the limited capacity of human beings to handle complexity and maintain attention. As a consequence, one often gets the impression that inventors or innovators have superhuman creative heuristics or abilities to "walk on water" (Van de Ven and Hudson 1985). *A more realistic view of innovation should begin with an appreciation of the physiological limitations of human beings to pay attention to nonroutine issues, and their corresponding inertial forces in organizational life.*

Physiological Limitations of Human Beings

It is well established empirically that most individuals lack the capability and inclination to deal with complexity (Tversky and Kahneman 1974; Johnson 1983). Although there are great individual differences, most people have very short spans of attention—the average person can retain raw data in short-term memory for only a few seconds. Memory, it turns out, requires relying on "old friends," which Simon (1947) describes as a process of linking raw data with pre-existing schemas and world views that an individual has stored in long-term memory. Most individuals are also very efficient processors of routine tasks. They do not concentrate on repetitive tasks, once they are mastered. Skills for performing repetitive tasks are repressed in subconscious memory, permitting individuals to pay attention to things other than performance of repetitive tasks (Johnson 1983). Ironically as a result, what most individuals think about the most is what they will do, but what they do the most is what they think about the least.

In complex decision situations, individuals create stereotypes as a defense mechanism to deal with complexity. For the average person, stereotyping is likely to begin when seven (plus or minus two) objects or digits are involved in a decision—this number being the information processing capacity of the average individual (Miller 1956). As decision complexity increases beyond this point, people become more conservative and apply more subjective criteria which are further and further removed from reality (Filley, House, and Kerr 1976). Furthermore, since the correctness of outcomes from innovative ideas can rarely be judged, the perceived legitimacy of the decision *process* becomes the dominant evaluation criterion. Thus, as March (1981) and Janis (1982) point out, as decision complexity increases, solutions become increasingly error prone, means become more important than ends, and rationalization replaces rationality.

It is generally believed that crises, dissatisfaction, tension, or significant external stress are the major preconditions for stimulating people to act. March and Simon (1958) set forth the most widely accepted model by arguing that dissatisfaction with existing conditions stimulates people to search for improved conditions, and they will cease searching when a satisfactory result is found. A satisfactory result is a function of a person's aspiration level, which Lewin et al. (1944) indicated is a product of all past successes and failures that people have experienced. If this model is correct (and most believe it is), then scholars and practitioners must wrestle with another basic problem.

This model assumes that when people reach a threshold of dissatisfaction with existing conditions, they will initiate action to resolve their dissatisfaction. However, because individuals unconsciously adapt to slowly changing environments, their thresholds for action are often not triggered while they adapt over time. In this sense, individuals are much like frogs. Although we know of no empirical support for the frog story developed by Gregory Bateson, it goes as follows.

> When frogs are placed into a boiling pail of water, they jump out—they don't want to boil to death.
> However, when frogs are placed into a cold pail of water, and the pail is placed on a stove with the heat turned very low, over time the frogs will boil to death.

Cognitive psychologists have found that individuals have widely varying and manipulable adaptation levels (Helson 1948, 1964). When exposed over time to a set of stimuli that deteriorate very gradually, people do not percieve the gradual changes—they unconsciously adapt to the worsening conditions. Their threshold to tolerate pain, discomfort, or dissatisfaction is not reached. As a consequence, they do not move into action to correct their situation, which over time may become deplorable. Opportunities for innovative ideas are not recognized, problems swell into metaproblems, and at the extreme, catastrophes are sometimes necessary to reach the action threshold (Van de Ven 1980b).

These worsening conditions are sometimes monitored by various corporate planning and management information units and distributed to personnel in quantitative MIS reports of financial and performance trends. However, these impersonal statistical reports only increase the numbness of organizational participants and raise the false expectation that if someone is measuring the trends then someone must be doing something about them.

When situations have deteriorated to the point of actually triggering people's action thresholds, innovative ideas turn out to be crisis management ideas. As Janis (1982) describes, such decision processes are dominated by defense mechanisms of isolation, projection, stereotyping, displacement, and retrospective rationalizations to avoid negative evaluations. As a result, the solutions that emerge from such "innovative" ideas are likely to be "mistakes."

Group and Organizational Limitations

At the group and organizational levels, the problems of inertia, conformity, and incompatible preferences are added to the above physiological limitations of human beings in managing attention. As Janis (1982) has clearly shown, groups place strong conformity pressures on members, who collectively conform to one another without them knowing it. Indeed, the classic study by Pelz and Andrews (1966) found that a heterogeneous group of interdisciplinary scientists when working together daily became homogeneous in perspective and approach to problems in as little as three years. Groups minimize internal conflict and focus on issues that maximize consensus. "Group Think" is not only partly a product of these internal conformity pressures, but also of external conflict—"out-group" conflict stimulates "in-group" cohesion (Coser 1959). Consequently, it is exceedingly difficult for groups to entertain threatening information, which is inherent in most innovative ideas.

Organizational structures and systems serve to sort attention. They focus efforts in prescribed areas and blind people to other issues by influencing perceptions, values, and beliefs. Many organizational systems consist of programs, which create slack through efficient repetitive use of procedures believed to lead to success (Cyert and March 1963). But as Starbuck (1983) argues, the programs do not necessarily address causal factors. Instead, the programs tend to be more like superstitious learning, recreating actions which may have little to do with previous success and nothing to do with future success. As a result, the older, larger, and more successful organizations become, the more likely they are to have a large repertoire of structures and systems which discourage innovation while encouraging tinkering. For example, strategic planning *systems* often drive out strategic thinking as participants "go through the numbers" of completing yearly planning forms and review cycles.

The implication is that without the intervention of leadership (discussed below), structures and systems focus the attention of organizational members to routine, not innovative activities. For all the rational virtues that structures and systems provide to maintain existing organizational practices, these "action generators" make organizational participants inattentive to shifts in organizational environments and the need for innovation (Starbuck 1983). It is surprising that we know so little about the management of attention. However, several useful prescriptions have been made.

Ways to Manage Attention

At a recent conference on strategic decision making (Pennings 1985), Paul Lawrence reported that in his consulting practice he usually focuses on what management is *not* paying attention to. Similarly based on his observations in consulting with large organizations, Richard Normann observed that well-managed companies are not only close to their customers, they search out and focus on their *most demanding customers.* Empirically, von Hippel (1977) has shown that ideas for most new product innovations come from customers. Being exposed face-to-face with demanding customers or consultants increases the likelihood that the action threshold of organizational participants will be triggered and will stimulate them to pay attention to changing environmental conditions or customer needs. In general, we would expect that *direct personal confrontations with problem sources* are needed to reach the threshold of concern and appreciation required to motivate people to act (Van de Ven 1980b).

However, while face-to-face confrontations with problems may trigger action thresholds, they also create stress. One must therefore examine the effects of stress on the innovative process. Janis (1985) outlines five basic patterns of coping with stress, and states that only the vigilance pattern generally leads to decisions that meet the main criteria for sound decision making. Vigilance involves an extended search and assimilation of information, and a careful appraisal of alternatives before a choice is made. Janis proposes that vigilance tends to occur under conditions of moderate stress, and when there may be sufficient time and slack resources to make decisions. Under conditions of no slack capacity or short-time horizons (which produce stress) the decision process will resemble crisis decision-making—resulting in significant implementation errors (Hrebiniak and Joyce 1984).

Argyris and Schon (1982) focus on single loop and double loop learning models for managing attention that may improve the innovation process. In single loop learning, no change in criteria of effective performance takes place. Single loop learning represents conventional monitoring activity, with actions taken based on the findings of the monitoring system. Because it does not question the criteria of evaluation, single loop learning leads to the organizational inertia which Starbuck (1983) indicates must be unlearned before change can occur. Double loop learning involves a change in the criteria of evaluation. Past practices are called into question, new assumptions about the organization are raised, and significant changes in strategy are believed to be possible.

While double loop learning can lead to change, it can also lead to low trust, defensive behavior, undiscussibles, and to bypass tactics. Thus, the management of attention must be concerned not only with triggering the action thresholds of organizational participants, but also of channeling that action toward constructive ends. Constructive attention management is a function of how two other central problems are addressed: part-whole relations and institutional leadership—which we will now discuss.

THE MANAGEMENT OF PART-WHOLE RELATIONSHIPS

Proliferation of ideas, people, and transactions over time is a pervasive but little understood characterstic of the innovation process, and with it come complexity and interdependence—and the basic structural problem of managing part-whole relations.

The proliferation of ideas is frequently observed in a single individual who works to develop an innovation from concept to reality. Over time the individual develops a mosaic of perspectives, revisions, extensions, and applications of the initial innovative idea—and they accumulate into a complex set of interdependent options. However, as the discussion of managing ideas into good currency implies, innovation is not an individual activity—it is a collective achievement. Therefore, over time there is also a proliferation of people (with diverse skills, resources, and interests) who become involved in the innovation process. When a single innovative idea is expressed to others, it proliferates into multiple ideas because people have diverse frames of reference, or interpretive schemas, that filter their perceptions. These differing perceptions and frames of reference are amplified by the proliferation of transactions or relationships among people and organizational units that occur as the innovation unfolds. Indeed, management of the innovation process can be viewed as managing increasing bundles of transactions over time.

Transactions are "deals" or exchanges which tie people together within an institutional framework (which is context). John R. Commons (1951), the originator of the concept, argued that transactions are dynamic and go through three temporal stages: negotiations, agreements, and administration. Most transactions do not follow a simple linear progression through these stages. The more novel and complex the innovative idea, the more often trial-and-error cycles of renegotiation, recommitment, and readministration of transactions will occur. Moreover, the selection of certain kinds of transactions is always conditioned by the range of past experiences and current situations to which individuals have been exposed. Therefore, people have a conservative bias to enter into transactions with parties they know, trust, and with whom they have had successful experiences. As a consequence, what may start as an interim solution to an immediate problem often proliferates over time into a web of complex and interdependent transactions among the parties involved.

There is an important connection between transactions and organizations. Transactions are the micro elements of macro organizational arrangements. Just as the development of an innovation might be viewed as a bundle of proliferating transactions over time, so also, is there proliferation of functions and roles to manage this complex and interdependent bundle of transactions in the institution that houses the innovation.

The prevailing approach for handling this complexity and interdependence is to divide the labor among specialists who are best qualified to perform unique tasks and then to integrate the specialized parts to recreate the whole. The objective, of course, is to develop synergy in managing complexity and interdependence with an organizational design where the whole is greater than the sum of its parts. However, the whole often turns out to be less than or a meaningless sum of the parts because the parts do not add to, but subtract from one another (Hackman 1984). This result has been obtained not only when summing the products of differentiated units within organizations, but also the benefits member firms derive from associating with special interest groups (Maitland 1983, 1985). Kanter (1983), Tushman and Romanelli (1983), and Peters and Waterman (1982) have shown that this "segmentalist" design logic is severely flawed for managing highly complex and interdependent activities. *Perhaps the most significant structural problem in managing complex organizations today, and innovation in particular, is the management of part-whole relations.*

For example, the comptroller's office detects an irregularity of spending by a sub-unit and thereby eliminates an innovative "skunkworks" group; a new product may have been designed and tested, but runs into problems when placed into production because R&D and engineering overlooked a design flaw; the development of a major system may be ready for production, but subcontractors of components may not be able to deliver on schedule or there may be material defects in vendors' parts. Typical attributions for these problems include: lack of communication or misunderstandings between scientific, engineering, manufacturing, marketing, vendors and customers on the nature or status of the innovation; unexpected delays and errors in certain developmental stages that complicate further errors and rework in subsequent stages; incompatible organizational funding, control, and reward policies; and ultimately significant cost over-runs and delayed introductions into the market.

Peters and Waterman (1982) dramatized this problem of part-whole relationships with an example of a product innovation which required 223 reviews and approvals among 17 standing committees in order to develop it from concept to market reality. Moreover, they state that

> The irony, and the tragedy, is that each of the 223 linkages taken by itself makes perfectly good sense. Well-meaning, rational people designed each link for a reason that made sense at the time. . . . The trouble is that the total picture as it inexorably emerged . . . captures action like a fly in a spider's web and drains the life out of it. (Peters and Waterman 1982, pp. 18–19).

This example clearly illustrates a basic principle of contradictory part-whole relationships—*impeccable micro-logic often creates macro nonsense,* and vice versa.

Is there a way to avoid having the whole be less than or a meaningless sum of its parts? Perhaps a way is needed to design the whole into the parts, as Gareth Morgan (1983a, b, 1984) has been pursuing with the concept of a *hologram*. He concluded that the brain, with its incredible complexity, manages that complexity by placing the essential elements of the whole into each of its parts—it is a hologram.

Most organizations, however, are not designed with this logic, but if possible ought to be. The hologram metaphor emphasizes that organization design for innovation is not a discrete event but a process for integrating all the essential functions, organizational units, and resources needed to manage an innovation from beginning to end. It requires a significant departure from traditional approaches to organizing innovation.

Traditionally the innovation process has been viewed as a sequence of separable stages (e.g., design, production, and marketing) linked by relatively minor transitions to make adjustments between stages. There are two basic variations of this design for product innovation. First, there is the technology-driven model where new ideas are developed in the R&D department, sent to engineering and manufacturing to produce the innovation, and then on to marketing for sales and distribution to customers. The second, and currently more popular, design is the customer or need-driven model, where marketing comes up with new ideas as a result of close interactions with customers, which in turn are sent to R&D for prototype development and then to engineering and manufacturing for production. Galbraith (1982) points out that the question of whether innovations are stimulated by technology or customer need is debatable.

> "But this argument misses the point." As reproduced in Figure 2-2, "the debate is over whether [technology] or [need] drives the downstream efforts. This thinking is linear and sequential. Instead, the model suggested here is

FIGURE 2-2   Linear Sequential Coupling Compared with Simultaneous Coupling of Knowledge

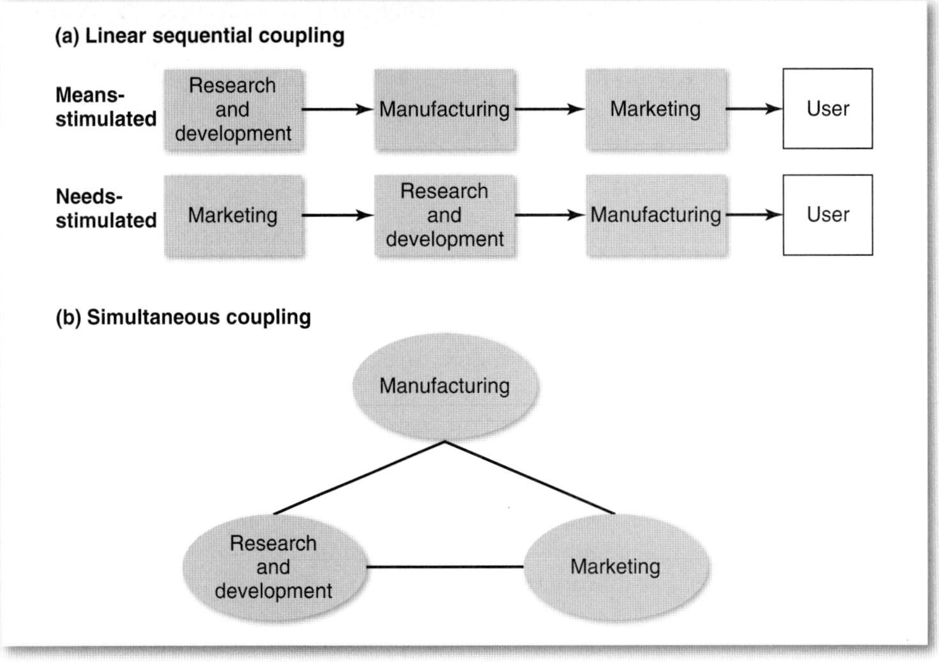

(a) Linear sequential coupling

Means-stimulated: Research and development → Manufacturing → Marketing → User

Needs-stimulated: Marketing → Research and development → Manufacturing → User

(b) Simultaneous coupling

Manufacturing — Research and development — Marketing

Source: Jay R. Galbraith (1982).

shown in Figure 2-2b. That is, for innovation to occur, knowledge of all key components is simultaneously coupled. And the best way to maximize communication among the components is to have the communication occur intrapersonally—that is, within one person's mind. If this is impossible, then as few people as possible should have to communicate or interact. (Galbraith 1982, pp. 16–17).

As Galbraith implies, with the hologram metaphor the innovation process is viewed as consisting of iterations of inseparable and simultaneously-coupled stages (or functions) linked by a major ongoing transition process. Whereas the mechanical metaphor of an assembly line of stages characterizes most current views of the innovation process, the biological metaphor of a hologram challenges scholars and practitioners to find ways to place essential characteristics of the whole into each of the parts.

Although very little is known about how to design holographic organizations, four inter-related design principles have been suggested by Morgan (1985) and others: self-organizing units, redundant functions, requisite variety, and temporal linkage.

First, the hologram metaphor directs attention to identifying and grouping together all the key resources and interdependent functions needed to develop an innovation into one organizational unit, so that it can operate as if it were an *autonomous unit.* (Of course, no organizational unit is ever completely autonomous.) The principle of autonomous work groups has been developed largely by Trist (1981), and is consistent with Thompson's (1967) logical design principle of placing reciprocally-interdependent activities closely together into a common unit in order to minimize coordination costs. By definition, autonomous groups are self-organizing, which implies that management follows the "principle of minimum intervention" (Hrebiniak and Joyce 1984, p. 8). This allows the group to self-organize and choose courses of action to solve its problems within an overall mission and set of constraints prescribed for the unit by the larger organization.

Second, flexibility and a capacity for self-organizing is needed by creating *redundant functions,* which means that people develop an understanding of the essential considerations and constraints of all aspects of the innovation in addition to those immediately needed to perform their individual assignments. Redundant functions does not mean duplication or spare parts as may be implied by the mechanistic metaphor, nor does it eliminate the need for people to have uniquely-specialized technical competencies. It means that all members of an innovation unit develop the capacity to "think globally while acting locally." The principle of redundant functions is achieved through training, socialization, and inclusion into the innovation unit so that each member not only comes to know how his or her function relates to each other functional specialty, but also understands the essential master blueprint of the overall innovation. The former is needed for interdependent action; the latter is essential for survival and reproduction of the innovative effort.

Third, following Ashby's (1956) principle of *requisite variety,* learning is enhanced when a similar degree of complexity in the environment is built into the organizational unit. This principle is a reflection of the fact that any autonomous organizational unit at one level is a dependent part of a larger social system at a more macro level of analysis. Requisite variety means placing critical dimensions of the whole environment into the unit, which permits the unit to develop and store rich patterns of information and uncertainty that are needed in order to detect and correct errors existing in the environment. The principle of requisite variety is not achieved by assigning the task of environmental scanning to one or a few boundary spanners, for that makes the unit dependent upon the "enactments" (Weick 1979) of only one or a few individuals whose frames of reference invariably filter only selective aspects of the environment. Requisite variety is more nearly achieved by making environmental scanning a responsibility of all unit members, and by recruiting personnel within the innovation unit who understand and have access to each of the key environmental stakeholder groups or issues that affect the innovation's development.

Whereas the principles of redundant functions and requisite variety create the slack needed to integrate members of the unit and between the unit and its environment (respectively), the principle of *temporal linkage* integrates parts of time (past, present, and future events) into an overall chronology of the innovation process. While innovations are typically viewed as making additions to existing arrangements, Albert (1984c) proposes another arithmetic for linking the past, present and future. Given a world of scarcity, Albert (1984a, b) notes that the implementation of innovations often results in eliminations, replacements, or transformations of existing arrangements. As a consequence, the management of innovation must also be the management of termination, and of transitioning people, programs, and investments from commitments in the past toward the future. In common social life, funerals and wakes are used to commemorate and bereave the passing of loved ones and to make graceful transitions into the future. As Albert suggests, there is a need to create funerals, celebrations, and transitional rituals that commemorate the ideas, programs, and commitments falling out of currency in order to create opportunities for ushering in those that must gain good currency for an innovation to succeed.

INSTITUTIONAL LEADERSHIP AND INNOVATION CONTEXT

Innovation is not the enterprise of a single entrepreneur. Instead, it is a network-building effort that centers on the creation, adoption, and sustained implementation of a set of ideas among people who, through transactions, become sufficiently committed to these ideas to transform them into "good currency." Following holographic principles, this network-building activity must occur both within the organization and in the larger community of which it is a part. *Creating these intra- and extra-organizational infrastructures in which innovation can flourish takes us directly to the strategic problem of innovation, which is institutional leadership.*

The extra-organizational context includes the broad cultural and resource endowments that society provides, including laws, government regulations, distributions of knowledge and resources, and the structure of the industry in which the innovation is located. Research by Ruttan and Hayami (1983) and Trist (1981) suggests that innovation does not exist in a vacuum and that institutional innovation is in great measure a reflection of the amount of support an organization can draw from its larger community. Collective action among institutional leaders within a community becomes critical in the long run to create the social, economic, and political infrastructure a community needs in order to sustain its members (Astley and Van de Ven 1983). In addition, as Aldrich (1979) and Erickson and Maitland (1982) indicate, a broad population or industry purview is needed to understand the societal demographic characteristics that facilitate and inhibit innovation.

Within the organization, institutional leadership is critical in creating a cultural context that fosters innovation, and in establishing organizational strategy, structure, and systems that facilitate innovation. As Hackman (1984, p. 40) points out, "an unsupportive organizational context can easily undermine the positive features of even a well-designed team." There is a growing recognition that innovation requires a special kind of supportive leadership.

> This type of leadership offers a vision of what could be and gives a sense of purpose and meaning to those who would share that vision. It builds commitment, enthusiasm, and excitement. It creates a hope in the future and a belief that the world is knowable, understandable, and manageable. The collective energy that transforming leadership generates, empowers those who participate in the process. There is hope, there is optimism, there is energy (Roberts 1984, p. 3).

Institutional leadership goes to the essence of the process of institutionalization. It is often thought that an organization loses something (becomes rigid, inflexible, and loses it ability to be innovative) when institutionalization sets in. This may be true if an organization is viewed as a mechanistic, efficiency-driven tool. But, as Selznick (1957) argued, an organization does not become an "institution" until it becomes infused with value; i.e., prized not as a tool alone, but as a source of direct personal gratification, and as a vehicle for group integrity. By plan or default, this infusion of norms and values into an organization takes place over time, and produces a distinct identity, outlook, habits, and commitments for its participants—coloring as it does all aspects of organizational life, and giving it a social integration that goes far beyond the formal command structure and instrumental functions of the organization.

Institutional leadership is particularly needed for organizational innovation, which represents key periods of development and transition when the organization is open to or forced to consider alternative ways of doing things. During these periods, Selznick emphasized that the central and distinctive responsibility of institutional leadership is the creation of the organization's character or culture. This responsibility is carried out through four key functions: defining the institution's mission, embodying purpose into the organization's structure and systems, defending the institution's integrity, and ordering internal conflict. Selznick (1957, p. 62) reports that when institutional leaders default in performing these functions, the organization may drift. "A set of beliefs, values and guiding principles may emerge in the organization that are counterproductive to the organization's mission or distinctive competence. As institutionalization progresses the enterprise takes on a special character, and this means that it becomes peculiarly competent (or incompetent) to do a particular kind of work" (Selznick 1957, p. 139). Organization drift is accompanied by loss of the institution's integrity, opportunism, and ultimately, loss of distinctive competence.

Lodahl and Mitchell (1980, pp. 203–204) insightfully apply Selznick's perspective by distinguishing how institutional and technical processes come into play to transform innovative ideas into a set of guiding ideals—see Figure 2-3. First there are the founding ideals for an innovation or an enterprise, followed by the recruitment and socialization of members to serve those ideas. Leadership and formalization guide and stabilize the enterprise.

When viewed as a set of technical or instrumental tasks, the process is operationalized into setting clear goals or ends to be achieved; establishing impersonal and universal criteria for recruitment, developing clear rules and procedures for learning

FIGURE 2-3 Institutional and Technical Processes

Institutional processes	Idea	Technical processes
Creation, elaboration of ideology	Founding ideals	Statement of organizational goals
Use of personal netwoks; selection based on values and ideals	Recruitment	Board search: use of universalistic criteria
Face-to-face contact with founders: sharing rituals, symbols	Socialization	Rules and procedures learned through colleagues
Charismatic, mythic images (transforming)	Leadership	Problem solving and consensus making (transactional)
Ideals paramount: structure tentative	Formalization	Early routinization; uncertainty reduction

Source: T. Lodahl and S. Mitchell (1980).

and socialization; analytical problem solving and decision making; and routinizing activities in order to reduce uncertainty. Institutional processes are very different from this well-known technical approach.

As Figure 2-3 illustrates, institutional processes focus on the creation of an ideology to support the founding ideals; the use of personal networks and value-based criteria for recruitment; socialization and learning by sharing rituals and symbols; charismatic leadership; and the infusion of values as paramount to structure and formalize activities.

Lodahl and Mitchell (1980, p. 204) point out that an innovation is an institutional success to the degree that it exhibits authenticity, functionality, and flexibility over time. Authenticity requires that the innovation embodies the organization's ideas; functionality requires that the innovation work; and flexibility requires that the innovation can incorporate the inputs and suggestions of its members. If these tests are met, organizational members will make a commitment to the innovation. In contrast, if institutional skills are not used while technical skills are in operation, the innovation may be an organizational success but an institutional failure. In that case, there will be evidence of drift and disillusionment. Such a result will be characterized by individual self-interest, differentiation, and technical efficiency.

These distinctions between institutional and technical processes have three significant implications for addressing the problems of managing attention, ideas, and part-whole relations discussed in previous sections. These implications draw upon cybernetic principles and the hologram metaphor, as Morgan (1983b, 1984) proposes.

First, organizational members can develop a capacity to control and regulate their own behavior through a process of *negative feedback,* which means that goals are achieved by avoiding not achieving the goal. In other words, deviations in one direction initiate action in the opposite direction at every step in performing an activity so that in the end no error remains. In order for learning through negative feedback to occur, an organization must have values and standards which define the critical limits within which attention to innovative ideas is to focus. Whereas technical processes focus attention on clear-cut goals and targets to be achieved, institutional processes define the constraints to avoid in terms of values and limits. Institutional leadership thus involves a choice of limits (issues to avoid) rather than a choice of ends. As Burgelman (1984, p. 1349) points out, "top management's critical contribution consists in strategic recognition rather than planning." As a result, a space of possible actions is defined which leaves room for innovative ideas to develop and to be tested against these constraints.

Second, whereas single loop learning involves an ability to detect and correct deviations from a set of values and norms, double loop learning occurs when the organization also learns how to detect and correct errors in the operating norms themselves. This permits an institution to adjust and change the ideas considered legitimate or to have good currency.

From an institutional view legitimate error stems from the uncertainty inherent in the nature of a situation. The major problem in dealing with uncertainty is maintaining a balance on organizational diversity and order over time (Burgelman 1984). Diversity results primarily from autonomous initiatives of technical units. Order results from imposing standards and a concept of strategy on the organization. Managing this diversity requires framing ideas and problems so that they can be approached through experimentation and selection. The process of double-loop learning is facilitated by probing into various dimensions of a situation, and of promoting constructive conflict and debate between advocates of competing perspectives. Competing action strategies lead to reconsideration of the organization's mission, and perhaps a reformulation of that mission.

Finally, although technical processes of formalization press to reduce uncertainty, institutional processes attempt to preserve it. Just as necessity is the mother of invention, preserving the same degrees of uncertainty, diversity, or turbulence within an organization that is present in the environment are major sources of creativity and long-run viability for an organization. Embracing uncertainty is achieved by maintaining balance among innovative subunits, each designed according to the holographic principles of autonomous groups, requisite variety, and redundant functions discussed above. Application of these principles results in mirroring the turbulence present in the whole environment into the decision processes and other activities of each of the organization's parts. As a consequence, innovation is enhanced because organizational units are presented with the whole "law of the situation."

CONCLUDING DISCUSSION

Innovation has been defined as the development and implementation of new ideas by people who over time engage in transactions with others within an institutional context. This definition is particularly relevant to the general manager for it applies to a wide variety of technical, product, process, and administrative kinds of innovations that typically engage the general manager. From a managerial viewpoint, to understand the process of innovation is to be able to answer three questions: How do innovations develop over time? What kinds of problems will most likely be encountered as the innovation process unfolds? What responses are appropriate for managing these problems? Partial answers to these questions can be obtained by undertaking longitudinal research which systematically examines the innovation process, problems, and outcomes over time. Undertaking this research requires a conceptual framework to guide the investigation. The main purpose of this paper has been to develop such a framework by suggesting what key concepts, problems, and managerial responses should be the guiding focus to conduct longitudinal research on the management of innovation.

As our definition of innovation suggests, four basic concepts are central to studying the innovational process over time: ideas, people, transactions, and context. Associated with these four concepts are four central problems in the management of innovation: developing ideas into good currency, managing attention, part-whole relationships, and institutional leadership. Although these concepts and problems have diverse origins in the literature, previously they have not been combined into an interdependent set of critical concepts and problems for studying innovation management.

An invention or creative idea does not become an innovation until it is implemented or institutionalized. Indeed by most standards, the success of an innovation is largely defined in terms of the degree to which it gains good currency, i.e., becomes an implemented reality and is incorporated into the taken-for-granted assumptions and thought structure of organizational practice. Thus, a key measure of innovation success or outcome is the currency of the idea, and a basic research question is how and why do some new ideas gain good currency while the majority do not? Based on work by Schon (1971), Quinn (1980), and others, we think the answer requires longitudinal study of the social and political processes by which people become invested in or attached to new ideas and push them into good currency.

But what leads people to pay attention to new ideas? This is the second major problem to be addressed in a research program on innovation. We argued that an understanding of this issue should begin with an appreciation of the physiological limitations of human beings to pay attention to nonroutine issues, and their corresponding inertial forces in organizational life. The more specialized, insulated, and stable an individual's job, the less likely the individual will recognize a need for change or pay attention to innovative ideas. It was proposed that people will pay attention to new ideas the more they experience personal confrontations with sources of problems, opportunities, and threats which trigger people's action thresholds to pay attention and recognize the need for innovation.

Once people begin to pay attention to new ideas and become involved in a social-political process with others to push their ideas into good currency, a third problem of part-whole relationships emerges. A common characteristic in the development of innovations is that multiple functions, resources, and disciplines are necessary to transform innovative ideas into reality—so much so that individuals involved in specific transactions or parts of the innovation lose sight of the whole innovative effort. If left to themselves, they will design impeccable micro-structures for the innovation process that often result in macro nonsense. The hologram metaphor was proposed for designing the innovation process in such a way that more of the whole is structured into each of the proliferating parts. In particular, application of four holographic principles was proposed for managing part-whole relationships: self-organizing groups, redundant functions, requisite variety, and temporal linkage.

However, these holographic principles for designing innovation units simultaneously require the creation of an institutional context that fosters innovation and that links these self-organizing innovative units into a larger and more encompassing organizational mission and strategy. The creation of this macro context for innovation points to the need to understand and study a fourth central problem, which is institutional leadership. Innovations must not only adapt to existing organizational and industrial arrangements, but they also transform the structure and practices of these environments. The strategic problem for institutional leaders is one of creating an infrastructure that is conducive to innovation and organizational learning.

Three cybernetic principles were proposed to develop this infrastructure. First, the principle of negative feedback suggests that a clear set of values and standards are needed which define the critical limits within which organizational innovations and operations are to be maintained. Second, an experimentation-and-selection approach is needed so that the organization develops a capacity for double-loop learning, i.e., learning how to detect and correct errors in the guiding standards themselves. Third, innovation requires preserving (not reducing) the uncertainty and diversity in the environment within the organization because necessity is the mother of invention. Embracing uncertainty can be achieved at the macro level through the principles of requisite variety and redundancy of functions.

It should be recognized that this has been a speculative essay on key problems in the management of innovation. Little empirical evidence is presently available to substantiate these problems, their implications, and proposed solutions. However, the essay has been productive in suggesting a core set of concepts, problems, and propositions to study the process of innovation over time, which is presently being undertaken by a large group of investigators at the University of Minnesota. A description of the operational framework being used in this longitudinal research is available (Van de Ven and Associates 1984). As this research progresses we hope to provide systematic evidence to improve our understanding of the central problems in the management of innovation discussed here.[1]

References

ALBERT, S., "A Delite Design Model for Successful Transitions," in J. Kimberly and R. Quinn (Eds.), *Managing Organizational Transitions,* Irwin, Homewood, Il., 1984a, Chapter 8, 169–191.

——, "The Sense of Closure," in K. Gergen and M. Gergen (Eds.), *Historical Social Psychology,* Lawrence Erlbaum Associates, 1984b, Chapter 8, 159–172.

——, "The Arithmetic of Change," University of Minnesota, Minneapolis, unpublished paper, 1984c.

ALDRICH, H., *Organizations and Environments,* Prentice Hall, Englewood Cliffs, N.J., 1979.

ARGYRIS, C. AND D. SCHON, *Reasoning, Learning, and Action,* Jossey-Bass, San Francisco, 1983.

ASHBY, W. R., *An Introduction to Cybernetics,* Chapman and Hall, Ltd., London, 1956.

ASTLEY, G. AND A. H. VAN DE VEN, "Central Perspectives and Debates in Organization Theory," *Admin. Sci. Quart.,* 28 (1983), 245–273.

BURGELMAN, R. A., "Corporate Entrepreneurship and Strategic Management: Insights from a Process Study," *Management Sci.,* 29, 12 (1983), 1349–1364.

COHEN, M. D., J. G. MARCH AND J. P. OLSEN, "A Garbage Can Model of Organizational Choice," *Admin. Sci. Quart.,* 17 (1972), 1–25.

COMMONS, J., *The Economics of Collection Action,* MacMillan, New York, 1951.

COOPER, A., "Strategic Management: New Ventures and Small Business," in D. Schendel and C. Hofer (Eds.), *Strategic Management,* Little, Brown and Company, Boston, 1979.

COSER, L., *The Functions of Social Conflict,* Routledge and Kegan Paul, New York, 1959.

CYERT, R. M. AND J. G. MARCH, *A Behavioral Theory of the Firm,* Prentice-Hall, Englewood Cliffs, N.J., 1963.

DAFT, R. AND S. BECKER, *Innovation in Organization,* Elsezier, New York, 1978.

ERICKSON, B. AND I. MAITLAND, "Healthy Industries and Public Policy," in Margaret E. Dewar (Eds.), *Industry Vitalization: Toward a National Industrial Policy,* Elmsford, N.Y., 1982.

FILLEY, A., R. HOUSE AND S. KERR, *Managerial Process and Organizational Behavior,* Scott Foresman, Glenview, Il., 1976.

GALBRAITH, J. R., "Designing the Innovating Organization," *Organizational Dynamics,* (Winter 1982), 3–24.

GILBERT, D. AND E. FREEMAN, "Strategic Management and Environmental Scanning: A Game Theoretic Approach," presented to the Strategic Management Society, Philadelphia, October 1984.

HACKMAN, J. R., "A Normative Model of Work Team Effectiveness," Yale School of Organization and Management, New Haven, Conn., Research Program on Group Effectiveness, Technical Report #2, 1984.

HELSON, H., "Adaptation-Level as a Basis for a Quantitative Theory of Frames of Reference," *Psychological Rev.,* 55 (1948), 294–313.

——, "Current Trends and Issues in Adaptation-Level Theory," *American Psychologist,* 19 (1964), 23–68.

HUBER, G., "The Nature and Design of Post-Industrial Organizations," *Management Sci.,* 30, 8 (1984), 928–951.

JANIS, I., *Groupthink,* 2nd ed., Houghton Mifflin, Boston, 1982.

——, "Sources of Error in Strategic Decision Making," in J. Pennings (Ed.), *Strategic Decision Making in Complex Organizations,* Jossey-Bass, San Francisco, 1985.

JOHNSON, PAUL E., "The Expert Mind: A New Challenge for the Information Scientist," In M. A. Bemmelmans (Ed.), *Beyond Productivity: Information Systems Development for Organizational Effectiveness,* North Holland Publishing, Netherlands, 1983.

KANTER, R., *The Change Masters,* Simon and Schuster, New York, 1983.

KIMBERLY, J., "Managerial Innovation," in Nystrom, P. and W. Starbuck (Eds.), *Handbook of Organizational Design,* Volume 1, Oxford University Press, Oxford, 1981, 84–104.

LAWRENCE, P. AND P. DYER, *Renewing American Industry,* Free Press, New York, 1983.

LEAVITT, H. J., "Applied Organizational Change in Industry: Structural, Technological, and Humanistic Approaches," Chapter 27 in J. March (Ed.), *Handbook of Organizations,* Rand McNally, Chicago, 1965, 1144–1170.

——, "Applied Organizational Change in Industry: Structural, Technological, and Humanistic Approaches," Chapter 25, in J. March (Ed.), *Handbook of Organizations,* Rand McNally, Chicago, 1965, 1144–1170.

LEWIN, ARIE Y., AND JOHN W. MINTON, "Organizational Effectiveness: Another Look, and an Agenda for Research," *Management Sci.,* 32, 5 (May 1986).

LEWIN, K., T. DEMBO, L. FESTINGER, AND P. SEARS, "Level of Aspiration," Chapter 10 in J. McV. Hunt (Ed.), *Personality and the Behavior Disorders,* Vol. 1, Ronald Press, New York, 1944.

LODAHL, T. AND S. MITCHELL, "Drift in the Development of Innovative Organizations," in J. Kimberly and R. Miles (Eds.), *The Organizational Life Cycle,* Jossey-Bass, San Francisco, 1980.

MAITLAND, I., "Organizational Structure and Innovation: The Japanese Case," in S. Lee and G. Schwendiman, *Management by Japanese Systems,* Prager, New York, 1982.

——, "House Divided: Business Lobbying and the 1981 Budget," *Research in Corporate Social Performance and Policy,* 5 (1983), 1–25.

——, "Interest Groups and Economic Growth Rates," *J. Politics,* (1985).

MARCH, JAMES G., "Decisions in Organizations and Theories of Choice," In A. Van de Ven and W. F. Joyce (Eds.), *Perspectives on Organizational Design and Behavior,* Wiley, New York, 1981.

——, AND J. P. OLSEN, *Ambiguity and Choice in Organizations,* Universitetsforlaget, Bergen, 1976.

——, AND H. SIMON, *Organizations,* Wiley, New York, 1958.

MILLER, G. A., "The Magical Number Seven, Plus or Minus Two: Some Limits on our Capacity for Processing Information," *Psychological Rev.,* 63 (1956), 81–97.

MORGAN, G., "Action Learning: A Holographic Metaphor for Guiding Social Change," *Human Relations,* 37, 1 (1983a), 1–28.

———, "Rethinking Corporate Strategy: A Cybernetic Perspective," *Human Relations,* 36, 4 (1983b), 345–360.

———, "Images of Organizations," York University, Downsview, Ontario, prepublication manuscript, 1986.

NORMANN, R., *Management for Growth,* Wiley, New York, 1977.

———, "Towards an Action Theory of Strategic Management," in J. Pennings (Ed.), *Strategic Decision Making in Complex Organizations,* Jossey-Bass, San Francisco, 1985.

OUCHI, W., *Theory Z,* Addison-Wesley, Reading, Mass., 1981.

PASCALE, R. AND A. ATHOS, *The Art of Japanese Management,* Warner Books, New York, 1981.

PELZ, D. AND F. ANDREWS, *Scientists in Organizations,* Wiley, New York, 1966.

PENNINGS, J., *Strategic Decision Making in Complex Organizations,* Jossey-Bass, San Francisco, 1985.

PETERS, T. AND R. WATERMAN, *In Search of Excellence: Lessons from America's Best-Run Companies,* Harper and Row, New York, 1982.

QUINN, JAMES BRIAN, *Strategies for Change: Logical Incrementalism,* Irwin, Homewood, Ill., 1980.

ROBERTS, N., "Transforming Leadership: Sources, Process, Consequences," presented at Academy of Management Conference, Boston, August 1984.

ROGERS, E., *Diffusion of Innovations,* 3rd ed., The Free Press, New York, 1982.

RUTTAN, V. AND HAYAMI, "Toward a Theory of Induced Institutional Innovation," *J. Development Studies,* 20, 4 (1984), 203–223.

SCHON, D., *Beyond the Stable State,* Norton, New York, 1971.

SCHUMPETER, J., *Capitalism, Socialism, and Democracy,* Harper and Row, New York, 1942.

SELZNICK, P., *Leadership in Administration,* Harper and Row, New York, 1957.

SIMON, H. A., *Administrative Behavior,* Macmillan, New York, 1947.

STARBUCK, W., "Organizations as Action Generators," *Amer. J. Sociology,* 48, 1 (1983), 91–115.

TERRYBERRY, S., "The Evolution of Organizational Environments," *Admin. Sci. Quart.,* 12 (1968), 590–613.

TRIST, E., "The Evolution of Sociotechnical Systems as a Conceptual Framework and as an Action Research Program," in A. Van de Ven and W. Joyce (Eds.), *Perspectives on Organization Design and Behavior,* Wiley, New York, 1981, 19–75.

TUSHMAN, M. AND E. ROMANELLI, "Organizational Evolution: A Metamorphosis Model of Convergence and Reorientation," in B. Staw and L. Cummings (Eds.), *Research in Organizational Behavior,* Vol. 7, JAI Press, Greenwich, Conn., 1985.

TVERSKY, A. AND D. KAHNEMAN, "Judgment under Uncertainty: Heuristics and Biases," *Science,* 185 (1974), 1124–1131.

UTTERBACK, J., "The Process of Technological Innovation within the Firm," *Acad. Management J.,* 14 (1971), 75–88.

VAN DE VEN, A., "Problem Solving, Planning, and Innovation. Part 1. Test of the Program Planning Model," *Human Relations,* 33 (1980a), 711–740.

———, "Problem Solving, Planning, and Innovation. Part 2. Speculations for Theory and Practice," *Human Relations,* 33 (1980b), 757–779.

———, "Strategic Management Concerns among CEOs: A Preliminary Research Agenda," Presented at Strategic Management Colloquium, University of Minnesota, Minneapolis, October 1982.

——— AND ASSOCIATES, "The Minnesota Innovation Research Program," Strategic Management Research Center, Minneapolis, Discussion Paper #10, 1984.

——— AND R. HUDSON, "Managing Attention to Strategic Choices," in J. Pennings (Ed.), *Strategic Decision Making in Complex Organizations,* Jossey-Bass, San Francisco, 1984.

VON HIPPEL, E., "Successful Industrial Products from Customer Ideas," *J. Marketing,* (January 1978), 39–40.

WEICK, KARL, *The Social-Psychology of Organizing,* Addison-Wesley, Reading, Mass., 1979.

WILSON, J., "Innovation in Organizations: Notes toward a Theory," in J. Thompson (Ed.), *Approaches to Organizational Design,* University of Pittsburgh Press, Pittsburgh, 1966.

ZALTMAN, G., R. DUNCAN AND J. HOLBEK, *Innovations and Organizations,* Wiley, New York, 1973.

Endnote

1. The author wishes to gratefully recognize the stimulation of ideas for this paper from faculty and student colleagues involved in the Minnesota Innovation Research Program. Helpful comments on earlier drafts of this paper were provided by George Huber, William Joyce, Arie Lewin, Kenneth Mackenzie, and Donald Schon. This research program is supported in part by a major grant from the Organizational Effectiveness Research Programs, Office of Naval Research (Code 4420E), under Contract No. N00014-84-K-0016. Additional research support is being provided by 3M, Honeywell, Control Data, Dayton-Hudson, First Bank Systems, Cenex, Dyco Petroleum, and ADC Corporations.

3

HOW ESTABLISHED FIRMS RESPOND TO THREATENING TECHNOLOGIES

Arnold C. Cooper
Purdue University

Clayton G. Smith
University of Notre Dame

EXECUTIVE OVERVIEW
Major product innovations that create new industries are considered from the perspective of established firms for whom the innovation poses a substitution threat. Based upon a study of eight young industries and twenty-seven leading "threatened firms," common patterns of industry development are considered, as are the participation strategies of those companies that decided to enter the new field. The challenges and pitfalls that were often encountered are examined and implications are developed for firms that choose to enter threatening young industries. While there are no assured success formulas, the discussion highlights some of the problems that can be encountered and suggests possibilities for avoiding them.

ARTICLE

The emergence of a new industry based on a major product innovation (such as the electronic calculator industry in the 1960s) often poses a threat of substitution to companies with a base in a more established industry (e.g., the producers of electro-mechanical calculators). During the early stages of industry development, the extent to which a substitution effect will occur is rarely clear. Nevertheless, managers of firms in the established, threatened industry must decide how to respond to an innovation that has the potential to alter or destroy their companies' existing business.[1]

This article considers the decisions confronting managers of firms in threatened industries and, in particular, the alternative of entering the emerging young industry. Such a response would seem to represent a natural extension of a company's existing business, one that, at a minimum, would allow the firm to build upon its established marketing resources and skills (including brand names, customer relationships, and channels of distribution). Further, at a time when it may be unclear whether the new product will substitute for the old, a strategy of participation in the young industry also provides a hedge, an opportunity to replace lost sales if the traditional product is displaced.

Our specific focus is on the challenges and pitfalls associated with this strategic response to a technological threat.[2] The analysis is based upon a study of eight young

TABLE 3-1 Summary of Industries and Firms Considered

Young Industry (Time Period)*	Established Industry Firms Considered	Young Industry (Time Period)	Established Industry Firms Considered
Ball-Point Pens (1945–1962)	Fountain Pens Eversharp Inc. Parker Pen Co. Sheaffer Pen Co.	Electronic Calculators (1962–1976)	Electromechanical Calculators Litton Industries (Monroe) SCM Corp. Singer Co. (Friden) Victor Comptometer Corp.
CT Scanners (1973–1979)	X-ray/Nuclear Medical Equip General Electric Co. G D Searle & Co. Technicare Corp.	Electronic Watches (1969–1980)	Mechanical Watches Bulova Watch Co. K Hatton & Co. (Seiko) Timex Corp.
Diesel-Electric Locomotives (1924–1953)	Steam Locomotives American Locomotive Co. Baldwin Locomotive Works	Microwave Ovens (1955–1983)	Gas/Electric Ovens General Electric Co. Magic Chef, Inc. Roper Corp. Tappan Co.
Electric Typewriters (1925–1965)	Mechanical Typewriters Remington Rand Royal Typewriter Co. Smith-Corona, Inc. Underwood Company	Transistors (1948–1968)	Receiving Tubes General Electric Co. RCA Raytheon Mfg Co. Sylvania Electric Products, Inc.

*Using decision rules which were based upon yearly changes in unit sales volume and industry development histories, the young industries and the firms were studied during the time period that roughly corresponded to the "introduction" and "rapid growth" stages of development.

industries and twenty-seven "threatened firms," with the firms being chosen based upon the strong competitive positions that they enjoyed in their home industries. Table 3-1 lists the industries, the firms, and the time periods during which the young industries were examined. (The young industries and the firms were studied during the period that roughly corresponded to the "introduction" and "rapid growth" stages of development.) In total, nearly 250 sources of information from the secondary literature were considered in the analysis.

Each young industry involved the commercialization of a major product innovation. The nature of each innovation was such that, while firms from the threatened industry were sometimes able to build upon their existing technical capabilities, important new capabilities were required that were not associated with the traditional product. For example, the CT scanner harnessed both x-ray and data processing technology. Thus, while entrants from the x-ray equipment industry were able to build upon existing technical capabilities, they also had to develop important new resources and skills pertaining to computer technology and product design. Indeed, several innovations were what has been termed "competence-destroying"—so fundamentally different that the technical capabilities for the traditional product were largely irrelevant for the new technology.[3] Finally, these new industries attracted not only firms from the threatened industries, but also start-up firms and companies from other industries as well.

Prior work has presented frameworks for analyzing the potential of new technologies, and the industry attributes that favor "first-movers" versus those who follow.[4] Other studies have found that where established firms enter threatening young industries, they do not pursue the new product aggressively, and that they continue to make substantial commitments to their old product even after its sales begin to decline,[5] the studies have largely attributed these patterns to the constraining effects of sunk costs and internal political difficulties. Recent research has examined the ways in which innovations may enhance or destroy existing competences, and has suggested that unrelated new technologies can be especially challenging.[6] However, little consideration has been given to the pitfalls that may be encountered by entrants from an established, threatened industry. In particular, the ways in which the historic experience of firms from a threatened industry can affect their perceptions of how to compete in the new field have received little attention.

We begin by considering the characteristics of young industries that typically develop around new technologies, characteristics that have important implications for companies

TABLE 3-2   Decisions Concerning a Strategy of Participation

Timing of Entry
Early ————————————————————————————————➤ Late
Magnitude of Commitments
Token ————————————————————————————————➤ Major
Degree of Organizational Separation
Close Linkages with Established Organization ————➤ Separate/Independent Organization
Competitive Strategy for New Business
Traditional Ways of Competing ————————————➤ New Ways of Competing

Note: The decisions outlined above range along a spectrum, such as from early to late entry, etc. Further, some decisions may change over time, with, for instance, a token early commitment followed by later commitments of greater magnitude.

that enter an emerging field. The participation strategies of the leading threatened firms that entered these new industries are then considered. As noted in Table 3-2, a strategy of participation involves decisions along a spectrum concerning the timing of entry and magnitude of commitments, as well as how the new business should be organized and the strategy it should follow. Our findings indicate that entrants from the threatened industries made these decisions in characteristic ways—and often encountered particular pitfalls in the process. Special attention is given in the discussion to these pitfalls, and to possible reasons for them. The implications of the analysis for decisions concerning a strategy of participation in a threatening young industry are examined in the final section. While there are no assured success formulas, our intention is to highlight some of the problems that can be encountered and suggest possibilities for avoiding them.

Young Industries and Technological Threats

Any assessment of a technological threat obviously involves an appraisal of the new technology and the extent to which it will have advantages in meeting user needs. What may be less obvious, however, is the necessity of appraising the nature of the industry that is likely to develop around a major product innovation, and how competition in the new field may differ from competition in the established, threatened industry.

What may be less obvious, however, is the necessity of appraising the nature of the industry that is likely to develop around a major product innovation, and how competition in the new field may differ from competition in the established, threatened industry.

Our study of these eight young industries highlights the common patterns of industry development—patterns that managers of threatened firms should be sensitive to if they consider entering an emerging field that poses a threat of substitution.

In the eight industries, the first commercial introduction of the new product was made by a firm from the established industry in three cases (electric typewriters, electronic watches, and transistors), firms from outside the industry introduced the others. But in every instance, early versions of the new product were crude and expensive, and there was great uncertainty about how rapidly the market would develop. For example, the first electronic watches were unreliable, and so bulky and unattractive that they were sometimes referred to as "quarter-pounders." Consumers were also deterred from purchasing early microwave ovens by the high price—roughly $1,500, in 1950s dollars—and the fact that microwave cooking left cold spots and changed food colors. In some instances, the initial lack of complementary products (e.g., cookbooks and cookware for microwave cooking) retarded the market's development as well.

In this context, early entrants invariably had to overcome substantial technical difficulties, and they often had to remain patient when the market developed slowly Indeed, in some instances, the new product may never gain widespread acceptance. But in all of the cases studied here, an industry did begin to emerge, and a time of rapid growth followed that promised substantial opportunities to participating firms. Beyond the prospect of significant increases in revenues, the environment created by burgeoning demand often limited competitive pressures and permitted lucrative profit margins. In addition to later entrants from the established, threatened industry, the growing promise of the new product encouraged start-up firms and established companies from other industries to enter the field as well.

Even in the "growth stage," however, these industries were characterized by high levels of uncertainty and risk. During this period, there usually was no clear success formula and firms often followed different strategies; only time proved—or disproved—the validity of the assumptions on which these strategies were based. Thus, steam locomotive producers found that their new competitor in the diesel-electric field, General Motors, disdained their traditional custom manufacturing methods and produced standard products for inventory instead. In fact, firms from the established industry and entrants from outside that industry often had different ideas about how to compete. In such cases, the traditional firms had to appraise and respond to the novel strategies that their new competitors chose to pursue.

During the time before "dominant designs" became established, there was much experimentation with different technical approaches and product designs.[7] In the transistor industry's early years, for example, it was not clear whether germanium or silicon transistors would prevail. Similarly, in the electronic watch industry, models with light-emitting diode (LED) and liquid crystal displays (LCDs) dueled for market acceptance Industry participants had to decide which approaches "to bet on," and some companies committed to what later proved to be blind alleys.

For firms from the established industry, long-standing competitive strengths did not necessarily provide an advantage in the new field. All of the industries required technical resources and skills that were not associated with the traditional product; in several cases, the traditional technical capabilities were largely irrelevant. For example, the ability of electromechanical calculator firms to produce precise mechanical parts was of little value for electronic calculators.

Rapid rates of change also characterized the industries. To stay in the game, participants often had to field successive generations of the product as the state of the art advanced; in CT scanners, four generations followed one another in almost as many years. Companies also had to cope with constant changes in manufacturing methods. In transistors, one vacuum tube firm blundered when it built the most automated plant for germanium transistors, shortly before silicon transistors and newer manufacturing processes came to dominate. And while the competitive environment was usually not intense initially, cut-throat competition often quickly emerged when the period of rapid growth began to wane—in some cases with little warning.[8] In this context, participating firms needed strong R&D and financial capabilities to remain competitive, and to absorb the inevitable setbacks and risks.

And surprisingly, even established marketing capabilities for the traditional product did not always provide a long-term advantage, as several vacuum tube firms discovered. While their distribution networks were important in the tube business as a means of quickly delivering replacement components, the value of this capability for transistors waned as the new product became more and more reliable.

In summary, these industries were characterized by high levels of uncertainty, new competitors that had different ideas about how to compete, alternative and unproven technical approaches and product designs, rapid rates of change and, in some cases, by the obsolescence of established technical and marketing capabilities for the traditional product. The characteristics of the young industries and the corresponding managerial implications are displayed in Table 3-3. A typical pattern of sales development for a

TABLE 3-3 Characteristics of Young Industries

Attribute	*Managerial Implications*
New product crude and expensive at first. Sometimes, an initial lack of complementary products	Difficult to judge rate at which market will develop. Often must overcome substantial technical difficulties, and remain patient if market develops slowly
Entrants often start-up firms and established firms from other industries	Difficult to predict competitors' actions. Must appraise and respond to "different" strategies
Alternative and unproven technical approaches and product designs	Risks associated with "betting on" particular approaches/designs
Rapid rates of change, especially in product and manufacturing methods	Strong R&D and financial capabilities needed to remain competitive over time
New technical resources and skills required. Existing technical/marketing capabilities sometimes of limited or little value	Established competitive strengths may not provide a long-term advantage

FIGURE 3-1   Transistor/Receiving Tube Unit Volume Comparison

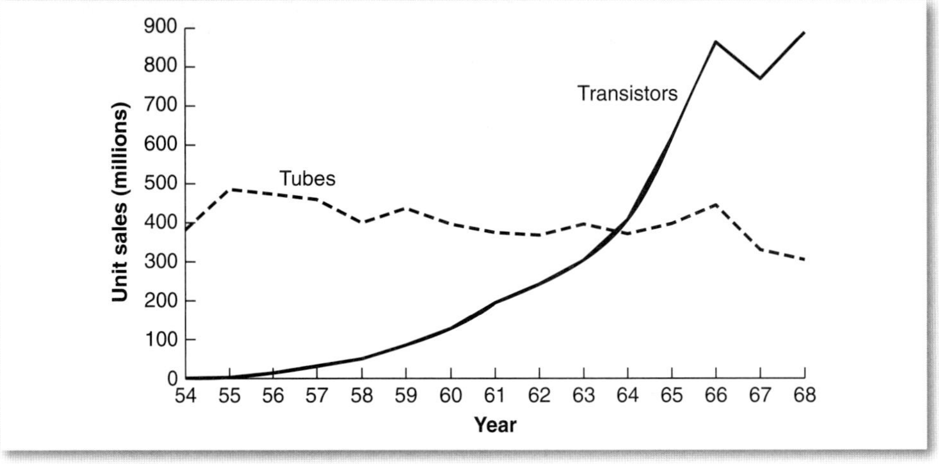

Sources: Business Week (various issues). Electronic Industries Association.

new technology (transistors), and its impact on the traditional counterpart (receiving tubes) is also shown in Figure 3-1. Because of their dynamic nature, competitive positions were often unstable; success was often transient. Commitment to these new technologies was like entering a poker game in which the stakes kept increasing and the rules were not at all clear. Overall, these industries differed markedly from the mature, relatively stable industries that were threatened.

The Strategy of Participation: Challenges and Pitfalls

We now consider the strategic issues confronting a firm that chooses to respond to a technological threat by entering the new field. A decision to participate in the young industry involves determinations concerning the (1) timing of entry; (2) magnitude of commitments; (3) degree of organizational separation between new and traditional product activities; and (4) competitive strategy for the new business. In the sections that follow, the participation strategies of the twenty-seven threatened firms are examined along these dimensions. Particular attention is given to the problems that many of the firms encountered, and to possible reasons for their occurrence.

Timing of Entry

Prior research indicates that early entry by established firms into a young industry is associated with higher levels of long-term performance.[9] Balanced against this, however, are the risks of an early entry, including the risk that the new product may never achieve commercial success. When faced with a major product innovation, a firm often must contend with the challenges of assessing the potential of an unproven technology and the speed with which market acceptance will occur. Further, it must appraise the resources and skills required to compete at a time when the requirements for success are not clear. Overall, a firm must decide whether and when to enter under rather uncertain circumstances.

There is a common view that established firms, when threatened by major product innovations, lack the vision and will to commit to the new technology. (For example, Levitt's classic, "Marketing Myopia," gives example after example of firms that failed to define their business broadly, and thereby missed opportunities or subsequently failed.)[10]

For example, Eversharp and Sheaffer, leading producers of fountain pens, were two of the earliest companies to introduce ball-point pens in 1946. Unfortunately, their new pens—and those of many new entrants as well—tended to skip, blot, and even leak into pockets. One industry observer condemned the early ball-point pen as "the

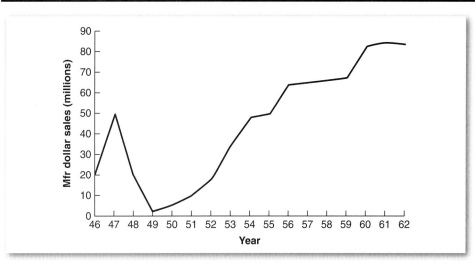

FIGURE 3-2 Ball Point Pen Sales

Source: Writing Instrument Manufacturers Association.

In reviewing these twenty-seven leading firms, however, it was found that all entered the young industries. Indeed, twenty-one entered relatively early, before sales of the new product began to grow rapidly. Far from ignoring the new technology, these firms seemed to recognize its possibilities at an early date. But, surprisingly, eight of these twenty-one early entrants made abortive commitments, in which they entered but then withdrew before achieving much success.

only pen which would make eight copies and no original." After an initial fad phase, public disenchantment set in, and the ball-point pen industry virtually disappeared. Eversharp and Sheaffer both withdrew from the market and many of the new entrants went bankrupt. In 1950, improved ball-point pens were introduced by a new firm, Papermate. Subsequently, the young industry began to develop rapidly, as shown in Figure 3-2.

Similar patterns were observed with producers of mechanical typewriters. Remington and Royal had electric typewriters as early as 1925. However, their initial offerings were bulky, noisy, and prone to break down; the two firms discontinued their efforts after three or four years. (IBM, which never made mechanical models, introduced the first commercially successful electric in 1934.) And American Locomotive introduced a number of experimental diesel-electric engines beginning in 1924. However, because of their high weight-to-power ratio and other difficulties, American subsequently ceased its development efforts. (In 1934, General Motors, which never produced steam locomotives, made the first successful introduction of a diesel-electric based upon improved diesel-engine technology developed in its laboratories.)

In several cases (e.g., Eversharp, Sheaffer, and Royal), it appeared that the firm had little in the way of an R&D orientation that might have provided experience in managing the process of introducing *and improving* major product innovations. While they recognized the new technology's potential, they seemed unable to make the further advancements that later led to commercial success. Further, in industries such as diesel-electric locomotives and electronic calculators, the new technology was so different from the traditional that the technical capabilities for the old product were largely irrelevant. At the outset, the firms may not have fully recognized the fact that their existing engineering/production capabilities would be of little value in the new field. But this fact undoubtedly made it more difficult for them to overcome the technical obstacles that all of the early entrants faced.

Of the eight firms whose initial entry was abortive, two companies resumed their commercial efforts within a year. However, on average, the other six firms did not do so for more than nine years. For example, American Locomotive did not renew its efforts with diesel-electrics until 1936, two years after General Motors made the first successful introduction of the new product. Having been "burned" once, these firms seemed content to leave the pioneering to others. With one exception (General Electric in microwave ovens), the six firms did not resume their commercial efforts until after the new product's viability had been demonstrated by other firms from outside the established industry.

Magnitude of Commitments

Where corporate management chooses to enter the new field, important decisions must be made over time concerning the magnitude of commitments. The firm's initial involvement could vary widely, ranging from a token effort with only a few prototypes to major and immediate investments. The magnitude of commitments may also change over time as the young industry evolves. Prior research has argued that major early investments should often lead to greater long-term success, as the firm reaps the benefits of a stronger competitive position.[11] However, such investments may also lead to substantial commitments to the "wrong" technical approach (e.g., germanium versus silicon transistors) or to a market that develops very slowly (e.g., microwave ovens).

Of the twenty-seven companies examined, twenty-four made substantial investments over time. But while four of the twenty-four firms took an aggressive stance from the start, the investments made over time by most of the remaining twenty were uneven. It was quite common for these latter firms to make a limited initial commitment (relative to their capabilities), and permit other companies—usually from outside the established industry—to lead in improving the new product and in gaining market acceptance for it. Typically, they would then mount a more vigorous effort as the industry developed. This approach had the virtue of delaying major investments until after many of the technical and market uncertainties had faded. However, as it turned out, the net effect in most cases was to fall behind and to make it much more difficult to establish a viable long-term competitive position.

During the microwave oven industry's early growth stages (1972–1975), for instance, there were challenges in stimulating primary demand, in teaching consumers how to cook with the new product, and in overcoming fears about radiation. Here, the conventional oven producers made very limited initial commitments relative to entrants from outside the range industry, notably Raytheon/Amana. As an example of this, Figure 3-3 displays company advertising expenditures for 1975 and 1977, the contrast in emphasis between the conventional range producers and Amana is striking. As sales growth accelerated further in the years after 1975, the conventional oven producers began to make more significant commitments. Still, it was through efforts of new entrants such as Amana that the image of the microwave oven was changed from that of an expensive "hot-dog cooker" to a legitimate cooking device.[12]

While Timex entered electronic watch manufacturing early, the firm continued to concentrate on mechanical watches in its marketing efforts. In fact, at a trade show in 1975, the firm's director of sales refused to be photographed holding a model from its electronic line, he said that the company's big push that year was still in traditional

FIGURE 3-3 1975/1977 Microwave Oven Advertising Expenditures

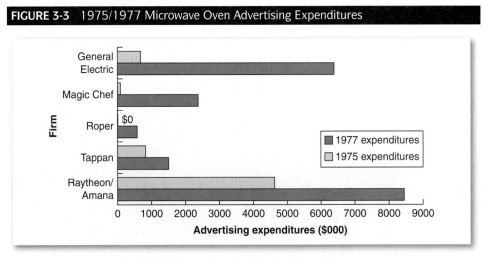

Source: Leading National Advertisers, Inc.

watches. The firm was also slow to develop internal R&D/manufacturing capabilities for semiconductor components (which were critical to the new product's performance, quality, and cost), preferring instead to rely on outside suppliers for its requirements. Only after prices for electronic watches began to tumble into the firm's low-price niche did Timex begin to make a strong commitment. However, the combination of increasing competition and a late start in mastering the technology proved to be a severe handicap, each time the firm introduced a newer watch line, other producers had already fielded superior models at lower prices. In 1980, after four years of heavy investments, Timex was still struggling to build and market electronic watches profitably.

Similarly, while Litton/Monroe and SCM entered the electronic calculator industry at an early date, their initial efforts largely took the form of marketing electronic desk-top models that were produced by Canon and Toshiba (firms that had never been active in electromechanical calculators). To a considerable degree, this was due to their belief that electronic calculators would be mainly used by scientists and engineers—small, specialized customer groups that had previously relied on large computers for computational needs. And as the division president of Monroe said later of his company's early participation, "Our effort in electronics, I think logically, was not to create competition for these electromechanical machines. It was not to take away the established base, but to seek new business over that base."[13]

Subsequently the broader applicability of the new product in the office equipment and other segments became more apparent, and Monroe and SCM began a serious effort to develop their own skills for electronic calculators. But by this time, Canon, Toshiba, and other new entrants had gained a formidable lead in the requisite technical and manufacturing capabilities, and were rapidly becoming established in the market under their own brand names.

Finally, while American and Baldwin Locomotive entered the market for diesel electrics, they continued to devote most of their energies to steam locomotives for several years while General Motors was gaining a foothold in the new field. (As late as 1938, American's president spoke to the Western Railway Club, saying, "For a century, as you know, steam has been the principal railroad motive power. It still is and, in my view, will continue to be.")[14] By the time they began to make a serious effort in diesel-electrics, General Motors had already gained a significant lead in product design and had developed facilities and methods for mass-producing its product. In addition, GM had also established a solid reputation and strong customer relationships with many of the major railroads in the United States.

> *At the same time, however, it is important to have decision makers who are enthusiastically committed to the new product, even though it may cannibalize sales of the traditional product.*

While most of the firms examined made substantial commitments over time, these investments were made only after the potential of the new product had become apparent. Such firms seemed to harbor the expectation (initially) that the new product would not penetrate the core markets of the traditional business. In several cases, there were also concerns that the new product's early imperfections could tarnish the firm's reputation, as such, there was a reluctance to make a full commitment until the product was "proven." In virtually every case, however, these companies appeared to underestimate the ability of firms from outside the established industry to overcome important technological obstacles, to gain market acceptance for the new product, and to establish a defensible competitive position. Only after the miscalculation became apparent did these firms begin to mount a more vigorous effort.

Degree of Organizational Separation

The third area to be considered concerns the degree of organizational separation between new and traditional product activities. In choosing to enter the young industry, it would be natural to consider using the established organization for the new product. Potentially, this arrangement could provide significant cost savings, facilitate the coordination of efforts with the traditional product, and permit the new business to benefit from the skills of executives from the traditional business. At the same time, however, it is important to have decision makers who are enthusiastically committed to the new product, even though it may cannibalize sales of the traditional product.[15]

Further, it may also be necessary to violate the conventional wisdom that has developed over time in the established organization.

Specific information on parent-business organizational decisions was available for seventeen of the twenty-seven firms; eleven of the seventeen appeared to have established close organizational linkages between new and traditional product activities. For example, based upon information obtained from secondary sources (e.g., annual reports, business articles, and industry studies), it appeared that Remington, Royal, Smith-Corona, and Underwood handled the production, sales, and distribution of electric typewriters through the departments that had been used for mechanical models. Similarly, Tilton's study of the transistor industry and other sources indicated that the entrants from the vacuum tube industry had placed their semiconductor operations in their tube divisions, where tube experts were the principal decision makers.[16]

However, in a number of cases where the new and traditional technologies were fundamentally different, decisions to use the established organization proved to be ill-advised. Thus, while other firms were lowering costs by building new manufacturing facilities, Victor Comptometer decided to use its existing organization and build electronic calculators at an old three-story plant in Chicago, where electromechanical machines were being made. Victor eventually made nearly everything for its electronic calculators but the semiconductor chips at this facility. Unfortunately, the net result was a line of high-priced, high-cost machines that brought little or no return. As an executive from a rival firm said later, "Victor failed to realize that its mechanical and technical expertise meant nothing in the electronics age."

More generally, when the new product was closely tied to the established organization, business strategy decisions were often constrained by concerns about the obsolescence of existing investments. This appears to have been true for RCA, where transistor activities were initially placed within the established vacuum tube division. In 1960, eight years after entering the new field, RCA recognized the problem and separated its tube and semiconductor operations. However, the two divisions were recombined three years later when the transistor unit began to experience losses. The latter decision, in addition to reintroducing the original problem, apparently undermined the morale of the semiconductor people, as their unit's strategic direction kept changing with each reorganization.[17]

These examples illustrate the fact that there were no easy answers to the question of how to organize the new business. There were tradeoffs between the synergies to be gained from having close linkages with the established organization, and the benefits of having the flexibility and drive of an independent management group. However, it appeared that the tendency among these firms was to forge close organizational linkages between activities for the new and traditional products. This decision may also have influenced the ways in which they chose to compete in the young industry, which we will now consider.

> *Even where an independent unit was created for the new product, other problems sometimes emerged. At Timex for example, the decision to establish a separate organization for electronic watches in 1976 led to fierce rivalry between the mechanical and electronic groups. One old-guard manager acknowledged that his people had stood by while new managers in the electronic unit made mistakes that the company had made years earlier. Indeed, the rivalry became so intense that the electronic people accused the mechanical group of withholding essential information, and senior management had to enter the fray to lay the charge to rest.[18] Needless to say, these organizational difficulties compounded the firm's competitive problems in the electronic watch market.*

Competitive Strategy for the New Business

The final issue to be examined concerns the strategy that is developed for competing in the young industry. In making decisions concerning competitive strategy, firms from the established, threatened industry have a substantial base of experience to draw upon. Particularly when the firm's strategy in the established industry has historically been successful, it would be natural to consider employing the same basic approach in the new field (essentially to fold the new product into the existing strategy). However, if the new technology requires, or makes possible, different product concepts or ways of competing, strategic approaches that are based on "the conventional wisdom" may be less likely to succeed.

In cases where a new product concept emerged, the traditional firms rarely pioneered the new design. For example, when Tappan and General Electric entered the infant microwave oven industry in the mid-1950s, they utilized product designs (built-in models and free-standing double ovens) that were quite similar to conventional models.

However, because such designs implied the replacement of a household's existing range and also since microwave ovens proved to be ill-suited for cooking meats and other foods, sales were very limited. Indeed, rapid market growth did not begin until after Raytheon/Amana entered the field with its countertop design in 1967—a configuration that was intended to supplement, not replace a household's existing range. Further, while other new competitors quickly followed Raytheon's lead, conventional oven producers were slow to respond to the promising countertop innovation. (Tappan and GE did not begin self-manufacture of countertop ovens until 1973 and 1974, respectively, more than half a decade after Raytheon/Amana pioneered the countertop design.)[19]

Similarly, where new ways of competing emerged, traditional producers were usually slow to recognize the implications. In electromechanical calculators, for example, direct-sales organizations and service networks had historically been important requirements for success. In fact, the leading producers of such machines each had approximately 1500 sales and service personnel in several hundred company-owned branches. As a senior executive at Friden said at the time, "You don't have a chance in this business without this capability." However, firms from outside the established industry chose to sell their electronic desk-top calculators through office equipment dealers. Because this permitted them to deal with a few hundred dealers rather than with thousands of end-users, a sales force of less than fifty people was sufficient.

If the new technology requires, or makes possible, different product concepts or ways of competing, strategic approaches that are based on "the conventional wisdom" may be less likely to succeed.

Office equipment dealers did not have the facilities for servicing electronic calculators. (Friden attempted to exploit this fact in magazine ads that were aimed at foreign producers of electronic calculators. The ads asked potential customers, "Does an imported repairman come with your imported calculator?") However, as the reliability of the new product (which had few moving parts) improved relative to electromechanical models (which had an average downtime of ten percent), the need for a strong service network waned. The new competitors also engaged in aggressive price competition, a practice that was uncommon in electromechanical calculators. As the new technology improved over time, market prices for most desk-top models fell to levels that made it difficult to cover the costs of direct-selling efforts. As a result, several firms from the established industry, such as SCM Corp., were eventually forced to develop a network of office equipment dealers for their electronic calculators.[20]

Analogous patterns were found in other industries as well. In ball-point pens, the concept of a throw-away pen was pioneered not by a fountain pen producer, but by BIC. In diesel-electric locomotives, it was General Motors that pioneered the concept of a standardized locomotive produced for inventory. And in transistors, firms from the vacuum tube industry emphasized process innovation in their business strategies, as they had in vacuum tubes. In contrast, young semiconductor firms, such as Texas Instruments, focused on product innovation—and sometimes obsoleted the designs of transistors that the vacuum tube companies were trying to produce in volume.[21]

These patterns suggest that the historic experience of threatened firms in the established industry often "colored" their perceptions of how to compete effectively in the emerging young industry.

These patterns suggest that the historic experience of threatened firms in the established industry often "colored" their perceptions of how to compete effectively in the emerging young industry. As noted previously, these firms were often among the earliest entrants in the young industries. But they rarely took the lead in developing new product concepts or ways of competing that might have allowed them to better capitalize upon the new technology's potential. Rather, they tended to use the same basic approaches that had been successful in the established industry.

Patterns of Performance

Given the difficulties that have been described, an obvious question is, "What were the overall patterns of performance for these twenty-seven firms?" To explore this issue, the firms were classified as "successful" or "unsuccessful," based upon their survival or non-survival in the given industry, market share data, and descriptive information concerning business performance obtained from secondary sources (e.g., annual reports, business articles, industry surveys, and stock reports). As noted earlier, these twenty-seven companies were all leading firms in the established industries that were threatened. However, despite their presumed advantages, twenty of the twenty-seven firms were unable to develop and sustain a strong competitive position in the young industries.[22]

The remaining seven firms were classified as having been successful, through the end of the study period. The firms were:

- Parker Pen (ball-point pens)
- General Electric (CT scanners)
- Technicare (CT scanners)
- Smith-Corona (electric typewriters)
- Litton/Monroe (electronic calculators)
- K. Hattori/Seiko (electronic watches)
- General Electric (microwave ovens)

For these companies, there was no single path to a strong competitive position, and they, too, encountered the problems that have been described (see Table 3-4). The entry of five of the seven firms either preceded or coincided with the "take-off" in market sales. Of the five firms, GE discontinued its microwave oven effort for several years when the slow rate of market development became apparent, K. Hattori/Seiko withdrew from electronic watches for nearly a year because of technical problems with its original offering. The two remaining firms, Parker Pen and Smith-Corona, were late entrants. Both had limited R&D and financial capabilities, but their late entry allowed them to avoid some of the technical challenges that earlier entrants faced. They also focused on niche markets (high-priced ball-point pens and portable electrics) and largely avoided the more competitive mainstream segments.

Despite their presumed advantages, twenty of the twenty-seven firms were unable to develop and sustain a strong competitive position in the young industries.

Relative to their capabilities, five of the firms made significant or strong commitments from the outset. While Litton/Monroe and General Electric (in microwave ovens) made only limited initial investments, their considerable R&D and financial capabilities enabled them to establish a strong position in the new field after they began to make a whole hearted effort. Regarding organizational decisions, three of the four firms for which data were available appeared to maintain a high degree of separation between new and traditional product activities. Finally, with respect to competitive strategy decisions, these firms rarely pioneered new product concepts or ways of

TABLE 3-4 The Successful Firms

Company (Young Industry)	Time of Entry	Magnitude of Commitments	Degree of Org. Separation	Competitive Strategy for New Business
Parker Pen Co. (Ball Point Pens)	Late Entrant	Strong Commitment	—	Traditional strategic approach employed (Ignored throwaway pen segment)
General Electric Co. (CT Scanners)	Entered at outset of growth stage	Strong Commitment	High	Traditional strategic approach employed
Technicare Corp. (CT Scanners)	Entered at outset of growth stage	Strong Commitment	High	Traditional strategic approach employed
Smith Corona, Inc. (Elec Typewriters)	Late Entrant	Significant Commitment	Low	Traditional strategic approach employed
Litton/Monroe (Electronic Cals)	Early Entrant	Ltd → Strong Commitment	—	Traditional strategic approach employed (Slow response to emergence of new distribution methods)
K. Hattori/Seiko (Electronic Watches)	Early Entrant Initial Entry Abortive	Strong Commitment	—	Traditional strategic approach employed
General Electric Co. (Microwave Ovens)	Early Entrant Initial Entry Abortive	Ltd → Strong Commitment	High	Traditional strategic approach employed (Slow response to countertop Innovation)

Note: These firms were all relatively successful as of the end of the study period. However, it should be noted that the fortunes of several subsequently waned when they later faced severe competitive pressures from overseas manufacturers or from still newer technologies.

TABLE 3-5 Pitfalls of Typical Strategy Decisions

Typical Strategic Decision	*Pitfalls Encountered*
Entered early (before market began to grow rapidly)	Often lacked resources and skills required to overcome initial technical obstacles, sometimes became disenchanted when market did not develop quickly
Limited initial commitment, mounted more substantial effort as industry developed	Often allowed new competitors to establish formidable technical lead; became much more difficult for firm to develop viable long-term competitive position
Established close organizational linkages between new and traditional product activities	Decision-making attuned to competition in established industry/needs of traditional business. Problem of divided loyalties sometimes constrained firm's actions in new field
Utilized product concepts/ways of competing that had been successful in established industry	Wedded to "conventional wisdom." Often slow to recognize potential/implications of new product concepts and ways of competing

competing. As it turned out, however, Parker Pen was able to ignore the throw-away pen because it never threatened its high-priced niche. And while GE and Litton were eventually compelled to respond to new product concepts and methods of distribution, they did so before their position was severely undermined.[23]

Avoiding the Pitfalls

The decision to enter an emerging young industry from a base in an established, threatened industry is clearly fraught with challenges and pitfalls. The "typical" participation strategy decisions of the firms examined, and the corresponding pitfalls are summarized in Table 3-5. The limited number of successful firms makes any discussion of assured success formulas problematic. Indeed, much may depend upon how a young industry develops, including the extent to which there prove to be sizable market segments that are not attacked by new competitors. But based upon the experiences of these twenty-seven firms, it is possible to highlight some of the potential problems that are associated with a strategy of participation, and to suggest possibilities for avoiding them.

In relation to the time-of-entry decision, most of the firms examined recognized the possibilities of the new technology at an early date, and entered the field before the market began to grow rapidly. There was little evidence that management "buried its head in the sand" and refused to recognize the new product's potential. However, some of the companies may not have appreciated the implications of an early commitment. These firms often lacked the resources and skills required to overcome the initial technical obstacles, and they sometimes became disenchanted when the market did not develop quickly.

The implication is that, in considering an early entry, management should carefully appraise the firm's technical capabilities relative to the challenges involved. The challenge is not simply to introduce the new product; it is to be able to make the further advancements in performance, quality, and cost that will be required for commercial success. Where the firm's capabilities are lacking, it should be understood that the inevitable technical obstacles will be especially difficult, developing the necessary competences will be a critical task. Further, management should consider the extent to which the firm has the patience and the will to overcome substantial technical difficulties, to work closely with early customers, and to make continuing investments even if the market develops slowly. If these qualities are lacking, a decision to enter early is likely to be regretted.

The challenge is not simply to introduce the new product; it is to be able to make the further advancements in performance, quality, and cost that will be required for commercial success.

In terms of the magnitude of commitments, these firms often made limited early commitments—but then mounted a more vigorous effort as the industry developed. Perhaps this was due to the high initial levels of technical and market uncertainty, or organizational resistance to more substantial investments. However, the result in most cases was to fall behind more aggressive entrants, usually from outside the threatened industry. Thus, where a limited early commitment is being considered, management should weigh the impact of this on the firm's ability to compete later in the industry's development, possibly when other firms have established a commanding technical lead. Deferring heavy investments may be possible if the firm has very strong R&D and financial capabilities that it can bring to bear (e.g., GE in microwave ovens), or if it can find markets where competition is not established (e.g., portable electrics for Smith-Corona). But, in general, limited early commitments seem likely to impair the firm's ability to establish a viable long-term competitive position.

Concerning the degree of organizational separation, close linkages between new and traditional product activities appeared to be fairly common among these firms. Indeed, there will often be synergies to be gained from utilizing the existing organization for the new product. But in considering this approach, management should recognize that decisions concerning the new product will take place within an administrative system and culture that is attuned to competition in the established industry, and the needs of the traditional business. Management should be especially sensitive to the problem of divided loyalties that may result if the existing organization is used, and of the constraining effect that this may have upon the firm's actions in the young industry. In addition, if the decision is made to create an independent unit for the new product, senior managers should recognize that a high level of sponsorship and protection on their part may be required for this arrangement to succeed.

Finally, with respect to the strategy that is developed for competing in the new field, there seemed to be a tendency for firms to use the same basic approaches that were successful in the established industry—to fold the new product into the traditional strategy. It may be that they viewed the new product simply as a new way of meeting needs they had previously served (for example, cooking food with a microwave oven rather than a gas or electric oven). Nevertheless, such firms seemed to be slow in recognizing possibilities for employing new product concepts and ways of competing that might have allowed them to capitalize upon the new technology's potential.

The implication is that management should be willing to allow new or experimental strategies, and should carefully monitor the approaches that are pursued by other entrants. Appraising the strategies of new competitors may be especially important, since they will often possess different resources and skills, different ideas about how to compete, and little interest in the status quo. Overall, the conventional wisdom may no longer apply. Those who view an emerging young industry through the lens of their experience in an established, threatened industry may see what is familiar more clearly than what is different. A sensitivity to the problems encountered by the firms studied here may increase the chances for success.

About the Authors

Arnold C. Cooper is Louis A. Weil, Jr. professor of management, Purdue University, and has been a member of the faculties at the Harvard Business School, Stanford University, Manchester Business School (England), and IMEDE Management Development Institute (Switzerland). He is the author or co-author of five books and has written a number of articles on entrepreneurship, strategic management, and the management of technology. Cooper has served on the Federal Advisory Committee on Industrial Innovation and the Indiana Employment Development Commission. He has been chairman of the Division of Business Policy and Planning of The Academy of Management and has served on a number of Editorial Boards. He was a recipient of the "Distinguished Scholar Award" of the International Council on Small Business.

Clayton Smith is assistant professor of management at the University of Notre Dame. Professor Smith holds the BBA degree from Pace University and the MS and PhD degrees from Purdue University. He is a member of the Academy of Management, the American Management Association, and the Strategic Management Society. Professor Smith's research interests and publications concern diversification by established firms into young industries (and the factors that affect their performance in that context), and technological substitution.

Endnotes

1. The potential impact of major product innovations upon established industries was described by Schumpeter, who spoke of the "creative destruction" which "strikes not at the margins of the profits and the outputs of existing firms, but at their foundations and their very lives." J. A. Schumpeter, *The Theory of Economic Development,* (Cambridge, MA Harvard University Press, 1934).

2. Other strategic options that are oriented toward defending the traditional product against a substitution threat (for example, by attempting to improve its performance cost, or by focusing on market segments that are less likely to adopt the new) are discussed by A. C. Cooper and D. Schendel. "Strategic Responses to Technological Threats," *Business Horizons,* 19(1), 1976, 61–69; and M. Porter, *Competitive Advantage,* (New York, NY The Free Press, 1985).

3. M. L. Tushman and P. Anderson, "Technological Discontinuities and Organizational Environments," *Administrative Science Quarterly,* 31, 1986, 439–465.

4. See M. E. Porter, op cit., 1985, and D. J. Teece, "Profiting from Technological Innovation. Implications for Integration, Collaboration, Licensing and Public Policy," in D. J. Teece (Ed.), *The Competitive Challenge Strategies for Industrial Innovation and Renewal* (Cambridge, MA Ballinger, 1987).

5. R. N. Foster, *Innovation: The Attacker's Advantage* (New York Summit Books, 1986); and A. Cooper and D. Schendel, op cit., 1976.

6. W. J. Abernathy and K. B. Clark, "Innovation. Mapping the Winds of Creative Destruction," *Research Policy*, 14, 3–22. M. L. Tushman and P. Anderson, op cit., 1986, and C. G. Smith. "Responding to Substitution Threats A Framework for Assessment," *Journal of Engineering and Technology Management,* 7(1), 1990, 17–36.

7. W. J. Abernathy and J. M. Utterback, "Patterns of Industrial Innovation," *Technology Review,* 80(7), 1978, 41–47.

8. In CT Scanners, for example, sales fell substantially after the advent of restrictive "certificate of need" legislation. (The legislation required health care providers accepting federal reimbursements for medical procedures to obtain prior approval for all capital expenditures in excess of $100,000.)

9. C. G. Smith and A. C. Cooper, "Established Companies Diversifying Into Young Industries: A Comparison of Firms with Different Levels of Performance," *Strategic Management Journal,* 9(2), 1988, 111–121.

10. T. Levitt, "Marketing Myopia," *Harvard Business Review,* 38(4), 1960, 26–37.

11. R. E. Biggadike, *Corporate Diversification. Entry, Strategy, and Performance* (Cambridge, MA Harvard University Press, 1979).

12. C. G. Smith, "Established Companies Diversifying into Young Industries. A Comparison of Firms With Different Levels of Performance," unpublished PhD dissertation. Purdue University, 1985.

13. B. A. Majumdar, "Innovations, Product Developments and Technology Transfers An Empirical Study of Dynamic Competitive Advantage. The Case of Electronic Calculators," unpublished PhD dissertation, Case Western Reserve University, 1977.

14. A Study of the Antitrust Laws, Hearings Before the Subcommittee on Antitrust and Monopoly of the Committee on the Judiciary, U.S. Senate, First Session, December 9, 1955, 3975.

15. R. N. Foster, op cit., 1986.

16. J. E. Tilton, *International Diffusion of Technology The Case of Semiconductors* (Washington, DC: Brookings Institute, 1971).

17. W. R. Soukup, "Strategic Response to Technological Threat in the Electronics Components Industry," unpublished Ph. D dissertation, Purdue University, 1979.

18. M. Magnet, "Timex Takes the Torture Test," *Fortune,* June 27, 1983, 112.

19. C. G. Smith, op cit., 1985.

20. Majumdar, op cit., 1977; and Creative Strategies International, *Electronic Calculators* (San Jose, CA: Creative Strategies, Inc., 1978).

21. J. E. Tilton, op cit., 1971.

22. Of these twenty firms, six withdrew from the given industry, and one surrendered its independence to become a division of another company. In each case, information obtained from secondary sources indicated that the decision was due to financial difficulties stemming from the firm's participation in the young industry. The other thirteen firms survived, but market share data and secondary source descriptions of business performance made it clear that they had been relegated to marginal or second tier positions by the end of the study period.

23. Interestingly, while GE was slow to respond to the countertop oven, it gradually learned what the customer was looking for. In 1978, the firm introduced the "Spacemaker" oven which was designed to be mounted below a kitchen cabinet. The design quickly gained acceptance among space-cramped apartment dwellers and helped GE to emerge as the industry leader in 1982.

4

THE ROLE OF CORE COMPETENCIES IN THE CORPORATION

Dramatic Growth Will Take Place When We Focus on the Organization—with Technology a Part—Rather Than on Technology Alone

C. K. Prahalad

OVERVIEW

The scorecard of Western firms—be it performance along dimensions such as quality, cycle time and cost, or growth and new business creation—has been less than satisfactory. We need a new approach to evaluating the value added by senior management. One such approach is outlined. It is argued that strategy must be seen as "stretch" and the critical role of senior management as creating the capacity to "leverage corporate resources." A set of concepts that enable managers to do this is outlined. Finally, the agenda for managers during this decade is seen as profitable growth—not just restructuring.

The debate about the competitiveness of Western firms in a wide variety of industries inevitably triggers debates about technology policy and investment levels in technology. While the preoccupation with investment in R&D and the list of "critical technologies" are important inputs to that debate, the real issue for most Western firms is internal capacity for new business development. Technology leadership is but an enabler.

Therefore, the debate on technology should benefit from a top management focus—the perspective of general management and, more importantly, that of the CEO. Such a perspective would provide a very different vantage point from which to examine the role of technology in the growth of the company; specifically, the underlying rationale and logic for growth in a globally competitive environment. The CEO perspective, as opposed to that of the chief technical officer (CTO), will allow us to put technology investment in a business perspective.

Prahalad, C. K. 1993. The role of core competencies in the corporation. Research-Technology Management (November–December): 40–47.

I shall illustrate my ideas with examples primarily drawn from high-volume electronics. I believe these concepts are equally applicable to industries as diverse as agricultural processing, chemicals, and, at least in some cases, defense electronics. I do not claim that the concepts presented here apply universally to all industries. I have found them useful in a wide variety of industries.

In this article, I present the conceptual framework. A previous article, by Presbylowicz and Faulkner, described a process for operationalizing these ideas in the context of a specific firm.[1]

THE MANAGEMENT SCORECARD

It will be useful to start with a scorecard for Western top management during the last 35–40 years. If we consider the period 1950–1980, immediately following World War II—in a wide variety of industries, from automotive, to semiconductors, to tires, to medical systems, to earth-moving equipment, and to reprographics—almost all the world leaders were Western companies. For example, in the automotive industry General Motors and Ford dominated the world. In the merchant semiconductor business Texas Instruments and Motorola were the leaders. However, if we consider the period 1980–1990 and ask: "Who is providing the intellectual leadership in these industries?" we come up with a very different list. For example, the intellectual leadership in the automotive industry is increasingly provided by companies such as Honda and Toyota, be it in terms of use of new technology, new features, new standards of quality, customer orientation and service, and price-performance relationships. The changing pattern of industrial leadership in a wide variety of industries is illustrated in Figure 4-1.

We should reflect on this change: *How did the intellectual and market leadership in so many industries shift in such a short period of time?* In view of the many advantages U.S. firms enjoyed during the period 1950–1980—such as superior technology, larger size, global distribution, reputation, and management know-how—how did the intellectual leadership slip away? If it had happened in just one industry, we could attribute the decline to a wide variety of external factors, including the role of MITI in Japan, the cost of capital, and the attitude of unions. But why and how did the U.S. lose leadership in so many industries during the 1975–1985 period?

This loss of intellectual leadership is just one part of the scorecard. Consider *internally generated growth* during the same period. Let us focus on the top 25 electronics companies during the decade of the 1980s. The giants of 1980 were IBM, GE, ITT, Philips, and Siemens. Most Japanese firms were small. Hitachi at around $12 billion was

Industry	Leaders 1950–1980	Challengers 1980
Automotive	GM Ford	Toyota Nissan Honda
Semiconductors	TI Motorola	NEC Toshiba Fujitsu Hitachi
Tires	Goodyear Firestone*	Michelin Bridgestone
Medical systems	GE Philips Siemens	Hitachi Toshiba
Consumer electronics	GE* RCA* Philips	Matsushita Sony
Photographic	Kodak	Fuji
Xerography	Xerox	Canon

FIGURE 4-1 Industrial Leadership Shifted in a Variety of Industries during 1975–1985

*Has been acquired

about half the size of IBM. Sony at $3 billion was one-fifth of Philips. And high-volume electronics was a "fortunate" industry during this decade. The industry overall experienced an average growth rate of 14 percent through the decade of the 1980s; but if we consider the rate of growth of various companies in this industry, we see wide variations: 12 percent for IBM, 11 for GE, 5 for Philips, 8 for Siemens. But Hitachi grew at 17 percent, Matsushita at 16, Toshiba at 15, NEC at 23. This is the annual compounded growth rate during the decade. The disparity in growth rates among firms, essentially in the same industry category, demands an explanation: Why do some firms grow at 5 percent and others at 20 percent for 10 years in the same industry?

Large Western firms have not fared well on the opportunity management (growth) dimension. Let us use a simple metric to evaluate the scorecard of a company's capacity to grow. Consider the period 1985–1991. If sales were 100 for the year 1985, the capacity-to-grow index during the period 1985–1991 can be computed as follows:

Capacity-To-Grow Index = (sales revenue for 1991 − acquisitions during the period 1985 to 1991 − inflation + divestments during the period 1985–1991).

By eliminating growth through acquisitions and inflation, this index measures *internal capacity to grow.* Unfortunately, for most large firms, the index is not very flattering. Top managers must ask themselves the following questions: What is the opportunity that we have lost? Why? Who is responsible for it? Who should pay the price for lost opportunities?

Let us take this analysis one step forward with a paired comparison of companies: Westinghouse, Hitachi and General Electric. Westinghouse grew from $8.5 billion to $12 billion during the decade. Westinghouse primarily divested itself of major businesses and acquired a few. GE also aggressively pursued a strategy of portfolio shuffling—acquisitions and divestments. However, Hitachi grew through internal development. This pattern is no different if we consider RCA, Sony and Matsushita, or GTE and NEC.

Why do some firms grow at 5% and others at 20% for 10 years in the same industry?

Paired comparisons allow us to further re-examine our scorecard. How can one company (Hitachi) grow from $12 to $50 billion, primarily through internal development, during a decade, while another company (Westinghouse), with a similar starting portfolio, grows from $8 billion to $12 billion only? The market opportunities were similar around the globe and the technological capabilities were comparable. In fact, all during the 1970s and 1980s, U.S. firms like Westinghouse led in technology in almost every field.

A reflection on this scorecard suggests that explanations must focus not on the differences in starting resource positions but on the differences in the ability of managers of firms to leverage corporate resources. We need answers to such questions as: Is our orientation to management and exploitation of technology and market opportunities appropriate? Is there a distinctly different underlying logic (as compared to the financial portfolio logic) to profitable growth? What is that logic? And what should top managers do in order to change their orientation from cost-cutting to opportunity management and growth?

RETHINKING THE SCORECARD

The real issue for the 1990s is *growth.* That is the agenda for top management—not down-sizing, not restructuring and de-cluttering of organizations. Restructuring without rethinking the role of management inevitably leads to further restructuring. Many large firms have restructured themselves more than once in the last ten years and the problems do not seem to go away. If growth and new business development are the real issues, *value creation* will be the scorecard for managers during this decade. This scorecard consists of two parts: 1. managing the *performance gap;* i.e., improving performance across a wide variety of dimensions such as quality, cost, cycle time, productivity, and profitability; 2. simultaneously, managers should focus on the *opportunity gap,* profitably deploying resources to create new markets, new businesses and a sense of broad strategic direction.

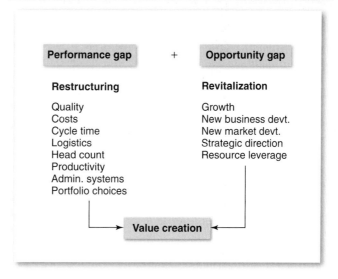

FIGURE 4-2   Value Creation Is Not Just Catching Up with the Performance—It Is the Active Management of the Opportunity Gap As Well

The twin aspects of value creation are illustrated in Figure 4-2. During the past decade, management attention has been primarily focused on the performance gap. It is the legitimate task of the management to fix problems of profitability, cost, quality, cycle time, logistics, and productivity. Managing the performance gap, if done well, ought to create a *large investment pool*. The question for managers, then, is how to redeploy the investment pool, created by focusing on the performance gap, in the pursuit of new opportunities for growth. To create value, concerns for operational improvement (performance gap) and strategic direction (opportunity gap), must coexist.

In this article, I focus on the opportunity gap through revitalization and growth. New business development, growth, new market development, and leveraging of corporate resources are an integral part of the value creation process. So I start with the assumption that value creation is not just catching up with the performance gap; it is the active management of the opportunity gap as well. Is there an underlying logic to opportunity management?

A NEW FRAMEWORK FOR VALUE CREATION

I suggest that the logic of opportunity gap management consists of at least four interlinked parts, as shown in Figure 4-3.

1. How can top managers establish an aspiration level (strategic intent) for the organization? Motivation for change results from an aspiration that all employees can identify with and feel committed to. Aspirations must represent a stretch and must by definition exceed the current resources of the company. Therefore, by design, strategic intent must cause a "misfit" between aspirations and current resources and current approaches to using resources. The aspiration must focus the energies of the organization toward innovation (changing the rules of the game) in the way the firm competes.

2. A high aspiration level (compared to the resources available) leads to the need for resource leverage. The issue for managers is: How do you create the capacity in a large organization to leverage corporate resources? The process of resource leverage is accomplished through the development of a *strategic architecture* (a way to capture the pattern of likely industry evolution), identifying *core competencies* and *core products*. Reusability of invisible assets,

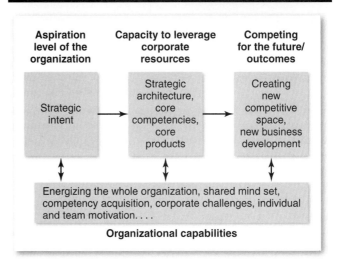

FIGURE 4-3   Opportunity Gap Management Begins with Establishing an Aspiration Level (Strategic Intent) for the Organization

as well as core products, in new and imaginative configurations to create new market opportunities is at the heart of the process of leverage.

3. An internal capacity to leverage resources is a prerequisite for inventing new businesses, creating *new competitive space.* This is competing for the future and requires a framework for identifying new opportunities, focusing on functionalities rather than on current products and services, and dramatically altering the price-performance relationships in an industry.

4. This new approach is not just a technical task or a senior management task—it is a task for the whole organization. The role of top management, therefore, is essentially one of energizing the whole organization—all people, at all levels, in all functions, and in all geographies. It involves developing a shared mindset and shared goals, and developing strategies for acquiring competency. Senior managers must focus on such questions as: How do we stretch the imagination of the total employee pool? How do we challenge the organization? How do we focus on individual and team motivation?

> *An internal capacity to leverage resources is a prerequisite for inventing new businesses.*

Using this framework, I will examine one building block at a time, starting with strategic intent.[2]

AN OBSESSION WITH WINNING

Strategic intent is a way of creating an obsession with winning that encompasses the total organization (all levels and all functions). It is a shared competitive agenda, sustained over a long period of time, for global leadership. Extraordinary accomplishment is often based on a clearly articulated strategic intent.

The U.S. has experienced the power of a clear strategic intent. Consider the Apollo program: "Man on the moon by the end of the decade" was a "stretch" target. It meant global leadership and the domination of space. The goal was competitively focused; Russians were the enemy. It was very clear. While the goal was clear, managers of the project had to discover the means, and a lot of new technologies had to be developed under enormous time pressure. How do we account for the inventiveness that was characteristic of the NASA efforts during the 1960s? Why is the "spirit" of the Apollo program not replicable in firms?

Consider some specific company examples, such as NEC's goal of *C&C* (computers and communications) or Kodak's strategic intent: to remain a *world leader in imaging,* not just chemical or electronic imaging, but the creative combination of both. Once *imaging* is accepted as the strategic intent, debate inside the company on whether chemical imaging is superior to electronic or vice versa, dies down. The focus shifts to creating new hybrids—products and services that creatively combine both capabilities. In Komatsu, the strategic intent was to encircle Caterpillar. Strategic intent may be stated in different ways in different firms—from C&C to Leadership in Imaging. But in all cases, it must represent an agenda for the whole company, not just for a function—be it manufacturing, marketing, top management, technologists, or sales.

Strategic intent provides a basis for stretching the imagination of the total organization and a focus for developing "barrier-breaking" initiatives.

FRAMEWORK FOR LEVERAGE

Once we have developed a shared aspiration, we need a framework for leveraging corporate resources that is consistent with the strategic intent. We start with a strategic architecture, which is a way of developing a point of view regarding the evolution of an industry. How will the interface with customers change? What are the new technological possibilities? How are our current and future competitors positioning themselves to approach this industry? Strategic architecture is a *distillation of a wide variety of information.* It is a way of capturing major discontinuities and trends in the industry. It does not attempt to identify a specific product or business opportunity, but captures the direction and major likely milestones. It provides a framework for focused resource allocation over a long period, allows managers to maintain consistency in their efforts, and provides a logic for managing linkages across business units in a large company.

> *Innovation is the fundamental job of a general manager.*

Strategic architecture can be used to identify targeted acquisitions, and alliance partners. Most important of all, it is a useful framework for effectively managing innovation. The underlying assumption is that innovation is a line job and not a staff job. Further, innovation cannot be left to skunk works or "off-line activities" such as internal entrepreneurship or internal venture teams. *Innovation is the fundamental job of a general manager.* We need to develop a framework in which innovation can be planned and managed. Strategic architecture provides one such framework for proactively managing the innovation process.

An example of strategic architecture is NEC's concept of C&C, or the convergence of computing and communications, shown in Figure 4-4. The evolution of computing driven by the need for decentralized processing as a trend, coupled with the changes in communication and component technologies, led to the convergence called C&C.[3] Obviously, in this architecture, there are no specific product plans, but the basic milestones are obvious. Accomplishing the aspiration of C&C is a stage-managed process. For over 15 years, the broad framework of C&C represented by the strategic architecture was used as an organizing idea. The value of such a framework to provide consistency and direction to technical resource allocation is obvious.

The fact is that anyone in this industry could have drawn this picture. However, even though all of us could visualize C&C, why didn't other companies use it as the organizing and stage-setting concept for mobilizing the efforts of the total company? Why did C&C not provide a logic for resource allocation? These are the critical questions. It is not enough for a small group of technical people to have a bold concept. There has to be widespread agreement and understanding of the concept. An architecture, such as C&C, can be easily developed by the technical community. But to get agreement among several levels of managers inside a company is an entirely different task. It is an effort that takes time and patience.

What is the benefit of this approach? Consider R&D expenditures. NEC's R&D budget, during the period 1980–1990, was considerably smaller than either IBM or AT&T. But NEC generated a 23 percent per year growth record, for over a decade, on

FIGURE 4-4   NEC's Strategic Architecture Is Its Concept of Computers & Communications (C&C). From Koji Kobayashi, *Computers and Communications.*

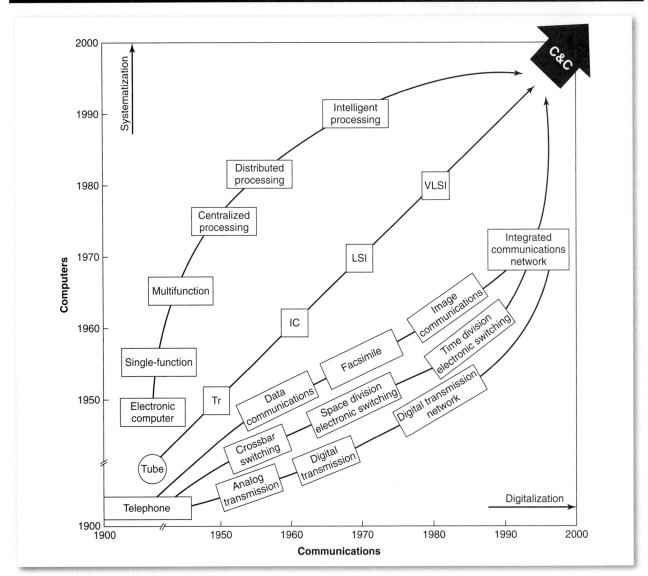

significantly less investments in R&D. NEC supplemented its investments in R&D by a series of carefully targeted alliances. Between 1965 and 1987, it was involved in more than 130 alliances. The logic for this network of alliances can be derived from the strategic architecture. In fact, one can track all the alliances between 1965 and 1987 and position them in the overall strategic architecture of the company. The strategic architecture also provided the motivation to learn from these alliances. It is important to recognize that NEC used its alliance partners as multipliers to its internal resources. NEC used its architecture not only as an organizing framework inside the firm but as a way of communicating to the rest of the world what it was all about. NEC's advertisements embodied the C&C theme.

The NEC portfolio encompasses enormous product variety. However, there is no problem in understanding the logic behind that diverse portfolio. They are all derivatives of C&C. This consistency—in strategic intent, architecture, alliance strategies, and businesses—contributed to NEC's ability to leverage its resources. NEC, in 1990, occupied one of the top five positions in telecom, computing and semiconductors worldwide. And it was a $3 billion company in 1980!

Other firms such as Vickers (a division of TRINOVA), Sharp, Colgate-Palmolive, Kodak, and others have developed similar strategic architectures to guide their managerial actions.

IDENTIFYING CORE COMPETENCIES

A strategic architecture allows managers to identify what core competencies we have and what we need to get. Core competencies are an important link in the process of leverage. The concept of core competencies tends to be confused with core technologies and/or capabilities. Core technologies are a component part of core competencies. Core competency results when firms learn to *harmonize multiple technologies.* For example, consider miniaturization, which has been the unique signature of Sony. Miniaturization requires core technologies, such as microprocessors, miniature power sources, power management, packaging, and manufacturing. It certainly also requires knowledge and understanding of user-friendly design and a knowledge of ergonomics. In addition, miniaturization is a result of deep sensitivity to emerging life styles. A core competency does not represent just technical capabilities in microprocessors, or packaging, or passive components; it also means understanding how to exploit life style knowledge using electronics. The point I want to stress is that it is not just technical capabilities that matter. What matters is the *creative bundling* of multiple technologies and customer knowledge and intuition, and managing them as a harmonious whole.

A core competency can be identified by applying three simple tests: 1) Is it a significant source of competitive differentiation? Does it provide a unique signature to

> *Core competency results when firms learn to harmonize multiple technologies.*

the organization, like miniaturization for Sony, or user-friendliness at Apple? 2) Does it transcend a single business? Does it cover a range of businesses, both current and new? 3) Is it hard for competitors to imitate? It is hard for someone to visit Matsushita or Sony and come back and outline why they are good at manufacturing or miniaturization, respectively. Competence permeates the whole organization, and it represents tacit learning in an organization.

The difference between technology and competence is that technology can be stand-alone (e.g., design of very-large-scale-integration). Competence, on the other hand, is getting consistently high yields in VLSI. This transcends design capabilities. The process of converting good designs into high yields requires that multiple levels (e.g., shop floor to product development engineers) and multiple functions (e.g., application engineers and manufacturing groups) work very closely. A lot of the understanding and learning is tacit. And the recognition that competence represents tacit as well as explicit learning and is the cumulative knowledge base involving a large number of people is critical to understanding core competence. Technical capabilities, as stand-alone skills, are not the key to understanding core competencies. Competence is embedded in the whole organization.

Miniaturization at Sony, network management at AT&T, billing at the regional Bell operating companies, user-friendliness at Apple, and high-volume manufacturing at Matsushita, are examples of core competencies.

Often, core competencies are confused with capabilities. Capabilities are, in some cases, prerequisites to being in a business. For example, "just-in-time" delivery is a prerequisite to be a Tier 1 supplier to the auto industry. It is the price one has to pay to get into the game. If one is a gambler, one may call it "table stakes." Capability is crucial for survival but, unlike a core competency, does not confer any specific differential advantage over other competitors in that industry.

COMPETENCE IS GOVERNANCE TOO

The key to understanding competence is that although it incorporates a technology component, it also involves the *governance process* inside the organization (the quality of relationships across functions, across business units), and *collective learning* across levels and functions) inside the company. We may conceptualize competence as follows: Competence = (Technology × Governance Process × Collective Learning).

We can examine the implications of this view with a hypothetical example. Consider a typical U.S. firm. The assumption is that if we pour a lot of money into technology the competitiveness problems will go away. Using the expression above, let us consider this hypothetical firm to be rich in technology, say 1,000 units of technology. However, let us assume that the various businesses within this corporation do not work together; Let's give them 20 units for the governance process—capability to work across business and functional unit boundaries. Let us also assume that in this firm the capacity for collective learning is low. So let us give it 5 units for this dimension. Using the formula above, we now have an overall competence score of 100,000 units.

Consider another company that is not blessed with as much technology. It qualifies for not more than, say, 200 units, using the same formula we used in considering the previous firm. However, this firm has fostered the capacity to work across organizational boundaries and is fully focused on organizational learning. Let us give it 100 units for governance and 500 for collective learning, leading to a competence of 10 million. The message is clear: Investments in technology, if they are not, in tandem, accompanied by investments in *governance* and *creation* of a *learning environment* at all levels in the organization will remain under-leveraged. So, the logical point of leverage for Western firms resides in investments to improve the *quality of organization.*

Honda has been an example of this kind of thinking. Honda's multiple businesses are built on the basis of a competence in engines. If every one of those business units, be it power tillers or lawn mowers, behaved as if it were a discrete and stand-alone business, and each business unit only focused on (and was willing to pay for) the functionalities it needed, Honda's engine competence could be easily compromised. For example, in power tillers, managers may demand and be willing to pay for a light and robust engine. However, noise reduction is not a major priority for power tiller managers as they target their products for use in villages in the developing world. On the other hand, the business unit manager developing lawn mowers for sale in the United States may need not only a light and robust engine but one with low noise level as well. Business unit managers can uniquely define the functionalities that they need. But if each one of them tends to optimize their needs without maintaining a perspective on the implications of their parochial approach for the protection and development of an overall competence—in this case, engines—the skill base will be eroded. Often, a single-minded focus on SBU (strategic business unit) structure without checks and balances can destroy the very basis of nurturing and exploiting core competencies.

If the only model we use represents the company as a portfolio of businesses, then cost reduction within those businesses appears to be the primary task, sometimes followed by focus on product line extensions. When we model the corporation as a portfolio of core competencies, we tend to focus on new application opportunities. This perspective enhances the focus of management on new business development.

The portfolio of businesses at Sharp, Sony and Canon makes the case for focus on core competencies. But in order to focus on growth based on core competencies, we need to create a new set of managerial capabilities—one where sharing knowledge and components across organizational boundaries is relatively routine and painless. For example, Canon has a wide variety of businesses (end products) like copiers, laser printers, fax machines, cameras, and camcorders. But those business units are fed by core products, such as lens systems, laser engines and miniature motors. These core products are supported by core competencies such as miniaturization, mechatronics and so on. Each business has an independent identity. It focuses on a specific set of customers and markets. But underlying that is a structure of shared core products and core competencies. As a result, within the firm, there is an opportunity for gaining economies of scale, an ability to provide new functionalities, and leverage.

Core products are often the physical embodiment of one or more core competencies. Compressors in Matsushita and laser printer engines in Canon are examples of core products. Canon not only uses its laser printer engine in several businesses, it also markets it outside. Firms such as Canon distinguish between their market share of end products (e.g., copiers), manufacturing share (e.g., share of market gained by providing manufactured products under private label to others), and share of core products (e.g., laser printer engines sold to others). Canon has gained a significant market share of over 85 percent worldwide in laser printer engines. It remains a small player in laser printers—the end product, worldwide. There is a market that is developing for core products. And we need to recognize that competition for core products is distinctly different from competition for end products and services.

The logical point of leverage for Western firms resides in investments to improve the quality of the organization.

We need to go beyond market share for end products. Consider the color television business, for example. In order to succeed, firms must have access to core products such as picture tubes, signal processing ICs, tuners, and line output transformers. If we disaggregate businesses at the core product level—be it TVs, VCRs, camcorders, or laptop computers—we find very few Western firms that dominate worldwide. This perspective allows us to evaluate competitive outcomes differently. For example, with this perspective we can explain why Matsushita and JVC won the battle for VCRs. Their combined market share for VHS VCRs was only 24 percent. However, manufacturing share was 41 percent, format share through licensing was 80 percent, and core product share for decks was 85 percent. Eight-five percent of the world's requirements for decks were made by one company!

We underestimate the power that accrues to these companies because they dominate core products. Managers tend to underestimate the power of core product dominance. The issue is who controls critical technologies. Technological superiority without competence may represent a hollow victory.

The emerging competitive picture should force senior managers to ask themselves such questions as: How long can this erosion of core product capability in the West be sustained? Who are the custodians of the technical virtuosity of our companies? While business unit managers have no natural inclination to concern themselves with core product share or competencies, should group and sector executives transcend the concerns of the business units and play a role in protecting the basis for long-term competitiveness of our firms? Who should protect the disciplines that require multiple business units to work together?

It is important to recognize that competition today takes place on multiple planes. First, there is competition for end product markets and services; that is, price-performance competition represented by market share battles for today's market. Managers have to fight in that arena. There is also a less visible battle for dominance in core products that create the capacity to lead in the development of new functionalities. Finally, there is competition for competence—the capacity to create new businesses. The three levels of competition are shown in Figure 4-5. We need to learn to compete on all three levels.

FIGURE 4-5 We Need to Learn to Compete on All Three Levels of Competition

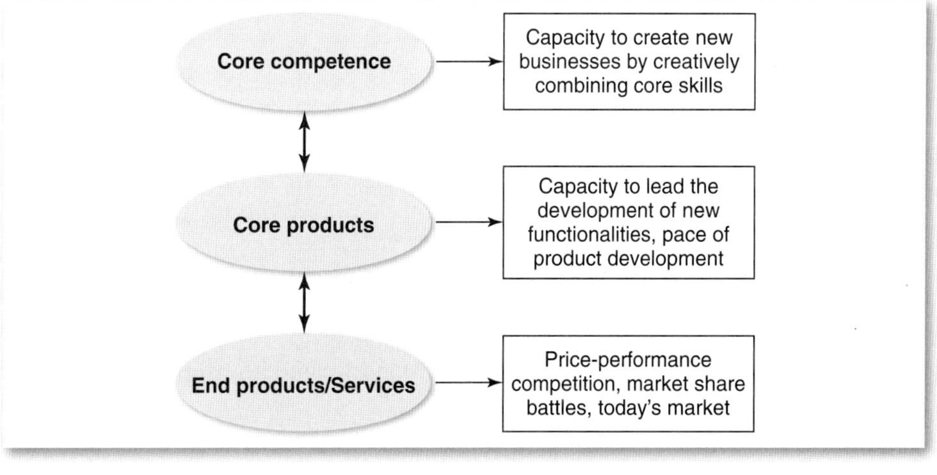

CREATING NEW COMPETITIVE SPACE

How can firms create totally new products and services? Consider new businesses such as personal fax, Global Positioning Satellites for hikers, photo CD, and camcorders. I believe the *opportunity list* for the next decade in high-volume electronics could be five pages long. The question for consideration by senior managers is: What do we have to do to capture our share of new business development?

I believe we need to develop a new mindset that is characterized by the following:

1. *Challenging existing price-performance assumptions.*—Why can't we create a color fax for $200? Why should it be $5,000? Canon in copiers, and Lexus or Honda in the luxury car segment are good examples of firms dramatically challenging the existing price–performance assumptions in the industry.

2. *Understanding the "meaning of customer-led."*—In most firms, this means listening to customers and giving them what they ask for. That's important, but it is also important to lead customers. As customers, many of us may not have anticipated our emerging dependence on a fax in our home 10 years ago. Being customer-led is important, but leading customers is what competing for the future is about: understanding functionalities and needs, and creating products with a price performance that makes it attractive for people to buy.

3. *Escaping the tyranny of the "served market" orientation among managers.*—A served market orientation puts too much emphasis on current businesses, and reduces the capacity to foresee new opportunities, especially opportunities that fall between two or more current business units. If we want to re-fire corporate imagination, we need to do the following:

   We must de-emphasize the served market orientation and emphasize an orientation that focuses on the opportunity horizon. Managing the served market is important, but exploiting the opportunity horizon is what leads to profitable growth. We must not just defend markets, but create markets. Instead of incrementalism in price-performance there must be stretch price–performance goals; instead of simply benchmarking, currently popular in many firms, we must outpace the competition. We want to move from satisfying needs to anticipating needs; from being close to customers to leading customers; from thinking in terms of products to focusing on functionality and rapid market incursions; from focusing on core business to diversifying around core competencies. This is a very different mindset.

   Managers have traditionally focused on current customers, product–markets, and corresponding business units. My research has convinced me that there is something beyond understanding business units and customers. We need to start with a *strategic intent, create a strategic architecture, understand core competencies and products,* such that there is a logic for business units, both current and new, and that leverage is based on continuous reconfiguration of these competencies.

   To realize both the stretch and the leverage that this set of ideas promotes, we need to develop a set of values and beliefs that are consistent with this orientation to profitable growth. What is the unit of analysis for resource allocation? How do we manage inter-business unit linkages, inter-functional linkages? How do we create organizational capabilities, such as global–local capability or cycle time? And then, how do we think about administrative processes such as budgeting or planning?

   The next challenge for senior management is: How do you connect individual employees' motivation and contribution with customers through a transparent process inside the company, where everybody understands what the shared aspirations are and how the various businesses interlink with each other, and the logic for nesting individual products and new initiatives? That, to me, is the next round of challenge.

I conclude with the following thoughts: 1) Growth is the agenda—not restructuring. 2) Dramatic growth will not take place if we focus on technology; it will take place when we focus on the organization, with technology as a part of it. 3) Dramatic growth requires a radical rethinking of current management paradigms.

About the Author

C. K. Prahalad is the Harvey C. Fruehauf Professor of Business Administration in the Graduate School of Business Administration at the University of Michigan, Ann Arbor, where he teaches corporate strategy and international business. His research interests center around the role and value added of top management in large, diversified, multinational firms. Prahalad's ideas have received widespread attention in academic and management circles. Two of the articles that he coauthored—"Strategic Intent" and "Core Competencies of the Corporation"—won the McKinsey Prize (first place and runner-up, respectively) for the best articles published in the *Harvard Business Review* during 1989 and 1990. He has consulted with top managements of firms such as Eastman Kodak, AT&T, Philips, Colgate Palmolive, Ahlstrom, Cargill, and Honeywell. He received his doctor of business administration degree from the Harvard Business School, and has taught at INSEAD, France, and at the Indian Institute of Management, in Ahmedabad. This article is adapted from his paper presented to the Industrial Research Institute Fall Meeting in Chicago, October 1991.

References

1. Przbylowicz, Edward P. and Faulkner, Terrence W. "Kodak Applies Strategic Intent To the Management of Technology." *Research Technology Management,* No. 1 (1993), pp. 31–38.

2. Hamel, Gary and Prahalad, C. K. "Strategic Intent." *Harvard Business Review,* No. 3 (1989), pp. 63–76; Prahalad, C. K. and Hamel, Gary. "The Core Competence of the Corporation." *Harvard Business Review,* No. 3 (1990), pp. 79–91; Hamel, Gary and Prahalad, C. K. "Corporate Imagination and Expeditionary Marketing." *Harvard Business Review,* No. 4 (1991), pp. 81–92.

3. Kobayashi, Koji. *Computers and Communications: A vision of C&C.* Cambridge, The MIT Press, 1986.

5

JAPAN'S MANAGEMENT OF GLOBAL INNOVATION: TECHNOLOGY MANAGEMENT CROSSING BORDERS

Kiyonori Sakakibara and D. Eleanor Westney

In the industries where Japan has become a major global competitor (such as computers, semiconductors, automobiles, consumer electronics), Japanese companies have developed the reputation for rapid commercialization of new product ideas and for effective and efficient incremental innovations in existing products (Rosenberg and Steinmueller 1988; Dertouzos, Lester, and Solow 1989, pp. 48–49; Stalk and Hout 1990). They have done so with relatively low investments in basic research, and with a very high degree of geographic concentration of their research and development organizations in Japan. Indeed, the success of these companies in designing in their home country laboratories products that meet the needs of customers in many different national markets has been greatly envied by U.S. firms.

These same Japanese firms, however, are now under increasing pressures to internationalize their research and development organizations and to increase their basic research activities. Japanese research managers are beginning to formulate new technology strategies to deal with these pressures and to assess the implications for institutionalized patterns of technology management.

NEW DIMENSIONS OF TECHNOLOGY STRATEGY

In the latter half of the 1980s, Japanese firms have increasingly confronted demands that they put more of their technology development activities overseas. Some of these pressures come from the governments and business communities within the countries which are Japan's major markets, the United States and Europe in particular, where policy makers are increasingly critical of Japanese firms' low level of local value-added, not only in manufacturing but also in product development and research (Ishikawa 1990). Western policy makers and businessmen also contend that Japan is not "pulling its weight" in investment in basic research to increase the global stock of scientific and technical knowledge (*The Economist,* 1989).

Sakakibara, Kiyonori and D. Eleanor Westney, (1992), "Japan's Management of Global Innovation: Technology Management Crossing Borders," in *Technology and the Wealth of Nations,* edited by N. Rosenberg, R. Landan, and D. Mowery, Stanford University Press, pp. 327–343. From Rosenberg, Nathan et al., eds TECHNOLOGY AND THE WEALTH OF NATIONS. Copyright © 1992 by the Board of Trustees of the Leland Stanford Jr. University.

70

However, much of the pressure for dispersing R&D geographically is self-generated: Japanese firms want to become "true" international companies, on the model of leading Western multinationals like IBM. In addition, Japanese managers anticipate a growing shortage of scientists and engineers within Japan itself, as the aging of the Japanese population lowers the numbers of university graduates and as they must increasingly compete for those graduates with the financial services sector (which is hiring more and more scientific and technical graduates) and with foreign firms establishing R&D facilities in Japan. A survey of 177 leading Japanese firms in 1988 (*Nihon Keizai Shimbun,* September 13, 1988) found that over 80 percent of the respondents were either actively working to establish R&D bases abroad or interested in doing so.

Japanese companies are by no means alone in seeing the internationalization of their technology development capacity as an important strategic challenge. A 1985 Booz Allen study of technology management found widespread agreement within the sixteen U.S., European, and Japanese multinationals they surveyed on the perception that

> "New technologies and the specialized talent that produces them will
> continue to develop locally in 'pockets of innovation' around the world.
> Nurturing those technologies, uprooting them, and cross-fertilizing them for
> commercialization and global distribution will continue to be major
> challenges in technology management." (Perrino and Tipping 1989, p. 13)

Tapping geographically dispersed "pockets of excellence"—which include government laboratories, cooperative R&D projects, and universities—can be undertaken in a variety of ways: technology scanning, cross-licensing, strategic alliances, and joint ventures. However, managers are increasingly realizing that even these can be most effectively supported by a local technology development capacity: that is, by a wholly owned critical mass of credible researchers who are part of the multinational corporation but who can function as insiders within the national technology system. More than five years ago, the Booz Allen study found a consensus that

> "What we have called the 'global network' model of technology management
> is clearly the 'wave of the future' when it comes to competing globally. This
> model consists of a network of technology core groups in each major
> market—the United States, Japan, and Europe–managed in a coordinated
> way for maximum impact." (Perrino and Tipping 1989, p. 13)

In a growing number of firms, this perception is leading to increasing efforts to internationalize R&D organization, and, in those U.S. and European multinationals that already have local product development centers, to enhance and integrate these dispersed facilities (Perrino and Tipping 1989, Herbert 1989, Hakanson and Zander 1986, De Meyer and Mizushima 1989).

Within Japan, the drive to expand basic research is rooted in internal pressures that are as strong as those behind the push for internationalization, if not stronger: Japanese managers increasingly emphasize the need to generate new technology within the company, as external sources become scarcer and harder to tap (MITI 1989). In contrast to the dominant patterns in the United States and Europe, industrial companies, not government or the universities, have assumed the primary role in expanding Japan's basic research activities (Sakakibara 1988). Between 1980 and 1985, over forty of the companies listed on the Tokyo Stock Exchange have established new research facilities, many of which are oriented to basic research rather than the more traditional product-oriented R&D. In a dramatic break from tradition, these have been built away from existing corporate research and manufacturing sites, to emphasize the autonomy of the new labs.

For some companies, the drive to expand basic research is integrally linked to their internationalization strategies. Otsuka Pharmaceuticals Co. Ltd., for example, has set up research facilities in Maryland and Seattle in the United States and in Frankfurt, West Germany; their mandates cover basic research as well as clinical development. NEC has established a basic research facility in Princeton, New Jersey. Ricoh Co. Ltd. recently established a center for research in artificial intelligence in California's "Silicon Valley."

Other firms are pursuing the two agendas simultaneously but independently, expanding basic research activities at home and setting up R&D facilities overseas with less ambitious mandates. Hitachi, for example, has set its top priority on establishing the basic research facility in Japan that it set up in 1985, but it is also working on plans to build research facilities in the United States and the United Kingdom.

INTERNATIONAL TECHNOLOGY STRATEGY OF JAPANESE FIRMS

Theories of the multinational corporation (MNC) developed in the 1960s and early 1970s, based primarily on the experience of U.S. firms, made the internationalization of production the defining criterion of the MNC. Japanese business scholars, reflecting their own national experience, have tended to focus more broadly on the internationalization of the firm, using a three-stage model (see, for example, Saito and Itami 1986). In the first stage, marketing and distribution organizations are set up offshore but other functions, including manufacturing, remain concentrated at home. The second stage centers on the establishment of production facilities in the firm's major markets abroad. And the third—the globalization of corporate management—involves the internationalization of core corporate functions such as finance and R&D. In terms of this model, Japan's leading industrial companies have moved beyond the first stage of internationalization. They are well advanced into the second stage ("classic" foreign direct investment in production facilities abroad), and they are now moving toward the third stage (Saito and Itami 1986).

The internationalization of the technology development function of large Japanese firms has been somewhat more complex, involving five stages. The first stage, technology scanning, is associated with the first stage of internationalization, in which Japanese companies manufacture products in Japan for sale abroad. In this stage the company focuses on developing organizational systems to collect scientific and technical information and product information for use in the product development organization back in Japan. Some companies have relied heavily on sending individual "scouts" on specific technology-gathering missions; others established separate offices in the United States and Europe that were explicitly charged with technology scanning. The companies relied primarily on their own nationals in staffing these offices.

The second stage involves the creation of an organizational system to support the transfer of technology to production facilities overseas. Most production transplants have set up a technology department, following a standard Japanese pattern, in which each major factory is supported by a technology department or laboratory capable of process technology development and some incremental product improvement. In some companies these technology departments have been capable of minor modifications of product technologies to suit local markets, although new product development remained concentrated in Japan. These offshore technology departments were usually heavily staffed by Japanese, although of course local engineers were also recruited (Trevor 1988, pp. 143–144).

The formal establishment of R&D laboratories marks the beginning of the third stage. However, for many Japanese companies, the overseas laboratory, despite being called an R&D center, has done very little actual research or product development. Instead it has been a base for performing a range of other activities: technical cooperation with suppliers, support for technology transfer into production facilities, cross-licensing support, and the supervision of contract research. The overseas research laboratories of several of the leading Japanese pharmaceutical companies exemplify this stage. Instead of carrying out research directly, they contract out research to independent laboratories and specialized drug testing companies that supervise the clinical trials necessary to satisfy local regulatory requirements. In addition, they monitor technological trends and evaluate emerging technologies and new products.

In the fourth stage, overseas research laboratories embark on new product development, which becomes their central mission. These laboratories epitomize what is

FIGURE 5-1   The Dimensions of International Technology Strategy

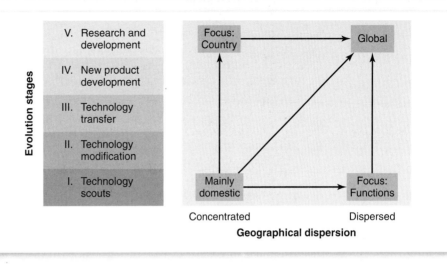

generally defined as the internationalization of R&D. The fifth stage extends the strategic mandate to encompass basic research, where the laboratory participates in an advanced, global division of technology development within the company.

Figure 5-1 summarizes the previous discussion and provides a way for mapping various companies' technology strategies, using two variables: the five stages of internationalization, and the geographic dispersion of the technology function (measured by the number of regions in which the company has developed a technology capability). The Y axis represents the stages of development of the strategic motivation behind the internationalization of technology strategy, and the X axis indicates the degree of geographical dispersion of technology-generating activities. The upper left corner maps a case in which all R&D for the company, including basic research, is carried out within one country; the lower right corner represents a case in which the activities associated with technology scanning are distributed among many countries. The upper right corner, where research activities are geographically dispersed and varied, represents the "global network" of technology development described in the Booz Allen study cited above (Perrino and Tipping 1989, p. 13).

Roughly speaking, most Japanese firms are in the process of shifting from Stage II to Stage III on the Y axis and are moving gradually out on the X axis. In the computer industry, for example, NEC has advanced farthest on the Y axis, with the establishment of its basic research facility in New Jersey in the spring of 1988. Hitachi is advancing into Stage IV and is moving farther than NEC along the X axis, with its plans to set up full-scale research facilities in both the United States and the United Kingdom. Fujitsu has relied primarily on its equity partnership with Amdahl to penetrate the North American technology system, and on its non-equity strategic alliance with ICL in the United Kingdom to penetrate the European system. To date, it has not made public any plans to support these activities through a wholly owned basic R&D presence in either region. Toshiba and Mitsubishi, in comparison, have yet to propose publicly any clear internationalization strategy for technology development in their computer businesses.

Otsuka Pharmaceutical Company is another of the handful of Japanese companies who have approached Stage V on the Y axis. Otsuka has built an international system for pharmaceutical product development, including basic science, that incorporates research institutes in Maryland (near the National Institutes of Health) and Seattle in the United States and in Frankfurt, West Germany.

The model of internationalization portrayed in Figure 5-1 differs somewhat from the model proposed by Robert Ronstadt on the basis of his research into the internationalization of technology development in U.S. multinationals, which has to date been the dominant typology in studies of the internationalization of R&D. Ronstadt identified four types of overseas technology facilities in the U.S. multinational corporation:

the TTU (Technology Transfer Unit), which supported the transfer of product and production technologies from the parent to a manufacturing subsidiary; the ITU (Indigenous Technology Unit), with a capacity for new product development for the local market; the GTU (Global Technology Unit), which had the capacity to develop new products for worldwide markets; and the CTU (Corporate Technology Unit), which carries out basic research to develop advanced technology that will be applied elsewhere in the multinational (Ronstadt 1978). Ronstadt was careful to say that his typology was not a model of evolutionary stages: some of the companies he studied showed a gradual progression over time from the TTU to the GTU or CTU, while others did not.

The typology of the internationalization of technology development in Japanese firms has some similarities with Ronstadt's model. Stage II corresponds to Ronstadt's TTU, and Stage V to his GTU. However, the Japanese internationalization trajectory has been strongly influenced by two factors: the much longer reliance on export-based strategies for penetrating international markets, and Japan's lengthy experience as a technology follower. In consequence, the earliest stage of technology internationalization for Japanese firms was the development of technology-gathering outposts in the highly industrialized nations. The long period of success in gathering technology for use in their home country's laboratories has not only given Japanese firms the capacity to develop products at home for world markets; it has become something of an impediment in their ability to develop local product development capacity. Even when top management develops a strategic commitment to develop a local product development capacity, the patterns institutionalized in Stages I and II lead the home country R&D organization to treat the developing research center as a "listening post" whose function is to report on local developments in technology and to host visiting technology scanners. In consequence, the facility finds it difficult to hire and keep good local technical people. This difficulty reinforces the belief of the home country organization that the local technical organization can never match the product development capacity in Japan.

Moving on to Stage IV and V therefore requires a very strong commitment on the part of top-level R&D managers as well as top-level general management. It often follows the development of a strong local production and marketing organization that is capable of breaking the long-established loop of gathering technical and local market information and transferring it back to Japan for embodiment in new products or product modifications, which are then transferred again to the local production organization. The lag in product development and improvement time inherent in this loop has been a major factor in stimulating Japanese and local managers to a commitment to develop a local product development capacity.

INTRAFIRM COORDINATION OF DISPERSED R&D

The establishment of R&D centers abroad expands the range of technological expertise on which the firm can draw effectively. However, establishing the relationships among the dispersed centers to ensure synergies in technology development strategies raises problems of internal coordination.

Figure 5-2 presents a range of configurations for intra-function coordination that develop in response to an international technology strategy. The circles represent country R&D centers (the numbers within the circles indicate different countries). The rectangles are groups of countries. In general, coordination becomes more difficult as the number of countries increases; the figure presents only a simplified set of models.

The first model is a "country-centered" approach, which concentrates all R&D activities in one country. Strictly speaking, it is not part of an international technology strategy, even though R&D is undertaken on a global scale for multiple countries. This model makes for the easiest type of intrafirm coordination, and it preserves economies of scope and scale in R&D. Many Japanese companies still pursue this approach.

The second model is "pooled," when R&D activities are conducted at several overseas bases, and half of the research is initiated by each base, making for simultaneous, parallel R&D within the company. In this mode, some firms clearly mandate a division

FIGURE 5-2 Configurations of R&D Activity Flow

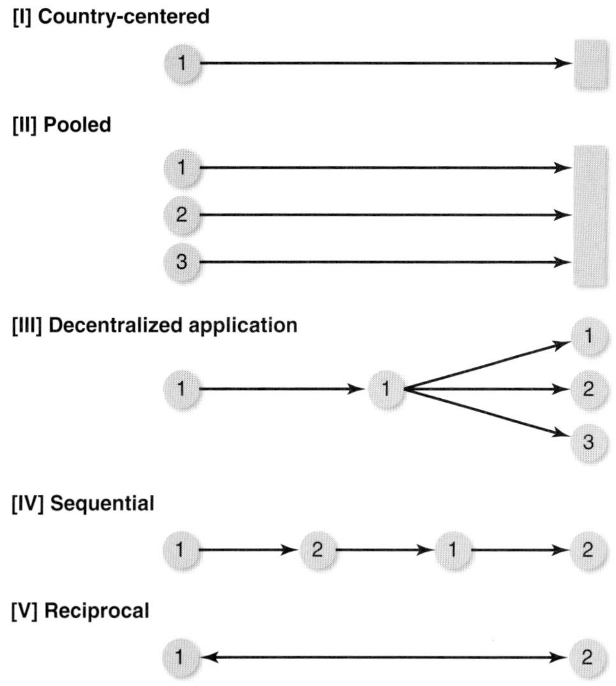

[I] Country-centered

[II] Pooled

[III] Decentralized application

[IV] Sequential

[V] Reciprocal

Note: Circles represent countries. Each number represents a different country. Rectangles represent plural countries.

of labor, so that each research base has a distinctive mandate (either by product or by project segment). Others permit some duplication of R&D among their overseas bases, but usually in the same way that they permit project duplication within their home country R&D organization: to select the most promising outcome for the corporation's technology pool.

This approach is relatively simple, and close horizontal coordination across the R&D bases is not a complex problem. However, it puts a heavy load on management control systems to prevent unnecessary duplication of R&D investment. In the extreme case, it might give rise to a multi-domestic strategy in which each R&D base develops a complete set of products for the national market in which it is located.

Otsuka Pharmaceutical is one example of a firm which has adopted this approach. Each overseas R&D base conducts its own basic and advanced research in the pursuit of original new pharmaceutical products. Interdependence with the home research organization is not expected; the products developed at each lab become part of the worldwide product line of the firm.

The third model is "decentralized application," in which the firm concentrates roughly half its R&D activities in Japan (particularly basic and advanced product development), and distributes the remaining half in offshore R&D centers, which focus on applied product development. The centralized part of R&D emphasizes the expansion of the basic technology portfolio of the firm; direct contact with local markets and associated local product development are pursued offshore. The actual ratio of centralized to decentralized R&D is a matter of strategic choice. If the centralized part grows too large, the R&D pattern approaches the first model described above ("country-centered"); if the offshore R&D centers come to dominate, it approaches the second model ("pooled").

This third model leads to increased complexity in managing the interdependence of the home country and local research centers. Nevertheless, many Japanese companies are taking this route. For instance, many IC makers put their custom IC development facilities abroad, where they can be closer to the customer. Several of the pharmaceutical companies test their new drugs in laboratories in Europe and the United States, close to local markets and local regulatory authorities.

The fourth model is the "sequential" strategy, in which dispersed R&D centers share their results on a continuous basis. A typical example is the joint development of software by Xerox in the United States and Fuji-Xerox in Japan. Since 1986, these companies have built up a satellite telecommunications network. At the end of each day, Fuji-Xerox engineers in Japan electronically send their files to their U.S. counterparts. The work then continues in the United States, and at the end of the U.S. working day, the process is reversed. The goal, obviously, is to minimize development time by mobilizing development expertise in both countries, and the most important advantage of this approach is speed of development. It requires the project organization and the technology to be highly standardized across locations, and perhaps works best with routine development work, such as debugging in software development.

The fifth and final model is the "reciprocal" approach, which also features a two-way exchange in the R&D process, but which is distinguished from the sequential model by a division of labor across sites. This is ideal for mobilizing complementary expertise, but it is the most difficult in terms of coordination. A good example is the joint development of a laptop computer, the DG One, by Data General in the United States and its subsidiary in Japan, Nippon Data General. The Japanese side was in charge of hardware and the U.S. side developed the software. The project was conceived and refined through interaction between the two sites, and there was a frequent two-way flow of information throughout the development process.

There are very few actual examples of the "sequential" and "reciprocal" modes, and even fewer successful cases. For example, while Data General's laptop computer featured many noteworthy technical accomplishments, the product itself was not a market success. Other firms were able to move quickly to match its distinctive features, and were quicker to produce incremental innovations to reduce its cost and improve its features. The geographic separation between the two parts of the product development project in Data General may have inhibited those subsequent incremental innovations. Nevertheless, the rapid improvement of international data communications networks will continue to ease the technical problems of cross-border communication and may well make these modes more possible and profitable in the future.

Of these five strategies, all but the first require some degree of coordination and interaction across borders within the technology function, and even the first requires cross-border interactions between the technology function and offshore production. One of the key challenges facing the Japanese firm in internationalizing technology development is the extent to which it adapts to other societies the organizational systems which have been so successful within Japan for managing product and process innovation and for linking product development and production. In their overseas production facilities that undertake considerable local value adding (beyond simple assembly), Japanese manufacturers have made greater efforts than their U.S. or European counterparts to transfer and adapt their home country production organization. As they move into higher value adding activities in technology development, efforts to do the same with the organization of product development and technology transfer are likely, in order to maintain their competitive advantages in design for manufacturability and quality, incremental innovation, and short design cycles. The challenges in adaptation are very great, especially in North America, because of the differences in technology management systems, to which we now turn.

TECHNOLOGY MANAGEMENT SYSTEMS IN JAPAN AND NORTH AMERICA

The most fundamental difference between Japanese and U.S. technology management is the locus of responsibility for the career of the technical employee: in North America, that responsibility rests primarily with the individual; in Japan, it rests with the company. This difference underlies the patterns of technology transfer, incremental innovation, and human resource development in large Japanese corporations.[1]

RECRUITMENT

The difference in systems begins with recruitment. Leading Japanese firms still hire their technical employees from among new university graduates; those hired to work on new product development are likely to have M.S. degrees. Even today, hiring researchers with experience in other companies is rare, and limited to cases where the firm is diversifying into new technology fields. In this process Japanese companies depend heavily on close, long-term relationships with universities and with key professors within those universities. The result is an annual intake of researchers of similar age, experience, academic background, and career orientation. This similarity is reinforced in the "freshman training" given to new recruits. Japanese companies in general maintain a well-organized program for new hires; the first one or two months is usually conducted in a special training facility. The next two years are closely supervised on-the-job training, with designated "mentors" within the research organization.

In most U.S. technology-intensive firms, the technical organization is made up of people who vary widely in age, job experience, academic background, and career orientation. Few U.S. firms use formal entry-level training programs to develop more homogeneous capabilities and orientations. Instead, college graduates are hired into specific research teams and undergo whatever training they receive with the help of team members.

On the other hand, both Japanese and U.S. firms offer considerable mid-career training. In our study of technical organization in the computer industry (Westney and Sakakibara 1985), for example, we found no great differences between the Japanese and U.S. companies in the opportunities for mid-career technical training courses. The motives behind enrollment in these courses, however, were quite different, as Table 5-1 shows.

In both countries, updating existing skills was an important motivation. But many more Japanese said that they took the program because they were assigned to the course by their company. Many U.S. researchers, on the other hand, cited such motives as "to add new skills," "to improve chances of promotion," and "to improve chances of assignment to more interesting activities." They hoped to use such courses for personal growth or career advancement. Their responses reflect the strong interest in—and responsibility for—designing their own careers. U.S. companies are expected to provide opportunities for education and to provide financial and managerial support for continuing training. But the responsibility for taking advantage of those opportunities rests with the individual. Supervisors can make suggestions to individuals; they can rarely assign them to courses, as is routinely the case in Japan.

TABLE 5-1 Comparison of Motives for Taking Courses

Question: "How important was each of the following motives for taking the additional scientific, engineering, or math courses since receipt of last degree?"

Motives	Japan (n = 51) Mean (S.D.)	U.S. (n = 56) Mean (S.D.)	t
To update existing skills	4.25 (1.01)	4.00 (1.21)	1.18
To add new skills	3.71 (0.97)	4.56 (0.68)	-5.09***
To improve chances of promotion	2.02 (1.09)	2.77 (1.26)	-3.23***
To improve chances of assignment to more interesting activities	2.30 (1.29)	3.18 (1.40)	-3.30***
Assigned to course by company	3.32 (1.44)	1.32 (0.89)	8.31***

Notes: (1) Mean score of 5-point Likert scale from 1 = unimportant to 5 = very important.
(2) ***$p < 0.01$

EVALUATIONS AND REWARDS

How technical employees are evaluated and rewarded differs dramatically between Japan and the United States, as indicated by the data in Table 5-2.

In Japan, evaluations are usually based on daily observations by managers. Some companies have elaborate formal systems that specify evaluation criteria and formats, but in practice evaluations are informal and are carried out with minimal direct feedback to the employee. The annual face-to-face evaluation meetings that play so important a role in U.S. research organizations are conspicuous by their absence in Japan. The opportunity that such interviews give employees to emphasize their accomplishments and for both parties to exchange information and receive feedback are replaced in the Japanese system by an annual written self-assessment that employees are required to give to their managers. But the employee receives no formal feedback during the process.

This kind of evaluation system works well if there is a strong, trust-based relationship between researchers and managers. Without such a relationship, frustration levels can rise, because there is no system to allow researchers to vent their dissatisfaction. Despite the prevailing image of dedicated, company-oriented researchers in Japan, the levels of frustration are growing, especially among younger and more ambitious researchers.

Frustration levels are growing over the reward system in Japanese technical organization. Even though most Japanese companies have adopted formally a more merit-based pay system, managers are reluctant to differentiate significantly among researchers in either base pay or bonuses. And they have no freedom to differentiate across functions: base pay in research laboratories is set by the same criteria as in manufacturing or marketing within that company. In consequence, job performance has relatively little impact on salary and bonus for the individual researcher (Table 5-2, item h). On the other hand, the Japanese system does evaluate researchers over a long

---

TABLE 5-2 Perceptions of Appraisal Process

Question: "The following questions concern your views about the appraisal of engineers in your organization. Please indicate how much you agree or disagree with the following statements."

	Percent indicating "agreement"	
Statements	*Japan (n = 98)*	*U.S. (n = 109)*
a. The performance of engineers is evaluated by the end results of their efforts rather than by the amount of effort itself.	71.4%	55.6%
b. Data collection on the performance of each engineer is highly mechanized, i.e., scoring systems exist for rating specific types of behavior.	7.1%	18.9%
c. The evaluation criteria for each engineer are individualized according to special circumstances, job and organizational situations.	64.3%	50.5%
d. In this organization judgmental or subjective appraisal by the engineer's superior is emphasized.	90.8%	59.8%
e. A regular formal face-to-face assessment interview is emphasized in the appraisal of engineers.	28.6%	70.4%
f. The performance of an engineer is evaluated over a period of five to ten years so that his potential capabilities can be taken into account.	48.0%	10.6%
g. In this organization encouragement and rewards usually outweigh criticism or negative sanctions.	34.7%	57.0%
h. In this organization people get financial rewards in proportion to the excellence of their job performance.	15.3%	55.1%

time period (Table 5-2, item f), and enables the company to assess and utilize the talents of each member of the technical organization.

One of the most significant rewards and incentives for Japanese researchers, therefore, is assignment to interesting and potentially important projects. But such assignments are firmly controlled by research managers in Japan, whereas in the United States researchers can seek out and volunteer for specific projects. Some U.S. companies have gone so far as to adopt an "internal market" whereby project positions are posted within the company and individual researchers encouraged to volunteer.

The greater voluntarism in the U.S. companies also leads to the possibility that researchers will leave team assignments during the project. Asked whether there was a chance of leaving their current project teams during the course of the research, 77.7 percent of the Americans said "of course" or "probably, although I might hesitate a bit." On the other hand, 71.4 percent of the Japanese respondents replied either "of course not" or "yes, but only under special conditions," meaning that in principle such departures were rare.

CAREER PATTERNS

Most Japanese researchers expect to move eventually into line management positions, even those whose interests and abilities lie primarily in technology and research. In interviews, we have found that Japanese researchers are more oriented than their U.S. counterparts to acquiring general managerial skills (as opposed to research management skills). In large part this is due to a widespread perception that the rewards and opportunities are much greater in the management track, and in part it is attributable to highly homogeneous expectations about the direction of careers.

A typical career path for a Japanese researcher who joins a corporate research facility is to remain there for the first seven to ten years as a researcher, usually on new product development, and then to move to a product division to work on incremental product improvement for a few years. The next step, after a few years in the divisional laboratory, is a promotion into line management in the product division. The move from the corporate to the divisional lab is usually an integral part of the technology transfer process: the researcher moves with a project on which he or she has been working, and personally follows the project through manufacturing to the market. In the divisional lab, the next few years are often spent in incremental product improvements on that same product, or a related product family. In the United States, in contrast, outlining a "typical" career for a researcher is an almost impossible task. But most researchers spend most of their working lives in the technical organization; relatively few move out into line management positions in production or general management, and even fewer aspire to do so.

IMPLICATIONS OF CHANGING TECHNOLOGY STRATEGIES

Clearly the Japanese system of technical management has worked extremely well in the past. The standardization of careers and the relatively low input from technical people in shaping those careers has meant that the company can move technical employees from product development into close interaction with production and assign them the responsibility for ongoing incremental improvements, regardless of individuals' personal interests and preferences. Resistance from employees is rare, because the pattern is so strongly institutionalized and taken for granted. The rewards are long term: they are enhanced prospects for advancing into the ranks of upper management. Only a very small number of the most outstanding senior researchers have a long-term career in the research organization. In consequence the corporate research organization is constantly renewed by the entry of new graduates and the movement outward of more experienced researchers.

On the other hand, the system faces challenges from the changing technology strategies of Japanese firms. Internationalization raises questions about whether the system can be transplanted and adapted to other societies. The move to basic research raises the question of whether a system so well-suited to close linkages with production and to continuous improvement of products can accommodate the different individual and managerial orientations required by a major commitment to basic research. One of the key strengths of the system is the homogeneity of technical careers. Japanese firms are beginning to struggle with a difficult dilemma: can they change their existing systems slightly to accommodate the new demands of internationalization and basic research, or must they add new units whose patterns are in sharp contrast to those in the parent technical organization? And if they choose the latter strategy, can they keep the newer patterns from eroding the patterns that have been so successful in the past?

The answers to these questions will only emerge over the next decade. Managers and scholars alike are becoming increasingly aware of the scope of the problems; the solutions still lie in the future.

References

De Meyer, Arnoud and Atsuo Mizushima. 1989. Global R&D Management. *R&D Management,* vol. 19, no. 2.

Dertouzos, Michael L., Richard K. Lester, and Robert M. Solow. 1989. *Made in America: Regaining the Productive Edge.* Cambridge, MA: M.I.T. Press.

Hakanson, Lars, and Udo Zander. 1986. *Managing International Research and Development.* Stockholm: Sveriges Mekanforbund.

Herbert, Evan. 1989. Japanese R&D in the United States. *Research-Technology Management,* vol. 32, no. 6, pp. 11–20.

Ishikawa, Kenjiro. 1990. *Japan and the Challenge of Europe 1992.* London: Pinter Publishers.

MITI (Tsusho Sangyosho Sangyo Seisaku Kyoku). 1989. *NichiBei no Kigyo Kodo Hikaku* (A Comparison of Japanese and U.S. Enterprise Behavior). Tokyo: Nihon Noritsu Kyokai.

National Research Council. 1989. *Learning the R&D System: University Research in Japan and the United States.* Washington, D.C.: National Academy Press.

Perrino, Albert C., and James W. Tipping. 1989. Global Management of Technology. *Research-Technology Management,* May/June, pp. 12–19.

Ronstadt, Robert. 1977. *Research and Development Abroad by U.S. Multinationals.* New York: Praeger.

Rosenberg, Nathan, and W. Edward Steinmueller. 1988. Why Are Americans Such Poor Imitators? *American Economic Review,* vol. 78, no. 2 (May), pp. 229–34.

Saito, Masaru and Hiroyuki Itami. 1986. *Gijutsu Kaihatsu no Kokusai Senryaku* (International Strategies for Technology Development). Tokyo: Toyo Keizai Shimposha.

Sakakibara, Kiyonori. 1988. Increasing Basic Research in Japan: Corporate Activity Alone Is Not Enough. Working Paper No. 8802, Graduate School of Commerce, Hitotsubashi University.

Stalk, George, Jr., and Thomas M. Hout, 1990. Competing Against Time: How Time-Based Competition Is Reshaping Global Markets. New York: The Free Press.

Trevor, Malcolm. 1988. *Toshiba's New British Company.* London: Policy Studies Institute.

Westney, D. Eleanor, and Kiyonori Sakakibara. 1985. A Comparative Study of the Training, Careers, and Organization of Engineers in the Computer Industry in Japan and the United States. M.I.T. Working Paper.

Endnote

1. The following discussion is based heavily on our study of the careers and organization of engineers in product development in three Japanese and three U.S. computer companies. A questionnaire was distributed to 98 Japanese and 109 U.S. engineers and interviews were conducted with individual engineers and research managers in those companies. The full research report is available as a working paper from the M.I.T.-Japan Science and Technology Program under the title of "A Comparative Study of the Training, Careers, and Organization of Engineers in the Computer Industry in Japan and the United States" by D. Eleanor Westney and Kiyonori Sakakibara.

6

MANAGING INNOVATION IN THE TRANSNATIONAL CORPORATION

Christopher A. Bartlett and Sumantra Ghoshal

Philips has long held a leading position in the mature but profitable electric shaver business. Its Philishave is sold world-wide, but has particularly strong sales in Europe and North America. In recent years, this rather traditional and stable product category has been shaken up by several product innovations brought to market primarily by Japanese companies trying to fight their way into an established business with new clearly differentiated product ideas. The most important innovations have been in the area of miniaturization, rechargeability, and most radically, the concept of wet shaving with an electric razor.

For Philips, the new technologies and product market concepts were important trends that had to be fully understood and closely monitored, and in this task Philips' Japanese subsidiary had a critical role. However, the subsidiary had neither the technological capabilities nor the marketing expertise to develop the appropriate response to these events, and had to pass its data on to the product group and development laboratories in Europe to decide what actions Philips should take and to undertake the actual technological development. Finally, while the company had to consider introducing a new product in Japan, its competitive exposure was far greater in Europe and the United States. It was vital to introduce the new product in these locations and the co-operation of the local subsidiaries was necessary to protect Philips' global leadership position in this business.

This example, one of the thirty-eight cases that we documented in some detail in the course of a large research project involving extensive discussion with over 230 managers in nine large companies,[1] illustrates the complexity of managing the innovative process in today's multinational corporations. Not only must the company have sensing, responding and implementing capabilities around the globe, it must be able to co-ordinate those activities and link them in a flexible yet efficient manner, despite the fact that interdependent units may be separated by enormous physical and cultural distances.

Bartlett, Christopher A. and Sumantra Ghoshal, (1990), "Managing Innovation in the Transitional Corporation," in *Managing the Global Firm,* edited by C. Bartlett, Y. Doz, and G. Hedlund, London: Routledge, pp. 215–255.

INNOVATIONS AS THE KEY SOURCE OF GLOBAL COMPETITIVE ADVANTAGE

Scholarly research on international corporations has long identified innovations as the *raison d'être* of multinationals. A firm invests abroad to make more profits out of innovations embodied in the products it has developed for the domestic market. The ticket for a firm to invest and manage its affairs in many different countries is its ability to innovate, i.e. to develop new products and processes, and to create an organization through which it can appropriate the benefits of its innovations more advantageously by operating as a multinational rather than selling or licensing its technology.[2]

In the current international environment, a company's ability to innovate is rapidly becoming the primary source of its ability to compete successfully. While once MNCs gained competitive advantage by exploiting global scale economies or arbitraging imperfections in the world's labour, materials or capital markets, such advantages have tended to erode over time. In most industries today, MNCs no longer compete primarily with numerous national companies, but with a handful of other giants who tend to be comparable in terms of size and geographic diversity. In this battle, having achieved global scale, international resource access and world-wide market position is no longer sufficient—many other MNCs will match such assets. The new winners are the companies that are sensitive to market or technological trends no matter where they occur, creatively responsive to the opportunities and threats they perceive world-wide, and able to exploit their new ideas and products globally in a rapid and efficient manner. Meanwhile, companies that are insensitive, unresponsive, or slow are falling victim to the rising costs of R&D, the narrowing technology gap between countries and companies and the shortening of product life cycles.

The Different Multinational Innovation Processes

World-wide competition has not only made innovations more important for MNCs, it has also made it necessary for them to find new ways of creating innovations. Traditionally, most MNCs have adopted one or both of two classic innovation processes. The first of these is what we describe as the 'centre-for-global' innovation process: sensing a new opportunity in the home country, using the centralized resources of the parent company to create a new product or process, and exploiting it world-wide. The other traditional process we have labelled 'local-for-local' innovation process: national subsidiaries of MNCs using their own resources and capabilities to create innovations that respond to the needs of their own environments.

While most MNCs have tried to develop elements of both processes, the tension that exists between them normally means that one will become the primary source of innovations in any particular company. Quite naturally, the centre-for-global process has been dominant in MNCs adopting what has been described elsewhere as the 'centralized hub' mode of operations while local-for-local innovations have been common in the 'decentralized federation' organizations.[3]

These traditional innovation processes also reflect the traditional mentalities of these two types of companies. The centre-for-global process tends to be associated with what may be described as the extreme global mentality which sees the diversity of international environments as an inconvenience whose effects must be minimized. Thus, these organizations modify their centre-for-global innovations reluctantly and only minimally to meet specific needs. On the other hand, the archetypal multinational mentality underlies the local-for-local innovation process wherein complete conformity to local needs is seen as an unavoidable price of admission to the market. To somewhat caricature these multinational mentalities, if the first reflects minimum compromise to meet local needs, the second implies unquestioning capitulation to the whims and fancies of local customers.[4]

In recent years, however, some of these traditional management attitudes have been changing. As a result, the innovative processes in some MNCs have been evolving. In the course of documenting innovation cases in our nine core companies, we have seen how successful MNCs are developing and managing some new ways of creating new products, technologies, and even administrative systems. These new approaches tend to fall into two broad categories which we have labelled 'locally-leveraged' and 'globally-linked' innovation processes. The first involves utilizing the resources of a national subsidiary to create innovations not only for the local market but also for exploitation on a world-wide basis. The second pools the resources and capabilities of many different components of the MNC—at both the headquarters and the subsidiary level—to create and implement an innovation jointly. In this process, each unit contributes its own unique resources to develop a truly collaborative response to a globally perceived opportunity.

Both of these new and much less frequently implemented innovative processes imply a very different attitude on the part of management—an attitude that constitutes what we call the transnational mentality. Rather than viewing the differences among international environments and the diversity of local demands as liabilities, managers with the transnational mentality see them as one of the company's greatest assets. By being exposed to a diversity of consumer needs, market trends, technological breakthroughs, and government demands, a company has a greater chance of stimulating new ideas internally.[5] By operating in different environments world-wide, the company has access to a broader range of resources and capabilities (particularly the scarcest resource of all—creative people) and is able to enhance its capacity for innovative response. Many companies in our sample tried to create new products, processes, and administrative systems through the two new innovation processes but it seemed that in the absence of this transnational mentality, such efforts rarely succeeded.

Some of the companies we studied, however, were in the midst of a transition to this transnational mentality. They were beginning to synthesize their learning from exposure to diverse environments. The new mentality led them to a new set of management processes that could integrate and focus their dispersed organizational capabilities, and thereby unlock the power of the new innovation processes. Why and how they have succeeded while many others have failed is the main topic of our discussion in this chapter.

MANAGING INNOVATIONS IN MNCs: THE MANAGEMENT CHALLENGE

While locally-leveraged and globally-linked innovations are becoming increasingly important, they are not substitutes for the more traditional innovation processes. In a competitive environment in which the ability to innovate is becoming the critical differentiating capability between the winners and losers, companies are recognizing the need to maximize the number of ways in which they can develop innovative products and processes. But as they try to develop all four of these innovative processes, managers have become aware of the advantages and disadvantages of each, and also of their mutually debilitating characteristics.

Centre-for-Global Innovations: Risk of Market Insensitivity

Centre-for-global innovations are necessary because certain key capabilities of the MNC must, of necessity, remain at the headquarters both because of the administrative need to protect certain core competencies of the company, and also to achieve economies of specialization and scale in the R&D activity. A good example is provided by Ericsson's development of the AXE digital switch.

Impetus for this came from early sensing of both shifting market needs and emerging technological changes. The loss of an expected order from the Australian Post Office combined with the excitement generated in a trade show by the new digital switch developed by CIT-Alcatel, then a small French competitor virtually unknown outside its home country, set in motion a formal review process within Ericsson's headquarters. The review resulted in a proposal for developing a radically new switching system based on new concepts and a new technology. The potential for such a product was high, but the costs and risks were also enormous. The new product was estimated to require over £50 million and about 2,000 man-years of development effort and take at least five years before it could be offered in the market. Even if the design turned out to be spectacular, diverting all available development resources during the intervening period could erode the company's competitive position beyond repair.

In sharp contrast to almost all the 'Principles of Innovation' proposed by Peter Drucker in his book *Innovation and Entrepreneurship,* corporate managers of Ericsson decided to place their bet on the proposal for the AXE switch, as the new product came to be called. They provided full authority and all resources so that Ellemtel, the R&D joint venture of Ericsson and the Swedish telecommunications administration, could develop the product as quickly as possible. For over four years, the technological resources of the company were devoted exclusively to this task. The development was carried out entirely in Sweden, and by 1976 the company had the first AXE switch in operation. By 1984, the system was installed in fifty-nine countries around the world.

The need to centralize the development process was driven by three main forces. First, management wanted to have control over a technology that was going to be at the very core of the company's long-term competitiveness. The cost of unco-ordinated or duplicated development in such a product is astronomical. Second, the effort required close integration between hardware and software development, and subsequently between the development and manufacturing functions. Such close co-ordination could best be provided at a central location. Finally, in a rapidly changing competitive environment, Ericsson knew it had to develop its new switch rapidly if it was to respond to tenders that had begun to specify digital capabilities. Centralizing development reduced the time and inefficiencies associated with more dispersed efforts.

The major risk of such a centralized development process is that the resulting innovations may be insensitive to market needs and may also be difficult to implement because of resistance from the subsidiaries in accepting a central solution. Ericsson was able to avoid many of these problems by seconding to the development a group of engineers from their Australian subsidiary who had recent and direct market experience in responding to the demands of one of the first tenders in the world to specify digital switching capabilities. Other companies, however, were not so fortunate and experienced some of the problems of centre-for-global innovation. For example, NEC designed NEAC 61 as a global digital switch, but with the primary objective of meeting the requirements of the US market. However, while the Japanese engineers at the corporate headquarters had excellent technical skills, they were not totally familiar with the highly sophisticated and complex software requirements of the independent telephone operating companies in the US. The result was that while everyone applauded the switch for the capabilities of its hardware, early sales suffered since the software did not meet some specific needs of end users that were significantly different from those of Japanese customers.

Local-for-Local Innovations: Risk of Needless Differentiation

Local-for-local innovations are essential for responsiveness to the unique attributes of each of the different national environments in which the MNC operates. Current fascination with globalization of markets tends to overlook the fact that while the forces of globalization have certainly strengthened in many industries, the need for responsiveness to national demands and local differences has not disappeared, and often has increased. For example, Unilever faces numerous pressures to develop globally standardized products. The cost and sophistication of R&D is increasing, economies of globally integrated operations are available, and competitive battles with major MNCs like P&G are forcing global responses. Yet, Unilever's ability to sense and respond in innovative ways to local needs and opportunities has been a major corporate asset. While advanced laundry detergents did not sell well in huge markets like India, where much of the laundry was done in streams, a local development that allowed synthetic detergents to be compressed into solid tablet form gave the company a product that could capture much of the bar soap market. Similarly, in Turkey, while the company's margarine products did not sell well, an innovative application of Unilever's expertise in edible fats allowed the local company to develop a that competed with the traditional local clarified butter product, ghee.

But, on the negative side, such innovations may also reflect the efforts of national subsidiaries to differentiate themselves to retain their identity and autonomy, without any real need, and may impose differentiation costs without any significant benefits. Also, they may lead to considerable reinvention of the wheel as each subsidiary finds its own solution to common problems. In the course of interviewing managers in the different companies, we came across scores of instances of such limitations of local-to-local innovations. In Philips, for example, the British subsidiary spent a large amount of resources to create a new TV chassis that would be specially suitable for the local market. The final product was almost indistinguishable from the standard European chassis that headquarters managers were trying to implement, and resulted in the company having to operate five instead of four television set factories in Europe. While this may have been an objective of the managers in the national organization, it clearly compromised Philips' overall efficiency and competitiveness.

Locally-Leveraged Innovations: NIH Risk

Locally-leveraged innovations permit management to take the most creative resources and innovate developments from its subsidiaries world-wide, and allow the whole company to benefit from them. In so doing, the company is often able to take the responses to market trends that emerge in one location and use them to lead similar trends in other locations. This kind of innovation requires management to develop and control a process of world-wide learning, but in so doing it allows the company substantially to leverage its world-wide innovative resources.

For example, Procter and Gamble created the fabric softener product category with a brand called Downy in the US and Lenor in Europe. Unilever's entrant in this fast-growing segment was Comfort, but after years of effort it had done little to shake P&G's dominant first mover advantage. Then, its German subsidiary developed a new brand with a product position and marketing strategy that proved enormously successful in gaining market share rapidly. Management soon recognized that at the heart of the success of Kusshelveich (literally Teddy soft) was the bear that the Germans had developed as the product's symbol and identity. Consumer research showed that not only did the bear do an excellent job in communicating the desired image of softness, it also evoked strong recognition and trusting association in consumers that gave the advertising promise great credibility. The German brand (appropriately translated) and their product market strategy were successfully transferred to other markets throughout Europe and eventually to the US where the teddy bear spokesman rapidly helped Snuggle to build a 25 per cent share in P&G's home market where Unilever's Comfort had been struggling for a decade.

Yet local innovations are not always so easily transferred. The main impediments include attempts to transfer products or processes that are unsuited to the new environment, the lack of suitable co-ordinating and transfer mechanisms (a particular problem with much of the technology transfer), and the barriers presented by the NIH syndrome.[6]

Despite the outstandingly successful transfer of its bear fabric softener, Unilever management was unable to transfer a zero phosphate detergent product developed by its German subsidiary to other European subsidiaries. Insisting that its market needs were different, the French subsidiary proceeded with its own zero-P project. Product co-ordination managers at the central office believed that a NIH attitude was at least as important a factor, particularly in an environment where national companies were struggling to maintain their local R&D budgets against pressures from the centre for more co-ordination.

Globally-Linked Innovation: Co-ordination Cost

The globally-linked innovation process is the one most suited to an environment in which the stimulus for an innovation is distant from the company's response capability, or where the resources and capabilities of several organizational units can contribute to developing the most innovative response to a sensed opportunity. By creating flexible linkages that allow the efforts of multiple units to be combined, a company can create synergies that can significantly leverage its innovation process. Like locally-leveraged innovations, the globally-linked process captures the MNC's potential scope economies and harnesses the benefits of world-wide learning.

One of the best examples we observed of this mode of innovation was the way in which Procter and Gamble developed its global liquid detergent. When Unilever's US success with Wisk demonstrated the potential of the heavy duty liquid detergent category, P&G and Colgate rushed to the market with competitive products (Era and Dynamo respectively), but with limited success. All three companies tested their products in Europe, but due to different washing practices and the superior performance of European powder detergents which contained levels of enzymes, bleach and phosphates not permitted in the US, the new liquids failed in all these test situations.

But P&G's European scientists remained convinced they could enhance the performance of the liquid to match the local powders. After seven years of work they developed a bleach substitute, a fatty acid with water softening capabilities equivalent to phosphate, and a means to give enzymes stability in liquid form. Their new product beat the leading powder in blind tests, and the product was launched as Vizir, establishing the heavy duty liquid segment in Europe.

Meanwhile, researchers in the US had been working on a new liquid to replace Era which had failed to establish a satisfactory share against Wisk. The challenge for liquids in the US was to deal with the high-clay soil content in dirty clothes, and this group was working on improving builders, the ingredients that prevent redisposition of dirt in the wash. Also during this period, the company's International Technology Co-ordination group was working with P&G's subsidiary in Japan and had developed a more robust surfacant (the ingredient that removes greasy stain) making the liquid more effective in the cold water washes that were common in Japan. Each unit had developed effective responses to its local needs, yet none of them was co-operating to share its break-throughs.

When the company's head of R&D for Europe was promoted to the top coporate research job, one of his primary objectives was to develop more co-ordination and co-operation among the diverse local-for-local development efforts. Through several important organizational changes, he was able to develop the means for co-operation, and the world liquid project became a test case. Plans to launch Omni, the new liquid the US group had been working on, were shelved until the innovations from Europe and Japan could be incorporated. Similarly, the Japanese and Europeans picked up on the new developments from the other laboratories. The result was the launch of Liquid Tide in the US (a brand that was able to challenge market leader Wisk), the successful launch of Liquid Cheer in Japan, and Liquid Ariel in Europe. All of these products incorporated the best of the developments created in response to European, American, and Japanese needs.

But this process also has its own limitations. It requires a degree of internal co-ordination that may be extremely expensive and wasteful. The complex interlinkages among different organizational components that are necessary to facilitate this process can also overwhelm a company because of ambiguity and excessive diffusion of authority. One of the companies participating in our study estimated that a new system of periodic meetings that had been instituted for more effective integration of its European production plants resulted in company managers having to spend 2,581 person-days in one year just on travel and in being physically present to attend the meetings. Similarly, ITT faced enormous problems in attempting to develop its System 12 digital telecommunications switch through a collaborative effort of its different European subsidiaries. Trying to co-ordinate the efforts of the different units that were responsible for developing different components of the switch proved to be extremely time consuming and costly, leading to delays and budget overruns. This effort to create a globally-linked innovation may well have been responsible for the failures that led to the company's exit from this business which has traditionally been its primary activity.

The Management Challenge

The challenge for MNC managers, therefore, is not one of promoting one or the other of these different innovation processes, but to find organizational systems and processes that will simultaneously facilitate all the different processes. In other words, they must, at one and the same time, enhance the effectiveness of central innovations, improve the efficiency of local innovations, and create conditions that will make the newer forms of transnational innovations feasible. To do so, however, requires that the companies overcome two related but different problems. First, for each innovation process, they must avoid the different pathologies we have described. Second, to develop innovations simultaneously through all the different processes, they must find ways to overcome the contradictions among the organizational factors that facilitate these processes.

None of the companies in our sample had solved both problems fully. However, some of them had developed special competencies in managing one or the other of the different innovation processes and in overcoming the pathologies of those processes. Their experiences suggest some ways in which MNC managers can overcome the first problem and these are described in the next part of this chapter.

A few of these companies had also made some progress in overcoming the inherent contradictions among the different processes. A special system of internal differentiation in the roles and responsibilities of different organizational units appeared to lie at the core of the solution they were in the process of developing. Instead of finding ways so that each unit could contribute equally to all the different processes, those companies were systematically differentiating among the units based on their capabilities and needs, and were creating an internally differentiated organization so that each unit could have attributes that facilitated its participation in the particular innovation process to which it could make the greatest contribution. In the concluding part of the chapter, we draw some lessons from the emerging practices of these companies to suggest how multinational managers can build an overall organizational system for creating and exploiting the local, central, and two transnational innovation processes.

MAKING CENTRAL INNOVATIONS EFFECTIVE: LESSONS FROM MATSUSHITA

The key strength on which Japan's Matsushita Electric Company has built the global leadership position of its well-known Panasonic and National brands in the highly competitive consumer electronics industry is its ability to create central innovations and to exploit them quickly and efficiently throughout its world-wide operations. This is not to say that it does not employ some of the other modes of innovation, but, of all the companies we surveyed, Matsushita is the champion manager of central innovations. As we tried to identify the organizational mechanisms that distinguish Matsushita's way of managing central innovations from those of the others, three factors stood out as the most important explanations of its outstanding success in managing this innovation process: gaining the input of subsidiaries into the process, ensuring development efforts are linked to market needs, and managing responsibility transfers from development to manufacturing and to marketing.

Gaining Subsidiary Input: Multiple Linkages

The two most important problems facing a company innovating centrally are that those developing the new product or process may not understand market needs, or that those required to implement the new product introduction are not committed to it. (Philips learned both lessons very well when it tried to introduce its technologically superb V2000 video recorder in competition with Matsushita's VHS system and Sony's Beta format.) Matsushita managers are very conscious of this problem and spend a great deal of time building multiple linkages between headquarters and overseas subsidiaries designed not only to give headquarters managers a better understanding of country-level needs and opportunities, but also to give subsidiary managers greater access to and involvement in headquarters' product development processes.

Matsushita recognizes the importance of market sensing as a stimulus to innovation and does not want its centrally driven development process to reduce its environmental sensitivity. Rather than trying to limit the number of linkages between headquarters and subsidiaries, or focus them through a single point, as many companies do for the sake of efficiency, Matsushita tries to preserve the different perspectives, priorities, and even prejudices, of its diverse groups world-wide, and ensure that they have linkages to those in the headquarters who can represent and defend their views.

The organizational systems and processes that connect different parts of the Matsushita organization in Japan with the video department of MESA, the US subsidiary of the company, are illustrative of these multifaceted interlinkages. The Vice President in charge of this department has his roots in Matsushita Electric Trading Company (METC), the organization which has overall responsibility for Matsushita's overseas business. Although formally posted to the United States, he continues to be a member of the senior management committee of METC and spends about a third of his time in Japan. This allows him to be a full member of the top management team of METC that finalizes overall product strategy for the US market, including priorities for new product development. In his role as the V.P. of MESA, he ensures that the local operation implements the agreed video strategy effectively. The General Manager of this department is a company veteran who has worked for fourteen years in the video product division of the corporate headquarters of Matsushita Electric, the production and domestic marketing company in Japan. He maintains strong connections with the central product division and acts as its link to the local US market. Two levels below the department's general manager is the Assistant Product Manager, the junior-most expatriate in the organization. Having spent five years in the company's main VCR plant in Japan, he acts as the local representative of the factory and handles all day-to-day communication with factory personnel.

None of these linkages is accidental. They are deliberately created and maintained and they reflect the company's open acknowledgement that the parent company is not one homogeneous entity, but a collectivity of different constituencies and interests, each of which is legitimate and necessary. Collectively, these multiple linkages enhance the subsidiary's ability to influence key headquarters decisions relating to its market, and particularly decisions about product specifications and design. The multiple links not only allow local management to reflect its local market needs, they also give headquarters managers the ability to coordinate and control implementation of their strategies and plans, including those of implementing their innovations.

Linking Development to Needs: Market Mechanisms

But Matsushita's efforts to ensure innovations are linked to market needs does not stop at the input stage. The company has created an integrative process that ensures that the researchers and technologists are not sheltered from the pressures, constraints and demands felt by managers in the front line of the operations. One of the key elements in achieving this difficult organizational task is the company's willingness to employ internal 'market mechanisms' for directing and regulating the activities of central researchers and development engineers. Because the system is unique, we will describe some of its key characteristics.

Research projects undertaken by the central research laboratories (CRL) of Matsushita can be categorized into two broad groups. The first group consists of 'company total projects' which involve developing technologies that are important for Matsushita's long-term strategic position and that may be applicable across many different product divisions. Such projects are decided jointly by the research laboratories, the product divisions, and top management of the company, and are funded directly by the corporate Board. The second group of CRL research projects consists of relatively smaller projects which are relevant to the activities of particular product divisions. The budget for such research activities, which amounts to approximately half of the total research budget of the company, is allocated not to the research laboratories but to the product divisions. This creates an interesting situation in which technologically driven and market-led ideas can compete for attention. Each year, the product divisions suggest a set of research projects that they would like to sponsor. At the same time, the various research laboratories hold annual exhibitions and meetings and also write specific proposals to highlight research projects that they would like to undertake. The Engineering and Development groups of the product divisions mediate the subsequent contracting and negotiation process through which the expertise and interests of the laboratories and the needs of the product divisions are finally matched. Specific projects are sponsored by the divisions and are allocated to the laboratories or research groups of their choice, along with requisite funds and other resources.

The system creates intense competition for projects (and the budgets that go with them) among the research groups, and it is this mechanism that forces researchers to keep a close market orientation. At the same time the product divisions are conscious that it is their money being spent on product development and they become less inclined to make unreasonable or uneconomical demands of R&D.[7]

The market mechanism also works to determine annual product styling and features. Each year the company has its merchandising meetings, which are in effect, giant internal trade shows. Senior marketing managers from Matsushita's sales companies worldwide visit their supplying divisions and see on display the proposed product line for the new model year. Relying on their understanding of their individual markets, these managers pick and choose among proposed models, order specific modifications for their local markets, or simply refuse to take products they feel are unsuitable. Individual products or even entire lines might have to be redesigned as a result of input from the hundreds of managers at the merchandizing meeting.

Managing Responsibility Transfer: Personnel Flow

In local-for-local innovations, the task of transferring responsibility from research to manufacturing and finally to marketing is facilitated by the smaller size and closer proximity of the units responsible for each stage of activity. This is not so where large central units take the lead role in the development of new products and processes, and Matsushita has built some creative means for managing these transitions. The systems rely heavily on the transfer of people. First, the careers of research engineers are structured so as to ensure that a majority of them spend about five to eight years in the central research laboratories engaged in pure research, then another five years in the product divisions in applied research and development, and finally in a direct operational function, usually production, wherein they take up line management positions for the rest of their working lives.[8] More importantly, each engineer usually makes the transition from one department to the next along with the transfer of the major project on which he has been working.

In other companies we surveyed it was not uncommon for research engineers to move to development, but not with their projects, thereby depriving the companies of one of the most important and immediate benefits of such moves. We also saw no other examples of engineers routinely taking the next step of actually moving to the production function. This last step, however, is perhaps the most critical in integrating research and production both in terms of building a network that connects managers across these two functions, and also for transferring a set of common values that facilitates implementation of central innovations.

Another mechanism that integrates production and research in Matsushita works in the opposite direction. Wherever possible the company tries to identify the manager who will head the production task for a new product under development and makes him a full-time member of the research team from the initial stage of the development process. This system not only injects direct production expertise into the development team, but also facilitates transfer of the innovation, once the design is completed. Matsushita also uses this mechanism as a way of transferring product expertise from headquarters to its world-wide sales subsidiaries. Although this is a common practice among many multinationals, in Matsushita it has additional significance because of the importance of internationalizing management as well as its products.

MAKING LOCAL INNOVATIONS EFFICIENT: LESSONS FROM PHILIPS

If Matsushita is the champion manager of central innovation, Philips, its arch rival in the consumer electronics business, is the master of local innovations. Again, this does not imply that they have not been successful at central innovations. Indeed, the company has a long list of products and processes that were developed in their Central Research Laboratories that extends from their earliest ventures in light bulbs to today's latest innovations in laser disc technology. In the present context, however, we would like to focus attention on why and how Philips has been able to foster a process of innovation at the national organization level to a degree unmatched by any other company of comparable size, diversity and maturity.

The first colour TV set of the company was produced and sold not in Europe, where the parent company is located, but in Canada, where the market had closely followed the US lead in introducing colour transmission. The K6 chassis introduced in Canada was designed in the company's central research laboratory in Holland, but the local subsidiary had played a major role in the development process and had an even greater input in designing the production system. The first stereo colour TV set of the company was developed by the Australian subsidiary; teletext TV sets were created by its British subsidiary; 'smart cards' by its French subsidiary, a programmed word-processing typewriter by North American Philips; the list of local-for-local innovations in Philips is endless.

Philips' ability to create such local innovations has been due in part to the administrative history that shaped the company's growth, and in part to a strong philosophy and explicit strategic choice to respond to the local market needs. The net result has been that, over a period of time, the company has accumulated substantial resources in its different national organizations which, in conjunction with the relatively high level of decentralization of authority, has made dispersed entrepreneurship one of its key organizational assets. Out of the many different factors that have facilitated local-for-local innovations in Philips, there are three that appear to have been the most significant—the company's use of a cadre of entrepreneurial expatriates, an organization that forced tight functional integration within a subsidiary, and the historical dispersion of resources and authority.[9]

A Cadre of Entrepreneurial Expatriates

Expatriate positions, particularly in the larger subsidiaries, have been very attractive for Philips managers for several reasons. With only 6 to 8 per cent of its total sales coming from Holland, many of the different national subsidiaries of the company have contributed much larger shares of the company's total revenues than the parent company. As a result, foreign operations have enjoyed relatively high organizational status compared to most companies of similar size with headquarters in the United States, Japan, or even the larger countries in Europe. Further, because of the importance of its foreign operations, the formal management development system of Philips has always required considerable international experience as a prerequisite for top corporate positions. Finally, Eindhoven, the small town in a rural setting that serves as the corporate headquarters of the company, is far from the sophisticated and cosmopolitan world centres that host many of its foreign subsidiaries. After living in London, New York, Sydney, or Paris, many managers find it hard to return to Eindhoven. Collectively, all these factors have led to the best and the brightest of Philips managers spending most of their careers in different national operations. This cadre of entrepreneurial expatriate managers has been an important facilitator of local-for-local innovations in the company.

Further, unlike companies such as Matsushita or NEC where an expatriate manager spends a tour of duty of three to five years in a particular national subsidiary and then returns to the headquarters, expatriate managers in Philips spend a large part of their careers abroad continuously, working for two to three years each in a number of different subsidiaries. This difference in the career systems results in very different attitudes on the part of these managers. In Philips, the expatriate managers follow each other into assignments and develop close relations among themselves. They tend to identify strongly with the national organization's point of view, and this shared identity makes them part of a distinct subculture within the company. In companies such as Matsushita, on the other hand, there is very little interaction among the expatriate managers in the different subsidiaries, and they tend to see themselves as part of the parent company temporarily on assignment in a foreign company. One result of these differences is that expatriate managers in Matsushita are far more likely to take a custodial approach which resists any local changes to standard products and policies, while expatriate managers in Philips, despite being just as socialized into the overall corporate culture of the company, are much more willing to be advocates of local views and to defend against the imposition of corporate ideas on national organizations.[10] This willingness to 'rock the boat' and openness to experimentation and change is the characteristic that fuels local innovations.

Furthermore, by creating this kind of environment in the national organization, Philips has had little difficulty in attracting very capable local management. In contrast to the experience in many Japanese companies where local managers have felt excluded from a decision-making process that encompasses headquarters management and the local expatriates only, local managers in Philips feel their ideas are listened to and defended in headquarters. This too, creates a supportive environment for local innovations.

Integration of Technical and Marketing Functions within Each Subsidiary

Historically, the top management in all national subsidiaries of Philips consisted not of an individual CEO but a committee made up of the heads of the technical, commercial, and finance functions. This system of three-headed management had a long history in Philips, stemming from the functional independence of the two Philips brothers, one an engineer and the other a salesman. Although this management philosophy has recently been modified to a system which emphasizes individual authority and accountability, the long tradition of shared responsibilities and joint decision-making has left a legacy of many different mechanisms for functional integration at multiple levels. These integrative mechanisms within each subsidiary enhance the efficiency of local-for-local innovations in Philips[11] just the same way that various means of cross-functional integration within the corporate headquarters facilitate centre-for-global innovations in Matsushita.

In most subsidiaries, these integration mechanisms exist at three organizational levels. First, for each project, there is an article team that consists of relatively junior managers belonging to the commercial and technical functions. It is the responsibility of this team to evolve product policies and to prepare annual sales plans and budgets. At times, sub-article teams may be formed to supervise day-to-day working, and to carry out special projects, such as preparing capital investment plans should major new investments be felt necessary for effectively manufacturing and marketing a new product.

A second tier of cross-functional co-ordination takes place at the product group level, through the group management team, which again consists of both technical and commercial representatives. This team meets once a month to review results, suggest corrective actions, and resolve any interfunctional differences. Keeping control and conflict resolution at this low level facilitates sensitive and rapid responses to initiatives and ideas generated at the local level.

The highest level co-ordination forum within the subsidiary is the senior management committee (SMC) consisting of the top commercial, technical, and financial managers in the subsidiary. Acting essentially as a local board, the SMC provides an overall unity of effort among the different functional groups within the local unit, and ensures that the national unit retains primary responsibility for its own strategies and priorities. Again, the effect is to provide local management with a forum in which actions can be decided and issues resolved without escalation for approval or arbitration.

Dispersed Resources and Decentralized Authority

Finally, perhaps the most important facilitator of local innovations in Philips is the dispersal of its organizational assets and resources, and the very high level of decentralization of authority which respectively enable and empower subsidiary managers to experiment and to seek novel solutions to local problems.

The decentralized organization structure and management philosophy have deep roots. From its inception in 1891, Philips has recognized the need to expand its operation beyond its small domestic market. In those early days, however, transport and communications barriers forced management to decentralize operations and delegate responsibilities within its far-flung empire. The forces of decentralization were reinforced by the protectionist pressures of the 1930s that made it practically impossible to ship products or components across different countries within Europe. During World War II, even R&D capabilities were dispersed to avoid the possibility of their falling into enemy hands and many corporate managers left Holland reducing the parent company's control of the world-wide operations. For all these historical reasons, Philips' national organizations developed a degree of autonomy and self-sufficiency that was rare among companies of its size and complexity.

It is said that for an innovation to arise, two factors are necessary. First, the innovation must be desirable for the local managers. Second, it must be feasible for them to create it.[12] Dispersed managerial and technological resources and effective integration among them have made local innovations feasible for Philips subsidiaries. Local autonomy and decentralized control over those resources, coupled with the leadership of a highly entrepreneurial group of expatriate managers have made such indications desirable for them.

MAKING TRANSNATIONAL INNOVATIONS FEASIBLE: LESSONS FROM L. M. ERICSSON

Innovations are created by applying required resources to exploit an opportunity, or to overcome a threat. In multinational corporations, however, the location of the opportunity (or threat) is often different from the location of the appropriate response resources. The transnational innovation processes (locally-leveraged or globally-linked) use linkages among different units of the organization to leverage existing resources and capabilities, irrespective of their locations, to exploit any new opportunity that arises in any part of the dispersed multinational company.

Among the companies we studied, there were several that were in the process of developing such organizational capabilities. A few appeared to have become quite effective in managing the required linkages and processes, and we were able to identify three organizational characteristics that seemed most helpful in facilitating the new integrated innovation processes. The first was an inter-dependence of resources and responsibilities among organizational units, the second was a set of strong cross-unit integrating devices, and the last was a pervasive management attitude of strong corporate identification and well-developed world-wide perspectives.

Interdependence of Resources and Responsibilities

Perhaps the most important requirement for facilitating global innovations is a need for the organizational configuration to be based on a principle of reciprocal dependence among units. Such an interdependence of resources and responsibilities breaks down the hierarchy between local and global interests by making the sharing of resources, ideas and opportunities a self-enforcing norm. To illustrate how such a basic characteristic or organizational configuration can influence a company's process of innovation, let us contrast the way in which ITT, NEC and L. M. Ericsson developed the electronic digital switch that would be the core product for each company's telecommunications business in the 1980s and beyond.

From its beginnings, in 1920, as a Puerto Rican telephone company, ITT built its world-wide operation on an objective described in the 1924 annual report as being 'to develop truly national systems operated by the nationals of each company'. For half a century ITT's national 'systems houses', as they were called within the company, committed themselves to meeting local interests and market needs. All but the smallest systems houses were established as fully integrated, self-sufficient units with responsibility for developing, manufacturing, marketing, installing and servicing their own products. All major innovations had their origins in the powerful and independent national companies, and even a product as important to the company's world-wide success as the highly regarded Pentaconta electromechanical switch was developed by ITT's French subsidiary.

These powerful, independent, and entrepreneurial national companies became the source of many important innovations, but management had never been able to co-ordinate or integrate the diverse efforts very effectively. After enormous frustrations in trying to co-ordinate development efforts and technical standards on the company's production in the electromechanical then early electronic (SPC) exchange switches, management recognized that establishing collaborative processes and co-ordinated efforts was all but impossible in an organization in which the key units were so strongly independent and autonomous. Yet the increasing cost of developing a new switch, and the shortening life cycle of successive generations of technology were forcing the company to take a more integrated approach.

The first sign that exchange switches built on a digital technology might replace recently introduced analog signal processing products occurred in the United States in the late 1970s when Northern Telecom's switch started creating what became referred to as 'digital fever' in North America. Despite the fact that ITT's British and French companies held the original patents for the process of sampling analog signals to convert them into digital form, European markets were being converted to ITT's existing analog switch and the local subsidiaries showed no interest in further developing and applying their pioneering digital research. At headquarters, the company's general technical director saw this as an opportunity to seize the initiative and create a company standard for this product that could then be developed in a co-ordinated global fashion. Consequently he assigned a team at the company's small Connecticut research centre to work on the project. But within a year, the Europeans were interested (and concerned) enough to send their own team of engineers to work with the headquarters group on the new System 12 switch. Their market knowledge and development experience allowed them to bend the researchers' global specifications better to reflect European needs. Soon after they convinced the company to take the responsibility for System 12 out of the hands of 'theoretical researchers in Connecticut' and transfer it to 'practical engineers close to the market'.

But the company wanted to ensure that the original work was not dissipated, diverted, and adapted by local systems houses, and created an International Telecommunications Center (ITC) in Brussels to lead, co-ordinate and control the development process of the System 12 switch. But the newly formed group and the staff managers responsible for it soon found they were no match for the powerful systems houses and the well-entrenched line managers who ran them. Although ITC management was able to allocate some development tasks and keep control over some standards, the large systems houses generally refused to rely on others for the development of critical parts of the system or accept standards that did not fit with their view of local needs. As a result, duplication of effort and divergence of specifications began to emerge, and the cost of developing the switch ballooned to over $1 billion. The biggest problems appeared when the company decided to take System 12 into the US market. In true ITT tradition, the US business wanted to assert its independence and launched a major new R&D effort, despite appeals from the chief technological officer that they risked developing System 13. After years of effort and hundreds of millions of dollars in costs, ITT acknowledged it was withdrawing from the US market. The largest and most successful international telecommunications company in the world was blocked from its home country by the inability to transfer and apply its leading edge technology in a timely fashion. It was a failure that eventually led to ITT's withdrawal from direct involvement in telecommunications.

If effective global innovation was blocked by the extreme independence of the organizational units in ITT, it was impeded in NEC by the strong dependence of national subsidiaries on the parent company. Like ITT, NEC managers first detected 'digital fever' in the US market. The Japanese manager in charge of the US company recognized the importance of this trend early but did not have the resources, the capability or the authority to take much action. His role was one of selling corporate products and developing a beachhead in the US market. In Japan, technical managers were wary about a supposed trend to digitalization that they saw nowhere else world-wide (they called it a passing fad). They were skeptical about the claims of digital's technological superiority, and they were hesitant about beginning developmental work on a new switch that would compete with NEC's existing electromechanical and electronic products.

When the US managers finally were able to elicit sufficient support, the new NEAC 61 digital switch was developed almost entirely by headquarters personnel. Even in deciding which features to design into the new product, the central engineering group tended to discount the requests of the North American sales company and rely on data gathered in their own staff's field trips to US customers. Although the NEAC 61 was regarded as having good hardware, its software was thought to be unadapted to US needs. Sales did not meet expectations.

Both ITT and NEC have recognized the limitations of their independent and dependent organization systems and have begun to adapt them. But the process of building organizational interdependence is a slow and difficult one that must be constantly monitored and adjusted. In our sample of companies, L. M. Ericsson was by far the most consistent and experienced practitioner of creating and managing a delicate balance of inter-unit interdependency. The way in which it did so suggests the value of a constant readjustment of responsibilities and relationships as a way of adapting to changing strategic needs while maintaining a dynamic system of mutual dependence.

Like ITT, Ericsson had built during the 1920s and 1930s a substantial world-wide network of operations sensitive and responsive to local national environments; but like NEC, it had a strong home market base and a parent company technological, manufacturing, and market capability that was available to support those companies. Keeping the balance between and among these units has been a consistent company objective. In the late 1930s, when management became concerned that the growing independence of its offshore companies was causing divergence in technology, duplication of effort, and inefficiency in the sourcing patterns, they pulled sales and distribution control to headquarters and began consolidating responsibilities under product divisions. In the early 1950s, when these divisions showed signs of isolation and short-term focus, corporate staff functions were given more power, particularly in R&D. This led to the company's development of a crossbar switch that was an industry leader. As the product design and manufacturing technology for this product became well understood and fully documented, Ericsson management was able to respond to the demands of increasingly sophisticated and aggressive host governments, and transfer more manufacturing capacity and technological know-how abroad. Because assembly of crossbar switches was so labour intensive, it could often be done more efficiently abroad, and offshore sourcing of components and subassemblies increased.

Following half a century of constant ebb and flow in the centralization and decentralization of various responsibilities, Ericsson had no hesitation and little difficulty in adjusting tasks and responsibilities in response to the coming of electronic switching in the 1970s. Development efforts and manufacturing responsibilities were pulled back to Sweden, but where national capabilities, expertise or experience could be useful in the corporate effort, the appropriate local personnel were seconded to headquarters. In this way, the work the Australian subsidiary had done on a digital group selector was incorporated into the company's AXE digital switch. The AXE was designed knowing that local modifications would be necessary. As a modular system with very clear specifications, it allowed national companies to make necessary adaptations without compromising the integrity of the system. Similarly, in manufacturing,

Ericsson's global computer-aided design and manufacturing system has allowed the delegation of component design and production to any national unit without the parent losing control.

With such central control, Ericsson has been willing to delegate substantial design, development, and manufacturing responsibilities to its subsidiaries and in recent years, the interdependence of units has increased. Primary responsibility for global development of peripheral products has been delegated (for example, Italy is the centre for transmission system development, Finland has mobile telephones, and Australia develops the rural switch). Further, headquarters has given some of these units responsibility for handling certain export markets (e.g. Italy's role in Africa). Increasingly, the company is moving even advanced software development offshore to subsidiary companies with access to more software engineers than it has in Stockholm.

By changing responsibilities, shifting assets and modifying relationships in response to evolving environmental demands and strategic priorities, Ericsson has maintained a dynamic interdependence between its operating units that has allowed it to develop entrepreneurial and innovative subsidiary companies that work within a corporate framework defined by a knowledgeable and creative headquarters group. This kind of interdependence, while hard to achieve rapidly, is the basis for global innovations.

Inter-Unit Integrating Devices

We have shown how central innovations require strong integrating mechanisms at headquarters, and how local innovations are facilitated by co-ordinative capabilities within national units. The two newer global innovation processes need a different kind of integration process—one that operates across units. Such organizational positions and devices are more difficult to develop and manage than the inter-unit mechanisms, and an examination of the approach taken by L. M. Ericsson may provide some insight into how it can be achieved.

Unlike ITT, where relationship among national companies was often competitive and where headquarter–subsidiary interactions were often of an adversarial nature, L. M. Ericsson has been able to develop an organizational climate that is more co-operative and collaborative. This is essential if units are to work together to develop and implement innovations, but is not easily achieved. There are three important pillars to Ericsson's success in inter-unit integration—a clearly defined and tightly controlled set of operating systems, a people-linking process employing such devices as temporary assignments and joint teams, and inter-unit decision forums, particularly subsidiary boards, where views can be exchanged and differences resolved.

Ericsson management feels strongly that its most effective integrating device is strong central control over key elements of its strategic operation. Unlike ITT, Ericsson has not had strong or sophisticated administrative systems (it only introduced strategic plans in 1983), but its operating systems have been carefully developed. As indicated earlier, AXEs product specifications are tightly controlled and the CAD/CAM systems allow close central co-ordination of manufacturing. Rather than causing a centralization of decision-making, management argues that these strong operating systems allow them to delegate much more freely; knowing that local decisions will not be inconsistent with or detrimental to the overall interests.

But, in addition to strong systems, inter-unit co-operation requires good interpersonal relations, and Ericsson has developed these with a long-standing policy of transferring large numbers of people back and forth between headquarters and subsidiaries.[13] It differs from the more common transfer patterns in both direction and intensity, as a comparison with NEC's transfer process will demonstrate. Where NEC may transfer a new technology through a few key managers, Ericsson will send a team of 50 or 100 engineers for a year or two; while NEC's flow is primarily from headquarters to subsidiary, Ericsson's is a balanced two-way flow with people coming to the parent not only to learn but also to bring their expertise; and while NEC's transfers are predominantly Japanese, Ericsson's multidirectional process involves all nationalities.

Australian technicians seconded to Stockholm in the mid-1970s to bring their experience with digital switching into the development of AXE developed enduring relationships that helped in the subsequent joint development of a rural switch in Australia a decade later. Confidences built when an Italian team of 40 spent 18 months in Sweden to learn about electronic switching in the early 1970s provided the basis for greater decentralization of AXE software development and a delegated responsibility for developing the transmission systems.

But any organization in which there are shared tasks and joint responsibilities will require additional decision-making and conflict-resolving forums. In Ericsson, often divergent objectives and interests of the parent company and the local subsidiary are exchanged in the national company's board meetings. Unlike many companies whose local boards are pro forma bodies whose activities are designed solely to satisfy national legal requirements, Ericsson uses its local boards as legitimate forums for communicating objectives, resolving differences and making decisions. At least one and often several senior corporate managers are members of each board and subsidiary board meetings become an important means for co-ordinating activities and channelling local ideas and innovations across national lines.

National Competence, World-Wide Perspective

If there is one clear lesson from ITT's experience with the development of its System 12, it is that a company cannot innovate globally if its managers identify primarily with local parochial interests and objectives. But NEC's experience shows that when management has no ability to defend national perspectives and respond to local opportunities, global innovation is equally difficult. One of the important organizational characteristics Ericsson has been able to develop over the years has been a management attitude that is simultaneously locally sensitive, and globally conscious.

At the Stockholm headquarters, managers will emphasize the importance of developing strong country operations, not only to capture sales that require responsiveness to national needs, but also to tap into the resources that are available through world-wide operation. Coming from a small home country where it already hires over a third of the graduating electrical and electronics engineers, Ericsson is very conscious of the need to develop skills and capture ideas wherever they operate in the world. But, at the same time, local managers see themselves as part of the world-wide Ericsson group rather than as independent, autonomous units. Constant transfers and working on joint teams over the years has helped broaden many managers' perspectives from local to global, but giving local units systemwide mandates for products has confirmed their identity with the company's world-wide operations.

MANAGING INNOVATION IN THE TRANSNATIONAL

As we highlighted earlier in the chapter, the challenge of managing innovation in world-wide organizations is two-fold; first, management must enhance the efficiency and effectiveness of each of the different innovation processes and, second, it must create conditions that allow innovations to come about through all the different processes simultaneously.

In the preceding part of the chapter, we have described some of the ways in which managers can achieve the first of these two tasks. However, to benefit from these specific suggestions we have made, managers must also ensure that efforts to strengthen one of the innovation processes do not drive out the others. And this task of achieving simultaneity of the different innovation processes often proves to be the great challenge because of the dilemma that organizational attributes which facilitate one of the innovation processes often tend to impede the others.

The Organizational Dilemma

Consider, for example, the organizational attributes that are required to facilitate local-for-local and centre-for-global innovations. As we have illustrated, the former process requires that national subsidiaries have certain slack resources, and the requisite autonomy for deployment of those resources for creating local innovations. But such independent and resource-rich subsidiaries also tend to become victims of what Rosabeth Kanter, the Harvard sociologist and author of best selling *Changemasters* calls the 'entrepreneurial trap'—a mentality in which 'the need to be the source, the originator, leads people to push their own ideas single-mindedly'. This mentality impedes the subsidiary's ability and willingness to adopt centre-for-global innovations. Philips has long suffered from this problem, just as companies like Matsushita have suffered from the reverse problem of sheer incapability or lack the motivation wherein perceived or actual scarcity of slack resources and local authority in the national organizations have led to efficient adoption of centre-for-global innovations, but have constrained the company's ability to facilitate local-for-local innovations.

Overcoming the Dilemma: The Transnational Organization

At the core of this dilemma lies an assumption that managers of most multinational companies make about their international organization: they assume that organizational structure and management processes must be symmetric and homogeneous. This assumption is common to companies with what we have described as the global and the multinational mentalities and appears to be extremely widespread in practice.

Although there are wide differences in importance of operations in major markets like Germany, Japan, or the United States compared with subsidiaries in Argentina, Malaysia, or Nigeria, for example, most multinationals treat their foreign subsidiaries in a remarkably uniform manner. One executive we talked to termed this approach 'the UN model of multinational management'. While the functions carried out by the different subsidiaries may be different, they are administratively created as similar and equal. Thus, it is common to see managers express subsidiary roles and responsibilities in the same general terms, apply their planning and control systems uniformly world-wide, involve country managers to a like degree in product development, and evaluate them against standardized criteria. This norm of symmetry and uniformity is inherent in the family metaphor that multinationals, irrespective of their origin, use persistently: Subsidiaries are children of the parent, and therefore there should be no discrimination—read differentiation—among them.

This symmetrical and homogeneous organizational approach encourages management to envision two roles in the multinational company: a local role for each subsidiary, and a global role for the headquarters. As a result, the relationship between the headquarters and the subsidiaries is also viewed in unidimensional terms. It is assumed that the relationship must be based on either dependence or independence of the subsidiary and, therefore, on either local autonomy or central control.

These assumptions and their administrative consequences constrain the flexibility of most multinational companies and imprison them into an either/or choice between central and local innovations. The very simplicity and clarity in these traditional organizational systems prevent the companies from developing the relatively more complex global innovation processes we have described and from achieving the even more difficult task of facilitating all the different local, central, and global innovation processes simultaneously.

These limitations of the symmetrical and homogeneous mode of operations have become increasingly clear to multinational corporations, and in many of the companies we surveyed, we found managers experimenting with alternative ways to manage their world-wide operations. And as we reviewed these various approaches, we saw a new pattern emerging that suggested a significantly different model of international organization based on some important new assumptions and beliefs. This organizational model we call the transnational and we have described the key characteristics of such organizations in a separate paper.[14] However, one attribute of the transnational—its ability and willingness to explicitly differentiate the roles and responsibilities of its different national subsidiaries—is of particular importance to our present discussions since this attribute appears to allow such companies to break out of central/local dilemma and to create an organizational infrastructure for managing central, local, and global innovations simultaneously and effectively.

Differentiated Subsidiary Roles for Different Innovation Processes

In most industries, a few key markets lead the industry's evolution. They are often the largest, most sophisticated and most competitive markets in which the nature of impending global changes is first mirrored. Results of competitive battles in such markets usually have a great deal of influence on the future world-wide competitive positions of firms. In the telecommunications switching business, for example, the United States is perhaps the principal lead market in the world. In the consumer electronics industry, in contrast, Japan, the United States, and a few of the major European markets share the lead position.

These are the markets that provide the stimuli for most global products and processes of a multinational company. Local innovations in such markets become useful elsewhere as the environmental characteristics that stimulated such innovations diffuse to other locations. Similarly, the technological, competitive, and market-sensing processes that are required as inputs for centre-for-global and globally-linked innovations must also be provided by local operations in these lead markets. Relatively speaking, the sensing task for global innovations is much less intense in other 'follower' markets in which the company operates.

While the sensing opportunities lie outside the company and are determined by the strategic importance of different national environments, capabilities required to respond to the stimuli through development of new products or processes lie inside the organization and are determined by the company's administrative history. Further, while environmental opportunities are footloose, shifting from location to location, organizational resources are not easily transferable within the same company due to various administrative, regulatory and other reasons. The result is a situation of environment-resource mismatches: The company accumulates excessive resources in some environments that are relatively non-critical, and very limited or even no resources in some critical lead markets that offer the greatest opportunities and challenges.

Such environment-resource mismatches are pervasive in multinationals. Ericsson has significant technological capabilities in Australia and Italy—relatively insignificant markets in the global telecommunications business—but almost no presence in the United States which not only represents almost 40 per cent of the world's telecommunications equipment demand, but is the source of much of the new technology. Procter and Gamble is strong in the United States and Europe, but not in Japan where important consumer product innovations have occurred recently and where a major global competitor is emerging. Matsushita has appropriate technological and managerial resources in Japan and the United States, but not in Europe—a huge market, and home of arch rival, Philips.

These differences in external environments and internal capabilities imply some significant differences in the contributions that different subsidiaries can potentially make to the different innovational processes we have described. Thus, instead of either choosing to facilitate innovativeness or adoption in all subsidiaries, or seeking to find the non-existent grand compromise between the two, managers of transnational companies allocate different roles to their different operating units, based on the contributions the units can make to the different innovation processes. While none of the companies we studied had developed an explicit set of criteria for allocation of such differentiated roles, Figure 6-1 shows a simple framework for such differentiation that reflects some of the norms that appeared implicitly to guide their various approaches.[15]

Some subsidiaries which are located in challenging and stimulating environments and which possess high levels of technological and managerial capabilities, are allocated the role we label as strategic leaders and these subsidiaries serve as the transnational's innovative spark plugs.[16] They create local-for-local innovations, many of which are subsequently diffused to the rest of the organization as locally-leveraged innovations

FIGURE 6-1 Managing Innovations in the Transnational Organization

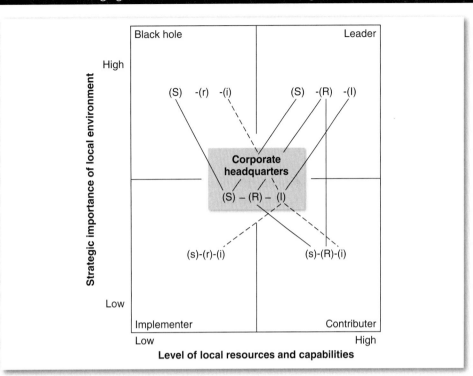

as the new technologies, tastes or business practices that first emerge in their environment diffuse around the world. Similarly, like the German organization of P&G that led the development of Vizir, they play key roles in creating globally-linked innovations. They also contribute to centre-for-global innovations, providing headquarters managers with the early warning signals of an emerging market need or opportunity and by serving as a learning ground for central managers to test their ideas and fine-tune their responses.

If, however, the subsidiary in a critical market does not have adequate internal capabilities to exercise the lead role, it can be designated the sensor role of serving as a scanning and monitoring unit to direct the global innovation processes. Such, for example, has been the role played by the Japanese subsidiaries of many North American companies, and of the US subsidiaries of many Japanese companies.

National subsidiaries with relatively high levels of resources in nonstrategic markets can, in the traditional organization forms of the multinational, become a major source of disruption for the global strategies of the companies. The normal tendency in such units is to utilize the excess resources to demand and justify greater local differentiation and autonomy.[17] In the transnational organization, these subsidiaries are allocated the contributor role through which these excess resources are channelled to global rather than local tasks. Specific tasks with regard to centre-for-global or globally-linked innovations are farmed out to them and their primary contribution to the company's innovation processes becomes one of response rather than sensing.

Finally, organizations with relatively low levels of resources in relatively nonstrategic markets are allocated the implementer role, in which their principal task is seen as one of adapting and implementing central and global innovations in the local context, creating in this process such local innovations as the adaptation task may require.

It is important to note, however, that these roles apply to specific businesses, functions, and product lines only, and not to all the activities of the subsidiary. Thus, a particular subsidiary may play a lead role for a specific product and an implementer or contributor role for others. For example, the UK subsidiary of Philips plays the lead role for the company's teletext TV sets, but an implementer role in the compact disc player business.[18]

Recognition of these differences in the potentials of its different organizational units to contribute to the different innovation processes lead to a set of clear norms in the transnational for deciding where and at what scale they should build the sensing, response, and implementation capabilities that are required to support the different innovation processes. In Figure 6-1 we provide a schematic representation of how such capabilities may be configured and linked within the transnational organization so as to enhance the overall innovation capacity of the company.

In the implementer subsidiaries, each of these capabilities may be built only to the extent that they are required to execute local tasks, including the task of creating and implementing local-for-local innovations. Such local level capabilities are represented by small letters in the diagram with (s), (r), and (i) standing for sensing, response, and implementation, respectively.

In the leader subsidiaries, in contrast, each of these capabilities is required in global scale to support its global roles. Recall, however, that these roles apply to specific businesses, functions, or product lines only, and not for all the activities of the subsidiary, and the global scale sensing, response, and implementation capabilities (represented by capital letters, (S), (R), and (I) respectively) are built in these units only with regard to the specific activities for which they carry the leadership role. Thus, if the French national organization in Philips is given this role for the 'smart card' business, the unit is made responsible for scanning the world-wide technological, competitive, and market environments of this business and not just the environment in France. Similarly, adequate development resources are also provided within the subsidiary to support its 'world product mandate', and appropriate production and marketing capabilities are also established locally so that the unit can serve as a world-scale source for the product as well as the driver for the company's global strategy for this business.

The sensor is not a viable strategic role, and the company's long-term goal should be to build up adequate resources and capabilities in such subsidiaries so that they can assume a leadership role in the relevant business. This process, however, is difficult and requires a long period of time. In the meanwhile such subsidiaries can and must serve as key sources of intelligence; collecting, interpreting, and circulating critical technological and competitive information on developments in its environment. Given the strategic importance and complexity of its local environment, this task requires a high level of sensing capability. Thus, while its response and implementation capabilities may be built up over time, advanced scanning capabilities must be built in such locations on high priority to support their global sensor roles.

The innovation process, however, requires that these dispersed and differentiated capabilities be interlinked so that the sensing, response, and implementation processes can function both sequentially and interactively. Thus, the sensing capabilities of the leader and the sensor subsidiaries must be linked by establishing mechanisms to ensure that intelligence acquired by the latter is passed on to the former. Similarly, the response capabilities of the contributor must also be integrated with those of the leader so as to capture the excess slack in the contributor organization to support the global level tasks that are carried out by the leader.[19] Even the implementation capabilities of the different subsidiaries may be interlinked, or they may be connected via the headquarters since all subsidiaries other than the leader carry only local-level responsibilities for this task.

In our description of the system we have assumed a situation where a national subsidiary plays the leadership role. However, this is not always necessary and the headquarters can and must play the leadership role for certain businesses, and in those cases the linkage among the dispersed sensing, response, and implementation capabilities must be established with the headquarters playing the nodal role. Even otherwise, in most companies, the centre retains the responsibilities for overall strategic direction and co-ordination, and has advanced sensing, response, and implementation capabilities either by design or as a result of historical evolution. Therefore, even for those activities for which the leadership role is allocated to a national subsidiary, the central capabilities must be linked with those of the leader to sustain the overall co-ordination role of the headquarters.

Let us illustrate how such a system might function. In L. M. Ericsson, the Australian subsidiary carries the leadership role for small rural switches built and marketed by the company. For this business, both the headquarters and the Italian subsidiary of the company act as sensors and as contributors. To support this way of operations, the Australian subsidiary has built a highly developed scanning capability and closely monitors world-wide developments in this particular business. The company also has a centralized scanning unit in Stockholm, and this unit passes on to Australia any information on the rural switch market that may come to its attention. Similarly, some of the development engineers in Italy are allocated specific tasks for designing rural switches and they, in effect, work for the Australian subsidiary, despite being located physically in Italy. The development process is co-ordinated through the company's CAD/CAM system which serves as the linking device for the response task. The headquarters co-ordinates the design activities being carried out in Italy and Australia, but the Australian subsidiary drives the entire process and considers itself responsible for the overall task of designing and developing new products to support this small but profitable business of the company.

CONCLUSION: ORGANIZATIONAL CAPABILITY IS KEY

In the course of our study, we found that managers in many companies see the task of managing innovations as one of committing the greatest possible resources for creating new products and processes. This view implied that creating innovations was a specialized function performed in isolation from the mainstream of company activities and that the role of top management was one of resource allocation. Innovation could be improved if R&D budgets were increased, or, if the allocation of funds was made more efficient.

The emerging transnational companies, on the other hand, take a very different view of this task. More than increasing resources or developing new capabilities, we found that managers in these companies consider the challenge to be one of enhancing and leveraging the company's existing assets; rather than focusing the innovative responsibility on a specialized group, they see the task to be one of involving all units of the organization in the process; and instead of developing one highly efficient process of innovation, they recognize the need to manage and integrate multiple processes.

In short, the challenge is much more one of developing organizational capabilities than one related to technological skills or resource allocation. Indeed, the two new transnational innovative processes are based on the ability to leverage existing innovative resources and capabilities by capturing synergies in their combined application or gaining scale and scope economies through broader exploitation of innovations. And to provide just one dramatic illustration of how organizational capabilities may triumph over resource commitments, recall that spending well over $1 billion on the development of its digital switch did not assure ITT success over L. M. Ericsson who spent only a third of that amount.

References

Bartlett, C. A. (1986) 'Building and managing the transnational: the new organizational challenge', in M. E. Porter (ed.), *Competition in Global Industries*, Boston: Harvard Business School Press.

Bartlett, C. A. and Ghoshal, S. (1986) 'Tap your subsidiaries for global reach', *Harvard Business Review*, vol. 64, No. 6, November–December.

_____. (1987a) 'Managing across borders: new strategic requirements', *Sloan Management Review*, Summer.

_____. (1987b) 'Managing across borders: new organizational responses', *Sloan Management Review*, Fall.

Buckley, P. J. and Casson, M. (1976) *The Future of Multinational Enterprise*, London: Macmillan.

Burns, T. and Stalker, G. M. (1961) *The Management of Innovation*, London: Tavistock.

Calvert, A. L. (1981) 'A synthesis of foreign direct investment theories and theories of the multinational firm', *Journal of International Business Studies*, Spring–Summer.

Doz, Y. L. (1979) *Government Control and Multinational Strategic Management,* New York: Praeger.

Doz, Y. L., Bartlett, C. A., and Prahalad, C. K. (1981) 'Global competitive pressures and host country demands: managing tensions in MNCs', *California Management Review,* Spring.

Drucker, P. F. (1985) *Innovation and Entrepreneurship,* New York: Harper & Row.

Edstrom, E. and Galbraith, J. R. (1977) 'Transfer of managers as a coordination and control strategy in multinational organizations', *Administrative Science Quarterly,* June.

Franko, L. G. (1976) *The European Multinationals,* London: Harper & Row.

Ghoshal, S. and Bartlett, C. A. (1987a) 'Innovation processes in multinational corporations', unpublished manuscript, Fontainebleau, France: INSEAD.

————. (1987b) 'Creation, adoption, and diffusion of innovations by subsidiaries of multinational corporations', unpublished manuscript, Fontainebleau, France: INSEAD.

Haspeslagh, P. (1982) 'Portfolio planning: uses and limits', *Harvard Business Review,* (January–February): 58–73.

Hedlund, G. (1984) 'Organization in-between: the evolution of the mother-daughter structure of managing foreign subsidiaries in Swedish MNCs', *Journal of International Business Studies,* Fall, vol. 15, No. 2.

————. (1986) 'The hypermodern MNC—a heterarchy?', *Human Resource Management,* Spring, vol. 25, No. 1.

Kanter, R. M. (1983) *The Change Masters,* New York: Simon & Schuster.

Katz, R. and Allen, T. J. (1982) 'Investigating the not invented here (NIH) Syndrome: a look at the performance, tenure, and communication patterns of 50 R&D project groups', *R&D Management,* 12.

Kogut, B. (1983) 'Foreign direct investment as a sequential process', in C. P. Kindelberger and D. B. Audretsch (eds), *The Multinational Corporation in the 1980s,* Cambridge, MA: MIT Press.

Levitt, T. (1983) 'The globalization of markets', *Harvard Business Review,* May–June: 92–102.

Mohr, L. B. (1969) 'Determinants of innovation in organizations', *American Political Science Review,* 63: 111–28.

Peters, T. J. and Waterman, R. H. (1982) *In Search of Excellence,* New York: Harper & Row.

Porter, M. E. (1986) 'Competition in global industries: a conceptual framework', in M. E. Porter (ed.), *Competition in global industries,* Boston: Harvard Business School Press.

Prahalad, C. K. (1975) 'The strategic process in a multinational corporation', unpublished doctoral dissertation, Graduate School of Business Administration, Harvard University, Boston.

Prahalad, C. K. and Doz, Y. L. (1981) 'An approach to strategic control in MNCs', *Sloan Management Review,* 22, No. 4, Summer.

————. (1987) *The Multinational Mission: Balancing Local Demands and Global Vision,* New York: Free Press.

Ronstadt, R. C. (1977) *Research and Development Abroad by US Multinationals,* New York: Praeger.

Rugman, A. M. and Poynter, T. A. (1982) 'World product mandate: how will multinationals respond?', *Business Quarterly,* October.

Van Mannen, J. and Schien, E. H. (1979) 'Toward a theory of organizational socialization', in B. Shaw (ed.), *Research in Organizational Behavior,* JAI Press.

Westney, D. E. and Sakakibara, K. (1985) 'The role of Japan-based R&D in global technology strategy', *Technology in Society,* No. 7.

White, R. E. and Poynter, T. A. (1984) 'Strategies for foreign-owned subsidiaries in Canada', *Business Quarterly,* Summer.

Vernon, R. (1966) 'International investment and international trade in the product cycle', *Quarterly Journal of Economics,* May.

Vernon, R. (1980) 'Gone are the cash cows of yesteryear', *Harvard Business Review,* November–December.

Endnotes

1. This research project consisted of three phases. The first aimed at identifying and describing the key challenges that are being faced by managers of multinational corporations and to document 'leading practice' in coping with these challenges. This was also the hypothesis-generating phase and the sample was selected to represent the greatest variety of strategic and organizational situations. We chose three industries: consumer electronics, branded packaged products, and telecommunications switching. Each of these businesses was highly international but represented a very different set of key strategic demands. The first offered the greatest benefits of globalization, the forces of national responsiveness were particularly strong in the second, and the third represented the situation where both global and local forces were strong. Within each industry, we selected a group of firms that represented the greatest variety of administrative heritages including differences in nationality, internationalization history, and corporate culture. Philips, Matsushita, and GE in consumer electronics; Kao, Procter and Gamble, and Unilever in branded packaged products; and ITT, NEC, and L. M. Ericsson in telecommunications switching were the obvious choices.

   Figure 6-2 provides a schematic representation of our sample in terms of the strategic characteristics of the industries, and the competitive postures of the firms. In this representation, we adopt the Global Integration–National Responsiveness framework proposed by Prahalad (1975) and subsequently developed by Doz (1979), Prahalad and Doz (1981), and Doz, Bartlett, and Prahalad (1981). For each box, the vertical axis represents the strength of globalizing forces in the industry or the extent of global integration in the company's strategic posture, and the horizontal axis represents the need for national responsiveness in the business or the extent of local differentiation in the company's overall competitive strategy (for a more detailed description of the strategic demands of these industries and administrative

FIGURE 6-2 Sample: Choice of Industries and Companies

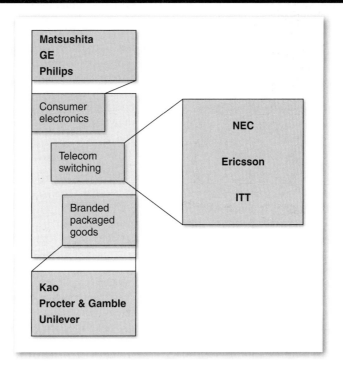

heritages of the companies, see Bartlett and Ghoshal 1987a).

In each of these companies, we tried to identify as many specific cases of innovations as possible, and to document the participants' views on the organizational factors that facilitated or impeded the innovation process. To this end, we interviewed about 230 managers in these companies, both at their corporate headquarters and also in their national subsidiaries in the US, UK, Germany, France, Italy, Taiwan, Singapore, Japan, Australia, and Brazil. None of the interviews lasted less than an hour, and some took as long as three to five hours. We also collected and analysed internal documents relating to the histories of these innovations. This effort led to identification of thirty-eight innovation cases which form the key data base for this article (these innovations have been listed and briefly described in Ghoshal 1987b).

In the next phase of the project, we conducted detailed questionnaire surveys in three of the nine companies. The principle objective of the survey was to carry out a preliminary test of some of the hypotheses that were generated from the first phase of clinical research, also to define the hypotheses more precisely, and to develop suitable instruments for testing them more rigorously. Approximately 160 managers from NEC, Philips, and Matsushita participated in the survey, the results of which broadly confirmed most of the ideas that were generated from the first phase of the study (see Ghoshal and Bartlett 1987a and b).

Finally, in the third phase of the study, the hypotheses were tested through a large sample mailed questionnaire survey that yielded usable data from sixty-six of the largest US and European multinational corporations.

The overall findings of the project are being reported in our book, *Managing Across Borders: The Transnational Solution* (Harvard Business School Press, 1989).

2. This argument is implicit in the Product Cycle Theory proposed by Vernon (1966). It has been stated more explicitly in the internationalization and appropriability theories of foreign direct investment: see Buckley and Casson (1976), Rugman (1982), and Calvet (1981).

3. See Bartlett (1986) for descriptions of centralized hub and decentralized federation modes of multinational operations. In the centralized hub mode, the key assets and capabilities of the company and key value-adding activities, such as product development and manufacturing, are retained at the centre, or are tightly controlled from the centre. The national subsidiaries of centralized hub organizations act primarily as delivery pipelines to supply centrally manufactured global products to the local markets, and their roles are limited to local sales and service tasks. In contrast, in companies operating in the decentralized federation mode, key assets and capabilities of the multinational are dispersed among the different subsidiaries, each of which is allowed to develop as a self-contained and autonomous operation that is able to respond to local demands and opportunities. In a loose sense, the centralized hub mode supports what Porter (1986) calls a 'pure global' strategy, while the decentralized federation corresponds to what he describes as 'multidomestic' strategy.

4. See Levitt (1983) for an interesting, if somewhat provocative, discussion of these two mentalities.

5. Vernon (1980) has highlighted the potential advantages that could accrue to a multinational through such a global scanning capability. The same point has also been made by Kogut (1983) and a number of other scholars in the field of international management.

6. The Not-Invented-Here (NIH) syndrome refers to the resistance of managers to accept ideas or solutions that have been generated elsewhere, and not by them. For a

discussion and elaboration of this syndrome, see Katz and Allen (1982).

7. Westney and Sakakibara (1985) have observed a similar system of internal quasi-markets governing the interface between R&D and operating units in a number of other Japanese companies.

8. See Westney and Sakakibara (1985) for a more detailed discussion of these transitions in the careers of research personnel in Japanese companies, and for a comparison of American and Japanese practices in this regard.

9. The organizational form we have described as the decentralized federation shares many common features with the mother-daughter organization that Franko (1976) described as representative of many large European multinationals. Hedlund (1984) showed that national subsidiaries of such companies typically develop strong and entrepreneurial local management teams and also accumulate relatively high levels of local resources—two attributes that we propose are key to the ability of such companies to foster local-for-local innovations.

10. See Van Mannen and Schein (1979) for a rich and theory-grounded discussion on how such differences in socialization processes and career systems can influence managers' attitudes towards change and innovation.

11. Much of the earlier research on organizational innovation has been focused on innovations that are conceived, created, and implemented within individual sub-units of large and multi-unit organizations. Burns and Stalker (1961), for example, state this explicitly: 'The twenty concerns which were subject of these studies were not all separately constituted business companies . . . (some of them) were small parts of the parent organization. . . . This is why we have used "concern" as a generic term.' Other researchers have similarly observed a district sales office of General Electric, or a department in the headquarters of 3M, or a divisional data processing office of Polaroid, but not the overall configuration of any of these companies. In essence, therefore, these studies have focused on what we call local-for-local innovations. And most of them have identified internal integration, local slack and decentralized authority as key factors that facilitate such innovations in organizations that have been variously described as 'organic', 'integrative', or simply 'excellent' (see, for example, Burns and Stalker 1962; Peters and Waterman 1982; Kanter 1983). To this extent, our findings regarding the factors that make local innovations efficient fully conform to the conclusions reached by earlier researchers. A major point of departure in our study, however, is that we view such local innovations as one of many different processes through which innovations may come about in complex organizations and suggest that the organizational factors that facilitate the different innovation processes are not only different, but may also be mutually contradictory.

12. See Mohr (1969).

13. The use of personnel transfers as an integration mechanism in multinational companies has been highlighted by many scholars, most notably by Edstrom and Galbraith (1977).

14. See Bartlett (1986) for a broad description of the transnational organization. Subsequently, some key attributes of such organizations have been described and illustrated in Bartlett and Ghoshal (1987b). Based on their own research in a wide range of companies, a number of other researchers have also identified this emerging trend of a very different organizational model being adopted by some major multinational companies around the world—a model that has been variously described as the multi-focal organization (Prahalad and Doz 1987), the hierarchy (Hedlund 1986) and the horizontal organization (White and Poynter in this volume). While there are some considerable differences among these different organizational models, there are also some significant similarities. In essence, all these observations point towards the emergence of a more complex organizational form in multinational companies, with significantly higher levels of internal differentiation and integration that are supported through the simultaneous use of a wide variety of structures and management processes.

15. Refer to Bartlett and Ghoshal (1986) for a more detailed description of these different roles of national subsidiaries and for some suggestion on how these roles can be allocated and managed.

16. Rugman and Poynter (1982) have observed a similar phenomenon in the trend toward assigning 'global product mandates' to mature national subsidiaries.

17. The potential of such a disruptive role being played by resource-rich subsidiaries in noncritical environments has been highlighted by White and Poynter (1984) based on their study of the Canadian subsidiaries of a number of large multinational corporations.

18. This is an extremely important point that we have elaborated in Bartlett and Ghoshal (1986) and therefore do not discuss in this paper. If the roles are not differentiated by product lines or businesses, a few subsidiaries will come to play the lead role in general while others will become implementers for all tasks. This can have some adverse motivational consequences, not unlike those described by Haspeslagh (1982) for companies that embraced the portfolio concept uncritically and allocated star roles to some businesses and cash cow, question mark, or dog roles to others.

19. The response capability can be of many different kinds: research and development, manufacturing, marketing, and general management competencies are but some of the capabilities that may be required to respond to a specific situation. In the specific context of R&D capabilities, the need for such linkages among dispersed facilities has been emphasized by Håkanson (see his paper, Chapter 10 of this volume) and also by Ronstadt (1977).

SECTION

II

PROGRESSION OF INNOVATION OVER TIME

Introduction

A primary purpose of the articles included in this section is to illuminate the relationship between innovation and time from a number of perspectives. These articles and book chapters offer insight into the potential lack of generalizeability of innovation research, the concept of the diffusion of innovations, an initial categorization of various types of innovation, an investigation into the association among different kinds of innovation, and how varieties of innovations themselves and the organizations in which they are produced change over time, especially as these innovation modes are related to the product life cycle concept. George Downs and Lawrence Mohr discuss reasons for what they perceive as the lack of generalizeability of innovation research over time, followed by a discussion of changes in innovation over the product life cycle by William Moore and Michael Tushman, and an explanation of the diffusion of innovations over time by Everett Rogers.

Section II begins with an article by George W. Downs, Jr., and Lawrence B. Mohr, in which they take issue with the progress and generalizeability of the findings of innovation research. Their research focuses on innovation from an adoption perspective. They note four categories of research instability that tend to plague the study of innovation. The first area of instability stems from the use of secondary rather than primary variables to classify innovations into typologies. Another area of instability is thought to be associated with the operationalization of the dependent variable—innovation. Employed measures have often been incompatible across studies. A third condition that can add instability to innovation research surrounds the creation of multiple innovation and multiple organization studies. These authors maintain that, even though multiple organizations and innovations might assist in the generalizeability of the findings, using multiple organizations and innovations compounds conceptual difficulties. A final area of instability is fostered by the employment of aggregated secondary data measures rather than primary data measures, and then attempting to infer to specific instances. They conclude their article by offering a set of seven prescriptions to assist innovation research.

The second article in Section II by Thomas Robertson in the late 1960s offers insight into the interface between the consumer of innovations and the innovation itself. Robertson attempts to categorize innovations from a product perspective with an emphasis on how a consumer's behavior might be influenced by an innovation's level of innovativeness or novelty. Robertson also posed a number of additional questions that he addresses in this article, such as: (1) can innovation be programmed?, and (2) can consumer "innovators" be identified and appealed to? This article presents another definition of innovator, which is from the vantage point of a consumer.

Three chapters are borrowed from James Utterback's investigation of innovation dynamics. He presents definitions and descriptions of three major types of innovation, including product, process, and organizational. These three innovation types also provide us with a typology of innovation and we have structured a number of our sections with this framework in mind. Utterback, by investigating many examples of innovations developed throughout history, has advanced the notion of the dominant design applicable to a category of products that he describes as "assembled" goods. This concept is pivotal in his analysis of changes that occurred in many industries during the past one hundred years and is implemented in the work of others such as Abernathy and Utterback (Section V) and Moore and Tushman (this section). The notion of a dominant design allows Utterback to illuminate turning points in the progress of firms and industries over time. Utterback also examines another category of product innovations, which he describes as "nonassembled" goods. He introduces another concept that is analogous to a dominant design but is pertinent to nonassembled goods: an enabling technology. With these concepts and a description of the marketplace in which such products compete, he formulated his three-factor model. He employs his three-factor model to attempt to understand important issues such as: (1) the longevity of a new product and firm, (2) where attacking new products will likely originate, and (3) how to transition from a small entrepreneurial firm to a mature company.

William L. Moore and Michael L. Tushman, as Utterback did, begin their thesis with the premise that there is a relatively predictable pattern in the amount and type of innovation that occurs over a product's life cycle. Moore and Tushman, rather than primarily focus on the market and competitive forces to the degree that Utterback did, concentrate on two primary issues: (1) the transitions that must be made from leading an entrepreneurial firm to managing an established, functionally oriented company, and (2) the retention of the ability to learn and innovate during the organization's mature years. To illuminate these transitions and investigate a firm's ability to retain an innovative spirit, Moore and Tushman describe in detail the managerial paradoxes that present themselves to the leaders of organizations, such as the ability to perform as an entrepreneur while transitioning to being the steward of a firm's assets.

One chapter from Everett M. Rogers' book, describing years of research relative to the diffusion of innovations, concludes this section. As noted by Robertson earlier in this section, the diffusion of innovations is as important as the innovation process or the innovation itself. Rogers describes the major findings that the research in this area has produced over the years. He also offers major definitions and descriptions of an individual's process of innovation adoption and how the adoption cycle relates to the process of diffusion through a target population. He details the five special attributes of innovations that tend to provide innovations with an advantage in a marketplace. For Rogers, a marketplace is anywhere anything is being sold. "Selling" in these "marketplaces" takes on a whole new meaning because it is defined broadly enough to encompass new goods such as cellular telephones sold in Chicago as well as new methods for people in third world countries to understand important health issues.

References

Downs, George W., Jr., and Lawrence B. Mohr. 1976. Conceptual issues in the study of innovation. *Administrative Science Quarterly* (21): 700–714.

Moore, William L. and Michael L. Tushman. 1982. Managing innovation over the product life cycle. In *Readings in the Management of Innovation*. Eds. Michael L. Tushman and William L. Moore. Boston, MA: Pitman.

Robertson, Thomas S. 1967. The process of innovation and the diffusion of innovation. *Journal of Marketing* 31(1): 14–19.

Rogers, Everett M. 1995. Diffusion of innovations, 4th ed. New York: The Free Press.

Utterback, James M. 1994. *Mastering the dynamics of innovation.* Boston, MA: Harvard Business School Press.

7

CONCEPTUAL ISSUES IN THE STUDY OF INNOVATION

George W. Downs, Jr., and
Lawrence B. Mohr

This paper discusses a number of complex and currently unresolved conceptual issues arising in research on innovation in complex organizations. In an effort to link the issues they are approached through an exploration of the factors responsible for instability in empirical findings. Four separate sources of instability are defined and their theoretical and methodological implications are treated at some length.

The analysis of the relative adoptability of innovations and the innovativeness of organizations are found to be related by mirror-image theoretical symmetry. The four sources of instability are seen to have the same implications for the development of a theory of adoptability. Seven prescriptions for research on innovation are suggested. Although this study suggests how one might arrive at a general theory of innovation, it does not actually construct any specific theory.

Innovation has emerged over the last decade as possibly the most fashionable of social science areas; a frequently short-lived and perhaps dubious distinction held in recent memory by small group research. Like the latter, the study of innovation has not been confined to any single discipline but is being explored in fields as diverse as anthropology and economics. This popularity is not surprising. The investigations by innovation research of the salient behavior of individuals, organizations, and polities can have significant social consequences. The latter imbue even the most obscure piece of research with generalizability that has become rare as social science becomes increasingly specialized. The act of innovating is still heavily laden with positive value. Innovativeness, like efficiency, is a characteristic we want social organisms to possess (cf. Nelson, 1972: 39). Unlike the ideas of progress and growth, which have long since been casualties of a new consciousness, innovation, especially when seen as more than purely technological change, is still associated with improvement.

Unfortunately, the theoretical value of the research that has been done is problematic. Perhaps the most alarming characteristic of the body of empirical study of innovation is the extreme variance among its findings, what we call instability. Factors found to be important for innovation in one study are found to be considerably less important, not important at all, or even inversely important in another study. This phenomenon occurs with relentless regularity.[1] One should certainly expect some variation of results in social science research, but the record in the field of innovation

Downs, George W., Jr., and Lawrence B. Mohr. 1976. Conceptual issues in the study of innovation. *Administrative Science Quarterly* (21): 700–714.

is beyond interpretation. In spite of the large amount of energy expended, the results have not been cumulative. This is not to say that the body of existing research is useless; when organized properly, when we know just how to examine it, it may well constitute a powerful source of evidence bearing on important theoretical elements. But progress toward what has been called integrative theory (see Rogers and Shoemaker, 1971: 346) will have to be made before much of this data will be useful.

This troubling instability results from a lack of clarity on several conceptual issues. We will therefore elucidate certain key conceptual difficulties in research and theory, showing their necessary effect on the stability of research results from study to study, and suggest what must be done to make research effort more cumulative. Our study focuses on innovation in complex organizations. We define four primary sources of instability: (1) variation among primary attributes, (2) interaction, (3) ecological inferences, (4) varying operationalizations of innovation; and we offer seven methodological prescriptions toward the development of an integrative theory. We will be employing the rather broad, conventional definition of innovation as the adoption of means or ends that are new to the adopting unit. Although we will mainly discuss the question of the relative innovativeness of organizations rather than the relative adoptability of different innovations, we will suggest that the two are closely related methodologically and that this relationship describes an important symmetry.

We would like to emphasize that we are not constructing a specific theory of innovation, but are describing how one might be arrived at through research and the rough form a general theory of innovation might take.

TYPOLOGIES OF INNOVATIONS

The purpose of investigating the reasons some organizations are more likely than others to adopt a given innovation has been to develop a general theory of innovation. Because previous research indicates that determinants important for one innovation are not necessarily important for others, these efforts have not yielded such a theory. In industry, for example, the large, successful firms have been found to lead in adopting some innovations (Mansfield, 1963), while the relatively unsuccessful firms were clearly the leaders with respect to others (Adams and Dirlam, 1966). In the public sector, Becker (1970: 275) found that the public health officials leading in the adoption of measles immunization were young, urban, liberal, and cosmopolitan, while the pioneers in the adoption of diabetes screening were old, rural, conservative, and parochial. The instability of the determinants from case to case frustrates theory-building efforts.

Perhaps the most straightforward way of accounting for this empirical instability and theoretical confusion is to reject the notion that a unitary theory of innovation exists and postulate the existence of distinct types of innovations whose adoption can best be explained by a number of correspondingly distinct theories (cf. Rowe and Boise, 1974: 289–290). These theories may include different variables, or they may contain the same explanatory variables while positing different interrelationships among them and different effects upon the dependent variable. The existence of empirically distinguishable categories of innovations and their associated models would help to explain why studies employing roughly the same predictors achieve widely varying R^2s and why the explanatory power of individual variables is unstable across them.

Even the suggestion that a single theory and set of determinants are applicable to the entire set of newly implemented techniques, programs, rules, and norms that are lumped under the generic heading *innovations* should be considered suspect. While most students of innovation might agree with this statement in the abstract, its implications have rarely been considered in either research or theory building. Most emphasis has been placed on uncovering the effect of centralization, executive ideology, or professionalization. Summaries are presented of those attributes of organizations or individuals associated with innovativeness but are unaccompanied by any hint that their impacts may depend on the innovation studied. When findings surrounding the impact of a variable on innovation are contradictory, the common reaction has been to view the matter as yet undecided and call for further study, rather than to explore the divergent studies in search of linkages between the kinds of results obtained and the kinds of innovations considered.

Examples of potentially fruitful categorization schemes or typologies of innovations are plentiful. For instance, the determinants of high-cost innovations would seem to be markedly different from those of low-cost innovations. Wealth or resources would clearly predict the former differently from the latter. Resource levels might explain much of the variation in the adoption of elaborate EDP systems by corporations but be relatively unrelated to the same corporations' adoption of new supervisory techniques or job enrichment programs. Similarly, variations in the communicability of an innovation would be expected to affect the impact of professionalism or cosmopoliteness on adoption. It may therefore not be merely coincidental that the role of resources and cosmopoliteness has varied a great deal from one study to another (see Rogers and Shoemaker, 1971: 361, 369).

Primary Attributes of Innovations

A typology dividing innovations into groups or categories must itself be based on a characteristic or attribute of the innovation. For example, it might be based on the cost of the innovation (high or low), or on its communicability (a simple innovation or a complicated one). Such characteristics may be either primary or secondary, and this distinction has important implications for how typologies should be employed and what may be their relationships to theory building. James Jeans (1966: 196) concisely explains the usage of these terms as follows:

> Galileo, Descartes, Locke, and others divided the qualities of objects and substances into two classes which Locke designated as primary and secondary. Secondary qualities are those which are perceived by the senses, and so may be differently estimated by different percipients; primary qualities are those which are essential to the object or substance and so are inherent in it whether they are perceived or not.

When a typology is based on a primary attribute, an innovation can be confidently classified without reference to a specified organization. Regardless of its size, wealth, complexity, decentralization, and so forth, each organization would place the innovation in the same cell of the typology. Thus, both rich and poor and large and small organizations would describe the innovation as type A. However, when a typology is based on a secondary attribute, the classification of the innovation depends on the organization that is contemplating its adoption. Large organizations, for example, might classify it as type A while small ones might classify the same innovation as type B.

Deciding whether or not there are purely intrinsic (primary) characteristics of innovations that are logically independent of the organizations which might adopt them is not essential for our purpose. What matters instead is constancy within an individual study. We define an attribute (for instance, cost) as primary in a given piece of research when there would be essentially no variation among the organizations studied in categorizing the innovation on that attribute—for example, it is a low-cost innovation to all. This lack of variation leads to a restricted ability to generalize from a given study of innovation.

The existence of such attributes is less relevant to the *design* of research than to its *interpretation*. The consequences for the evaluation of research and for theory building are great, since at least some instability can be explained by differences among innovations in their primary attributes. For example, some findings of research into the determinants of high-cost[2] innovations are generalizable only to other high-cost innovations. Variation among studies in the cost of the subject innovation will cause variation among the coefficients of certain independent variables, and there is little that can be done about this instability other than to understand and accept it. There would be no point in trying to generalize about the impact of a variable like wealth on innovativeness because wealth would not have a constant impact. It is no doubt an important determinant of the adoption of high-cost innovations but may have no bearing at all upon the adoption of low-cost innovations. The challenge to the theorist is, by comparing studies of disparate innovations, to determine the coefficient on wealth as a function of cost, so that, given the cost of the innovation, theory is definite.

In addition to cost, there may be several other characteristics of innovations that are candidates for the basis of a primary-attribute typology. There is the danger in all scientific research that such constants place unknown limits upon generalizability. Moreover, it is an obstacle to science that the constants that matter are generally difficult to divine, so that the limits often go unrecognized.

Variation of a characteristic of an innovation between one study and another but not within the respective studies is almost certainly an important source of instability in innovation research. If such a characteristic were a true, Lockean primary attribute (that is, actually intrinsic to the innovation), then this instability could not be resolved. We would need as many theories of organizational innovativeness as there were categories of such primary attributes. However, if the characteristic were in truth a secondary attribute, different theories would not be needed. It would be possible to manage the resulting instability with a general theory by postulating interaction among independent variables. Fortunately, most if not all characteristics upon which one might consider basing a typology turn out to be secondary attributes of innovations.

Secondary Attributes of Innovations

While there have been few attempts to categorize innovations by primary characteristics, several social scientists have suggested typologies based on secondary attributes of innovations. The rationale behind these categorization schemes is identical, in that the determinants of adoption are different for different categories of innovations. Some examples from the literature are problem versus slack, routine versus radical, variation versus reorientation, major versus minor, and means versus ends (see Cyert and March, 1963; Knight, 1967; Normann, 1971; Wilson, 1966). What these categorization schemes have in common is that the same innovation may be classified in different categories for different organizations, for example, an innovation might be seen as minor or routine by some organizations but as major or radical by others. When we think in terms of a continuous dimension, such as the extent to which an innovation is compatible with the organization's present mode of operation, the amount of variance across organizations is even more conspicuous. Winter (1968) has made the point forcefully that an innovation is rarely the same thing to two organizations. Secondary attributes are no doubt more numerous by far than primary attributes.

Because an innovation's classification in a secondary-attribute typology can vary from organization to organization, we face a situation where two or more theories are presumably applicable to the adoption of the *same innovation.* If researchers ignore this fact and proceed with analysis, the result with respect to a single innovation would often be similar to arbitrarily taking an average of the findings among high-cost and low-cost innovations. That is, if different organizations in a study cause the same innovation to be classified differently, the coefficient of an independent variable that possesses differential impact within two categories of the typology would be a misleading average of the values obtaining in each category. The value that actually emerges from a regression analysis would therefore depend upon the proportion of organizations in the sample that considered the innovation major (or a reorientation, and the like) as opposed to those that considered it minor. As to correlation coefficients, which are frequently employed, the mixing or superimposing of one causal function upon another in this fashion almost always acts to increase the variance of the dependent variable (innovation) relative to the independent variable (for instance, executive ideology), so that the correlation coefficient will almost always be smaller than it would be in any single category of the typology. This may possibly help to show why the explanatory power of some variables thought to be theoretically relevant has been low.

The existence of secondary-attribute typologies would appear to have implications for research design. The crucial difference between secondary and primary attributes—that any secondary attribute of an innovation may vary from organization to organization—is not necessarily a liability. It indicates that we must build the idea of statistical interaction into our models of innovation. When we recognize that different organizations classify the same innovation into different categories, and also that determinants vary in existence or strength depending upon the category into which the innovation is classified, we are by these very facts recognizing the existence of interaction. Further, the interaction may be built into our designs and used to advantage.

Suppose that executive ideology is a more important determinant of the adoption of reorientation innovations than it is of variations. If we are studying an innovation that would be a reorientation for some organizations and a variation for others, all we need do is insert a variable which measures how compatible[3] the innovation is to each organization in the sample. This would provide us with even more information than we would obtain from separate studies of variations and reorientations. Specifically, we can obtain the following four types of information. (1) By including the organization's compatibility with the innovation as a separate independent variable, we can determine the extent to which this in itself affects the adoption of the innovation—note that to make compatibility an independent variable we must transform it from a property of the innovation to a property of the organization, and that this can easily be done. (2) By employing one or more interaction terms—for example, the product of compatibility and executive ideology—we can determine the differential importance of a variable, such as executive ideology, for innovation, given any particular level of compatibility. (3) We can also investigate which characteristic or set of characteristics of the organization determines the classification of the innovation. (4) If, for the sake of discussion, size is found to play such a determining role, then we might also investigate the interaction of size and executive ideology as predictors of innovation. This may be an interesting and prescriptively valuable finding that could not be expected to emerge from the separate study of variations and reorientations.

There is no reason for developing separate models of innovation for different categories of secondary attributes. Instead, the secondary attribute may simply be measured as an organizational property and then used in the ways described. Should there be more than one secondary attribute responsible for variation among the determinants of adoption—and this may well be true, given the number of typologies that have been suggested—there is of course the requirement that new interaction terms be added and that, therefore, sample sizes be larger. The consequence of hypothesizing interaction in this fashion should be an increased understanding of the determinants of innovation, greater explanatory power, and less randomness in the appearance of results.

Secondary Attributes of Organizations

Just as many characteristics turn out to be secondary attributes of innovations, so also may a great many well known variables function as secondary attributes of organizations. Centralization, for instance, is a loose term for the degree to which authority and influence regarding decisions are consolidated in higher echelons rather than being spread among lower ones. It is commonly considered to be a general property of an organization and it used to be measured in global, nonspecific terminology (see for example, Hall, 1963). However, organization theorists have long since recognized that centralization varies within organizations as well as between. It is still included in analysis as though it were an organization-wide property, but it is measured by aggregating the responses to questions or observations about several different kinds of decisions—personnel, purchasing, and so forth (Pugh, *et al.,* 1968: 102–104; Child, 1972; Negandhi and Prasad, 1971). Thus, it is recognized in measurement procedures that centralization differs depending upon what is being decided, and this observation clearly extends into the realm of innovation. For a variety of reasons, in any given organization some innovation decisions might be made at a high level and others at a lower one; some might be taken with broad organizational input and some with the involvement of only one or two persons. Centralization, in sum, is a secondary attribute. Its measured value depends upon the innovation being considered. The same is true of complexity, formalization, integration (conflict-resolution mechanisms), specialization, professionalization, traditionalism, and no doubt many other factors that in some sense help to determine innovation (see Hage and Aiken, 1967; Zaltman *et al.,* 1973: 134–154).

THE INNOVATION-DECISION DESIGN

It is apparent that much of the conceptual and methodological complexity surrounding the issue of instability is brought about by the existence of secondary attributes. Because this category of variables seems to be composed of a large portion of the most important predictors of innovation, the strategy of increasing stability by simply eliminating secondary attributes from our models would hardly appear a viable one.

One way of coming to grips with secondary attributes is to think of them not as being composed wholly of characteristics of the innovation or the organization but as characterizing the *relationship* between the two. The unit of analysis is no longer the organization but the organization with respect to a particular innovation, no longer the innovation, but the innovation with respect to a particular organization. Neither the organization nor the innovation would be described as compatible, for example, but rather the pair taken in conjunction. From this perspective, secondary attributes can be viewed as variables that characterize the circumstances surrounding a particular decision to innovate.

In order to integrate this perspective into the research on innovation, it is helpful to employ an innovation-decision design, a consideration of the unit of analysis as an organization in relation to an innovation. If we were studying the adoption of 10 innovations by 100 organizations, we would be working with a sample of 1,000. This design eliminates any confusion that might stem from volatile secondary attributes. It would no longer seem inappropriate to assign a particular organization one set of scores with respect to its perceived profit, level of centralization, formalization, and so forth in connection with innovation X and another set of scores for these same dimensions in connection with innovation Y. As for primary attributes, the organization's scores would by definition remain constant across the set of innovations.[4]

A benefit of employing the innovation-decision design is that it serves to remind us of the dangers of thinking in terms of something called the organization, a reification with constant properties whose probability of adoption never varies, regardless of the kind of innovation it considers. Rather, it focuses our attention on the shifting incentives and constraints that are relevant to the decision to innovate.

The innovation-decision design is an extension of the single-innovation design. It has all of the advantages of the latter, plus the greater generalizability that results from considering many innovations rather than one. Furthermore, we will show that it connects the study of innovation with the study of adoptability in a manner that is both illuminating and efficient. We therefore highly recommend its adoption for innovation research.

MULTIPLE-INNOVATION RESEARCH

From the standpoint of theory building and conceptual issues, what are the advantages and disadvantages of treating several innovations at once, not as in the innovation-decision design, but as an aggregate? The strategy has been employed in scores of studies (such as Mansfield, 1963; Hage and Aiken, 1967; Mohr, 1969; Walker, 1969, 1971), the apparent motive being to increase the reliability and generalizability of findings over a single-innovation study. But does it work?

In a multiple-innovation study, we encounter dependent and independent variables in a form such as "number of technological innovations adopted" and "average perceived profitability," respectively. The only clue indicating the extent to which the differential profitability of a given innovation for various organizations determines the order in which they adopt it is the relationship of these two aggregate measures. The clue might or might not be a good one, depending upon certain properties of theory and data; if it is not good in a certain case, if the inference from the collective or ecological level to the individual level is either biased or intolerably variable, then the inference is often termed an "ecological fallacy." In innovation research, this kind of cross-level inference is very likely to be incorrect. There are two reasons for this. One is that, given the interactions we have discussed and that almost certainly exist, the impact of a variable like profitability upon individual instances of innovation varies substantially from one organization to another. This connotes the ecological difficulty generally called aggregation bias (see Theil, 1971: 556–566). The other is that the grouping by organization of the values of independent variables such as expected profitability is almost necessarily inefficient; it would be most efficient if all of the highly profitable expectations were concentrated in some organizations and the unprofitable expectations in others, rather than a mixture in each (see Prais and Aitchison, 1954; Cramer, 1964; and Hannan and Burstein, 1974). The bias and variability resulting from these sources can be quite large and may either aggrandize or understate the true coefficient. We can be misled easily in innovation research by aggregate statistics.

It should be noted that an ecological fallacy can occur only when the independent variable involved is a secondary attribute of the organization, one whose value differs from one innovation to another so that averaging these values becomes necessary. Profitability and similar motivational forces are obviously in this category, as are variables like organizational compatibility, the organizational counterparts of important attributes of innovations. We have seen that centralization and complexity are secondary attributes as well, even though they might not be recognized as such in measurement procedures. So are certain resources relevant to innovation, such as professionalization and expertise. Thus, correlation and regression coefficients involving such variables will be unstable in multiple-innovation designs; they will fluctuate mysteriously around the true microlevel values that they are supposed to represent. But these variables are extremely important for the development of theories of innovation. We cannot rely solely on primary attributes such as raw organizational wealth and the age and cosmopoliteness of the chief executive. Since secondary attributes must be prevalent in broadly applicable models, interpretation based on aggregate data will be grossly misleading.

A question remains, however, whether this difficulty might not be offset by the gains in generalizability that are realized when multiple- rather than single-innovation designs are used.

It is not meaningful to offset an evil of one kind with a good of another. The central disadvantage of the multiple-innovation design is so serious as to be incapacitating. Furthermore, generalizability is not better attained by the multiple-innovation design. The dependent variable, aggregate adoption of a mixture of innovations, generally represents a large variety of values on both primary and secondary attributes of the innovations considered, all blended together so as to obscure totally the special implications of each. There is in fact nothing to generalize to. We learn nothing about variations and reorientations, high and low cost, and so forth. The innovation-decision design, on the other hand, does accomplish what has been sought in multiple-innovation research. It is a combination, in a sense, of the single- and multiple-innovation designs. It uses many innovations and so has substantial generalizability, but it does not aggregate them. It considers them as discrete units, thereby preserving the special theoretical implications of each.

Some might consider that studying the aggregate adoption or nonadoption of a number of new ideas is a reasonable substitute for studying extensiveness of commitment to any given new idea. That is clearly not the case. It is quite possible for organizations to adopt a great many innovations at the most superficial level. In fact, in at least one empirical study (Mohr, 1969: 121), this propensity was found to exist among the larger organizations.

It might also be considered that aggregate adoption or nonadoption may substitute for time-of-adoption as a dependent variable or that one can at least infer relative earliness to adopt from relative number of innovations adopted. This is no more true of multiple- than of single-innovation studies. If organization A has adopted n innovations and organization B has adopted $n + 2$, we know only that B has adopted two innovations earlier than A, but nothing about the time at which either adopted the other n. If we were awarding points for earliness of adoption, A could accumulate many more points than B by having adopted the n innovations earlier. We should not hastily classify as early adopters organizations that have adopted many innovations.

We conclude that the multiple-innovation design is undesirable for investigating the basic theoretical question "What are the determinants of the adoption of an innovation?" Despite its drawbacks, however, it might be considered that the multiple-innovation design is uniquely capable of tapping an entirely different dimension of innovation. Consider the aggregated or macrolevel measure of innovativeness as a dependent variable in its own right, rather than as a substitute for some microlevel concept. There does, after all, appear to be something different about adopting lots of innovations as opposed to adopting one, and we would benefit from a model that predicts the former as well as the latter. Again, however, a multiple-innovation study is not the appropriate way to accomplish this end. It presumes that the adoption of one blended set of innovations follows the same laws as the adoption of another, regardless of the kinds of innovations included in each. The assumption is not valid. Should we actually wish to predict the adoption of a given set of innovations, the correct method is to plug the appropriate values of primary and secondary attributes for each innovation into a statement of the theory and then to aggregate the individual equations.

Thus, we find that the multiple-innovation design solves no problems in the study of innovation, but only compounds conceptual difficulties.

THE MEASUREMENT OF INNOVATION

Another potential source of instability in innovation research involves the operationalization of the dependent variable. Just as the results of studies of different kinds of innovations are commonly considered together in general discussions of what determines innovation, so are the results of studies in which quite different behaviors are being explained. There are three principal, interrelated operationalizations of innovation found in the literature. The first, and by far the most common, is the assignment to each organization of an innovation score based on its time of first adoption or use. The second is a simple, dichotomous adoption or nonadoption. This may be seen as merely a crude measure of the time of adoption, allowing many ties. The third operationalization is determined by the extent to which an organization has implemented an innovation, or the degree to which an organization is committed to it.

The prevalence of the first operationalization over the third can probably be attributed to the relative ease with which pertinent data can be gathered and to the light shed by its analysis on the nature of the diffusion process. It is considerably easier to learn approximately when a physician or hospital first used an experimental drug, or when a legislature passed affirmative-action legislation, than it is to discover the proportion of eligible patients who received the drug or the proportion of jobs filled in accordance with the new regulation. In addition, innovation research has traditionally manifested great interest in the manner and rate by which an innovation is spread through a population. A knowledge of the order in which members of a population first employed an innovation is a necessary prerequisite to inferences about their search patterns, communication processes, reference-group behavior, and so forth. Extensiveness of use contributes little to such discussion.

On the other hand, it is often the case that operationalizing innovation by the extent of implementation comes closer to capturing the variations in behavior that we really want to explain. While it is useful to know what determined the sequence in which states first experimented with a new hybrid strain of corn, it is much more desirable that the researcher uncover what determines variation across states in the *extent* to which the hybrid strain has replaced the traditional strain (see Griliches, 1957). Of course, there are some innovations in which virtually no variation in the extent to which they are adopted is possible. An individual either purchases soft contact lenses or does not, a city fluoridates its water or it doesn't. In the cases where such variation is possible, it is frequently this variation rather than time of first usage that we would like to account for.

The two operationalizations are functionally related only if we assume that all units first employ the innovation at the same level and that each then increases its utilization at the same rate. This may be true of some portion of innovations, but we suspect that the assumption is generally tenuous. Few would agree to the even weaker generalization that the first organization to adopt an innovation will be the one found to have implemented it to the greatest extent at any point in the diffusion process; most students of innovation are familiar with a number of cases where early adopters do not have the highest degrees of commitment to the innovation.

Reinforcing this belief that the two operationalizations are tapping different aspects of innovation is the suspicion that the determinants of the time of adoption are not the same as the determinants of the depth of adoption. For example, because a certain amount of prestige is known to be extended to organizations and individuals who are among the first to adopt new innovations, we might hypothesize that the desire for prestige will be a more powerful predictor of the time of adoption than of the extent (cf. Mohr, 1969: 121–123). We might also expect organizational slack to be a better predictor of how quickly an organization adopts than of how extensively the innovation is employed (Cyert and March, 1963: 278–279), something that may depend heavily on motivational variables. This is the same sort of differential impact of organizational variables that is responsible for instability in connection with primary characteristics, and the effect is the same here. Further, unless a clear and consistent relationship can be established between the two operationalizations, which is unlikely, the results of research on them are simply irreconcilable. *It would be wise to conceive of the two operationalizations as two different behaviors to be explored,* not because they are invariably independent of one another, but because of the need to avoid biased, muddled generalizations.

If one attempts to ignore the instability and generalize impressionistically about the impact of a specific variable across a number of studies that operationalize innovation differently, the result will be an unenlightening average that would depend on the proportion of studies having employed each operationalization. Since the major proportion of studies have used time of adoption as the operationalization of innovation, that interpretation would be emphasized. This would no doubt inflate the role of variables related to organizational slack and a desire for prestige.

THE ADOPTABILITY OF INNOVATIONS

We have simplified our study by considering one important research aim in detail while neglecting another one, that is, we have postponed the question of the relative adoptability of innovations. Our justification is that what holds for the first should hold for the second by mirror-image symmetry; the two theories are not independent but are essentially two sides of the same coin.

What makes one innovation more likely than another to be adopted by any given organization?

Just as there may be typologies of innovations, so may there be typologies of organizations, and these may also be based either on primary or secondary attributes. Primary-attribute typologies of organizations would function here just as primary-attribute typologies of innovations. Just as organizational wealth would undoubtedly be a better predictor of the adoption of a high-cost than a low-cost innovation, so would the cost of innovations be a better predictor of their adoption in a poor organization than a rich one. Wealth would therefore appear to be a primary attribute upon which organizations should be classified for development of a general theory of adoptability. How important this primary attribute is and whether there are others of importance (for instance, public versus private sector) is a question that must be addressed in future research. There has been little work bearing upon the question, and the complexities that it raises are formidable enough that it is difficult even to volunteer a speculative response.

The study of innovation meets the study of adoptability in the concept of secondary attributes. The secondary attributes of innovations are essentially the same phenomena as the secondary attributes of organizations. For example, just as the technical and procedural requirements of the innovation are highly (or minimally) compatible with the structure and activities of the organization, so is the organization by that fact precisely as compatible with the innovation. In the same sense, what we have called an organization's benefits are identical to what is called the relative advantage of an innovation (Rogers and Shoemaker, 1971: 138–145). By the nature of secondary attributes, we always refer to only one organization and one innovation at a time, and once the pair is joined, properties such as expected benefit and relative advantage are identical.

The possibility of a variety of operationalizations of the dependent variable has identical significance in research on adoptability as on innovation. We are studying different, though overlapping, phenomena depending upon which dependent variable is employed, and there is no *a priori* reason to believe that the explanatory theories of the three will be congruent.

Shall we use one organization or many in our research on adoptability? This is a most interesting question, largely because "many" has been the answer given by every investigator who has published on this subject, to the best of our knowledge. This differs markedly from the study of innovation, where the single-innovation design has been used frequently (hybrid corn, Gammanym, and so forth). It would be difficult to say why this difference in practice exists, perhaps because there has frequently been a strong practical interest in the diffusion of a particular innovation, such as hybrid corn, whereas there has rarely been a comparable interest in the innovativeness of a particular organization. Whatever the reason, it would not appear adequate to justify the common, multiple-adopter study in which both independent and dependent variables are aggregate measures.

All of the difficulties with multiple-innovation studies apply to the multiple-organization design in adoptability research. Once again, the problems of secondary attributes and ecological inferences are of particular concern. We simply cannot be certain from a strong correlation between "average complexity rating" and "proportion who have adopted" that those who did not find the innovation complex are the same as those who adopted. These studies have frequently used correlation designs, and the obtained correlations are in general quite high (Fliegel and Kivlin, 1966; Petrini, 1966; Singh, 1966). But correlations based on aggregated measures are notoriously inflated over the true microlevel relationships (Cramer, 1964). The less consistency there is among potential adopters in their ratings of a trait—such as the complexity of an innovation—the less confidence we should have in the strength of the correlation involving that trait.

The symmetry and close relation among the theories of innovation and adoptability are best demonstrated by considering the innovation-decision design, the design in which the sample size is equal to the number of innovations times the number of organizations. Assume that we wish to study both innovation and adoptability. Because the measured secondary attributes of the innovations are identical to those of the organizations, these need be measured only once. Given a single data set based on the innovation-decision design, we can study *adoptability* simply by eliminating the primary attributes of organizations; reinserting those primary attributes, we can study *innovation* by eliminating the primary attributes of innovations.

We suggest, then, that both single-organization and innovation-decision designs should be afforded extensive trial in the study of adoptability.

CONCLUSION

We conclude by offering a set of prescriptions for research on innovation suggested by our analysis.

1. Use studies of different innovations to expose the impact of primary-attribute variation on models of innovation. This will involve observing and reporting the primary attributes of innovations and restricting generalizations from a given study to innovations in the same category of a primary-attribute typology rather than expecting all results to be identical.

2. Measure the secondary attributes of innovations (compatibility, relative advantage, and so forth) with respect to each organization and consider them as characteristics of adopters.

3. Use interactive models. In terms of the development of integrated theory, this would probably be the single most important departure from current practice.

4. Use the innovation-decision design as the basis for analysis. It is essentially a single-innovation design, which explicitly recognizes that a great many organizational characteristics are secondary attributes, that is, they can be validly measured only in relation to a particular innovation.

5. Do not conduct multiple-innovation studies in which the organization is assigned an aggregate score for innovation.

6. Recognize that extent of adoption and time of adoption are distinct conceptualizations of innovation. Do not generalize from one dependent variable to the other. Do not use either as a comprehensive measure of innovativeness. There is not a single, unitary theory, but rather different theories to explain different aspects of innovation.

7. Study the adoptability of innovations by using either many innovations in relation to one single organization or by using the innovation-decision design.

About the Authors

George W. Downs, Jr., is an assistant professor in the Department of Political Science, University of California at Davis. Lawrence B. Mohr is an associate professor in the Department of Political Science and an associate research scientist in the Institute of Public Policy Studies, University of Michigan.

References

Adams, Walter, and Joel B. Dirlam, 1966. "Big steel, invention, and innovation." Quarterly Journal of Economics, 80: 167–89.

Becker, Marshall H., 1970. "Sociometric location and innovativeness: reformulation and extension of the diffusion model." American Sociological Review, 35: 267–82.

Child, John, 1972. "Organizational structure and strategies of control: a replication of the Aston study." Administrative Science Quarterly, 17: 163–77.

Coleman, James, Elihu Katz, and Herbert Menzel, 1957. "The diffusion of an innovation among physicians." Sociometry, 20: 253–70.

Cramer, J. S., 1964. "Efficient grouping: regression and correlation in engel curve analysis." Journal of the American Statistical Association, 59: 233–250.

Cyert, Richard M., and James G. March, 1963. A Behavioral Theory of the Firm. Englewood Cliffs, N.J.: Prentice-Hall.

Downs, George W., Jr., 1976. Bureaucracy, Innovation, and Public Policy. Lexington, Mass.: D. C. Heath.

Fliegel, Frederick C., and Joseph E. Kivlin, 1966. "Attributes of innovations as factors in diffusion." American Journal of Sociology, 72: 235–248.

Griliches, Zvi, 1957. "Hybrid com: an exploration in the economics of technological change." Econometrica, 25: 501–22.

Hage, Jerald, and Michael Aiken, 1967. "Program change and organizational properties: a comparative analysis." American Journal of Sociology, 72: 503–519.

Hall, Richard H., 1962. "The concept of bureaucracy: an empirical assessment." American Journal of Sociology, 69: 32–40.

Hannan, Michael T., and Leigh Burstein, 1974. "Estimation from grouped observations." American Sociological Review, 39: 374–392.

Jeans, James H., 1966. Physics and Philosophy. Ann Arbor: University of Michigan Press.

Knight, K., 1967. "A descriptive model of the intra-firm innovation process." Journal of Business, 40: 478–496.

Mansfield, Edwin, 1963. "The speed of response of firms to new techniques." Quarterly Journal of Economics, 77: 290–309.

Menzel, Herbert, 1966. "Innovation, integration, and marginality: a survey of physicians." American Sociological Review, 25: 704–713.

Menzel, Herbert, and Elihu Katz, 1955. "Social relations and innovation in the medical profession: the epidemiology of a new drug." Public Opinion Quarterly, 19: 337–352.

Mohr, Lawrence B., 1969. "Determinants of innovation in organizations." American Political Science Review, 63: 111–126.

Negandhi, Anant R., and S. Benjamin Prasad, 1971. Comparative Management. New York: Appleton-Century-Crofts.

Nelson, Richard R., 1972. "Issues and suggestions for the study of industrial organization in a regime of rapid technical change." In Policy Issues and Research Opportunities in Industrial Organization, V. Fuchs (ed.). National Bureau of Economic Research. New York: Columbia University Press.

Normann, R., 1971. "Organizational innovativeness: product variation and reorientation." Administrative Science Quarterly, 16: 203–215.

Petrini, Frank, 1966. The Rate of Adoption of Selected Agricultural Innovations. Reprint 53. Uppsala: Agricultural College of Sweden.

Prais, S. J., and J. Aitchison, 1954. "The grouping of observations in regression analysis." Review of the International Statistical Institute, 22: 1–22.

Pugh, D. S., D. J. Hickson, C. R. Hinings, and C. Turner, 1968. "Dimensions of organization structure." Administrative Science Quarterly, 13: 65–106.

Roessner, J. David, 1974. Designing Public Organizations for Innovative Behavior. Paper delivered at the Thirty-fourth Annual Meeting of the Academy of Management, Seattle, Washington.

Rogers, Everett M., and F. Floyd Shoemaker, 1971. Communication of Innovation: A Cross-Cultural Approach. New York: The Free Press.

Rowe, Lloyd A., and William B. Boise, 1974. "Organizational innovation: current research and evolving concepts." Public Administration Review, 34: 284–392.

Singh, Ram N., 1966. Characteristics of Farm Innovations Associated with the Rate of Adoption. Reprint 14. Guelph: Ontario Agricultural Extension Education Reprints.

Theil Henri, 1971. Principles of Econometrics. New York: John Wiley.

Walker, Jack L., 1969. "The diffusion of innovations among the American states." American Political Science Review, 63: 880–899.

1971. "Innovations in state politics." In Politics in the American States—A Comparative Analysis, 2nd ed., Herbert Jacobs and Kenneth Vines (eds.). Boston: Little, Brown and Co.

Warner, Kenneth E., 1974. "The need for some innovative concepts of innovation: an examination of research on the diffusion of innovations." Policy Sciences, 5: 433–451.

Wilson, James Q., 1966. "Innovation in organization: notes toward a theory." In Approaches to Organizational Design, James D. Thompson (ed.). Pittsburgh: University of Pittsburgh Press.

Winter, Sidney G., Jr., 1968. Toward a Neo-Schumpeterian Theory of the Firm. Publication No. P-3802. Santa Monica: Rand Corporation.

Zaltman, Gerald, Robert Duncan, and Jonny Holbek, 1973. Innovations and Organizations. New York: John Wiley.

Endnotes

1. Of 38 propositions bearing directly on the act of innovation cited by Rogers and Shoemaker (1971: 350–376), 34 were supported in some studies and found to receive no support in others. The 4 propositions with a consistent record were treated in very few studies.

2. We use discrete categories such as "low-cost" and "high-cost" as a matter of terminological convenience. Actually, cost is a continuum and its impact is such that there is a slightly different curvilinear relationship of wealth, for example, to innovation at each point on the continuum.

3. The attribute, "compatibility," has been used extensively in research as a determinant of the rate of adoption of innovations (Rogers and Shoemaker, 1971: 145–154). Its meaning is actually quite close to Normann's (1971) "variations-reorientations," but perhaps not precisely the same. We use the two dimensions interchangeably simply for terminological convenience.

4. For example, the organization might score large with respect to all innovations in the study. But generalizability need not be completely constrained even here because we might also have a small organization in the study facing the same or a similar set of innovations. It is as though we conducted some studies of large organizations and some of small ones and then compared the results. The same logic would obtain with respect to primary attributes of innovations. Providing this sort of variety within a single study is one way in which the innovation-decision design is an improvement over the ordinary single-innovation research.

8

THE PROCESS OF INNOVATION AND THE DIFFUSION OF INNOVATION

Thomas S. Robertson

"Innovate or Perish" is the marketer's cry of the 1960s. And "Perish as You Innovate" could well be the marketing slogan of the 1970s.

But several questions arise.

Can innovation be programed to occur? What is the nature of the diffusion process? Can consumer "innovators" be identified and appealed to? How do advertising and personal influence compare in effectiveness for new product diffusion?

Here are some answers to these questions.

Journal of Marketing, Vol. 31 (January, 1967), pp. 14–19.

Theories of innovation in business have stemmed mainly from the work of economist Joseph A. Schumpeter.[1] He viewed innovation as distinctly different from invention, which he held occurred in isolation of innovation and which could or could not be coupled with innovation.

He further envisioned innovation as being characterized by: (1) construction of new plants and equipment, (2) introduction of new firms, and (3) the rise to leadership of new men. From this point of view, innovation is a *discontinuous* event.

Only in the last few years have behavioral scientists devoted much attention to the subject of innovation, although the literature certainly abounds with discussions on creativity—especially as to how the creative process occurs within the self.

Anthropologist H. G. Barnett alludes to innovation as the basis of cultural change, and defines innovation as "any thought, behavior, or thing that is new because it is qualitatively different from existing forms."[2] This is a considerably broader definition than Schumpeter's "setting up of a new production function."[3] Sociologist Everett M. Rogers broadens the definition even further by referring to innovation as "an idea perceived as new by the individual."[4]

The present article outlines the *process* by which innovation occurs. Schumpeter's distinction between invention and innovation merely produces the illusion of separate events.

Innovation takes place via a *process* whereby a new "thought, behavior, or thing," which is "qualitatively different from existing forms," is conceived of and brought into reality.[5] Given the innovation, we then need to pay particular attention to its diffusion. By this is meant the process by which the innovation spreads from its source of invention to its ultimate users or adopters.

THE INNOVATION PROCESS

Several theories have been proposed to account for the innovation process. Predominant in the literature of economics has been the "transcendentalist" approach, which attributes innovation to the "inspiration of genius."[6] Such an approach is typified by

Robertson, Thomas S. 1967. The process of innovation and the diffusion of innovation. *Journal of Marketing* 31(1): 14–19.

the following observation: "While at all times there live creative men . . . no prediction is possible as to *where* they will appear in any particular moment or how they will act. The creative entrepreneur being a deviant, he and his work are unpredictable."[7]

In sociological thinking, there is the "mechanistic" theory, which emphasizes that innovation represents "an accumulation of many individual items over a relatively long period of time."[8] Barnett asserts that "No innovation springs full-blown out of nothing: it must have antecedents . . ."[9]

Economist Abbott Payson Usher combines both views to a certain extent, while rejecting the validity of either view standing alone. He points out that innovation is not an accidental affair, as believed by the "transcendentalists," but that neither is it a mechanistic affair, as this view would overlook the discontinuities inherent in the process of innovation. Usher proposes the "cumulative-synthesis" approach—that major inventions are the result of the cumulative synthesis of "many individual items of novelty as well as many familiar elements."[10] To him, the "act of insight" in the synthesis is the crucial stage.

The innovation process which Usher proposes consists of four steps:

1. *Perception of the problem.* In order for innovation to occur, a problem must first be felt to exist.
2. *Setting of the stage.* Some particular configuration of events is brought together.
3. *The act of insight.* Here the solution is found. Insight is needed, due to the uncertainty involved and because of the various possible solutions.
4. *The critical revision.* The innovation is analyzed, to determine how practical it is.

Empirical Studies

The innovation process has been studied empirically in several instances. Of particular value is a study of the machine-tool industry by William H. Brown, whose hypothesis is that innovation in this industry is a *planned* attempt to increase demand for machine tools.[11] His analysis indicates that innovation occurs when the demand for machine tools falls, and furthermore that innovation need not be discontinuous in nature, as economists such as Schumpeter have suggested. Rather, he holds that innovation can in fact be *programed to occur.*

Both sociological thinking, which emphasizes that an innovation is merely a recombination of old innovations, and Usher's "cumulative-synthesis" approach also indicate that innovation need not be discontinuous. When a manufacturer finds through research that a more convenient breakfast drink than a frozen drink is demanded by consumers, he can program the occurrence of such an innovation. Once the problem is perceived, he can bring together in his laboratory all the drinks presently available—from frozen drinks to powdered drinks, and so on. Via an act of insight and a regrouping of the basic elements involved, he can innovate a new soft drink by combining some of the ingredients of a soft drink already in existence with Vitamin C, orange flavoring, and other available ingredients. Market testing and critical revision of the product then follow.

Framework for Classifying Innovations

Is it possible to develop a conceptual framework for classifying innovations as to their effects on established patterns? The following is representative of such a framework.

Innovations may be classified as (1) *continuous* innovations, (2) *dynamically continuous* innovations, and (3) *discontinuous* innovations.

1. A *continuous* innovation has the least disrupting influence on established patterns. Alteration of a product is involved, rather than the establishment of a new product. Examples: fluoride toothpaste; new-model automobile changeovers; menthol cigarettes.
2. A *dynamically continuous* innovation has more disrupting effects than a continuous innovation, although it still does not generally alter established patterns. It may involve the creation of a new product or the alteration of an

existing product. Examples: electric toothbrushes; the Mustang automobile; Touch-Tone telephones.

3. A *discontinuous* innovation involves the establishment of a new product and the establishment of new behavior patterns. Examples: television; computers.

Returning to Brown's study of the machine-tool industry and relating it to the innovation process proposed by Usher, we realize that the perception of the problem in the machine-tool industry (a fall in demand) implies the need for an innovative answer. The stage is then set for innovation to occur. A "shelf" or series of design ideas is common to firms in this industry. "The shelf is made up of suggestions, complaints, basic ideas, reports on research done outside the firm, etc."[12] Thus, the configuration of events from which the solution will be drawn is quite readily available.

The act of insight and the critical revision stages in the innovation process were outside the scope of Brown's study; but, as indicated earlier, a whole body of literature is built around the concept of "creativity" or the "act of insight." This literature remains to be related to the total innovation concept.

Much innovation today is programed innovation. This is true for both industrial goods and for consumer goods, where marketers are constantly trying to differentiate products via innovation in order to increase their market share. The annual automobile "change-over" is an excellent example of psychological obsolescence, or, in the present terms, programed innovation.

THE DIFFUSION PROCESS

Given the innovation, the problem becomes that of diffusion. However, a theoretical model of the diffusion process is difficult because of the tremendously large number of variables involved.

The questions posed are numerous: Does diffusion occur in some predictable manner? Is there such a person as a consumer-innovator, and can he be identified? (Innovator here is used to refer to the earliest adopter in the diffusion process, rather than the creator or inventor of the product.) How to advertising and personal influence compare in effectiveness for new product diffusion?

If these questions alone could be answered, considerable waste would be avoided in the marketing of new products. For example, if we knew that a set of innovators existed for automobiles, manufacturers could concentrate on this innovative set in introducing a new product and avoid expensive mass-media advertising until the innovator-level of penetration had been achieved and the mass market was ready to adopt the product.

We cannot pretend to arrive at an all-encompassing theory of diffusion here. But we can attempt to build a general model of the diffusion process, and discuss some of the key variables involved.

How the Process Occurs

The diffusion process is looked on by sociologist Everett M. Rogers as an orderly sequence of events.[13] He proposes a diffusion curve, which is essentially a normal curve of distribution, as shown in Figure 8-1.

Rogers is referring specifically to the adoption of an innovation by farmers over a given period of time. His reference to innovators is to those who are *first* in the adoption process, which actually stretches from innovators to laggards, or those who adopt last. The question is whether the Rogers model, which assumes 100% adoption, is a valid model to describe diffusion of marketing innovations.

First, let us compare Rogers' rural-diffusion model with an industrial-diffusion process described in a 1961 study of the rapidity with which 12 innovations spread among firms in the bituminous coal, iron and steel, brewing, and railroad industries.[15] This study confirms the Rogers model to a considerable extent. The investigator, Edwin Mansfield, found that the proportion of firms already using an innovation

FIGURE 8-1 Adopter Categories Based on Relative Time of Adoption of Innovation.[14] Innovators 2.5%, Early Adopters 13.5%, Early Majority 34.0%, Late Majority 34.0%, Laggards 16.0%

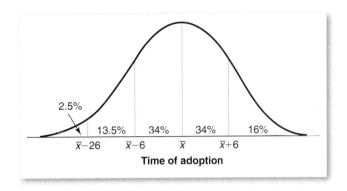

would increase the rate of adoption, in other words, that competitive pressures would create a "bandwagon" effect.[16] This corresponds closely to the Rogers model, where diffusion occurs slowly until the early majority stage and then "snowballs."

Now, let us turn to an empirical investigation of the diffusion of an innovation among physicians in four cities.[17] Here again the Rogers model of stages of diffusion appears to be validated. The study indicates that the socially integrated physicians in the community—that is, those best accepted by their peers—tended to adopt in a "chain-reaction" manner.

The studies referred to do not account for the diffusion of all innovations, of course. In fact, they account for the diffusion process of only a small percentage of innovations—those that are decidedly better than existing forms and where it is only a matter of time before most people adopt. For example, the innovation of concern in the study of physicians was a "miracle drug" which was actually superior to previous drugs then on the market. Most farming innovations studied—hybrid corn, for example—could be proved superior by objective measures of crop yield.

For most marketing innovations, however, *not everyone* will adopt, because the product will not be actually superior to existing forms or brands—or not seemingly so in the mind of the consumer, because of the lack of objective measuring criteria.

An ever-incomplete curve of adoption is, therefore, the case for innovations in marketing. And yet the conceptual sequence proposed is a considerable aid to understanding the diffusion process.

ADVERTISING COMPARED WITH PERSONAL INFLUENCE

What are the effects of advertising as compared with personal influence?

The model portraying the impact of mass media advertising has undergone some drastic changes over the years. In the 1920s, the structure of the model was such that the millions of people who read their newspapers or listened to their radios assumedly were aroused to action because of exposure to powerful buying stimuli. In other words, a "vertical" model of communication supposedly existed, whereby the audience was viewed as "a mass of disconnected individuals hooked up to the media but not to each other. . . ."[18]

A study in Albany in 1940 during the course of the presidential campaign showed that this was far from a correct view. This was the first of a series of studies that "rediscovered" the *primary group* and its influence upon voting, buying, and other forms of behavior.

Radio and the printed page were found to have "only negligible effects on actual vote decisions and particularly minute effects on *changes* in vote decisions."[19] The

FIGURE 8-2   A Schematic Representation of the Roper Model of Concentric Circles

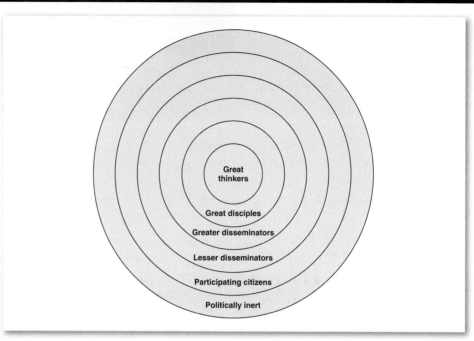

individual's primary group held the greatest influence over him. Voting decisions, particularly those involving a change in voting behavior, were found to be most often influenced by "other people." Further analysis indicated that those individuals more influential than others in affecting voting behavior were more often influenced by mass media than those who were less influential. Thus, a "two-step flow of communication" model was derived.

The "two-step flow of communication" implies basically that the mass media actually influence opinion-leaders, who in turn influence the less-influential people. Furthermore, opinion-leaders are scattered throughout society at all social-class levels, in all occupations, and in all communities.[20]

In their 1945 Decatur study, Katz and Lazarsfeld specifically analyzed the effects of mass-media advertising as compared with personal influence in the areas of fashion, public affairs, and movies. Again, justification was found for the greater importance for most people of personal influence than for advertising.[21]

Other models of the diffusion effect of the mass media also exist. Elmo Roper has proposed the "concentric-circle" theory, as to how ideas flow throughout society.[22] See Figure 8-2.

According to the Roper theory, ideas diffuse in circles, much as ripples on the water after a pebble has disturbed the surface. The "Great Thinkers" are the idea men, and these ideas eventually reach the "Politically Inert" who form the bulk of society, approximately 70% of the people. Roper says, "There is some evidence that ideas can be communicated to the Politically Inert by way of the mass media. But I think it is an assumption worthy of greater research that the Politically Inert come to accept ideas more readily from their Participating Citizen neighbors. . . ."[23] His concentric-circle theory does not conflict with the two-step model, but in a sense is an extension of it.

Some sociologists hold that "the average person is likely to be affected more strongly by social pressures, group associations, and the attitudes of 'opinion leaders' he knows than by direct use of the mass media."[24] If this is true, we should hypothesize that a company, in introducing an innovation, should advertise less to the masses and more to opinion leaders. It should use specialized media to reach group influentials, rather than using mass media to reach the masses.

However, there are practical difficulties. For the most part, advertisers have not oriented their product-messages in line with a two-step theory of communication. Part of the difficulty is due to the fact that different opinion-leaders may exist for different consumption systems. Clothing may be looked upon as a consumption system, as well as entertainment or food. Influentials may exist for each such system; but finding out specifically who the influentials are for any one system would be difficult, to say the least.

Advertisers can question the two-step model, arguing that it may be effective in the dissemination of ideas, but that it is not valid in the dissemination of information about products and services because everyone is interested in them.

The value of the two-step theory comes in realizing that mediating factors do exist between the product message and the act of adoption. Other people are a major factor in the communications-flow. Where it is possible to take advantage of personal-influence channels, this should be done. Media selection is only one part of the total possible communications mix.

SOCIAL INTEGRATION OF INNOVATORS

In a study referred to earlier regarding physicians, it was concluded that "the degree of a doctor's integration among his local colleagues was strongly and positively related to the date of his first use of the new drug," and that "the more isolated doctors, on the average, introduced (the product) considerably later than the socially more integrated doctors."[25]

However, findings concerning social integration are not consistent. Rogers' conclusions imply that innovators are "marginal" members of the community—the least socially integrated of all. States Rogers, "Agricultural innovators were perceived as deviant by other members of their local social system. . . . Thus, innovators *are* in step with a different drummer."[26]

Says anthropologist Barnett, "There are biographical determinants for the lack of satisfaction that is characteristic of individuals who are predisposed to accept a substitute for some accustomed idea . . ."; and "acceptance probabilities are weighted on the side of the dissenter."[27]

Can the differences in findings be reconciled? Elihu Katz concludes that whether innovators will be socially integrated or not is a function of the *risk* in adoption and the *norms* of the social system.

In regard to the study of physicians, Katz reasons that "innovation in medicine is risky business." He continues: "A new drug represents a highly ambiguous stimulus. . . . In this kind of situation, communication among colleagues serves to spread, and thus to reduce, the individual risk."[28] Furthermore, there is no question for the doctor, as there is for the farmer, of emancipation from local primary groups as a prerequisite to the acceptance of innovation."[29]

In agriculture, risk in purchase is considerably reduced through the scientific efforts of the Agricultural Extension Service. Even commercial sources frequently offer financial proof of greater farm productivity for many innovations. Such is not the case in the realm of physicians. In agriculture, the normative structure typically has been considered more traditional than that existing in the rest of society. Whereas the farming innovator must "emancipate" himself from such traditional norms, the physician innovator need not.

How socially integrated will marketing innovators be? Purchase of an innovation can seldom amount to a financial saving. At the most, the consumer can hope for a savings in time or energy. Raymond A. Bauer has considered the topic of risk in marketing and concludes, "Consumer behavior involves risk in the sense that any action of a consumer will produce consequences which he cannot anticipate with anything approximating certainty, and some-of which at least are likely to be unpleasant."[30]

Consumers, like physicians, are faced with an "ambiguous stimulus." Sources of objective communication are scarce. Communication with other consumers, however, can reduce risk in the purchase decision; and socially-integrated persons are in a more advantageous position than others to engage in such communications and to innovate.

The overall norms in marketing favor innovation, as evidenced by the American consumer's fascination with new products and the advertiser's continued emphasis upon "new." Accordingly, the marketing innovator should be aware of the socially integrated, since such individuals are the most norm-conscious and norm-abiding.[31]

IN CONCLUSION

Innovation has been defined as a process whereby a new thought, behavior, or thing is conceived of and brought into reality. Several conclusions can now be drawn:

1. An innovation *can be programed to occur.*
2. An innovation *can be classified according to its effects on established patterns,* from almost no disrupting influence to establishment of new behavior-patterns.
3. In many ways personal influence *may be superior to advertising*; but it is difficult to utilize personal-influence channels.
4. When significant *risk* is present in the purchase situation and when the *norms* of the group favor innovation, the innovators will be socially-integrated members of the community.

About the Author

Thomas S. Robertson is Assistant Professor of Business Administration at the University of California at Los Angeles. A graduate of Detroit's Wayne State University, he recently completed concurrently an M.A. in Sociology and a Ph.D. in Marketing at Northwestern University.

The author's doctoral dissertation, "An Analysis of Innovative Behavior and Its Determinants," under a grant from Illinois and Michigan Bell Telephone Companies, provides further insights into the diffusion process of innovations of consumer goods.

MARKETING MEMO

A Basic Organizational Concept . . .

The work of mankind is done through three principal groupings, the family, the state, and in between, the groups that willingly join to achieve common purposes. Primitive and feudal societies knew little of the vast resources that are represented by sustained voluntary group action. It is this unforced coming together of human energy and effort, outside the family and apart from political instrumentalities, which has fueled material progress and expanded the range of personal choice in what have come to be identified as pluralistic societies. Of all voluntary associations, the business corporation is today perhaps the most significant.

—Courtney C. Brown, "Nothing Less Than the Entire Human Condition," *Columbia Journal of World Business,* Vol. 1 (Fall, 1966), pp. 7–12, at p. 7.

Endnotes

1. Joseph A. Schumpeter, *Business Cycles* (New York: McGraw-Hill Book Company, 1939), Vol. 1.
2. H. G. Barnett, *Innovation: The Basis of Cultural Change* (New York: McGraw-Hill Book Company, 1953), p. 7.
3. Schumpeter, same reference as footnote 1, at p. 87.
4. Everett M. Rogers, *Diffusion of Innovations* (New York: The Free Press of Glencoe, 1962), p. 13.
5. Barnett, same reference as footnote 2.
6. Abbott Payson Usher, *A History of Mechanical Inventions* (Cambridge: Harvard University Press, 1954), p. 60.
7. Fritz Redlich, "Innovation in Business," *American Journal of Economics and Sociology,* Vol. 10 (April, 1951), pp. 285–291, at p. 291.
8. Usher, same reference as footnote 6, at p. 61.
9. Barnett, same reference as footnote 2, at p. 181.
10. Usher, same reference as footnote 6, at p. 68.
11. William H. Brown, "Innovation in the Machine Tool Industry," *Quarterly Journal of Economics,* Vol. 71 (August, 1957), pp. 406–425.
12. Same reference as footnote 11, at p. 409.
13. Rogers, same reference as footnote 4, at p. 162.
14. Same reference as footnote 4, at p. 162.
15. Edwin Mansfield, "Technical Change and the Rate of Imitation," *Econometrica,* Vol. 29 (October, 1961), pp. 741–766.
16. Same reference as footnote 15, at p. 746.
17. James Coleman, Elihu Katz, and Herbert Menzel, "The Diffusion of an Innovation Among Physicians," *Sociometry,* Vol. 20 (December, 1957), pp. 253–270.
18. Elihu Katz, "The Two-step Flow of Communication: An Up-to-date Report on an Hypothesis," *Public Opinion Quarterly,* Vol. 21 (Spring, 1957), pp. 61–78, at p. 61.
19. Elihu Katz and Paul F. Lazarsfeld, *Personal Influence* (Glencoe, Illinois: The Free Press, 1955), p. 31.
20. Katz, same reference as footnote 18, at p. 63.
21. Katz and Lazarsfeld, same reference as footnote 19, at pp. 309–320.

22. Elmo Roper, "Reaching the General Public," *Public Relations,* Vol. 1 (October, 1945), pp. 1–6.

23. Katz and Lazarsfeld, same reference as footnote 19, at p. xix.

24. Edwin Emery, Phillip Ault, and Warren Agee, *Introduction to Mass Communications* (New York: Dodd, Mead and Company, 1960), p. 14.

25. Coleman, Katz, and Menzel, same reference as footnote 17, at pp. 257 and 267.

26. Rogers, same reference as footnote 4, at p. 207.

27. Barnett, same reference as footnote 2, at pp. 379, 381.

28. Elihu Katz, "The Social Itinerary of Technical Change: Two Studies on the Diffusion of Innovation," *Human Organization,* Vol. 20 (Summer, 1961), pp. 70–82, at p. 79.

29. Katz, same reference as footnote 28, at p. 80.

30. Raymond A. Bauer, "Consumer Behavior as Risk Taking," *Proceedings of the National Conference of the American Marketing Association,* Robert S. Hancock, Editor (Chicago: American Marketing Association, 1960), pp. 389–398, at p. 390.

31. Katz, same reference as footnote 28, at p. 73.

9 | THE DYNAMICS OF INNOVATION IN INDUSTRY

James M. Utterback

There is an idea that will revolutionize business.
—Henry Benedict to Philo Remington on the Sholes typewriter

In the summer of 1874, Mr. Samuel Clemens (Mark Twain) had come from Hartford to Boston to deliver a series of readings. He and a friend, humorist "Petroleum" V. Nasby, were out for a walk one afternoon when they spied a new contraption called a "type writing machine" in a store window. Clemens was a great fan of American ingenuity in any form and had a weakness for the gadgets and inventions that sprang from the minds and workshops of his countrymen. In today's parlance, Clemens was a "lead user," invariably the first in his circle to have the latest technical gizmo.

Entering the store, Clemens asked to see how the device worked. The sales clerk was happy to oblige and offered that it could write 57 words per minute. He had a young lady demonstrate the machine, and her performance so astonished Clemens and Nasby that they asked her to do it again, this time while they timed her work on their pocket watches. Clemens was impressed, and he bought the machine on the spot.

Back in Hartford, he pecked out a letter to his brother Orion:

TRYING TO GET THE HANG OF THIS NEW FANGLED
MACHINE . . . [it] COSTS 125 DOLLARS. THE MACHINE HAS
SEVERAL VIRTUES. I BELIEVE IT WILL PRINT FASTER THAN I CAN
WRITE . . . IT PILES AN AWFUL STACK OF WORDS ON A PAGE.[1]

MR. CLEMENS'S NEW MACHINE

The machine Clemens purchased was a Remington No. 1, the first ever offered to the general public. The large, cumbersome device came mounted on its own platform, enclosed in a japanned black metal case, with a keyboard and a roll of paper on top. It could print only uppercase letters and had no tabs. Still, many today would recognize this first commercial typewriter for what it was.

The Remington machine was actually a synthesis of many existing technologies and mechanical elements in widespread use at the time. Clockwork suggested the idea of the *escapement*—i.e., moving the carriage one letter at a time. The keys and their connecting arms were adaptations of the telegraph key. A sewing machine pedal returned the carriage, and the piano suggested a model for the free-swinging arms and hammers that struck the letter to the paper.[2] It was noisy, in the words of its inventor going "thump, thump at every letter" and "back with a crash sufficient to wake the dead."

Utterback, J. (1994), *Mastering the Dynamics of Innovation,* Boston, MA: Harvard Business School Press. (pp. 1–21)

This chapter considers the case of the typewriter as an assembled product innovation. Here we will see how an innovation often draws from existing technologies and models for its application but uses these elements creatively in combination with new ones to form a uniquely different product. We will see how the characteristics of the innovation are molded by forces of competition, invention, and customer use until they crystallize into a product with a certain standardized form, set of features, and technical capability. Most important, we will extend the case of the manual typewriter to its successor forms—the electric typewriter, the dedicated word processor, and the personal computer—each of which appeared as a new wave of technological innovation washing through the industry with tremendous effects on the nature of competition.

The Remington No. 1 typewriter purchased by Samuel Clemens was based on the invention of a former Milwaukee newspaper editor named Christopher Latham Sholes. Like most other inventions, Sholes's was part of a stream of inventions. As early as 1714, an English engineer named Henry Miller had obtained a patent for a "writing engine," of which all descriptions are now lost. In the United States, William Burt of Mt. Vernon, Michigan patented a crude "typographer," which apparently interested almost no one. The government official who gave Burt his patent document wrote it out in longhand, of course, attesting to the need for some kind of mechanical writing device, but Burt's contraption did not fit the bill. A good writer with a pen could not do more than 30 words per minute—the official speed record in 1853. This, and the fact that telegraphers and shorthand stenographers of the time could now take down information at speeds of up to 130 words per minute, created the imperative for an effective fast writing machine. Dozens of prototypes appeared and received patents between the time of Burt and the Sholes inventions, but none were put into commercial use.[3]

Sholes had first developed a machine using narrow wooden keys that connected to the type hammers by means of wires. An ink-saturated ribbon passed beneath. He made improvements using telegraph-like keys that dispensed with the wires of the older model, and he received patents in July 1868.[4] Sensing the need for a partner with the money and the moxie to take his invention into successful commercial development, Sholes in 1869 took on as partner a burly, swaggering, salesman character named James Dunsmore. Dunsmore did not have two nickels to rub together, but he had plenty of grit and saw in the typing machine a chance to make a fortune. First, however, he wanted Sholes to improve the crude device, and he imposed on the inventor for a succession of some 50 models—each reflecting some minor improvement—before he had the machine he wanted. At that point, Dunsmore began approaching manufacturers.

After an unsuccessful attempt to sell exclusive manufacturing rights to Western Union Company for a reported $50,000, Dunsmore and an associate approached Mr. Philo Remington, president of the Remington Company. With the boom times of the Civil War behind it, Remington had been trying to diversify into other areas, and by then had gone into farm machinery, sewing machines, horse-drawn fire engines, and cotton gins—generally with disastrous results.[5] The idea of the typewriter appealed to Philo Remington and his associates; their plant in Ilion, New York was underutilized, and they wanted to expand their line of consumer products. In 1873, Remington agreed to be exclusive manufacturer of the Sholes typewriter and dedicated two top mechanics to the problem of perfecting the machine for production in a section of its Ilion plant.[6]

THE NEW MACHINE MEETS THE PUBLIC

By July 1874, the first production models, including the one purchased by Samuel Clemens, were in stores across the country. They had some unusual operating characteristics. The keys of the No. 1 struck the paper *inside* the machine, making it impossible for the operator to see his or her work until the first four rows were typed, at which time the paper began emerging from the machine. And, of course, no one knew how to type.

The fact that it had only uppercase letters did not endear the No. 1 to users or readers, which is made clear in many letters of the time. The uppercase script led some early readers to believe that the letters sent to them were in fact printed handbills—that is, junk mail—which they tossed out without reading. Still others, like this Texas banker, took offense at the first typewritten correspondence:

> I realize, Mr. John, that I do not possess the education which you have. However, until your last letter I have always been able to read the writing. I do not think it necessary to have your letters to me taken to a printer and set up like a handbill. I will be able to read your writing and am deeply chagrined to think you thought such a course necessary.[7]

Even Clemens, who was committed to making a go of the new writing machine, grew frustrated with it. "I DONT KNOW WHETHER I AM OGING TO MAKE THIS TYPE-WRITING MACHINE GO OR NTO," he wrote to his Cambridge literary friend, W.D. Howells, after a short time with the new machine. Six months later he shipped the beast to Howells, preceding it with a note that warned, "You just wait a couple of weeks & if you don't see the Type-Writer come tilting along toward Cambridge with the raging hell of an unsatisfied appetite in its eye, I lose my guess." The typewriter did arrive, and Howells kept it, returning at least two witty letters to

---

HOW THE TYPEWRITER KEYBOARD GOT THAT WAY

The development of the QWERTY, or Universal, keyboard is subject to some debate. Both Sholes and Dunsmore had experience as printers. Thus, according to one explanation, they were familiar with the type case, the sectioned box in which the printer's pieces of type were arranged. Because letters such as A, E, and I were used more often than others, the type case was arranged not alphabetically, but in a way that made picking out the most frequently used letters more convenient. The typewriter inventors supposedly used this principle as they experimented with various keyboard layouts. One problem they encountered was the jamming together of type bars as an operator's speed increased. Sholes and Dunsmore found that they could minimize this problem by altering the arrangement of the keys so that letters frequently struck in close succession would converge from opposite sides of the machine.

Historian Bruce Bliven disputes the type case story. According to Bliven's sources, Sholes originally laid out the keyboard alphabetically (the FGH and JKL sequences are surviving relics). As Sholes struggled through many model changes, he reportedly made modifications to keep the keys from jamming up. According to Bliven, the machine offered to Remington for manufacture in 1873 bore this keyboard arrangement:[1]

    2 3 4 5 6 7 8 9 - ,
    Q W E . T Y I U O P
    Z D F G H J K L M
    A X & C V B N ? ; R

Whichever story was accurate, the inventors were aware that keyboard standardization would be important to successful adoption of the new machine.

Typing a letter to his stepson on a new keyboard arrangement that he and Sholes had just concocted, Dunsmore complained, "I had to unlearn as well as learn" the new arrangement. This concern has made the modern QWERTY keyboard, named after the order of the top left-hand row of letters, a standard (except in France), despite subsequent attempts to improve typing efficiency through keyboard redesign.[2] Paul David, who has considered the effect of the keyboard arrangement on competing alternatives offers these comments:

> Under competitive conditions, and in the absence of public policy interventions, the existence of significant increasing returns to scale, or analogous positive feedback mechanisms such as "learning by doing," and by "using," can give the result that one particular formulation of a network technology—VCRs, or QWERTY-formatted keyboard—will be able to drive out other variants and so emerge as the de facto standard for the industry. By no means need the commercial victor in this kind of systems rivalry be more efficient than the available alternatives.[3]

Paul David and others have pointed to the persistence of the QWERTY keyboard as an example of how high "switching costs" from one design standard to another make it possible for less efficient artifacts—like the original Sholes key layout—to persist, even though more efficient alternatives exist. They point out that technological changes in typing (with respect both to the change from type bars to type balls and daisy wheels on modern typewriters and to the digital underpinnings of computer-based typing) have virtually eliminated the problem of jamming keys. The Dvorak keyboard, introduced by August Dvorak in 1936 as a more ergonomically efficient system that balanced the frequently used letters between the two hands and loaded the strong fingers more heavily, is often pointed to as *the* better system that high switching costs have effectively kept off the market. The fact that so many individuals and business establishments have an investment in QWERTY skills and equipment, the reasoning goes, has prevented adoption of the Dvorak keyboard. This same switch-cost issue is important in other fields where product innovations are rapid.[4]

The latest salvo in the continuing argument about QWERTY versus Dvorak keyboards and the power of design standards comes from S.J. Liebowitz and Stephen E. Margolis, who challenge the entire notion of the superiority of the Dvorak design. According to these scholars, the assumption of the Dvorak superiority has never been established by scientific tests. To Liebowitz and Margolis, the persistence of the QWERTY design is not an indication of market failure due to an entrenched product standard, but an indication that the Dvorak design failed to prove its superior value in an open marketplace.[5] They point to the high variety of typewriter designs in the early days of the industry, the many typing contests that pitted the performance of one design against another, and the economic incentives for modern corporations to invest in switching to improve typing systems as an indication of the inherent fitness of the QWERTY design and an explanation for its persistence over time.

Notes

1. Bruce Bliven, *The Wonderful Writing Machine* (New York: Random House, 1954), p. 143.
2. Richard Nelson Current, *The Typewriter: And the Men Who Made It* (Champaign, Ill.: University of Illinois Press, 1954), pp. 55–58.
3. Paul A. David, "Heroes, Herds and Hysteresis in Technological History," *Industrial and Corporate Change*, vol. 1, no. 1 (1992), p. 139.
4. See Paul A. David, "Clio and the Economics of QWERTY," *American Economic Review*, 75 (May 1985), pp. 332–337; and "Understanding the Economics of QWERTY: The Necessity of History," in W.N. Parker, ed., *Economic History and the Modern Economist* (New York: Basil Blackwell, 1986).
5. S.J. Liebowitz and Stephen E. Margolis, "The Fable of the Keys," *The Journal of Law & Economics,* vol. XXXIII (1) (April 1990), pp. 1–25.

Clemens in payment, both at the expense of the Remington device: "I have begun several letters to My d ar lemans, as it prefers to spell your respected name. . . . It's fascinating, in the meantime, and wastes my time like an old friend." After a few years with the typewriter, Howells could tell Clemens that "The wretch who sold you that typewriter has not yet come to a cruel death."[8]

Sales of the No. 1 were slow. Impeded by its high price and poor performance, Remington managed to sell only 400 during the first six months. But the company made improvements in both the product and its manufacturing process, and by 1877 it had sold 4,000 machines. In 1878, the company introduced a new machine, the No. 2, with the now-familiar double typeface and shift keys, making lowercase writing possible. This machine did much better, selling 100,000 units during its lifetime.[9] Remington catalogs described the wonders of its new machine in glowing terms—"A Machine To Supersede the Pen," they proclaimed. And "Persons traveling by sea can write with it when pen writing is impossible."[10]

The typewriter was on its way, and over the course of the next 30 years it would create a totally new industry with many competitors offering a variety of innovative products. Old methods of writing in newsrooms, offices, and homes gave way to typewriting. It was helped along by the expansion of business enterprise in general and the growing requirements for written documents, reports, and records. Even the rudimentary Remington No. 1 could produce up to 75 words per minute in the hands of an expert typist.[11] The literary community caught the spirit; Samuel Clemens delivered the first typewritten manuscript—*Life on the Mississippi*—to his publisher, and others followed suit.

THE NEW PERSON IN THE OFFICE

The typewriter was soon a ubiquitous fixture of the workplace. As early as 1887 it would be said that "its monotonous click can be heard in almost every well-regulated business establishment in the country."[12] It would make broad ripples of change in the social environment of the office, creating, as JoAnne Yates has documented, "a whole new class

TABLE 9-1 Typists and Stenographers in the United States	
1890	33,000
1900	134,000*
1910	387,000
1920	786,000

*Starting in 1900, this occupational category included secretaries.

of clerical workers"—largely female—to handle the production of written documents.[13] U.S. Bureau of the Census figures on occupations, begun in 1890 and cited by Yates, tell the story of the expanded role of typewriting in the American economy (Table 9-1).

A major consequence of this development was the opening of the office workplace to women. Women had shared the work of men on America's farms for hundreds of years, and their daughters left those farms for work in the textile mills of New England in the mid-nineteenth century. But the office had always been a male bastion of managers who ruled and male clerks who were ruled over, hoping to be managers one day. The demand for typists changed that situation permanently; men still ruled the bastion, but women were now let in. Typewriters did for the office what automated equipment did for the mill—it separated thinking from doing. Now the manager could do all the thinking, and the typist could manually transcribe those thoughts into documents. By 1890, 64 percent of all typists were women; by 1920, the percentage had risen to 92.[14]

The aptitude of women for the new occupation of typist was hotly debated, even in the presuffrage era of the 1880s and 1890s. "Women," it was claimed in their favor, "are superior to men, their greater quickness of perception and motion giving them obvious advantages," while men were decried as "more frequently absent because of their vices."[15]

Natural abilities aside, pay levels probably had much more to do with the recruitment of women for the boom in typing jobs. Then, as now, women were usually paid less for the same work—perhaps by 25 percent in those times. But at $15 per week in 1886, the typist's pay was far better than what could be had in the factory or the retail shop, and the working environment was said to be much better.

NEW COMPETITORS AND INNOVATIONS

The commercial possibilities of the typewriter were not lost on potential competitors, and before long a number had entered the field with machines of many designs. The first of these was the Yost Caligraph, a cheap version of the Sholes machines offered by the former sales agent of Remington. Dunsmore had a financial interest in this operation as well. In 1881, the Caligraph No. 2 came onto the market with upper- and lowercase functions; but unlike the Remington, the Caligraph did not use a shift key—it had two entirely separate keyboards. In 1885, the Crandell, the Hammond, and the Hall machines appeared—each based on a uniquely different design for striking type to paper.[16]

By 1886, *Scientific American* estimated that 50,000 typewriters of all makes had been produced; and by 1888, Remington Standard Typewriting Company[17] was turning out some 1,500 machines each month. Its Ilion plant had adopted mass-production techniques to reach this level. Specialized departments performed the die-casting, tempering, forging, annealing, plating, and assembly operations. Specialized equipment was developed and brought on line, and skilled workers assembled each machine individually.

Remington knew that it had the best-made and most functional machine and was aggressive in letting the public know about it. In 1888, the company's sales agency put up a "$1,000 Challenge" to Caligraph and the handful of other competitors, proposing a public contest with impartial referees to determine which machine was the fastest. Caligraph did not shrink from this challenge, but sent its typing champion with the double-keyboard machine to take on Remington in a highly publicized event in Cincinnati in July 1888. Caligraph was soundly thrashed.

If Remington's public victory confirmed its position as top dog in the typewriting world, it did nothing to stop a torrent of new competitors from entering the field, particularly as Sholes's patents began to expire. Between 1885 and 1890, the number of firms doubled to ten. A community of some 20 supplier firms grew up in their shadow, and collectively, in 1890, they employed some 1,800 people and produced $3.6 million in finished goods sales.[18] But the real threat to Remington's dominance was a yet-unhatched innovation by Franz X. Wagner. Wagner had designed the Caligraph machine for Yost, and now he and his brother had a new design with an important new feature: visible type. The Wagner design had the type arms swing out and strike the paper front and center, where the operator could observe any mistake and correct it immediately. John T. Underwood and his father, who were in the ribbon and carbon business, saw the virtue of this innovation. They bought the design from Wagner and put the new machine into production in 1895.

The Underwood No. 1 was an immediate success, and was followed in short order by several models that refined its basic design, the most important of which was the Model 5 (1899). The Model 5 had the look and feel of the modern manual typewriter that anyone today who has ever used such a device (a vanishing breed) would quickly recognize and feel comfortable with; it had visible type, a light touch, a tab function, quiet operation, and a design that made corrections easy. Its placement of the type bars—like its predecessor models—represented a successful departure from the design of competing machines. So successful was this machine that Underwood immediately shifted production to a larger factory in Hartford to meet the skyrocketing demand. With its market leadership decimated by the new challenger, Remington rushed out its Monarch model in 1901; L.C. Smith & Brothers—another big producer—followed with its No. 8 (1908). From photographs, it is clear that these competitors were look-alikes of the design pioneered by Underwood.[19] Imitation, however, did nothing to shore up their sales, and by 1920 Underwood had a lock on the business, selling as many machines as all of its rivals combined.[20]

The Royal Company (1904), was perhaps the last of the new entrants to gain any real standing, but this did not prevent other startups from joining the fray. Some 89 manufacturers had tried their luck in the American market by 1909, but almost all were marginal operations, and many came and went quickly. Underwood, Remington, Royal, and L.C. Smith & Brothers (later merged with Corona) were to dominate the American market until the next chapter was opened. With everyone settled on the design and features of the typewriter, the pace of product innovation slowed dramatically, and the big producers concentrated on manufacturing and costs.

THE ELECTRIC AGE

In 1933, one of the fringe players in the industry—Electrostatic Typewriters, Inc.—was purchased by International Business Machines (IBM). Both Remington and Underwood had passed up the opportunity to buy it; both had disappointing experiences with electrics as early as 1925. Electric-powered typewriters had been around since 1906 but had never made a dent in the market—home or office. The 1930s were not good years for the industry anyway. The Great Depression decimated economic growth, and with it expenditures for office equipment. Of the four leaders, only Royal had a positive growth rate, and its was anemic. Firms were leaving the business at a high rate.

IBM was not in the typewriter business, but it did make record-accounting and tabulating machines and thought it might acquire some useful keypunch technology from the Electrostatic acquisition.[21] There is little information about the early IBM electric machines, except that the War Department gave the company a great many orders during the war, while requiring its principal competitors to forego typewriter production altogether in favor of military production. This gave IBM years of design and manufacturing experience that put it well down the learning curve. In the postwar economic boom, demand for the IBM electrics was poised to intensify.[22]

Electrics did not represent a radical innovation so much as a mixing of two well-understood technologies to provide better performance: more uniform print, better-quality copies, and less physical stress on the typist over long periods. But the business market was not yet convinced. Perhaps secretaries found these early electrics too

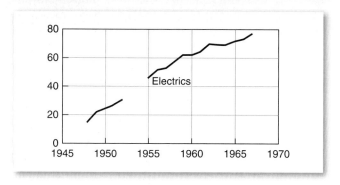

FIGURE 9-1   Electrics as a Percentage of Office Typewriter Sales, 1948–1967

Note: No data for years 1954 and 1955.

Source: Based on data in George Nichols Engler, *The Typewriter Industry: The Impact of a Significant Technological Innovation,* Ph.D. diss. (Los Angeles: University of California at Los Angeles, 1970), pp. 276–277.

crude and too noisy; perhaps they did not find their virtues overwhelming. For whatever reason, electrics were slow to catch on; but once they did, they rapidly displaced manual office typewriters (Figure 9-1).

In terms of total machine sales, both office and nonoffice, a similar picture prevailed. In 1950, electrics had only 10 percent of the total office/nonoffice market, but by 1965 they were capturing 50 percent of all sales. By 1970, only 24 percent of total machine sales went to manuals, mostly for the home market.

By 1967, IBM controlled 60 percent of the electric market and 74 percent of the high-end, full-featured electric market. SCM, Royal, and Olivetti-Underwood each had about 10 percent. Remington was barely on the map. The stage was now set for an invasion of the office market by another wave of innovation, this time something so radical that Sholes, Dunsmore, Wagner, and other pioneers of the typewriter business would have had trouble understanding it, but which Mr. Samuel Clemens would surely want to get his hands on.

THE SMARTER MACHINES

At the time that the business community was excitedly buying Underwood's Model 5, there were about 5 million office workers in America—about 20 percent of the working population. Today, more than 55 million are white-collar workers—clerical and professional—and they represent about half of all employed people in the United States.[23] By all accounts they are not the most productive workers, and no one has been able to measure any appreciable rate of productivity increase over many years. Thus, with half of the working population in a state of productive lethargy, and some four-fifths of office costs going for labor, any technologies that suggested improvements in white-collar productivity were welcomed.

The office-machines industry was ripe for radical change, but when change first appeared it was as an adaptation of a new technology to an old form. The IBM Magnetic Tape Selectric, introduced in 1964, combined electric typewriter technology with digital computing technology to make text editing possible for the first time. By the early 1970s, stand-alone "word processors" with CRTs for true text editing began to appear and replace standard office typewriters.[24] A group of new companies, some from unrelated industries, read the tea leaves and determined that what the "office of the future" needed was an integrated system of dedicated word processors—that is, smart typewriters with CRTs, microprocessor systems, and text-processing software— that would improve productivity. Wang, Xerox, Exxon, ITT, AT&T, Olivetti, IBM, and others (as many as 55 by one count[25]) developed elaborate and expensive systems that intended to do for text processing what Henry Ford had done for auto assembly. Exxon alone, in its bid to diversify from the oil business, spent an estimated $2 billion on its office equipment division, developing such fanciful products as Vydec word processors, Qwip fax machines, and Qyx electronic typewriters. All signs pointed to big success, and by 1975, some 200,000 word-processing devices had been installed. By 1986, over 4 million word processors had been sold in the United States alone.

But the electronic office proved not to be the factory of the future. The millions spent on word processors could not be shown to generate any productivity improvements, except in law offices and other establishments where boilerplate documents were heavily used. Secretaries dreaded the prospect of being corralled into word-processing "centers" like so many assembly-line drudges; managers sensed they would be lost without their secretaries; and companies that organized word-processing pools faced heavy reorganizing efforts and costs. Office workers wanted something else, and when they found it, the word-processor firms took big losses. Wang went belly up. Exxon retreated to the oil patch after selling its product line to Lanier for pennies on the dollar. ITT and AT&T pulled back. The "something else" that office workers wanted was the personal computer.

THE NEXT WAVE OF INNOVATION

Like the innovation of the typewriter a century earlier, the personal computer was destined to draw from many existing technologies of the time, came in a variety of designs offered by many competing firms, and ultimately crystallized around a fairly uniform set of product features and specifications. And, like the Sholes/Remington typewriter, it was an innovation destined to both create a major industry and affect the way people did their work. Further, the personal computer represented a wave of technological innovation that swept through the same market occupied by the typewriter and the dedicated word processor. These pattern similarities support the earlier contention that the study of older innovations is not just a form of academic recreation, but a way to enrich our understanding of developments taking place today.

Development of the PC Industry

The first device that deserved the name "personal computer" was the Altair 8800, designed by a small electronic kit maker in Albuquerque (MITS), and offered to the public for $395. How this machine was invented and the early history of the personal computer industry are engagingly told in *Fire In the Valley*[26] and other books. The Altair 8800 was an instant hit among electronic gadgeteers and the new breed of digital enthusiasts; by 1977, there were at least 30 firms making personal computers, including Apple, Commodore, Tandy (Radio Shack), and Heathkit.[27] That year, the Apple II was introduced—a 16K RAM machine that sold for $1,195 without a monitor. Its skyrocketing sales were encouraged by the development of the spreadsheet and word-processing software that would eventually create a business market for it and other machines. By 1981, an estimated half-million personal computers had found their ways to the business market.[28] A comparable number were being used by students, scientists, and hobbyists. Interestingly, the first Apple II computers produced many of the same annoying features that afflicted the original typewriter. They would create only capital letters; there was no tabulation feature or number pad; the format seen on the screen was not necessarily the format that would be printed out (the "what you see is what you get" of the personal computer appeared in the market only with the introduction of the Macintosh).

The landmark event for the personal computer was the August 1981 introduction of the IBM PC. For a list price of about $3,000, IBM offered a conservatively designed desktop computer based on the Intel 8088 microprocessor. In the judgment of most experts, the IBM PC was no technological breakthrough, but that fact did not stop it from quickly grabbing 30 percent of the business market. In the last three months of 1981 alone, IBM shipped 13,000 of its new machines; over the next two full years 40 times that number would be sold.[29] Despite its technical shortcomings, IBM's machine legitimized the personal computer industry. As Stan Augarten observes in his history of computers, ". . . the PC has had a stabilizing influence on the youthful personal computer industry, providing a focal point for manufacturers and customers alike."[30] IBM's use of an open architecture and policy of making operating system information available to the public created a center of gravity for applications software developers. The fact that it was built largely from nonproprietary components opened the door to many imitators who created "IBM compatible" machines and peripherals. Before long, the vast majority of personal computer users were operating equipment that shared the same operating characteristics as the dominant IBM PC.

Personal computers—of all makes and models—very quickly assumed a form that was recognizable and accepted by consumers. This consisted of a monitor, a standard QWERTY keyboard, an underlying operating system, a processing unit, a disk drive (and eventually an internal hard drive), and a bus-architecture of one or another type.[31] Each of these forms affected the way the user fed data into the machine and how data in the machine was made available to the user. What happened inside the machine—once the user made his keystrokes, or popped her disk into the machine's drive—was a function of microprocessors and software.

Apple Computers remained the sole major holdout from the IBM-driven movement. Apple, too, offered the standard outward features of monitor, keyboard, disk drive, operating system, processing unit, and bus, but its steadfastness in maintaining a closed architecture, proprietary operating system and bus, and reliance on Motorola microprocessors isolated Apple from the larger universe of DOS-based, Intel chip machine users. Despite the greater elegance of the Apple Macintosh machine, the company's share of market in 1993 remained stuck at 13 percent. At the same time, intense price competition within the entire industry cut deeply into its profit margins.

The Brains and the Box

For the typical user, the internal interaction of microprocessors and software was largely transparent and of little concern; what went in and what came out were the things that interested the user. But microprocessors and software very quickly established themselves as the technological soul of the machine, its unique identity, and the source of major improvements in the personal computer industry. In contrast, the business of designing and assembling the machines took on all the characteristics of a commodity business—like television sets and other electronic appliances—commanding lower margins and lower stock valuations. Remarkably, in 1993, the total combined market value of Intel and Microsoft—the two leading vendors of microprocessors and software, respectively—exceeded the market value of the IBM corporation. The suppliers had become more valuable than their customer. They were supplying the brains; IBM and manufacturers of IBM-compatible machines were supplying the boxes the brains were sold in. Clearly, the brains were more highly valued.

Growth of the Personal Computer Industry

The versatility of the personal computer allowed clerical workers and professionals to write and edit text, run spreadsheets, and create graphics—all the things that their typewriters could not do and that the old word processors had failed to accommodate. By 1987, personal computers—of all manufacturers—were outselling word processors by 4.5 times.[32] Unit sales to business in 1991 were projected to reach 20 million. But the growth in sales only led to a great industry shakeout. In 1983, a year in which the market grew by 50 percent, many important competitors exited the industry. Commodore, Atari, and Texas Instruments experienced serious business problems; Timex-Sinclair, Osborne, Coleco, and Mattel vanished from the industry. In 1984, 62 percent of total personal computer sales to business firms went to IBM (49) and Apple (13) alone.[33] T. Modis and A. Debecker point to 1982–1983 as the peak, in terms of numbers of different models and new companies entering the personal computer industry. They cite 125 distinguishable new PCs per year introduced by almost 18 new companies per year. Within five years those rates dropped to 82 new models for 14 companies.[34]

Today, more and more office workers are having personal computers put on their desks at great expense to their employers. It is not at all clear if these are improving the workers' productivity; indeed, many believe that they have simply created more and needless revisions of text and have wasted time on out-of-the-blue spreadsheet forecasts. The one thing that is clear is that employees want them, just as secretaries wanted electric typewriters through the 1960s.

A BACKWARD GLANCE

As a means of putting words on paper, the new computer technology represented a great advance over the crude mechanical instrument that Samuel Clemens and his pal Petroleum Nasby encountered that summer day in 1874. A safe bet is that it in turn will be displaced by something better in the future, as likely as not developed and manufactured by some entity unknown to us today.

The story of the typewriter was not recounted here simply as a quaint tale; rather, the invention of the device, its transformation over time, and the rise and fall of its various manufacturers underscores many of the themes to be developed in detail in this book. Looking back at this business of printed documents, we can see a number of distinct developments:

- *New innovations from old capabilities.* The Sholes typewriter was a synthesis of a number of existing mechanical technologies. Joined together, they created something new. The early electrics likewise joined together familiar components (small electric motors and manual typewriters) to create a new machine. Even the very radical leap to personal computer technology carried with it the old and the familiar: the QWERTY keyboard, typing conventions, and so forth. Although not mentioned here, the personal computer itself was built from available components created by other sectors of the electronics industry: television monitors, printed-circuit boards, memory chips, semiconductors, and the like.
- *Dominant design.* After an initial period of intensive churning of product innovations—different modes of striking the paper (type bar, type wheel, type sleeve), hidden and visible types, dual keyboards versus single boards with shift keys, and so forth—a dominant design emerged in the manual typewriter industry. At that point, experimentation with the fundamental systems of the machine tapered off. Manufacturers and customers had a clear idea in their minds as to what a typewriter should be and how it should operate. No substantial innovation took place until 25 years later, when electric machines began to attract interest. A similar phenomenon is seen in the personal computer industry, in which a tremendous amount of product variety was very quickly crystallized by the emergence of the IBM PC, whose great success enforced a good deal of design and operating uniformity.
- *A shifting ecology of firms.* From the days when only Remington and two or three other firms were in the market, there was an explosion of competing firms followed by an implosion later. We will see in the next chapter that the rapid exit of firms from a young industry is closely related to the emergence of a dominant design. In this case, the emergence of the IBM PC was followed shortly by the exit of many previously important competitors.
- *Waves of technological change.* One hundred and twenty-five years of innovation in typewriters, word processors, and personal computers had one fundamental objective: to put words on paper neatly and efficiently. Over that period we have witnessed the shift from handwriting to manually operated machines, a dramatic shift to electric machines, and the introduction of a radically different technology—digital technology. Each change reflects the fundamental objective, but each represents a different way of achieving it. Each is based on a different technology, which requires in turn a different set of skills on the part of producer firms.
- *Changing leadership at breakpoints in technology.* Remington's monopoly crumbled rapidly with the innovation of visible typing. Underwood, a newcomer, took the lead and held it for the next three decades. When the electric machine

came in, a virtual outsider (IBM) rode it to the top while traditional leaders stuck with the old technology and fell on hard times. The leap to digital technology brought in other unknown firms, particularly when word processors were riding high. The regaining of leadership by IBM's personal computer is unusual in this respect, as this firm was a dominant force in both the electric typewriter and PC waves of innovation. Some might argue that IBM was merely the packager or distributor of the truly important innovations underlying the PC industry—software and microprocessors. Here leadership rested in Microsoft, designer of the ubiquitous DOS operating system, and Intel, whose chips were the heart and soul of the machine. Recent developments, particularly the rising fortunes of these two firms and the declining fortunes of IBM, seem to support this argument.

- *The invasion of an alien technology.* Electric typewriters have almost totally displaced manual machines in the workplace, and one might speculate that the same has happened in the home market. The appearance of personal computers in the 1970s represents an invasion by a truly alien technology, and all of its purveyors—hardware, software, printer manufacturers, and so forth—have come from outside the original manual typewriter tradition; only IBM had any position in electrics. As we will see in later chapters, looking for industry-shattering innovation among the current players in an industry might be misdirected effort; most of the important innovations occur in unexpected places, and when they do, the current leaders often react in inappropriate ways and lose their dominant positions in the industry.

There is much to be learned by looking backward through time at industries that have run their full course of birth, growth, maturity, and decline, as we have done here with the typewriter industry. Subsequent chapters continue this method, in each case choosing industries that are familiar and not so complex that they will lose the reader in a thicket of technical details. These case studies are intended to be entertaining as well as enlightening. Looking at a number of innovation-driven industries helps us see common patterns from which a general model can be constructed.

Endnotes

1. Samuel Clemens's correspondence, cited in Richard Nelson Current, *The Typewriter: And the Men Who Made It* (Champaign, Ill.: University of Illinois Press, 1954), p. 72.
2. George Nichols Engler, *The Typewriter Industry: The Impact of a Significant Technological Innovation,* Ph.D. diss. (Los Angeles: University of California at Los Angeles, 1970), pp. 20–21.
3. Bruce Bliven, *The Wonderful Writing Machine* (New York: Random House, 1954), p. 34.
4. Current, *The Typewriter,* pp. 1–22.
5. Engler, *The Typewriter Industry,* p. 20.
6. Bliven, *The Wonderful Writing Machine,* pp. 55–56.
7. From *The Story of the Typewriter, 1873–1923,* (Herkimer, N.Y.: Herkimer County Historical Society), pp. 74–75.
8. Correspondence cited in Kenneth E. Eble, *Old Clemens and W.D.H.* (Baton Rouge: University of Louisiana Press, 1985), pp. 56 and 81.
9. George Carl Mares, *The History of the Typewriter* (London: Guilbert Pitman, 1909), p. 58.
10. Herkimer County Historical Society, *Story of the Typewriter,* p. 72.
11. Bliven, *The Wonderful Writing Machine,* p. 66.
12. "Penman's Art Journal," 1887, as cited in Current, *The Typewriter,* p. 110.
13. JoAnne Yates, *Control Through Communication: The Rise of System in American Management* (Baltimore: Johns Hopkins University Press, 1989), p. 43.
14. Shoshana Zuboff, *In the Age of the Smart Machine* (New York: Basic Books, 1989), p. 116.
15. Unattributed remarks cited in Current, *The Typewriter,* p. 119.
16. Remington used a type-bar design; Hammond and Hall both used a type wheel; and the Crandell machine used a design called the type sleeve, in which the letters and numbers were arranged on a long, slender cylinder that formed the outer sleeve of the key-driven movement.
17. Philo Remington and his brothers were forced to sell their interests in the typewriter in reorganization proceedings. The early success of their typewriter could not cover their losses from other business lines, and eventually they were bankrupt. The Remington name was sold with the company's interests and manufacturing facilities.
18. Current, *The Typewriter,* p. 112.
19. See *The Evolution of the Typewriter* (New York: The Royal Typewriter Company, 1921), pp. 41–45.
20. Engler, *The Typewriter Industry,* p. 30.
21. Ibid., p. 129.
22. Ibid., pp. 131–133.

23. Tom Forester, *High-Tech Society* (Cambridge, Mass.; MIT Press, 1987), p. 195.

24. "The Revolution in the Office," condensed from *Data Processing,* May 1978, in Tom Forester, ed., *The Microelectronics Revolution* (Cambridge, Mass.: MIT Press, 1981), pp. 232–243.

25. Walter A. Kleinschrod, *Critical Issues in Office Automation* (New York: McGraw-Hill, 1986), p. 8.

26. Paul Freiberger and Michael Swaine, *Fire in the Valley: The Making of the Personal Computer* (Berkely, Calif.: Osborne/McGraw-Hill, 1984).

27. Stan Augarten, *Bit by Bit: An Illustrated History of Computers* (New York: Ticknor & Fields, 1984), pp. 270–273.

28. Kleinschrod, *Critical Issues,* p. 12.

29. Freiberger and Swaine, *Fire in the Valley,* p. 279.

30. Augarten, *Bit by Bit,* p. 281.

31. Hidetaka Kai, *Competitive Strategy Under Standardization in the Personal Computer Industry and Its Influence on New Entrants,* unpublished S.M. thesis (Cambridge, Mass.: MIT Alfred P. Sloan School of Management), May 1992.

32. "Personal Computers Invade the Office," *Business Week,* August 8, 1983.

33. Survey data cited in James K. Loebbecke and Miklos Vasarhely, *Microcomputers* (Homewood, Ill.: Irwin, 1986), p. 4.

34. T. Modis and A. Debecker, "Innovation in the Computer Industry," *Technological Forecasting and Social Change,* vol. 33 (1988), pp. 267–278.

10 | INNOVATION AND INDUSTRIAL EVOLUTION

James M. Utterback

Innovation in the typewriter industry, in the electric lighting industry, and in those industries profiled in Chapter 2 suggests a dynamic relationship among product innovation, the marketplace, and the firms that emerge and compete on the basis of particular innovations.

In examining the early life of the typewriter it is impossible to separate interactions between producing firms, ongoing experiments with machine designs and features, and the growing cadre of typists. The first decades of incandescent lighting present a similar web of relationships. Edison was more than just a clever inventor working in isolation from other technologists and potential customers. He drew heavily from the work of others in his bid to create a practical incandescent bulb, and the market dimensions of the project were never far from his mind. Even his great moment of success—when the first incandescent lamp burned through the night at Menlo Park—was just one more step in a long process of innovation that emerged with arc lighting, with Wallace's powerful generator, with the development of insulated copper wire, and with dozens of other supporting technologies. As incandescent lighting was accepted in the lighting industry, the focus of innovation in Edison's company and in the companies of his competitors changed as well, but the links among competition, customers, and the innovative process were never shaken loose.

These dynamic relationships remain a part of the innovative process in industry today. For example, even though the dust has far from settled in the personal computer industry, it is clear that the pace and direction of innovation has been heavily determined by a complex web of interrelated events taking place among integrated circuit producers, software companies, disk drive manufacturers, and others. And their progress has not been made in isolation from the market, but has had to factor in the work habits, skills, and expectations of millions of users—many of whom formed their habits and skills in the age of the typewriter.

Unfortunately, academic studies and models of innovation have failed to capture the richness of this system. Instead, we have seen it in fairly linear terms—as something that begins with a company possessing a certain technology, investing in that technology and accompanying ideas, and implementing them in the market. This approach assumes that all innovations occur in the same way in all companies; it misses the important differences and powerful interactions between the subjects of study; and it generally disregards the fact that organizations change throughout their lifetimes. Earlier research also failed to distinguish between product and process innovations, each of which follows a different path yet affects the other. In short, the interaction of

Utterback, J. (1994), *Mastering the Dynamics of Innovation,* Boston, MA: Harvard Business School Press (pp. 79–102).

technological change, organizations, and the competitive marketplace is much more complex and dynamic than most models describe.

The model presented in this chapter attempts to capture those important dynamic relationships. It describes how change in product and process innovation and in organizational structure occurs in patterns that are observable across industries and sectors. The model incorporates marketplace realities and allows consideration of the different conditions required for rapid innovation and for high levels of output and productivity. This model is based on historical studies of innovations in their organizational, technical, and economic settings. The data gathered from such studies—particularly those of more contemporary industries—are necessarily incomplete, but they nevertheless add to the richness of our insights.

THE DYNAMICS OF INNOVATION

This model has its origins in work begun in 1974 in collaboration with the late William Abernathy at the Harvard Business School and continued over the years. As a result, it is more familiar to many scholars than to the industrial managers who have the most to gain from it. Bill Abernathy was one of those rare people who successfully bridged the chasm between the academy and industry. This fact, along with his energy and creativity, inspired a new generation of researchers whose work in the areas of technological change, innovation, and industrial management today enriches the tradition of inquiry of which Abernathy was a true pioneer. Some of their important contributions to this tradition are discussed later in the chapter.

The model describes the changing rates of product and process innovation, and considers in connection with these the business-oriented characteristics that mark their ebbs and flows.

Product Innovation

We have already observed the richness of product innovation that prevailed in the early years of the typewriter, the personal computer, and electric lighting industries. Unencumbered by universal technical standards or by uniform product expectations in the marketplace, the early participants in these new industries experimented freely with new forms and materials. This same sense of pioneering prevailed in the early, pre-Model-A years of the auto industry, when any number of uniquely designed vehicles emerged from hundreds of American and European workshops.

We also observed that this flurry of radical product innovation eventually ends with the emergence of a dominant design. With the marketplace forming its expectations for a product in terms of features, form, and capabilities, the bases on which product innovation can take place become much fewer, and the focus of R&D narrows to incremental innovations on existing features. A good example of this was seen in the case of the incandescent lamp. Once the ensemble of necessary features for a commercially effective lamp was introduced by Edison, product innovation downshifted dramatically. The same was observed with the introduction of the Underwood Model 5 and a number of other products mentioned in Chapter 2. Figure 10-1 is a representation of this phenomenon.

Several studies have shown that somewhere along the product innovation curve the performance criteria that serve as a primary basis for competition change from ill defined and uncertain to well articulated.[1] At the same time, forces that reduce the rate of product change and innovation begin to build up. As obvious improvements are introduced, it becomes increasingly difficult to better past performance; users develop loyalties and preferences, and the practicalities of marketing, distribution, maintenance, and so forth demand greater standardization. Innovations leading to better product performance become less likely unless they are easy for the customer to evaluate and compare. Firms attempt to maximize their sales and market shares by defining their development initiatives in terms that clearly matter to potential customers.

But even as the energies that characterize the period of greatest product innovation begin to fade, other creative activities awaken and assume their place.

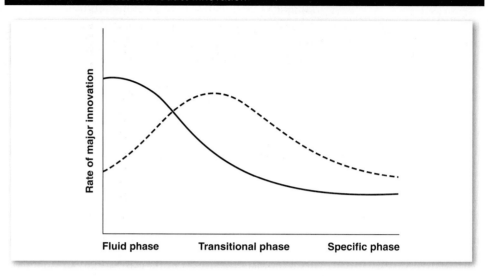

FIGURE 10-1   The Rate of Product Innovation

Process Innovation

During the formative period of a new product technology, the processes used to produce it are usually crude, inefficient, and based on a mixture of skilled labor and general-purpose machinery and tools. Thus, in the first few years of commercially produced incandescent lamps, Edison's products were made by laborious processes in a building adjacent to the laboratory in which they were first conceived. There were no specialized tools, machines, or dedicated craft traditions for incandescent bulb making. It was the product itself, at this point, that mattered to innovators and to those customers venturesome enough to try it out.

But product innovation and process innovation are interdependent; as the rate of product innovation decreases, it is common to observe a growing rate of process innovation (Figure 10-2). In the case of incandescent lighting we noted the innovation of specialized glass-blowing equipment, high-capacity vacuum pumps, and other manufacturing improvements. The number of steps in the manufacturing process dropped from 200 to 30 between 1880 and 1920. Skilled labor using common tools gave way to specialized equipment operated by workers who were less skilled. Lamp production moved from the making of individual units, to batches, to semicontinuous production.

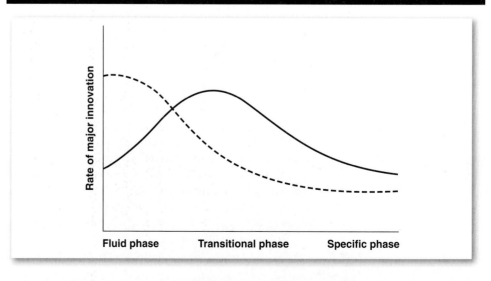

FIGURE 10-2   Rate of Process Innovation

Organizational Change

Essentially, the organization of a firm formed around an innovation goes through the familiar transformation that entrepreneurial organizations experience as they become successful and shift their focus from innovative products to larger-scale production of standardized offerings. This transformation is characterized by the following:

- Informal control gives way to an emphasis on structure, goals, and rules.
- Structure become hierarchical and rigid, and tasks become formal.
- Major innovations—once the life-blood of the firm—are less and less encouraged; continuous incremental improvements become the order of the day.

Not only do changes in products and processes occur in the systematic pattern described earlier, but organizational requirements may also be expected to vary according to a similar pattern. During periods of high market and technical uncertainty, a productive unit must be focused to make progress; for a group to be successful in an uncertain environment, individuals in the organization must act together. This type of structure is called *organic*[2] and emphasizes, among other things, frequent adjustment and redefinition of tasks, limited hierarchy, and high lateral communication. An organic firm is appropriate to uncertain environments because of its increased potential for gathering and processing information for decision making.

The relative power of individuals in the organic firm is related to their assumption of entrepreneurial roles. The rewards for radical product innovation in these firms are substantial and are generally valued by the entrepreneur to a much greater degree than are salary rewards. Realization of potential rewards depends on the survival and growth of the firm, which in turn depends largely on the ability of the entrepreneur to generate a superior product and to capture a share of an emerging market. The innovative capacity of such an organization is high.[3]

As the firm loses its organic character, the relative power of individuals begins to shift from those with entrepreneurial ability to those with management skills. A different set of skills is required for the growth and structuring of the organization. Often the original entrepreneur or entrepreneurial group departs (as did Steve Jobs of Apple, Robert Noyce of Fairchild, and Henry Kloss of Acoustic Research) to start other, smaller enterprises (Next, Intel, and KLH and Advent, respectively). As the transition away from a high rate of product innovation begins, individuals and units in the firm lose their organic connections and become more sequentially interdependent; coordination and control becomes correspondingly more important. Thus, during the transition, organizations are often structured according to products or regions, each division replicating in some respects the earlier entrepreneurial form.

As a dominant design emerges and production operations expand rapidly in response to increased demand, the focus of rewards shifts to those who are able to expand production operations, marketing functions, and so forth. Rewards may be provided in more traditional terms of bonuses, stock options, and other managerial perquisites.

These changes will cause moderation of the innovative capacity of an organization. As a product becomes more standardized and is produced in a more systematic process, interdependence among organizational subunits gradually increases, making it more difficult and costly to incorporate radical innovations.

Once a production process and a set of market relationships and expectations become highly developed with respect to a specified and standardized product, organizational control is provided through structure, goals, and rules. When the business environment is better known and operations become routine, it is seen as necessary to provide more rigid coordination that establishes consistent routines and rules to minimize inefficiency and costs in operations. This type of structure is known as *mechanistic*.

The power and influence of individuals who show administrative ability increases in a mechanistic organization. When the technical and market environment becomes stable—and when growth of a productive unit relies more on stretching existing products and processes—the ability to hold a steady and consistent course is highly valued. Rewards in a stable environment are centered on financial results and on predictable, incremental performance in product and process change that builds on past investments. Ideas that threaten to disrupt the stability of the existing process will be discouraged, and ideas that extend the life of existing products and technology will be encouraged and rewarded, probably in a highly structured manner.

The innovation capacity of such a productive unit tends to be low. When production processes are highly integrated within a system, and a high degree of interdependence exists among subprocesses, the disruption and cost associated with major changes becomes a primary concern. Innovation and change—prized in the organic firm—are a threat and expensive nuisance in the mechanistic firm.

Market Characteristics

When a technology is in its infancy and many producers are rushing to join the industry the market shares of each firm are highly unstable. For example, Klein has shown that between the inception of the auto industry at the beginning of the century and the appearance of its dominant design in 1923, market shares varied rapidly. Klein concludes that "on the basis of 1903 sales it would have been impossible to pick the top ten in 1924," and further that "the positions of the leading makes oscillated greatly during this period."[4] Conversely, during periods of primarily incremental change a chart of market shares consists of mostly horizontal lines with little fluctuation.[5] At the same time, one would expect market feedback to be rapid during this fluid period of inception, and expect performance, features, and functionality of the product to be much more important than price to its demanding "lead users."[6] Perhaps a better way to phrase this is to say that price is more influenced by value in use than by direct cost of production. Both development efforts and costs and profit margins may be relatively high.

After a dominant design or standard is determined, products are likely to become more commoditylike and undifferentiated in terms of function and features. The key functions required of a car, a typewriter, a personal computer, or a light bulb will be widely agreed, and not to have the full set of features and functions means not to be competitive in most of the market. Stable market shares will generally imply the existence of only a few significant and dominant producers. Market feedback will tend to be slow, and direct contact with customers relatively less compared to analysis of statistics and industry information. Price, performance, features, and service will tend to be at parity over the long run with small changes serving as stimuli to take marginal market share from rivals. Incremental changes in products made by competitors will tend to be copied rapidly. The emphasis of innovation, however, will tend to be process improvements that are less easily copied. Price and quality will strongly influence competitiveness, and price will depend heavily on direct manufacturing costs. It is important to note that the rigid situation described here is probably as much or more the result of managerial attitudes and organizational factors as it is to technical factors. Klein contends that "when firms begin to act on the assumption of a lower rate of progress there is likely to be both an increase in the degree of organization and a decline in the degree of competitive interaction."[7]

The Competitive Environment

As this process of decreasing product innovation and increasing process innovation moves forward, it is not uncommon to observe important changes in the competitive environment.

We have already seen how the absence of consensus on product capabilities and features introduces tremendous uncertainty for both customers and producers. Once consensus crystallizes around a particular product, however, that product can enjoy large market share for an extended period. The case of the DC-3 aircraft provides an example of how that consensus can be achieved in one product. The DC-3 is not the most familiar example to readers who have grown up in the jet age, but this aircraft was a culmination of previous innovations and it set the standard for commercial aircraft for two decades.[8] It was not the largest, or the fastest, or the longest-range aircraft to fly when it was introduced, but it was simply the *only* economical, large, fast plane able to fly long distances. The DC-3 satisfied combined market needs so well, in fact, that it provided the basic concepts of commercial aircraft design from the time of its introduction in the mid-1930s until jet-powered aircraft appeared in the late 1950s. Some design concepts introduced in the DC-3 continue in use today.

But as product capabilities and features are crystallized through the emergence of a dominant design, competition between rival firms stabilizes. The number of competitors drops off quickly after this landmark event for the industry, and the bases of competition shift to refinements in product features, reliability, and cost. From this crystallization, a set of efficient producers usually emerges.

The appearance of a dominant design shifts the competitive emphasis to favor those firms with a greater skill in process innovation and process integration and with more highly developed technical and engineering skills. When this happens, many firms are unable to compete and effectively fail. Others may possess special resources and thus merge successfully with the ultimately dominant firms. Weaker firms may merge and still fail.

Eventually the competitive environment reaches a point of stability in which there are only a few firms—four or five is a typical number from the evidence reviewed to date—producing standardized or slightly differentiated products with stable sales and market shares. A number of small firms may remain in the industry serving specialized market segments, but compared with the small firms entering special segments early in the industry, they have little growth potential. Thus it is important to distinguish between small surviving firms and small firms that are new entrants, and to keep in mind that the term "new entrants" includes existing larger firms moving from their established market or technological base into a new product area.

Mueller and Tilton were among the first to present this hypothesis in its entirety.[9] They contend that a new industry is created by the occurrence of a major process or product innovation and develops technologically as less radical innovations are introduced. They further argue that the large corporation seldom provides its people with incentives to introduce a development of radical importance; thus these changes tend to be developed by new entrants without an established stake in a product market segment. In their words, neither large absolute size nor market power is a necessary condition for successful competitive development of most major innovations.

Mueller and Tilton further contend that once a major innovation is established, a rush of firms enters the newly formed industry or adopts a new process innovation. They hold that during the early period of entry and experimentation immediately after a major innovation, the science and technology on which it depends are often only crudely understood and that this reduces the advantage of large firms. However:

> As the number of firms entering the industry increases and more and more R&D is undertaken on the innovation, the scientific and technological frontiers of the new technology expand rapidly. Research becomes increasingly specialized and sophisticated and the technology is broken down into its component parts with individual investigations focusing on improvements in small elements of the technology.[10]

Clearly, the situation Mueller and Tilton describe works to the advantage of larger firms in the expanding industry and to the disadvantage of smaller entrants. Reese Jenkins studied this explicitly in the case of photography and found that as the product became standardized, smaller firms consolidated and the industry went through a phase of large and small firms fighting for market share, followed by a phase dominated by an oligopoly of large firms.[11]

Staples, Baker, and Sweeney have summarized several clear parallels between our model and Mueller and Tilton's hypotheses:

> The Utterback and Abernathy model holds implications for organizational structure, just as Mueller and Tilton's does for the composition of an industry. A comparison of the two will show a number of similarities. Both describe a

continuum. The stages roughly correspond. Both emphasize the shift of the basis of competition from performance and technological characteristics to price and cost considerations. In both, the evolution is accompanied by an expanding market, increasing importance of production process investment, and a progression from radical to incremental product and process innovation. In general, they describe a progression from a state of flux with rapid technological progress to an ordered situation with cumulative incremental changes. Although they emphasize different aspects of innovation from different perspectives, the models are consistent.[12]

Both this work and that of Mueller and Tilton contend that as an industry stabilizes—that is, as technological progress slows down and production techniques become standardized—barriers to entry increase. The most attractive market segments will already be occupied. As process integration moves forward, the cost of production equipment usually rises dramatically. Product prices fall concurrently, so that firms with the largest market shares are the ones to benefit from further expansion. Product differentiation usually forms around the technical strengths and R&D organization of the existing firms. Strong patent positions established by earlier entering firms become difficult for later entrants to circumvent. Finally, an existing distribution network may also be a powerful barrier to entry, particularly to foreign firms.

Another hallmark of stability is the emergence of a set of captive suppliers of equipment and components. Although such suppliers can be an initial source of innovation and growth, they may ultimately become a conservative force, further stabilizing the competition and change within the product market segment and creating yet another barrier to entry.

A final characteristic of the evolution toward stability is a concerted drive among the surviving firms toward vertical integration from materials production to sales. Integration may take various forms. Firms producing the product can reach backward to furnish more of their own components, subassemblies, and raw materials; or firms producing components can reach forward to do more of the assembly and production of final goods for the market. Such dramatic changes have ripple effects on firms that buy from or sell to the evolving set of productive units. It is just at the point of stability where firms get locked into narrow positions that they also ultimately increase their vulnerability. An existing distribution network can suddenly be threatened by a new technology that requires sharply reduced servicing or maintenance, or by the entrance of a large product line. An existing patent may expire. Although Mueller and Tilton contend that industries become stable when patent positions expire, this seems more likely to be a period of invasion of the industry by a new wave of product and process change—or, in a few cases, the revitalization of the dominant technology itself.

In the early days of an industry, when products are unique in design and capabilities, competition has more to do with winning over customers to the new technology embodied in an unrefined product than in crossing swords with rival innovators. Thus innovators compete as much against their own product inadequacies and market skepticism as against their rivals. This explains the great optimism that spread among companies such as Apple and Tandy when IBM first entered the personal computer field. Far from trembling out of fear for Big Blue's clout as a potential rival, these firms understood that the real enemy was public skepticism about the value of personal computers; they understood clearly that IBM's entry to the field would give the industry the credibility it was struggling to engender with the general population.

THE MODEL SUMMARIZED

We might summarize the model thus far as exhibiting interdependent rates of product and process innovation over time, and these in turn are linked to important transformations in the characteristics of product, process, competition, and organization. These relationships are combined in Figure 10-3.

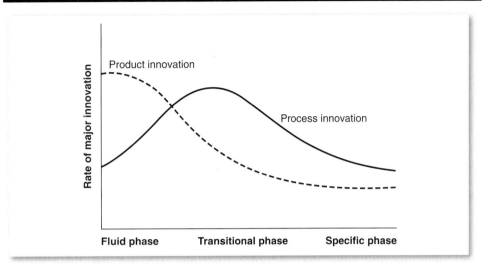

FIGURE 10-3   The Dynamics of Innovation

Product	From high variety, to dominant design, to incremental innovation on standardized products
Process	Manufacturing progresses from heavy reliance on skilled labor and general-purpose equipment to specialized equipment tended by low-skilled labor
Organization	From entrepreneurial *organic* firm to hierarchical *mechanistic* firm with defined tasks and procedures and few rewards for radical innovation
Market	From fragmented and unstable with diverse products and rapid feedback to commodity-like with largely undifferentiated products
Competition	From many small firms with unique products to an oligopoly of firms with similar products

PHASES WITHIN THE MODEL OF INNOVATION DYNAMICS

This model attempts to capture the dynamic processes that take place both within an industry and within its member firms over time. It is a model that attempts to cut through two dimensions: 1) the components of product innovation, process innovation, the competitive environment, and organizations; and 2) the life cycle of the industry itself. It is toward this second dimension that we now turn.

Social and natural scientists often segment the subjects of their analyses into chronological or developmental periods. European historians have the Dark Ages, the Middle Ages, the Renaissance, and modern times; developmental psychologists have early childhood, adolescence, adulthood, and old age. These are largely categories of convenience that facilitate discussion and generalization, even though specific cases stubbornly fail to fall into these categories. They also help us to understand patterns and implication for action.

Developmental phases are also used in this model of industrial innovation, if only as a matter of analytical convenience. These phases are here called *fluid, transitional,* and *specific.* Because this is a dynamic model, these phases are associated with both the rate of innovation and the underlying dimensions of product, process, competition, and organization. In effect, these phases slice the model a different way, each cutting across those dimensions.

Significant characteristics in each of the three phases—as they apply to product, process, competition and organization—are briefly stated in Figure 10-4. While this listing is by no means complete, it does nevertheless give a sense of what is going on within an industry as it passes through three stages of development.

FIGURE 10-4 Significant Characteristics in the Three Phases of Industrial Innovation

	Fluid phase	*Transitional phase*	*Specific phase*
Innovation	Frequent major product changes	Major process changes required by rising demand	Incremental for product and with cumulative improvements in productivity and quality
Source of innovation	Industry pioneers; product users	Manufacturers; users	Often suppliers
Products	Diverse designs, often customized	At least one product design, stable enough to have significant production volume	Mostly undifferentiated, standard products
Production processes	Flexible and inefficient, major changes easily accommodated	Becoming more rigid, with changes occurring in major steps	Efficient, capital intensive, and rigid; cost of change high
R&D	Focus unspecified because of high degree of technical uncertainty	Focus on specific product features once dominant design emerges	Focus on incremental product technologies; emphasis on process technology
Equipment	General-purpose, requiring skilled labor	Some subprocesses automated, creating islands of automation	Special-purpose, mostly automatic, with labor focused on tending and monitoring equipment
Plant	Small-scale, located near user or source of innovation	General-purpose with specialized sections	Large-scale, highly specific to particular products
Cost of process change	Low	Moderate	High
Competitors	Few, but growing in numbers with widely fluctuating market shares	Many, but declining in numbers after emergence of dominant design	Few; classic oligopoly with stable market shares
Basis of competition	Functional product performance	Product variation; fitness for use	Price
Organizational control	Informal and entrepreneurial	Through project and task groups	Structure, rules, and goals
Vulnerabilities of industry leaders	To imitators, and patent challenges; to successful product breakthroughs	To more efficient and higher-quality producers	To technological innovations that present superior product substitutes

The Fluid Phase

The fluid phase is one in which a great deal of change is happening at once and in which outcomes are highly uncertain in terms of product, process, competitive leadership, and the structure and management of firms.

In the fluid phase of a technology's evolution, the rate of product change is expected to be rapid. The new product technology is often crude, expensive, and unreliable, but it is able to fill a function in a way that is highly desirable in some niche markets. In the batch of examples presented through Chapter 3, the Remington No. 1 typewriter was just such an expensive and inelegant contraption. Mark Twain's complaints about his infernal new machine did not overshadow his need to churn out text at a rapid pace—which even this early typewriter successfully accomplished. Likewise, the high initial cost and experimental nature of incandescent lighting did not inhibit the builders and owners of the *S.S. Columbia* from installing Edison's first system. Its unique benefits for lighting in closed spaces where fumes and fire dangers were important considerations made it preferable to the existing technologies of gas and oil lamps. The first personal computers were also crude and relatively expensive versions of what would emerge over the following decade, but dedicated lead users were undeterred by these drawbacks and stayed with the new technology through its many early forms.

Product innovation in the fluid phase proceeds in the face of both *target* and *technical* uncertainties. Target uncertainty refers to the fact that most early innovations do not enjoy an established market. Markets, in fact, tend to grow around these innovations. The emergence of an entirely new market and occupation—like typist—testifies to the power of technological innovations to create markets; discussion in Chapter 8 of George Eastman's innovation of roll film and the subsequent rise of amateur photography will help to reinforce this point. But in the early years, it is not always clear who the target market is or what product features will best serve its interests.

Technical uncertainty results from the diffused focus of research and development during the fluid phase. When the technology is in a state of flux, firms have no clear idea where to place their R&D bets. Many, in fact, concentrate on product technologies that ultimately will be ignored by the marketplace in favor of others. Custom designs and user-adapted designs are common during the fluid phase, and we see them essentially as experiments in the marketplace.

To reiterate, process innovation generally takes a back seat to product innovation in this early fluid stage. Frequent and major changes in product design and specifications impede the development of linked process innovation. The inputs in terms of materials are off the shelf; manufacturing uses general-purpose equipment and skilled labor and is conducted in small-scale plants, generally located close to the source of the technology. While this is not efficient in terms of modern production standards, it does make the cost of process flexibility low; and process change is frequent at this stage owing to the rapid evolution in product technology.

Functional product performance is the basis for competition during the fluid phase. Since most producers are unknown quantities, brand names count for little. As we observed in Chapter 2, the number of competitors is small at this stage, but rises as the product technology gains a market that encourages new entrants with different approaches to lifting technical constraints. Fluid phase firms retain their entrepreneurial character and often reflect the personalities of their founders, who are generally technical entrepreneurs.[13] Among the set of competitors are, inevitably, one or more imitators. Both Sholes and Edison—and, as we will see later Eastman—worked feverishly to acquire and protect patents to their innovations to assure their technological superiority against a field of imitators.

The Transitional Phase

If the market for a new product grows, the industry may enter what could be termed a transitional phase. Market acceptance of a product innovation and the emergence of a dominant design are its hallmarks. Competitive emphasis in this phase is on producing products for more specific users as the needs of those users become more clearly understood. The focus of firms begins to shift from the inventor's workbench to the factory floor, where the large-scale production of innovative products must be worked out.

It is in this phase that product and process innovations start to become more tightly linked. Materials become more specialized; expensive specialized equipment is brought into the manufacturing plant; islands of automation begin to appear; managerial controls are suddenly seen as important. The growing rigidity of these aspects of operations means that changes in the product can be accommodated only at increasingly greater cost.

The Specific Phase

The term "specific" rather than "mature" is used here because the manufacturing of assembled products aims over time at producing a very specific product at a high level of efficiency. Here, the value ratio of quality to cost becomes the basis of competition. Products in the specific phase become highly defined, and the differences between products of competitors are often fewer than the similarities. Even automobiles, very complex products, tend to follow very similar design and manufacturing protocols, having essentially the same aerodynamic shape, similar engines, interiors, and so forth.

The linkages between product and process are now extremely close. Any small change in either product or process is likely to be difficult and expensive and require a corresponding change in the other. Even what may seem like a small change—such as shifting production from manual to electric typewriters—is viewed as revolutionary by manufacturing, which by now has fully automated operations geared to highly efficient, low-unit-cost production of highly specified products.

Organizationally, the day of the inventor has given way in the specific phase to the tenders—that is, those who monitor and control the smooth working of the production system. This term does not refer exclusively to laborers but to managers and engineers as well, people whose jobs and skills tend to mirror those of labor and whose roles are equally altered by technological change.[14]

BREAKING OUT OF THE SPECIFIC PHASE

In terms of this model, the firm that produces in the specific phase has entered a final state from which only a radical departure in product or process can liberate it. In his landmark study of the U.S. automobile industry up to the early 1970s, William Abernathy documented the extent to which product and process innovations—over time—led that industry into a trade-off between technological innovation and production efficiency,[15] a situation in which innovation had come in a distant second. At the time Abernathy conducted his study and published his findings, complex production methods and specialized machinery had reduced the direct labor hours required to produce a car from some 4,600 hours (roughly the time required to build an average house) to less than 100.[16] This amazing progress, however, was shown to be accompanied by overwhelming standardization and uniformity among producers, prompting one auto executive to comment that the last important automotive innovation had been the automatic transmission—a feature introduced in the 1930s.

Is the specific phase of production the "end of history" for an industry? Is there a way to break out of this highly capitalized, highly controlled, and generally uninnovative mode of production? Recent innovations in flexible manufacturing by Japanese auto manufacturers have enabled them to defy the iron rule of mass production: that long production runs of standard products and low unit costs are necessarily bound together. As James Womack, Daniel Jones, and Daniel Roos have documented in *The Machine That Changed The World,*[17] Japanese auto companies can retain low unit cost while producing greater variety in smaller runs. Their unique capability to produce

---

ABERNATHY'S PRODUCTIVITY DILEMMA

Looking at auto engine plants during a long period extending through 1973, William Abernathy made the following observations:

- An overall reduction in mechanical novelty occurred; while auto options proliferated, variety decreased.

- Major innovations were self-limiting, reducing the need for future innovations.

- While product line diversity had increased, for individual plants diversity had actually decreased.

- The tasks and skills of labor had evolved with the evolution in equipment "from craft skills to operative skills to systems-monitoring skills."

Abernathy's study of the auto industry included a focused look at the Ford Motor Company. There he found that innovation, evolution, and competitive factors had been responsible for creating two different environments: an engine plant that was so highly automated that response to change was extremely difficult; and an assembly plant much less complete that demonstrated a course of evolution from fluid to specific phase and was still more dependent on large amounts of manual labor than on specific machinery because of its annual struggle to accommodate model changes.

Thus a single industry, indeed a single company, can support productive units in distinctly different phases of industrial evolution. As Abernathy said of the Ford assembly plant he studied and observed to move toward the specific stage under pressure from foreign producers, "The long period in which the stage of development remained flexible shows that a productive unit need not progress toward either extreme [fluid or specific] unless the overall competitive environment requires a change."

Source: William J. Abernathy, *The Productivity Dilemma: Roadblock to Innovation in the Automobile Industry* (Baltimore and London: The Johns Hopkins University Press, 1978), pp. 112–113, 145.

small lots makes this possible. This brand of flexible manufacturing acts as an enabler for a business strategy based on a high level of product variety and near custom-tailoring of products to the specification of individual customers. Joe Pine has described this strategy in *Mass Customization: The Next Frontier of Business Competition.*[18] The strategy of mass customization uses both flexible manufacturing and the creation of unique products from standard platforms to satisfy customer requirements more fully. Among the examples of firms already following this strategy, Pine cites National Bicycle Company of Japan, which has made it possible for a customer to order a bicycle with any of over 11 million configurations of model, color, frame size, and components, and receive it at the local bike shop within ten days.

Flexible manufacturing and the strategy of mass customization seem to offer an escape hatch from the innovative dead end of the specific phase. Just as the quality revolution has exploded the idea that quality and low cost are mutually exclusive characteristics that must be traded off, these new notions seem to break the mutually exclusive ends of product variety and low production costs. However, flexible manufacturing and mass customization may also be a trap resulting in products with little commercial potential and in unwanted product variety. For example, Abernathy and Clark have shown this may be true for highly specialized auto engines, and White has shown that it may be true more generally.[19]

THE NEXT WAVE OF INNOVATION

Most technology-based innovations are in fact part of a continuum of change. We have already seen how the typing of documents has gone through waves of innovation; the same happened in lighting and will be found to have happened in many other industries. How, then, does this model accommodate these waves of innovation?

Experience with a number of industries supports the notion that each wave of innovation repeats the pattern of interlinking product and process innovation and the importance of dominant design on the number of firms that the industry can support at one time. Each new wave of innovation has its fluid, transitional, and specific phases; each sees the rate of product innovation peak more or less early and experiences a surge of process innovation even as product innovation declines; each is characterized by a peak in the number of competing firms sometime around the emergence of the dominant design, with a decline thereafter.

Figure 10-5 illustrates these familiar patterns, but adds something new. In the top two quadrants are the product and process innovation curves for two waves of innovation at the level of the firm. In both cases the rate of product innovation reaches a high point very early. The dominant design appears around this time. The rate of process innovation continues to increase, but it too declines as the innovation and the firm enter the specific phase.

The lower quadrants relate the innovative activities of firms to the number of firms participating. In both cases, the number of firms reaches a zenith around the time that the dominant design first appears and drops rapidly thereafter. What is worth noting here is the overall lower number of firms participating in the second wave of innovation. Thus, while there might be many firms making incandescent lamps (the first wave in electric lighting), there would be fewer trying to break into the fluorescent lamp business (the second wave).

We could speculate that this pattern would repeat itself in any subsequent wave of lighting technology. It should be mentioned that this point is intuitive and not based on empirical findings. Still, the pattern rings true with experience: we know that there were many more manual typewriter makers than there were electric typewriter firms; there were many more incandescent lamp firms than there were fluorescent lamp makers; more competitors were in the dry-emulsion photographic plate business than were in the succeeding celluloid roll-film industry (treated in Chapter 8). When and if automobiles powered by noninternal combustion engines take the roads in larger numbers, we would expect that far fewer than the hundred firms that emerged in the United States during the first auto age will vie for dominance in the new industry.

FIGURE 10-5 Model Extended to the Next Wave of Innovation

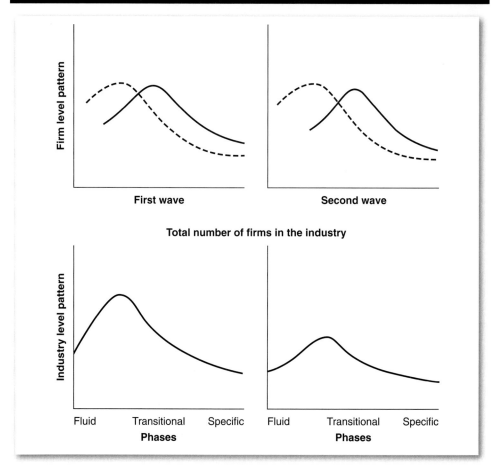

The reason for this drop-off in the number of competing firms in later waves is no doubt related to the fact that markets are often well defined by the first wave of innovation, and established firms develop the distribution channels and production facilities to serve these markets, limiting the number of possible firms that can reform the industry—even with a superior technology.

This hypothesis does not hold up when the new wave of innovation substantially broadens or alters the market. The innovation of computer-based typing, for example, so altered the way this mundane task was accomplished that barriers to new firms tumbled, and dozens of computer and software firms entered the industry. These last points will be treated in greater detail in Chapter 9, though they are speculative and need a good deal more research.

Endnotes

1. J.S. Frischmuth and T.J. Allen, "A Model for the Description of Technical Problem Solving," *IEEE Transactions on Engineering Management,* May 1969, pp. 79–86.
2. See T. Burns and G.M. Stalker, *The Management of Innovation* (London: Tavistock, 1961).
3. For an excellent discussion of the background, personality, and motivation of the entrepreneur, see Edward B. Roberts, *Entrepreneurs in High Technology* (New York: Oxford University Press, 1991), in particular pp. 251–259.
4. Burton H. Klein, *Dynamic Economics* (Cambridge, Mass.: Harvard University Press, 1977), pp. 100–101.
5. Ibid., p. 108.
6. See for example, Eric von Hippel, *The Sources of Innovation* (Oxford: Oxford University Press, 1988).
7. Klein, *Dynamic Economics,* p. 108.
8. See Almarin Phillips, *Technology and Market Structure: A Study of the Aircraft Industry* (Lexington, Mass.: Lexington Books, 1971).
9. D.C. Mueller and J.E. Tilton, "R&D Cost as a Barrier to Entry," *Canadian Journal of Economics,* vol. 2 (November 1969), p. 576.
10. Ibid.

11. Reese V. Jenkins, *Images & Enterprise: Technology and the American Photographic Industry, 1839–1925* (Baltimore & London: The Johns Hopkins University Press, 1975).

12. E.P. Staples, N.R. Baker, and D.J. Sweeney, "Market Structure and Technological Innovation: A Step Towards a Unifying Theory," Final Technical Report," NSF Grant RDA 75-17332, November 1977, p. 12.

13. Edward B. Roberts, *Entrepreneurs in High Technology* (Oxford: Oxford University Press, 1991).

14. See James R. Bright, *Automation and Management* (Boston, Mass.: Division of Research, Harvard Business School, 1958) for a thorough discussion of this generally overlooked relationship.

15. William J. Abernathy, *The Productivity Dilemma: Roadblock to Innovation in the Automobile Industry* (Baltimore and London: The Johns Hopkins University Press, 1978), p. 112.

16. By 1990, this had shrunk to 20 hours per vehicle in the leading plants, or even less in a few instances. See James P. Womack, Daniel Jones, and Daniel Roos, *The Machine That Changed the World* (New York: Rawson Associates, 1990).

17. Ibid.

18. B. Joseph Pine II, *Mass Customization: The Next Frontier of Business Competition* (Boston: Harvard Business School Press, 1993).

19. William J. Abernathy and Kim B. Clark, "Mapping the Winds of Creative Destruction," *Research Policy,* vol. 14, no. 1 (January 1985), pp. 3–22; and M. Abdelkader Dagfous and George R. White, "Information and Innovation," *Research Policy* (forthcoming).

11 ‖ INNOVATION AND CORPORATE RENEWAL

James M. Utterback

Even the casual observer of industrial enterprise must be struck by the cycle of development, growth, maturity, and decline through which many individual firms pass. Growth companies eventually run out of steam, or are eclipsed by new competitors. Solid blue chip companies that once seemed permanent fixtures of the economic scene suddenly fall under a weight of problems. Their descents from market leadership are often public and painful, marked by massive financial losses and employment dislocations. Some blame widening global competition for the difficulties of beleaguered firms, while others see them as victims of macroeconomic and structural shifts beyond the clear control of government and corporate managers. Overshadowed by the troubles of these firms are the many small victories won by new firms, and by individual divisions of the troubled giants.

The examples and arguments in the preceding chapters should have convinced the reader that a strong technological base is as critical to the prosperous survival of a firm as a good understanding of markets and a strong financial position. They should also have sown doubts about the permanence of a competitive position, no matter how strong it may seem on a national or an international scale to contemporary observers. Indeed, one of the advantages of choosing examples spread over so great a span of time is that the vulnerabilities of prominent current industries can easily be recognized by an analogy. At the same time, it is clear that there are few or no general answers to the challenges that technological changes pose to a leading large firm. Solutions will depend on the circumstances of both the firm and its industry, the types of products produced, and the sources of added value, and even the path by which the firm reached its current status. I believe that the illustrations and patterns discussed in this book will be helpful, even provocative, for managers dealing with the opportunities and crises produced by technological change and innovation.

Firms owe it to themselves to improve and extend the lives of profitable product lines. These represent important cash flows to the firm and links to existing customers. They provide the funds that will finance future products. At the same time, managers must not neglect pleas that advocate major commitments to new initiatives. Typically top management is pulled by two opposing, responsible forces: those that demand commitment to the old, and those that advocate for the future. Unfortunately, advocacy tends to overstate the market potential of new product lines and understate their costs. Management, then, must find the right balance between support for incremental improvements and commitments to new and unproven innovations. Understanding and managing this tension perceptively may well separate the ultimate winners from the losers.

Utterback, J. (1994), *Mastering the Dynamics of Innovation*, Boston, MA: Harvard Business School Press (pp. 215–232).

Clearly, there are important lessons in this book for the entrepreneurial founders of new firms. Starting a firm with a new product in a new industry involves much borrowing of diverse elements from others and synthesizing them creatively. We have seen that the winners are often the ones that are the most experimental and flexible in matching the early forms of the product with unexpected demands and opportunities and that think through the development of their innovation in the most thorough and systematic way. As we have seen, firms that stay the course must be prepared to shift their strategic and competitive postures at several points along the way. That entrepreneurs must prepare themselves to address global markets and prepare to meet competitors from many fronts is also a truism, evident even in the earliest cases discussed. However, it seems that the larger and more well-established firms face the more difficult problems. They must constantly renew, even regenerate, their businesses, and it is to them that this chapter is primarily addressed. First I will address the need for the constant improvement and renewal of established products, and the issues of how to encourage ceaseless incremental innovation. In the second section of the chapter I will conclude the discussion, begun in Chapter 9, of the issues facing the firm beset by the challenges of radical innovation.

CONTINUOUS RENEWAL OF ESTABLISHED PRODUCTS

Incremental innovation is clearly of critical economic and competitive importance. We have seen that the firms that perfected the typewriter and invested in large-scale plants to become low-cost producers stayed at the top of their industry for half a century. Incremental product improvements raised the efficiency of the incandescent electric light, while process improvements reduced the cost of production one-hundredfold. Similarly, dramatic efficiencies in production were accomplished in the first thirty years of the harvested ice industry. These cumulative changes moved typewriters, electric lighting, and ice refrigeration from being luxury items for the few to being commonplace in businesses and homes. The same can be said about plate glass, photographic film, rayon, and countless other products.

Success in continuous incremental improvement requires equal emphasis on product and process design, which must be closely integrated. This was a novel idea when William Abernathy and I first proposed it, but it has become widespread today as simultaneous engineering and design for manufacturing. Moreover, process advances often enable further improvements in products, particularly in reliability and cost. Leadership in incremental improvement requires persistence in measuring product and process performance, and in seeking improvement from any source. Savings may come from better use of materials, energy, and labor, but are often the result of reductions in the number of parts, product complexity, and process steps as well. Value may also be added by finding simple ways to do complex jobs (as in the use of "getters" to remove the last bit of oxygen from light bulbs) and making product use simple (as in Eastman's pre-loaded camera).

The challenge of renewing the vitality of an established firm should not be thought of as limited to technical choices or effective research and development. Innovation entails much more for the firms that adopt it. As Lewis Branscomb has pointed out,

> . . . technologies must be mastered, reduced to practice, supported by cost effective production processes, and introduced to the market. Then that market position must be sustained by appropriate complementary assets, by effective channels of distribution, and by responsive customer service. Even that, however, is not enough, for many innovating products have found strong initial markets, only to see other firms—sometimes other nations—capture the lion's share of the market growth through incremental functional improvements, cost reductions, quality superiority, and better marketing and service.[1]

Over the past decade business leaders have adopted a number of panaceas for extending their period of leadership. By right sizing and refocusing, by removing layers of management and building teams, by installing total quality management and lean manufacturing, and by striving toward time-based competition, today's corporations are attempting to bolster lagging sales, productivity growth, and profitability. More recently, managers have been urged to listen to the voice of the customer, to mass customize their products, and to reengineer their corporations. Although each of these approaches to corporate maintenance have merit, and many have demonstrated remarkable effects, they are, nevertheless, limited solutions. They help companies be more effective in their current lines of business for a time, but they do little to help them if the changes prescribed are made in isolation or if, as is often the case, they have little staying power.

Charles Baden-Fuller and John Stopford have recommended that managers view each action they take for change as a step on a strategic staircase. Although an organization can seldom attend to more than one campaign for change at a time, it is equally important to be sure that the just-completed and dearly won campaign not be reversed by the next one. Thus, Baden-Fuller and Stopford suggest that managers consider ways to mount the entire staircase of changes with cumulative effect, rather than simply bumping along the floor.[2] Branscomb, Baden-Fuller and Stopford, and this book argue against any one suggestion or solution as *the* key to sustained corporate success in the face of technological change. Clearly, the key is the thoughtful and persistent development of the firm's capabilities and resources, and, even more important, the balance among them. As we have seen in the cases and examples described, the balance required is dynamic and constantly shifting; achieving it is somewhat akin to riding a bicycle.

A fundamental approach to renewal then is the development of core capabilities. C. K. Prahalad and Gary Hamel have suggested that a firm's ability to identify, nurture, and exploit its basic strengths as "core products" is both directly related to competitiveness and provides a new perspective on organizational form and process.[3] They have suggested that instead of examining their firms as portfolios of businesses, executives should view them as portfolios of core competencies that transcend specific strategic business unit boundaries. These competencies are defined as "the collective learning in the organization," especially as they coordinate diverse production skills and integrate multiple streams of technologies. Such competencies, according to Prahalad and Hamel, become the basis for multiple market applications, are difficult to imitate, and provide a substantial part of the design in final products that solve customers' perceived problems and needs. The core products needed for the firm's thrust toward new markets flow from organizational strengths. Prahalad and Hamel provide neither methods to measure the concept of core competencies nor data, but their argument is nonetheless compelling.

CHOOSING THE RIGHT CAPABILITIES

The idea of fortifying the core competences of a firm as a means of increasing its survivability is not in itself a solution; it merely provokes two further questions. First, which competences should the firm develop? The ones it already has? The ones it expects to need in the future? Or some of both? The harvested ice industry of New England invested heavily in its core competences. Over time it learned better ways to score and cut cakes of ice; it became expert at storing ice over several years; it developed its capabilities to transport a heavy, perishable product efficiently over great distances. It reduced costs from 10 or 20 *dollars* per ton to 10 or 20 *cents* per ton and owned world markets. It was the most competent ice harvesting industry ever. These efforts were essential. But none of those competences assured its survival when technology changed. With the rise of mechanical ice making, competence in cutting blocks of ice became irrelevant. With electric refrigeration, what was the value of competence in storing and transporting blocks of ice? What was the value of a house-to-house ice delivery system once most people had acquired electric refrigerators?

The failure to keep up with innovation is really the failure to develop and focus core competences in the direction of change and progress. And that direction is often unclear except in hindsight. The U.S. tire industry represents another case in which firms increased their core competence, but not in a direction that had a promising future. Tire producers continued to develop their ability to manufacture bias-ply tires when they should have been learning to design and manufacture the new radials being produced in Europe. The bias-ply producers had every reason to continue in their old direction: they had tremendous investments in fixed assets, distribution arrangements, and specialized knowledge. Just as important, their best customers, the Big Three U.S. automakers, manufacturers of vehicle suspensions that would not run smoothly on radial tires, discouraged them from pursuing the new technology through their requirements for traditional bias-ply tires.[4]

Unfortunately, there is no easy answer as to how firms should choose the core competences that will assure their progress and survival. Certainly it is essential to anticipate discontinuities and to try to act in advance of their full impact. Doing so requires constant monitoring of the firm's external environment to notice forerunners of significant change. We have seen that most firms look in exactly the wrong places for vital signs of technological change: namely, their universe of traditional rivals. Large and similar competitors are the focus today of vigorous benchmarking efforts by many firms. Benchmarking is an excellent source of information to guide evolutionary change and continuous improvement, but probably a poor source for signals of discontinuities. Looking toward more obscure new entrants and unconventional sources of competition is more fruitful, although these sources are more diffuse and difficult to monitor.[5] Technological and market uncertainty, however, implies that no one can act with clear anticipation or forecasts. Among equally capable generals the one with the best contingency plans will usually win the battle. Unexpected departures from the anticipated plan are almost certain to arise, and in the best of cases they will open the way to greater opportunities than at first imagined. This is crucial in the choice of capabilities to foster.

THE QUESTION OF FOCUS

The second important question to answer is: How narrowly or how broadly should a firm construe its core competences? Here again, there is no simple answer. Each firm must make that determination in light of the trade-off between the virtues of having broad competences and those of having a more concentrated set of technical and market skills.[6] A broad set of related and unrelated competences hedges the future of the firm against many possible technological changes, but leaves it with no strong suit. A highly focused set of competences concentrates a firm's powers of knowledge, but in a narrow range, making it vulnerable to radical innovation. Like other living organisms, the firm that becomes too highly specialized—too keenly adapted to the peculiarities of its environment of technologies, production processes, and markets—is in danger of extinction if that environment changes even slightly.

One possible way to finesse this problem is to build core capabilities into diverse product lines. Consider, briefly, the case of the incandescent light bulb, the low-cost manufacture of which required a very specific set of competences: the ability to draw thin-walled glass bulbs by mass production, to insert a fragile wire filament, to create a vacuum and seal the bulb, and so on. For bulb producers, the development of the vacuum tube for use in radio and electronic equipment provided a test of their abilities to diversify into an area where many of their core competences could be directly transferred. This resulted in an entirely new market for bulb makers. For those that went into vacuum tubes, the innovation of the transistor represented a true technological discontinuity. Transistors were a substitute product for vacuum tubes and eventually nearly drove them from the marketplace. The transistor was a radical innovation, and few of the tube makers' competences helped them cross over to it. A similar chasm confronted transistor makers with the appearance of integrated circuits, which represented a synthesis of old competences and new ones.

Renewal of well-established products does not create new industries, however, nor will it save established firms from decline when their markets are invaded by radical innovations. This is the lesson of the typewriter industry, oil, and then gas illumination, photography, and harvested ice. Simply becoming better and better with current technology will not, in the long run, keep new firms with new technology from absorbing markets and relegating unresponsive established firms to the scrap heap of industrial history. It is this second type of innovation radical innovation, that is so necessary for the regeneration of a corporation's business, yet it is the most painfully difficult to master.

Although sustained leadership in innovation and business clearly requires persistence and continuous improvement, examination of radical change suggests that most firms persist in defending well-established products and ways of making them too ardently, even when the seeds of far more effective new alternatives are clearly in evidence.

RADICAL INNOVATION AND CORPORATE REGENERATION

As individuals, each of us are keenly aware of our own mortality. We know we will die some day, but when and how are almost never certain. Corporate managers know that their products, like people, are mortal. And like people, the future for those products is seldom knowable, except in retrospect. A product's life could end quite suddenly with the appearance of a radical new competing product that invades and quickly conquers the market. Or the end might come gradually, allowing time to prepare and launch new products. Whatever the case, managers are faced with tough decisions for which there are no pre-determined or universal answers.

Not many firms have the dexterity to retool their capabilities in order to survive successive waves of innovation. A striking fact drawn from earlier chapters is that over the life of a product, few of the firms that enter the market to produce it survive. Ironically, just as a firm seems most successful in its chosen product and market, that product generation is often challenged by a newer generation. In the resulting contest even fewer of the firms that produce the older version survive in the market to produce the new generation.[7] Firms holding the largest market share in one product generation seldom appear in the vanguard of competition in the next.

These are grim facts, yet examples exist of firms that have successfully defied the odds and leaped from one generation of product or process technology to the next, making it clear that no morbid natural law of predetermined failure is in force. Motorola is an example of one of these survivors, having successfully made the transition from the age of vacuum-tube car radios to the new era of cellular communications and computer chips. Hewlett-Packard, whose beginnings go back to the late 1930s as a maker of video oscillators and electrical testing equipment, is now a world leader in precision plotters, laser printers, computer workstations, professional calculators, and medical analytic devices—all products based upon technologies unimagined just two decades ago.

Looking back over the descriptions of industry evolution and of individual firms that have successfully mastered several generations of technological change, we can see that the idea of developing and balancing core competences as the key to success seems more credible than any number of current management philosophies and fashions. Ford and Kodak started early in developing their competence in distribution with early market entry in Europe and Japan. Kodak and General Electric were among the first firms in the world to set up central laboratories to advance their understanding of the principles of their products' operation—both clear examples of the deliberate enhancement of core competences. Black & Decker and Canon have been pioneers in modular design. Thomas Edison and Sony's Akio Morita, though generations apart, both set overarching goals for their enterprises and painstakingly and persistently pursued them for decades. Thomas Watson, Jr., transformed IBM when he announced that all new developments would be based on solid-state electronics, abandoning a generation of expertise and accepted product designs and leading the way to the System 360, one of the most successful products of all times. Many of the characteristics that these firms exhibit seem timeless, rooted in a respect for the value of human resources and skills and their continuing development.

In summary, the most important change of all would seem to lie in top managements' renewed appreciation of the people who build and sustain their firms and in their ability to learn and to adapt to changing and challenging circumstances.

ORGANIZATIONAL IMPEDIMENTS TO RADICAL INNOVATION IN ESTABLISHED FIRMS

To understand why established firms find radical innovation so difficult, we need to look at their organizational behavior and at the priorities of their leaders. Established firms with massively profitable businesses are almost invariably more conservative and risk averse than are fledgling competitors with none. Staffs of planners and analysts, and review committees and controllers all serve as bulwarks protecting the known, identifying and quantifying the risks associated with proposed changes. As firms grow larger, their top managers necessarily function more as conservators than as creators; they have income-producing products that must be nurtured and preserved to continue the benefits of shareholders and fellow employees. They see themselves as conscientious servants, implementing wise choices, and in many respects they are. Many attempts by newcomers to break into an industry and unseat the leading competitors will fail. Therefore in this regard conservatism usually has a positive survival value.

We have seen how Thomas Edison, whose reputation is synonymous with change and new ideas, could become a change resister—as he was in the cases of alternating current and metal filament bulbs—once he had deep commitments to earlier technologies. Similarly, Henry Ford, whose innovations of the Model T and production of the paced assembly line made him the richest man in America, stubbornly resisted changes to the Model A, believing that he had perfected the automobile. In fact defense of the one idea was correct, while defense of the other was not. Ford's process innovations rewarded the firms that extended it for decades. Trying to defend the product failed, while Ford's process ideas succeeded brilliantly. In this regard Ford exemplifies both sides of the story.

These very human and organizationally induced flaws turn the one-time creator into a change resister. In a stable and effective but conservative organizational environment the reward for improving existing technology, products, and processes is greater than the incentive to turn the world on its head. Thus ground breaking changes are viewed as difficult, disruptive, unpredictable, and risky, while incremental innovations are seen as reliably producing more predictable results more quickly. It is a great irony that wisdom for many firms that derive current good fortune from radical innovations of the past lies in erecting barriers to these same types of innovations today. Indeed, for some, the development projects that made them wealthy would be rejected if presented to current corporate staffers. "Too risky," they would say. "The projected stream of cash flows is too small to meet our internal rate-of-return hurdle." "The market is too small." Taken by itself, the decision not to abandon well-worn products in a timely manner is transitory. It leaves much greater risks for the business down the line and increases chances of failure. Doing only incremental innovation leaves the firm closer to the inevitable end of its business, but with no preparation for the future.

Incremental innovation, then, is a wise path of least resistance for the established firm, but sustained success in this form of innovation forms a trap for management. When radical innovation is plausible, according to Donald Frey, constant incremental innovation can create myopia in the ranks of top management. Frey contends that after decades of success, chief executives tend to become bureaucratic and process oriented, viewing their core businesses and competences as givens; board members who share similar backgrounds reinforce this tendency. "Successful chief executives," according to Frey, "are products of a bureaucratic selection process run with the wrong paradigms. When companies get into trouble late in their principal business life cycle, they cannot cope with the ambiguity of a new future, and their analytical tools can't predict an uncertain future."[8] To survive, firms must prepare to cope with an emerging new future, even though when action is needed, the form of the future will be far from clear.

Arnold Cooper and Clayton Smith recently examined 27 firms in 8 industries that were threatened by radical innovations. They found that the strengths of these firms did not necessarily provide an advantage in the new technology, and that in every case some new skills were required to enter. More important, the established firms tended to closely tie their entry into the new to the old (for example, transistors being placed under the vacuum tube division). This often led to a situation of divided loyalties, meaning that the effort to enter the new was often undertaken half-heartedly, even when the established firm was among the early entrants. Usually the new product was essentially folded into the existing strategy, which, however appropriate for the old product was seldom suited for the new one.[9] The result is not surprising, given these findings and those of Chapter 9. Only seven of the 27 threatened firms were successful. But the irony is that these firms all made the right decisions to enter with the threatening innovation. They were simply blocked by organizational impediments and the constraints of established patterns of thought and action.

INVESTMENT IN RADICAL INNOVATION IS DIFFICULT TO JUSTIFY

The medical dictum to "never take a well patient into surgery" finds its parallel in modern business: "When you have a good thing going, don't change it." Similarly, money spent on development of technologies that could potentially undermine existing profitable product lines is generally seen as counterproductive, "shooting oneself in the foot," or otherwise misdirecting funds from incremental improvement of the existing business. Obviously, this is a problem that the bias-ply tire producers must have confronted when the European technology for radial tires appeared likely to emerge in the United States.

Another important barrier is the mathematical logic of discounted cash-flow analysis, a useful method for evaluating and ranking competing projects, but a method that favors modest near-term rewards of high probability to extravagant long-term possibilities of high uncertainty. Discounted cash flow tends to favor investments in incremental change, where cost dimensions and payoffs are more reliably forecasted, than investments in radical innovation, which are by nature long term, unfamiliar, and questionable. Discounted cash-flow analysis provides no room for the unexpected surprises that destroy existing businesses. The earlier testimony of Alastair Pilkington with respect to his company's tremendous investments in the float process of making plate glass reminds us how public companies, which must report earnings that please analysts and shareholders on a quarterly basis, are constrained in their abilities to invest heavily, or otherwise "bet the company" on unproven technology.

Investments in incremental change may produce measurable benefits in the short term, but they cannot save established firms when their markets are demolished. These firms will not find their long-term vitality renewed, but will follow the lead of the gas lighting industry, the ice harvesters of New England, and others who have failed to make the bold leap across chasms of technological discontinuity.

THE FAILURE OF PIECEMEAL APPROACHES TO THE FUTURE

The analogy of technological discontinuity as a chasm between the present and the future is useful. On one side of the chasm stands the established technology and the firms that embrace it; on the other side we find the radical new technology, its adherents, and a budding market. Often the former represents the present and the latter represents the future for the industry. Once they recognize their peril, firms on the established side of the chasm must find a way across if they hope to stay in the game. But what forms the bridge across the chasm?

Established businesses have adopted any one of several piecemeal approaches for managing their way to the future:

- Diversified portfolios of R&D projects and technology
- Mergers, acquisitions, alliances, and joint ventures
- Dual strategies

A portfolio approach to managing innovation ranks prospects in terms of predictable returns. The result is too often a grab bag of minor process and product improvements considered one by one, each judged on its own financial merits without sufficient consideration given to the long-run strength and competence of the firm in the face of change.

Mergers and acquisitions very often have unsatisfactory outcomes. When a large firm acquires a small entrepreneurial company to get its technology, it often finds that it has bought an empty box. The real assets were the brains of the entrepreneurs, who find the culture of the new company stifling and quickly leave. The current fashion of alliances and joint ventures among firms having complementary skills is also less than adequate as a solution for corporate revitalization. The motivation for this solution, particularly for both small technology-based firms and large established firms, is obvious; each has something the other desperately needs. New firms in technology product industries are often closer to the frontiers of progress than are established firms, while established firms have the financial, manufacturing, and distribution clout that the new firms lack almost entirely. The flaw in the seemingly idyllic marriage of these parties is the substantial cultural differences that set them apart. The new firms are entrepreneurial and unburdened by organizational controls; the established firms are just the opposite. And these differences tend to undermine the benefits of the relationship. Alliances will not correct the flaws in management posture that Frey describes. Moreover, they are often used by larger companies to justify reductions in research staffs and costs. Alliances may be of value, but they are no panacea for the problems of flagging corporate vitality. Only commitment by top management to renewing the business of the firm—and patience and persistence in that commitment—will have a chance to succeed.

Dual strategies have already been mentioned in Chapter 9, in the case of Sun and DEC. DEC's dual strategy of addressing the needs of current customers while simultaneously moving to a more modern computer architecture did not prove satisfactory. Dual strategies also carry the danger of creating destructive turf battles within the firm, as partisans of different strategies compete for power and scarce resources. A dual strategy essentially is an attempt to stand with one foot on each side of the chasm—a seemingly untenable position in the best of circumstances.

ORGANIZING SEPARATE DIVISIONS AND ALLIANCES TO BRIDGE TECHNOLOGICAL DISCONTINUITIES

As preceding chapters have made clear, the struggle for corporate survival in industry is unceasing. Further, the challenge of survival appears to take place in a series of successive tests: first at the level of the fluid phase of a product or process technology—just as the 80 or so manual typewriter firms in North America battled for position and survival; and, again, at the breakpoints between waves of technologies—as when the surviving manual typewriter companies had to make the leap to electrics, and again to computer-based word processing. Each of these tests eliminates industry participants and opens the door to others, and each has a bias against long-term survival. These tests may appear in many forms over time.

Preceding chapters indicate the necessity for businesses to rejuvenate themselves as changes in markets and technological discontinuities come their way. Although many firms fail this test, some have passed it successfully. They seem able to introduce dynamic, distinctive new products time and time again, while many others quickly exhaust their ability to keep generating new products that are competitive and the basis of sustained success. The main difficulty for established firms seems to be their reluctance to abandon old positions and embrace new ones when radical innovations invade their markets and undermine them. Some firms may be strong in product development yet fail to gain commercial rewards from their technical efforts, while their more successful counterparts exhibit the right mix of skills and capabilities not only in product design and implementation, but also in understanding user needs, in manufacturing, and in distribution. Thus a viable strategy for corporate renewal may be to build on established competences in marketing and distribution to renew a firm's line of business in its chosen market. Another might be to build on its strengths in product development and manufacturing to address new markets.

Organizing especially to meet the challenge may also be part of the solution. There are a number of cases in which established firms gained a foothold in markets generated by radical technology by reorganizing their efforts. In dealing with discontinuities, where the fluid-phase attributes of organizational flexibility and entrepreneurial spirit are required, managers of large established firms can either set up autonomous, independent units or forge alliances with the small firms that typically appear in the vanguard of an invading new technology. If they choose the latter course, they should do so with the knowledge that these arrangements are not always successful.

Cooper and Smith found that even in the rare instances in which a large firm did decide to organize separately to pursue a radical idea, other problems sometimes emerged. These included intense conflicts between organizational units and tacit attempts to derail the new initiative by withholding critical support and experience when needed.[10] William Hamilton and Harbir Singh have shown in their study of corporate capabilities and emerging technologies that neither established firms nor upstart competitors have all the competences needed to make a success of revolutionary technology, at least in its early stages. Both attempt to develop these over time.[11] Ironically, the competences of these rivals in the early stage are, according to Hamilton and Singh, highly complementary: the established firms have financial, marketing, and manufacturing resources in abundance and the emerging firms generally possess greater technical know-how. The result is that alliances often benefit both firms. The problems of these alliances, however, have been noted above, and need to be recognized and dealt with.

Chapter 1 described how IBM successfully entered the personal computer market through a separate dedicated unit set up far from the firm's headquarters; later in the book we saw an independent Team Taurus put Ford Motor Company back on the map and how General Motors entered the small-car market through the Saturn Motor Company. In each instance, the task of creating the competences needed to successfully bridge into chosen markets hinged on creating organizations with clear mandates and a great deal of independence from the staffs, committees, and other encumbrances of their parent companies.

Organizational separation, however, does not always lead to success. Xerox's attempt to revitalize itself through its Xerox Palo Alto Research (PARC) facility is a notable example. Xerox PARC was a paragon of inventive genius, creating the technology for a truly superior personal computer, the facsimile machine, Ethernet™, and the laser printer. Few of these ideas accrued to Xerox's benefit, however. Most found their way to the marketplace via new firms.[12]

SUMMARY

Innovation is not just the job of corporate technologists, but of all major functional areas of the firm. And the support of radical innovation by these areas must be managed with boldness and persistence from the top. Here the responsibility of management is nothing less than corporate regeneration in the face of radical innovation.

Little success will result from any program of innovation, of course, unless the people of the firm are properly deployed, given sufficient resources, and provided with a climate that encourages and rewards new thinking and risk taking. For radical innovation to occur, traditional organizational controls must loosen. Capital-budgeting procedures that push projects with long-term horizons and uncertain payoffs to the back of the line must be reevaluated. Committee systems and organizational requirements that diffuse responsibility too broadly need to be recalibrated. Investors must be educated to the new direction of the firm, and reminded that greater rewards are only associated with greater risks. Otherwise new initiatives will almost inevitably be starved for resources, allowing competitors to establish formidable positions at the expense of the once-preeminent industry leaders. Attending mainly to the needs of the established business will ensure that entering the new area will be done with strategies well honed for the old but compromised or flawed for the new. For success certainly these efforts should at least be equally balanced and emphasized.

The importance of leadership should never be underestimated. Historian Arnold Toynbee concluded in his famous *Study of History* that the decline of a civilization can be arrested or reversed when strong leaders come forward to meet the challenges of their times—be the challenges from outside invaders or from internal decay. "Challenge and response" was for Toynbee the dynamic process through which the fortunes of great past civilizations were sorted out. Similarly, managers of established industrial firms eventually find themselves faced with threats to their continued prosperity and survival, either from the invasion of radical innovations or from the gradual deterioration of the potency of their own core businesses. In either case the effect is the same: firms lose their ability to satisfy their traditional market. To stem the eventual tide of decline, they must either find new markets for existing products or regenerate themselves.

From the viewpoint of a new firm radical change gives it its only chance to enter a business and grow at the expense of powerful existing rivals. We have seen that the first versions of a new product are crude and expensive. This often catches stronger firms unaware because the nascent threat seems objectively so absurd. Entrepreneurial firms, though, can be more nimble and experimental and find a niche market for the new technology from which to grow, often rapidly. From the viewpoint of the established firm it is patently foolish to give up the development and production of the old product and technology. The new will arguably be a long time growing to be of any importance, if ever, and this conservative position is probably more often right than wrong. Only the prospective and imminent loss of the established business can justify a shift by a major firm, but this often seems impossible or incredible to them, even when it is clearly beginning. The problem is that we cannot judge or predict which of many threats will have such potency, but the cases and examples developed in this work show that even the strongest product and business strategy will eventually be overturned by technological change. The central issue is not when or how this will happen, but that it will happen for sure. In the final analysis only that understanding will allow a firm to bridge a discontinuity, because only a total commitment will win the day.

Endnotes

1. Lewis M. Branscomb (ed.), *Empowering Technology: Implementing a U.S. Strategy* (Cambridge, Mass.: MIT Press, 1993), p. 269.
2. Charles Baden-Fuller and John M. Stopford, *Rejuvenating the Mature Business: The Competitive Challenge* (Boston: Harvard Business School Press, 1994).
3. C. K. Prahalad and Gary Hamel, "The Core Competence of the Corporation," *Harvard Business Review,* May–June, 1990, pp. 79–91.
4. As mentioned in the previous chapter, this point is disputed by Donald Frey, formerly at Ford, who says that Ford persistently sought radial tires from its reluctant suppliers.
5. James M. Utterback and James W. Brown, "Monitoring for Technological Opportunities," *Business Horizons,* October 1972, pp. 5–15; and James M. Utterback and Elmer H. Burack, "Identification of Technological Threats and Opportunities by Firms," *Technological Forecasting and Social Change,* vol. 8 (1975), pp. 7–21.
6. One is reminded here of the complaint that our society has developed two classes of people: generalists and specialists. The generalists spend their time learning less and less about more and more; the specialists are committed to learning more and more about less and less. Ultimately, we will have one group that knows nothing about everything, and another that knows everything about nothing.

7. Arnold Cooper and Dan Schendel, "Strategic Responses to Technological Threats," *Business Horizons,* vol. 19, no. 1 (February 1976), pp. 61–69.

8. Donald Frey, correspondence with the author.

9. Arnold C. Cooper and Clayton G. Smith, "How Established Firms Respond to Threatening Technologies," *Academy of Management Executive,* vol. 6, no. 2 (May 1992), pp. 55–70.

10. Ibid., p. 64.

11. William Hamilton and Harbir Singh, "The Evolution of Corporate Capabilities in Emerging Technologies," *Interfaces,* vol. 22, no. 4 (July–August 1992), pp. 13–23.

12. Douglas K. Smith and Robert C. Alexander, *Fumbling the Future* (New York: William Morrow, 1988).

12

MANAGING INNOVATION OVER THE PRODUCT LIFE CYCLE

William L. Moore
Michael L. Tushman

There exists a relatively predictable pattern in the amount and type of innovation over the product class life cycle. Changes in innovation lead to systematic differences in competitive emphases which necessitate that strategies and organization structures and processes must also evolve over time. Not only do these new strategies, structures, and processes have to be articulated, but also, the transition from old to new needs to be explicitly managed.

The successful development and commercialization of innovation in both product itself and the manufacturing process is crucial to the health of firms, industries and our national economy. The efficient use of research, development, and engineering (RD&E) funds can have a significant impact on productivity increases and, therefore, on the rate of inflation in the medium and long run (Mansfield 1980). However, the management of a stream of innovations over time is exceptionally complex. Most new products or new businesses fail, many successful small firms do not make the transition to more mature larger organizations, and many large firms become ever more bureaucratized thereby stifling their ability to innovate.

The problem in developing and commercializing new products and processes does *not* arise from a lack of usable technology; the vast majority of failing innovations are due to marketing and organizational pathologies (Booz, Allen and Hamilton, Inc. 1968, Mansfield and Wagner 1975, Myers and Marquis 1969, Myers and Sweezy 1978). Furthermore, if one considers not just single innovations, but the entire stream of innovations that are required for success over a large portion of the product life cycle, strategic and organizational concerns play a dominant role in the success or failure of a business unit. This implies that marketing's concern with innovation must go beyond that of making sure that each innovation is directed at solving customer problems or fulfilling needs. Specifically, the marketing strategist must realize the impact that present decisions with regard to product and process innovation have on future strategic alternatives.

This paper shall focus on the interrelationships between marketing strategy and a range of organizational factors. We argue that different strategies and organizational forms are appropriate at different times (and inappropriate at other times), that management must be able to manage these substantively different kinds of organizations, and be prepared to manage the transitions between relatively incompatible strategies, structures and organizational processes which are required at different points in the product life cycle.

Moore, William L, and Michael L. Tushman, (1982). "Managing Innovation Over the Product Life Cycle," in *Readings in the Management of Innovation,* eds. Michael L. Tushman and William L. Moore, Boston, MA: Pitman.

Innovation refers to any product or process new to a business unit (firm). While many associate research and development and innovation only with major advances (e.g., transistors, xerography), the vast majority of successful innovations is based on the cumulative effects of small, incremental changes in either product or process (Myers and Marquis 1969). Furthermore, as anyone who could not afford the original HP calculator at $400 can attest, the continuing stream of incremental innovations (both in the product itself and in the manufacturing process) over the product life cycle (PLC) can be every bit as important as the initial breakthrough.

Most generally, innovation can be seen as the synthesis of a market need with the means to achieve and produce a product to meet that need (Schmookler 1966). Thus innovation requires the coordination of Research and Development, Marketing and Production. Moreover, we argue that the number and types of innovations and the relative importance of the different functional areas are systematically different at different points in the product life cycle.

While there has been substantial research on innovation, much of it has had a static focus. For example, Miles and Snow (1978) and Ansoff and Stewart (1967) focus on the relationship among decisions made in research and development, manufacturing and marketing at a point in time, while Burns and Stalker (1965) and Lawrence and Lorsch (1967) focus on the design problem at a point in time. Even more generally, much of the organization and marketing literatures focus on achieving consistency or fit at a single point (for example, see Nadler and Tushman 1980). However, this paper suggests that fit/consistency is a necessary, but not sufficient condition for successful innovation over time. We argue that strategies and actions which are optimal in one period may not be in the next. The paper draws on concepts from marketing, operations management, management of technology and organization behavior to discuss a general pattern of the amount and type of innovation over the product life cycle. Changes in this pattern of innovation will be associated with systematic changes in the bases of competition and in the strategies, structure, and process of successful firms. We extend Wright's (1974) work at the firm level, Abernathy and Utterback's (1976, 1978) work on production processes and Galbraith and Nathanson's work (1978) on stages of growth of the single business unit over time. This review will not cover processes of adoption and diffusion; as most readers are familiar with them. (See Howard 1980 for an integration of buyer behavior theory with some of the concepts discussed here.)

The framework for this paper is the *product class life cycle,* rather than that of a product form or brand life cycle (Polli and Cook 1967). Thus, we are focusing on the life cycle of automobiles, cigarettes, or integrated circuits—not on forms such as convertibles, filter cigarettes, or MOS devices, and not on brands such as Citations, Winstons, or Intel's 8080 microprocessor. This framework has been chosen because when a new brand is introduced into a mature market (e.g., Ford's Escort) the manufacturing process and organization associated with it are typically going to be much more similar to the mature brands (e.g., Ford's Granada) than to the manufacturing process and organizations associated with a new brand early in the history of the product class (e.g., Ford's Model A of 1901–1903).

The unit of analysis will not be just the product. Abernathy and Utterback (1976, 1978) indicate that since the product produced and the manufacturing process used become so interdependent that the relevant unit of analysis should be the productive unit: "the product line and its associated production process" (1978, p. 43). However, the required synthesis of market/user needs with technical possibilities renders Abernathy and Utterback's focus on the productive unit as too narrow. We use the term business unit to refer to the product line and the smallest part of the firm which has some control over marketing, manufacturing, and research, development and engineering. This unit may share a sales force, manufacturing plant, or research and development laboratory, but it is able to exercise some control over these functions. This is similar to the concept of a strategic business unit and the product line it produces.

Using the product class life cycle as the basic framework, the following section describes systematic differences in (1) strategy and competitive emphasis; (2) the nature and rate of innovation; (3) the role and functions of functional areas; (4) the nature of the formal organization and organizational processes and (5) the role and philosophy of senior management. The final section discusses the problem of managing transitions between stages.

STAGES IN THE PRODUCT LIFE CYCLE

Introductory Stage

This stage begins with the development and introduction of a product innovation that starts a new product class life cycle, and runs until many of the products start to be manufactured in higher volume. This latter point typically corresponds to the time when the sales curve first starts to climb rapidly. The basis of competition here is product performance; does this product meet an existing or emerging need, or does it provide significant performance advantages over other products. The business units are typically small entrepreneurial ventures. Their strategy is to take an incompletely understood technology and an ill-defined market to produce a product with superior functional performance, even if the product is expensive. This phase of the product life cycle is inherently entrepreneurial (see, for example, the early stages of xerography, Dessauer 1975).

Innovation

A new product life cycle is initiated by a radical or discontinuous product innovation; an innovation which has the potential to substantially affect life-styles (for example, automobiles, computers, frozen foods). The recognition of a need, which may be latent or just unmet, often stimulates an entrepreneur to search for ways to meet this need. Several studies suggest that as much as 80 percent of major innovations are a response to a market need (Carter and Williams 1957; Sherwin and Isenson 1967; Utterback 1974). For market or user driven innovation, basic research is usually not directly relevant. Rather, entrepreneurial firms take existing knowledge and technologies and combine them in novel ways. For market driven innovation, basic research and new knowledge, then, enters the innovation process indirectly through education (Allen 1977; Myers and Marquis 1969). Still, approximately 20 percent of major product innovations are technology driven and emerge more directly from research and development (e.g., transistor, xerography).

First applications of the new innovation are typically in very specialized niches where the old technology is not appropriate (e.g., the wireless radio was first used in ship-to-shore communication). The innovation usually has cost and reliability drawbacks when compared to existing products. Performance disadvantages and transition costs are probably the main reason why firms in the existing industry are slow to react (Cooper and Schendel 1976).

The product initially introduced is usually crude. Feedback from vendors and innovative users must be used to improve the product. For example, early gasoline powered cars (prior to 1900) were inferior to steam and electric cars, but by 1904 gasoline powered cars were clearly superior performers. Similarly, Xerox's original 914 copier was severely flawed, but by 1962 the 914's were clearly superior to wet-copying. At this early point in PLC, competition is based primarily on product performance. Thus competition occurs both between the new and old technology, and between different versions of the new technology. There is substantial experimentation during this phase of the product life cycle, and few units are made of any one model. For example, between 1944–50 over three-fourths of the computer models were one or two of a kind, by 1953 under half were one or two of a kind, and by 1960 less than 10 percent were made in such small volumes (Knight 1963).

As a result of this experimentation, a "dominant design" emerges. This is an "optimal" product configuration that does not undergo any major changes for some time. Usually, this is an evolutionary design, i.e., each of the major features of the design may have been incorporated in previous models, but this particular *combination* of features has not been present in any previous model. For example, a number of features that were embodied in virtually all cars between 1920 and 1970 were present in the early 1900's: longitudinally mounted engine in front connected to rearwheel drive via torque tube, steering wheel on the left, "H" transmission, water cooled engine, independent body and chassis design, and the essential driver controls of today. Yet no single car employed all of these design features (Abernathy 1978). While Ford's Model T may not have been the first to incorporate all of these, it was an early model that did. Based on a large number of experimental designs, this design appeared to be optimal. Similarly, the DC-3 has been regarded as a dominant design in the aircraft industry. No major innovations were introduced into aircraft design for the next 15 years. Again, all the essential design features that made the DC-10 so successful were present in previous models, but this was the first time they were all combined in one airplane (Phillips 1971).

The dominant design is an extremely important event in the product life cycle of an industry in that it fundamentally changes the nature of innovations, the bases of competition, manufacturing processes, and therefore marketing strategy and organizational design. Before considering these implications of the dominant design, we shall discuss characteristics of a successful business unit at this stage of the PLC.

Business Unit and Functional Areas

In the introductory stage of the product life cycle the primary form of innovation is major product innovation. Competitors are experimenting with designs that may be radically different from each other. Because of the experimental nature of each model, production volumes are very low and a real product line does not exist.

The primary functional areas are marketing and research and development. Marketing's job includes stimulating primary demand, searching for niches where the product has a differential advantage, and determining who the early adopters are. Moreover, marketing must learn what levels of various attributes are most desirable. Finally, marketing must undertake the often substantial job of educating the consumer (Howard 1977, 1980). Von Hipple (1978) has suggested that in a number of industrial product settings innovative users generate many innovations. In these instances, marketing needs to set up the structure to collect these ideas.

The role of research and development changes dramatically during this phase of the PLC. In the early introductory period, market needs are ill-defined and relevant technologies are not clear. The primary focus is on producing a new product that works. Given market uncertainties and the product push, there is relatively little incentive for early-on organized research and development. However, as a dominant design is approached and relevant dimensions-of-merit emerge, as user needs become clearer and as relevant technologies arise from early product experimentation, organized research and development becomes very important. Research and development can be focused on market and technical opportunities (Abernathy and Utterback 1978). Under these conditions, research and development must develop new and use existing knowledge to improve the product's functional performance. At this stage of the product life cycle, more successful laboratories will have extensive contact with suppliers, vendors and customers as well as with universities and professional societies (Tushman 1979; Cooper 1973). Laboratories at this stage will be relatively small and informally organized with strong links to marketing (Tushman 1979).

During this period, manufacturing efficiency is relatively less important than later in the product life cycle. However, Sommers (1979) points out the need for product and process design to go hand in hand. The high level of product innovation requires a job shop or a jumbled flow process run by skilled workers utilizing general purpose equipment. As this type of manufacturing process requires slack resources in workers, inventories and equipment, it is a high cost operation. High unit cost is the price paid for product flexibility.

As the volume of products is low and the size of the unit is small, the formal organization is relatively unimportant now. Whether the organization is independent or part of a venture unit within a parent corporation, the organization is usually managed by a powerful entrepreneur whose vision, enthusiasm and energy dominate the infant organization. The organization is ad hoc; the boundaries between functional areas are not substantial (Dessauer 1975). Communication is widespread and face-to-face, there are few rules and regulations, decisions are made quickly and informally, and control is achieved by the direct personal action of the entrepreneur. Key roles which must be fulfilled at this stage include the entrepreneur, technical innovators and market and technological gatekeepers (individuals who link their unit to market and technological domains). These roles may well be filled by the same person early in the units' existence (Roberts and Frohman 1972).

In summary, in the introductory stage of the product life cycle small entrepreneurial organizations produce a low volume of relatively expensive experimental products using highly skilled labor and general purpose equipment. This phase ends as firms begin to increase volume production of their dominant design. Large companies seldom generate radical innovations in their own industry. Most frequently, the innovators are totally new entrants (for example, DEC in minicomputers or Fairchild, IBM and TI in the early semiconductor industry).

Growth Stage

Dominant Design and Competitive Emphasis

The decision to standardize the product and to begin to rationalize the production process signals the start of the second phase of the PLC from the innovation standpoint, a phase of transition from primarily product innovation to process innovation (Abernathy and Utterback 1976, 1978). While this transition phase need not correspond exactly to the growth stage of the PLC, there is enough commonality in the time they start to discuss them that way. Once sales have started to grow rapidly, it will usually be only a short time before it is no longer possible to manufacture the product in a job shop process. Conversely, a certain volume must be attained before it is economical to buy special purpose equipment.

During this phase, major process innovations begin to increase the interdependence between the product and the manufacturing process, and decisions made in one area start to have a large impact on the other. For example, as soon as a piece of special purpose equipment has been purchased, the number of product modifications are limited if one wants to continue to use that piece of equipment. This interdependence leads to more incremental product changes.

The decision to standardize the product is of great strategic importance to the business unit. As pointed out earlier, (1) it is only in retrospect that one realizes that a design is dominant and (2) the dominant design is the result of a number of experimental forerunners. Thus, at some point, a firm makes the decision that more can be gained by concentrating on one design and starting down the experience curve at a steeper slope than can be gained through continued experimentation. Furthermore, it is quite possible that a firm will decide to standardize too early, with a design that is not dominant. In a study of the early period of the semiconductor industry, Tilton (1971) found that the firms that were also in the vacuum tube market (divisions of General Electric, Philco, and RCA) concentrated on process innovations, while the new entrants (IBM, Fairchild, and TI) focused on product innovations. It appears that concentrating on further product improvements was the more viable competitive strategy at that time. Ironically, TI has been faulted recently for settling on an LED electronic watch and attempting to make it in volume instead of waiting for the perfection of the LCD watch (*Business Week* 1980).

Some combination of three forces determines the dominant design: technical superiority, market acceptance, and company strategy. By 1904 it was evident that automobiles powered by gasoline engines would be technically superior to electric and steam cars given the environment in the foreseeable future. Similarly, in the 1920's several other developments interacted to make the V-8 design dominant (Abernathy 1978). The DC-3 was technically superior to its competitors as it was the most economical fast plane to fly long distances in its time.

Alternatively, it may be a decision of the market, for example the success of the two competing videodisc systems may hinge much more on the availability of a wide range of discs than on the technical merits of the system. When a semiconductor memory device is chosen as the industry standard, it is not always done with just performance characteristics in mind. Also, decisions on standard record speeds, widths of railroad tracks, radio broadcasting methods or measurement systems are not necessarily based on performance characteristics as much as the need to have a standard.

Finally, choice of a standard design may be the result of a strategic decision. If the market starts to grow rapidly and one decides to grow with it, the only possible way may be by moving from a job shop to a more rational manufacturing process. This necessitates a more standardized product. Similarly, when Ford made the strategic decision to market a car for the masses, this required that the car be manufactured at a low cost. Consequently, he did not make any fundamental changes in the chassis for the next 18 years.

As products become more standardized and superior designs are copied, competition becomes *more* price oriented. This is because the differences in performance narrow, the products are becoming more commodity-like. This is also a period of major process innovations as the manufacturing operation passes from that of a job shop to a batch system, to some type of jumbled assembly line as volume permits. During this stage of the PLC, the emphasis is usually on maintaining or increasing share of a growing market (which may be the primary segment or a fairly small niche). Several authors (e.g., Abell and Hammond 1979, Boston Consulting Group 1972) have suggested that it is easier to gain share at this point than in a stagnant market and that gains in this stage allow a longer period to enjoy the benefits of high market share.

While all companies are attempting to rationalize their production process, the degree of efficiency achieved should be based on a strategic decision. Increased sales volume requires that all business units rationalize their manufacturing process to some extent. Similarly, the standardization of the product will push everyone down the experience curve. However, these facts obscure the crucial strategic decisions that must be made at this point. A company may attempt to achieve a high market share by becoming the lowest cost producer. This can be accomplished by (1) "buying" market share to move down the experience curve as fast as possible and (2) making the experience curve as steep as possible. One could increase the slope of the experience curve by integrating backwards for some components, specializing the labor force, buying or building special purpose (and usually automated) production equipment, and by introducing product innovations only when they lower the cost of the product. This might move a company down a 70 percent experience curve.

On the other hand, a competitor might attempt to achieve a high market share by virtue of superior quality. If this strategy is followed, the company would have to keep its production process more flexible. This necessitates the use of more general purpose equipment and more highly skilled labor. Performance enhancing components might be introduced even if they raise the cost. This might move a company down a 90 percent experience curve.

It should be noted that the high quality strategy is not necessarily incompatible with low prices. It is possible that product innovations will result in lower priced products (e.g., the cost of storing one bit of information has been decreasing for many years due to denser chips). It is also possible that the higher volume resulting from a quality product will result in greater cumulative experience and/or economies of scale. For example, GM was not as fully integrated as Ford between 1920 and 1945, but by the end of that period, it was the lower cost manufacturer because of economies of scale.

However, it should be noted that a strategy focusing on product innovation is incompatible with a steep experience curve (Abernathy and Wayne 1974).

Business Unit and Functional Areas

During the growth phase we can first talk about a product line. Prior to this, a very small number of each model is made. Now a much larger volume of one, or a small number of models, is produced. The most obvious change this causes is in the manufacturing process—it becomes more rationalized. At the start of the growth phase, this may mean a switch from a job shop to a batch process—making a number of units of one model at once. As volume permits labor can become more specialized, concentrating on smaller jobs. This allows faster learning of the task and the development of specialized tools (e.g., a drill with multiple spindles that drills a number of holes simultaneously). These tools must usually be devoted to one operation. As this stage progresses, the logical extention of the specialization of labor is a continued breakdown of jobs into smaller steps, then the substitution of machines for workers. This process has been speeded up with the advent of numerically controlled machine tools and more sophisticated robots. These changes allow the production process to become more rationalized, so that the product moves in a linear fashion during manufacture and assembly, rather than being routed back to the same location several times.

However, beyond this general trend toward specialization and rationalization there *can* be a great diversity of production organizations within an industry. Unfortunately, as observed by Skinner (1969, 1974, 1978) few companies tailor their production systems to be consistent with business unit strategy. Specifically, "Most top executives and production managers look at their production systems with the notion of 'total productivity' or the equivalent 'efficiency'. They seek a kind of blending of low costs, high quality, and acceptable customer service. The view prevails that a plant with reasonably modern equipment, up-to-date methods and procedures . . . will be a good plant" (Skinner 1969, p. 139). These people are not realizing that trade-offs must be made, that a given plant cannot perform well on every yardstick. Skinner (1974) suggests that the factory needs to be "focused" on the one key manufacturing task. This is done by translating the overall business unit strategy into what it means for manufacturing. This describes the key manufacturing tasks that must be carried out to support the business unit strategy. What is the one job that must be done right?

As mentioned earlier two alternative strategies are high quality and low price. The difference between the manufacturing focus of these two strategies goes beyond just that of automation and job specialization. It includes such things as size and location of plants, inventory levels, and wage and control systems. Furthermore, these differences may be seen in the basic organizational structure of manufacturing. Hayes and Schmenner (1978) contrast a product and process focused manufacturing organization. The product-focused organization typically includes most staff functions in each plant, it is highly decentralized, quite flexible, but may not achieve the economies of scale that a process-focused organization would. The product-focused organization tends to be more suited when flexibility and innovation are more critical than control and lower costs. Conversely, a process-focused organization requires a large central staff to coordinate the plants with each other and with other functional areas. This focus does not tend to be as good for the rapid introduction of product innovations.

During the growth phase the task of marketing shifts from stimulating primary to stimulating selective demand. Also market segmentation becomes more important. As different distinct market segments develop with the maturity of the product, marketing may become organized around products and markets (termed a bilateral structure by Corey and Star 1971). For example, if one product can be sold in a number of markets, like a main frame computer sold to manufacturing or retailing/wholesaling companies, hospitals, and universities, different marketing organizations may be required to sell to each of these segments. Still some integrated emphasis needs to be placed on the product in the area of product planning. So some parts of the marketing organization must be organized by product and some by market. Similarly, when DuPont first introduced one of their synthetic fibers, the marketing organization was organized by product as the customer needed a large amount of specific information about that fiber. However, as the market grew and uses for the various fibers began to overlap, the marketing organization needed to be organized by markets. For example, a manufacturer of men's clothing wanted to see one person from DuPont who could discuss the pros and cons of each of their fibers and suggest which one would be best in this particular application rather than having a different salesman call for each fiber.

Research and development increases in importance during the growth phase. As the firm's technical core is clear (for example, hydraulics at Technicon or coating and bonding at 3M) and market needs are more clear, the firm can direct its investment in R&D with greater certainty. Typically during this phase of growth the laboratory specializes in distinct work areas. A small portion of laboratory personnel (typically between 5–10 percent) work on basic research in disciplines which are or may be of importance to the firm. The rest of the laboratory is focused on applied development, engineering, and technical service work. This work is aimed directly at putting existing knowledge to work in developing new or improved products or processes.

During the growth phase, management must facilitate both disciplinary specialization as well as the ability to develop integrated products. Scientists and engineers must be hired, socialized and developed so that they remain both technically competent and highly motivated (Ritti 1971; Pelz and Andrews 1966). Depending on the rate-of-change of the technology and average program length, the laboratory will be organized either by discipline or by program (Allen 1977). When technologies are substantially different and there are multiple programs, a matrix organization is appropriate (Galbraith 1974). Throughout this phase, development and technical service areas must be strongly linked to both marketing and manufacturing, while researchers must be well linked to sources outside the organization. Given the importance of new product and process change during this phase and given the number of distinct functional areas involved, the unit must develop program selection and evaluation systems as well as a relatively common program development process.

During this period the unit grows rapidly and develops specialized functions. This combination of growth and specialization, in the context of increased price competition, produces a need for coordination, control and planning. Where the business unit was small and ad-hoc, it is now larger and in need of systems, policies, procedures and organization that do not rely on the personal judgment of the entrepreneur. The managerial thrust during this period is, then, one of integration and administration; the development and implementation of procedures, controls and policies which standardize and systematize functional and inter-functional processes (Adizes 1979). The philosophy of the more successful firms at this stage is of continued growth, but growth based on planning and organization.

Reflecting the need for competitive new products, marketing and R&D are relatively more influential than manufacturing at this stage of the product life cycle (Wright 1974; Lawrence and Lorsch 1967). Critical roles in the innovation process beyond those of entrepreneur, technologist, and gatekeeper are those of project manager and sponsor. As the unit is larger and more heterogeneous, a sponsor's role is to provide protection and to advocate positions of less organizationally influential technologists or entrepreneurs. A project manager is one who can focus on the specifics of program development and who can coordinate needed efforts. Where in the introductory phase many of the roles could be fulfilled by one person, as the organization grows and becomes more complex these roles are played by different individuals in different parts of the organization (Maidique 1980; Roberts 1977).

In summary, in the growth phase of the product life cycle the firm focuses on a dominant design and related product differentiation. The rate of product change decreases, while the rate of process change increases. The organization grows substantially and develops and staffs specialized functions for dealing with the unique and complex problems in marketing, manufacturing, R&D and planning. Given the degree of differentiation, the unit invests substantial energy in conflict resolution and integration.

Mature Stage

Strategy

Classically, the mature stage is a time of little or no sales growth. Abernathy and Utterback (1978) talk about a specific phase, characterized by standardized products manufactured in high volumes with efficient techniques. It is a time when both product and process innovation are incremental. These two stages will typically overlap, even though they need not begin at the same time. For example, companies may still be developing major process innovations even though growth has stopped. Conversely, the pool of major process innovations may dry up before the growth slows. Still, these two stages will be discussed as if they occurred simultaneously.

With product innovation becoming very incremental, Abernathy and Utterback (1978) view price reduction as the dominant competitive focus. This view is in accord with that of BCG who feels that the company with lowest cost (most experience) will be able to control the market when the growth slows. These observations are based on the assumption that products become more commodity-like over their life cycle. Obviously, there is less variation in U.S. cars, beer, and coffee now than there was at the turn of the century. Several forces are driving this phenomenon. Manufacturers are attempting to sell to the national (or world) market. Only a relatively standard product which can take advantage of mass production and distribution, can effectively sell in a large and heterogeneous market (Chandler 1977). Second, good ideas are copied over time. Finally, the reward for major innovation diminishes over time, since it is increasingly difficult to make any but incremental changes. Successful designs, then, are copied over time and no one has a real incentive to look for new changes. With product differences decreasing, competition tends to focus more on price.

However, a number of researchers have suggested that it is still possible to pursue a high quality strategy (e.g., Hall 1980; Harrigan, 1980; Hamermesh and Silk 1979). Hall (1980) looked at 8 industries with low growth (e.g., cigarettes, tires, and long haul trucks) and found higher performers in each. The common denominator of success was one of the following strategies: (1) achieve the lowest delivered cost position relative to the competition, (2) achieve the highest product/service quality differentiated position, or (3) follow both strategies simultaneously. The simultaneous strategy is not as incompatible as it seems at first glance. As Levitt has demonstrated in a number of articles (e.g., 1980), the differentiating characteristic does not have to be the physical product. Thus, one can combine low cost manufacturing with an excellent distribution or service system, or a low cost manufacturing system with a quality image maintained through promotion. Similarly, Hamermesh and Silk (1979), using the PIMS data base, show good returns associated with medium and high levels of R&D/sales and with high product quality in low growth industries. In addition to the two successful strategies found by Hall, they suggest further segmentation of the market and concentration on high growth segments. Beyond price and/or quality strategies, the business unit may also attempt to directly manipulate its environment. These external strategies are directed at creating a more stable set of suppliers, vendors and customers (McMillan 1978). There are, then, several possible profitable strategies at this point in the product life cycle.

Innovation

Product innovation during this phase is minimal. On the other hand, to the extent possible by volume and homogeneity of customer/user tastes, the production process becomes substantially more efficient. Islands of automation emerge (process change) and are linked together through automatic work feeding, removal and material handling devices (that is, further process innovation). As plants become more capital intense and rigid, the interdependence between product and process becomes even greater. It becomes more and more difficult to make any changes in the product without making very costly changes in the production process. For example, prior to 1951, automotive manufacturers assembled all car models in most assembly plants, and manufactured most engine models in every engine plant. However, after this time, plants became more rigid and assembled one, or at most a small number of closely related models (e.g., the X-cars) at a given plant. On a corporate basis, the models/plant ratio did not change significantly, but it declined dramatically at the plant level. These changes made it much harder to shift production mixes quickly with changing consumer tastes. However, this stream of incremental process innovation can have a large impact on cost; e.g., incandescent lights (Bright 1947), airline operating costs (Miller and Sawers 1970) and the Model T (Abernathy and Townsend 1975). Similarly, Hollander (1965) found that most of the reduction in cost of producing rayon was due to incremental changes that could not be classified as formal R&D projects, and Enos (1967) found that incremental developments in petroleum refining often achieved greater cost reductions than improvements gained from the original innovation.

Business Unit and Functional Areas

As volume and product homogeneity increase, the manufacturing process becomes more and more capital intensive, more specialized and more efficient. Manufacturing becomes more formalized with an abundance of rules, regulations and standard operating procedures as the production process moves from islands of automation to assembly lines to continuous flow operations (Woodward 1967). Decision making is pushed to highest levels in manufacturing, while production employees become ever more involved in overseeing operations of their specialized equipment (Hayes and Wheelwright 1979A, 1979B).

However, this general movement to more automated processes obscures the potential diversity of the industry. A firm that is pursuing a strategy of quality needs some of its operations to be more flexible. They cannot all be too flexible as costs will be driven too high, but the critical operations must be able to produce differential quality. Abernathy (1978) suggests that the various operations be managed as a portfolio where some are quite flexible and others are very efficient. Hayes and Schemenner (1978) counsel separating the "quality" and "efficiency" operations organizationally.

R&D is less important and more focused during the mature phase than in earlier periods. The laboratory must focus on technical service work and on process changes which become more and more incremental over time. For this kind of pragmatic work, more effective laboratories are more centralized, rely on more rules and SOP's, and have less contact with external information areas. Communication with other functional areas is mediated by supervisors (Tushman 1979). During this mature phase, the business unit is most resistant to new ideas and new technology from research or development areas. Given this emphasis on short-term problem solving and incremental process improvement, engineers and scientists hired and socialized during earlier periods may become de-motivated (Schein 1978).

Marketing also has a somewhat diminished role in the mature phase as annual plans reflect few changes from the previous year's plan. However, they do have the responsibility to continually look for ways to differentiate their product. Equally, they must at least coordinate an environmental scanning process to detect the emergence of new technologies that may impact their business.

As the business unit's product becomes more and more commodity-like, the unit faces less and less uncertainty: product and process technologies are well understood and user needs are well known (in that industry). More effective units become more bureaucratic. Rules and SOP's are introduced to handle repetitive procedures, decisions are made at senior levels of the hierarchy, more and more communication is transferred through formal mechanisms, and control is achieved through formal bureaucratic mechanisms. Conflict is relatively rare as the unit takes advantage of yesterday's efforts and the unit's climate emphasizes greater formality, stability and a business-as-usual orientation. The dominant managerial philosophy in this stage is one of stewardship (Wright 1974; Adizes 1979). Given the emphasis on the status quo, the innovative roles (that is, gatekeepers, entrepreneurs, creative technologists, etc.) so important in the introductory and growth phases are not rewarded.

In sum, in the mature phase of the product life cycle, the business unit focuses on costs and efficiency through sales service and manufacturing. It is a period of increasing product volume and organizational size (although increasing at a decreasing rate), and increasing bureaucratization. Consistent with the greater contextual and task certainty, this is a period of relatively little interfunctional conflict and an increasing emphasis on stability and the status quo. As there is less intra-unit differentiation, fewer integration mechanisms are used and there is greater emphasis on senior management decision making.

INNOVATING AND MANAGING TRANSITIONS

The magnitude and rate of product and process innovation change systematically over the product life cycle. To produce a stream of product then process innovations over time, the business unit itself must evolve as different types of organizations and strategies are appropriate at each stage of the product life cycle. We have, then, discussed organizational statics; bases of competition, the nature and function of functional areas and organizational processes to deal with different contexts and work requirements at a point in time. This is highlighted in Figure 12-1.

Several questions arise from this approach to innovation. Do all successful business units move as discussed here; will all successful firms shift their patterns of product and process change similarly? We shall argue that these are modal patterns in an industry, but that there will be systematically different behaviors by firms with different business unit strategies. Finally, if business units must have systematically different characteristics over the product life cycle, then a key managerial responsibility is to manage these transitions. What are some of the difficulties in making the transitions from an effective organization at one time to an equally effective organization at a later time? Are each of the transitions over the product life cycle equally difficult? We shall argue that basic aspects of the unit must change if it is to successfully make these transitions and that not all of the transitions are equally difficult.

Product-Process Strategies

There is a relatively predictable pattern of the amount and type of innovation over the product life cycle. In the introductory stage there is a relatively large amount of product innovation. At the start of the growth stage the total amount of innovation starts to decrease and the type of innovation shifts to a combination of major process innovation and more incremental product innovation. This pattern continues until the product and its associated production process become so intertwined that only incremental process innovation is possible.

Some industries, or parts of industries, may never reach the mature phase of the process life cycle. Because of a lack of standardization of consumer requirements and the concomittant lower volumes, production processes may still be job shop even if the market has matured (for example, printing shops or some foundries). Similarly, low volume for certain mature products, such as the largest mainframe computers or the larger airplanes, may be too small to justify a continuous flow production process. At the firm level, while some changes are natural (for example, cost reduction through learning is almost automatic), there are wide variations in the nature and type of innovation by firms within the same industry. This intra-industry variability is not random but a consequence of a set of managerial decisions at the business unit level. These patterns of decisions flow from either an explicit or implicit innovation strategy (Steele, 1978; Mintzberg 1978).

Hayes and Wheelwright (1979A, 1979B) develop a product-process matrix to discuss strategic alternatives at the firm level (see Figure 12-2). As one moves across (or down) the matrix, general stages in a product (or process) life cycle are encountered; these stages are, in turn, associated with their own unique strategic and organizational requirements. The most typical product-process combinations are found on the diagonal. There are, however, other possible product-process combinations. For example, a firm's strategy might place it slightly above (or to the right of) the diagonal, thereby emphasizing quality and flexibility. A strategy emphasizing price (and therefore efficient manufacturing) would place the firm below (or to the left of) the diagonal.

FIGURE 12-1 Variation of Strategic and Organizational Factors over the Product Life Cycle

	PRODUCT LIFE CYCLE STAGE								
	INTRODUCTION				*GROWTH*		*MATURE*		
TYPE OF INNOVATION	MAJOR PRODUCT INNOVATION	—			INCREMENTAL PRODUCT/MAJOR PROCESS INNOVATION	—	INCREMENTAL PRODUCT/ PROCESS INNOVATION		
LOCATION OF INNOVATION	ENTREPRENEUR	—	MARKETING/ R & D	—	MARKETING/ PRODUCTION	—	PRODUCTION		
BASES OF COMPETITION	PRODUCT PERFORMANCE	—			PRODUCT DIFFERENTIATION PRICE	—	PRICE IMAGE MINOR DIFFERENCES		
PRODUCTION PROCESS	JOB SHOP	—	BATCH	—	ISLANDS OF AUTOMATION	—	ASSEMBLY LINE	—	CONTINUOUS FLOW
DOMINANT FUNCTION	ENTREPRENEUR	—	MARKETING/ R & D	—	MARKETING/ PRODUCTION	—	PRODUCTION/ SALES (PROMOTION)		
MANAGEMENT ROLE	ENTREPRENEUR	—	SOPHISTICATED MARKET MANAGER	—	ADMINISTRATOR/ INTEGRATOR	—	STEWARD		
MODES OF INTEGRATION	INFORMAL COMMUNICATION	—	INFORMAL COMMUNICATION TASK FORCES TEAMS	—	INFORMAL COMMUNICATION TEAMS PROJECT MANAGER	—	FORMAL COMMUNICATION SENIOR MANAGEMENT COMMITTEES		
ORGANIZATIONAL STRUCTURE	FREE FORM	—	FUNCTIONAL ORGANIC	—	PROJECT/ MATRIX	—	FUNCTIONAL/ BUREAUCRATIC		

FIGURE 12-2   The Product-Process Life Cycle (Adapted from R.H. Hayes and S.C. Wheelwright, *Harvard Business Review,* January–February, 1979, p. 135.)

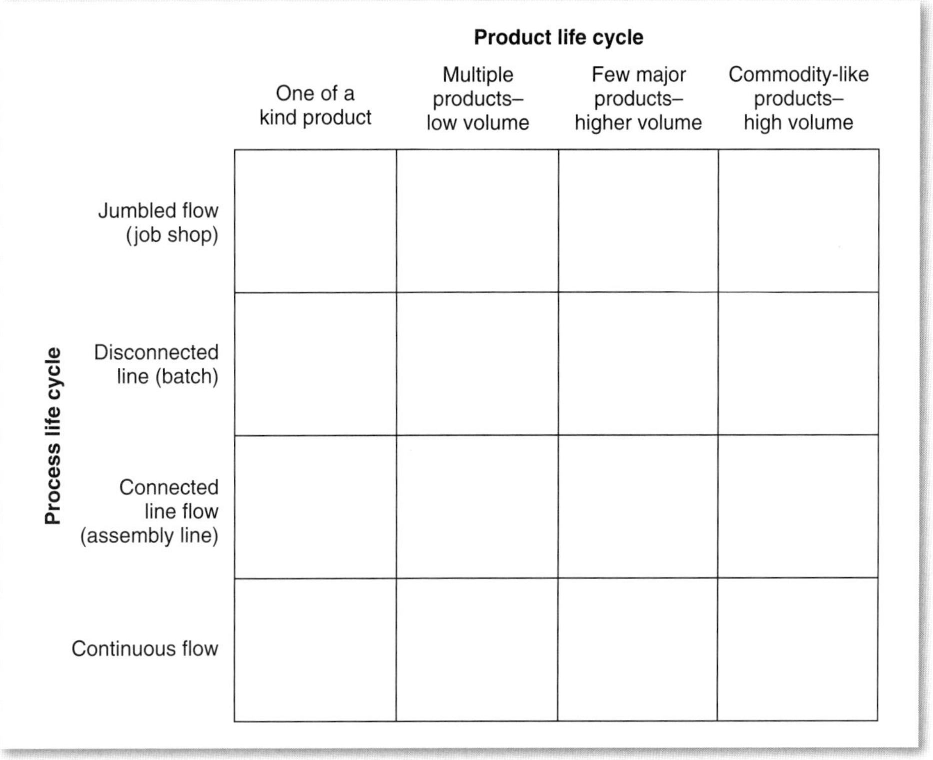

	Product life cycle			
	One of a kind product	Multiple products– low volume	Few major products– higher volume	Commodity-like products– high volume
Jumbled flow (job shop)				
Disconnected line (batch)				
Connected line flow (assembly line)				
Continuous flow				

(Process life cycle is the vertical axis label.)

In both the growth and maturity stages of the product life cycle, there appear to be two viable strategies: noticeable quality difference or lowest delivered cost. The former strategy is consistent with remaining above the diagonal, while the latter is consistent with moving below the diagonal. On the other hand, a position of average quality combined with average price almost insures poor performance. This suggests that moving down the diagonal (industry average) may be a disaster path. Moreover, it is hypothesized that the longer one remains on the diagonal, the harder it will be to move to a position of either highest perceived quality or lowest delivered cost. So while the general cycle is fairly natural, just moving with the industry is asking for trouble. However, the two "success paths" entail risks of their own.

If some environmental force causes a change in the type of product demanded, firms below the diagonal will have a much harder time reacting than other firms. By the same token, this kind of change creates an opportunity for firms above the diagonal. An oft-cited example is that of Ford's Model T. The incremental changes made to the car body between 1914 and 1924 added weight, which was not compensated with increased power, causing performance to decline over time. During this time, there was a growing number of used cars which offered better performance at a price comparable to that of the Model T. Furthermore, innovations in steel making led to the introduction of enclosed steel bodies, also adding weight and decreasing performance. Thus, a series of environmental changes rendered a design no longer dominant. Ford's very efficient manufacturing process required a shutdown of 18 months to respond to these changes (Abernathy and Wayne, 1974). On the other hand, Zenith has consistently positioned itself above the diagonal of television manufacturers. This was an appropriate strategy when Japanese sets were perceived to be of inferior quality. However, changing consumer perceptions rendered Zenith's high cost position more vulnerable than some of the more traditional competitors.

Environmental change, then, will have a greater impact on firms off the diagonal than those firms that are closer to the diagonal. Not only is the impact greater, but it is more difficult to take corrective action because of the amount of change required going forward (e.g., Zenith) and because, when going backward, the firm is moving against the natural tendencies toward greater production efficiency (e.g., Ford).

Managing Transitions

The problem of managing transitions is particularly complex. While successful organizational change is always difficult, it is even more so when the business unit attempts to move from one successful condition to a relatively unknown future state (Beckhard and Harris 1977). Organizational characteristics and individual behaviors which are vital at time one are precisely wrong and dysfunctional at time two. This mismatch in organizations over time requires that the organization move through periods of stability punctuated by periods of instability which lead to a new basis for organizing (Greiner 1972). The organization must be capable of accommodating mutually inconsistent strategies, structures and processes over time.

In our opinion, the two most critical management problems are (1) managing the transition from a successful entrepreneurial firm to an established, functionally oriented company and (2) the retention of the ability to learn and innovate during the mature phase.

In the introductory phase, the organization is small and entrepreneurial. Given its size and substantial technical and market uncertainty, the organization is informal and very loosely structured. These firms are often dominated by an entrepreneur whose energy, enthusiasm and intuition drive the organization. These infant organizations quickly begin to learn about their environments and core technologies, and are flexible enough to adapt to changing conditions.

If successful and sales begin to grow rapidly, the unit must deal with several profound consequences. Increased sales volume will be associated with the development of specialized functional areas, an increase in functional specialists and professionals, increased external competition, increased number of employees, and an increased need for coordination and control. The "garage shop" mentality so appropriate earlier can now kill the business; the loving embrace of the entrepreneur now becomes a stranglehold and chaos ensues (Adizes 1979).

The style and substance of the firm must change as it approaches the transition from the introductory to the growth phase. Alternative business strategies must be articulated, a consistent structure and set of processes and controls must be developed, and individuals must be hired and promoted who can thrive in this more systematic and professional organization. The informal climate must move from ad-hoc and intuitive to one which encourages contention and collaboration between functional areas.

At the introductory-to-growth phase transition, senior management must invest time and energy into administration and integration. The organization must retain its entrepreneurial energy but complement this with administrative energy. This transition is very difficult; many firms fail here or underperform and get bought out. For the entrepreneur there seems to be profound clinical difficulties in recognizing the need to shift styles and being able to change organizational processes (Levinson 1974; Clifford 1972). Similarly, members of the entrepreneurial organization may find it difficult to make the transition from the close-knit organization to the larger and more impersonal professional organization (Levinson 1970).

Those business units making this transition invest substantial resources in reducing or controlling uncertainty. As process innovation increases and product innovation decreases, the organization begins to drive out more and more uncertainty (Thompson 1967; Chandler 1977). Inter-functional conflict, an important source of creative energy early in the growth phase, gradually reduces as the degree of differentiation decreases and as product/process changes become incremental. The mature organization is, then, a logical extension of processes initiated during the growth phase. The organization learns how to plan, organize and control during this period; this learning is translated into SOP's and related processes which are optimized over time. As volume increases and the organization pursues cost reduction, the organization's momentum pushes it into the mature phase of the product life cycle.

There are profound psychological and organization consequences of this extensive and detailed learning. As individuals become committed to a stabilized mode of operation they become more rigid, more insulated, more alike, and they sharply restrict their information processing (Katz 1980). At the organization level, subunits also restrict their information processing, rely more heavily on prior knowledge, and move towards more centralized and formalized structures (Salancik 1977). These inherent consequences of becoming larger and more bureaucratic are functional as long as the unit does not have to change. However, if the unit's technical or market environment changes, it has almost no ability to learn and to adapt to these changes. Indeed, a mature organization's response to substantial threat is to fixate on its routinized behaviors and to further restrict information and control (Abernathy 1978A; Kimberly 1979). This rigidity and inability to learn not only hinders the mature organization's ability to innovate into new technologies or markets, but also makes it very difficult to successfully diversify through acquisition. Mature organizations, with their emphasis on procedures, budgets and rituals, frequently suffocate small entrepreneurial firms (Kitching 1967; Hill and Hlavacek 1977; Quinn 1979).

There are, then, several contradictory forces an organization must deal with to be innovative over the product life cycle. In the introductory phase, the growing organization must begin to systematize and routinize its processes; continued chaos will kill the entrepreneurial firm. As the entrepreneurial organization approaches the growth phase, senior management must seed the organization with individuals who can develop and manage a more professional organization. As the transition approaches, management must legitimize administrative changes and convene a transition team to build, develop and implement the new organization and its associated processes. A climate must be established which balances the entrepreneurial one with the more professional orientation and which tolerates diversity and conflict.

The mature organization has a very different set of problems. Instead of centralizing and further systematizing, the mature organization must create the conditions for an entrepreneurial firm, venture or acquisition to grow; it must permit decentralization and flexibility. Senior management must permit the mature organization to evolve *and* create the conditions for an entrepreneurial unit to grow and develop unencumbered by what the mature business has learned. As this entrepreneurial unit is so different from the dominant business, it must be kept independent and managed systematically different than the dominant business (Galbraith 1974).

In sum, to successfully manage innovation over time, senior management must balance several paradoxes; these paradoxes shift over the product life cycle. Senior management must balance stability with change, consistency with inconsistency, centralization with decentralization, order with disorder, commitment with a tolerance for ambiguity, entrepreneurs with stewards. Those firms who can master these paradoxes over time will be most successful. The role of a manager goes beyond that of a social engineer and a human relations expert to that of an artist; an individual who can creatively synthesize paradoxical demands over the product life cycle.

Research Working Paper No. 380A, November 1980. This work was supported by a grant from the Columbia University Research Fund. The authors wish to thank Morris B. Holbrook and Avi Meshulach for comments on an earlier draft of this paper.

References

Adizes, I. "Organizational Passages: Diagnosing and Treating Life Cycle Problems of Organizations." *Organizational Dynamics*. 8, 1979, 2–25.

Abell, Derek F. and John S. Hammond. *Strategic Marketing Planning*. Englewood Cliffs, N.J.: Prentice-Hall, Inc., 1979.

Abernathy, William J. *The Productivity Dilemma: Roadblock to Innovation in the Automotive Industry*. Baltimore: Johns Hopkins University Press, 1978.

Abernathy, William J. and Phillip J. Townsend. "Technology Productivity and Process Change." *Technological Forecasting and Social Change*, 1975, (7), pp. 379–96.

Abernathy, William J. and James M. Utterback. "Innovation and the Evaluation of Technology in the Firm," working paper #75-18R, Harvard Business School, June, 1976.

Abernathy, William J. and Utterback, James M. "Patterns of Industrial Innovation." *Technology Review,* 1978, (80), pp. 41–47.

Abernathy, William J. and Kenneth Wayne. "Limits of the Learning Curve." *Harvard Business Review,* 1974, (52), pp. 109–19.

Allen, T. J. *Managing the Flow of Technology.* Cambridge: MIT Press, 1977.

Ansoff, H. Igor and John M. Stewart. "Strategies for a Technology-based Business." *Harvard Business Review,* 1967, (45), November–December, pp. 71–83.

Beckhard, R. and R. Harris. *Organizational Transitions.* Reading, Massachusetts: Addison-Wesley, 1977.

Booz-Allen & Hamilton, Inc. *Management of New Products.* New York: Booz-Allen & Hamilton, Inc., 1968.

Boston Consulting Group. *Perspectives on Experience.* Boston: Boston Consulting Group, 1972.

Bright, Arthur A., Jr. *The Electric-Lamp Industry: Technological Change and Economic Development from 1800 to 1947.* New York: MacMillan Co., 1949.

Burns, Tom and G. M. Staulker. *The Management of Innovation.* London: Tavistok Publications, 1961.

Business Week. "Texas Instruments Shows U. S. Business How to Survive in the 1980s." September 18, 1978, pp. 66–76.

Business Week. "Japanese Heat on the Watch Industry." May 5, 1980, pp. 92–106.

Carter, E. and B. Williams. *Industry and Technical Progress.* London: Oxford University Press, 1957.

Chandler, A. *The Visible Hand.* Cambridge, Massachusetts: Harvard University Press, 1977.

Clifford, D. "The Case of the Floundering Founder." *Organizational Dynamics,* 1976, 21–33.

Cooper, Arnold C. "Technical Entrepreneurship: What Do We Know?" *R & D Management,* 3, February, 1973, pp. 59–64.

Cooper, Arnold C. and Dan Schendel. "Strategic Responses to Technological Threat." *Business Horizons,* 1976, (19), pp. 61–69.

Corey, E. Raymond and Steven H. Star. *Organizational Strategy: A Marketing Approach.* Boston: Division of Research, Harvard Business School, 1971.

Dessaur, J. *My Years with Xerox.* New York: Manor Books, 1975.

Enos, John L. *Petroleum Progress and Profits: A History of Process Innovation.* Cambridge, Massachusetts: MIT Press, 1962.

Freeman, Christopher. *The Economics of Industrial Innovation.* Baltimore: Penguin, 1974.

Galbraith, J. *Organization Design.* Reading, Massachusetts: Addison-Wesley, 1974.

Greiner, Larry E. "Evaluation and Revolution as Organizations Grow." *Harvard Business Review,* (50), July–August, 1972, pp. 37–46.

Hall, William K. "Survival Strategies in a Hostile Environment." *Harvard Business Review,* (58), September–October, 1980, pp. 75–85.

Hammermesh, Richard G. and Steven B. Silk. "How to Compete in Stagnant Industries." *Harvard Business Review,* (57), September–October, 1979, pp. 161–168.

Harrigan, K. *Strategies For Declining Businesses.* Lexington, MA.: D.C. Heath, 1980.

Hayes, Robert H. and Roger W. Schmenner. "How Should You Organize for Manufacturing?" *Harvard Business Review,* 1978, pp. 105–118.

Hayes, Robert H. and Steven C. Wheelwright. "Link Manufacturing Process and Product Life Cycles." *Harvard Business Review,* (57), January–February, 1979, pp. 133–140.

Hayes, Robert H. and Steven C. Wheelwright. "The Dynamics of Process Product Life Cycles." *Harvard Business Review,* (57), March-April, 1979, pp. 127–135.

Hill, R. and Hlavacek, J. "Learning from Failure." *California Management Review.* 1977, (14), pp. 5–16.

Hlavacek, James D. "Towards More Successful Venture Management." *Journal of Marketing,* (38), October, 1974, pp. 55–60.

Hollander, Samuel. *The Sources of Increased Efficiency: A Study of DuPont Rayon Plants.* Cambridge, Massachusetts: MIT Press, 1965.

Howard, John A. *Consumer Behavior.* New York: McGraw-Hill, 1977.

Howard, John A. "Management of the Product Market" (working paper), Columbia University, Graduate School of Business, October, 1980.

Kantrow, Alan K. "The Strategy-Technology Connection." *Harvard Business Review,* (57), July–August, 1980, pp. 6–21.

Katz, R. "Time and Work: Toward an Integrative Perspective." In B. Staw and L. Cummings (eds). *Research in Organizational Behavior,* (2), 1980, pp. 81–127.

Kimberly, J. "Issues in the Creation of Organizations." *Academy of Management Journal,* (22), 1979, pp. 437–457.

Kitching, J. "Why Do Mergers Miscarry." *Harvard Business Review,* November, 1967, pp. 84–101.

Knight, Kenneth E. "A Study of Technological Innovation— The Evolution of Digital Computers." Unpublished Ph.D. dissertation, Carnegie Institute of Technology, 1963.

Lawrence, Paul R. and Jay W. Lorsch. *Organization and Environment: Managing Differentiation and Integration.* Boston: Division of Research, Harvard Business School, 1967.

Levinson, H. "A Psychologist Diagnoses Merger Failures." *Harvard Business Review,* April, 1970, pp. 139–147.

Levinson, H. *The Great Jackass Fallacy.* Boston: Harvard University Press, 1973.

Levitt, Theodore. "Marketing Success Through Differentiation of Anything." *Harvard Business Review,* (58), January–February, 1980, pp. 83–91.

MacMillan, I. *Strategy Formulation: Political Concepts.* New York: West Publishing, 1978.

Maidique, Modesto A. "Entrepreneur Champions and Technological Innovation." *Sloan Management Review,* Winter, 1980.

Mansfield, E. "Research and Development, Productivity, and Inflation." *Science,* (209), 1980, pp. 1091–1093.

Mansfield, E. and S. Wagner. "Organizational and Strategic Factors Associated with Probabilities of Success in Industrial Research." *Journal of Business,* (48), 1975, pp. 179–198.

March, J. and H. Simon. *Organizations.* New York: Wiley and Co., 1958.

Miles, R. and C. Snow. *Organizational Strategy, Structure and Process.* New York: McGraw-Hill, 1978.

Miller, R. E. and D. Sawers. *The Technical Development of Modern Aviation.* New York: Praeger Publishers, 1970.

Mintzberg, H. "Patterns in Strategy Formulation." *Management Science,* (24), 1978, pp. 934–948.

Myers, Sumner and Donald G. Marquis. *Successful Commercial Innovations NSF 69-71.* Washington, D. C.: National Science Foundation, 1969.

Nadler, D. and M. Tushman. "A Congruence Model for Diagnosing Organizations" *Organizational Dynamics.* Winter 1980.

Nystrom, Harry. *Creativity and Innovation.* New York: John Wiley & Sons, 1979.

Pelz, D. and F. Andrews. *Scientists in Organizations.* New York: Wiley and Co., 1966.

Phillips, Almarin. *Technology and Market Structure: A Study of the Aircraft Industry.* Lexington, Massachusetts: Heath Lexington Books, 1971.

Polli, Rolando and Victor Cook. "Validity of the Product Life Cycle." *Journal of Business,* October, 1969, pp. 385–400.

Quinn, James Brian. "Technological Innovation, Entrepreneurship and Strategy." *Sloan Management Review,* Spring, 1979, pp. 19–29.

Ritti, R. *The Engineer in the Industrial Corporation.* New York: Columbia University Press, 1971.

Roberts, Edward B. "Generating Effective Corporate Innovation." *Technology Review,* 1977, pp. 27–33.

Roberts, Edward B. "New Ventures for Corporate Growth." *Harvard Business Review,* (57), July–August, 1980, pp. 134–142.

Roberts, E. and A. Frohman. "Internal Entrepreneurship: Strategy for Growth." *Business Quarterly,* 1972, pp. 71–78.

Salancik, J. "Commitment and the Control of Organizational Behavior and Belief." In Staw, B. and J. Salancik (eds). *New Directions in Organizational Behavior.* Chicago: St. Clair Press, 1977.

Schein, E. *Career Dynamics.* Reading, Massachusetts: Addison-Wesley, 1978.

Schmookler, J. *Invention and Economic Growth.* Cambridge: Harvard University Press, 1966.

Sherwin, C. and R. Isenson. "Project Hindsight." *Science,* (156), 1967, 1571–1577.

Skinner, Wickham. "Manufacturing—Missing Link in Corporate Strategy." *Harvard Business Review,* May–June, 1969, pp. 136–145.

Skinner, Wickham. "The Focused Factory." *Harvard Business Review,* May–June, 1974, pp. 113–120.

Skinner, Wickham. *Manufacturing in the Corporate Strategy.* New York: John Wiley and Sons, Inc., 1978.

Sommers, William P. *Product Development: New Approaches in the 1980's.* New York: Booz-Allen & Hamilton, Inc., 1979.

Steele, L. *Innovation in Big Business.* New York: Elsevier-North Holland, 1975.

Thompson, J. *Organizations in Action.* New York: McGraw-Hill, 1967.

Tilton, John E. *International Diffusion of Technology: The Case of Semiconductors.* Washington, D. C.: Brookings Institute, 1971.

Time. "Detroit's Uphill Battle." September 8, 1980, pp. 46–54.

Tushman, Michael L. "Managing Communication Networks in R & D Laboratories." *Sloan Management Review,* 1979, pp. 37–49.

Tushman, Michael L. and David A. Nadler. "Information Processing as an Integrating Concept in Organizational Design." *Academy of Management Review,* July, 1978, pp. 613–624.

Utterback, James M. "Innovation and the Difficulty of Technology." *Science,* (183), 1974, pp. 620–26.

Utterback, James M. "The Dynamics of Production Process Innovation in Industry." In Hill, Christopher T. and James Utterback (eds.) *Technology Innovation for a Dynamic Economy.* New York: Pergamon Press, 1980, pp. 40–65.

Von Hipple, Eric. "Successful Industrial Products from Customer Ideas." *Journal of Marketing,* January, 1978, pp. 39–49.

White, George R. "Management Criteria for Executive Innovation." *Technology Review,* February, 1978, pp. 15–23.

White, George R. and Margaret B. W. Graham, "How to Spot a Technological Winner." *Harvard Business Review*, (56), March–April, 19 ** pp. –146.

Woodward, Joan. *Industrial Organization: Theory and Practice.* London: Oxford University Press, 1965.

Wright, Robert V. L. *A System For Managing Diversity.* Cambridge, Massachusetts: Arthur D. Little, Inc., 1974.

13

ELEMENTS OF DIFFUSION

Everett M. Rogers

> There is nothing more difficult to plan, more doubtful of success, nor more dangerous to manage than the creation of a new order of things. . . . Whenever his enemies have the ability to attack the innovator they do so with the passion of partisans, while the others defend him sluggishly, so that the innovator and his party alike are vulnerable.
>
> —Niccolò Machiavelli, *The Prince*

Getting a new idea adopted, even when it has obvious advantages, is often very difficult. Many innovations require a lengthy period, often of many years, from the time they become available to the time they are widely adopted. Therefore, a common problem for many individuals and organizations is how to speed up the rate of diffusion of an innovation.

The following case illustration provides insight into some common difficulties facing diffusion campaigns.

WATER BOILING IN A PERUVIAN VILLAGE: DIFFUSION THAT FAILED

The public health service in Peru attempts to introduce innovations to villagers to improve their health and lengthen their lives. This change agency encourages people to install latrines, to burn garbage daily, to control house flies, to report cases of infectious diseases, and to boil drinking water. These innovations involve major changes in thinking and behavior for Peruvian villagers, who do not understand the relationship of sanitation to illness. Water boiling is an especially important health practice for villagers in Peru. Unless they boil their drinking water, patients who are cured of infectious diseases in village medical clinics often return within a month to be treated again for the same disease.

A two-year water boiling campaign conducted in Los Molinas, a peasant village of 200 families in the coastal region of Peru, persuaded only eleven housewives to boil water. From the viewpoint of the public health agency, the local health worker, Nelida, had a simple task: to persuade the housewives of Los Molinas

to add water boiling to their pattern of daily behavior. Even with the aid of a medical doctor, who gave public talks on water boiling, and fifteen village housewives who were already boiling water before the campaign, Nelida's diffusion campaign failed. To understand why, we need to take a closer look at the culture, the local environment, and the individuals in Los Molinas.

Most residents of Los Molinas are peasants who work as field hands on local plantations. Water is carried by can, pail, gourd, or cask. The three sources of water in Los Molinas include a seasonal irrigation ditch close to the village, a spring more than a mile away from the village, and a public well whose water most villagers dislike. All three sources are subject to pollution at all times and show contamination whenever tested. Of the three sources, the irrigation ditch is the most commonly used. It is closer to most homes, and the villagers like its taste.

Although it is not feasible for the village to install a sanitary water system, the incidence of typhoid and

---

other water-borne diseases could be greatly reduced by boiling the water before it is consumed. During her two-year campaign in Los Molinas, Nelida made several visits to every home in the village but devoted especially intensive efforts to twenty-one families. She visited each of these selected families between fifteen and twenty-five times; eleven of these families now boil their water regularly.

What kinds of persons do these numbers represent? We describe three village housewives—one who boils water to obey custom, one who was persuaded to boil water by the health worker, and one of the many who rejected the innovation—in order to add further insight into the process of diffusion.

Mrs. A: Custom-Oriented Adopter. Mrs. A is about forty and suffers from a sinus infection. The Los Molinas villagers call her a "sickly one." Each morning, Mrs. A boils a potful of water and uses it throughout the day. She has no understanding of germ theory, as explained by Nelida; her motivation for water boiling is a complex local custom of "hot" and "cold" distinctions. The basic principle of this belief system is that all foods, liquids, medicines, and other objects are inherently hot or cold, quite apart from their actual temperature. In essence, hot-cold distinctions serve as a series of avoidances and approaches in such behavior as pregnancy, child-rearing, and the health-illness system.

Boiled water and illness are closely linked in the norms of Los Molinas; by custom, only the ill use cooked, or "hot" water. Once an individual becomes ill, it is unthinkable to eat pork (very cold) or drink brandy (very hot). Extremes of hot and cold must be avoided by the sick; therefore, raw water, which is perceived to be very cold, must be boiled to make it appropriate to consume.

Villagers learn from early childhood to dislike boiled water. Most can tolerate cooked water only if a flavoring, such as sugar, cinnamon, lemon, or herbs, is added. Mrs. A likes a dash of cinnamon in her drinking water. The village belief system involves no notion of bacteriorological contamination of water. By tradition, boiling is aimed at eliminating the "cold" quality of unboiled water, not the harmful bacteria. Mrs. A drinks boiled water in obedience to local norms, because she perceives herself as ill.

Mrs. B: Persuaded Adopter. The B family came to Los Molinas a generation ago, but they are still strongly oriented toward their birthplace in the Andes Mountains. Mrs. B worries about lowland diseases that she feels infest the village. It is partly because of this anxiety that the change agent, Nelida, was able to convince Mrs. B to boil water.

Nelida is a friendly authority to Mrs. B (rather than a "dirt inspector" as she is seen by other housewives), who imparts useful knowledge and brings protection. Mrs. B not only boils water but also has installed a latrine and has sent her youngest child to the health center for a checkup.

Mrs. B is marked as an outsider in the community of Los Molinas by her highland hairdo and stumbling Spanish. She will never achieve more than marginal social acceptance in the village. Because the community is not an important reference group to her, Mrs. B deviates from village norms on health innovations. With nothing to lose socially, Mrs. B gains in personal security by heeding Nelida's advice. Mrs. B's practice of boiling water has no effect on her marginal status. She is grateful to Nelida for teaching her how to neutralize the danger of contaminated water, which she perceives as a lowland peril.

Mrs. C: Rejector. This housewife represents the majority of Los Molinas families who were not persuaded by the efforts of the change agents during their two-year water-boiling campaign. In spite of Nelida's repeated explanations, Mrs. C does not understand germ theory. How, she argues, can microbes survive in water that would drown people? Are they fish? If germs are so small that they cannot be seen or felt, how can they hurt a grown person? There are enough real threats in the world to worry about—poverty and hunger—without bothering about tiny animals one cannot see, hear, touch, or smell. Mrs. C's allegiance to traditional village norms is at odds with the boiling of water. A firm believer in the hot-cold superstition, she feels that only the sick must drink boiled water.

WHY DID THE DIFFUSION OF WATER BOILING FAIL?

This intensive two-year campaign by a public health worker in a Peruvian village of 200 families, aimed at persuading housewives to boil drinking water, was largely unsuccessful. Nelida was able to encourage only about 5 percent of the population, eleven families, to adopt the innovation. The diffusion campaign in Los Molinas failed because of the cultural beliefs of the villagers. Local tradition links hot foods with illness. Boiling water makes water less "cold" and hence, appropriate only for the sick. But if a person is not ill, the individual is prohibited by village norms from drinking boiled water. Only individuals who are unintegrated into local networks risk defying community norms on water boiling. An important factor regarding the adoption rate of an innovation is its compatibility with the values, beliefs, and past experiences of individuals in the social system. Nelida and her superiors in the public health agency should have understood the hot–cold belief system, as it is found throughout Peru (and in most nations of Latin America, Africa, and Asia). Here is an example of an indigenous knowledge system that caused the failure of a development program.

(Continued)

Nelida's failure demonstrates the importance of interpersonal networks in the adoption and rejection of an innovation. Socially an outsider, Mrs. B was marginal to the Los Molinas community, although she had lived there for several years. Nelida was a more important referent for Mrs. B than were her neighbors, who shunned her. Anxious to secure social prestige from the higher-status Nelida, Mrs. B adopted water boiling, not because she understood the correct health reasons, but because she wanted to obtain Nelida's approval. Thus we see that the diffusion of innovations is a social process, as well as a technical matter.

Nelida worked with the wrong housewives if she wanted to launch a self-generating diffusion process in Los Molinas. She concentrated her efforts on village women like Mrs. A and Mrs. B. Unfortunately, they were perceived as a sickly one and a social outsider, and were not respected as social models of appropriate water-boiling behavior by the other women. The village opinion leaders, who could have activated local networks to spread the innovation, were ignored by Nelida.

How potential adopters view the change agent affects their willingness to adopt new ideas. In Los Molinas, Nelida was perceived differently by lower- and middle-status housewives. Most poor families saw the health worker as a "snooper" sent to Los Molinas to pry for dirt and to press already harassed housewives into keeping cleaner homes. Because the lower-status housewives had less free time, they were unlikely to talk with Nelida about water boiling. Their contacts outside the community were limited, and as a result, they saw the technically proficient Nelida with eyes bound by the social horizons and traditional beliefs of Los Molinas. They distrusted this outsider, whom they perceived as a social stranger. Nelida, who was middle class by Los Molinas standards, was able to secure more positive results from housewives whose socioeconomic level and cultural background were more similar to hers. This tendency for more effective communication to occur with those who are more similar to a change agent occurs in most diffusion campaigns.

Nelida was too "innovation-oriented" and not "client-oriented" enough. Unable to put herself in the role of the village housewives, her attempts at persuasion failed to reach her clients because the message was not suited to their needs. Nelida did not begin where the villagers were; instead she talked to them about germ theory, which they could not (and probably did not need to) understand. These are only some of the factors that produced the diffusion failure in Los Molinas. Once the remainder of the book has been read, it will be easier to understand the water-boiling case.

This case illustration is based on Wellin (1955).

WHAT IS DIFFUSION?

Diffusion is the process by which an innovation is communicated through certain channels over time among the members of a social system. It is a special type of communication, in that the messages are concerned with new ideas. *Communication* is a process in which participants create and share information with one another in order to reach a mutual understanding. This definition implies that communication is a process of convergence (or divergence) as two or more individuals exchange information in order to move toward each other (or apart) in the meanings that they give to certain events. We think of communication as a two-way process of convergence, rather than as a one-way, linear act in which one individual seeks to transfer a message to another in order to achieve certain effects (Rogers and Kincaid, 1981). A linear conception of human communication may accurately describe certain communication acts or events involved in diffusion, such as when a change agent seeks to persuade a client to adopt an innovation. But when we look at what came before such an event, and at what follows, we often realize that the event is only one part of a total process in which information is exchanged between the two individuals. For example, the client may come to the change agent with a problem, and the innovation is recommended as a possible solution to this need. The change agent–client interaction may continue through several cycles, as a process of information exchange.

So diffusion is a special type of communication, in which the messages are about a new idea. This newness of the idea in the message content gives diffusion its special character. The newness means that some degree of uncertainty is involved in diffusion.

Uncertainty is the degree to which a number of alternatives are perceived with respect to the occurrence of an event and the relative probability of these alternatives. Uncertainty implies a lack of predictability, of structure, of information. In fact, information is a means of reducing uncertainty. *Information* is a difference in matter–energy that affects uncertainty in a situation where a choice exists among a set of alternatives (Rogers and Kincaid, 1981, p. 64). By differences in matter–energy we mean inked letters on paper, sound waves traveling through the air, or an electrical current in a copper wire. Information can thus take many forms, as matter or energy. A technological innovation embodies information and thus reduces uncertainty about cause–effect relationships in problem-solving. For instance, adoption of residential solar panels for water heating reduces uncertainty about future increases in the cost of fuel.

Diffusion is a kind of *social change,* defined as the process by which alteration occurs in the structure and function of a social system. When new ideas are invented, diffused, and are adopted or rejected, leading to certain consequences, social change occurs. Of course, such change can happen in other ways, too, for example, through a political revolution, through a natural event like a drought or an earthquake, or by means of a government regulation.

Some authors restrict the term "diffusion" to the spontaneous, unplanned spread of new ideas, and use the concept of "dissemination" for diffusion that is directed and managed. In this book we use the word "diffusion" to include both the planned and the spontaneous spread of new ideas.

CONTROLLING SCURVY IN THE BRITISH NAVY: INNOVATIONS DO NOT SELL THEMSELVES

Many technologists believe that advantageous innovations will sell themselves, that the obvious benefits of a new idea will be widely realized by potential adopters, and that the innovation will therefore diffuse rapidly. Seldom is this the case. Most innovations, in fact, diffuse at a disappointingly slow rate.

Scurvy control illustrates how slowly an obviously beneficial innovation spreads (Mosteller, 1981). In the early days of long sea voyages, scurvy was a worse killer of sailors than warfare, accidents, and all other causes of death. For instance, of Vasco de Gama's crew of 160 men who sailed with him around the Cape of Good Hope in 1497, 100 died of scurvy. In 1601, an English sea captain, James Lancaster, conducted an experiment to evaluate the effectiveness of lemon juice in preventing scurvy. Captain Lancaster commanded four ships that sailed from England on a voyage to India; he served three teaspoonfuls of lemon juice every day to the sailors in one of his four ships. Most of these men stayed healthy. But on the other three ships, by the halfway point in the journey, 110 out of 278 sailors had died from scurvy. The three ships constituted Lancaster's "control group"; they were not given any lemon juice. So many of these sailors became sick that Lancaster had to transfer men from his "treatment" ship in order to staff the three other ships.

The results were so clear that one would expect the British Navy to adopt citrus juice for scurvy prevention on all its ships. But it was not until 1747, *about 150 years later,* that James Lind, a British Navy physician who knew of Lancaster's results, carried out another experiment on the *HMS Salisbury.* To each scurvy patient on this ship, Lind prescribed either two

oranges and one lemon, or one of five other diets: A half-pint of sea water, six spoonfuls of vinegar, a quart of cider, nutmeg, or seventy-five drops of vitriol elixir. The scurvy patients who got the citrus fruits were cured in a few days, and were able to help Dr. Lind care for the other patients. Unfortunately, the supply of oranges and lemons was exhausted in six days.

Certainly, with this further solid evidence of the ability of citrus fruits to combat scurvy, one would expect the British Navy to adopt this technological innovation for all ship's crews on long sea voyages, and in fact, it did so. *But not until 1795, forty-eight years later.* Scurvy was immediately wiped out. And after only *seventy more years,* in 1865, the British Board of Trade adopted a similar policy, and eradicated scurvy in the merchant marine.

Why were the authorities so slow to adopt the idea of citrus for scurvy prevention? A clear explanation is not available, but other, competing remedies for scurvy were also being proposed, and each such cure had its champions. For example, Captain Cook's reports from his voyages in the Pacific did not provide support for curing scurvy with citrus fruits. Further, Dr. Lind was not a prominent figure in the field of naval medicine, and so his experimental findings did not get much attention in the British Navy. While scurvy prevention was generally resisted for years by the British Navy, other innovations like new ships and new guns were accepted readily. So the Admiralty did not resist all innovations.

This case illustration is based on Mosteller (1981).

Obviously more than just a beneficial innovation is necessary for its diffusion and adoption to occur. The reader may think that such slow diffusion could happen only in the distant past, before a scientific and experimental approach to evaluating innovations. We answer by calling the reader's attention to the contemporary case of the nondiffusion of the Dvorak typewriter keyboard.

NONDIFFUSION OF THE DVORAK KEYBOARD

Most of us who use a typewriter or who do word processing on a computer do not realize that our fingers tap out words on a keyboard that is called "QWERTY," named after the first six keys on the upper row of letters. The QWERTY keyboard is inefficient and awkward. This typewriter keyboard takes twice as long to learn as it should, and makes us work about twenty times harder than is necessary. But QWERTY has persisted since 1873, and today unsuspecting individuals are being taught to use the QWERTY keyboard, unaware that a much more efficient typewriter keyboard is available.

Where did QWERTY come from? Why does it continue to be used, instead of much more efficient alternative keyboard designs? QWERTY was invented by Christopher Latham Sholes, who designed this keyboard to slow down typists. In that day, the typebars on a typewriter hung down in a sort of basket, and pivoted up to strike the paper; then they fell back in place by gravity. When two adjoining keys were struck rapidly in succession, they jammed. Sholes rearranged the keys on a typewriter keyboard to minimize such jamming; he "anti-engineered" the arrangement to make the most commonly used letter sequences awkward. By thus making it difficult for a typist to operate the machine, and slowing down typing speed, Sholes' QWERTY keyboard allowed these early typewriters to operate satisfactorily. His design was used in the manufacture of all typewriters. Early typewriter salesmen could impress customers by pecking out "TYPEWRITER" as all of the letters necessary to spell this word were found in one row of the QWERTYUIOP machine.

Prior to about 1900, most typists used the two-finger, hunt-and-peck system. Later, as touch typing became popular, dissatisfaction with the QWERTY typewriter began to grow. Typewriters became mechanically more efficient, and the QWERTY keyboard design was no longer necessary to prevent key jamming. The search for an improved design was led by Professor August Dvorak at the University of Washington, who in 1932 used time-and-motion studies to create a much more efficient keyboard arrangement. The Dvorak keyboard has the letters A, O, E, U, I, D, H, T, N, and S across the home row of the typewriter. Less frequently used letters were placed on the upper and lower rows of keys. About 70 percent of typing is done on the home row, 22 percent on the upper row, and 8 percent on the lower row.

On the Dvorak keyboard, the amount of work assigned to each finger is proportionate to its skill and strength. Further, Professor Dvorak engineered his keyboard so that successive keystrokes fell on alternative hands; thus, while a finger on one hand is stroking a key, a finger on the other hand can be moving into position to hit the next key. Typing rhythm is thus facilitated; this hand alternation was achieved by putting the vowels (which represent 40 percent of all letters typed) on the left-hand side, and placing the major consonants that usually accompany these vowels on the right-hand side of the keyboard.

Professor Dvorak was thus able to avoid the typing inefficiencies of the QWERTY keyboard. For instance, QWERTY overloads the left hand, which must type 57 percent of ordinary copy. The Dvorak keyboard shifts this emphasis to 56 percent on the stronger right hand and 44 percent on the weaker left hand. Only 32 percent of typing is done on the home row with the QWERTY system, compared to 70 percent with the Dvorak keyboard. The newer arrangement requires less jumping back and forth from row to row; with the QWERTY keyboard, a good typists' fingertips travel more than twelve miles a day, jumping from row to row. These unnecessary intricate movements cause mental tension, typist fatigue, and lead to more typographical errors.

One might expect, on the basis of its overwhelming advantages, that the Dvorak keyboard would have completely replaced the inferior QWERTY keyboard. On the contrary, after more than 50 years, almost all typists are still using the inefficient QWERTY keyboard. Even though the American National Standards Institute and the Equipment Manufacturers Association have approved the Dvorak keyboard as an alternate design, it is still almost impossible to find a typewriter or a computer keyboard that is arranged in the more efficient layout. Vested interests are involved in hewing to the old design: Manufacturers, sales outlets, typing teachers, and typists themselves.

No, technological innovations are not always diffused and adopted rapidly. Even when the innovation has obvious, proven advantages.

As the reader may have guessed by now, the present pages were typed on a QWERTY keyboard.

Details on resistance to the Dvorak keyboard may be found in Dvorak and others (1936), Parkinson (1972), Lessley (1980), and David (1986a).

FOUR MAIN ELEMENTS IN THE DIFFUSION OF INNOVATIONS

Previously we defined *diffusion* as the process by which an *innovation* is *communicated* through certain *channels* over *time* among the members of a *social system.* The four main elements are the innovation, communication channels, time, and the social system (Figure 13-1). These elements are identifiable in every diffusion research study, and in every diffusion campaign or program (like the diffusion of water-boiling in a Peruvian village).

The following description of these four elements in diffusion constitutes an overview of the main concepts that will be detailed in Chapters 2 through 11.

The Innovation

An *innovation* is an idea, practice, or object that is perceived as new by an individual or other unit of adoption. It matters little, so far as human behavior is concerned, whether or not an idea is objectively new as measured by the lapse of time since its first use or discovery. The perceived newness of the idea for the individual determines his or her reaction to it. If the idea seems new to the individual, it is an innovation.

Newness in an innovation need not just involve new knowledge. Someone may have known about an innovation for some time but not yet developed a favorable or unfavorable attitude toward it, nor have adopted or rejected it. "Newness" of an innovation may be expressed in terms of knowledge, persuasion, or a decision to adopt.

Among the important research questions addressed by diffusion scholars are (1) how the earlier adopters differ from the later adopters of an innovation (Chapter 7); (2) how the perceived attributes of an innovation, such as its relative advantage or compatibility affect its rate of adoption, whether relatively rapidly (as for Innovation I in Figure 13-1) or more slowly (Innovation III), as is detailed in Chapter 6; and (3) why the S-shaped diffusion curve "takes off" at about 10- to 25-percent adoption, when interpersonal networks become activated so that a critical mass of adopters begins using an innovation (Chapter 8). It should not be assumed that the diffusion and adoption of all innovations are necessarily desirable. Some harmful and uneconomical innovations are not desirable for either the individual or the social system. Further, the same innovation may be desirable for one adopter in one situation, but undesirable for another potential adopter in a different situation. For example, mechanical tomato-pickers

FIGURE 13-1 Diffusion Is the Process by Which (1) An *Innovation* (2) Is *Communicated* Through Certain *Channels* (3) Over *Time* (4) Among the Members of a *Social System*

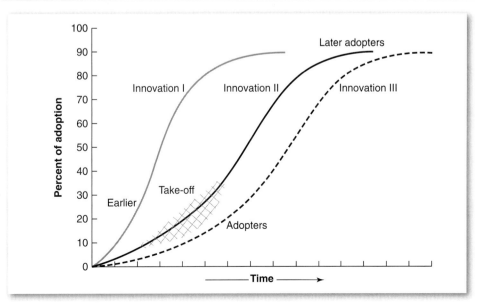

have been adopted rapidly by large commercial farmers in California, but these machines were too expensive for small tomato growers, and thousands of farmers have thus been forced out of tomato production.

Technological Innovations, Information, and Uncertainty

Most of the new ideas analyzed in this book are technological innovations, and we often use the word "innovation" and "technology" as synonyms. A *technology* is a design for instrumental action that reduces the uncertainty in the cause-effect relationships involved in achieving a desired outcome.[1] A technology usually has two components: (1) a *hardware* aspect, consisting of the tool that embodies the technology as a material or physical object, and (2) a *software* aspect, consisting of the information base for the tool. For example, we often speak of (1) "computer hardware" consisting of semiconductors, transistors, electrical connections, and the metal frame to protect these electronic components, and (2) "computer software" consisting of the coded commands, instructions, and other information aspects of this tool that allow us to use it to extend human capabilities in solving certain problems. Here we see an illustration of the close relationship between a tool and the way it is used.

The social embedding of the hardware aspects of a technology is usually less visible than its machinery or equipment, and so we often think of technology mainly in hardware terms. Indeed, sometimes the hardware side of a technology is dominant. But in other cases, a technology may be almost entirely composed of information; examples are a political philosophy like Marxism, a religious idea, a news event, a rumor, assembly-line production, and quality circles. The diffusion of such software innovations has been investigated, although a methodological problem in such studies is that their adoption cannot be so easily traced or observed in a physical sense.

A number of new products involve a hardware component and a software component, with the hardware purchased first so that the software component can then be utilized. Examples are VCRs and videotapes, cameras and film, and compact disc players and CDs. Often a company will sell the hardware product at a relatively low price in order to capture market share, and then sell the software at a relatively high price in order to recover profits (Bayus, 1987). An example is the Nintendo game-player, which is sold at a fairly low price (about $100), but with each Nintendo video game sold at a relatively high price (about $60). This is sometimes called a shaver-and-blades strategy.

Some innovations only have a software component, which means they have a relatively lower degree of observability and thus a slower rate of innovation. Such idea-only innovations have seldom been studied by diffusion scholars, perhaps because their spread is relatively difficult to trace.

Even though the software component of a technology is often not so easy to observe, we should not forget that technology almost always represents a mixture of hardware and software aspects. According to our definition, technology is a means of uncertainty reduction that is made possible by information about the cause-effect relationships on which the technology is based. This information often results from scientific R&D activities when the technology is being developed. A technological innovation usually has at least some degree of benefit for its potential adopters. This advantage is not always very clear-cut, at least not to the intended adopters. They are seldom certain that an innovation represents a superior alternative to the previous practice that it might replace.

So a technological innovation creates one kind of uncertainty (about its expected consequences) in the mind of potential adopters, as well as representing an opportunity for reduced uncertainty in another sense (reduced by the information base of the technology). The latter type of potential uncertainty reduction (from the information embodied in the technological innovation itself) represents the possible efficacy of the innovation in solving an individual's perceived problem; this advantage provides the motivation that impels an individual to exert effort in order to learn about the innovation. Once such information-seeking activities have reduced the uncertainty about the innovation's expected consequences to a tolerable level for the individual, a decision concerning adoption or rejection will be made. If a new idea is used by an individual, further evaluative information about its effects is obtained. Thus, the innovation-decision process is essentially an information-seeking and information-processing activity in which the individual is motivated to reduce uncertainty about the advantages and disadvantages of the innovation (see Chapter 5).

We distinguish two kinds of information in respect to a technological innovation.

1. *Software information,* which is embodied in a technology and serves to reduce uncertainty about the cause-effect relationships in achieving a desired outcome.

2. *Innovation-evaluation information,* which is the reduction in uncertainty about an innovation's expected consequences.

The main questions that an individual typically asks in regard to software information are, "What is the innovation?" "How does it work?" and "Why does it work?" In contrast, an individual usually wants to know such innovation-evaluation information as, "What are an innovation's consequences?" and "What will its advantages and disadvantages be in my situation?"

Technology Clusters

An important conceptual and methodological issue is to determine the boundaries around a technological innovation. The practical problem is how to determine where one innovation stops and another begins. If an innovation is an idea that is perceived as new, this boundary between innovations ought to be determined by the potential adopters who do the perceiving. In fact, this approach is used by diffusion scholars and by market researchers in positioning studies (described in Chapter 6). For example, a California study of the diffusion of recycling found that households that recycled paper were also likely to recycle bottles and cans, although many families only recycled paper (Leonard-Barton and Rogers, 1980); presumably the two recycling behaviors represented two innovations that were part of an interrelated cluster of recycling ideas. A *technology cluster* consists of one or more distinguishable elements of technology that are perceived as being closely interrelated. Some change agencies promote a package of innovations because they find that the innovations are thus adopted more rapidly. An example of a technology cluster was the package of rice- or wheat-growing innovations that led to the Green Revolution in the Third World countries of Latin America, Africa, and Asia. In addition to the so-called miracle varieties of rice or wheat, the cluster included chemical fertilizers, pesticides, and thicker planting of the seeds.

Past diffusion research has generally investigated each innovation as if it were independent from other innovations. This is a dubious assumption, in that an adopter's experience with one innovation obviously influences that individual's perception of the next innovation to diffuse through the individual's system. In reality, a set of innovations diffusing at about the same time in a system are interdependent. It is much simpler for diffusion scholars to investigate the spread of each innovation as an independent event, but this is a distortion of reality.

Characteristics of Innovations

It should not be assumed, as it sometimes has in the past, that all innovations are equivalent units of analysis. This assumption is a gross oversimplification. While consumer innovations like mobile telephones or VCRs may require only a few years to reach widespread adoption in the United States, other new ideas such as the metric system or using seat belts in cars require decades to reach complete use. The characteristics of innovations, as perceived by individuals, help to explain their different rate of adoption.

1. *Relative advantage* is the degree to which an innovation is perceived as better than the idea it supersedes. The degree of relative advantage may be measured in economic terms, but social prestige, convenience, and satisfaction are also important factors. It does not matter so much if an innovation has a great deal of objective advantage. What does matter is whether an individual perceives the innovation as advantageous. The greater the perceived relative advantage of an innovation, the more rapid its rate of adoption will be.

2. *Compatibility* is the degree to which an innovation is perceived as being consistent with the existing values, past experiences, and needs of potential adopters. An idea that is incompatible with the values and norms of a social system will not be adopted as rapidly as an innovation that is compatible. The adoption of an incompatible innovation often requires the prior adoption of a new value system which is a relatively slow process. An example of an incompatible innovation is the use of contraceptive methods in countries where religious beliefs discourage use of family planning, as in Moslem and Catholic nations. Previously in this chapter we saw how the innovation of water boiling was incompatible with the hot-cold complex in the Peruvian village of Los Molinas.

3. *Complexity* is the degree to which an innovation is perceived as difficult to understand and use. Some innovations are readily understood by most members of a social system; others are more complicated and will be adopted more slowly. For example, the villagers in Los Molinas did not understand germ theory, which the health worker tried to explain to them as a reason for boiling their drinking water. New ideas that are simpler to understand are adopted more rapidly than innovations that require the adopter to develop new skills and understandings.

4. *Trialability* is the degree to which an innovation may be experimented with on a limited basis. New ideas that can be tried on the installment plan will generally be adopted more quickly than innovations that are not divisible. Ryan and Gross (1943) found that every one of their Iowa farmer respondents adopted hybrid seed corn by first trying it on a partial basis. If the new seed could not have been sampled experimentally, its rate of adoption would have been much slower. An innovation that is trialable represents less uncertainty to the individual who is considering it for adoption, as it is possible to learn by doing.

5. *Observability* is the degree to which the results of an innovation are visible to others. The easier it is for individuals to see the results of an innovation, the more likely they are to adopt it. Such visibility stimulates peer discussion of a new idea, as friends and neighbors of an adopter often request innovation-evaluation information about it. Solar adopters often are found in neighborhood clusters in California, with three or four adopters located on the same block. Other consumer innovations like home computers are relatively less observable, and thus diffuse more slowly.

Innovations that are perceived by individuals as having greater relative advantage, compatibility, trialability, observability, and less complexity will be adopted more rapidly than other innovations. Past research indicates that these five qualities are the most important characteristics of innovations in explaining the rate of adoption.

Re-Invention

For the first several decades of diffusion research, it was assumed that an innovation was an invariant quality that did not change as it diffused. I remember interviewing an Iowa farmer years ago about his adoption of 2,4-D weed spray. In answer to my question about whether or not he had adopted this innovation, the farmer described in some detail the particular and unusual ways in which he used the weed spray on his farm. At the end of his remarks, I simply checked "adopter" on my questionnaire. The concept of re-invention was not yet in my theoretical repertoire, so I condensed the farmer's experience into one of my existing categories.

In the 1970s, diffusion scholars began to study the concept of *re-invention,* defined as the degree to which an innovation is changed or modified by a user in the process of its adoption and implementation. Some researchers measure re-invention as the degree to which an individual's use of a new idea departs from the mainline version of the innovation that was originally promoted by a change agency (Eveland and others, 1977). Once scholars became aware of the concept of re-invention and began to measure it, they began to find that a considerable degree of re-invention occurred for many innovations. Some innovations are difficult or impossible to re-invent; for example, hybrid seed corn does not allow a farmer much freedom to re-invent, as the hybrid vigor is genetically locked into the seed for the first generation in ways that are too complicated for a farmer to change. Certain other innovations are more flexible in nature, and they are re-invented by many adopters who implement them in a wide variety of different ways. An innovation is not necessarily invariant during the process of its diffusion. And adopting an innovation is not necessarily the passive role of just implementing a standard template of the new idea.

Given that an innovation exists, communication must take place if the innovation is to spread. Now we turn our attention to this second element in the diffusion process.

Communication Channels

Previously we defined *communication* as the process by which participants create and share information with one another in order to reach a mutual understanding. Diffusion is a particular type of communication in which the message content that is exchanged is concerned with a new idea. The essence of the diffusion process is the information exchange through which one individual communicates a new idea to one or several others. At its most elementary form, the process involves (1) an innovation, (2) an individual or other unit of adoption that has knowledge of the innovation or experience with using it, (3) another individual or other unit that does not yet have experience with the innovation, and (4) a communication channel connecting the two units. A *communication channel* is the means by which messages get from one individual to another. The nature of the information-exchange relationship between a pair of individuals determines the conditions under which a source will or will not transmit the innovation to the receiver, and the effect of the transfer.

Mass media channels are often the most rapid and efficient means to inform an audience of potential adopters about the existence of an innovation, that is, to create awareness-knowledge. *Mass media channels* are all those means of transmitting messages that involve a mass medium, such as radio, television, newspapers, and so on, which enable a source of one or a few individuals to reach an audience of many. On the other hand, interpersonal channels are more effective in persuading an individual to accept a new idea, especially if the interpersonal channel links two or more individuals who are similar in socioeconomic status, education, or other important ways. *Interpersonal channels* involve a face-to-face exchange between two or more individuals.

Diffusion investigations show that most individuals do not evaluate an innovation on the basis of scientific studies of its consequences, although such objective evaluations are not entirely irrelevant, especially to the very first individuals who adopt. Instead, most people depend mainly upon a subjective evaluation of an innovation that is conveyed to them from other individuals like themselves who have previously adopted the innovation. This dependence on the experience of near peers suggests that the heart of the diffusion process consists of the modeling and imitation by potential adopters of their network partners who have adopted previously. So diffusion is a very social process (see Chapter 8).

Heterophily and Diffusion

An obvious principle of human communication is that the transfer of ideas occurs most frequently between two individuals who are similar, or homophilous. *Homophily*[2] is the degree to which two or more individuals who interact are similar in certain attributes, such as beliefs, education, social status, and the like. In a free-choice situation, when an individual can interact with any one of a number of other individuals, there is a strong tendency to select someone who is very similar.

Homophily occurs because similar individuals belong to the same groups, live or work near each other, and share the same interests. This physical and social propinquity makes homophilous communication more likely. Such communication is also more likely to be effective, and thus to be rewarding. *More effective communication occurs when two or more individuals are homophilous.*[3] When they share common meanings, a mutual subcultural language, and are alike in personal and social characteristics, the communication of new ideas is likely to have greater effects in terms of knowledge gain, attitude formation and change, and overt behavior change. When homophily is present, communication is therefore likely to be rewarding to both participants in the process.

One of the most distinctive problems in the diffusion of innovations is that the participants are usually quite heterophilous. A change agent, for instance, is more technically competent than his or her clients. This difference frequently leads to ineffective communication as the participants do not talk the same language. In fact, when two individuals are identical regarding their technical grasp of an innovation, no diffusion can occur as there is no new information to exchange. The very nature of diffusion demands that at least some degree of heterophily be present between the two participants. Ideally, they would be homophilous on all other variables (education and social status, for example) even though they are heterophilous regarding the innovation. Usually, however, the two individuals are heterophilous on all of these variables because knowledge and experience with an innovation are highly related to social status, education, and the like.

Time

Time is a third element in the diffusion process. Much other behavioral science research is timeless in the sense that the time dimension is simply ignored. The inclusion of time as a variable in diffusion research is one of its strengths, but the measurement of the time dimension (often by means of the respondents' recall) can be criticized (Chapter 3). The time dimension is involved in diffusion (1) in the innovation-decision process by which an individual passes from first knowledge of an innovation through its adoption or rejection; (2) in the innovativeness of an individual or other unit of adoption—that is, the relative earliness/lateness with which an innovation is adopted—compared with other members of a system; and (3) in an innovation's rate of adoption in a system, usually measured as the number of members of the system that adopt the innovation in a given time period.

The Innovation-Decision Process

The *innovation-decision process* is the process through which an individual (or other decision-making unit) passes from first knowledge of an innovation to forming an attitude toward the innovation, to a decision to adopt or reject, to implementation and use of the new idea, and to confirmation of this decision. We conceptualize five main steps in the innovation-decision process: (1) knowledge, (2) persuasion, (3) decision, (4) implementation, and (5) confirmation. *Knowledge* occurs when an individual (or other decision-making unit) learns of the innovation's existence and gains some understanding of how it functions. *Persuasion* occurs when an individual (or other decision-making unit) forms a favorable or unfavorable attitude toward the innovation. *Decision* occurs when an individual (or other decision-making unit) engages in activities that lead to a choice to adopt or reject the innovation. *Implementation* occurs when an individual (or other decision-making unit) puts an innovation into use. Re-invention is especially likely to occur at the implementation stage. *Confirmation* occurs when an individual (or other decision-making unit) seeks reinforcement of an innovation-decision that has already been made, but the individual may reverse this previous decision if exposed to conflicting messages about the innovation.

Previously we stated that the innovation-decision process is an information-seeking and information-processing activity in which an individual obtains information in order to decrease uncertainty about the innovation. At the knowledge stage, an individual mainly seeks software information that is embodied in the technological innovation, information that reduces uncertainty about the cause-effect relationships involved in the innovation's capacity to solve an individual's problem. At this stage the individual wants to know what the innovation is and how and why it works. Mass media channels can effectively transmit such software information.

But increasingly at the persuasion stage, and especially at the decision stage, an individual seeks innovation-evaluation information in order to reduce uncertainty about an innovation's expected consequences. Here an individual wants to know the innovation's advantages and disadvantages in his or her own situation. Interpersonal networks with near-peers are particularly likely to convey such evaluative information about an innovation. Subjective evaluations of a new idea from other individuals are especially likely to influence an individual at the decision stage, and perhaps at the confirmation stage.

The innovation-decision process can lead to either *adoption,* a decision to make full use of an innovation as the best course of action available, or to *rejection,* a decision not to adopt an innovation. Such decisions can be reversed at a later point; for example, *discontinuance* is a decision to reject an innovation after it has previously been adopted. Discontinuance may occur because an individual becomes dissatisfied with an innovation, or because the innovation is replaced with an improved idea. It is also possible for an individual to adopt an innovation after a previous decision to reject it. Such later adoption and discontinuance occur during the confirmation stage of the innovation-decision process.

The innovation-decision process involved time in the sense that the five steps usually occur in a time-ordered sequence of knowledge, persuasion, decision, implementation, and confirmation. Exceptions to the usual sequence of the five stages may occur, such as when the decision stage precedes the persuasion stage. The *innovation-decision period* is the length of time required to pass through the innovation-decision process.

The present discussion of the innovation-decision process is mainly at the level of a single individual, and thus to the case of individual-optional innovation-decisions. But many innovation-decisions are made by organizations or other types of adopting units, rather than by individuals. For example, an organization may decide to implement an electronic mail system on the basis of a staff decision or an official's authority decision; the individual office worker in the organization may have little or no say in the innovation-decision. When an innovation-decision is made by a system, rather than by an individual, the decision process is more complicated because a number of individuals are involved (see Chapter 10).

So time is an important dimension in the innovation-decision process.

Innovativeness and Adopter Categories

Innovativeness is the degree to which an individual or other unit of adoption is relatively earlier in adopting new ideas than the other members of a system. Rather than describing an individual as "less innovative than the average member of a social system," it is handier and more efficient to refer to the individual as being in the "late majority" or in some other adopter category. This short-hand notation saves words and contributes to clearer understanding. Diffusion research shows that members of each of the adopter categories have a good deal in common. If the individual is like most others in the late majority category, he or she is of low social status, makes little use of mass media channels, and learns about most new ideas from peers via interpersonal channels. In a similar manner, we shall present a concise word picture of each of the other four adopter categories (in Chapter 7). *Adopter categories,* the classifications of members of a social system on the basis of innovativeness, include: (1) innovators, (2) early adopters, (3) early majority, (4) late majority, and (5) laggards.

Innovators are active information-seekers about new ideas. They have a high degree of mass media exposure and their interpersonal networks extend over a wide area, reaching outside of their local system. Innovators are able to cope with higher levels of uncertainty about an innovation than are other adopter categories. As the first to adopt a new idea in their system, they cannot depend upon the subjective evaluations of the innovation from other members of their system.

The measure of innovativeness and the classification of a system's members into adopter categories are based upon the relative time at which an innovation is adopted.

Rate of Adoption

There is a third specific way in which the time dimension is involved in the diffusion of innovations. The *rate of adoption* is the relative speed with which an innovation is adopted by members of a social system. When the number of individuals adopting a new idea is plotted on a cumulative frequency basis over time, the resulting distribution is an S-shaped curve. At first, only a few individuals adopt the innovation in each time period (such as a year or a month, for example); these are the innovators. But soon the diffusion curve begins to climb, as more and more individuals adopt in each succeeding time period. Eventually, the trajectory of adoption begins to level off, as fewer and fewer individuals remain who have not yet adopted the innovation. Finally, the S-shaped curve reaches its asymptote, and the diffusion process is finished.

Most innovations have an S-shaped rate of adoption. But there is variation in the slope of the "S" from innovation to innovation; some new ideas diffuse relatively rapidly and the S-curve is quite steep. Other innovations have a slower rate of adoption, and the S-curve is more gradual, with a slope that is relatively lazy. One issue addressed by diffusion research is why some innovations have a rapid rate of adoption, while others are adopted more slowly (see Figure 13-1).

The rate of adoption is usually measured by the length of time required for a certain percentage of the members of a system to adopt an innovation. Therefore, we see that the rate of adoption is measured using an innovation in a system, rather than an individual, as the unit of analysis. Innovations that are perceived by individuals as possessing greater relative advantage, compatibility, and the like, have a more rapid rate of adoption (as discussed previously).

There are also differences in the rate of adoption for the same innovation in different social systems. Many aspects of diffusion cannot be explained by just individual behavior. The system has a direct effect on diffusion through its norms and other system-level qualities, and also has an indirect influence through its individual members.

A Social System

A *social system* is defined as a set of interrelated units that are engaged in joint problem-solving to accomplish a common goal. The members or units of a social system may be individuals, informal groups, organizations, and/or subsystems. The system analyzed in a diffusion study may consist of all the peasant families in a Peruvian village, medical doctors in a hospital, or all the consumers in the United States. Each unit in a social system can be distinguished from other units. All members cooperate at least to the extent of seeking to solve a common problem in order to reach a mutual goal. This sharing of a common objective binds the system together.

Diffusion occurs within a social system. The social structure of the system affects the innovation's diffusion in several ways. The social system constitutes a boundary within which an innovation diffuses. Here we deal with how the system's social structure affects diffusion, the effect of norms on diffusion, the roles of opinion leaders and change agents, types of innovation-decisions, and the consequences of innovation. These issues involve relationships between the social system and the diffusion process that occurs within it.

Social Structure and Diffusion

To the extent that the units in a social system are not all identical in their behavior, structure exists in the system. We define *structure* as the patterned arrangements of the units in a system. This structure gives regularity and stability to human behavior in a system; it allows one to predict behavior with some degree of accuracy. Thus, structure represents one type of information, in that it decreases uncertainty. An illustration of this predictability is provided by structure in a bureaucratic organization like a government agency; there is a well-developed social structure in such a system, consisting of hierarchical positions, giving officials in higher-ranked positions the right to issue orders to individuals of lower rank. They expect their orders to be carried out. Such patterned social relationships among the members of a system constitute *social structure,* one type of structure.

In addition to this formal structure among the units in a social system, an informal type of structure also exists in the interpersonal networks linking a system's members, determining who interacts with whom and under what circumstances. We define such *communication structure* as the differentiated elements that can be recognized in the patterned communication flows in a system. Previously we defined homophily as the degree to which two or more individuals in a system talk with others who are similar to themselves. A communication structure is thus often created in a system in which homophilous sets of individuals are grouped together in cliques. A complete lack of communication structure in a system would be represented by a situation in which each individual talked with equal probability to each other member of the system. Such a situation might occur when a set of complete strangers first come together. However, regularized patterns soon begin to occur in the communication network of the system. These aspects of communication structure predict, in part, the behavior of individual members of the social system, including when they adopt an innovation.

The structure of a social system can facilitate or impede the diffusion of innovations in a system. The impact of the social structure on diffusion is of special interest to sociologists and social psychologists, and the way in which the communication structure of a system affects diffusion is a particularly interesting topic for communication scholars. Katz (1961) remarked, "It is as unthinkable to study diffusion without some knowledge of the social structures in which potential adopters are located as it is to study blood circulation without adequate knowledge of the veins and arteries."

Compared with other aspects of diffusion research, however, there have been relatively few studies of how the social or communication structure affects the diffusion and adoption of innovations in a system. It is a rather tricky business to untangle the effects of a system's structure on diffusion, independent from the effects of the characteristics of individuals that make up the system. Consider an illustration of *system effects,* the influences of the structure and/or composition of a system on the behavior of the members of the system. An example is provided by a study of the diffusion of family planning in Korea (Rogers and Kincaid, 1981). Two Korean women are both illiterate, married, have two children, and are twenty-nine years of age. The husbands of both women are high school graduates, with farms of five acres. One might expect that both women would be about equally likely, or unlikely, to adopt a contraceptive method.

But the women are different in one crucial respect: They live in different villages, one in Village A and one in Village B. The rate of adoption of family planning methods is 57 percent in Village A, and only 26 percent in Village B. The social and communication structures of these two villages are quite different regarding the diffusion of contraceptives, even though these innovations had been promoted equally in both villages by the national family planning program in Korea. We predict that the woman in Village A is more likely to adopt a contraceptive method than her counterpart in Village B because of system effects: Mrs. A's friends and neighbors are more likely to encourage her to adopt since they themselves have adopted, and the village leaders in Village A are especially committed to family planning, while in Village B they are not.

This example shows how a system's structure can effect the diffusion and adoption of innovations, over and above the effect of such variables as the individual characteristics of the members of the system. Individual innovativeness is affected both by individuals' characteristics, and by the nature of the social system in which the individuals are members.

System Norms and Diffusion

The Korean investigation by Rogers and Kincaid (1981) also illustrates the importance of village norms in affecting the rate of adoption of innovations. For example, this study of twenty-four villages found large differences from village to village, both in the level of adoption of family planning and in the adoption of particular types of family planning methods. One village had 51 percent adoption of the IUD (intrauterine device) and only one vasectomy adopter. Another village had 23 percent adoption of vasectomy. Yet another was a "pill village" in which all the adopters chose to use contraceptive pills. These differences were not due to the nature of the national family planning program in Korea, which promoted the same "cafeteria" of contraceptive methods in all villages for ten years prior to our data-gathering. The main explanation for the different contraceptive behavior from village to village was these systems' norms.

Norms are the established behavior patterns for the members of a social system. They define a range of tolerable behavior and serve as a guide or a standard for the members' behavior in a social system. The norms of a system tell an individual what behavior is expected.

A system's norms can be a barrier to change, as in the example of water-boiling in a Peruvian community. Such resistance to new ideas is often found in norms on food habits. In India, for example, sacred cows roam the countryside while millions of people are malnourished. Pork is not consumed by Moslems and Jews. Polished rice is eaten in most of Asia and the United States, even though whole rice is more nutritious. These are examples of cultural and religious norms. Norms can operate at the level of a nation, a religious community, an organization, or a local system like a village.

Opinion Leaders and Change Agents

The most innovative member of a system is very often perceived as a deviant from the social system, and is accorded a somewhat dubious status of low credibility by the average members of the system. This individual's role in diffusion (especially in persuading others about the innovation) is therefore likely to be limited. Other members of the system function as opinion leaders. They provide information and advice about innovations to many in the system.

Opinion leadership is the degree to which an individual is able to influence other individuals' attitudes or overt behavior informally in a desired way with relative frequency. This informal leadership is not a function of the individual's formal position or status in the system. Opinion leadership is earned and maintained by the individual's technical competence, social accessibility, and conformity to the system's norms. When the social system is oriented to change, the opinion leaders are quite innovative; but when the system's norms are opposed to change, the behavior of the leaders also reflects this norm. By their close conformity to the system's norms, opinion leaders serve as an apt model for the innovation behavior of their followers. Opinion leaders thus exemplify and express the system's structure.

Any system may have both innovative opinion leaders and also leaders who oppose change. Influential persons can lead in the spread of new ideas, or they can head an active proposition. When opinion leaders are compared with their followers, they (1) are more exposed to all forms of external communication, and thus are more cosmopolite, (2) have somewhat higher social status, and (3) are more innovative (although the exact degree of innovativeness depends, in part, on the system's norms). The most striking characteristics of opinion leaders is their unique and influential position in their system's communication structure: They are at the center of interpersonal communication networks. A *communication network* consists of interconnected individuals who are linked by patterned flows of information. The opinion leader's interpersonal networks allow him or her to serve as a social model whose innovative behavior is imitated by many other members of the system. The respect with which the opinion leader is held can be lost, however, if an opinion leader deviates too far from the norms of the system. Opinion leaders can be "worn out" by change agents who overuse them. Opinion leaders may be perceived by their peers as too much like the professional change agents and may therefore lose their credibility with their former followers.

Opinion leaders are members of the social system in which they exert their influence. In some instances individuals with influence in the social system are professionals who represent change agencies external to the system. A *change agent* is an individual who influences clients' innovation-decisions in a direction deemed desirable by a change agency. The change agent usually seeks to obtain the adoption of new ideas, but may also attempt to slow down diffusion and prevent the adoption of undesirable innovations. Change agents use opinion leaders in a social system as their lieutenants in diffusion campaigns.

Change agents are often professionals with a university degree in a technical field. This professional training, and the social status that goes with it, usually means that change agents are heterophilous from their typical clients, thus posing problems for effective communication about the innovations that they are promoting. Many change agencies employ change agent aides. An *aide* is a less than fully professional change agent who intensively contacts clients to influence their innovation-decisions. Aides are usually homophilous with the average client, and thus provide one means of bridging the heterophily gap frequently found between professional change agents and their client audience.

Types of Innovation-Decisions

The social system has yet another important kind of influence in the diffusion of new ideas. Innovations can be adopted or rejected (1) by an individual member of a system, or (2) by the entire social system, which can decide to adopt an innovation by a collective or an authority decision.

1. *Optional innovation-decisions* are choices to adopt or reject an innovation that are made by an individual independent of the decisions of the other members of the system. Even in this case, the individual's decision may be influenced by the norms of the system and by interpersonal networks. The decision of an individual housewife in Los Molinas to adopt or reject boiling water was an optional innovation-decision, although this choice was influenced by community-level factors, like the hot-cold complex. The distinctive aspect of optional innovation-decisions is that the individual is the unit of decision making, rather than the social system.

   The classical diffusion model evolved out of early diffusion investigations of optional innovation-decisions: The diffusion of hybrid corn among Iowa farmers, the spread of a new antibiotic drug among medical doctors, and the like. In more recent decades, however, the scope of the diffusion paradigm included collective and authority innovation-decisions.

2. *Collective innovation-decisions* are choices to adopt or reject an innovation that are made by consensus among the members of a system. All of the units in the system usually must conform to the system's decision once it is made. For example, in Southern California, all organizations employing more than 100 workers are required by a state law to gradually increase the average number of riders per vehicle over a five-year period, or else pay a stiff fine. The purpose is to reduce traffic congestion in Los Angeles, and thus to cut down on the smog caused by vehicle emissions. A work organization may choose to raise parking fees, encourage the use of mass transportation, or to provide car pools and van pools to employees. Freedom of choice is allowed the individual as long as the goal of reducing the number of commuter vehicles is served.

3. *Authority innovation-decisions* are choices to adopt or reject an innovation that are made by a relatively few individuals in a system who possess power, status, or technical expertise. The individual member of the system has little or no influence in the authority innovation-decision; he or she simply implements the decision. For instance, the president of a large U.S. computer corporation some years ago decided that all male employees should wear a white shirt, conservative necktie, and a dark suit; this authority decision had to be followed by every man who worked for the computer company.

These three types of innovation-decisions range on a continuum from optional decisions (where the adopting individual has almost complete responsibility for the decision), through collective decisions (where the individual has a say in the decision), to authority decisions (where the adopting individual has no influence in the innovation-decision). Collective and authority decisions are much more common than optional decisions in formal organizations, such as factories, schools, or government organizations, in comparison with other fields like agriculture and consumer behavior, where most innovation-decisions by farmers and consumers are optional.

Generally, the fastest rate of adoption of innovations results from authority decisions (depending, of course, on how innovative the authorities are). Optional decisions can usually be made more rapidly than collective decisions. Although made more rapidly, authority decisions may be circumvented during their implementation.

The type of innovation-decision for a given idea may change or be changed over time. Automobile seat belts, during the early years of their use, were installed in autos as optional decisions by the car's owner, who had to pay for the cost of installation. Then, in 1966, a federal law was passed requiring that seat belts be included in all new cars in the United States. An optional innovation-decision thus became a collective decision. But the decision by a driver or passengers to fasten the belts when in the car was still an optional decision—that is, except for 1974 model cars, which a federal law required to be equipped with a seat belt-ignition interlock system that prevented the driver from starting the engine until everyone in the auto's front seat had fastened their seat belts. So for one year, the decision to fasten seat belts became a collective authority-decision. The public reaction to this draconian approach was so negative that the U.S. Congress reversed the law, and the fastening of auto seat belts again became an individual-optional decision. Then, during the 1980s, many states passed laws requiring seat belt use; if the police apprehend someone not using a seat belt, they issue a traffic citation.

There is yet a fourth type of innovation-decision that is a sequential combination of two or more of the three types we just discussed. *Contingent innovation-decisions* are choices to adopt or reject that can be made only after a prior innovation-decision. For example, an individual member of a social system may be free to adopt or not adopt a new idea only after his/her system's innovation-decision. In the example just discussed, until the 1966 law (a collective innovation-decision by elected legislators representing the public), it was difficult for a vehicle owner to make an optional decision to install seat belts.

One can imagine other types of contingent innovation-decisions in which the first decision is of an authority sort followed by a collective decision. The distinctive aspect of contingent decision making is that two (or more) tandem decisions are required; either of the decisions may be optional, collective, or authority.

The social system is involved directly in collective, authority, and contingent innovation-decisions.

Consequences of Innovations

A social system is involved in an innovation's consequences because certain of these changes occur at the system level, in addition to those that affect the individual (Chapter 11).

Consequences are the changes that occur to an individual or to a social system as a result of the adoption or rejection of an innovation. There are at least three classifications of consequences:

1. *Desirable* versus *undesirable* consequences, depending on whether the effects of an innovation in a social system are functional or dysfunctional.
2. *Direct* versus *indirect* consequences, depending on whether the changes to an individual or to a social system occur in immediate response to an innovation or as a second-order result of the direct consequences of an innovation.
3. *Anticipated* versus *unanticipated* consequences, depending on whether the changes are recognized and intended by the members of a social system or not.

Change agents usually introduce innovations into a client system that they expect will have consequences that will be desirable, direct, and anticipated. But often such innovations result in at least some unanticipated consequences that are indirect and undesirable for the system's members. For instance, the steel ax was introduced by missionaries to an Australian aborigine tribe (Sharp, 1952). The change agents intended that the new tool would raise levels of living and material comfort for the tribe. But the new technology also led to a breakdown in family structure, the rise of prostitution, and "misuse" of the innovation itself. Change agents can often anticipate and predict an innovation's *form,* the directly observable physical appearance of the innovation, and perhaps its *function,* the contribution of the idea to the way of life of the system's members. But seldom are change agents able to predict an innovation's *meaning,* the subjective perceptions of the innovation by the clients.

DIFFUSION OF HYBRID CORN IN IOWA

The Ryan and Gross (1943) study of the diffusion of hybrid seed corn in Iowa is the most influential diffusion study. The hybrid corn investigation includes each of the four main elements of diffusion that we have just discussed, and serves to illustrate these elements.

The innovation of hybrid corn was one of the most important new agricultural technologies when it was released to Iowa farmers in 1928. The new seed ushered in a whole set of agricultural innovations in the 1930s through the 1950s that amounted to an agricultural revolution in farm productivity. Hybrid seed was developed by agricultural scientists at Iowa State University and at other state land-grant universities. The diffusion of hybrid seed was heavily promoted by the Iowa Agricultural Extension Service and by salesman from seed corn companies. Hybrid corn yielded about 20 percent more per acre than the open-pollinated varieties that it replaced. It was also more drought-resistant and better suited to harvesting with mechanical corn-pickers. The seed lost its hybrid vigor after the first generation, so farmers had to purchase hybrid seed each year. Previously farmers had saved their own seed, selected from their best-looking corn plants. The adoption of hybrid corn meant that an Iowa farmer had to make important changes in his corn-growing behavior.

When Bryce Ryan, fresh from his Ph.D. studies at Harvard University, arrived at Iowa State University in 1939, he chose hybrid corn as the innovation of study in his investigation of social factors in economic decisions. This interest drew him to study how an Iowa farmer's social relationships with his neighbors influenced the individual's decision to adopt hybrid corn. Ryan had read anthropological work on diffusion while he was at Harvard, so he cast his Iowa study of hybrid corn in a diffusion framework. But unlike the qualitative methods used in anthropological studies of diffusion, the Iowa investigation mainly utilized quantitative data from survey interviews with Iowa farmers about their adoption of hybrid corn seed.

In the summer of 1941, Neal Gross, a new graduate student in rural sociology, was hired as a research assistant on the hybrid corn diffusion project. Ryan and Gross selected two small Iowa communities located west of Ames, and proceeded to interview personally all of the farmers living in these two systems. Using a structured questionnaire, Neal Gross, who did most of the data gathering, interviewed each respondent as to when he decided to adopt hybrid corn (the year of adoption was to become the main dependent variable in the data analysis), the communication channels used at each stage in the innovation-decision process, and how much of the farmer's corn acreage was planted in hybrid (rather than open-pollinated seed) each year. In addition to these recall data about the innovation, the two rural sociologists also asked each respondent about his formal education, age, farm size, income, travel to Des Moines and other cities, readership of farm magazines, and other variables that were later correlated with innovativeness (measured as the year in which each farmer decided to adopt hybrid corn).

Neal Gross was from an urban background, and initially felt somewhat uncomfortable interviewing Iowa farmers. Someone in Ames told Gross that farm people got up very early in the morning, so on his first day of survey data gathering, he arrived at a respondent's home at 6:00 AM, while it was still half-dark. By the end of the day, Gross had interviewed twenty-one respondents, and he averaged an incredible fourteen interviews per day for the entire study! Today, a survey interviewer who averages four interviews per day is considered hard-working. During one personal interview, an Iowa farmer asked Gross for advice about controlling horse nettles. Gross had never heard of horse nettles. He told the farmer that he should call a veterinarian to look at his sick horse (horse nettles are a kind of noxious weed).

Neal Gross personally interviewed 345 farmers in the two Iowa communities, but twelve farmers operating less than twenty acres were discarded from the data analysis, as were seventy-four respondents who started farming after hybrid corn began to diffuse. Thus, the data analysis was based on 259 respondents.

When all the data were gathered, Ryan and Gross coded the farmers' interview responses into numbers. The diffusion researchers analyzed the data by hand tabulation and with a desk calculator (computers were not available for data analysis until some years later). Within a year, Neal Gross (1942) completed his Master's thesis on the diffusion of hybrid corn, and shortly thereafter Ryan and Gross (1943). published their research findings in the journal, *Rural Sociology* (this article is the most widely cited publication from the study, although there are several others).

All but two of the 259 farmers had adopted hybrid corn between 1928 and 1941, a rather rapid rate of adoption. When plotted cumulatively on a year-by-year basis, the adoption rate formed an S-shaped curve over time. After the first five years, by 1933, only 10 percent of the Iowa farmers had adopted. Then, the adoption curve "took off," shooting up to 40 percent adoption in the next three years (by 1936). Then the rate of adoption leveled off as fewer and fewer farmers remained to adopt the new idea.

(*Continued*)

Farmers were assigned to adopter categories on the basis of when they adopted the new seed (Gross, 1942). Compared to later adopters, the innovators had larger-sized farms, higher incomes, and more years of formal education. The innovators were more cosmopolite, as measured by their number of trips to Des Moines (Iowa's largest city, located about seventy-five miles away).

Although hybrid corn was an innovation with a high degree of relative advantage over the open-pollinated seed that it replaced, the typical farmer moved slowly from awareness-knowledge of the innovation to adoption. The innovation-decision period from first knowledge to the adoption-decision averaged about nine years for all respondents, a finding that the innovation-decision process involved considerable deliberation, even in the case of an innovation with spectacular results. The average respondent took three or four years after planting his first hybrid seed, usually on a small trial plot, before deciding to plant 100 percent of his corn acreage in hybrid varieties.

Communication channels played different roles at various stages in the innovation-decision process. The typical farmer first heard of hybrid seed from a salesman, but neighbors were the most frequently cited channel leading to persuasion. Salesmen were more important channels for earlier adopters, and neighbors were more important for later adopters. The Ryan and Gross (1943) findings suggested the important role of interpersonal networks in the diffusion process in a system. The farmer-to-farmer exchange of their personal experiences with hybrid seed was at the heart of diffusion. When enough such positive experiences were accumulated by the innovators and early adopters, and exchanged with other farmers in the community, the rate of adoption took off. This threshold for hybrid corn occurred in 1935. After that point, it would have been impossible to halt the further diffusion of hybrid corn. The farm community as a social system, including the networks linking the individual farmers within it, was a crucial element in the diffusion process.

In order to understand the role of diffusion networks and opinion leadership, Ryan and Gross (1943) should have asked sociometric questions[4] of their respondents, such as, "From which other farmers have you obtained information about hybrid corn?" The sample design, which consisted of a complete enumeration in two communities, would have made the use of sociometric questions appropriate. But "information was simply collected from all community members as if they were unrelated respondents in a random sample" (Katz and others, 1963).

Even without sociometric data about diffusion networks, Ryan and Gross (1943) sensed that hybrid corn spread in the two Iowa communities as a kind of social snowball: "There is no doubt but that the behavior of one individual in an interacting population affects the behavior of his fellows. Thus, the demonstrated success of hybrid seed on a few farms offers new stimulus to the remaining ones." The two rural sociologists intuitively sensed what later diffusion scholars were to gather more detailed evidence to prove: That the heart of the diffusion process consists of interpersonal network exchanges and social modeling between those individuals who have already adopted an innovation and those who are then influenced to do so. Diffusion is fundamentally a social process.

Study of the invisible college of rural sociologists investigating diffusion as of the mid-1960s identified the researchers who first utilized a new concept and/or methodological tool in studying diffusion (Crane, 1972). Ryan and Gross launched fifteen of the eighteen most widely used intellectual innovations in the rural sociology diffusion research tradition. So Bryce Ryan and Neal Gross played key roles in forming the classical diffusion paradigm. The hybrid corn study has left an indelible stamp on the history of diffusion research.

This case illustration is based on Ryan and Gross (1943), Gross (1942), Ryan and Gross (1950), and Valente and Rogers (1994).

SUMMARY

Diffusion is the process by which an innovation is communicated through certain channels over time among the members of a social system. Diffusion is a special type of communication concerned with the spread of messages that are perceived as new ideas. *Communication* is a process in which participants create and share information with one another in order to reach a mutual understanding. Diffusion has a special character because of the newness of the idea in the message content. Thus some degree of uncertainty is involved in the diffusion process. An individual can reduce the degree of uncertainty by obtaining information. *Information* is a difference in matter-energy that affects uncertainty in a situation where a choice exists among a set of alternatives.

The main elements in the diffusion of new ideas are: (1) an *innovation*, (2) which is *communicated* through certain *channels*, (3) over *time*, (4) among the members of a *social system*. An *innovation* is an idea, practice, or object perceived as new by an individual or other unit of adoption. Almost all of the new ideas discussed in this book are technological innovations. A *technology* is a design for instrumental action that reduces the uncertainty in the cause-effect relationships involved in achieving a desired outcome. Most technologies have two components: (1) *hardware*, consisting of the tool that embodies the technology as a material or physical object, and (2) *software*, consisting of the knowledge base for the tool. The software information embodied in a technology serves to reduce one type of uncertainty, that concerned with the cause-effect relationships involved in achieving a desired outcome. But a technological innovation also creates another kind of uncertainty because of its newness to the individual, and motivates him or her to seek information by means of which the new idea can be evaluated. This *innovation-evaluation information* leads to a reduction in uncertainty about an innovation's expected consequences.

The characteristics of an innovation, as perceived by the members of a social system, determine its rate of adoption. Five attributes of innovations are: (1) relative advantage, (2) compatibility, (3) complexity, (4) trialability, and (5) observability.

Re-invention is the degree to which an innovation is changed or modified by a user in the process of its adoption and implementation.

A *communication channel* is the means by which messages get from one individual to another. Mass media channels are more effective in creating knowledge of innovations, whereas interpersonal channels are more effective in forming and changing attitudes toward a new idea, and thus in influencing the decision to adopt or reject a new idea. Most individuals evaluate an innovation, not on the basis of scientific research by experts, but through the subjective evaluations of near-peers who have adopted the innovation. These near-peers thus serve as role models, whose innovation behavior tends to be imitated by others in their system.

Another distinctive aspect of diffusion as a subfield of communication is that some degree of heterophily is present. *Heterophily* is the degree to which two or more individuals who interact are different in certain attributes, such as beliefs, education, social status, and the like. The opposite of heterophily is *homophily*, the degree to which two or more individuals who interact are similar in certain attributes. Most human communication takes place between individuals who are homophilous, a situation that leads to more effective communication. Therefore, the heterophily that is often present in the diffusion of innovations leads to special problems in securing effective communication.

Time is involved in diffusion in (1) the innovation-decision process, (2) innovativeness, and (3) an innovation's rate of adoption. The *innovation-decision process* is the mental process through which an individual (or other decision-making unit) passes from first knowledge of an innovation to forming an attitude toward the innovation, to a decision to adopt or reject, to implementation of the new idea, and to confirmation of this decision. We conceptualize five steps in this process: (1) knowledge, (2) persuasion, (3) decision, (4) implementation, and (5) confirmation. An individual seeks information at various stages in the innovation-decision process in order to decrease uncertainty about an innovation's expected consequences. The decision stage leads (1) to *adoption*, a decision to make full use of an innovation as the best course of action available, or (2) to *rejection*, a decision not to adopt an innovation.

Innovativeness is the degree to which an individual or other unit of adoption is relatively earlier in adopting new ideas than other members of a social system. We specify five *adopter categories*, classifications of the members of a social system on the basis of their innovativeness: (1) innovators, (2) early adopters, (3) early majority, (4) late majority, and (5) laggards. *Rate of adoption* is the relative speed with which an innovation is adopted by members of a social system.

A *social system* is a set of interrelated units that are engaged in joint problem-solving to accomplish a common goal. A system has *structure*, defined as the patterned arrangements of the units in a system, which gives stability and regularity to individual behavior in a system. The social and communication structure of a system facilitates or impedes the diffusion of innovations in the system.

Norms are the established behavior patterns for the members of a social system. *Opinion leadership* is the degree to which an individual is able to influence informally other individuals' attitudes or overt behavior in a desired way with relative frequency. A *change agent* is an individual who attempts to influence clients' innovation-decisions in a direction that is deemed desirable by a change agency. An *aide* is a less than fully professional change agent who intensively contacts clients to influence their innovation-decisions.

We distinguish three main types of innovation-decisions: (1) *optional innovation-decisions,* choices made by an individual independent of the decisions of other members of the system to adopt or reject an innovation, (2) *collective innovation-decisions,* choices made by consensus among the members of a system, and (3) *authority innovation-decisions,* choices made by relatively few individuals in a system who possess power, status, or technical expertise. A fourth category consists of a sequential combination of two or more of these types of innovation-decisions: *Contingent innovation-decisions* are choices to adopt or reject that are made only after a prior innovation-decision.

A final way in which a social system influences diffusion is *consequences,* the changes that occur to an individual or to a social system as a result of the adoption or rejection of an innovation.

Endnotes

1. This definition of technology as information is based upon Thompson (1967) and Eveland (1986), who stress the uncertainty-reduction aspect of technology, and thus the important role of information, a view of technology that has not been widely recognized. Technology is information and transfer is a communication process, and so technology transfer is the communication of information (Eveland, 1986).

2. This concept and its opposite, heterophily, were first called to scientific attention by Lazarsfeld and Merton (1964). *Heterophily,* the opposite of homophily, is defined as the degree to which two or more individuals who interact are different in certain attributes.

3. A further refinement of this proposition includes the concept of *empathy,* defined as the ability of an individual to project into the role of another. *More effective communication occurs when two individuals are homophilous, unless they have high empathy.* Heterophilous individuals who have a high degree of empathy are, in a socio-psychological sense, really homophilous. The proposition about effective communication and homophily can also be reversed: *Effective communication between two individuals leads to greater homophily in knowledge, beliefs, and overt behavior.*

4. *Sociometry* is a means of obtaining and analyzing quantitative data about communication patterns among the individuals in a system by asking each individual to whom he or she is linked.

SECTION III

HISTORICAL PERSPECTIVE OF INVENTION, INNOVATION, AND PRODUCT TECHNOLOGY

Introduction

The selections contained in this section portray the development of invention and innovation thought over time. This section focuses on some of the early but truly remarkable works related to invention and innovation. The book chapters and one article that form this section were written between 1929 and 1966. Themes contained in this section include:

- Where do inventive and innovative thoughts originate?
- Who are the innovators or entrepreneurs?
- What impact do innovations have on economies and societies?

In these early years, primary perspectives for innovation study were often from a historical perspective and grounded in the theories related to technology and economics. The four major contributors in this section are Usher (1929), Schumpeter (1949), Jewkes and associates (1958), and Schmookler (1966). Abbott Payson Usher begins this section with thoughts about the place of technology in economic history and relates innovation, and in particular mechanical invention, to a number of unsuspecting roles in society. Usher is followed by Joseph Schumpeter, who presents the innovation and the innovator, the entrepreneur and creator of new combinations, as the preeminent force in the process of innovation. Jewkes and associates focused on inventors as well as their inventions. These authors describe both the connections among inventors in addition to their approach to the "process" of invention. Jacob Schmookler, writing in the mid-1960s, concludes with his thoughts about the relationship between invention and economic growth. He has a somewhat different assessment from that of Schumpeter, particularly related to the sources of innovations.

The first two works included in this section consist of two book chapters created by Abbott Payson Usher published in 1929. He begins his work with thoughts about the place of technology in economic history. He implies that there are several types of innovation and that they reside in many walks of life, such as in the careers of statesmen, artists, scientists, and scholars. He portrays innovation as a learning process, a necessity for each individual. He then settles into a discussion of what mechanical invention is and an analysis of how it fits into the overall process of innovation. He explains the concept of discovery and describes how it supports the inventive and innovative processes. Usher reinforces thoughts that were highlighted earlier in this book by Holt. Specifically, that invention begins with a consciously felt want and proceeds because of the inventor's "total experience." This is what Holt termed the "corridor principle." Usher seems to believe that the "felt need" is sensed only by the inventor, or at least that the inventor is the only individual who can adequately fulfill that need. He ends this portion of his work with the thought that inventive effort concludes with the creation of a new "configuration" of elements, one that never existed before.

The third selection in this section is a book chapter written by Joseph Schumpeter (1949). Schumpeter offers his thoughts relative to the association of economic history and economic development. A portion of Schumpeter's theory of economic development is described in his chapter entitled "The Fundamental Phenomenon of Economic Development." It is an important part of the thesis of this chapter to describe the difference between the "circular flow" of economics, the steady-state condition of supply and manufacturing, and, the "economic development process," the demand, purchase, and utilization of currently devised products. He notes that the economic development process is exceedingly different from the circular flow. And, it embodies the creative process that is at the center of the development of economies in general. An important concept that Schumpeter emphasizes here is that economic development originates within the economy itself. It is not a phenomenon occurring outside of the economy that happens to have a significant affect on the economy. Schumpeter entitles the changes that are manifest in innovations, product or process, "new combinations." He notes that new combinations grow out of the circular flow and can cause major disruptions of that flow due to the resources that are diverted to new uses. In Schumpeter's terminology, new combinations are revolutionary, not evolutionary. He describes innovations as spontaneous and discontinuous changes in the circular flow. He points out that these innovations do not derive from new wants that arise out of consumers, but that new innovations typically begin in production directly beside "old" methods of want fulfillment.

The next two book chapters selected for this section are by John Jewkes, David Sawers, and Richard Stillerman (1958). Jewkes and associates almost humorously point out in retrospect what many have said over the years about invention and inventions. They note that it is almost impossible to select a period in which many people do not have the impression that everything that is going to be invented has already been invented. In other words, there can never again be anything that is truly new. Moreover, many new processes and innovations are feared due to their potential for evil and destruction. This assumption is frequently derived from the uncertainty or lack of familiarity that people, often of a particular age, have with new technology. For example, it was thought that automation would create great unemployment; that lasers were the embodiment of death rays; and that robots would take over the world. Fortunately, new innovations will continue to arise from invention and it is hoped that most of these innovations will be used for practical purposes. Jewkes, Sawers, and Stillerman also describe a process of invention. In their second chapter offered here, they wrestle with three major questions:

- To what degree is the inventor's work based on scientific knowledge?
- How methodical is the inventor's approach to invention?
- Does the inventor seek assistance from (other) scientists?

The authors scrutinized several inventors and their inventions in various industries of the nineteenth century and reached the following conclusions. First, inventors during this time, and, perhaps others, appear to have many linkages with the scientific community. The author's review of history indicates that many mechanical inventions of the nineteenth century were thought to be "empirical" or created by accident. The authors believe that the chemical inventions of the twentieth century are more likely to be categorized as "empirical" than most mechanical inventions because of the need to envision "why" a mechanical invention does what it does prior to its design, as opposed to many chemical inventions that are known to perform but the fundamental reasons for their performance remain a mystery. Moreover, the inventors of this period appear to be more than just familiar with other inventors. They appear to have a reasonably close-knit association.

In his second writing in this section, Joseph Schumpeter (1965) describes how an innovation is developed through entrepreneurs or innovators, and how these individuals differ significantly from capitalists. With the clarification of the concept of the innovator or entrepreneur, Schumpeter then explains how entrepreneurial profits differ from that of rent or interest. Schumpeter goes on to describe the reasons for economic change. He suggests that it is not the increase of either the population or the existing factors of production. In fact, he points out that both of these variables are probably the results of entrepreneurial endeavors as opposed to the sources of them. It is in this area where he presents his thoughts regarding "creative destruction" as it relates to the processes of the destruction and reconstruction of industrial structures that relentlessly occur. Schumpeter also points out in this piece that because providing capital is not a defining function of an entrepreneur, the bearing of risk should not be a primary function or descriptor of entrepreneurial activity either. These discussions paved the way for a review of why economic development differs so significantly from that of the circular flow. Here he discusses the entrepreneur as distinct from the entrepreneurial function. This discussion illuminates the premise that typically an entrepreneur is not a career path title. Entrepreneur or innovator is a title for people performing a particular process (the entrepreneurial process) and when the process is complete the titles are inapplicable.

The final selection in this section, composed of two chapters developed by Jacob Schmookler (1966), presents another picture of the relationship between invention and economic growth. In his first book chapter, Schmookler presents detailed definitions of technology and technical change, and provides us with a modified definition of innovation. Schmookler allows a firm to be an innovator, as well as an imitator, of technical progress, an innovator being the newest provider of an innovation, whereas an imitator is seen as an implementer or follower in terms of technical change. Schmookler also furnishes an altered definition for "development," which differs from that employed by Schumpeter. Schmookler uses development to refer to the specific development of a product, whereas Schumpeter employs development to indicate a product that is a dramatic departure from anything currently found in the market. Schmookler relates patents to inventions, but only those he construes to belong to a category of inventions that are not obvious. This view is consistent with the current philosophy regarding patent protection law. Schmookler also discusses the reasons for invention. In this context, he presents arguments for both the influence of demand as well as supply on invention. He suggests that the process of invention embraces a state that can be described as inventing what we can invent and having the capability to invent what people want. This philosophy differs from that of Schumpeter in that Schmookler suggests that invention is primarily pursued for gain, which comes in the form of sales. Sales are driven by customer demand. This is especially accurate for consumer products, for which Schmookler indicates that demand determines the allocation of inventive resources.

References

Jewkes, John, David Sawers, and Richard Stillerman. 1958. *The Sources of Invention.* London: MacMillan & Company Limited.

Schmookler, Jacob. 1966. *Invention and Economic Growth.* Cambridge, MA: Harvard University Press.

Schumpeter, Joseph A. 1965. Economic theory and entrepreneurial history. In *Explorations in Enterprise.* Ed. Hugh G. J. Aitken. Cambridge, MA: Harvard University Press.

Schumpeter, Joseph A. 1949. The fundamental phenomenon of economic development. in *The Theory of Economic Development.* Cambridge, MA: Harvard University Press.

Usher, Abbott P. 1929. *A History of Mechanical Inventions.* Cambridge, MA: Harvard University Press.

14

THE PLACE OF TECHNOLOGY IN ECONOMIC HISTORY

Abbott Payson Usher

I

Economic history is deeply concerned with the development of various associated subjects, but in particular with geography and the technological sciences. These disciplines deal with basic elements in economic history and without a just appreciation of the precise nature of their contributions no adequate interpretation of economic history is possible. The fact has long been recognized as a matter of abstract truth, but the materials of these allied subjects have been very imperfectly worked into the text of economic history. Economic history is the story of the mutual transformations taking place between human societies and their environment. Geography, broadly conceived, furnishes an account of the environmental factors that inevitably mould social life in many ways. The technological sciences furnish the account of the most important single factor in the active transformation of environment by human activity. Both of these sources must be utilized by the economic historian and the results effectively worked into the organized presentation of the historical record. The fact that these materials come from different sources is itself of assistance, for they indicate modes of arrangement that will do the least possible violence to the data of the record. These different factors must be separately analyzed and dealt with as specific elements because they are somewhat self-contained units in the story. We must deal with them separately because we feel them separately. But it must be evident that these two classes of material are equally important. Unfortunately, it has not yet been possible to secure a well-balanced consideration of these fundamental elements.

Economic geography has made great progress during the last 50 years. The notable accomplishments of the vigorous French school were from the first significantly supplemented by the work of individuals in other countries, and latterly the recognition of the value of this direction of attention has made such headway that general position is thoroughly established in all countries. The essential principles are effectively formulated for instruction and methods of analysis are well established, though much remains to be done in applying these methods to the earlier historical periods. These results have been responsible for much extravagant geographical determinism; on the part of the specialists, no less than among the lay readers. Significant studies of the geographical data are frequently disfigured by naïve misconceptions of the relation of the phenomena to economic activity. The simplicity of the deterministic concept leads some economic historians to find the explanation of all economic changes in the simple facts about climate, minerals, or soil exhaustion. Class-room presentation of geographic factors is extremely difficult because of the likelihood of misinterpretation.

Usher, Abbott Payson, (1929), *A History of Mechanical Inventions*, New York: McGraw-Hill Book Company, Inc. (pp. 1–7)

The natural antidote to these dangers is of course to be found in the materials of the technological sciences, and the development of these contacts is thus especially important to economic history at the present moment. Balanced judgment of the complex social phenomena of history will be easily achieved only when the different classes of material are presented with measurably equal effectiveness. We must have all the elements of the social process clearly presented to the mind; the geographical data bearing mainly upon passive adaptation to environment; the technological data, concerned with the process of active transformation of the environment through human agencies.

The adaptations with which economic geography deals are only in part historical phenomena. They are the spatial phenomena of social life; the analysis of the geographical data throws light chiefly upon the relations of different regions to each other at a given time, and upon the detail of settlement within particular regions. None of these matters can be ignored, but they obviously have to do with the description of conditions as of particular dates; and this is, of course, only one item in the historical record, just as the individual picture is an item of the series embodied in an entire moving-picture film. The geographical data are a part of history, but in reality they are so small a part that they do not in themselves throw much light on the nature or character of the changes embodied in the total historical movement.

Geographical phenomena are, however, closely associated with one phase of social change; the growth of population and the consequent redistributions over the areas involved. Particular regions disclose progressive increases in density up to levels which can be explained largely in terms of differences in climate and resources. This growth seems to be somewhat independent of technical improvement, though the densities achievable are, at times, profoundly affected by technological advance.

These phenomena in their entirety involve the development of frontiers through the discovery of new habitable areas and ultimate redistributions of the massing of populations in the various areas by differential rates of growth or by actual migration. These phenomena are among the most complex of any presented to the historian. They involve all the factors operating in economic history and at present we are scarcely in position to attempt more than a preliminary analysis. It is clear that some of these changes are closely related to changes in the technique of transportation. It is very likely that the rapid extension of the effectively habitable area exerted some influence upon the development of technique in the first millenium of the Christian era. During that period, technological development seems to have been very slow; we are tempted to regard the predominance of frontier conditions as an explanation, because the economic pressure would be a less significant factor on the frontiers than in maturely settled regions. But it is possible to create presumptions in favor of the thesis that more technological development occurred in frontier regions than in the mature regions of dense settlement in the Near and Middle East. This situation might be explained on the grounds that the relative scarcity of labor on the frontier made it more necessary to utilize every possible mechanical device, and made it possible to utilize effectively devices that would have been too imperfect to be useful in a region in which skilled labor was relatively abundant and cheap.

It is obviously unwise to attempt to explain the "slow" rate of technical change in this or any other period until it is established that progress was "slow" in relation to some significant standard of judgment. In the present stage of our knowledge we are in no position to make such a judgment; for there can be only one sound basis for comparison—the maximum achievement intellectually possible. This involves an extremely close judgment of the internal obstructions to invention in the total body of philosophic and scientific thought. There are grounds for believing that these obstructions were very great, but, obviously, it is not wise to attempt to deal with the more complex problems until the simpler and more objective problems have been tolerably well settled. Consequently, it is for the present wiser to confine attention to those matters that do not involve many interactions of the various factors. We need clear conceptions of the nature of the processes of invention and achievement. We need some measurable knowledge of the actual chronology of the development of the technique of industry and commerce, in its purely scientific aspects, as well as in its practical applications.

II

The purely geographic phenomena of history are essentially spatial, and for this reason they are not only deterministic in their bearings, but essentially unhistorical. The technological problems with which economic history is concerned present a sharp antithesis to these geographic factors. Changes in technique involve series of individual innovations that are finally embodied in practical accomplishments. These series or sequences of relatively independent inventions are among the most intense manifestations of the dynamic processes of history.

Each step in the sequence is a necessary part of the process; each step must needs be taken in the given order; consequently these processes of technological development are in form as well as in content the very essence of history. They are sequences of events which are intelligible only when read forward. They are sequences which can be interpreted adequately only after the events have occurred. They are thus deeply imbedded in time; they must be conceived as taking place in a kind of extension distinguishable from space which by nature admits of movement in any direction, indifferently. For some purposes of scientific thought, spatialized concepts of time are used without serious consequences, but in formal historical study it is essential to recognize that the record of history must be read forward. Historical process is a forward-moving development, incapable of prediction, but yielding rational meaning when the full sequence of events is organized as an orderly progression from a demonstrable beginning to a significant end. Technical progress is historical process in this sense, and must be regarded as the essential and vital feature of economic history, for it is around these technical changes that all the phenomena of economic history must be grouped. There is a special value, too, in a separate study of the technological problems without regard for the moment to the detailed economic consequences of particular changes. The development of all these ultimate consequences would require a whole series of separate and measurably independent narratives, involving the activities of many different types of men and an amount of detail in which the larger elements of perspective over long periods of time would be irretrievably lost.

Economic history has been weakened in the past by the impersonality of its record. It has dealt so largely with classes, movements, and materialistic interpretations that the accomplishments of individuals have been lost. Few heroes have been put forward for popular admiration, and no little uncertainty has been shown as to the kinds of heroes to seek. The English empiricists were inclined to look to inventors and even the spiritually minded Carlyle said noble things of them. The German nationalists and the Socialists have given more attention to statesmen and political leaders, and this has been the prevailing view. This notion of economic statecraft as a socially creative activity finds itself in many logical and historical difficulties. The substantive benefits conferred by these "great men" are not easily pointed out and after a generation or two it is painfully obvious that the idols have feet of clay. The instincts of the empiricists were essentially trustworthy. The true heroes of economic history are the scientists, the inventors, and the explorers. To them is due the actual transformation of social life. Carlyle made only one error—he assumed that the movement of history could be attributed to the efforts of a very small number of uniquely gifted leaders. He failed to realize that the processes of history in their entirety involve not only the few who find themselves in strategically important positions, but also the many obscure and unrecognized innovators whose efforts were essential but not immediately significant or conspicuous. When it is recognized that the total achievement is the cumulative accomplishment of many men of considerable gradations in natural ability, the processes of history become more comprehensible. Human accomplishment can then be presented as the result of continuous activity of common mental processes. It is no longer necessary to think in terms of intermittent manifestations of a mysterious transcendental power exhibited rarely and somewhat capriciously in men of genius. The process of innovation is relatively continuous.

Properly understood, the newer concepts of historical processes do not diminish the fame and honor of the great figures that have been esteemed in the past; but to their number many new names are added, some of equal talent, others of lesser talent, all worthy of honor.

The attribution of the function of innovation to the scientists, inventors, and explorers does not diminish the significance of the role of the statesman, but it conceives the character of his task in a different fashion. Instead of thinking of his work as creative innovation, it is presented in the light of a difficult task in the adaptation of the legal framework of society to changes in economic circumstance. This work becomes the last phase in the process of social change. First the technological changes, then the development of the consequences, finally the revision of law or custom. There is innovation involved in a measure, but these accomplishments are dominated to such a degree by current circumstance that their quality is more justly felt as an adaptation than as an innovation. The element of novelty has become diluted through many transformations and has acquired the status of a present fact. The statesman faces a "condition"; he is dominated by an external necessity. The inventor is dominated by his unfulfilled wish. Consequently, despite elements in common, the creative factors in the art of statecraft are subordinated to the adaptive. Of the important acts in history, the choices of the statesmen are the most elaborately conditioned by external circumstance.

The statesman, therefore, plays a part in economic history, but it is not the creative part attributed to him by the mercantilist, the nationalist, or the socialist. The actual role may seem to call for less originality of thought, and for a lower order of talent. In fact it is not less difficult, but different. The task is critical, rather than creative; it requires courage and social responsibility rather than brilliant, but possibly irresponsible, originality.

The presentation of economic history as being primarily a phase of the organized activity of the state thus laid the emphasis in the wrong place. The policies of state are not the chief elements in economic development, nor are the statesmen the chief actors. George Unwin was perhaps carried rather far in his reaction against the political concepts of history embodied in the famous dictum of Seeley. "History is past politics; politics is present history." Unwin left the statesman a very subordinate role in any phase of history; quite possibly a smaller part in the total accomplishment than is just. But however that may be, the primary concept of Unwin is a notable contribution to historical thought. He finds the outcome of history in no particular form of church or state; whether Catholic or Protestant; absolute monarchy or republic; empire or national state. "The political outcome of today," he says, "cannot be justified as a creation. It bears a closer resemblance to that primeval anarchy before the light was divided from the darkness." The true outcome of history is to be found not in particular institutions, but in "the inward possessions and experiences of mankind—religion, art, literature, science, music, philosophy—but, above all, the ever widening and deepening communion of human minds and souls with each other." The chief creators of this result are to be found in the whole body of the people; in the reformers, the artists, the scientists, the scholars, the inventors.

Such a view carries us close to the deeper realities of history, and opens up new judgments of men and events which will make it easier for the historian to achieve the ultimate ideal of all historical writing—the presentation of a record in which we shall "see life without rearrangement."

15

THE PROCESS OF MECHANICAL INVENTION

Abbott Payson Usher

I

The process of innovation has frequently been held to be an unusual and mysterious phenomenon of our mental life. It has been long regarded as the result of special processes of inspiration that are experienced only by persons of the special grade called men of genius. This mystical account of these phenomena is, however, gradually yielding ground before the growing body of psychological analysis, and we are beginning to realize that these phenomena of innovation are neither more nor less mysterious than the most humble and commonplace phases of our mental life. In the past we have underestimated the complexity of the processes of thought and behavior applied to the daily business of living, and we have failed to perceive the continuity of the gradation of mental activity from the most commonplace to the most distinguished accomplishments. The elements of difference do not consist in the development or application of essentially new types of mental activity; the processes that can be identified in the simpler and more immediate acts of living are applied to new and more remote objectives which can be achieved only by the finer perceptions and more fertile imagination of individuals that rise above the general level of the mass.

Innovation is an integral part of the process of learning, an inescapable necessity for the individual as for the group as a whole. It is doubtless true that our attention is commonly centered upon the conservative and imitative elements of the process of learning, so that we are likely to think of learning as a passive acceptance by the individual of a group tradition. But even in those societies where the weight of tradition is heaviest, there remain many daily problems that demand new judgments and responses on the part of the individual. No tradition is so complete as to be proof against the subtle transformations wrought by new precedents. The common law, which by theory is a comprehensive and pure tradition, is not in practice a rigid and unchanging body of rules, but in fact the most fluid of all legal systems. It is based upon recorded precedent, but inasmuch as cases arise for which there is really no precedent, the process of innovation is ever a constructive force. It is so with all learning: there is a need of mastery of tradition, and there is also need of incessant innovation. False concepts of education and exaggerated respect for the canons of classical authority may obscure the actuality and significance of the learning of new things, but at the worst they do no more than obstruct and retard an inevitable process. The most skilfully contrived system of education can merely provide the most harmonious adjustment between these somewhat inconsistent and irreconcilable ends. It is truly difficult to impress upon the individual that necessity of facing both past and future symbolized in the image of

Usher, Abbott Payson, (1929), *A History of Mechanical Inventions,* New York: McGraw-Hill Book Company, Inc. (pp. 8–19)

Janus contemplating with equal attention both the eternity that is accomplished and the eternity that is to be.

Our powers of innovation are mysterious and in their entirety inexplicable; but so too are the other phases of the process of learning. The building of unorganized impulses and needs into a coherent personality of any grade or quality is no less mysterious in its processes than the most noted achievements of genius. Personality building is a persistent feature of all social life, and in some measure we must presume that all these processes reach back to the origins of human societies. In this respect, they are a commonplace phenomenon, but they are not for that reason the less mysterious. The discovery of similar mental processes at both extremes of mentality does not, therefore, withdraw the veil of mystery; rather is it spread impartially over the humblest commoner as over the greatest genius.

Throughout these gradations our mental processes fall into two types; the synthetic, constructive, and creative activities concerned with innovation; the analytical, imitative, and conservative activities concerned with the formulation and imposition of tradition. A comprehensive theory of innovation would involve by necessity all the synthetic activities, but it could not be confined to them because the analytical activities are called into play at several stages in the process. The data of experience must be organized and worked into consciously defined configurations or patterns. Some of these achievements in organization may obstruct particular innovations, but on the whole the enlargement of our significant experience is dependent upon systematic analysis and organization. The unorganized content of the mind also plays an important part in innovation, and thus consideration of perception, memory, and imitation becomes an essential part of the study of innovation. Because the impulses to invention and discovery are deeply involved in the emotions, a comprehensive account must of necessity include the study of the emotional life from this special point of view. The innovating activities of the mind are thus synthetic not merely as regards the form in which their results are expressed. They are a synthesis of all the faculties of conscious life. Strictly speaking, any adequate theory of innovation would be an analysis of all the activities of the mind from a somewhat special point of view. The naïve error of common sense lies in the presumption that a specific and unusual process is responsible for accomplishments that express in a peculiarly intense degree the entire mental activity of admittedly unusual personalities. No single generalization or formula can summarize the process of innovation.

II

Mechanical invention, with which we are especially concerned, is only one phase of the innovating activities of the mind. A wide range of phenomena is included in the field as a whole, including the creative work of artists, scientists, and inventors. Although the work of exploration is a factor in the changing circumstances of economic life, it can hardly be considered a mental activity. When more than physical adventure is involved, it becomes a special phase of scientific or technological innovation. The true mental phenomena are highly complex both as regards the detail of the processes and as regards the objectives concerned, but at least two distinct types may be distinguished.

Discovery consists in the perception of relations existing in nature that were not previously recognized. Strictly speaking, the arrangements exist independently of our minds though obscured in many ways by the complexity of the phenomena. The perception of such relations turns largely upon eliminations and simplifications of the items of experience that may distract attention from the orderly patterns that are finally recognized. Many accomplishments of art and science are of this type. Scientific generalizations are the most obvious case, and we commonly speak of them as discoveries. In this case common sense requires no correction. The more realistic accomplishments in art are essentially similar. The landscape painter "discovers" a time of day and a point of view from which certain harmonies of mass, and color can be perceived. The more difficult task is the making of a record in which elimination of irrelevant detail and simplification of masses make the objects as seen by him evident to less-gifted perceptions. The sculptor discovers the beautiful pose. The musician discovers his themes. Elements of gradation are involved in these different phases of phenomena of discovery, ranging from the perception of relations that are always present down to relations which are only rarely present. In the lower ranges, the distinction between certain kinds of discovery and certain types of invention may not be very sharp. It is possible that careful analysis might establish the thesis that the process of invention is a development out of the process of discovery, and that in early stages of evolution we deal only with discoveries and not with inventions. But if this be the case, the distinction between the two types must have emerged at an early stage, for the apes of the laboratory at Teneriffe clearly seem to be capable of a limited range of inventive accomplishment.

Invention finds its distinctive feature in the constructive assimilation of preexisting elements into new syntheses, new patterns, or new configurations of behavior. The objectives may vary through a wide range: including at one extreme, creations intended to gratify æsthetic desires; and at the other, mechanical devices for the more facile gratification of material wants. Invention thus establishes relationships that did not previously exist. In its barest essence, the element of innovation lies in the completion of an incomplete pattern of behavior or in the improvement of a pattern that was unsatisfactory and inadequate. Innovation of this type appears in its lowest form in the learning of an act of skill which may not require any implements at all. Some significant innovation in behavior occurs when the directness of action characteristic of the wholly naïve animal is qualified by the power to substitute roundabout methods whenever the direct method of gratification is obstructed.

The simplest demonstration of this type of behavior is provided by the detour problems that have been used in some experiments with animals and children. This type of problem should be carefully distinguished from the maze tests that are sometimes used. The detour test when properly staged makes it possible for the animal to see clearly all the elements of the problem, differing in this respect from the maze in which the general elements of the problem are not within the possible field of direct observation. The test consists of bringing the animal within a three-sided enclosure and offering food outside the enclosure on the side directly opposite the opening. Care must obviously be exercised to avoid suggesting the opening to the subject of the experiment. Lower animals, such as hens, are practically powerless to solve such a test except by accident. Their behavior is largely restricted to motion in a direct line to the objective, and if that is obstructed they can modify their course of action only by luck. Young apes and dogs solve such tests with decision under most circumstances, but they may be puzzled and even made to fail completely if the food is placed so near the barrier that their attention becomes fixed upon the apparent accessibility of the object by the direct method of approach. The choice of the indirect, rather than the direct, means to the end involves in reality a substantial innovation in behavior; it presents in its simplest form the problem of surmounting obstacles to the gratification of wants which is the characteristic element in all invention. New patterns or modes of behavior must be established in such cases; and, if attention is given to the inner content of the case rather than to the external features, these new patterns are "invented" no less than the more complex patterns which include the use of instruments in the new solution. The addition of elements external to the animal merely makes the case somewhat more complex.

A modification of the detour problem tried with apes at Teneriffe is suggestive in this connection. Food is placed in a low three-sided enclosure in such a manner that the apes must first push it away from themselves with a stick in order to get it around the obstacle. Even after they had become thoroughly familiar with the use of a stick in procuring food, this test proved rather difficult and some could not solve the problem at all if the opening in the low enclosure were directly opposite. The angle at which they could solve the problem afforded apparently a measure of the relative intelligence of the different apes. Although, in such a test, the ape always had a clear view of all the elements of the problem, it was evidently more difficult for them than the detour problem in which they turned themselves completely around to avoid the obstacles. To adopt a somewhat indirect route to food was not a very difficult problem, but the necessity of pushing away something they really wanted encountered very serious resistances in their ordinary modes of behavior.

At the moment, the significant feature of the case lies in the fact that the increased resistance is not primarily due to the necessity of using an implement. The stick is merely an integral part in a pattern of behavior. Some new patterns involving a stick were quickly learned, but each new obstruction is a separate problem. There is thus ground for the opinion that the simplest form of invention is the establishment of new patterns of behavior; or more concretely, the acquisition of skill in meeting new situations.

Running and boxing, though they do not require any special instruments, are acts of skill no less than pole vaulting or rowing. The development of proficiency in any of these activities involves a transformation of behavior that is built up partly by the selection of new and effective modes of action that have been discovered, partly from inventions of new patterns. The instruments used are merely parts of an established system or pattern of events which cannot be divided.

Inventive activity extends through a wide range. In its more immediate forms it deals with the data of directly perceived experience. Both ends and means are explicitly present. In its more complex forms it appears in the field of the imagination, where its materials are the shifting complex of the images furnished by fancy or by the memory of actual experiences. Although the range is wide, throughout its full extent there is an actual identity in the processes involved. In all cases, the element of novelty consists in the assimilation of particular data into a pattern previously recognized as incomplete. The dominant fact is the gratification of obstructed wants. But in the more complex forms a distinction appears between the initial completion of the pattern in thought and the ultimate gratification of the want.

This element in the process appears clearly in the account we possess of the initial conception of the condensing chamber of the steam engine. In 1763, Watt was called upon to repair a model of Newcomen's engine belonging to the University. He had already been making a systematic study of some of the problems of heat and on that account made an attempt to determine the practical efficiency of the engine. After experiments he reached the conclusion that not less than three-fourths of the heat supplied by the engine was wasted by the alternate heating and cooling of the cylinder. The crucial idea did not come to him until 2 years after his first work on the engine and 6 years after his first deliberate studies in the problems of heat. He describes the experience in these words:

"I had gone to take a walk on a fine Sabbath afternoon. I had entered the Green and passed the old washing house. I was thinking of the engine at the time. I had gone as far as the herd's house when the idea came into my mind that as steam was an elastic body it would rush into a vacuum, and if a connection were made between the cylinder and an exhausting vessel it would rush into it and might there be condensed without cooling the cylinder. I then saw that I must get rid of the condensed steam and injection water if I used a jet, as in Newcomen's engine. Two ways of doing this occurred to me: First, the water might be run off by a descending pipe, if an offlet could be got at the depth of 35 or 36 feet, and any air might be extracted by a small pump. The second was, to make the pump large enough to extract both water and air . . . I had not walked farther than the Golf-house, when the whole thing was arranged in my mind."[1]

The experience described is clearly the conclusion of the cycle of events which constitute the act of invention in the narrower sense. This imaginative perception of the final solution is the essential act of innovation. But such an experience is obviously different in its consequences from an experience at the level of bare perception. At that level the completion of the pattern results in the final gratification of the want. The ape Sultan gets his banana as soon as he solves his detour problem, or as soon as he perceives that a stick may be used to procure food lying outside the cage beyond the reach of his arm. When the incomplete pattern is filled out by an act of the imagination, the achievement consists in the perception of the means by which the want may ultimately be gratified. At the level of perception, therefore, the act of innovation is complete and final; at the level of the imagination, the essential act necessarily engenders further striving to attain the still relatively remote goal. Invention is at that stage no longer identical with achievement, if we think of achievement in its literal sense of an explicit gratification of a want. Much confusion of thought is due to the failure to distinguish sufficiently between the act of invention and the ultimate achievement based upon the imaginative act.

III

It will now be desirable to give more attention to the details of the experiences involved in the process of invention. The experience is closely associated with the disposition of the mind to see things whole. We do not first perceive all the separate elements of an experience, and then subsequently combine them into an organized group. The whole mass of data is experienced as a unit, more or less satisfactory and complete. Such is the view of an important school of psychologists represented by Kurt Koffka, R. M. Ogden, and others. The thesis is clearly stated by Professor Ogden.

"A perception is any experienced circuit of events. In time it has a beginning and an end, although in the mesh of continuous happening, in which different strands are constantly overlapping, it is often difficult, if not impossible, to determine either an absolute beginning or a finite end; which leads us to wonder if time in its ever onflowing course, is really the safest guide in the analysis of experience. If it is not, then the conception of a circuit in which a want is satisfied is perhaps the truer description of adjustment. In turning full circle the end coincides with the beginning; in satisfying a want a gap is filled, and the want disappears."[2]

It is a great misfortune that there is no wholly adequate term to apply to this notion. In German the word *gestalt* is used; in English, *configuration*: but neither of these terms is sufficiently vivid or certain in its connotation. The school maintains that such perceptions possess inherently a unity that defies analysis. When we do succeed in breaking them up into their component parts, it is only by deliberate and, at times, protracted effort. Synthesis is more natural than analysis. The crude data of the imagination doubtless owe their structure to this essential unity of the things perceived. Such images present the inherent unity and the absence of separately perceived details which characterize the original experience. We perceive things as wholes.

The synthetic quality of experience, however, does not preclude wide gradations in the degree to which the various elements in a circuit make up a satisfactory and complete whole. Gratification is not always complete; the need or want may be wholly obstructed or satisfied incompletely. Innovation is thus in its primary features an attempt to complete or improve some configuration felt by the mind to be unsatisfactory. There is thus an essentially æsthetic element involved in the selection of the most fitting or satisfactory method of completing particular circuits. Two wants are gratified: the desire explicitly felt; the desire to have a satisfying configuration.

The requirements of historical analysis of the development of mechanical appliances do not impose upon us the task of minute examination of the internal aspects of the mental processes. It will be sufficient for our purpose if we can secure a comprehensive description of the external features of the process by which the new configuration is reached.

We must think of the process as beginning with the recognition of a new or an incompletely gratified want. In most instances, we are concerned with improvements in the gratification of commonly recognized wants; but though the specific want is generally present, it does not necessarily follow that the inadequacy of current modes of gratification is always recognized. There are certainly many instances in which some of the distinctive contributions of the individual inventor lie in the perception of the inadequacy of current methods. This was true in part in the case of Watt's work with the steam engine: neither the nature nor the extent of the mechanical inefficiency of the Newcomen engine was generally known. In all probability there is some progressive change in the degree to which the need of an invention is obvious and commonly known. The problem, as such, is perhaps more obvious in later stages; but it is dangerous to follow such a theme very far. We may profitably consider the problem in a concrete case. Grinding was accomplished by mortars or saddle stones (see *infra*) until the third century B.C. when the rotary mill or quern was invented. How much direct gain in efficiency was there in such a change? How keenly or how generally were people dissatisfied with saddle stones and mortars? May we not presume that some special powers of perception were involved in the mere recognition that something better could perhaps be devised. The original inventor of the quern could hardly have foreseen the remoter consequences of the change: the possibility of applying animal power, water power, and ultimately wind power. We begin then with a consciously felt want; and though it may seem to be a commonplace beginning, it is not a point of departure that is certainly self-evident.

The second element in the establishment of a new configuration consists in the total experience of the individual inventor. The telephone and the phonograph are variants of a particular problem; the recreation of sound by mechanically controlled diaphragms. It is doubtless more than a matter of chance that we find Edison producing solutions of both phases of the problem. In part, this will reflect the general body of contemporary knowledge; but in nearly all cases the experience of the inventive individual is richer than usual along the lines of his special interests, and these differences are likely to play a decisive part in inventive accomplishments. Many illustrations can be found in the lives of George Stephenson, Bessemer, and Edison. Early work served significantly in furnishing their minds with interests and experiences which were turned to especially good account in the later and more commonly known inventions. These factors are largely responsible for vague elements of unity in the work of particular inventors—their work falls within certain limits, and reveals a style and quality which may be highly individualized.

These elements in the process of invention are fairly obvious. The next step may not at first seem necessary. Many may presume that the invention flows directly from the combination of a special problem with the highly individualized experience of the gifted inventor. The invention seems to be a mere putting together of the want and the experience. The biographies of inventors, however, show clearly that something else is involved. Popular opinion gives an entirely mystical explanation. Inspirations come to some men but not to others. Close attention to the detailed accounts of particular inventions affords a clue to the general character of the circumstances that promote the achievement of a new configuration. It is well-nigh indispensible that certain data of experience should be presented to the mind of the inventor in such a fashion as to suggest their connection with the problem. All the elements essential to the accomplishment must be brought together sufficiently to facilitate their organization into a new circuit or configuration.

In experimental work with the apes at Teneriffe, the results of the experiments were found to depend in no small measure upon the arrangement of the materials. In work concerning the use of sticks, everything depended upon the location of the stick with reference to the banana used as an object of desire. *The stage had to be set* with meticulous care, and conscious attention had to be given every detail both in planning the experiment and in interpreting the results.

All inventive accomplishment involves some special setting of the stage. This phase of events is conspicuous in all "discoveries," and it is surely present in the work of invention. Edison's work with the incandescent lamp is somewhat of a border-line case between discovery and invention. Strictly speaking, the discovery of the properties of a carbon filament was a necessary condition of the invention of the lamp. The critical achievement was thus a discovery rather than an invention. He began experimenting with the problems of incandescence in 1878. Early work was based on platinum wire. The general fact of the lighting properties of incandescent wires had, of course, long been known, but all the experiments with metal wire had failed to give adequate results because the filaments were too short lived to be of any practical use. Some trials had been made with carbon rods. Edison's experiments with the incandescent light were contemporaneous with his work on the carbon transmitter for the telephone and the final achievement was actually based upon the casual presence on his laboratory table of lamp black that had been used in the telephone work. The story of the invention as told some months later in New York papers implies that the new association came to Edison as a result of his absent-mindedly rolling up between his thumb and forefinger some of the lamp black mixed with tar that was lying on the table. He had worked it into a kind of filament when the thought struck him that such a carbon element might solve the problem of his lamp. An experiment was finally tried with laboriously prepared apparatus and results were achieved which led to protracted experiment with various kinds of carbon filaments. These carbon products combined all the essential properties: resistance, infusibility and indestructibility. After prolonged experimentation with different kinds of vegetable fiber, filaments were turned out which ran to over 1,500 hours of life. From that stage the success of the general project was assured.

In this particular case, the carbon came as definitely into the line of vision between Edison and his projected lamp as the stick provided for the use of the ape Sultan came between the ape and his objective. It is difficult to secure wholly reliable illustrations of this special stage in the process of invention. Accounts are rather sketchy and many stories are based on memories and second-hand accounts. Furthermore, nearly all contemporaneous stories are involved in the extreme complexities of modern accomplishments which present a substantial series of inventions rather than the specifically single act involved in the completion of a single configuration. Any account of this setting of the stage, therefore, must be accepted subject to some qualification, but there are certainly grounds for presuming that the circumstances of the staging of the scene are a crucial bridge between the past experience of the individual and the actual completion of the new configuration. Subsequent discussion of the nature of the obstructions to new configurations will afford further suggestions as to the importance of the circumstances involved in the setting of the stage.

Little remains to be said, beyond explicit and repeated emphasis upon the fact that the unity involved in the individual act of invention is brought to a close with the achievement of a single new concept, design, pattern, or configuration. The variety of words that may be used is indicative of the difficulty of adequately conveying the full connotation of the technical term "configuration."

Endnotes

1. THURSTON, "Steam Engine," p. 87.

2. OGDEN, "Psychology and Education," p. 124.

16 | THE FUNDAMENTAL PHENOMENON OF ECONOMIC DEVELOPMENT

Joseph A. Schumpeter

I

The social process, which rationalises[1] our life and thought, has led us away from the metaphysical treatment of social development and taught us to see the possibility of an empirical treatment; but it has done its work so imperfectly that we must be careful in dealing with the phenomenon itself, still more with the concept in which we comprehend it, and most of all with the word by which we designate the concept and whose associations might lead us astray in all manner of undesirable directions. Closely connected with the metaphysical preconception—more precisely with the ideas which grow out of metaphysical roots and become preconceptions if, neglecting unbridgeable gulfs, we make them do the work of empirical science—even if not itself such a metaphysical preconception, is every search for a "meaning" of history. The same is true of the postulate that a nation, a civilisation, or even the whole of mankind, must show some kind of uniform unilinear development, as even such a matter-of-fact mind as Roscher assumed and as the innumerable philosophers and theorists of history in the long brilliant line from Vico to Lamprecht took and still take for granted. Here, too, belong all kinds of evolutionary thought that centre in Darwin—at least if this means no more than reasoning by analogy—and also the psychological prejudice which consists in seeing more in motives and acts of volition than a reflex of the social process. But the evolutionary idea is now discredited in our field, especially with historians and ethnologists, for still another reason. To the reproach of unscientific and extra-scientific mysticism that now surrounds the "evolutionary" ideas, is added that of dilettantism. With all the hasty generalisations in which the word "evolution" plays a part, many of us have lost patience.

We must get away from such things. Then two facts still remain: first the fact of historical change, whereby social conditions become historical "individuals" in historical time. These changes constitute neither a circular process nor pendulum movements about a centre. The concept of social development is defined by these two circumstances, together with the other fact: that whenever we do not succeed in adequately explaining a given historical state of things from the preceding one, we do indeed recognise the existence of an unsolved but not insoluble problem. This holds good first

"The Fundamental Phenomenon of Economic Development" reprinted by permission of the publisher from THE THEORY OF ECONOMIC DEVELOPMENT: AN INQUIRY INTO PROFITS, CAPITAL, CREDIT AND INTEREST IN THE BUSINESS CYCLE by Joseph A. Schumpeter, translated from the German by Redvers Opie, pp. 57–94, Cambridge Mass: Harvard University Press, Copyright © 1934 by the President and Fellows of Harvard College, Copyright © 1962 by Redvers Opie.

of all for the individual case. For example, we understand Germany's internal political history in 1919 as one of the effects of the preceding war. It also holds good, however, for more general problems.

Economic development is so far simply the object of economic history, which in turn is merely a part of universal history, only separated from the rest for purposes of exposition. Because of this fundamental dependence of the economic aspect of things on everything else, it is not possible to explain *economic* change by previous *economic* conditions alone. For the economic state of a people does not emerge simply from the preceding economic conditions, but only from the preceding total situation. The expository and analytical difficulties which arise from this are very much diminished, practically if not in principle, by the facts which form the basis of economic interpretation of history; without being compelled to take a stand for or against this view, we can state that the economic world is relatively autonomous because it takes up such a great part of a nation's life, and forms or conditions a great part of the remainder; wherefore writing economic history by itself is obviously a different thing from writing, say, military history. To this must be added still another fact which facilitates the separate description of any of the divisions of the social process. Every sector of social life is, as it were, inhabited by a distinct set of people. The heteronomous elements generally do not affect the social process in any such sector directly as the bursting of a bomb "affects" all things which happen to be in the room in which it explodes, but only through its data and the conduct of its inhabitants; and even if an event occurs like the one suggested by our metaphor of a bursting bomb, the effects only occur in the particular garb with which those primarily concerned dress them. Therefore, just as describing the effects of the Counter Reformation upon Italian and Spanish painting always remains history of art, so describing the economic process remains economic history even where the true causation is largely non-economic.

The economic sector, again, is open to an endless variety of points of view and treatments, which one can array, for example, according to the breadth of their scope—or we might just as well say according to the degree of generalisation which they imply. From an exposition of the nature of the economic life of the Niederaltaich monastery in the thirteenth century to Sombart's exposition of the development of economic life in western Europe, there runs a continuous, logically uniform thread. Such an exposition as Sombart's is theory, and indeed theory of economic development in the sense in which we intend it for the moment. But it is not economic theory in the sense in which the contents of the first chapter of this book are economic theory, which is what has been understood by "economic theory" since Ricardo's day. Economic theory in the latter sense, it is true, plays a part in a theory like Sombart's, but a wholly subordinate one: namely, where the connection of historical facts is complicated enough to necessitate methods of interpretation which go beyond the analytic powers of the man in the street, the line of thought takes the form offered by that analytical apparatus. However, where it is simply a question of making development or the historical outcome of it intelligible, of working out the elements which characterise a situation or determine an issue, economic theory in the traditional sense contributes next to nothing.[2]

We are not concerned here with a theory of development in this sense. No historical evolutionary factors will be indicated—whether individual events like the appearance of American gold production in Europe in the sixteenth century, or "more general" circumstances like changes in the mentality of economic men, in the area of the civilised world, in social organisation, in political constellations, in productive technique, and so forth—nor will their effects be described for individual cases or for groups of cases.[3] On the contrary, the economic theory the nature of which was sufficiently expounded to the reader in the first chapter will simply be improved for its own purposes, by building onto it. If this were also to enable this theory to perform better than hitherto its service to the other kind of theory of development, the fact would still remain that the two methods lie in different planes.

Our problem is as follows. The theory of the first chapter describes economic life from the standpoint of a "circular flow," running on in channels essentially the same year after year—similar to the circulation of the blood in an animal organism. Now this circular flow and its channels do alter in time, and here we abandon the analogy with the circulation of the blood. For although the latter also changes in the course of the growth and decline of the organism, yet it only does so continuously, that is by steps which one can choose smaller than any assignable quantity, however small, and always within the same framework. Economic life experiences such changes too, but it also experiences others which do not appear continuously and which change the framework, the traditional course itself. They cannot be understood by means of any analysis of the circular flow, although they are purely economic and although their explanation is obviously among the tasks of pure theory. Now such changes and the phenomena which appear in their train are the object of our investigation. But we do not ask: what changes of this sort have actually made the modern economic system what it is? Nor: what are the conditions of such changes? We only ask, and indeed in the same sense as theory always asks: how do such changes take place, and to what economic phenomena do they give rise?

The same thing may be put somewhat differently. The theory of the first chapter describes economic life from the standpoint of the economic system's tendency towards an equilibrium position, which tendency gives us the means of determining prices and quantities of goods, and may be described as an adaptation to data existing at any time. In contrast to the conditions of the circular flow this does not mean in itself that year after year "the same" things happen; for it only means that we conceive the several processes in the economic system as partial phenomena of the tendency towards an equilibrium position, but not necessarily towards the same one. The position of the ideal state of equilibrium in the economic system, never attained, continually "striven after" (of course not consciously), changes, because the data change. And theory is not weaponless in the face of these changes in data. It is constructed so as to be able to deal with the consequences of such changes; it has special instruments for the purpose (for example the instrument called quasi-rent). If the change occurs in the non-social data (natural conditions) or in non-economic social data (here belong the effects of war, changes in commercial, social, or economic policy), or in consumers' tastes, then to this extent no fundamental overhaul of the theoretical tools seems to be required. These tools only fail—and here this argument joins the preceding—where economic life itself changes its own data by fits and starts. The building of a railway may serve as an example. Continuous changes, which may in time, by continual adaptation through innumerable small steps, make a great department store out of a small retail business, come under the "static" analysis. But "static" analysis is not only unable to predict the consequences of discontinuous changes in the traditional way of doing things; it can neither explain the occurrence of such productive revolutions nor the phenomena which accompany them. It can only investigate the new equilibrium position after the changes have occurred. It is just this occurrence of the "revolutionary" change that is our problem, the problem of economic development in a very narrow and formal sense. The reason why we so state the problem and turn aside from traditional theory lies not so much in the fact that economic changes, especially, if not solely, in the capitalist epoch, have actually occurred thus and not by continuous adaptation, but more in their fruitfulness.[4]

By "development," therefore, we shall understand only such changes in economic life as are not forced upon it from without but arise by its own initiative, from within. Should it turn out that there are no such changes arising in the economic sphere itself, and that the phenomenon that we call economic development is in practice simply founded upon the fact that the data change and that the economy continuously adapts itself to them, then we should say that there is *no* economic development. By this we should mean that economic development is not a phenomenon to be explained economically, but that the economy, in itself without development, is dragged along by the changes in the surrounding world, that the causes and hence the explanation of the development must be sought outside the group of facts which are described by economic theory.

Nor will the mere growth of the economy, as shown by the growth of population and wealth, be designated here as a process of development. For it calls forth no qualitatively new phenomena, but only processes of adaptation of the same kind as the changes in the natural data. Since we wish to direct our attention to other phenomena, we shall regard such increases as changes in data.[5]

Every concrete process of development finally rests upon preceding development. But in order to see the essence of the thing clearly, we shall abstract from this and allow the development to arise out of a position without development. Every process of development creates the prerequisites for the following. Thereby the form of the latter is altered, and things will turn out differently from what they would have been if every concrete phase of development had been compelled first to create its own conditions. However, if we wish to get at the root of the matter, we may not include in the data of our explanation elements of what is to be explained. But if we do not do this, we shall create an apparent discrepancy between fact and theory, which may constitute an important difficulty for the reader.

If I have been more successful than in the first edition in concentrating the exposition upon essentials and in guarding against misunderstandings, then further special explanations of the words "static" and "dynamic," with their innumerable meanings, are not necessary. Development in our sense is a distinct phenomenon, entirely foreign to what may be observed in the circular flow or in the tendency towards equilibrium. It is spontaneous and discontinuous change in the channels of the flow, disturbance of equilibrium, which forever alters and displaces the equilibrium state previously existing. Our theory of development is nothing but a treatment of this phenomenon and the processes incident to it.[6]

II

These spontaneous and discontinuous changes in the channel of the circular flow and these disturbances of the centre of equilibrium appear in the sphere of industrial and commercial life, not in the sphere of the wants of the consumers of final products. Where spontaneous and discontinuous changes in consumers' tastes appear, it is a question of a sudden change in data with which the businessman must cope, hence possibly a question of a *motive* or an opportunity for other than gradual adaptations of his conduct, but not of such other conduct itself. Therefore this case does not offer any other problems than a change in natural data or require any new method of treatment; wherefore we shall neglect any spontaneity of consumers' needs that may actually exist, and assume tastes as "given." This is made easy for us by the fact that the spontaneity of wants is in general small. To be sure, we must always start from the satisfaction of wants, since they are the end of all production, and the given economic situation at any time must be understood from this aspect. Yet innovations in the economic system do not as a rule take place in such a way that first new wants arise spontaneously in consumers and then the productive apparatus swings round through their pressure. We do not deny the presence of this nexus. It is, however, the producer who as a rule initiates economic change, and consumers are educated by him if necessary; they are, as it were, taught to want new things, or things which differ in some respect or other from those which they have been in the habit of using. Therefore, while it is permissible and even necessary to consider consumers' wants as an independent and indeed the fundamental force in a theory of the circular flow, we must take a different attitude as soon as we analyse *change*.

To produce means to combine materials and forces within our reach (cf. *supra,* Chapter 1). To produce other things, or the same things by a different method, means to combine these materials and forces differently. In so far as the "new combination" may in time grow out of the old by continuous adjustment in small steps, there is certainly change, possibly growth, but neither a new phenomenon nor development in our sense. In so far as this is not the case, and the new combinations appear discontinuously, then the phenomenon characterising development emerges. For reasons of expository convenience, henceforth, we shall only mean the latter case when we speak of new combinations of productive means. Development in our sense is then defined by the carrying out of new combinations.

This concept covers the following five cases: (1) The introduction of a new good— that is one with which consumers are not yet familiar—or of a new quality of a good. (2) The introduction of a new method of production, that is one not yet tested by experience in the branch of manufacture concerned, which need by no means be founded upon a discovery scientifically new, and can also exist in a new way of handling a commodity commercially. (3) The opening of a new market, that is a market into which the particular branch of manufacture of the country in question has not previously entered, whether or not this market has existed before. (4) The conquest of a new source of supply of raw materials or half-manufactured goods, again irrespective of whether this source already exists or whether it has first to be created. (5) The carrying out of the new organisation of any industry, like the creation of a monopoly position (for example through trustification) or the breaking up of a monopoly position.

Now two things are essential for the phenomena incident to the carrying out of such new combinations, and for the understanding of the problems involved. In the first place it is not essential to the matter—though it may happen—that the new combinations should be carried out by the same people who control the productive or commercial process which is to be displaced by the new. On the contrary, new combinations are, as a rule, embodied, as it were, in new firms which generally do not arise out of the old ones but start producing beside them; to keep to the example already chosen, in general it is not the owner of stage-coaches who builds railways. This fact not only puts the discontinuity which characterises the process we want to describe in a special light, and creates so to speak still another kind of discontinuity in addition to the one mentioned above, but it also explains important features of the course of events. Especially in a competitive economy, in which new combinations mean the competitive elimination of the old, it explains on the one hand the process by which individuals and families rise and fall economically and socially and which is peculiar to this form of organisation, as well as a whole series of other phenomena of the business cycle, of the mechanism of the formation of private fortunes, and so on. In a non-exchange economy, for example a socialist one, the new combinations would also frequently appear side by side with the old. But the economic consequences of this fact would be absent to some extent, and the social consequences would be wholly absent. And if the competitive economy is broken up by the growth of great combines, as is increasingly the case to-day in all countries, then this must become more and more true of real life, and the carrying out of new combinations must become in ever greater measure the internal concern of one and the same economic body. The difference so made is great enough to serve as the water-shed between two epochs in the social history of capitalism.

We must notice secondly, only partly in connection with this element, that whenever we are concerned with fundamental principles, we must never assume that the carrying out of new combinations takes place by employing means of production which happen to be unused. In practical life, this is very often the case. There are always unemployed workmen, unsold raw materials, unused productive capacity, and so forth. This certainly is a contributory circumstance, a favorable condition and even an incentive to the emergence of new combinations; but great unemployment is only the consequence of non-economic events—as for example the World War—or precisely of the development which we are investigating. In neither of the two cases can its existence play a fundamental rôle in the explanation, and it cannot occur in a well balanced circular flow from which we start. Nor would the normal yearly increment meet the case, as it would be small in the first place, and also because it would normally be absorbed by a corresponding expansion of production within the circular flow, which, if we admit such increments, we must think of as adjusted to this rate of growth.[7] As a rule the new combinations must draw the necessary means of production from some old combinations—and for reasons already mentioned we shall assume that they *always* do so, in order to put in bold relief what we hold to be the essential contour line. The carrying out of new combinations means, therefore, simply the different employment of the economic system's existing supplies of productive means—which might provide a second definition of development in our sense. That rudiment of a pure economic theory of development which is implied in the traditional doctrine of the formation of capital always refers merely to saving and to the investment of the small yearly increase attributable to it. In this it asserts nothing false, but it entirely overlooks much more essential things. The slow and continuous increase in time of the national supply of productive means and of savings is obviously an important factor in explaining the course of economic history through the centuries, but it is completely overshadowed by the fact that development consists primarily in employing existing resources in a different way, in doing new things with them, irrespective of whether those resources increase or not. In the treatment of shorter epochs, moreover, this is even true in a more tangible sense. Different methods of employment, and not saving and increases in the available quantity of labor, have changed the face of the economic world in the last fifty years. The increase of population especially, but also of the sources from which savings can be made, was first made possible in large measure through the different employment of the then existing means.

The next step in our argument is also self-evident: command over means of production is necessary to the carrying out of new combinations. Procuring the means of production is one distinct problem for the established firms which work within the circular flow. For they *have* them already procured or else can procure them currently with the proceeds of previous production as was explained in the first chapter. There is no fundamental gap here between receipts and disbursements, which, on the contrary, necessarily correspond to one another just as both correspond to the means of production offered and to the products demanded. Once set in motion, this mechanism works automatically. Furthermore, the problem does not exist in a non-exchange economy even if new combinations are carried out in it; for the directing organ, for example a socialist economic ministry, is in a position to direct the productive resources of the society to new uses exactly as it can direct them to their previous employments. The new employment may, under certain circumstances, impose temporary sacrifices, privations, or increased efforts upon the members of the community; it may presuppose the solution of difficult problems, for example the question from which of the old combinations the necessary productive means should be withdrawn; but there is no question of procuring means of production not already at the disposal of the economic ministry. Finally, the problem also does not exist in a competitive economy in the case of the carrying out of new combinations, if those who carry them out have the necessary productive means or can get them in exchange for others which they have or for any other property which they may possess. This is not the privilege of the possession of property *per se,* but only the privilege of the possession of disposable property, that is such as is employable either immediately for carrying out the new combination or in exchange for the necessary goods and services.[8] In the contrary case—and this is the rule as it is the fundamentally interesting case—the possessor of wealth, even if it is the greatest combine, must resort to credit if he wishes to carry out a new combination, which cannot like an established business be financed by returns from previous production. To provide this credit is clearly the function of that category of individuals which we call "capitalists." It is obvious that this is the characteristic method of the capitalist type of society—and important enough to serve as its *differentia specifica*—for forcing the economic system into new channels, for putting its means at the service of new ends, in contrast to the method of a non-exchange economy of the kind which simply consists in exercising the directing organ's power to command.

It does not appear to me possible to dispute in any way the foregoing statement. Emphasis upon the significance of credit is to be found in every textbook. That the structure of modern industry could not have been erected without it, that it makes the individual to a certain extent independent of inherited possessions, that talent in economic life "rides to success on its debts," even the most conservative orthodoxy of the theorists cannot well deny. Nor is the connection established here between credit and the carrying out of innovations, a connection which will be worked out later, anything to take offence at. For it is as clear *a priori* as it is established historically that credit is primarily necessary to new combinations and that it is from these that it forces its way into the circular flow, on the one hand because it was originally necessary to the founding of what are now the old firms, on the other hand because its mechanism, once in existence, also seizes old combinations for obvious reasons.[9] First, *a priori:* we saw in the first chapter that borrowing is not a necessary element of production in the normal circular flow within accustomed channels, is not an element without which we could not understand the essential phenomena of the latter. On the other hand, in carrying out new combinations, "financing" as a special act is fundamentally necessary, in practice as in theory. Second, historically: those who lend and borrow for industrial purposes do not appear early in history. The pre-capitalistic lender provided money for other than business purposes. And we all remember the type of industrialist who felt he was losing caste by borrowing and who therefore shunned banks and bills of exchange. The capitalistic credit system has grown out of and thrived on the financing of new combinations in all countries, even though in a different way in each (the origin of German joint stock banking is especially characteristic). Finally there can be no stumblingblock in our speaking of receiving credit in "money or money substitutes." We certainly do not assert that one can produce with coins, notes, or bank balances, and do not deny that services of labor, raw materials, and tools are the things wanted. We are only speaking of a method of procuring them.

Nevertheless there is a point here in which, as has already been hinted, our theory diverges from the traditional view. The accepted theory sees a problem in the existence of the productive means, which are needed for new, or indeed any, productive processes, and this accumulation therefore becomes a distinct function or service. We do not recognise this problem at all; it appears to us to be created by faulty analysis. It does not exist in the circular flow, because the running of the latter presupposes given quantities of means of production. But neither does it exist for the carrying out of new combinations,[10] because the productive means required in the latter are drawn from the circular flow whether they already exist there in the shape wanted or have first to be produced by other means of production existing there. Instead of this problem another exists for us: the problem of detaching productive means (already employed somewhere) from the circular flow and allotting them to new combinations. This is done by credit, by means of which one who wishes to carry out new combinations outbids the producers in the circular flow in the market for the required means of production. And although the meaning and object of this process lies in a movement of goods from their old towards new employments, it cannot be described entirely in terms of goods without overlooking something essential, which happens in the sphere of money and credit and upon which depends the explanation of important phenomena in the capitalist form of economic organisation, in contrast to other types.

Finally one more step in this direction: whence come the sums needed to purchase the means of production necessary for the new combinations if the individual concerned does not happen to have them? The conventional answer is simple: out of the annual growth of social savings plus that part of resources which may annually become free. Now the first quantity was indeed important enough before the war—it may perhaps be estimated as one-fifth of total private incomes in Europe and North America—so that together with the latter sum, which it is difficult to obtain statistically, it does not immediately give the lie quantitatively to this answer. At the same time a figure representing the range of all the business operations involved in carrying out new combinations is also not available at present. But we may not even start from total "savings." For its magnitude is explicable only by the results of previous development. By far the greater part of it does not come from thrift in the strict sense, that is from abstaining from the consumption of part of one's regular income, but it consists of funds which are themselves the result of successful innovation and in which we shall later recognise entrepreneurial profit. In the circular flow there would be on the one hand no such rich source, out of which to save, and on the other hand essentially less incentive to save. The only big incomes known to it would be monopoly revenues and the rents of large landowners; while provision for misfortunes and old age, perhaps also irrational motives, would be the only incentives. The most important incentive, the chance of participating in the gains of development, would be absent. Hence, in such an economic system there could be no great reservoirs of free purchasing power, to which one who wished to form new combinations could turn—and his own savings would only suffice in exceptional cases. All money would circulate, would be fixed in definite established channels.

Even though the conventional answer to our question is not obviously absurd, yet there is another method of obtaining money for this purpose, which claims our attention, because it, unlike the one referred to, does not presuppose the existence of accumulated results of previous development, and hence may be considered as the only one which is available in strict logic. This method of obtaining money is the creation of purchasing power by banks. The form it takes is immaterial. The issue of bank-notes not fully covered by specie withdrawn from circulation is an obvious instance, but methods of deposit banking render the same service, where they increase the sum total of possible expenditure. Or we may think of bank acceptances in so far as they serve as money to make payments in wholesale trade. It is always a question, not of transforming purchasing power which already exists in someone's possession, but of the creation of new purchasing power out of nothing—out of nothing even if the credit contract by which the new purchasing power is created is supported by securities which are not themselves circulating media—which is added to the existing circulation. And this is the source from which new combinations *are* often financed, and from which they would have to be financed *always,* if results of previous development did not actually exist at any moment.

These credit means of payment, that is means of payment which are created for the purpose and by the act of giving credit, serve just as ready money in trade, partly directly, partly because they can be converted immediately into ready money for small payments or payments to the non-banking classes—in particular to wage-earners. With their help, those who carry out new combinations can gain access to the existing stocks of productive means, or, as the case may be, enable those from whom they buy productive services to gain immediate access to the market for consumption goods. There is never, in this nexus, granting of credit in the sense that someone must wait for the equivalent of his service in goods, and content himself with a claim, thereby fulfilling a special function; not even in the sense that someone has to accumulate means of maintenance for laborers or landowners, or produced means of production, all of which would only be paid for out of the final results of production. Economically, it is true, there is an essential difference between these means of payment, if they are created for new ends, and money or other means of payment of the circular flow. The latter may be conceived on the one hand as a kind of certificate for completed production and the increase in the social product effected through it, and on the other hand as a kind of order upon, or claim to, part of this social product. The former have not the first of these two characteristics. They too are orders, for which one can immediately procure consumption goods, but not certificates for previous production. Access to the national dividend is usually to be had only on condition of some productive service previously rendered or of some product previously sold. This condition is, in this case, not yet fulfilled. It will be fulfilled only after the successful completion of the new combinations. Hence this credit will in the meantime affect the price level.

The banker, therefore, is not so much primarily a middleman in the commodity "purchasing power" as a *producer* of this commodity. However, since all reserve funds and savings to-day usually flow to him, and the total demand for free purchasing power, whether existing or to be created, concentrates on him, he has either replaced private capitalists or become their agent; he has himself become the capitalist par excellence. He stands between those who wish to form new combinations and the possessors of productive means. He is essentially a phenomenon of development, though only when no central authority directs the social process. He makes possible the carrying out of new combinations, authorises people, in the name of society as it were, to form them. He is the ephor of the exchange economy.

III

We now come to the third of the elements with which our analysis works, namely the "new combination of means of production," and credit. Although all three elements form a whole, the third may be described as the fundamental phenomenon of economic development. The carrying out of new combinations we call "enterprise"; the individuals whose function it is to carry them out we call "entrepreneurs." These concepts are at once broader and narrower than the usual. Broader, because in the first place we call entrepreneurs not only those "independent" businessmen in an exchange economy who are usually so designated, but all who actually fulfil the function by which we define the concept, even if they are, as is becoming the rule, "dependent" employees of a company, like managers, members of boards of directors, and so forth, or even if their actual power to perform the entrepreneurial function has any other foundations, such as the control of a majority of shares. As it is the carrying out of new combinations that constitutes the entrepreneur, it is not necessary that he should be permanently connected with an individual firm; many "financiers," "promotors," and so forth are not, and still they may be entrepreneurs in our sense. On the other hand, our concept is narrower than the traditional one in that it does not include all heads of firms or managers or industrialists who merely may operate an established business, but only those who actually perform that function. Nevertheless I maintain that the above definition does no more than formulate with greater precision what the traditional doctrine really means to convey. In the first place our definition agrees with the usual one on the fundamental point of distinguishing between "entrepreneurs" and "capitalists"—irrespective of whether the latter are regarded as owners of money, claims to money, or material goods. This distinction is common property to-day and has been so for a considerable time. It also settles the question whether the ordinary shareholder as such is an entrepreneur, and disposes of the conception of the entrepreneur as risk bearer.[11] Furthermore, the ordinary characterisation of the entrepreneur type by such expressions as "initiative," "authority," or "foresight" points entirely in our direction. For there is little scope for such qualities within the routine of the circular flow, and if this had been sharply separated from the occurrence of changes in this routine itself, the emphasis in the definition of the function of entrepreneurs would have been shifted automatically to the latter. Finally there are definitions which we could simply accept. There is in particular the well known one that goes back to J. B. Say: the entrepreneur's function is to combine the productive factors, to bring them together. Since this is a performance of a special kind only when the factors are combined for the first time—while it is merely routine work if done in the course of running a business—this definition coincides with ours. When Mataja (in Unternehmergewinn) defines the entrepreneur as one who receives profit, we have only to add the conclusion of the first chapter, that there is no profit in the circular flow, in order to trace this formulation too back to ours.[12] And this view is not foreign to traditional theory, as is shown by the construction of the *entrepreneur faisant ni bénéfice ni perte,* which has been worked out rigorously by Walras, but is the property of many other authors. The tendency is for the entrepreneur to make neither profit nor loss in the circular flow—that is he has no function of a special kind there, he simply does not exist; but in his stead, there are heads of firms or business managers of a different type which we had better not designate by the same term.

It is a prejudice to believe that the knowledge of the historical origin of an institution or of a type immediately shows us its sociological or economic nature. Such knowledge often leads us to understand it, but it does not directly yield a theory of it. Still more false is the belief that "primitive" forms of a type are also *ipso facto* the "simpler" or the "more original" in the sense that they show their nature more purely and with fewer complications than later ones. Very frequently the opposite is the case, amongst other reasons because increasing specialisation may allow functions and qualities to stand out sharply, which are more difficult to recognise in more primitive conditions when mixed with others. So it is in our case. In the general position of the chief of a primitive horde it is difficult to separate the entrepreneurial element from the others. For the same reason most economists up to the time of the younger Mill failed to keep capitalist and entrepreneur distinct because the manufacturer of a hundred years ago was both; and certainly the course of events since then has facilitated the making of this distinction, as the system of land tenure in England has facilitated the distinction between farmer and landowner, while on the Continent this distinction is still occasionally neglected, especially in the case of the peasant who tills his own soil.[13] But in our case there are still more of such difficulties. The entrepreneur of earlier times was not only as a rule the capitalist too, he was also often—as he still is to-day in the case of small concerns—his own technical expert, in so far as a professional specialist was not called in for special cases. Likewise he was (and is) often his own buying and selling agent, the head of his office, his own personnel manager, and sometimes, even though as a rule he of course employed solicitors, his own legal advis-er in current affairs. And it was performing some or all of these functions that regular-ly filled his days. The carrying out of new combinations can no more be a *vocation* than the making and execution of strategical decisions, although it is this function and not his routine work that characterises the military leader. Therefore the entrepreneur's essential function must always appear mixed up with other kinds of activity, which as a rule must be much more conspicuous than the essential one. Hence the Marshallian definition of the enterpreneur, which simply treats the entrepreneurial function as "management" in the widest meaning, will naturally appeal to most of us. We do not accept it, simply because it does not bring out what we consider to be the salient point and the only one which specifically distinguishes entrepreneurial from other activities.

Nevertheless there are types—the course of events has evolved them by degrees—which exhibit the entrepreneurial function with particular purity. The "promoter," to be sure, belongs to them only with qualifications. For, neglecting the associations rela-tive to social and moral status which are attached to this type, the promoter is fre-quently only an agent intervening on commission, who does the work of financial technique in floating the new enterprise. In this case he is not its creator nor the dri-ving power in the process. However, he *may* be the latter also, and then he is some-thing like an "entrepreneur by profession." But the modern type of "captain of industry"[14] corresponds more closely to what is meant here, especially if one recognis-es his identity on the one hand with, say, the commercial entrepreneur of twelfth-century Venice—or, among later types, with John Law—and on the other hand with the village potentate who combines with his agriculture and his cattle trade, say, a rural brewery, an hotel, and a store. But whatever the type, everyone is an entrepreneur only when he actually "carries out new combinations," and loses that character as soon as he has built up his business, when he settles down to running it as other people run their businesses. This is the rule, of course, and hence it is just as rare for anyone always to remain an entrepreneur throughout the decades of his active life as it is for a businessman never to have a moment in which he is an entrepreneur, to however modest a degree.

Because being an entrepreneur is not a profession and as a rule not a lasting condi-tion, entrepreneurs do not form a social class in the technical sense, as, for example, landowners or capitalists or workmen do. Of course the entrepreneurial function will *lead* to certain class positions for the successful entrepreneur and his family. It can also put its stamp on an epoch of social history, can form a style of life, or systems of moral and aesthetic values; but in itself it signifies a class position no more than it presuppos-es one. And the class position which may be attained is not as such an entrepreneurial position, but is characterised as landowning or capitalist, according to how the proceeds of the enterprise are used. Inheritance of the pecuniary result and of personal qualities may then both keep up this position for more than one generation and make further enterprise easier for descendants, but the function of the entrepreneur itself cannot be inherited, as is shown well enough by the history of manufacturing families.[15]

But now the decisive question arises: why then is the carrying out of new combina-tions a special process and the object of a special kind of "function"? Every individual carries on his economic affairs as well as he can. To be sure, his own intentions are never realised with ideal perfection, but ultimately his behavior is moulded by the influence on him of the results of his conduct, so as to fit circumstances which do not as a rule change suddenly. If a business can never be absolutely perfect in any sense, yet it in time approaches a relative perfection having regard to the surrounding world, the social conditions, the knowledge of the time, and the horizon of each individual or each group. New possibilities are continuously being offered by the surrounding world, in particular new discoveries are continuously being added to the existing store of knowledge. Why should not the individual make just as much use of the new possibilities as of the old, and, according to the market position as he understands it, keep pigs instead of cows, or even choose a new crop rotation, if this can be seen to be more advantageous? And what kind of special new phenomena or problems, not to be found in the established circular flow, can arise there?

While in the accustomed circular flow every individual can act promptly and rationally because he is sure of his ground and is supported by the conduct, as adjusted to this circular flow, of all other individuals, who in turn expect the accustomed activity from him, he cannot simply do this when he is confronted by a new task. While in the accustomed channels his own ability and experience suffice for the normal individual, when confronted with innovations he needs guidance. While he swims with the stream in the circular flow which is familiar to him, he swims against the stream if he wishes to change its channel. What was formerly a help becomes a hindrance. What was a familiar datum becomes an unknown. Where the boundaries of routine stop, many people can go no further, and the rest can only do so in a highly variable manner. The assumption that conduct is prompt and rational is in all cases a fiction. But it proves to be sufficiently near to reality, if things have time to hammer logic into men. Where this has happened, and within the limits in which it has happened, one may rest content with this fiction and build theories upon it. It is then not true that habit or custom or non-economic ways of thinking cause a hopeless difference between the individuals of different classes, times, or cultures, and that, for example, the "economics of the stock exchange" would be inapplicable say to the peasants of to-day or to the craftsmen of the Middle Ages. On the contrary the same theoretical picture[16] in its broadest contour lines fits the individuals of quite different cultures, whatever their degree of intelligence and of economic rationality, and we can depend upon it that the peasant sells his calf just as cunningly and egotistically as the stock exchange member his portfolio of shares. But this holds good only where precedents without number have formed conduct through decades and, in fundamentals, through hundreds and thousands of years, and have eliminated unadapted behavior. Outside of these limits our fiction loses its closeness to reality.[17] To cling to it there also, as the traditional theory does, is to hide an essential thing and to ignore a fact which, in contrast with other deviations of our assumptions from reality, is theoretically important and the source of the explanation of phenomena which would not exist without it.

Therefore, in describing the circular flow one must treat combinations of means of production (the production-functions) as data, like natural possibilities, and admit only small[18] variations at the margins, such as every individual can accomplish by adapting himself to changes in his economic environment, without materially deviating from familiar lines. Therefore, too, the carrying out of new combinations is a special function, and the privilege of a type of people who are much less numerous than all those who have the "objective" possibility of doing it. Therefore, finally, entrepreneurs are a special type,[19] and their behavior a special problem, the motive power of a great number of significant phenomena. Hence, our position may be characterised by three corresponding pairs of opposites. First, by the opposition of two real processes: the circular flow or the tendency towards equilibrium on the one hand, a change in the channels of economic routine or a spontaneous change in the economic data arising from within the system on the other. Secondly, by the opposition of two theoretical *apparatuses:* statics and dynamics.[20] Thirdly, by the opposition of two types of conduct, which, following reality, we can picture as two types of individuals: mere managers and entrepreneurs. And therefore the "best method" of producing in the theoretical sense is to be conceived as "the most advantageous among the methods which have been empirically tested and become familiar." But it is not the "best" of the methods "possible" at the time. If one does not make this distinction, the concept becomes meaningless and precisely those problems remain unsolved which our interpretation is meant to provide for.

Let us now formulate precisely the characteristic feature of the conduct and type under discussion. The smallest daily action embodies a huge mental effort. Every schoolboy would have to be a mental giant, if he himself had to create all he knows and uses by his own individual activity. And every man would have to be a giant of wisdom and will, if he had in every case to create anew all the rules by which he guides his everyday conduct. This is true not only of those decisions and actions of individual and social life the principles of which are the product of tens of thousands of years, but also of those products of shorter periods and of a more special nature which constitute the particular instrument for performing vocational tasks. But precisely the things the performance of which according to this should involve a supreme effort, in general demand no special individual effort at all; those which should be especially difficult are in reality especially easy; what should demand superhuman capacity is accessible to the least gifted, given mental health. In particular within the ordinary routine there is no need for leadership. Of course it is still necessary to set people their tasks, to keep up discipline, and so forth; but this is easy and a function any normal person can learn to fulfil. Within the lines familiar to all, even the function of directing other people, though still necessary, is mere "work" like any other, comparable to the service of tending a machine. All people get to know, and are able to do, their daily tasks in the customary way and ordinarily perform them by themselves; the "director" has his routine as they have theirs; and his directive function serves merely to correct individual aberrations.

This is so because all knowledge and habit once acquired becomes as firmly rooted in ourselves as a railway embankment in the earth. It does not require to be continually renewed and consciously reproduced, but sinks into the strata of subconsciousness. It is normally transmitted almost without friction by inheritance, teaching, upbringing, pressure of environment. Everything we think, feel, or do often enough becomes automatic and our conscious life is unburdened of it. The enormous economy of force, in the race and the individual, here involved is not great enough, however, to make daily life a light burden and to prevent its demands from exhausting the average energy all the same. But it is great enough to make it possible to meet the ordinary claims. This holds good likewise for economic daily life. And from this it follows also for economic life that every step outside the boundary of routine has difficulties and involves a new element. It is this element that constitutes the phenomenon of leadership.

The nature of these difficulties may be focussed in the following three points. First, outside these accustomed channels the individual is without those data for his decisions and those rules of conduct which are usually very accurately known to him within them. Of course he must still foresee and estimate on the basis of his experience. But many things must remain uncertain, still others are only ascertainable within wide limits, some can perhaps only be "guessed." In particular this is true of those data which the individual strives to alter and of those which he wants to create. Now he must really to some extent do what tradition does for him in everyday life, viz. consciously plan his conduct in every particular. There will be much more conscious rationality in this than in customary action, which as such does not need to be reflected upon at all; but this plan must necessarily be open not only to errors greater in degree, but also to other kinds of errors than those occurring in customary action. What has been done already has the sharp-edged reality of all the things which we have seen and experienced; the new is only the figment of our imagination. Carrying out a new plan and acting according to a customary one are things as different as making a road and walking along it.

How different a thing this is becomes clearer if one bears in mind the impossibility of surveying exhaustively all the effects and counter-effects of the projected enterprise. Even as many of them as could in theory be ascertained if one had unlimited time and means must practically remain in the dark. As military action must be taken in a given strategic position even if all the data potentially procurable are not available, so also in economic life action must be taken without working out all the details of what is to be done. Here the success of everything depends upon intuition, the capacity of seeing things in a way which afterwards proves to be true, even though it cannot be established at the moment, and of grasping the essential fact, discarding the unessential, even though one can give no account of the principles by which this is done. Thorough preparatory work, and special knowledge, breadth of intellectual understanding, talent for logical analysis, may under certain circumstances be sources of failure. The more accurately, however, we learn to know the natural and social world, the more perfect our control of facts becomes; and the greater the extent, with time and progressive rationalisation, within which things can be simply calculated, and indeed quickly and reliably calculated, the more the significance of this function decreases. Therefore the importance of the entrepreneur type must diminish just as the importance of the military commander has already diminished. Nevertheless a part of the very essence of each type is bound up with this function.

As this first point lies in the task, so the second lies in the psyche of the business-man himself. It is not only objectively more difficult to do something new than what is familiar and tested by experience, but the individual feels reluctance to it and would do so even if the objective difficulties did not exist. This is so in all fields. The history of science is one great confirmation of the fact that we find it exceedingly difficult to adopt a new scientific point of view or method. Thought turns again and again into the accustomed track even if it has become unsuitable and the more suitable innovation in itself presents no particular difficulties. The very nature of fixed habits of thinking, their energy-saving function, is founded upon the fact that they have become subconscious, that they yield their results automatically and are proof against criticism and even against contradiction by individual facts. But precisely because of this they become drag-chains when they have outlived their usefulness. So it is also in the economic world. In the breast of one who wishes to do something new, the forces of habit rise up and bear witness against the embryonic project. A new and another kind of effort of will is therefore necessary in order to wrest, amidst the work and care of the daily round, scope and time for conceiving and working out the new combination and to bring oneself to look upon it as a real possibility and not merely as a day-dream. This mental freedom presupposes a great surplus force over the everyday demand and is something peculiar and by nature rare.

The third point consists in the reaction of the social environment against one who wishes to do something new. This reaction may manifest itself first of all in the existence of legal or political impediments. But neglecting this, any deviating conduct by a member of a social group is condemned, though in greatly varying degrees according as the social group is used to such conduct or not. Even a deviation from social custom in such things as dress or manners arouses opposition, and of course all the more so in the graver cases. This opposition is stronger in primitive stages of culture than in others, but it is never absent. Even mere astonishment at the deviation, even merely noticing it, exercises a pressure on the individual. The manifestation of condemnation may at once bring noticeable consequences in its train. It may even come to social ostracism and finally to physical prevention or to direct attack. Neither the fact that progressive differentiation weakens this opposition—especially as the most important cause of the weakening is the very development which we wish to explain—nor the further fact that the social opposition operates under certain circumstances and upon many individuals as a stimulus, changes anything in principle in the significance of it. Surmounting this opposition is always a special kind of task which does not exist in the customary course of life, a task which also requires a special kind of conduct. In matters economic this resistance manifests itself first of all in the groups threatened by the innovation, then in the difficulty in finding the necessary cooperation, finally in the difficulty in winning over consumers. Even though these elements are still effective to-day, despite the fact that a period of turbulent development has accustomed us to the appearance and the carrying out of innovations, they can be best studied in the beginnings of capitalism. But they are so obvious there that it would be time lost for our purposes to dwell upon them.

There is leadership *only* for these reasons—leadership, that is, as a special kind of function and in contrast to a mere difference in rank, which would exist in every social body, in the smallest as in the largest, and in combination with which it generally appears. The facts alluded to create a boundary beyond which the majority of people do not function promptly by themselves and require help from a minority. If social life had in all respects the relative immutability of, for example, the astronomical world, or if mutable this mutability were yet incapable of being influenced by human action, or finally if capable of being so influenced this type of action were yet equally open to everyone, then there would be no special function of leadership as distinguished from routine work.

The specific problem of leadership arises and the leader type appears only where new possibilities present themselves. That is why it is so strongly marked among the

Normans at the time of their conquests and so feebly among the Slavs in the centuries of their unchanging and relatively protected life in the marshes of the Pripet. Our three points characterise the nature of the *function* as well as the *conduct* or behavior which constitutes the leader type. It is no part of his function to "find" or to "create" new possibilities. They are always present, abundantly accumulated by all sorts of people. Often they are also generally known and being discussed by scientific or literary writers. In other cases, there is nothing to discover about them, because they are quite obvious. To take an example from political life, it was not at all difficult to see how the social and political conditions of France at the time of Louis XVI could have been improved so as to avoid a breakdown of the *ancien régime*. Plenty of people as a matter of fact did see it. But nobody was in a position to *do* it. Now, it is this "doing the thing," without which possibilities are dead, of which the leader's function consists. This holds good of all kinds of leadership, ephemeral as well as more enduring ones. The former may serve as an instance. What is to be done in a casual emergency is as a rule quite simple. Most or all people may see it, yet they want someone to speak out, to lead, and to organise. Even leadership which influences merely by example, as artistic or scientific leadership, does not consist simply in finding or creating the new thing but in so impressing the social group with it as to draw it on in its wake. It is, therefore, more by will than by intellect that the leaders fulfil their function, more by "authority," "personal weight," and so forth than by original ideas.

Economic leadership in particular must hence be distinguished from "invention." As long as they are not carried into practice, inventions are economically irrelevant. And to carry any improvement into effect is a task entirely different from the inventing of it, and a task, moreover, requiring entirely different kinds of aptitudes. Although entrepreneurs of course *may* be inventors just as they may be capitalists, they are inventors not by nature of their function but by coincidence and vice versa. Besides, the innovations which it is the function of entrepreneurs to carry out need not necessarily be any inventions at all. It is, therefore, not advisable, and it may be downright misleading, to stress the element of invention as much as many writers do.

The entrepreneurial kind of leadership, as distinguished from other kinds of economic leadership such as we should expect to find in a primitive tribe or a communist society, is of course colored by the conditions peculiar to it. It has none of that glamour which characterises other kinds of leadership. It consists in fulfilling a very special task which only in rare cases appeals to the imagination of the public. For its success, keenness and vigor are not more essential than a certain narrowness which seizes the immediate chance and *nothing else*. "Personal weight" is, to be sure, not without importance. Yet the personality of the capitalistic entrepreneur need not, and generally does not, answer to the idea most of us have of what a "leader" looks like, so much so that there is some difficulty in realizing that he comes within the sociological category of leader at all. He "leads" the means of production into new channels. But this he does, not by convincing people of the desirability of carrying out his plan or by creating confidence in his leading in the manner of a political leader—the only man he has to convince or to impress is the banker who is to finance him—but by buying them or their services, and then using them as he sees fit. He also leads in the sense that he draws other producers in his branch after him. But as they are his competitors, who first reduce and then annihilate his profit, this is, as it were, leadership against one's own will. Finally, he renders a service, the full appreciation of which takes a specialist's knowledge of the case. It is not so easily understood by the public at large as a politician's successful speech or a general's victory in the field, not to insist on the fact that he seems to act—and often harshly—in his individual interest alone. We shall understand, therefore, that we do not observe, in this case, the emergence of all those affective values which are the glory of all other kinds of social leadership. Add to this the precariousness of the economic position both of the individual entrepreneur and of entrepreneurs as a group, and the fact that when his economic success raises him socially he has no cultural tradition or attitude to fall back upon, but moves about in society as an upstart, whose ways are readily laughed at, and we shall understand why this type has never been popular, and why even scientific critique often makes short work of it.[21]

We shall finally try to round off our picture of the entrepreneur in the same manner in which we always, in science as well as in practical life, try to understand human behavior, viz. by analysing the characteristic motives of his conduct. Any attempt to do this must of course meet with all those objections against the economist's intrusion into "psychology" which have been made familiar by a long series of writers. We cannot here enter into the fundamental question of the relation between psychology and economics. It is enough to state that those who on principle object to *any* psychological considerations in an economic argument may leave out what we are about to say without thereby losing contact with the argument of the following chapters. For none of the results to which our analysis is intended to lead stands or falls with our "psychology of the entrepreneur," or could be vitiated by any errors in it. Nowhere is there, as the reader will easily satisfy himself, any necessity for us to overstep the frontiers of observable behavior. Those who do not object to *all* psychology but only to the *kind* of psychology which we know from the traditional textbook, will see that we do not adopt any part of the time-honored picture of the motivation of the "economic man."

In the theory of the circular flow, the importance of examining motives is very much reduced by the fact that the equations of the system of equilibrium may be so interpreted as not to imply any psychic magnitudes at all, as shown by the analysis of Pareto and of Barone. This is the reason why even very defective psychology interferes much less with results than one would expect. There may be rational *conduct* even in the absence of rational *motive*. But as soon as we really wish to penetrate into motivation, the problem proves by no means simple. Within given social circumstances and habits, most of what people do every day will appear to them primarily from the point of view of duty carrying a social or a superhuman sanction. There is very little of conscious rationality, still less of hedonism and of *individual* egoism about it, and so much of it as may safely be said to exist is of comparatively recent growth. Nevertheless, as long as we confine ourselves to the great outlines of constantly repeated economic action, we may link it up with wants and the desire to satisfy them, on condition that we are careful to recognise that economic motive so defined varies in intensity very much in time; that it is society that shapes the particular desires we observe; that wants must be taken with reference to the group which the individual thinks of when deciding his course of action—the family or any other group, smaller or larger than the family; that action does not promptly follow upon desire but only more or less imperfectly corresponds to it; that the field of individual choice is always, though in very different ways and to very different degrees, fenced in by social habits or conventions and the like: it still remains broadly true that, within the circular flow, everyone adapts himself to his environment so as to satisfy certain *given* wants—of himself or others—as best he can. In *all* cases, the *meaning* of economic action is the satisfaction of wants in the sense that there would be no economic action if there were no wants. In the case of the circular flow, we may also think of satisfaction of wants as the normal *motive*.

The latter is not true for our type. In one sense, he may indeed be called the most rational and the most egotistical of all. For, as we have seen, conscious rationality enters much more into the carrying out of new plans, which themselves have to be worked out before they can be acted upon, than into the mere running of an established business, which is largely a matter of routine. And the typical entrepreneur is more self-centred than other types, because he relies less than they do on tradition and connection and because his characteristic task—theoretically as well as historically—consists precisely in breaking up old, and creating new, tradition. Although this applies primarily to his economic action, it also extends to the moral, cultural, and social consequences of it. It is, of course, no mere coincidence that the period of the rise of the entrepreneur type also gave birth to Utilitarianism.

But his conduct and his motive are "rational" in no other sense. And in *no* sense is his characteristic motivation of the hedonist kind. If we define hedonist motive of action as the wish to satisfy one's wants, we may indeed make "wants" include any impulse whatsoever, just as we may define egoism so as to include all altruistic values too, on the strength of the fact that they also mean something in the way of self-gratification. But this would reduce our definition to tautology. If we wish to give it meaning, we must restrict it to such wants as are capable of being satisfied by the consumption of goods, and to that kind of satisfaction which is expected from it. Then it is no longer true that our type is acting on a wish to satisfy his wants.

For unless we assume that individuals of our type are driven along by an insatiable craving for hedonist satisfaction, the operations of Gossen's law would in the case of business leaders soon put a stop to further effort. Experience teaches, however, that typical entrepreneurs retire from the arena only when and because their strength is spent and they feel no longer equal to their task. This does not seem to verify the picture of the economic man, balancing probable results against disutility of effort and reaching in due course a point of equilibrium beyond which he is not willing to go. Effort, in our case, does not seem to weigh at all in the sense of being felt as a reason to stop. And activity of the entrepreneurial type is obviously an obstacle to hedonist enjoyment of those kinds of commodity which are usually acquired by incomes beyond a certain size, because their "consumption" presupposes leisure. Hedonistically, therefore, the conduct which we usually observe in individuals of our type would be irrational.

This would not, of course, prove the absence of hedonistic motive. Yet it points to another psychology of non-hedonist character, especially if we take into account the indifference to hedonist enjoyment which is often conspicuous in outstanding specimens of the type and which is not difficult to understand.

First of all, there is the dream and the will to found a private kingdom, usually, though not necessarily, also a dynasty. The modern world really does not know any such positions, but what may be attained by industrial or commercial success is still the nearest approach to medieval lordship possible to modern man. Its fascination is specially strong for people who have no other chance of achieving social distinction. The sensation of power and independence loses nothing by the fact that both are largely illusions. Closer analysis would lead to discovering an endless variety within this group of motives, from spiritual ambition down to mere snobbery. But this need not detain us. Let it suffice to point out that motives of this kind, although they stand nearest to consumers' satisfaction, do not coincide with it.

Then there is the will to conquer: the impulse to fight, to prove oneself superior to others, to succeed for the sake, not of the fruits of success, but of success itself. From this aspect, economic action becomes akin to sport—there are financial races, or rather boxing-matches. The financial result is a secondary consideration, or, at all events, mainly valued as an index of success and as a symptom of victory, the displaying of which very often is more important as a motive of large expenditure than the wish for the consumers' goods themselves. Again we should find countless nuances, some of which, like social ambition, shade into the first group of motives. And again we are faced with a motivation characteristically different from that of "satisfaction of wants" in the sense defined above, or from, to put the same thing into other words, "hedonistic adaptation."

Finally, there is the joy of creating, of getting things done, or simply of exercising one's energy and ingenuity. This is akin to a ubiquitous motive, but nowhere else does it stand out as an independent factor of behavior with anything like the clearness with which it obtrudes itself in our case. Our type seeks out difficulties, changes in order to change, delights in ventures. This group of motives is the most distinctly anti-hedonist of the three.

Only with the first groups of motives is private property as the result of entrepreneurial activity an essential factor in making it operative. With the other two it is not. Pecuniary gain is indeed a very accurate expression of success, especially of *relative* success, and from the standpoint of the man who strives for it, it has the additional advantage of being an objective fact and largely independent of the opinion of others. These and other peculiarities incident to the mechanism of "acquisitive" society make it very difficult to replace it as a motor of industrial development, even if we would discard the importance it has for creating a fund ready for investment. Nevertheless it is true that the second and third groups of entrepreneurial motives may in principle be taken care of by other social arrangements not involving private gain from economic innovation. What other stimuli could be provided, and how they could be made to work as well as the "capitalistic" ones do, are questions which are beyond our theme.

They are taken too lightly by social reformers, and are altogether ignored by fiscal radicalism. But they are not insoluble, and may be answered by detailed observation of the psychology of entrepreneurial activity, at least for given times and places.

Endnotes

1. This is used here in Max Weber's sense. As the reader will see, "rational" and "empirical" here mean, if not identical, yet cognate, things. They are equally different from, and opposed to, "metaphysical," which implies going beyond the reach of both "reason" and "facts," beyond the realm, that is, of science. With some it has become a habit to use the word "rational" in much the same sense as we do "metaphysical." Hence some warning against misunderstanding may not be out of place.

2. If economists, nevertheless, have always had something to say on this theme, this is only because they did not restrict themselves to economic theory, but—and indeed quite superficially as a rule—studied historical sociology or made assumptions about the economic future. Division of labor, the origin of private property in land, increasing control over nature, economic freedom, and legal security—these are the most important elements constituting the "economic sociology" of Adam Smith. They clearly relate to the social framework of the economic course of events, not to any immanent spontaneity of the latter. One can also consider this as Ricardo's theory of development (say in Bücher's sense), which, moreover, exhibits the line of thought which earned the characterisation of "pessimist" for him: namely the "hypothetical prognosis" that in consequence of the progressive increase of population together with the progressive exhaustion of the powers of the soil (which can according to him only temporarily be interrupted by improvements in production) a position of rest would eventually appear—to be distinguished *toto coelo* from the ideal momentary position of rest of the equilibrium of modern theory—in which the economic situation would be characterised by an hypertrophy of rent, which is something totally different from what is understood above by a theory of development, and still more different from what we shall understand by it in this book. Mill worked out the same line of thought more carefully, and also distributed color and tone differently. In essence, however, his Book IV, "Influence of the Progress of Society on Production and Distribution," is just the same thing. Even this title expresses how much "progress" is considered as something non-economic, as something rooted in the data that only "exercises an influence" upon production and distribution. In particular his treatment of improvements in the "arts of production" is strictly "static." Improvement, according to this traditional view, is something which just happens and the effects of which we have to investigate, while we have nothing to say about its occurrence *per se*. What is thereby passed over is the subject matter of this book, or rather the foundation stone of its construction. J. B. Clark (Essentials of Economic Theory), whose merit is in having consciously separated "statics" and "dynamics," saw in the dynamic elements a disturbance of the static equilibrium. This is likewise our view, and also from our standpoint an essential task is to investigate the effect of this disturbance and the new equilibrium which then emerges. But while he confines himself to this and just like Mill sees therein the meaning of dynamics, we shall first of all give a theory of these causes of disturbances in so far as they are more than mere disturbances for us and in so far as it seems to us that essential economic phenomena depend upon their appearance. In particular: two of the causes of disturbance enumerated by him (increase of capital and population) are for us, as for him, merely causes of disturbance, however important as "factors of change" they may be for another kind of problem just indicated in the text. The same is true of a third (changes in the direction of consumers' tastes) which will later be substantiated in the text. But the other two (changes in technique and in productive organisation) require special analysis and evoke something different again from disturbances in the theoretical sense. The non-recognition of this is the most important single reason for what appears unsatisfactory to us in economic theory. From this insignificant-looking source flows, as we shall see, a new conception of the economic process, which overcomes a series of fundamental difficulties and thus justifies the new statement of the problem in the text. This statement of the problem is more nearly parallel to that of Marx. For according to him there is an *internal* economic development and no mere adaptation of economic life to changing data. But my structure covers only a small part of his ground.

3. Therefore one of the most annoying misunderstandings that arose out of the first edition of this book was that this theory of development neglects all historical factors of change except one, namely the individuality of entrepreneurs. If my representation were intended to be as this objection assumes, it would obviously be nonsense. But it is not at all concerned with the concrete factors of change, but with the method by which these work, with the *mechanism of change*. The "entrepreneur" is merely the bearer of the mechanism of change. And I have taken account not of one factor of historical change, but of none. We have still less to do here with the factors which in particular explain the changes in the economic organisation, economic custom, and so on. This is still another problem, and although there are points at which all these methods of treatment collide, it means spoiling the fruit of all if they are not kept apart and if each is not allowed the right to grow by itself.

4. The problems of capital, credit, entrepreneurial profit, interest on capital, and crises (or business cycles) are the ones in which this fruitfulness will be demonstrated here. Yet it is not thereby exhausted. For the expert theorist I point, for example, to the difficulties which surround the problem of increasing return, the question of multiple points of intersection between supply and demand

curves, and the element of time, which even Marshall's analysis has not overcome.

5. We do this because these changes are small per annum and therefore do not stand in the way of the applicability of the "static" method. Nevertheless, their appearance is frequently a condition of development in our sense. But even though they often make the latter possible, yet they do not create it out of themselves.

6. In the first edition of this book, I called it "dynamics." But it is preferable to avoid this expression here, since it so easily leads us astray because of the associations which attach themselves to its various meanings. Better, then, to say simply what we mean: economic life changes; it changes partly because of changes in the data, to which it tends to adapt itself. But this is not the only kind of economic change; there is another which is not accounted for by influence on the data from without, but which arises from within the system, and this kind of change is the cause of so many important economic phenomena that it seems worth while to build a theory for it, and, in order to do so, to isolate it from all the other factors of change. The author begs to add another more exact definition, which he is in the habit of using: what we are about to consider is that kind of change arising from within the system *which so displaces its equilibrium point that the new one cannot be reached from the old one by infinitesimal steps.* Add successively as many mail coaches as you please, you will never get a railway thereby.

7. On the whole it is much more correct to say that population grows slowly up to the possibilities of any economic environment than that it has any tendency to outgrow it and to become thereby an independent cause of change.

8. A privilege which the individual can also achieve through saving. In an economy of the handicraft type this element would have to be emphasised more. Manufacturers' "reserve funds" assume an existing development.

9. The most important of which is the appearance of productive interest, as we shall see in Chapter V. As soon as interest emerges somewhere in the system, it expands over the whole of it.

10. Of course the productive means do not fall from heaven. In so far as they are not given by nature or non-economically, they were and are created at some time by the individual waves of development in our sense, and henceforth incorporated in the circular flow. But every individual wave of development and every individual new combination itself proceeds again from the supply of productive means of the existing circular flow—a case of the hen and the egg.

11. Risk obviously always falls on the owner of the means of production or of the money-capital which was paid for them, hence never on the entrepreneur *as such* (see Chapter IV). A shareholder *may* be an entrepreneur. He may even owe to his holding a controlling interest the power to act as an entrepreneur. Shareholders *per se,* however, are never entrepreneurs, but merely capitalists, who in consideration of their submitting to certain risks participate in profits. That this is no reason to look upon them as anything but capitalists is shown by the facts, first, that the average shareholder has normally no power to influence the management of his company, and secondly, that participation in profits is frequent in cases in which everyone recognises the presence of a loan contract. Compare, for example, the Graeco-Roman *foenus nauticum.* Surely this interpretation is more true to life than the other one, which, following the lead of a faulty legal construction—which can only be explained historically—attributes functions to the average shareholder which he hardly ever thinks of discharging.

12. The definition of the entrepreneur in terms of entrepreneurial profit instead of in terms of the function the performance of which creates the entrepreneurial profit is obviously not brilliant. But we have still another objection to it: we shall see that entrepreneurial profit does not fall to the entrepreneur by "necessity" in the same sense as the marginal product of labor does to the worker.

13. Only this neglect explains the attitude of many socialistic theorists towards peasant property. For smallness of the individual possession makes a difference only for the petit-bourgeois, not for the socialist. The criterion of the employment of labor other than that of the owner and his family is economically relevant only from the standpoint of a kind of exploitation theory which is hardly tenable any longer.

14. Cf. for example the good description in Wiedenfeld, *Das Persönliche im modernen Unternehmertum.* Although it appeared in Schmoller's Jahrbuch in 1910 this work was not known to me when the first edition of this book was published.

15. On the nature of the entrepreneurial function also compare my statement in the article "Unternehmer" in the Handwörterbuch der Staatswissenschaften.

16. The same *theoretical* picture, obviously not the same sociological, cultural, and so forth.

17. How much this is the case is best seen to-day in the economic life of those nations, and within our civilisation in the economics of those individuals, whom the development of the last century has not yet completely drawn into its stream, for example, in the economy of the Central European peasant. This peasant "calculates"; there is no deficiency of the "economic way of thinking" (Wirtschaftsgesinnung) in him. Yet he cannot take a step out of the beaten path; his economy has not changed at all for centuries, except perhaps through the exercise of external force and influence. Why? Because the choice of new methods is not simply an element in the concept of rational economic action, nor a matter of course, but a distinct process which stands in need of special explanation.

18. Small disturbances which may indeed, as mentioned earlier, in time add up to great amounts. The decisive point is that the businessman, if he makes them, never alters his routine. The usual case is one of small, the exception one of great (*uno actu* great), disturbances. Only in this sense is emphasis put upon "smallness" here. The objection that there can be no difference in principle between small and large disturbances is not effective. For it is false in itself, in so far as it is based upon the disregard of the principle of the infinitesimal method, the essence of which lies in the fact that one can assert of "small quantities" under certain circumstances what one cannot assert of "large quantities." But the reader who takes umbrage at the large-small contrast may, if he wishes, substitute for it the contrast adapting-spontaneous. Personally I am not willing to do

this because the latter method of expression is much easier to misunderstand than the former and really would demand still longer explanations.

19. In the first place it is a question of a type of *conduct* and of a type of *person* in so far as this conduct is accessible in very unequal measure and to relatively few people, so that it constitutes their outstanding characteristic. Because the exposition of the first edition was reproached with exaggerating and mistaking the peculiarity of this conduct, and with overlooking the fact that it is more or less open to every businessman, and because the exposition in a later paper ("Wellenbewegung des Wirtschaftslebens," Archiv für Sozialwissenschaft) was charged with introducing an intermediate type ("half-static" businessmen), the following may be submitted. The conduct in question is peculiar in two ways. First, because it is directed towards something different and signifies doing something different from other conduct. One may indeed in this connection include it with the latter in a higher unity, but this does not alter the fact that a theoretically relevant difference exists between the two, and that only one of them is adequately described by traditional theory. Secondly, the type of conduct in question not only differs from the other in its object, "innovation" being peculiar to it, but also in that it presupposes aptitudes differing *in kind* and not only in degree from those of mere rational economic behavior.

Now these aptitudes are presumably distributed in an ethically homogeneous population just like others, that is the curve of their distribution has a maximum ordinate, deviations on either side of which become rarer the greater they are. Similarly we can assume that every healthy man can sing if he will. Perhaps half the individuals in an ethically homogeneous group have the capacity for it to an average degree, a quarter in progressively diminishing measure, and, let us say, a quarter in a measure above the average; and within this quarter, through a series of continually increasing singing ability and continually diminishing number of people who possess it, we come finally to the Carusos. Only in this quarter are we struck in general by the singing ability, and only in the supreme instances can it become the characterising mark of the person. Although practically all men can sing, singing ability does not cease to be a distinguishable characteristic and attribute of a minority, indeed not exactly of a type, because this characteristic—unlike ours—affects the total personality relatively little.

Let us apply this: Again, a quarter of the population may be so poor in those qualities, let us say here provisionally, of economic initiative that the deficiency makes itself felt by poverty of their moral personality, and they play a wretched part in the smallest affairs of private and professional life in which this element is called for. We recognise this type and know that many of the best clerks, distinguished by devotion to duty, expert knowledge, and exactitude, belong to it. Then comes the "half," the "normal." These prove themselves to be better in the things which even within the established channels cannot simply be "dispatched" (erledigen) but must also be "decided" (entscheiden) and "carried out" (durchsetzen). Practically all business people belong here, otherwise they would never have attained their

positions; most represent a selection—individually or hereditarily tested. A textile manufacturer travels no "new" road when he goes to a wool auction. But the situations there are never the same, and the success of the business depends so much upon skill and initiative in buying wool that the fact that the textile industry has so far exhibited no trustification comparable with that in heavy manufacturing is undoubtedly partly explicable by the reluctance of the cleverer manufacturers to renounce the advantage of their own skill in buying wool. From there, rising in the scale we come finally into the highest quarter, to people who are a type characterised by super-normal qualities of intellect and will. Within this type there are not only many varieties (merchants, manufacturers, financiers, etc.) but also a continuous variety of degrees of intensity in "initiative." In our argument types of every intensity occur. Many a one can steer a safe course, where no one has yet been; others follow where first another went before; still others only in the crowd, but in this among the first. So also the great political leader of every kind and time is a type, yet not a thing unique, but only the apex of a pyramid from which there is a continuous variation down to the average and from it to the sub-normal values. And yet not only is "leading" a special function, but the leader also something special, distinguishable—wherefore there is no sense in our case in asking: "Where does that type begin then?" and then to exclaim: "This is no type at all!"

20. It has been objected against the first edition that it sometimes defines "statics" as a theoretical construction, sometimes as the picture of an actual state of economic life. I believe that the present exposition gives no ground for this opinion. "Static" theory does not assume a stationary economy; it also treats of the effects of changes in data. In itself, therefore, there is no necessary connection between static theory and stationary reality. Only in so far as one can exhibit the fundamental form of the economic course of events with the maximum simplicity in an unchanging economy does this assumption recommend itself to theory. The stationary economy is for uncounted thousands of years, and also in historical times in many places for centuries, an incontrovertible fact, apart from the fact, moreover, which Sombart emphasised, that there is a tendency towards a stationary state in every period of depression. Hence it is readily understood how this historical fact and that theoretical construction have allied themselves in a way which led to some confusion. The words "statics" and "dynamics" the author would not now use in the meaning they carry above, where they are simply short expressions for "theory of the circular flow" and "theory of development." One more thing: theory employs two methods of interpretation, which may perhaps make difficulties. If it is to be shown how all the elements of the economic system are determined in equilibrium by one another, this equilibrium system is considered as not yet existing and is built up before our eyes *ab ovo*. This does not mean that its coming into being is genetically explained thereby. Only its existence and functioning are made logically clear by mental dissection. And the experiences and habits of individuals are assumed as existing. How just these productive combinations have come about is not

thereby explained. Further, if two contiguous equilibrium positions are to be investigated, then sometimes (not always), as in Pigou's Economics of Welfare, the "best" productive combination in the first is compared with the "best" in the second. And this again need not, but may, mean that the two combinations in the sense meant here differ not only by small variations in quantity but in their whole technical and commercial structure. Here too the coming into being of the second combination and the problems connected with it are not investigated, but only the functioning and the outcome of the already existing combination. Even though justified as far as it goes, this method of treatment passes over our problem. If the assertion were implied that this is also settled by it, it would be false.

21. It may, therefore, not be superfluous to point out that our analysis of the rôle of the entrepreneur does not involve any "glorification" of the type, as some readers of the first edition of this book seemed to think. We do hold that entrepreneurs *have* an economic function as distinguished from, say, robbers. But we neither style every entrepreneur a genius or a benefactor to humanity, nor do we wish to express any opinion about the comparative merits of the social organisation in which he plays his rôle, or about the question whether what he does could not be effected more cheaply or efficiently in other ways.

17

MODERN VIEWS ON INVENTION

John Jewkes, David Sawers, and Richard Stillerman

> All philosophers who find
> Some favourite system to their mind,
> In every point to make it fit
> Will force all nature to submit.
>
> —Thomas Love Peacock, *Headlong Hall*

There is one type of mind which finds it tempting to stress the contrast between the world of today and that of yesterday and to think of change as a series of big fresh starts: there is another type congenitally disposed to believe that there is nothing new under the sun, that all that has been said and done has happened before. As between these two extremes, both likely to give a distorted perspective, there can be little doubt that the greater part of modern writing about invention and technical progress strongly inclines to the view that we live in a new world in which thinking of the present or the future in terms of past experience is largely irrelevant, and that our ideas must be recast and our institutions reformed to fit fresh surroundings. Social scientists are now tending to speak with more confidence about the scale on which inventions will be made and the sources from which they will arise. There have, indeed, been some odd switches of thought since the end of the First World War. In the early 1930's it was widely believed that technical progress would normally be so swift and disturbing that a high level of 'technological' unemployment would be usual and inevitable. In the later thirties, due mainly to the failure of the American economy to continue to expand at an unbroken rate, the view gained currency that technical progress would usually be too sluggish to create sufficient profitable investment openings for the savings arising under full employment: secular stagnation and chronic unemployment were inevitable, in the absence of public intervention, because technical progress would never be on a large enough scale.[1]

The period following the Second World War with its general shortage of capital, its full employment and the impact upon the public mind of the discovery of atomic energy, has brought forth a fresh crop of generalisations which, compared with the pessimistic views of the inter-war period, are oddly sanguine in tone.[2] Unbroken and rapid technical advance, it is thought, can now be taken for granted; the causes of it, the institutions which best foster it, are understood, and understood so well that society may be within measurable distance of the power deliberately to control it or, failing that, to predict with a high degree of certainty what the future holds.

Jewkes, John, David Sawers, and Richard Stillerman, (1958), *The Sources of Invention,* London: MacMillan and Company Limited (pp. 27–34).

This new and fashionable doctrine, subscribed to by many scientists, technologists, economists, statesmen, business men and popular writers, does not seem anywhere to have been expounded in final or authoritative shape. Nor is it difficult to pick out inconsistencies between its varying formulations. The mainspring is sometimes held to be the growing power of science, sometimes the increasing skill and eagerness with which technologists pick up and use scientific knowledge. By some, inventions are now thought to be easier to make than formerly; there is a gathering momentum, an 'auto-catalytic process,' driving things on. Others believe that inventions have now become more difficult to make because all the easy inventions have already been made. 'Necessity', to some is still 'the mother of invention'; to others, inventions are thought to pour out almost automatically and prodigally in an ever-increasing stream in the richer industrial communities where needs are least urgent. Some hold that there never was a time when inventions were more eagerly seized upon by industry for commerical exploitation; others that there is still a great deal of 'resistance to change.'

Whatever the discrepancies and dissensions, there appears to be a broad area of agreement among those who adhere to the spectacular view of modern invention. A few quotations, drawn from a vast literature, will serve to indicate the gist of the doctrine.

James B. Conant:[3]

As theory developed in physics and chemistry and penetrated into practice, as the degree of empiricism was reduced in one area after another, the inventor was bound to disappear. Today the typical lone inventor of the eighteenth and nineteenth centuries has all but disappeared. In his place in the mid-twentieth century came the industrial research laboratory and departments of development engineering.

J. K. Galbraith:[4]

A benign Providence . . . has made the modern industry of a few large firms an almost perfect instrument for inducing technical change. . . . There is no more pleasant fiction than that technical change is the product of the matchless ingenuity of the small man forced by competition to employ his wits to better his neighbour. Unhappily, it is a fiction. Technical development has long since become the preserve of the scientist and the engineer. Most of the cheap and simple inventions have, to put it bluntly, been made.

W. R. Maclaurin:[5]

We have now reached a stage in many fields where inventions are almost made to order, and where there can be a definite correlation between the numbers of applied scientists employed (and the funds at their disposal) and the inventive results. But one really gifted inventor is likely to be more productive than half a dozen men of lesser stature.

Walton Hamilton and Irene Till:[6]

Most discoveries patented today can be anticipated. . . . For the most part, technicians are not self starters. The bulk of them in fact are captives; those in corporate employ are told by business executives what problems to work on. . . . The solo inventor's real opportunity is to seize or blunder upon a pioneer idea; as a technology foliates from its base, his self reliance is hardly a match for a bevy of experts who can be kept on the job. . . . A captive technology offers no chance to invent except to those already in control, or to others on such terms as those in control dictate.

W. B. Kaempffert:[7]

It is not difficult to predict the effect of industrial group research on invention. As organised invention and discovery gain momentum the revolutionist will have no chance in explored fields. He will have to compete with more and more men who have at their disposal splendidly equipped laboratories, time and money, and who may work for three or four years before producing a noteworthy result. Only the exceptionally brilliant trained scientist will be able to meet these explorers on their own ground. Possibly Edison may be the last of the great heroes of invention.

J. D. Bernal:[8]

Many intelligent non-scientific people still think of science as it appeared to be in the nineteenth century, as the product of individual efforts of men of genius, instead of, as it now is, a highly organised new profession closely linked with industry and government. . . . It is almost as difficult in an age of vast engineering and chemical factories, each furnished with its own research department, to recall the intimate traditional and practical character of the old workshops and forges from which the modern giants are descended.

A. Hunter:[9]

The days when one individual's inventiveness and enterprise could transform an industry are in the past. In this context the big firm again shows to advantage. Perhaps we are labouring the obvious. These are all well known facts of economic life. . . .[10]

The pith of the modern view is, therefore, that in the nineteenth century most invention came from the individual inventor who had little or no scientific training, and who worked largely with simple equipment and by empirical methods and unsystematic hunches. The link between science and technology was slight. Manufacturing businesses did not concern themselves with research. In the twentieth century the characteristic features of the nineteenth are rapidly passing away. The individual inventor is becoming rare; men with the power of originating are largely absorbed into research institutions of one kind or another, where they must have expensive equipment for their work. Useful invention is to an ever-increasing degree issuing from the research laboratories of large firms which alone can afford to operate on an appropriate scale. There is increasingly close contact now between science and technology, both through the closer association of the workers in the two fields and because the borderline between the two formerly separate functions is becoming obliterated. The consequence is that invention has become more automatic, less the result of intuition or flashes of genius and more a matter of deliberate design. The growing power to invent, combined with the increased resources devoted to it, has produced a spurt of technical progress to which no obvious limit is to be seen. It will be noted that statements of the kind quoted above assert facts, imply causes and express satisfaction as to results. Something is actually occurring in the world of technology which is heartily to be welcomed, or is inevitable, and which is bringing about improved standards of living.

This, then, is the sharp contrast drawn between an earlier heroic age of clumsy individual pioneering and a modern age in which highly trained, closely organised teams of technologists, fortified by an easily accessible and constantly expanding body of scientific knowledge, move forward with deliberation to results which can largely be predetermined. Not all modern writers, however, share this view about nineteenth-century invention. Whitehead once wrote[11] that—

The greatest invention of the nineteenth century was the invention of the method of invention. . . . The whole change has arisen from the new scientific information. . . . It is a great mistake to think that the bare scientific idea is the required invention. . . . One element in the new method is just the discovery of how to set about bridging the gap between the scientific ideas and the ultimate product.

That is to say he claimed for the nineteenth century those very achievements which other writers attribute uniquely to the twentieth.

It is perhaps even more significant that some writers in the nineteenth century did not picture their own century as twentieth-century writers now often describe it. In 1808, in a paper presented to the Manchester Literary and Philosophical Society,[12] Ewart challenged the view that invention was, or could effectively be, carried on without scientific knowledge and contacts. A knowledge of the principles of mechanics, he argued, must help the inventor and assist him to distinguish real from illusory improvements. Nor would he allow that the history of mechanical discoveries supported the contrary opinion. Both Huygens and Hooke, he pointed out, had been scientists and, if they had not, they might not have invented the balance. Smeaton had used theoretical knowledge in his inventions. Watt also was a man of scientific attainments, but for which he might not have invented his improvements to the steam engine. Charles Babbage in his *Decline of Science in England,* published in 1830, stressed the importance of science in technical progress and alleged that the failure of official bodies to support science was endangering industrial expansion. Professor Tyndall, in a lecture on the electric light[13] in 1879, quoted with approval Cuvier as saying:

> Your grand practical achievements are only the easy application of truths not sought with a practical intent. . . . Your rising workshops, your peopled colonies, your vessels which furrow the seas; this abundance; this luxury, this tumult, all come from discoveries in science.

It is clear that at this time the potential use of scientific discoveries, and the manner in which the inventor could base his work upon them, were recognised in many quarters.

Some experts in the nineteenth century were even prepared to argue that invention had already become 'a social process' in which the contribution of no one individual could be crucial. Engineers such as I. K. Brunel and Sir William Armstrong made this their chief argument for the abolition of the patent system; all inventions, they claimed, were merely improvements or adaptations of existing knowledge. And, in developing their case, they employed arguments that modern writers have employed about the twentieth century: that most inventions were made simultaneously by several people; that inventions are called for by the existence of a need and that, since so much knowledge was already available, the need would always be met and probably by more than one person.

It is, therefore, of more than ordinary interest to try, as a first step, to put into proper perspective invention and the inventors of the nineteenth century; the next chapter is devoted to this subject.

Endnotes

1. By much more cautious and scientific methods Professor Simon Kuznets (*Economic Change*, chap. 9) has suggested that in each industry taken separately, technical progress will tend to slacken after a time. The suggestion, of course, carries with it no support for theories of secular stagnation of whole economies. And it seems that, by extending the cases beyond those chosen by Mr. Kuznets, exceptions to his tentative hypothesis are to be found. The whole subject, however, is well worth more study than it has received since the publication of the original stimulating article in 1929.

2. Although alarms have been sounded about the unemployment which might arise from 'automation.' These fears seem similar to those which arose in the 1920's about 'rationalisation' and in the 1930's about 'technocracy.'

3. Speaking in May 1951.

4. *American Capitalism* p. 91.

5. 'The Sequence from Invention to Innovation,' *Quarterly Journal of Economics,* Feb. 1953.

6. *Law and Contemporary Problems,* vol. 13 (1945), p. 252.

7. *Invention and Society,* p. 30.

8. *Science and Industry in the Nineteenth Century,* p. 4.

9. 'The Control of Monopoly,' *Lloyds Bank Review,* Oct. 1956.

10. Even at the risk of repetition the following ought to be quoted: 'It has become generally established that scientific progress is the result of well-organised research teams. The day of the garret scientist, working alone in a near-bare loft by the flickering light of an oil lamp is almost past. For the scope of knowledge in any one field is so vast that few individuals can fully master it. In addition, an individual effort is dwarfed by the large

scale attack on the frontiers of our technical knowledge by incalculable numbers of scientific workers in many great laboratories with unlimited facilities. Even in purely theoretical contributions, the facilities available in these million dollar laboratories are almost indispensable to original work; in experimental investigations the facilities of large laboratories are even more essential.' (A. Coblenz and H. L. Owens, *Transistors, Theory and Application,* p. 1.)

11. *Science and the Modern World,* pp. 120, 121.

12. 'On the Measure of Moving Force,' *Memoirs of the Literary and Philosophical Society of Manchester,* Second Series, vol. 2. Ewart was a well-known engineer who had been apprenticed to Rennie and then worked for Boulton and Watt, becoming a lifelong friend of Watt. In 1792 he became Samuel Oldknow's partner in his cotton business; the following year he set up as a cotton spinner in Manchester on his own. In 1835 he left this business to become Chief Engineer and Inspector of Machinery in H. M. Dockyards.

13. *Proceedings of the Royal Institution,* vol. 9 (1879–81), pp. 22, 23.

18

THE DEVELOPMENT OF INVENTIONS

John Jewkes, David Sawers, and Richard Stillerman

The writer may derive a more delicate satisfaction from the free confession of his ignorance, and from his prudence in avoiding that error, into which so many have fallen, of imposing their conjectures and hypothesis on the world for the most certain principles.

—David Hume

I

THE ISSUES

Although when this work was started it was not intended to say anything in detail about the development of inventions, it subsequently became increasingly apparent that some comment on it was unavoidable. For even those who are prepared to accept the description and analysis of invention as given in the foregoing pages might well protest that this is, after all, the less important part of the story of technical progress and that the real determinants of the rate of advance will be the scale and the speed of the efforts made to perfect new commodities and devices and to contrive ways of producing them cheaply and in quantity.[1]

This, in effect, is a variation, much more convincing than the original, of the doctrine outlined in Chapter II. It can perhaps fairly be summarised as follows. The costs of carrying inventions forward to final use are high and are steadily increasing; development is very much a new function, only recently has it become a separable and important task for business. These costs are now so large that only a big firm can afford them. Indeed, the advantages of size may persist to the point at which a few firms, or even only one, within an industry can operate to the best effect. The risks are now so great that speedy and effective development is only likely where it is nourished by monopoly profits. Patent rights are one form of protection but over and beyond these, a firm which finds little rivalry in its special field of manufacturing, and therefore has less to fear from technical developments closely parallel to its own, will carry out development most confidently and therefore with the greatest effect.

These contentions are obviously germane to policy; they imply that the future will lie with the bigger firms and that monopoly has its merits. The whole complicated subject is, indeed, worthy of thorough examination. It has not been possible here to undertake such a study nor to bring to bear any information beyond that acquired

Jewkes, John, David Sawers, and Richard Stillerman, (1958), *The Sources of Invention,* London: MacMillan and Company Limited (pp. 197–222).

incidentally in the present narrower enquiry. What follows, therefore, is an attempt, not to reach settled conclusions, but to pose questions and clarify issues.

The most important specific questions seem to be these:

(a) Are the costs of developing inventions becoming progressively greater? If so, why?

(b) Can the outstanding twentieth-century successes in development usually be attributed to large firms?

(c) An invention once made, are there reasons for assuming that the development will more readily be entered upon and more whole-heartedly pursued where one or a very limited number of firms can enter the field and share in the profits? Is monopoly the most favourable environment for development?

II

DEFINITION

One reason why systematic knowledge of development seems so scrappy, a few generalisations passing on unchanged and unchallenged from author to author, lies in the awkward problem of definition. We speak of the development of some revolutionary idea, such as the jet engine or the Pescara free-piston engine, meaning the building of one machine which establishes the fact that results can be obtained by the new principle. At the other extreme we speak of the development of a new aircraft design, which of itself embodies no radical innovation, meaning the systematic testing and modifying in numerous minor ways of the design to satisfy standards of performance and safety for the special conditions which the aircraft will encounter. And, between the two extremes, of course, there are to be found innumerable intermediate conditions.

Even if study is confined to development in the first sense, to the work following closely upon and directly connected with the original innovation, useful lines of demarcation are not easily drawn. Sometimes development consists of finding ways of producing on a large scale the same thing—or broadly the same thing—as has been produced already on a small scale; a new man-made fibre, for instance. But the development of the jet engine, in the course of which power and reliability were increased, also involved changes in the physical form of the product.

Assuming this hurdle is surmounted, how are the costs of development to be ascertained? If they are wholly incurred by one firm which brings the development to a successful conclusion the task is easier than where a number of firms have pursued the same development, one or more successfully and others perhaps fruitlessly. Some of the heaviest development costs have probably been spent in wholly abortive efforts, such as the attempts to store electricity in large quantities or to make perpetual motion machines. In assessing the costs of the final success in transmuting metals, would it be necessary to include all the expenses of all the alchemists of the past fifteen hundred years?

For practical purposes, the important thing is to fix upon the 'period' of development. In one sense this period has no end—at least until the process, commodity or machine has completely disappeared from use. Improvements were still being made to the sailing ship right up to the end of the nineteenth century; indeed the competition of the steamship stimulated numerous improvements in the sailing ship. In this chapter, the discussion is confined to that period, intimately associated with an invention which ends when commercial utilisation appears at least to some people to be feasible.[2]

III

DEVELOPMENT IN THE NINETEENTH CENTURY

The contrast between the relative cheapness of inventing and the heavy costs of perfecting and developing was frequently remarked upon in the nineteenth century. The United States Commissioners of Patents frequently refer to it in their reports and it is one point on which the witnesses before the House of Lords Committee on the Patent Law Amendment

Bills of 1851, the Royal Commission on Patent Law of 1865, and the Commons Committee on Letters Patent of 1871, were almost unanimous. The views of Sir William Armstrong are typical. He told the Royal Commission in 1865 that 'mere conception of primary ideas in invention is not a matter involving much labour, and it is not . . . a thing demanding a large reward; it is rather the subsequent labour which a man bestows in perfecting the invention, a thing which the patent laws at present scarcely recognize.'

In the middle of the century, Goodyear is known to have spent some $130,000 on the vulcanisation of rubber, mainly in evolving a satisfactory process for commercial use. Richard Roberts, the inventor of the self-acting mule, said that he had spent thousands of pounds on perfecting it; there were many inventions on which very large sums had to be spent, 'for there are many things which cannot be seen through all their parts without experiment'. The Bessemer process was an invention which required the solution of certain development tasks before it could be used, especially those arising out of the presence of phosphoric pig-iron in the convertor. Bessemer told the 1871 Committee that he had spent £16,000 on solving this problem. He argued that no man would go to the expense of introducing a new process without patent protection; they would let another have that expense. Sir William Siemens, another witness, referred to the great expense and delay involved in developing a process; without patent protection men would not go to this expense. E. K. Muspratt, the alkali manufacturer, said that in the chemical industry an idea had to be elaborated by practical men for several years, often with a very large expenditure, before it became practical.

Towards the end of the century, it is known that Parsons spent considerable sums, perhaps in the neighbourhood of £100,000, on the development of the steam turbine. The development of viscose rayon from the first patent in 1892 to the first commercial marketing in 1910 in Great Britain by Courtauld's seems to have cost, including the first manufacturing plant, not less than £250,000. The patents were also licensed to German and French firms, which are known to have incurred heavy expenditure for the same purpose.

IV

THE GROWTH OF DEVELOPMENT COSTS

Development costs were, therefore, sometimes heavy in the nineteenth century, and it is unfortunate that more detailed comparisons are not available, for example, of the costs of development of the steam turbine and the gas turbine, of the first aniline dyes and the later ones, of the Solvay process for producing soda ash and polyethylene; of the Bessemer steel-making process and the Kroll titanium process; of the methods of making aluminium and those for producing magnesium.

Even in the absence of such studies, however, it seems difficult to escape the conclusion that there is nothing in the nineteenth century to match some of the spectacular cases of costly development to be found in the twentieth. Many of the figures quoted are, indeed, unduly swollen by the inclusion of the cost of the final manufacturing plant. But it appears that about $6 million was spent on the research and development of nylon; some £4 million was spent on the development of Terylene (although this figure apparently includes the cost of pilot plants, some part of the product of which was sold commercially). The Radio Corporation of America, one of a number of American firms engaged in the task, spent 2\frac{1}{2}$ million on research and advanced development of television; in Great Britain, E.M.I. is said to have spent £550,000 for the same purpose.[3] The cost of development of penicillin ran into millions of dollars; that of the hot cathode fluorescent lamp is given as $170,000; of the long-playing record, $250,000; of the Houdry catalytic cracking process, $2 million.

Is there, then, some general law arising out of the nature of modern science, the character of modern technology or the pattern of modern markets, indicating that a new idea of a given inventive content will increasingly cost more to develop? If so, this would in one sense be surprising, for it might be supposed that scientific and technical advance would make for economy in the effort of development; that costly empirical testing could be replaced by cheaper and quicker scientific calculation; that cul-de-sacs could be perceived before they had been pursued too far; that scientific market research would render less hazardous the commercial introduction of a new product. Why should technical progress make everything cheaper except the process of development?

Nevertheless, the grounds for assuming that development steadily becomes a more formidable, intricate and costly task are strong. They will be discussed, first in terms of technical forces and then in respect of market factors.

The cost of perfecting an invention will depend partly upon how far a small-scale experiment or model will suffice to provide adequate knowledge for conducting operations on a larger scale. Whether the one will reveal reliable data for the other and how far this can be known beforehand are matters on which there has long been dispute.[4] Although it is only too easy to find exceptions to any generalisation, it appears that there are significant differences, for instance, between engineering at its various levels, where quite small models will often provide as much useful working knowledge as full-scale machines and where the cost of even a full-scale machine may be relatively modest, and the chemical industries, where relatively large pilot plants are often needed for the empirical accumulation of 'know-how.' In so far, therefore, as the growing industries, such as chemicals, are those where very large scale experiments are a condition precedent to commercial operation, development costs will tend to increase.

Development consists of applying existing technical knowledge to exploit some new idea. It follows that the greater the stock of technical knowledge, the wider the range of effort which may be brought to bear upon any development task. There are now more different possible routes for reaching a predetermined target; more ways of spending money which offer some chance of success. This, of course, gives heightened value to a new type of judgment, the choice of the methods combining in the best way the highest chances of success and the lowest cost. (Conversely, it is probably easier to waste money in industrial development than it has ever been.) But so long as technical knowledge accumulates, it seems reasonable to suppose that potentially worth-while avenues of expenditure will increase in number.

Much development, especially in the field of chemistry and chemotherapeutics, has in this century consisted of empirical search and observation in wide new fields suddenly opened up by one crucial discovery or invention. When the success of penicillin drew attention to the possible virtues of moulds, then the area of search for new strains of penicillin or other moulds with similar qualities became virtually unlimited. Of course, the opening up of one new field of search might simultaneously close down another—doubtless the success of penicillin brought to an end much more traditional work on antiseptics. But it seems that frequently the new fields of effort are additional to, and not a complete substitute for, the old.

The accumulation of technical knowledge is a two-edged weapon; it helps to determine what is possible but it may also define what is impossible. With the area of probable successful search narrowed down, firms may be more ready to risk development expenditures which, though great, appear tolerable. Suppose, for example, it were known that a satisfactory method of synthesising insulin existed as one among 10,000,000 possibilities. The risk involved in a systematic search, which might not reach success until the 10-millionth experiment had been performed, might be too great for any firm to undertake. Under these circumstances, of course, a firm might be prepared to try to find the answer without a systematic search: it might be prepared to devote a limited sum to a search for the answer, relying upon intuition or the possibility of a lucky shot. In that case the firm would have to be prepared to spend with the chance of a nil return. But if, through increased technical knowledge, it became known that the correct answer must be found as one within 100,000 possibilities, the firm might be prepared to spend a large sum knowing that a systematic search must bring success, even if the chance of getting the winner at an early stage in the search be completely discounted.

Finally, on the technical side, the increased costs of modern development may be attributable to the greater caution of manufacturers in not taking their problems out of the laboratory or moving beyond a pilot plant stage until they are convinced that full-scale manufacture is wholly feasible. The absence of such discretion in the nineteenth century sometimes led to mistakes and back-tracking, and consequent loss of time and money.[5]

Market factors, it is argued, will also tend to increase the cost of development. The more discriminating becomes the taste of the consumer the more important is it that a new commodity should not be put on to the market until its quality and reliability can be guaranteed. The producer now searches in the laboratory for weaknesses which might in earlier times have been discovered by putting the commodity on the market and allowing the consumer to discover the defects through use. New commodities must force their way into markets against the resistance of competing traditional types of goods. If they are launched prematurely while still imperfect, their reputation may be finally and fatally damaged. Perfecting in the laboratory cannot always be made a substitute for testing through widespread use but it will probably become increasingly so.

It seems, too, with many modern processes and commodities, that the handling of the materials can be extremely dangerous, calling for special security devices and most scrupulously standardised procedures. This helps to explain the high development costs inseparable from work in atomic energy or in the manufacture and mass application of drugs such as polio vaccine.

On occasions, a new commodity may have to be put on the market on a minimum scale if it is to make an appropriate impact.[6] An advertising campaign to break down the initial resistance of the consumer is an overhead cost which it is desirable to spread as widely as possible. A car manufacturer might be reluctant to introduce a new form of transmission unless it could be embodied in at least one full assembly line. The older commodity, presumably, is already being manufactured on the scale which brings lowest costs; the introduction of a new competing commodity will meet additional obstacles unless it can also be manufactured from the outset on an economical scale. The more extensive the scale on which the new product must initially be manufactured, the more formidable may be the task of development.

But the most important reason for these heavy expenditures on development seems to be one in which technical and market factors are both involved: the high competitiveness of an economic system where technical progress is general and rapid and where, in consequence, one invention may quickly supplant another. The point can best be established by considering the puzzles which confront a business trying to decide whether or not to develop an invention and, if the development be decided upon, how much should be spent and at what rate.

Such a firm is faced by a group of questions, the answer to each being mutually dependent upon the answers to all the others. The discussion can, therefore, begin at any point. The firm might first ask: is the development technically feasible? But the feasibility of development will, at least in part, turn on the resources made available for it. The second question would be: the development once successfully completed, is it likely that a profitable market will be available for the final product? The answer here will of course depend upon a whole series of guesses: the probable cost of production, the probable volume of sales (which will help to determine cost per unit) and so on. But the answer to this second question pushes the firm back to the answer to the first question: for the probable cost of production of the finished product will depend upon how successful the developers are in devising cheap methods of production, and this, in turn, may be a function of how much the firm is prepared to spend on development.

The firm, therefore, finds itself arguing in a circle. If it knew how cheaply a commercial product would finally be put on the market it would know whether development was worth while. But whether development is likely to be successful will partly turn on how much is spent on development. And the costs of development may help to determine the price at which the final product can be sold.

Practically every important decision on the development of a new product represents a heavy plunge by the firm concerned; there can be no precision or certainty in what is done. Let it be supposed, however, that the firm has actually decided that development is technically feasible and that, with expenditures of an acceptable magnitude, it seems that the final article can be put on the market at a price which will give a volume of sales providing a margin over cost (cost including the cost of development) yielding a return on investment probably larger than that obtainable by investment in any other possible direction.

The firm decides to spend up to a given sum on development, always of course hoping that good fortune will be on its side in that the cost of development will prove to be less than expected, or the final product will have unexpected merits. Another question then arises: how quickly should this money be spent? Rapid expenditure may be wasteful Pressure for swift development may bring quicker results but cost more finally. To gather together quickly a group of technologists of second-best quality when more deliberate methods would have made possible the appointment of more able men; to plunge a large number of technologists into a task before the real problems have been clearly perceived (which may partly be a function of time); to pursue simultaneously likely and unlikely avenues when it would have been more economical to try out the more likely first;[7] to attempt to make progress at the same time in the different stages of development which could more conveniently be carried out successively; to have research groups standing by in case they may be needed: these are all forcing tactics, justifiable in emergency, which can rapidly produce decreasing returns to cost. Speedy development, therefore, is likely to be expensive.

On the other hand, speed may have its attractions whatever its cost. Development consummated over five years rather than ten brings profitable sales all the sooner: the firm is standing out of its money for only half the time. There may be other good though less tangible reasons for haste: the excitement of an all-out effort may itself be a stimulus and may contribute to results; the shorter the period of development the less hazardous will be the guesses about the potential future market.

The main reason for haste, however, seems to be the fear of competition. The most favourable circumstances in which the firm could find itself would be where it had fallen upon an invention so novel in character that it was unlikely to be challenged or superseded for a long time; where the firm held what seemed to be an unbreakable master patent; where it felt confident that by secrecy or subsequent patenting it could keep to itself the fruits of development, and where it possessed skills and experience in the relevant manufacturing processes enjoyed by few or no other manufacturing firms.

Although instances are to be found of firms which have in fact enjoyed such good fortune, they are likely to be few; in even fewer cases will the firm believe, before the event, that its luck will hold to this degree.[8] Even a firm with good master patents, power to defend them and to retain exclusive use of its know-how will face the future with some trepidation. Those who have taken out a patent have given a hostage to fortune; for the secret, thereby publicly revealed, will set other minds working along related, and perhaps non-infringing lines, to ends which no one can foresee. Beyond that, there is always the chance that an invention, along entirely different routes, will bring onto the market a competitive final product. Where the strategical and tactical position of the firm is less favourable than the ideal pictured above (which surely must very often happen), the natural anxieties of the firm lest it be supplanted will be all the greater.

Firms which once set their hand to development will usually be anxious to produce results quickly, even if this means a higher total development cost. Whether they feel simply that their own innovations will breed competition against them or whether they fear generally that the constant forward pressure of technical knowledge on a wide front will in some unpredictable way bring rivalry, time will appear to them to be of the essence for successful exploitation. If it is true that in these days there is a greater chance than formerly of one invention being superseded by another moving in from an entirely different direction, this would help to explain the upward trend in development costs.

To reduce its risks, therefore, the firm will increase the speed of development, and this will enlarge the annual, and perhaps the total, expenditures, in respect of any one invention. The greater the risks the stronger the justification for higher development investment. But it is part of the tantalising antithesis of this subject that if the risks are *too* great, if the chances of being supplanted *too* palpable, the development may not be attempted at all. A small wind may fan the flames but a strong wind extinguish them completely.

V

SOME CONTRARY DATA

The solid value of heavy development expenditure in many instances cannot be denied; further supporting testimony is provided by a number of cases where development was suddenly speeded up by a heavy increase in the funds devoted to it, as with

Terylene when taken over by I.C.I. and du Pont, the jet engine when taken up in Britain by Rolls-Royce and the diesel electric locomotive in the United States when developed by General Motors.

On the other hand, particularly in the earlier phases of development, much progress has often been made by the use of very moderate means. Even with the jet engine:

> The total cost of Power Jets' work from its beginning in 1936 to the middle of 1939, when it had definitely shown that the turbo-jet was not a dream but a practical new type of propulsive system, was only some $100,000. The total cost of Heinkel's development over the same period of time was little if any greater than this.[9]

Of the sixty cases studied in detail in this volume, successful development appears to have been carried out by individuals or smaller firms without enormous cost in air conditioning, automatic transmissions, bakelite, cellophane tape, electric precipitation, magnetic recording, power steering, quick freezing, shell moulding and the synthetic light polariser. The discovery of the crease-resisting process for textile fabrics merits special attention.[10] This was a path-breaking discovery which has been universally employed and has long remained unchallenged, where the invention and development was carried through by a firm of medium size with expenditures very much smaller than those normally associated with twentieth-century chemical inventions.

There are also a number of striking instances outside the sixty cases where development has been carried out successfully by a small firm. One of them is the development of the piloted ram-jet aircraft by René Leduc in France. The development of the Pescara free-piston engine in Britain is another case where such work has been successfully executed by a small firm.

Again, instances are not unknown where firms of different size have pursued parallel tasks of development and the victory has not always gone to the large battalions. In the evolution of the cotton picker one large combine and two smaller firms reached results at about the same time.[11] Television provides an extremely interesting illustration.[12] By 1932 it had been clearly established that mechanical systems offered little prospect of further advance and that the future lay with electronic systems. Zworykin, working in the laboratories of the Radio Corporation of America had already produced his 'iconoscope,' perhaps the crucial invention in the emergence of modern television. From then on, the search for the perfection of a practical electronic television system went forward in several quarters. Farnsworth and his associates, with more limited resources than R.C.A., contributed much to the final results. And in Great Britain in 1936 the first regular system of high-definition television broadcasting in the world was established as the result of the work of a small team in Electrical and Musical Industries Ltd. under the direction of I. Shoenberg. Comparisons of this kind can, of course, never be exact or conclusive. In this instance, it would have to be pointed out that the system introduced by R.C.A. in the United States was one of 525 lines as compared with that of 405 of E.M.I.; that in the United States the task of producing a satisfactory system was complicated by the great distances involved; that E.M.I. held licences under the Zworykin patents. Even so, it should counter any facile assumption that the size of a firm is the sole determinant of its commercial imagination or its power in development.

VI

MONOPOLY AND DEVELOPMENT

The grounds for believing that inventions will be most actively developed under conditions of monopoly are various: they may amount to little more than a plea for the merits of the patent system; they may constitute simply a case for the economies of large-scale development for, if the bigger the better, the best will be where an industry consists of only one firm; monopoly then appears as an incident to size.

But a third and more sweeping suggestion is now to be examined; that the more sheltered and exclusive the position of the firm the more likely it is to embark upon, and succeed in, development. To put it concretely, that the ideal industrial organization for snapping up and transmuting inventions into serviceable products is that where the firm holds a master patent on an important invention, is confident it can rope off for itself the fruits of development, and is dominant in the relevant field of manufacture.

At this point scepticism appears pardonable. For if, as suggested earlier, the large development costs of modern times arise partly out of the threat of competition, it seems inconsistent to assert at the same time that only under the security of monopoly will these large sums be spent.

The case for competition, even in the process of development, would run as follows. Competition is in itself a stimulus. The knowledge on the part of one firm that other firms are on the same track forces them all to move more rapidly, the prize lies in what can be gained from priority and, transient as the lead may be, it still remains a powerful motive. Development under such conditions, to be sure, may mean overlapping of effort, it may result in much waste, but it brings about a larger total effort and, carried out by different firms pursuing different lines, may not only make success swifter but sometimes make the difference between success and complete failure. Why, it may be asked, should the knowledge on the part of one firm that success will bring to them the whole of a long-continuing reward, be a sharper spur to effort than the recognition on the part of a number of firms that opportunity beckons but only to a relatively short-lived reward, the size of which depends on their own forcefulness and skill?

Whether a radical invention is more likely to be developed swiftly and effectively if the industry most directly concerned consists of one very large firm holding a secure patent than if the industry consists of a substantial number of small firms and the patent is in the public domain or is freely under licence, will depend partly upon factors other than the degree of monopoly: whether business men are temperamentally disposed to competition; the character of the invention; the apparent feasibility of the development; whether a market seems to be there for the taking or would have to be built up against the solid resistance of existing commodities; whether it is possible for firms to retain the secrets of accumulated know-how; whether firms of the same size are roughly equal in the facilities they possess for development; and how each firm may rate its chances against others in a struggle for technical and commercial priority. General reasoning, that is to say, cannot carry us to a final conclusion. Undoubtedly the *capacity* of the monopolist to carry through development is greater than that of any one of the firms in the second set of conditions, for any one or all of these firms might find it impossible to take the risks involved. But it is relevant to consider not merely the *power* to do something, but also the *will* to do it.

At this point there seems to be no choice but to have recourse to actual experience. This provides some support for three conclusions:

(**a**) that certain examples, frequently put forward as proof of the virtue of monopoly, can bear interpretations different from those normally placed upon them and, in any case, are hardly typical;

(**b**) that there are a large number of instances of development occurring under keenly competitive conditions;

(**c**) that the fewness of the producers in an industry where an important invention arises may in itself constitute a block to development.

These conclusions will be illustrated in turn.

The Case of Nylon

The case of nylon is perhaps the most commonly quoted as proof of the success of a one-firm development. There, a very large firm with a dominating position in the chemical industry supported for several years in its research laboratories a brilliant scientist whose chances of success must at times have appeared depressingly slight. In the event, a remarkable discovery was made, the first synthetic fibre was produced upon which du Pont obtained patents and to the development of which it devoted very large sums. Within a short period the product was available commercially in quantity.

It is not surprising that this story should excite the imagination and colour the popular view of how progress can most expeditiously be effected. In fact, however, it is reasonable to assume that potential competition played some part in determining the policy of du Pont. Their patents were strong but it was known at the time that at least one German firm had made progress in parallel work on synthetic fibres. In the event, the progress of the German technologists proved slower than might have been expected. The war interrupted their efforts and they encountered unexpected obstacles in development. The German fibre, Perlon, however, came on to the market after the war and has since enjoyed large sales in Europe.

Beyond that, the nylon case, it might be argued, is untypical. There can hardly ever have been another example in industrial history where, the discovery once made, so large and obvious a peace-time market presented itself if only the invention could be successfully developed. In the case of nylon the market was that for women's stockings. Fashion had long decreed that women in the Western world should wear thin stockings of light shades; cotton and wool fibres were unsuitable for this purpose; silk itself was expensive, artificial silks of various types were suitable but had a very short life and stood up badly to frequent washing. Stockings of the new fibre were an answer to a multitude of prayers;[13] for nylon could be drawn very fine, was relatively hard-wearing and was easy to wash. When it is further added that the fibre by good fortune proved very suitable for use on the knitting machine, and that, once the first fibre had been produced, the tasks of development, while formidable, did not appear insuperable, there can have been little doubt that here was a windfall of great magnitude.[14]

Further, and without in any way seeking to belittle the great achievements of du Pont, is it unreasonable to suggest that, if Carothers had made his discovery in a university instead of in the du Pont laboratories, and if non-exclusive licences had been available or the patents had been in the public domain, many chemical or other firms would have been prepared, in competition, to devote large sums to its development? And, if this had happened, might not successful development have resulted just as quickly as it actually did?

Development under Competition

From the very large number of instances which might be quoted where firms have been prepared to take the risks of competition in development a few of the most interesting may be referred to here.

The first practicable method of producing *Titanium* was evolved by an individual inventor, who found the chemical and metallurgical firms extremely lukewarm about the potentialities of his discovery.[15] The early stages of development were carried through during the Second World War by a United States Government research agency. The problem of the companies at first was to find a market for this remarkable metal, but, from 1950 onwards, this was partly solved for them by the demands of military agencies for titanium for use in aircraft. By far the greater part of the output is still absorbed by the fighting services, both in the United States and Great Britain, under contracts very favourable to the producers. In Great Britain I.C.I. appears to be the only firm in production, using its own sodium process after experimenting with and discarding the original Kroll magnesium reduction process. In the United States, however, there are now more than a score of firms, some of them government-financed and some acting independently, who have taken substantial risks in the production of the metal and in research directed both towards the further development of the Kroll process and to improvements upon it. Undoubtedly military needs gave an early forced draught to this development, but, even if this cannot be regarded as falling within 'the traditional folk-lore of invention in the free capitalist economy,' the present position is one of vigorous competition in development springing largely from the work of an individual inventor.

Shell Moulding was a brilliant invention whereby castings can be produced with smoother surfaces and more accurate dimensions, thus enormously reducing the need for machining. It was invented by a German during the Second World War; after the war it was found by the Allied technical teams and was published as belonging to the public domain. Its potentialities were so great and so obvious that dozens of firms, large and small, old and new, vigorously took up the perfection of the idea.[16]

Polyethylene was discovered in the research laboratories of Imperial Chemical Industries, which took out patents on it before the Second World War. Their method of manufacture involved the use of very high pressures. After the war two new processes, which seem to have some similarities, were discovered in which high pressures were no longer required. Of these, one was discovered by Professor Ziegler of the Max Planck Institute. The Ziegler process has been eagerly seized upon for development by a number of firms in the United States, Germany and Great Britain. In the United States licences have been taken out by du Pont, Union Carbide, Koppers, Monsanto and other chemical companies. In Great Britain an exclusive licence was taken out by Petro-Chemicals Ltd., a firm afterwards absorbed by Shell.[17]

The development of the *Jet Engine*[18] is perhaps not a clear-cut case, for the engine was badly needed for war purposes and the firms concerned undoubtedly took a wider view of their national responsibilities than would have been determined by purely commercial considerations, but very vigorous competition occurred and, of course, still continues.

Insulin in Great Britain is a highly relevant case.[19] Between 1922 and 1941, five British concerns held licences to develop and manufacture insulin; there was no technical collaboration between them. There was further competitive prodding from abroad in the form of improvements principally arising from the brilliant work of Dr. Hagedorn of the Nordisk Laboratorium in Copenhagen.[20] Under these conditions rapid progress was made. With improvements in the method of manufacture, the price of the standard insulin pack was brought down from 25s. in April 1923 to 1s. 6d. in July 1935. In 1941, however, these conditions changed, originally because of war-time needs. Since that year, with one short break, the manufacturers of insulin have engaged in the fullest exchange of technical information and have collaborated at every stage in research, development and production and have fixed common prices. But it would be misguided to exaggerate the improvements that accompanied co-operation after 1941 and ignore the more spectacular improvements that went along with competition in development before 1941.

There are other instances, too numerous to describe in detail here,[21] of successful development under competitive conditions: the cotton picker, air conditioning, the ballpoint pen, television, automatic transmissions, the catalytic cracking of petroleum, the new forms of three-dimensional films, the electron microscope, the hardening of liquid fats, magnetic recording, acrylic fibres, power steering and synthetic detergents.

Security as a Block to Development

The very *fewness* of the firms in an industry may (it would be going too far to say will) result in delay in exploiting new ideas or even in their permanent loss to society. Here we move again among the intangibles. A firm with a dominating position, conscious of its power to pounce if its position should suddenly be put into jeopardy, may be so confident of being able to deal with incipient competition as to become sluggish.[22] And the general knowledge that it can so pounce may deter potential rivals and thus leave the field empty.

In an industry with one or a few firms the chances are obviously greater that a new thing may be missed either simply because it is overlooked or, even where it is known about, because it happens not to excite the imagination Illustrations are easy to come by. In the 1930's the large oil companies moved slowly until Houdry, an outsider, with his catalytic cracking process forced the pace and finally galvanised the industry into action. In the United States the big firms were slow to take up and exploit the invention of power steering for passenger cars; in Great Britain they have been tardy in the development of automatic transmissions for the lighter motor cars. For a long time the large photographic firms ignored the possibilities of xerography. For a number of years the leading companies in the non-ferrous and electrical industries showed no interest in ideas for producing ductile titanium which have since been taken up eagerly.

The case of taconite is especially relevant. Taconite is a rock which forms the underlying bed of the Mesabi deposits of high-grade ore in the United States and constitutes an almost unlimited reserve of iron. Quite recently it has been increasingly mined by a number of American companies as an important supplement to the dwindling domestic supplies of iron ore. But much of the credit for the final achievement must be given to one man, E. W. Davis, a scientist in the University of Minnesota, who began in 1912 what proved to be a lifelong struggle to arouse interest in the possible use of taconite and to solve the highly intractable problems of extracting the iron from the rock. An experimental plant was set up in 1916 but closed down in 1922. Davis, however, persisted and made great progress both in the breaking down of the rock and the forming of the ore into pellets for use in furnaces. But most of his funds were obtained from public bodies, for the big eastern steel companies were unresponsive. It was not until 1943 that they started their own development on the basis of his work. Since 1948 the scale of development has enormously increased, although even now it is by no means clear that the pace is being set by the largest iron and steel companies.

The presence of a significant number of possibly interested firms can be expected to bring about the trial of a wider range of innovations than where fewness is the rule. Society may thereby avoid the putting of too many of its eggs in the one basket. A dominating firm in an industry may well be confronted with an embarrassment of riches; such firms frequently assert that they have many more promising ideas than they can possibly afford to develop. If they are disposed, for reasons already enlarged upon, to choose a limited number of innovations and to push these on at great cost with the utmost speed, this may be to the detriment of the chances of other new methods and products ever seeing the light of day.

The dangers of fewness can, of course, be exaggerated. It must not be supposed that every alleged case of resistance to change is a mistake: it may represent a perfectly legitimate reluctance to embark on projects where the balance of economic advantage is against action. And there are always safety valves: an innovation may be taken up by a firm outside the industry where it might have been expected to be developed, and many new firms have come into an industry for the sole purpose of exploiting an idea which established interests had set on one side. But there are enough instances since the beginning of the nineteenth century of the neglect, sometimes prolonged, of potentially fruitful ideas, to indicate that there is a real risk of loss through development being pursued on too narrow a front.

VIII

Against the claim that the prerogative in development should always rest with the biggest and the most securely established industrial organisations, may be set, therefore, the advantages of the attack from many angles. The tasks of development are themselves of such diversity and of so varying a scale that it may be a great and a dangerous over-simplification to suppose that they can always be best handled by any single type of institution. It may be that the happiest situation for a community, the condition most effectively contributing to general liveliness, will be found where the variety in form and outlook in industrial institutions matches that of the problems with which they have to deal; firms of varying size, some disposed to pursue plans deliberately and with an eye on the distant future and others inclined to plunge heavily for quick results; some mainly concerned with holding an established status and others prepared to dare much to restore a lost position or to break into a new industry; some that regard their forte as lying in rapid innovation and others which feel that their strength is found in following up and improving. It may well be that there is no optimum size of firm but merely an optimum pattern for any industry, such a distribution of firms by size, character and outlook as to guarantee the most effective gathering together and commercially perfecting of the flow of new ideas.

Endnotes

1. Thus *The Economist,* May 5th, 1956, speaking of titanium: 'Even though Dr. Kroll, back in the thirties, may certainly fit the stereotype of the individual inventor, it is hard to fit the whole titanium exploit, including the last chapter of it that forms I.C.I.'s titanium venture, into the traditional folklore of invention in the free capitalist economy. But it may well epitomise the ruling pattern of innovation in our time.'

2. Thus the first stage of development of Terylene or nylon might be thought to end with the pilot plant stage; that of the jet engine when the Germans and British put fighters into operation; that of high-altitude rockets when the V2's started to fall with some regularity on London that of the steam-turbine around 1900; that of viscose rayon around 1910. But when it was announced in 1955 that the first British diesel electric locomotive had been 'developed' at a cost of £500,000, nearly ten years after all the main-line locomotives in the U.S. had become diesel electrics, this clearly is a reference to a later phase of development.

3. Lord Brabazon of Tara, *The Brabazon Story,* pp. 151–2.

4. Thus Leonardo da Vinci: 'Vitruvius says that small models are of no avail for ascertaining the effects of larger ones: and I here propose to prove that this conclusion is false.'

5. J. M. Cohen, *The Life of Ludwig Mond,* p. 218, points to this as the cause of some of the vicissitudes in the early business career of Ludwig Mond.

6. In the case of both nylon and Terylene in Great Britain an output of about 10 million pounds per year was considered the minimum commercially desirable.

7. For a very interesting account of how, in the efforts to get quick results, a good deal of wasted effort has necessarily to be tolerated, see the account of the development of the I.C.I. sodium process for the making of titanium. R. B. Mooney and J. J. Gray, 'I.C.I.'s New Titanium Process,' *I.C.I. Magazine,* June 1956. Of course the outstanding example of prodigal expenditure in the interests of speed is that of the development of the first atom bomb.

8. Note that anyone who has solved a puzzle by methods which after the event seem simple, finds it difficult to believe that others will not also discover the critical clues. That was the terrifying anxiety in the minds of most atomic scientists on the Allied side during the war.

9. R. Schlaifer and S. D. Heron, *Development of Aircraft Engines and Fuels,* p. 90.

10. See pp. 286–90.

11. See pp. 282–6.

12. See pp. 384–8.

13. During and immediately after the war when nylon stockings were not produced in Europe, the scale of smuggling in them and their commerce on the black market were both enormous.

14. The scale of the commercial scoop can be judged by the fact that the nylon stocking, where available, rapidly replaced all others. In the United States in 1954, 97 per cent of the women's stockings produced were of nylon. From 1939 until 1955 du Pont was the only maker of nylon type yarns in the United States. Nylon 66, the type du Pont first chose, has remained unchallenged among the different types available. Nylon has proved to be by far the greatest of du Pont's products by sales and almost certainly by profits; in 1954 it may have accounted for one-third of du Pont's a total profits.

15. See pp. 395–8.

16. See pp. 363–5.

17. See pp. 339–42.

18. See pp. 314–21.

19. The authoritative story is told in the report of the Monopolies and Restrictive Practices Commission, *Report on the Supply of Insulin,* 1952.

20. An import duty was imposed on insulin, but, as a result of public agitation, the Government was forced to remove it in 1934.

21. But some detail is given in the cases recorded in Part II.

22. A. A. Bright, *The Electric Lamp Industry,* p. 389, has pointed out that General Electric, content with its dominating position in artificial lighting, was sluggish in taking up the development of fluorescent lighting, but that, once it was aroused by the presence of other pioneers in the field, its bountiful resources and the assistance it derived from the innovating work of others, quickly enabled it to reassert its predominance. Similarly R. Schlaifer, *Development of Aircraft Engines,* pp. 100–3, suggests that the monopoly possessed between the wars by Stromberg in aircraft carburettors and by General Electric in superchargers delayed improvements.

19

ECONOMIC THEORY AND ENTREPRENEURIAL HISTORY

Joseph A. Schumpeter

In the areas of economic theory and entrepreneurial history, I propose to deal with three topics. First, I shall present a brief survey of the history, within economic literature, of the notions that economists have formed at various times on the subject of entrepreneurship and economic progress (I). Secondly, I shall deal with some aspects of enterprise as it actually evolved through the ages (II). And, thirdly, I shall briefly comment on the possibilities of what might be termed "general economic history" as viewed from the standpoint of the phenomenon of economic enterprise (III). The first topic will also provide the conceptual apparatus to be used in the treatment of the other two.

I

In the field to be discussed, as in others, early economic analysis started from the notions evolved by common experience of everyday life, proceeding to greater precision and refinement of these notions as time went on. From the first, the businessman was a familiar figure that did not seem to call for elaborate explanation at all. The particular forms of business enterprise that every particular environment produced—the artisan, the trader, the moneylender, and so on—took a long time in merging into the general concept of businessman. But by the end of the 17th century this modest generalization was pretty much accomplished. It is, however, worth noting that at least from the beginning of the 15th century on, the scholastic doctors in their economics had a very definite idea of the businessman and his functions, and that in particular they distinguished clearly between the specific *industria* of the merchant and the *labor* of the workman. The same applies to the laic successors of the scholastic doctors, "the philosophers of natural law," and still more to all those pamphleteers of the "mercantilist" age that laid the foundations of classic economics. Cantillon's work, which is usually, though not quite correctly, described as the first systematic treatise on economics, then introduced the term "entrepreneur." It is worth our while to note that Cantillon defined this entrepreneur as the agent who buys means of production at certain prices in order to combine them into a product that he is going to sell at prices that are uncertain at the moment at which he commits himself to his costs. I think that this embryonic analysis was not infelicitous. Besides recognizing business activity as a function *sui generis,* it emphasizes the elements of direction and speculation that certainly do enter somehow into entrepreneurial activity. Like most of Cantillon's ideas, including the idea of the *tableau économique,* this one was accepted by the physiocrats as a matter of course. Since directly and through the physiocrats Cantillon's teaching continued to be known in France, it seems fair to say that J. B. Say only continued the French tradition by developing this analysis further. In this he was greatly helped by the fact that, knowing from experience what business practice really is, he had a lively vision of the phenomenon which most of the other classic economists lacked. With him, then, the entrepreneur is the agent that combines the others into a productive organism. It could be shown both that this definition might be expanded into a satisfactory theory of entrepreneurship by analyzing what this combining of factors really consists in, and that Say himself did not do much with it beyond stressing its importance. Let us note in passing, however, that he put the entrepreneur into the center of both the productive and the distributive theory which, though it is disfigured by many slips, first adumbrated the analytic structure that became fully articulate in the hands of Walras, Marshall, Wicksell, Clark, and the Austrians. Still more clearly the nature and importance of entrepreneurship were perceived by Jeremy Bentham. It is a curious fact (curious, that is, considering the tremendous influence that Bentham exerted in other respects) that his views on this subject—which were not fully given to the public until the posthumous publication of his collected works—remained almost unnoticed by professional economists.

In spite of the great influence of the physiocrats and of Cantillon upon Adam Smith, English thought took a quite different line. To be sure, Adam Smith repeatedly talked about the employer—the master, the merchant, and the undertaker—but the leading or directing activity as a distinctive function played a surprisingly small role in his analytic scheme of the economic process. His reader is bound to get an impression to the effect that this process runs on by itself. Natural law preconceptions led Adam Smith to emphasize the role of labor to the exclusion of the productive function of designing the plan according to which this labor is being applied. This shows characteristically in his turn of phrase that asserts that "capitalists" hire "industrious people," advancing them means of subsistence, raw materials, and tools, and letting them do the rest. What the businessman does in the system of Adam Smith is, therefore, to provide real capital and nothing else: the identification of the capitalist's and the entrepreneur's function was thus accomplished. Let us note: first, that this picture of the industrial process is entirely unrealistic; but that, considering the prevalence at Adam Smith's time of the putting-out system, and also for other historical reasons, this identification was then less absurd than it became fifty years later; and that Smith's authority explains why it survived so well into times that presented different patterns. Since capital, according to Adam Smith, is the result of saving, and since providing capital is the only essential function of the businessman, the latter's profit was essentially interest to be explained on the lines of either an exploitation or an abstinence theory. Adam Smith elaborated neither, but no doubt suggested both.

With Ricardo and Marx the processes of production and commerce are still more automatic. The designing, directing, leading, co-ordinating function has practically no place at all in their analytic schemata. To avoid misunderstandings, let me emphasize that there is no doubt but that, if pressed, both Ricardo and Marx (and this goes for a majority of the writers of the classic period) would certainly have recognized the importance of entrepreneurship or business management or however they would have called it, for the success or failure of the individual concern. But it is possible to recognize this and to hold, nevertheless, that for the social process as a whole individual differences in this respect are of no great moment. John Stuart Mill who, at an early age, had experienced the influence of Say, abandoned Ricardianism in this as he did in other points. He emphasized the function of direction in the productive process and went out of his way to say that very often it required "no ordinary skill." His perception of the importance of entrepreneurial activity shows among other things in the fact that he regretted that there is no good English word for the French "entrepreneur," but this was all. When we observe that he analyzed the entrepreneur's profits into wages of management, interest on owned capital, and premium of risk, we wonder why he should not have been content with the perfectly good English term "business management," which was in fact to satisfy Marshall. For, after all, his entrepreneur does a type of non manual work that does not essentially differ from other types, and therefore reaps a return that is analogous to wages. There should be no need for a distinctive term.

Just as the understanding of the phenomenon of rent of land was facilitated by the English land system that showed up the distinction between the owner of land and the agricultural producer with unmistakable clearness, so the distinction between the entrepreneur and the capitalist was facilitated in the second half of the nineteenth century by the fact that changing methods of business finance produced a rapidly increasing number of instances in which capitalists were no entrepreneurs and entrepreneurs were no capitalists. Though the owner-manager remained for a time still the ruling type, it became increasingly clear that a link between owning and operating the physical shell of industry is not a necessary one. Economists accordingly began to emphasize distinctions between the two functions and to devote more attention to the specifically entrepreneurial one. Fundamental change in the analytic setup was very slow, however. Among other things, this shows in the survival of the risk theory of entrepreneurial profit. If providing the capital is not the essential or defining function of the entrepreneur, then risk bearing should not be described as an essential or defining function either, for it is obviously the capitalist who bears the risk and who loses his money in case of failure. If the entrepreneur borrows at a fixed rate of interest and undertakes to guarantee the capitalist against loss whatever the results of the enterprise, he can do so only if he owns other assets with which to satisfy the creditor capitalist when things go wrong. But, in this case, he is able to satisfy his creditor because he is a capitalist himself and the risk he bears he bears in this capacity and not in his capacity of entrepreneur. To this point I shall return below. The economists, therefore, who went on to emphasize the entrepreneurial function more and more, such as Francis A. Walker in the U.S., Marshall in England, Mangoldt and others in Germany, added very little to its analysis.

Two lines of thought that issued in distinctive theories of entrepreneurial profits as distinguished from interest should not go unmentioned. Mangoldt, following up a generalization of the rent concept that may be traced to Samuel Bailey, defined the particular element of total receipts that goes to the entrepreneur as a rent of ability. The underlying idea is very plausible. All current disturbances of the economic process, the whole task of adaptation to ever changing situations, impinges primarily upon the heads of business concerns. Obviously this is a very personal task of which some people acquit themselves very much better than others. There is a common-sense impression to the effect that there is such a thing as a distinct business ability, which includes aptitude for efficient administration, for prompt decision, and all that sort of thing; and it is very generally recognized in spite of some votes to the contrary (in this country, mainly from economists of Veblenite persuasion) that successful survival of difficult situations and success in taking advantage of favorable situations is not merely a matter of luck. The concept of a rent of ability expresses the element involved quite well. Again the cognate idea that business decisions in a world that is full of uninsurable risks ("uncertainty") will in general produce results that diverge more or less widely from the expected ones and thus lead sometimes to surplus gains and sometimes to losses, is one that common experience presses upon us very strongly. This idea may be but need not be added to the element of business ability and is of course, still more obviously, not quite the same as the element of risk: but we need not stress these relations. So far as I know, Böhm-Bawerk was the first to make use of this notion for the purpose of explaining entrepreneurial profits as distinct from interest. But this line of thought culminates in the work of Professor Knight.

It does not seem far-fetched, however, to analyze the entrepreneurial function in a different direction which moreover leads to a result that comprises also some of the elements of other theories. I shall try to convey this analysis by starting from two different standpoints. The first standpoint to start from is given by Say's definition of the entrepreneurial function. If production in the economic, as distinguished from the technological, sense consists essentially in transforming or combining factors into products, or as I have put it above, in providing the design of production, then we certainly have in this combining or planning or directing activity distinct function before us. But this function would be an exceedingly simple matter and essentially a matter of administration if the combinations that have been carried into effect in the past had to be simply repeated or even if they had to be repeated subject to those adaptations which common business experience suggests in the face of conditions that change under the influence of external factors. Administrative or managerial activity of this kind, however necessary, need not be distinguished from other kinds of non manual labor; but if we confine Say's definition to cases in which combinations that are *not* inherited from the past have to be set up anew, then the situation is obviously different and we do have a distinctive function before us. Naturally, to some extent, even current decisions contain elements that have not been contained in inherited routine. There is, therefore, no sharp dividing line between entrepreneurial activity in this restricted sense and ordinary administration or management, any more than there is a sharp dividing line between the *homo neanderthalis* and the types which we recognize as full-fledged human beings. This does not, however, prevent the distinction from being possible and useful. And the distinctive element is readily recognized so soon as we make clear to ourselves what it means to act outside of the pale of routine. The distinction between adaptive and creative response to given conditions may or may not be felicitous, but it conveys an essential point; it conveys an essential difference.

The other standpoint from which to get a realistic understanding of the entrepreneurial function comes into view when we try to analyze the nature and sources of the gains that attend successful entrepreneurship. This can be done in many ways, for instance, by analyzing the sources of a sufficient number of industrial fortunes. We find immediately that industrial activity in established lines and by established methods hardly ever yields returns that are much greater than is necessary to secure the supply of the factors required. Furthermore, we find that the earning capacity of almost any industrial concern peters out after a time that varies from a few months to a few decades. And, finally, we find that the great surplus gains are in general made in new industries or in industries that adopt a new method, and especially by the firms who are the first in the field. These propositions await scientific investigations in order to be fully established, but are strongly suggested by universally known facts.

If then we have, on the one hand, a distinctive function and, on the other hand, a distinct return on the exercise of this function, we can start with the task of conceptualization. First, we need a word. I have myself suggested that the word "entrepreneur" be harnessed into service, but it is quite clear, of course, that since this "entrepreneurial function" is not a neologism other meanings are bound to creep in. I should, therefore, have no objection to some such expression as "business leader" or simply "innovator" or the like. The essential thing is the recognition of the distinct agent we envisage and not the word.[1] Secondly, in applying our conception to reality we find, as we do in other such cases, that real life never presents the function in and by itself. Even the English landlord is not merely the owner of a natural agent but does various other things besides. In the case of the entrepreneur it is even difficult to imagine a case where a man does nothing but set up new combinations and where he does this all his life. In particular an industrialist who creates an entirely new setup will, in a typical case, then settle down to a merely administrating activity to which he confines himself more and more as he gets older. On the other hand, the entrepreneurial element may be present to a very small extent even in very humble cases and in these the entrepreneurial function may be all but drowned in other activities. It will be seen, however, that while this makes it difficult to deal with entrepreneurship irrespective of the other types of activity of the same individual and while Professor Cole is therefore quite right in emphasizing the necessity of considering business activity as a whole, the distinctive element and its *modus operandi* should not and need not be lost from sight.

Thirdly, since entrepreneurship, as defined, essentially consists in doing things that are not generally done in the ordinary course of business routine, it is essentially a phenomenon that comes under the wider aspect of leadership. But this relation be-tween entrepreneurship and general leadership is a very complex one and lends itself to a number of misunderstandings. This is due to the fact that the concept of leadership itself is complex. Leadership may consist, as it does in the arts, merely in doing a new thing, for instance, in creating a new form of pictorial self-expression, but in other cases it is the influencing of people by methods other than example that is more im-portant. Take, for instance, the phenomenon that we call the ability of being obeyed. Here it is not so much example as a direct action upon other people that matters. The nature and function of entrepreneurial leadership, its causes and effects, therefore constitute a very important subject of investigation for our group.

Fourthly, the distinctive return to entrepreneurship presents difficulties of its own. It is certainly a return to a personal activity. In this sense we might be tempted to call it a form of wages as has in fact been done in the past by many economists. Furthermore, it is clear that if all people reacted in the same way and at the same time to the pres-ence of new possibilities no entrepreneurial gain would ensue: if everybody had been in a position to develop the Watt condenser, prices of products to be produced with the new steam engine would have adjusted themselves instantaneously and no surplus over costs would have arisen for the firm of Boulton and Watt. Therefore, entrepre-neurial gain may also be called a monopoly gain, since it is due to the fact that com-petitors only follow at a distance.[2] But if we called it either wages or monopoly gains we should be obscuring very important characteristics that do not apply to other wages or to other monopoly gains. Moreover, the entrepreneurial gain does not typically con-sist, and in any case does not necessarily consist, in a current surplus *per se*. If a man, for instance, sets up a new industrial organization such as United States Steel, the value of the assets that enter into this organization increases. This increase no doubt embodies, at least ideally, a discounted value of the expected surplus returns. But it is this increase in asset values itself rather than the returns that constitute the entrepre-neurial gain, and it is in this way that industrial fortunes are typically created—another subject to be investigated.

Finally, as has been often pointed out, the entrepreneurial function need not be embodied in a physical person and in particular in a single physical person. Every social environment has its own ways of filling the entrepreneurial function. For instance, the practice of farmers in this country has been revolutionized again and again by the introduction of methods worked out in the Department of Agriculture and by the Department of Agriculture's success in teaching these methods. In this case then it was the Department of Agriculture that acted as an entrepreneur. It is another most important point in our research program to find out how important this kind of activity has been in the past or is in the present. Again the entrepreneurial function may be and often is filled co-operatively. With the development of the largest-scale corporations this has evidently become of major importance: aptitudes that no single individual combines can thus be built into a corporate personality; on the other hand, the constituent physical personalities must inevitably to some extent, and very often to a serious extent, interfere with each other. In many cases, therefore, it is difficult or even impossible to name an individual that acts as "the entrepreneur" in a concern. The leading people in particular, those who carry the titles of president or chairman of the board, may be mere co-ordinators or even figureheads; and again a very interesting field of research opens up into which I do not wish to go, however, since this problem is in no danger of being forgotten.[3]

We have now briefly to advert to the relation that exists between economic change (usually called economic progress if we approve of it) and the entrepreneurial activity. At present there is, as has been stated above, a whole range of differences of opinion on this subject that extends from a complete or almost complete denial of any impor-tance to be attached to the quality of leading personnel to the equally reckless asser-tion that the creative individual is nothing less than everything. It need hardly be pointed out that most of these opinions carry the stamp of ideological preconception. It is no doubt part of our work to put provable results into the place of such ideologies. The fundamental question is one of fact, but the necessity of a theoretical schema to start with is nevertheless obvious. I submit that the material under observation may be classed into two masses: on the one hand, there are the given data of the physical and social (including political) environment and, on the other hand, there are the observable reactions to these environmental conditions. But it is better perhaps to include those facts that may be independently observed concerning the quality of leading personnel among the conditions in order to display the interrelation between this and the other factors and to emphasize from the first that on principle there are never any causal chains in the historical process but only mutual interaction of distinguishable factors.

We can then attempt to construct an analytic model of the mechanism of economic change or else, for different countries and periods, different such schemata or models. Let us, in order to visualize this method, consider for a moment the situation that existed in England around 1850. A unique set of historical conditions had produced a uniquely able political sector, the bulk of the members of which hailed from a distinct social class. This sector, while very efficient in certain respects, was entirely unfit and unwilling to undertake anything that we now call economic public management or economic planning. Neglecting for the rest the agrarian sector, we find industry, trade, and finance substantially left to themselves; and if we add a number of other unique historical circumstances we are pretty much able to draw the picture of economic change that is in fact drawn in the ordinary text-book of economic history. In this process of change it is possible to identify a number of factors and events that are entirely impersonal and in some cases random. But looking more closely we see not only that these factors do not determine outcomes uniquely but also that they do not tell us how the actual changes such as the tremendous increase in exports actually came about. In order to make headway with this problem we must investigate how the thousands of individuals actually worked whose combined action produced these results. And for this purpose it is useful as a first step to assume all the environmental factors to be constant and to ask the question what changes we might expect under this assumption. We immediately see that simple increase of population and of physical capital does not constitute the answer. It is not simply the increase of the existing factors of production but the incessantly different use made of these factors that matters. In fact much of the increase in factors and particularly of physical capital was the result rather than the cause of what we may now identify as entrepreneurial activity. What we observe is rather a behavior pattern, possibly supplemented by a schema of motivation; a typical way of giving effect to the possibilities inherent in a given legal and social system both of which change in the process; the effects of entrepreneurial activity upon the industrial structure that exists at any moment; the consequent process of destruction and reconstruction that went on all the time. All these things may be conceptualized in a more or less complicated schema, every time of which has to be nourished with facts and corrected and amplified under their influence. And this is all.

I shall add, however, that in investigations of this kind the notion of an economic process that merely reproduces itself and shows neither decay nor progress has been found to be of considerable use. It is called the stationary state, and plays two distinct roles in economic theory. On the one hand, economists, ever since Adam Smith and perhaps earlier times, have envisaged the possibility that the energetic advance they were witnessing would some day subside into what we now call a stagnating or mature economy. John Stuart Mill differed from Ricardo not in his expectation that a stationary state would one day emerge but in the optimistic view he took of its features—a world without what he considered an unpleasant bustle, a world much more cultured and at ease than the one he observed. Now, as everybody knows, this "stagnationist thesis" has emerged once more, but it has emerged with two differences. First, the stationary state is by some authors not looked upon as something that looms in the far future but as something on which we are actually about to enter. Let us note in passing that the experiences of the crises 1929–1932 may have a lot to do with the emergence of this frame of mind. Secondly, a problem has arisen which did not worry the classics at all. Smith or Ricardo did not anticipate any particular difficulties that would arise from the very process of settling down into stationality: rates of change would

converge towards zero in a slow and orderly way. But our modern stagnationists anticipate difficulties in this process of settling down. Keynes in particular anticipated that
habits of saving to which equally strong or still stronger propensities to invest corresponded would run on in spite of the fact that there would be no longer any investment
opportunities left. With everything indicating now that a new period of unheard-of
"progress" is at hand it might be thought that we need not greatly worry about this. But
I do not think that we can entirely overlook the problem and history's contribution to it.

II

Whether we define the entrepreneur as an "innovator" or in any other way, there remains the task to see how the chosen definition works out in practice as applied to historical materials. In fact it might be argued that the historical investigation holds
logical priority and that our definitions of entrepreneur, entrepreneurial function, enterprise, and so on can only grow out of it *a posteriori*. Personally, I believe that there
is an incessant give and take between historical and theoretical analysis and that,
though for the investigation of individual questions it may be necessary to sail for a
time on one tack only, yet on principle the two should never lose sight of each other.
In consequence we might formulate our task as an attempt to write a comprehensive
history of entrepreneurship.

So far as the institutional framework is concerned we are, comparatively speaking, well of. The social, legal, technological, and other conditions in which entrepreneurship has run its historical course, from the primitive tribe to the modern
large-scale corporation, have been on the whole satisfactorily worked out already. But
until relatively recent times it is this framework only that is really known: the actual
activity of the entrepreneur, what he really was and did at various stages of historical
development, is largely construction. It is true that this construction is in many cases
quite safe. For instance, when we know the trade routes in the Near East during the
first ten centuries A.D., the commodities that were transported, the political history of
the territories through which they were transported, it is not very difficult to imagine
the kind of tasks and difficulties that the trader met on these routes and the kind of
chap he must have been in order to overcome them. When we know the history of the
later trading companies such as the Trading Company of Ravensburg, we again have
little difficulty in complementing this by a picture of the kind of man that a member
of this company must have been. And to a certain extent we might hope to answer the
question directly how environment, public authority, corporate action, and individual
initiative must have co-operated and what relative weight we are to attach to each.
However, these are favorable cases. In others, much digging may have to be done before we arrive at reliable results. Let us then note that the forms of organization of
trade and later on of manufacturing are an acquired asset all along. The same applies
largely to the fields and methods of what provisionally we should call entrepreneurial
activity. That is to say we know or readily understand that at some times under certain
conditions entrepreneurial activity must have consisted largely in trading and transporting, in manufacturing and organizing and financing at others. Finally, the history
of entrepreneurial types and of the nature of entrepreneurial performance, the action
of these types on the social organization and the reaction of the social bodies on the
entrepreneurial impulse should not be too difficult to analyze. Having thus adumbrated my ideas about what that history of entrepreneurship should do, I want now briefly
to touch upon a number of problems and stumbling blocks that will inevitably be met
with on this road.

The first of all these stumbling blocks is that most of us do not approach the material with a perfectly unbiased mind. In other words, every age and every social organization approaches these problems from an *a priori* of its own, that is to say, from a
conviction (all the more dangerous if subconscious) that individual initiative in the
matter of economic development counts for almost everything or else for almost nothing, and it is easy to see how such a conviction supplies the basic colors of the picture.

For some of us the problem of economic development is all but solved so soon as natural and social conditions and political measures are stated—the rest follows automatically, and if entrepreneurs have anything to do with what actually happens they are a sort of beast of prey withholding the fruits of technological advance from the community and sabotaging progress in their own interest. It is needless to point out that this attitude is very prevalent in this country and that any attempt to take another view is for many a modern economist stigmatized as apologetics. Nevertheless, it should be clear from even a superficial survey of facts that this view is as wrong as is the exactly opposite one and that careful discussion of ever more numerous situations is the only method of arriving at a more tenable one.

Secondly, in connection with this we frequently meet with an attitude that is indeed a necessary prerequisite for the "theory" just alluded to. This attitude may be expressed by saying that the entrepreneur or money-maker simply does nothing but take advantage of technological progress, which therefore appears, implicitly or explicitly, as something that goes along entirely independently of entrepreneurial activity. Now how far is this true? It is perhaps not difficult to understand that technological progress, so obvious in some societies and so nearly absent in others, is a phenomenon that needs to be explained. For instance, it is necessary to find out whether the rational or rationalist attitude to life has or has not been formed by the type of mind that pervades bourgeois society. In this ease technological progress would be related to entrepreneurial action in a way that may not always be obvious but would be very important all the same. I have always emphasized that the entrepreneur is the man who gets new things done and not necessarily the man who invents. As a matter of history, the entrepreneur is almost as often an inventor as he is a capitalist but it seems to me that analysis shows that neither of these capacities is essential to him. I can adduce plenty of examples by which to illustrate what seems to me to be the true relation, but only extensive research can present really reliable results.

Thirdly, let us consider a very old problem that has played more of a role in economic literature than it does now under the title of "original accumulation." Some command over physical and personal factors is no doubt necessary in order to start any enterprise: but how is such command acquired in the first place? The old classical answer, that resources came from savings, was understandably unpopular with socialists and is equally unpopular with modern radicals. And it is quite true that, however great the role of self-financing may be in the course of the development of an enterprise, the original nucleus of means has been but rarely acquired by the entrepreneur's own saving activity—which in fact is one of the reasons, and a significant one, for distinguishing the entrepreneur as sharply as I think he should be distinguished from the capitalist. One important source of the means for early enterprise is no doubt to be found in the fact that such means were available in the hands of extra-bourgeois strata and in particular in the hands of temporal and spiritual lords. As everybody knows, this source has been particularly stressed by Sombart and drew so much critical fire that Sombart himself practically surrendered it. But the last word has certainly not been spoken on this affair and if we command co-operation from medieval historians we might well ask them to go into the matter. Another explanation is in the fact that for many types of enterprise the minimum of means to start with was very small: a shack which a man could put up with his own hands, very simple tools, and very few assistants were sometimes all that was required. Means of that order of magnitude many people would possess for a variety of reasons. A third source was tapping the savings of other people and "created credit." The roles of these two last-mentioned sources, though in a general way obvious, also deserve further research. "Credit creation" introduces banks and quasi-banking activities. Here we meet with the difficulty that orthodox banking theory, emphasizing as it does current financing of current trade transactions as the main function of banks, did its best to obliterate all that banks had to do with bringing into existence new industries. French and German experience offers a rich field for the study of this phenomenon, and the common saying that in the United States enterprise developed so well because its banking system was so bad also indicates an important truth: after all, we should not simply shut our eyes or sanctimoniously disapprove when we find that in certain cases even railroad building was financed by the issue of bank notes. Fourthly, it stands to reason that a bank which finances the overhead of a new enterprise must at the very least supervise very closely the behavior of the enterprise founded. That is to say, the necessity of supervising customers which exists to some extent even for the most ordinary routine business acquired in the case envisaged a novel importance. In consequence, two phenomena are observable which are so essential for capitalist life that they are well worth our attention. On the one hand, banks have, though to a very different extent in different countries, established themselves as a social organ of entrepreneurial activity. What this supervision actually consisted in, what the means were by which it was actually carried out, and the success with which it was exerted, has been frequently discussed but quite inadequately, even if we neglect the fact that many social critics have seen nothing in this institution (and it is an institution of later capitalism) but abuse. On the other hand, entrepreneurs and industrialists generally have fought against the restrictions imposed upon their freedom of action by bankers' interference, and important features of modern industrial policy are precisely explainable by the wish of industrialists to free themselves from it. For instance, this has been an important feature of industrial policy in this country during the first World War and in the 1920's. But an entrepreneur can also gain freedom from interference by bankers by turning into a banker himself. John Law and the brothers Pereire are outstanding examples. They illustrate also something else, namely, the fact that the economic and social meaning of this kind of activity has been almost invariably misunderstood.

However, if we could poll business leaders, we should, I am convinced, establish that according to their opinion it is self-financing from earnings which constitutes the soundest method of providing the means for raising an enterprise to its full size. This method, too, is highly unpopular with modern economists and its investigation is a matter of urgent necessity—as is, by the way, the opposite phenomenon, namely, the phenomenon that expenditure on current replacement of equipment is very often financed on credit. The actual results of the method of self-financing, for instance, the question whether or not it involves malallocation of resources, are so much blurred by preconceptions that a reopening of the case promises to add considerably to our knowledge of how modern business works.

III

In the enterprise economy the entrepreneur will inevitably exert some influence on things in general; hence the study of his interests, positions, and so on necessarily constitutes one of the possible approaches to an understanding of economic history or even of history in general. A recent paper by Professor Cochran may be referred to for the general philosophy of this approach as against the approach embodied in what he calls the "presidential synthesis."[4]

It has been emphasized above that when we speak of the entrepreneur we do not mean so much a physical person as we do a function, but even if we look at individuals who at least at some juncture in their lives fill the entrepreneurial function it should be added that these individuals do not form a social class. They hail from all the corners of the social universe. For instance, if we list all the entrepreneurs mentioned in Mantoux's work on the Industrial Revolution we find among them the Duke of Bridgewater and we may, starting from him, go through practically the whole extent of the social ladder until we reach men who rose to entrepreneurship from the ranks of manual labor. This seems to me a very important fact. How important precisely it is can again be only said after extensive research. However, all the men who actually do fulfill entrepreneurial functions have certain interests in common and, very much more important than this, they acquire capitalist positions in case of success. The modern corporation has not entirely done away with inheritance of this capitalist position and so we may say that entrepreneurs do in the end land in the capitalist class, at first as a rule in its most active sector until they wind up in its less active and finally in its decaying sector. I believe that this statement can be supported successfully but I do confess to a wish to see it established.

Now the man whose mind is entirely absorbed by a struggle for entrepreneurial success has as a rule very little energy left for serious activity in any other direction—some philanthropy and some more or less well-advised collector's interests usually fill the bill. From where then stems the influence or the power which most economists and historians attribute to him? I shall state frankly that I consider power to be one of the most misused words in the social sciences, though the competition is indeed great. So firmly entrenched in our popular psychology is the idea that entrepreneurs or else the capitalist class into which they merge are the prime movers of modern politics that it is very difficult to make headway against it and to point out how very little foundation there is to this opinion. Let me take an example that is far enough removed from us to be looked at with something like detachment: Ehrenberg's book on the Fuggers.[5] There, the rise and decline of that industrial, commercial, and financial family is in my opinion described in a perfectly responsible way. Among other things, the report itself clearly shows that in the time of Charles V the two Fuggers who came into contact with the imperial policy and especially its financial needs exerted no influence on this imperial policy other than is implied in their getting various concessions, especially mining concessions, in the Emperor's Latin territories. For the rest, however, they were ruthlessly exploited, so much so in fact that their wealth declined in consequence, and there is no sign whatever that they influenced the Emperor's policy in such matters as his attitude toward the Protestants, toward France, toward the Turks, and so on. Although all this is quite clear from Ehrenberg's own report, he is, nevertheless, so imbued with the idea that in a capitalist age the capitalists rule as to emphasize repeatedly what he considers to be the proud position of power of that family. Now this instance could be multiplied as everyone knows and at the end of a long list of instances, if I could present it, I should mention a conversation I had with an otherwise quite intelligent lawyer who defended the legislation that was to subject the insurance companies to federal control on the ground that "we cannot allow the insurance companies to run the country."

It seems to me that at the outset it is necessary to distinguish two entirely different things. Naturally, as has been pointed out above, the mere emergence of a quantitatively significant number of entrepreneurs presupposes, and its existence, contributes to, a certain type of civilization and a certain state of the public mind. Entrepreneurs will be few and without great importance in situations where this activity is despised and frowned upon, and entrepreneurial success in turn will tend to change such a situation. If I had space to develop this point, I should end up by saying that to some extent entrepreneurial activity impresses the stamp of its mentality upon the social organism. In any cultural history, therefore, the entrepreneurial factor will have to come in as one of the explaining elements, but this is not the same as saying that the wishes and interests of entrepreneurs or even of the capitalist class into which they merge is a political factor that counts by direct influence or else at the polls. It is quite true that in individual cases, for reasons of self-defense primarily, individual entrepreneurs need to acquire and do acquire political positions of their own. But the importance of these positions seems to be limited, and the way to show this is to analyze the means at their disposal in order to exert influence, such as contributions to politicians' war chests, or ownership of newspapers, and so on. I think it can be shown that the influence that can be acquired in these and other ways is much smaller than it is usually supposed to be. In fact, little more is necessary in order to convince one's self of this than to look at the modern situation in practically all countries. Methodological questions of great interest arise in the course of an attempt to investigate these matters. To begin with, we should have to have a much more realistic theory of politics than any that has been developed so far, but this is not enough. In order to see what entrepreneurs or the capitalist class as a whole can and cannot do, it is necessary to establish facts which are extremely difficult to get at and the appraisal of which requires a kind of experience of life which, even in those cases in which it is present in a research worker, is confined to individual environments, inferences from which may easily mislead.

The attitude of the state to entrepreneurial activity is a most fascinating study and raises questions of interpretation such as these: what was the nature of that amphibial condition of society that culminated in the state of Louis XIV? The court and the bureaucracy which ruled that state were no doubt alive to the fact that in order to spend as they did they needed adequate objects of taxation and that the most promising of these objects was a powerful community of traders and manufacturers. Thus a large group of measures find a ready explanation in the wishes to further the wealth and taxable capacity of the bourgeoisie. But what precisely does this mean and how would all parties concerned fare as a result? Colbert has had among historians his fervent admirers. To my immense amusement, I have also found that Sir John Clapham described him as a big, stupid, brutal fellow, who never had an idea in his life. Whatever else such judgments prove or do not prove they certainly establish one thing: that the nature and amount of influence exerted by public administration in the period in question really is no more than a big question mark; and if we leave the time of Louis XIV and transfer ourselves into our own I feel that the question mark is still bigger.

IV

Students interested in the history of economic thought and in the writings upon economic development will draw two important, though variant conclusions from their inquiries as far as entrepreneurship and entrepreneurial history are concerned. First, I believe that they would be justified in the view that theories of past economists relative specifically to entrepreneurship will not form a very firm support for future investigations of facts. New hypotheses and the marshalling of factual data, old and new, must proceed together.

Secondly, I would commend to economic historians—and, for that matter, to economic theorists, if they will interest themselves in the problem—that they examine the already available secondary literature for data upon entrepreneurial characteristics and phenomena. A miscellany of such writings—from general economic histories to biographies of businessmen, and from local histories to studies of technological change—all hold information, which sifted and arranged with definite hypotheses in mind will carry us a goodly distance toward our goal. New facts will doubtless be needed in the end, but already we have a multitude that have as yet not been digested.

In the handling of old and new facts, the historian will gain from keeping in touch with theorists. Neither group should ever be distant from one another—but here the promise from collaboration is particularly great for both parties. As I have said before, the study of economic change is an area of research where "economic historians and economic theorists can make an interesting and socially valuable journey together, if they will."[6]

Endnotes

1. The difficulty of naming our function is of course greatly increased by the fact that such words as "management" or "administration" from which we are trying to distinguish our function have with many authors also caught some of the meanings that we wish to reserve for the term "entrepreneur."

2. The rate of speed at which competitors follow is another very important point for our research program, as are the means at the disposal of the successful entrepreneur for holding his own against would be competitors (patents and other practices).

3. It is extremely interesting to observe that for a long time and occasionally even now economic theorists have been and are inclined to locate the entrepreneurial function in a corporation with the shareholders. However little the individual small shareholder may have to do with the actual management or else with the entrepreneurial function in the corporation, they hold that the ultimate decision still lies with them to be exerted in the shareholders' meeting. All I wish to say about this is first, that the whole idea of risk-taking in this way takes on a further lease of life and, second, that such a theory is about as true as is the political theory that in a democracy the electorate ultimately decides what is to be done.

4. Cochran, Thomas, C., "The presidential synthesis in American history," American Historical Review, vol. 53 (1948), pp. 748–59.

5. Ehrenberg, Richard, "Das Zeitalter der Fugger" (Jena, 1896). 2 v.

6. Cf, my "Creative Response in Economic History", Journal of Economic History, vol. 7(1947), p. 149.

20 THE SETTING OF THE PROBLEM

Jacob Schmookler

TECHNOLOGICAL PROGRESS AND ECONOMIC GROWTH

What laws govern the growth of man's mastery over nature?

When we can answer this question a great gap will be closed in our understanding of the rise of civilization and of the way in which mankind trades old problems for new.

To help answer it, this book examines the causes of variations in invention over time in a given industry and at a moment of time between industries. Inventions are among the most important and specific and least predictable of the intellectual creations man uses to increase his dominion over his environment. Accordingly, understanding the inventive process is a step toward understanding technological progress generally.

We begin our examination in this chapter first by sketching some connections between technological progress and economic development. We next differentiate invention from other forms of technological progress. Then, having established the larger context of our topic, we conclude by stating the leading possible determinants of variations in invention.

The reader who wishes to concentrate on the book's principal substantive findings can omit Chapter II, which discusses the data used.

Technology is the social pool of knowledge of the industrial arts. Any piece of technological knowledge available to someone anywhere is included in this pool by definition. That portion of existing technology which a people commands, "weighted" by its distribution among the labor force, may be called the nation's *technological capacity*. Its technological capacity, which is conceptually analogous to the capacity of its physical plant, is unquestionably a nation's most important economic resource. By the same token, the rate at which its technological capacity grows sets what is probably the most important ceiling on its long-term rate of economic growth.

The rate of growth of a nation's technological capacity depends jointly on the rate at which it produces new technology and the rate at which it disseminates the old. We shall call the rate at which new technology is produced in any period the *rate of technological progress,* and the rate at which technology in existence at the beginning of a period is disseminated, the *rate of replication*. Hence, as defined here, an element of technology affects the rate of technological progress only once and only at one point on the globe, but it may enter the rate of replication at an indefinitely large number of places and over an indefinitely long period. Moreover, since much learning by a new generation of workers merely replaces knowledge passing out with the old, for some purposes it is essential to distinguish the *net* from the *gross* rates of replication.

The economic return to any investment in either technological progress or replication comes only when the resulting knowledge is used. Technological knowledge may be used to produce either more knowledge or ordinary goods and services. A method of producing a given good or service is a *technique.* When an enterprise produces a good or service or uses a method or input that is new to it, it makes a *technical change.*[1] The first enterprise to make a given technical change is an *innovator.* Its action is *innovation.* Another enterprise making the same technical change later is presumably an *imitator* and its action, *imitation.* Since new technological knowledge is usually produced for use, technological progress is associated with innovation as thought to deed. And since replication is likewise usually undertaken with the same objective, replication is similarly linked to imitation. Because technical change is the ultimate purpose of technological change, the former will necessarily enter our account on occasion, even though our direct concern is only with invention, that is, with one aspect of technological change.

Society generally uses far more of its resources to disseminate technology than to advance it. This is plain from the far greater manpower, including that of students, devoted to formal and informal technological education than to discovery and invention. Indeed, the task of imprinting existing technology on each new generation seems to grow in size and complexity with each increase in the stock of knowledge. Since the opportunities for further advance seem also to grow as the stock increases, and since those best qualified to make the advance are also usually among those who can best communicate existing technology to others, the competition between research and invention on the one hand and teaching on the other seems to increase with the progress of society.

The stationary state of classical economics is an economy in which only replication occurs, and any isolated society which elected to enlarge its technological capacity only by replication would tend to approach that state. While the analysis of a strictly replicating economy, that is, an economy without technological progress, is helpful in understanding many economic phenomena, its utility in the study of economic development is limited. The vast economic changes since the Stone Age, or for that matter during recent centuries in the West, were possible only because of technological progress.

Unfortunately, neoclassical as well as classical economics seems better adapted to the analysis of replication than to that of technological change. Technological change is the *terra incognita* of modern economics. Economists and noneconomists have only the most general ideas about what determines it, and if the findings of this book are to be credited, some of those ideas are wrong. We do not even have an agreed-upon set of terms. Indeed, it is by no means uncommon to find in a work by a distinguished economist phrases like "technological change" used to signify sometimes the production of new technological knowledge, sometimes a combination of research, development, invention, innovation, and imitation, sometimes a subset of these.[2]

This state of affairs reflects the characteristic preoccupation of economists with the practical problems of their time. While economic development was an issue in Adam Smith's time and has become one in our own, in the interim the problems of the day concerned the tariff, monopoly, trade unions, business cycles, monetary and fiscal policy, and so on, and it was during this period and to solve these problems that the present formal apparatus of economic theory was developed.

In that theory technological progress is assumed to be exogenous, that is, to be determined by noneconomic forces. For some economists, this assumption is only a methodological convenience; for others, it is a matter of conviction. But few have given the question serious thought. While it drastically simplified the analysis of traditional problems, the assumption also relieved the profession of any sense of obligation to explain technological change. Hence, except for a few economists, largely those of a heterodox stripe preoccupied with problems of economic development, like Marx, Veblen, Schumpeter, and Kuznets, technological change was generally ignored until the last decade or so.

In consequence, when economists reared in the neoclassical tradition shifted their attention to economic development under the stimulus of the post-World War II liberation of the colonies and the East-West confrontation, most of them seemed to think that increased physical capital (that is, physical plant and equipment) per worker was the main cause of increased output per worker in the long run. The reasons for this expectation are plain. Saving and the production function are among the leading features of the received theory. From saving arises the accumulation of capital. If capital accumulates faster than labor grows, as has been the historical tendency, then output per worker will rise provided production functions have the properties usually assumed. Economists, of course, were quite aware that technological change could also raise output per worker. However, since technological change has to be introduced into the traditional analysis *ad hoc,* like war or an earthquake, it was easy and natural to assume that capital accumulation was the prime factor in development.

But it was, unfortunately, also wrong. For, as intimated above and as several independent studies in the last dozen years have shown, the accumulation of *intellectual* capital—reflected in the production of better products and the use of better methods—has been much more important than the accumulation of physical capital in explaining the rise of output per worker in advanced countries when the period studied covers several decades. Intellectual capital, of course, is but another term for technological capacity. Over any given period it increases, as noted previously, by the creation of new technological knowledge and the more widespread dissemination of the old.

On the whole the dissemination of pre-existing technological knowledge, that is, replication, can be analyzed by applying traditional economic theory. This is intuitively apparent from the term "investment in human capital," commonly used to describe that analysis. However, the study of technological progress seems far different, for in this instance we have little understanding of *where* the impulse for it originates or why it is sustained.[3] It is to these questions that this book is addressed.

INVENTION AND TECHNOLOGICAL PROGRESS

Before we discuss these issues further, we should distinguish our focus, invention, from related phenomena. Specifically, we wish to differentiate inventions from other kinds of technological knowledge, and inventive activity from other kinds of technology-producing activities.

In this book we shall understand technology to consist of applied science, engineering knowledge, invention, and subinvention. "Applied science" as used here consists of tested generalizations, used in industry, which concern how things "are." Such generalizations may take the form either of theories or laws, or of systematized empirical observations about nature or the works of man. By "engineering knowledge" I mean tested generalizations, whether theories, laws, or systematized observations, about how a class of economic goods, such as bridges or electric motors, can be made, or how a class of technical industrial processes, such as electrolytic reactions or electric currents, can be controlled by man.[4] Thus, as used here, the bodies of knowledge represented by applied science and engineering are included in technology. Both consist of generalizations, the one oriented toward understanding, the other toward control.

Whereas engineering knowledge deals with *classes* of products and processes, invention and subinvention relate to *individual* products and processes. We can define "invention" simply as a prescription for a producible product or operable process so new as not to have been "obvious to one skilled in the art" at the time the idea was put forward, or we can add to the requirement of novelty the additional one of *prospective utility*. We shall defer the choice between these definitions until later in the chapter when some of the significance of the decision can be explored.

By "subinvention" I mean an "obvious" change in a product or process. Subinventions result both from relatively straightforward applications of engineering knowledge and from acts of skill by workers, supervisors, users, and so on. The term is intended to include what Robert S. Merrill terms "routine innovation"—a modification which a skilled practitioner in the art can be expected to make in a product or process to adapt it to minor changes in materials, function, site, and so on. Thus the average house designed by an architect, though differing in detail from all others, would be a "routine innovation," that is, a species of subinvention. The distinction between invention and subinvention corresponds to that between a new product or process which would receive a patent at the United States Patent Office and one which would not.[5]

Given the foregoing definition of technology, technological progress itself necessarily consists of additions to knowledge in any of these four categories. Thus, not only invention but also additions to applied science, engineering, and subinvention constitute technological progress. Inventions and subinventions, however, constitute the payoff, the only forms in which scientific and engineering progress can directly affect economic activity. In this sense scientific and engineering knowledge are intermediate products, while inventions and subinventions are final products.[6] (Many inventions and subinventions, of course, are made without scientific or engineering knowledge behind them.)

Having indicated briefly the different kinds of knowledge which comprise technology, we shall turn to technology-producing activities. The central concepts relevant to the latter are "research," "development," and "inventive activity." Of these three terms only "research" has a generally accepted meaning, signifying a relatively systematic quest for new knowledge about a *class* of phenomena. Used in this sense, research may yield new knowledge in science or engineering.

By contrast, "development" has two principal meanings. It is *usually* used to signify the creation of a new industrial product or process, beginning with the conception of the idea and ending with its readiness for production. This is a curious usage since one does not ordinarily expect development to occur until *after* the thing to be developed has been created. For this reason, others limit "development" to the improvement of an idea after it has been shown to be basically sound. The latter, *uncommon* meaning of the term thus signifies the effort expended in making a patentable invention suitable for production.[7] While the National Science Foundation has adopted the wider meaning of the term, it is more convenient for our purposes to use the narrower one.

Like "development," "inventive activity" can be given a wide or a narrow meaning. It can designate technology-producing effort of any sort, or its meaning can be confined only to work specifically directed toward the formulation of the essential properties of a novel product or process. The latter, narrower meaning thus excludes both research, which attempts to *discover* properties of classes of objects or processes, and postinvention *development,* which (as defined here) refines and perfects individual inventions. The second definition has both advantages and disadvantages. For our purposes, however, the advantages are overriding and we shall therefore use it. To begin with, there is a functional difference between invention on the one hand and both discovery and refinement on the other. This difference is not only commonly recognized, but indeed is reflected in the fact that they are made not only by different individuals, but usually by different *kinds* of individuals.[8] The kind of talent required for good scientific research or engineering development is not necessarily that best suited for inventing new products or processes. Second, the narrower definition of inventive activity emphasizes the element common to both older style, empirical invention and modern industrial research and development.[9] Given an historically oriented investigation such as ours, this is a considerable advantage. The latter definition enables us to consider a more homogeneous phenomenon than otherwise. This advantage is heightened by the fact that the patent statistics, which provide the core of the data to be used here, relate more to the narrow than to the broad definition of inventive activity.

On the other hand, a practical penalty is paid for this restrictive definition. While the functional distinctions between inventive activity on the one hand and research and development on the other, as these terms were defined above, seem clear, inventive activity is often so intertwined with research and development today that a scientist or engineer might have trouble deciding which function he was performing at a given moment.[10] However, the practical difficulties of distinguishing inventive activity from other phases of modern research and development are, for our purposes, outweighed by the conceptual merits of the distinction and by the practical advantages of a concept which links modern to older style inventing.

In brief, we distinguish for our purposes and define in particular ways three kinds of technology-producing activities: research, inventive activity, and development; and four kinds of technological progress: discoveries in applied science, discoveries in engineering, inventions, and subinventions. The general lines of association between these activities and products are obvious. Research which affects technological progress yields discoveries in applied science or engineering, inventive activity yields inventions, and development, subinventions.[11]

Within this frame of reference we can now begin our investigation of the causes of variations in inventive activity.

THE CAUSES OF INVENTION

The very definition of an invention suggests the leading possible determinants of variations in invention. Every invention is (a) a new combination of (b) pre-existing knowledge which (c) satisfies some want. Each element of the definition calls to mind a set of distinctive phenomena, and each set constitutes a possible determinant of invention. Thus, the first element of the definition, by emphasizing the novelty of the product, suggests that unique characteristics of the inventor, his circumstances, or both may have played an important part in bringing the invention into being; for to create a product or process so novel as not to be obvious to one skilled in the art, the inventor must either possess extraordinary ability, motivation, or resources, be the focus of special pressures, or the observer of a happy, insight-yielding accident. These considerations imply that the events which bring a problem before a man who can solve it, which commit him to solving it once he has identified it, or which evoke "the flash of genius" that provides the key to its solution, may be partly chance in nature.

Since this research deals primarily with inventions in clusters, not with them as individual cases where alone "accidental" or "unique" features are observable, we shall not throw much light on the role of chance. Of course, this does not mean chance is unimportant. Rather it signifies only that we will not focus on it until a later chapter.

Whereas the first element of the definition, by emphasizing uniqueness, suggests the influence of a peculiar concatenation of forces, the other two elements summon up thoughts of "social forces," that is, factors common to groups of individuals. Thus, "pre-existing knowledge" is part of society's intellectual heritage, some elements of which are necessarily used in fashioning any given invention. It therefore relates to an invention's *intellectual past* and to the industry whose products have been built on that past. On the other hand, the presumptive, want-satisfying quality of an invention centers our attention on its intended, *socio-economic, functional future,* and therefore on the consumption activity or industry expected to use the new product. In doing so this characteristic of invention directs our attention to the world of functioning men with their material and psychological wants, transient or permanent, and to the social order which conditions and gives effect to those wants.

The foregoing suggests that, chance factors aside, the joint determinants of invention are (a) the wants which inventions satisfy, and (b) the intellectual ingredients of which they are made. The inventor's problem arises in the world of work and play, rest and action, frustration and satisfaction, health and sickness, and so on. That world, together with his estimate of the difficulty of solving the problem, provides the basis for his judgment that the solution is worth seeking. On the other hand, in order to analyze the problem, to imagine possible solutions to it, to estimate their relative cost and difficulty, and to reduce one or more to practice, the inventor must use the science and technology bequeathed by the past. Thus, in a fundamental sense, both wants and accumulated knowledge are necessary to invention. Neither alone is sufficient. Without wants no problems would exist. Without knowledge they could not be solved.

If this formulation is appropriate, it would appear that, once having gone outside the conventional province of economics to study invention, we confront the possible necessity of examining still another phenomenon outside the conventional province of economics—wants. For just as we have traditionally thought of technological change as playing across the domain of the traditional economic variables to affect wants via changes in supply, the analysis in the preceding paragraph implies the additional possibility that wants and changes in them can likewise play across that domain to affect technology, via demand.

Does man simply invent what he can, so that the inventions he makes in any period are essentially those which became possible in the previous period? Or is it to man's wants with their different and changing intensities, and to economic phenomena associated with their satisfaction, that one must primarily look for the explanation? In short, *are inventions mainly knowledge-induced or demand-induced?* In the parlance of economics, are they primarily the outgrowth of changes in the conditions of their supply, or do they largely reflect changes in the demand for them?

Presumably, what we invent is the joint product of what we want and what we know. That we cannot invent all that we want is certain. That we invent all that we can seems improbable. Roughly speaking, we invent what we can, and, in some sense, want badly enough.

Thus, as a first approximation, imagine that there exists at some point in time a set of inventions that a people could make, and another set of inventions that they would want to make. Then the inventions actually made during the following period presumably consist of the intersection of the two sets—that is, of inventions that are both possible and desirable. From this construction it follows that the changing character of inventions from period to period can be viewed as the net effect of the interaction of the changing set of possible inventions with the changing set of desired ones. Considered in this light, this book is an attempt to explore some interesting aspects of this interaction.

In order that the results of that exploration may be seen in proper perspective, it seems desirable first to refine the intuitive concepts just advanced. Specifically, what attributes would it be analytically useful for the set of desired inventions and the set of possible inventions to have?

The specification of the set of desired inventions seems simple: If there is an existing product, we want it made cheaper and better; if there is an existing want that is unfulfilled, we want a way to satisfy it. We want better and cheaper food, clothing, and shelter; faster, safer, and cheaper transportation, including transportation to the stars; faster, better, and cheaper education; cheaper and better cures for curable diseases and cures for diseases now incurable, and so on. Such a list presumably would be enormous, with the desired effects indicated in great detail—a way of prolonging the life of this particular kind of lathe, a way of increasing the reliability of that kind of transistor, a cheaper way of attaching the soles of shoes to uppers—for the list of desired inventions consists essentially of a list of those unfulfilled wants of man which could conceivably be met by technical means. It is not really a list of inventions. It is a list of problems that would require technical means to solve.

What is the list of possible inventions? To answer this we must first settle an issue left unresolved above. What is an invention? Is it simply a novel product or process, or is it rather a novel *and prospectively useful* one? If we settle for the former, then the list of possible inventions at any time is virtually infinite. Just as there exists a hopelessly large number of ways for me to go from my house to the one next door—via Hong Kong, through the chimney, and so on, so the number of novel ways of doing almost anything must be very large, and getting larger all the time. To regard clearly inferior ways of doing something as inventions merely because they are novel seems absurd, which of course explains why humorists sometimes create them.

Common sense, the patent law, and the courts unite in affirming that "an invention is prima facie an improvement."[12] Except to entertain, no one would intentionally create a novelty inferior in all respects to existing alternatives, although, since invention is a risky business, this often turns out to be the case inadvertently. Accordingly, we shall require that an invention be not only new but also prospectively useful.

The fact that we expect men to produce *useful* inventions implies that every item on the list of possible inventions matches an item on the list of desired inventions. The reason for this is simply that, by definition, something would be on the list of possible inventions only if it promised to serve some useful purpose, and, also by definition, if it served a useful purpose, that purpose would appear on the list of desired inventions.

Now, if possible inventions are also desired ones by definition of their being useful, and if it were strictly true, as suggested above, that those inventions are made which are both desired and possible, then it would follow that all possible inventions are made.

Whether this inference is reasonable depends partly on how one defines "possible." If he had put his mind to it, Edison might have been able to invent a better mattress than anyone else in his time. Was that mattress a possible invention? Plainly, if the list of possible inventions consists of all those which the flesh and blood men of the society in question could make, each invention being considered separately without regard to alternative uses for the manpower needed to make it, then the entire list considered as a totality may be impossible: The men who could make some items on the list may be the same as those needed to make others, and life may be too short for them to make both sets. Inventive men also have other work besides invention to which they may devote their talents. In brief, since creative manpower is scarce, the necessity to allocate it between invention and other uses and between one invention and another means that some of the new and useful ideas which that manpower could create may go unmade. Since this allocative process is a crucial aspect of the phenomenon we wish to examine, it seems appropriate to say that an invention is possible if it is intellectually attainable by the men of the society in question.

The word "possible" also suggests another interesting problem in the present context. Suppose Edison, but nobody else, could have invented a better phonograph than he did had he known more of the physics and mathematics of his time. Was that phonograph possible? It seems analytically convenient to think so. The inventive process is often described in terms of scientific discoveries triggering important inventions, and of the latter triggering minor ones. The inventions thus induced become, in a sense, possible once the knowledge that led to them was created. By regarding inventions as possible as soon as all the knowledge needed to create them exists—all the knowledge, that is, except that produced by the creative leap—we are forced to think about the process by which inventors acquire the knowledge they need to make their inventions, and to consider whether the acquisition of indispensable new knowledge plays the "triggering" role just mentioned.

In sum, it is analytically helpful to say that the possible inventions at a given moment consist of those inventions which somebody in the society could make with the talent he has and the knowledge that anybody has. This set of possible inventions we shall call the *inventive potential*. We may say that an invention enters the inventive potential the moment the last bit of knowledge needed to make it—except for the knowledge produced by the creative leap itself—is created.

Defined in this way, the inventive potential of any period may not be fully realized. Men may not make some of the inventions that they think of because they find more profitable uses for their resources. That is, they do not want the inventions badly enough. Other inventions may not be made because the men who might make them do not acquire the knowledge that would enable them to do so.

Stated in more positive terms, at least six steps are critical in the occurrence of an invention:

1. The entry of the invention into the inventive potential: the production somewhere of the last bit of knowledge needed for the creative leap to be possible.[13]
2. The acquisition by a potential inventor of the last bit of knowledge he would need for him to be able to make the invention. This step is distinct from Step 1 both because he may acquire the necessary bits in an order different from that in which they appear historically, and because he may require more knowledge to make the given invention than would the most gifted inventor referred to in the preceding note.
3. The development of a desire on the part of the inventor (or his backer) for the effect the invention would produce.
4. The decision to try to make the invention.
5. The creation or recognition by the inventor of the root idea of the invention.
6. The reduction of the invention to operable form.

The numbering of the steps should not be taken to indicate a necessary sequence—except of course that Step 6 is always last. Otherwise, the desire for the effect (Step 3) may occur first, followed by a tentative decision to try to accomplish the end sought

(Step 4), the production by the inventor himself of the knowledge he needs (Step 2 and perhaps Step 1, if the latter was not accomplished long before), and finally by Steps 5 and 6. In other instances, Steps 1 and 2 may have occurred well beforehand, and some accident may place the root idea of the invention (Step 5) under the inventor's nose. Only then may he develop a desire for the effect (Step 3) and decide to make it (Step 4).

While all six steps must occur before an invention is made, Steps 1 and 2 are often regarded as somehow jointly or separately crucial, the remaining steps taking place more or less automatically. Technological progress is thus regarded as some kind of self-generating process which expresses either the inexorable working of laws governing the growth of knowledge or the response of creative men to essentially intellectual stimuli. In Chapters III–V, we shall explore these views in greater detail and consider some evidence bearing on them. In the process indirect light will be shed on other steps.

Since the inventions produced in one period are indeed based on knowledge produced earlier, there is a genetic pattern evident in the growth of ideas, inventions included. However, in other genetic phenomena an enormous selection process is observable, and the number of offspring that are born and survive is only a small fraction of the total number of potential progeny. In the case of invention the selecting factor is man himself. The phenomenon of selection suggests that the common emphasis on the inventive potential and intellectual stimuli may be misplaced, and indicates instead that it may be desirable to view invention not only as an aspect of the growth of knowledge in general but also, and perhaps even more, as an example of economic choice made in the context of economic change. In effect, this implies shifting our attention from Steps 1 and 2 to Steps 3–6, particularly 3 and 4. This possibility will be examined in the later chapters of the book.

Before dealing with such substantive problems, however, we must first examine the properties of the peculiar data we are forced to rely primarily on, patent statistics.

Endnotes

1. This definition departs from another often used. The latter limits "technical change" to changes in technique resulting from the acquisition of knowledge new to the enterprise and excludes thereby changes in technique occasioned by price changes. While these distinctions are well worth making, the terminology chosen seems inappropriate. It seems only natural to define any change in technique as a technical change. The alternative definition can result in the paradox that a technological change (change in knowledge) which becomes economical only after a change in relative prices will never result in a "technical change" (change in practice) no matter how widespread the use of the knowledge in question becomes.

2. See, for example, *Economic Report of the President* (Washington, D.C., 1964), Ch. IV.

3. Interestingly enough, the other social sciences also seem insecure in their apprehension of the creation of knowledge—witness the low state of development of the psychology of creativity, and of the sociology and history of science and technology.

4. The term "generalization" here is intended to include the theory of engineering design, which usually consists of a highly conceptualized model of real objects, the model itself being used to guide an engineer in synthesizing a system from such objects.

5. Patentable invention "is a concept or thing evolved from the mind, and is not a revelation of something which existed and was unknown, but the creation of something which did not exist before" *(Pyrere Mfg. Co. v. Boyce,* C.C.A.N.J., 292 F. 480). "'Invention' consists of the conception of the idea and of the means for putting it in practice and producing the desired result" *(Burson v. Vogel,* 29 App. D.C. 388, 395). "There can be no patent upon an abstract philosophical principle" *(Boyd v. Cherry,* 50 F. 279, 282). Patentable invention is, therefore, differentiated from scientific principles (and the recognition of their technological significance) in two ways: (1) patentable invention is the creation by the human mind of something which did not exist before, and not the discovery of something which existed but was unknown; (2) patentable invention must constitute a specific physical means for the attainment of a result, or be itself a specific physical product.

A patentable invention must have as its subject matter an "art, machine, manufacture, or composition of matter" (U.S. Code, Title 35, sec. 31). In the terminology of the patent law, the words "art, machine, manufacture, or composition of matter" mean either a physical result which is patentable or a patentable physical means for attaining some result, physical or otherwise *(Waldman v. Swanfeldt,* C.C.A. Cal., 66 F (2nd) 294, 295; *Cochrane v. Deener,* 94 U.S. 780, 788; *Pittsburgh Reduction Co. v. Cowles Electric Smelting and Aluminum Co.,* 55 F. 301, 316; *Boulton v. Bull,* 2 H.B1., 463, 471; 48 *Corpus Juris* 24). But a nonphysical or rather a purely human means for attaining a result, physical or otherwise, is not patentable. "Conception of mind is not 'invention' until represented in some physical form" (*Smith v. Nevin,* Cust. and Pat. App. 73 F. (2nd) 940, 944). "A system of transacting business disconnected from the means for carrying out the system is not, within the most liberal interpretation of the term, an art" *(Hotel Security Checking Co. v. Lorraine Co.,* 160 F. 467, 469). "The non-patentability of a system—i.e., a connected view of the principles of some department of knowledge or action—has been sufficiently shown" (*Guthrie v. Curlett et al.,* 10 F. (2nd) 725, 726).

The distinction between patentable invention and subinvention is solely in the degree of novelty involved. "'Invention' is the antithesis of evolution and connotes necessarily the unexpected" (*Less Car Load Lots v. Pennsylvania R. Co.,* D.C.N.Y., 10 F. Supp. 642, 648).

6. Designating inventions and subinventions as final products, and engineering and scientific knowledge as intermediate products, obviously implies no hierarchy of merit. Rather it reflects an economist's effort to structure the relationship between these kinds of knowledge from the standpoint of their bearing on his primary interest, economic change.

7. For an example of the first use of the term, see James B. Quinn, *Yardsticks for Industrial Research* (New York: Ronald Press Co., 1959), p. 5; Dean E. Woolridge, "The Effective Utilization by Industry of the Results of Research," in *Proceedings of the Seventh Annual Conference on the Administration of Research* (Berkeley, 1953), p. 29; and National Science Foundation, *Science and Engineering in American Industry: Final Report on a 1956 Survey,* NSF 59-50 (Washington, 1959), p. 95. The more restricted use of the term is exemplified by F. Russell Bichowsky, *Industrial Research* (Brooklyn: Chemical Publishing Co., Inc., 1942), p. 26; and Simon Kuzne's, "Inventive Activity: Problems of Definition and Measurement," in R. R. Nelson, ed., *The Rate and Direction of Inventive Activity: Economic and Social Factors* (Princeton: Princeton University Press, 1962).

8. Cf. Donald W. MacKinnon, "Intellect and Motive in Scientific Inventors: Implications for Supply," *ibid.*

9. John Jewkes argues, and I am inclined to agree from my limited knowledge, that nineteenth-century invention rested more and twentieth-century invention rests less on science than is commonly supposed (see John Jewkes, David Sawers, and Richard Stillerman, *Sources of Invention,* New York: St. Martins Press, 1958, Ch. III). However, it is still probably true not only that the dependence of invention on science is now greater than before, but, what is more to our purpose, that inventive activity now must, more often than formerly, be preceded by scientific research either by the inventor himself or by others in the same organization. This is an inevitable consequence of the shifts from mechanical to electrical, electronic, chemical, and nuclear invention, and from small- to large-scale products and processes, shifts which make preliminary scientific explorations more economical.

10. Thus a scientist, while studying a given phenomenon, may begin to think about a particular possible industrial application. At this point we might say inventive activity has begun. He may then attempt to create this potential application on a laboratory scale. If he makes the attempt, and finds that his application does not work as expected, he may return to do more research (thereby temporarily terminating his inventive activity) in order to find out why his invention is not working properly. Later, armed hopefully with a better understanding, he may return to his model (beginning his inventive activity again) to try again. While these shifts in role may be difficult to keep track of as a practical matter, the roles, as suggested above, are *different:* understanding a phenomenon is one thing; creating an industrial process or product based on that understanding is another.

11. A brief comment on the peculiar relation between engineering progress and invention seems in order here. On the one hand, since engineering knowledge deals with classes of products and processes, it follows that the more fully developed that knowledge is, the more obvious will be any improvements made in the products or processes to which that knowledge pertains. Engineering research and inventive activity are thus to some extent substitutes. Engineering knowledge indeed is so advanced in some fields that it can be programmed for computers which can thereafter be used to design products or processes in those fields to specification. Some of these products or processes would be patentable were they not "obvious" to the computer. On the other hand, since systematized knowledge about a class of products or processes is hard to develop until the class has members, it seems unlikely that engineering progress will ever render inventive activity obsolete. Moreover, given a highly developed body of engineering knowledge in one or more related fields, it seems reasonable to expect that creative men will conjecture about and work toward the creation of products or processes beyond those immediately derivable from existing knowledge. While some needed elements for such inventions can be directly developed from current engineering knowledge, other elements or the general configuration of elements either will be impossible to produce without the exercise of the inventive faculty, or can be produced more cheaply via inventive activity than through further research. Moreover, it often happens that the products resulting from excessive substituting of engineering for inventive effort are more complex, more expensive, and less efficient than similar ones developed through inventive activity. I understand that this difference has sometimes been critical in the case of different missile guidance systems.

Thus, the relation between inventive activity and research (scientific as well as engineering) is complementary as well as substitutive. On the one hand, invention helps create the classes of products or processes with which engineering research is concerned. On the other hand, the results of that research help provide the basis for later inventive effort.

The interdependence of inventive activity and engineering research suggests three conjectures which, while they will not be pursued in this work, are nonetheless relevant to some aspects of it. (1) The mix between engineering research and inventive activity is likely to be affected by the mix between public and private funds expended in advancing technology. The reason for this is simply the presumption that research, because it focuses on classes of phenomena, is likely to yield more external benefits, that is, benefits to enterprises not engaged in the research. This reasoning is reinforced by the fact that inventions are patentable while discoveries are not, so that the inventor or his backer has a better chance of capturing part of the social gain from his efforts than does the researcher. (2) For obvious reasons there probably exists some tendency, by now perhaps quite small, to keep secret the results of engineering research conducted by private enterprise. (3) To the degree that business-conducted engineering research results are published, publication is likely to be delayed at least until applications on important inventions based thereon have been filed. Otherwise, the inventions covered by the applications might be regarded as "obvious" by the Patent Office and the courts, and therefore construed as unpatentable for want of novelty.

12. *William Schwarzwaelder and Co. v. City of Detroit* (77 F. 886, 891).

13. Note that since men vary in creative ability, the pre-existing knowledge that would enable the most gifted inventor to make the invention may not suffice for others to make it. For conceptual purposes it seems best to consider Step 1 completed when the last bit of knowledge needed by the most gifted inventor has been produced. This definition compels us to recognize that an invention can vanish from the inventive potential if the most gifted inventor dies and is succeeded by a lesser talent.

21

INVENTION AND ECONOMIC GROWTH: SUMMARY AND CONCLUSIONS

Jacob Schmookler

SETTING OF THE PROBLEM

Long-term economic growth is primarily the result of the growth of technological knowledge—the increase in knowledge about useful goods and how to make them. Such knowledge increases in two different ways: (1) what was known before becomes more widely known, and (2) knowledge never known before by anyone is produced. For our purposes, new technological knowledge can be subdivided into two broad categories: (a) knowledge, commonly denoted by the terms "engineering" and "applied science," about whole classes of technical phenomena, and (b) knowledge about particular products or processes.

The distinction between an industry's production technology and its product technology is critical. The former relates to the knowledge used to produce its products—the machines, materials, and processes it uses to fabricate the goods it sells to others. The product technology relates to the knowledge used in creating or improving the products themselves. Thus, the hydraulic press is part of the automobile industry's production technology, while power steering is part of its product technology. Since each industry buys inputs (products) from other industries, the production technology of the former consists to a large extent of the product technologies of the latter.

New technological knowledge about particular products or processes can be classified according to degree of novelty. Thus, "invention" is a prescription for a product or process so new as not to have been "obvious" to one skilled in the art at the time; operationally the term denotes an idea which would be patentable at the United States Patent Office; while "subinvention" is an improvement obvious to those skilled in the art.

This book has tried to explain variations in invention—in the same industry over time, and between industries at a moment of time. It has focused therefore on the determinants of the rate of production of one class of new knowledge. The relations of invention to other technological knowledge and of inventive activity to research and development were briefly explored.

The very definition of an invention as a novel combination of pre-existing knowledge to satisfy some want better suggests the possible causes for its occurrence. Since it is novel, accident may play a role. Since it is based on prior knowledge, the received stock of knowledge must also play a role. And since it is calculated to better serve human wants, these too must also affect invention. Because of the nature of the data used and because our concern was primarily with relative numbers of inventions classified by industry of use, chance received little attention in our enterprise. Rather, our chief inquiry concerned the comparative influence of wants and past knowledge on the inventive process.

THE DATA USED

The study was based primarily on two kinds of data—chronologies of important inventions made throughout the world since 1800 in petroleum refining, paper making, railroading, and agriculture; and annual statistics of United States patents granted (usually counted as of the date of application) in many industries. Of course, not all inventions are patented, and some of those patented; though relevant, were inadvertently omitted from our series. Moreover, inventions differ greatly in quality. The problems arising from these deficiencies were examined in detail. It was concluded that the deficiencies of these data are probably less than is commonly assumed, and that in any case, if used carefully they can illuminate phenomena of interest here as no other presently available body of data can.

Thus, the nonpatenting of inventions seemed serious only after 1940. Moreover, about half of all inventions patented have been used commercially in recent decades, and indirect evidence suggests that the proportion so used in the past, though smaller, was also appreciable. Hence a random collection of patents is likely to represent economically significant knowledge. The presumptive utility of the data is suggested by the high correlation between corporate spending on Research and Development in 1953 and patent applications filed by the firms in question. It is also suggested by the correspondence of patent statistics with other knowledge concerning the course of independent invention and of corporate invention until World War II, the shift of invention from empirical toward scientific fields, the shift from invention by individuals in a wide variety of occupations toward invention by scientists and engineers, and the shift from part- to full-time invention.

These data obviously are imperfectly correlated with each of the dimensions of invention in which we might be interested, and lacking independent measures of any of these dimensions, it is impossible even to say how closely patent statistics are associated with any of them. Unfortunately, in most instances the choice is not between patent statistics and better data, but between patent statistics and no data. The general conformity of patent statistics to expectations derived from other knowledge suggests that it is sensible to regard the data as an "index of the number of private inventions made for the private economy in different fields and periods." The term "index" implies in this context that only "large" differences are likely to be significant. The data are construed to relate to private rather than government-financed invention, since the latter only infrequently results in patents. However, while Chapter II shows that the data usually perform as one would expect, the final judgment on the utility of these data must rest on the results achieved in using them.

Other data on invention relied on here derive from the study of over nine hundred important inventions. The inventions that we studied in detail either were economically important in themselves or provided the intellectual basis for later inventions which were economically important. While more commonly accepted than are patent statistics, such data present serious problems of their own. Since the importance of an invention depends on how it fits its environment and not entirely on its own attributes, statistics of important inventions may relate more to changing conditions in the environment than to the progress of invention proper. Equally important, such data are generally derived from technical and trade journals or from economic and industrial histories. Each of these sources is subject to such demonstrable and often substantial bias that it is doubtful that our chronologies, exhibited in appendices' represent the class of important inventions which we sought to study as well as patent statistics represent the class of all inventions. Despite the difficulties, these data also provided results of considerable interest.

THE ROLE OF INTELLECTUAL STIMULI

The knowledge produced in the past can influence the inventions made today in three ways. (1) It can limit what inventions are made. This it must do, since if an invention is "beyond the present state of the art," it is by definition impossible. (2) The *use* of knowledge formerly unused or formerly used less extensively necessarily changes economic, social, and political conditions, and these altered conditions may induce men to make inventions which somehow enable them to benefit from, or ameliorate untoward consequences of the altered conditions. (Some aspects of this phenomenon are discussed in Chapter IV and Sections 4 and 12 below.) And (3) each addition to knowledge may constitute an intellectual stimulus that prompts someone to make another addition to knowledge. Thus, it is sometimes thought, inventions are commonly made because men are stimulated to think of them by some other invention or scientific discovery.

This possibility has interest not only because of the frequent assertion that this indeed is the normal state of affairs, but also because this explanation is perhaps most congruent with the even more common (if unsupported) assertion that technology tends to grow at an exponential rate.

Despite the popularity of the idea that scientific discoveries and major inventions typically provide the stimulus for inventions, the historical record of important inventions in petroleum refining, paper making, railroading, and farming revealed not a single, unambiguous instance in which either discoveries or inventions played the role hypothesized. Instead, in hundreds of cases the stimulus was the recognition of a costly problem to be solved or a potentially profitable opportunity to be seized; in short, a technical problem or opportunity evaluated in economic terms. In a few cases, sheer accident was credited.

In part this result may reflect the fact that for most of the inventions the record was silent on the nature of the stimulus. In part it may result from a tendency of inventors to minimize their intellectual dependence on the work of others. However, many of the important inventions scrutinized used no scientific knowledge at all, and many of those that did used science that was old at the time. Hence, the conception of invention as an immediate and direct outgrowth of scientific discovery seems incorrect, at least with respect to the four industries studied.

Even in more science-based fields that view of the inventive process seems in error. Aggregate research and development expenditures in individual firms do not seem substantially influenced by individual scientific discoveries. Even in the comparatively few instances in which a scientific discovery leads directly to a radical invention, its application creates technical and economic problems and opportunities which, as with most of the important inventions covered by our survey, provide the stimulus for further invention in the field. Thus, while discoveries in pure science—those unmotivated by technological objectives—sometimes provide the stimulus for inventions in science-based industries, most of the inventions in such industries probably derive from the same sorts of stimuli which led to invention in the fields we studied in detail. Indeed, two of these, petroleum refining and paper making, are themselves substantially science-based.

The negligible effect of individual scientific discoveries on individual inventions is doubtless due to the orientation of the typical inventor, even those well trained in science and engineering, to the affairs of daily life in the home and industry rather than to the life of the intellect. The result, however, does not mean that science is unimportant to invention, particularly in recent times. Rather it suggests that, in the analysis of the effect of science on invention, the conceptual framework of the Gestalt school of psychology is perhaps more appropriate than is that of the mechanistic, stimulus-response school. The growth of the *body* of science conditions the course of invention more than does each separate increment. It does this by making inventors see things differently and by enabling them to imagine different solutions than would otherwise be the case. The effect of the growth of science is thus normally felt more from generation to generation than from one issue of a scientific journal to the next.

Given the practical orientation of inventors, the appearance of an important invention seems more likely to stimulate other inventors than does the publication of a scientific discovery. Yet, while instances of this can be suggested from other fields, we were unable to find examples among important inventions in the four fields we surveyed. While the completeness of this failure probably reflects the incompleteness and biases in the record, the overwhelming frequency with which the documents cite as the initiating stimulus the recognition and economic valuation of a technical problem or opportunity suggests that only a small minority of inventions are made in response to other varieties of stimuli, including the announcement of striking inventions. What makes this inference strong, however, is the synchronization of inventive activity with economic phenomena associated with it, as discussed in Section 6 below.

THE USE OF IMPORTANT INVENTIONS AS A CAUSE OF FURTHER INVENTION

Although any phase of life can stimulate invention, one of the most commonly cited sources is technical change—the continually changing character of the machines and products which man uses. Generally, it is the few major inventions rather than the many minor ones that are thought to have that effect. As a very incomplete test of this hypothesis, in Chapter IV we compared the trend and long-swing behavior of the number of important inventions with the total number of patented inventions in each of the four fields for which data on important inventions had been prepared. The test is valid only on the assumptions that the average important invention of one period had roughly the same diffusion pattern with respect to use as the average important invention in any other period, that the effect of this diffusion pattern in stimulating invention was not so complex as to evade detection by crude statistical methods, and that the effect of widening use of an important invention in an industry would be observable in inventive activity in the same industry. The implausibility of these assumptions may explain the negative results.

In petroleum refining, important inventions and total patents exhibited similar trends—two growth cycles in each, one associated with the kerosene phase of the industry, the other with its gasoline phase. In the other three industries, the all-time peaks in important inventions occurred from two to ten decades before the corresponding peaks in patents in the respective industries. Since good reasons exist for believing that the important invention data in the petroleum field are more reliable than those in the other three, the implications of the variability in the trend relationships between the two classes of invention in the four fields are not clear.

The results of the long-swing comparisons were less ambiguous: at least as good a case could be made from the evidence for the proposition that long swings in all inventions in a field *induce* long swings in important inventions in the same field, as for the opposite proposition. And this was despite the fact that the timing of long swings in the patent series was chosen in a fashion biased in favor of the hypothesis being considered.

The generally negative if somewhat ambiguous results of this crude approach to an exceedingly complex phenomenon suggest that, if indeed the use of old inventions somehow is the main factor leading to the making of new ones, then perhaps (a) the new ones are made in response partly to inventions used in *other* industries, a factor that we were unable to take into account; (b) the impact of the use of many minor inventions on the making of the few major ones approximates that of the use of the few major inventions on the making of the many minor ones; and/or (c) since each invention is unique, its diffusion path and consequences are likewise unique, or at least too variable for the simple approach followed to reveal the relationship sought between important inventions and all inventions in a field.

PRODUCTIVITY ADVANCE: A CASE OF SUPPLY AND DEMAND?

While individual additions to knowledge of the recent past in themselves seem minor influences as stimuli which lead men to invent, the entire body of received knowledge necessarily limits what inventions are possible at any given time. Moreover, nature's laws insure that some accomplishments are forever impossible. Some scholars have called upon these two facts to explain two others: (1) the tendency for the output of any given product to grow at a declining percentage rate in any given economy; and (2) the tendency for the number of inventions made in any given field first to rise and then to decline. The authors in question evidently believe that the technology of any given field is perfectible and that it rather quickly approaches perfection; hence, ultimately fewer important inventions can be made in it, and inventors leave the field because of diminishing returns to their efforts; in consequence, the rate of technological progress (progress in knowledge), and therefore the rate of technical progress (progress in actual practice), tends to decline over time; the result, presumably transmitted through a declining rate of fall in product price, is that output tends to grow at a declining rate. In short, the inventive potential of the industry's production technology tends to become exhausted.

The question is whether this explanation is consistent with the facts. Perhaps the *cost* of a given percentage increase in productivity does rise as an industry grows, as assumed. On the other hand, it is also logically possible that the *value* of such an increase declines as the industry grows.

Indeed it is precisely the latter which the behavior of statistics of patents suggests. While the concept of the horseshoe is ancient and simple, the annual number of inventions relating to horseshoes in the United States increased throughout the nineteenth century and declined only when the use of the horse declined. Inventions relating to the horseshoe calk, a device attached to the shoe to prevent slipping, continued advancing until World War I, presumably because paving of streets and roads made the slippage problem worse.

Perhaps more persuasive on the issue is the evidence that the patterns of invention in two or more different technologies used by a single industry, such as railroad track and nontrack inventions, exhibit very marked similarities, both in the long run and the short. There is no special reason to suppose that different technologies serving the same industry would approach perfection at the same time. Hence, there is no reason why the long-run decline of invention in them should occur at the same time, if the cost of productivity advance in a field controls inventive activity in it. Yet the long-run declines are simultaneous in the case of track and nontrack railroad inventions. This fact, as in the case of horseshoes, suggests that the changing value, not the changing cost, of invention dominates its temporal path. The same inference is suggested by the short-run synchronization of invention in different branches of shoe manufacturing technology, and by the fact that differences in the onset of the secular decline in the different branches of shoemaking technology are explicable on economic grounds. Similar results were observed in different branches of farm and building technology respectively.

Finally, marked long- and short-run similarities were observed in the number of inventions in railroading, building, and "all other" fields in the United States, with only such significant differences in trend behavior as variations in the economic fortunes of these fields would account for. Thus, both the similarities and the differences in invention in these substantial economic sectors suggest that the principal determinant of the volume of invention in a field is not its cost but its value. Moreover, the observed synchronization of invention in such broad but distinct fields is inconsistent with the view that invention is primarily a response to intellectual stimuli, since the influence of the latter should be more localized as to field.

A major implication of these results is that the S-shaped long-run growth curve for individual industries, in which output tends to grow at a declining percentage rate, usually reflects demand, not supply, conditions. The concomitant retardation in each industry's rate of technical progress is to be explained by the retardation in the rate of growth, not vice versa, although there is, of course, some feedback. Thus, a given percentage cut in costs probably does not become progressively more difficult or costly to achieve over time. Rather, the return from achieving it declines. If this is correct, it suggests that demand functions may ordinarily have the property that both income- and price-elasticity decline, because of a saturation phenomenon. This is an appreciably more restrictive property than the law of diminishing marginal utility or diminishing marginal rate of substitution. To be sure, the historically observable retardation in the rate of growth of output of a given good may also reflect the rise of substitute products. However, since old and new goods are often complementary, the advent of new goods seems insufficient to explain the general phenomenon.

Moreover, demand factors may also prove the most common cause of the invention of a radically new product, for example, a product of the sort for which separate output statistics are prepared by public agencies or trade associations.

THE AMOUNT OF INVENTION AND THE EXTENT OF THE MARKET

The foregoing serves to introduce the most striking and most significant result of the entire study. This result concerns the relation of capital goods output to the number of capital goods inventions. The relation is evident in time series involving a single industry, and in cross sections relating to several industries. When time series of investment (or capital goods output) and the number of capital goods inventions are compared for a single industry, both the long-term trend and the long swings exhibit great similarities, with the notable difference that lower turning points in major cycles or long swings generally occur in capital goods sales before they do in capital goods patents. This result was observed in comparisons of railroad gross investment (and railroad stock prices) and railroad patents, with data running far back into the nineteenth century, and in annual data going back to about 1860 or 1870 in individual varieties of railroad equipment. It was likewise observed with respect to trends in investment and capital goods invention in petroleum refining. While difficulties in securing suitable data precluded trend comparisons in building, the long swings in building activity and building patents exhibited the same relation as did those in railroad investment and railroad invention.

Moreover, Chapter VI, which described the foregoing results, also showed that the railroads' share of gross national capital formation and their share in total patents had similar trends and long swings. A similar relation was observed with respect to long swings in the share of the building industry in total investment and total patents.

The cross-section comparisons of Chapter VII confirmed the impressions derived from comparisons of the share of railroading and building in total investment and total patents. When the logarithm of investment in each of over twenty industries in 1939 and then in 1947 was correlated with the logarithm of capital goods patents in the succeeding three years, very high correlations were obtained. Since the regression coefficients did not differ significantly from unity, interindustry differences in the number of capital goods inventions tend to be proportional to corresponding differences in capital goods sales in the immediately preceding period. The degree of association between the number of patents (in logarithm form) and investment (also in logarithm form) increases as the period in which the patent applications are filed is shifted from the years immediately before to those immediately following the year when the investments occur. For example, the successful capital goods patent applications filed in 1940–1942 are more closely correlated with 1939 investment than are those filed in 1936–1938.

These close correlations, moreover, were not the by-product of mere differences in industry size, since the introduction of the number of workers in each industry as an additional variable failed either to improve the correlation or to alter significantly the value of the regression coefficient for investment.

Lacking investment data for a significant number of industries for earlier years, we used value added as a proxy. This enabled us to carry the analysis back to 1899, with a succession of sixteen cross-section analyses, each involving fourteen or more industries. In these too the regression coefficient of the logarithm of value added was always close to unity, again suggesting that the number of capital goods inventions in different industries tends to be distributed among them in proportion to capital goods sales.

EXPLANATION OF THE RELATION

The most reasonable explanation for the relation, an explanation consistent with the kinds of stimuli that led men to make important inventions, is probably the simplest. It is that (1) invention is largely an economic activity which, like other economic activities, is pursued for gain; (2) expected gain varies with expected sales of goods embodying the invention; and (3) expected sales of improved capital goods are largely determined by present capital goods sales. This at least seems the first approximation to the truth. The rather considerable implications of this explanation will be discussed shortly. Before coming to them, however, it seems desirable first to indicate why alternative explanations seem to fall far short of the facts.

One possible alternative explanation is that the phenomenon somehow reflects patenting, not inventing. While patenting decisions relating to inventions already made undoubtedly contribute to the result observed, their influence must be minor. It is hard to believe that an industry with ten times as many patents as another did not also have far more inventions, or that an industry with ten times as many patents in one period as in another period did not have far more inventions in the first period than in the second. Moreover, since the incentives to invent are much the same as those to patent, whatever forces affect patenting would tend to affect inventing in the same direction.

The possibility that the results reflect the effect of capital goods invention on capital goods sales is grossly implausible. In the time series comparisons, trend turning points tend to occur in sales before they do in patents, and long-swing troughs in sales generally precede those in patents. Moreover, trends and long swings in investment in the industries examined are adequately explained on other grounds. In the cross-section comparisons, this explanation is contradicted by the simple fact noted above that the industrial distribution of investment in a given year is more highly correlated with the industrial distribution of capital goods invention of later years than with that of earlier years. Indeed, the interindustry differences in investment levels of the industries in our cross sections were far too great to be accounted for by any imaginable differences in invention among them in the years immediately preceding the investments.

Thus, while other phenomena may help cause the relation observed, its chief cause seems to lie in the simple fact that invention—and in all probability technological change generally—is usually not apart from the normal processes of production and consumption but a part of them. It expresses something not adventitious to a nation's economic life but an inherent part of it. Reflection suggests that man's efforts to satisfy his wants better should be, as the evidence indicates that they are, intimately related to the ways in which he satisfies his wants now. Since invention is usually costly—in time if not in money—its volume is bound to be somewhat sensitive to the returns expected from it. In this respect, only the apparently great sensitivity of invention to expected returns suggested by the study is occasion for surprise. In all likelihood, the continuation and completion of inventive work are more sensitive to profit expectations than is its initiation, but this aspect of the problem was not investigated.

TECHNOLOGICAL CHANGE AS AN ECONOMIC VARIABLE

The fact that inventions are usually made because men want to solve economic problems or capitalize on economic opportunities is of overwhelming importance for economic theory. Hitherto, many economists have regarded invention—and technological change generally—as an *exogenous,* and, some even thought, an *autonomous,* variable. It was exogenous in the sense that it was not controlled by economic variables. According to some, it was exogenous in a particular sense: it was autonomous, its own past entirely determining its future.

These views, insofar as they were of a substantive nature rather than merely a methodological convenience, are no longer tenable. We shall, it is true, often and for a long time continue to treat technological change as an exogenous variable simply as a methodological necessity,[1] partly because we still have so much to learn about it and sometimes simply because it is not germane to the problem at hand. But the belief that invention, or the production of technology generally, is in most instances essentially a noneconomic activity is false. Invention was once, when strictly a part-time, *ad hoc* undertaking, simply a *nonroutine* economic activity, though an economic activity nonetheless. Increasingly, it has become a full-time, continuing activity of business enterprise, with a routine of its own. That routine is, of course, quite different from the routine of the circular flow traditionally contemplated by economists for assistance in the study of the problems which concerned them. But the production of inventions and much other technological knowledge, whether routinized or not, when considered from the standpoint of both the objectives and the motives which impel men to produce them, is in most instances as much an economic activity as is the production of bread.

The propriety of this view was recognized long ago. John Stuart Mill, for example, wrote, "The labour of Watt in contriving the steam-engine was as essential a part of production as that of the mechanics who build or the engineers who work the instrument; and was undergone, no less than theirs, in the prospect of a remuneration from the produce."[2]

The economic character of such activity is evident not only from the fact that inventors choose economic objectives to achieve, or from the related fact that the intensity of their pursuit of those objectives varies with the magnitude of the gains they expect to make. It is equally apparent in the behavior of those inventors who, unlike those making the important inventions we studied in Chapter III, take their initial cues from laboratory findings or theoretical results and then proceed to choose from among alternative applications those which promise the greatest returns.

While our ignorance may dictate the continued treatment of technological change as an exogenous variable *in our economic models,* it is plain that *in the economic system* it is primarily an endogenous variable. Even the state of knowledge at a point in time in "intellectually coherent fields" of technology, and therefore the inventive potentials of those fields, are economic variables, for the rate at which each such field is cultivated is primarily determined by the promise it holds of yielding useful knowledge. The selection of the means for achieving an economic end is itself an economic process. Hence, the present state of an intellectually coherent field is largely the end product of a history of economizing decisions made in the process of achieving economic ends.

If this general line of reasoning is accepted, it follows that economists should study invention—and other forms of technology production—not only because they greatly affect economic development, but also simply because they are forms of economic activity.

INVENTIONS CLASSIFIED BY USE VERSUS INVENTIONS CLASSIFIED BY INTELLECTUALLY COHERENT FIELD

The continued increase in the annual number of horseshoe inventions until the horseshoe declined in economic significance suggests that hardly any field is likely to develop so much that no further room for improvement exists. On the other hand, this hardly warrants the inference that inventions are equally costly to make in all fields. Some inventions are forever impossible, and others are impossible until adequate prior knowledge has developed. What is more, one can reasonably define fields in such a way that marked differences in the difficulty or cost of inventing in them would exist, even though invention in any of them is possible.

The high correlations between investment (or value added) and invention in different industries at the same time, therefore, pose a serious puzzle, for they suggest that interindustry differences in the cost of invention were small. The answer suggested to this puzzle is that the inference is sound, at least for modern times, if inventions are classified according to use, for example, capital goods for industry X, but not if they are classified according to intellectually coherent field, that is, according to conventional academic disciplines. The point is that, while a marketable improvement in envelope-making equipment is probably about as easy to make as one in glass making, it may be easier today to make an improvement in either field via electronic means than through some mechanical change. This interpretation of the results is consistent with the dramatic rise of great, science-based industries during the last century.

Partly because so much of modern science and engineering knowledge is applicable to many industries, and partly because progress in one branch of science or engineering has been more or less matched by progress in some other branches, the results indeed suggest that mankind today possesses, and for some time has possessed, a *multi-purpose knowledge base*. We are, and evidently for some time have been, able to extend the technological frontier perceptibly at virtually all points. This does not mean that, measured in terms of advance in physical productivity, the possible extensions have been necessarily equal at all points along the frontier, or that one branch of science or engineering could serve as well as any other at any given point in making an advance.

What it does suggest is that, at least for the period and fields studied here, even if there exists an upper limit to the number of possible improvements in a production technology, that limit has been too remote from the frontier to affect inventive effort. This is the other major assumption required to complete the explanation offered of the relation between investment and capital goods invention. Without this assumption it is difficult to see why the number of capital goods inventions in an industry is so sensitive to investment in that industry, regardless of which industry it is, and regardless of the industry's age.

The distinction between a production technology and a product technology becomes important here. As noted above, an industry's production technology is improved to a large extent by changing its inputs, that is, the products it buys from other industries. If differences exist in the richness of the different inventive potentials of the product technologies of different supplying industries, the pressure to improve an industry's production technology tends to be met by the creation of relatively more new products in supplying industries with richer product inventive potentials. For example, if new electrical machines are easier to invent than are nonelectrical machines, then the aggregate demand for new machinery tends to induce relatively more electrical than nonelectrical machinery inventions. In brief, inventors tend to select the most efficient means for achieving their ends, and at any given moment, some means are more efficient than others. This approach would appear to have substantial implications for interindustry analysis.

The point suggests the following view of the rise of the chemical and electrical industries during the past century or so. These industries sell most of their output to other industries, and while it is not obvious that the inventive potentials of their production technologies were far richer than those of other industries, it seems plain that the inventive potentials of their product technologies were usually richer than those of their rivals. In consequence, the demand for productivity advance in the industries that were or could become customers of the electrical or chemical industries has tended to be supplied relatively more by them than by other industries. For this reason, as we saw in Chapter VIII, these two industries have a higher ratio of patents to sales than other industries.

Thus the current variety of goods each industry produces constitutes the useful residue of past invention, and reflects the richness of the inventive potential of each industry's product technology in the past relative to the richness of the product technologies of rival industries. By the same token, the current additions to each industry's product mix reflect the richness of its product inventive potential relative to the richness of the product inventive potentials of rival industries.

The determinants of the richness of the inventive potential of an industry's product technology are probably complex and would seem to merit serious investigation rather than casual observation. However, it seems certain that a leading reason why it may grow over time is that the scientific and engineering knowledge relating to it grows. This has clearly been the case with respect to chemicals and electrical equipment and some other product fields. However, it is important to note, as discussed in Chapter VIII, that the prospect of practical uses also largely accounted for the growth of scientific and engineering knowledge in these fields.

In addition, as suggested in Chapter VIII, it may be an over-simplification to credit only the relatively greater improvement in their scientific and engineering underpinnings for the fact that inventive activity in them exceeded that in other fields (relative to the economic size of the industries concerned). Specifically, it seems plausible to believe that with the rise of mass production, the standardized quality of chemically produced materials tended to become relatively more preferred than formerly; while the same development, coupled with the increase in the cost of labor in relation to that of capital and the increased cost of space tended to favor the use of electrical power and machinery and electrical or electronic means of communication and control. Any good is a collection of properties, and the relative value of different properties may have shifted over time in ways favorable to electrical and chemical products.

The combination of a richer knowledge base underlying the product technologies of some industries and possible shifts in the characteristics desired in inventions thus results in substantial interindustry variation in the patent—sales ratio, as observed in Chapter VIII. Nonetheless, the over-all relation between these two variables is also linear across industries, just as when capital goods inventions classified according to using industry were regressed on capital goods purchases, and interindustry differences in sales "explain" about 40 per cent of the differences in the number of product inventions made. Moreover, the patent—employment ratio is about the same for all durable goods industries as for all nondurable goods industries.

Thus, a million dollars spent for one economic function is likely to evoke as many inventions, whether of substitutes or of complementary goods, as the same sum spent for any other. However, while the new goods invented tend to be made by the same industries whose existing products currently fulfill the given function, this tendency is weakened by the fact that at any given time the product technologies of rival industries are not equally expansible along lines desired by the market.

CONSUMER GOODS INVENTIONS

The fundamental conclusion that demand determines the allocation of inventive effort among alternative uses probably applies to consumer goods. Impressionistic evidence suggests that inventive activity has tended to respond to differential shifts in consumer demand resulting from differences in income elasticity of demand, changes in geographic distribution of population, in the degree of urbanization, the status of women, the age distribution of the population, and so on.

The principal implication of this is that consumer demand probably plays a role in the "dynamic" aspects of economic development comparable to the role assigned to it in the theory of a static economy. It not only guides the allocation of economic resources in the production of existing goods. It also guides their allocation between the production of existing goods and the production of technological knowledge, and between the production of one kind of technological knowledge and another. Thus, the received conceptual framework of economic theory seems more widely applicable than is customarily assumed. However, to apply it effectively to the rise of new goods, economists may have to link their discipline to others, such as the psychology of motivation, in order to uncover the nature of the link between wants and the goods that satisfy them. Only by this step does it seem possible to formulate a theory of the process of economic development which encompasses the rise of new goods.

In this spirit we note the possibility that important differences may exist in the size of the inventive potentials of different classes of consumer goods. Convention, psychological symbolism, and the constants of human physiology may limit the range of acceptable variation more in some classes than in others. Diffusion rates and hence inventive profits also may differ because of differences in the chance for the "demonstration effect" to work. Thus, unlike capital goods inventions, consumer goods inventions may not be distributed in proportion to expected sales of all goods in each class.

FURTHER IMPLICATIONS

If the general view presented here is correct, then it follows that those troubles that come with the advancement and use of new technological knowledge express in one way or another the conflicts inherent in man and society. Man's wants often conflict, not only because they compete for scarce resources but also because satisfying one may make the satisfaction of another impossible regardless of the resources available. I cannot enjoy the opportunities of the big city and the beauties of the countryside simultaneously, and I cannot eat the entire steak and still have room for the pie à la mode. Life forces us always to choose. Yet each choice conditions the next by shaping both the new situation we confront and the preferences we confront it with.

And, of course, because each man lives among other men and is obligated to satisfy the wants of others in order to satisfy his own, another major by-product of the discovery and use of new technological knowledge is the continual disruption of economic and social relations. Those who make, use, and benefit from new technological knowledge—and therefore, essentially, those who demanded and supplied any given bit of it—are not the only ones affected by its use. Hence, while invention, and presumably technological and technical change generally, represent an effort to satisfy wants better, the wants to be satisfied are usually not the wants of all men but those of only some. Third party effects, favorable and unfavorable, are constantly with us, and their changing shape and intensity, too, condition the course of further change.

Thus, seldom able fully to predict the consequences of our choices, compelled always to pass by attractive alternatives, our lives deflected by the repercussions of the use of new knowledge that others sought, we need have little wonder that the myth of Sisyphus, the craftiest of Greeks, doomed forever to roll a big stone up a hill in Hades only to have it always roll down before it reached the top, strikes such a responsive chord in us.

If modern men at the same time see technological progress as an inevitable consequence of the endowment of life with creative intelligence, it is only because they forget the examples of the ascetics on the one hand, and of those medieval craft guilds that for centuries suppressed invention, on the other. From this vantage point, the pervasiveness of technological progress in modern times appears not so much a consequence of man's nature, though it certainly expresses an important aspect of it, but perhaps even more an outgrowth of the importance attached to material wants in modern times and of the indefensible military position of societies centered on other values. The increase in our capacity to wage war, thermonuclear and conventional, which has accompanied the increase in our capacity to satisfy our private wants may in the end justify the position of the ascetics.

Finally, as argued in Chapter X, to account for the number of inventions in a field in terms of "social forces" of whatever sort, as we have done, provides no support for the sociological determinist thesis, recently exhumed by Merton, that individual inventions are inevitable. The evidence thus far advanced to support that thesis has been misinterpreted. The "duplicate" inventions cited as proof are not duplicates at all. Chance often plays a role in the inventive process itself. Some inventions require creative ability that is extremely rare. And most inventions are made in response to changing economic and technical conditions. Hence, to argue that individual inventions are inevitable because of the accumulation of knowledge and the pressure of social needs seems to go too far. The thesis requires stability in economic and technical conditions, a large number of men with sufficient creative ability seeking to make the invention, and a sufficiently large number of chance events in the laboratory. To say that only those inventions are inevitable for which these conditions are fulfilled is obviously mere tautology. All that present knowledge permits us to say is that the probability that any given invention will be made varies between zero and one *inclusive!* On the other hand, if our results have been correctly interpreted, we can now predict within comparatively narrow limits the *number* of inventions that will be made in capital goods fields, and there is reason to suppose that, with further research, a similar statement about invention in consumer goods fields will also prove possible.

This obviously does not mean that particular inventions are inevitable in the sense that if they were not made by one man, they would certainly be made by another. Indeed, even when genuine duplication occurs, as shown in Chapter X, the fact of duplication does not prove inevitability on the most liberal construction of the term.

It is also of interest to note, as discussed in Chapter X, that even if accepted Merton's formulation of the inevitability of inventions doctrine leads to a rejection of any kind of historical determinism that is based exclusively on social forces.

Endnotes

1. What now seems needed is an empirically validated theory that links the *number* of changes in technology—the problem illuminated in this study—with the magnitude of the resulting change. Once this gap is closed, a new and far more useful theory of the industry should be within reach.

2. John Stuart Mill, *Principles of Political Economy* (New York: D. Appleton and Co., 1890, from the 5th London ed.), Vol. I, p. 68. Mill continues, "In a national, or universal point of view, the labour of the savant, or speculative thinker, is as much a part of production in the very narrowest sense, as that of the inventor of a practical art."

SECTION IV

PRODUCT INNOVATION

Introduction

This section investigates the definition and development of product innovations. Product innovation is viewed from a scholarly as well as a practical perspective, in that scholarly model construction is depicted in addition to practical research that relates to both consumer and industrial goods. The first article, by Donald Heany, offers a new product typology. The following article presents a review of factors that are associated with new product success by Johne and Snelson. The next article in this section is a model building and evaluation work related to the development of new products by Billie Jo Zirger and Modesto Maidique. The fourth article by Cusumano and associates investigates how a second entrant with a lesser technology can win a battle for market share. The final article by Cooper and Kleinschmidt explores differences between firms led by managers who possess conservative or entrepreneurial management philosophies and implications for the different directions that firms can take based on such radically different management perspectives.

New products come in various shades, flavors, and degrees. In the initial article in this section, Donald Heany notes that managers often come to realize that product differentiation is temporary and that it fades with time as anything that is new eventually does. The purpose of Heany's article is to point out the importance of the varying *shades* of "new" products. Heany segments new products into six categories based on product and market properties. These categories are defined as:

1. New products for markets as yet undefined and undimensioned
2. New products for established markets
3. New products for currently served markets
4. Product line extensions
5. Product improvements
6. Style changes

Heany points out that the type of product, amount of work, and risk varies depending upon the category in which a new product is placed. In conjunction with the work and risk involved in bringing a new product to market, there also is the attendant strategy that must support the product to give it the best possible opportunity for market success.

In the next article, F. Axel Johne and Patricia Snelson review several factors associated with the success of newly developed products. They employ the McKinsey 7 Ss framework used to analyze organizations to assist in the analysis and structure of their presentation. Their focus is product development at the program level and is especially germane to what they denote as "bread and butter" or those product developments that are based on current technologies. The 7 Ss framework incorporates the following factors: skills, strategy, structure, shared values, style, staff, and systems. They also review the skills required for new product planning, idea generation, idea screening, technical analysis, market planning, and launch planning. In addition, they explore the strategies and structures necessary for new product success. They investigate the shared values deemed appropriate from a cultural perspective for success. Moreover, they explore management styles, such as risk-taking and hands-off, that might facilitate new product success. The staff and organizational systems necessary for success are also analyzed to determine what procedures and personal qualities are more likely to lead to successful new products.

The third article involves a research report by Billie Jo Zirger and Modesto Maidique that describes the building and evaluation of a model of new product development. Many new products were investigated to be able to test the concepts and relationships comprising their model. The major elements of their new product development model include the market in terms of lead customers, research and development (R&D) and engineering, and manufacturing. In this model, the market, marketing, and R&D and engineering are connected, and only marketing and R&D and engineering are connected to manufacturing. Management is seen as an integral function that operates between the three areas of marketing, manufacturing, and R&D and engineering. Eight hypotheses were formulated and tested as part of this research project. Important findings include: management excellence and commitment are crucial to new product success, the development of new product strategies contribute significantly to new product success, and new products must provide major improvements over previous offerings to be successful.

Michael Cusumano, Yiorgos Mylonadis, and Richard Rosenbloom explore the evolution of the dynamics and strategic maneuvering required in the creation of standard or dominant designs in mass markets. The authors investigate and analyze the history of the videocassette recorder industry in an attempt to determine the factors related to the conquest of Beta by the VHS video format. They investigate many of the players, both competitors and partners, of Sony and JVC to ascertain how a second entrant with a lesser technology attained the dominant market position. They conclude that the two major factors associated with the demise of Sony's Beta format offering were JVC's timely alliance with the resource-laden Matsushita and JVC's humility and versatility in forming licensing alliances, whereas Sony's market strategy was based on reputation and product commitment.

The fifth article by Robert G. Cooper and Elko J. Kleinschmidt identifies nine lessons derived primarily from earlier research entitled the NewProd Studies. Moreover, their current research discusses these lessons with respect to a new process for new product management and development success entitled the Stage Gate Systems process. The nine lessons for new product success include: developing unique, superior products; creating a strong market orientation; focusing more on predevelopment stage activities; defining product concepts and benefits clearly and early; organizing a new product team; developing effective new product evaluation "screens"; controlling the innovation process; observing limits to project acceleration; and implementing a multitasking new product development process such as the Stage Gate Systems process. The authors describe the Stage Gate Systems process as a progression of four to six predetermined phases in which prescribed, multifunctional, and parallel activities are performed. They note that each succeeding stage of this process is more costly than the stage before it. They conclude by suggesting that their plan allows new product developers to be "reading from the same page of the same book" (Cooper and Kleinschmidt, 1993, p. 29).

References

Cooper, Robert G. and Elko J. Kleinschmidt. 1993. Stage Gate Systems for new product success. *Marketing Management,* 1(4): 20–29.

Cusumano, Michael A., Yiorgos Mylonadis, and Richard S. Rosenbloom. 1992. Strategic maneuvering and mass market dynamics: The triumph of VHS over Beta. *Business History Review* 66 (Spring): 51–94.

Heany, Donald F. 1983. Degrees of product innovation. *Journal of Business Strategy* 3 (Spring): 3–14.

Johne, F. Axel and Patricia A. Snelson. 1988. Success factors in product innovation: A selective review of the literature. *Journal of Product Innovation Management* 5(2) (June): 114–128.

Zirger, Billie Jo and Modesto A. Maidique. 1990. A model of new product development: An empirical test. *Management Science* 36(7): 867–884.

22 | DEGREES OF PRODUCT INNOVATION

Donald F. Heany

Donald F. Heany is with The Strategic Planning Institute, Cambridge, Mass.

Product innovation can run the gamut from new products and product-line extensions to product improvements and style changes. Business managers need to understand this entire spectrum of product innovation in order to be able to compete effectively in the marketplace.

Every businessman realizes that product differentiation is temporary. The differentiation established between one business's products and those of its leading competitors will generally erode with the passage of time. This erosion may result from new-product introductions by some of the competitors. Other competitors may improve the relative quality of their traditional offerings. Still others may make price concessions to hold their customer base.

Product differentiation can also decay because of market factors. For instance, shifts in life-styles can impact relative product quality. In the United States, the current concern with bodily health has dramatically increased sales of sugarless gum, natural cereals, low-calorie beverages, athletic togs and low-cholesterol food products.

Businessmen must be sensitive to such market and industry dynamics. A failure to react might cause their products to become commodities. Since businesses offering commodity products rarely yield a respectable return on investment, many try to resist these profit pressures by product innovation. They:

- Introduce new products based upon their own R&D programs.
- Enhance the quality of their existing products.
- Search for new markets for their existing products.
- License new products developed by other businesses, and/or acquire another business with high-quality products.

Such strategic and tactical moves may or may not find favor with customers.

The primary purpose of this article is to direct attention to the danger of semantic inflation with respect to product innovation. Every well-informed person is aware that there is a big difference between a style change in a product and a change in the product's technological base. Nonetheless, we smile indulgently when promotional literature applies the label "new product" to both.

Unfortunately, such careless use of the English language can have serious consequences within a business. It prompts some managers and strategic planners to build castles in the air. They underestimate the time required to launch a really new product.

Heany, Donald F., (1983), "Degrees of Product Innovation," *Journal of Business Strategy,* 3, (Spring), 3–14.

They overestimate the income stream of innovations that are mislabeled "new products."

This, perhaps, is enough justification for reexamining some very basic semantic distinctions with respect to product innovation. Some readers may have learned these distinctions long ago but often fail to bear them in mind when formulating strategy or designing tactical programs.

A second purpose of this article is to share some empirical evidence illuminating the contributions that new products (properly defined) can make to business strategy. This evidence comes from the PIMS data base. It relates to established businesses and to start-up business.

THE SPECTRUM OF PRODUCT INNOVATION

It is helpful for businessmen to view product innovation as a spectrum. The least risky form of product innovation is a style change in an established product. The functional repercussions are localized and often predictable. By contrast, at the other end of the spectrum, one finds major innovations that have the potential of creating new markets and new industries. Such product innovations place major strains on all or most functional areas. When launched, the manager feels he or she is betting the company. No amount of market research can dissipate the uncertainty.

Between these end points of the product-innovation spectrum, one can identify four other types of innovation (Table 22-1). Specifically, these are:

- Product-line extensions.
- Product improvements.
- New products for the current market served.
- New products for an established market in which the business offering the innovation is not now recognized as a vendor.

Each category within this product-innovation spectrum triggers a functional shock wave with its own distinctive signature. We will illustrate the functional impacts for a manufactured product. No doubt an equivalent description can be given for innovations in service and software.

New Products for Markets as Yet Undefined and Undimensioned

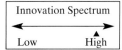

The most ambitious type of product innovation entails development of a new product for a market that, in the strict sense of the term, does not yet exist. Inventors such as Henry Ford, Alexander Graham Bell, Thomas Edison, and George Westinghouse developed new products for markets whose size and growth rate they could not quantify. The initial applications of their products were only the forward edge of an evolving market or series of related markets. These entrepreneurs were people of faith. Had they had a planning staff, they might have been deterred from their strategic course.

TABLE 22-1   The Spectrum of Product Innovation

Is the Market for Product Established?	*Is the Business Already Serving Market?*	*Do Customers Know Functions and Features?*	*What Is the Design Effort?*		*Then Innovation Is a*
			Product?	*Process?*	
Yes	Yes	Yes	Minor	Nil	Style change
Yes	Yes	Yes	Minor	Minor	Product-line extension
Yes	Yes	Yes	Significant	Minor	Product improvement
Yes	Yes	Yes	Major	Major	New product
Yes	No	Yes	Major	Major	Start-up business
No	No	No	Major	Major	Major innovation

Modern examples of this type of product innovation include:

- Computers for the home.
- Private air-express services featuring overnight delivery for small parcels.
- Wide-screen television displays.
- Unmanned vehicles for delivering parts to work on an assembly line or in an office.
- A temporary, worldwide network for broadcasting sporting events to locations where people pay for the privilege of watching these events.

Obviously, the downside risks associated with this type of product innovation are very high. There is new expertise to acquire in all functional areas. A new organization has to be created and staffed. This is the domain of venture capitalists. Out of 100 proposals, they participate in ten. They regard themselves as fortunate if one out of the ten proves to be a bonanza.

Even billion-dollar firms are leery of this type of product innovation. The average chief executive becomes cautious when told that the entry price will exceed $50 million. If the development cycle is predicted to be over eight years, he or she will call for more documentation and analysis.

New Products for an Established Market

A second category on the product innovation spectrum consists of new products for a market that has already been developed. Customers are already using products equivalent in function to the one you propose to introduce. Your business, however, is not recognized by them as a qualified vendor.

Table 22-2 lists familiar examples of this type of innovation. The label "start-up" business is often attached to the source of such innovations. This label is apt. It dramatizes that a great deal of expertise has to be acquired in many functional areas. One might imagine that such expertise can be pirated away from established competitors. Unfortunately, there is a big difference between "acquiring an expert" and "internalizing expertise."

Start-up businesses report stress in several of the functional areas. For example:

- *Engineering.* Some new products are built around a product concept that has never been tested except in the laboratory. As a result, product designers relearn Murphy's Law every day. This has prompted General Electric to transfer researchers to line components charged with the responsibility to commercializing their research results.

TABLE 22-2	Examples of Start-Up Businesses Based on New Products Offered to an Established Market
Xerox	Offered a word processor to Fortune 1000 firms and to governmental agencies in direct competition with IBM's magnetic-card typewriter
IBM	Introduced a copier for offices in direct competition with Xerox's line of copiers
Polaroid	Offered a movie camera in direct competition with Kodak's movie camera; Polaroid's viewer enabled the user to see the results instantly; previously, Polaroid had offered single-frame instant cameras
Texas Instruments	Offered electronic watches and electronic calculators for the U.S. mass market; TI previously concentrated on electronic components for the military and original-equipment manufacturers' market
Procter & Gamble	Introduced a line of paper diapers in direct competition with Scott Paper's products; P&G previously offered packaged goods for the home
Dannon	Offered U.S. consumers a yogurt with fruit, packaged in a single-serving container
Timex	Entered the U.S. watch market via the mass merchant and drug store channel; its product design and manufacturing process differed greatly from that of U.S. or Swiss watch manufacturers

- *Distribution.* Sometimes the primary stress develops in the distribution channel. Think of the difficulty of creating a catalog store in a shopping area dominated by venerable department stores and discount chains.
- *Marketing.* The penetration of a new market is anything but automatic even when you have a trained sales force familiar with the targeted customers. Recall the problems Olivetti had when it first attempted to market electronic computers. Think of the different skills required to market minicomputers to small businesses when the sales team has been calling on the Fortune 500.

One problem of start-up businesses is that their product designers and process engineers do not share a common knowledge base. No doubt each is an accomplished engineer. But, start-up businesses are dependent on teamwork, not on solo performances. This means that the general manager of a fledgling business must work at developing individual and organizational relationships. It is one thing for a manager/engineering to articulate the general nature of the new product that is to become the cornerstone of the new business. It is quite a different thing for a collection of individuals to absorb that information and then produce the new product at a quality level and a unit cost that assure a profit [1]. Many a start-up business has underestimated the magnitude of the effort required.

Start-up businesses represent an organizational headache. Some large, diversified companies try to minimize the difficulties by loosely attaching a start-up to an established business. The individual in charge of the start-up or product section has all the prerogatives of a general manager or managing director. The staff, however, is heavily weighted toward the technical expertise relevant to problems associated with the new product. Other skills (e.g., finance, personnel, etc.) are available on call from the host business.

Another major problem with start-up businesses is that the targeted customers do not recognize them as vendors. The publicity surrounding their entry into the market may not have reached the ears of purchasing agents. Some customers will have heard the news but refuse to place an order until others testify that the new product is "safe." The larger the customer's volume of production, the greater the reluctance to experiment with a new vendor.

New products are typically protected by patents. It is no simple matter to decide:

- What to patent.
- When to file for a patent.
- In what countries to file.

Competitors follow such registrations very closely. They can often infer from your filings a great deal about the state of your product development and your strategic intentions. Thus, the quest for patent protection may engender an undesired competitive attack or squander a technological lead.

New Products for the Currently Served Market

A business may call upon its engineering staff to develop a new product for customers it is already serving. Such products constitute another category on the product-innovation spectrum. Table 22-3 illustrates this form of innovation.

These new products may be indistinguishable from those offered by a start-up business. Yet, we place them in a separate category because they are designed and manufactured by an established business. Such a business can assemble a team of talented engineers with long-term work relationships.

Nonetheless, new products set up change-action patterns that reverberate throughout many areas of the business. The reasons are clear. A new product may entail:

- Elaborate market test programs.
- A major advertising campaign to draw the customer's attention to the innovation and to explain where, how, and why to use the new product.
- Major changes in the product logic. This triggers the design of new parts and assemblies, experimentation with new materials and new vendors.

TABLE 22-3 Examples of New Products for the Currently Served Market

Currently Served Market	Current Product(s)	New Product
U.S. households	Camera capable of producing a black-and-white picture within one minute	Camera capable of producing instant color pictures
U.K. camera buffs	Discrete lenses for 35 mm camera	A "zoom" lens
Housewares for the Common Market	Toasters, coffee percolators, electric fry pans, etc.	Smoke alarm, toaster oven, coffee "system"
U.S. homeowners with workshops	Electric hand tools (drills, sanders, etc.)	Cordless power tools
Canadian households	Electric oven	Microwave oven
Engineers, scientists, and students attending technical institutes in Western Europe, the U.S., and South America	Electronic hand calculators with small memories; keyboard entry	Calculators responding to programs encoded on magnetic strips
Thrift market	Savings account	Life insurance

- Major changes in the production process. New work stations have to be added and, sometimes, new feeder lines. The old work procedures and work standards may have to be scrapped. Radically different assembly drawings will have to be made and worker training initiated.

In addition, the manufacturer may have to make substantial investments in:

- R&D programs.
- Production prototypes.
- Plant and equipment.
- Logistical systems.
- Warehouse modifications.

If there is a debate as to whether a product innovation deserves the label "new product," it does not qualify as one.

When new products are developed for customers already being served by the business, managers spend a great deal of time picking the right entry point. Some direct the new product at those segments of the served market believed to be most disposed toward experimentation and to those customers most likely to appreciate the new product's features and functions.

Another major question uppermost in a manager's mind is the impact of the new product on sales of other, older products in the line. In some instances, the substitution possibilities loom very large. Think of the effect of color television on the sale of black-and-white television sets. When color sets were available in quantity, the demand for black-and-white sets dropped and prices plummeted. More recent examples of this substitution effect can be found in the tire industry (radial versus bias), in typewriters (electronic versus electric), and in housewares (food processors versus mixers).

The new product may differ so in function, features, and use patterns that a significant change in customer behavior is required. For example, initially one had to explain that a roast cooked in a microwave oven was "done" even if it did not have the color of a roast cooked in a conventional oven. In short, marketing departments play a key role in new product development. It is up to them to get both the immediate customer and the end user to understand and value the newly established degree of product differentiation.

Typically, new products move through the same distribution channel as existing products in the line.

The launching of a new product may or may not be visible in the organization chart of an established business. Some new products do cause organizational changes, particularly if the process technology needed is dramatically different from that in use.

The risk associated with a new product is high. The determinants of risk vary from product to product. First, the development cycle is longer. It is not unusual for new-product R&D to span three to five years. In extreme cases, the technological problems and engineering bugs are banished—but only a few years before the patent covering the innovation expires!

Businessmen are ingenious when it comes to reducing or sharing R&D-related risks. For instance:

- They can shift some risks to their vendors.
- They license innovations by other firms.
- They participate in jointly funded development projects.

A second source of risk is linked to customer behavior. For example, government purchasing agents have traditionally selected air-conditioning equipment on the basis of unit price. Obviously, a manufacturer who develops a new product—a heat pump—that cools and heats the room, plus operates at a lower cost over the life of the product, will not immediately be swamped with government orders. Purchasing agents may require years to comprehend, and then be prepared to act upon, the implications of the new heat pump's operating characteristics. The difference between the price of a heat pump at the time of purchase and that of a conventional air-conditioning unit is large enough to make them hesitate.

New products for original-equipment manufacturers (OEM) raise a completely different risk, namely, that borne by the purchaser. The purchaser will not incorporate any vendor's new product into a system unless and until multisourcing is arranged. The risk that a strike or fire might interrupt the flow of the new product to an OEM is not always established by doing a cost analysis or by making price comparisons with existing, competing products. The new product may qualify for a premium price because it enables OEMs to simplify their own products or improve their production systems.

No one questions that a successful new product can provide a bountiful harvest. Take the case of Tide, Procter & Gamble's initial laundry detergent. This new product helped to create and maintain P&G's leadership position in an established U.S. market—that for soap powders.

The Tide story is interesting for several reasons.[1] It underscores the necessity of assessing accurately the character of each product innovation. P&G clearly saw Tide as a "new product for an established market." Its competitors, on the other hand, believed that a detergent would not perform well in hard water. They were content to make style changes in their traditional soap powders. Today, we know that a style change was tepid response. To be effective, competition must take place within the same category on the product innovation spectrum.

Previous to Tide, P&G's profits had been significantly influenced by cyclical swings in the price of a key raw material for soap—animal fat (tallow).[2] In some years, P&G profited from variations in commodity prices. In other years, its earnings were depressed by unanticipated swings in the price of tallow.

Fortunately, Tide freed P&G from its dependence upon oscillations in the price of tallow. Tide was manufactured from a heavy-duty synthetic, a substance that was in plentiful supply. As a consequence, P&G's shift in product technology—from animal fat to a synthetic material—dramatically reduced its downside risk.

The Tide story is also a vivid reminder that end users will experiment with new products. They have traditional purchase patterns, yet they will respond if a new product addresses customer wants that established products neglect. As proof of this point, recall that Tide was only the first in a series of detergents. In time, other competitors imitated Tide. Today, detergents have penetrated the original laundry-soap market to a level of 95 percent. Animal fats are now used only for specialized washing requirements. Thus, Tide not only had an impact on P&G, it also revolutionized an entire industry.[3]

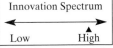

Product-Line Extensions

The term "product-line extension" covers a class of new models that derive directly from product-design principles visible in the business's existing products. Table 22-4 lists some familiar examples.

TABLE 22-4 Examples of Product-Line Extensions

Current Product Line	*Product-Line Extension*
Dishwasher permanently installed in a kitchen	A mobile dishwasher
Breakfast cereals	Fortified cereals appealing to those preferring natural foods
Canned fruit	Dietetic canned fruit
2-slice toaster	4- and 6-slice models
Knitted sweaters for tennis players	Knitted sweaters for skiers
Retail bank services	Credit card

Product-line extensions do not require serious modifications in customer behavior. Initially, they are tailored to the perceived needs of customers constituting a segment of the currently served market. Consequently, product-line extensions move through the current distribution channels.

The functional impact of product-line extensions is relatively minor and localized. They can be produced on the existing production line. Engineers do prepare a separate set of drawings and bill of materials, yet many of the parts, components, and subassemblies of older products are incorporated into a product-line extension. No elaborate, specialized marketing programs need to be drawn up to help customers see where and how to use the new model. Their familiarity with that class of product is sufficient for them to decide such questions without outside help.

Thus, the downside risk associated with product-line extensions is generally[4] small because (1) the level of engineering effort is relatively modest,[5] (2) engineers are proficient in the tasks to be done, (3) the dollar expenditures often lie within the discretionary limits of the general manager of that business, (4) the relevant technological expertise is nearly identical to that underlying existing products, and (5) no significant changes in marketing are required.

Marketing is often the prime mover behind product-line extensions. Sales representatives dream of a line of products broad enough to include a customized product for each and every customer. The vice-president of marketing cannot afford to fund that kind of variety. He or she will lobby for product-line extensions that have special appeal to particular segments of the currently served market. For example, a business selling a line of television consoles for use in the family's living room may regard smaller television sets for the den, patio, kitchen, beach, or children's room as an ideal way to respond to the saturation of their original market.

Some business plans explicitly provide for an orderly progression of product-line extensions. The designers of the original product are instructed to anticipate an evolution in models. Physical space is reserved for new features that will be added in the event it is necessary to rekindle the customer's interest or to respond to an innovation introduced by a competitor. When it comes time to offer a product-line extension, it will be easy and relatively inexpensive to accommodate the necessary product-design changes. This technique may entail a slight overdesign for the initial models, but over the longer term, the total design cost is less.

The decision to offer a product-line extension may prompt a business to experiment with one or more style changes as well. Should these prove popular with the targeted market segment, they will be incorporated when the full line is restyled.

Product Improvements

Innovation Spectrum

←———————→
Low   High

Probably the most common type of product innovation involves a change in one or two end-product characteristics of models that have already been offered to the currently served market. The basic appearance of the product may or may not change, but changes are made in function, features, packaging, or warranty. Table 22-5 lists some familiar examples.

TABLE 22-5	Examples of Product Improvements
Product	**Change**
Telephone	Subscriber is alerted to the fact that another caller is ringing that number. Handset enables subscriber to put the first caller on "hold" and talk to the second caller.
Light bulb	A 20% reduction in power consumption; a 10% increase in life expectancy
FM radio	Add feature to prevent "drift"
Electric mixer	Add the capability of kneading bread dough as well as whipping cream, mixing cake ingredients, beating eggs, etc.
Automobile	Reduce weight of car so as to improve gasoline consumption by purchasing plastic rather than metal parts from your vendors
Typewriter	Add an "erasing" capability
Hi-fi system	Extend warranty to two full years
Car insurance	Automatic coverage for a 30-day period after the purchase of a new car
Commercial banking services	Deposit and withdrawal at any hour of the day or night via a terminal

Product improvements should not be dismissed as trivial changes. They can involve a significant amount of engineering design. Think only of the investment and engineering effort required by changes in automobile emission standards, in safety standards (e.g., the air-bag controversy), or the desire of some governmental officials to require bus manufacturers to make their vehicles more accessible to the handicapped. Fuel economy has also posed a real challenge for auto manufacturers.

Product improvement can require substantial promotional campaigns. For example, when manufacturers of television sets switched from electromechanical to solid-state components they effected a real product improvement. They did not, however, expect any of their customers to take the backs off of the new sets and applaud the improvement. Instead, they launched a major advertising campaign to explain that the product improvement just made translated into a higher level of reliability and lower service costs.

Product improvements should not be dismissed as trivial changes.

The impact of a product improvement on process design depends on the nature of the improvement and the skill of the product designers. Some businesses make every effort to alert their product designers to the impact their design decisions are likely to have on the current production systems and hence on profitability.[6]

Any improvement in relative product quality as perceived by immediate customers or the end user is, by definition, a product improvement. Thus, some changes in packaging can legitimately be labeled product improvements. Consider, for example:

- The substitution of paper milk containers for glass bottles.
- Throw-away bottles for soft drinks versus the once conventional, reusable glass containers.
- Hanes' decision to display L'Eggs hosiery in egg-shaped containers.

In some industries, product improvements are designed by specialists in advertising and promotion. They can influence customer perceptions with little or no change in the end-product characteristics that are of interest to product designers.

Product improvements do not produce major functional shock waves. Their impacts tend to be localized. A newly improved product will be offered to the same served market and move through the same distribution channel. It can be made in the same facility and often produced on the same production line as older products. No specialized marketing programs are required in order to help the purchaser understand how to use the improved product. Furthermore, no organizational adjustments need to be made to accommodate the improved product. The necessary work can be performed by existing employees, functioning in existing organizational components and using standard procedures and routines.

A product improvement may or may not:

- Replace older products.
- Incorporate style changes as well as new functions and/or features.
- Require changes in packaging.
- Be given a brand name.

For the sake of completeness, it might be useful to recognize those innovations that improve product performance yet are never publicized. For example, an improvement in the design of an electric blanket may decrease the risk that it malfunction and cause a fire. The vice-president/marketing would not want this design change to be publicized as customers might begin to associate fire with electric blankets. Similarly, no seller of smoke alarms will want to admit that the 1982 model is more sensitive to smoke than the 1981 model.

In other cases, the product's characteristics are changed, yet go unmentioned by the manufacturer because the changes do not affect performance. The improvements accrue to the manufacturer, not to the user. For example, it is standard practice in some engineering components to audit their product designs periodically in an effort to detect products that:

- Offer functions or features customers do not find valuable.
- Use materials that are no longer cost-effective (e.g., metal parts may be more expensive than plastic parts, yet function no better than plastic parts) [2].
- Fail to capitalize upon design principles that can simplify fabrication or reduce the number of defects per batch.

Occasionally, a product improvement goes unmentioned because it is based on proprietary processes. There is no way to call these improvements to the attention of the customer without also alerting one's competitors. This form of competition is very important in high-volume businesses. Changes in product design, process design, or in the operation of the production line may enable the business to offset increases in the cost of labor and and materials. A business that can innovate in this manner and maintain prices in an inflationary period puts great pressure on less efficient, less innovative competitors.

A business must be attentive to the opportunities for hidden product improvements as well as for publicized improvements. Both require a commitment of resources and both expose the business to risk.

Style Changes

> Innovation Spectrum
> ←————————▲——→
> Low   High

The most modest type of product innovation entails a change in the esthetic features of a product. Manufacturers can take an existing product and, without altering its basic functions, change its shape or color. Such changes are popular in consumer-goods markets. For example:

- Ladies' apparel. The hemline of dresses are lengthened or shortened.
- Automotive. Tail fins are added or removed, bumpers are redesigned, more chrome strips are added.
- Furniture. The Spanish style may be featured one year, only to give way to a modern, functional style the next.
- Watches. The wrist band may be made more attractive; the watch may be sold in a box that appears more luxurious to the purchaser.

These changes are designed to attract the attention and catch the fancy of customers. They do not require customers to effect major changes in their behavior patterns.

The functional impact of model changes based on esthetics is usually minimal. The work triggered by style changes is well-defined and familiar to current employees. The incremental investment is small by comparison to that required for a brand new product. The change in product and process technology is also minimal [2], so the business risk is not great.

The frequency of stylistic changes varies from industry to industry. The weather cycle stimulates some clothing manufacturers to restyle their lines twice a year. In the U.S. automative market, the custom of a model change each year is well-established.

Businesses can resort to style changes even when the customer or the industry does not call for annual or seasonal model introductions. For example, banks are becoming market-driven. They have restyled their staid black checkbooks and offer checks in a variety of colors and designs. Now they are restyling the customer's monthly statement in order to make the information more comprehensible and the task of account reconciliation easier. Even public utilities are discovering the importance of style. Telephone companies now feature colored units that blend with the decor of each room in the house.

One can think of businesses where esthetics has always been the key to success. Jewelers and watch manufacturers have excelled in this regard. Manufacturers who deal with customers that buy on impulse also devote a great deal of attention to styling innovations. They know that the cost of their product does not justify the time or effort needed to discriminate between valid and invalid product claims. Products with an attractive design will move quickly and capture the attention of new customers.

CLASSIFICATION PROBLEMS

In defining categories on the product-innovation spectrum, we must expect grey areas. They can occasion a great deal of debate, as discussed below.

Requisitioned Products

It is customary for manufacturers of large-scale capital goods, measuring instruments, controls, laboratory equipment, and the like to respond to product specifications set down either by the purchaser or by specifying engineers engaged by the purchaser. Each order is different and in that sense each product is shipped new. For purposes of cross-sectional analysis, however, we would not classify all requisitioned products as new products.

To the functional specialist working on these products, the work is conventional and proceeds in accordance with long-established procedures. A new requisition does not trigger any significant organizational changes. The customer is using products of the same type and requires no special marketing program to learn how or where to use them.

A Shift in Product Technology

A question may arise when a company that has addressed a given market elects to offer its customers a product that performs the same basic functions via different technological principles. Nuclear-powered turbine-generator sets are a case in point.

A switch from fossil fuel to nuclear fuel necessitates such major shifts in product design that a separate business should be established to develop and market such new power-generating equipment. We would classify it as a start-up in an established market. The functional and organizational impacts are too pervasive to treat such an innovation as a "new product in the current market" or as a "product-line extension." Specialized marketing programs are required. The level of R&D and the product-design effort required to switch technology is massive. The changes in the production process are also major.

Leased Products

Business manufacturing and leasing hardware can make sequential and incremental product improvements while the hardware is out on lease. Other improvements are made after a product comes off lease and before it is reentered into the lease base.

We would not classify lease revenues derived from a factory-rebuilt product as "new-product sales."

Software

The arrival of programmable hardware presents a new source of product innovations. For example, new software can be written to extend both the range of stitch patterns and the functions of an electronic sewing machine. An equivalent change would have been more costly a decade ago when the manufacturer relied chiefly on electromechanical designs.

We would classify such software-dependent changes as "product improvements."

Businessmen must be sensitive to market and industry dynamics.

Business Definition

For many years, the pioneers in business policy were content to focus on the firm. They gave little attention to profiling individual businesses making up the firm.

Managers of manufacturing businesses have recognized the need to survey business boundaries with great care. Product innovation can complicate these surveys. For example, are "powdered coffee" and "freeze-dried coffee" examples of new products for the established market or the foundations for a start-up business?

This is not the place to debate these important questions. They are included only to point out that some product innovations have profound effects on business strategy. At their inception, new products were of concern to the technical staff. As the development cycle unfolded, they entered into the domain of business policy.

Mandated Innovations

Manufacturers may not be able to restrict innovations to their own products. To reach the customer, an innovation in logistical systems carrying those new products to the end user may be necessary. If the businesses now designing such logistical systems are loath to invest in their piece of the total innovation, the manufacturer may have to assume this type of pioneering in addition to the product innovation.

These one-time innovations are not classified as "new products" because they are not actively offered to the manufacturer's served market or to customers in other markets.

THE LINK BETWEEN INNOVATION AND BUSINESS STRATEGY

It is not enough for managers to position their technical innovations on the spectrum defined above. They must commercialize them.

In the nineteenth century, the inventor of a new product doubled as manager and strategist. Thomas A. Edison's success at Menlo Park helped to sever this connection. Today, innovators in large diversified companies turn their innovations over to others to market.

This division of labor, between scientists and engineers on the one hand and specialists and managers in charge of commercialization on the other, underscores the need for empirical data on the merits of alternate ways of converting an innovation into a profitable business or a profitable line of products quickly. Such data are becoming available. The PIMS program of the Strategic Planning Institute initiated the collection of cross-sectional data from lines of business in 1972. Data collection has continued. Today, the PIMS data base contains the strategic and tactical experiences of more than 1,790 established businesses. In addition, the data base contains information on 168 start-up businesses.

Table 22-6 identifies key data elements pertinent to product innovation that PIMS collects. The respondents also provide much other strategic and tactical information.

We present a few of the relationships between new products, tactical choices, and business performance. In furnishing these data, respondents were asked to exclude product-line extensions, product improvements, and style changes. Only "new products" were counted.

Table 22-7 is constructed from data from 1,795 established businesses. These were ordered, by revenue, from products introduced in the previous three years. The PIMS software attempted to subdivide these observations into five equal groups. This proved to be impossible. Little or no reliance upon new products was reported by 1,891 businesses. The entries in Table 22-7 are four-year averages.

Table 22-8 indicates the level of new-product sales by type of manufacturing business. Clearly, these data suggest that the innovative spirit is not uniformly distributed.

TABLE 22-6 Some PIMS Data Elements Pertinent to Product Innovation

Type of business?	Entry of major competitor?
Age of product?	Relative breadth of product line?
"Life cycle" stage of product category?	Product R&D/sales?
Type of market entry (Early? Close follower? Late?)	Process R&D/sales?
	Newness of plant and equipment?
Patents on product?	Gross book value of P&E/revenue?
On process?	Market share?
Standard or customized products?	Relative market share?
Frequency of product changes?	Number of competitors?
Major technological change?	New-product sales
Development time for new products?	• by the business?
Exit of major competitor?	• by the "Big 3" competitors?

TABLE 22-7 Some Linkages Between New Products and Other Business Characteristics

	Sales of New Products (% of Total Sales)[*]				
	Very Low	Low	Medium	High	Very High
No. of observations	691	271	288	270	275
Return on investment (%)	22	26	23	23	18
Cash flow/investment (%)	3.8	5.1	4.9	2.2	−4.5
Market share (%)	24	25	25	22	21
Relative market share (%)	66	66	68	61	58
Relative product quality (%)	22	25	26	29	32
Industry long-term growth rate (% per year)	8.2	8.6	9.0	9.4	11.6
Real market growth (% per year)	2.7	3.5	4.4	4.1	8.9
Real sales growth (% per year)	4.7	4.7	5.8	7.0	15.4
Selling-price growth rate (% per year)	8.7	8.2	8.2	7.7	5.8
Product R&D/sales (%)	0.9	1.3	1.7	1.8	3.0
Process R&D/sales (%)	0.4	0.5	0.6	0.5	0.8
Sales force experience/sales (%)	4.3	5.4	5.6	5.9	6.4
Advertising and promotional experience/sales (%)	1.8	1.9	2.0	2.1	2.6
Media advertising experience/sales (%)	0.7	0.7	0.8	0.6	1.0
Market experience/sales	7.5	9.3	9.6	10.0	11.8
New-product sales by "Big 3" competitors (% of sales)	1.3	3.2	6.4	11.0	30.7
Gross book value of plant and equipment (% of sales)	52	41	45	42	39
Capacity utilization (%)	78	76	75	76	73

*Cut points: 0.01, 3.4, 8.6 and 18.6.

PIMS research has dramatized that the factors influencing profitability are complex and sometimes quite subtle. We cannot explore the many ties between new products and profitability in this article. We can, however, illustrate two approaches, namely one generic and one customized.

Generic Approach

Cross-classification is a standard tool of analysis. Table 22-9 probes for the connection between new products and profitability, given different levels of real market growth and different levels of competitive position.

TABLE 22-8 New-Product Sales by Type of Manufacturing Business

	New-Product Sales (% of Total Sales)
Consumer-products manufacturing	
Durable	10
Nondurable	8
Capital goods	15
Raw or semifinished goods	6
Components	9
Supplies	6

TABLE 22-9 Linkage Between Profitability, New Products, Growth, and Competitive Position

Businesses With Market Share Less Than 19%[*]

		ROI		
		Low	Medium	High
New Products[**] (% of Total Sales)	Few	15	15	19
		19	22	18
	Many	17	12	11

Businesses With Market Share Over 19%

		Low	Medium	High
New Products[***] (% of Total Sales)	Few	26	28	29
		24	28	37
	Many	26	32	28

[*]Real market growth rate (% per year).
[**]Cut points: –0.2 and 6.7.
[***]Cut points: 0.01 and 7.5.

The exhibit indicates that the effect of competitive position on profitability is much stronger than the effect of either new products or growth.

Note the evidence in favor of moderation in new-product introductions when competitive position is strong and real market growth rapid. These businesses averaged a pretax preinterest rate of return on investment (at net book value of plant and equipment) of 37 percent.

There are 641 businesses in the PIMS data base with at least six years of data. Thus, it is possible to explore lagged relationships. Table 22-10 is a single illustration. It shows the tie between the following:

- Average market share in years 1 and 2.
- Average new-product sales in years 3 and 4.
- The difference in average ROI, years 5 and 6, less average ROI, years 1 and 2.

These data also suggest that innovation is likely to be much more profitable when pursued by businesses with strong competitive positions.

Customized Approach

PIMS has written software to enable members of the Strategic Planning Institute to customize their probes of the empirical relationship between new products and business strategy and/or tactics. Managers are invited to define their "strategic look-alikes" (i.e., those businesses that have equivalent or very similar profiles to those of the

TABLE 22-10 Lagged Relationship Between Change in Profitability, Competitive Position, and New-Product Sales				
		Market Share, Yrs. 1 + 2[*] *Change in ROI* *(Yrs. 5 + 6) − (Yrs. 1 + 2)*		
		Low	*Medium*	*High*
New Products Yrs. 3 + 4 (% of sales)[**]	Few	0.1	8.2	−1.0
		1.6	1.3	4.9
	Many	2.4	3.7	7.4

[*]Cut points: 13 and 27.
[**]Cut points: 0.01 and 7.99.

businesses under study). To do so, they select eight to twelve PIMS data elements (or transformations) and give each an appropriate weight. The ROLA software then retrieves a sample of look-alikes from the entire PIMS data base. The sample comes with more than 100 items of information. Thus, one can study how other businesses, operating in markets and industries similar to one's own, have managed their new products. Consider a simple example. A general manager takes over a business with the following profile:

- Gross plant and equipment (58% of sales)
- Real market growth rate (3% per year)
- Number of competitors (51 +)
- Market share (20%)
- Combined share of the three largest competitors (48%)
- New-product sales (18% of total sales)

He or she can call for a sample of twenty-four "look-alikes" and examine their tactical choices along with their profitability, cash flow, and change in market share. Specifically, what was their level of:

- Sales force expenses?
- Advertising and promotion expenses?
- Finished-goods inventory?
- Process R&D expenses?
- Product R&D expenses?

A second step is often taken. For example, extract from the PIMS data base two samples of look-alikes: one that effected a significant improvement in market share, and one that did not. The intent is to identify significant differences—what tactical moves differentiated the winners (those who gained market share) from the losers (those who failed to gain share)?

PIMS has developed still more powerful information-retrieval software called the "dynamic report on look-alikes" (DROLA), which examines repeated samples from the data base. During a DROLA analysis, a single matching criterion (change in market share) is varied by small increments; other matching criteria are held constant. This enables one to sweep the data base and study how business performance and tactics of the winners differ from those of the losers, given various changes in market share. Specifically, when one sweeps one change in market share, one obtains look-alike businesses for each of some 20 points on a change-in-market share spectrum with end points of −5 percent and +6 percent. The user obtains all PIMS data on each sample of look-alikes. Thus, it is possible to study the contribution of new products to share gains (or losses) along with other tactical options. The amount of computer time to complete a DROLA analysis is substantial.

CONCLUSION

The conventional wisdom is that product innovation is required in order to stimulate growth in the U.S. economy and to regain the competitive edge we once enjoyed. If so, it behooves us to review the quality of management in this area.

We have proposed that one drag on managerial effectiveness is semantic inflation. The type of work required to accomplish a product innovation varies depending on where one is on the product-innovation spectrum. For this reason, we have urged managers and strategic planners to employ the words "new products," "product-line extensions," "product improvements," and "style changes" as reserved words.

Second, we have pointed to new empirical data that can illuminate the relationship between product innovation on the one hand and business strategy and tactics on the other. Managers responsible for new-product introductions need not rely exclusively on their personal experience. They can leverage the experience of others.

References

Biggadyke, R., "The Risky Business of Diversification," *Harvard Business Review,* May–June 1979, pp. 103–111.

Miles, L.D., *Techniques of Value Analysis and Engineering* (2d ed.; New York: McGraw-Hill, 1972).

Vinson, W.D., and Heany, D.F., "Is Quality Out of Control?" *Harvard Business Review,* Nov.–Dec. 1977, pp. 114–122.

Endnotes

1. Alden Clayton supplied a great deal of the information on Tide.
2. Some observers suspected that, prior to Tide, P&G's profits depended as much on successful speculation in the commodity market as on earnings from soap.
3. Leica cameras had a similar impact on hand-held cameras and film.
4. There are exceptions. The classic example is the Edsel. The root of that problem lay with (1) highly automated, integrated production processes and (2) the complex, interdependent systems and subsystems within a modern automobile.
5. An "extension" may entail removing functions or features from an existing product.
6. See [3] for a discussion of methods for integrating manufacturing, product design, and market requirements.

23

SUCCESS FACTORS IN PRODUCT INNOVATION: A SELECTIVE REVIEW OF THE LITERATURE

F. Axel Johne and Patricia A. Snelson

In today's increasingly competitive climate, more and more managers are having to update themselves on the range of factors that determine product innovation success. Such successes can be measured at the project (product) level or at the program level. Axel Johne and Patricia Snelson have prepared a review of factors associated with achieving success in a high proportion of recently developed new products.

The authors address practical questions, such as the following: To what extent can product innovation be planned? Should development tasks be scheduled sequentially or in parallel? What is the proper degree of formality in effective new product decision making? What are the optimal organizational arrangements?

The article concentrates on recent writings, drawing chiefly from journal articles published after 1980, including a large number from the *Journal of Product Innovation Management*. Factors contributing to success are ordered according to the now well-known McKinsey 7 Ss framework popularized by Peters and Waterman in their book *In Search of Excellence*. Detailed development tasks are considered according to the schema advanced by Crawford in his book *New Products Management*.

Published research findings have revealed that many factors influence product innovation (or development) success. The long list of factors results from analytical and empirical research undertaken from the vantage point of four main analytical perspectives. First, from considering the market and operating environment of the firm; second, from considering the actions or attributes of the firm as a whole; third, from considering the group of people within a firm involved in development work; and fourth, from considering particular individuals who are or ought to be involved. Each resulting set of factors provides the manager with insights. However, when the basis of the analytical perspective is not stated clearly, the mix of factors frequently presents a confusing picture. Further, some analysts do not state clearly whether they are speaking about project (individual product) success or whether they are addressing program success.

In this article we use and build on the McKinsey 7 Ss framework popularized by Peters and Waterman [60] to review factors that affect success at the program level. The aim is to help managers in manufacturing businesses to check what has been

Johne, F. Axel and Patricia A. Snelson, (1988), "Success Factors in Product Innovation: A Selective Review of the Literature," *Journal of Product Innovation Management*, 5(2), (June), 114–128.

F. Axel Johne, The City University Business School, Frobisher Crescent, Barbican Centre, London, EC2Y 8HB United Kingdom.

written recently about factors over which they have direct control when aiming to develop new products more efficiently and quickly. Accordingly, we focus on internal or endogenous factors.

On their own, endogenous factors cannot account for success or lack of it in the case of individual projects, nor for program success. This is because success will be determined also by exogenous factors over which managers have little or no control, such as, for example, a sudden downturn in economic activity or an unexpected competitive reaction that may cause sales of a new product to be much lower than anticipated. However, even accepting that they have limited control over exogenous factors, managers can increase the chances of launching new products successfully by ensuring that development work is undertaken efficiently. So, at the risk of repetition, we will concentrate in this review on factors that have been shown to be necessary for efficient and speedy in-house product development, even though these factors are unlikely on their own to be sufficient to ensure success for each and every new product launch.

The following key questions arise in managing product innovation.

- How quickly do existing product lines need to be replaced by newer ones and can this decision be planned?
- How quickly do new products need to be developed; should the emphasis be on undertaking the needed tasks in parallel or in series? (Undertaking the tasks sequentially is usually cheaper but usually takes longer.)
- If some responsibility for product development is delegated by the chief executive of a business, how much authority is also to be delegated?
- What should be the composition and seniority of teams set up to manage and progress development projects?
- What specialist skills are needed?

Before surveying what the published literature has to offer in answer to this sort of specific question, it is important to reflect on the different types of product innovation open to a manufacturing business. Broadly, there are three: (1) developments of existing product lines (i.e., old product development); (2) developments of new product lines in areas of current technological expertise (i.e., new product development based on known technology) and (3) developments of a new product lines in areas in which a business has little or no technological expertise (i.e., new product development based on new technology).

In this article we confine ourselves to old product development and also to the development of new product lines based on technology in which the business is already skilled. In other words, the sort of bread-and-butter type of developments that can keep a business competitive in the face of market change. Success in these types of product developments can, of course, involve more than improving technical performance capabilities. It might involve quite the opposite, as is illustrated by the recent launch of new microprocessor controlled products, many of which have entered a more mature phase in their life cycle. The British firm Amstrad, for example, in the early 1980s developed new lower-specification word processors targeted at clearly identified markets and has sold these successfully using a penetration pricing policy.

While incremental market-led product innovation is insufficient and, indeed, even dangerous when a major technological leap occurs, it is important on two main counts: first, because continual in-house product development is often an effective competitive weapon during the period in which a technology matures; second, because streamlined procedures aimed at staying abreast of product developments based on existing technology can help alert a business in good time to threats and opportunities associated with the shift to a new technological plateau.

WHAT DO WE MEAN BY PRODUCT DEVELOPMENT SUCCESS?

Most empirical investigations have measured factors associated with success at the project level [21, 24, 51, 55, 67, 69, 80]. Far fewer have set out to measure factors specifically associated with success at the program level. The difference between these two measures of success is important. Gluck and Foster [35] showed long ago that it is all too easy to claim short-run success for individual new product developments, particularly when these are of a low-risk nature, while jeopardizing the long-run future of a business.

As far as program success is concerned Cooper [19] has identified three main measures: (1) *relative track record,* which is the proportion of successful developments as opposed to those killed before launch; (2) *relative impact,* which is the extent to which product developments account for a certain proportion of current sales and profits, and (3) *relative performance* in terms of the strategic success of the product innovation program.

In this review of the literature we concentrate on relative impact as the criterion for product development success. This particular measure reflects the ability of a business to enhance its existing products and to develop new product lines. The measure is of great importance for managers competing in fast-moving product markets because studying its determinants can provide insights into: (1) procedures aimed at growing a business organically, (2) how the needed tasks can be undertaken efficiently so that a high proportion of current sales stem from enhanced or new products, and (3) how the needed tasks can be undertaken speedily, that is to say, as fast as or faster than competitors.

While the impact measure of program success is concerned with important aspects of efficiency in product development, it needs to be stressed that it is an incomplete and imperfect measure. It is incomplete because it considers only one of three important aspects of program performance as has been explained. It is imperfect because high impact can be achieved by many new products or by one or more fluke new products, which after introduction happen to account for a high proportion of company sales. We must emphasize that our review does not address factors underlying success in occasional one-off big bang product developments. The task we have set ourselves in this selective review is to highlight factors that contribute to success (after launch) of the sort of regular product developments that need to be undertaken by businesses that compete in fast-moving market environments.

THE ELEMENTS OF EFFICIENT PRODUCT DEVELOPMENT

Many writers have stressed that the development of new products cannot be divorced from the management of existing products [3, 27, 70]. After all, a major question that needs to be addressed by managers is whether to invest in product development as opposed to improving the efficiency of on-going operations. Some analysts have gone further: they suggest that the management of new products can usefully be viewed as an extension of the management of existing products [91]. If one accepts these arguments then the factors that determine efficiency in managing an existing business will be broadly similar to those underlying efficiency in product development.

There are available now comprehensive analytical schemas or checklists of factors that allow examination of efficient management practice. Perhaps the best known of these schemas is the McKinsey 7 Ss framework [60]. This framework has the advantage of parsimony: efficiency factors are encompassed under only seven headings all of which are readily understood by and meaningful to practitioners. They are summarized in Table 23-1.

TABLE 23-1   A Framework for Organizational Analysis—The 7 Ss

Skills	the distinctive capabilities of key personnel
Strategy	the plan leading to the allocation of resources
Structure	the characteristics of the organization chart
Shared values	the goals shared by organizational members
Style	the cultural style of the organization
Staff	the type of functional specialists employed
Systems	the nature of proceduralized control processes

Source: Peters and Waterman [60].

TABLE 23-2 Principal Factors Underlying Efficient Product Development in the Form of Relevant Questions

Skills	What specialist knowledge and techniques are applied for executing product development tasks?
Strategy	Is there a product development strategy that defines the sort of new products to be developed and the resources to be released for the purpose?
Structure	What type of formal organization structures are used to implement product development activities?
Shared values	Is there a shared belief in the need to pursue product development for the purpose of growing the business?
Style	Does top management provide active support for those involved in key product development tasks, or is a divide and rule management style practiced in which individual functions are left to slug it out between themselves?
Staff	What type of functional specialists are there for executing product development tasks?
Systems	What type of control and coordination mechanisms are used for executing product development tasks?

Source: Adapted from Pascale and Athos [58] and Peters and Waterman [60].

While the 7 Ss framework was developed originally to appraise the workings of a total organization, it can be applied with equal effectiveness to analyzing and enhancing understanding at the business unit level, that is to say, the level in the organization at which particular activities are actually carried out. Indeed, Crawford [26] has emphasized that product innovation is second only to corporate strategy in the way it involves all aspects and all functions of management. Table 23-2 shows how the 7 Ss framework has been adapted for the purpose of analyzing product development procedures at the business unit level.

Before moving on to consider detailed activities involved in undertaking product developments, it is necessary to reflect on the validity of invoking the McKinsey 7 Ss framework. After all, the framework is merely an analytical tool, so one cannot be confident that the relatively small number of factors in it captures the full complexity of what underlies the operations of a business. However, in just the way in which the workings of a business are complex, so are the activities involved in product development. In answer to these potential criticisms it is important to remember that the purpose of using the McKinsey framework is to help make sense of complexity rather than to understand each and every aspect of that complexity.

THE PRODUCT DEVELOPMENT SEQUENCE

An important feature of the complex product innovation process is the separate and distinct activities that need to be performed. The essentials of what is involved have been variously described; a review of the suggested steps has been provided by Saren [71]. One of the most popular conceptualizations is that provided by Crawford [26], who splits product development into the following key tasks:

1. New product planning
2. Idea generation
3. Screening and evaluation
4. Technical development
5. Market appraisal
6. Launch

The above are essential tasks. Each task will, of course, include its own set of specialist sub-activities. A useful listing of the likely span of operational subactivities is provided by Cooper and Kleinschmidt [23]:

1. Initial screening
2. Preliminary market assessment
3. Preliminary technical assessment
4. Detailed market study/market research
5. Business/financial analysis
6. Product development

7. In-house product testing
8. Customer tests of product
9. Test market/trial sell
10. Trial production
11. Precommercialization business analysis
12. Production startup
13. Market launch

It is an open question whether or to what extent operational subactivities need to be followed in step-wise sequence. Takeuchi and Nonaka [81] have argued that in the development of certain high technology products it can be advantageous to undertake activities in parallel in order to complete developments ahead of competitors. Other authors [18, 63] also show that new product development is, by its very nature, a creative process of convergent and divergent activities that requires feedback, reworking of stages and multiple approaches. These arguments call into question the validity of the sequential approach.

It is important to note that Cooper and Kleinschmidt [23] have found that project success and completeness of the development process are correlated. This is an important finding because it means that despite the possible need to undertake some subactivities in a nonsequential way, each will nonetheless have to be undertaken to a minimum level of acceptability. In this connection recent evidence collected by Moore [53] indicates an increasing use of formal product development procedures. Further empirical work is urgently required in this important operational area.

Any conceptualization of the product development process needs to take cognizance of the dilemma between the requirements of practical efficiency and thoroughness. In Figure 23-1 we present our own schema for analyzing the essential

FIGURE 23-1 The Product Development Sequence

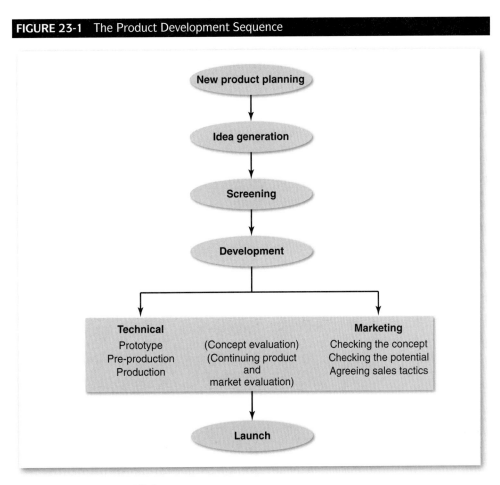

Source: Based on Crawford [26].

tasks involved. The schema is based on that originally advanced by Crawford [26]. It is our contention that efficiency in performing each of the essential tasks can and, for operational purposes, needs to be checked against each of the 7 Ss identified in Table 23-2.

Our representation of the essential tasks involved in product development shows that while tasks are initially sequential, the important development process is best viewed as a parallel set of subactivities in which the technical and marketing disciplines interact to evaluate and develop further the product concept. We start our review by considering first the skills required for each essential task.

SKILLS

For New Product Planning Purposes

Many authors stress the need for new product planning to be an intrinsic element of the corporate planning system [26, 27, 90]. Crawford [25] advocates the formulation of a new product charter as a spin-off from the corporate plan in order to give strategic direction to innovation. Such a charter needs to define the strategic arena for innovation, the goals of the new product activity and the program to achieve those goals.

However, while a rich body of knowledge has now been built up on strategic corporate planning [39, 62], specific new product planning techniques have received far less attention. More research is urgently required on the question of how different business strategy options do and might translate into new product development plans. Indeed, as Hamermesh [39] points out, one of the most fashionable corporate planning techniques, portfolio planning, does not generate adequate information for new product development planning purposes. After all, portfolio planning identifies the need for new products but does not identify which market areas offer opportunities for developing these. Dickson and Gigliero [30] show that portfolio planning advocates the spread of risk through diversification, whereas effective new product planning frequently capitalizes on the advantages of synergy with the technical, production and marketing skills that the firm already possesses [91]. Recognizing these and other practical limitations to portfolio planning, Day [27] has advocated a new product planning system which incorporates such questions as the degree to which new products should be related to existing business activities, internal growth versus acquisition and innovation versus imitation.

For Idea Generation Purposes

Studies have shown that the majority of successful product innovations arise in response to the recognition of a need of one sort or another, that is, need-pull, as opposed to the recognition of a new technological development, that is, technology-push [51, 80]. Indeed, as the work of von Hippel [92] and Parkinson [57] demonstrates, in the industrial marketplace, the customer is frequently the main source of innovative ideas. The implications are that idea generation should be rooted in the assessment of market needs.

However, several writers have stressed that while good marketing skills are an essential element of successful idea generation, these skills need to go beyond basic market research because this invariably attempts to assess and build solely on the needs of existing customers. As has been pointed out powerfully by Hayes and Abernathy [40], most customers will couch their needs in terms of the products they know, which can lead suppliers into a spiral of imitative me-too products. Tauber [82] has shown that basic market research techniques may actually inhibit product innovation because customers find it particularly difficult to articulate future demands and needs.

It is important to accept that good marketing skills alone will not pick up major developments in the technical environment. A company's technical resource cannot be left to be triggered by marketing input. As has been stressed by Brockhoff [11], Cooper [20], Schmitt [72] and Tushman and Moore [84], truly successful product innovators ensure the interplay and balance between highly skilled marketing inputs and highly skilled technical inputs. This is achieved during the initiation activities by permitting potential new product ideas to originate in the technical skill base of the firm but ensuring that they are fused with marketing input to ensure a need-pull for the new product. Similarly, feedback from the marketplace is related carefully to existing and future technological developments to ensure that the most up-to-date technological solutions are applied.

Many analysts have focused on the uses and limitations of the various idea generating techniques available to practitioners [8, 34, 88]. Their work highlights the need for multifunctional participation in the idea generation process to generate the diversity of information required to recognize gaps in product performance and derive possible solutions. Top management participation in particular is stressed by Conway and McGuinness [15].

For Screening Purposes

The process of screening and evaluating new product ideas had attracted much attention in recent product innovation literature. In this, both studies into the factors underlying successful innovation, and those that examine the innovation process itself suggest that the screening decision is of pivotal importance in the development procedure. Several studies show that managers, in actuality, use text-book–type screening models such as checklists and scoring models [22, 28]. However, marketing criteria tend to take a secondary role to financial considerations and to the level of corporate, production and technical synergy achieved with the new product proposal. The dominance of the latter factors tend to lead to the development of low-risk, incremental product updates that most nearly fit existing business activities, as was pointed out long ago by Gluck and Foster [35].

In contrast, Cooper [21] demonstrates that the screening decision should concentrate on such factors as the new product's advantage and superiority, the economic advantage to the end-user and the growth of the market to which it is being targeted. These factors are derived from earlier studies into successful innovations that particularly emphasize the importance of the market advantages that the new product offers [17].

Many writers have concentrated on the uses and limitations of the different screening models that are available [5, 7, 77]. These studies demonstrate that traditional screening models (such as scoring, checklist and benefit measurement models) do not handle adequately factors such as risk, opportunity costs, the relationship with other product developments, and nonmonetary aspects such as human and organizational behavioral influences. Souder [77] has argued that different combinations of these models should be used according to the nature of the project and its significance to the corporation. Taking up this point, Muncaster [54] stresses that the criteria in a screening model should be weighted according to their instrumental importance in meeting company objectives.

It is important to emphasize that many authors stress that the screening effort should be a process continuing throughout product development and not merely a discrete decision at one key point in the process. It is for this reason that we have considered screening and evaluation simultaneously. Cooper [21] stresses that the screening process is an important diagnostic tool that serves to isolate problem-areas in particular product proposals and their development. Similarly, Muncaster [54] suggests a venture screen that becomes an action plan to solve particular problems as the development unwinds.

For Technical Development Purposes

Studies into successful product development highlight the necessity for a reliable and technically sound product [51, 67, 80]. In developing the technical aspects of the project, many authors stress that efficiency in this process is promoted by multiple and/or competing developments. Quinn [63] demonstrates that many large innovative companies have parallel prototype programs, so that if one possible technical solution proves to be less appropriate, another can be invoked. Such parallel approaches generate the most creative technical problem-solving, despite the risk of duplicating technical effort. Similarly, Peters and Austin [59] show that the most innovative companies develop a rapport with leading edge customers. These customers are willing to test out prototype models that are derived from live use situations and to input design modification into the technical development process.

Goltz's [36] research concentrates on the new product development process from the technical point of view. He shows that the development process involves a series of activities that seek to generate a number of development options from which the optimum is chosen. He stresses that the technical development process should be guided by a clear statement of corporate and project goals and should elicit top management support.

For Marketing Development Purposes

The generation, evaluation and testing of marketing options based on market forecasting and product testing is a crucial strand of the development process. However, with the prominent exception of Shanklin and Ryans [73], relatively little attention has been focused on how and why traditional marketing techniques can most usefully be adapted to new product development. As Shanklin and Ryans demonstrate, the techniques of identifying customer needs and targeting market segments are most suited to a market situation in which the producer can identify the broad user groups for the new product. However, with truly innovative new products, there is usually no extant market demand from which to gather such information and to formulate a strategy. In this, the marketer has to adopt a more creative and entrepreneurial approach that often involves the interpretation of wider socioeconomic and industrial trends in order to identify potential applications for new products.

The subject of test marketing has attracted considerable attention in the literature [13, 46, 95]. Many of these authors stress the pitfalls of test marketing in terms of cost, competitor awareness of new product efforts, and the difficulties of analyzing and interpreting the data generated from the test market exercise. Such problems have led to an increasing interest in pre–test-marketing models such as concept testing, historical regression, laboratory tests and sales wave experiments. However, many authors stress that these models themselves have drawbacks and are applicable only to particular types of new product innovation [74, 83, 95]. More specifically, many of these techniques are dependent on historical information concerning similar previous product developments and therefore do not deal adequately with truly innovative new products.

For Launch Purposes

Considering how often poor execution of the product's launch has been cited by managers as a reason for ultimate failure [17], surprisingly little attention has been paid to the launch process in the literature. However, several authors do demonstrate that a crucial element of a successful launch is the identification of innovative customers who provide a bridgehead market from which further market penetration is developed [6, 73]. Identifying and targeting innovative business customers is made easier by the fact that those which tend to be more innovative and venturesome in their own end-user marketplace also tend to be the most innovative in adopting new products [44].

To secure deeper market penetration, marketing techniques that reduce the perceived risks of purchase by less innovative segments of the market can be utilized [73]. Such techniques center on communicating the new product's benefits and assisting laggard purchasers in the efficient usage of the product. They include trade press coverage, face-to-face demonstrations and efficient after sales service [33, 68, 73, 93]. Crawford [26] emphasizes that as market penetration is achieved, different marketing techniques should be brought into play, in particular, as market size increases: mass advertising, distribution and branding techniques. Crawford also stresses the need to develop tracking systems to monitor whether the product is meeting marketing expectations and to gather feedback on possible product modifications.

Choffray and Lilien [14] have examined the effectiveness of different launch strategies. They argue that the launch strategy should be tailored to the type of new development involved. Simple line extensions are best launched via the sales-force using a customer base with which it is already familiar, while more innovative new products require an aggressive market introduction strategy. Choffray and Lilien also stress that the new product's diffusion through the marketplace is linked strongly to the level of sales support and the overall innovative image of the company. This aspect has been developed further in the work of Wind and Mahajan [96] who speak of marketing hypes to engender interest and excitement at this stage.

The above review of the skills needed for efficient product development makes obvious that factors other than the inherent or acquired abilities of staff will contribute to success. We shall, therefore, now consider each of the other factors in the McKinsey 7 Ss framework in turn. We start with strategy and will thereafter deal with structure, shared values, style, staff and systems.

STRATEGY

Nystrom [56] has usefully categorized fundamental business strategies as being either positional—where the emphasis is on achieving efficiency with present products, or entrepreneurial—where the emphasis is on new product or new business development. As far as product development strategies are concerned a business has four main choices open to it, as is shown in Table 23-3. New product development strategy options can also be categorized using market-entry timing variables such as Ansoff and Stewart's [2] First to the Market, Follow the Leader and Me-Too alternatives which is a useful amplification of the four main strategies.

Many authors have stressed that particular product innovation strategies will suit businesses in different circumstances [2, 20, 26, 86]. Nominally, a business that wants to grow and whose products are based on technology that is still not obsolescent can choose any one of the four strategies shown in Table 23-3. But in circumstances when product technology is very fast moving many writers have stressed the potential advantages of pursuing a proactive strategy [19, 16, 32]. It has been asserted that a delay of 6 to 12 months in launching a new product in certain fast-moving sectors of the electronics components industry can mean foregoing up to 50% of the potential profits [64, 89]. If these assertions are anywhere near the truth, then there are clear advantages in choosing a proactive strategy in circumstances where a premium price can be charged early in the life of a new product. It is doubtless this phenomenon that has led analysts to assert that in conditions of rapid technological and market change regular product development forms the leading edge of business strategy.

The way that strategy choice in new product development pivots around the technological turbulence of a firm's existing and related markets suggest that technological analysis should be the fundamental drive behind product innovation strategy formulation. Indeed many authors have stressed the importance of keeping abreast of product technology to avoid the risk of missing out on those developments that revolutionize the nature of products [16, 32, 35, 94]. Moreover, as Foster [32] demonstrates, the effects of technological turbulence are not confined to industries with products of a

TABLE 23-3 Principal Organic Product Development Strategies

Proactive Strategies	*Reactive Strategies*
1. Broad-span leader undertaken for leading in several market segments	3. Reactor undertaken (sometimes very fast) in response to successful competitive launches
2. Narrow-span leader undertaken for leading in a particular market segment	4. Responder undertaken (usually with some reluctance) in response to competitive pressure

high technological content. Process technology can revolutionize the product offerings of many industries with a low technology content to their products, such as food and packaging manufacture. However, Cooper's [20] analysis of strategy performance demonstrates that a strategy that is solely technology-led does not always guarantee success. More successful are balanced strategies that seek to marry technological sophistication and marketplace needs.

Irrespective of the type of product innovation strategy selected for competitive reasons many writers have stressed the importance to a business of an explicit strategy, derived directly from corporate strategy [4, 26, 27, 86]. For example, the Booz, Allen and Hamilton [10] study found that successful businesses had not just an explicit corporate strategy but also an explicit plan as far as their whole product development program is concerned. Similarly, Crawford's [25] research identified how successful innovators develop product innovation charters that give specific direction to business unit product development activities.

It is, of course, important to emphasize that the overall product innovation strategy of a business may well have different product development components. Booz, Allen and Hamilton's [10] study found that successful businesses often assign specific strategic roles for individual new product developments. For instance, one new product development may be designated to defend market presence (an example of a reactive strategy), while another may seek to establish a new competitive edge, or even to develop a new market (an example of a proactive strategy). Different performance variables can then usefully be formulated according to the strategic role assigned to particular product developments. Cooper's [19] research also shows that companies need to decide what kind of success they want from their product innovation programs. For example, companies can look for a high percentage of sales generated by new products; low marketplace failure rate, or good performance relative to objectives or competitors. In this respect, Cooper's work is most important because it shows that each type of performance outcome is generated by a different strategy package.

STRUCTURE

The impact of corporate structure on a firm's innovative capability has become a central issue in research. The debate centers on the need for different structural forms for managing the ongoing operation on the one hand and the need for change on the other. It is widely accepted that functional and stratified organization structures are efficient for managing current business activities but less suited to effecting change. Kolodny [47] argues that matrix structures are conducive to innovation. Such structures allow for the integration of the many functional inputs required for innovation and can encourage creative problem-solving. Likewise, Hull and Hage [42] have shown that organic structures, with flat hierarchies and low-level centralization, foster a high rate of innovation.

The need for an organization structure to foster change is one reason for the current fashion for free-standing strategic business units. As has been pointed out by Hamermesh [39], this form of overall structuring has the advantage of focusing the minds of business managers on the current and future needs of customers, which can lead to the efficient development of updated and new products. Frequently SBUs in large firms whose businesses are related in some way are coordinated as far as product innovation is concerned by a central policy group or group vice-president. Such coordination has the advantage of reducing the risk of duplication in technological developments and can provide the SBU with technical expertise and resources for innovation outside its nominal capability. SBUs of large conglomerates are, by contrast, often left to sink or swim, with the only possibility for help being recourse to corporate funds for expansion purposes.

Considerable attention has been given in the literature to the formal structures suited to the day-to-day management of new product development. Many writers have concentrated on the advantages and disadvantages of such organizational devices as new product development departments, managers and task groups [9, 41, 70]. A common theme in this analytical work is the recognition that different organizational mechanisms are appropriate to different types of new product development. Souder [76] shows that turbulence in the market and technological environment will determine the nature of the task group mechanism for managing product development. Similarly Benson and Chasin [9] and McTavish [52] demonstrate that the product development organization is contingent on the size of the firm and the similarity of its product lines.

Many writers have emphasized the need to keep radical new product activities shielded from those of the on-going operation. For example, as early as 1976, Cooper and Schendel [16] stressed the advantages of separating product innovation activities organizationally from on-going activities. The exigencies of the current operation can easily eclipse the longer-term and more complex task of innovation unless managers are released full-time to address new product development. Quinn [63] stresses the importance of establishing separate organizational task groups to by-pass the inevitable bureaucracy of the existing organization. Moreover, new product development requires different skills and talents from those of managing existing business. Acceptance of this philosophy has led some businesses to establish new product managers to work alongside existing product managers. For more important product developments, Smale [75] argues for the establishment of separate business teams.

While separating product innovation activities from the mainstream organization provides tangible benefits, it also creates new problems of coordination and control. Tushman and Nadler [85] emphasize that innovating organizations utilize linking mechanisms (committees, central policy groups, etc.) that ensure that the different components of the organization are coordinated into a workable whole.

While the importance of addressing particular tasks efficiently is widely acknowledged, organizational devices such as task groups set up on a temporary basis for the purpose of pursuing particular developments are difficult to show on a formal organization chart. This has led certain analysts to place less emphasis on formal structure as an important factor determining success in product innovation in favor of newer free forms of structuring where the emphasis is on shared values [48]. Specific newer organizational forms that aim for the advantages of small business within a large firm have been popularized by Burgelman [12] and by Pinchott [61].

Moreover, as far as the organization of business units is concerned, the problem is that formal structure reflects only the trappings and not the substance of what is intended to happen. As is well known, how an organization actually functions may be quite different from what is portrayed in its organization chart. For example, a business may have appointed a new products manager with formal responsibility for product development, yet the chief executive may permit that manager very little authority to act independently without referring back constantly to the strategic apex. True, the lateral position of the new products manager on the organization chart will give some indication of his likely authority, but this is by no means certain because of hidden factors that concern operating norms and management style.

SHARED VALUES

Many writers have stressed that a prerequisite for successful product development is the acceptance at all levels of an organization of the need for change [65, 78, 85]. After all, most product development activities are disruptive of on-going activities and are therefore likely to meet resistance within the mainstream organization. Abernathy and Wayne [1] report that neither R&D nor marketing can successfully follow an innovative program if the rest of the organization's work is concerned with cost minimization. Many studies have cited the part played by key individuals in product development, people such as product managers, new product managers, technical champions, executive champions and the like [50, 51, 66, 68, 78, 80]. The implication is that without their strong personal commitment to and enthusiastic and sometimes bloody-minded support for an innovation, many new product developments would not have materialized in firms where the values for change were not fully shared. After all, for a business to rely on a few exceptional individuals to force change through a resisting organizational culture is a high-risk approach where much is left to chance and the personalities involved.

It is difficult for analysts to grapple with issues that deal with the more intangible aspects of an organization such as culture and atmosphere. However, it is clear that it is precisely these factors that distinguish successful innovator firms from the less successful. As Booz, Allen and Hamilton report [10], successful innovators have an operating philosophy that incorporates a commitment to growth through new product development. They point out that the work of new product task groups and individuals can be nullified if other areas of an organization do not accept the validity of their work.

Inculcating an acceptance of change within an organization is a long and complex process and is likely to vary according to the organization's history, existing beliefs and management background. Many studies have shown that an innovating culture is fostered by an openness and interchange between different units and functions operating at all levels of the organization [37, 81, 85]. Such interchange is promoted by a number of different policies and operating norms, including staff training in the main functions [81] and cross-functional job design and rotation [85]. Experience in different functions fosters creativity by inculcating multiple perspectives in the approach to work and facilitates effective cooperation in managing innovation where different functions and personalities have to be brought together. Highly innovative organizations display diverse and informal communication networks both within their internal and external environments [33, 65, 85] that bring a wider understanding of the changing market and industrial scene.

The innovating culture of the organization can be supported by tangible symbols such as mission statements [26] and the elevation of new product development as a central tenet of corporate strategy. Similarly, Souder [78] argues that entrepreneurial behavior can be encouraged by appropriate tangible rewards for change agents within an organization.

STYLE

All recent major studies into product innovation management have shown that a crucial factor in bringing a new product to the marketplace successfully is top management support [10, 32, 33, 51, 68]. Conversely, top management isolation from a project and preoccupation with short-term business performance is characteristic of failed innovation [63]. Interestingly, Maidique and Zirger [51] discovered that general managers did not think their support was important in the successful execution of innovative projects, while functional line managers stressed the significance of top management backing.

Rothwell [68] argues that top managers need to have an open, imaginative and creative management style to encourage middle management to function effectively in product innovation. Booz, Allen and Hamilton [10] argue that top management of innovating firms provide a supportive environment in which risk-taking and experimentation are encouraged. Considering its crucial role, surprisingly little attention has been given to the precise characteristics of the leadership style most appropriate to and supportive of innovation.

Such top management support is not a matter of direct hands-on control over projects; indeed, studies have shown that over-meddling by top management actually delays and upsets the innovation process [10, 63, 69]. Takeuchi and Nonaka [81] argue that top management should exert a subtle control over innovation. Top management should set the broad goals for innovation but give the organization's change agent or task group freedom to operate how they wish in respect of fulfilling these goals. Similarly, Souder's [78] research shows that top management encouragement of entrepreneurial behavior involves endowing change agents with a formal license and clearly defined discretionary powers to carry out their work.

Top management's role in innovation would appear to center on inculcating an acceptance of change within the organization and determining the strategic direction for change and then openly to promote and encourage the efforts of the change agents

[50]. In this, top managers particularly need to support risk-taking and to tolerate mistakes that inevitably result from it. Indeed, as Tushman and Nadler [85] show, the top management's role in the innovation process should be one of envisioning, energizing and enabling the innovation program.

STAFF

The type of staff and functional specialists needed to execute new product developments successfully has been treated only obliquely in the literature. However, the nature of the roles individuals adopt and the breadth of functional specialism applied to the innovation task can be identified as two central issues in the staffing of the innovation process.

Roberts [66] identifies key staff roles that must be fulfilled if innovative ideas are to be generated and developed: a creative scientist is needed to originate the idea, while an entrepreneur and project manager are needed to promote respectively and coordinate the development of the product. The SPRU [80] study found that the existence of various types of innovator roles discriminated between successful and unsuccessful innovations. A technical innovator (who originates the concept), a business innovator (who promotes the project from a senior level in the organization) and a product champion (who actively supports the project's progress through its critical stages), were all present in successful projects. Takeuchi and Nonaka [81] show that firms that are successful at innovation reassign individuals who have been key agents of change in previous developments to new projects. Through the process of osmosis the firm transfers and accumulates experience in managing product innovation.

The psychological qualities of the individuals who fill key roles in the innovation process is a largely unresearched area. However, as Roberts [58] has argued, different talents and types of people are likely to be needed to fulfill these different roles. Kanter [45] describes people who lead innovation in an organization as change masters. These have the ability to cope with uncertainty and to think in a kaleidoscope way, using new angles and perspectives on existing business problems. Such change masters also tend to be participative managers who are good at team building and generating commitment for a project. Characteristically, individuals who are agents of change within an organization do not tend to adopt the psyche of one particular functional specialism. Takeuchi and Nonaka [81] show that some Japanese firms encourage certain individuals to adopt a multifunctional perspective by providing these with basic training in all functional skills.

Many studies stress that the organization mechanism or task group charged with innovation should be a composition of different functional specialists [9, 26, 80]. Similarly, Cooper [18] shows that the new product development process should be a vehicle for multifunctional cooperation and coordination. Involving many functional specialists in the innovation process fosters the diversity of inputs required for creative new product development and builds cross-functional commitment for a project. Not only do marketing and R&D need to be involved from the project's initiation, but the design, manufacturing and service arms of the firm do also [26, 33].

SYSTEMS

There is wide recognition in the literature of the importance of effective integration between the separate functional inputs required during the product innovation process. Most recent research has focused on the R&D/marketing interface. For example, Gupta, Raj and Wilemon [38] have identified 19 key areas where integration is important, spanning from the setting of product development objectives to post-launch feedback from customers.

Souder [79] found that in many firms power and prestige imbalances arise between the R&D and marketing functions, stemming from differentials in decision-making prerogatives, budgetary powers and discretionary spending authorities. When severe disharmony occurred it was organizationally disruptive, requiring much time for moderating disputes. Not surprisingly, product development failure rates were found to be higher under the severe disharmony state.

Gupta, Raj and Wilemon [38] report that despite the wide recognition of the importance of R&D/marketing integration, high technology firms frequently lack a systematic approach to this problem. The biggest barrier to achieving effective integration is, of course, lack of communication. While effective communication between R&D and marketing personnel is important throughout the product innovation process, its importance during the development phase is critically important because cooperation is often required on a daily basis.

The type of coordination and control suited for achieving integration during the product innovation process has long been the subject of conjecture. The debate centers on the tension between the necessity to formalize the innovation task within the firm for efficiency and the advantages of keeping the process open and flexible to promote creativity. Many authors stress that the innovation process, by its very nature, is not conducive to formalized procedures and control [37, 63, 65]. Formal control tends to stifle creativity and trial-and-error experimentation, which are essential elements of innovation. On the other hand, leaving the innovation efforts of the organization to develop in a lopsided way is likely to be insufficient given the cost and complexity of the innovation process. A successful new product development program needs to be managed and controlled so that a stream of new products are launched into the marketplace at the right time to counter competitive threats and to ensure the firm's survival and growth [41].

Two studies have demonstrated how successful innovators have come to terms with the necessity for both formality and flexibility. In a study of experienced and less experienced product innovators, Johne [43] shows how experienced innovators apply largely informal and non-standardized procedures in the initiation phase of the innovation process. In this, the tasks of idea generation, screening and concept development are carried out in a flexible way, promoting creative problem-solving and feedback. However, once the product proposition is crystallized, more formal and rigid controls are exercised as the development reaches its prelaunch and launch stages. Here tight coordination and control are necessary in order to time the launch into the marketplace successfully.

In their study of Japanese innovators, Takeuchi and Nonaka [81] show how project teams are left to create their own mode of operation within the broad context of the firm's overall goals. Once procedures developed in this way have proved to be successful, they become standardized in the firm's repertoire of project control devices. Such standardization is only instituted for procedures that are not project-specific. In other words, there is a recognition that some controls are only successful and conducive to innovation management in particular circumstances.

Many authors have focused on the uses and limitations of the various project management techniques that have been developed to cope with the control and coordination of complex projects [29, 31, 49, 87]. From these studies it is clear that such techniques as PERT and CPM enjoy only a relatively low level of use in product development. R&D managers are reported as perceiving their operating environment as being unique and therefore not amenable to generic management science models [49]. Where project management techniques have been used, they have frequently proved to be cumbersome and unwieldly, in some instances causing delay and inefficiency in a project's development.

CONCLUSION

In this review it has been our intention to provide students of product innovation, particularly practicing managers, with a roadmap through the many factors that influence success. We have chosen to concentrate on the determinants of program success and have confined ourselves to high impact success achieved with bread-and-butter types of product developments. The decision to focus on the likely determinants of this type of product innovation success is forced upon us by space limitations. To have attempted to address all or most aspects of success, even at the program level, would require a book. We hope, however, within these necessary limitations, to have provided managers with insights based on recent analytical and empirical enquiries that will help them formulate answers to the many and oftentimes confusing questions that surround efficient and speedy product development.

The authors wish to acknowledge the financial assistance provided by the Economic and Social Research Council, London, England for a study of product innovation management practices in U.S. and British firms of which this article represents the initial review of the published literature. They also wish to thank two anonymous *JPIM* reviewers of the original draft for their helpful comments and advice.

About the Authors

Frederick (Axel) Johne is Director of the Innovation Research Unit at the City University Business School, London, England. He received his Ph.D. in marketing from Strathclyde University, Scotland. His teaching and research interests are in the area of innovation management in established firms. Prior to entering academic work he was engaged in product management and research with Imperial Chemical Industries PLC in Europe. His book, *Industrial Product Innovation* (New York: Nichols; London: Croom Helm), received the 1986 International Award from the European Association of Marketing and Sales Experts, Geneva.

Patricia A. Snelson is currently Research Fellow in the Innovation Research Unit. She received her MBA, specializing in marketing, from the City University Business School, London, England. She is a doctoral candidate working in the area of product innovation management. Prior to entering academic work she was engaged as a marketing manager with the British Post Office.

References

1. Abernathy, W. J. and Wayne, K. Limits of the learning curve. *Harvard Business Review.* 52:109–119 (September–October 1974).

2. Ansoff, H. I. and Stewart, J. M. Strategies for a technology based business. *Harvard Business Review.* 45:71–83 (November–December 1967).

3. Avlonitis, G. J. The product elimination decision and strategies. *Industrial Marketing Management.* 12:31–43 (1983).

4. Ayal, I. and Rothberg, R. G. Strategic control of R&D resource allocations in diversified businesses. *Journal of Product Innovation Management.* 3:238–250 (1986).

5. Baker, K. J. and Albaum, G. S. Modelling new product screening decisions. *Journal of Product Innovation Management.* 3:32–39 (1986).

6. Baker, M. J. *Marketing New Industrial Products.* London: MacMillan, 1975.

7. Baker, N. R. and Freeland, J. R. Recent advances in R&D benefit measurement and project selection methods. *Management Science.* 20:1164–1175 (June 1975).

8. Baker, N. R., Winkofsky, E. P., Langmeyer, L. and Sweeney, D. J. Idea generation: A procrustian bed of variables, hypotheses and implications. In *Management of Research and Innovation,* Dean, B. V. and J. L. Goldhar (eds.). New York: North Holland, 1980, pp. 30–51.

9. Benson, G. and Chasin, J. *The Structure of New Product Organization.* New York: AMACOM, 1976.

10. Booz, Allen and Hamilton. *New Products Management for the 1980s.* New York: Booz, Allen and Hamilton, 1982.

11. Brockhoff, K. *Produktpolitik.* Stuttgart/New York: Gustav Fischer Verlag, 1981.

12. Burgelman, R. A. Designs for corporate entrepreneurship in established firms. In *Strategy and Organization–a West Coast Perspective.* Carroll, G. and Vogel, D. (eds.) Boston, Massachusetts: Pitman, 1984, pp. 145–157.

13. Cadbury, N. D. When, where and how to test market. *Harvard Business Review* 53:96–105 (May–June 1975).

14. Choffray, J. M. and Lilien, G. L. Strategies behind the successful industrial product launch. *Business Marketing* 69:85–94 (November 1984).

15. Conway, H. A. and Mc Guinness, N. W. Idea generation in technology-based firms. *Journal of Product Innovation Management,* 3:276–291 (1986).

16. Cooper, A. C. and Schendel, D. Strategic responses to technological threats. *Business Horizons* 19:61–69 (February 1976).

17. Cooper, R. G. The dimensions of industrial new product success and failure. *Journal of Marketing.* 43:93–103 (Summer 1979).

18. Cooper, R. G. A process model for industrial new product development. *IEEE Transactions in Engineering Management* EM-30. 1:2–11 (February 1983).

19. Cooper, R. G. How new product strategies impact on performance. *Journal of Product Innovation Management.* 1:5–18 (1984).

20. Cooper, R. G. New product strategies: what distinguishes top performers? *Journal of Product Innovation Management.* 1:151–164 (1984).

21. Cooper, R. G. Selecting winning new product projects: Using the NewProd system. *Journal of Product Innovation Management.* 2:34–44 (March 1985).

22. Cooper, R. G. and Ulrike de Bretani Criteria for screening new industrial products. *Industrial Marketing Management.* 13:149–156 (1984).

23. Cooper, R. G. and Kleinschmidt, E. J. An investigation into the new product process: steps, deficiencies, impact. *Journal of Product Innovation Management.* 3:71–85 (1986).

24. Cooper, R. G. and Kleinschmidt, E. J. New products: What separates winners from losers? *Journal of Product Innovation Management.* 4:169–184 (1987).

25. Crawford, C. M. Defining the charter for product innovation. *Sloan Management Review* 22:3–12 (Fall 1980).

26. Crawford, C. M. *New Products Management.* Homewood, Illinois: Richard D. Irwin, 1983.

27. Day, G. S. A strategic perspective on product planning. *Journal of Contemporary Business* 4:1–34 (Spring 1975).

28. de Bretani, Ulrike. Do firms need a custom-designed new product screening model? *Journal of Product Innovation Management* 3:108–119 (1986).

29. Dean, B. V. and Chaudhuri, A. K. Project scheduling: A critical review. In: *Management of Research and Innovation.* Dean, B. V. and J. L. Goldhar (eds.). New York: North Holland, 1980, pp. 215–233.

30. Dickson, P. R. and Gigliero, J. J. Missing-the-boat and sinking-the-boat: A conceptual model of entrepreneurial risk. *Journal of Marketing* 50:58–70 (July 1986).

31. Dunne, E. J. How six management techniques are used. *Research Management* 26:35–40 (March–April 1983).

32. Foster, R. N. *Innovation: The Attacker's Advantage.* London: MacMillan, 1986.

33. Gardiner, P. and Rothwell, R. *Innovation: A Study of the Problems and Benefits of Product Innovation.* London: Design Council, 1985.

34. Geschka, H. Creativity techniques in product planning and development: A view from West Germany. *R&D Management.* 13:169–183 (1983).

35. Gluck, F. W. and Foster, R. N. Managing technological change: A box of cigars for Brad. *Harvard Business Review* 53:139–150 (September–October 1975).

36. Goltz, G. E. A guide to development. *R&D Management.* 16:243–249 (1986).

37. Gresov, C. Designing organizations to innovate and implement: Using two dilemmas to create a solution. *Columbia Journal of World Business* 19:63–67 (Winter 1984).

38. Gupta, A. K., Raj, S. P. and Wilemon, D. L. R&D and marketing dialogue in high-tech firms. *Industrial Marketing Management* 14:289–300 (1985).

39. Hamermesh, R. G. Making planning strategic. *Harvard Business Review* 64:115–120 (July–August 1986).

40. Hayes, R. H. and Abernathy, W. J. Managing our way to economic decline. *Harvard Business Review.* 58:67–77 (July–August 1980).

41. Hopkins, D. S. The roles of project teams and venture groups in new product development. *Research Management.* 18:7–12 (January 1975).

42. Hull, F. and Hage, J. Organizing for innovation: beyond Burns and Stalker's organic type. *Sociology.* 16:563–577 (1982).

43. Johne, F. A. How experienced product innovators organize. *Journal of Product Innovation Management.* 1: 210–223 (December 1984).

24

A MODEL OF NEW PRODUCT DEVELOPMENT: AN EMPIRICAL TEST

Billie Jo Zirger

Department of Industrial Engineering and Engineering Management, Stanford University, Stanford, California 94305

Modesto A. Maidique

Florida International University, University Park, Miami, Florida 33199

This paper reports on the culmination of a four-year study of high technology product innovation. During the course of this research, we examined over 330 new products in the electronics industry in order to better understand the factors that differentiated successful from unsuccessful product development efforts.

This paper presents the conclusions from the final phase of the research. In this study we empirically test a model of product development that incorporates our findings from the earlier exploratory survey and case study phases of our research. The model identifies the critical organizational subunits, development activities and communication channels that influence product outcome, as well as, external factors such as characteristics of the product and the competitive environment.

Our findings suggest the following key factors affect product outcome: (1) the quality of the R&D organization, (2) the technical performance of the product, (3) the product's value to the customer, (4) the synergy of the new product with the firm's existing competences, and (5) management support during the product development and introduction processes. Also important but less significant were the (6) competence of the marketing and manufacturing organizations and market factors, such as the (7) competitiveness and the (8) size and rate of growth of the target market.

(PRODUCT DEVELOPMENT PROCESS; PRODUCT SUCCESSES; INNOVATION PROCESS; PRODUCT INTRODUCTIONS)

INTRODUCTION

Success in product development is a critical management issue for the modern firm, especially those in technology driven industries. Clearer understanding of the factors that drive product outcome can help a firm focus valuable R&D resources, better

Zirger, Billie Jo and Modesto A. Maidique, (1990), "A Model of New Product Development: An Empirical Test," *Management Science,* 36(7), (July), 867–884. Courtesy of The Institute of Operations Research and the Management Sciences (INFORMS), 7240 Parkway Drive, Suite 310, Hanover, MD 21076 USA.

utilize resources dedicated to the product delivery process and increase the market demand for a firm's new products.

Research has shown that new product introductions are vital to most manufacturing firms' growth and prosperity. A Booz, Allen and Hamilton study of over 700 Fortune 1000 companies estimated that new products would provide over 30 percent of these firm's profits during a five-year period from 1981–1986. For technology driven industries such as the information processing and instruments and controls industries, the contribution to profits of new products was over 40 percent. The same study suggested that the number of new products introduced by these firms were expected to double compared to the previous five-year period (Booz Allen & Hamilton 1982).

This paper reports on the culmination of a four-year study of high technology product innovation. During the course of this research, we examined over 330 new products in the electronics industry in order to understand the factors that differentiated successful from unsuccessful product development efforts. In this final phase of the research, we empirically test a model of product development that incorporates our findings from the earlier exploratory survey and case study phases of our research (Maidique and Zirger 1984). The model identifies the critical organizational subunits, development activities and communication channels that influence product outcome, as well as such external factors as characteristics of the product and the competitive environment. In the first section of the paper, we briefly review prior research on new product development emphasizing those studies that have compared product successes and failures.

R&D IN NEW PRODUCT DEVELOPMENT

New product development has been studied using several methodologies. Case studies of the development of specific new products constitute the earliest research (Morison 1966, Sorenson 1971, Baruch and Kiser 1973, Baruch and Barbour 1971, 1972, Rosenbloom 1976). This early research provided detailed descriptions of each phase of the development process, but lacked the statistical validity of a large, systematic sample study. Thus, researchers began to study larger samples, usually focusing on groups of either successful or alternatively unsuccessful products.

One of the earliest studies of new product successes was Myers' and Marquis' (1969) (Marquis 1969) landmark study of 567 product and process innovations. These innovations had been developed by 121 firms representing five manufacturing industries. Their most important finding, the importance of identifying and understanding the user's needs, has been confirmed by numerous researchers in the subsequent studies. New products were more successful if they were designed to satisfy a perceived need than if they were developed to simply take advantage of a new technology.

Another key finding of the Myers and Marquis study was the importance of organizational communication, both internal and external. According to their study, information generated and diffused internally represented a major portion of the information required to develop the innovations. This finding suggests the need for strong interfaces between the functional groups, particularly between R&D and marketing.

Other researchers have focused on product failure as the unit of analysis. Explaining the failure of new products has been the focus of several studies including the Conference Board study of new U.S. products (Hopkins 1980) and Cooper's (1975) examination of 114 Canadian industrial product failures from 66 industrial firms. These two studies identified the principal causes for failure as ineffective product marketing and poor market research. They also identified other marketing problems such as inadequate assessment of market potential, poor understanding of competitor's strengths and weaknesses, and inaccurate product pricing. Apart from these studies' focus on failure, a common denominator for success also emerged from this stream of research. Successful innovation was found to be strongly influenced by the firm's understanding of its "customers' needs" and its effectiveness in marketing.

Notwithstanding the important insights generated by these studies, conclusions reached by the isolated study of successes or failure must be viewed as tentative. A study that focuses on only successful or only unsuccessful new products will provide a list of influencing factors characteristic of the type of products in the sample. Nonetheless, if several of the influencing factors are common to both the success and failure samples, this approach will not provide a means to differentiate successful from unsuccessful product development.

Therefore, studies of either successes or failures may not provide a full understanding of the differences in the product development processes, internal organizational structure, firm strategies, external environments, or other factors that may influence a product's outcome. For example, if a factor is present in a success group and not in a failure group while all other study variables are constant, we can then suggest that this factor differentiates successful product development from an unsuccessful effort. Such concerns about methodology led researchers to use an approach that directly compared product successes and product failures.

The Scientific Activity Predictor from Patterns of Heuristic Origins (SAPPHO) study, the first comparative study of product success and failure, was conducted during the early seventies in the United Kingdom (Rothwell et al. 1974, Rothwell 1972). The SAPPHO investigators identified 43 product success and failure pairs in the chemical and scientific instruments industries. The products were selected from two unrelated industries in order to identify possible industry effects. The SAPPHO study concluded that product success was primarily related to the following five factors:

1. understanding of user needs,
2. attention to marketing and publicity,
3. efficiency of development,
4. effective use of outside technology and external scientific communication, and
5. seniority and authority of the managers' responsible for the development of the product (Rothwell et al. 1974, Rothwell 1972).

The SAPPHO findings confirmed three of prior researchers' findings, and introduced two new success factors both of which were related to characteristics of the organization and the team that developed the successful products. First, R&D teams must be efficient and effective in their development efforts. R&D efficiency and effectiveness was defined as the ability to (1) identify product defects prior to the product launch, (2) assess the feasibility of projects and select the most promising ones, (3) appropriately allocate both capital and labor resources, and (4) efficiently utilize the available resources. The second new factor, one that was also confirmed in several subsequent studies, was the need for an executive champion, a senior member of the firm with power and authority who fought for the product. Researchers have suggested that product champions facilitate the allocation of resources to the development effort, and stimulate cooperation and communication between the functional groups, other important factors in product success.

Other studies of success and failure products in European and Japanese markets followed SAPPHO. A study of Hungarian electronics products by Szakasits (1974) confirmed the SAPPHO findings and emphasized communication, technical competence and proficiency market understanding and synergy, product planning and management support. Kulvik's (1977) study in Finland also had similar results to the SAPPHO conclusions. A study of West German products by Gerstenfeld (1976) found that market pull products were more successful than technology push, and that monitoring the product development process was essential to ensure minimal resources were allocated to project failures. Finally, Utterback et al. (1976) in his study of European and Japanese products emphasized the importance of a competitive advantage, patent protection, regulatory constraints and project urgency.

A study of 103 projects developed by U.S. industrial firms was conducted by Rubenstein et al. (1976). This research focused on the innovation process at the project level. They concluded internal management factors were primary influences on product success and that government policies, actions and regulations were secondary. They suggested organizations concentrate on improving communication, particularly between the functional groups, and upgrade data collection, analysis and decision making processes for projects.

More recently, a major study of 200 product innovations, Project NewProd, was conducted in Canada by Robert Cooper (Summer 1979) (Cooper 1979). In his research Cooper studied pairs of product successes and failures that had been developed by the same firm and for the same industry. The SAPPHO study, by comparison, kept the industry constant, but not the firm for each product pair. Cooper's methodology allowed him to identify differences relating to characteristics of the organization and the project team.

The NewProd data were collected using a mailed survey sent to a senior person in the firm, usually the general manager. The respondent was asked to rate the successful and failed products along 77 dimensions that described the environment, the organization, and characteristics of the development process. Cooper found that the most critical determinants of new product success were:

1. having a product unique or superior in the eyes of the customer,
2. having marketing knowledge and proficiency,
3. having technical and production synergy and proficiency,
4. avoiding markets in which many new products are introduced,
5. being in a high need, high growth, large market,
6. avoiding pricing the product higher than competitive alternatives,
7. having marketing and managerial synergy,
8. avoiding markets which are very competitive and where customers are very satisfied,
9. avoiding products, markets, customers, and technologies which are new to the firm (Cooper 1979).

Cooper and Kleinschmidt (1987) later followed NewProd with another study of 203 Canadian product winners and losers. He concluded that the three most important success factors were:

1. product superiority which included features such as unique benefits to the customer, product quality, reduced customers' costs, product innovativeness, and providing a solution to a customer's problems,
2. project definition and "up front" activities,
3. marketing and technological synergy.

Cooper's results suggest two new dimensions of successful product development. The first is that market conditions such as a market segment's potential size and growth are positively related to successful product development programs. Cooper's market factor combines market need with market attributes such as growth and size. The role of market need or pull has also been identified by several other researchers (Marquis 1969, Rubenstein et al. 1976, Globe et al. 1973). Nonetheless, market attributes had not been previously found to be as significant. The second new dimension suggested by Cooper's study was the importance of developing a product that is technically superior and innovative. Technical superiority and uniqueness in his study is defined as a product having higher quality, unique benefits and features and one that allows the customer to reduce his costs. In addition, Cooper suggested that to succeed new products should capitalize not only on market expertises but also on R&D and production capabilities.

Cooper did not, however, test two factors that have been identified as significant by other researchers: the importance of interfaces between functional groups such as marketing and R&D, and the influence of key sponsors such as senior managers and product champions. Interfaces between the functional groups are important (Rubenstein et al. 1976, Souder and Chakrabarti 1978, Gupta et al. 1985) because they provide the mechanisms for transferring information such as customer needs and wants, product pricing points, and market timing and positioning. Myers' and Marquis's (1969) and the SAPPHO results (Rothwell 1972) referred to the need for strong internal communication. Numerous studies, including the work previously mentioned and other studies such as Rubenstein et al.'s (1976), Globe et al.'s (1973), and the Hungarian SAPPHO type study (Rothwell 1974), have confirmed the importance of sponsorship.

Remarkably, despite this considerable research foundation, the literature on new product success does not include a major comparative study of U.S. industrial products. Yet, industrial product development, especially in the research intensive industries, is of fundamental importance to the U.S. economy for several reasons. Technological innovation has been a potent factor in U.S. productivity growth during the last 50 years (Mueser 1985, Avard et al. 1982). Product life cycles are shorter in high technology firms, and for most of these firms a significant portion of their revenues are derived from new product introductions. High development costs are a third reason managers and researchers alike should study technological innovation. R&D investment for technology firms average 4%–6% of sales and may range as high as 10%–15%. Lastly, in part due to the rapidly changing nature of product and process technology, it is critical to the competitiveness of U.S. electronics firms that managers better understand the factors that influence new product success. All of these considerations provided the impetus for this research project.

A MODEL OF PRODUCT DEVELOPMENT & HYPOTHESES DEVELOPMENT

This research project began in 1982, and includes field data on over 330 electronics product successes and failures. The research is divided into three parts: two exploratory surveys (158 products), a case study validation (21 cases), and an empirical testing of our model of the factors that influence product outcome. The findings from our two exploratory surveys and the case studies were reported in two earlier articles (Maidique and Zirger 1984, 1985). The conclusions from the earlier phases of this study are important because they provide the basis for our model of the factors that influence product outcome. We found from these studies that new product success was likely to be greater under the following circumstances.

1. The firm has an in-depth understanding of its customers and the marketplace.
2. The firm markets proficiently and commits a significant amount of its resources to selling and promoting its successful products.
3. The firm's R&D is efficiently planned and well executed.
4. The firm's R&D, production and marketing functions are well coordinated.
5. The firm provides a high level of management support for the product from the development stage through its launch to the marketplace.
6. The product has a high performance to cost ratio.
7. The product benefits significantly from the firm's existing market and technology strengths.
8. The product provides a high contribution margin to the firm.
9. The market has few competing products (Maidique and Zirger 1984).

A simple listing of the critical factors necessary to develop successful new products is useful, but not a strong guide for managerial action. For this reason, we sought to move beyond this stage and create a model of the critical influences on a new product's development that could then be tested. Developing quantifiable constructs of this model and empirically testing it is the subject of this paper.

Using the findings from the earlier phases of the study (Maidique and Zirger 1984, 1985) and the research literature as a guide, we refined our model of the critical influences on the product development process. This model (Figure 24-1) is based on our interpretation of the process of new product development in a technology-based industry as a *change-producing activity that is usually blocked at key transfer points by the tendency at each stage of the process to resist change* (Lawrence 1969, Schon 1967). In the following section we explain the significant attributes of the model followed by the hypotheses we developed to test the influence of each of these attributes on product outcome.

The model describes the development process in terms of the organizational and external entities that influence product outcome. Internal to the organizational are three primary groups involved in a new product's development: R&D, manufacturing

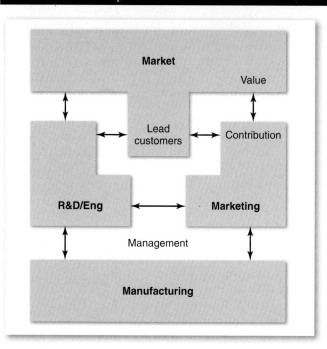

FIGURE 24-1   Critical Elements of the New Product Development Process

and marketing. Prior research indicated that three factors relating to these functional groups influenced product outcome. First, the competence of the functional groups. Product success was more likely if development was conducted by a competent and skilled R&D, manufacturing (Cooper 1987) and marketing team. Second, it was important that the development process was well-planned and capably executed (Cooper 1987). Often this included the assistance of a product champion (Rothwell et al. 1974, Rubenstein et al. 1976) who promoted the product to senior management, to other functional groups and to customers throughout the development and introduction cycle. Finally, successful development relies on strong communication links and cooperation between the functional groups (Rubenstein et al. 1976, Souder and Chakrabarti 1978, Souder 1981, Gupta 1985) in order to effectively manage the transition of the product through the various design and development stages. The implicit barrier between the functional groups is represented in the model by physical separations between the entities. Without conscious efforts by the organization to bridge these gaps, information critical to the product's form and function are likely to be lost, particularly as an organization grows in complexity and diversity. These findings led to the following hypotheses that represent the importance of competent functional groups and strong internal and external communication.

> *Hypothesis* 1. R&D competence and management is positively related to product success and negatively related to product failure.
>
> *Hypothesis* 2. Marketing and manufacturing competence and coordination is positively related to product success and negatively related to failures.

Another important attribute and one that plays an important role in overcoming these internal organizational barriers is management support (Rothwell et al. 1972, Utterback et al. 1976, Souder and Chakrabarti 1979). Management support is shown in the model as a force that pulls the functional groups together. Management impetus provides organizational support for change and assures sufficient allocation of resources. This is not to say that product champions, the focus of much prior research, are not important, especially for radical innovations (Booz Allen & Hamilton 1968, Schon 1963). But, for our sample, which was largely composed of incremental and significant enhancements, their role was secondary compared to managerial sponsorship.

Hypothesis 3. General management support of the product development effort is positively related to product success and negatively related to failure.

Understanding customers' needs was also critical to developing a product success. With indepth knowledge of their customer's problems, a firm can develop solutions that provide a significant value (Utterback et al. 1976, Cooper et al. 1987). Value can be manifested in terms of the product's cost savings, quality (Buzzell and Gale 1987), performance advantages or a combination of features. For example, one product success in our sample was priced 20% less than competitive products, and provided a three-fold performance advantage. Since value in high technology markets is often measured in terms of product performance, we also tested whether product success was more likely to occur when products were technically superior in some aspect of their performance.

Hypothesis 4. A product providing a significant value (performance to cost) to the customer is positively related to successful products and negatively related to failures.

Hypothesis 5. A technically superior product is positively related to successful outcomes and negatively related to failures.

Another one of our principal findings and that of other researchers (Cooper 1979, Souder and Chakrabarti 1979, Kulvik 1977) was that products are more likely to be successful if they build upon existing technological and market strengths. Entry into new markets or technologies generally requires the establishment of new customer/company connections (i.e., new lead customers), and if new personnel are brought in, new patterns of coordination during the product's development. Thus, the established communication networks and the coordination required in the new product development loop can be significantly disrupted by the organizational restructuring that entry into new markets and technologies generally requires (Tushman and Romanelli 1985). In addition, entering new markets or using new technologies requires that the firm develop new competencies, a process that can be riskier and more time consuming than building upon an existing base. It is for these reasons that established teams entering markets that are closely related to their organization's current businesses have the best change of succeeding with a new venture (Cooper 1979).

Hypothesis 6. Products that build upon the firm's existing market, technology and product competences are positively related to successes and negatively related to failures.

Finally, two market characteristics were found to influence product outcome. First, firms who enter markets where competition is weak have a better chance of providing a significant value to the customer. For example, in a newly created market, new entrants can pursue niche strategies by developing product enhancements that extend the applications of a product in ways no previous competitor has conceived. Also, in the early stages of a new product's development, competitors are struggling against each other to establish their product as the industry standard. Alternatively, new entrants in established markets with innovative technologies or creative approaches to solving the customer's problems often have a good chance at shaking up the market positions of existing competitors if these firms are insecure. Our earlier work (Maidique and Zirger 1984) suggested that the competitiveness of the market influenced product outcome in contrast to Cooper and Kleinschmidt's (1987) results that indicated no relationship between outcome and market competitiveness.

Hypothesis 7. Weak competitive environments are positively related to product successes and negatively related to failures.

Also products entering large and growing markets are also more likely to be winners. As the market rapidly expands, existing competitors may have difficulty ramping up to supply market needs at the quality and reliability levels the customer demands. In these situations, the strongest competitors usually focus on the market with the largest market share and/or profit potential. This leaves lucrative market niches available for others. Market expansion could also be triggered by new applications for the product or new capabilities, in many cases these innovative approaches are offered by new entrants trying to establish a foothold in the market. In contrast, Cooper and Kleinschmidt (1987) tested for market attractiveness and potential and determined it was not related to product outcome.

> *Hypothesis* 8. Markets that are large and growing are positively related to successful outcomes and negatively related to failures.

Using our model of new product development as a guide, we have presented eight hypotheses that we believe represent the key influences on new product outcome. Our next step was to test these hypotheses in a large sample study of product successes and failures. The objective of this final test and analysis was to confirm the significance of these hypotheses in influencing product outcome and determine the relative importance of each of the factors. The research methodology and the results of the test of our hypotheses follows.

RESEARCH METHODOLOGY

The unit of analysis for the study was a product pair, one success and one failure, and the sample consisted of 172 electronics products. Only products that were technically feasible and for which at least one unit has been manufactured were included in the database. Two products were selected by each company that participated in the study, one product considered to be success and one a failure. Respondents were asked to choose a pair of products that were financial extremes. The degree of a product's success and failure was measured on a ten-point scale ranging from a major financial loss to a major profitability contributor with financial breakeven at its midpoint. The success and failure ratings were graphed and the results are shown in Figure 24-2. In the aggregate success and failure ratings did overlap, but for any pair of products in the sample, successes were always more financially lucrative than failures. Also, the correlation between a success and a failure outcome was low, 0.05, and a *t*-test of the success and failure means indicated a significant difference ($p < 0.001$). The product success and failure pair within each company were developed within five years of each other and were introduced into the same or similar market. The sample distribution by market is as follows: (1) computer hardware, peripherals, software and related equipment (30%), (2) test, measurement and process control instruments (22%), (3) telecommunications and communication systems and equipment (16%), (4) electronic components, materials and equipment (16%), and (5) other (16%).

FIGURE 24-2 Innovation Financial Success (Percent of Total)

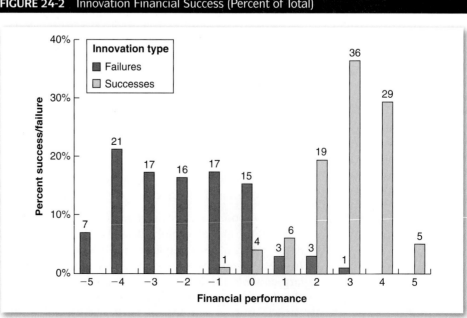

The data were collected using a survey of senior managers participating in a general management program for senior executives in electronics companies. The respondents were either general managers, presidents, or chief executive officers of their firms or functional vice-presidents of a division of a Fortune 1000 company. All the data were collected prior to the participants' participation in the program to minimize program bias. Respondent bias due to functional and educational background differences was tested, and found to be insignificant for those subgroups that were large enough to be statistically tested.

The same questionnaire was administered twice, the first time in 1983 to 33 respondents and a second in 1984 to 53 different managers resulting in 86 different product pairs. Due to the small sample size for each individual year, it was desirable to combine the two years of data into one sample. To test the likeness of the two data sets, a MANOVA test was conducted that compared the statistical similarity of the mean value for each item in the 1983 survey with the corresponding item mean value in the 1984 survey. The F significance using the Hotelling and Wilks test was 0.348 indicating no significance item difference in the two years of data. Twenty-four of the original 172 products was later excluded because of incomplete data. The final analysis included 77 successful innovations and 71 failures.

The questionnaire used for data collection was divided into three parts. The first part of the survey instrument asked for background data on the respondent and his firm or division. In the second section of the survey, we asked the respondent to select and describe two innovations, one success and one failure. Any supplementary literature such as product brochures, technical bulletins or advertisements relating to the product were collected for background purposes. The respondent was also asked to evaluate the degree of each product's success on a ten-point scale.

The third and final section of the survey consisted of 23 items (see Appendix 1) that we had determined from our previous survey (Maidique and Zirger 1984) and case study work (Maidique and Zirger 1985) and the research of others, influenced new product outcome. These items describe the basic elements of our model of the product development process as shown in Figure 24-1. Each respondent in the sample group was asked to determine to what degree both the success's and the failure's development was influenced by each item. The 23 items were each rated on a seven-point Likert-type scale with endpoints labelled strong agreement (7) and strong disagreement (1).

While the 23 items provided the foundation for our empirical test of the product development process, we felt these items could be reduced to a smaller set of underlying constructs. In order to reduce the data set, we conducted numerous SPSS exploratory factor analyses varying the extraction technique, the number of factors and the rotation methods. The factor analysis resulted in an eight-factor solution (principal components, varimax rotation). We believe the eight-factor solution provides a good description of the underlying constructs for the following reasons: (1) the factor loadings of the variables averaged more than 0.69, (2) the amount of common factor variance explained by the eight factors was 70%, (3) different factoring and rotation techniques gave us largely the same variable groupings for each factor, and (4) the variable groupings matched our intuitive conceptualization of the hypothesized constructs. All except one factor had a eigenvalue greater than one, a common rule of thumb used by practitioners. Since there is no one correct method to determine the number of factors in the data set (Kim and Mueller 1978), one factor with an eigenvalue less than one was included because of its contribution to our intuitive model. The factors and their loadings are shown in Table 24-1.

Constructs were developed from the factors. These constructs are shown in Table 24-1 and their names correspond to the factor labels determined for each factor group. The items measuring each construct are also shown in Table 24-1. For example, R&D Excellence consisted of seven measures and Product Value was measured by three items. The value for each construct was determined by calculating the numeric average of the scale values for the items in each construct. Table 24-2 shows the intercorrelations between the constructs, the reliabilities, the means and standard deviations for the constructs. One factor, management support, was described by only one variable, therefore, its construct has no reliability measure.

TABLE 24-1 Factor Analysis Results

Factor & Variable Description	*Factor Loadings*
R&D Excellence	
— Product had superior quality and reliability.	0.76
— Product was developed by a highly competent engineering organization.	0.75
— Product development process was well planned.	0.70
— Product was strongly supported by project management.	0.65
— Coordination between engineering and manufacturing was good.	0.63
— A clearly identified individual was an activist in promoting the product's development throughout the product development and the introduction cycle.	0.52
— Product was a good match with the customer's needs.	0.41
Eigenvalue: 6.5 Percent of variance: 28.3	
Marketing and Manufacturing Competence	
— Coordination between marketing and manufacturing was good.	0.74
— Product was manufactured by a highly competent manufacturing organization.	0.73
— Product was introduced by a highly competent sales and marketing organization.	0.72
Eigenvalue: 1.9 Percent of variance: 8.2	
Synergy with Existing Competences	
— Product benefitted from its closeness to the company's existing products.	0.86
— Product benefitted from its closeness to the company's existing markets.	0.77
— Product benefitted from its closeness to the company's technologies.	0.63
Eigenvalue: 1.7 Percent of variance: 7.3	
Superior Technical Performance	
— Coordination between marketing and engineering was good.	0.60
— Product had superior technical performance.	0.63
Eigenvalue: 1.5 Percent of variance: 6.7	
Large and Growing Market	
— Product was developed for a large market.	0.84
— Product was developed for a rapidly growing market.	0.77
Eigenvalue: 1.3 Percent of variance: 5.8	
General Management Support	
— Product was strongly supported by general management.	0.81
Eigenvalue: 1.3 Percent of variance: 5.6	
Weak Competitive Environment	
— Product was first to the market.	0.80
— Product was developed for a market with few strong competitors.	0.77
Eigenvalue: 1.0 Percent of variance: 4.5	
Product Value	
— Product was priced lower than competitive alternatives.	0.84
— Product provided superior benefit to cost.	0.50
— Product concept developed from frequent interactions between the product development team, introduction team, and the customers.	0.41
Eigenvalue: .87 Percent of variance: 3.8	

The first construct, R&D Excellence, consisted of seven items with a scale mean for successful products of 5.74 and a failure mean of 4.11 (Table 24-2). The Cronbach's alpha of the R&D Excellence scale was 0.83. The Marketing and Manufacturing Competence scale had a 4.85 and 4.13 mean value for successes and failures respectively, and an internal consistency measure of 0.70. The Product Value and Product Synergy

TABLE 24-2 Intercorrelations, Reliabilities, Means and Standard Deviations

	Intercorrelations and Reliabilities							
	1	*2*	*3*	*4*	*5*	*6*	*7*	*8*
1 R&D Excellence	1.00							
2 Mkt & Mfg Competence	0.50***							
3 Product Value	0.43***	0.19						
4 Technical Performance	0.64***	0.50***	0.41***					
5 Management Support	0.30***	0.18	0.16	0.36***				
6 Product Synergy	0.36***	0.29***	0.26**	0.34***	0.20			
7 Weak Competitive Env.	0.18	0.11	0.20	0.22**	0.06	0.13		
8 Large & Growing Market	0.25**	0.20	0.13	0.20	0.22	0.16	−0.08	
Reliabilities	0.83	0.70	0.52	0.67	a	0.73	0.53	0.59

**p ≤ 0.01.
***p ≤ 0.001.
aOnly one variable used in this scale.

	Successes		*Failures*		*Total Sample*	
Variable	*Mean*	*Std Dev*	*Mean*	*Std Dev*	*Mean*	*Std Dev*
R&D Excellence	5.74	0.81	4.11	1.23	4.96	1.31
Mkt & Mfg Competence	4.85	1.30	4.13	1.37	4.50	1.38
Product Value	4.87	1.13	3.72	1.30	4.32	1.34
Technical Performance	5.61	1.09	3.91	1.59	4.79	1.60
Management Support	6.20	1.18	5.20	1.76	5.70	1.57
Product Synergy	5.91	1.12	4.93	1.48	5.44	1.39
Weak Competitive Env.	5.21	1.62	4.30	1.67	4.77	1.70
Large & Growing Market	5.64	1.15	4.87	1.71	5.27	1.49

scales each had three measures and had reliability values of 0.52 and 0.73. Product Value had a success mean of 4.87 and a failure of 3.72. The Product Synergy scale had a 0.98 difference between the mean value of the success rating for the scale, 5.91, and the failure rating of 4.93. Technical performance was measured by a two-item scale with a reliability of 0.67, and the mean value of successful products, 5.61, was greater than the unsuccessful products mean by 1.7. Finally, the market descriptor scales, market size and growth and weak competitive environment, had reliability indexes of 0.59 and 0.53 respectively, and were each measured by two items. The mean value for successful products using the market size and growth scale was 5.64 and the failure mean was 4.87. The competitiveness of the environment scale was similar with a success average of 5.21 and failure of 4.30.

ANALYSIS AND RESULTS

A linear discriminant analysis was conducted, a technique that produces a discriminant function that distinguishes statistically between two groups of cases (i.e. successes and failures). It is an empirically robust technique (Efron 1975, Lachenbruch 1975, Lee and Bayus 1985) and is well suited to our study's central question, what distinguishes between successful and unsuccessful product development. Discriminant analysis has finite statistical properties, therefore, produces coefficients and *R*-square values that are readily interpretable.

The cases were grouped by product outcome, success or failure, and the discriminant function included eight variables. Wilks method was used for selecting variables for the model and their order of inclusion. The structure coefficients are shown in Table 24-3 and indicate the correlation between the discriminant function and each variable. They are used for interpreting the model because in cases where the correlation between the variables is significant (see Table 24-2), the magnitude and sign of

TABLE 24-3 Results of Hypotheses Tests Based on Multiple Discriminant Analysis

Variable Description		Structure Coefficients	Split Sample[b] Structure Coefficients
Excellent R&D Organization		0.80***	0.77***
Superior Technical Performance		0.64***	0.60***
Product Value		0.48***	0.44***
Synergy with Existing Competences		0.38***	0.48***
Management Support		0.35***	0.34**
Competent Marketing & Manufacturing		0.28**	0.27**
Weak Competitive Environment		0.28**	0.22*
Large & Growing Market		0.27**	0.16
Group Centroids:	Failure	−1.023	−1.106
	Success	0.943	0.968
Canonical Correlation		0.70	0.72
Eigenvalue:		0.978	1.100
Wilks' Lambda:		0.51**	0.48**

*$p \leq 0.05$.
**$p \leq 0.01$.
***$p \leq 0.001$.
[b]Since the percent correct prediction is overestimated due to the use of the same cases in deriving the classification function, the analysis was rerun using half the data to derive the function and the remainder to test the function's classification accuracy. (Klecka 1984, pp. 51–52.)

the standardized coefficients may be misleading. The F values for all of the variable constructs were high, and they were all highly significant ($p < 0.01$). The canonical correlation is high (0.70) indicating a strong relationship between the groups and the function, and Wilks' lambda is significant suggesting strong discrimination among the two groups (Klecka 1984).

A split sample analysis was also done to assess the extent of bias induced by using the same cases for both determining the function and the predictive accuracy for the function (Green 1978, Klecka 1984). As shown in Table 24-3, the split half sample had very similar coefficient magnitudes and rankings compared to the full sample model.

As a predictor of a success and failure outcome, the discriminant model was quite good, and correctly predicted success or failure in 88% of the *original* samples (Table 24-4). The classification accuracy was very significant based on a z statistic of 9.01 (Joy and Tollefson 1975). Similarly, the split sample predicted outcome well.

All of our individual hypotheses were supported. R&D competence (Hypothesis 1) was positively related to product success. When the R&D group was competent and the product development was well planned, coordinated and executed, the product was more likely to be financially successful. Marketing and manufacturing competence (Hypothesis 2) and Management support (Hypothesis 3) were also predictors of success. Product characteristics, Product Value (Hypothesis 4) and Technical Superiority

TABLE 24-4 Discriminant Analysis Classification Tables

Actual Group	# of Cases	(Predicted Group)		Percent Correctly Classified[c]
		Successes	Failures	
Total Sample				
Successes	77	93.5%	6.5%	87.8%[d]
Failures	71	18.3%	81.7%	
Split Sample				
Successes	37	86.5%	13.5%	83.6%
Failures	36	19.4%	80.6%	

[c]Classification accuracy, z: 9.01 ($p \leq 0.001$).
[d]Classification accuracy was computed using a z statistic (Joy and Tollefson 1985).

(Hypothesis 5) were positively related to product success. Products that did not provide a significant value to the customer and were "me-too" products were more likely to be failures in this sample. Product and market choices were also important. Firms that built upon their existing market, product and technology strengths (Hypothesis 6) were more likely to have a product success. Finally, market characteristics also predicted product outcome. Failures were more likely for products introduced into highly competitive (Hypothesis 7), and small, stagnant markets (Hypothesis 8).

DISCUSSION

Five major points arise from this study. *The first key finding is that managerial excellence is critical to product success.* Products are more likely to be successful if they are planned and implemented well. Project planning should include all phases of the development process; research, development, engineering, manufacturing and market introduction. The functional groups should interact and coordinate activities during the development process. Particularly important are the links between R&D and the other functional groups, marketing and manufacturing. One critical reason for a strong link with marketing is to ensure the firm understands user needs and effectively translates these needs into solutions for the customer. The connection with manufacturing is emphasized because of the increasing importance of efficient and effective operations, a goal that cannot be reached unless design for manufacturing is part of the product's development objectives. To ensure goals are clearly set a priori and agreed upon between the functional groups, Crawford (1984) suggested that firms negotiate a new product protocol.

Development does not have to be a linear process (Takeuchi and Nonaka 1986). Many phases of the process can overlap and personnel can move with the product to smooth the transition and communicate learnings. The process should also be regularly and formally monitored throughout the life of the project (Cooper and Kleinschmidt 1987). Cooper et al. (1985) found that product success was linked to consistent adherence to a new product process; one that included market studies, initial screening and preliminary market assessment. Note that two of the three activities they flagged were related to understanding the market. An essential part of effective product development is understanding customer needs and embodying solutions to those needs in the product.

Finally, many have found the use of product champions as important enablers of the process. Product champions are one or more individuals who build technical and financial sponsorship throughout the organization and nurture the project through development and introduction.

Our second major conclusion is that new products must provide significant value to the customer. Value can be measured in several ways. It can be superior technical performance, a characteristic of many of the successes in our sample. Value can be provided by a lower cost design, one that allows pricing the product lower than competitive alternatives or, it can also be provided by a product that provides a set of unique features. Superior product quality and reliability was another form of value for the customer. All of these measures of value, either singly or in combination, translate into a product that provides a superior benefit to cost for the customer. In order to understand the value of particular features to customers, the developing firm must have close contact between the development team and the end user. Often developing firms had frequent interactions with lead customers (Von Hippel 1986), particularly with customers who were trend setters in their industry and could provide insightful and innovative suggestions during product development.

The third primary contributor to product success is strategic focus. Firms should choose projects that build upon the firm's existing technological, marketing, and organizational competences. Related products allow firms to use and further develop existing technological competences, and take advantage of communication sources and networks both internal and external to the firm. "Sticking to your knitting" (Peters and Waterman 1982) has been a common theme in the popular general management literature. Notwithstanding this synergy benefit, we do not suggest that a firm never venture into new technical or market arenas. Without occasional ventures in new directions, the firm will soon exhaust the technical potential of current product lines particularly in rapidly changing high technology markets. It is, however, important that when new ventures are undertaken, the firm consider and perhaps minimize where possible one or more dimensions of newness.

Management commitment is also essential to product success. Without management support, the scarce staffing and capital resources necessary to develop the product are not likely to be approved. Securing the support of management is materially aided if, early in the development process, the development team can demonstrate significant market demand for their product.

A fifth and final, albeit weaker, contributor to new product success is the market environment. Products that are first to the market and experience little competition are more successful. This is consistent with our finding that technically superior, first to the market products were winners. Also, introducing products into relatively large and growing markets is more likely to result in product success. Technological leadership, however, is very risky. Innovators must have indepth customer communication and customer understanding. Technology leaders generally find that they must educate potential customers about the uses and applications of a new product. As the customer uses the new product, the developing firm must understand how customer needs change and mature, and then redesign the product accordingly. Additionally, leaders must try to establish industry standards, if they plan to be a major player in the market and lead the procession down the learning curve. Ripe, untouched markets are enticing for product developers, but entry must be carefully planned and well-executed to avoid a product failure.

CONCLUSION

During the five years of this project we have investigated over 330 new electronics products. We have conducted two exploratory surveys, numerous case studies at company sites, and successfully developed and tested a model of new product development. The findings in this paper represent our understanding of the critical components affecting the successful launch of a new high technology product. It is hoped that these findings can be a guide to further research, as well as, useful to practitioners who are managing product development programs in the ever increasingly competitive electronics market. Religious adherence to these success factors—managerial excellence, superior benefit to cost, strategic focus, managerial commitment and early entry into large and growing markets—cannot, unfortunately, ensure a firm of a new product winner. On the other hand, we are convinced that careful attention to the areas that our extensive research has identified will lead to enhanced probabilities of success for new product developers and will assist subsequent researchers in their own contributions to our field.[1]

Appendix 1. List of Study Items
1. The product development process was well planned.
2. Coordination between engineering and manufacturing was good.
3. The product was developed by a highly competent engineering organization.
4. The product was developed for a rapidly growing market.
5. The product was strongly supported by project management.
6. The product had superior technical performance.
7. The product was a good match with the customer needs.
8. The product benefitted from its closeness to the company's technologies.
9. The product was manufactured by a highly competent manufacturing organization.
10. The product was developed for a market with a few strong competitors.
11. The product was strongly supported by general management.

12. The product was priced lower than competitive alternatives.

13. The product concept developed from frequent interactions between the product development and introduction team and customers.

14. Coordination between marketing and engineering was good.

15. The product was introduced by a highly competent sales and marketing organization.

16. The product benefitted from its closeness to the company's existing markets.

17. A clearly identified individual was an activist in promoting the product's development throughout the product development and the introduction cycle.

18. Coordination between marketing and manufacturing was good.

19. The product was developed for a large market.

20. The product benefitted from its closeness to the company's existing products.

21. The product had superior quality and reliability.

22. The product provided superior benefit to cost ratio.

23. The product was first to the market.

Endnote

1. This research was funded by the Department of Industrial Engineering and Engineering Management while both authors were at Stanford University. The authors wish to thank Warren Hausman, Industrial Engineering and Engineering Management, Stanford University, for his encouragement and support during this investigation.

References

AVARD, S., V. CATTO AND M. DAVIDSON, "Technological Innovation-Key to Productivity," *Research Management,* (July 1982).

BARUCH, J. AND E. BARBOUR, *Pilkington Float Glass (A),* Harvard Business School Case Services, Boston; #9-672-069, 1971.

———— AND ————, *Pilkington Float Glass (B),* Harvard Business School Case Services, Boston; #9-673-042, 1972.

—— AND D. KISER, *Advent Corporation (C),* Harvard Business School Case Services, Boston; #9-674-027, 1973.

BOOZ ALLEN & HAMILTON, *Management of New Products,* Booz Allen & Hamilton, New York, 1968.

————, *New Products Management for the* 1980s, Booz Allen & Hamilton, New York; 1982.

BUZZELL, R. D. AND B. T. GALE, *The PIMS Principles: Linking Strategy to Performance,* Free Press, New York, 1987, 103–134.

COOPER, R. G., "The Dimensions of Industrial New Product Success and Failure," *J. of Marketing,* 43 (Summer 1979), 93–103.

————, "Identifying Industrial New Product Success: Project NewProd," *Industrial Marketing Management* 8 (1979), 124–135.

————, "Why New Industrial Products Fail," *Industrial Marketing Management,* 4 (1975), 315–316.

—— AND E. J. KLEINSCHMIDT, "An Investigation into the New Product Process: Steps, Deficiencies, and Impact," *J. Product Innovation Management,* 3 (1987), 71–85.

—— AND ————, "New Products: What Separate Winners from Losers? *J. Product Innovation Management,* 4 (1987), 169–184.

CRAWFORD, C. M. "Protocol: New Tool for Product Innovation," *J. Product Innovation,* 2 (1984), 85–91.

DILLON, W. R. AND M. GOLDSTEIN, *Multivariate Analysis: Methods and Applications,* Wiley, New York; 1984, 69.

EFRON, B., "The Efficiency of Logistic Regression Compared to Nominal Discriminant Analysis," *J. Amer. Statist. Assoc.,* 70 (1975), 892–898.

GERSTENFELD, A., "A Study of Successful Projects, Unsuccessful Projects and Projects in Process in West Germany," *IEEE Trans. Engineering Management,* 23 (August 1976), 116–123.

GLOBE, S., G. W. LEVY AND C. M. SCHWARTZ, "Key Factors and Events in the Innovation Process," *Research Management,* (July 1973), 8–15.

GREEN, P. E., *Analyzing Multivariate Data,* Dryden Press, Hinsdale, IL, 1978, 83–84.

GUPTA, A. K., S. P. RAJ AND D. WILEMON, "The R&D-Marketing Interface in High Technology Firms," *J. Product Innovation Management,* 2 (1985), 12–24.

HOPKINS, D. S., *New Product Winners and Losers,* The Conference Board, Report #773, 1980.

JOY, O. M. AND J. D. TOLLEFSON, "On the Financial Applications of Discriminant Analysis," *J. Financial and Quantitative Anal.,* 10 (1975), 723–739.

KIM, J. AND C. W. MUELLER, *Factor Analysis: Statistical Methods and Practical Issues,* Sage, Beverly Hills, 1978, 41–45.

KLECKA, W. R., *Discriminant Analysis,* Sage, Beverly Hills, 1984.

KULVIK, H., *Factors Underlying the Success and Failure of New Products,* University of Technology, Report No. 29, Helsinki, Finland, 1977.

LACHENBRUCH, P., *Discriminant Analysis,* Hafner, New York, 1975.

LAWRENCE, P. R., "How to Deal with Resistance to Change," *Harvard Business Rev.,* 47, 1 (January-February 1969), 166–176, 16–22.

LEE, H. AND B. BAYUS, "A Comparison of the Predictive Reliability of Discriminant Analysis and the Logic Model," Working Paper, Stanford University, Stanford, CA, 1985.

MAIDIQUE, M. A. AND B. J. ZIRGER, "The New Product Learning Cycle," *Research Policy,* 14, 6 (December 1985), 299–313.

——— AND ———, "A Study of Success and Failure in Product Innovation: The Case of the U.S. Electronics Industry," *IEEE Trans. Engineering Management,* EM-31, 4 (November 1984), 192–203.

MARQUIS, D. G., "The Anatomy of Successful Innovations," *Innovation,* 1 (November 1969), 28–37.

MORISON, E., *Men, Machines and Modern Times,* Chapter 2, MIT Press, Cambridge, MA.; 1966, 17–24.

MUESER, R., "Identifying Technical Innovations," *IEEE Trans. Engineering Management,* EM-32, 4 (November 1985), 158–176.

MYERS, S. AND D. G. MARQUIS, "Successful Industrial Innovations," National Science Foundation, Technical Report NSF 69-17, 1969, 1–117.

PETERS, T. J. AND R. H. WATERMAN, JR., *In Search of Excellence,* Harper & Row, New York, 1982.

ROSENBLOOM, R. S., *Advent (D),* Harvard Business School Case Services, Boston; #9-676-053, 1976.

ROTHWELL, R., "Factors for Success in Industrial Innovations,"*Project SAPPHO—A Comparative Study of Success and Failure in Industrial Innovation,* S.P.R.U., 1972.

ROTHWELL, R., "The Hungarian SAPPHO: Some Comments and Comparison," *Research Policy,* 3 (1974), 30–38.

———, C. FREEMAN, A. HORLEY, V. I. P. JERVIS, A. B. ROBERTSON AND J. TOWNSEND, "SAPPHO Updated-Project SAPPHO, PHASE II," *Research Policy,* 3 (1974), 258–291.

RUBENSTEIN, A. H., A. K. CHAKRABARTI, R. D. O'KEFFE, W. E. SOUDER AND H. C. YOUNG, "Factors Influencing Innovation Success at the Project Level," *Research Management,* (May 1976), 15–20.

SCHON, D. A., "Champions for Radical New Innovations," *Harvard Business Rev.,* 41, 2 (1963), 77–86.

———, *Technology and Change,* Dell, New York; 1967.

SORENSON, R. Z., *Gould, Incorporated, Graphics Division,* Harvard Business School Case Services, Boston; #9-571-071, 1971.

SOUDER, W. E. AND A. K. CHAKRABARTI, "Industrial Innovations: A Demographical Analysis," *IEEE Trans. Engineering Management,* 26, 4 (November 1979), 101–109.

—— AND ——, "The R&D/Marketing Interface: Results from an Empirical Study of Innovation Projects," *IEEE Trans. Engineering Management,* 25 (November 1978), 88–93.

SZAKASITS, G. D., "The Adoption of the SAPPHO Method in the Hungarian Electronics Industry,"*Research Policy,* 3 (1974), 18–28.

TAKEUCHI, H. AND I. NONAKA, "The New New Product Development Game," *Harvard Business Rev.,* 1 (January–February 1986), 137–146.

TUSHMAN, M. L. AND E. ROMANELLI, "Organizational Evolution: A Metamorphosis Model of Convergence and Reorientation," *Organizational Behavior,* 7 (1985), 171–222.

UTTERBACK, J. M., T. J. ALLEN, J. H. HOLLOMON AND M. A. SIRBU, JR., "The Process of Innovation in Five Industries in Europe and Japan," *IEEE Trans. Engineering Management,* 23, 1 (February 1976), 3–9.

VON HIPPEL, E., "Lead Users: A Source of Novel Product Concepts," *Management Sci.,* 32, 7 (July 1986), 791–805.

25

STRATEGIC MANEUVERING AND MASS-MARKET DYNAMICS: THE TRIUMPH OF VHS OVER BETA

Michael A. Cusumano, Yiorgos Mylonadis, and Richard S. Rosenbloom

ABSTRACT (ARTICLE SUMMARY)

The videocassette recorder (VCR) industry featured a standardization rivalry between 2 similar but incompatible formats: 1. Betamax, introduced by the Sony Corp. in 1975, and 2. VHS (Video Home System), introduced in 1976 by the Victor Co. of Japan (JVC). No single producer of VCRs was strong enough to impose a worldwide standard, and since repeated efforts to bring producers to an agreement failed, the marketplace set the standard. The industry's global mass market characteristics and the product's technical complexity meant that clear market preferences would require years to develop. The standardization contest was ultimately decided by complementary product alliances and bandwagon effects largely shaped by the strategic maneuvering of the VHS producers. Despite being first to the home market, the Beta format fell behind in market share in 1978 and declined thereafter. Sony has ceased production of the Beta models.

This article explores the evolution of a dynamic mass market and the strategic maneuvering to establish a product standard among firms that commercialized the videocassette recorder (VCR) for household use. The VCR was only one of several consumer electronics products (others include televisions, radios, stereos, audio tape recorders, and miscellaneous items ranging from digital watches to calculators) whose basic technology and initial applications came from within the United States or Europe. In each case, Japanese firms mastered the essentials of consumer-oriented product design and then went on to develop superior capabilities in mass production and mass distribution. As a result, during the 1970s and 1980s Japanese industry came to dominate the global consumer electronics business. In the U.S. market, for example, of an estimated $30 billion in sales for 1986, American firms accounted for merely 5 percent, compared to nearly 100 percent of U.S. sales in the 1950s.[1]

After its first appearance in the early 1970s, the VCR surpassed color television to become the largest single consumer electronics product in terms of sales by the early 1980s. One format, the U-Matic, developed primarily by the Sony Corporation, soon emerged as the dominant design for professional and educational uses, replacing other

Cusumano, Michael A., Mylonadis, Yiorgos, Rosenbloom, Richard S. *Business History Review*. Boston: Spring 1992. Vol. 66, Iss. 1; pg. 51, 44 pgs kinds of video players and recorders. By the mid-1970s, variations of this machine embodying more integrated electronics and narrower (1/2-inch) tape resulted in two formats designed exclusively for home use: the Betamax, introduced in 1975 by Sony, and the VHS (Video Home System), introduced in 1976 by the Victor Company of Japan (Japan Victor or JVC) and then supported by JVC's parent company, Matsushita Electric, as well as the majority of other firms in Japan, the United States, and Europe.[2] Despite their common ancestry and technical similarities, Beta and VHS machines remained incompatible, because they used different tape-handling mechanisms and cassette sizes, as well as coding schemes for their video signals that varied just enough so that tapes were not interchangeable.

Beta was the first compact, inexpensive, reliable, and easy-to-use VCR; it accounted for the majority of VCR production during 1975–77 and enjoyed steadily increasing sales until 1985. Nonetheless, it fell behind the VHS in market share during 1978 and steadily lost share thereafter. By the end of the 1980s, Sony and its partners had ceased producing Beta models, with Sony promoting another similar but incompatible standard using a smaller (8 mm) tape, primarily for home movies. The outlines of this competition have been discussed before, both in English and in Japanese.[3] This study examines how and why the VCR rivalry unfolded as it did.

The literatures on both management and economics contain discussions of the strategic challenges that a new large-scale industry poses to innovators and later entrants. Of importance to this story, given the particular characteristics of the VCR product and market, are the roles of first movers versus other technological pioneers and later entrants. The first movers—the first firms to commercialize a new technology—often benefit from superior technology and reputation, which they may sustain through greater experience or a head start in patenting. Being first often provides a unique opportunity to shape product definitions, forcing followers to adapt to a standard or to invest in order to differentiate their offerings.[4] The first movers may also exploit opportunities for the early acquisition of scarce critical resources, as exotic as specialized production equipment or as mundane as retail shelf space; they can accumulate above-average profits if they enjoy a de facto monopoly position, as occurred in the early days of the industrial video recorder used by television stations (invented and commercialized by Ampex), the mainframe business computer (commercialized most successfully by IBM), and the plain-paper copier (commercialized by Xerox).[5] Rather than to inventors, however, the largest payoffs may actually go to the that lead in creating the necessary systems and investments for successful mass production and mass distribution.[6]

With technologies and markets that require years to develop, being the inventor or first mover in commercialization may not be as useful as coming into the market second or third, as long as the rapid followers have comparable technical abilities, which usually result from having been among the pioneers who participated in developing the technology for commercial applications.[7] These firms, which, along with the inventors, are also technological pioneers, may follow the first mover quickly enough to neutralize its advantages while still exploiting the benefits that come from being a leader in creating the set of complementary assets in manufacturing, marketing, and distribution needed for market dominance.[8] For example, rapid followers who are also pioneers should be able to copy the best features of the first product while adding others to differentiate their offerings. They may have better information about buyer preferences after watching early consumer reactions and have more time to plan for manufacturing, distribution, licensing, or the use of complementary products and services. Follower pioneers and later entrants may also exploit investments made by the first mover, such as in solving engineering and manufacturing problems (if the solutions become public knowledge) or in educating buyers in the use of a new product (as occurred with the video recorder and the personal computer). They may benefit as well from the mistakes or inflexibility of the first mover as the market develops and the technology changes.[9]

In a mass consumer market, the time required to create a dominant standard may be so great that first-mover advantages are minimal, especially for products subject to what economists and others have termed "bandwagon" effects and "network externalities." The bandwagon effect refers to situations where early sales or licensing of a particular product lead (either accidentally or deliberately) to rising interest in that product. A momentum builds up that encourages other potential licensees, distributors, and customers to support the product that seems most likely to become the industry standard, regardless of whether it is technically superior, cheaper, or "better" in other ways than alternatives. The support for one standard over another can become especially dynamic and self-reinforcing if, for reasons apart from the main product itself (such as the need for and relative availability of a complementary product like software programs for computers or prerecorded tapes for VCRs), customers perceive value in owning the standard that becomes the most commonly available in the industry. Network externalities refer to whether or not there is a usage pattern that depends on such a complementary product, as well as to how and how much customers use it with the main product.[10]

While a market is unfolding, both early and later entrants can maneuver to establish a sustainable winning position before the game is decided. Each has particular advantages and disadvantages associated with the timing of decisions and the extent of commitments. Each can affect, at least in part, whether or not support for its standard occurs and how much it continues. In the case of the VCR, the potential global market measured hundreds of millions of units. Its very scale created a window of opportunity lasting a few years, during which firms with comparable engineering and manufacturing capabilities could challenge Sony, the first mover in refining the technology for consumers as well as in making preparations to exploit the mass market. As demand grew at rates outstripping the supply capabilities of Sony or any one producer, rapid followers who were also technological pioneers stimulated the occurrence of a first bandwagon that affected the formation of alliances for production and distribution. The emergence of demand for a complementary product—prerecorded tapes (usually movies)—set off a second bandwagon in the 1980s, as retail outlets for tape rental chose to focus on stocking tapes in the format being adopted by a majority of users, even though Sony's original format still enjoyed substantial acceptance. Of particular interest to historians, economists, and students of management strategy is how the initial moves of the main rivals shaped their long-term competitive positions as well as their eventual success or failure in this market.

INVENTORS, PIONEERS, AND STANDARD-SETTERS

Magnetic video recording technology was created in the United States, but numerous European and Japanese companies competed and collaborated in the 1960s and 1970s to adapt the technology to the requirements of a mass market. Ampex Corporation, a small California company, invented a video recorder for broadcasting applications in 1956.[11] This came after several years of competition with Radio Corporation of America (RCA) to use magnetic tape (as earlier used in audio tape recorders) to record television signals, and freed the broadcast industry from a reliance on live performances or on a clumsy system of film recording. In the late 1950s, Sony, JVC, and Matsushita, as well as several other Japanese firms, began studying and improving on the $50,000-plus Ampex machine, employing novel recording-head mechanisms and solid-state electronic circuits, as well as other product and process innovations, which allowed them to miniaturize the video recorder and to reduce its price dramatically.

Design technology for video recording had been difficult for Ampex to master but proved more difficult to protect from a select handful of companies that had made audio tape recorders and then invested in the development of video recording. Although Amp*ex* retained control of important patents, Japanese firms challenged these in Japanese courts and also explored ways to invent around them. By the mid-1960s, several firms in Japan, along with Ampex in the United States and Philips in Europe, had accumulated considerable expertise in video recording design and manufacture.

Despite a series of products through the 1960s that did not appeal to consumers because of high prices, poor picture quality, bulky housings, and inconvenient reel-to-reel formats, the Japanese pioneers continued to improve their machines until, in 1971, Sony succeeded in designing a cassette model with 3/4 inch-wide tape. This machine, called the U-Matic, was still too large and expensive for regular home use. Nonetheless, it found a market among schools and other institutions, and it embodied the core design concepts that served as the basis for both the Beta and VHS formats.[12] In conjunction with an agreement to adopt Sony's U-Matic as a standard for institutional machines, three Japanese firms that later competed for the home video standard—Sony, Matsushita, and JVC—signed a cross-licensing agreement for video recording patents in 1970.[13] Philips did not join this group and pursued its own distinctive VCR design.

Although engineers and managers recognized that a standard format would be better for consumers and producers (who would benefit from expansion of the market), agreement on a single home video format proved impossible to reach. In fact, Sony's experience with the U-Matic had made its engineers particularly reluctant to cooperate in establishing or refining a new standard. As early as 1970, Sony had appeared ready to introduce a smaller machine that used a more sophisticated (azimuth) recording system and that might have proved popular with consumers. Since Matsushita and JVC were not yet ready to mass produce this type of machine, the U-Matic ended up as a compromise design, requiring a wide tape and a large cassette. The compromise thus forced Sony, by agreeing to support what became the industry standard for institutional machines, to miss a potential opportunity to enter even earlier into the home market.[14]

Utilizing nearly two decades of experience with video recorder design, engineering, and manufacturing, Sony and JVC both proceeded to develop 1/2 inch-wide tape VCRs for the home and introduced them in 1975 and 1976. Meanwhile, other companies, including Ampex, RCA, Matsushita, Toshiba, Sanyo, and Philips, introduced or experimented with alternative formats. Unlike the Sony and JVC designs, both of which resembled the effective U-Matic design, the other VCRs were based on distinctive design concepts that proved to be inferior to Beta and VHS.

In addition, just as Sony's Betamax was essentially a miniaturization of the U-Matic but with a more advanced recording technique, the VHS closely resembled the U-Matic (and thus the Betamax), even though the recording format, tape-handling mechanisms, and cassette sizes remained different. Accordingly, it proved difficult for Sony and JVC, and the firms that carried their machines, to differentiate their products through basic features. Hence, neither Beta nor VHS could gain a technological advantage in design or manufacturing that could be sustained long enough to gain a dominant market position. Sony did establish an advantage in reputation if not in actual design and manufacturing skills because of its unique history as an innovator in home video and as primary inventor of the U-Matic As discussed later in this article, however, Sony's first-mover role and strategic initiatives did not result in a sustainable advantage. Its chief competitors also had superb technical skills, and domination of the huge global market required cooperation with other firms in mass production, licensing, and distribution of both hardware and software. It was by no means certain, however, that the VHS—which came to market after Betamax and was backed by a small firm JVC) with limited manufacturing and distribution capabilities—would prove superior in the global marketplace.

THE GLOBAL MASS MARKET

Demand for a novel consumer-electronics product can rise rapidly as masses of new customers appear each year. In home video, for example, everyone with a television set was a potential customer. In contrast, professional video had been a very limited market. Machines for broadcast use were expensive and complex, and the number of buyers equaled the number of television stations—hundreds, not millions, in the United States, Japan, and Europe combined. As a result, one firm was able to supply most of the new and replacement demand for many years. For example, Ampex had produced approximately 75 percent of all video recorders in use worldwide in 1962, and it was able to dominate the broadcast market for two decades after its invention of the video recorder in 1956.[15]

The Beta and VHS models opened up a true mass market, allowing video recorders to parallel and then in the early 1980s to pass color television sets to become Japan's (and the world's) top consumer electronics product in production value.[16] The vast size and worldwide structure of this new demand made it nearly impossible for any one firm to accommodate it. Annual production of home videocassette recorders in Japan exceeded one million as early as 1978, having commenced only in 1975, and continued to double each year until 1981. Japanese firms exported 53 percent of the video recorders they produced in 1977 and approximately 80 percent from 1979 onward. The top export destination was the United States during 1979, but European exports consumed larger share during 1980–82, as VCR sales boomed with the increasing availability of prerecorded tapes.[17] Europe was probably a more favorable market in which to promote the use of software than the United States because of the smaller number of television stations and available broadcast programs.

Thus, the characteristics of home video—the market's "mass" and global nature, as well as the product's technical complexity meant that efficient mass production capacity, broad distribution channels, and clear market preferences would require years to emerge. An early mover into the market had no guarantee of a sustainable advantage from simply being first, but needed an effective strategy to capitalize on its position. The need for strategic action was especially strong because other pioneers, after observing customer reactions to the initial product offering, had the option of moving in with a comparable product, lower prices, better features, or superior distribution. In fact, Matsushita was known for competing in that manner: monitoring a broad range of technical developments and gradually building up in-house skills while waiting for Sony, JVC, or other innovative consumer-electronics firms to introduce a new product. Matsushita would then enter the market six months to a year later with a similar but lower-priced version, usually manufactured more efficiently because of Matsushita's mass production skills and willingness to invest to achieve scale economies where they proved useful. The scale of Matsushita manufacturing reflected broad distribution guaranteed through an enormous domestic sales network, which marketed products under brand names that included Panasonic, Technics, National, and Quasar. Matsushita also could schedule large production runs because of its willingness to sell finished products to original equipment manufacturers (OEMs) in Japan and abroad for sale under their labels.[18]

THE ARGUMENT

A VCR by itself is worthless. Users can employ it only in conjunction with a complementary product, the videotape cassette, that is designed to conform to the interface specification of the VCR. This is a common characteristic of contemporary information technologies, such as the personal computer (PC) and its software programs, compact disc (CD) players and discs, or TV receivers and broadcast signals. Interface standards for innovative products of this sort can be established by various means: government regulation (the Federal Communications Commission for television), formal agreement among a large number of producers of the primary product (CD players), or implicit acceptance by producers reflecting the market power of a sponsor (IBM PC).

In the case of the VCR, since no single producer or coalition was strong enough to impose a worldwide standard, and since repeated efforts to bring producers to an agreement failed, the marketplace set the standard. Furthermore, the existence of a "network externality" had two important consequences. First, given rival products of approximately equal cost and capabilities, buyers will tend to choose the one that has been chosen, or appears likely to be chosen, by a greater number of other buyers. Second, this creates a dynamic system with a "positive feedback": the perceived benefit of choosing a given standard increases as more buyers choose it, thus increasing the probability of purchase by others not yet in the marketplace. An early lead in this sort of contest, however achieved, may become self-reinforcing.

In the drama of the VCR standardization battle, there were three sets of principal players: 1) the main protagonists, JVC, and Philips, sponsors of the three principal rival formats and major producers of the core product, the VCR; 2) the remaining consumer electronics producers, each of whom would adopt one of the standard formats for production and/or distribution; and 3) the producers and distributors of an important complementary product, prerecorded software.

As it played out, the crucial battle was between Beta and VHS, Sony and JVC. (Although Philips held on to a different standard in Europe for a decade, it never posed a serious challenge to the other two.) The facts are simple: Beta reached the market first, took 58 percent of the market in 1975–77, and fell behind VHS in 1978. For the next six years, sales of Beta-format VCRs increased every year, even as its share of the worldwide market fell every year. After being outsold four-to-one by VHS in 1984, Beta began a rapid decline to extinction.

The figures show how quickly the VHS format turned a slight early lead in sales into a dominant position. Chance events might have produced that early lead, and, as the theory suggests, that might be enough to explain the outcome. The thesis of this article, however, is that the early lead and the eventual outcome reflect the deliberate actions of the main players. Strategic maneuvering by the principal protagonists in 1975–77 led to an alignment of producers of the core product and to the exploitation of mass production and distribution capabilities sufficient to account for the early dominance of VHS sales. In a second phase of rivalry, in the 1980s, the strategic alignment of producers of complementary products reinforced the VHS advantage and hastened the demise of Beta, which might otherwise have survived as a second format.

EMERGENCE OF THE VCR STANDARD

A three-year period, from mid-1974 to 1977, proved decisive in determining the outcome of the standardization battle that would rage on for another decade. At the start of this period, diversity characterized the positions of the world's largest consumer electronics companies with respect to home video, a market that remained wholly speculative in 1974. VCR designs based on six different incompatible formats were in late stages of development at rival companies, and three of the majors, Hitachi, Sharp, and Zenith, had no commitments at all to home video development. By mid-1977, the pattern had changed sharply, as all ten of the biggest firms were marketing home VCRs, and the industry had divided into three "families," supporting either Sony's Beta, JVC's VHS, or the Philips format.

The decisive factors in the standards battle were few. First, of the six designs being developed around the world in 1974, four were significantly flawed and destined to fail. The Philips N-1500, Sanyo-Toshiba V-Code, and Matsushita VX designs were marketed vigorously yet fell short, despite the introduction of improved second-generation models in each case. RCA's VCR design never got past the prototype stage, since management abandoned the project after seeing the Betamax. Although a later Philips model, the V-2000, had many fine technical features, it proved complex and costly to manufacture and was introduced too late to capture a viable market share. Like RCA, Philips also had a video disc system under development, which distracted management attention away from the VCR; JVC and other Japanese firms also had disc systems under development but concentrated on refining and marketing their VCR machines.

Because of the common technical heritage in the U-Matic, the Beta and VHS designs were closely comparable in cost and performance. Sony had a clear lead primarily in timing; it would take JVC roughly two more years to match the stage that Sony had achieved by late 1974. But moving first was not sufficient, in itself, to win the prize in this market; how Sony moved and what its principal rivals did also mattered. In retrospect, as Akio then Sony's president, later acknowledged, he and Masaru Ibuka, then chairman, made a "mistake" and "should have worked harder to get more companies together in a 'family' to support the Betamax format."[19] JVC, in the number two position, did "try harder" and was more effective at forming alliances in support of VHS.

JVC's more effective campaign to form an alliance behind VHS produced a coalition that matched the Beta family in global market power. JVC and its principal ally (and parent), Matsushita, followed that with strategic commitments that gained a decisive edge in market share for VHS, beginning in 1978. Matsushita exploited its generic skills in mass production and substantial previous experience in VCR manufacture by establishing production capacity for the VHS that exceeded the combined capacities of all other Japanese VCR producers. JVC, meanwhile, moved aggressively to bring leading European consumer electronics firms into the VHS family, almost preempting that market from Beta.

STRATEGIC ALIGNMENT OF PRIMARY PRODUCERS

A set of assumptions that proved to be in conflict shaped Sony's strategy for commercializing the Betamax. Sony's leaders believed that the Beta design was good enough to be a winner, and they knew that they were ahead of their rivals in VCR development. But they also understood that no producer, on its own, could establish a VCR format, however good the design, as a recognized global standard. Thus, Sony set out to interest other VCR pioneers in adopting the Beta format, concentrating especially on winning the allegiance of Matsushita, its most formidable rival. But two premises hampered their ability to recruit allies. As Japan's leading developer of video technology, Sony believed that it should not have to delay commercialization of the Betamax in order to cooperate, and probably compromise, on the development of an industry standard with other firms. Sony managers and engineers felt that their earlier willingness to compromise on the U-Matic had been a competitive error. Consequently, Sony went ahead and began manufacturing preparations for the Betamax in the fall of 1974, before approaching other firms to discuss the prospect of their adopting the Sony machine as an industry standard (see Appendix A).

Furthermore, Sony was reluctant to build VCRs for its licensees. Sony had always been uniquely innovative with consumer products that incorporated advanced electronics. Its management had never before agreed to ship Sony products to other companies for distribution under their labels, preferring to build up the Sony name and reputation and to avoid sharing the benefits of Sony innovations with too many levels of distributors. For example, Sony developed and marketed Japan's first audio-tape recorder (1950), stereo audio system for broadcasting (1952), transistorized radio (1955), transistorized video-tape recorder (1958), and transistorized micro-television (1959), as well as unique products such as the Trinitron television, whose picture-tube technology did not follow the industry standard established by RCA.[20] Thus, although Sony managers realized that they would have to license the Beta format to ensure its widest distribution, they were unwilling to compromise on their standard or to help potential licensees with OEM shipments.

Sony first demonstrated the Betamax to representatives of RCA, an American video pioneer, in September 1974. At the same time, Sony began talking to JVC and Matsushita, its U-Matic partners, about "joint development" of a home video format. But Sony did not manage these relationships well. When it approached the other firms, Sony had already begun tooling up for the Betamax, signaling to prospective partners a commitment to proceed with mass production irrespective of their support. Sony thus acted as a true first mover, perhaps believing that its lead in the market would convince other firms to follow. At the same time, having begun manufacturing preparations also made Sony less flexible, because altering the design of its machine would require expensive changes in manufacturing equipment.

The 1974 discussions with RCA accomplished one of Sony's objectives by persuading RCA to kill its own VCR development program, but they also brought to light the most vulnerable aspect of the initial Beta design, its limited playing time. RCA had given two hundred of its own VCRs to U.S. customers in a market test during early

1974 and concluded that a minimum two-hour playing time was necessary for commercial success."[21] RCA executives knew from the Betamax demonstration that their efforts to develop VCR technology had been far surpassed by the innovative Japanese, and they terminated their own program. But they decided to wait for further progress in the technology, especially for longer playing times, before making a commitment to market a particular VCR.

When Sony demonstrated the Betamax to Matsushita and JVC in December 1974, Matsushita also questioned the adequacy of a one-hour playing time.[22] These negative reactions to the Betamax then convinced managers at JVC that a successful machine would have to offer at least two hours of playing time and strengthened their commitment to the VHS, whose development had always proceeded on that assumption. JVC now joined RCA and Matsushita in declining to adopt the Beta format.[23]

Sony managers eventually realized that they were not in a strong bargaining position and decided to modify the Betamax for two-hour recordings. Sony postponed further licensing negotiations, losing valuable time and opportunities to continue attempts at enlisting licensees. In particular, when Hitachi, another major producer of consumer electronics products, showed an interest in July 1975 in licensing the Betamax, Sony managers refused, insisting that the Betamax was not yet perfected and thus not available for licensing.[24] It seems that Sony managers were still primarily interested in persuading Matsushita to adopt the Beta standard, rather than Hitachi; they knew by this time that JVC was working on a competing format, which, because of JVC's position as a Matsushita subsidiary, Matsushita was likely to support if Sony did not make a special effort to persuade them to adopt the Beta format.

Moreover, Sony sought partners who could quickly manufacture VCRs on their own rather than requiring Sony to provide complete machines. Sony chairman Akio Morita was unequivocal about this strategy, declaring early in 1976 that "Sony is not an OEM manufacturer."[25] In this regard, Matsushita, which had a large manufacturing capability for VCRs based on previous unsuccessful products, was a better fit than Hitachi, which had made only a few broadcast-use VCRs through a subsidiary and needed an OEM relationship before it could establish in-house production.[26]

Sony resumed seeking partners as soon as it revised the Betamax to play for two hours. Top executives from Sony and Matsushita met again in March 1976 to discuss adopting Beta as the common standard. In July, Sony demonstrated the latest machine to Matsushita, JVC, Hitachi, Sharp, Mitsubishi, Toshiba, and Sanyo and also appealed to Japan's Ministry of International Trade and Industry (MITI) for support. MITI officials tried to negotiate a settlement and favored Sony in these discussions, since it already had a machine in the market. Toshiba and Sanyo eventually agreed to back Beta, but the other firms decided to wait for the VHS, which JVC announced publicly in September 1976.[27]

In contrast to Sony, JVC followed a strategy aimed at forming as large a group as possible, aggressively pursuing both licensing and OEM agreements, including exports.[28] Management first established a group of adherents in Japan who could boost JVC's manufacturing and marketing capabilities—before completing the design and its own preparations for manufacture. JVC initiated this process in the spring of 1975, shortly after Sony's initial demonstration of the Betamax, and by the end of 1976 had lined up Hitachi, Mitsubishi, and Sharp, in addition to Matsushita. JVC also proposed an OEM relationship to Matsushita, which turned it down because JVC did not have enough capacity to supply Matsushita's huge distribution network and also because Matsushita was capable of producing the VHS machine on its own within a few months.[29] In addition, JVC agreed to provide machines to Hitachi, whereas Sony would not; JVC began shipments to Hitachi in December 1976. In January and February 1977, JVC also began supplying VCRs to Sharp and Mitsubishi, which Hitachi had helped to recruit.[30]

As a second step, toward the end of 1976, JVC moved to establish a footing in the U.S. market by negotiating with RCA. The U.S. company rejected this offer for an OEM relationship because of JVC's small production capacity.[31] Yet, rather than giving up on OEM agreements outside Japan, JVC turned toward European firms, which would be satisfied with smaller quantities than RCA needed. JVC pursued these European alliances far more actively and effectively than any other VHS or Beta producer, even after establishing a large production base and gaining worldwide recognition for its brand name.

In addition, to entice other firms to support VHS, JVC was willing to let other companies participate in refining the standard, such as moving from two hours to longer recording times or adding new features. JVC also provided considerable assistance in manufacturing and marketing.[32] Yet another important difference from Sony proved to be style: JVC managers approached prospective partners in an exceedingly "polite and gentle" manner, and encouraged them to adopt as the common VCR standard "the best system we are all working on," rather than the VHS per se.[33] One outcome of JVC's approach was that prospective manufacturing partners truly believed they would have some stake in the future evolution of VHS features.[34] Allowing partners to share in development also improved the VHS in ways that JVC might not have pursued itself. For example, after JVC exhibited the VHS prototype to Matsushita in spring 1975, Matsushita provided technical feedback that sped the completion of the new VCR.[35] Matsushita also took the lead in increasing recording and playback time after consulting with RCA.

JVC also strengthened the position of the VHS family by moving aggressively to line up European distribution. Philips, the leader in the consumer electronics market in Europe, still commanded less than 25 percent of the market for color television in the region. With its German ally, Grundig, the number two producer, Philips was producing home VCRs based on its 1972 technology, now outmoded by the Beta and VHS innovations. Most of the other European consumer electronics firms had earlier marketed VCRs produced by Philips and Grundig but by 1975 all of them had dropped the product. In contrast to RCA's reaction to the Japanese innovations, Philips determined to surpass the new designs with an innovative machine, for which they launched development in 1975. Meanwhile, Philips and Grundig persisted with the old design, upgraded in 1977 to provide two-hour recordings. The Philips V-2000 reached the market in 1980 but, despite impressive technical features, it was too expensive and too late.

JVC exploited this opportunity to recruit Telefunken, Thomson, Thorn, Nordmende, and other strong European brands into the VHS family. Moving quickly with its Japanese partners, JVC had defined the technical standards for a PAL (the European color standard) VCR in 1977. JVC's readiness to supply machines on an OEM basis as well as to help firms prepare for manufacturing in Europe, plus the evident superiority of VHS over the current Philips offering, won commitments in rapid order from the remaining major European firms.[36]

The marketing clout wielded by the rival families is worth close analysis, because all the participants understood that VCRs would be sold as adjuncts to television and audio equipment. A rough proxy for market power in that industry in the mid-1970s was a company's share of the color television receiver market. At one level, the rivals appear evenly balanced. Among the world's top ten consumer electronics companies, the VHS and Beta groups were evenly matched, each selling slightly more than one-quarter of the color sets sold in 1976, whereas Philips and Grundig together accounted for less than one-sixth. But the VHS family was more successful in gaining the allegiance of smaller brands. Hence, within each of the three major geographic markets, VHS started out with a market share advantage. The VHS family—Matsushita, JVC, Hitachi, Sharp, and Mitsubishi—accounted for nearly 60 percent of color TV sales in Japan in 1976, compared to only 37 percent for Sony, Toshiba, and Sanyo. In the U.S. market, the VHS brands, led by RCA, had a 49 percent share of color TV sales in 1976, compared to only 41 percent for Zenith, Sony, Sears, and the rest of the Beta family. And by 1978, almost all the European brands not committed to the Philips format adopted VHS, leaving Beta in a minority position.

In 1975 and 1976, all the world's leading consumer electronics producers entered the home video market. Those that had bet wrong on video development, choosing an inferior design approach, or electing not to invest at all, reversed their positions and adopted one of the three contending formats. In the course of these two years, JVC, by adroit maneuvering (and with a major boost from Matsushita), transformed the structure of the rivalry to establish a standard format for home VCRs. In mid-1975, Sony had stood out in a field of diverse contenders, including rival VCRs as well as potential alternatives such as videodisc. Its Beta design was the only format both ready for market and capable of performing at the level required for a mass market. By mid-1977, VHS could challenge it from a position of parity, both in product cost and functionality and in the market power of the VHS family.

PRODUCT DIFFERENTIATION

Did the market performance of VHS result from differentiating features, price, or quality? A comparison of models introduced during 1975–85 by Sony, JVC, and Matsushita, the major home VCR producers, indicates some differences in all three dimensions. In general, however, at no time did either format establish more than a transient advantage in features, prices, or picture quality.

For example, although Sony's initial models played for one hour and VHS machines two hours, Sony increased its machine's capacity to two hours merely five months after JVC entered the market and several months before Matsushita appeared. Sony offered more low-priced models until 1980, when Sanyo introduced inexpensive Beta models. Nevertheless, Matsushita quickly surpassed Sony in share once it entered the VHS market in 1977, and the VHS standard was dominant worldwide by the end of 1978. Beta and VHS offered basic models at similar prices; the VHS group included more brand names, yet Sony led in the introduction of most new features even as it was losing market share to the VHS group. Between 1977 and 1983, Sony was the first company to offer wireless remote control, half-speed and one-third speed machines, multifunction machines (scan, slow, and still), high fidelity (hi-fi) sound, and a one-unit movie camera (camcorder). But, as can be seen in Table 8, Matsushita or JVC usually matched Sony's new features within a few months, and sometimes more quickly. JVC also was first with several innovations, such as slow/still functions, a portable VCR, and stereo recording (which Matsushita marketed at the same time).

Differences in picture quality are more difficult to assess, but VHS did not have a reputation as being superior to Beta, and the truth may indeed have been the opposite.[37] In addition, physical differences existed in the machine weights and cassette sizes, but it remains unclear how these affected the course of events, except that the smaller Beta cassette made it more difficult for Sony to increase recording or playing time simply by putting more tape into its cassettes.[38]

The key issue here is that Beta machines still might have survived as an alternative format used for high-quality recording of broadcast programs off the air or for home movies (the market niche Sony has exploited with 8 mm camcorders). To have achieved this with Beta, Sony would have had to distinguish its VCR through special effects or features that made it especially convenient or superior to VHS in performance. Yet, as with basic features and prices, Sony was unable to differentiate Beta models for a significant length of time because of the technical skills and initiatives of JVC and Matsushita, as well as those of their partners in the VHS group.

It also seems that Matsushita was able to counter Sony in the Japanese and U.S. markets by utilizing its huge engineering and manufacturing resources to offer a product line with more combinations of features and prices. Compared to Sony, Matsushita introduced both less and more expensive VCRs between 1978 and 1981 and manufactured about twice the number of model types Sony produced during the same time period. Other marketing measures helped VHS firms overcome Sony's image for high quality and reliability; for example, RCA and Matsushita (which marketed Panasonic and Quasar brands in the United States) both offered an extended labor warranty for their machines.

MASS PRODUCTION AND MASS DISTRIBUTION

By 1978, the VHS family had gained a significant edge in manufacturing capability, as well as in market power. Both the Beta and VHS machines were complex to manufacture, compared to other consumer electronics products such as radios, televisions, or audio equipment, in particular because they required high precision for machining the heads and sophisticated assembly skills for building the tape-handling mechanism and other components. The difficulty of designing and then mass-producing an inexpensive VCR kept Ampex and RCA from entering this segment of the market in the 1970s, even though both designed home VCR prototypes in their laboratories.[39] Philips, in addition to difficulties with product reliability, also had to price its VCRs 20 to 30 percent higher than VHS and Beta machines.[40]

Both Sony and JVC mastered the problems of mass production engineering and manufacturing, benefiting from experiences gained through earlier video recorder production. They also relied on integrated development teams for the Beta and VHS projects that brought together members with both design and operations backgrounds. JVC, which had less experience making VCRs than Sony, paid special attention to making its VCR easy to manufacture and service by creating a relatively simple, low-cost design with fewer components and assembly steps than the Betamax—characteristics that also appealed to companies wishing to license a VCR for in-house manufacturing. In contrast, although Sony had the manufacturing expertise to produce the Betamax economically, potential licensees appeared concerned over their ability to mass produce the Beta design.[41]

Matsushita also made low-cost production a major priority as it modified the VHS design and prepared its own plants. The company spent at least fourteen months studying manufacturing issues before formally adopting the VHS standard in January 1977. Matsushita engineers knew what problems to expect, because they had accumulated invaluable experience producing earlier VCR machines, including a cartridge model once made in a plant with 1,200 workers and a monthly capacity of 10,000 units, as well as the VX cassette model, which Matsushita had made in 1976 before switching to the VHS.[42] Matsushita not only emphasized a reduction in parts but also invested in manufacturing automation and scheduled large production runs, anticipating that its vast distribution system would enable it to sell a great number of VCRs.[43] Matsushitas's ability to deliver low-priced VCRs with an increasing variety of features also helped it undercut Sony prices and win contracts to supply machines to overseas distributors-arrangements that further increased Matsushita's scale of operations and ability to justify additional investments in product development and automation.[44]

Managers at Matsushita believed that the manufacturer who would dominate the world market would be the company that captured the largest share of the U.S. market, where the major VCR distributors were likely to be RCA and Zenith, the leaders in color television sales.[45] Sony moved first after developing a two-hour model by establishing a relationship with Zenith, after having been rebuffed by RCA. RCA intended to lead in the market for home video players but wanted lower-priced machines as well as a longer recording time. Meanwhile, Matsushita took a strong interest in RCA's distribution resources. These mutual interests brought RCA and Matsushita together in negotiations for an OEM agreement after discussions broke down between RCA and JVC, which did not have the manufacturing capacity to supply RCA with the volume of machines it wanted.

As RCA managers pondered which Japanese producer with which to link up, they reconsidered the issue of tape length. In February 1977, apparently to the astonishment of Matsushita executives, RCA requested a VCR that "could record a football game." This meant a recording time of at least three hours. Rather than ending the negotiations, Matsushita launched an intensive effort to double playing time from two to four hours by using the approach Sony had taken to double the playing time of its one-hour machine: halving the width of each recording track (called the track pitch) as well as slowing the recording speed. Matsushita put seventy engineers on this project alone and achieved the increase in playing time in merely two months; it then set up production capacity for 10,000 units per month within six months. By the end of March 1977, Matsushita had an agreement to supply RCA with approximately 50,000 four-hour VCRs by year's end.[46]

A large part of the VHS advantage came from the sheer ability to deliver more VHS machines than Beta producers could make early on in the competition. Even in 1978, because of Matsushita's massive capacity, the VHS group accounted for approximately percent of the total Japanese VCR production capacity of 191,000 units per month. Matsushita—not JVC—thus proved instrumental in winning over RCA and pushing the VCR competition toward the areas where *Sony* was weakest: low prices and mass distribution, as well as longer playing and recording times. JVC personnel opposed a doubling of the playing time, arguing that this constituted a "bastardization" of the VHS (that is, a compromise in picture quality), and they refrained from collaborating with Matsushita in pursuing this feature. JVC eventually built a two-speed (two- and four-hour) machine in August 1977, primarily to satisfy its OEM partners, but not until July 1979 did it introduce such a machine commercially under the JVC brand name.[47] JVC, which had about one-tenth the sales volume of Matsushita, also took six months to build a machine with four-hour play and twelve months to achieve a monthly capacity of 10,000 units.[48]

Most important, the nature of competition changed as a result of Matsushita's alliance with RCA. First, momentum clearly built up for VHS in the U.S. market, as General Electric, Sylvania, Magnavox, and Curtis Mathes scrambled to join this group in 1977, under the rationale that the format RCA supported would probably become the dominant machine in the American market.[49] U.S. distributors initially had been indifferent to the choice of standards and appeared to be waiting for clearer market signals before selecting a format. Second, because of the longer playing time, Matsushita and its distributors, and later other firms in the VHS group, were able to establish an image of the Beta machine as deficient with respect to this basic feature. Sony increased the Betamax's playing time to three hours in October 1978, but not until March 1979, a year and a half after Matsushita introduced the four-hour VHS, did Sony introduce a 4.5-hour machine.

Thus, by spring 1977 Matsushita was able to plan a large-scale entry into the worldwide VCR market and to begin exploiting its skills and investments in low-cost manufacturing and mass distribution. These assets, in turn, helped RCA, which had brand recognition as well as extensive distribution channels, to offer reliable products at low prices. The effective Matsushita-RCA combination then damaged Sony's competitive position in both the U.S. and Japanese markets, not only because Sony's market share and distinctiveness declined. Shortly after RCA's announcement of a reduction in prices to undercut Sony in August 1977, Zenith demanded a renegotiation of its OEM agreement with Sony, to whom it was paying $100 more for Beta machines than RCA paid Matsushita for VHS machines.[50] After a lag of more than two months, Sony and Zenith responded by matching RCA's prices.[51] Yet these moves portended a difficult future: Sony would now play the game on terms that Matsushita and RCA had set, and play it poorly. In fact, Sony had trouble matching the prices of both Matsushita and JVC in the low end of the VCR market between 1979 and 1981. Sanyo took over as the primary supplier of the lowest-priced Beta machines, but it did not have the range of alliances or the distribution channels to which Matsushita had access.

STRATEGIC ALIGNMENT FOR COMPLEMENTARY PRODUCTS

Of the three principal functions of the VCR—namely, "time-shifting" (recording broadcast programs for later viewing), making and viewing home movies, and playing prerecorded cassette programs—only in the last one did the greater availability of VHS prove to be a significant factor for consumers. Blank cassettes used for time-shifting and movies were readily available for both machines. The format did represent a potential constraint on the sharing of these tapes among households, once recorded, but such use remained small. On the other hand, users quickly perceived that prerecorded tapes were more available in VHS than in Beta, and that difference appeared very salient to users intending to rent or buy programs.

Until the early 1980s, that difference did not matter much in the marketplace. The VCR was broadly perceived to be a niche product, appealing primarily to certain demographic segments. In 1980 and 1981, with VCR ownership in only 5 to 10 percent of television households in most advanced countries, forecasts typically projected a leveling of demand at penetration levels of 15 to 30 percent in the late 1980s.[52] Users gave little evidence of interest in prerecorded tapes. In the United States in the late 1970s, three-quarters of all VCR owners bought no prerecorded tapes.[53] In 1983, several years after the beginning of the tape-rental business, 40 percent of VCR owners never used such tapes and only 8 percent identified them as "important."[54] With a small installed base of players and low consumer interest, producers and distributors of programs had little incentive to invest heavily in prerecorded tapes and video rental stores.

All that changed in the mid-1980s. Confounding the forecasts, the VCR turned into a mass-market product, reaching 30 percent of American homes by 1985, five years ahead of most forecasts, and still climbing. Sales and rentals of prerecorded cassettes began to grow exponentially, doubling each year from 1982 to 1986. Although at least one leading U.S. firm concluded in 1982 that tape rentals would not be accepted by U.S. consumers and that the economics of the rental business would not support a large industry, entrepreneurs flocked to open rental stores in every neighborhood.[55]

Europe stood at the leading edge of this change. VCRs began to achieve mass-market penetration in Europe earlier than elsewhere, apparently due to the availability of fewer broadcast channels there. In 1983, when penetration had reached 10 percent in the United States and 12 percent in Japan, it was 29 percent in the United Kingdom and still growing. Because TV set rental was a common practice in Britain, extended readily to VCRs, the practice of renting programs on tape was a natural adjunct. The linkages formed by JVC and Hitachi with Thorn and Cranada, the leading British TV-rental operations, led those distributors to emphasize the VHS format in tape rental as well. Program producers and distributors, observing the preponderance of European brands adopting VHS, tended to emphasize it over Beta and Philips formats. One pioneer in tape production, Magnetic Video, in 1980 had three times as much capacity in Europe for VHS production as for either Beta or V-2000.[56]

In the United States, aggressive steps by RCA in the late 1970s contributed significantly to the momentum behind the VHS standard, which still did not overtake Beta decisively until the mid-1980s. Because of its ambitious videodisc venture, RCA had well-developed ideas about the consumer market for recorded video programming. To promote its VCR in 1978, RCA developed an important alliance with Magnetic Video Corporation of America (MV). MV was a leader in prerecorded video (primarily used then for education and training) and was the first to offer feature films on cassette. RCA supplied two MV program cassettes free with each VCR in 1978, along with a membership in the MV "club." MV, which soon found most of its growth coming in the VHS format, expanded capacity to enable it to duplicate 2.4 VHS tapes for every Beta tape. Matsushita facilitated this by developing equipment or high-speed duplication and by rapidly making low-cost decks available to MV and others. When the British firm, Granada, began opening rental shops in the United States in 1980, it offered only VHS players and cassettes.

Sony matched most of these moves, but with a lag and with less effect. In 1979 Sony linked up with Video Corporation of America (VCA), but this firm continued to promote VHS as well. Sony also proved less effective than Matsushita in supplying equipment for duplication of tapes in the Beta format. As a consequence of these and other moves, by 1980 the VHS format clearly dominated Beta in the channels for prerecorded tapes. According to one estimate, VHS then accounted for 70 to 90 percent of the revenues of cassette dealers in the United States.[57]

As the mass market began to grow in subsequent years, VHS sustained and multiplied this initial advantage. The greater abundance of VHS program material gave buyers greater incentive to choose VHS players, which then led tape distributors to stock more VHS tapes, in a reinforcing pattern. By 1984, contrary to most forecasts made as recently as 1980 or 1981, the sale and rental of prerecorded tapes was a billion-dollar business in the United States, dominated by the VHS format.[58] When Zenith, the leading U.S. color TV brand, switched from Beta to VHS in 1984, the end was in sight for the Beta format.

CONCLUSIONS

The VCR story provides a classic example of the dynamics possible in a standardization contest affected by bandwagons and complementary products. The evidence cited here also shows this case to be an important illustration of how strategic maneuvering can harness the dynamic power of a special marketplace—the mass-consumer market—to make a winner out of a second mover with extensive technological skills but a weak starting position in manufacturing and distribution capabilities.

In April 1975, Sony enjoyed what looked like an insurmountable lead. Its Betamax, already on the market in Japan, was clearly superior to VCRs being offered by major rivals—Matsushita, Sanyo, Toshiba, and Philips. The company had a lustrous reputation globally as an innovator and leader in consumer electronics. JVC, a minor factor in the industry, was still struggling to perfect VHS prototypes that seemed to offer few evident technological advantages. Matsushita was struggling with its poorly received VX product. Two years later, though Beta still enjoyed a lead, VC, supported by Matsushita, set in motion the fundamental forces that would continually erode, and then extinguish, Beta's share of a massive global market.

In retrospect, it is possible to identify the key events and to "explain" the outcome in terms of a few factors. But as events were unfolding, the implications of each strategic move must have been more difficult to discern. Each of the key protagonists acted in a way that made sense in context. Sony's behavior followed patterns that had brought it great success over two decades. JVC, the underdog could not reasonably have been less humble or flexible in its relationships. Matsushita, along with Toshiba, Sanyo, and Philips, were actually failed first movers, since they introduced unsuccessful VCRs at nearly the same time as the Betamax. Matsushita, however, exhibited its usual mixture of caution and flexibility. Had the market grown more slowly, as nearly all observers expected, Sony might have been able to respond more effectively to its early mistakes and to the actions of its key competitors.

A few important moves made the difference. JVC created a winning alignment of VCR producers in Japan by the way its managers conducted the formation of alliances, showing versatility and humility, whereas Sony pressed commitment and reputation. The alliance with the giant Matsushita brought huge added benefits. Matsushita's management waited until VHS seemed likely to be a viable alternative to Betamax before abandoning its own VX model and then quickly switched over to the new machines, investing massively in capacity in advance of demand while pushing the product technology to meet RCA's requirements of a longer recording time. JVC completed the sweep by moving ahead of Sony to enlist a huge number of European partners behind VHS.

JVC's early success in aligning itself with Matsushita and other Japanese producers allowed the company to gain a decisive edge in the race for distribution rights. Sony's reluctance to be an OEM supplier, and its underestimation of the threat from VHS, left Beta in a minority position for potential market power in North America and Western Europe as well as in Japan. As the theories discussed in this article suggest, once VHS took the lead, it became more and more likely that it would continue to gain share year after year. The final contest, among producers and distributors of video software, accelerated this process. Even without the growing importance of software, the outcome probably would have been the same in the long run. Nonetheless, the dominance of VHS in tape-rental channels hastened the demise of Beta and made certain it would not survive even as a second format.

Louis Pasteur said that "chance favors the prepared mind." Chance no doubt played a role in the dynamic growth of the VCR industry and the eventual success of VHS. But the alliances that JVC formed for production and distribution and the timely strategic commitments of its ally, Matsushita, proved to be the decisive factors in the triumph of VHS over Beta.

APPENDIX A: VCR INDUSTRY CHRONOLOGY, 1974–1978

Year/Month

1974/9—Sony proposes to Matsushita and JVC that they jointly adopt the Sony VCR under development, although development was largely completed and Sony already had begun setting its manufacturing dies and making other production preparations. Sony also shows the Betamax prototype to RCA, in the hope of persuading the U.S. firm to adopt it. (RCA subsequently abandons an attempt to develop its own VCR but rejects the Betamax because of its short 1-hour recording and playing time.) Toshiba and Sanyo introduce their own VCR, the V-Code I, with 30-minute and 1-hour tapes.

/12—Sony shows the Betamax prototype to Matsushita and VC, but still receives no commitment from them.

1975/4—Sony introduces the Betamax SL-6300 in Japan, priced at 229,800 yen (ca. $800); 1-hour recording time.

JVC announces to Matsushita that it has a competing VCR under development, the VHS.

/7—Hitachi approaches Sony as a potential licensee of the Betamax, but is rebuffed as Sony prefers to wait for Matsushita and modify the Betamax for 2 hours.

/9—Matsushita introduces its own VCR model, the VX-100, with 1-hour tape. JVC also completes a VHS prototype and demonstrates this to Matsushita and later to other firms.

/12—Hitachi adopts the VHS format.

1976/1—JVC asks Sharp and Mitsubishi Electric to adopt the VHS format; they agree by fall 1976.

/2—Sony introduces the Betamax (SL-7200) in the U.S.

/3—Hitachi, acting on behalf of JVC, asks Toshiba and Sanyo to join the VHS group. Sony again approaches Matsushita and asks that it adopt the Betamax and Matsushita shows the VHS prototype to Sony for the first time.

/4—Toshiba and Sanyo introduce the V-Code II with a 2-hour tape.

/5—Matsushita introduces the VX-2000, with a 100-minute tape.

JVC begins manufacturing preparations for the VHS.

/6—Sony and JVC each ask the Ministry of International

/7—Trade and Industry (MITI) to back their standards. MITI proposes that

/8—JVC adopt the Betamax, or that the two firms negotiate on a standard, adopt one or the other or a combination, but these suggestions fail to be accepted.

/10—JVC introduces the VHS for commercial sale in Japan with a 2-hour tape.

/12—Hitachi begins marketing VHS machines supplied by JVC.

1977/1—Sharp begins marketing VHS machines supplied by JVC. Matsushita publicly adopts the VHS format.

/2—Sanyo, Toshiba, and Zenith adopt the Betamax format.

/3—Sony introduces a 2-hour color version of the Betamax (SL-8100), although it is not compatible with the 1-hour Betamax.

Matsushita introduces a 4-hour version of the VHS for export to RCA, Magnavox, Sylvania, CE, and Curtis.

/4—Pioneer and Aiwa adopt the Betamax format.

/8—Sanyo reaches an agreement with Sears-Roebuck to supply it with Betamax machines.

/10—The VHS group settles on a European standard, followed by export agreements to several European distributors.

/11—NEC adopts the Betamax format.

1978/1—Hitachi begins in-house production of the VHS

/5—Mitsubishi begins in-house production of the VHS for export

Sources: Primarily Nihon Keizai Shimbunsha, ed., Gekitotsu: Soni tai Matsushita: bideo ni kakeru soryokusen Crash! Sony versus Matsushita: the all-out war wagered on video! (Tokyo, 1978) and Sony Corporation, "Table of Sony VTR History," unpublished memorandum, 16 Aug. 1977.

About the Authors

Michael A. Cusumano is associate professor of management at the Sloan School of Management of the Massachusetts Institute of Technology. YIORCOS MYLONADIS is assistant professor in the Department of Management at the Wharton School of the University of Pennsylvania. RICHARD S. ROSENBLOOM is David Sarnoff Professor of Business Administration at the Harvard Graduate School of Business Administration.

This research would not have been possible without the cooperation of many individuals at JVC, *Sony Corporation,* and Matsushita Electric. We particularly thank JVC's Yuma Shiraishi and Junko Yoshida for their assistance over many years. James Utterback of *MIT,* as well as Steven Tolliday and two anonymous referees for the Business History Review, offered useful suggestions for revisions. The Division of Research at the Harvard Business School and the Leaders for Manufacturing Program at MIT both provided funding that contributed to this project.

References

1. Michael L. Dertouzos, Richard K. Lester, and Robert M. Solow, Made in America: Regaining the Productivity Edge (Cambridge, Mass., 1989), 216–18.

2. Betamax is a trademark of the Sony Corporation. VHS is a trademark of the Victor Company of Japan.

3. In English see, for example, James Lardner, Fast Forward: Hollywood, the Japanese, and the VCR Wars (New York, 1987); and P. Ranganath Nayak and John M. Ketteringham, Breakthroughs! (New York, 1986); in Japanese see, for example, Nihon Keizai Shimbunsha, ed., Gekitotsu; Soni tai Matsushita: bideo ni kakeru soryokusen Crash! Sony versus Matsushita: the all-out war wagered on video! (Tokyo, 1978); and Itami Hiroyuki, Nihon no VTR sangyo: naze sekoi o seiha dekita no ka Japan's VTR industry: why it was able to dominate the world! (Tokyo, 1989).

4. Marvin B. Lieberman and David B. Montgomery, "First-Mover Advantages," Strategic Management Journal 9 (1988): 41–58; and Michael A. Porter, Competitive Advantage: Creating and Sustaining Superior Performance (New York, 1985), 18–89.

5. For discussions of these cases, see Richard S. Rosenbloom and Karen J. Freeze, "Ampex Corporation and Video Innovation," in Research on Technological Innovation, Management, and Policy, ed. R. S. Rosenbloom (Greenwich, Conn., 1985), 2: 1186; Franklin M. Fisher, James W. McKie, and Richard B. Mancke, IBM and the U.S. Data Processing Industry: An Economic History (New York, 1983); and Gary Jacobson and John Hilkirk, Xerox: American Samurai (New York, 1986).

6. This definition of "first movers" is used in Alfred D. Chandler, Jr., Scale and Scope: The Dynamics of Industrial Capitalism (Cambridge, Mass., 1990).

7. Richard S. Rosenbloom and Michael A. Cusumano, "Technological Pioneering and Competitive Advantage: The Birth of the VCR Industry." California Management Review 1, 4 (1987): 51–76.

8. David I. Teece, "Profiting from Technological Innovation: Implications for Integration, Collaboration, Licensing, and Public Policy," in The Competitive Challenge, ed. David J. Teece (Cambridge, Mass., 1987), 185–219.

9. Lieberman and Montgomery, "First-Mover Advantages"; Porter, Competitive Advantage; and Richard N. Foster, Innovation: The Attacker's Advantage (New York, 1986).

10. See, for example, M. L. Katz and C. Shapiro, "Technology Adoption in the Presence of Network Externalities," Journal of Political Economy 94 (1986): 822–41; J. Farrell and G. Saloner, "Installed Base and Compatibility: Innovation, Product Preannouncements, and Predation," American Economics Review 76 (1986): 9455; and W. Brian Arthur, "Positive Feedbacks in the Economy," Scientific American, Feb. 1990, 92–99.

11. See Rosenbloom and Cusumano, "Technological Pioneering and Competitive Advantage," and Rosenbloom and Freeze, "Ampex Corporation and Video Innovation."

12. Useful discussions of the concept of a dominant design as well as "architectural" variations, which seem to describe VHS and Beta as refinements of the U-Matic, can be found in Kim B. Clark, "The Interaction of Design Hierarchies and Market Concepts in Technological Evolution," Research Policy 14 (1985): 235–51; and Rebecca M. Henderson and Kim B. Clark, "Architectural Innovation: The Reconfiguration of Existing Product Technologies and the Failure of Established Firms," Administrative Science Quarterly 35 (1990): 9–30.

13. Nihon Keizai Shimbunsha, ed., Gekitotsu; and Rosenbloom and Cusumano, "Technological Pioneering and Competitive Advantage."

14. Nihon Keizai Shimbunsha, ed., Gekitotsu; Nomura Management School, "VTR Sangyo noto" VTR industry note! (Tokyo, 1984); and Richard S. Rosenbloom interviews with Nobutoshi Kihara and Masaaki Morita, Senior Managing Directors, Sony Corporation, July 1980.

15. Rosenbloom and Freeze, "Ampex Corporation and Video Innovation."

16. Katz and Shapiro, "Technology Adoption in the Presence of Network Externalities."

17. Arthur, "Positive Feedbacks in the Economy."

18. Nihon Keizai Shimbunsha, ed., Gekitotsu, 151–54.

19. Akio Morita, Made in Japan (New York, 1986).

20. Nick Lyons, The Sony Vision (New York, 1976).

21. Lardner, Fast Forward, 84; and TV Digest, 21 April 1975.

22. Nihon Keizai Shimbunsha, ed., Gekitotsu, 13–17.

23. Nayak and Ketteringham, Breakthroughs! 37–38.

24. Nihon Keizai Shimbunsha, ed., Gekitotsu, 33–34; Lardner, Fast Forward, 156.

25. Quoted in TV Digest 16 Feb. 1976.

26. Yoichi Yokomizo, "VCR Industry and Sony" (MS Thesis, MIT, Sloan School of Management, 1986), 79–80.

27. Nihon Keizai Shimbunsha, ed., Gekitotsu, 59–72.

28. See Appendix A and Tables 5, 6, and 3 (Tables omitted); Nayak and Ketteringham, Breakthroughs! 42; Nomura Management School, "VTR Sangyo noto"; and "Innovations Spur Boom in VCR Sales," The New York Times, 11 Dec. 1984, D1.

29. Nihon Keizai Shimbunsha, ed., Gekitotsu, 54.

30. JVC committed to supplying Hitachi on an OEM basis although this entailed that a large portion of its production capacity of about 2,000–3,000 units per month would be diverted to that end. This portion would have been significantly smaller for Sony which, at the time, had a production capacity of more than 7,000 units per month. See Nomura Management School, "VTR Sangyo noto"; and TV Digest, 21 April 1975 and 13 Dec. 1976.

31. Nayak and Ketteringham, Breakthroughs! 46.

32. Michael A. Cusumano interview with Susumu Gozu, Manager, Domestic Sales Dept., Video Products Division, Victor Company of Japan, July 1989.

33. Kokichi Matsuno, message to employees in taking over as JVC President in 1975, and Shizuo Takano, JVC's Video Department manager, both quoted in Navak and Ketteringham, Breakthroughs! 41. Susumu Gozu, in his interview with Cusumano, gave a similar account of JVC's approach.

34. Nayak and Ketteringham, Breakthroughs! 32–33; also, Gozu interview.

35. Lardner, Fast Forward, 148–49.

36. Alan Cawson et al., Hostile Brothers: Competition and Closure in the European Electronics Industry (New York, 1990).

37. "VCRs; Coming on Strong," Time, 24 Dec. 1984, 48; "Selecting the First VCR—Some Questions to Keep in Mind." The New York Times, 18 Dec. 1983, H38; Tony Hoffman, "How to Buy a VCR." Home Video, April 1981, 48–55.

38. Nihon Keizai Shimbunsha, ed., Gekitotsu; Yanagida Kunio, "VHS kaihatsu dokyumento" Documentation of VHS development!, Shukan gendo, May 1980; Richard S.

Rosenbloom interviews with Nobutoshi Kihara and Masaaki Morita, Senior Managing Directors, Masaru Ibuka, Honorary Chairman, and Akio Morita, Chairman, Sony Corporation, July 1980.

39. Rosenbloom and Cusumano, "Technological Pioneering and Competitive Advantage"; Rosenbloom and Freeze, "Ampex Corporation and Video Innovation"; and Margaret B. W. Graham, RCA & the VideoDisc: The Business of Research (New York, 1986).

40. Nomura Management School, "VTR Sangyo noto," 4.

41. Rosenbloom and Cusumano, "Technological Pioneering and Competitive Advantage"; Yanagida Kunio, "VHS kaihatsu dokyumento"; Michael A. Cusumano interview with Gozu of JVC as well as with Tak Matsumura, Assistant Director, Video Recorder Division, Matsushita Electric, July 1989.

42. Nihon Keizai Shimbunsha, ed., Gekitotsu, 21–24, 54; Lardner, Fast Forward, 159.

43. Yokomizo, "VCR Industry and Sony," 39–40.

44. TV Digest, 4 April 1977.

45. Itami Nihon no VTR sangyo.

46. Lardner, Fast Forward, 1613; Nayak and Ketteringham, Breakthroughs! 47.

47. TV Digest, 11 July 1979.

48. Ibid., 29 Aug. 1977.

49. Ibid., 30 May, 27 June, 7 Nov. 1977.

50. Ibid., 4 April 1977.

51. Ibid., 29 Aug., 3, 31 Oct., 7 Nov. 1977.

52. Bruce C. Klopfenstein, "Forecasting the Market for Home Video Players: A Retrospective Analysis" (Ph.D. diss., Ohio State University, 1985).

53. TV Digest, 9 Sept., 16 Oct. 1978, 12 April.

54. Klopfenstein, "Forecasting the Market for HomeVideo Players," 141.

55. Richard S. Rosenbloom, personal interviews at RCA, 1982.

56. TV Digest, 6 Oct. 1980.

57. Ibid, 8 Dec. 1980.

58. The Wall Street Journal, 21 April 1986, 20D.

26 STAGE GATE SYSTEMS FOR NEW PRODUCT SUCCESS

Robert G. Cooper and
Elko J. Kleinschmidt

Here's a new game plan to boost your odds on the innovation battlefield.

Product innovation has become the decisive corporate battlefield, vital to success, prosperity, and even corporate survival. Witness the companies doing well today; chances are, they are succeeding because of sound new product decisions made in the last decade or two. Losing the battle spells disaster. Companies simply disappeared because they failed to innovate, failed to keep their product portfolio current and competitive, and were surpassed by more innovative competitors.

Here, we first look at past victories and defeats on that battlefield and draw nine key lessons for new product success. They are based on rigorous research, including our own *NewProd* studies which address the question, "What separates winners from losers?" (See "The *NewProd* Studies," on page 366.)

Those nine lessons lead us to a game plan—a process template for driving new products to market quickly and efficiently—which a number of leading firms in North America and Europe have used successfully.

PRODUCT SUPERIORITY MATTERS

Lesson 1: The number one success factor is a unique superior product—a differentiated product that delivers unique benefits and superior value to the customer.

Superior products delivering real and unique benefits to users succeed far better than "me too" products with few positive elements of differentiation. Figure 26-1 shows the relationships. When we compared the top 20% of products in terms of product superiority to the bottom 20% (the least differentiated), the superior products had five times the success rate, in terms of the manufacturer's success criteria. Here, we define success and failure from a financial, or profitability, standpoint: the degree to which the new product's profits exceeded or fell short of the firm's hurdle rate for this type of investment.

Superior products with unique benefits outscored the others on every other measure of performance as well, by considerable margins, as assessed by knowledgeable managers and project teams. They captured much higher market share, by more than 40 share points. They enjoy higher profitability; managements rate them 8.4 out of 10 on profitability, compared to only 2.6 for "me too" products. Superior products were much more likely to meet company sales and profit objectives.

Cooper, Robert G. and Elko J. Kleinschmidt, (1993), "Stage Gate Systems for New Product Success," *Marketing Management,* Vol. 1, No. 4, pp. 20–29.

EXECUTIVE BRIEFING

New products are critical to the growth, prosperity, and survival of the modern corporation. Nine key lessons for new products success improve the chances of winning and reduce the time-to-market. The prescriptions are drawn from the *NewProd* studies of more than 1,000 new product launches, successful or otherwise, in hundreds of firms. The stage gate system, a new tool for managing the product innovation process, builds on those nine lessons. Stage gate models have been successfully implemented in many leading U.S. and foreign companies in the last half-dozen years.

Such results, no surprise to leading product innovators, apparently are not obvious to everyone. We've found that "tired products" and "me too" offerings are the rule rather than the exception in many firms' new product efforts—and 82% of such efforts fail!

What did superior products with real customer benefits have in common? They offer unique features not available on competitive products. They meet customer needs better than competitive products. They have higher relative product quality, and solve problems customers had with competitive products. They reduce the customer's total costs, providing high value-in-use. And they are innovative, the first of their kind on the market.

CUSTOMER FOCUS IS ESSENTIAL

Lesson 2: A Strong market orientation—a market-driven and customer-focused new product process—is critical to success.

A thorough understanding of customers' needs and wants, the competitive situation, and the nature of the market is an essential component of new product success. Virtually every study of product success factors supports that finding. Need recognition, understanding user needs, market need satisfaction, constant customer contact, strong market knowledge, undertaking market research, quality of marketing execution, and more spending on up-front marketing activities are recurring themes throughout the many studies that have probed what makes a new product a winner.

Conversely, failing to adopt a strong market orientation in product innovation, an unwillingness to undertake essential market assessments, and leaving the customer out of product development spells disaster. Insufficient resources, poor market research, inadequate market analysis, weak market studies, and lackluster test marketing and

FIGURE 26-1 Impact of Product Superiority on Success

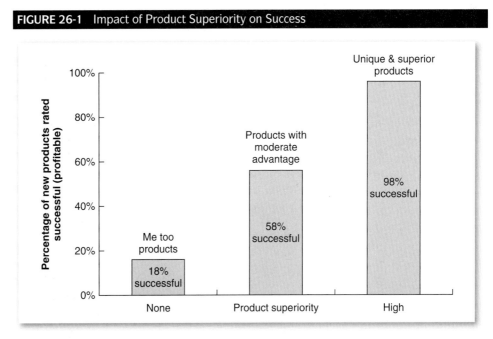

Source: Based on *NewProd* studies of 203 industrial products

product launches are common weaknesses found in virtually every study of why new products fail.

In our *NewProd* studies, we have focused on what actually happened during the new product project, examining 13 key activities in particular, from initial screening through product launch. Figure 26-2 shows the mean "quality of execution" self-assessment ratings that project managers assigned to these 13 actions, for product successes vs. failures. We also looked at how much money and effort went to each activity.

Particularly notable is how much marketing actions discriminated between winners and losers.

- For the five marketing actions listed in Figure 26-2, quality of execution was rated higher for the successful products than for the failures. This was especially true for four marketing activities: the preliminary market assessment, the detailed market study, test market or trial sell, and the launch itself.
- Companies devoted three times as many person-days and twice as much money to preliminary market assessments for successful projects, compared to failures.
- Companies spent twice as much on market research, in both dollars and person-days, in successful projects than in failures.

Sadly, a strong market orientation is missing in the majority of firms' new product projects. For example, we found that 75% of new product projects' studies omitted a detailed market study. Marketing activities were rated the poorest of all steps of the entire new product process. Typically they scored much lower than technical issues on our zero-to-ten "quality of execution" index in Figure 26-2.

Moreover, companies spend relatively few resources and little money on marketing actions: only 16% of the effort and 32% of dollar expenditures in the typical project. (About 81% of that money goes to the launch.)

FIGURE 26-2   Quality of Execution—13 Key Activities

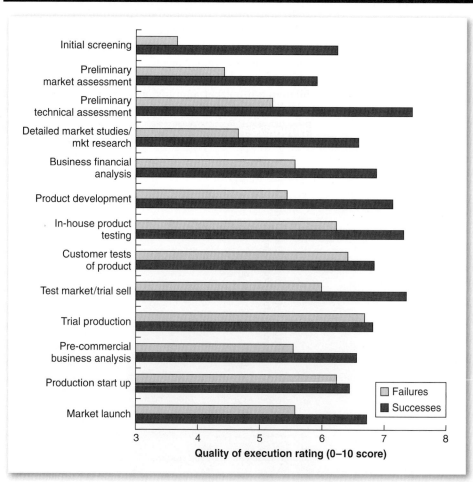

DO THE HOMEWORK

Lesson 3: More predevelopment work must be done before product development gets under way.

Homework is critical to winning. *NewProd* and other studies reveal that the steps preceding the actual design and development of the product—screening, market studies, technical feasibility assessment, and building the business case—are key factors separating winners from losers.

In Figure 26-2, the greatest differences between winners and losers occur in the top half of the diagram with the up-front or homework activities that precede development. The quality of execution of the predevelopment steps—initial screening, preliminary market and technical studies, market research, and business analysis—is closely tied to the product's financial performance. And successful projects have more than 1.75 times as many person-days spent on predevelopment steps as do failures.

Japanese innovators, for example, devote substantial effort to the planning stage of the new product process. As described by researchers, "Japanese developers make a clear distinction between the 'planning' and the 'implementation' phases of a new technology initiative. . . . The objective of planning is complete understanding of the problem and the related technology before a 'go' decision is made. It is reported to be an unrushed process which might look agonizingly drawn out to Western eyes."[1]

Also, Booz Allen & Hamilton's 1982 study, *New Product Management for the 1980s,* found that Japanese firms and successful U.S. companies apply considerably more time to the homework stages before entering development than does the average U.S. firm.

Threadbare Excuse

Surprisingly, most companies acknowledge serious weaknesses in the predevelopment steps of their new product activities. The *NewProd* evidence on resources spent shows pitifully small amounts of time and money devoted to these critical steps: only 7% of the dollars and 16% of the effort.

"More homework means longer development times," is a frequent complaint. It is a valid concern, but experience has shown that homework pays for itself in reduced development times as well as improved success rates, primarily for three reasons:

1. Product failure is much more likely if the homework is omitted. So the choice is between a slightly longer project or greatly increased odds of failure.
2. Better project definition, the result of sound homework, actually speeds up the development process. One of the major causes of time slippage is poorly defined projects entering the development phase as vague targets and moving goalposts. This is often the result of weak predevelopment activities.
3. Given the inevitable product design evolution that occurs during the life of a project, the time to make the majority of design improvements or changes is not as the product is moving out of development and into production. More homework up front anticipates changes and encourages them to occur earlier in the process, rather than later, when they are more costly.

DEFINE THE PROJECT EARLY

Lesson 4: Sharp and early product definition is one of the key differences between winning and losing at new products.

How well the project is defined before entering the development phase is a key success factor. Managers should consider including what Professor Merle Crawford has called the "protocol step," in which all parties involved in the project agree on specific product requirements before beginning development.[2]

The *NewProd* studies find that successful products had much sharper definition before development and were more than three times as likely to be successful. They

FIGURE 26-3 Impact of Early and Sharp Product Definition on Success

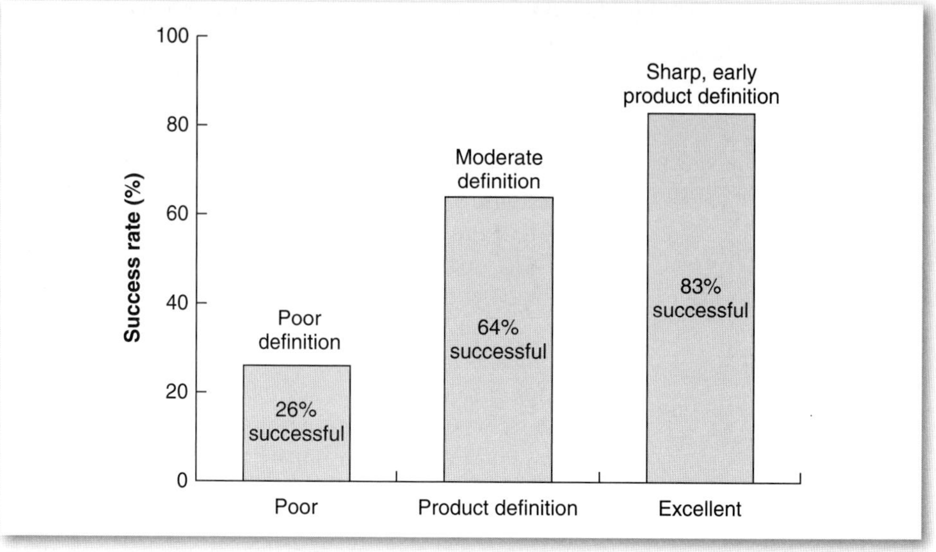

Source: Based on *NewProd* studies of 203 industrial products

achieved higher market share, by 38 points on average, they were rated 7.6 out of 10 in terms of profitability (compared to 3.1 for poorly defined products), and they tended to meet company sales and profit objectives much more often than lesser efforts (see Figure 26-3). Getting the product definition right was also the number one factor in success identified in a 1991 internal study by Hewlett-Packard.

Definition Criteria

Some companies devise an excellent product and project definition before the door is opened to a full development program. Their definitions:

- Specify target markets, the intended users.
- Describe the product concept and the benefits to be delivered.
- Delineate the positioning strategy.
- Prioritize product features, attributes, requirements, and specifications by "must have" and "would like to have" criteria.

Unambiguous project definitions before development focus more attention on predevelopment activities and objectives. Definitions guide each functional area involved in the project, engendering their commitment to it.

PROMOTE CROSS-FUNCTIONAL EFFORT

Lesson 5: The right organizational structure is a key factor in success.

Product innovation is not a one-department show, but a multidisciplinary, cross-functional effort. The evidence is compelling. Our most recent *NewProd* studies in the chemical industry show projects were more likely to be successful when they were handled by cross-functional teams dedicated to the projects, accountable for them from idea to launch, and led by strong leader-champions having top management support. Studies of U.S. high-technology firms, and Japanese new product programs, find similar cross-functional patterns unfettered by traditional functional barriers.

How does one design a process that integrates many activities and multifunctional inputs? And how does one ensure quality of execution? One answer is to develop a systematic approach to product innovation, a game plan that cuts across departmental boundaries and forces the active participation of people from different functions, such as the stage gate approach we will explain later in this article.

Organizational design is just as important. The traditional functional organization structure does not suit many of the needs of product innovation. Indeed, functional and functional matrix approaches led to the least new product success, according to one extensive study on new products.[3]

Companies must move to team approaches that cut across functional lines. Three approaches that appear to work well are the *balanced matrix,* the *project matrix* and the *project team* methods, which emphasize the autonomy of the team, and the responsibility and independent authority of the project leader.

In the balanced matrix, a project manager oversees the project and shares responsibility and authority with functional managers. There is joint approval and direction.

The project matrix approach assigns a project manager who takes primary responsibility and authority for the venture. Functional managers assign personnel as needed to provide technical expertise to the project.

In the project team, the project manager heads a core group of people drawn from several functional areas. Functional managers do not have formal involvement.

These approaches contrast with functional designs, in which functional managers retain responsibility and authority for their segments of the projects, and the project leader role is minimal or doesn't exist.

SCREEN WITH A WINNER

Lesson 6: New product success is predictable, and the profile of a winner can be used to make sharper project selection decisions.

Most companies suffer from a lack of effective project evaluation and priorities. As a result, they waste scarce resources on the wrong projects and starve the truly meritorious ones. Solving that allocation problem requires that management make tough go/kill and priority decisions.

In too many firms, however, project evaluations are either weak, deficient, or nonexistent. Our *NewProd* studies find that initial screening was one of the most poorly handled activities of the entire new product process. In 88% of the projects studied, project management judged the screening decision point to be deficient: the decision involved only one decision maker, or there were no criteria used to screen projects. And 37% of projects did not undergo a business or financial analysis before the development phase; 65% did not include a pro forma business analysis.

In many cases, managers confessed that ventures simply aren't killed once they're into development: "Projects get a life of their own," as one put it, and become like "express trains, slowing down at the stations, but never with the intention of stopping until they reach their final destination, market launch."

Often the problem of poor project evaluation boils down to a lack of criteria against which to judge projects. Fortunately, new product success is fairly predictable; certain project characteristics consistently separate winners from losers, and should be used as evaluation criteria for other projects.

For instance, three important factors which consistently differentiate successful from unsuccessful projects in our *NewProd* investigations include *product superiority, synergy,* and *market attractiveness.* Those three factors, and the list of items that comprise them, should be an integral part of firms' screening and project evaluation decisions. (For example, a computer-based new product screening and diagnostic model, the *NewProd Model,* has been constructed from the *NewProd* results and is available from the authors.)

CONTROL THE PROCESS

Lesson 7: New product success is controllable. More emphasis is needed on completeness, consistency, and quality of execution.

Quality of execution of the project is *the* key to success. Note the major impact of factors that capture quality of execution of technological, marketing, and predevelopment activities in the *NewProd* studies, illustrated in Figure 26-4. Here we look at

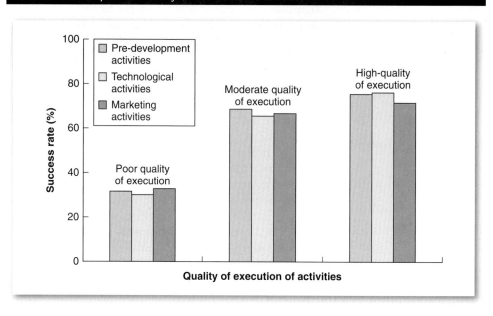

FIGURE 26-4 Impact of Quality of Execution on Success

"quality of execution" across groups of activities, comparing the top 20% of projects to the bottom 20%. Projects with well-executed marketing actions were 2.2 times as successful as those receiving weak marketing. Those with well-executed technological activities were 2.6 times as successful. Projects with predevelopment activities executed in a quality fashion were 2.4 times as successful.

Sins of Omission

Certain key activities such as those shown in Figure 26-2, cited earlier, are strong correlates of success. But as the *NewProd* studies reveal, managers frequently omit many of those activities altogether. For example, 76% of projects featured no market research or detailed market study: 37% had no precommercialization business and financial analysis; 33% had no customer tests or trials; and 77% did not include a test market or trial sell.

Quality of execution ratings were also low. No activity came close to receiving a "10 out of 10" rating. Rather, the mean quality of execution score across all activities was a mediocre 6.42 out of 10, with initial screening, preliminary market assessments, and detailed market studies scoring particularly low.

The men and women controlling new product projects must strive for significant improvements in the way the innovation process unfolds. The solution that some firms have adopted is to treat product innovation as a process with quality-of-execution checkpoints. They design quality into their game plan by making mandatory certain key activities and actions that are often omitted, yet are central to success.

OBSERVE SPEED LIMITS

Lesson 8: Speed is everything! But not at the expense of quality of execution.

Speed is the new competitive weapon. Speed yields competitive advantage—the first on the market. It means launching products with less likelihood that the market or competitive situation has changed. It results in quicker realization of profit.

But while the goal of reducing the development cycle time is admirable, it is only an interim objective, a means to an end. Many of the practices naively employed in order to reduce time-to-market ultimately cost the company money; they achieve the interim objective but fail to reach the ultimate objective, profitability.

An example is moving a product to market quickly by shortening the customer test phase, only to incur product reliability problems after launch, lost customer confidence, and substantial warranty and servicing costs. Be careful in your quest for cycle time reduction. Too often the methods used to reduce development time yield precisely the opposite effect. In many cases they are very costly and are at odds with sound management practice.

Reducing Cycle Time

Here are five sensible ways to reduce cycle time—ways that are totally consistent with sound management practice and are derived from our lessons for success. They not only will increase the odds of winning, but also will reduce the time-to-market.

- Do it right the first time. Build in quality of execution at every stage of the project. The best way to save time is by avoiding having to do it again. (See Lesson 7.)
- Do the up-front homework and provide clear project definition, based on fact rather than hearsay and speculation. That saves time downstream, requiring less recycling back to get the facts or redefine the product requirements. (See Lesson 3.)
- Organize around an empowered multifunctional team. "Rip apart a badly developed project and you will unfailingly find 75% of slippage attributable to (1) 'siloing,' or sending memos up and down vertical organizational 'silos' or 'stovepipes' for decisions, and (2) sequential problem solving," writes consultant Tom Peters in his book, *Thriving on Chaos.* Sadly, the typical project resembles a relay race, with each function or department carrying the baton for its stretch, then handing off to the next runner or department. (See Lesson 5.)
- Parallel process. The rugby game is a better model, with activities proceeding concurrently rather than sequentially.[4] More gets done per unit time as each part of the team—marketing, R&D, manufacturing, and engineering—work together simultaneously. Because parallel play is a lot more complex than a series approach, the new product process demands a disciplined game plan. (See Lesson 9.)
- Prioritize and focus. The best way to slow projects down is to spread limited resources and people too thinly across too many projects. Concentrating on the truly meritorious projects will improve the quality and speed of the work. That means tough choices, however, and perhaps killing some promising projects. One must apply the right criteria for making go/kill decisions. (See Lesson 6.)

MULTITASKING THE PROCESS

Lesson 9: Companies that follow a multistage, disciplined new product game plan fare much better.

A game plan or formal new product process—a "stage gate system"—is the solution to which many firms have turned to overcome deficiencies plaguing their new product programs. Strong evidence supports the approach. Booz Allen & Hamilton found that companies with such game plans are more successful; those with the longest experience at it were even more successful.

In one of out studies, we examined what happened at 21 divisions in leading firms that implemented stage gate plans. The results were dramatic.

- Improved teamwork: Managers reported significant improvements in cross-functional teamwork. The fact that formal new product processes stress multifunctional activities and stages and use multifunctional criteria at each gate or decision point promotes teamwork.
- Less recycling and less rework: The amount of time spent going back and doing it again was greatly reduced. Stage gates have a number of quality checks built in to ensure that all actions are executed in a quality fashion.
- Improved success rates: Managers reported that a higher proportion of new products succeeded and that resulting profitability was better. Stage gates

require sharper project evaluation and focus, and highlight the activities that result in success.

- Earlier failure detection: Potential disasters were spotted earlier, and either killed outright or modified. Stage gates with tough go/kill criteria help sharpen project evaluations.
- Better launches: Marketing planning and other marketing activities are an integral part of stage gate new product processes, resulting in more involvement in new products by marketing people.
- Shorter cycle times: This result was both surprising and reassuring. Better teamwork, more cross-functional involvement, sharper and earlier market and product definition and less recycling all served to shorten the idea-to-launch time.

THE STAGE GATE GAME PLAN

Many leading firms have developed a systematic stage gate process for moving a new product project through the various steps from idea to launch. Most important, they have built into their road map the key lessons for new product success in order to improve the effectiveness and timeliness of their programs.

Stage gate systems break the innovation process into a predetermined set of stages, each consisting of prescribed, multifunctional, and parallel activities. Figure 26-5 illustrates the process flow. The entrance to each stage is a decision gate, a checkpoint for a go or kill decision. Many other names have been used to describe similar formats, among them "product delivery process," "new product process," "gating system," and "product launch system."

The stage gate concept is based on the experiences, suggestions, and observations of a large number of managers and firms, and on our own and others' research in the field. What happened in over 60 case histories laid the foundation for it. Since the stage gate system first appeared in print, it has been implemented in whole or in part by dozens of firms in North America, including Exxon Chemicals, Procter & Gamble, Du Pont, Polaroid, US West, B.F. Goodrich, Corning Glass, Labatts, Westinghouse, the Royal Bank of Canada, and Rohm & Haas—all of which have provided an excellent laboratory setting to further refine and improve the concept. In Europe, firms such as ICI, Waven division of Shell, Courtalds, and Lego provide similarly successful examples, as have many other firms worldwide.

The stage gate system breaks the new product project into discrete and identifiable stages, typically four, five, or six in number. Each is designed to gather information needed to move the project to the next decision point.

Each stage is multifunctional. There is no "R&D stage" or "marketing stage": each consists of parallel activities by people from different functional areas within the firm. Commitment at each stage costs more than the preceding one.

A go/kill decision gate precedes each stage. Gates are the scrums or huddles on the rugby field, the points during the game when the team converges and where all new

FIGURE 26-5   A Typical "Stage Gate" New Product Process or Game Plan

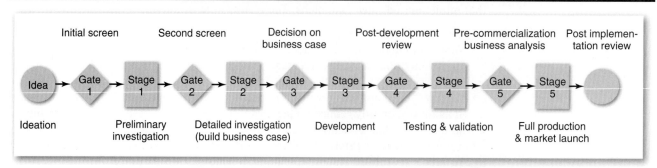

information is brought together. Gates serve as checkpoints for quality control and for choosing the next play.

Gates are predefined, specifying sets of "must meet" project requirements and "should meet" desirable characteristics. And they designate an output—what comes next. Senior managers from different functions, who "own" the resources the project requires, usually man the gates.

Process Overview

As shown in Figure 26-5, Gate 1 screens ideas which originate in basic research, come out of seed or unfunded projects, and are generated from a variety of customer-based and creativity techniques. Initial screening is the first decision to commit resources to the project, signaling a tentative commitment to it. Gate 1 criteria tend to be qualitative and few in number; strategic alignment; technical feasibility; competitive advantage; and opportunity attractiveness.

Stage 1—Preliminary investigation: This first and inexpensive stage determines the project's technical and marketplace merits. Stage 1 is a quick review of the project, often completed in 10 to 20 person-days' work effort. Its activities include a *preliminary market assessment* (a "quickie" study to determine market size, market potential, and possible market acceptance) and a *preliminary technical assessment* (an in-house appraisal of the proposed product's development and manufacturing feasibility).

The project then moves to Gate 2, a second and somewhat more rigorous screen. If the decision is go at this point, the project becomes more expensive, so Gate 2 criteria tend to be more rigorous than in Gate 1. In addition to again invoking the "must meet" criteria of Gate 1, the project must satisfy "should meet" yardsticks applied at Gate 2. Those standards often take the form of a scoring model for synergies, market attractiveness and competitive situation, elements of product advantage, and profit potential.

Stage 2—Detailed investigation: This is where management develops the business case that defines the product and verifies the attractiveness of the project before heavy spending in the next stage, development. It is the critical homework stage, the one research shows is so often weakly handled. Typical Stage 2 activities include:

- A user needs-and-wants study to determine the customer's desires and define the ideal new product.
- Competitive analysis.
- Concept testing, where a representation of the proposed new product is presented to potential customers to gauge likely acceptance.
- Technical appraisal, which focuses on the feasibility of the project from an economic and technological viewpoint.
- Manufacturing (or operations) appraisal, in which issues of manufacturability, costs to manufacture, and investment required are investigated.
- Legal, patent, and regulatory assessment, in order to remove risks and to map out legally required action.
- Detailed financial analysis, the justification which typically involves a discounted cash flow forecast complete with sensitivity analysis of "what if" risks.

Gate 3, the decision following the work in Stage 2, is the final gate before the development stage. It is the last point at which the project can be killed before incurring heavy spending. Gate 3 also yields a "sign off" on the product definition. Criteria for a pass should be tough and include a rigorous repeat of the Gate 2 "must" and "should" criteria as well as a critical financial and risk-return review.

Stage 3—Development: The "deliverable" at the end of Stage 3 is a lab-tested prototype of the product. Stage 3 emphasizes technical work, while marketing and manufacturing activities also proceed in parallel. For example, market analysis and customer feedback continue, with constant customer opinion sought as the product

THE *NEWPROD* STUDIES

Over the last 20 years, the NewProd research investigations have probed the causes of new product failure and what distinguishes new product successes from failures. The database now includes more than 1,000 new product projects—products which went to market and whose commercial outcomes are known—from more than 300 firms in North America and Europe.

Each project has measured a myriad of characteristics, including factors thought to be important to success as well as various performance gauges. While some of the studies have been private, in company research, most of the results are public and have been published in numerous articles. The cases studied have been largely industrial goods in moderate-to-high technology industries, the most recent study being of the chemical industry in four countries.

The majority of the NewProd results referred to in the current article are based on a study of 203 industrial new product projects. Detailed results have been published in a 1990 American Marketing Association monograph by the authors: New Products: The Key Factors in Success.

takes shape during development. It's an iterative process. Meanwhile, detailed market test plans, market launch programs, and production and operations plans take shape. At the same time, the innovation team updates its financial and legal analyses.

At the post-development review of Gate 4, planners recheck the continued attractiveness of the project. Has work proceeded in a quality fashion? Does the developed product conform to the original definition specified at Gate 3?

Stage 4—Testing and validation: This stage tests and validates the entire project—the product itself, the production process, customer acceptance, and the economics. Stage 4 requires a number of activities.

- In-house product tests check product quality and performance under controlled or lab conditions.
- User or field trials verify that the product functions under actual use conditions, and generates customer purchase intent.
- Trial, limited, or pilot production debugs the production process and determines more precise production costs and throughputs.
- Pretest market, test market, or trial sell gauges customer reaction, measures the effectiveness of the launch plan, and determines expected market share and revenue.
- Revised financial analysis checks on the continued economic viability of the project, based on new and more accurate revenue and cost data.

The precommercialization business analysis of Gate 5, the final gate, opens the door to full commercialization: a market launch and full production or operations start-up. It is the final point at which the project can still be killed. Criteria to pass Gate 5 focus largely on the quality of efforts to date, on the appropriateness of the production and launch plans, and on the financial viability of the product.

Stage 5—Full production and market launch: This final stage involves putting the marketing launch plan and the production or operations plan in motion. Given a well-thought-out plan of action backed by appropriate resources and barring unforeseen events, it should be clear sailing for the new product. Another new product success!

Post-Implementation Review

Following commercialization, often 6 to 18 months, the company terminates the new product project and disbands the team. The product has become a "regular" in the line. At this point, management reviews the project's performance to assess its strengths and weaknesses. A major question is what the company can learn from the project and do better the next time. The project team and leader remain responsible for the success of the project through this post-launch period, right up to the point of the post-implementation review.

WHAT THE STAGE GATE SYSTEM IS NOT

Let's deal with some potential misconceptions. The stage gate game plan is designed to facilitate development and speed products to market. Here are some of the things the system is not:

1. *Stage gate is not a functional, phased-review system.*

The game plan of the '90s is not the traditional "phased-review" process of the '60s. Phased review, endorsed by NASA and others, broke the innovation process into stages, each reporting to a function or a department. Implemented with the best of intentions, the process nonetheless managed to nearly double development times. It scheduled activities in sequence rather than in parallel, as one team or function passed the project on to the next department. And, as with any relay race, there are the inevitable fumbles and dropped batons. With no one group committed to the project from beginning to end, there was no accountability.

2. *Stage gate is not a rigid system.*

The game plan or new product process outlined in Figure 26-5 is fairly typical. Most companies tailor the model to their own circumstances and build flexibility into it.

For example, not all projects pass through every stage or gate of the model. In some firms, management defines two or three categories of projects, based on project scope, investment, and risk level. These range from sales developments or product modifications (relatively simple, short time frame and low-risk projects) to major projects involving heavy expenditures and high risks. Management chooses appropriate routes for each type of project, with lower-risk projects typically leapfrogging some stages and gates.

In any one project, stages, gates, and activities can be omitted or bypassed. Similarly, activities can be moved from one stage to another—moving an activity ahead one stage in the event of long lead time, for instance. The point is that the game plan is a guide or road map, and that deviations or detours are made consciously and deliberately, with full awareness of the facts, consequences, and risks. Decisions to skip over, delete, or shift activities or gates are not ad hoc, arbitrary, and made for the wrong reasons. They are decided thoughtfully, with the agreement of the gatekeepers at the preceding gate.

3. *Stage gate is not a bureaucratic system.*

Properly implemented, the stage gate system fosters all the attributes of a timely, successful development effort: a clearly visible road map with defined deliverables and objectives; a cross-functional team approach with empowerment; and defined decision points with criteria spelled out. Sadly, some managers consider any system an opportunity to impose more paperwork, more meetings, and more red tape.

'READING FROM THE SAME PAGE'

Many investigations, including our *NewProd* studies, have provided clues and insights into product innovation. We have translated them into the skeleton of a carefully crafted new product process—a game plan which provides a disciplined focus on quality of execution, up-front homework, strong market orientation, and backing by appropriate resources.

Stage gate is the blueprint for successful innovation, visible, relatively simple, and easy to understand and communicate. As one manager exclaimed, "At least we're all reading from the same page of the same book."

About the Authors

Robert G. Cooper is a leading researcher and consultant in the field of new products, and has published more than 50 articles and books on the subject. He is the Lawson Mardon Chaired Professor of Industrial Marketing and Technology Management at the Michael De Groote School of Business, McMaster University, Hamilton, Ont.

Bob is also Professor of Marketing and Chair of the Marketing, International Business and Policy Areas at the university, and Director of Research of the Canadian Industrial Innovation Centre, Waterloo, Ont. A former Associate Dean of McGill University's Faculty of Management, Montreal, he holds bachelor's and master's degrees in chemical engineering, and an MBA and a PhD in business administration.

Parts of this article are condensed from his latest book, *Winning at New Products: Accelerating the Process from Idea to Launch,* which Addison-Wesley will publish in 1993.

Elko J. Kleinschmidt is Associate Professor of Marketing and International Business at the Michael De Groote School of Business, McMaster University, Hamilton, Ont. He is an active researcher and consultant in both North America and Europe in the fields of international marketing and product innovation, with an emphasis on international comparative studies of new product practices.

Elko has published extensively on those topics in the *Journal of Product Innovation Management* and other journals. His most recent research includes a study into formal new product processes, an analysis of new product success factors; and a study of how innovativeness affects performance.

He holds a bachelor's degree in mechanical engineering, and an MBA and PhD in business administration.

Endnotes

1. See research as cited in Everett M. Rogers, "The R&D/Marketing Interface in the Technological Innovation Process," in Massoud M. Saghafi and Ashok K. Gupta, eds., *Managing the R&D/Marketing Interface for Process Success: The Telecommunications Focus, Vol. I, Advances in Telecommunications Management* (Greenwich, Conn., JAI Press Inc.)

2. C.M. Crawford, "Protocol: New Tool for Product Innovation," *Journal of Product Innovation Management,* 2, 1984, pp. 85–91.

3. E.W. Larson and David H. Gobeli, "Organizing for Product Development Projects," *Journal of Product Innovation Management,* 5, 1988, pp. 180–190.

4. Bro Uttal, "Speeding New Ideas to Market," *Fortune,* March 1987, pp. 62–66.

SECTION

V PROCESS INNOVATION

Introduction

In this section we transfer from our discussion of product innovation to an examination of the processes related to the production of those product innovations. The articles selected focus on process innovations as manufacturing pieces of equipment in addition to process innovation as a process in and of itself. We present an analysis of radical as opposed to incremental innovation relative to process equipment in the shoe industry by Robert Dewar and Jane Dutton, followed by a study investigating the general relationship between product and process innovation by Kornelius Kraft. Next, we offer an exploration of process innovation in process and non-process industries by Wickham Skinner. E. Celse Etienne then describes the interaction between R&D and process technology, followed by an investigation of methods that can be used to improve process technology by Hatch and Mowery.

Robert Dewar and Jane Dutton present an empirical study that tests different models that can be used to predict the adoption of technical process innovations that contain either a high degree of new knowledge or novelty (radical innovation) or a low degree of new knowledge or novelty (incremental innovation). It is important to note that this study is finely tuned to focus on a manageably sized sample of 40 industrial firms; that only process innovations are investigated; that only the adoption of innovations is of interest; and that the innovation is an industrial manufacturing product. Their findings suggest that knowledge depth or many technical specialists are required for the adoption of incremental as well as radical innovations, but larger firms are more likely to have more technical specialists and, therefore, have the capability to adopt a greater number of radical innovations.

In the second selection in this section, Kornelius Kraft furnishes a study that investigates the relationship between product innovation and process innovation. Kraft created a simultaneous regression equations model to perform his study. He investigated the determinants of both product and process innovation, including his measure of process innovation in his equation for product innovation. He found from this study that product innovation had a significant impact on process innovation, but the reverse relationship was not found to be significant. Kraft also included a measure for market structure, which is associated with the degree of market competition, as well as a measure of an industry's operating barriers to entry in both equations. When the product innovation construct was included in his equation for process innovation, the coefficients for the aforementioned variables (market structure and operating barriers) became insignificant. He interpreted these results to mean that market structure and competitive forces are associated with process innovation *through* its relationship with product innovation. It is clear that this is not a test of causality, but it does pave the way for further investigation.

Wickham Skinner in our third selection offers a perspective of the implementation of process innovations in both "process" and "non-process" industries. He examines successes that occurred after the implementation of process innovations as well as major problems that are often associated with process innovation implementation. He concludes by noting three major points. First, management must trust in and have in place a strategy grounded in the belief that competitive leadership can be attained by process superiority. Second, process innovation in either process or non-process industries requires a management team that has a high level of technical sophistication. Third, process innovation in non-process industries must be performed in large numbers of linked processes and, therefore, the procedure for such implementation requires intense management commitment and involves a high level of risk.

As we continue our pursuit to understand process innovation, we offer an article by E. Celse Etienne. Etienne extensively employs the product life cycle concept, which supports two selections we offered in Section II, one by Moore and Tushman and the other by Utterback. In the current article, Etienne brings together two streams of thought. One stream relates to the traditional product life cycle that attempts to explain how sales and profits vary over time. The other stream describes a conceptualization of a process life cycle that is defined by the relationship between the productive or manufacturing forces associated with product development and how those forces change with the passage of time. The author notes that there are three fundamental variables that form the basis of the product life cycle concept. The three variables suggested by this author include the pattern of sales, the pattern of competitive strategies, and the pattern of product innovation. The author proposes three stages of development in a manufacturing process. The first stage is an uncoordinated stage in which the process is kept fluid so that product changes can be easily made. The second stage is entitled segmental, in which the manufacturing process becomes more routinized to reduce costs while capitalizing on a more standardized product design. The third stage is the systemic stage in which few product changes are anticipated and the process of product manufacturing reaches the ultimate in sophistication. Whether applied to products or processes, Etienne notes it is innovation that ensures that firms will be competitive. The author concludes by pointing out that the interdependence among marketing, production, and R&D should be managed and reviewed in light of a firm's competitive strategy and position because the weaknesses that may be tolerable at one point in time may spell disaster at another. It is also important to note that this author suggests that strategy reviews are becoming more important as product life cycles shrink.

In the final selection, Nile W. Hatch and David C. Mowery develop and test a model of "learning by doing." Their research examines one of the most important firm-specific capabilities related to competitiveness in the semiconductor industry and, perhaps others. This capability involves a firm's capacity to develop, introduce, and expand production with newly developed manufacturing processes. They point out that in some industries, such as the semiconductor industry, process technology change is often as problematic, or more so, than product design and innovation. This is frequently due to the vast number of parts to be produced, the rate of production, and the tightness of the specifications that must be maintained in these industrial processes. These authors assert that process technology is extremely important to many industries, especially to industries such as the memory or commodity branches of the semiconductor industry, in which new products demand price premiums for a woefully short period of time. Therefore, being first to market is significantly important to the profit levels of firms in these industries. In the semiconductor industry, there appears to be two major types of product loss. The one that is the most important from the perspective of the Hatch and Mowery study is parametric loss, which results from an incomplete understanding of the parameters of the process technology that can influence manufacturing processes. For example, the authors note that semiconductor die yields, which is a measure of product and process success, represent a prime example of "learning by doing" in the semiconductor industry. Any process technology that can increase yields is considered beneficial. They conclude by pointing out that many prior studies have indicated that learning curves with their attendant cost reductions and decreased cycle times have pointed to the fact that yield increases were incidental byproducts of such reductions. This study, on the other hand, notes that the same magnitudes of cost reductions and decreases in cycle times can be the result of deliberate managerial activities. Moreover, the important factors of dedicated developmental process facilities, the close proximity between the process development and manufacturing facilities, and the duplication of equipment in both the developmental area and manufacturing facility can significantly increase manufacturing performance when new process technology is introduced. One further finding of this study is the authors' conclusion that it may be necessary but not sufficient to hire the most skilled personnel from competitive firms to "reverse engineer" and introduce new manufacturing processes. This is because the capabilities that are employed by firms to manage new process introductions cannot be solely reduced to differences in human capital, but appear to be due in part to organizational differences.

References

Dewar, Robert D. and Jane E. Dutton. 1986. The adoption of radical and incremental innovations: An empirical analysis. *Management Science* 32(11): 1422–1433.

Etienne, E. Celse. 1981. Interactions between product R&D and process technology. *Research Management* 24(January): 22–27.

Hatch, Nile W. and David C. Mowery. 1998. Process innovation and learning by doing in semiconductor manufacturing. Part 1 of 2. *Management Science* 44(11): 1461–1477.

Kraft, Kornelius. 1990. Are product- and process-innovations independent of each other? *Applied Economics* 22(August): 1029–1038.

Skinner, Wickham. 1992. The shareholder's delight: Companies that achieve competitive advantage from process innovation. *International Journal of Technology Management* 7(1–3): 41–48.

27

THE ADOPTION OF RADICAL AND INCREMENTAL INNOVATIONS: AN EMPIRICAL ANALYSIS *

Robert D. Dewar and Jane E. Dutton

J. L. Kellogg Graduate School of Management, Northwestern University, Evanston, Illinois 60201
Graduate School of Business Administration, New York University, New York, New York 10006

This paper proposes and empirically tests whether different models are needed to predict the adoption of technical process innovations that contain a high degree of new knowledge (radical innovations) and a low degree of new knowledge (incremental innovations). Results from a sample of 40 footwear manufacturers suggest that extensive knowledge depth (measured by the number of technical specialists) is important for the adoption of both innovation types. Larger firms are likely to have both more technical specialists and to adopt radical innovations. The study did not find associations between the adoption of either innovation type and decentralized decision making, managerial attitudes toward change, and exposure to external information. By implication, managers trying to encourage technical process innovation adoption need not be as concerned about modifying centralization of decision making, managerial attitudes and exposure to external information as would managers trying to encourage other types of innovation adoption, e.g., innovations in social services where these factors have been found to be important. Instead, investment in human capital in the form of technical specialists appears to be a major facilitator of technical process innovation adoption.
(PROFESSIONALIZED ENGINEERING; INNOVATIONS; DECENTRALIZED DECISION MAKING; RADICAL; INCREMENTAL)

INTRODUCTION

The current state of innovation theory is undergoing a critical but necessary change. Unstable results from innovation adoption and diffusion models call into question the validity and generalizability of innovation studies (Downs and Mohr 1976; Kimberly

---

*Accepted by Burton V. Dean; received March 27, 1985. This paper has been with the authors 1 month for 1 revision.

Dewar, Robert D. and Jane E. Dutton, (1988), "The Adoption of Radical and Incremental Innovations: An Empirical Analysis," *Management Science,* 32(11), (Nov.), 1422–1433. Courtesy of The Institute of Operations Research and the Management Sciences (INFORMS), 7240 Parkway Drive, Suite 310, Hanover, MD 21076 USA.

1981). One criticism of innovation research concerns the assumption that a universalistic theory of the innovation process can be developed that applies to all types of innovations. The search for a universalistic theory may be inappropriate given the fundamental differences that exist across innovation types (Downs and Mohr 1976). Empirical support for this conclusion is accumulating (Damanpour 1984; Kimberly and Evansiko 1981; Moch and Morse 1977).

This paper addresses and tests the efficacy of developing theoretical models for the adoption of two different types of innovations. Although there may be innovations in products, services, social structure or technology, this paper concentrates on the adoption of technological innovations involved in a firms' production processes. Theoretical arguments are made for the differential effects of organizational variables on the adoption of radical and incremental technical process innovations.

We define an innovation as an idea, practice, or material artifact *perceived to be new* by the relevant unit of adoption (Zaltman, Duncan and Holbek 1973). However, their definition does not emphasize that innovations vary in the degree of newness to an adopting unit. This distribution is captured, in part, by the notion of radicalness. Radical and incremental describe different types of technological process innovations. Radical innovations are fundamental changes that represent revolutionary changes in technology. They represent clear departures from existing practice (Duchesneau, Cohn and Dutton 1979; Ettlie 1983). In contrast, incremental innovations are minor improvements or simple adjustments in current technology (Munson and Pelz 1979). The major difference captured by the labels radical and incremental is the degree of novel technological process content embodied in the innovation and hence, the degree of new knowledge embedded in the innovation. This distinction is consistent with those researchers who define technology in terms of its knowledge component (Dutton and Thomas 1985). Although radical and incremental pertain to distinctions along a theoretical continuum of the level of new knowledge embedded in an innovation, the middle values of this continuum are difficult to interpret. For this reason, we focus on the two polar types of innovations.

The distinction between radical and incremental innovations is easier to intuit than to define or measure. Kaluzny, Veney and Gentry (1972) define radical innovations in terms of risk. Since the radical incremental distinction is one of the perceived degree of new knowledge embodied in the technology, managers are likely to differ in their judgment of an innovation based on their level of familiarity and experience. Furthermore, innovations change their classifications over time, e.g., steam locomotives were once thought quite novel, but today, unfortunately, they are mere historical curiosities. The distinction between radical and incremental innovations, then, is not one of hard and fast categories. Instead, there is a continuum of innovations that range from radical to incremental (Hage 1980). An innovation's placement on this continuum depends upon perceptions of those familiar with the degree of departure of the innovation from the state of knowledge prior to its introduction.

THEORETICAL FRAMEWORK

This paper tests whether the correlates of the adoption of radical versus incremental innovations are different. While previous researchers have documented different predictors of administrative vs. technological innovations (Kimberly and Evanisko 1981), technical vs. administrative (Damanpour 1984), and differences in the adoption of innovations compatible vs. incompatible with the interests of lower level participants (Moch and Morse 1977), this research focuses on correlates of the adoption of technologies that incorporate different levels of new knowledge. The research follows the work of Ettlie (1983), who has also documented the importance of the radical and incremental distinction. It differs insofar as it includes in the theoretical model three kinds of variables thought to be associated with innovation adoption. The first concerns of the distribution of knowledge, i.e., the depth and diversity of knowledge and extent exposure to information obtained from external sources. The second category contains the attitudes of the organization's management, namely the value they place on changed. The third category contains dimensions of organizational structure. Here our interest is in the effects of centralization upon adoption behavior.

The selection of variables from these categories is not exhaustive. Instead, variables were chosen that are widely regarded as being associated with innovation adoption. Our endeavor is distinctive in that it examines whether or not these variables have different relationships with adoption depending on the degree of new knowledge contained in the innovation.

Distribution of Knowledge in the Organization

For radical innovations which incorporate a large degree of new knowledge, organizational complexity (the number of different occupational specialties) and the depth of the organization's knowledge resources (the number of technical or engineering personnel) should strongly relate to their adoption. The different points of view, backgrounds, and types of training inherent in a mix of diversified knowledge types generate new and broader perspectives (Kimberly and Evanisko 1981), a synthesis through the contrast, the thesis and antithesis of different ideas (Hage 1980). This synthesis of different perspectives permits a better understanding of new technical processes, encouraging their adoption. Consequently, the more different types of knowledge that are present, i.e., the more complex or specialized the organization, the higher the rate of radical innovation adoption.

The depth of organizational knowledge should also covary with the adoption of radical innovations. The greater the number of specialists, the more easily new technical ideas can be understood and procedures developed for implementing them. This argument assumes, however, that the specialists are concentrated so that they can easily communicate with one another. The concentration provides a greenhouse effect for the development of and support of new ideas—particularly important when these new ideas represent major modifications in the conceptualization of a production process.

Several researchers in the innovation area have noted the effect of complexity on the innovation process (Carroll 1966; Hage and Aiken 1970; Zaltman *et al.* 1973). Hage and Aiken (1970) present evidence that knowledge depth, measured as the extent of professional training, is associated with innovation utilization. There are a few findings showing a relationship between the existence of indepth knowledge residing in a group of specialists and innovations adoption (see Bigoness and Perrault 1982; Ettlie 1983).

In contrast, complexity and knowledge depth should be less important for incremental innovations because adoption of these types require less knowledge resources in the organization for development or support. Instead, adoption of these kinds of changes should be facilitated by mere exposure to the innovation through contact with the external environment. Exposure may occur through membership in trade or professional associations or contact with manufacturer's representatives. These represent means for organizations to keep abreast of developments for improving current operations (Webster 1970). Numerous researchers have found that communication frequency is an important facilitator of innovation (Allen 1970; Utterback 1974).

Radical innovation ideas and examples also circulate in the environment. Few of these ideas will be adopted, however, unless the organization has the internal knowledge resources (complexity and knowledge depth) to interpret and absorb them. Consequently, exposure to external information is expected to be more important for the adoption of incremental rather than radical innovations, while complexity and depth of knowledge should be more important for radical and not incremental innovation adoption.

Managerial Attitudes

Upper management may have different attitudes toward innovation. They may be conservative, preferring to use standard methods and procedures no matter what the nature of the problem, or they may encourage change. Whatever their attitudes, upper management is a potent force in the organization, especially if decision making power is concentrated in their hands.

The relationship between managerial attitudes and innovation is complex, since the effect of attitudes toward change depends on whether management retains the power to make adoption decisions. In a highly decentralized organization, it is more difficult to convert attitudes towards change into action than in a centralized one. In formal terms, centralization is hypothesized to moderate the relationship between managerial attitudes and the adoption of radical innovations.

The potentially disruptive and threatening characteristics of radical innovations mean that pro-change managerial attitudes are needed to support adoption. Hage (1980) argues that, even if management favors innovation, in a more decentralized organization, there is a greater potential for powerful interest groups to dilute proposed changes. For incremental innovation adoption, there is less need to mobilize organizational power to overcome potential resistance since these innovations are less costly and have more predictable outcomes.

Centralization of Authority

The hypothesis that centralization accelerates the effects of managerial attitudes toward change on radical innovation adoption does not address whether there is a direct effect of centralization on the adoption of either innovation type. Such an effect has clearly been proposed in the literature: one argument posits a positive and the other a negative relationship. This discrepancy emerges because of a failure to distinguish different stages of the innovation process. In the initiation stage, a decentralized structure in which lower levels participate in decisions (Hage and Aiken 1970) facilitates the circulation of information, exposing decision makers to new technological innovations. During the implementation phase, a more centralized authority structure facilitates the adoption process by reducing conflict and ambiguity (Zaltman *et al.* 1973). If both of these arguments are correct, the effects may cancel each other, leaving centralization with no effect on innovation.

Our argument is that centralization will have a direct negative effect on the adoption of incremental innovations. When decentralization gives individuals at lower levels increased power over their work, they will acquire a sense of work ownership and propose changes for improvement. As long as these changes involve little new knowledge content, there should be limited opposition, and concentrated power is unnecessary for adoption. Centralization, on the other hand, will facilitate radical innovation adoption because more concentrated power may be needed to overcome opposition to these kinds of changes (Normann 1971).

There is some indirect empirical support for this argument. Hage and Aiken (1970) found a positive relationship between the rate of successfully adopted innovations and decentralization, innovations that Hage (1980) later described as incremental. Kimberly and Evanisko (1981) found that the adoption of technical innovations in hospitals was greater for more decentralized organizations. The innovations included in their research were incremental technologies. The proposed associations are summarized in Figure 27-1.

FIGURE 27-1 Predicted Associations for Radical and Incremental Innovation Adoption

A. Fundamental Innovations
  (1) External Exposure—no association with adoption of fundamental innovations
  (2) Complexity—a positive association with adoption of fundamental innovations
  (3) Depth of Knowledge—a positive association with adoption of fundamental innovations
  (4) Management attitudes favoring change—a positive association with adoption of fundamental innovations
  (5) Centralization—a positive association with adoption of fundamental innovations
  (6) Centralization also accelerates the positive association between management attitudes favoring change and the adoption of fundamental innovations.
B. Incremental Innovations
  (1) Complexity—no association with adoption of incremental innovations
  (2) Depth of Knowledge—no association with adoption of incremental innovations
  (3) Management attitudes favoring change—no association with adoption of incremental innovations
  (4) Centralization—a negative association with adoption of incremental innovations
  (5) External Exposure—a positive association with adoption of incremental innovations

---

METHODS AND PROCEDURES

Data Collection

The data were collected from a random sample of domestic footwear manufacturers stratified by size, geographic location and product types (Duchesneau *et al.* 1979). The sample distributions by region and company size (number of employees) were generally within two percentage points of the total industry's distributions (U.S. Bureau of the Census 1977). Measures of the dependent variables were collected from January to May 1977. Measures for the independent variables were collected from the same firms in 1975. From an original sample of 50 firms that were contacted, complete data sets were collected from 40 firms.

Measurement of the Variables

The variables were measured by a combination of newly developed and replications of previous measures. Radical and incremental innovation rates were based on adoptions of innovations from 1973 to 1977. From an original sample of 12 innovations (identified a priori by a panel of industry experts as radical and incremental innovations in the domestic footwear industry), a subsample of six innovations was selected that met three criteria: (1) there was a perceived difference in the rating of the type of innovation on a radical-incremental scale; (2) the innovation had been commercially introduced after 1970; and (3) the innovation had been adopted by more than one organization. Six of the original twelve innovations were eliminated based on these selection criteria. The six technical process innovations used are listed in Table 27-1.

The two categories of innovations were established by using 56 judges' ratings of the degree of new knowledge embodied in each innovation. The innovations were rated on a three-point scale indicating whether each innovation: (1) had no new knowledge contained in the machine or process; (2) represented an improvement over existing technology; or (3) represented a major technological advance. The judges were persons designated as most knowledgeable in their organization about the acquisition of new technology. The higher the score received by an innovation, the more radical it was perceived to be. Using the average rating of each innovation across the 56 judges, three innovations were classified as radical and three as incremental. A *t*-test performed on the mean scores indicated that the two innovation types were significantly different from each other ($t = 4.63$, $p \le 0.01$).

Having classified innovations as incremental or radical, we scored each firm's adoption pattern by devising two unique innovation scores based upon the simple sum of the scaled values of incremental and radical innovations adopted (see Table 27-1 for the scale values for each innovation). A firm was scored as adopting the innovation if it was in use in at least one of the firm's plants. For example, a firm that adopted the computer pattern generating system, the numerically controlled stitcher, and the flat lasting system received a 5.15 and 2.26 on the radical and incremental scores, respectively. A single score based on a count of innovations was not used, since it could not indicate

TABLE 27-1 Comparison of Innovations on the Perceived Radicalness Scale[1]

Radical Innovations	Judges' Average Innovativeness Score[2]	*Incremental Innovations*	Judges' Average Innovativeness Score
1. Flow Molding	2.65	1. Goodyear Welt Lasting System	2.19
2. Computer Pattern Generating System	2.60	2. Flat Lasting System	2.26
3. Numerically Controlled Stitcher	2.55	3. Automatic Needle Positioner and Thread Trimming Machine	2.42

[1]The Radicalness Score is computed on a three-point scale.
[2]Number of judges = 56.

whether the innovation pattern was more radical or incremental. The innovation measure used captures differences in radicalness in a more finely-grained way than a simple innovation count as used by previous researchers (e.g., Ettlie *et al.* 1984).

The independent variables were measured in late 1975. Complexity of knowledge resources was operationalized as the number of distinct occupational specialties in the organization (Hage and Dewar 1973). Degree of centralization was measured using Hage and Aiken's (1970) measure for participation in decision making (Cronbach's $\alpha = 0.7$). Managerial attitudes towards change were measured using Neal's battery (1965) for values in favor of change. For this three-item scale, a high score indicated values that favored change (Cronbach's $\alpha = 0.47$). Depth of knowledge resources were operationalized as the total number of persons employed full-time in technical or engineering groups—a modified version of a measure of the presence of technical groups used in previous studies (Ettlie 1983). While he used a categorical measure, this study uses a continuous one. Exposure to external information was operationalized as the average number of managerial memberships in trade organizations. This measure, while valid, is incomplete, since there are many more sources of external information available to a firm. Still, interviews with respondents indicate that trade associations were an important source of technical information for this industry.

Measures of the variables were collected from both key informants and respondents. The number of informants per firm ranged from 1 to 50: the size of these organizations ranged from 100 to 20,000 employees. While Seidler (1974) has demonstrated that key informant results on controversial issues are less reliable with a small number of informants per case, Phillips (1982) has shown that reliability can be increased by selecting informants for their expertise. Several procedures ensured that knowledgeable informants were selected. The number of occupational specialties and number of personnel employed in technical or engineering groups were described by the informant designated as the person "most knowledgeable about general company operations." The dependent innovation measures were obtained from the informant designated as "most knowledgeable about capital equipment purchases." The remaining variables (attitudes toward change, attendance at trade shows and centralization) were respondent-based measures. A random sample of half the managers from each organization received a mailed questionnaire. Overall, the response rate to this questionnaire was 66%. Responses were aggregated by their level in the formal hierarchy based on information from an organizational chart for each firm (see Hage and Aiken 1970).

To test whether the respondent-based measures were sensitive to the number of respondents reporting for each organization, reliabilities were calculated for the scales omitting all firms with less than five respondents per case (32 out of 46 organizations).[1] The reliability on the centralization scale increased (Cronbach's $\alpha = 0.77$ with $N = 46$ and 0.84 with $N = 32$), indicating that the inclusion of firms with fewer than five informants did not seriously affect the measure's reliability. The reliability of the managerial attitudes scales decreased from $\alpha = 0.47$ ($N = 46$) to $\alpha = 0.39$ ($N = 32$). However, the reliability of this scale is generally poor, and results using it must be regarded as tentative.

Analysis

We had originally intended to predict adoption patterns from 1970 through 1977, since we had data for this period and because Hage and Aiken (1970) have argued that structural conditions conducive to innovation should be associated with adoption rates prior and subsequent to measurement of the structural variables. We decided not to use the entire period's innovations (1970–1977) because we had no way to test whether innovation rates affected subsequent levels of structural variables in ways opposite to those we predicted. There is some reason to be concerned with this problem. Dewar and Duncan (1977) have argued that high rates of innovation adoption may lead to more mechanistic structures, in which case some structural variables might be positively associated with innovation adoption rates prior to their measure and negatively associated with those subsequent to it. Consequently, we used a shorter time period. Our dependent variable is the adoption rate for the two-year period immediately preceding and following the measurement of the independent variables (i.e., 1973 to 1977).

TABLE 27-2 Zero Order Correlation Coefficients, Means and Standard Deviations of the Independent and Dependent Variables (*N* = 40)

	1.	*2.*	*3.*	*4.*	*5.*	*6.*	*7.*	*8.*	*9.*	$\bar{x}$	σ
1. Radical Innovation Adoption	—									0.9	1.8
2. Incremental Innovation Adoption	0.61***	—								1.9	2.4
3. Complexity	0.71***	0.60***	—							10.8	5.6
4. Depth of Knowledge	0.77***	0.55**	0.60***	—						1.7	5.1
5. Exposure to External Information	−0.08	0.07	−0.10	−0.05	—					0.9	0.61
6. Managerial Attitudes Toward Change	0.07	0.04	0.21*	0.04	0.26*	—				3.7	0.4
7. Centralization	0.14	0.07	0.28*	0.01	−0.01	−0.08	—			2.1	0.8
8. Centralization Attitudes	0.16	0.32**	0.35**	0.02	0.06	0.21*	0.95***	—		7.9	2.9
9. Log Size	0.74***	0.52***	0.71***	0.62***	−0.02	0.20	0.11	0.17	—	6.3	1.3
	1.	*2.*	*3.*	*4.*	*5.*	*6.*	*7.*	*8.*	*9.*		

*⇒ $p \leq 0.10$.
**⇒ $p \leq 0.05$.
***⇒ $p \leq 0.01$.

Zero order correlations, means and standard deviations for the variables are shown in Table 27-2. We excluded the interaction of managerial attitudes and centralization in our regression models because the interaction term was highly correlated with centralization ($r = 0.95$) and second, when we ran regressions (not shown here) with the interaction term but excluding the main effect terms and controlling for the other independent variables, it did not have a significant effect on either type of innovation adoption. We find, then, no support for our hypothesis that centralization accelerates the effects of managerial attitudes toward change on the adoption of radical innovations.

Although we did not hypothesize any direct effects, we included the log of firm size as an independent variable, as the zero order correlations indicated it was closely related to both types of innovation adoption as well as to complexity and depth of knowledge resources. Size was measured as the log of the number of employees to reflect the expectation that a curvilinear relationship best captured the link between size and innovation adoption (Kimberly 1976). When using the Kimberly and Evansiko (1981) technique comparing the correlations between size, log size, and the adoption of both innovation types, no significant differences were found. The log size measure was retained to be consistent with previous researchers' practice.

Size was so highly related to the other variates that multicollinearity again was a concern (see Table 27-3). Consequently, we ran models including and omitting firm size. Thus, the results were assessed by regressing both types of innovation adoption on two sets of independent variables. Model 1 represents the full model with size and all other independent variables included. Model 2 is a reduced form model that excludes size due to the multicollinearity problems cited above.

DISCUSSION OF RESULTS

The regression equations in Table 27-3 for the most part do not confirm our hypotheses, but do offer support for our general contention that the predictors of radical and incremental innovation adoptions differ. We had much more success predicting radical adoption patterns than incremental ones, largely because of the unanticipated effects

TABLE 27-3 Regression of Radical and Incremental Innovations on the Independent Variables ($N = 40$)

Part A. Radical Innovations

	Adjusted R^2	Complexity	Depth of Knowledge	External Exposure	Managerial Attitudes	Centralization	Log Size
Model 1	0.67***	0.17	0.43***	−0.08	−0.01	0.02	0.36***
Model 2	0.61***	0.35	0.53***	−0.07	0.02	0.01	omitted

Part B. Incremental Innovations

	Adjusted R^2	Complexity	Depth of Knowledge	External Exposure	Managerial Attitudes	Centralization	Log Size
Model 1	0.38***	0.27	0.34**	0.08	0.18	0.16	0.05
Model 2	0.40***	0.31***	0.36	0.08	0.18	0.16	omitted

*$\Rightarrow p \le 0.10$.
**$\Rightarrow p \le 0.05$.
***$\Rightarrow p \le 0.01$.

of size on the former. The depth of knowledge resources (i.e., the number of persons in engineering specialties) had a stronger effect on radical than on incremental adoption with or without the effects of size controlled.

Part A of Table 27-3 indicates that the principal predictors of radical innovation adoption are the depth of knowledge resources and size. Exposure to external information did not predict radical innovation adoption. Centralization and managerial attitudes favoring change were expected to affect this kind of adoption and did not. In the case of centralization, it may be that the previously discussed contradictory effects on innovation are cancelling each other. Other researchers have reported similar findings for centralization (e.g., Miller and Friesen 1982). The profile that emerges for the adoption of radical innovations is one of large organizations that can afford large numbers of engineers to experiment with and absorb innovations containing a substantial new knowledge component.

Complexity has a weak and insignificant effect when size is controlled. These findings are different from Hage and Aiken's (1970) results where complexity was one of the most important predictors. By applying the distinction between types of innovation, this discrepancy may be resolved. Hage and Aiken examined social service innovations, while this study concentrated on changes in the technical process. Unlike technical process changes, with social service innovations, the outcomes are difficult to demonstrate (i.e., they are more uncertain). It is possible that a knowledge generation process is more important for both incremental and radical social service innovation adoption, while a knowledge storage and manipulation process is more important for production process innovations. Large numbers of engineers may not be particulary creative, but they facilitate technical process innovation because engineers have easy access to state of the art ideas (knowledge storage) and can test these ideas and their variations (knowledge manipulation). All six innovations included in this study were invented before the organizations adopted them, so the innovation process involved copying and adapting these changes rather than inventing them. In contrast, with social service innovations, a think tank approach representing the combination of diverse professional viewpoints may be the more important innovation generator. Again, there is a need to distinguish innovation types in determining important predictors.

Finally, the effects of size on the adoption of more radical innovations cannot be denied. Increased size leads to more engineers and, most likely, to more research equipment, larger labs, and more slack to permit failures (March 1981). As more experiments and trials are made, the number of failures increases, but so does the number of successes (Peters and Waterman 1982). Larger size permits more risk-taking, a necessary condition for the consideration and adoption of more radical innovations.

We had far less success predicting incremental innovation adoption (see Table 27-3, Part B). The variance explained is half of that explained for the more radical types. Size in this model was unimportant. Centralization and managerial attitudes favoring change had small, insignificant positive effects. The failure to find an effect of attitudes favoring change makes our results differ from those of Hage and Dewar (1973) who found that these attitudes were important determinants of innovative performance. This discrepancy may be because in smaller organizations, such as the 16 social service agencies, managerial attitudes would be expected to have a larger effect, since these managers have more direct contact with operations. Exposure to new incremental developments in technology through trade show membership was not important in promoting incremental innovation adoption. Again, the only consistent predictor of incremental innovation adoption is the depth of knowledge resources. Although its effect on incremental innovations is less than its effect on the radical type, we must conclude that large numbers of engineers are also important for adopting this innovation type.

CONCLUSIONS

Conclusions regarding causality from this research must be tempered because measures of adoption that took place two years prior to measurement of the independent variables were included in the innovation measures. However, confidence in our findings is enhanced by direct comparison with the only other study published that explicitly assesses the determinants of radical vs. incremental innovation adoption (Ettlie *et al.* 1984). By comparing the results of research based on a sample of domestic footwear manufacturers with similar research conducted in a sample of firms from the food processing industry (i.e., Ettlie *et al.* 1984), the generalizability of the findings can be evaluated. Several key variables were the same across both studies: organizational size, depth of knowledge resources, complexity and decentralization. Table 27-4 summarizes the comparable results.

In both types of firms, depth of knowledge resources was an important predictor of the adoption of radical and incremental innovations. Ettlie *et al.* provide several insights into why this relationship is so important. Their research on adoption of radical process innovations suggests that an aggressive technological policy, defined as "a preemptive, long-range strategy for technological innovation" (Ettlie *et al.* 1984, p. 684) tends to encourage a structural arrangement consisting of a concentration of technical specialists. Both studies use log numbers of employees to measure size. This suggests that larger organizations up to some threshold are associated with this structural form. Their research suggests that the existence of extensive knowledge in the form of technical specialists translates into radical innovation adoption. The existence of a technical group promotes the existence of innovation champions and creates the perception of greater economic congruence between an innovation and the organization adopting it.

TABLE 27-4   Comparison of Results from Two Studies of Radical and Incremental Innovation Adoption

Organizational Variables	Adoption in the Domestic Footwear Industry[1]		Adoption in the Food Processing Industry	
	Incremental Innovation Adoption	*Radical Innovation Adoption*	*Incremental Innovation Adoption*[2]	*Radical Innovation Adoption*
Organizational Size (Natural logarithm of number of year-round employees)		***	**	**
Depth of knowledge Resources (Presence of Technical Engineering Groups)	**	***	**	**[3]
Complexity (Number of Occupational Specialities)				
Centralization				

*$p \le 0.05$.
**$p \le 0.01$.
***$p \le 0.001$.

[1]Used results from the model to summarize the effects on innovation adoption.
[2]Results for new product introduction are included in effects on incremental innovation adoption as in Ettlie et al. (1984).
[3]A significant positive correlation was found between depth of knowledge resources and the adoption of a radical packaging adoption ($r = 0.46$, $p \le 0.01$), but the correlations with adoption of a radical process innovation were not significant.

Organizational size was an important predictor of radical innovation adoption in both the shoe and food packaging industries, although it was also an important predictor of incremental innovation adoption in Ettlie *et al.*'s (1984) research. Firm complexity and a decentralized structure were not significant predictors of adoption of either innovation type when other variables, such as firm size, were controlled. Thus, the direct comparison of these two studies in different industries, but examining the same distinction between the two innovation types, begins to build a foundation of comparative research that points to very similar managerial implications.

IMPLICATIONS OF THE FINDINGS FOR THE MANAGER

It is an inherent risk with any empirical undertaking that hypotheses developed with reasonable logic will fail to be supported. Such is the case with the links between either type of innovation adoption and centralization, exposure to external information, and managerial attitudes conducive to change. Furthermore, the findings regarding complexity are weaker than expected. These "nonfindings" involving variables managers could manipulate make it difficult to draw a large number of practical implications.

It would be tempting for managers to dismiss these variables. The results of other studies, however, in which they have been found to have effects on innovation suggest caution in concluding they are unimportant. Perhaps a distinction between service and technical process innovations needs to be drawn. While service innovations may be highly dependent on a think tank of specialties supported by managerial attitudes conducive to change, and in which idea generators have some authority to implement their ideas (decentralization), innovations in technical processes probably depend more on acquiring a critical mass of engineers.

Large size is conducive to the acquisition of this critical mass of expertise. In this study, the log of size was highly correlated ($r = 0.62$) with the depth of knowledge. It is apparently easier, then, for larger organizations up to some point to bury the expense of extra specialists in their budgets, facilitating the adoption of more radical innovations. Economies of scale may also operate, allowing larger organizations to take the financial risk entailed in radical changes of their technical processes. We found that radical innovations are somewhat less likely to be adopted by smaller firms. In the case of incremental innovations, large size has no adoption advantage. Finally, the number of different specialties has a weak positive effect on radical innovation adoption and a somewhat stronger one on incremental innovations. From this finding flows an implication that a think tank approach to technical change cannot be ruled out entirely. Consequently, hiring different types of specialties may still be conducive to innovation adoption.

SUMMARY

We hypothesized and found that radical and incremental innovations have different predictors. These findings support the arguments of others that differences across innovation types need to be acknowledged and measured. While the depth of knowledge resources in an organization is more important for radical innovation adoption and less so for incremental, organizational size is clearly important only for radical innovation adoption. The discrepancy between our results regarding the effect of complexity and others' caution researchers may need to make a distinction between the predictors of machine technology and people-changing innovations. This conclusion also receives support from studies that document the differences in the predictors of technological vs. service innovations.[2]

References

ALLEN, T. J., "Roles in Technicago Communication Networks" in Carnot E. Nelson and Donal K. Pollack (Eds.) *Communication Among Scientists and Engineers,* Heath, Lexington, Mass., 1970, 191–208.

BIGONESS, W. AND W. D. PERRAULT, "A Conceptual Paradigm and Approach for the Study of Innovators," *Acad. Management J.,* 24 (1982), 68–82.

CARROLL, J., "A Note on Departmental Autonomy and Innovation in Medical Schools," *J. Business,* 49 (1966), 531–534.

DAFT, R. L. AND S. W. BECKER, *Innovation in Organization,* Elsevier, New York, 1978.

DAMANPOUR, FARIBORZ, "The Adoption of Technological, Administrative and Service Innovations: Impact of Organizational Factors," Working paper, LaSalle University, 1984.

DEWAR, R. D. AND R. B. DUNCAN, "Implications for Organizational Design of Structural Alterations as a Consequence of Growth and Innovation," *Organization and Administrative Sci.,* 7 (1977), 203–222.

DOWNS, G. W. AND L. B. MOHR, "Conceptual Issues in the Study of Innovation," *Admin. Sci. Quart.,* 21 (1976), 700–714.

DUCHESNEAU, T. D., S. COHN AND J. DUTTON, *A Study of Innovation in Manufacturing, Determination, Processes and Methodological Issues.* Vol. I, Social Science Research Institute, University of Maine, Orono, 1979.

DUTTON, JOHN AND ANNIE THOMAS, "Relating Technological Change and Learning by Doing," in R. Rosenbloom (Ed.), *Research on Technological Innovation, Management and Policy,* JAI Press, Greenwich, Conn., 1985, 2, 187–224.

ETTLIE, J. E., "Organizational Policy and Innovation Among Suppliers to the Food Processing Sector," *Acad. Management J.,* 26 (1983), 27–44.

———, W. P. BRIDGES AND R. D. O'KEEFE, "Organization Strategy and Structural Differences for Radical vs. Incremental Innovation," *Management Sci.,* 30 (1984), 682–695.

HAGE, J., *Theories of Organization,* Wiley Interscience, New York, 1980.

——— AND M. AIKEN, *Social Change in Complex Organizations,* Random House, New York, 1970.

——— AND R. DEWAR, "Elite Values versus Organization Structure in Predicting Innovation," *Admin. Sci. Quart.,* 18 (1973), 279–290.

KALUZNY, A. D., J. E. VENEY AND J. T. GENTRY, "Innovation in Health Services: A Comparative Study of Hospitals and Health Departments," Paper presented at the University of North Carolina Health Services Symposium, Innovation in Health Care Organizations, Chapel Hill, N.C., May 18–19, 1972.

KIMBERLY, J. R., "Managerial Innovation," In *Handbook of Organization Design,* P. Nystrom & W. Starbuck (Eds.), Oxford University Press, 1981, 203–225.

———, "Organizational Size and the Structuralist Perspective: A Review, Critique and Proposal" *Admin. Sci. Quart.,* 21 (1976), 571–597.

——— AND M. J. EVANISKO, "Organizational Innovation: The Influence of Individual, Organizational and Contextual Factors on Hospital Adoption of Technological and Administrative Innovations," *Acad. Management J.,* 24 (1981), 689–713.

KNIGHT, K. E., "A Descriptive Model of the Intra-Firm Innovation Process," *J. Business,* 40 (1967), 478–496.

MARCH, JAMES G., "Footnotes to Organizational Change," *Admin. Sci. Quart.,* 26 (1981), 563–577.

MILLER, D. AND P. H. FRIESEN, "Innovation in Conservative and Entrepreneurial Firms: Two Models of Strategic Momentum," *Strategic Management J.,* 3 (1982), 1–25.

MOCH, M. K. AND E. T. MORSE, "Size, Centralization and Organizational Adoption of Innovations," *Amer. Sociological Rev.,* 42 (1977), 716–725.

MUNSON, F. C. AND D. C. PELZ, "The Innovating Process: A Conceptual Framework," Working paper, University of Michigan, 1979.

NEAL, S. A., *Values and Interest in Social Change,* Prentice Hall, Englewood Cliffs, N.J., 1965.

NORMANN, R., "Organizational Innovativeness: Product Variation and Reorientation," *Admin. Sci. Quart.,* 16 (1971), 188–207.

PELZ, D. C. AND F. C. MUNSON, "Originality Level and the Innovating Process in Organizations," *Human Systems Management,* 3 (1982) 173–187.

PETERS, T. J. AND R. H. WATERMAN, *In Search of Excellence,* Harper & Row, New York, 1982.

PHILLIPS, L. W., "Assessing Measurement Error in Key Informant Reports: A Methodological Note on Organizational Analysis in Marketing," *J. Marketing Res.,* 18 (1982), 395–415.

SIEDLER, J., "On Using Informants," *Amer. Sociological Rev.,* (1974), 816–831.

U.S. Bureau of the Census, *Census of Manufacturers,* 1972 (Washington: U.S. Government Printing Office), 1977.

UTTERBACK, JAMES M., "Innovation in Industry and the Diffusion of Technology," *Science,* 183 (1974), 620–626.

WEBSTER, F. E., "Informal Communications in Industrial Markets," *J. Marketing Res.,* (1970), VII, 48–53.

ZALTMAN, G. N., R. B. DUNCAN AND J. HOLBEK, *Innovations and Organizations,* John Wiley & Sons, New York, 1973.

Endnotes

1. Measures of the independent variables were available for 46 firms. The 40 firms on which the analysis is based include firms for which measures of both dependent and independent variables were available.
2. The data and tabulations utilized in this manuscript were made available by the Social Science Research Institute of the University of Maine at Orono. The data were originally collected as part of an interdisciplinary study of innovation funded under NSF Grant RDA-7423651, Thomas D. Duchesneau, Principal Investigator. Neither the principal investigator, the Social Science Research Institute, nor the National Science Foundation bear any responsibility for the analyses or interpretation presented here.

The authors are equally responsible for this paper. The second author was directly involved in the original data collection, the first was not. The authors gratefully acknowledge the helpful comments of Fariborz Damanpour and three anonymous reviewers of earlier drafts of this manuscript.

28

ARE PRODUCT- AND PROCESS-INNOVATIONS INDEPENDENT OF EACH OTHER?

Kornelius Kraft

*Department of Economics, University of Kassel, Nora-Platiel-Strasse 4,
P.O. Box 10 13 80, D-3500 Kassel, Federal Republic of Germany*

This paper studies the relationship between product- and process-innovation. After discussing the determinants of product- and process-innovation, a simultaneous equation model is estimated. A positive impact of product-innovation on process-innovation can be proved, but no evidence for a reverse effect can be found. Coefficients of other variables explaining process-innovation are sensitive with respect to the inclusion of product-innovation.

INTRODUCTION

In the last few years a considerable number of empirical studies on the determinants of innovative activity have been undertaken.[1] Within these investigations the difference between product- and process-innovation is mostly neglected. One reason for this neglect is the frequent use of proxy variables for innovative activity like R&D expenditures, employees working in R&D departments or the total number of patents, which make a differentiation into product- and process-innovation difficult or even impossible.

The few empirical studies, which explicitly look both at process- and product-innovation, rarely discuss in detail whether the determinants of these two kinds of innovation might differ. In the empirical test usually the same set of exogenous variables is applied to explain both dependent variables, and the question of a possible relationship between the two kinds of innovative activity is neither discussed nor tested.

The implicit assumption that these two ways of technological advance are independent but determined by the same variables seems to be questionable. A company's intention to develop a new product can well lead to a simultaneous development of a new technology. The topic of this paper is the discussion and empirical investigation of the determinants of product- and process-innovation. It is empirically tested whether the two regarded kinds of innovation influence one another in a simultaneous equation model. The result of this estimation is that product-innovation stimulates process-innovation, but there is no evidence of a reverse effect.

DETERMINANTS OF PRODUCT- AND PROCESS-INNOVATION

There are obvious reasons why product- and process-innovation do not have to be independent of each other. Frequently the manufacturing of a new product will only be possible if a new process is implemented. The development of a new product can initiate reflections on the used production technology and, as a consequence, this technology might well be judged as being inadequate. Even if in principle an innovative good could be produced with an already established process, management may use this opportunity of a change in the product line to modify the production technology as well. A reverse causality is also possible, but has less plausibility. An innovative process might lead to a product improvement as a side effect, but in principle the product policy is too important to be mainly determined by the used technology. Nevertheless, the possibility that such an influence exists cannot be rejected *a priori*.

If one of the discussed simultaneous effects is present but neglected, the analysis may suffer from an omitted variable bias. Assume for a moment that product-innovation determines process-innovation. In this case, variables connected with product-innovation can be significant in a regression explaining process-innovation without having a true impact. The reason for this can be that variables like concentration are determining product-innovation, but the variable product-innovation itself is missing in this equation. The impact product-innovation has on process-innovation is, in this case, measured by the coefficients of the variable correlated with product-innovation (according to this example concentration). This will lead to biased coefficients and standard errors, and to conclusions about relations between the exogenous variables and the dependent variable process-innovation which are counterfactual.

An econometric study of the relationship between product- and process-innovation has to consider the determinants of each of the two kinds of technological progress. A major issue in most empirical studies is the relationship of market structure to innovation. Schumpeter (1975) hypothesized a positive relationship between these two variables, but the empirical evidence is rather mixed. The intensity of competition seems to be more relevant for product-innovation than for process-innovation. The introduction of a new product obviously becomes known fairly quickly, especially, as consumers have to be informed about its existence. Rivals can easily compare this product with their own goods, and imitation can only be prevented by patents. This is, however, not necessarily true for process-innovation. Such a modification, and especially the particular features of the process-innovation, can be kept secret as no outsiders have direct contact with it. Over time, of course, secrets will leak out, but nevertheless there is a difference with respect to information properties of product- and process-innovation.

The second hypothesis of Schumpeter was that innovative activity rises overproportionally with firm size. It is not obvious that firm size should have a different impact on one of the regarded kinds of innovation.

Aside from these frequently considered determinants of innovative activity, other factors can be discussed. Exports can enhance product-innovations, as German products will be—due to the relatively high wages—only competitive if they are technologically advanced. The relation to the process is less clear. Zimmermann (1987) points out that exports should increase competitive pressure and should therefore—if Schumpeter's analysis is correct—have a negative influence on innovative activity. This is of course a valid argument, if market structure is measured on a domestic level. As it will be shown in the empirical section, competition is, however, measured here on an international level and therefore the impact of exports can be investigated without the indirect influence of competition.

Managerial capitalism states that managers without capital ownership will tend to maximize their own utility and are not strict profit maximizers. Income as one determinant of the utility of managers can be dependent on size, which leads to the hypothesis that firms led by managers grow faster than firms managed by the owners themselves.

Growth is among other factors determined by product-innovation. This argument implies that firms led by managers will, on average, put more emphasis on product-innovation than other firms. On the other hand, one can also argue that managers are not usually laid off because of mediocrity but because of large mistakes. The risk of being laid off in this case rises with every product-innovation because of the uncertain outcome of R&D projects. Given that in Germany the salary of managers is mostly fixed, capital owners will benefit from the high returns of a successful innovation to a greater degree than managers. An investment in a R&D project that fails reduces profits and increases the managers' risk of being laid off. Hence the losses from unsuccessful R&D projects have to be borne by both capital owners and managers, while the profits of a successful project will mostly go to the capital owners' benefit. This asymmetric payout situation speaks in favour of a risk-averse and therefore reluctant innovation policy by managers.

The risk connected with process-innovation will presumably be lower than that connected with product-innovation, because in the latter case the reaction of the market to the introduction of the innovation is crucial for its success but usually unknown. Hence, risk will be of lower importance with respect to the question of an introduction of a process-innovation and the growth aspect can be dominant. Low unit costs due to an advanced production technology might benefit growth and perhaps the income of the managers. But one has to admit that it is unknown whether the theory of managerial capitalism is relevant for Germany at all.

Another factor, which possibly determines innovative activity, is the qualification level of employees. The management literature (e.g. Wildemann, 1986) has pointed out that especially for process-innovation but also for product-innovation, the skill level of the workforce and training expenditures are of relevance.[2]

EMPIRICAL SPECIFICATION

Data from 56 West German firms for 1979 have been used for the empirical test. All firms were operating in the metal-working industry, were of medium size and were not obliged to publish any financial data. Of course, the application of data from just one particular industry reduces on the one hand the number of observations but has, on the other hand, the advantage that firms are relatively homogeneous. Given that the technical opportunity for innovations presumably differs considerably, an aggregation of observations from different industries is not without problems.[3]

In practice, it is difficult to identify innovations exactly. Many studies use R&D expenditures or the number of patents as proxy variables for innovative activity. The use of total R&D expenditures is not helpful in the given context, as their differentiation into process- and product-innovation is of prime interest. Patents could, in principle, be divided into process- and product-innovations, but Kamien and Schwartz (1982) note some shortcomings of patent statistics. They point out that many patents have never been commercialized, are only used for minor modifications of existing products and that many innovations are not patented at all.[4]

In the light of these problems, product-innovation is measured here as the share of sales that can be attributed to products newly developed during the last five years. Thereby not only the number of new products but also their success on the market is taken into account.[5] Investigated firms were questioned in such a way that minor modifications could be ruled out. Compared to R&D expenditures or patent statistics the measurement used here gives a low weight to those firms actually developing innovative products which are, however unimportant with respect to overall sales. In the latter case, variables like technology or capital ownership have a limited explanatory power.

With respect to process-innovation measurement problems arise as well. To accomplish a standardization of innovative activity, firms were asked whether the degree of innovativeness of their technology was below, equal or above the level of competitors. The position of the regarded firm in relation to competitors was used to avoid, as far as possible, a bias from subjective answers. If an absolute scaling had been applied, the possibility of inappropriate classification would have been much more severe. Assuming that the sample is randomly chosen, there should be as many answers indicating that technology is 'below average' as those stating 'above average.' This is, however, not the case. Only seven percent of the firms say that their innovativeness is below average, whereas about 57% pretend that their innovative activity is above the level of competitors. Although this is troublesome with respect to the validity of an econometric study, it is not surprising given that this evaluation must be necessarily subjective, as naturally nobody would like to confess to being 'below average.' Despite these problems of subjective evaluation, there is no other way than to transfer the responses to the question 'is innovative activity above the level of what competitors do?' to a variable indicating a high level of process-innovation.

Compared to patents on process-innovations this variable has the disadvantage of being subjective and the advantage of excluding minor modifications of technology. Hence the relative strength of both dependent variables used in this study is that they take into account whether the innovative activity is actually relevant for a significant part of output and technology. This aspect is important insofar as the firm's characteristics presumably only have an impact with respect to innovative activity if technological advance is significant for the whole company. Furthermore, in the context of this study it is particularly important to identify the relative importance of process- and product-innovation, as the influence of one variable on the other is considered. For example, product-innovations will probably only affect process-innovations if these products form a sizable proportion of overall output. As stated above, the disadvantage is clearly the somewhat subjective determination of the variables in question. A bias from the application of the described variables is, however, not obvious. Despite the fact that this study addresses a specific question, the results presented below do not deviate from those obtained in related investigations using other variables.

An important explanatory variable is concentration. Most studies use the three- or four-firm concentration or the Herfindhal index to control for influences of a market structure. Here as an exogenous variable, the inverse of the number of main competitors of the regarded firm operating in the major markets (MS) is taken. Clearly the use of this variable is limited due to the neglect of the size distribution of the competitors. On the other hand, this variable has the advantage that the level of competition is measured as being as disaggregated as possible. The firms have to define their relevant market themselves. This means, if a company is for some reason only operating in a particular region, only the number of rivals actually competing in this area will be considered. Firms, which on the other hand export a significant share of their production to other countries, were asked also to take into account the number of those foreign competitors. Hence this study has tried to measure the degree of competitive pressure, as it is actually perceived on the firm level.[6]

Connected with concentration are barriers to entry. Barriers to entry can only be proxied but not directly observed. Here, capital intensity KAPIN is taken as an indicator for barriers to entry. Personal interviews by Zörgiebel (1983) with managers of firms operating in the metal working industry support the view that capital requirements act as a barrier to entry. Capital intensity can be regarded as a barrier to entry in regressions explaining product innovation, but this variable is questionable in estimations with process-innovation as the dependent variable. Technical progress is frequently connected with capital intensity and, therefore, in the latter regression KAPIN can presumably be more reasonably interpreted as a necessary precondition for process-innovation.

As mentioned above, Zimmermann (1987) investigates the effect of international trade on innovative activity. One would expect that exports give rise to the intensity of competition if market structure is measured only on a national level. In this case the hypotheses of Schumpeter would speak in favour of a negative effect of exports on innovative activities. Zimmermann (1987) also points out that international trade can lead to a more intensive quality competition which, in turn, should enhance (product-) innovation. In this study the effects of exports on innovation can be investigated without the indirect impact that exports have on competitive pressure, as the market structure takes international competition into account. The variable exports EXP is measured as the share of sales delivered to other countries.[7]

Resources available for an internal financing of innovations are taken into account by the cash-flow CASH. It has been hypothesized that internal financing is of high relevance for innovations, as external financing requires disclosure of information and eases imitation. The Schumpeterian viewpoint also suggests that firm size should be included in the analysis which is measured in this study by the total number of employees.

The structure of capital ownership is taken into consideration by the use of a dummy variable CTOP, which has the value one if the management holds 25% of equity or more The qualification level of the employees is measured by the variables AKAD, the ratio of employees who have an academic degree to all employees; TREX, training expenditures employee; WAGE, average wage per employee;[8] and WHITE, the ratio of white-collar workers to blue-collar workers. The last mentioned variable has an ambiguous interpretation, as a high number of white-collar workers, aside from a high qualification level of the workforce, can also express a bureaucratic and hierarchical structure. White-collar workers are employed to fulfil administrative tasks and a high share of white-collar workers may indicate an orientation towards administration instead of innovation.

Innovative activity has, of course, to do with production technology. This is obvious and needs no explanation as far as process-innovation is concerned, but a relation to product-innovation can also be present. By including those variables describing the type of technology used (not the level of technological progress), it is intended to control the technological opportunity a firm is faced with. Two variables are used. The dummy variable FLOW has the value one if the regarded firm produces with a flow-technology. The application of flow-technology most likely reduces the flexibility of production and renders a frequent modification of the product line more difficult. Furthermore, flow-technology is mostly used for a mass production of low quality products, while innovative-products are sold in the beginning in small quantities. A hypothesis with respect to the most preferable process of production cannot be easily developed. The introduction of a flow-technology may lead management to use an advanced technology, but once installed it may be expensive to modify.

The second technology variable INC measures the ratio of piece-rates to total wage payments. Piece-rates will usually be applied as incentives, if the work is not very demanding and the workforce is not highly qualified. A technologically advanced process is hardly compatible with unambitious tasks of the workforce. Therefore a negative coefficient can be expected. The connection with the product is not obvious. Empirical tests did not show a significant impact and thus, for the purpose of identification, this variable was omitted from the regression explaining product-innovation. To control for specific subindustry effects, two industry dummies IND 1 and IND 2 are included according to the classification of the German Statistical Office.

The main issue of this paper is an investigation of a possible joint determination of product- and process-innovation. Therefore a simultaneous equation model has to be used. However, in this particular context it is not possible to apply a standard simultaneous equation approach. The variable 'process innovation' is a dummy variable (unit value if a firm innovates 'above the level of competitors'), and therefore an estimation procedure for limited dependent variables has to be used. In this case a simultaneous Probit-model is estimated.[9] One of the endogenous variables is the probability that the firm uses a production function technology which is more advanced than that of competitors. The other dependent variable is the share of sales which can be attributed to newly developed products. For identification purposes some variables have to be excluded from the estimations. Likelihood-ratio and *F*-tests respectively have been applied to determine those variables which have to be either included or excluded from the two equations. For example, CTOP was excluded from the Probit-model, as no influence of capital ownership on process-innovation could be proved. This approach leads to the following:

$$\text{PRODUCT IN} = f(\text{MS, SIZE, KAPIN, FLOW, EXP, WHITE, CASH,}$$
$$\text{AKAD, CTOP, }\widehat{\text{PROCESS IN}}) \tag{1}$$

$$\text{PROCESS IN} = g(\text{MS, SIZE, KAPIN, FLOW, EXP, CASH, INC, TREX,}$$
$$\text{WAGE, IND 1, IND 2, }\widehat{\text{PRODUCT IN}}) \tag{2}$$

The expressions $\widehat{\text{PROCESS IN}}$ and $\widehat{\text{PRODUCT IN}}$ stand for the instrumented values of the two endogenous variables. Instrumental variables are all right-hand side variables (i.e. estimating the reduced-form equations). Equation 2 (as well as the reduced form equation to predict $\widehat{\text{PROCESS IN}}$) is estimated by Probit. In order to remove heteroscedasticity in the error variances, Equation 1 is estimated by Weighted Least Squares (WLS).

RESULTS

The results of the simultaneous equation model are displayed in Table 28-1, rows 1 and 2.[10] In addition, the results of a single equation model with a dependent variable process-innovation, but without product-innovation as an explanatory variable, are shown in row 3.

The most important result is that product-innovation has a significant impact on process-innovation, but the reverse is not the case. This result is, however, consistent with the expectation that product-innovation can lead to the introduction of new technology. The second tested possibility, that process-innovation influences product-innovation, is obviously less plausible.

Another striking result is the strong impact of the additional variable product-innovation on the coefficients of the explanatory variables market structure MS and KAPIN. Both coefficients are much smaller and lose their significance. One is tempted to interpret these results as if product-innovation not market structure determined process-innovation. This argumentation would lead to a recursive model, in which market structure determines product-innovation and this, in turn, influences process-innovation.[11] This makes sense intuitively, as market structure seems to be more relevant for product-innovation than for process-innovation because of the information properties discussed above. If this interpretation is correct, an omission of product-innovation from a regression explaining process-innovation leads to an omitted variable bias. The impact of product-innovation would be attributed to other variables like market structure correlated with product-innovation.

However, a simultaneous equation model is not a causality test. Several statistical reasons could be responsible for these results. Clearly, all included variables are highly correlated with one another, and in such a small sample, the addition of the variable product-innovation can simply lead to insignificant coefficients because of multicollinearity (but the coefficients are unbiased). In addition, standard errors are always larger in simultaneous equation models compared with single equation models. Both arguments suggesting that the results are caused by a 'statistical' reason are supported by a single-equation Probit-estimation with product-innovation (not instrumented) as an explanatory variable.

In this estimation product-innovation, MS and KAPIN are significant, although the *t*-values of the latter two variables are somewhat smaller than those reported in row 3. This estimation may, however, suffer from a simultaneous equation bias and the results are thus—at least with respect to the coefficients—less reliable than the ones displayed.

The other results are mostly according to expectations. Capital intensity has a positive impact on product-innovation, and like the result for the MS variable points to the relevance of Schumpeter's hypotheses. Manager-owners tend to be more active with respect to product-innovation than managers who have no share of equity. These results are consistent with the theory exposed above on risk and risk-aversion of managers.

WHITE has a strong negative effect on product-innovation leading to the interpretation that a high share of white-collar workers let firms become inflexible and are uninterested in innovating.

By jointly including the variables, exports and MS in the regression, it is possible to determine the effects of international trade without the possible influence of exports on competition. EXP has an insignificant coefficient in the regression explaining product-innovation and a negative one in the Probit-model. These results are in contrast to the ones obtained by Zimmermann (1987) and cannot be easily explained.

TABLE 28-1 Determinants of Product- and Process-Innovation

Independent Variables	Dependent Variable		
	(1) *Product In*	**(2)** *Process In*	**(3)** *Process In*
Constant	21.87 (2.65)**	−4.89 (−2.71)**	−2.49 (−1.95)*
MS	82.48 (4.72)***	2.17 (0.89)	4.26 (1.97)*
SIZE	0.04 (1.48)	0.0008 (2.14)**	0.0008 (2.19)**
KAPIN	0.35 (3.02)***	0.001 (0.10)	0.02 (1.71)*
FLOW	−27.92 (−3.73)***	2.76 (2.57)**	1.48 (1.76)*
EXP	−0.14 (−1.18)	−0.04 (−2.38)**	−0.03 (−2.58)**
WHITE	−17.69 (−5.50)***		
CASH	−3.74 (−0.61)	−0.58 (−0.90)	−0.44 (−0.72)
AKAD	−113.12 (−0.92)		
CTOP	13.77 (2.68)***		
Process In	−1.33 (−0.47)		
INC		−0.13 (−3.22)***	−0.12 (−3.25)***
TREX		0.36 (0.59)	−0.11 (−0.22)
WAGE		0.08 (1.87)*	0.03 (1.06)
IND 1		−0.19 (−0.18)	0.37 (0.39)
IND 2		1.40 (1.23)	1.65 (1.52)
Product In		0.06 (2.18)**	

t-values in parentheses.
*Significant at the 10% level (two-tailed test).
**Significant at the 5% level (two-tailed test).
***Significant at the 1% level (two-tailed test).

Intuitively the opposite result would have been expected. Finally, the coefficients of the technology variables FLOW and INC as well as WAGE have their expected signs (as far as a sign can be predicted) and are significant.

CONCLUSION

The main issue of this paper is an investigation of the relationship between product- and process-innovation. The empirical results point to a recursive model, where product-innovation leads to process-innovation. A reverse relationship cannot be proved. Although these results are consistent with theoretical expectations, econometric exercises like this cannot test causality and have to be treated with some care.

Nevertheless it is demonstrated that a relationship between both kinds of innovation can exist. This result implies that by the use of aggregate data on both product and process innovation, for example information on expenditures for R&D may get lost, one part of this variable may determine the other. In this case disaggregated data seem to be superior compared with aggregate data, however, the empirical model must be carefully specified in order to estimate the relationship between the exogenous and endogenous variables correctly.

Acknowledgements

I am indebted to Doro Lütticke and an anonymous referee for helpful comments.

References

Angelmar, R. (1985) Market structure and research intensity in high-technological-opportunity industry. *Journal of Industrial Economics,* **34,** 69–79.

Bartel, A. P. and Lichtenberg, F. R. (1987) The comparative advantage of educated workers in implementing a new technology. *Review of Economics and Statistics,* **69,** 1–11.

Bresnahan, D. F. and Schmalensee, R. (1987) The empirical renaissance in industrial economics: an overview. *Journal of Industrial Economics,* **35,** 371–8.

Cohen, W. M., Levin, R. C. and Mowery, D. C. (1987) Firm size and R&D intensity: a re-examination. *Journal of Industrial Economics,* **35,** 543–65.

FitzRoy, F. R. and Kraft, K. (1987) Efficiency and internal organization: works councils in West-German firms. *Economica,* **54,** 493–504.

Kamien, M. E. and Schwartz, N. L. (1982) *Market Structure and Innovation,* Cambridge, Mass. Cambridge University Press.

König, H. and Zimmermann, K. F. (1986) Innovations, market structure and market dynamics. *Journal of Institutional and Theoretical Economics/Zeitschrift für die gesamte Staatswissenschaft,* **142,** 184–99.

Kraft, K. (1986) Exit and voice in the labor market: an empirical study of quits. *Journal of Institutional and Theoretical Economics/Zeitschrift für die gesamte Staatswissenschaft,* **142,** 697–715.

Kraft, K. (1989) Market structure, firm characteristics and innovative activity. *Journal of Industrial Economics,* **37,** 329–336.

Levin, R. C., Cohen, M. W. and Mowery, D. C. (1985) R&D appropriability, opportunity, and market structure: new evidence on Schumpeterian hypotheses. *American Economic Review, Papers and Proceedings,* **75,** 20–4.

Lunn, J. (1986) An empirical analysis of process and product patenting: a simultaneous equation framework. *Journal of Industrial Economics,* **34,** 319–30.

Lunn, J. (1987) An empirical analysis of firm process and product patenting. *Applied Economics,* **19,** 743–51.

Maddala, G. S. (1983) *Limited Dependent and Qualitative Variables in Econometrics,* Cambridge, Mass: Cambridge University Press.

Neumann, M, Böbel, I. and Haid, A. (1982) Innovations and market structure in West-German industries. *Managerial and Decision Economics,* **3,** 131–9.

Scherer, F. M. (1980) *Industrial Market Structure and Economic Performance,* Chicago: Rand McNally, 2nd edn.

Scherer, F. M. (1982) Inter-industry technology flows and productivity growth. *Review of Economics and Statistics,* **64,** 627–34.

Scherer, F. M. (1983) Concentration, R&D and productivity change, *Southern Economic Journal,* **50,** 221–5.

Schumpeter, J. A. (1975) *Capitalism, Socialism and Democracy,* New York: Harper and Row, 3rd edn.

Wildemann, H. (1986) Einführungsstrategien für neue Produktions-technologien—Dargestellt an CAD/CAM-Systemen und flexiblen Fertigungssystemen, *Zeitschrift für Betriebswirtschaft,* **56,** 337–69.

Zimmermann, K. F. (1987) Trade and dynamic efficiency, *Kyklos,* **40,** 73–87.

Zörgiebel, W. W. (1983) *Technologie in der Wettbewerbsstrategie,* Berlin: Erich Schmidt Verlag.

Endnotes

1. Cf. the studies surveyed by Scherer (1980), Kamien and Schwartz (1982), and more recently work by Neumann, Böbel and Haid (1982); Angelmar (1985); Levin, Cohen and Mowery (1985); König and Zimmermann (1986); Cohen, Levin and Mowery (1987); Zimmermann (1987); Lunn (1986, 1987) and Scherer (1982, 1983).

2. Bartel and Lichtenberg (1987) argue that the reverse causality is also possible. As it becomes very difficult to control for this simultaneity in addition to the central one of product- and process-innovation, this possible feedback effect is ignored.

3. Problems associated with interindustry studies are discussed in general by Bresnahan and Schmalensee (1987) and with regard to innovation by Cohen, Levin and Mowery (1987).

4. The view that patents are unimportant for innovating firms is suggested by Zörgiebel (1983, p. 225), who bases his conclusion on a case study in the metal working industry.

5. Alternatively, firms were asked in the interviews whether a significant innovation has been developed internally during the last five years. It turned out that over 90% of

the approached firms answered positively, and therefore this variable is not very meaningful. Innovation is a vague concept in practice and some standardization is necessary in order to make a comparison possible.

6. If—as it is practised in similar studies—the concentration index on the two digit industry level had been applied, this variable would have had only three different values. The chosen variable MS has, however, 24 different values and it is therefore hypothesized that a measurement of concentration on the firm level can describe the market structure better than an industry-wide classification.

7. It should be noted that EXP is a potentially endogenous variable. Firms that are innovative may also be able to compete on the international market and, therefore their share of exports can be large. The consideration of several endogenous variables is, however, difficult with such a relatively small sample, as multicollinearity then becomes a serious problem.

8. Human capital theory predicts that the returns of investment in specific qualifications are shared between the firm and the employees. Therefore, a high wage is frequently used as proxy for accumulated specific human capital.

9. Cf. for a description of this method Maddala (1983) and for applications Kraft (1986) as well as FitzRoy and Kraft (1987).

10. An estimation without the endogenous variable process-innovation and the dependent variable product-innovation leads to almost similar coefficients and standard errors and is therefore omitted.

11. Frequently it is argued that concentration is an endogenous variable. The use of an instrumental variable approach does, however, not change the result. (Cf. Kraft, 1988.)

29 | THE SHAREHOLDER'S DELIGHT: COMPANIES THAT ACHIEVE COMPETITIVE ADVANTAGE FROM PROCESS INNOVATION

Wickham Skinner

Harvard Graduate School of Business, Box 282, St. George, ME 04857, USA

ABSTRACT

Process innovation strategies are rare in traditionally 'non-process' industries. Why do non-process industries appear to be so slow to learn from successful innovation in the process industries. What are the principal concepts and practices of process innovation? This paper examines some examples of success in process innovation strategies in several process industries. Similar successes in non-process industries are also described. Managerial policies in the two types of industry are compared, and a number of ideas for the management of process innovation in the non-process industries are offered.

KEYWORDS

Process industries, process innovation, non-process industries, technology management.

INTRODUCTION

Companies which successfully develop innovative production processes typically enjoy powerful, sustainable competitive advantages. Process superiority enables firms to produce a better or lower priced product or improved service, thereby creating a superb strategic posture for gaining an unassailable market position.

In the process industries, such as chemicals, plastics, steel and paper, process based strategies are common and typically successful. But, outside the process industries, those few companies which do in fact invest in process innovation as a cardinal foundation on which to base a successful competitive strategy are rare. Yet when such strategies succeed, the companies become precious jewels to their owners, museum piece exhibits of shareholder value crafted by a masterful yet unusual corporate strategy.

This article addresses why such strategies in the non-process[1] industries are so rare in spite of the clear appeal of such results and many well publicized examples of

Skinner, Wickham. 1992. The shareholder's delight: Companies that achieve competitive advantage from process innovation. *International Journal of Technology Management* 7(1–3): 41–48.

extraordinary competitive victories thus gained. Why do the non-process industries seem to be so slow to learn from the process industries? Could not executives outside the process industries benefit from certain management concepts and practices concerning process innovation which are so frequently employed in the process industries? What are those concepts and practices?

It is paradoxical that process innovation strategies are so unusual in the non-process industries considering the evidence that when they are successful they create one of the most formidable competitive advantages possible. If we can produce a product or service which our competitors cannot produce, or if they cannot produce the product with equally superior specifications or quality or reliability or performance, or if they are unable to provide the same service and customer reliability and delivery . . . we have built a position which will be most difficult to attack.

The results of a successful process innovation strategy are usually overwhelming. Ministeel mills, for example, have succeeded during the last fifteen years due almost entirely to their development of radically different steel mills from the large integrated conventional mills. McDonalds' origin and rapid growth was based on innovative development of a total process for cooking and presenting fast foods. The rise and present predominance of the Japanese in the semiconductor industry is due in large part to their ability to produce semi-conductors with outstanding performance, because of the production processes they developed. Wholecloth process innovation in the Japanese auto industry has accounted for much of its success.

This article is based on the author's research in both process and non-process industries, supplemented by case research by colleagues, principally at the Harvard Business School. We first examine some examples of success in process innovation strategies in several process industries, developing some lessons from the winners. We next turn to successes in non-process industries, and compare management policies to those in the process industries. To avoid any impression that process innovation strategies are easy, we then offer a sober look at the problems, costs, and risks in carrying out such intrepid operations strategies. From this analysis we offer in conclusion a number of ideas for managers in the non-process industries for developing and implementing a competitive strategy based on process innovation.

WINNING WITH PROCESS INNOVATION

A big winner in the late eighties was a large papermaker in the US Midwest. A new manufacturing strategy was explicitly aimed toward turning manufacturing into a competitive advantage. After analysing company papermaking processes and the services provided to customers, and recognizing how the manufacturing system design substantially impacted customer service, they totally redesigned manufacturing systems. Products were switched between the seven plants, physical modifications were introduced in various banks of equipment, and major changes were made in the uses of inventories, material flows, order quantities, and delivery methods for all customer product lines. This new process design so improved the service of the company that several competitors dropped out. The company's performance since this set of radical internal changes has been outstanding in its industry.

Borg-Warner's ABS plastics business strategy was formed around the concept of focusing the plants to maximize customer satisfaction. This meant a wide product line, customer colour specials, and short delivery cycles. In plastics resin production this represented a technological challenge because of the scale economies of large orders and the difficulties of short ones. The challenge was met by developing processes which could be economical on short runs and providing unusual flexibility by custom colour mixing in specially designed mixers and extruders. Customers were served by a production organization which consistently invested in process improvement toward better product in terms of moldability, finish, strength and colour, and better service and delivery to customers. The growth of Borg-Warner in the ABS business is one of the outstanding industrial stories of recent times. They greatly increased the total market for ABS and inexorably came to dominate the industry, driving out several major competitors to finally command an overwhelming market share.

To these examples from process industries can be added the rise of the mini-steel firms mentioned earlier and many similar examples from the chemical, pharmaceutical, and metals industries. In the process industries, it is easy to understand that the processes employed are a central key to the competitive strength of the firm. Process innovation is carried on more or less continuously and process research is apt to demand investment levels akin to product research. Process engineers are given high organizational stature. Executives at high levels, as well as middle managers, are typically competent and knowledgeable concerning process technologies at their companies, at competitors, and in engineering research literature.

These are the important lessons from the process industry: that processes are central to the competitive position of the firm; that process innovation and continuous improvement are essential to survival; and that the very organization and management focus of the company must be such as to provide excellent production processes. Sensitivity to comparative process performance is virtually a management mindset.

In non-process industries, cases where substantial, across-the-plant process innovation has been attempted are relatively scarce by comparison. Successful ones are those precious jewels, even more rare. Copeland is one such example.

The Cinderella story of the Copeland Corporation in Sydney, Ohio illustrates the competitive impact of a successful total process turnaround. This manufacturer of one horsepower and larger air conditioning and refrigeration compressors held about a 15% market share in the industry ten years ago. Now that share is over 50% worldwide. What did they do?

A new CEO took a look around the industry as his first step in deciding how to improve Copeland's position. He observed that there was not a single new plant within the industry, even including such companies as Tecumseh, Crane, General Electric, and Whirlpool. All refrigeration compressors were being made in old, depreciated factories with ancient machine tools and assembly methods.

By developing an entire new process and equipment technology using his own engineers and vendors, a great deal of imagination and about $45 million, most of which the company had to borrow, Copeland built the first new plant in the industry in twenty years. Based on innovative new processes, within two years the plant had established a formidable competitive advantage. While lower costs were partly offset by the sizeable high capital investment in the new plant, the main advantage was derived from producing products which were more predictably reliable and dependable. Within a few years, by pursuing the same approaches in other plants and in an old home office plant (each of which was focused on a specific market and entire new manufacturing systems developed), the company grew and prospered in each of its various industry segments.

This strategy was based entirely on manufacturing. They changed manufacturing processes and systems as well as the approaches, premises and systems by which all of their products were manufactured. As a result, financial performance such as margins, inventory turnover, return on investment, and share of market were impressively improved. Years later, officers revealed that the directors had recognized that they were 'betting the company' on the first new plant.

A second example comes from the fast food industries. McDonalds and Benihana restaurants transformed their industries by process innovation. The processes by which McDonalds hamburgers and other foods were made and delivered and customers handled were all part of a services process innovation which made McDonalds an outstanding performer in its industry.

Benihana restaurants demonstrated a similar ingenuity in a service industry. At Benihana, the preparation of the food, its delivery, the layout of the restaurant, and the subsidiary facilities and the sizing of each part of the restaurant, including the tables, grills and preparation areas, all made up a tailored, coordinated system by which delicious food can be delivered with surprisingly low cost and great presentation.

Of course there are other 'winners' cases. Certainly General Electric's dishwasher and locomotive plants are exemplars of total process innovation which transformed their industries. Now the General Motors Saturn subsidiary is on the line to be tested for its strategic payoff from process innovation.

Notwithstanding these happy examples, process innovation is not an easy road in any industry. We turn now to look at some of the hazards and difficulties involved.

PROBLEMS ATTENDING PROCESS INNOVATION STRATEGIES

Probably the most negative fact limiting the penetration of competitive strategies based on gaining advantage from process development is simply that they are indeed difficult to bring about. A great deal of time and sustained effort is usually involved. To be successful, personnel who innovate process improvements generally have to be some of the best in the industry. Their work needs continuity. It usually takes years to develop competence and expertise in any industrial sector. Managers and engineers in this work must be imaginative. Dogged and daring champions are usually part of any success. It takes time and this means money and investing with patience over many years.

Of course this typically amounts to a considerable capital investment; and to carry on that capital investment over a period of time requires a clear company strategy. A state of mind or philosophy which consistently encompasses the belief that the company can and should become first rate in process competence is critical. This implies an atmosphere within the company which values extraordinary ability in process technology. It also requires that the men and women involved in this work are outstanding concerning not only the company processes but also concerning the state of the industry's production processes. What is going on elsewhere in the industry is one part of this knowledge, but even more difficult is to look ahead and identify new, potentially excellent scientific advances still in the laboratory stage.

These are unusual skills and attitudes within most companies. Awareness of the strategic power of advanced processes requires both a business point of view and technological confidence. More often than not engineers are aversive to business, and top managers are aversive to technology. But continued investment in process development through years of thick and thin payoffs requires support from both.

A further problem for companies seeking process superiority is that in many industries their processes are controlled by vendors who must be relied upon for process development. In the metalworking industry, process capabilities are largely determined by the machine tool industry. In many other industries, such as plastic moulding, textiles, shoes, furniture, and to a large extent the auto industry, the primary processes are supplied by vendors. If a company in such an industry decides upon a process innovation strategy, either achieving independence from vendors or establishing a close partnership with them is a prerequisite and represents another big hurdle.

To add to this recounting of problems and uncertainty, process innovation strategies are extremely risky. The history of technology is replete with examples of new technologies seldom working just right when they are first employed. Ordinarily it takes months or years to work out the "bugs" in a new process and, in the meantime, it is difficult, costly and often disastrous to be dependent on that new process.

Further, the costs of capital at risk for major process innovations are tending to become ever higher because, with the systems concept demanded to take advantage of computer-linked processes, the investment chunks are bigger.

The plot thickens when the time dimension is factored into the issue. One of the problems of sustaining a process innovation advantage is that it does not last forever. Over some period of time it can be copied, or in various ways acquired or developed by competitors.

The chief timing risk centres on the question, 'Shall we try to be first or let somebody else put up their money?' The advantage of being first can be very short-lived and, if so, it might have been wise to wait until the first company develops the process. Then through the literature and other forms of industrial research, the trailing company can move fast to catch up, ordinarily spending only 10 to 20% of the outlay of the innovating firm.

The rarity of successful strategies based on process innovation in the non-process industries is heightened by the problem of process span. It is usually difficult to get a payoff of major competitive importance from isolated process developments such as, for example, in 'islands of automation.' It is tempting to develop a great new process for operation No. 4 of a ten-operation factory, and then to be disappointed by only gaining modest benefits because it has to be fed from operation 3 and delivered to operation 5. Maintaining operational interfaces so as to be productive and effective is difficult when the process in one operation is changed and others are not.

Similarly, maintaining capacity and production balance within the factory after a process change in part of the facility can be difficult. In the long run, when all operations or all the islands are automated, the picture can be entirely different. But the problem is that to automate or modernize all operations at once is apt to be excessively expensive and risky. Indeed, from a technical standpoint in most complex factories such as farm equipment or machine tool or multistage chemical plants, experience has shown the hazards of taking simultaneous technological leaps across a broad variety of production processes in one new or overhauled facility. This 'catch 22' is only answered by a thorough long-range plan with incremental investments and top management staying power.

So there are great risks of loss of capital, poor short-term performance, and costly expenditures of time in attempting a process innovation strategy. Clearly a process innovation strategy is a rough and risky road.

But what about those 'rare jewels' who do attempt it and then pull it off successfully? Do these exceptions prove some rules? Could there not be many more of these 'precious jewels'? What can be learned from the process industries, where process innovation seems to be a way of life?

TOWARD MORE PRECIOUS JEWELS

Successful process innovation strategies in the non-process industries are rare because few companies even try such strategies and because those who try subsequently may meet many of the difficulties cited, and then are rebuffed and disappointed. Thus, the negative cycle is reinforced, resulting in fewer firms which attempt process innovation strategies.

Since the literature of technology management offers useful insights into handling the problems of introducing new process technologies, we have chosen to focus on the major and more challenging issue in a time of extraordinary breakthroughs in operations process development. The question is: why don't more companies try?

In most industries, the motivation is certainly present in the form of severe domestic and often global competition. The technology is there in automation, servomechanisms, flexible manufacturing systems, lasers, robots, exotic material handling systems, computer-integrated manufacturing, and the list goes on. But outside of the process industries, competitive strategies are far more often based instead on product innovation, marketing policies, and financial wizardry.

Look first at the process industries. What can we learn from the many examples, such as Borg-Warner ABS plastics and the midwestern paper company? First off, interviews up and down the executive ladder make it unmistakably clear that in the process industries nearly everyone believes that process capability is considered critical to success. Second, from the same interviews, managers tend to be technology literate and interested. Technology is perceived as providing strategic opportunities. The 'mind-set' is toward process research and development on a substantial and continual basis as representing wise and prudent management stewardship.

What about the non-process industries? Not surprisingly, interviews and case analyses reveal quite the opposite executive interests, assumptions, and capacities. Technology aversion at all levels is frequent. It is common to hear, 'Let the manufacturing engineers worry about processes. And our vendors. It's to their own advantage to do the process development and offer us the best. Let the market prevail.'

Operations are seen frequently as a kind of necessary evil and, if the firm could buy more and make less, not even always so necessary. With these kinds of premises, it is not surprising that innovative and often risky process investment is seldom undertaken. Operations managers, probably wisely, hesitate to champion major process investments in such an environment, sensing the imbalance in the personal risk-payoff equation.

Is all this kind of behaviour irrational? Are the process industry managers so much smarter? Of course, the answers must be, 'no.' There is a very real and understandable problem for the non-process industry managers. *It is that there is no such thing as a non-process industry!* Every industry has a production process, but in the non-process industries there are generally a dozen or more processes compared to one to three in most process industries. In the non-process industries, the processes start out with materials and parts or components at vendors, then involve operators, tools, materials handling, scheduling and shop floor controls, and inventory management, materials processing, sub-assemblies and assembly in the company's operation.

Is it any wonder that company executives feel less than competent and eager toward process innovation in the non-process industries? What 'process' are we talking about? They are all related. Who and how is the executive to take leadership in 'process change,' other than piecemeal, starting with one that looks a bit inefficient, the Taylor approach of improving the factory detail by detail? So one big lesson from comparing process and non-process industries is that, in managerial terms, there is almost no comparison. It's an entirely different problem.

The successful innovators in the non-process industries, such as Copeland, appeared to recognize that changes in processes which create competitive advantage can range from many small ones to a few big ones. Process changes can take place from the most microscopic, small hand movements of an operator to improvement of tools and fixtures and workplaces, plant layout, materials handling, machine tools, basic process equipment that affects entire factories and, ultimately, new, totally rebuilt or greenfield factories.

There are opportunities along this entire range. It is a value-added chain with all links being interactive. For the same reason, to achieve major, leveraged improvements, many processes, rather than one, must be addressed together so that the entire set is improved as a unit. The successful companies studied seemed to recognize the linkages, whereas the less successful companies tended to concentrate on isolated processes at random.

The required span of processes to be improved as a unit varies by industry. Similarly, the managerial focus demanded ranges from attacking few, but capital intensive, processes in the chemical industry to many, by comparison, generally inexpensive processes in, say, the textile or the electrical machinery industries.

From the standpoint of developing a process-based competitive strategy, *all industries are 'process industries.'* The industries usually thought of as process industries simply have fewer processes which must be improved to create a competitive advantage. The other industries which we have called non-process industries, involve more, usually many more, processes and therefore are a much more complex entity in which to innovate change to improve performance.

Seen in this way, the rarity of Copeland type across-the-value-chain improvements which create powerful strategic advantage should not be surprising. Such innovation is inherently intellectually complex. In the conventional, barrier-packed, functional organization, many walls and conflicting professional objectives militate against an executive or a functional department assuming the risks and tackling such a bundle of connected changes.

Analysis of these cases suggests three principal conditions to be requisite for this near-miracle to happen. The 'shareholder's delights' are apparently developed only under these conditions:

Condition 1: The company has a clear and explicit operations strategy. Such a strategy is based on the concept that operations structured to meet corporate strategic objectives can create a formidable competitive weapon. Without this premise and set of understandings about focused operations policies, it is virtually impossible for a 'non-process' company to place an emphasis on process innovation successfully. This is because without an operations strategy there is seldom the vision at top levels of what major process changes could do for the firm. Changes are apt to be made piecemeal and dominated by professional experts separated by the usual functional barriers. An operations strategy supplies the vision without which linked process innovations across the value chain do not happen.

Condition 2: The second condition relates to the skills and mind-sets of managers. Regardless of the industry, major process innovation seldom comes about without many executives from the top down who are technology literate and generally competent and comfortable in the process technologies of their industry. This is common in the process industries, but it is a much bigger task and hence very rare in the non-process industries, where a large variety of processes make up '*the process*' of their industry. Such managers generally know how each competitor is competing process-wise, and are current on process developments in the industry and university laboratories.

Condition 3: Because process innovation which creates competitive advantage in the non-process industries requires addressing whole blocks of linked processes in the value chain, it is inherently difficult technically and organizationally, as well as in the magnitude of risk. For these reasons, the third condition observed in the successful companies is that their top managers were strongly motivated to take the plunge.

At Copeland, the CEO saw process innovation as the only way to get out from under the domination of much larger and better financed companies. He was backed by the major shareholder, who was equally convinced.

General Motors' Saturn facility is clearly motivated by the need of GM to experiment in a big way outside of the regular corporation as they urgently seek to stem the tide of declining market share.

Is desperation the only motivator which works to get top managers in non-process industries to get their operations people to examine their many processes as 'our process for making the product?' In this research, only one substitute for desperation emerged and that was in a handful of firms where the CEO and several dynamic, upper level managers recognized—from their own experience, or from the manufacturing strategy literature, or from courses or consultants—the enormous leverage of process superiority. The substitute for desperation was knowledge, which produced a certain vision. And, ultimately, a shareholder's delight.

Reference

Reference to this paper should be made as follows: Skinner, W. (1992) 'Precious jewels: companies that achieve competitive advantage from process innovation,' *Int. J. Technology Management,* Special Issue on Strengthening Corporate and National Competitiveness through Technology, Vol. 7, Nos 1/2/3, pp. 41–48.

Endnote

1. The term 'non-process industries' which is used in this article is clearly a 'no-brainer,' for every industry more or less by definition has a 'process.' The consumer electronics industry, for example, has at least five major processes. Nevertheless, it is a useful term to distinguish between the industries commonly known as 'process industries' and all others, and we beg the reader's indulgence.

30 | INTERACTIONS BETWEEN PRODUCT R&D AND PROCESS TECHNOLOGY

E. Celse Etienne

Product market strategy formulation and implementation require integration of marketing, production technology and R&D.

Marketing literature postulates the existence of a product life cycle that purports to show how sales of a product evolve over time. In its simplest form, the product life cycle concept divides the life of a product into four stages—introduction, growth, maturity and decline. More recently, some advances have been made in conceptualizing a process life cycle, one that attempts to show how the productive segment that produces the product evolves over time, partially in response to product market needs, fundamental product characteristics and process technology constraints.

The present paper is an attempt to identify and elaborate upon the wider managerial implications of the two streams of thought. The underlying thesis is that product markets, product and process technologies and the commensurate competitive strategies employed by the firm interact heavily over time. Consequently, the major objective of the paper is to elaborate upon these interactions and to map out their implications for the behavior of the firm with respect to product and process innovation.

PRODUCT LIFE CYCLE

Three fundamental variables are recognized here to form the basis of describing the product life cycle phenomenon: the pattern of sales, the pattern of competitive strategies and the pattern of product innovation.

Pattern of sales—This represents the most simple statement of the product life cycle concept. Briefly, it postulates that the level of sales achieved by a product class varies systematically over time and can be classified into four stages:

1. *Introductory stage*—The product is new and consumer acceptance is low if only because of lack of knowledge of the existence of the product. Lack of knowledge may also be with respect to the applicability of the product or the range of its problem solving capability. In any event, sales are very low.

E.C. Etienne is assistant professor in the School of Business Administration, University of Montreal, Canada.

Etienne, E. Celse. 1981. Interactions between product R&D and process technology. Research Management 24(January): 22–27.

399

2. *Growth Stage*—Knowledge of the product has diffused rapidly on the basis of successful trials by innovative customers. The problem solving capability of the product is being better understood and new fields of application are being found. Sales are growing very rapidly, partly because more firms have perceived the potential of the product and are moving in to try to establish a position in the market.

3. *Maturity Stage*—The product is widely accepted and sales are stable or growing just in line with the economy as a whole. At this point, efforts may be made to rejuvenate the product by deliberately seeking new applications or by incremental innovation. If rejuvenation fails, the stage is set for entry into the next stage in the development of the product.

4. *Decline Stage*—Sales of the product start to decrease chiefly because a new and better product has entered the market to fulfill the same generic need.

Pattern of competitive strategies—This involves two strategies as expressed by Utterback and Abernathy:

1. *Performance maximizing*—"In the early phases of the product life cycle, the rate of product change is expected to be rapid and margins to be large. A firm with a performance maximizing strategy might be expected to emphasize unique products and product performance, often in the expectation that a new capability will expand customer requirements."

2. *Cost minimizing*—"At the maturity and decline phases of the cycle, the product is standardized so that product differentiation is difficult. Consequently, firms must compete on price and the appropriate strategy is one that minimizes cost."[1]

Pattern of Product Innovation—Both the nature and rate of product innovation change over the life of the product. During the early stages of the product, when firms are competing on the basis of performance maximizing the objective is to produce a technology that is superior in terms of meeting functional product specifications. Innovative activity is very high and so is the rate of innovation. The latter is stimulated by perception and definition of the market need. Innovative activity is largely aimed at generating alternative technologies to improve product performance market need. Innovation is largely aimed at bringing basic product performance closer to the technological promise or surpassing it if possible.

Sales maximizing firms operate in Stage II, when there are only a few competing versions of the product. By that time, the basic technological promise has been fulfilled and it is difficult to increase generic product performance. Consequently, the rate of innovation has slowed down and most of it is aimed at making the firms product unique within the generic product performance.

Product standardization brings a rapid decrease in the rate of product innovation; if any innovation in the product occurs it tends to be very incremental in nature. Radical innovation usually results in a new product with consequent death of the old one. Innovation is aimed at reducing product cost.

The essential character of the product life cycle is shown in Figure 30-1.

STAGES OF PROCESS DEVELOPMENT

Attempts have been made to demonstrate the theoretical validity of a process development cycle. The underlying assumption is that since product and process are symbiotically related in the production system, then fundamental changes in the one must incite and parallel fundamental changes on the other. An effort to put a theoretical framework around this concept has been attempted by Abernathy and Townsend.[2] Development of that theoretical frame was based upon five critical hypothesis of which four are of central concern here:

Firstly, the proposition is advanced by these authors that production processes evolve toward greater predictability and more ordered or systematic relationships. Secondly, that development requires that progress be made at four different levels in

FIGURE 30-1   Product Life Cycle.

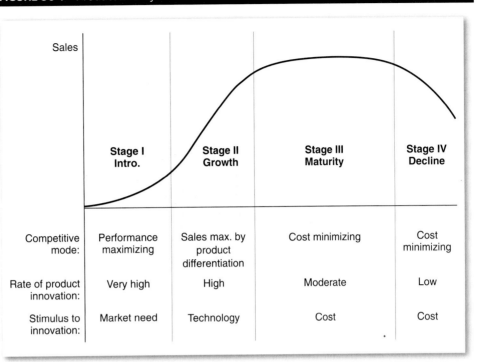

	Stage I Intro.	Stage II Growth	Stage III Maturity	Stage IV Decline
Competitive mode:	Performance maximizing	Sales max. by product differentiation	Cost minimizing	Cost minimizing
Rate of product innovation:	Very high	High	Moderate	Low
Stimulus to innovation:	Market need	Technology	Cost	Cost

the production process: process continuity and predictability, product improvement and standardization, process scale and material inputs. And thirdly, that the level of innovation or utilization of product and process technology is heavily influenced by the level of development that has been attained within the productive segment.

The authors then elaborate three stages in the development of a manufacturing process:

> *Uncoordinated*—the process is composed of unstandardized, general purpose equipment, with a high degree of flexibility and slack. This occurs because the product is new and changing so that the process must be kept fluid.
> *Segmental*—The production system is designed to achieve higher levels of efficiency so as to capitalize on increasing product standardization. The process becomes integrated and elaborated through automation and process control. The essential element is that some processes are highly integrated while others are still loose and flexible.
> *Systemic*—At this stage, the process has reached the ultimate in terms of level of integration and balance between various process elements. Developments in the product have led to such a high level of standardization that every conceivable process task can be pinpointed and well described. With such predictability in the product, the most efficient and specialized process can be built.

Implicit in the argument thus far and derivable from other building blocks of the model is the proposition that the rate of process innovation staged by a particular productive segment, varies over the process life cycle. During the uncoordinated stage it is quite low. Utterback and Abernathy argue:

> "During the uncoordinated stage, most technological applications are to the products that the productive segment will produce. Few are to process improvement, and those that do occur tend to be simple in application and to address single needs. Complex technological systems of process equipment do not take well when the recipient process is ill defined, uncertain and unstructured."[3]

FIGURE 30-2 Innovation and Stage of Development.

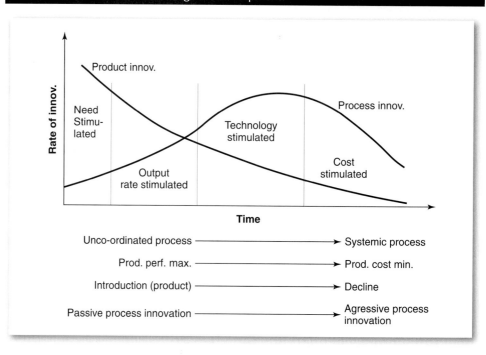

Process innovation by the productive segment reaches its zenith in the segmental stage and declines rapidly as the segment enters the systemic stage. At this final stage, the process is so well integrated and balanced that change is disruptive and costly. Innovations to process are only justifiable if they offer large economic advantage.

The patterns of product and process innovation together with their stimuli are important notions for this paper. Their essential nature as proposed by Utterback and Abernathy are adapted and presented schematically below. In addition to the notions developed by Utterback and Abernathy, the schema recognizes that the dominant thrust of process innovation also changes over the product/process life cycle. In the early stages, process innovation supports product innovation and the firm does only enough of the former to allow it to stage the latter. This can be conceptualized as passive process innovation. During the maturity stage, however, process innovation drives the competitive thrust of the firm, since it is the most fruitful avenue for cost reduction. Hence, the term aggressive process innovation.

Thus, from the point of view of innovation, its fundamental characteristics and consequences, it is clear that there is a symbiotic relationship between the evolution of product and process in a productive segment, and the firm's response to such evolution. These relationships have been elaborated during presentation of the models, and synthesized schematically in Figure 30-2. They will be drawn upon collectively in subsequent sections, when the implications of the framework for this paper are being mapped.

SOME FUNDAMENTAL IMPLICATIONS

Extension of the theoretical underpinnings of the integrated framework of product and process development can be done to explain the range of process acquisition modes over the life of the production segment and is based upon two conclusions: one of these is amply recognized and elaborated upon by Utterback and Abernathy.

"The locus of innovation shifts with the stage of development. During the unconnected stage in the development of a process, innovative insight comes from those individuals or organizations that are intimately familiar with the recipient process, rather than those intimately familiar with new technologies. Later in the systemic stage, needs are well defined, system-like and easily articulated. These needs lend themselves to complex technological solutions and the innovator will frequently be one that brings new technological insights to the problem."[4]

The second conclusion is that the degree of uncertainty inherent in innovation varies over the life of the productive segment. It has already been argued that innovation is an inherently uncertain act. The greater the rate of innovation, the greater the degree of uncertainty that the innovating firm must face. Hence, as far as process innovation is concerned, uncertainty is low in the uncoordinated and systemic stages and high in the segmental stage. Correspondingly, the degree of innovation related uncertainty characterizing the environment of the productive segment is low in the introductory stage, high in the growth stage and low in the maturity and decline stages of the product life cycle.

The proposition that the innovation insight in the uncoordinated stage comes from those intimately familiar with the recipient process is a statement as to the range of feasible process acquisition modes;

1. When the product is new, good specification of process needs are developing and have not been broadcast. Intimate understanding of the process need can only be development on the basis of knowledge of the product and interactions between product and process in the productive segment. These two essential requirements exclude the possibility or at least substantially reduces it, that supplier organizations will be in a position to know and understand process needs.
2. Innovation requires the fusion of an accurate definition of a need and technological possibility into a design concept. Supplier organization, even though they have the process technology capability will not be able to bring about fusion. Moreover, they are not in a position to evaluate the applicability of that capability to the problem of the product innovating firm. Therefore supplier firms are not in a position to stage process innovation.
3. User organizations are familiar with needs via the operations (manufacturing) group. Moreover, to stage product innovation calls for a minimum amount of process development (since product and process are symbiotically related). Hence, the fact that a new product has been launched is sufficient evidence that process related technical skills exist.
4. Consequently both need definition and technology skills exist in the innovating organization and can easily be fused together. Thus, the user organization is in a position and will most likely undertake process innovation.

Explanation of the phenomenon operative in the systemic stage (maturity stage) will be undertaken as follows:

1. Maturity of the product means that knowledge of product related technology has been broadcast, process needs are well articulated and their nature can be diffused on an economy or industry wide basis.
2. Organizations or groups that are interested in the product can have sufficient access both to the product technology and the nature of existing processes. Therefore, they are in a position to have accurate perceptions of need.
3. With needs well defined and having a constellation of concrete ideas as to the nature of the existing processes, non-user organizations can undertake search, research and development activity to build a process related technical base.
4. Continued development of a process technology base opens the way for fusion to occur at an opportune time. Hence, supplier organizations external to the user firm are now in a position to stage process innovation.

Following from the above arguments are the important observations that in the uncoordinated (introductory) stage of the process life cycle, the most likely process acquisition mode that will be used by the firm is acquisition by internal performance of the entire sequence of innovative activities. (Note: For our purposes, the process acquisition activities are process research, process development, process design, engineering design and process manufacture.)

Conversely, during the systemic stage, both supplier and user organizations can fruitfully stage process innovation; thus the process acquiring firm (user) can potentially acquire by performing all innovative activities internally or externally.

Standardization of the product in the systemic stage carries the fundamental result that the range of applicable process alternatives has been grossly reduced. Simultaneous reduction in the risks of innovation in the limited range of possibilities also means potentially that there is a wider market for the process. Suppliers can fruitfully stage innovation.

However, it is not obvious as to what will happen to process innovation by the user organization. On the surface, a user organization innovating for its own needs would find it difficult doing a more effective job than a specialized supplier. But specialization is limited by the extent of the market and so are the benefits to specialization. Hence, whether or not the user organization will continue to innovate will depend on three basic factors:

1. The attitude of user organizations as to accessibility of their innovation by competitive users. If these are available to others, the potential market is expanded thus diluting the fixed costs of innovating and the commensurate risk.
2. The size of the market for the process. Where the process market is small, no one supplier will benefit substantially from specialization.
3. The relationship between product and process innovation. As explained by Meyers and Marquis, some product innovations require the firm to undertake process innovations because product and process are so intimately bound that change in one necessitates change in the other.[5] Under such circumstances, the firm may be forced to undertake process innovation in order to protect its product innovation advantage.

Any of these eventualities reduces the net advantage of a specialized supplier.

BEHAVIOR OF THE FIRM

However, four questions remain to be answered. These are:

1. What will be the behavior of firms with respect to product innovation over the product/process life cycle?
2. Will all firms be affected equally by and respond in the same way to process innovation over the life cycle?
3. How do the differing temporal rates of product/process innovation affect different firms?
4. What innovation related skills does the firm need to undertake innovation at each stage?

It is the thesis of this paper that the critical factor affecting the innovative behavior of firms is risk. Hence, to answer these questions, one must have an image of how innovation related risk evolves over the life cycle and the options open to the firm to reduce risk to manageable proportions. The firm can reduce risk by one of three ways. It can decide to focus on one or other of product and process innovation or it can decide to reduce the risk of product innovation by performing less than the full range of product innovation activities of research, development, manufacture. For example, the firm could eliminate research and or development by procuring a license. Or, in the case of process innovation, it can use a supplier to perform some of the innovative activities of process research, process development, process manufacture.

Product innovation—the fact that the firm is competing in the introductory stage means that it had previously undertaken product research and development. In addition, the firm will also have undertaken some process innovation, since it needs the latter to stage product innovation in the introductory stage. Hence, a license to manufacture is very unlikely because the product innovating firm has not established the performance advantage of the product. Neither is the licensee likely to seek a license because of its relative ignorance as to process needs.

Both the risk level of product innovation and the lack of process technology capability coupled with the absence of the licensing option, preempt entry into the product market by small firms. Some aggressive medium sized firms following the extremely high risk strategy of product introduction can compete in this market, but, on the whole, the latter is dominated by large, aggressive firms.

The critical skill for the firm is a strong product R&D capability buttressed by strong process development support from manufacturing engineering. Such firms also need strong interfunctional communication so as to be able to link product market needs with product design concepts and process technology characteristics. Moreover, communication must be accompanied by influence.

Innovation involves bringing together expert knowledge of a diverse character to form a consistent, unified package that can be made to culminate into a problem solving artifact. The various technical expertise have very different modi operandi, assume very different time frames, and are characterized by very different types of uncertainty environments. These differences show up in the radically different motivations of the respective technical groups and thus their ways of perceiving the problems that arise in innovation. Somehow, these groups have to be made to see the innovating task in the same way, and, further, each must be allowed to influence and be influenced by the task of the others. The task is to get each group to understand the requirements, constraints and objectives of each other group and to take explicit consideration of these in accomplishing its own task.

In the growth stage, the firm still requires strong support from manufacturing engineering. However, it can reduce the risk of product innovation by the medium of a license, thus eliminating the need for product research and possibly a large part of product development. The critical technological skills required exist at the level of product design based upon firm development data, buttressed by a moderately strong process technology capacity. Consequently, most medium sized firms and some aggressive small firms can enter the market with large firms, the former having a tendency to rely heavily on product licensing.

At the maturity stage, all firms can enter the market since neither product technology nor process technology is a barrier to small firms. At this point, the supplier market for the process is well developed, so that firms can acquire their process technology requirements across the market and can undertake process innovation by adoption. Firms that are aggressive in seeking a competitive advantage via the application of new process technology will invest in process innovation related skills, the level of such investment varying with the ability of the firm to bear innovation related risk.

Process innovation—During the introductory and growth stages, process innovation is a support to product innovation and the former draws its information as to need definition from the latter. Process innovation by firms not competing in the product market is usually both difficult and superfluous. Consequently, process innovation is the domain of large firms.

The critical development in the maturity phase is the fact that process needs are well defined and broadcast. Consequently, any firm can undertake process innovation if it can support investment in the innovative activities. Such investment need not be high since process options have been reduced, because of process research and development conducted by firms in the introductory and growth phases. Moreover, the firm can reduce the investment required either by relegating some of the process innovation activities to a supplier market or by the purchase of proprietary information. These practices are used extensively in the petroleum refining and similar industries. Hence, most firms can fruitfully undertake process innovation.

The foregoing discussion underscores the fact that both markets and technologies change over time, and so must skills of the firm. The task for the firm is to match markets and technologies in a dynamic time frame. That idea is crystallized in Figure 30-3.

Innovation is what prepares the firm for the future. It is innovation, whether applied to products or to processes, that ensures that the firm which is competitive in

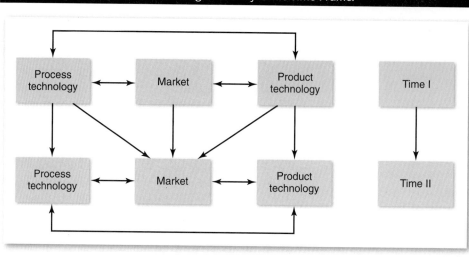

FIGURE 30-3 Markets and Technologies in a Dynamic Time Frame.

Time I will remain competitive in Time II. But the firm must organize its innovative effort around an accurate formulation of what the product market will demand, what constraints will be imposed by the process market, and what skills it can and needs to develop to compete in the market, given the resources at its disposal. There is no one way to approach deploying the firm's innovative effort. Rather, there are choices to be made, as has been argued, and they must be seen in relation to the product market, the process market and the technical skills of the firm.

CONCLUSION

The arguments developed in this paper give further support to the notion that product market strategy formulation and implementation require the integration of marketing, production and research and development. Moreover, that relationship is characterized by interdependence rather than dependence and they should be managed so as to culminate into interfunctional support. The model also argues for the need to appraise the firms innovative strategy periodically, since the technical strengths of the firm vis-a-vis the product market are time bound. Not only this, but the weaknesses that can be tolerated at one point in time may turn out to be catastrophic to the competitive stance of the firm once the product has moved through a different stage of development. This is the essence of the timing question in strategy formulation and implementation and its importance cannot be overemphasized.

Clearly, also, the chief executive officer needs a minimum understanding of the dynamics of process technology in order to do an effective job of strategy formulation and implementation. This requirement is particularly critical in modern societies, where both the product gestation period and the life cycle continue to shrink. The latter means that there must be more frequent reviews of the firms competitive stance. In addition, it also implies that mistakes are more costly, since there is much less time to make up for these.

References

1. Utterback, James, M., and William J. Abernathy, "A Dynamic Model of Product and Process Innovation," Omega, Vol. 3 #6 (1975).
2. Abernathy, William, J., and Philip Townsend, "Technology, Productivity and Process Change," Technological Forecasting and Social Change," 7, (1976).
3. Ibid.
4. Ibid.
5. Meyers, S., and Marquis, D.G., Successful Industrial Innovations, National Science Foundation, NSF 69 17, (1969).

PROCESS INNOVATION AND LEARNING BY DOING IN SEMICONDUCTOR MANUFACTURING

Nile W. Hatch

Department of Business Administration, University of Illinois at Urbana-Champaign, Champaign, Illinois 61820

David C. Mowery

Haas School of Business, University of California, Berkeley, Berkeley, California 94720

This paper analyzes the relationship between process innovation and learning by doing in the semiconductor industry where improvements in manufacturing yield are a catalyst for dynamic cost reductions. In contrast to most previous studies of learning by doing, the learning curve is shown here to be the product of deliberate activities intended to improve yields and reduce costs, rather than the incidental byproduct of production volume. Since some of the knowledge acquired through learning by doing during new process development is specific to the production environment where the process is developed, some knowledge is effectively lost when a new process is transferred to manufacturing. We find that dedicated process development facilities, geographic proximity between development and manufacturing facilities, and the duplication of equipment between development and manufacturing facilities are all significant in improving performance in introducing new technologies. Once in manufacturing, new processes are shown to disrupt the ongoing learning activities of existing processes by drawing away scarce engineering resources to "debug" the new processes.

(*Process Technology Development; Process Technology Transfer; Learning Curves*)

INTRODUCTION

The speed and effectiveness with which new products are developed and introduced into large-volume production is an important influence on competitiveness in manufacturing. The alleged failures of many U.S. firms to manage product development effectively have been frequently cited as a critical contributor to declining U.S. international competitiveness (see Dertouzos et al. 1988). In the semiconductor industry,

Hatch, Nile W. and David C. Mowery, (1998), "Process Innovation and Learning by Doing in Semiconductor Manufacturing," *Management Science*, vol. 44, no. 11, Part 1 of 2, pp. 1461–1477. Courtesy of The Institute of Operations Research and the Management Sciences (INFORMS), 7240 Parkway Drive, Suite 310, Hanover, MD 21076 USA.

manufacturing process technology is often as great an obstacle to bringing new products to market as product development. Unfortunately, the importance of developing and introducing new processes into manufacturing has received little attention. Pisano (1997) is an important exception.

This paper analyzes new process introduction in semiconductors, an industry characterized by extraordinary complexity in process technology. We develop a model of "learning by doing" in the new process development and introduction into the manufacturing environment of new process technologies. We use a dataset that tracks yield improvements for new manufacturing processes to test this model, which links the learning curve and process innovation. Specifically, we examine two broad issues: (1) the factors affecting superior performance in the introduction of new manufacturing processes into firms' semiconductor fabrication facilities (*fabs*), and (2) the factors that influence the rate of improvement, i.e., the rate of *learning,* in the early stages of production with a new manufacturing process. In both of these areas, firm-specific differences in performance are significant, and they reflect different approaches to management of new process introduction. Our empirical analysis of yield improvement shows that learning in the early stages of manufacturing is a function of the allocation of engineering resources, rather than an exogenous result of increasing production volumes. This paper sheds new light on manufacturing management in a technology-intensive industry and suggests the need for further work on models of learning-based improvement in manufacturing.

Since much of our analysis concerns learning in manufacturing, the next section of this paper surveys the vast literature on "learning by doing." Section 3 discusses semiconductor manufacturing technology. Following this, we discuss the sources and characteristics of our data. Section 5 develops our model of learning in new process development and the "learning losses" associated with the transfer of new process technologies into the manufacturing environment. In Section 6, we test the predictions of our basic model, and in Section 7 we examine the influence of product-specific effects on our results. Section 8 presents concluding comments.

LITERATURE REVIEW

In his pioneering article, Wright (1936) found that the direct labor cost of manufacturing an airframe fell by 20% with every doubling of cumulative output. Many subsequent studies corroborated Wright's findings in a variety of industries.[1] In addition to identifying learning by doing in a wide variety of industries, subsequent authors have broadened the analysis to show that costs other than direct labor also decrease with experience. Another branch of this empirical literature seeks to identify the best proxy for firm-specific experience. Time and cumulative investment are among the most common alternatives to the traditional cumulative volume measure (Arrow 1962; Rapping 1965; Sheshinski 1967; Stobaugh and Townsend 1975; Lieberman 1984).

Several authors have described the factors that influence a firm's learning performance, but these studies rarely test the importance of specific factors in a model.[2] A major obstacle to such statistical analyses of the determinants of the learning curve is the difficulty researchers face in gaining access to the required cost and manufacturing operations data, which many firms treat as sensitive, proprietary information. As a result, relatively little research has focused on the mechanisms that underpin learning by doing (an important exception is Adler and Clark [1991] who rely on case study data). The model of learning by doing presented in this paper examines these mechanisms in statistical tests that link learning to the management by firms of the introduction of new process technologies into manufacturing.

SEMICONDUCTOR MANUFACTURING

There are good reasons to suspect that the management of new process introduction is if anything even more important to competitive performance in semiconductors than is true in other industries such as automobiles. Semiconductor manufacturing processes are among the most complex production processes in industry. The fabrication of an integrated circuit with feature sizes and linewidths of less than 0.25 micrometers (mm) requires more than one hundred steps (patterning, coating, baking, etching, cleaning, etc.). The development of many of these steps is based on art and know-how rather than science; they are not well understood or easily replicated on different equipment or in different facilities; and they impose demanding requirements for a particle-free manufacturing environment. Product innovation in semiconductors depends on process innovation to a greater extent than is true of many other industries, since semiconductor product innovations frequently require major changes in manufacturing processes. Moreover, imperfect scientific understanding of semiconductor manufacturing means that changes in process technologies demand a great deal of experimentation.

Management of process technology is critical to firm strategy in semiconductors. Particularly in "commodity-product" segments of the industry like memory chips, a new product commands a price premium for a relatively brief period, and being first to market is important to profitability. Alvarez (1994) notes that the shrinkage of product cycles in the semiconductor industry means that rapid and smooth introduction of new manufacturing processes now is more important to competitive performance.[3]

A brief overview of semiconductor manufacturing processes is necessary to understand our data and model. Integrated circuits are manufactured in ultra-clean environments known as *clean rooms* within a fab. The process steps are performed on *wafers* of silicon ranging in diameter from four to eight inches. The manufacturing process technology produces the conductive and insulating regions that create the array of transistors comprising the integrated circuit. Before the integrated circuits (or semiconductors) are packaged, they are known as *dice*. Depending on the size of the die, the number of integrated circuits on each wafer ranges from dozens to thousands.[4]

Yield losses are an integral part of semiconductor manufacturing. Overall yield losses reflect losses in *line yield*, which measures the proportion of wafers that are not discarded as scrap, and *die yield*, the proportion of die on a successfully processed wafer that pass tests for functionality and performance. For a completed wafer, the cost of manufacturing a chip is the same whether it functions or not. As a result, the cost of good chips is inversely proportional to the die yield. Die yield losses can be attributed to two sources: unwanted random particles and parametric processing problems. The first source of die yield losses occurs when particles in the manufacturing environment land on critical areas of the die, destroying its functionality.[5] For new manufacturing processes, however, parametric problems are a more important source of die yield losses than random particles. Yield losses due to parametric problems result from an incomplete understanding of the parameters of the process technology as well as insufficient process control.[6]

Die yield improvement is one of the primary mechanisms of learning by doing in the semiconductor industry. Fabs devote substantial resources to the identification and elimination of the sources of die yield losses.[7] For both types of die yield losses, yield improvements are the result of engineering experiments and analysis of production data. Most particles are removed from the ambient air using air-filtration systems, but processing wafers on new equipment (or in some cases, using new recipes on existing equipment) generates new particles that typically can be observed only through their effects on die yield. Analysis of production data by engineers allows the identification of yield losses and the sources of the particles. Solutions to parametric problems also require engineering analysis of production data, which improves understanding of process parameters and the process control necessary to increase the likelihood that inputs are applied within the acceptable range.

In our model of new process introduction, learning by doing in the early stages of a new manufacturing process is the result of engineering analysis of production data that enables resolution of parametric and (to a lesser extent) particle-induced yield losses. Rather than testing the performance of various proxies for fab-level experience, we analyze the relative contributions of cumulative production volume and engineering resources to learning in the context of new process introduction.

In addition to problem solving on new processes once they are in volume production, performance in new process introduction also is affected by firms' management of the development and transfer of a new manufacturing process to the production fab. The uncertainties of many aspects of semiconductor manufacturing technology mean that many producers employ a dedicated development fab for new process development.[8] The development fab provides a facility for experimentation and research on process technologies in a setting designed to replicate manufacturing conditions. In an effort to achieve this goal, a number of the fabs in our sample require duplication within the receiving production facility of the equipment set used for a new process in the development facility. But even in the face of stringent requirements for equipment duplication, the manufacturing environment may differ in important respects from that of the development fab.[9] In addition, the complexity and "tacitness" of much of the knowledge and know-how associated with a new process technology mean that firms using development fabs face a significant challenge in transferring a new process into the manufacturing fab. In many cases, development personnel are temporarily transferred to the manufacturing site along with the new process technology in order to communicate the necessary know-how to manufacturing managers, engineers, and operators.

DATA

The data underlying this paper are drawn from a large dataset on the manufacturing performance of individual manufacturing plants operated by U.S. and foreign semiconductor firms in the U.S. and offshore.[10] These data primarily concern operations within an individual production facility (commonly called a "fab"), rather than within the entire firm. Moreover, the data are restricted largely to fabrication operations—the packaging of individual integrated circuits typically is not included in our data.

Data were collected through written questionnaires, the responses to which were verified and elaborated through a field visit from members of the research team. Our database includes detailed information on the characteristics of a given fab and its products and processes, as well as the results of researchers' observations of fab operations and summaries of extensive interviews with fab managers, engineers, and operators for more than 30 fabs in the global semiconductor industry. We collected detailed data on die yields, production volumes, and other characteristics for a number of "major process groups" in each fab (defined as the process groups accounting for at least 75% of the output of the fab) over the history of these processes. Most of the fabs in our sample provided historical data from the inception of a given process group, allowing us to construct time series on the performance of the fab during the introduction of a new process.[11]

Based on our field research and other information, we focused on die yield as the critical index of improvements in manufacturing performance. Because die yield is sensitive to die size, we normalized die yield for differences in die size by employing a model that converts die yield into a measure of the "density" of defects per cm². There are a variety of defect density models available, but our analysis uses the "Murphy model":

$$DY = \left[\frac{1 - e^{-A \cdot DD}}{A \cdot DD} \right]^2 \qquad (1)$$

where A is the die area and DD is the defect density parameter.[12]

Table 31-1 displays initial defect density and early-stage rates of improvement in defect density for the new processes in our sample. We have separated these processes into two line width classes, and our sample of fabs is not equally distributed across all these classes.[13] Superior performance in managing new process introduction should be revealed in relatively low initial defect densities. In the submicron class of processes, initial defect densities are more than 20 times larger in the worstperforming fab than in the best performer, substantially greater than the differences among

TABLE 31-1   Performance Measures for New Processes

Fab	Initial Defect Density (per cm²)	Average Quarterly Rate of Reduction in Defect Density
Submicron Processes		
A	1.290	−3.8180%
B	0.769	14.1638%
C	0.572	10.5913%
D	1.191	9.7213%
D	0.746	−0.5490%
D	2.447	14.6494%
E	0.700	8.0261%
E	0.377	0.3196%
F	1.010	−1.3923%
G	4.918	30.0464%
G	8.412	53.8064%
H	2.919	25.5009%
I	0.520	18.5136%
I	0.800	16.1611%
I	3.090	39.6154%
J	0.668	2.1271%
K	6.519	18.8139%
K	3.525	17.0226%
L	0.395	−25.4615%
M	2.597	30.2656%
M	1.107	3.9566%
N	0.614	2.0910%
O	6.089	59.4945%
O	0.164	11.8935%
1.0–1.2 μm Processes		
C	1.116	19.3749%
D	0.559	−6.6940%
D	0.924	−3.8160%
D	0.739	3.6401%
H	0.645	5.1361%
M	0.823	2.9346%
M	1.470	9.5943%
M	0.828	8.2739%
N	0.504	3.2236%
P	2.076	2.5960%
Q	1.306	11.6606%
R	1.428	18.2075%

fabs in the 1–1.2 micron class. The most dramatic differences among fabs' performance thus occur in the most advanced manufacturing processes. Firm-specific capabilities differ most substantially for the most advanced forms of this complex manufacturing technology, much of which is not well-codified or easily transferred among or within firms.

Lagging fabs face greater obstacles to "catching up" to the leaders' defect density performance in more advanced manufacturing processes. More mature manufacturing technologies are those in which firm-specific or fab-specific knowledge is most likely to "leak out" and diffuse among competitors, reflecting labor-force turnover, the widespread availability of engineering consultants and advanced equipment, etc. At the technological frontier, however, such fab-specific know-how disseminates more gradually among establishments, and the penalties associated with a poor introduction are likely to be more significant and enduring.

The second performance measure that we expect to be sensitive to management of new process introduction is the rate of improvement in manufacturing performance, measured for each fab as the average quarterly percentage decrease in defect densities during the first year of operation of a new process (column 3 of Table 31-1). This measure also reveals the largest differences among fabs for the smaller line width (submicron) processes. The fabs with the highest initial defect densities (a poor starting point) are among those with the highest rates of improvement. Careful management of improvement in manufacturing performance can overcome at least some of the performance penalties associated with poorly managed process transfer and/or introduction, especially in more mature processes. Conversely, some new processes experience yield declines following their introduction. This deterioration in defect density performance is apparent in several other manufacturing processes in Table 31-1, and may reflect the impact of rapid expansion in production volumes before a new process is fully stabilized or characterized. A similar association between low initial defect density and negative early-stage rates of improvement in defect density is apparent in the 1.0–1.2 micron linewidth class.

A MODEL OF LEARNING BY DOING

Our model of learning by doing draws on Hatch and Reichelstein (1997), where improvements in yield are driven by engineering analysis of production volume. We extend their analysis to include the effect of transferring a new process from development to manufacturing on knowledge acquisition and yields. In particular, we focus on the share of the knowledge that is acquired during the development of a new process technology that can be successfully transferred to the manufacturing fab, and the effects on this knowledge transfer of process development and transfer practices.

We denote the level of process-specific knowledge in the semiconductor firm at time t as K_t. L_t denotes the level of process-specific knowledge in the manufacturing fab at time t. In the case of mature processes, the manufacturing site has acquired virtually all of the relevant knowledge about the process. Thus, $K_t = L_t^m$, where L_t^m refers to the learning index for a mature process.

When a new process is transferred into the manufacturing fab, some of the knowledge acquired during development is not relevant in the manufacturing fab because of differences between the development and manufacturing environments. The firm does not lose knowledge, but the manufacturing fab must acquire new knowledge to operate the new process at the defect density levels obtained in the development fab before the process transfer. Even in the unlikely case that the production environment of the development fab (including production volumes) is identical to that of the manufacturing fab, some knowledge is lost in the transfer of the manufacturing process technology from one group of employees to another. For new processes, we define the learning index as $L_t^n = K_t + xfer$ where $xfer$ measures the knowledge that could not be appropriated during the transfer to the manufacturing fab plus the effect of managerial practices on the transfer. In particular, we hypothesize that

$$xfer = x_0 + x_1\text{dev} + x_2\text{prox} + x_3\text{dup} + x_4\text{fab}_1 \qquad (2)$$

where dev refers to processes developed in a separate development fab, prox denotes processes manufactured in fabs on the same site as the development fab, dup refers to processes transferred to manufacturing fabs where the equipment set of the development fab was duplicated, and fab_1 refers to processes transferred to manufacturing fabs that were the first to receive the new process.

Consistent with our description of learning by doing in Section 4, we hypothesize that process-specific knowledge is acquired through engineering analysis of production volume to identify and eliminate sources of yield loss. Then, denoting cumulative volume at time t as CV_t and cumulative engineering at time t as CE_t, the learning index for mature processes is

$$K_t = L_t^m = a \cdot CV_t + b \cdot CE_t + L_0^m, \qquad (3)$$

FIGURE 31-1   Effect of a Process Transfer on the Defect Density Curve

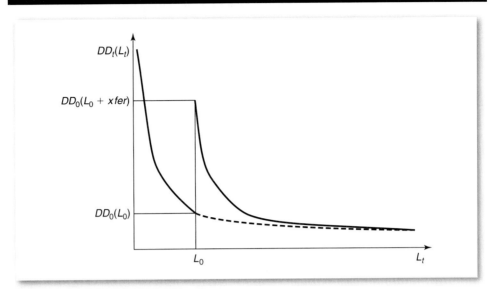

For new processes, it is

$$L_t^n = a \cdot CV_t + b \cdot CE_t + L_0^n. \tag{4}$$

where L_0 is the value of the index at the beginning of the sample and $L_0^n = L_0^m + xfer$.[14] The learning index for all processes is

$$L_t = a \cdot CV_t + b \cdot CE_t + npi \cdot xfer + L_0, \tag{5}$$

where *npi* is a dummy variable taking on a value of 1 for new processes and $L_0 = L_0^m$.

Learning by doing facilitates tighter process control and reductions in random particles, resulting in lower defect density. Figure 31-1 depicts the effects of a process transfer on the defect density parameter. Transferring the process (in period L_0) renders some of the process-specific knowledge that was acquired prior to the transfer irrelevant in the new manufacturing environment. The transfer causes a one-time increase in the defect density that is gradually ameliorated by learning by doing in the manufacturing fab. Eventually, the new defect density path converges to the path that would have been obtained in the absence of a transfer. Differences between the two nevertheless may persist for some time (Hatch and Reichelstein 1997).

To link learning by doing to reductions in defect density, we first assume that the defect density curve is additively separable into a dynamic (learning by doing) component and a static component:

$$DD_t = h_1(L_t) + h_2(\cdot) \tag{6}$$

where L_t is the unobservable "learning index" defined in Equation (5). The second term in (6) includes the influence of variables that do not directly affect the rate of learning by doing but exercise a constant influence over improvements in the defect density. Among these variables we include the process line width LW, number of mask layers ML, the cleanliness of the clean room CR (measured by the number of particles of per cubic foot), and the equipment vintage Vin.[15] The number of particles per cubic foot in the clean room influences the incidence of fatal defects due to particulate contamination. The line width measures the width of the metal strips that connect the transistors throughout the die, and is a good measure of process complexity.[16] The number of mask layers is a measure of the total number of steps in the process—more process steps increase the probability of a fatal defect in the die. The equipment vintage provides information about process capabilities of the equipment in the fab. In general, newer manufacturing equipment provides superior process control, which should reduce yield losses due to parametric processing errors.[17]

Since we cannot observe the learning index directly, we solve for L_0 in Equation (6) in terms of the initial defect density value, DD_0, and substitute the result. First, we specify the functional forms of $h_1(L_t)$ and $h_2(\cdot)$:

$$h_1(L_t) = \gamma + \psi e^{-\delta \cdot L_t};$$

$$h_2(\cdot) = cCR + lLW + mML + vVin_t. \tag{7}$$

In the initial period, i.e., when $t = 0$, the defect density curve is

$$DD_0 = \gamma + \psi e^{-\delta \cdot L_0} + h_2(\cdot).$$

Solving for L_0 gives

$$L_0 = \frac{-\ln\left[\dfrac{DD_0 - \gamma - h_2(\cdot)}{\psi}\right]}{\delta}.$$

Finally, substituting the previous expression into (5) and (7) gives us the defect density curve with the observable DD_0:

$$
\begin{aligned}
DD_t = {} & \gamma + \exp(-(\alpha \cdot CV_t + \beta \cdot CE_t + npi \cdot xfer)) \\
& \cdot (DD_0 - \gamma - (cCR + lLW + mML + vVin_0)) \\
& + cCR + lLW + mML + vVin_t
\end{aligned}
\tag{8}
$$

where $\alpha = \delta \cdot a$, $\beta = \delta \cdot b$, and $xfer = \delta \cdot xfer$.

Most fabs in the semiconductor industry manufacture more than one product within a fab through the simultaneous operation of several different process technologies on different production lines. The introduction of a new process into a multiproduct manufacturing fab therefore may affect the performance of the fab's other manufacturing processes. Engineers devote much of their attention to analysis of the new process technology to understand it quickly and expand its production. The resulting diversion of engineering attention from existing processes may slow yield improvement in these mature processes. Figure 31-2 shows how the rate of learning for a mature process may decline for a time when a new process is introduced at L_0.

FIGURE 31-2   Effect of a Process Transfer on Existing Processes in the Fab

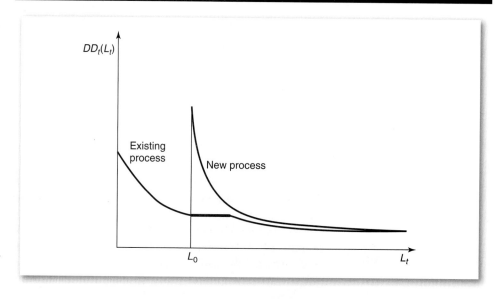

Incorporating the effect of a new process introduction on existing processes is straightforward. Let *fnpi* denote whether a new process is being introduced in the manufacturing fab. Then the learning index L_t becomes

$$L_t = a \cdot \text{CV}_t + b \cdot \text{CE}_t + fnpi(a_f \cdot \text{CV}_t + b_f \cdot \text{CE}_t + c_f)$$
$$+ npi \cdot xfer. \tag{9}$$

Based on Equation (9), the defect density curve is expressed as follows:

$$\text{DD}_t = \gamma + \exp(-(\alpha \cdot \text{CV}_t + \beta \cdot \text{CE}_t$$
$$+ fnpi(\alpha_f \cdot \text{CV}_t + \beta_f \cdot \text{CE}_t + c_f) + npi \cdot xfer))$$
$$\cdot (\text{DD}_0 - \gamma - (c\text{CR} + l\text{LW} + m\text{ML} + v\text{Vin}_0))$$
$$+ c\text{CR} + l\text{LW} + m\text{ML} + v\text{Vin}_t. \tag{10}$$

where $\alpha_f = \delta \cdot a_f$, $\beta_f = \delta \cdot b$, and $\text{C}_f = \delta \cdot c_f$.

EMPIRICAL ANALYSIS

Most of the data used in our empirical analysis are obtained from the questionnaires returned by the participating firms. The cumulative volume variable in the learning by doing equations is constructed from the number of "wafer starts" reported in the production data and is scaled to units of 1,000 wafers. Unfortunately, the fabs in our dataset were unable to provide information on the number of engineers working on individual processes. To estimate the influence of cumulative engineering on the path of defect density, it is necessary to employ a rule to allocate the engineering staff to processes. If there are no new processes in the fab, each process is allocated a share of total engineering time that is equal to its share of total fab volume. When a new process has been introduced, we assume that the new process receives 75% of the engineering time for the first year and then receives a share of engineering manpower in proportion to its relative volume. This allocation scheme is ad hoc, but consistent with what fabs report their engineers are doing, namely focusing attention on their most serious production problems. When there are no new processes in the fab, our allocation rule is conservative with respect to estimating the effect of engineering on learning, because newer processes generally have relatively low volumes but require a great deal of engineering effort to identify process boundaries.

Results of estimation of Equations (8) and (10) are reported in Table 31-2. A nonlinear maximum likelihood estimator was used to estimate the unknown coefficients. Because we use a panel of time series data, we assume autocorrelation and employ the appropriate correction (Judge et al., 1988). The estimated autocorrelation coefficient ρ is reported in Table 31-2 along with the number of observations and R^2.

The results in Table 31-2 support our hypothesis that learning is driven through engineering analysis of production volume. In all of the regression equations, the coefficients associated with the cumulative volume and cumulative engineering variable are significant and have the expected (positive) sign.[18] This result suggests that learning by doing is not solely an exogenous byproduct of growth in production volume, but is influenced by managers' investments in problem-solving for new manufacturing processes. The cumulative volume and cumulative engineering coefficients provide guidelines to relative effectiveness of production volume and engineering volume in reducing defect density. The coefficients are similar in magnitude; given the scaling of the cumulative volume variable, these estimates indicate that an additional engineering FTE is worth approximately 1,000 wafers of production volume.

Our primary interest is the impact of process innovations on the learning curve. When the process is first transferred to the manufacturing fab, we expect defect density to rise. Indeed, the estimated coefficient x_0 is statistically significant and negative,

TABLE 31-2 Learning Curve Estimates with Process Innovations

Coefficient	Equation (8)	Equation (10)
Dynamic (Learning by Doing) Component		
γ	9.5330	9.3536
$h_1 (\cdot)$ Constant	(4.8553)	(5.1126)
α	0.005703	0.005761
Cumulative Volume	(2.0245)	(2.0985)
β	0.005451	0.005999
Cumulative Engineering	(11.172)	(11.956)
Impact of New Process Introduction Variables		
x_0	−1.0521	−1.2731
Transfer Constant	(−4.7771)	(−5.6924)
x_1	0.31912	0.25712
Proximity	(2.7570)	(2.0856)
x_2	0.59474	0.68737
Development Fab	(3.9065)	(4.4581)
x_3	0.41227	0.49671
Equipment Duplication	(3.3886)	(4.1578)
x_4	0.02919	0.20089
First Manufacturing Fab	(0.2165)	(1.3665)
Interaction of New Processes with Learning Parameters of Existing Processes		
α_f		−0.001951
Cumulative Volume $\times$ *fnpi*		(−0.6129)
β_f		−0.001708
Cumulative Engineering $\times$ *fnpi*		(−3.7305)
c_f		−0.040411
Fab Transfer Constant $\times$ *fnpi*		(−0.9708)
Static Component		
c	0.000013	0.000010
Clean Room Grade	(1.3918)	(1.1977)
l	−0.038625	−0.017984
Line Width	(−0.4211)	(−0.1980)
m	0.006499	0.005581
Mask Layers	(1.0236)	(0.9515)
v	−0.10255	−0.1005
Equipment Vintage	(−4.6278)	(−4.8781)
ρ	0.76785	0.74255
R^2	0.9561	0.9578

Number of observations = 793.

Number of processes = 52.

Values in parentheses are asymptotic *t*-statistics.

signifying an increase in defect density associated with the process transfer. Firm-specific differences in the management of new process development and transfer, however, partially offset the loss of accumulated learning resulting from process transfers. In particular, the use of a development fab improves the defect density significantly. In addition to the use of a development fab, having the development fab on the same site as the manufacturing fab reduces the loss of relevant information in a process transfer. As expected, if the equipment set in the development fab is duplicated in the manufacturing fab, more of the knowledge acquired in the development fab can be used in the manufacturing fab since there are fewer differences between them. Finally, we hypothesize that if the manufacturing fab is the first commercial fab to receive the process, the defect density parameter should be larger. When the process is transferred from one commercial-scale fab to another, more process-specific knowledge moves with the process than is true of a transfer from a development fab with limited manufacturing experience with the process. This reflects the greater similarity in manufacturing environments, as well as the greater maturity of the process technology. In fact, however, the opposite effect is apparent, although the estimated coefficient is not significantly different from zero.

The coefficient estimates for the clean room grade, line width, and number of mask layers all have the expected sign but are not significant. In contrast, the significant coefficient estimates from both equations for the vintage variable point out the important effects of equipment vintage on defect density (newer equipment increases the average equipment vintage and defect density falls). This result underscores the importance of parametric processing errors as a source of die yield losses. Newer equipment (once fully "debugged") operates with tighter process controls and greater precision, reducing parametric yield losses.[19]

Equation 10, in the second column of Table 31-2, includes variables that seek to capture the disruptive effects of new process introduction on the processes already in operation in the fabs in our sample. The most interesting and important result here is the negative (increasing defect density) and statistically significant coefficient for cumulative engineering. Recalling that we have assumed that fully 75% of available engineering hours are allocated to new process introduction in the receiving fab, this coefficient suggests that new process introduction has a major negative impact on engineering problem-solving for mature processes, slowing the rate of defect density improvement in these products. New process introduction also influences defect density reduction in mature processes that is associated with expansion in volume and "shocks" to defect density improvements in existing processes, as revealed in the coefficients for cumulative volume $\times fnpi(\alpha_f)$ and the fab transfer constant (c_f). Unfortunately, neither variable's coefficient approaches statistical significance.

The results reported in Table 31-2 suggest that the effects of new technology development and transfer management practices are significant and sizeable. To illustrate the magnitude of these effects, we simulate the unit cost curve for a representative new manufacturing process based on our model of learning by doing, the estimates from Table 31-2, and average sample values for the remaining variables in the cost model. The model is based on the assumption of a constant unit cost of production, whether the product is functional or not. The average variable cost of output falls as yields improve.[20] What do these simulated cost curves reveal about the additional costs imposed on each unit of output and the cost savings gained through the process development and transfer practices described earlier?

The results of the simulation are presented in Figure 31-3, where the cost per unit of "experience" is shown. The "experience" variable is a weighted average index of volume and engineering resources that we employ for convenience.[21] The "baseline" for the analysis is the projected manufacturing cost assuming that the process is not transferred. The curve labeled "Basic Transfer" shows the additional cost associated with transferring a new process from development to the high-volume manufacturing environment. The constant cost of production is assumed to be $1.00. At the transfer date (Experience = 0), the baseline cost is $3.61 and the average variable cost of the transferred process is $8.93. The difference between the two ($5.32) gives the intercept for the "Basic Transfer" curve. Note that the unit cost of manufacturing with the transferred process is almost 2.5 times the unit cost without transfer, *ceteris paribus*. The other curves show how the process development and transfer practices discussed earlier reduce these cost penalties. Each curve shows the average variable cost for a process that was transferred using a specific process introduction practice. The use of a separate development fab is the single most effective management tool in reducing the transfer penalty, followed by equipment duplication, and colocation of development and manufacturing fabs.

FIGURE 31-3   Cost Savings from Management of New Process Introductions

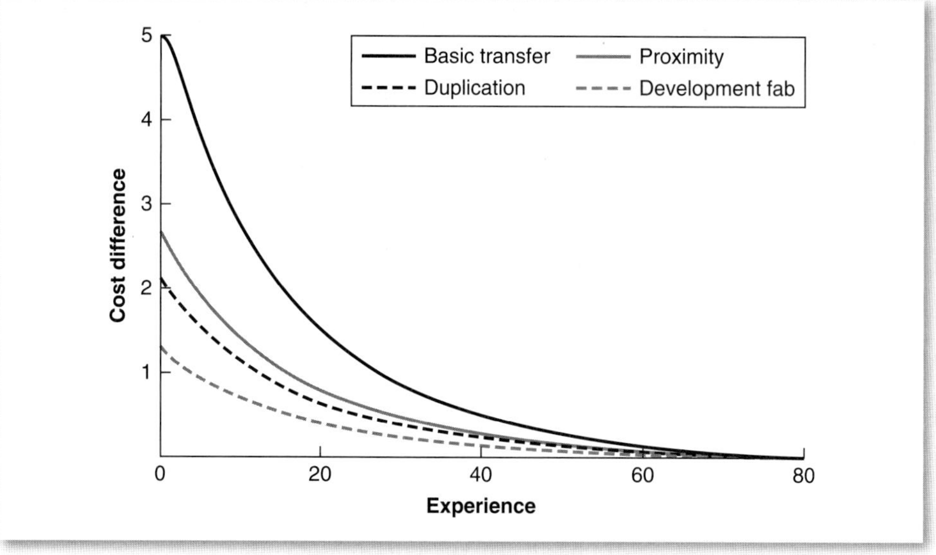

PRODUCT SPECIFIC EFFECTS

Numerous studies have identified firm and product-specific differences in learning curves.[22] In Section 4, we described how development and transfer activities may differ across such products as ASICs and DRAMs. These product-specific effects should influence both the rate of learning and performance in the development and transfer of new processes. This section presents empirical analyses of learning by doing and new process introduction for the ASIC and DRAM subsets of our sample.

ASIC Processes

Manufacturers of ASIC products develop a portfolio of manufacturing processes that are used to produce customized devices, often for customers that lack their own manufacturing facilities. Many ASIC fabs provide design services to customers to ensure that product designs can be produced with the processes in the fab. Rather than competing in the rapid introduction of new generations of ICs, ASIC fabs more often compete on the cost-effectiveness and reliability of their delivery commitments, which in turn places a high premium on the reliability of their process technology. As a result, process innovation in the ASIC segment is more incremental in character than is true of the memory or logic segments. Instead of changing manufacturing processes to accommodate a sharp jump in product requirements and functions, ASIC fabs more often strive for the gradual improvement and evolution of their manufacturing technologies, steadily upgrading their product offerings as a result. New process introduction thus is a continuous activity, with more introductions in the course of a given year, but each new manufacturing process results in a less significant "jump" in process capabilities.

These characteristics of product competition and new process introduction in ASICs affect the management of process development and transfer. Development fabs are much less common in firms that specialize in ASIC production, and equipment duplication should be less important for a process that is effectively developed in the manufacturing fab. Moreover, the disruption of existing processes in the fab should be less significant, and the new process introduction will place fewer demands on fab engineering talent.

TABLE 31-3 Estimates for ASIC Processes

Coefficient	Equation (8)	Equation (10)
Dynamic (Learning by Doing) Component		
γ	24.999	20.540
$h_1(\cdot)$ Constant	(6.5331)	(3.7850)
α	0.018642	0.015827
Cumulative Volume	(4.7703)	(4.5773)
β	−0.000420	−0.000544
Cumulative Engineering	(−0.8950)	(−1.1714)
Impact of New Process Introduction Variables		
x_0	−0.47181	−0.49421
Transfer Constant	(−0.6670)	(−0.75824)
x_2	−0.45136	−0.39961
Development Fab	(−0.73201)	(−0.66492)
x_3	−0.020304	−0.09466
Equipment Duplication	(−0.0324)	(−0.15461)
x_4	0.4397	0.43413
First Manufacturing Fab	(0.7179)	(0.9534)
Interaction of New Processes with Learning Parameters of Existing Processes		
α_f		0.002881
Cumulative Volume $\times$ *fnpi*		(0.5292)
β_f		0.000405
Cumulative Engineering $\times$ *fnpi*		(0.9028)
c_f		0.11182
Fab Transfer Constant $\times$ *fnpi*		(1.3681)
Static Component		
c	0.000084	0.000059
Clean Room Grade	(3.5538)	(2.0306)
l	0.33597	0.34508
Line Width	(2.5443)	(3.0244)
m	0.035243	0.049124
Mask Layers	(2.1304)	(3.0463)
ν	−0.28724	−0.23743
Equipment Vintage	(−6.5828)	(−3.8377)
ρ	0.7257	0.6670
R^2	0.8138	0.8189

Number of observations = 364.

Number of processes = 26.

Values in parentheses are asymptotic *t*-statistics.

The results in Table 31-3 are broadly consistent with our portrayal of new process introduction in ASICs as an activity whose characteristics differ somewhat from those of new process introduction in other semiconductor product classes. The first column of the table, which reports the results for the basic specification, shows that the cumulative volume of ASIC production is a more significant contributor to learning in new process improvement—the coefficient, which is statistically significant, is nearly three times as large as the estimated coefficient for this term in Table 31-2.

In addition, and consistent with our discussion immediately above, cumulative engineering volume is much less important in the early-stage improvement of new

ASIC manufacturing processes. None of the first specification's coefficients for the variables in the second panel of the Table are statistically significant. In particular, the lack of statistical significance (but correct sign) for the "transfer constant" variable is consistent with our hypothesis that new process introduction assumes a more incremental form than is true in logic or memory products. In contrast to the results in Table 31-2, the estimated coefficients for the "technical difficulty" variables in the fourth panel of Table 31-3 are all statistically significant, although the coefficient for line width has the "wrong" sign. The greater statistical significance of these variables lends support to our hypothesis that in new ASIC processes, the more incremental nature of the changes associated with new process introduction leave little learning by doing to be done.

In the second column of Table 31-3, we add to our original specification the variables that attempt to capture the impact of new process introduction on the existing processes in the fab. There are some interesting differences between these results and those for the overall sample in Table 31-2. In the first place, the effects of new process introduction on the improvement impact of cumulative volume are positive (although the coefficient for this variable is not statistically significant), the opposite of the result in Table 31-2. Consistent with our discussion above, the negative effects of new process introduction on existing processes are far less significant in ASICs than in the overall sample (revealed in the size and statistical nonsignificance of this variable's coefficient). A more puzzling result is that the "fab transfer constant" in this specification has a negative coefficient that approaches statistical significance. The coefficient estimate suggests that far from impairing the yield improvement trends in existing processes, the introduction of a new ASIC manufacturing process accelerates yield improvement in these manufacturing processes. Overall, however, these results for the existing processes are broadly consistent with our characterization of ASIC new process introduction as an activity that proceeds more incrementally than is true of new process introduction in logic or memory devices.

DRAM Processes

Our final set of specifications focuses on DRAM devices. Based on interviews and reviews of the data collected from the semiconductor firms in our sample, we anticipate that new process introduction in DRAM devices differs from this activity in logic or ASICs for several reasons. First, during the period covered by these data, DRAM devices placed the greatest demands on process capabilities, requiring smaller line widths and lower particle counts than any other devices. Second, DRAM devices typically are produced in high volumes, increasing the returns to the introduction of a well-characterized, stable manufacturing process whose output can be rapidly expanded. The importance of rapid "ramping" to high volumes in DRAMs is reinforced by the low level of firm-specific product differentiation, which distinguishes DRAMs from logic or ASICs. Finally, despite their demanding process requirements, memory devices have highly simple design parameters, consisting of numerous identical cells in each die. As a result, engineering problem-solving activities should be relatively productive in solving parametric yield problems, and we anticipate that the learning curve for memory devices will be steeper than those for other products.

Since DRAM manufacturing processes are generally at the technological frontier, manufacturers often avoid the simultaneous introduction of a new process and a new generation of DRAM by incrementally redesigning (often, shrinking the die size) an older DRAM product to run on the new process.[23] The introduction of a new process with an older product design allows for the exploitation of intrafirm spillovers. Knowledge from manufacturing experience in the fab for an older product design improves manufacturing performance for the new process. In contrast, new processes manufacturing "first-generation" products are likely to suffer from greater parametric problems when transferred. To incorporate the influence of multiple generations into our model of learning by doing, we add a "first generation" component to the learning index. Solving for the defect density curve as before gives the following defect density curve for DRAM processes:

$$DD_t = \gamma + \exp(-(\alpha \cdot CV_t + \beta \cdot CE_t$$
$$+ gen_1(\alpha_1 \cdot CV_t + \beta_1 \cdot CE_t + c_1) + npi \cdot xfer))$$
$$\cdot (DD_0 - \gamma - (cCR + lLW + mML + vVin_0))$$
$$+ cCR + lLW + mML + vVin_t, \tag{11}$$

where gen_1 denotes processes with first generation DRAM devices. α_1 and β_1 show how the slope of the learning curve differs for processes manufacturing first generation products and c_1 shifts the first generation learning curve relative to the curve for n^{th} generation DRAMs. The dev and prox variables are dropped from the equation, because all the processes were developed in development fabs at other locations. Equation (10) is similarly modified to get

$$DD_t = \gamma + \exp(-(\alpha \cdot CV_t + \beta \cdot CE_t$$
$$+ gen_1(\alpha_1 \cdot CV_t + \beta_1 \cdot CE_t + c_1)$$
$$+ fnpi(\alpha_f \cdot CV_t + \beta_f \cdot CE_t + c_f) + npi \cdot xfer))$$
$$\cdot (DD_0 - \gamma - (cCR + lLW + mML + vVin_0))$$
$$+ cCR + lLW + mML + vVin_t. \tag{12}$$

Estimates of the coefficients of these equations are reported in Table 31-4. The results of the regressions are consistent our earlier the description of DRAM manufacturing. In particular, for the basic specification of the model (column 1 in Table 31-4) we see that the learning curve for DRAM processes is nearly flat—the estimated coefficients are relatively small and not significantly different from zero. This is consistent with the observation that DRAMs are more likely to be more fully characterized before transfer in order to produce at high volumes from the start. They are so well characterized that less remains to be learned.

The estimates of the learning coefficients for first generations contrast with those for later generations. It appears that first generation processes are so difficult that they require intense engineering effort to eliminate parametric problems—the cumulative engineering coefficient is positive and significantly different from zero while the cumulative volume coefficient is negative and insignificant. Furthermore, the coefficient for the "1st generation" shift parameter shows that there is a significant increase in defect density for processes with first generation products. Estimates for the transfer variables are consistent with the earlier results for all processes. The "transfer constant" is unexpectedly positive but insignificant. Equipment duplication improves defect densities in new processes, and manufacturing fabs that are first to receive the new processes have significantly higher defect densities. The coefficient for the clean room grade has the expected sign but is insignificant and line width continues to have the "wrong" sign but is marginally significant. Increasing mask layers raise defect density significantly. In the third column of the DRAM specification results, we see that the introduction of new processes has little impact on the rate of improvement in mature processes in the fab. This is not surprising since most DRAM processes are producing n^{th} generation products that are well characterized and for which the potential learning opportunities are nearly exhausted.

These estimates extend the analysis of Irwin and Klenow (1994) concerning *intergenerational spillovers* (i.e., knowledge spillovers among successive generations of DRAM "families"). They find no significant intergenerational spillovers between firms for the 4 MB and 16 MB DRAM families. Our discussion of new process introduction for DRAMs provides an explanation for this finding, since the intergenerational knowledge spillovers happen almost entirely within firms. For new processes introduced on established product designs, the accumulated stock of process-specific knowledge is applicable to the next product modification. There is little left to be gained from internal learning by doing, let alone from interfirm intergenerational spillovers, in the production of successive modifications of established DRAM designs.[24]

TABLE 31-4   Estimates for DRAM Processes

Coefficient	Equation (11)	Equation (12)
Dynamic (Learning by Doing) Component		
γ	−7.2342	−6.6866
$h_1(\cdot)$ Constant	(−2.4792)	(−2.3623)
α	0.001286	0.004545
Cumulative Volume	(0.3385)	(0.9847)
β	0.000636	0.000242
Cumulative Engineering	(1.4323)	(0.4268)
Interaction of First Generation New Processes with Learning Parameters		
α_1	−0.35498	−0.40444
Cumulative Volume $\times$ gen_1	(−0.7199)	(−1.0604)
β_1	0.024534	0.024236
Cumulative Engineering $\times$ gen_1	(6.5243)	(5.0188)
c_1	−0.78501	−0.71605
1st Generation Shift	(−5.5673)	(−3.7929)
Impact of New Process Introduction Variables		
x_0	0.083982	0.24808
Transfer Constant	(0.56539)	(0.9775)
x_3	0.23344	0.11221
Equipment Duplication	(2.3231)	(0.7045)
x_4	−0.18382	−0.27530
First Manufacturing Fab	(−1.9013)	(−1.6204)
Interaction of New Processes with Learning Parameters of Existing Processes		
α_f		−0.0013684
Cumulative Volume $\times$ *fnpi*		(−0.6691)
β_f		0.000118
Cumulative Engineering $\times$ *fnpi*		(0.2849)
c_f		−0.057067
Fab Transfer Constant $\times$ *fnpi*		(−0.4901)
Static Component		
c	0.002497	0.0061367
Clean Room Grade	(1.6131)	(3.0487)
l	1.3588	1.2071
Line Width	(1.9368)	(1.3815)
m	0.18154	0.15376
Mask Layers	(1.9601)	(1.7451)
ν	0.02497	0.027892
Equipment Vintage	(0.7406)	(0.8974)
ρ	0.5249	0.5467
R^2	0.9790	0.9795

Number of observations = 115.

Number of processes = 6.

Values in parentheses are asymptotic *t*-statistics.

CONCLUSIONS

Students of firm-level capabilities emphasize the persistence of differences in performance, as well as behavior, among firms in the same industry that are not well addressed by other approaches, such as neoclassical economics or the structure-conduct approach to strategy developed by Porter (1980). Although the "resource-based" view of the firm (Teece et al. 1997) appeals to intuition and casual empiricism, it has proven difficult to test. Measures of firm-specific capabilities are difficult to collect on a large scale, and the performance consequences of differences in such capabilities are not easily determined. This paper has examined one of the most important firm-specific capabilities for competition in the semiconductor industry: the ability of firms to develop, introduce, and expand production with new processes. Although semiconductors assuredly is a high-technology industry, scientific understanding of many semiconductor manufacturing processes is limited, and their performance cannot be predicted without extensive experimentation.

This characteristic of the process technology means that firm-level differences in managing new process introduction are likely to persist and will have important consequences for performance. The capabilities that are exploited by firms to manage new process introduction cannot be reduced to differences in human capital; they seem to be organizational, rather than exclusively individual. One firm's hiring the most skilled process engineers of another firm may be necessary, but it is not sufficient, to "reverse engineer" and introduce a new manufacturing process.

The results presented in this paper indicate that the improvement of manufacturing performance through learning is not an exogenous result of output expansion but is influenced primarily by the systematic allocation of engineering labor to problem-solving activities. In other words, learning is subject to managerial discretion and control. Furthermore, the characteristics of learning for new processes differ significantly from those for mature processes, reflecting significant differences between the environments within which new processes are developed and those in which high-volume production takes place. Individual fabs' performance in new process introduction also is amenable to managerial actions that seek to reduce these differences and thereby reduce the knowledge loss associated with the transfer of a new manufacturing process.

Finally, our analysis considered the extent and significance of differences in new product introduction among product classes. Consistent with our qualitative characterization of this product group, ASICs exhibit less significant differences between learning in established and new processes. Moreover, the disruptive effects of new process introduction in this product category are also modest. Although their statistical significance is limited, our results for ASICs suggest that new process development and introduction in this segment is incremental, gradual, and less disruptive than in other product categories. DRAMs, by contrast, require far more problem-solving investment and careful management of new process introduction. Interestingly, however, the most difficult new process introduction activity by far in this product category is that for the "first generation" of a specific DRAM design; much if not all of the potential for learning in the new process introduction is exhausted with this first generation.

Although learning in manufacturing has been examined in an extensive literature, this literature has focused primarily on improved measurements or proxies for cumulative production experience, rather than testing models of the processes that underpin learning by doing. This paper provides and tests such a model. In addition, we consider the effects of the introduction of new processes into a production facility on learning for existing processes, and we find that these disruptive effects are very significant. Moreover, and consistent with our characterization of the sources of learning in semiconductor manufacturing, these disruptive effects operate through their effects on scarce engineering resources, forcing the reallocation of engineering talent away from problem solving on mature processes to "debugging" of the new manufacturing processes. These results thus establish an empirical linkage between the empirical work on new process introduction and that on learning that has received little attention.[25]

TABLE 31-5 Assumptions and Values for Cost Simulations

Unit production cost (w)	$1.00	Clean room grade (CRG)	100
Wafers (thousands)/engineers	6.67	Line width (LW)	1.0
Line yield (LY(t))	0.75	Mask layers (ML)	15
Die size (a cm^2)	0.75	Vintage (Vin$_t$)	88.0
Starting defect density (DD$_0$)	1.5	Starting vintage (Vin$_0$)	87.6

Appendix

The cost simulations in §6 are based on Hatch and Reichelstein (1997). Using the regression estimates of §6, we project the average variable cost of a good die and examine the influence of a process transfer and the management of new process introduction on average variable cost. We begin with the assumption that the cost of manufacturing a wafer is constant. Therefore, the cost of producing an individual chip, whether it functions or not, depends on the wafer size and the die size. Let the wafer size be denoted A cm^2 and let the area of the die be a cm^2, then the gross number of die on the wafer x is A/a. If we denote the manufacturing cost of a wafer as W, then the unit cost per die is $w = W/x = (W \cdot a)/A$.

Now we introduce the influence of yield losses on manufacturing cost. If we let $Y(t)$ denote the manufacturing yield at time t and q denote the number of functional die produced, then $x \cdot Y(t) = q$, by definition.[26] Since the good output must bear the cost of yield losses, the manufacturing cost can be represented as $w \cdot x = c \cdot q$, where c is the average variable cost of good output. The unit cost of production, including the cost of yield losses, at time t is

$$c(t) = \frac{w}{Y(t)} = \frac{w}{\text{LY}(t) \cdot g(a, \text{DD}(t))} \tag{13}$$

where LY(t) represents the line yield, DD(t) gives the defect density, and $g(\cdot)$ is the defect density model. Since we do not estimate the line yield curve, we substitute an average value into (13) and assume it is constant over time. We also insert average values for the die size and the variables in the defect density function given in Equation (8). Estimates from the first column of Table 31-2 are used in connection with a one dimensional "experience" variable that combines cumulative volume and cumulative engineering as was described in endnote 21. Table 31-5 gives the sample average values used in the simulation.

References

Adler, P. S. and K. B. Clark. 1991. Behind the learning curve: A sketch of the learning process. *Management Sci.* **37** 3 267–281.

Alchian, A. 1963. Reliability of progress curves in airframe production. *Econometrica* **31** 679–693.

Alvarez, A. R. 1994. Process requirements through 2001. Presented at the Second International Rapid Thermal Processing Conference, Monterey, California.

Arrow, K. 1962. The economic implications of learning by doing. *Rev. Econom. Studies* **29** 155–173.

Baloff, N. 1971. Extension of the learning curve. *Oper. Res. Quart.* **22** 329–340.

Carlton, J. 1995. Apple, IBM, Motorola Power PC group issues blueprint for a common computer. *Wall Street Journal,* **33** Nov. 15. 86.

Conway, R. and A. Schultz. 1959. The manufacturing progress function. *J. Indust. Engr.* **10** 39–53.

DeJong, J. 1957. The effects of increasing skill on cycle time and its consequences for time standards. *Ergonomics.* **1**(1) 51–60.

Dertouzos, M., R. Lester, and R. Solow. 1988. *Made in America,* MIT Press, Cambridge, Massachusetts.

Dick, A. R. 1991. Learning by doing and dumping in the semiconductor industry. *J. Law Econom.* **34** 133–159.

Dudley, L. 1972. Learning and productivity changes in metal products. *Amer. Econom. Rev.* **62** 662–669.

Gruber, H. 1992. The learning curve in the production of semiconductor memory chips. *Appl. Econom.* **24** 885–894.

Hatch, N. W. and S. Reichelstein. 1997. Learning effects in semiconductor fabrication. Unpublished manuscript, University of Illinois at Urbana-Champaign.

Hirsch, W. Z. 1952. Progress functions of machine tool manufacturing. *Econometrica* **20**(1) 81–82.

Hirschmann, W. B. 1964. Profit from the learning curve. *Harvard Bus. Rev.* **42**(1) 125–139.

Hollander, S. 1965. *The Sources of Increased Efficiency: A Study of the DuPont Rayon Plants*, MIT Press, Cambridge, Massachusetts.

Irwin, D. A. and P. J. Klenow. 1994. Learning-by-doing spillovers in the semiconductor industry. *J. Political Economy* **102**(6) 1,200–1,227.

Jarmin, R. S. 1994. Learning by doing and competition in the early rayon industry. *RAND J. Econom.* **25**(3) 441–454.

Judge, G. G., R. C. Hill, W. E. Griffiths, H. Lutkepohl, and T.-C. Lee, 1988. *Introduction to the Theory and Practice of Econometrics,* second edn, John Wiley & Sons, New York.

Kilbridge, M. 1962. A model for industrial learning. *Management Sci.* **8**.

Leachman, R. C. 1997. The competitive semiconductor manufacturing survey: Third report on the results of the main phase. Technical report, Engineering Systems Research Center, University of California, Berkeley.

Levy, F. 1965. Adaptation in the production process, *Management Sci.* **11** B136–B154.

Lieberman, M. 1984. The learning curve and pricing in the chemical processing industries. *RAND J. Econom.* **15**(2) 213–228.

Murphy, B. 1964. Cost-size optima of monolithic integrated circuits. *Proceedings of the IEEE* **52**(1) 1537–1545.

Okabe, T., M. Nagata, and S. Shimada. 1972. Analysis of yield integrated circuits and a new expression for the yield. *Electr. Eng. in Japan* **92** 135–141.

Pisano, G. P. 1997. *The Development Factory: Unlocking the Potential of Process Innovation.* Harvard Business School Press, Boston, Massachusetts.

Porter, M. E. 1980. *Competitive Strategy.* Free Press, New York.

Preston, L. and E. Keachie. 1964. Cost functions and progress functions: an integration. *Amer. Econom. Rev.* **54**(2) 100–107.

Rapping, L. 1965. Learning and World War II production functions. *Rev. Econom. Statis.* **47** 81–86.

Sheshinski, E. 1967. Tests of the learning by doing hypothesis. *Rev. Econom. Statis.* **49**(4) 568–578.

Stapper, C. H. 1973. Defect density distribution for lsi yield calculations, *IEEE Trans. Electron Devices* **ED-20** 655–657.

Stapper, C. H. 1989. Fact and fiction in yield modeling. *Microelectronics J.* **20**(1–2) 129–151.

Stobaugh, R. and P. Townsend. 1975. Price forecasting and strategic planning: The case of petro chemicals. *J. Marketing Res.* **12** 19–29.

Takahashi, D. 1997. Intel plans deeper price cuts on chips in an effort to ward off competitors. *Wall Street Journal* **B2** April 11, '97, pg B5.

Teece, D. J., G. Pisano, and A. Shuen. 1997. Dynamic capabilities and strategic management. *Strategic Management J.* **18**(7) 509–533.

Webbinck, D. 1972. The semiconductor industry: A survey of structure, conduct, and performance. Staff Report to the Federal Trade Commission, U.S. Government Printing Office, Washington, D.C.

Wright, T. 1936. Factors affecting the cost of airplanes. *J. Aeronautical Sci.* **3**(4) 122–128.

Zimmerman, M. 1982. Learning effects and the commercialization of new energy technologies: The case of nuclear power. *Bell J. Econom.* **13** 297–310.

Accepted by Ralph Katz; received November 1996. This paper has been with the authors 3 months for 1 revision.

Endnotes

1. For example, learning by doing has been documented in airframes (Wright 1936; Alchian 1963), automobile assembly (Baloff 1971), chemical processing (Lieberman 1984), clerical activities (Kilbridge 1962), housing construction (DeJong 1957), machine tools (Hirsch 1952), metal products (Dudley 1972), nuclear plant construction (Zimmerman 1982), petroleum refining (Hirschmann 1964), printing and typesetting (Levy 1965), radar (Preston and Keachie 1964), rayon (Jarmin 1994), and semiconductors (Webbinck 1972, Dick 1991, Gruber 1992, Irwin and Klenow 1994).

2. See, for example, Conway and Schultz (1959) and Hollander (1965).

3. According to A. R. Alvarez, the vice president for R&D at Cypress Semiconductor, "Industrial success in the year 2001 will depend as much on the methods by which process development is conducted as it will on the results of process development" (Alvarez 1994, p. 1). Indeed, the failure thus far of the PowerPC's challenge to Intel's dominance of desktop computers has been directly affected by Motorola's inability to expand output of the PowerPC microprocessor more rapidly. Simultaneously, Intel has relied on rapid development and "ramping" of new manufacturing processes to accelerate its introduction of a succession of improved versions of the Pentium and "Pentium Pro" microprocessors, making Motorola's challenge even greater (Carlton 1995). More recently, competition between Intel's Pentium and the "K6" microprocessor developed by Advanced Micro Devices (AMD) has been affected by AMD's inability to ramp production rapidly (Takahashi 1997). Rather than a "capacity race," which was hypothesized to characterize US-Japan competition in DRAM manufacture (e.g., Steinmueller 1982), this competition between architectures is driven by capacity utilization, which in turn is a function of success in new process introduction.

4. Currently, most fabs are producing with wafers that are eight inches in diameter, although four-, five-, and six-inch wafers are sometimes used. Die sizes vary much more than wafer sizes—ranging from 0.1 cm^2 to 2.5 cm^2 and even larger.

5. To protect against unwanted particles in the manufacturing environment, air-filtration systems are installed that reduce the number of particles in the air. Particles are also generated by the manufacturing equipment and personnel, however, and additional precautions, such as protective enclosures for equipment and protective clothing for personnel, are taken to reduce the amount of contaminants introduced by the equipment and personnel.

6. Each "ingredient" in the recipe for processing steps must be utilized within a given range for the input to have the desired effect. Parametric processing errors occur when ingredients fall outside the acceptable range. Many process steps are too complex to permit identification of the optimal ranges for all the ingredients. As a result, unexpected interactions between inputs can destroy the functionality of the die. Even if the limits of the process technology were perfectly known, the production equipment is limited in its process control, meaning that the ingredients are applied with some variance around the target level. When the acceptable range is sufficiently small and/or the variance is sufficiently high, the ingredient levels will randomly fall outside the acceptable range and the chip will fail. Given their random occurance, parametric processing errors may affect only one chip while leaving the next one unimpaired.

7. Due to data limitations on line yield, we will restrict our attention to die yield losses.

8. The development fab serves a function in this industry that resembles that of the pilot plant in the chemicals industry, providing a stable environment for experimentation and testing that nonetheless has equipment and other characteristics that resemble those of the manufacturing facility.

9. In the case of DRAM products, for example, the differences in production volumes between economically feasible development fabs and the manufacturing facilities of leading producers are so great that development fabs cannot fully replicate manufacturing conditions and therefore cannot fully characterize new manufacturing processes. This factor has contributed to efforts by some leading DRAM manufacturers to move new processes out of their development fabs and into manufacturing more rapidly, albeit at lower levels of process characterization.

10. The data were collected as part of a large empirical investigation of semiconductor manufacturing performance undertaken by the College of Engineering and the Haas School of Business at the University of California, Berkeley, under the direction of former Dean David Hodges and Professor Robert Leachman of the College of Engineering.

11. The semiconductor firms that participated in this study were chosen to provide a representative sample of producers across product types (logic, memory, and ASIC) as well as geography (US., Asia, and Europe). The specific fab was chosen in consultation with the firm to identify a facility with world-class technology together with a sufficiently long history to perform longitudinal analysis. Most firms that were contacted have agreed to participate, providing us with a representative sample of top-performing fabs. For a more detailed description of the Berkeley Competitive Semiconductor Manufacturing project, see Leachman (1996).

12. The list of commonly used models includes the Poisson model, the Murphy model (1964), and the negative binomial model (Okabe 1972, Stapper 1973). Murphy extended the Poisson model to account for the observed clustering of defects on wafers. In particular, his model assumes a triangular approximation of the Gaussian distribution. See Stapper (1989) for an overview of the defect density literature.

13. In the table, *submicron* refers to the line width of the smallest circuit feature. As we note below, line width is a widely accepted measure of the sophistication of product and process technology in integrated circuits.

14. Note that Equations (3) and (4) imply that learning by doing occurs at the same rate for mature and new processes. This is consistent with the notion that transferring a process to manufacturing reduces the amount of process-specific knowledge available to the manufacturing environment, although overall knowledge acquisition continues at the same rate as it did before.

15. The equipment vintage is measured by the weighted average purchase date of the photolithography equipment (aligners and steppers) in the fab. We consider only photolithography equipment to avoid comparison problems across equipment types and because photolithography has historically been considered the most challenging process step. In the few cases where fabs acquired used equipment, Vin was adjusted to reflect the original purchase date of the machine.

16. Current manufacturing processes have line widths as small as 0.25 μm which imposes tolerance limits of ± 0.07 μm for the resolution of patterns printed on the wafer. By comparison, the average human hair is 50–100 μm.

17. Unlike the other variables in the static ($h_2 (\cdot)$) portion of the learning curve, the equipment vintage varies over time as fabs acquire new equipment and/or discard old equipment.

18. For variables in the dynamic component ($h_1 (\cdot)$) of Equation (8), a positive coefficient implies that defect density is decreasing, while in the static component ($h_2(\cdot)$) a positive coefficient indicates increasing defect density.

19. We regressed all of the specifications in this study with controls for fixed effects, but since the results are unaffected, we do not report the estimates here.

20. A more detailed description of the learning curve simulation is given in the Appendix.

21. The experience variable is computed assuming a constant ratio between volume and engineering FTEs over time. In this case, the ratio of wafers to engineers is 1000:6.67 and the average fab accumulates 3 units of "experience" per month.

22. Adler and Clark (1991) address this, as do Gruber (1992), Jarmin (1994), Lieberman (1984), and Webbinck (1972). In particular, the product-specific effects of learning by doing have been studied in memory products by Webbinck (1972) and Gruber (1992).

23. For example, the process developed for the 16 MB DRAM would be introduced into the manufacturing fab to produce a second generation 4 MB DRAM.

24. Irwin and Klenow (1994) find significant intergenerational spillovers in early (4 K–16 K and 256 K–1 M) generations. This result is not surprising because it appears that the competitive pressures that have given rise to the practice of introducing new processes with previous-generation products began fairly recently.

25. Research for this paper was funded by the Alfred P. Sloan Foundation and the U.S. Air Force Office of Scientific Research. The data and interpretations contained in this paper draw on a larger research project, the Berkeley *Competitive Semiconductor Manufacturing* research project, but its conclusions and interpretations are solely those of the authors. We are indebted to Professor David Hodges, Professor Robert C. Leachman, Melissa Appleyard, and Sean Cunningham, among many others, for invaluable assistance and guidance in gathering and analyzing the data on which this paper is based. We also thank Ernst Berndt, Timothy Bresnahan, and seminar participants at the American Economics Association meetings, U.C. Berkeley, Brigham Young University, Harvard University, University of Illinois at Urbana-Champaign, and Utah State University of helpful comments.

26. We make yield a function of time to allow for yield improvements. Of course yield is not really just a function of time but rather depends on product and process design, process development and transfer characteristics, and manufacturing practices.

SECTION
VI

DEVELOPING AND MANAGING SERVICE INNOVATION

Introduction

The intent of this section is to present the state of innovation relative to services and service provision industries. This is an increasingly important area since services account for approximately three-quarters of all of the economic activity in the United States. The articles included here provide insight into service-related areas such as the relationship between service provision and service consumption, the theory underlying the development and offering of services, the process related to the development of new services, the actual design of service provision from a tactical perspective, some thoughts about the acceleration of new service development and implementation, and the eventual management of services as new products.

Christian Grönroos in the first article of this section offers insights into the solutions to customer problems in a service context and a variety of implications for service marketing from the perspective of the service consumer. Much of Grönroos' thesis is based on the premise that a service is process consumption rather than outcome consumption. This implies that the service experience is derived from the service process. The author notes that one service provider often cannot differentiate his or her service offering outcome from the outcomes offered by competitors. In this light, it is important to note that there are two methods of quality differentiation available to service providers. The first relates to the experience and the process of delivering the service (called functional quality; how service is provided), and the second, relates to the outcome of the service process or the benefit of the service process itself (called technical quality; what is provided). The author concludes his discussion by relating services to long-term relationship marketing associations. He points out that from a long-term marketing perspective it is far better to position a business as a service, because what customers are looking for is "service," and, therefore, any goods that are offered become service elements related to the provision of quality service.

In the next article, Richard Barras offers his theory of innovation in services. This is a foundation article that assists our overall understanding of service innovation. Barras suggests in his theory of services that capital goods, those services related to capital goods, and growth cycles, often called Kondratiev or long cycles, are related. Barras builds a theory of services by beginning with its foundation in the development of capital goods. The basis of this theory is fully supported by writings presented earlier such as that of Moore and Tushman, Utterback, and Etienne. It is purported here that capital goods progress through a process or evolution that includes three stages of development. These stages include a take-off or introduction stage with an emphasis on product innovation, a growth stage with an emphasis on process innovation, and a maturity stage in which both product and process innovation are usually limited to incremental changes. Barras notes that the initial stage, based on product innovation, is one in which employment increases and can, therefore, be thought of as a "capital widening" period of time. Whereas, the second stage, in which process innovation, standardization, and cost reduction take the position of primary importance, can be thought of as a stage of "capital deepening" or a time for investment in process machinery. Barras includes a fourth stage that he entitles transition which leads to the next cycle of innovation. Barras then proposes a "reverse cycle," that represents the "user" community of the capital goods sector. This reverse cycle, which operates in a direction opposite to the typical product cycle, forms the heart of his theory of services. In addition, Barras suggests an interesting distinction between a service itself (the product) and a service's mode of delivery (the process by which the service is provided) so as to ensure a comparative basis for goods and services. He concludes his discussion by noting that his portrayal of two out-of-phase innovation cycles helps to explain long wave fluctuations, which are symptomatic of successive Schumpeterian technological revolutions.

Christopher H. Lovelock, in an article related to developing new services, proposes a "new service development process" and offers some insight into the similarities and differences between new "good" and "service" development. Lovelock bases his investigation of new service development on the progress that has taken place in new goods development in the manufacturing sector. Lovelock refers to the "goods" categories that were presented by Donald Heany in his article that we included in Section IV. After a careful review of the various levels of novelty that can be associated with innovations and the way goods progress through the product life cycle, Lovelock focuses on the developmental process for new products. In doing so, he notes that a new product development process should proceed through a deliberate set of steps to ensure that all exigencies are accounted for in the process. He points out that goods as well as services should proceed in such a manner but, perhaps, not through the same steps or, perhaps, the same steps but not with the same degree of intensity during each step. Moreover, Lovelock reviews the roles of individuals, such as product champions, that have been associated with successful new product developments. He indicates that all eight roles that have been espoused by researchers such as Urban and Hauser are applicable to services as well as goods. He agrees with Yoram J. Wind, who has indicated that it might be prudent for service developers to progress directly from concept testing to test marketing or a similar process due to the inability to patent or in any way protect new services from competitive me-too products moving ahead in market entry. This admonition suggests that new service developers need to place an emphasis on the early stages of the development process to ensure that the new service has a distinct role, that there is a good product-market fit, and that the new service fits with the objectives of the firm. The author notes that new service developers must not only compare their new service to comparable services, but also that new services often compete with the benefits offered by goods. Lovelock concludes by warning that new product developers must be vigilant to avoid regarding services as homogeneous. Services need to be tailored to both the producing organization and the market for which they are developed.

The fourth article, by Michael R. Bowers, supports Lovelock's contention that new service development is somewhat different from the development of new "goods" and he tests some of these contentions empirically in this piece.

Bowers points out that new service developers appear to be more successful the more they understand the environment in which the new service will be deployed. It was distressing to Bowers to find that new service developers did not rely on the customer for input into the new service development (NSD) process to any great extent. He points out that the development steps employed by new "goods" developers to remain in contact with customers are often ignored by new service developers. He notes that the first time a new service is seen by customers is often at commercialization. His study also indicates that new service developers are likely not to participate in formal idea generation processes, product development, or market testing. Therefore, Bowers concludes that service developing firms frequently execute incomplete new product development processes. Bowers concludes with a plea to new service developers to progress to a more complete new product development process that is based on sound business strategies and is more sensitive to customers' desires.

G. Lynn Shostack and Jane Kingman-Brundage share their ideas regarding how to develop a service in their book chapter that is offered here as the fifth selection in this section. They view the development of new services as the creation of new processes as opposed to the construction of "bricks and mortar." Their work focuses on what they suggest is a blueprint of a service. Such a blueprint represents a road map or operational diagram for developing a service. Not only do service blueprints describe new services in terms of pointing out all customers' encounter or touch points, therefore directly addressing a service's and customers' benefits, but blueprints also describe a service's delivery process as suggested by Barras in an earlier article. These authors first describe major differences between goods and services to set the stage for their discussion of service design and development. They explain what facilitating goods are and how they fit into the service design picture. They also lay out a five-step process for service creation and checkout. Moreover, they agree with Bowers in that many of the new services that they are aware of are put together in very haphazard ways.

In the sixth article in this series, Eric Stevens and Sergios Dimitriadis present an investigation of new services development (NSD) from the perspective of organizational learning and based on the 4Is (Intuiting, Interpreting, Integrating, and Institutionalizing) Organizational Learning (OL) model. They employed a longitudinal case study methodology in their assessment of two NSD projects from the retail and banking industries in France to arrive at research propositions related to their suggested model of the NSD process and the learning activities that occurred during the process described. The authors focus on the development of a service process, which includes customer interaction, as opposed to the results or success of such a process in the marketplace. Their approach to the NSD process pays special attention to the "service concept," or the interweaving of service production and service delivery in their depiction of the NSD process. They make note that both of these NSD investigations covered a time span of over two and one-half years, which in terms of many current new product development projects is rather long. The authors' data suggest a three-stage process including the Initiation, Formal Development, and Implementation of the new service and an overlay of the 4Is model processes. Moreover, the authors note that in both the retail and banking cases there is a reliance on similar learning loops. In their discussion, the authors point out that in both projects analyzed, many of the participants in the NSD process had strong specializations and, therefore, none of them were capable of delivering the entire offering. This provides significant support for the coordination of internal functions or divisions in addition to the appointment of an established leader for such NSD projects. New service developers also need to ensure that the links between the 4Is model stages are maintained since, for example, the Interpretation and Integration stages contribute to Organizational Learning (OL) and successful new service launches. Finally, this article suggests that an NSD process, unlike an NPD process, can necessitate many more changes in the behavior of an organization's personnel.

References

Barras, Richard. 1986. Towards a theory of innovation in services. *Research Policy* 15(4): 161–173.

Bowers, Michael R. 1987. The new service development process: Suggestions for improvement. In *The Services Challenge: Integrating for Competitive Advantage,* ed. John R. Czepiel, Carole A. Congram, and James Shanahan. Chicago, IL: American Marketing Association Proceedings.

Grönroos, Christian. 1998. Marketing services: The case of the missing product. *Journal of Business and Industrial Marketing* 13(4/5): 322–338.

Lovelock, Christopher H. Developing and implementing new services. In *Develop New Services,* ed. William R. George and Claudia E. Marshall. Chicago, IL: American Marketing Association Proceedings.

Shostack, G. Lynn and Jane Kingman-Brundage. 1991. How to design a service. In *The AMA Handbook of Marketing for the Service Industries.* Ed. Carole A. Congram and Margaret L. Friedman. New York: American Management Association.

Stevens, Eric and Sergios Dimitriadis. 2004. New service development through the lens of organizational learning: Evidence from longitudinal case studies. *Journal of Business Research* 57(10): 1074–1084.

32 MARKETING SERVICES: THE CASE OF A MISSING PRODUCT

Christian Grönroos

Professor of Marketing, CERS *Center for Relationship Marketing and Service Management, Hanken Swedish School of Economics, Helsinki, Finland*

INTRODUCTION

In the service marketing literature, services are frequently described by characteristics such as intangibility, heterogeneity, inseparability of consumption from production and the impossibility to keep services in stock. Many of these, for example the first two, are not specific for services, and others, for example the last two, follow from the most important characteristic of services, i.e. the process nature of services. Physical goods are preproduced in a factory, whereas services are produced in a process in which consumers interact with the production resources of the service firm. Some part of the service may be prepared before the customers enter the process, but for service quality perception the crucial part of the service process[1] takes place in interaction with customers and in their presence. What the customer consumes in a service context is, therefore, fundamentally different from what is the focus of consumption in the context of physical goods.

Discussing Solutions to Customer Problems

The purpose of the present article is to discuss solutions to customer problems—and at the same time the objects of marketing—in a service context and the implications for service marketing that follow from the characteristic of service consumption. The analysis is based on the research tradition of the Nordic School of marketing thought (see Grönroos and Gummesson, 1985), which has been recognized as one of three major research streams in service marketing (Berry and Parasuraman, 1993).

PROCESS AND OUTCOME CONSUMPTION

A central part of service marketing is based on the fact that the consumption of a service is *process consumption* rather than *outcome consumption*, where the consumer or user perceives the production process as part of the service consumption, not just the outcome of that process as in traditional marketing of physical goods. When consuming a physical product customers make use of the product itself, i.e. they consume the outcome of the production process. In contrast, when consuming services customers perceive the process of producing the service to a larger or smaller degree, but always to a critical

Grönroos, Christian. 1998. Marketing services: The case of the missing product. *Journal of Business and Industrial Marketing* 13(4/5): 322–338.

extent, moreover taking part in the process. The consumption process leads to an outcome for the customer, which is the result of the service process. Thus, the consumption of the service process is a critical part of the service experience. As service quality research demonstrates, perception of the process is important for the perception of the total quality of a service, even though a satisfactory outcome is necessary and a prerequisite for good perceived quality. In many situations the service firm cannot differentiate its outcomes from those of its competitors. In some situations the customers take the quality of the outcome for granted, but in other situations it is difficult for the customer to evaluate the quality of the outcome of the service process. However, in all situations customers take part in the production process and sometimes more, sometimes less actively interact with the employees, physical resources and production system of the service organization. Because of this inseparability of the service process and the consumption of a service, the process can be characterized as an open process. Hence, regardless of how the customer perceives the outcome of a service process, service consumption is basically process consumption.

Thus service consumption and production have interfaces that are always critical to the customers' perception of the service and consequently to their long-term purchasing behavior. In the service marketing literature, the management of these interfaces is called interactive marketing (Grönroos, 1982, 1990). If a service firm wants to keep its customers, interactive marketing, i.e. the marketing effect of the simultaneous service production and consumption processes, must be positive. Hence, for the long-term success of a service firm the customer orientation of the service process is crucial. If the process fails from the customers' point of view, no traditional external marketing efforts, and frequently not even a good outcome of the service process, will make them stay in the long run. Only a low price may save the situation, at least for a while.

Traditional Product Marketing

In traditional product marketing, the physical goods, that is the products that are the outcomes of the production process, are the key variable around which the other marketing activities revolve. According to the 4P model, there has to be a preproduced product that can be priced, communicated about, and distributed to the consumers. However, when there is no such product, marketing becomes different, because there is no ready-made, preproduced object of marketing and consumption. There is only a process that cannot begin until the consumer or user enters the process.

In the following sections we will first discuss the nature of traditional marketing of physical goods, i.e. product marketing which is traditionally based on outcome consumption. Next we will explore how the nature of marketing changes when outcome consumption is replaced by process consumption as is the case with services. As a means of illustrating the nature of marketing we use the marketing triangle. This way of illustrating the field of marketing is adapted from Philip Kotler (1991), who uses it to illustrate the holistic concept of marketing suggested by the Nordic School approach to services marketing and management.

OUTCOME CONSUMPTION AND THE NATURE OF PRODUCT MARKETING

A Closed Process

A product in the traditional sense, is the result of how various resources, such as people, technologies, raw materials, knowledge and information, have been managed in a factory so that a number of features that customers in target markets are looking for are incorporated into it. The production process can be characterized as a closed process, where the customer takes no direct part. Thus, a product evolves as a more or less preproduced package of resources and features that is ready to be exchanged. The task of marketing (including sales) is to find out what product features the customers are interested in and to give promises about such features to a segment of potential customers through external marketing activities such as sales and advertising campaigns. If the product includes features that the customers want, it will almost by itself fulfill the promises that have been given to the customers. This marketing situation is illustrated in the product marketing triangle in Figure 32-1.

FIGURE 32-1 The Product-oriented Perspective: Outcome Consumption and Marketing

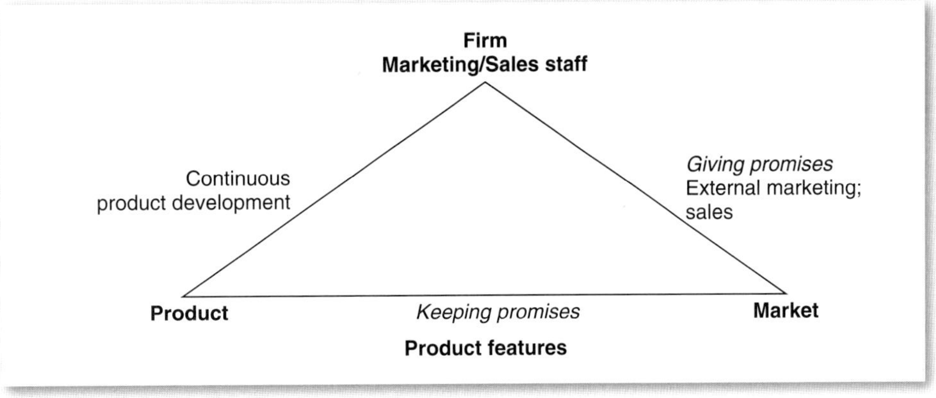

Source: Adapted from Grönroos (1997, p. 414)

Three Key Parties of Marketing

In Figure 32-1 the three key parties of marketing in a physical good or product context are shown. These are the firm, represented by a marketing and/or sales department, the market, and the product. Normally, marketing (including sales) is the responsibility of a department (or departments) of specialists or full-time marketers (and salespeople). Customers are viewed in terms of markets of more or less anonymous individuals. The market offering is a preproduced physical product. Along the sides of the triangle three key functions of marketing are displayed, viz. to give promises, to fulfil promises, and to enable promises. Calonius (1988) has suggested that the promise concept, and marketing's role in giving and fulfilling promises should be given a central position in marketing models. Recently Bitner (1995) added the expression "enabling promises" in the context of internal marketing. Promises are normally given through mass marketing and in business to business contexts also through sales. Promises are fulfilled through a number of product features and enabled through the process of continuous product development based on market research performed by full-time marketers and on technological capabilities of the firm. Marketing is very much directed toward giving promises through external marketing campaigns. The value that customers are looking for is guaranteed by appropriate product features, and the existence of a product with the appropriate features will make sure that promises given are also kept. "The idea of marketing as a sequence of activities giving and fulfilling promises is not expressed explicitly in the . . . [product] marketing literature, probably because it is taken for granted that the products are developed with such features that any promises which external marketing and sales have given are kept" (Grönroos, 1996, p. 9).

Process Consumption

The view of marketing illustrated in the product marketing triangle of Figure 32-1 is based on the notion of outcome consumption. Customers consume a product as a preproduced package of features that does not change during the consumption process. Different customers may perceive the product in different ways, but the product is the same. However, the situation changes when this type of outcome consumption is replaced by process consumption, as is the case with services. Next we will examine how the nature of marketing changes when we move to process consumption.

PROCESS CONSUMPTION AND THE NATURE OF SERVICE MARKETING

For a service firm the scope and content of marketing become more complicated. The notion of a preproduced product with features that customers are looking for is too limited to be useful in a service context. Also, in the context of business-to-business marketing the traditional product construct is too restrictive, as has been demonstrated, for example, in the network approach to marketing in business relationships (cf. Håkansson and Snehota, 1995; Mattsson, 1997) and in the relationship marketing approach (cf. Grönroos, 1996; Sheth and Parvatiyar, 1995). Even in the early 1980s Levitt (1983) argued for an extended product concept. However, in the present article we focus on service contexts only, either the marketing of service firms or service organizations of manufacturing firms. In another context we have analyzed the need to expand the product construct in a relationship marketing context (Grönroos, 1997).

Adjusting Resources

In many cases it is not known at the beginning of the service process what the customer wants and expects in detail, and consequently what resources should be used and to what extent and in what configuration they should be used. For example, the service requirements of a machine that has been delivered to a customer may vary, the need to provide training of the customer's personnel and the need to handle claims may vary. Thus the firm has to adjust its resources and its ways of using its resources accordingly.

In Figure 32-2 (the service marketing triangle), marketing in a service context is illustrated in the same way as product marketing was in Figure 32-1. As can be seen, most elements in the figure are different.

The most important change from the product marketing situation is the fact that the product is missing. In the case of process consumption, no preproduced bundle of features that constitutes a product can be present. Only preparations for a service process can be made beforehand and partly prepared services can exist. In many service contexts, such as fast-food restaurants or car rental services, also physical product elements with specific features are present as integral parts of the service process. These product elements are sometimes, as in the case of car rental, preproduced, and sometimes, as in the case of the hamburger in a fast-food operation, they are partly preproduced, partly made to order. However, such physical products have no meaning as such, unless they fit the service process. They become one type of resource among many other types that have to be integrated into a functioning service process. A bundle of different types of resources creates value for the customers when these resources are used in their presence and in interaction with them. Even if service firms try to create products out of the resources available, they do not come up with more than a more or less standardised plan that guides the ways of using existing resources in the simultaneous service production and service consumption processes. "They (service firms) only have a set of resources and, in the best case scenario, a well-planned way of using these resources as soon as the customer enters the arena"

FIGURE 32-2 The Service-Oriented Perspective: Process Consumption and Marketing

Source: Adapted from Grönroos (1997, p. 415)

(Grönroos, 1996, p. 10). Customer-perceived value follows from a successful and customer-oriented management of resources relative to customer sacrifice, not from a preproduced bundle of features.

Treated Individually

The firm may still have a centralised marketing and sales staff, the full-time marketers, but they do not represent all the marketers and salespeople of the firm. In most cases the service firm has direct contacts with its customers, and information about each and every customer can be obtained on an individual basis. Moreover, in many cases customers, organizational customers and individual consumers and households alike, like to be treated much more individually than before. In principle, no customer must remain anonymous to the firm if this can be justified from an economic or practical standpoint (cf. Peppers and Rogers, 1993) or if the customer does not want to stay anonymous (cf. Grönroos, 1997).

In Figure 32-2 the resources of a firm are divided into five groups: personnel, technology, knowledge and information, customer's time and the customer. Many of the people representing the firm create value for customers in various service processes, such as deliveries, customer training, claims handling, service and maintenance, etc. and some of them are directly engaged in sales and cross-sales activities. Thus, they are involved in marketing as part-time marketers, to use an expression coined by Gummesson (1991). He observes that in industrial markets and in service businesses, the part-time marketers typically outnumber the full-time marketers of the marketing and sales departments several times over. Furthermore, he concludes that "marketing and sales departments (the full-time marketers) are not able to handle more than a limited portion of the marketing as their staff cannot be at the right place at the right time with the right customer contacts" (Gummesson, 1990, p. 13).

Technological Resources

In addition to the part-time marketers, other types of resources influence the quality and value perceived by the customer and hence are important from a marketing perspective as well. Technologies, the knowledge that employees have and that is embedded in technical solutions, and the firm's way of managing the customer's time are such resources. Physical product elements in the service process can, for example, be viewed as technological resources. Moreover, the customers themselves as individual consumers or as users representing organizations often become a value-generating resource. The impact of customers on the final development or design of a technical solution or on the timeliness of a service activity may be critical to the value perceived by them.

In summary, from the customers' point of view, in process consumption the solutions to their problems are formed by a set of resources needed to create a good customer-perceived service quality and value. In addition, the firm must have competencies to acquire and/or develop the resources needed and to manage and implement the service process in a way that creates value for each customer. Thus, a governing system is needed for the integration of the various types of resources and for the management of the service process.

Promises given by sales and external marketing are fulfilled through the use of the various types of resources. In order to prepare an appropriate set of resources continuous product development in its traditional form is not enough, because the service process encompasses a large part of the activities of the service firm. Instead internal marketing and a continuous development of the competencies and of the resource structure of the firm are needed.

Customer-Perceived Value

The conclusion of the discussion so far is that service firms, or service organizations of manufacturing firms, do not have products (understood as preproduced bundles of resources and features); they only have processes to offer their customers. Of course, these processes lead to an outcome that is also important for the customer. However, as the outcome of, for example, a management consultancy assignment or an elevator maintenance process cannot exist without the process, and because from the customers' perspective the process is an open process, it is fruitful to view the outcome as a part of the process. Both the process and its outcome have an impact on the perception of the quality of a service and consequently on customer-perceived value. In contrast, in the case of preproduced physical products, it is only the outcome of the process of production that counts for the customers.

IN SEARCH OF THE MISSING PRODUCT: THE PERCEIVED SERVICE QUALITY CONCEPT

Within the Nordic School research tradition, attempts to conceptualize the phenomenon of the missing product of service firms were made as early as the late 1970s (e.g. Gummesson, 1977) and in the early 1980s (e.g. Grönroos, 1982). The characteristics of the service process—for example, its heterogeneity and the inseparability of production from consumption—made it difficult to conceptualize easily the service process and its outcome as a solution to customer problems and as marketing objects. Instead, studying the quality of the service as perceived by the users offered a possible way of understanding the marketing situation. Hence, the question "How is the quality of a solution to problems or needs perceived by consumers or users of services?" was addressed. By taking such a consumer-oriented approach, the conceptualization of the service process could be achieved and the missing product of service firms be replaced by a genuinely service-based, and moreover, customer-oriented construct.

Basic Perceived Service Quality

Based on some previously suggested aspects of the quality of services (Gummesson, 1977) and on perspectives from cognitive psychology (cf. Bettman, 1979), the concept of perceived service quality was developed as a solution to the problem of the missing product of service firms (Grönroos, 1982, 1984). In Figure 32-3 the basic perceived service quality model is illustrated. The original perceived service quality model from 1982 is (a), and shown in the extended model where the quality dimensions and the disconfirmation notion of the model are put into their marketing context, is illustrated in (b). The extended model includes the same phenomena as the "giving promises" and "keeping promises" sides of the service marketing triangle in Figure 32-2.

FIGURE 32-3   Perceived Service Quality

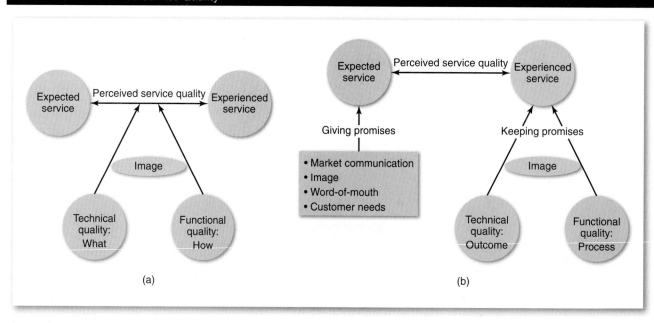

Source: Adapted from Grönroos (1983, p. 28; 1990, p. 47)

The disconfirmation concept was introduced, because it seemed theoretically obvious that quality perception is a function of what the customer expects of the process as well as of what in fact is experienced. In the model customers' perceptions of the process are divided into two dimensions, the process dimension or how the service process functions and the output dimension or what the process leads to as a result of the process. In the perceived service quality model (Grönroos, 1982, 1984), these two quality dimensions were called functional quality (how the service process functions) and technical quality (what the service process leads to for the customer in a "technical" sense). Image, on a company and/or local level was introduced in the model as a filter that influences the quality perception either favorably, neutrally or unfavorably depending on whether the customer considers the service firm good, neutral or bad. As the image changes over time depending on the quality perceptions of a given user of a service, the image component adds a dynamic aspect to the model, which in other respects is static (cf. Grönroos, 1993).

An Abductive Research Process

The perceived service quality model emerged in what now would be called an abductive research process (see Coffey and Atkinson, 1996, pp. 155–6), that is in a process where theoretical deduction and a qualitative case study in the context of industrial services supported each other. In a major quantitative study in the service sector (Grönroos, 1982), where among other service marketing elements perceived service quality was empirically studied, the "how" and "what" dimensions of the model as well as the image component were clearly supported. This study also indicated that the perception of the process (functional quality, how) frequently seemed to be at least as important to the total perception of the quality of a service as the outcome (technical quality, what). Subsequently these findings have been supported by a number of studies about service quality in business-to-business markets as well as in consumer markets (e.g. Brown and Swartz, 1989; Chandon *et al.*, 1997; Crosby *et al.*, 1990; Lapierre, 1996; Lehtinen and Lehtinen, 1991; Palmer, 1997; Price *et al.*, 1995). Of course, the importance of the process dimension does not contradict the position of the outcome dimension as a prerequisite for good service quality.

A Theoretical Construct

The perceived service quality model was never intended to be an operational model of service quality. It was developed and introduced as a theoretical construct to help academics and practitioners understand the nature of the missing product of service firms, i.e. to understand the service process itself as the solution to customer problems—the object of marketing—in order to develop a consistent service marketing model and well-functioning marketing programs in service firms. How good the quality of the service was perceived to be by customers was expected to be measured using customer satisfaction approaches.

However, the introduction of the perceived service quality model created an interest in measuring service quality instead of only measuring customer satisfaction as traditionally was done. The best measurement instrument is the SERVQUAL model developed by Berry, Parasuraman and Zeithaml (Parasuraman *et al.*, 1988, 1994). When operationalizing the perceived service quality model it has become evident that the expectation construct is complicated and difficult to measure in a valid way. For example, customers' expectations after the service process may be different from their expectations before the process (cf. Boulding *et al.*, 1989; Gardial *et al.*, 1994; Grönroos, 1993). Furthermore, expectations that change during the service consumption process may also affect how the service is perceived. Based on their empirical findings, Boulding *et al.* (1989) note that "a person's expectations color the way he or she perceives reality" (p. 11). They suggest two types of expectations: predictive "will" expectations and normative "should" expectations, and finally observe that "though we suggest conceptually, and demonstrate empirically, that customers update their expectations and perceptions, interesting aspects of this process have not been investigated" (p. 25).

Recent research by Johnson and Matthews (1997) suggests that customers' experiences influence the formation of "will" expectations but not of "should" expectations.

More Than One Comparison Standard May Be Used

Tse and Wilton (1988) propose that more than one comparison standard may be used by customers. In a study in the service sector of how several comparison standards function in a disconfirmation approach Liljander (1995) showed that the best approximation of perceived service quality is achieved by omitting the expectation variable and other comparison standards altogether and only measuring the service experience. This is in line with the observations of Teas (1993) and Cronin and Taylor (1994). Theoretically the disconfirmation concept still seems to make sense for the understanding of how service quality is perceived (Grönroos, 1993; see also Cronin and Taylor, 1994). However, even the theoretical value of the disconfirmation concept has been questioned in a recently published study of the validity of the perceived service quality construct (Persson and Lindquist, 1997).

Here and Now Perception

As the original perceived service quality model was intended to be a replacement of the preproduced product that is missing in service contexts, it is obvious that this quality construct relates to one single service process and one single service experience. Hence, it is not a long-term quality perception. It is the quality perception here and now. From this follows clearly that the perceived service quality construct cannot be a synonym of customer satisfaction. In addition to the perception of a service, satisfaction with a service is also at least dependent on the sacrifice incurred by a customer for this service. Because the perceived service quality construct has often been interpreted as something else and more than the perception of quality of a given service process here and now (with the outcome of the process as an integral part of it), there has been substantial confusion about the relationship between perceived quality and satisfaction in the service marketing and service quality literature. Sometimes service quality is considered to influence customer satisfaction (e.g. Parasuraman *et al.,* 1985), sometimes again service quality is considered a long-term concept, whereas customer satisfaction is described as something that is perceived on the basis of a specific service encounter (cf. Cronin and Taylor, 1994 citing research conducted by Parasuraman *et al.* reported in Parasuraman *et al.* 1988). Teas (1993) argues that service quality comes before customer satisfaction and suggests two service quality concepts, a transaction-specific quality concept that influences customer satisfaction and a relational quality concept that is a long-term concept. Spreng and Mackoy (1996) draw the following conclusion: "There seems to be great deal of similarity between these two concepts (service quality and customer satisfaction), yet researchers are usually careful to state that these are different constructs" (p. 201). (For a further discussion of the relationship between service quality and customer satisfaction see, for example, Oliver, 1993.)

Perceived Quality Comes First

However, if the perceived service quality construct had been understood as a construct that replaces the missing product in a service marketing context, this rather confusing debate could have been avoided. Perceived service quality comes first, then satisfaction with quality (and the value of this given quality). From this also follows that perceived service quality can be viewed as a concept for the understanding of how to develop services, whereas customer satisfaction is a concept for the evaluation of how successfully these services are fulfilling the needs and desires of customers.

MANAGING THE MISSING PRODUCT

In order to create good perceived quality of a service, the firm must manage the service process as well as all resources needed in that process. As previously was observed, this process is an open process, where the customer not only sees and experiences how the

FIGURE 32-4   The Service System

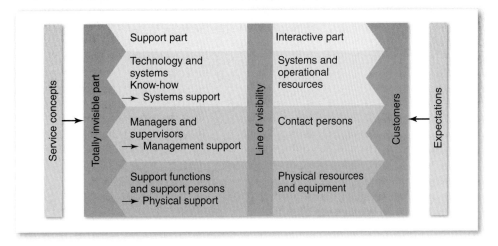

Source: Adapted from Grönroos (1990, p. 208)

process functions but also takes part in it and interacts with the resources that the firm directly controls. In Figure 32-2 these resources were systematized as personnel, technology, knowledge, the customer's time as well as the customer. A system has to be developed so that these resources are used in a way that leads to good perceived quality. As early as the 1970s Eiglier and Langeard in France developed a structure for the understanding of these resources and of the system for managing the them (Eiglier and Langeard, 1976; see also Eiglier and Langeard, 1981). In Figure 32-4 a service process model based on the earlier work by the two French researchers as well as by Lehtinen in Finland (Lehtinen, 1983) is developed (cf. Grönroos, 1990).

Contact Persons

In the service process model the resources that are interacting in the company/customer interface, the interactive part of the system, are contact persons with certain knowledge about how to perform their tasks and how to interact with the customers, with systems and operational resources as well as physical resources and equipment. The customers themselves are also important resources in the service process. They should know how to perform in the system, and they have a given amount of time at their disposal which they expect the firm to make effective use of. The service process and its functional and technical quality impact depend on how this service system functions. If it functions well, the equivalent of the physical product in a service context is good. The four parts of the interactive system, including the customer as one part, have an impact on each other. For example, the systems and the physical resources used have a direct influence on the quality perception of customers, as have the attitudes and behaviors of the contact personnel. The contact persons' style of performance must match the style of consumption of the customers (Lehtinen, 1983). If the customers feel comfortable with the systems, the resources and the personnel, these resources are probably service oriented and will produce a good perceived quality. On the other hand, systems and physical resources, as well as customers, may have a negative impact on the employees, who thus easily create a negative quality perception.

Support Part

The interactive part of a service system cannot function well without the support of a back office, which in Figure 32-4 is called a support part. This part of the service system produces various types of support to the interactive system. From the user's perspective it is hidden beyond a line of visibility. Customers seldom see what is going on behind this line, and they often do not realize the importance to the quality of a service of the part of the service process that takes place there. Especially the technical quality is supported by activities behind the line of visibility. However, there is also an interaction between the back office and the interactive process. Too often good technical quality that is founded on the support process of the back office is destroyed by bad functional quality created in the interactive process in front of the line of visibility.

As is illustrated in Figure 32-4, the perceived service quality is dependent on systems support, management support and physical support from the support system. For example, the service provider has to know how to develop and use a comprehensive customer database in order to be able to create such a support system (systems support), managers and supervisors must support and encourage the contact personnel to perform well (management support), and information systems and people running such systems must produce accurate and timely input for the interactive system (physical support).

Behind the support part a totally invisible part of the service system exists. This part has no direct or indirect impact on the perceived quality of the service process and its outcome. Frequently, there are surprisingly few parts of a service firm that are truly invisible in this respect.

Sometimes the service process becomes even more complicated, for example when a service firm uses the support of an outside partner or subcontractor to perform some parts of the support system or the interactive system. This of course makes it more complicated to manage the service system and the resulting perceived service quality, because all resources are not under the immediate control of the service firm.

A CASE ILLUSTRATION: ELEVATOR REPAIR AND MAINTENANCE

Good Service Quality

As an illustration of how the missing product of a service organization was replaced by a quality-generating service system so that good service quality was created, the study of a case of elevator repair and maintenance services will be presented. The case company is the largest repair and maintenance provider on the Scandinavian market. Its business had, however, been unprofitable for some time and it was losing more service contracts annually than it managed to replace.

Diagnosing the Problem

To find out the reason for the loss of customers, a large-scale survey among the firm's customers was conducted. The questionnaire was based on the assumption that the case company offered a product that more or less could be described as the result of repair and maintenance activities. This quantitative study indicated that the product of the firm was of low quality and that the price of this product was high. This result led to a substantial amount of consternation among top management of the firm and the marketing and sales group, because they knew that the firm as the largest service provider on the market had by far the best trained service technicians, the best possible tools and equipment for taking care of any repair and maintenance job, and the widest possible assortment of spare parts. No other company could handle an equally large number of repair and maintenance problems. Everybody in the firm considered it to have the best product on the market, and hence they could not understand that the quality of the repair and maintenance services was considered low by customers. High price was easier to understand, because being a large company it had high overhead costs and had to maintain a high price level.

A Second Qualitative Study was Initiated

Because top management had difficulties in accepting the results of the study, a second, qualitative study was initiated. One hundred former customers, representing mostly business markets such as office buildings and institutions but also markets such as residential buildings, were interviewed in an unstructured fashion. The main interview question could be phrased as "What went wrong?". In spite of some variations in the results, the average lost customer expressed the following opinion:

> We realize that you have the best capabilities on the market to repair and maintain elevators, and in most cases you do a good job in this respect. However, we do not feel comfortable with the way you are doing the job. We cannot trust your service technicians to start doing the repair or maintenance task according to what has been promised, and quite often you do not give exact promises about when the job will start. Although some of your people are attentive and show an interest in our concerns regarding the elevator and its problems, most of them could not care less about us and the need of information that we sometimes have. Sometimes we do not even recognize them as your employees. Quite often the service technician just leaves an unfinished job and we do not know for what reason or when he will be back to finish the job. Because we cannot always trust your way of doing the job and because it, therefore, is complicated for us to be your customers, we think that the quality of your services is low and that we, therefore, pay too much for it.

The implications of the second study were quite obvious. Top management and the marketing and sales group thought that the company had products, the results of repair and maintenance, whereas the customers considered the company to be offering processes. Furthermore, although the customers recognized that the processes have to include a successful outcome, their concerns regarding the repair and maintenance services were associated with the process and with problems occurring in the process.

Technical and Functional Quality

Understanding the Service and the Quality of the Service

It was understood that the object of the elevator repair and maintenance business was the service process, and that it really was the case of a missing product. It was realized that the solution to the customers' problems consisted of the outcome as well as the process itself. The outcome has to be of an acceptable quality, but when this is the case it becomes transparent in the minds of the customers and the process itself becomes the issue. Both the outcome and the process have to be carefully planned and well implemented, if the repair and maintenance service is to be considered good. The service has to lead to both good quality of the outcome (technical quality; what) and good quality of the process (functional quality; how), where the former is perceived by the customers as a prerequisite and where in the final analysis it is the quality of the process that counts.

The technologies and knowledge required to create a good outcome of the repair and maintenance processes already existed. However, the systems as well as the attitudes and skills of the employees necessary for implementing the process well were lacking. Hence, a new service system was developed and subsequently implemented. In the rest of this section the changes in the interactive and the support parts of the service system and their impact on the service process are presented and discussed.

Service Technicians

Systems and Operational Resources

Previously the supervisor of a regional or local service group (covering a smaller city or part of a bigger city) every morning allocated the repair and maintenance objects to the service technicians available every morning, without considering the previous history of the various customers or whether a given service technician had any previous experience of the customers and elevators that were assigned to him. In this way no relationship between the two parties, a given customer and a given service technician could develop, and moreover, the service technicians did not develop a knowledge of and responsibility for any of the customers. After the second study this was changed, so that every service technician was given long-term responsibility for the same customers. A back-up system to be used in case the regular technician fell ill was also developed.

A Specific Systems Knowledge

In order for the company to change the operational system, a specific systems knowledge had to be developed. This was not an easy process because of the history of how to organize the workflow in the company. However, by developing the new understanding of how the operational systems should function, a systems support was created that enabled the service technicians to get a far better knowledge of the history of the elevators they were responsible for as well as to feel more responsible for the customers they had been assigned to.

Favorable Impact on Operational System Used

Physical Resources and Equipment

Moreover, previously the service technicians had had a limited stock of spare parts and a limited assortment of tools in their vans. In case they needed something else, they had to leave the job and get the missing spare part or tool from a central depot. This was one of the reasons why customers once in a while were left wondering where the service technician had gone and why he left the job unfinished. Now a decision to invest in new and bigger vans and to keep more spare parts and tools in stock was taken. (A decision to renew the car park had already been taken, but instead of purchasing the vans that originally had been planned the company bought bigger vans.) This made it possible for the service technicians to finish almost all jobs without interruptions. Hence, this decision did not only improve the usefulness of the physical resources used in the service process, it also had a favorable impact on the operational systems used in the process.

By changing the technology used, the company created an additional systems support that made it possible for the service technicians to perform in a more customer-oriented fashion.

Contact Persons

It was quite obvious that the service technicians were preoccupied with the outcome of the repair and maintenance tasks, whereas they were much less concerned with the way they were doing their jobs and with their interactions with people representing the customers. Furthermore, the operational systems and the management support from supervisors had been outcome oriented and had not encouraged an interest in the process itself. As a result of the study an internal marketing process was initiated, where the objective was to focus the interest of service technicians as well as their supervisors and upper-level managers on the quality perceptions of the customers and especially on the importance of the functional quality perception of the process. The reasons for the changes in systems and equipment were explained. By this internal marketing process the management wanted to achieve a change in the attitudes of all categories of employees toward the customers and toward their jobs, so that a more customer-oriented performance in the service process would be achieved.

Process Perspective

Traditionally the focus of supervisors and managers had been on the outcome of the service process—a product orientation—whereas the understanding of how to support and manage the process of repair and maintenance from a quality perspective had been neglected. The use of elevator repair and maintenance had been thought of as solely outcome consumption, but as the extended study demonstrated, in reality it was a case of process consumption. Now a process perspective was taken, supported by the internal marketing process. Hence, management support by supervisors and upper-level managers was created.

In the back office a support function responsible for information about customers already existed. Through more customer-oriented market research, more accurate physical support in the form of better customer information was achieved.

Positive Results

Customers

The new service system was intended to make it easier for the customer to interact with the service technicians. Customers would feel that their viewpoints are recognized and that they more effortlessly get answers to questions that they may have. Also, the customers' time could be expected to be used more effectively, because unnecessary stops in the repair and maintenance jobs could be avoided in the future.

The results of the development of the service system were positive. The customer defection rate went down, while the company managed to maintain its premium price level. The business turned profitable.

CONCLUSIONS

From the case presented in the previous section as well as from the analysis of the particular characteristics of the object of marketing in a service firm the following conclusions can be drawn:

1. Service firms do not have products in the form of preproduced solutions to customers' problems; they have processes as solutions to such problems.
2. From a customer's perspective the process has two dimensions, viz. the process itself and the outcome for the customer that it leads to.
3. The process as the object of marketing (instead of a product as the object of marketing) can be analyzed in terms of its quality implications, viz. the functional quality perception (how well the process functions) and the technical quality perception (what outcome for the customer the process results in). In addition, the image of the service provider has an impact on the overall quality perception.
4. As successful marketing of physical goods requires that the object of marketing (the product) is good enough, successful marketing of services requires that the process is good enough. Thus, even if it may lead to a good outcome, an inferior process (poor interactive marketing) jeopardizes the long-term success of service marketing.
5. Although the development of products with certain product features to be produced in a factory can be done in a product development department, the development of the processes of service firms is much more complicated. It requires decisions and actions in a number of departments: internal marketing as well as investments in people, tools and equipment and the development of all parts of the interactive and support parts of the service system (including investment in the serviscape, to use a term introduced in Bitner, 1992).

Understanding the Services

As the discussion has shown, understanding the services requires a different logic than understanding physical goods. Important reasons for this are the fact that the consumption of services can be characterized as process consumption, whereas the consumption of physical goods can be understood as outcome consumption, as well as the observation that services are processes, not preproduced products. However, from a marketing point of view it is in many cases no longer meaningful to keep up a strict borderline between goods and services. Most firms offer both goods and services, and increasingly often they do so in a long-term relationship with their customers. The concept of relationship marketing is especially relevant for situations where firms offer their customers solutions that include the provision of both goods and services (cf. Christopher *et al.,* 1992; Grönroos, 1996; Gummesson, 1995; Sheth and Parvatiyar, 1995).

However, one of the key observations in relationship marketing is that regardless of whether its business traditionally is service-oriented or goods-oriented, a firm that adopts a relationship marketing approach has to define itself as a service business (Webster, 1994). In a long-term relationship the customer is looking for service, and the goods that are exchanged in the relationships become a service element among others in a continuous relationship (Grönroos, 1996). For example, in the production of physical goods, such as cars, customers can be drawn into the planning of the goods and the processes of the factory, among other things through the use of the internet and modern design techniques. In such cases the customers' interactions with the production process become part of their consumption process, and the consumption of the physical product becomes partly process consumption. What the firm is offering in a situation like this is a factory-related service element in the solution to customer problems. The physical goods become more and more service oriented, and service marketing and management knowledge are required to manage the business successfully.

Understanding Services Process

Thus it seems inevitable that understanding services processes is becoming an imperative for all types of businesses, not just for what used to be called service businesses.

References

Berry, L.L. and Parasuraman, A. (1993), "Building a new academic field—the case of services marketing," *Journal of Retailing,* Vol. 69 No. 1, pp. 13–60.

Bettman, J.R. (1979), *An Information Processing Theory of Consumer Choice,* Addison-Wesley, Reading, MA.

Bitner, M.J. (1992), "Serviscapes: the impact of physical surroundings on customers and employees," *Journal of Marketing,* Vol. 56, April, pp. 57–71.

Bitner, M.J. (1995), "Building service relationships: it's all about promises," *Journal of the Academy of Marketing Science,* Vol. 23 No. 4, pp. 246–51.

Boulding, W., Kalra, A., Staelin, R. and Zeithaml, V.A. (1989), "A dynamic process model of service quality: from expectations to behavioral intentions," *Journal of Marketing Research,* Vol. 30, February, pp. 7–27.

Brown, S.W. and Swartz, T.A. (1989), "A gap analysis of professional services quality," *Journal of Marketing,* Vol. 54, April, pp. 92–8.

Calonius, H. (1988), "A buying process model," in Blois, K. and Parkinson, S. (Eds), *Innovative Marketing—A European Perspective, Proceedings of the XVIIth Annual Conference of the European Marketing Academy,* University of Bradford, England.

Chandon, J.-L., Leo, P.-Y. and Philippe, J. (1997), "Service encounter dimensions—a dyadic perspective. Measuring the dimensions of service encounters as perceived by customers and personnel," *International Journal of Service Industry Management,* Vol. 8 No. 1, pp. 65–86.

Christopher, M., Payne, A. and Ballantyne, D. (1992), *Relationship Marketing. Bringing Quality, Customer Service and Marketing Together,* Butterworth, London.

Coffey, A. and Atkinson, P. (1996), *Making Sense of Qualitative Data. Complementary Research Strategies,* Sage Publications, Thousand Oaks, CA.

Cowell, D. (1985), *The Marketing of Services,* Heinemann, London.

Cronin, J.J. Jr and Taylor, S.A. (1994), "SERVPERF versus SERVQUAL: reconciling performance-based and perceptions-minus-expectations measurement of service quality," *Journal of Marketing,* Vol. 58, January, pp. 125–31.

Crosby, L.A., Evans, K. and Cowles, D. (1990), "Relationship quality in personal selling: an interpersonal influence perspective," *Journal of Marketing,* Vol. 54, July, pp. 68–81.

Eiglier, P. and Langeard, E. (1976), *Principes Politiques de Marketing pour les Enterprises de Service,* Working paper, Institute d'Administration des Enterprises, Université d' Aix-Marseille, Decembre.

Eiglier, P. and Langeard, E. (1981), "A conceptual approach of the service offering," in Larsen, H., Hanne, H. and Søren (Eds), *Proceedings of the Xth EAARM Annual Conference,* Copenhagen School of Economics and Business Administration, May.

Gardial, S.F., Clemons, D., Woodruff, D.W., Schumann, D.W. and Burns, M.J. (1994), "Comparing consumers' recall of prepurchase and postpurchase product evaluations experiences," *Journal of Consumer Research,* Vol. 20, March, pp. 548–60.

Grönroos, C. (1982), *Strategic Management and Marketing in the Service Sector,* Swedish School of Economics Finland, Helsingfors, published in 1983 in the USA by Marketing Science Institute and in the UK by Studentlitteratur/ Chartwell-Bratt.

Grönroos, C. (1984), "A service quality model and its marketing implications," *European Journal of Marketing,* Vol. 18 No. 4, pp. 36–44.

Grönroos, C. (1990), *Service Management and Marketing. Managing the Moments of Truth in Service Competition,* Lexington Books, Lexington, MA.

Grönroos, C. (1993), "Toward a third phase in service quality research," in Swartz, T.A., Bowen, D.A. and Brown, S.W. (Eds), *Advances in Services Marketing and Management Vol. 2,* JAI Press, Greenwich, CT, pp. 49–64.

Grönroos, C. (1996), "The relationship marketing logic," *Asia-Australia Marketing Journal,* Vol. 4 No. 1, pp. 7–18.

Grönroos, C. (1997), "Value-driven relational marketing: from products to resources and competencies," *Journal of Marketing Management,* Vol. 13 No. 5, pp. 407–19.

Grönroos, C. and Gummesson, E. (1985), "The Nordic School of Service Marketing," in Grönroos, C. and

Gummesson, E. (Eds), *Service Marketing—Nordic School Perspectives,* Stockholm University, Sweden, pp. 6–11.

Gummesson, E. (1977), *Marknadsföring och inköp av konsulttjänster* (Marketing and Purchasing of Professional Services), Akademilitteratur, Stockholm, Sweden.

Gummesson, E. (1990), *The Part-Time Marketer,* Center for Service Research, Karlstad, Sweden.

Gummesson, E. (1991), "Marketing revisited: the crucial role of the part-time marketers," *European Journal of Marketing,* Vol. 25 No. 2, pp. 60–7.

Gummesson, E. (1995), *Relationsmarknadsföring. Från 4 P till 30 R (Relationship Marketing. From 4P to 30 R)*, Liber-Hermods, Stockholm, Sweden.

Håkansson, H. and Snehota, I. (1995), *Developing Relationships in Business Networks,* Routledge, London.

Johnson, C. and Mathews, B.P. (1997), "The influence of experience on service expectations," *International Journal of Service Industry Management,* Vol. 8 No. 4, pp. 290–305.

Kotler, P. (1991), *Marketing Management. Analysis, Planning, and Control,* 7th edition, Prentice-Hall, Englewood Cliffs, NJ.

Lapierre, J. (1996), "Service quality: the construct, its dimensionality and measurement," in Swartz, T.A., Bowen, D.E. and Brown, S.W. (Eds), *Advances in Services Marketing and Management Vol. 5,* JAI Press, Greenwich, CT, pp. 45–70.

Lehtinen, J.R. (1983), *Asiakasohjautuva palveluyritys (Customer-driven Service Firm)*, Weilin+Göös, Espoo, Finland.

Lehtinen, U. and Lehtinen, J.R. (1991), "Two approaches to service quality dimensions," *The Service Industry Journal,* Vol. 11 No. 3, pp. 287–303.

Levitt, T. (1983), "After the sale is over," *Harvard Business Review,* Vol. 61, September–October, pp. 87–93.

Liljander, V. (1995), *Comparison Standards in Perceived Service Quality,* Diss., Research report A:63, CERS Center for Relationship Marketing and Service Management, Swedish School of Economics Finland, Helsingfors.

Mattsson, L-G. (1997), "'Relationship marketing' and the 'market-as-networks approach': a comparison analysis of two evolving streams of research," *Journal of Marketing Management,* Vol. 13 No. 5, pp. 447–61.

Oliver, R.L. (1993), "A conceptual model of service quality and service satisfaction: compatible goals, different concepts," in Swartz, T.A., Bowen, D.A. and Brown, S.W.

(Eds), *Advances in Services Marketing and Management Vol. 2,* JAI Press, Greenwich, CT.

Palmer, E. (1997), *Aspects of Professional Service Quality: A Focus on Customer Satisfaction including Relationship Impacts,* diss., The University of Auckland, New Zealand.

Parasuraman, A., Zeithaml, V.A. and Berry, L.L. (1985), "A conceptual model of service quality and its implications for further research," *Journal of Marketing,* Vol. 49, Fall, pp. 41–50.

Parasuraman, A., Zeithaml, V.A. and Berry, L.L. (1988), "SERVQUAL: a multiple-item scale for measuring consumer perceptions of service quality," *Journal of Retailing,* Vol. 64 No. l, pp. 12–37.

Parasuraman, A., Zeithaml, V.A. and Berry, L.L. (1994), "Reassessment of expectations as a comparison standard in measuring service quality: implications for future research," *Journal of Marketing,* Vol. 58, January, pp. 111–24.

Peppers, D. and Rogers, M. (1993), *One-to-One Future: Building Relationships One Customer at a Time,* Currency/Doubleday, New York, NY.

Persson, J.E. and Lindquist, H. (1997), *Kundupplevd kvalitet i tjänsteverksamheter. En analys och kritik av den företagsekonomiska dialogen (Customer Perceived Quality in Services. Analysis and Criticism of the Dialogue in Business Research)*, Lund University, Sweden.

Price, L.L., Arnould, E.J. and Tierney, P. (1995), "Going to extremes: managing service encounters and assessing provider performance," *Journal of Marketing,* Vol. 59, April, pp. 83–97.

Sheth, J.N. and Parvatiyar, A. (1995), "The evolution of relationship marketing," *International Business Review,* Vol. 4 No. 4, pp. 397–418.

Spreng, R.A. and Mackoy, R.D. (1996), "An empirical examination of a model of perceived service quality and satisfaction," *Journal of Retailing;* Vol. 72 No. 2, pp. 201–14.

Teas, R.K. (1993), "Expectations, performance evaluation, and consumers' perception of quality," *Journal of Marketing,* Vol. 57, October, pp. 18–34.

Tse, D.K. and Wilton, P.C. (1988), "Models of consumer satisfaction formation: an extension," *Journal of Marketing Research,* Vol. 25, May, pp. 204–12.

Webster, F.E. Jr (1994), "Executing the new marketing concept," *Marketing Management,* Vol. 3 No. 1, pp. 9–18.

Endnotes

1. We use the term *service process* for the process that, in the service marketing and management literature, is frequently called service production process or service delivery process.

33 | TOWARDS A THEORY OF INNOVATION IN SERVICES

Richard Barras

Technical Change Centre, 114 Cromwell Road, London SW7 4ES, U.K.

Final version received April 1986

The paper sets out some foundations for a theory of innovation in service industries, and indicates the role that such innovation may play in the generation of growth cycles. The discussion starts with the origins of a major new technology in the capital goods sector, and its subsequent development according to the normal product cycle theory. This is followed by a consideration of the transmission process by which the new technology is taken up in user industries within the consumer goods and services sector. A "reverse product cycle" is then proposed to describe the innovation process which takes place in user industries such as services, once the new technology has been adopted. This cycle starts with process improvements to increase the efficiency of delivery of existing services, moves on to process innovations which improve service quality, and then leads to product innovations through the generation of new types of services. Finally, the existence of two out of phase innovation cycles in the capital and consumer sectors, deriving from a technology transmission process which causes disequilibrium in technical progress between the two, is put forward as a mechanisms helping to create the long wave fluctuations in economic development associated with Schumpeterian technological revolutions.

INTRODUCTION

The current debate on long waves, or growth cycles, has not so far paid enough attention to the process of transmission by which major new technologies originating and developing in the capital goods sector are taken up through applications in the consumer goods and services sector. An understanding of this transmission process requires a more complete view of technological innovation and diffusion than is provided by the traditional demand-pull model; as is recognised in the more recent innovation literature, such a view must encompass both the supply of a new technology by its producers and the demand for that technology by its users or adopters. It is argued here that examination of the technology transmission process helps to explain the underlying dynamics of the growth cycle, in terms of a disequilibrium in the rates of innovation achieved in the capital goods (producer) sectors and the consumer goods (adopter) sectors.

Barras, Richard. 1986. Towards a theory of innovation in services. *Research Policy* 15 (4): 161–173.

This view of the innovation process, and the role of technology transmission in the growth cycle, can further offer insights into the likely course of events during the new technological revolution now beginning, sometimes labelled the "fifth Kondratiev." There is a widespread consensus that this new revolution will be based on the emergent information technologies; what has so far been less recognised is that the key adopter sectors in this revolution are likely to be the service industries, rather than the manufacturing sectors which have dominated previous technological revolutions. From this supposition it can be argued that the application of information technology in a wide variety of previously "pre-industrial" service activities will provide the motor for the next major wave of expansion of output and employment in advanced industrialised economies, and that an understanding of this new source of economic growth requires the development of a theory of innovation in services.

There has been a growing awareness in recent years of the importance of service industries within advanced industrialised economies, though this realisation has perhaps been rather belated given that in such economies services already typically account for at least 50 percent of total output and employment [2]. With this growing awareness there has begun to emerge a body of applied research into services, such as the work of Gershuny [18] and [19]. However, there has so far been virtually no consideration of the particular nature of innovation in services within economic theory, which incorporates innovation models drawn almost exclusively from analysis of the manufacturing process. The aim of this paper is to lay some foundations for building such a theory of innovation in services. In trying to lay these foundations, a theoretical model of the innovation process in services is proposed, based upon the idea of a "reverse product cycle" operating in service industries. This model has been developed out of a quite extensive programme of empirical research into technical innovation in services; this research has focused primarily on the adoption and impact of information technology in service industries and has involved a mixture of econometric and case study analysis of current trends, as well as some more speculative and less formal forecasting of likely trends over the next ten years (Barras [3], [4], [5] and [6]; and Barras and Swann [7], [8], [9] and [10]). Nevertheless, given the relative lack of previous research in this area, and the still emergent nature of many of the service innovations which are described, a great deal more empirical testing needs to be undertaken before any claim can be made to have constructed a complete theoretical edifice on these foundations.

THE ORIGIN AND DEVELOPMENT OF NEW TECHNOLOGY

The origins of a major new technology such as information technology can be located in the capital goods sector, where fundamental product innovations such as computers are produced, after what may be a long period of research and development in industries such as electronics, business equipment and telecommunications, for example (see, for example, Mansfield et al. [24], on the industrial R&D process). If a cluster of related innovations emerge, and if their combined influence on other branches of economic activity is potentially very pervasive, then the foundations of a major new technology are established, particularly if reinforced by the establishment of an infrastructure such as a digital telecommunications network suitable for opening up a wide range of markets to the influence of the technology. The importance of such product innovations in capital goods supply industries have been touched upon by several authors (see, for example, Abernathy and Townsend [1]; Rosenberg [27]; and Metcalfe [25]); while the long wave literature stresses the central role of the new technologies associated with these innovations in creating the Schumpeterian "technological revolutions" underlying successive growth cycles (see Freeman et al. [17]; van Duijn [15]; and Coombs [11]).

Once the new technology has been established and embodied in a set of emergent products, the development of the new capital goods industries set up to manufacture these products can be described according to the by now standard product cycle theory first expounded by Kuznets [23] and subsequently elaborated by authors such as

Utterback [28]. Three phases of development can be identified. The first, take-off or introduction phase, corresponding to the period of major product innovation during the establishment of the new industries, is characterised by rapid technical advances and a diversity of new products; labour intensive, relatively high cost flexible production methods are applied to low volumes of output; and the competitive emphasis is laid on product performance to capture new markets. In the second, growth phase, the competitive emphasis shifts to major process innovations designed to improve the quality of a decreasing range of products; production methods become more standardised and automated with increasing capital intensity; and production volumes increase as user markets continue to expand. The third, maturity phase, sees a further shift in competitive emphasis towards more incremental process improvements designed to reduce the unit costs of a relatively narrow range of standard products in markets nearing saturation; production methods reach their highest stage of automation, with intensifying concentration in larger production units and high rates of labour saving investment progressively raising the costs of further innovation.

The progression through these phases of the product cycle is accompanied by a shift from the early predominance of product innovations, which on balance generate increased employment through investment which is "capital widening," to later process innovations, which on balance displace employment through investment which is "capital deepening." Furthermore, once the maturity phase is reached, the by now established technology, and the established capital goods industries which produce it, become increasingly vulnerable to competition from new and more advanced technologies, leading to a fourth, transitional, phase in which the whole cycle begins again as the old industries decline and new industries begin to emerge.

While the main phases recognised by this theory are plausible, it is essential to beware of too simplistic an interpretation of the mechanisms involved. Thus several authors stress that the cycle does not involve a strictly linear, sequential process, but rather there exists close interaction and feedback between process and product innovations at each stage (see Abernathy and Townsend [1]; Utterback [28]; and Kline [22]). This interaction and feedback can be seen very clearly in the development of the computer industry since the 1960s. Successive generations of the technology (mainframes, minis; micros), each represent an important product innovation which has then been extensively improved by a sequence of subsequent process innovations, during a period when the industry as a whole has moved from the take-off to the growth phase. It is also too simplistic to assume that either "technology push" or "demand pull" is the single dominant driving force for innovation throughout the product cycle, since both are operating and interacting at each stage. Nevertheless it is not unreasonable to suggest that in the early phase of major product innovations, technology push pressure resulting from an earlier phase of fundamental research and development is the predominant driving force, whereas in the later phases of more incremental innovations, the demand pull pressures created by users of the technology become increasingly dominant. Since in the case of information technology, the majority of these users consist of service industries, then an understanding of their role in the innovation process becomes essential.

THE TRANSMISSION OF TECHNOLOGY

The transmission of a major new technology such as information technology, from the capital goods sector in which it is produced to the user sectors, and particularly the service sectors, in which it is applied, occurs slowly over a considerable period of time. Two types of delays occur. The first consists of the adoption delays which are widely discussed in the innovation diffusion literature, corresponding to the lag between the availability of capital goods embodying the new technology, and their take-up by potential users. The second, and less widely recognised, type of delay consists of the lags between the installation of the capital goods, such as computers, and the realisation of the potential benefits to be derived from them in terms of new or improved applications within the user industries, for example, office automation in services. This second type of delay is closely related to the innovation process within the new industries themselves.

Starting with the familiar "adoption delays," the literature recognises three main types of factors which regulate the rate of adoption or diffusion of a technology: the first is the trade-off between price and technical performance, which influences both the investment cost and the profitability of adopting the new technology; the second is the risk or uncertainty attached to the investment; and the third is the market structure of the adopter industry (see, for example, Mansfield et al. [24]). As far as the price-performance trade-off is concerned, Rosenberg [27] points out that there is often a considerable delay between the attainment of technical feasibility for a fundamental product innovation in the producer sector, and the achievement of economic feasibility for potential users through a whole series of subsequent incremental improvements by the producers—particularly if the older, competing technologies are also subject to continuing improvement. In a similar vein, Metcalfe [25] discusses the crucial role of the price mechanism in creating a "balanced diffusion path," such that the declining price of the product balances the growth in demand as adoption increases in parallel with the growth in production capacity in the supply industry. As Metcalfe points out, this model can be extended to allow for the decline in unit production costs as further technical improvements are introduced into the supply industry. The effect of continuous product and process improvements on the price-performance trade-off is illustrated dramatically by the computer industry, in which it is estimated there has been an average 20–25% percent per annum decrease in the price of hardware of constant equivalent performance over the past 25 years, leading to an average growth of over 40 percent per annum in the installed value of computers of constant performance in UK user industries over the period [8].

The second factor identified as regulating the rate of adoption of the technology, the expectation of risk or uncertainty which users attach to its adoption, is one which Klein [21] has considered in detail. He distinguishes two types of uncertainty—that associated with the performance of the technology itself, and that associated with the likely actions of other competitor firms within the user sector. This latter type of uncertainty links to the third factor identified as regulating the rate of adoption, which is the market structure of the user industries. This is an issue to which Schumpeter paid considerable attention, formulating his view that an oligopolistic market structure produces the optimal conditions for the adoption of a new technology, whereby large user organisations with secure market shares and considerable investment resources are able to risk uncertainty and indulge in "technological competition" rather than price competition (see Heertje [20]). In contrast, Klein considers that the optimal conditions for innovation are offered by a market structure characterised by "dynamic competition," consisting of competition between a large number of innovative, risk-taking firms, and an absence of institutional barriers or price controls. Such conditions of dynamic competition have prevailed during the very rapid development of microcomputer technology in the past 5–10 years, whereas Schumpeter's model of oligopolistic competition seems more appropriate to explain the leading role taken by financial institutions such as banks and insurance companies in the adoption of computer technology over the past 20 years. It could, therefore, be argued that dynamic competition offers the best conditions for innovation in the early stages of the product cycle associated with the development of a major new technology in the capital goods sector, whereas oligopolistic competition provides the best conditions for its early adopted by user industries.

Having examined the main factors which regulate the rate of adoption of a new technology within a user industry, it is equally important to recognise the factors which contribute to "realisation delays" in the rate at which innovative applications are generated through the use of the technology within that industry, once it is introduced. Again, three main types of factors can be identified as affecting the rate of realisation of the potential of the technology. The first factor is "opportunity," defined as the suitability of the activities carried out within the user sector for applications of the new technology. This of course affects the rate at which the technology is initially adopted within an industry, but more important in the longer term, it affects the rate at which process and product innovations can be generated once the technology has been introduced. In the case of computer technology, opportunity is another factor contributing to the leading role of financial institutions in the use of computers, since financial transactions of all types are ideally suited to computerisation. The second factor is the "usability" of the technology, which in recent years has become a far more critical constraint on the rate of innovation in the use of computers than the technical performance of the hardware. Here usability is defined to cover both the availability and quality of software, which provides the direct embodiment of service sector applications of the technology, and the "user friendliness" of the system's basic operating procedures. The final factor affecting the realisation of the potential of a technology is the "adaptability" of the organisations installing the equipment; this includes workforce or managerial resistance to the introduction of new technology; the extent to which working procedures can be adjusted; and the rate at which the workforce can be trained in the necessary skills to use the technology.

In combination, therefore, the influence of price-performance, uncertainty and market structure, are all assumed to determine the rate of adoption of a new technology in user industries, while opportunity, usability and adaptability together determine the rate at which the innovative potential of the technology can subsequently be realised. The path taken by this adoption and diffusion process can be described by the familiar S-shaped, logistic diffusion curve (see Davies [12] for a review of such models) or, perhaps more usefully, by the concept of a "natural trajectory" of innovation first put forward by Nelson and Winter [26]. Different trajectories in different user industries reflect a combination of the common price-performance characteristics of the technology, and the differing market structures and types of applications to be found in each industry, all of which define the selection environment for user adoption and innovation. With the adoption and innovation. With the adoption of computer technology, the most dynamic influence on the diffusion process has been provided by the very rapid rate of technical progress in the production of computers, which as already indicated is creating a continuous expansion of the "technological frontier" defined by the price-performance characteristics of the equipment, and thus a parallel expansion of the user markets being penetrated by the technology.

Case studies of the application of computers in three different sectors (insurance, accountancy and local government) illustrate how innovation trajectories develop in service industries ([7], [9] and [10]). Each of the sectors shows a broadly similar pattern of progression through successive generations of the hardware, but significant divergences can be identified in relation to differences in the service functions to which the technology is applied, ranging from the computerisation of insurance policies and claims, through computer audit in accountancy, to corporate financial systems in local government. These case studies also illustrate how the market structure of both the capital equipment supply industry and the service user industries influence the adoption and innovation process. Thus given the pervasive influence of technical change in the production of computer equipment, the suppliers are in a powerful position to influence the rate of adoption and application of the technology in user industries through their development and marketing strategies, particularly when the supply industry is becoming increasingly dominated by one multinational company. In contrast, no one adopter organisation can dictate the trajectory of innovation within a particular user industry, and indeed it appears that individual organisations move along the trajectory in a rather irregular manner, at some stages implementing "leading edge" applications which quite often prove costly or inefficient, followed by periods when they fall behind the vanguard in order to consolidate their position.

So far two sets of factors have been identified as determining the rate of adoption of new technology in user industries, and the innovation trajectories which develop in these industries. The first set can loosely be characterised as "technology push" factors associated with the capital goods embodying the technology, i.e. their price-performance characteristics, the uncertainty about their performance, and their usability; the second set can be characterised as "demand-pull" factors stemming from the nature of the user industries and their applications of the technology, i.e. the market structure of each industry, the opportunities to apply the technology, and the adaptability of the user organisations. However, these factors tell only half the story, since they are concerned with the transmission of the technology from the capital goods producer industries to the consumer goods user industries. The second half of the story concerns the innovation process within the user industries themselves, which determines how the technology is applied in the production of consumer goods and services as a result of both "technology push" pressures originating within these industries, and "demand pull" pressures originating within the consumer markets for their products.

THE REVERSE PRODUCT CYCLE

The argument has now arrived at the central question addressed in this paper—how does innovation occur in user industries such as services? The answer which is proposed here relies upon a model of innovation which mirrors the theory of the product cycle, as it has been applied to the production of goods embodying a new technology, but which assumes that in the user industries which adopt the technology, the cycle operates in the opposite direction. This model, derived from empirical study of the adoption of information technology in service industries ([7], [9] and [10]), has been termed the "reverse product cycle." In summary, the three phases of the reverse product cycle consist of a first stage in which the applications of the new technology are designed to increase the efficiency of delivery of existing services; a second stage in which the technology is applied to improving the quality of services; and a third stage in which the technology assists in generating wholly transformed or new services. Furthermore, this sequence of phases in the reverse product cycle within user industries will tend to parallel the succession of phases of the normal product cycle within capital goods industries such as the computer industry which are producing the technology. Both innovation processes will steer the innovation trajectories within service industries, and there will be considerable feedback and interaction between the two processes, as for example when innovations in service delivery create new demands upon the performance of computer equipment, leading to secondary innovations in their design.

Each phase of the proposed reverse product cycle can now be considered in more detail, using illustrations derived from the case study research into the adoption and impact of information technology in three selected service sectors (Table 33-1). During the first phase of the cycle, adopter organisations in the user sectors will tend to concentrate their early applications of the new technology on incremental process innovations designed cumulatively to transform the mode of delivery of established services, thereby achieving significant cost savings and increased efficiency. Almost inevitably, given the labour intensive nature of typically "pre-industrial" service activities, these early applications are of a labour saving, capital deepening nature, such that the first phase of technical progress in services tends to have a strong labour saving bias [5]. While these labour saving effects may be masked in industries experiencing a continued

TABLE 33-1 Illustrations of the Stages of the Reverse Product Cycle in Computer Applications.

Cycle Stage	1. Improved Efficiency	2. Improved Quality	3. New Services
Period	1970s	1980s	1990s
Computer Technology	Mainframes	On-line Systems; Minis&Micros	Networks;
Sector applications			
a. Insurance	Computerised policy records	On-line policy quotations	Complete on-line service
b. Accountancy	Computer audit; Internal time recording	Computerised magnagement accounting	Fully automated audit&accounts
c. Local government	Corporate financial systems (e.g. payroll)	Departmental service delivery (e.g. housing allocation)	Public information services (e.g. Viewdata)

Sources: Barras [6] and Barras and Swann [7], [9] and [10].

growth in demand for their services, the competitive pressures to use new technology to shed labour and restructure the organisation of production are typically strongest in established sectors suffering from saturated or even shrinking markets.

The early 1970s applications of mainframe computer technology in service organisations were certainly directed towards improved efficiency, and they usually led to the shedding of a considerable amount of clerical labour. Examples from the case study research (Table 33-1) include the use of corporate financial systems to computerise internal administration functions such as personnel records and payroll, in a wide variety of sectors such as local government [10], the development of computer audit techniques in accountancy [9], and the computerisation of policy records in insurance [7]. The rate at which such efficiency improvements could be realised was considerably enhanced by the extraordinary rate of cheapening of computer equipment which was occurring due to technical progress in the supply industry, which as already noted led to very high rates of user investment in such equipment [3]. Furthermore, the full cost-saving potential of these applications has in many cases only become fully realised with the onset of recession after 1979, which has forced a major restructuring and labour shakeout in service industries such as general insurance which have been suffering from over-capacity [7].

As the first phase efficiency impacts of the new technology are realised, the reverse product cycle moves to the second phase in which the technology is directed towards more radical process innovations which improve the effectiveness rather than the efficiency of delivery of services, leading to improvements in quality rather than reductions in cost. Given the intangible nature of most service products, increases in quality are at least as important as increases in quantity when it comes to measuring the output of service industries [3]. Consequently, this second stage movement towards a qualitative improvement in services can be viewed as an interim "transition phase," between the improved efficiency of delivery of existing services, and the generation of new types of services. These quality improvements begin to encourage some expansion of markets for the improved products, while the competitive emphasis on quality may typically be accompanied by corporate diversification or integration among the service providers. Furthermore, while investment in the capital equipment embodying the technology continues at a high rate, there is a shift towards a more neutral form of technical progress, with the capital widening impact being at least as strong as the capital deepening effects, and the net impact on labour utilisation also being broadly neutral.

These effects can clearly be seen in the more recent applications of mini and micro computer technology in service industries in the last few years. The focus of applications has moved from central corporate systems directed towards internal administration, towards departmental applications on machines dedicated to the provision of improved services in sectors where there is growing consumer demand. For households, much of the growth in demand in recent years has been for improved public services, and in some sectors such as local government, the providers of these services are beginning to respond by using information technology to improve the quality of services delivered, for example by computerising the processing of housing waiting lists [10]. In the private sector, quality improvements have been particularly prominent in expanding sectors of the financial and business services industry such as life insurance and accountancy, with the introduction of on-line policy quotations in insurance branch offices [7], and computerised management accounting and book-keeping services in accountancy [9] providing two obvious examples (Table 33-1). These applications have not led to a significant displacement of labour, and in some cases such as accountancy they appear to have sustained continued employment growth through the expansion of markets for the services provided by the industry. A clear connection can also be observed between the latest applications of computer technology and the current "revolution" occurring in the financial sector, with distributed processing and local area networks offering the capability for greatly enhanced information handling, which is encouraging the emergence of financial and business services conglomerates offering a much wider range of different services than hitherto [8].

The third phase of the reverse product cycle involves a shift from qualitative improvements in services to the generation of wholly new service products. At this stage, product rather than process innovations become dominant, as the competitive emphasis shifts to product differentiation and product performance in order to open up and capture new markets. New industries and organisation emerge, in parallel with the further diversification of existing organisations, in order to supply the growing range of new services. The overall impact on output and employment is expansionary, investment in new technology becomes predominantly capital widening in effect, and the bias in technical progress may even tend towards capital saving, reinforcing the employment generating effects of this stage of the cycle.

Now some confusion surrounds the concept of product innovation in services, and in particular what constitutes a "new service." Because of the intangibility of services, economic literature often assumes that they are by definition processes—yet this confuses the "product" which is the service consumed by a firm or household, and the "process" which is the mode of delivery of the service. Furthermore, it is often argued that radical applications of new technology do not generate new service products, but rather they provide new ways of delivering existing services. This is true in the strict sense that such activities continue to fulfil the same functions which are defined by basic social needs such as health, education, travel, entertainment and the exchange of goods. However, using an analogy with the contrast between a horse and a motor car as a means of transportation, these new service applications are so different in nature and mode of delivery from more traditional forms of services that they can meaningfully be described as new service products.

A further problem that arises in trying to define product innovation in services is that in terms of the impact of information technology on services, this third stage of the reverse product cycle has hardly begun. Consequently, both the precise form of the new products and the extent of the markets for them can only be a matter of speculation at present [6]. What does seem clear, however, is that a necessary, though not sufficient, condition for a major wave of IT-based product innovation in services is the installation of a suitable digital telecommunications infrastructure, such as broad band cable, linking all domestic and business users via a network of computer terminals [19]. The development of such an infrastructure seems likely to proceed by stages, starting with the existing telephone networks and proceeding by progressive digitalisation to a broad band network capable of transmitting text, data, voice and live pictures [6]. Such a network will provide the means of production and delivery for a range of new interactive, electronic services, opening up whole new markets for such services in the same manner that the construction of the railways opened up new markets for manufactured goods in the mid-nineteenth century [4].

Once this IT infrastructure is installed, new service products are feasible in most current fields of service activity, for example home banking and shopping, electronic corporate banking and other financial services, network information services for domestic and business users, computer aided education and training, and expert systems for medical diagnosis. More precisely, the potential for such services can already be distinguished in the case study sectors which have been examined in detail (Table 33-1). Thus in insurance, the provision of a universal IT infrastructure would allow access to a complete on-line insurance and investment service by both domestic and business users [7]: in accountancy such an infrastructure could be used to link clients' and accountants' computers directly, so allowing for the provision of a fully automated audit and accounts service [9]; while in local government, experiments are already underway to use view-data systems to offer public information services to local residents [10]. What appears to distinguish these new services is a combination of three types of changes compared with existing services. The locus of delivery shifts from the point of production (e.g. the insurance office) to the point of consumption (the home or business); the qualitative nature of the service changes, with an emphasis on increased flexibility and improved information for consumers; and the nature of the producer–consumer relationship changes, with the growing computerisation of knowledge particularly affecting the role of service professionals such as teachers, accountants and insurance underwriters.

The rate at which new markets will develop for such services will depend upon a variety of factors influencing demand, such as the costs of the new services compared with those of their established equivalents, the ease with which these network-based services can be accessed, and the elimination of various social and institutional barriers to their adoption [6]. However, once the new services become established, it seems reasonable to suppose that their further development may follow a path similar to that of the normal product cycle outlined for the capital goods embodying the original technology. In other words, the transition phase which began in the previous phase of the cycle will extend to cover the period between the achievement of technical feasibility in the delivery of the new services, for example with the installation of a telecommunications infrastructure suitable for home banking and shopping, and the achievement of economic feasibility in competition with older established service equivalents such as existing banking and retailing services. Thereafter, as the "new service" industries win an increasingly dominant position within their respective consumer markets, their further development will involve a shift from product innovations to major process innovations during the growth stage, and thereafter a further shift to incremental process improvements as they reach maturity. At this stage a new wave of technology may emerge within the capital goods sector, suitable for transmission to the service sector and thus triggering the start of a new reverse product cycle among the by now mature service industries which originated during the previous cycle.

INNOVATION AND THE GROWTH CYCLE

The theoretical model developed in previous sections has articulated the innovation process in the capital goods sector and the consumer goods and services sector in terms of what van Duijn [15] calls "innovation life cycles," based on the theory of the product life cycle. Furthermore, the model has assumed the emergence of a cluster of related innovations in the capital goods sector which are so fundamental and so pervasive in their impacts that their combined effect, particularly when reinforced by the development of an appropriate infrastructure, is to establish a major new technology, or as Freeman et al. term it, a "new technology system" [17]. As already indicated, much of the long wave literature affords a central role to the emergence of these major new technologies as the driving force underlying successive growth cycles; this tradition started with Schumpeter's original formulation of a theory of "technological revolutions," and continues through to recent discussions of the discontinuities in growth and innovation trajectories caused by the emergence of new "technological paradigms" [14].

Thus the First Kondratiev cycle is associated with the convergence of steam power and textile manufacture in the early nineteenth century; the Second Kondratiev with the industries associated with iron and steel, engineering and railways in the second half of the nineteenth century, the Third Kondratiev with the emergence of electric power, automobiles and chemicals manufacture in the early part of this century; and the Fourth Kondratiev with the post-war boom based on industries such as consumer electronics, synthetic materials and pharmaceuticals (Freeman et al. [17]). The thrust of this paper has been that the next and Fifth Kondratiev will be associated with new service activities based on information technology, and it can be argued that these activities qualify as a "new technology system" for three reasons—because of the interlinkages created by the convergence of established technologies (computing, electronics, and telecommunications), because of their pervasive impact on other established industries due to the increase information content of all branches of production, and because of the reinforcing effect of a digital telecommunications infrastructure in transmitting the new services and opening up new markets for them.

Now while there is considerable consensus as to the central role of major new technologies in successive growth cycles, there is considerable dispute about the mechanisms by which innovation causes regular cyclical fluctuations in the secular trend of economic growth. Delbeke [13] provides a review of the alternative theories, all of which he characterises in terms of assumptions about alternating scarcity and abundance of different factors of production in the upswing and downswing phases of the cycle, whether they be theories based on variations in the rate of innovation, in the intensity of capital goods production, or in the availability of labour or raw materials. More specifically related to the discussion in this paper, Coombs [11] reviews some of

TABLE 33-2 The Phases of the Growth Cycle.

| Growth Cycle Phase | Capital Sector | | Consumer Sector | |
	Stage in Innovation Cycle	Products	Stage in Innovation Cycle	Products
Prosperity	Transition	Emergent	Growth	Improved
Recession	Introduction	New	Maturity	Cheaper
Depression	Growth	Improved	Transition	Emergent
Recovery	Maturity	Cheaper	Introduction	New

the conflicting theories in terms of what they have to say about the relationship between innovation in the capital goods and consumer goods sectors. What is proposed here is a rather different perspective on the growth cycle mechanism derived from the dynamics of the technology transmission process, whereby a new technology is transferred from the capital goods sector to the consumer goods and services sector, creating a disequilibrium in technical progress due to the juxtaposition of two out-of-phase innovation life cycles in the two sectors. This mechanism helps to explain the cyclical fluctuations in capital productivity and profitability which occur during the long wave [17], and which have themselves been employed as explanatory factors in some long wave theories. The model can be explained schematically in terms of the four stages of the long wave identified by Schumpeter—prosperity, recession, depression and recovery—with conditions at each stage being determined predominantly by conditions in the larger consumer goods and services sector (Table 33-2). In practice, the course of events is naturally far more complex, with considerable variations between technologies, sectors and national economies at each stage of the long wave.

For convenience, consider first the conditions prevailing during the prosperity phase of the long wave. The industries in the consumer goods and services sector are in their growth phase, with the quality of existing products being improved through process innovations in the use of established technologies originating in the previous growth cycle. Output and labour productivity are growing strongly to satisfy demand in expanding consumer markets, employment is stabilising at its peak level, and there is a continued strong growth in capital investment, which increases the capital intensity of production while stabilising capital productivity and the rate of profit. During this phase, technical progress is concentrated principally within the consumer sector, and it is broadly neutral in its impact. Within the capital goods sector, on the other hand, a transition phase between successive "technological paradigms" prevails, with little further improvement possible in the technologies establishes in the previous cycle, while the next wave of technology is still in the research and development phase, generating "emergent products" which may have reached technical feasibility but are as yet of limited economic feasibility. Such was the stage reached in the emergent computer industry during most of the 1960s, at the peak prosperity phase of the post war boom generated by the previous wave of technologies established in the 1930s and 1940s.

Once the emergent technologies in the capital goods sector have reached the stage at which it is economically feasible for the consumer sector to begin widespread adoption of the new capital goods embodying these technologies, then the growth cycle moves into its recession phase. Now the focus of technical progress shifts to the capital goods sector, where major product innovations are being generated in the take-off or introduction phase of the normal product cycle of innovation which has already been described. These product innovations create a rapid rate of cheapening of the new capital goods, which encourages a similarly rapid expansion of their markets among the by now maturing consumer goods and services industries. Within these industries the first applications of the new technology are directed towards achieving cost-cutting efficiency improvements through incremental process improvements in the production of existing goods and services. The first stage of the reverse product cycle in the consumer sector is thus launched, in parallel with the start of the normal product cycle in the capital goods sector. Since the consumer sector has now reached its maturity phase, overall output growth is slowing down as markets near saturation; the rapid rate of investment in the new technology is thus predominantly labour saving and capital deepening in its effects, so that while labour productivity continues to increase, though perhaps at a lower rate, employment, capital productivity and profitability all enter a period of decline. Such were the conditions of recession prevailing during most of the 1970s when, despite the recession, the computer industry experienced very high rates of growth and of product innovation in its major take-off phase, while the first wave of applications of the technology among mature consumer industries, especially service industries, began on a wide scale.

As the normal product cycle in the capital goods sector, and the reverse product cycle in the consumer sector, move into their second phases, the economy moves from recession to depression. Innovation in the capital goods sector moves from the introduction to the growth phase, with the emphasis shifting from rapid and diversifying product innovations to process innovation which by improving the quality of product ranges sustain continued market growth among the consumer industries while consolidating the position of the capital goods industries themselves. In the consumer sector, the emphasis shifts from using the technology to increase the efficiency of production of existing products towards improving the quality of goods and services. Now these improved products, especially in the service industries, represent an intermediate stage between the old established products which dominated the previous, recession, phase and the new products which will be produced in the coming recovery phase. As already indicated, this second phase of the reverse product cycle in the consumer sector can therefore be termed a "transition phase" during which new products begin to emerge, at least in embryo form, though they may not yet have reached the stage of technical feasibility and they have certainly not reached economic feasibility.

Consequently, the limited expansion of markets created by product improvements in the consumer sector, even when combined with the strong growth in the capital goods sector producing the new technology, is not sufficient to offset the decline in already mature consumer goods and services sectors which are suffering from saturated markets and a limited scope for further process improvements using by now outmoded technologies. The economy thus suffers a phase of depression, with output levels static or only slowly rising, maintaining high levels of unemployment and under-utilised capacity, even though the decline in employment levels does tail off. Capital investment is now broadly neutral in its effects, halting the decline in profitability and capital productivity; this new investment is accompanied by extensive scrapping in the mature consumer industries of underutilised capacity embodying obsolete technologies, giving an apparent boost to average labour productivity across the sector as a whole. These are the conditions which are prevailing in the 1980s, in some sectors at least, with the computer and related information technology industries having entered their growth and consolidation phase; applications of computer technology in the consumer sector, and especially in services, having begun to shift from efficiency improvements to transitional quality improvements; but with the major part of the consumer sector suffering a prolonged period of depression and restructuring.

To complete the stages of the long wave, attention now shifts to the consumer sector, where the achievement of widespread economic feasibility among the new products which began to emerge in the transition phase leads to a major new phase of product innovation. New products and new consumer industries are established, serving new consumer markets and creating the base for sustained economic recovery. These new consumer industries make extensive use of the products of the now mature capital goods industries which are producing the dominant technology, particularly once a suitable infrastructure is installed to accelerate its transmission and open up new markets. This investment is predominantly capital widening, with a possibly capital saving tendency as the relative price of the technology begins to increase, so that as output levels expand, so does employment, capital productivity and profitability. Hereafter, the now established technology installed in the consumer sector provides the motor for further product and process innovations within the new industries, as the consumer sector moves towards its growth phase, the capital goods sector moves towards another transition phase, and the cycle begins over again. These were the conditions prevailing in the 1950s, during the period of postwar economic recovery, when the mature technologies established in the 1930s and 1940s helped to launch a major new consumer boom. This is also the current prospect offered by the maturing information technology industries—the generation of a services-led boom in the 1990s once a suitable, universal telecommunications infrastructure is installed at national and international level to act as the catalyst for the establishment of the new service industries.

CONCLUSIONS

The argument which has been developed in this paper starts with an examination of the origins of a major new technology in the capital goods sector, and its subsequent development according to the product life cycle theory. Consideration is given next to the transmission process by which this new technology is taken up by user industries in the consumer goods and services sector, identifying the factors which contribute both to delays in the adoption of the technology and to delays in the realisation of its potential, and discussing how these factors shape the innovation trajectories which emerge in the user industries. The central thrust of the argument is then directed towards the nature of the innovation process in the user industries, concentrating in particular upon the innovations in services currently being generated by the adoption of information technology. A "reverse product cycle" is proposed to describe the innovation process in these industries, running in parallel to the normal product cycle in the capital goods sector, but operating in the opposite sequence of stages. Finally, the existence of two out of phase innovation cycles in the capital and consumer sectors, deriving from a technology transmission process which causes disequilibrium in technical progress between the two, is put forward as a dynamic mechanism helping to create the long wave fluctuations in economic activity which are symptomatic of successive Schumpeterian "technological revolutions."

The theoretical model of innovation in services which has been proposed in the paper, based upon the idea of a "reverse product cycle," does appear to correspond to empirical observation of how the innovation process has been operating in three case study service sectors over the past twenty years, as a result of the introduction of computer technology. However, far more applied research is needed to test the model fully across a wider range of sectors, and such a programme of research would have to stretch over several years to allow for the gradual emergence of the electronically-based "new services" which in most cases are still no more than a product of speculation. This research would need to address general questions as to how precisely the innovation mechanism works in service industries, examining the innovation trajectories in different sectors in some detail. There are also more specific questions to be answered as to how the operation of the reverse product cycle varies according to differences in technology, in service applications and in national economic conditions. Once the operation of the proposed reverse product cycle is established and fully understood, then its interaction with the normal product cycle in capital goods industries could be investigated empirically, to ascertain how important is the disequilibrium between the innovation life cycles in the two sectors as a mechanism contributing to long waves of economic growth.

Beyond these theoretical considerations, it seems vital to pursue the line of investigation indicated here, since the arguments which have been advanced in the paper offer some optimistic pointers to the possible emergence in the 1990s of a services-led boom based upon the universal application of information technology. A necessary initial condition is the establishment of a digital telecommunications network which is capable both of transmitting the vast volumes of information which will be generated and of opening up new domestic and international markets among household and business consumers. Once such an infrastructure is installed, there is enormous potential for the generation of new service products in a wide variety of fields such as financial and business services, retail and wholesale distribution, entertainment and leisure, education and health, and public administration. The development of such services is likely to be further assisted by current software developments in "expert" or "knowledge based" systems. While the precise form of these new network-based services is difficult as yet to predict, the indications are that they could generate a major wave of capital saving, employment-generating output growth. Furthermore, they could be produced by high skill, relatively labour intensive and more decentralised organisations, using the IT infrastructure as their main means of production and so perhaps generating more modest capital requirements, particularly for expensive buildings, than those of today's major service providers. Of course, such predictions beg a whole series of questions about the distributional impacts of a new growth cycle based on information technology, but these lie outside the scope of this paper. A separate paper does, however, consider some of the broader implications of a new services-led boom, which is likened to a "Services Revolution" comparable in scope and importance to the nineteenth century Industrial Revolution in manufacturing, and draws out some pointers for government policies which can encourage this boom, with a view to promoting the much sought-after recovery towards full employment in the advanced industrialised economies [4].

References

1. W.J. Abernathy and P.L. Townsend, Technology, Productivity and Process Change, *Technological Forecasting and Social Change* 7 (1975) 379–396.
2. Bank of England, Services in the UK economy, *Bank of England Quarterly Bulletin* 25 (3) (September 1985).
3. R. Barras, *Growth and Technical Change in the UK Service Sector.* Research Report TCCR-83-015 (Technical Change Centre, London, 1983).
4. R. Barras, Information Technology and the Service Revolution, *Policy Studies* 5 (4) (1985) 14–24.
5. R. Barras, A Comparison of Embodied Technical Change in Services and Manufacturing Industry, *Applied Economics* 18 (1986), 941–958.
6. R. Barras, *New Technology and the New Services: Towards an Innovation Strategy for Europe* (Technical Change Centre, London, 1986).
7. R. Barras and J. Swann, *The Adoption and Impact of Information Technology in the UK Insurance Industry.* Research Report TCCR-83-016 (Technical Change Centre, London, 1983).
8. R. Barras and J. Swann, Information Technology and the Services Sector: Quality of Services and Quantity of Jobs, in: P. Marstrand (ed.) *New Technology and the Future of Work and Skills* (Frances Pinter, London, 1984).
9. R. Barras and J. Swann, *The Adoption and Impact of Information Technology in the UK Accountancy Profession.* Research Report TCCR-84-008 (Technical Change Centre, London, 1984).
10. R. Barras and J. Swann, *The Adoption and Impact of Information Technology in UK Local Government.* Research Report TCCR-85-005 (Technical Change Centre, London, 1985).
11. R.W. Coombs, Innovation, Automation and the Long-wave Theory, in: C. Freeman (ed.) *Long Waves in the World Economy,* pp. 115–125.
12. S. Davies, *The Diffusion of Process Innovations* (Cambridge University Press, 1979).
13. J. Delbeke, Recent Long Wave Theories, A Critical Survey, in: C. Freeman (ed.) *Long Waves in the World Economy,* pp. 1–12.
14. G. Dosi, Technological Paradigms and Technological Trajectories, in: C. Freeman (ed.) *Long Waves in the World Economy,* pp. 78–101.
15. J.J. van Duijn, *The Long Wave in Economic Life* (George Allen and Unwin, 1983).
16. C. Freeman (ed.) *Long Waves in the World Economy* (Francis Pinter, London, 1984).
17. C. Freeman, J. Clark and L. Soete, *Unemployment and Technical Innovation* (Frances Pinter, London, 1982).
18. J.I. Gershuny, *After Industrial Society: the Emerging Self-Service Economy* (Macmillan, London, 1978).
19. J.I. Gershuny and I.D. Miles, *The New Service Economy* (Frances Pinter, London, 1983).
20. A. Heertje, *Economics and Technical Change* (Weidenfeld & Nicolson, London, 1977).
21. B.H. Klein, *Dynamic Economics* (Harvard University Press, Cambridge, MA, 1977).
22. S.J. Kline, Innovation Is Not a Linear Process, *Research Management* 28 (4) (1985) 36–45.
23. S. Kuznets, *Economic Change* (Norton, New York, 1953).
24. E. Mansfield, J. Rapoport, A. Romeo, E. Villain, S. Wagner and F. Husic, *The Production and Application of New Industrial Technology* (Norton, New York, 1977).
25. J.S. Metcalfe, Impulse and Diffusion in the Study of Technical Change, in: C. Freeman (ed.), *Long Waves in the World Economy,* pp. 102–114.
26. R.R. Nelson and S.G. Winter, In Search of a Useful Theory of Innovation, *Research Policy* 6 (1977) 36–76.
27. N. Rosenberg, *Perspectives on Technology* (Cambridge University Press, 1977).
28. J.M. Utterback, The Dynamics of Product and Process Innovation in Industry, in: C.T. Hill and J.M. Utterback, *Technological Innovation for a Dynamic Economy* (Pergamon, Oxford, 1979).

34 | DEVELOPING AND IMPLEMENTING NEW SERVICES

Christopher H. Lovelock

Harvard University

ABSTRACT

Service marketers can learn much about the new product development process from existing studies of innovation management in the manufacturing sector. However, distinctive issues for managers in service organizations include understanding the factors that motivate or facilitate new service development, searching for new service ideas, evaluating new product "fit," blueprinting the design of the new service and its delivery system, and managing the implementation process as it relates to integrating different management functions and obtaining the desired behavior from customers.

INTRODUCTION

The topic of developing and introducing new products has long been regarded as very important among both marketing academics and professionals. The literature on this topic is enormous, reflecting extensive research and widespread sharing of insights from experience. Virtually every marketing principles text devotes an obligatory chapter—or at least a major section of a chapter—to new products.

This fact poses some problems for a symposium on developing new services, where the natural desire of many participants is to focus on issues that are distinctive to services rather than to rehash generalizations from past research that focused almost exclusively on new manufactured goods. However, I think it would be a mistake to ignore the useful conceptual frameworks that we already have.

Instead, I'd like to begin by reviewing some key concepts and frameworks from the general literature and then considering what other writers have had to say about new services development. From that starting point, I'll proceed to raise additional issues tailored to the concerns of service organizations and offer some insights for managers of specific types of services.

DEGREES OF PRODUCT INNOVATION

The word "new" is perhaps one of the most overused in the marketer's lexicon. Heany (1983) rightfully calls attention to the danger of semantic inflation with regard to product innovation. He proposes six categories of product innovation within a spectrum

Lovelock, Christopher H., (1984), "Developing and Implementing New Services," in *Developing New Services,* editors William R. George and Claudia E. Marshall, Chicago, IL: American Marketing Association Proceedings Series.

461

that runs from major innovations to style changes. These categories are described below with service sector examples added.

1. *Major Innovations* are new products for markets as yet undefined and undimensioned. Past examples include the first broadcast television services and Federal Express's introduction, of nationwide, overnight small package delivery service. These innovations involve a high degree of uncertainty, not least in terms of market response.

2. *Start-up Businesses* consist of new products for a market that is already served by existing products that meet the same *generic* needs. Service examples include: the creation of health maintenance organizations to provide an alternative form of health care delivery; Merrill Lynch's creation of the Cash Management Account that combines brokerage, debit card, and bank checking services in a single package; and the entry of telecommunication companies into the long-distance household telephone call market previously restricted to the Bell System.

3. *New Products for the Currently Served Market* represent an attempt to offer existing customers of the organization a product not previously available there (although it may be available elsewhere). Examples include: retail banks that add insurance services or money-market funds, or museums that add restaurants or shops to their exhibit facilities.

4. *Product Line Extensions* represent an augmentation of the existing product line, such as adding new menu items for a restaurant, new routes for an airline, new courses of study at a university. Offering a new self-service option, such as an automatic teller machine (ATM) at a bank or a self-serve island at a gas station effectively constitute product-line extensions.

5. *Product Improvements* represent perhaps the commonest type of product innovation, involving a change in certain features for products that are already on offer to the currently served market. In the service sector these may include not only improvements to the core service, such as faster execution of service, but also peripheral changes such as automatically providing bank customers with their account balances after each deposit and withdrawal at an ATM, or improvements in service delivery achieved by extending hours of availability or increasing the number of outlets.

6. *Style Changes* represent the most modest type of product innovation, although they are often highly visible. Thus an airline may paint its aircraft in a new color scheme, a hotel may put its employees into new uniforms, or a bank may refurbish its branch interiors or introduce a new design of checks.

When speaking of new product development, we need to be clear what level of innovation is being discussed. As a generalization, the higher the level of innovation, the greater the risks and expenses entailed and the more difficult the managerial task. All innovations require effort in evaluation planning, and execution. The resources allocated to these efforts should reflect the degree of uncertainty involved, the downside risks, the upside potential for the organization, the extent of management coordination involved, and the time horizon required for effective implementation.

PRODUCT EVALUATION AND LIFE CYCLE

In nearly all successful marketing organizations, the composition of the product portfolio is slowly but continuously evolving. Likewise, the characteristics of the individual products making up that portfolio are themselves undergoing change. Both processes reflect the need to be responsive to the dynamics of the marketplace, since external factors in the environment—the economy, technology, government policies, social structures and values, and competitive forces—are constantly changing.

As each planning cycle begins—and sometimes more frequently if sudden external changes occur—the marketing manager needs to consider the following issues.

1. Are we offering the appropriate mix of products in our portfolio or is a shift in emphasis needed? Should new products be added or existing ones deleted?

2. Are we currently offering (or planning to introduce) products with the right characteristics to appeal to our target market segments, or are changes needed in product attributes?

3. Do the other elements in the current marketing-mix strategy for each product—distribution and delivery systems, monetary prices and nonmonetary costs, and communication efforts—reflect a cost-efficient (and, where appropriate, competitive) approach to marketing the product to our target market segments? If not, what changes should we be making in our marketing mix?

It is important to remember that no decision can be taken on product strategy without reference to how that product should be priced, delivered, and communicated to its effective market segments. Effective marketing strategy requires consistency and synergy between each element of the marketing mix; hence decisions concerning any one element must be evaluated against their impact on—and must fit with—the other three. As will be shown, there is often an extremely close link in service organizations between the product and its delivery system.

Product Evolution

Marketing theorists are constantly looking for conceptual frameworks that will help practicing managers better understand the nature of the problems and opportunities they face.

One intriguing approach is to consider the evolution of species, as described by the theory of natural selection, as a model for the evolution of products in a competitive marketplace (Gross 1968). Appraising this analogy, Wind remarks:

> The basic concepts of the Darwinian natural selection theory and marketing concepts are strikingly similar. The individual organism in the evolution theory is analogous to a product (not product class . . .). The concept of a *variation of species* is analogous to the differences among products and brands. The concept of overpopulation relates to the tremendous production capacity for most products. The *struggle for existence* and *survival of the fittest* are quite descriptive of the product marketplace in which only few new products ever make it. The result of overcapacity (overpopulation) is competition among species (products). In this competition, those best suited to the *environment* (the marketplace) have the best chance for success (survival and growth). (Wind 1982, p. 64).

A number of useful managerial insights are suggested by this analogy. For instance, specialization (typically entailing a carefully designed product-positioning strategy) undoubtedly offers an advantage under conditions of strong competition. However, as the environment changes, the characteristics that determine suitability also change, requiring evolutionary development of the product so that it may adapt; this emphasizes the need for long-range product planning. When the environment changes suddenly—reflecting such factors as significant technological, economic, or political developments—highly specialized products that were well adapted to the old environment may be less capable of adjusting to the change than less specialized products. "This conclusion," says Wind, "suggests the intriguing hypothesis that products aimed at narrow market segments or very specialized applications have shorter 'life cycles' than more broadly-based products."

Recent rethinking of Darwinian theory suggests that evolution may have been less gradual than Darwin believed, consisting more of a series of sudden, discontinuous spurts in response to dramatic environmental changes. This is also, perhaps, a better model of the marketplace for the products of service organizations, faced as they are with sudden shifts of the regulatory environment, changes in professional association standards, the ups and downs of the economy, and the periodic advent of new technology. The key difference between animal species and product species lies in the fact that animals can only react to change. Managers, however, can anticipate change and take proactive steps to enhance their products' prospects for future survival. The sum of all the products offered by an organization is the organization itself; that, too, must evolve and change over the years if it is to survive as an entity.

The Product Life Cycle

Complementing the product-evolution model is another conceptual framework, the product life cycle (PLC), which is based on the biological life cycle of birth, growth, maturity, decline, and death. It can be applied to an individual product or to an entire class of related products produced by a number of different competing organizations. Most marketing theorists divide the PLC into four stages.

1. *Introduction.* A period of typically slow growth in sales volume following the launch ("birth") of the product. At this point, an innovative organization that is the first to market the product may have the field to itself. However, extensive communication efforts are often needed to build consumer awareness.
2. *Growth.* Demand for the product begins to increase rapidly, reflecting repeated use by satisfied customers and broadening awareness among prospective customers who now try the product for the first time. Competition develops as other organization introduce their own version, transforming a single product into a product class of competing brands. Since few service organizations are able to obtain patent protection for their innovations, competition often develops very rapidly in the service sector.
3. *Maturity.* This is often an extended period (except for fad and fashion products) during which sales volume for the product class stabilizes and astute marketers seek to position their own product offerings in ways that will differentiate them from those of competing organizations.
4. *Decline.* Sales volume for the product class declines as a result of environmental forces such as changing population profiles, changing consumer preferences, new legislation, or competion from new types of products that meet the same generic need. Some competitors, anticipating the death of the entire product class, kill off their own entries in the market.

The appeal of the PLC concept to marketers is that it provides a marketing-strategy prescription tailored to the stage in the life cycle that the product has currently reached. However, a quick review of the PLC literature reveals that its prescriptive insights are directed primarily at consumer packaged goods.

PRODUCT-LINE ADDITIONS, DELETIONS, AND MODIFICATIONS

Few service organizations face a static, unchanging market for their products. Most marketplaces are dynamic—changes in customer needs and behavior and in the number and mix of customers occur; competitors enter and exit; technological changes influence product features and delivery systems. Products that advanced the institutional mission well 10 years ago may be outmoded, uncompetitive, or even irrelevant today. Some will need to be discarded and others improved or reconstituted. To fulfill the mission well 10 years (or less) from now may require development of new product offerings that will be attuned to the needs and opportunities of the times.

NEW PRODUCT DEVELOPMENT

Many new products prove to be a disappointment to their sponsors, failing to advance the institutional mission, diverting management time and attention, generating a new cash drain on the organization's finances—or perhaps all of these. Managers who have had bad luck with new products in the past often become averse to risk as a result. But no organization can afford to stagnate, and not introducing any new products at all may prove as damaging to the institution's health as selecting the wrong new products or botching the introduction process.

FIGURE 34-1   New-Product-Development System (From Wind 1982)

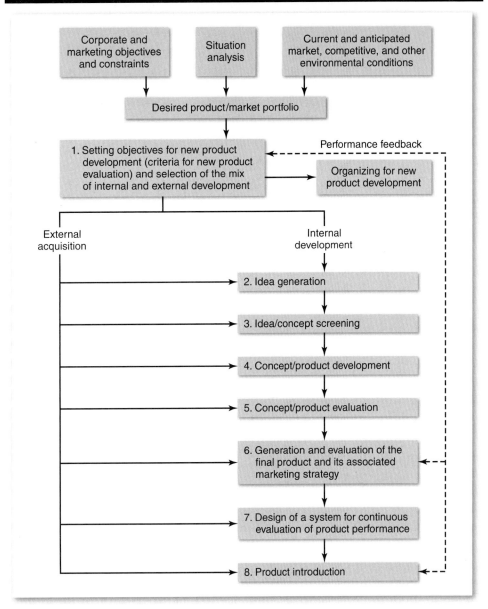

The issue of designing and marketing new products has attracted great interest from both managers and academics. Excellent syntheses and new insight are provided by Urban and Hauser (1980) and Wind (1982). There is generally agreement that the new-product-development process should proceed systematically through a series of steps, beginning with a review of corporate (institutional) objectives and constraints and continuing through to product introduction. Figure 34-1 (drawn from Wind 1982) summarizes these steps in diagrammatic form. As can be seen, there are three major sets of inputs:

1. Corporate and marketing objectives.
2. The organization's strengths and weaknesses—assessed by conducting a marketing audit (see Kotler, Gregor, and Rodgers 1977).
3. Information on the current and anticipated market, the competitive situation and other environmental factors (also assessed via the marketing audit).

From these inputs, management can derive an indication of what the desired product portfolio for the organization should look like. By comparing this "ideal" with the current portfolio, gaps and opportunities can be quickly identified. Objectives can then be set for new-product development and suitable criteria established for evaluating prospective candidates. Later we will look at some specific factors spurring innovation in the service sector.

New products can be developed entirely in-house or through external acquisition. Thus a merger might take place between two service businesses with complementary products, or a service firm that was strong in one geographic area might seek to acquire similar firms in other geographic areas. In either case, a carefully managed process is needed, first, to ensure that good ideas are not overlooked and, second, to subject the ideas that are generated to a rigorous screening process.

Ideas that pass the initial screening (stage 3 or the sequence in Figure 34-1) then move to a more formal conceptualization and are developed into a specific product proposal (Step 4). At this point, the proposed product is still likely to be in conceptual form but should be sufficiently clearly defined that consumer reactions can be sought to specific features and a management evaluation made of the proposed product's technical feasibility, economic implications, market potential, and congruence with management objectives (Step 5). Truly innovative new products are particularly at risk during this stage since they involve higher risks, are less likely to be compatible with current procedures and objectives, and may not be readily understood by prospective customers.

Step 6 is a difficult one. As Wind (1982) writes, "The transformation of new product concepts (which survived the screening and evaluation stages) into actual products is one of the most challenging tasks in the new product development process. This transformation typically involves the conversion of verbally stated (and occasionally pictorially presented) product features into a product prototype, package, brand name, and associated services such as warranty or after sales services" (p. 338). As we will show, it is often difficult to develop prototypes of services since such products are basically processes or performances, rather than things or objects. This stage involves not only definition of the final product but also specification of how that product will be priced, distributed, and communicated to target customers.

The last two stages in Wind's version of the new product development process involve design of a system for continuous evaluation of product performance and, finally, product introduction.

Evaluating Product Fit

Throughout the new-product-development process the product must be evaluated in terms of how well it fits the marketing environment. This evaluation should continue at regular intervals throughout the product's life. There are two basic dimensions to product fit:

1. Product-organization fit.
2. Product-market fit.

Product-organization fit raises such questions as how well the product matches the institutional mission and what its impact will be on the organization's financial situation. There are also questions relating to the fit with other existing resource inputs, including labor, management skills, and physical facilities. Lastly, the product must be evaluated against each element in the organization's current marketing mix, requiring consideration of such questions as:

- Is the proposed new service a logical extension of the existing product line? Will it complement existing products or "cannibalize" them by eating into their sales?
- Are the monetary price and payment terms compatible with those for existing products? What are the implications for a public or nonprofit organization of introducing (say) a fee-based service when previously all its services have been offered free of charge?
- Can existing channels of distribution or delivery systems be used, or will it be necessary to add new outlets and new intermediaries?

- What communications strategies will be needed to inform prospective customers about the product? Is it possible to "piggyback" information about the product on existing sales calls or advertising messages, or must new communications programs be developed—perhaps requiring use of unfamiliar media and communication techniques?

Product-market fit is concerned with how well the new product matches customer needs, interests, and purchase/adoption procedures. Unless the product represents a significant innovation, the question must be asked: does it have sufficient advantages over already established competing products that customers will be prepared to switch? Can the organization reach prospective customers with the information they need about the product? Can customers afford the cost in terms of money and time? Will they be turned off by the facilities, by other customer using the service, or by some other perceived psychic costs associated with the product? Are customers likely to patronize the locations in which the product will be distributed at the specific times that it is scheduled to be available? Even if the product appears to fit well with prospective customers, do competing products fit even better? Will introduction of the product result in a competitive retaliation to which the organization cannot adequately respond?

ORGANIZING AND MANAGING THE DEVELOPMENT EFFORT

Urban and Hauser (1980) and Wind (1982) devote considerable space in their books to how best to organize and manage new product development efforts. Both recognize the importance of top management involvement and the need for interfunctional coordination and continuity over time. Both present alternative formal organization models but recognize the significance of informal roles and relationships in successful execution. Urban and Hauser identify eight informal roles that need to be filled and played well:

1. *Champion*—an advocate who champions the new product and sells it internally, overcoming objections and generating the energy and resources necessary to see it through.
2. *Protector*—a senior manager who defends the champion's right to advocate the new product, facilitates the latter's efforts to sell the concept internally, and provides legitimacy and maturity for the product development effort.
3. *Auditor*—an individual who balances the champion's enthusiasm by ensuring that the product will meet corporate objectives and that sales forecasts are realistic and accurate.
4. *Controller*—an individual responsible for watching schedules and budgets. The controller should be willing to treat past inputs to a project as sunk costs, allocating new funds solely on the basis of anticipated future results.
5. *Creator/Inventor*—creative managers and scientists who will design and market new products if nourished and supported in an environment that doesn't impose too many constraints.
6. *Leader*—the manager (not necessarily the champion) who recruits, teaches, and motivates the new product development team, as well as interfacing with other parts of the organization by acting as a translator and integrator.
7. *Strategist*—the new product development effort requires a senior manager or planner who possesses a long-run managerial perspective. This individual recognizes that innovation is needed not for its own sake but for its ability to help the organization achieve its long-term goals.
8. *Judge*—an individual who resolves differences of opinion concerning new product introduction in situations where consensus cannot be arrived at through mediation.

These roles seem as appropriate for innovations from the service sector as from manufacturing. In my view, the roles of champion, protector, and leader may be particular important for new services when the initiative for the innovation comes from marketing and is resisted by operations personnel.

The literature on new service development is limited, especially when it comes to developing generalizations across service industries. The principal studies of interest are by Wind (1982), Shostack (1981), and Langeard *et al.* (1981).

Wind (1982)

Although most of Wind's book is based on studying new consumer goods, he indicates that most goods require some supporting services and that services often have marketing characteristics similar to goods. Hence, the principles of new product development should be equally applicable to services. However, Wind cites a few distinctive characteristics of services that are likely to have an impact on new service research and development systems (pp. 550–551).

Specifically, he cites the *intangibility* of services as making in-home tests not very meaningful for services that don't require supporting physical goods and suggests that it may be more appropriate to move directly from concept testing to test marketing or its alternatives. Then he notes that *difficulty in patenting services* increases the ease of competitive entry, reducing the incentive for large R&D investments and focusing new service development efforts on "me-too" products or improvements to existing services. *Problems in achieving standardization,* he says, make it difficult to develop accurate concept descriptions and increase the uncertainty involved in projecting market performance from concept test results.

A further distinction concerns the *direct relationships between client and service provider* found in many services; this argues for conducting research that can obtain information on clients' desired interaction with the service delivery system. Finally, says Wind, the lack of clear demarcation lines between the *outlet and product components* of many services poses difficulties for concept/product testing, since customers must combine new product decisions with choices of outlet. Will people adopt a new service from a new supplier, possibly purchasing all their service needs from the innovator, as opposed to waiting for the existing supplier to add the new service later?

Shostack (1981)

Shostack's past contribution to our understanding of new service development focuses on the product evaluation stage. Although a mock-up or prototype can be made of a physical good or of a facility associated with the delivery of a service, the actual service performance can only exist in blueprint form until the concept is made operational. Essentially, the marketer must understand what processes must take place for the service to be performed satisfactorily for prospective customers in each of the segments targeted. Figure 34-2, adapted from Shostack, displays a blueprint for a simple service such as a corner shoeshine, standard execution times for each step, the customer's estimated tolerance for delays in execution, and specification of the facilitating goods and services required.

Describing this model, Shostack writes: "The basic requirements of a service blueprint are three. First, since processes take place in time, the blueprint must, like PERT charting, show time dimensions in diagrammatic form.

"Second, like methods engineering, the blueprint must identify and handle errors, bottlenecks, recycling steps, etc.

"Finally, usually after research, the blueprint must precisely define the tolerance of the model, i.e., the degree of variation from the blueprint's standards that can be allowed in execution without affecting the consumer's perception of overall quality and timeliness."

Langeard, Bateson, Lovelock, and Eiglier (1981)

Langeard *et al.* examine several different services—retail banking, restaurants, travelers' checks, airline travel, lodging, and gasoline service stations—with primary emphasis on the first two. Their study emphasizes innovations in service delivery procedures that require customers to perform certain services for themselves, rather than having service

FIGURE 34-2 Blueprinting a Simple Service: A Street Corner Shoeshine (Expanded from Shostack 1981)

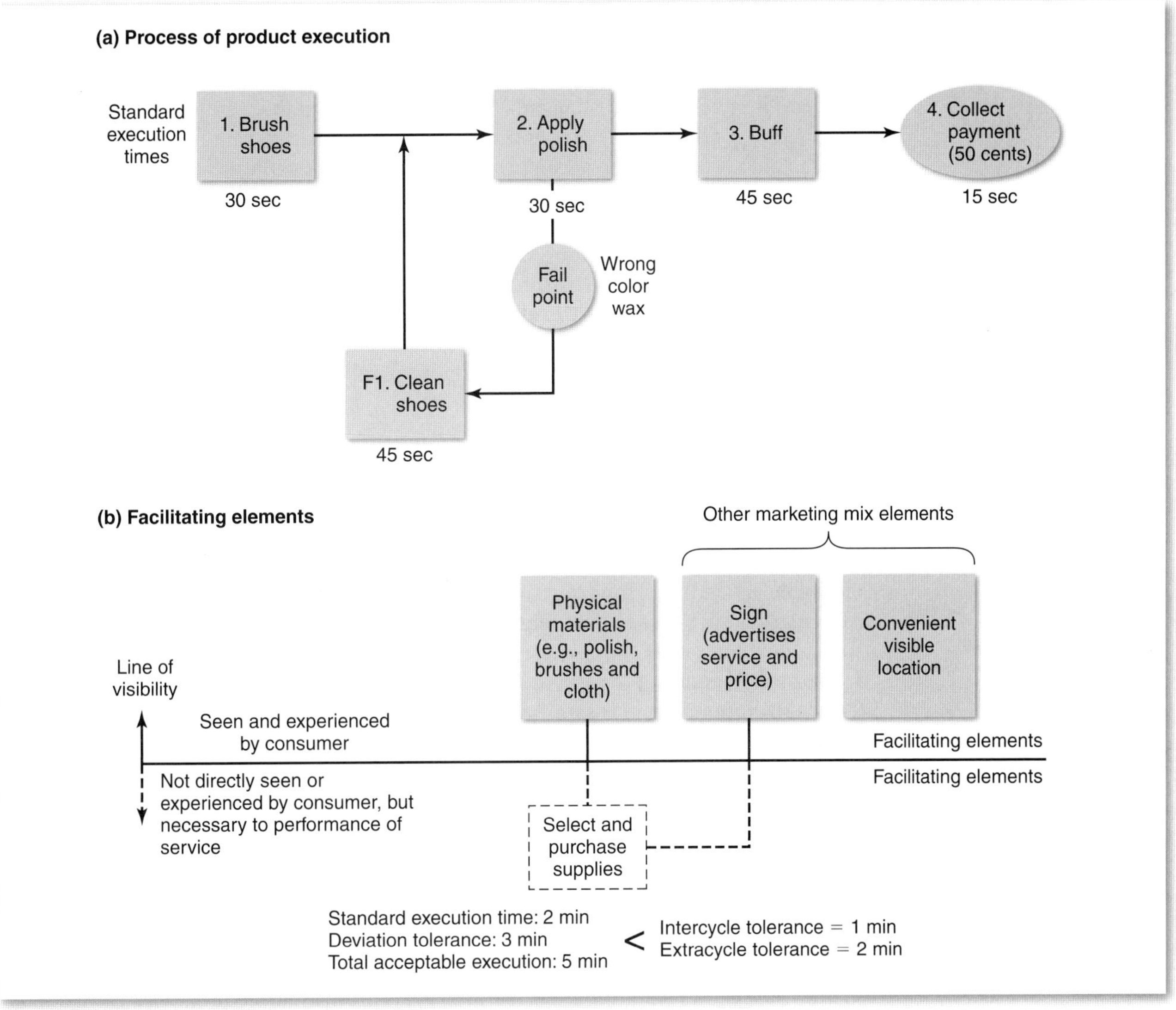

(a) Process of product execution

Standard execution times

1. Brush shoes — 30 sec
2. Apply polish — 30 sec
3. Buff — 45 sec
4. Collect payment (50 cents) — 15 sec

Fail point — Wrong color wax

F1. Clean shoes — 45 sec

(b) Facilitating elements

Other marketing mix elements

Line of visibility

Physical materials (e.g., polish, brushes and cloth)

Sign (advertises service and price)

Convenient visible location

Seen and experienced by consumer — Facilitating elements

Not directly seen or experienced by consumer, but necessary to performance of service — Facilitating elements

Select and purchase supplies

Standard execution time: 2 min
Deviation tolerance: 3 min
Total acceptable execution: 5 min

< Intercycle tolerance = 1 min
Extracycle tolerance = 2 min

personnel do it for them. These innovations include automatic teller machines (ATMs), quick service restaurants, travelers' check dispensing machines, and self-service gasoline pumps. The authors examine not only consumer attitudes towards adoption but also views on implementation by both head office and field managers.

This study draws a distinction between the *service operations system,* which is divided into those aspects of the production process that are visible to consumers and those that are invisible, and the *service delivery system,* which comprises visible operations personnel and facilities plus other customers using the service at the same time. As far as the customer is concerned, the service delivery system is the product.

Among the conclusions reached by Langeard *et al.* are the following:

1. Consumer willingness to consider the self service innovation is strongly dependent upon situational factors (such as time of day, presence of absence of others accompanying the decision-maker, type of clothes worn, and so forth). Concept testing must include definition of relevant situational variables, otherwise prospective consumers are likely to respond simply that "it all depends. . . ."

2. Both time savings and monetary savings are important motivators, either singly or jointly, for using the self service option.

3. Management's perceptions of consumer preferences and intentions are frequently inaccurate, emphasizing the importance of conducting research as opposed to simply relying on managerial judgments.
4. Whereas the emphasis for technologically innovative delivery systems in banking (such as ATMs) often comes from operations, the impetus for new menu items in chain restaurants tends to come from marketing. The former function tends to focus on opportunities for cost savings and improved efficiency, the latter on adding value for consumers without full understanding of the operational implications.
5. New services involving customer interaction with equipment can be tested under laboratory conditions, using prototypes of the equipment operated by a sample of representative prospective users. Unobtrusive observation and subsequent interviews are useful research devices.
6. Successful development and implementation of a new service requires effective coordination of efforts between marketing and operations.

DISTINCTIVE ISSUES FOR SERVICE MARKETERS

The discussion thus far has emphasized that service marketers can learn much about the new product development process from existing concepts, analytical frameworks, and strategic insights based primarily upon studies of innovation management in the manufacturing sector. However, recent research indicates that services do have some distinctive characteristics that require modification of traditional approaches to new product development.

In the remainder of this paper, I want to offer some further thoughts about the new service development process as these relate to the following aspects of that process:

- Understanding the factors that motivate or facilitate new service development
- Searching for new service ideas
- Evaluating new product "fit"
- Blueprinting the design of the new service and its delivery system, and
- Managing the implementation process as it relates to integrating different management functions and obtaining the desired behavior from customers

Factors Motivating or Facilitating New Service Development

Most of the factors initating a need for new goods also apply to services. Urban and Hauser (1980) list corporate objectives such as financial goals, sales growth, competitive standing, and extension of product life cycle, as well as technology, invention, regulation, material costs and availability demographic and lifestyle changes, and customer requests. I'd like to comment on a couple of these and add some additional ones.

Technology creates opportunities for new or enhanced services in several ways: (1) new goods—such as videotape recorders or CAT scanners—are developed and a rental service may grow up to make them more widely available; (2) new equipment, such as automatic teller machines or supersonic aircraft, makes possible new or faster delivery systems for existing services: (3) electronic data banks, coupled with suitable updating, search, and access systems, allow creation of information retrieval services; (4) on-line connections to centralized data banks allow creation of electronic delivery channels to remote locations where financial and other information-based services can be delivered in real-time through branches, intermediaries, or self-service machines; (5) new technologies present a need for expert consulting, repair, and maintenance services.

Deregulation

Partial or complete deregulation in the U.S. of such service industries as banking and other financial services, transportation, and telecommunications has allowed firms to enter new geographic markets, offer products previously prohibited to them, and spurred innovations such as bundling of several related services into a synergistic package (e.g. the Cash Management Account that combines brokerage, checking, and debit card facilities).

Elimination of Professional Association Restrictions

Changes in legal, medical, accounting, and architectural codes of "professional ethics" to allow advertising have spurred development of new services and innovative delivery systems such as health maintenance organizations, franchise chains of small business accounting services, and legal clinics in shopping malls.

Growth of Franchising

As one-time "Mom & Pop" service outlets are displaced by or absorbed into large franchise chains, a centralized management function is created. This spurs formal research into service innovations, product line extensions, product enhancement, and opportunities for new delivery systems. The consolidation of information into a centralized data bank may also have the effect of creating an information service of value to customers. Examples include nationwide real estate or employment listing services for geographically mobile clients.

Balancing Supply and Demand

Capacity-constrained services that face significant fluctuations in demand find themselves in a feast or famine situation: either business is turned away because demand exceeds supply, or expensive equipment and staff stand idle because demand is well below the operation's capacity. This situation provokes a need to develop new, countercyclical services that will use productive capacity in periods of previously low demand (e.g. Alpine slides in summer to stimulate use of chair-lifts that carry skiers in winter). It also encourages development of reservation services (often supplied by intermediaries) and services that occupy customers' time while they are queuing (e.g. a bar for restaurant patrons waiting for a table to become available).

Searching for New Service Ideas

Many services fall into one of the following three categories: (1) rental of equipment and/or facilities that the customer doesn't own; (2) hire of labor or expertise that the customer does not possess (or choose to exercise); (3) rental of both equipment and/or facilities, and the personnel required for their operation. In each instance, using the service is an alternative to owning the item or doing the work oneself. Thinking constructively about such alternatives may suggest opportunities for new services that perform the task better or more economically.

Figure 34-3, taken from Lovelock (1984) illustrates how services often compete with manufactured goods to deliver the same generic benefits.

In this diagram, the examples shown are for consumer goods and services, but comparable industrial/institutional products—such as truck fleets and computers—could

FIGURE 34-3

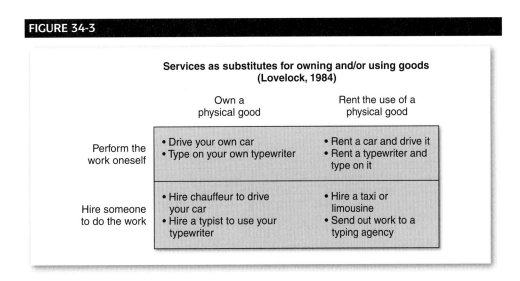

Services as substitutes for owning and/or using goods
(Lovelock, 1984)

	Own a physical good	Rent the use of a physical good
Perform the work oneself	• Drive your own car • Type on your own typewriter	• Rent a car and drive it • Rent a typewriter and type on it
Hire someone to do the work	• Hire chauffeur to drive your car • Hire a typist to use your typewriter	• Hire a taxi or limousine • Send out work to a typing agency

easily be substituted. The Yellow Pages are full of firms both large and small that rent equipment and expertise as an alternative to owning it and doing it in-house.

Another source of new service ideas comes from manufacturing firms with in-house service departments (such as repair and maintenance, education, advertising services, research, credit, consulting, and so forth). A number of firms which developed these services to facilitate the sales of their own manufactured goods have since sought to make them available to customers who did not purchase original equipment from the firm. As a result, new profit centers or subsidiary companies may be set up. Successful examples include firms such as GE Credit Corporation, several former in-house advertising agencies or consulting firms, repair shops that once only serviced a specific brand, and company educational facilities that are now open to students from outside.

This approach to new product development requires that the initiating company examine carefully its internal resources and ancillary services to determine whether they could perform competitively if made more widely available. (Sometimes, of course, the result of such an analysis may be a decision to contract out the service to another supplier!)

Evaluating New Product "Fit"

The nature of the delivery system for many services means that there is often a high degree of interdependence between existing and new services. As a result, the failure of a new service can also blacken the reputation of existing ones. This is particularly likely to occur when customers are actively involved in the production system, such that the visible portion of the service operations system is large and other customers are encountered during service delivery. For instance, if a hotel introduces services designed to attract a new customer segment, it may not be possible to separate the old and new segments. Incompatibility between the two could discourage both groups from patronizing the hotel in the future. Even if different customer segments do not encounter each other (this would be unlikely in situations where the service firm was trying to develop counter-cyclical business), the new service may not fit well with either the existing facilities or service personnel. Expensive modifications and retraining (or new hiring) may be needed as a result.

Manufacturing firms that enter the service sector often find that they lack the operations and marketing expertise necessary for success in the new context. For instance, existing channels of distribution enable many manufacturers to maintain an arms-length relationship with consumers. Marketing a service may require managing retail outlets and customer contact personnel directly or else getting into franchising. Inventories can no longer be relied upon to balance supply and demand. And quality control is likely to be much more difficult.

Blueprinting Service Design and Delivery

Shostack's (1981) discussion of service blueprinting has already been mentioned. Such a blueprint can quickly become very complex for a service that involves multiple actions taken in sequence with various feasible outcomes. Many service operations, especially those involving numerous company-owned or franchise outlets, codify certain aspects of the blueprint in an operations procedures manual that defines how each task is to be performed. Quality control supervisions acting overtly (or perhaps covertly as "mystery shoppers") then check the performance of service personnel against the criteria laid down in the manual.

The danger with such procedures manuals is that they can be dominated by operational concerns for efficiency that crowd out marketing concerns aimed at satisfying the customer. However, many service firms have essentially redrawn their blueprints to incorporate customer-oriented actions ("make eye-contact with customer, greet customer by name, smile, determine customer need for complementary product and attempt to cross sell, thank customer according to prescribed format" and so forth).

In a very real sense, two sets of blueprints are required for each service. One should describe procedures and systems from the firm's perspective, including what happens behind the scenes. The second should describe the service encounter from the *customer's* perspective.

Although it may be difficult to test a prototype of a service in its entirety, certain aspects of the blueprint may lend themselves to laboratory testing. Thus mock-ups of a proposed new service facility can be built and tested on prospective customers, employees can rehearse service delivery procedures and problematic customer encounters during training programs, and new services can be test-marketed in limited locations before full commercialization is authorized. The world of entertainment uses dress rehearsals, pre-Broadway "tryouts," and "sneak previews"; banks have evaluated ATM installations in a single branch before going system wide; and Merrill Lynch first test-marketed its Home Equity Account (offering automatic borrowing privileges against customers' net equity in their homes) in California before entering other states with this new service.

The word "blueprinting" has strong architectural and engineering connotations. Yet services are not just processes, they are also frequently human performances. "Screenplay" and "choreography" are two words that may better capture the definition of the human actions within the broader operational blueprint.

Managing the Implementation Process

Although marketing has assumed greater importance in recent years, the operations function still dominates line management in most service institutions. Operations managers are responsible not only for operating equipment and procedures behind the scenes, but also for retail outlets and other facilities used by customers. In labor-intensive services, operations managers direct the work of large numbers of employees, including many who serve the customers directly.

In multi-site service businesses, implementation may take place at numerous local outlets, each of which essentially combines the characteristics of a "factory in the field" and a retail store. It is rare to find marketing managers in the service sector who can exercise line authority at the outlet level. In service organizations with a fairly standardized product line, the best opportunities to exercise control may come from marketing inputs to service manuals that prescribe the standards and procedures to be followed in creating and delivering a new service. However, such an approach is less feasible for customized services.

As service organizations change and adopt a stronger marketing orientation in relation to product enhancement and new product development, there is increased potential for conflict between the marketing and operations functions. As one executive in a service firm commented:

> "Marketing's role is typically seen as constantly adding superiority to the product offering so as to enhance its appeal to customers and thereby increase sales. Operations sees its role as paring these elements back to reflect the reality of service constraints—staff, equipment, and so forth— and the accompanying need for cost containment" (Langeard *et al.* 1981).

Under these circumstances, operations personnel whose performance is measured against cost-related criteria are likely to resist the introduction of new products because they will add to the expenses incurred by their division, branch, or outlet. One approach to dealing with this problem is to decentralize revenue responsibility by transforming cost centers into profit centers. When profit responsibilities are pushed down to the field level, potentially profitable new services take on an appeal they previously lacked for these managers. In a sense, field operations managers find themselves transformed into general managers and become more aware of consumer concerns and of the need for proactive marketing efforts.

There are a number of ways in which service firms are seeking to reduce the interfunctional stress generated by development and introduction of new services. One approach into transfer managers from one functional department to another to ensure better understanding of differing perspectives and also perform an educational role.

A related approach is to create a "task force" to plan and manage the implementation process. Task forces offer a way of integrating functional viewpoints into an environment that is at least partially insulated from the pressures and distractions of day-to-day management activities. The participants are in a position to create a microcosm of the organization to focus attention on the task at hand, and to discuss and resolve many of the problems likely to occur during the development and commercialization of an innovative service. There needs, of course, to be an external mechanism for settling any disputes which members of the task force cannot resolve among themselves.

Service innovations must be designed with customer needs and concerns in mind, requiring a strong orientation toward the marketplace. But there is also an *internal* marketplace, in that innovations usually affect service employees, too. Sometimes innovations involve just minor changes in operating procedures; at other times, they may require major procedural changes, and retraining or displacement of employees.

Gaining acceptance of service innovations among management and staff members is a human relations problem. Formation of a task force is one way of moving the project off the drawing board and into the development phase—"dimensioning the dream." But final implementation requires that members of the task force interact with operating personnel in the field. Winning the acceptance of unit or branch personnel requires that senior field management sell the project to people at the branch or unit level. Sometimes this requires field visits and one-on-one training sessions; at other times, it may be accomplished through use of sophisticated training films.

CONCLUSION

Service marketers have much to learn from existing knowledge of the new product development process derived from the study of innovations in manufactured goods. More recent research now offers insights that speak directly to issues distinctive to developing and introducing new services. This paper offered a number of observations on factors that stimulate new service development, sources of new service ideas evaluating how well proposed new services fit the existing operation, blueprinting and testing the design of new services, and managing the implementation process. One key caveat in all this is not to regard services as homogeneous. Managers should look outside their industries for insights from organizations that have faced (and resolved) similar problems. However, they should recognize that there are limits to the value of generalizations on new service development when it comes to working on highly specific issues.

References

Gross, I. (1968), "Toward a General Theory of Product Evolution: A Rejection of the 'Product Like Cycle' Concept," Marketing Science Institute Working Paper, 43–10.

Heany, Donald F. (1983), "Degrees of Product Innovation," *Journal of Business Strategy* 3; (Spring), 3–14.

Kotler, Philip, William Gregor, and William Rodgers, (1977), "The Marketing Audit Comes of Age," *Sloan Management Review* (Winter), 35–43.

Langeard, Eric, John E.G. Bateson, Christopher H. Lovelock, and Pierre Eiglier (1981), *Services Marketing: New Insights from Consumers and Managers,* Cambridge, MA: Marketing Science Institute.

Lovelock, Christopher H. (1984), *Services Marketing,* Englewood Cliffs, NJ: Prentice Hall.

Shostack, G. Lynn (1981), "How to Design a Service," In J.H. Donnelly and W.R. George, *Marketing of Services,* Chicago: American Marketing Association.

Urban, Glen L. and John R. Hauser (1980), *Design and Marketing of New Products,* Englewood Cliffs, NJ: Prentice-Hall.

Wind, Yoram J. (1982), *Product Policy: Concepts, Methods, and Strategy,* Reading, MA: Addison-Wesley.

35

THE NEW SERVICE DEVELOPMENT PROCESS: SUGGESTIONS FOR IMPROVEMENT

Michael R. Bowers

University of Alabama at Birmingham

ABSTRACT

Service organizations tend to use an incomplete means of developing new services. The result is a lack of attention to the needs of the marketplace. A model for developing new services is suggested that allows greater input on the part of the service recipients.

INTRODUCTION

For many service organizations the marketplace today is rapidly changing. Old ways of doing business are no longer adequate, services once popular are no longer in demand. There has been massive changes in the areas of regulation and consumer demand for services. These changes have to a large extent antiquated existing services and created a tremendous demand for new and innovative services. Service companies attempting to serve yesterday's product to today's consumer will not remain competitive.

Despite the importance of developing new services for today's market, little is understood about how new services are or should be developed. The purpose of this article is to report the results of preliminary research on the process of new service development; how it differs among service industries and how it might be improved.

LITERATURE REVIEW

The services marketing literature was reviewed for insight into how developing new services had been addressed by other authors. Table 35-1 presents a listing of publications written since 1980 that deal with aspects of the new service development process. The articles tend to focus on a particular component of new service development such as concept testing (Murphy and Robinson 1981), or service design (Shostack 1981, 1984a and Chase 1983). Distinction is made as to the role of service employees in developing new services (Schneider and Bowen 1984; Zimney 1984). Two articles address the process of new service development in a systematic and holistic fashion (Lovelock 1984; Shostack 1984b).

Bowers, Michael R. 1987. The new service development process: Suggestions for improvement. In *The Services Challenge: Integrating for Competitive Advantage,* ed. John R. Czepiel, Carole A. Congram, and James Shanahan. Chicago, IL: American Marketing Association Proceedings.

TABLE 35-1   New Service Development Literature Since 1980

Author	Theory Development	New Product Development Process–Strategy	Idea Generation	Screening and Evaluation	Business Analysis	Product Development	Testing: Product Market	Commercial-ization
Beckwith & Fitzgerald, 1981	Design flexibility into delivery system							
Murphy & Robinson, 1981				Concept Testing				
Sandeman, 1981						Molecular model for new services		
Shostack, 1981						Blueprinting new services		
Chase, 1983						Modeling service process		
Dixon & Smith, 1983	Customer perspective							
Langeard & Eiglier, 1983		Multi-site multi-service typology						
Robinson, 1983					Business analysis of services			
Lovelock, 1984		New service development process						
Pleyers, 1984	Managerial influences of innovation							
Schneider & Bowen, 1984		Employee's role						
Schwartz, 1984	Role of culture in service innovation							
Shostack, 1984		(b) New Service development process				(a) Designing new services		
Zimney, 1984								Employee's role

Lovelock argues that there is no need to discard useful concepts developed from research into manufactured goods. Therefore he suggests that with modification, the principles of new product development derived from manufacturing fit new service development as well. With regard to the process of developing new products Lovelock (1984 p. 50) states, "There is general agreement that the new-product-development process should proceed systematically through a series of steps, beginning with a review of corporate (institutional) objectives and constraints and continuing through product introduction."

Shostack (1984b) has developed a model of new service development based on her own work experience. To a certain extent, the steps in the Shostack model mirror the elements of product development models formulated by other researchers (Booz-Allen & Hamilton 1982, Urban and Hauser 1980, and Wind 1982). For example, First Phase Definition is essentially the same as concept testing, First Phase Analysis is equivalent to concept screening, and First Phase Implementation is equal to product testing.

To summarize, new service development has been treated as an extension of the product development process. Writers have accepted generally recognized stages of goods development and provided a service oriented corollary. Except for Lovelock's (1984) and Shostack's (1984b) articles, new service development has not been addressed as a total system.

METHODOLOGY OF THE STUDY

Three service industries were chosen as the sampling frame for the study; banks, hospitals and insurance companies. These service industries were chosen because they are active innovators in new service development. Johne's findings indicate that experienced product innovators develop new products differently from inexperienced ones. On average, companies in this sample have introduced twelve new services over the past five years, or one every six months.

A total sample size of nine hundred was drawn for this study; three hundred randomly selected from each of the three service industries. The questionnaire was mailed to individually identified marketing managers or hospital administrators within each firm. If the addressee felt there were others more qualified to answer questions about new service development in their organization they were asked to forward the questionnaire to those individuals. Beyond operating in the specified industry, no other organizational characteristics were stipulated.

Respondents were asked how often they engaged in a series of well established new product development activities. The activities mirror those steps identified in the Booz-Allen & Hamilton (1982) model of new product development. The Booz-Allen & Hamilton model incorporates the essential activities of other new product development models and is empirically derived from a large sample of both consumer goods and industrial manufacturers.

Participants in the study indicated the frequency in which their organization engaged in a given activity on a five point scale. Possible responses ranged from Never (1) to All the Time (5) Table 35-2 through Table 35-4 provide brief descriptions of the activities as well as the means of the responses for the three individual service industries. These statistics were used to identify differences in the process among the sample's service industries.

Table 35-5 presents the unweighted mean of the means for the activities of new product development, derived from the sample. These were calculated in order to

---

TABLE 35-2 Mean Scores for Banks on the Activities of New Product Development[a]

	Banks
Develop a Business Strategy (Long-term strategic direction)	3.70
Develop a New Product Strategy (Plan that outlines the type of new products to be developed)	3.13
Idea Generation (Formal process for soliciting ideas for new products)	2.70
Concept Development and Evaluation (Refining and developing the concept of the new product)	3.26
Business Analysis (Determining the profitability and feasibility of the new product)	3.83
Product Development and Testing (Developing and testing prototypes)	2.38
Market Testing (Limited testing of both the product and the marketing mix variables)	2.22
Commercialization (Full-scale introduction to the public)	3.86

[a]A score of three is midpoint on a five point scale. Therefore, a mean less than three indicates the sample participants are more likely to *not* engage in a given activity than they are to perform the activity.

TABLE 35-3 Mean Scores for Insurance Companies on the Activities of New Product Development

	Insurance Companies
Develop a Business Strategy (Long-term strategic direction)	3.80
Develop a New Product Strategy (Plan that outlines the type of new products to be developed)	3.51
Idea Generation (Formal process for soliciting ideas for new products)	3.10
Concept Development and Evaluation (Refining and developing the concept of the new product)	3.29
Business Analysis (Determining the profitability and feasibility of the new product)	3.77
Product Development and Testing (Developing and testing prototypes)	2.97
Market Testing (Limited testing of both the product and the marketing mix variables)	2.58
Commercialization (Full-scale introduction to the public)	3.38

TABLE 35-4 Mean Scores for Hospitals on the Activities of New Product Development

	Hospitals
Develop a Business Strategy (Long-term strategic direction)	3.93
Develop a New Product Strategy (Plan that outlines the type of new products to be developed)	3.24
Idea Generation (Formal process for soliciting ideas for new products)	3.05
Concept Development and Evaluation (Refining and developing the concept of the new product)	3.50
Business Analysis (Determining the profitability and feasibility of the new product)	4.10
Product Development and Testing (Developing and testing prototypes)	2.02
Market Testing (Limited testing of both the product and the marketing mix variables)	2.20
Commercialization (Full-scale introduction to the public)	3.50

TABLE 35-5 Mean of the Means for the Three Service Industries on the Activities of New Product Development

	Unweighted Means
Develop a Business Strategy (Long-term strategic direction)	3.81
Develop a New Product Strategy (Plan that outlines the type of new products to be developed)	3.29
Idea Generation (Formal process for soliciting ideas for new products)	2.95
Concept Development and Evaluation (Refining and developing the concept of the new product)	3.35
Business Analysis (Determining the profitability and feasibility of the new product)	3.90
Product Development and Testing (Developing and testing prototypes)	2.46
Market Testing (Limited testing of both the product and the marketing mix variables)	2.33
Commercialization (Full-scale introduction to the public)	3.58

understand the general pattern of new service development across industries without the bias of unequal sample size.

CHARACTERISTICS OF THE RESPONDENTS

An initial and follow up mailing yielded 253 useable questionnaires, for a response rate of 28%. Individual industry response rates were: a) banks—109 questionnaires returned (36.3%); b) insurance companies—83 questionnaires returned (27.7%); hospitals—61 questionnaires returned (20.3%).

The sample organizations varied tremendously in the number of employees. The smallest company had 20 employees, the largest had over 14,000. The mean number of employees for the sample was 1097 with a standard deviation of 2018. When asked about the geographic range of their operations 48.36% of the respondents stated they were local. Over 28% of the sample participants claimed they operated on a statewide or regional level. Almost 23% of the respondents said they operated at a national or international level.

The sample firms were asked to rate themselves in terms of competitive strength. About 58% of the respondents felt they were above average in comparison to their competition. Approximately 42% felt they were average or below average relative to their competitors.

RESULT FROM THE STUDY

From studying Table 35-2 through Table 35-5, it is apparent that the service industries of hospitals, banks and insurance companies differ from the Booz-Allen & Hamilton (1982) model in developing new services. Responding service organizations tend to not engage in formalized idea generation, product development and testing or marketing testing. Development of a business strategy and business analysis are the two most likely activities to be undertaken. Development of a new product strategy, concept development and evaluation, and commercialization occur in moderate amounts.

An analysis of variance combined with Fisher's test of Least Significant Difference (LSD) on the means from the three service industries reveals that banks are significantly less likely to engage in idea generation than insurance companies or hospitals (alpha = .05). This is not surprising given the tendency for the banking industry to rely upon regulatory agencies for new product initiatives. The same type of analysis indicates that insurance companies are significantly more likely to perform product development and testing than hospitals or banks (alpha = .05). Even though this is statistically significant, the performance of product testing and evaluation among insurance firms is an occasional event.

Results from an earlier study (Bowers 1985) indicates that the more service firms seek to understand their environment, the greater the success rate of their new services. It is therefore distressing to note the lack of customer exposure a new service receives before being released on the market. The activities which the sample respondents tend to *not* engage in are those activities which manufacturers use to insure they stay in touch with the market.

Manufacturers often solicit new product ideas from their salesforce (those who deal with the marketplace) or directly from consumers. Product testing is frequently performed by selected consumers to identify unforeseen strengths and weaknesses of the product. Market testing is done to see how the product, in conjunction with the other marketing mix variables, will fare in a controlled exposure to market forces. From the results of this study, it appears likely that the first time a new service is seen by consumers is during commercialization.

RECOMMENDATIONS

It is widely assumed that new product development is a critical function of any firm. Yet a general conclusion of this study is that service firms are doing an incomplete job of managing the process. It does not seem wise to develop new services in a vacuum, without input from the marketplace. The Normative Model presented in Figure 35-1 suggests the answer to this problem in three ways.

First, a formal process of searching for ideas, outside as well as inside the organization should be established (Idea Generation). Active searching for new service ideas will allow the innovative firm to stay in touch with changes in the environment. The firm might be able to anticipate the moves of regulatory agencies and gain time on their competitors. More importantly, they may be able to creatively repackage existing services into more meaningful products or develop innovative new services within existing regulatory constraints.

There are many avenues for new product ideas. Competitive shopping and focus groups with consumers are popular means of discovering new ideas outside of the company. Using focus groups, a homogenous collection of consumers are asked how existing products could be made better and how their needs could be better satisfied with new products. The important point here is that the search for new service ideas should be made a routine part of the product development process.

Second, the Normative Model suggests that prior to substantial investments in creating the product itself, a rigorous definition of the policies, procedures and standards of performance should be created (Service Development and Evaluation). This document should then be evaluated not only by those associated with the new service project, but also by line personnel and consumers. Input from those charged with creating the service as well as those consuming it will validate the viability of the new product. It is much easier to make changes in this document than to correct errors once the service is operational. As a consequence, a critical look should be given for potential operating problems.

Third, a major source or risk for new products is the failure of marketing mix variables. It is possible to gauge consumer reaction to advertising, sales promotions and personal selling campaigns as well as sensitivity to price. The results of this research suggest that determining consumer reaction to marketing mix variables is one of the most underutilized means of improving the chances for success of new services (Market Testing).

When possible, the Normative Model suggests that testing the service is appropriate in the context of a market test. This allows the service to be evaluated in comparison with the other marketing mix variables. Market testing the service permits the

---

FIGURE 35-1 A Normative Model of New Service Development[a]

1. Develop a Business Strategy
   (a long-term strategic direction for the firm)
2. Develop a New Service Strategy
   (a plan that outlines the type of new products to be developed)
3. Idea Generation
   (a formal process for soliciting ideas for new services)
4. Concept Development and Evaluation
   (refining and expanding the concept of the new service)
5. Business Analysis
   (determining the feasibility and profitability of the new service)
6. Service Development and Evaluation
   (establishing standards for performance of the new service)
7. Market Testing
   (testing of the marketing mix variables and of the service itself)
8. Commercialization
   (introduction to the public)

---

[a]Based on the Booz-Allen (1982) Model of New Product Development

organization to judge the impact and interaction of the marketing mix. Market testing occurs after the service has passed all the other less expensive screening mechanisms. Marketing testing should take place only for the most promising new services.

SUMMARY

This research suggests that service organizations employ a process of new service development that is not open to marketplace influences. The path to developing better new products appears to lie in a systematic process of new service development that is sensitive to external change and incorporates consumer reactions and criticisms.

Three ways are suggested to carry out this improvement. First, routinely search for new product ideas outside of the organization. Second, completely define, develop and evaluate the service with the assistance of contact personnel and consumers. Third, put the new service in a market test to determine how well the marketing mix will work in the marketplace. By allowing new services to face the crucible of the market before commercialization, better new products will be introduced.

References

Beckwith, Neil E. and Thomas J. Fitzgerald (1981) "Marketing of Services: Meeting of Different Needs," *Marketing of Services,* James H. Donnelly and William R. George, eds., Chicago: American Marketing Association, 239–241.

Booz-Allen & Hamilton (1982), *New Product Management for the 1980s,* New York: Booz-Allen & Hamilton.

Bowers, Michael R. (1985), *An Exploration into New Service Development: Process, Organization and Structure,* a dissertation, College Station Texas: Texas A&M University.

Chase, Richard B. (1983), "Modeling Service Processes," *Emerging Perspectives on Services Marketing,* Leonard L. Berry, G. Lynn Shostack and Gregory D. Upah, eds., Chicago: American Marketing Association, 137–138.

Dixon, Donald F. and Michael F. Smith (1983), "Theoretical Foundations for Services Marketing Strategy," *Emerging Perspectives on Services Marketing,* Leonard L. Berry, G. Lynn Shostack and Gregory D. Upah, eds., Chicago: American Marketing Association, 77–81.

Johne, Frederic A. (1984), "How Experienced Product Innovators Organize," *Journal of Product Innovation Management,* Volume 1, Number 4 (December), 210–223.

Langard, Eric and Pierre Eigler (1983), "Strategic Management of Service Development," *Emerging Perspectives on Services Marketing,* Leonard L. Berry, G. Lynn Shostack and Gregory D. Upah, eds., Chicago: American Marketing Association, 68–72.

Lovelock, Christopher (1984), "Developing and Implementing New Services," *Developing New Services,* William R. George and Claudia E. Marshall eds., Chicago: American Marketing Association, 44–64.

Meyers, Patricia (1984), "Innovative Shift: Lessons for Service Firms from a Technology Leader," *Developing New Services,* William R. George and Claudia E. Marshall, eds., Chicago: American Marketing Association, 217–220.

Murphy, Patrick E. and Richard K. Robinson (1981), "Concept Testing Services," *Marketing of Services,* James H. Donnelly and William R. George, Eds., Chicago: American Marketing Association, 217–220.

Robinson, Richard K. (1983), "New Service Development: The Cable TV Connection," *Emerging Perspectives on Services Marketing,* Leonard L. Berry, G. Lynn Shostack and Gregory D. Upah eds., Chicago: American Marketing Association, 73–76.

Sandeman, Graham (1981), "Implications of the Molecular Marketing Model in the Design of Retail Concepts," *Marketing of Services,* James H. Donnelly and William R. George, eds., Chicago: American Marketing Association, 230–235.

Schneider, Benjamin and David Bowen (1984), "New Services Design, Development and Implementation and the Employee," *Developing New Services,* William R. George and Claudia E. Marshall, eds., Chicago: American Marketing Association, 82–101.

Schwartz, Howard (1984), "Developing a Climate for Innovation of New Services," *Developing New Services,* William R. George and Claudia E. Marshall, eds., Chicago: American Marketing Association, 1–8.

Shostack, G. Lynn (1981), "How to Design a Service," *Marketing of Services,* James H. Donnelly and William R. George, eds., Chicago: American Marketing Association, 221–229.

_____ (1984a), "Designing Services that Deliver," *Harvard Business Review,* January–February, 133–139.

_____ (1984b), "Service Design in the Operating Environment," *Developing New Services,* William R. George and Claudia E. Marshall, eds., Chicago: American Marketing Association, 27–43.

Urban, Glen L. and John R. Hauser (1980), *Design and Marketing of New Products,* Englewood Cliffs, New Jersey: Prentice Hall.

Wind, Yoran J. (1982), *Product Policy: Concepts, Methods, and Strategy,* Reading, Maine: Wesley.

Zimney, Stephen A. (1984), "New Services Development and the Employee," *Developing New Services,* William R. George and Claudia E. Marshall, eds., Chicago: American Marketing Association, 68–81.

36

HOW TO DESIGN A SERVICE

G. Lynn Shostack

Jane Kingman-Brundage

Service design can be thought of as a form of architecture, but an architecture dealing with processes instead of bricks and mortar. The objective is the creation of a complete blueprint for a service concept that can be translated into a soundly functioning service. What makes service development unique is the number and complexity of issues that must be dealt with in order to plan and manage a service concept from conception to realization.

WHY SERVICE DESIGN IS DIFFERENT

A service is not something that is built in a factory, shipped to a store, put on a shelf, and then taken home by a consumer. A service is a dynamic living process. A service is something that is executed on behalf of, and often with the involvement of, the consumer. A service is performed. A service is rendered. A service is motion and activity—not pieces or parts. The "raw materials" of a service are time and process—not plastic or steel. A service cannot be stored or shipped—only the means for creating it can. A service cannot be held in one's hand or physically possessed. In short, a service is not a thing.

The important fact about a service is that it cannot be disassembled. Every part of the system is interrelated. A service is a "real-time" occurrence. In a metaphysical sense, the service only "exists" when it is being rendered. Otherwise, a service is simply a collection of machines, paper, or bodies at rest.

PLANNING THE TOTAL SYSTEM IS THE KEY

Every service is a complex system. To design and manage any service, all parts of the system must be addressed simultaneously. It is important to know that most of the needed methodologies already exist in the managerial tool kit: The methods are not themselves exotic. What *is* rare is a new managerial perspective—the habit of looking at a service as an integrated whole.

Consider the simple service of the corner shoeshine stand. In Figure 36-1, we can see that four actions, proceeding left to right in time, constitute the primary processes of the service. But clearly there is more to the service than simply these functional

FIGURE 36-1   Blueprint for a Simple Service: The Corner Shoeshine Stand

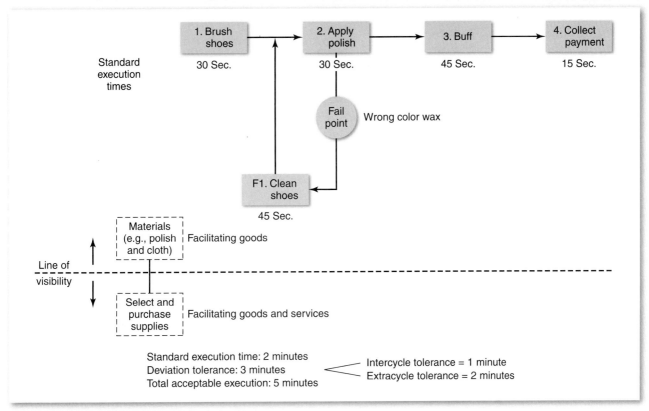

procedures. Every service requires *setup,* even so simple an action as purchase of supplies and arrangement of the shoeshine stand. Many services also require *follow-up,* actions taken to complete the service after the customer departs.

In Figure 36-1 a "line of visibility" separates actions observable to the customer from those which, although necessary to the functioning of the service system, are nonetheless invisible to the customer. In large service systems, these "back office" or "invisible" parts of the system can have enormous impact on quality, image, and function.

If, for example, a computer program is redesigned in such a way that a different account statement is produced for banking customers, this new piece of evidence may affect service image and other perceptions of price/value as well. Thus, even invisible processes must be planned and monitored by the marketer.

A facilitating good—wax—is necessary to the rendering of shoeshines. If this good is not selected and managed with care, the overall service will suffer.

The system also includes a person who renders the service. This person not only must be functionally competent, but also must be socially competent. Thus, his or her manner and appearance also are part of the system, representing physical "evidence" of service quality to the customer. The system has time and material costs, and it has "fail points," where potential breakdowns in service execution are most likely to occur. The service has an environment in which it is performed and, finally, the entire service system has a result or benefit, which we can describe as "shiny shoes" or perhaps "a smile on one's face."

FIGURE 36-2 Modified Design for Shoeshine Stand, Incorporating New Service Cycle, Service Evidence, and Product Elements

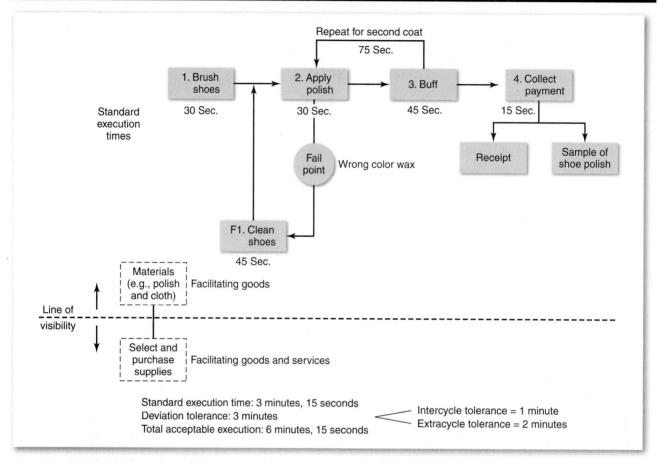

This "simple" service can take many unique forms. Figure 36-2 shows a different "design" with different constraints, prices, and marketability.

Not only can shoeshine service take many forms, whole new constellations of services or service "packages" can be created by combining various designs, including products. Figure 36-3 shows three different service "packages," derived from arrangement of basic service elements: additional service (repair) and product (shoe-care items and even shoes themselves).

Similarly, as Figures 36-4 and 36-5 show, the service of flower arranging can have as many unique designs as there are providers. In Figure 36-4, every arrangement is unique. The variability is infinite—constrained only by the imagination of the flower arranger. In Figure 36-5, the service design *predefines* the eight outcomes (arrangements).

From a service design perspective, it is harder to control for consistent, high quality on a discrete number of known outcomes than to control for quality by securing the service of a single master performer. The sources of difficulty are numerous. First, it is not easy to define standard outcomes, which are also desirable to consumers. Second, it is not easy to plan the *means* (goods and tasks) by which specified outcomes are to be achieved. Finally, variability in the skills of individual service providers may, at the last moment, thwart the best design. Trade-offs in quality, volume, and price follow naturally. For these reasons, service design demands a comprehensive approach to planning all elements of the service system.

FIGURE 36-3   Three Alternative Product/Service Combinations for a Shoeshine Operation

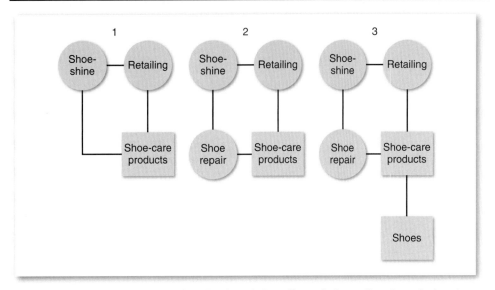

Source: Reprinted from "How to Design a Service," G. Lynn Shostack, *Proceedings From the American Marketing Association Services Marketing Conference* (Orlando, Florida), published by the American Marketing Association, 1981.

FIGURE 36-4   Service Design for a Park Avenue Florist

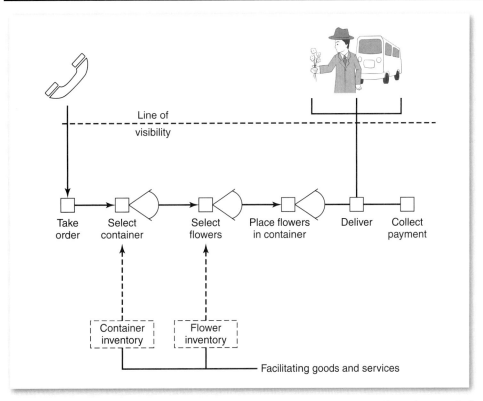

Source: Reprinted from "Service Positioning Through Structural Change," G. Lynn Shostack, *Journal of Marketing* 51, no. 1, published by the American Marketing Association, January 1987.

FIGURE 36-5 Alternative Service Design for the Florist

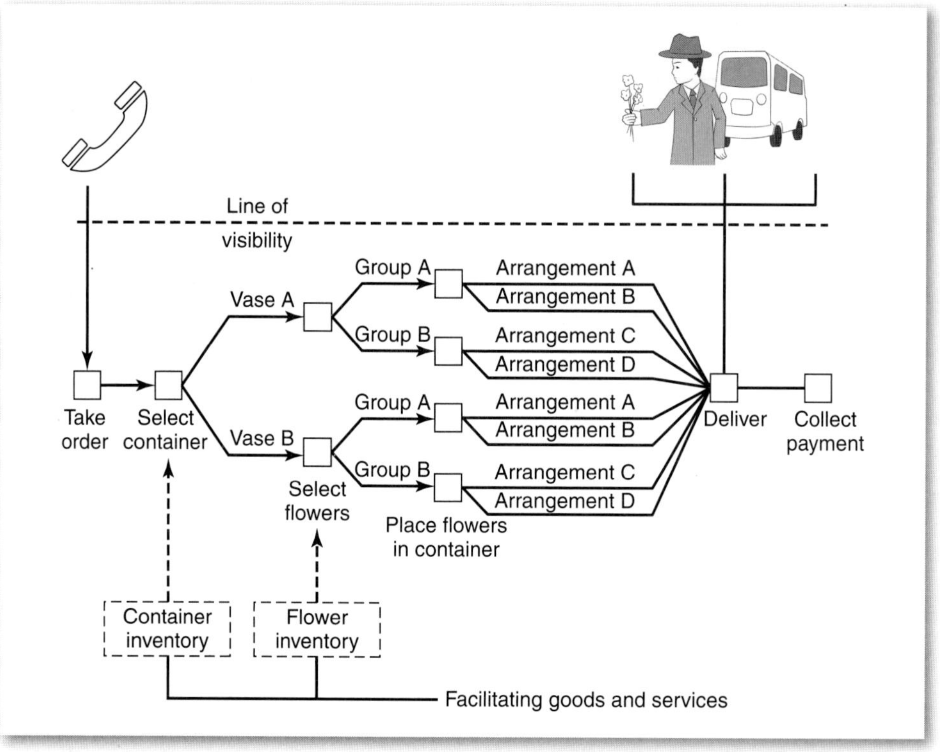

Source: Reprinted from "Service Positioning Through Structural Change," G. Lynn Shostack, *Journal of Marketing* 51, no. 1, published by the American Marketing Association, January 1987.

HOW TO USE THE PLANNING/DEVELOPMENT MODEL

Figure 36-6 shows the stages involved in designing and introducing a service. The model is a progressive step-by-step process that results in a fully defined, operational service.

Five Steps to Success

Five primary activities constitute the service development process:

Step 1: Design. Design is a mental plan or scheme in which means to an end are laid down. Service system design is the iterative act of defining and refining an initial service concept. As shown in Figure 36-6, reaching a master design involves repeating the cycle of definition, analysis, and synthesis many times. Even after a master design is finalized, the design function remains a permanent part of managing any service system. Design modifications and adjustments are a continuing necessity, based on consumer input, competitive conditions, and operational change.

Step 2: Implementation. Implementation means translating a master service design into the operating tasks, functions, and requirements that are necessary to introduce and operate the service. These tasks are ultimately performed by others who constitute the living service system.

Step 3: Documentation. Documentation represents specification, at the detailed level, of all the operating standards, instructions, schedules, rules, and outputs of the service system, so that other people know how the system is supposed to function.

Step 4: Introduction. Introduction is the actual "turning on" of the service system to interact with consumers.

Step 5: Audit. Audit is a series of feedback mechanisms and controls that allow fine-tuning or necessary modification of the service. The audit function is responsible for maintaining design integrity and is an essential ongoing monitoring activity.

FIGURE 36-6 Service Design and Development

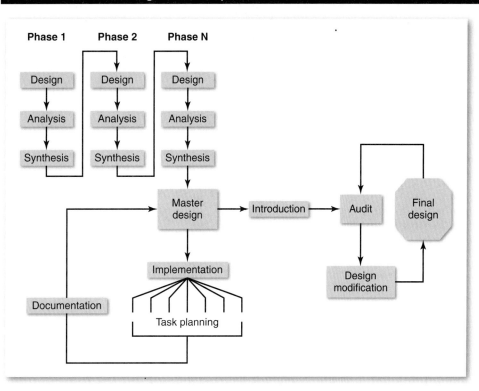

WHY A DIVERSIFIED TEAM IS IMPORTANT

Service development requires the participation and involvement of many individuals who bring different expertise and experience to the process.

In assembling a development team, one person should be designated the captain or team leader. He or she is responsible for pulling together all the people and expertise needed to address issues related to design, implementation, documentation, introduction, and audit. The team itself should be structured around four critical functions: Design, Process, Means, and Evidence. Figures 36-7 and 36-8 show these functions of and relationship among the team members.

> *Design.* This team member will be the keeper of the service design itself as it progresses through changes and refinement. He or she will also be responsible for incorporating market research into the design specifications, integrating consumer and operational feedback into the design, and analyzing the impact of all proposed changes in process, means, or evidence.
> *Process.* This team member will focus on operational issues and constraints that affect the design, and will oversee operational implementation.
> *Means.* The means by which services are rendered are only two: people and goods. This team member will concentrate on people issues (skills requirements and training) and facilitating goods and services, such as computers and other goods and services needed to execute the service.
> *Evidence.* This team member will address all consumer encounter points. Service evidence means everything the consumer will be exposed to regarding the service. It includes advertising, collateral material, telephone dialogues, person-to-person interaction, environments, direct mail, and all other forms of visible, aural, or tangible evidence.

Team members may not carry the titles described previously, but may be drawn from marketing, operations, personnel, information services, and other areas in the

FIGURE 36-7 Service Development Functions of the Team

Design management Process management Means management Evidence management

FIGURE 36-8 Functional Interfaces of the Team

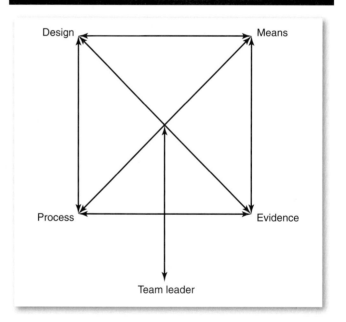

company. However, by organizing the team around these categories—design, process, means, evidence—developmental issues will cluster together naturally in a way that corresponds to the main elements of all service systems. The four areas relate logically to one another. This logical relationship helps ensure that no important issue is omitted as cross-boundary tasks emerge. As development progresses, others with even more specialized knowledge will be drawn into the process.

The Importance of Shared Understanding

Because many people will ultimately be involved, service design requires a high degree of shared understanding at each developmental stage. To provide a basis for this understanding, a technique called *service blueprinting* is suggested and described throughout this chapter. It is a way of diagramming and describing the total system and total concept to ensure that all issues and areas necessary to the successful development of a service are addressed.

BENEFITS OF SERVICE BLUEPRINTS

The benefits associated with service blueprints can be understood in terms of the traditional management tasks—planning, organizing, directing, and controlling:

1. A service blueprint is a *planning* tool for visualizing or depicting the service concept in concrete terms, thus facilitating market research and concept testing.
2. The service blueprint is an *organizing* tool for assisting managers in assembling appropriate resources for effective implementation of the service concept:
    * *Human resource:* By answering the question, "What exactly will service providers do?" blueprints provide a task-oriented basis for job descriptions and employee selection criteria.
    * *Technological resource:* By answering the question, "How will the service be provided—that is, using what equipment?" the blueprint guides selection and design of appropriate equipment. In the event the service system design process *begins* with innovative technology, the blueprint assists managers with the process of developing rational, systematic human support (work flows, procedures) designed to maximize the technological benefits.
    * *Evidence:* By answering the question, "What evidence do consumers require to (1) select the service in the first place; (2) have service experiences consistent with their expectations; (3) select the service again?" a service blueprint guides the development of advertising and promotion, visual environment, consumer materials, printed forms, and even suggested "scripts" for verbal interactions.
    * *Process:* By answering the question, "How does the service work?" a service blueprint is the objective basis for development of service policy, work-flow design, and operating procedures.
3. The service blueprint is a *communication* and *training* tool that helps service providers relate their specific job to the service overall. By answering the question, "How does my job serve consumers?" a service blueprint can foster employee commitment to the marketing task.
4. The service blueprint is a *control* device that makes it possible to structure monitoring and feedback devices at job, system, and management levels. Service blueprints facilitate quality control through analysis of fail points, which is the first step in identifying meaningful checkpoints for statistical control of quality.

The service blueprint is thus a technique for assisting marketers to identify and manipulate service elements in order to create barriers to entry by the competition. Similarly, the service blueprint enables marketers to isolate the explicit elements that distinguish competitive service offerings.

HOW TO BLUEPRINT A SERVICE

In the beginning of a service project, the service definition is usually vague and only a skeletal indication of what the final service will be. Often no written definition exists at this first stage, only a verbal or mental concept. Even when a written description does exist, it is frequently a brief, abstracted statement. The definition usually describes the main results or benefits of the service concept, rather than what service delivery entails. As shown in Figure 36-6, an iterative service design and development process is required to realize the service concept.

Phase 1 Design

To initiate development, the team should begin by writing as complete a description of the concept as possible. A preliminary blueprint should also be created, even though it will appear primitive.

FIGURE 36-9 Definition for a Discount Brokerage House in Phase 1

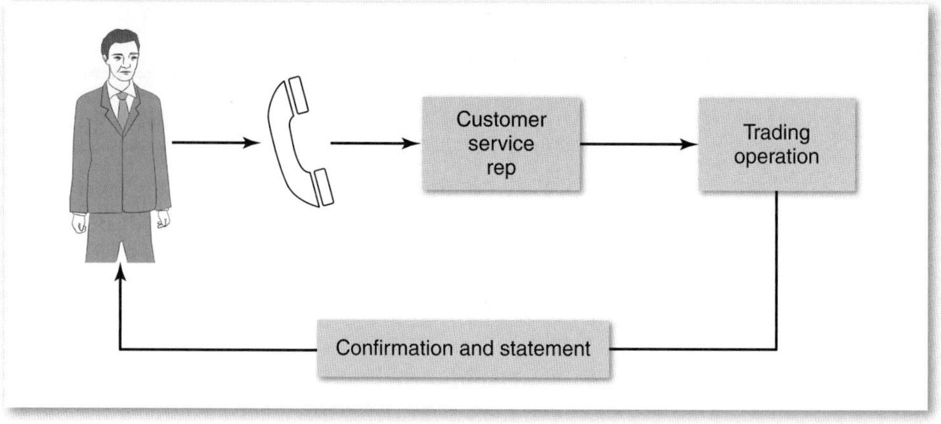

To illustrate the stages of the process, we will use the discount brokerage example.

This service concept might be stated as follows: Discount brokerage is a service through which people buy and sell stocks without paying for brokerage advice. The concept might be blueprinted as shown in Figure 36-9. To proceed from this stage to the creation and successful introduction of a new service requires a progressive program of refinement and detail.

Phase 1 Analysis

Having defined the concept, the information-gathering process begins. A search is made for data and examples relating to the proposed service concept. Competitors are analyzed. Various approaches to implementation are identified. Dialogue with knowledgeable internal and external parties is initiated. As alternative approaches and features for the service are identified and as new ideas surface, the inadequacy of the Phase 1 definition becomes apparent.

Phase 1 Synthesis

At this stage, basic boundaries for the service are drawn. A considerable amount of dialogue and discussion must take place in order to sort out the many alternatives and, more important, to achieve a common understanding of the basic profile of the service to be built. The project team should meet on a regular basis, so that the viewpoints of various parties can be clarified. The team will make a number of decisions at this stage. The cumulative effect of these decisions is to clarify the service definition and limit the issues that remain to be considered.

Some of the many decisions requiring definition, analysis, and synthesis in discount brokerage include choosing among the wide variety of securities that are potential candidates for inclusion. Each type of security requires staff expertise, has cost implications, and involves computer systems development time. Some possibilities require joint effort with other operating areas.

Decisions about whether all or part of the service should be done in-house are needed. In one alternative, custody of customer securities would remain with an external broker. In another, it is maintained in-house. Automatic cash sweep to a money market fund is a possibility, but requires contracting with outsiders. Literally hundreds of issues, small and large, will surface in Phase 1.

Phases 2 Through N

These three steps—design, analysis, and synthesis—must be repeated until the team has developed a complete and detailed service system blueprint. Shortcuts in the design phase inevitably lead to problems in implementation and introduction due to oversight, hasty conclusions, and erroneous assumptions.

FIGURE 36-10 Service Development Checklist.

Design Questions to Ask

* Have we described all the steps necessary to execute this service?
* Have we described completely the *order of* and *connections between* these steps?
* Have we described the *means* by which these steps will be rendered (i.e., people, computers, consumers)?
* Have we identified each point at which the service could fail?
* Have we described all the consumer encounter points identified with this service?
* Have we identified all the tangible evidence this service will present to the consumer?
* Have we defined all the facilitating goods and services required by this service?
* Have we identified the time/cost components of the service?

Analysis Questions to Ask

* What consumer research can assist us in evaluating this service?
* What do we know about competitive services (quality, price, evidence, structure)?
* How do we know our operational design will work?
* What kind of people are needed in this system?
* What kind of technologies or facilitating goods are needed?
* Are our cost/time assumptions valid?
* Is our choice of encounter points optimal?
* Have we chosen the best forms of evidence?

Synthesis Questions to Ask

* What parts of the blueprint have to be changed as a result of our definition and analysis?
* What impact do these changes have on other parts of the service system?
* What additional definition and analysis do we need to do?
* Have we revised the blueprint?

The use of the service development checklist shown in Figure 36-10 can help team members ensure that they have considered all aspects of the service system. The process of answering questions on the list requires team members to refine and clarify the service system as a whole.

Each of these phases demands thorough and careful work. Different team members may focus on parts of design that match their areas of expertise, which is one reason why a diversified team is important. From these exercises come creative answers and unique solutions that lead to differentiated and successful introductions.

The reason for such thoroughness in the design stage is that no two services are the same. Even when the outward or superficial evidence appears similar, every service is different. Services are processes. As such, they are variable. Two firms offering the same service will, upon investigation, be found to have established different designs, and each design will pose different constraints and opportunities for changing, expanding, and controlling the service.

For example, the choice of computer system to produce customer statements may seem to be a mechanical rather than a marketing issue. Yet one computer may allow linkage to other service systems, while another does not. Computer linkage can allow new service combinations to be created, which can differentiate an organization's offerings to the market. One computer may allow free-form statement messages, while another does not. One may use a laser printer, while another does not. One may be formatted to fit window envelopes, while another requires that envelope labels be produced. Each of these choices affects the final service's design, and each is a marketing issue.

One firm's customer contact employees may be required to fill out forms, while another firm's employees enter information directly into the computer. Each requires different training and different process standards, and potentially will yield different employee morale and different customer satisfaction levels. This seemingly small difference in computer use as a facilitating good may affect pricing and competitive position and will certainly affect evidence.

Pricing Issues

Pricing issues deserve special mention because pricing a service is different from pricing a packaged good. Marketers are familiar with the cost components employed in a manufacturing setting: raw materials, labor, and overhead. In a manufacturing context, labor is understood to be the number of widgets produced in a given time frame. Marketers, however, sometimes encounter difficulties in costing services because they do not recognize anything on the service side comparable to the "widgets" manufactured in the factory.

A different method is required to cost the labor associated with creation of a service. In Figure 36-1 each step in the shoeshine process has been timed. For each step, *standard execution* plus *deviation tolerance* yields a *total acceptable execution*. These discrete steps are comparable to factory widgets; taken as a whole, they comprise the labor cost associated with the total service. Service blueprints enable managers to develop accurate labor costs because blueprints depict the individual steps that make up a service.

For tasks and steps in which time cannot be rigidly controlled or measured as, for example, data entry, an acceptable norm must be developed based on average execution standards. Costing norms would apply to such variable tasks as customer dialogues, problem resolution, and other steps calling for diagnosis, judgment, and choices among possible courses of action.

Facilitating goods and services can then be amortized into the cost structure based on expected levels of service production. Evidence will be similarly costed.

These techniques will yield a blueprint cost at various production levels of the service, which will later be compared with actual costs under live conditions. To then set a price for the service, the marketer can begin by establishing a price based on a satisfactory profit margin or return. Next, the marketer should evaluate competition and, if the new service has unique advantages, decide whether these "value-added" elements might justify higher pricing. Research can be very helpful at this stage. Because all pricing is, at some level, partly subjective, the potential price flexibility of a service often is dramatically affected by customer perceptions of the total service's benefit. Whenever a service may be perceived as unique by the market, care must be taken not to underprice it at the outset.

How a Completed Blueprint Looks

In the case of the discount brokerage house, Figure 36-11 shows a condensed version of the completed blueprint for the concept. Clearly, there is a big difference between this and the initial definition.

At each stage, the service proposal should be widely circulated, so that its specifics can be critiqued. Attention should be focused on operational factors, as well as on the identification of flaws in the design and any remaining issues or problems. The more detailed the blueprint, the easier it will be to respond with constructive and specific feedback.

Exposing the proposal to the rigor of criticism is vital. If the design is critiqued in a vacuum or in a "planning" laboratory, not only are the conclusions likely to be biased toward the planners' preconceived wishes, but the service is very likely to encounter implementation problems.

Use Research to Help You Design

Focused market research should also be conducted to give prospective customers an opportunity to respond to the service concept and provide input to the design process. Market research done at very early stages is usually worthless, because it only provides reaction to a vague abstraction.

When prospective customers are invited to respond to a service blueprint, however, abstractions give way to the concrete actions proposed to make up the service. A service blueprint used in a market research context enables prospective customers to enter imaginatively into the service process. Actionable feedback—valuable insights into customer needs and perceptions—is the likely result when the market is given actionable input in the form of a service blueprint.

FIGURE 36-11 Blueprint for the Discount Brokerage House.

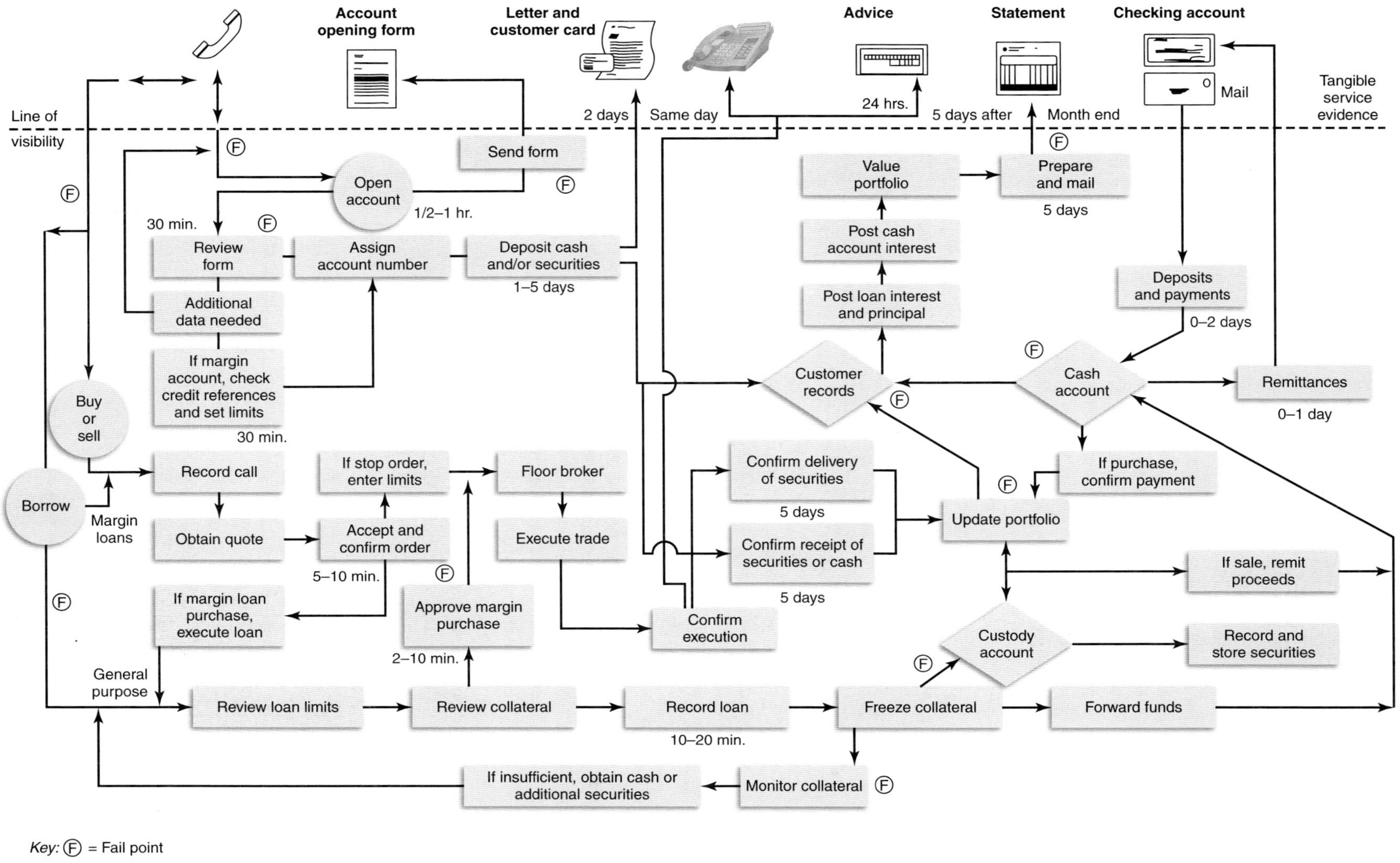

Source: Reprinted by permission of *Harvard Business Review*, exhibit from "Designing Services That Deliver" by G. Lynn Shostack, January/February 1984 issue. Copyright © 1991 by President and Fellows of Harvard College; all rights reserved.

From concept testing to price testing, from testing consumer response to statements to testing consumer response to uniforms on service representatives, each stage of development and operation benefits from well-crafted research.

WHAT GOES INTO A MASTER DESIGN

This stage represents the final pre-implementation blueprint. At this stage, the blueprint should be translated into a written document that includes a structural description of how the service system works, a pro forma financial projection based on pricing strategies derived from cost analysis of the functional design, an implementation plan that includes staff requirements, training, control and auditing standards, a market positioning and introduction strategy, including advertising/promotion, and a list of remaining issues. At this stage, issues become more and more specific, reaching to detailed levels such as design of customer statements, telemarketing, time/motion performance standards, selection of technologies, and mobilization of operating units. Even at this stage, hundreds of decisions remain to be made before the service reaches its final form.

The Master Design will trigger the preparation of detailed implementation subplans. A new team will be formed, consisting of all the accountable parties. Each area that will be involved in rendering the service will work from the final service blueprint, translating it to grass-roots levels in the organization.

The Master Design also triggers preparation of performance standards and development of Service System Audit instruments at both consumer and employee levels. The Service System Audit may be thought of as a series of still shots taken of the service system from a variety of angles and perspectives. The measurement devices mentioned here are commonplace. What distinguishes a Service System Audit is the *integration* of results geared to produce a comprehensive picture of service performance. The manager of design synthesizes audit measures to produce a composite evaluation of service performance overall.

In developing the Service System Audit, managers rely on performance standards enunciated in the Master Design. Development of the Service System Audit is a team effort. Managers of evidence and process prepare a Consumer Audit that focuses on pre- and posttesting of consumer encounter points, service fail points, and evidence. Managers of process and means prepare an Employee Audit that not only measures productivity (time and throughput) and quality (accuracy and timeliness) but zeroes in on internal, nonprocess issues as well. These issues involve assessment of the *means* by which the service is created: systems, facilitating goods, and support service provided internally across departmental lines.

It should be noted that the Employee Audit mirrors the Consumer Audit. Where consumers express dissatisfaction with a given factor or service step, employees are in a position to identify *why* they were unable to perform as specified. Perhaps a computer system is inadequate, or a piece of evidence is missing or deficient. Because they are on the front lines of creating a service, employees are an indispensable source of service improvements.

The Service System Audit is the management tool for monitoring performance as conformance or deviation from standards established by the service system blueprint. Used imaginatively, the Service System Audit is also a useful tool for providing important performance feedback to employees. Such feedback lies at the heart of the self-monitoring of performance, which is often required in sophisticated service systems.

The blueprint will now be frozen until the post-implementation audit.

GET READY FOR IMPLEMENTATION

In this stage, the operational pieces of the service are put in place. Implementation requires a separate plan drawn from the Master Design. This sub-plan includes time and deliverable schedules based on working backward from the desired introduction date. As is true in all other phases of service design, hundreds of specific issues must be addressed, and every detail must be seriously considered. Staff must be housed and trained, procedures written, performance standards defined, and the entire process debugged. It is in this phase that delays, such as in telephone installations and delivery of the wrong equipment, occur.

If possible, pre-implementation planning should include an operating test of the service, using actual prospective customers. This is similar to product testing or market testing in a manufacturing environment.

BE SURE YOU DOCUMENT

After the entire implementation plan is established, the service is ready for market introduction. In this stage, advertising, direct mail, publicity, and service evidence such as customer statements are prepared. As is true throughout the service design and development cycle, each phase represents many complex processes. The development of advertising/promotion programs, for example, is a full-time activity that, for some services, may consume as much time as the design itself.

All standards for the system must now be specified, usually in the form of operating manuals, media programs, training plans, parallel computer tests, volume throughput standards, and such. Prices are set, quality expectations are defined, and evidence is produced. It is against this documentation that success or failure will be measured.

YOU ARE READY TO INTRODUCE THE SERVICE

The service goes live. Telephones ring, inquiries are answered, accounts are opened, customers visit, representatives perform. Transactions are executed.

During the first stages of market introduction, it is vitally important that all parts of the service be closely monitored, which means that every phone call must be recorded and followed up to determine why accounts are or are not being opened. It means that every transaction is logged, every employee's performance is tracked, every glitch is isolated. This research should continue long enough to cover at least several complete cycles of the service. If the customer requires six months to experience all aspects of the service, then monitoring should continue six months before the next phase is reached.

Many services are thrown haphazardly into the marketplace. Whether they function as designed, or function well or poorly, seems to be of little concern. Considering the extraordinary labor involved in creating a service, it is unfortunate when a service is abandoned at the point of its birth. There are product analogs for this sort of sloppiness, but they are rare among goods companies, which have learned the value of and practice highly refined post-introduction research.

In this stage, data gathered in the Consumer and Employee Audits during the implementation stage are synthesized, and corrections to the service are made. Also at this stage, the next steps for modifying or enhancing the service are identified, and the design/development cycle begins again.

SUMMARY

The process of designing and developing a service is exceedingly complex. The description of actual events given in this chapter is a condensed one.

The first lesson to learn about services is that they are complex systems. All parts of the system must be addressed when developing a new service.

Second, the process is iterative and largely definitional. The objective of service design is to establish a totally specific and rational definition of the total system. Through iteration, decisions are made that make the profile increasingly specific, until all the means for creating the service have been laid down in an explicit plan.

Third, a great deal of the process is verbal. As the service is developed, an expanding circle of people becomes involved. This process and the dialogue that accompanies serve to construct successive and more refined service portraits.

It is important to control this expanding circle, so that each stage is properly completed before new parties are brought into the design process. One characteristic of projects that do not do well seems to be that too many people are involved in early phases. Conversely, projects that are developed entirely by staff or "planners" usually do not do well either. The key appears to be to start with a limited number of people and to add others only when their roles can be clearly defined. At each stage, the importance of translating verbal input into pictorial or quantitative terms is critical. This provides the objective benchmark for subsequent input and keeps the service clearly defined.

Fourth, every service is unique. The design process itself shows that the probabilities of any two services arriving at precisely the same design are virtually nil. Many factors—from environments to people—add variations. These subtle differences can be points of differentiation.

Finally, whether the process is fully documented or not, good service design seems to require that all stages be completed. Projects that fail often skip stages or gloss over them. And service problems appear to be traceable directly to stages that were not properly or thoroughly executed.

In sum, the design and development of a service can be made rational, objective, methodological, and precise. Such an approach to developing service systems is of great utility to all service marketers in ensuring success and quality in the marketplace.

About the Authors

G. Lynn Shostack serves as chairman and president of Joyce International, Inc., a private $350 million company. She is a recognized authority on services marketing and the financial services industry. Ms. Shostack currently writes a column on innovation and entrepreneurship for *The Journal of Business Strategy*.

Jane Kingman-Brundage is founding principal of Kingman-Brundage, Inc., a management consulting firm that is situated in North Salem, New York, and that emphasizes service system design and implementation. She specializes in the service blueprinting technique and has employed it on behalf of clients in major banks, investment institutions, and *Fortune* 500 companies.

37

NEW SERVICE DEVELOPMENT THROUGH THE LENS OF ORGANISATIONAL LEARNING: EVIDENCE FROM LONGITUDINAL CASE STUDIES

Eric Stevens*

Groupe ESCEM, 1 rue Léo Delibes, 37205 Tours, France

Sergios Dimitriadis

Athens University of Economics and Business, Patission 76, 10434 Athens, Greece

ABSTRACT

The paper examines the interest and limits of an organisational learning (OL) model for better understanding the new service development process. Based on the literature linking new service development and OL, the opportunity to use Crossan et al.'s [Acad. Manage. Rev. 24 (1999) 3.] 4I multilevel learning model in studying new service development process is discussed. In order to test the interest and limits of the model, a longitudinal and comparative case study methodology is described, using two cases of new service development process, the restructuring of the nonfood department of a supermarket and the launch of a new retail bank service package. The empirical findings support the overall interest of the 4I OL model, since several actions and loops of learning were observed, such as intuition, interpretation, integration and institutionalisation. These exploratory results encourage further research to study new service development through an OL lens and provide managers with insights for facilitating learning during the new service development process.
© 2003 Elsevier Inc. All rights reserved.

KEYWORDS

New service; Development process; Organisational learning; Model testing; Longitudinal research.

INTRODUCTION

The growing service economy, accounting for more than 70% of the GNP and of the employment in most developed countries, places service activities in the first place of growth drivers and makes new service development a critical issue for firms' success.

*Corresponding author. Tel.: +33-24771-7190; fax: +33-24771-7307. *E-mail addresses:* estevens@escem.fr (E. Stevens), dimitria@aueb.gr (S. Dimitriadis).

Stevens, Eric and Sergios Dimitriadis, (2004), "New Service Development Through the Lens of Organisational Learning: Evidence from Longitudinal Case Studies," *Journal of Business Research*, vol. 57, no. 10, pp. 1074–1084.

Yet, although the new product development (NPD) has very early attracted the attention of researchers, the development of new services remains a much less investigated research field. This seems even more surprising considering that from the early 1980s it has been underlined that services are fundamentally different from products (Berry, 1980; Shostack, 1984) and that their study requires specific frames of analysis—particularly systemic frameworks (Fitzsimmons and Fitzsimmons, 2001; Langeard and Eiglier, 1987; De Bandt, 1994).

The literature on new services is scarce, mainly marketing-driven and mostly focused on the financial sector. Empirical findings do not result in a theoretical framework that could support the understanding of the phenomenon (Johne and Storey, 1998; Johnson et al., 1999). Moreover, some authors suggested that empirical findings are more or less contradictory (De Brentani, 1989, 1991, 1993; Sundbo, 1997). Given the lack of consistency in empirical results, this article attempts to introduce an organisational learning (OL) approach in new service development research. It investigates the relevance of the 4I OL model (Crossan et al., 1999) in describing and understanding the new service development process.

The article is organised as follows. The Background section reviews previous theory and empirical evidence on new service development and organisation learning and concludes with the research propositions. The Methodology section presents the longitudinal case study research design and the two projects studied. The Results section describes the new service development process and the learning activities that took place during it. The Discussion section elaborates on the usefulness and limits of the tested model and draws implications of these preliminary results. The paper concludes on key findings and their contribution to existing knowledge.

NEW SERVICE DEVELOPMENT BACKGROUND

As services are generally defined as deeds, acts or performances that may be tangible or intangible (Berry, 1980; Gronroos, 1990; Gupta and Vajic, 2000), it is widely accepted that the very nature of a service leads to studying service production and delivery in a systemic approach. This approach has also been described as the "service concept" and formalized through blueprints by which service providers design the way the service offering is to be delivered (Shostack, 1984; Edwardsson et al., 2000; Fitzsimmons and Fitzsimmons, 2001). The transformation of any service offering—what the customer receives—either incremental or radical, will require the transformation of some elements of the service concept.

In line with the recommendations of Menor et al. (2002) about the potential fields of investigation, the present article adopts a managerial perspective and focuses on the development of new services that affects in some way the interaction process with the customer. It aims at understanding how the service organisation develops or redefines its service concept—not how the outcome of this process, the new service offering, performs on the market. Given this focus, the following sections review research on organisational issues of new service development, present the OL model that has been used in our field study and set the research propositions.

Organisational Issues in New Service Development

There is a lot of evidence on how new service development (hereafter abridged NSD) involves organisational issues and on how the organisation itself transforms during or after an NSD process. Thwaites (1992) and Edgett (1996) stated that the NSD process is based on multifunctional teams, specifically created for this task and that new services seem to be the result of this cooperation. Several authors mentioned that the level of personal contact maintained by the product manager, the commitment of the senior managers, the cross-functional team and the interaction process established all along the NSD influence the speed and effectiveness of the NSD (Edgett and Jones, 1991; Lievens et al., 2000; Froehle et al., 2001). Similarly, Hart and Service (1993) established that efficient NSD required a "functional integrative perspective," setting up less formal organisation, more communication, shared information and decision making.

Moreover, empirical evidence provided by Edgett and Jones (1991), Hart and Service (1993), Raesfeld Meijer et al. (1996), Jallat (1992) highlighted that the successful development of a new service entails changing the organisation itself, such as the creation of a new department or the restructuring of the distribution network.

Summarizing this body of literature it seems that (a) the NSD process appears as a cooperative, interactive, not very formalized process, involving actors from different departments of the company and (b) the organisational structure, the communication networks and the working processes are transformed by the NSD process. It may thus be argued that OL approaches can be useful in understanding the NSD process, as it has already been done to a certain extent for products by Van de Ven and Polley (1992).

New Service Development and OL

Initial statements that linked innovation to knowledge were made at a macroeconomic level and can be found in Nelson and Winter's (1982) evolutionist theory. At a micro level, Olson et al. (1995) investigated the links between NPD and learning. Maidique and Zirger (1990) revealed, through the analysis of 158 new products, that successes led to the creation of new knowledge while failures resulted in the unlearning of the processes which lead to success. Similarly, Simon (1991, p. 183) considers innovation as a classical OL process. The research of Van de Ven and Polley (1992), and Van de Ven and Chen (1996) find no support for a model of trial-and-error learning during the initial period of innovation development, but strong support for such model during the ending development period when innovations where being introduced to the market. More explicitly, Madhavan and Grover (1998) stated that development teams are engaged in a knowledge-producing activity that will be embodied in the new products.

Further on, innovation has been described as a process of reduction of uncertainty, anchored within groups and social networks (Pearson, 1991; Akrich et al., 1998). The research on interfunctional communication flows (Lievens and Moenaert, 2000; Lievens et al., 2000) demonstrated that the codification of knowledge, as well as the nature of the established network, will determine the communication among the members of a development team. Moorman and Miner (1997) argued that the organisational memory affects the NPD by influencing the interpretations of the incoming information and the development procedures.

Finally, Nonaka (1994) demonstrated the existence of links between NPD and a learning process. According to his research, it is because teams produce new inferences that they are able to create new products. It is through the production and testing of inferences and through mutual adjustment of representations that the development team is able to design a result in accordance with its expectations.

This important stream of research pointing that OL can be an important component of NPD or NSD justifies the empirical test of a formal but theoretical OL model as suggested by Brown and Eisenhardt (1995) and Trott (1998).

The OL Model

The literature on OL is flourishing due to the complexity of a concept that links individual learning with organisational behaviour and organisational change. Koenig (1994) has defined OL "as a collective process of acquisition and creation of competencies, which will modify the way situations are managed and will transform the situations themselves." Due to this intrinsic complexity of the OL, very few models have attempted to combine the individual and the OL in an integrative approach. Based on the previous work of Argyris and Schon (1996), Kim (1993), Nonaka and Takeuchi, (1995), Crossan et al. (1999) developed a detailed model integrating the learning at the different levels of the organisation. The building of collective knowledge is based on four subprocesses: intuiting, interpreting, integrating and institutionalising, which are supposed to occur at different organisational levels (individuals,

FIGURE 37-1   Organisational Learning as a Dynamic Process (Crossan et al., 1999)

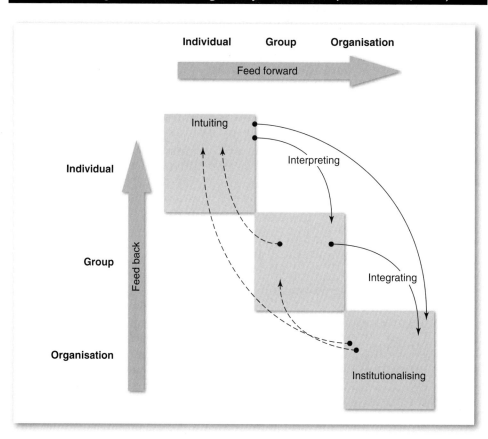

groups and organisation). The dynamic aspect of such a process of OL is shown in Figure 37-1 as the 4I's model. The model suggests that the organisation must manage the tension between what has been previously institutionalised and the emergence of new knowledge as highlighted by March (1991).

Compared to previous works (March and Olsen, 1975; Argyris and Schon, 1996; Daft and Weick, 1984; Nonaka and Takeuchi, 1995), this model presents many interests. While it is consistent with previous models, it provides a framework, which explains the links among individual, group and organisation levels. Moreover, it describes OL as a process: the main stages are identified; the interactions among the different levels of the organisation are recognized; the respective influence of the individuals on the creation of routines is described; the feedback effects of the routines previously created on the individual intuiting and interpreting are highlighted. This approach reveals the importance of the institutionalisation for the entire process as demonstrated by Argyris (1999) in many case studies.

The 4I model also appears to be of great interest for our research. First, it provides an extensive interpretation framework that encompasses the research previously quoted on the communication flows, organisational memory and structure. Second, it adds the idea that learning while innovating does not concern only the development team. The model encompasses the return effects of the previous knowledge that could either enhance or prevent further developments. Third, the systemic nature of the service concept advocates the use of a model that captures the multilevel actions required to perform a service. Finally, this model provides explanations on the links between the creation of knowledge and its transformation into standards, deeds, acts and performance.

Research Propositions

Following the arguments presented above, the research aims at testing whether during the NSD process there is an OL process occurring in the way the 4I model describes it.

If so, the empirical data must relate the following set of events: (1) NSD is achieved through many stages, (2) occurring at different levels of the organisation, (3) in the following sequence of events: at the initiation stage of NSD, changes in context, "routinised actions," procedures and "rules of thumb" result into cognitive conflicts at individual level. Due to those cognitive conflicts, individuals will develop new intuitions resulting from their own tacit experience. They will produce new inferences by linking expected gains to the implementation of a new set of procedures. Those individual intuitions will be tested and/or shared. Thus, convergence of representations is achieved through confrontations of diverging opinions. The creation of a formal and informal social network will support the convergence of representations. Those new inferences, which are tested and shared, may result into the implementation of a new set of procedures, which will be institutionalised in the case of perceived success. The transfer of newly created routines to other parts of the organisation will induce a new OL process.

Although these events may not capture all actions and forms of learning, if they occur as predicted by the 4I model, one could conclude that (a) OL is happening during an NSD process and (b) it happens at the levels and with the type of actions the 4I model suggests.

RESEARCH METHOD

Research Design and Data Collection

To make the observations, a comparative longitudinal case study research approach was used. It appeared to be the most appropriate method in order to identify the main sequences of events of NSD processes while they happen and to avoid the "ex-post rationalisation" phenomena (Van de Ven and Poole, 1990; Van de Ven and Huber, 1990). They also provide insights on decision before, during and after the events. Another reason of this methodological choice is that a research on learning entails a causal perspective on behaviour (Cohen and Manion, 1994) in which if something is learned at one moment of the process, the behaviours will be modified at another point of the process.

Data collection was based on multiple semidirective interviews all along the development process at different hierarchical levels, observation, text analysis of internal and external documents such as market reports, reports from consultants, reports from the internal meetings advertisements and promotional leaflets, procedures charts and routines supporting the production of the service. The interview protocol items are provided in Appendix A.

The interviews were recorded on tapes and transcribed on paper. Notes were taken during the different meetings and observations were written in a research diary. Verbal declarations were triangulated by crossing different sources (Stake, 1995; Yin, 1994).

The unit of analysis of the research was defined as the NSD project itself. Thus, the investigations focused on the content of the new services, the NSD process, as well as the organisational features of the company before, during and after the NSD. Finally, the firm's environment was encompassed in the observation by gathering information from the staff and from the reports and information they used. This approach is justified, in a constructivist perspective; by the need to understand the decision-making process during the development from the actor's perspective.

The Choice of the Companies and the NSD Projects

Two different sectors have been selected, retailing and banking. Changes in the competitive context, in the existing know-how, in the portfolio of existing services, in the organisation charts and in the strategic intends, provided opportunities to establish cross case patterns in the development process. By doing so, a theoretical sampling strategy was adopted to reinforce external validity (Eisenhardt, 1989; Yin, 1994; Huberman and Miles, 1994). Two NSD projects, one in each sector, were investigated.

In order to observe the expected events, ongoing development projects were selected. The investigations covered two years and a half for each project. The two selected companies had an NSD project in progress and were interested in being part of this research. They accepted to give free access to all documents, data and actors we thought relevant to the research. This collaboration was an additional criterion for the selection of the companies.

The Retailer Project

Cora is a well-known retailer in France. The global turnover of this company was nearly 10 billion euros in 1998. We focused our research on Cora's hypermarkets in France, where there are 60 outlets with an average size of $8700\,m^2$. The "Universe" project aimed at increasing the store's attraction in relation to specialised retailers through improvement of the nonfood part of the store. The project began in September 1994 and was supposed to be finished by the beginning of 1999.

The Bank Project

Crédit Mutuel was created in 1882 in the east part of France and currently ranked third level of all French banks in terms of its distribution network. The bank is managed according to its cooperative principles but the portfolio of financial products is very similar to the one offered by the competitors. We observed the innovative process of the Anjou federation, which accounts for more than 230,000 clients and over 12.7 billion francs of deposits. The initial idea of the project was to replace detailed and complicated billing with a predefined package. This resulted in a major change for both bankers and clients. Packages had to be transformed to be attractive and useful by defining the kind of products that should be included. Moreover, the bank had to decide how many packages to propose in order to satisfy the different categories of clients. Lastly, it had to construct the process to placate and gain support from their most important clients.

Both projects aimed at designing a new standardised process with low customer involvement in the delivery process, having noticed that the development process for nonstandardised offers may be impossible to compare (Shostack, 1987; Lovelock, 1983). Moreover, the two companies had a significant network of outlets. This allowed us to observe the way the development team and the other levels of the organisation interacted with front office staff, specifically during the crucial implementation stage. The two projects were of similar importance. The reimplementation of two thirds of a store for 60 hypermarkets meant the transformation of at least 300,000 m^2 of sales area. The transformation of the client contracts with Crédit Mutuel clients meant negotiating them with more than 230,000 customers in the federation of Anjou. Due to their importance, those projects entailed the participation of all organisational levels with a similar potential involvement. The general management was concerned by the strategic aspect of the project as well as by the organisational consequences of change. Similarly, the operational local level had to implement decisions made by top management.

The two projects have since then been launched on the market and are considered to be successful by the management of the respective companies. Although the early results were too limited to assess the impact on market share and profitability, the managers were satisfied regarding both customer expectations (demand exceeded the initial forecasts) and internal adoption. Our investigations stopped 3 months after the launching stage.

RESULTS

The analysis of the two NSD processes produced extremely rich and insightful information. The overall statement that emerged from the comparison of the two processes is that, apart from learning loops, none of the stages, actions or decisions can be considered similar. Contexts, organisations, people and results from the past led each institution to adopt singular solutions. However, the adoption of learning strategies, implicit or explicit, was common in both cases. Thus, the results detail the learning actions and the factors that supported or prevented them along three broad stages of the NSD: the initiation of the process, the formal development and the implementation stage.

The Initiation of the NSD Process

The first observation was that no specific department in either organisation was formally in charge of NSD. Also, there was no organised process systematically reviewing all ideas and aiming at generating new concepts, which is consistent with previous evidence (Thwaites, 1992; Scheuing and Johnson, 1989; Edgett, 1996).

The beginning of the learning process in both cases found its source in the occurrence of a cognitive conflict. Moscovici and Doise (1992) called cognitive conflict as the discrepancy occurring between the expectations of an output made by an actor and the actual result. In both projects, the initial cognitive conflict resulted from a decrease in the results achieved by the organisation. The market share of the retailer was decreasing as nonfood competitors were setting up a large number of new outlets. The bank's profitability was falling continuously during the 1990s. Furthermore, some actors added other unsatisfactory results. In retailing, the purchase manager who developed the initial project had to cope with coordination problems with the stores and found some opportunity to improve this situation. As a result, they changed their own representations of what a store might be in order to achieve better results. At this stage, the new representations were considered as intuitions in the sense that they were not tested. The actors interpreted data, events and facts as signals that something was not working as they expected. Based on their intuitions, they progressively built informal proposals, which entailed changing the existing causal links. Those proposals were somewhat vague and at this stage could not constitute a solution in themselves.

During this first stage, which precedes any formal development, the sole statement of the individual intuition is not sufficient to lead to the creation of a development group, mainly because the decision processes involved many individuals. This suggests that the position of the individuals concerned with the problem had a great influence on the creation of the development group. In both cases, the projects were initiated by the middle management, which had enough power to refer to a higher committee. Furthermore, they had enough power to implement their initial intuition in order to test it, which they did. Finally, they had learned from previous situations and strategic perspectives adopted by general management.

This meant that very quickly, initial intuitions were transferred to the group level, as the 4I model predicts. The test of intuitions was achieved through informal conversations in the personal networks and had two purposes. First, sharing the initial idea aimed to create of an informal network of people sharing similar concerns. The importance of this network, and the position of each of its members, strongly affected the recognition of a problem within the organisation. Second, each trial contributed to reducing uncertainty. The creation of a development project, without having made any experiments before, seemed impossible. As a result, through the use of informal discussions, interested people contributed to a shared definition of the problem the organisation faced. These observations are in line with the research on social networks and interfunctional communication of Hart and Service (1993), Pearson (1991), Lievens and Moenaert (2000).

The comparisons of the two cases revealed that, even though the contexts, decisions and organisations were different, the emergence of both projects relied on a similar loop of learning which led to the identification of development opportunities, the appointment of project leader and the creation of a formal working group.

The Formal Development Stage

The observation of intermediate and final results, the number of stages and the kind of actors involved in the NSD revealed no linear development pattern as those proposed by Cooper (1994) and Edgett and Jones (1991), but rather a weakly structured NSD process (Edgett, 1996; Salleh and Easingwood, 1993). Learning processes constituted the rationale behind the main stages. For example, the selection of team members (a), the interactions that occurred all along the development (b), as well as the formalisation of procedures (c) could be explained by using the learning framework. This section will detail those three major aspects of the observed NSD.

The composition of development teams changed constantly along the processes. No members were directly involved in the entire process, from its very beginning to the launching. Even the project managers changed along the different stages. In retailing, the initiator of the project changed after 1 year due to a change of function in the same organisation. Then the second project manager changed after another year of tests, due to the return of the previous manager. Then, the people in charge of the communication joined the development group and created the first promotional leaflet based on the concept of the "universe of interior." Having achieved the first promotional test of the concept, the initial team was replaced by staff members in charge of the implementation in the stores.

In both cases, the nomination of a project manager required consideration of his competencies and his position in the structure. Though the criteria themselves differed in the two cases due to the difference of the internal context, the choices were based on the same kind of reasoning. In both cases, the choices relied strongly on the identification of the kind of problems expected to arise. The leader was chosen according to his competencies to solve the kind of problems that were likely to happen. If those competencies were expected to diverge, many project managers may be chosen.

Most decisions were taken after a learning process had occurred, mainly through interactions among staff members. The confrontation of divergent points of view on the same problem led to modifications of the initial framework by the integration of major objections. This occurred through formal and informal conversations, mails, telephone calls, meetings and reports. The sharing of the ideas enriched the initial framework of all participants. This transformation corresponds to the creation of a new representation that could result in a new procedure or design. In the case of retailing, the dialogues resulted in the drawing of a first map of the "universe concept" that has been progressively refined according to the comments of the participants. Because the options were decided through the confrontation of ideas, the staff excluded from the interaction processes could not contribute to the refinement of initial ideas leading to launch delays. In both cases, the computer department was not involved in the initial discussions. As a result, the development team discovered new problems during the late stages of the development process. For the bank, the initial launch date had to be delayed due to the time required to develop programs. Similarly for the retailer, the development team discovered at the end of the process that a change of categories involved rewriting the entire computer program, since all the reporting systems based on gap analysis was threatened. This process delayed the launch by 1 year demonstrating that with no interaction, the OL process could not occur.

Further, it was observed that the interaction process as well as the testing of the ideas could not occur without formalisation of the ideas. In the case of banking, the writing of procedures led to discussions on the invoicing process of the new service package. Without such formal presentation of ideas, people could not react and thus, could not contribute to the improvement of the draft by adding their knowledge. All along the process, multiple documents were produced detailing parts of the new offers, and the interaction with clients. Those documents were used during meetings and interactions in order to detail the options and processes, until a relative consensus was achieved. Finally, the two developments resulted in a written document that described for the retailing of the new product categories and, for the bank, the scenarios of interaction with clients. Those descriptions were used to redesign the information systems, the facilities and the training of the employees for the implementation stage.

Beyond the establishment of the learning process itself (Nonaka and Takeuchi, 1995; Crossan et al., 1999), these observations confirmed (a) the importance of cooperation, integration and a broad scope of competencies inside the development group, and (b) the negative impact of the lack of communication on the effectiveness of the

NSD process (Lievens et al., 2000), that results in an absence of learning (Maidique and Zirger, 1990).

The Implementation Stage

After the decision to implement the concept, the development team had to imagine different ways to replicate the concept in all outlets. The means used to constrain the interaction process were multiple: information meetings, personnel training, publication of internal documents and reports describing the service, redefinition of the individual goals and the measurement of gaps, organisation charts using the information system, furniture and warehouse disposal, and promotional actions. Although such a list appeared to be very long, all of those means were adopted during the implementation of both services. The most significant of them will be discussed below.

First, the information system appeared to be one of the most efficient ways to institutionalise the new service. For the bank, once the electronic office integrated the concept, employees were forced to follow the programmed procedure. Due to the use of the electronic office, procedures were directly frozen during the programming. "Institutionalisation" results from compulsory use of the information system.

Second, the promotional means provided an explicit description of the final outcomes and parts of the delivery process. Thus, they created client's expectations and forced employees and the organisation to produce an offer similar to the description.

Third, the routinisation of the processes appeared as another institutionalisation means, though mostly unconscious. The routinisation of behaviours occurred each time the first trials produced satisfactory results. In this case, the people repeated the initial sequence without having to follow a detailed, analytical and step-by-step process. The memorisation of the sequence resulted in less use of the explicit procedures linked to its achievement. After some successful repetitions, the individual went directly to the prescribed behaviour without having to think of the different steps. By avoiding time-consuming mechanisms, the individual performed a faster process. But in this case, he also forgot the detailed processes. This process, which Nonaka and Takeuchi (1995) called the interiorisation, provided one of the most efficient means to institutionalise the new procedures.

The last means used to institutionalise the new service was the social network, made of the individuals who supported the delivery process. As routinisation, social network is not easily perceived as a means in itself and may be mixed up with the organisational change. The study of the implementation of the "universe" in the stores revealed that the department managers had to coordinate their actions with new actors. Rather than remaining specialised within the same department, they had to exchange information and know-how in order to achieve a good performance. Each time this new network did not function, for personal reasons, for example, the department managers were less efficient. The repetition of the information sharing through interaction resulted in the reinforcement of the network supported by the existence of well-established relationships among individuals. In this way, the social network contributed to institutionalising the new service. Such findings are consistent with the multiple observations of Raesfeld Meijer et al. (1996), Hart and Service (1993), Jallat (1992), Lievens et al. (2000), Froehle et al. (2001) who suggested that NSD may transform organisational features.

DISCUSSION AND IMPLICATIONS

Interest of the OL 4I Model

The 4I's model asserted that OL is achieved through a process of four broad actions: intuiting, interpreting, integrating and institutionalising, occurring at an individual, group and organisational level. Observations of the two development processes provided repeated evidence for these actions at each stage of the NSD process. A brief summary of some evidence is provided in Appendix B. Intuiting appears throughout the development process as one of the pivotal activities of individuals. A good illustration of this is the names of the projects themselves, which changed intentionally in order to express the managerial intuition. The Cora team, after having called the project "nonfood refurbishing," adopted the vocable "Universe project." The use of "Universe" referred both to categories regrouping similar families of products, to the space and design and to the future of the store. At the individual level, the use of this metaphor, its vagueness itself, forced new ways of interpretation and stimulated individual intuitions.

The second stage required having a social activity of interpreting, which was usually the implicit purpose of the development meetings. Far from the initial agenda, the teams devoted a lot of time to discuss the issue of the projects. They used examples from other sectors in order to clarify a common goal. The banking team used multiple references to the packages used in the mobile phone industry. The retailing team used the vocabulary from theatre. Those meetings typically closed when all the participants agreed on the vocabulary and thus, on the actions that must be implemented to achieve the definition adopted.

Discussion occurred also when adjustments were required. Given their strong specialisation, none of the actors were able to deliver the entire offer. Therefore, the major purpose of the discussions was to adjust actors' behaviours, to adapt the solution to the department's constraints and/or to adapt the department so that it could produce the output. The 4I model suggests that a failure in the interpreting and integrating stage will prevent OL. As described above, we observed such a failure when the computer departments were involved very late in the development process. Moreover, these departments developed a separate culture and their own vocabulary, far from the one shared in the development groups. As a result, the two projects had to be postponed for more than 1 year. This time was used by the computer engineers in order to understand the project (create a joined vocabulary) and to adjust their own actions to the rest of the group.

Finally, the 4I model predicts that a successful experience will be inscribed in the organisational memory through an institutionalising stage. In the retailing case, the creation and implementation of the "Universe" required transforming the organisational chart, modifying databases and programs used by the information systems, to reorganise the storage of products. Similarly, the launching of the new packages led to entirely rewriting the account management, adjusting the task performed by the sellers in the network of outlets, redesigning the back office organisation and, by doing so, transforming the organisational chart. This stage appeared as a key point for most managers, as they pointed out that without such kind of action, the new service simply could not exist.

The fit of our findings with the 4I model indicates that its multilevel perspective can provide an extensive framework that includes multiple dimensions of the systemic services production process. By doing so, the model gives sense to previous findings that were difficult to understand otherwise. This explains the stated relationship between communication flows and efficiency of the developments (Lievens and Moenaert, 2000). Translated into the vocabulary of 4I's model, communication flows support the interpretation and integration stages and therefore contribute to the creation of OL. Similarly, the work of Raesfeld Meijer et al. (1996) revealed that the exclusion of one member of the organisation explained the failure in the launching of a new service. The 4I's model suggests that learning is strongly linked to the creation of social networks that support the interpretation and integration stages.

Implications for Future Research

The 4I's model may contribute to extending the field of the research on NSD in several ways. By underlining the institutionalisation stage, it strongly indicates that the management of development projects encompasses the management of organisational changes that are required to embed knowledge into the organisational features. Links between organisational change and the ability to develop new services may thus be investigated. Moreover, the feedback effects of previous learning on acquisition of knowledge could bring further explanations on the factors that prevent innovation.

The 4I's model can also provide an interesting alternative to the linear process made of predefined and successive stages (Cooper, 1994) that has been invalidated for services (Scheuing and Johnson, 1989; Salleh and Easingwood, 1993; Jallat, 1992; Roth et al., 1997). It suggests that the main stages of development are justified by the need to transform the initial intuitions into a body of routines and procedures embedded in the organisational features. Also, the occurrence, role and impact of OL on NSD processes could further be tested through a quantitative approach, which would enhance the validity of our findings. Finally, as noted in the Limits of Research section, the dilemma between the benefits and the cost of learning may become an additional direction for future research.

Implications for Managers

The validation of a learning model as a framework for analysing NSD offers new perspectives for service managers. By facilitating the occurrence of the learning as described above, people in charge of the project could improve the efficiency of the development process. For instance, our findings suggest that project managers should focus their attention on the individual competencies involved in the development team: integrating the right skills and people at the right stage of NSD may be considered as a success factor that will save time, energy and reduce costs. A second recommendation emphasises the importance of informal communication within the development groups. Expression of the individual intuitions, conversations within the group, confrontations of individual points of view should result in the creation of innovative results. This way of building solutions through social interactions should lead to frequent iterations in the development process.

Finally, the NSD process should benefit from the implementation of all the learning actions available. Instead of fearing failure, all individuals and groups involved in the development process should be encouraged to find new ideas through testing and learning through making mistakes. Such experimentation is possible only if the organisation actively supports such attitudes that contribute to enriching the experience. It seems impossible to achieve such a result without having a support from the general management.

Limits of the Research

However, both the model itself and the methodology used imply several limits to our findings. As far as the model is concerned, many decisions could not be interpreted as resulting from a learning process. In the banking project, after an initial profitability and costs analysis, the project manager decided that the bill would be sent together with the other administrative documents by mail. This meant that the consumer would be charged at the moment that he received the bill. The general manager, who adopted the principle of "transparency towards the client," according to which the consumer must be informed before being charged, invalidated this decision. Because the decision was based on a principle, one cannot speak about a learning process. One reason for this non-learning functioning was the perceived duration and cost of learning: each learning loop necessitates spending time in the experimentation of the results and in the analysis of the outcomes.

Another weak point of the model is that it fails to integrate the resistance to change factors. It asserts that, due to the building of a learning process at the individual and group levels, the organisation will adopt new features. Our observations pointed out that this result could not be systematically achieved. For example, many stores delayed the implementation of the "Universe" due to managerial or planning constraints. Though the model includes the return effect of previous knowledge, it does not mention the resistance to change that could prevent the institutionalisation or even the interpretation and integration stage.

Finally, the qualitative methodologies present the well-recognised problem of external validity and generalisation of the findings. In-depth case studies may be considered very context specific. Consequently, our findings should be considered as exploratory, needing to be confirmed in a larger context.

CONCLUSION

The purpose of the present article was to examine the relevance and the interest of an OL model in better describing and understanding the NSD process. The evidence from the two longitudinal case studies revealed that learning activities occurred throughout the process at different levels: individual, group and organisational. Although the consequences of OL on the efficiency of the NSD process are limited, it seems that learning enriched, facilitated and contributed positively to the successful progress of the process, while nonlearning caused delays. The OL process was not linear and neither was the NSD process, as several learning loops and many revisions were observed until the very last stages of implementation.

To our knowledge, this is the first attempt to test empirically an OL model in the context of NSD. In the light of our exploratory findings, it can be suggested that, by completing the existing frameworks, the OL in general, and the Crossan et al. (1999) model in particular, seem to have important potential to enhance the understanding of the management of new services and may constitute a major investigation field for the next few years.

Acknowledgements
The authors thank the anonymous reviewers whose detailed and constructive comments contributed to significantly enhance the quality of the initial manuscript.

APPENDIX A. PROTOCOL FOR THE SEMIDIRECTIVE INTERVIEWS

About Interviewees

In the retailing project, we conducted interviews with two chief executives, one head of purchasing department, one head of communication department and three purchase managers at the corporate level, then five store managers, four department coordinators and five department managers at the store level. Questionnaires were administrated to department coordinators as well as to the store and department managers. In the bank project, the interviews concerned: chief executives, federation coordinator, sales manager, organisation manager, head of the software development, head of the administrative department, head of marketing department.

About Interview Protocol

Longitudinal methodology entails adopting two kinds of protocol, according to the stage of the survey. The first interviews were focused on the contextual data. The following interviews aimed at gathering all the events linked to the development process itself.

(A) First, we provided a short and vague description of the research topic:

> As this research is about innovation, we would like to understand how service companies develop new services. Our purpose is to gather data about perceptions of people in charge of the project, the way they are taking decisions, the main stages that they observed and the factors that facilitate or prevent, from their point of view, the development. Having checked the reports, I noticed you have been involved in the project. What interests us is your perception of what happened.

(B) Then we moved to questions more related to the development, with four broad kind of topics linked (a) to the history of the project as it is perceived by the interviewee, (b) to the content of the change linked to the NSD, (c) to the decision-making process and (d) to the uncertainty of the process:

> Could you describe the history of the project as you perceived it? What triggered the development? Which stages did you distinguish? Which

decisions were taken? By who? Do you know why those persons were involved in the development process? From your own perspective, which are the potential pitfall and opportunities? . . . What was transformed by this decision (when mentioned by the interviewee)? How formal was the decision? Was there an impact to the decision? Could you justify this decision? Did you agree or not? Did you use specific material to make the decision?

(C) We paid attention to keep a nondirective approach during the investigations. As we did repetitive interviews with the persons in charge of the development process, we repeated more or less those four broad kinds of questions. What changed with time is the fact that we concentrated on specific stages that had just finished or began.

APPENDIX B. SAMPLE EVIDENCES SUPPORTING THE 4I MODEL UTILITY

Stages of the 4I Model	*Events and Evidences from the Case Studies*	*Contribution of 4I's Model in Understanding What Happened*
Intuiting	(A) The management of the retailer chose an ambiguous name for the project: "the universe," which is an ambiguous term, opening significations to space, to groups of products (in French), to consumption activities. (B) The management changed the name of the head of department to head of the Universe, during the project, and then came back to head of the department.	(A) By choosing ambiguous names, the management opened space for new ideas to come up. This way of doing prevented the organisation from restraining the individual perception to what had been institutionalised earlier. (B) Those choices were deliberately adopted in order to change the job description of the head of the department. The use of ambiguity contributes to redesign the function by fostering a new approach through individual contributions.
Interpreting	(A) Contradictory debates occurred about what could be the "universes" of consumption for retailing, the kind of products they must gather, the kind of needs they must cover. (B) For the Bank, there have been many and passionate debates about the content of the package as well as the process of billing the client.	As the organisation opened the space for interpretation with ambiguous vocabulary, the individuals produced their own interpretations of what must be done. As a result, a flow of diverging assumptions rose to the point that only discussions and tests could lead progressively to convergence. Each debate appeared to transform the individual intuitions of one or two protagonists. A successful development process appeared to be a process where the interpretations led to convergence.
Integrating	(A) There was a strong interaction among the different parts of the organisation in order to design the body of rules and procedures. (B) Both organisations created multifunctional teams for the project.	Organising a complete process requires multiple competencies. The organisation selected the team members according to their competencies to solve the kind of problems which were expected to occur. As predicted at this stage by the 4I model, the development team integrated the constraints of the different contributors to the offer.
Institutionalising	Both organisations introduced the computer department into the project during the latest stages of the development.	As programming does not accept uncertainties and changes, the introduction of the computing department meant that the process is entirely formalised and that the stage of debates is over. Thus, having programmed the information in the system, it becomes very costly to change rules and procedures. This constitutes one way to institutionalise what has been designed.

References

Akrich M, Callon M, Latour B. A quoi tiennent les innovations. Ann Mines, Gérer Compr 1998 June;4–29.

Argyris C. On organisational learning. 2nd ed. Blackwell: Oxford; 1999.

Argyris C, Schon DA. Organisational learning: II. Theory, method and practice. Addison-Wesley: Boston; 1996. p. 13.

Berry LL. Service marketing is different. Business 1980 May–June;24–8.

Brown SL, Eisenhardt KM. Product development: past research, present findings and future directions. Acad Manage Rev 1995;20(2):343–78.

Cohen L, Manion L. Research methods in education. Routledge; 1994.

Cooper RG. Winning at new products. Addison-Wesley: Boston; 1994.

Crossan MM, Lane HW, White RE. An organisational learning framework: from intuition to institution. Acad Manage Rev 1999;24(3):522–37.

Daft RL, Weick KE. Toward a model of organisation as interpretation systems. Acad Manage Rev 1984;9:284–95.

De Bandt J. De l'Economie des Biens à l'Economie des Services: la Production de Richesses dans et par les Services. In: Gadrey J, De Bandt J, editors. Relations de service, marchés de service. Paris: CNRS; 1994. p. 309–38.

De Brentani U. Success and failure in new industrial services. J Prod Innov Manag 1989 December;6:239–58.

De Brentani U. Success factors in developing new business services. Eur J Mark 1991;25(2):35–59.

De Brentani U. The new product process in financial services: strategy for success. Int J Bank Mark 1993; 11(3):15–22.

Edgett S. The new product development process for commercial financial services. Ind Mark Manage 1996;25: 507–15.

Edgett S, Jones S. New product development in the financial service industry: a case study. J Market Manag 1991;7: 271–84.

Edwardsson B, Gustavsson A, Johnson MD, Sanden B. New service development and innovation in the new economy. Lund (Sweden): Studentlitteratur; 2000.

Eisenhardt KM. Building theories from case study research. Acad Manage Rev 1989;14(4):540.

Fitzsimmons JA, Fitzsimmons MJ. Service management, operation, strategy and information technology. 3rd ed. McGraw-Hill: New York; 2001.

Froehle CM, Roth AV, Chase RB, Voss CA. Antecedents of new service development effectiveness: an exploratory examination of strategic operations choices. J Serv Res 2001;3(1):3–17.

Gronroos C. Service management and marketing. Lexington Books; 1990. p. 26–7.

Gupta S, Vajic M. The contextual and dialectic nature of experiences. In: Fitzsimmons JA, Fitzsimmons MJ, editors. New service development, creating memorable experiences. Sage: London; 2000. p. 25–43.

Hart SJ, Service LM. Cross functional integration in the new product introduction process: an application of action science in service. J Serv Manag 1993;4(3).

Huberman AM, Miles MB. Qualitative data analysis. 2nd ed. London: Sage; 1994.

Jallat F. Management de l'innovation dans les entreprises de service au particulier: concept, processus et performances. Thèse de Doctorat de l'niversité de Aix-Marseille III, Juin, 1992.

Johne A, Storey C. New service development: a review of literature and annotated bibliography. Eur J Mark 1998;32(3):184–251.

Johnson SP, Menor U, Chase RB, Roth AV. A critical evaluation of the new services development process: integrating service innovation and service design. In: Fitzsimmons JA, Fitzsimmons MJ, editors. New service development, creating memorable experiences. Sage: London; 1999. p. 15–24.

Kim DH. The link between individual and organisational learning. Sloan Manage Rev 1993;37–50.

Koenig G. L'apprentissage organisationnel: repérage des lieux. Rev Fr Gest 1994;76–83.

Langeard E, Eiglier P. Servuction: le marketing des services. Paris: McGraw-Hill; 1987.

Lievens A, Moenaert RK. New service teams as information-processing systems: reducing innovative uncertainty. J Serv Res 2000;3(1):46–65.

Lievens A, Moenaert RK, Caeldries F, Wauters E. Communication flows in international product innovation teams. J Prod Innov Manage 2000 September [New York].

Lovelock C. Classifying services to gain strategic marketing insights. J Mar 1983 Summer;47:9–20.

Madhavan R, Grover R. From embedded knowledge to embodied knowledge: new product development as knowledge management. J Mark 1998 October;62:1–12.

Maidique M, Zirger BJ. A model of new product development: an empirical test. Manage Sci 1990;36:867–83.

March JG. Exploration and exploitation in organisation learning. Organ Sci 1991;2:71–87.

March JG, Olsen JP. The uncertainty of the past: organisational learning under ambiguity. Eur J Polit Res 1975;3:147–71.

Menor LJ, Takikonda MV, Sampson SE. New service development: area for exploitation and exploration. J Oper Manag 2002;20:135–57.

Moorman C, Miner A. The impact of organisational memory on new product performance and creativity. J Mark Res 1997. p. 91–107.

Moscovici S, Doise W. Décision et consensus: une théorie générale des décisions collectives. Paris: PUF; 1992. p. 244.

Nelson RR, Winter S. An evolutionary theory of economic change. Boston (MA): Harvard Univ. Press; 1982.

Nonaka I. The dynamic theory of organisational knowledge creation. Organ Sci 1994 February;5:14–37.

Nonaka I, Takeuchi H. The knowledge creating company. London: Oxford Univ. Press; 1995.

Olson EM, Walker OC, Ruekert JR. Organising for effective new product development: the moderating role of product innovativeness. J Mark 1995;59:48–62.

Pearson AW. Managing innovation: an uncertainty reduction process. In: Walker D, Henry J, editors. Managing innovation. Sage: London; 1991. p. 18–27.

Raesfeld Meijer A, De Ruyter K, Cabo P. Cooperation in new service development: a social dynamic approach. Adv Serv Mark Manag 1996;5:193–214.

Roth AV, Chase R, Voss C. Service in America: progress awards global service leadership. London: Pilluns and Wilson Greenaway; 1997.

Salleh M, Easingwood C. Why European financial institutions do not test market new consumer products. Int J Bank Mark 1993;11(3):23–8.

Scheuing EE, Johnson EM. A proposed model for service development. J Serv Mark 1989;3(2):25–34.

Shostack LG. Designing services that deliver. Harv Bus Rev 1984 January/February;62(1):133–139.

Shostack LG. Service positioning through structural change. J Mark 1987 January;51:34–43.

Simon HA. Bounded rationality and organisational learning. Organ Sci 1991 February;2(1):175–87.

Stake RE. The art of case study research. London: Sage; 1995.

Sundbo J. Management of innovation in services. Serv Ind J 1997;432–55 [London].

Thwaites D. Organisational influences on the new product development process in financial services. J Prod Innov Manag 1992;9:303–13.

Trott P. Innovation management and new product development. Prentice-Hall: New Jersey; 1998.

Van de Ven AH, Huber GP. Longitudinal field research methods for studying processes of organisational change. Organ Sci 1990;1(3):213–9.

Van de Ven AH, Polley D. Learning while innovating. Organ Sci 1992 February;3(1):92–116.

Van de Ven AH, Poole MS. Methods for studying innovation development in the Minnesota Research Program. Organ Sci 1990 August;1(3):313–35.

Van de Ven AH, Chen YT. Learning the innovation journey: order out of chaos. Organ Sci 1996;7(6):593–614.

Yin RK. Case study research: design and methods. London: Sage; 1994.

SECTION

VII ORGANIZATIONAL INNOVATION

Introduction

This section includes works involving organizational innovation, which is often recognized as the third "leg" or domain of innovation. Organizational innovation aligns itself with the areas of product and process innovation to form a three-dimensional cluster of innovation thought that is crucial to the success of modern-day businesses. Whereas product and process innovation refer to the goods and/or services developed and sold by firms and the manufacturing processes used to produce such goods and services, organizational innovation refers to changes in human processes, organizational structures, and political environments that can significantly impact a firm's success. The articles included in this section relate to these issues. Self-directed teams and new organizational structures for the twenty-first century are described. Differences between entrepreneurially and conservatively managed firms are discussed with a focus on extreme situations in which innovation can be performed for innovation's sake as opposed to situations in which little to no innovation occurs. This section also considers the differences and similarities between the sources of innovations such as innovations that emanate from the administration of organizations versus innovations that are derived from the technological bases of firms. Another area of interest examined in this section involves a review of alternative organizational structures in situations of high and low innovation and environments that are thought to be highly volatile or relatively stagnant.

The first article of this section was written by Thomas A. Stewart. He points out that what is known as the post-hierarchical organization is being developed at the confluence of three research streams. The first stream involves high involvement workplaces, the second focuses on business and technological processes, and the third emphasizes the information technology explosion. Stewart notes that firms boasting major business successes have taken some risk in the area of organizational innovation. High levels of success have not accrued to those firms that only rearranged the boxes on their organizational charts but to those that dramatically rethought their reporting and delegating routines in addition to their organizational structures. He offers many statistics, including one describing firms that have instituted some form of employee self-management and have increased productivity by 40 percent. A major focus of this article involves the development of business structures built around business processes. In these scenarios, rather than creating hierarchical structures that group people who have similar skills and interests, flat, flowing structures are generated grouping people who have comparatively different skills and, perhaps, interests, but form an integral work force relative to major processes associated with the production of a firm's goods and services. It is thought that organizing around major business processes results in manufacturing plants that have as great a success rate as those that are known as "high-involvement" factories. Stewart points out that one of the "old" organizational innovations (structuring around one or very similar businesses, or the creation of strategic business units [SBUs]), apparently continues to be thought of as a formidable weapon. Innovative business thought takes the SBU process one step further by creating factories that specialize in a single product or business. As a final note, Stewart suggests that in the future these specialized firms will be bound together by networks of alliances to achieve their objectives. The information revolution that we are in the midst of will continue to drive this process.

The second article, by William E. Souder, is based on the premise that the study and use of one vehicle associated with innovation, a firm's organizational structure, has not kept pace with changes in the environment. The author divides the innovation process into two sections. The first is initiation, which includes idea generation and development. The second section he refers to is implementation, which involves the commitment of organizational resources to an idea to commercialize it. Souder poses many characteristics of innovative organizations, such as a willingness to change, a long-term commitment to technological progress, a willingness to take calculated risks, the ability to confront and handle conflict, an external orientation, and a general sense of slack or freedom. Souder then describes both the classical and modern organizational points of view. Some of the tenets of the classical point of view are: communications are largely initiated by superiors; economic efficiency is the primary goal; conflict is suppressed; authority operates vertically; and tasks are subdivided and rigidly defined. He describes the modern philosophy as very different and almost directly opposed to that of the classical philosophy. For example, in the modern philosophy lateral communications exist, conflict is valued and managed, and there is a continual redefinition of tasks that are often performed by generalists. Based on these qualities and philosophies, he develops four organizational structures. Each organizational structure can be evaluated based on two variables: stable or dynamic markets and environments, and a low or high need for innovation. He concludes that only the Type IV organization, the organization developed for dynamic environments with high requirements for innovation, has the capability of meeting the life cycle needs of firms as they grow and mature.

In the next article, Richard L. Daft investigates the sources of innovation in organizations in an attempt to explain more fully the innovation processes found in such organization. He performed his exploration in suburban high school districts by analyzing innovation adoptions. He suggests that there are two primary sources of innovation, suggesting that there are two groups that primarily generate and adopt innovations. One is the administrative source and the other is the technological source. He points out that administrative personnel primarily adopt administrative innovations and that the technological personnel primarily adopt technological innovations. Using this framework, Daft proposes a dual core model of innovation to describe the two organizational processes operating in firms. One process operates in a top-down mode and the other operates in a bottom-up mode. He expected each group to initiate innovations pertinent to their own area and the division of labor to heighten as professionalism and organizational size increased. He found only a small number of innovations that originated with students and school boards. These findings confirmed his suspicion that innovations often originate with task experts/faculty in organizations. District innovativeness was found to be related to teacher professionalism or the number of teachers having master's degrees. District size had no affect on the process of administrative innovation. Daft found that most major innovations that were proposed were adopted. Therefore, he concluded that the innovation process found in specific organizations is contingent upon the type of innovation under consideration and the degree of employee professionalism.

The fourth article in this section was prepared by Danny Miller and Peter H. Friesen. These researchers proposed that there are differences between determinants of innovation in firms that are operated under two radically different philosophies. The two opposing operating philosophies comprise an entrepreneurial perspective and a conservative perspective. Miller and Friesen note that momentum is a pervasive force in organizations and that if left unchecked can force firms to continually evolve in a particular direction and, perhaps, reach a dysfunctional condition. Their conservative model description suggests that firms will innovate only when there are severe pressures from the environment, there is information about these pressures, there is an ability to innovate, and there is a decision-making capability to support the innovation project. The entrepreneurial model, in sharp contrast to the conservative model, suggests that innovation itself is a useful process and that firms will innovate unless there are powerful obstacles to stop them. Miller and Friesen found that their entrepreneurial sample of firms displayed many of the characteristics that were presupposed to exist such as high degrees of environmental hostility, organizational differentiation, heterogeneity, and technocratization. The conservative firms, on the other hand, exhibited low innovation forces such as non-hostile environments, few scientists and engineers, low levels of internal differentiation among groups, and a tendency to adhere to past products and practices. These authors concluded that innovation is primarily the product of strategy and the result of organizational philosophy. Therefore, innovativeness can be controlled and managed. Moreover, Miller and Friesen warn managers not to allow innovation to become an end in itself or allow it to progress beyond its point of usefulness.

In this section's final article, Kim B. Clark and Steven C. Wheelwright present descriptions of four types of new product development teams. The authors focus on one type, which is known as the "heavyweight" new product development team. The name of this type of an organization is derived from the abundance of power given to individuals leading new product development teams relative to the managers that manage traditional functional organizations. Functional new product development teams, the second approach, are found in organizations that can be described as traditional, larger, and mature. In such organizations, employees are often grouped in functional categories dictated by the type of work that is required. Each function is then managed by an individual who usually reports to a senior manager responsible for the entire function's operation within the firm. In a sense, no genuine teams are formed since the work of one department is often "thrown over-the-wall" for the next function to continue the new product development work. A major advantage of such an organization lies in its ability to bring specialized technical expertise to bear on key technological problems. The coordination and integration of subdivided tasks often represents a primary disadvantage of this approach. The lightweight team approach is the third technique discussed. This team approach places project leaders in liaison capacities. This structure dictates that functional managers retain control over major resources including the individual members of the team. An advantage of the "lightweight" team structure is having someone to coordinate the tasks of project personnel. However, this structure also has major disadvantages in that "lightweights" are often tolerated at best and totally ignored at worst. The autonomous team or Tiger team structure is one in which a new product development team is given free reign to plan and execute its strategy. The advantages of this structure lie in its focus and ability to control people and other resources. Disadvantages include problems such as team members not being able to gracefully return to their functional organizational units upon task completion. The "heavyweight" team structure provides a balance between the "lightweight" team and the Tiger team configurations. Some of the advantages of Tiger teams accrue to the "heavyweight" teams, but many of the disadvantages are mitigated.

References

Clark, Kim B. and Steven C. Wheelwright. 1992. Organizing and leading "heavy-weight" development teams. *California Management Review* 34(3): 9–28.

Daft, Richard L. 1978. A dual-core model of organizational innovation. *Academy of Management Journal* 21(2): 193–210.

Miller, Danny and Peter H. Friesen. 1982. Innovation in conservative and entrepreneurial firms: Two models of strategic momentum. *Strategic Management Journal* 3(January/March): 1–25.

Souder, William E. 1983. Organizing for modern technology and innovation: A review and synthesis. *Technovation* (Netherlands) 2(February): 27–44.

Stewart, Thomas A. 1992. The search for the organization of tomorrow. *Fortune* 125 (May 18): 92–98.

38

THE SEARCH FOR
THE ORGANIZATION
OF TOMORROW

Thomas A. Stewart

Are you flat, lean, and ready for a bold new look? Try high-performance teams, redesigned work, and unbridled information.

Lawrence Bossidy, CEO of Allied-Signal, predicts "organizational revolution" for corporate America. Says David Nadler, president of Delta Consulting Group, who works with the chiefs of AT&T, Corning, and Xerox, among others: "CEOs feel that companies need to be structured in dramatically different ways." In outfits as diverse as Eastman Kodak, Hallmark Cards, and General Electric—even the San Diego Zoo—the search for the organization perfectly designed for the 21st century is going ahead with the urgency of a scavenger hunt.

From many quarters we hear that hierarchical organization must wither away. In this view of the future middle managers have the life expectancy of fruit flies. Those who survive will not be straw bosses but Dutch uncles, dispensing resources and wisdom to an empowered labor force that designs its own jobs. Enabled, to use a trendy term, by information technology and propelled by the need to gain speed and shed unnecessary work, this flat, information-based organization won't look like the Pharaonic pyramid of yore but like—well, like what? Like a symphony orchestra, Peter Drucker suggests. No, a jazz combo, some say. More like a spider web, others offer.

Hamlet: Or like a whale?
Polonius: Very like a whale.

Gee, thanks. But where's my desk? What do I do eight hours a day—or ten, or 12? Who gives me my annual review? When do we start?

Good questions, which as yet have not had good answers. Says H. James Maxmim, the CEO of Laura Ashley Holdings: "We're just beginning to explore the post-hierarchical organization. We don't know what it looks like yet." Some hints, however, are emerging.

The 21st-century organization arises at the confluence of three streams. One is described by the term "high-involvement workplace," meaning operations with self-managing teams and other devices for empowering employees. Novelties once, these participative mechanisms have proved they can consistently deliver jaw-dropping gains in productivity, quality, and job

General Electric offers workers in Bayamón, Puerto Rico, self-management and a pay plan that rewards learning and performance. Says the plant manager: "I'm going to have the best work force in all GE."

satisfaction. A second productivity turbocharger is a new emphasis on managing business processes—materials handling, say—rather than functional departments like purchasing and manufacturing. Third is the evolution of information technology to the point where knowledge, accountability, and results can be distributed rapidly anywhere in the organization. The trick is to put them together into a coherent, practical design. Then you have the company yours may become, and the one your sons and daughters will work for.

At the end of this rainbow, say those, who have peeked, is a whole kettleful of gold. Advises Bossidy, who until last summer was vice chairman of General Electric: "Look at GE Appliances." In that $5.4-billion-a-year business, redesign has brought with it a $200 million drop in average inventory. McKinsey & Co. principal Douglas Smith, one of the blue-chip consulting firm's experts on organization, figures that a company applying the new principles of organization design can cut its cost base by a third or more. Smith bases his claim on results from companies that have already reorganized parts of their operations: an industrial goods manufacturer that cut costs and raised productivity more than 50%, a financial services company where costs fell 34%, and others.

Results like that come from changing a company in profound ways, not just tinkering with the boxes on an organization chart. For years, Smith says, the basic question about how best to arrange people and jobs stayed the same: "Do we centralize or decentralize—and where do we stick international?" The answer was never satisfactory. Companies were set up by product, or by customer, or by territory, and then switched when those arrangements stopped working. All that rejiggering missed the point, says Smith: "It mattered only to the top people in the company. Below them you found the same functional, vertical organization. For the 90% of the people who serve customers and make product, all that changed was the boss's name."

No longer. The Kodaks, GEs, and their ilk have first retailored the work people do, then management structures, with startling results. To make sense out of the rush of experimentation, McKinsey's Smith and his colleague Frank Ostroff are polishing a paper that lays out what Ostroff calls "perhaps the first real, fundamentally different, robust alternative" to the functional organization (see Figure 38-1). In the months since Ostroff released an early draft to his consulting colleagues, it has proved the document most often requested inside the firm.

There's nothing new about self-managing teams—they were "discovered" 43 years ago at the bottom of a coal mine in Yorkshire by a researcher from the Tavistock Institute of Human Relations in London. Since then, forms of worker self-management have been adopted at countless sites. Marvin Weisbord, an expert on organizational development, notes that all rely on one basic idea: "The people who do the work should have in their hands the means to change to suit the customer." That means workers should have the incentive and the power to respond to whoever buys their output—at times someone else within their organization—not just whoever cuts their paychecks. Weisbord adds that self-management *typically* delivers 40% increases in output per man-hour.

To see how it's done, skip the blackjack table next time you're in Puerto Rico and pay a visit to Bayamón, outside San Juan, where a new General Electric factory has been running for a year and a half. The place makes arresters, which are surge protectors that guard power stations and transmission lines against lightning strikes.

Bayamón is the godchild of Philip Jarrosiak, manager of human resources for GE's capacitor and power protection operations. Once a minor-league infielder, Jarrosiak joined GE when he was 20, landing an hourly job making aircraft engines in Rutland, Vermont. In the 32 years since, he put himself through college at night and worked his way into management ranks, where he specializes in designing high-performance workplaces at both green-field and established sites. Bayamón is his newest and, Jarrosiak says, "an opportunity to put in everything I know."

The facility employs 172 hourly workers and just 15 salaried "advisers," plus manager R. Clayton Crum. That's it: three layers, no supervisors, no staff. A conventional plant, Jarrosiak says, would have about twice as many salaried people. Every hourly worker is on a team with ten or so others; they meet weekly. Each team "owns" part of the work—assembly, shipping and receiving, etc. But team members come from all

FIGURE 38-1

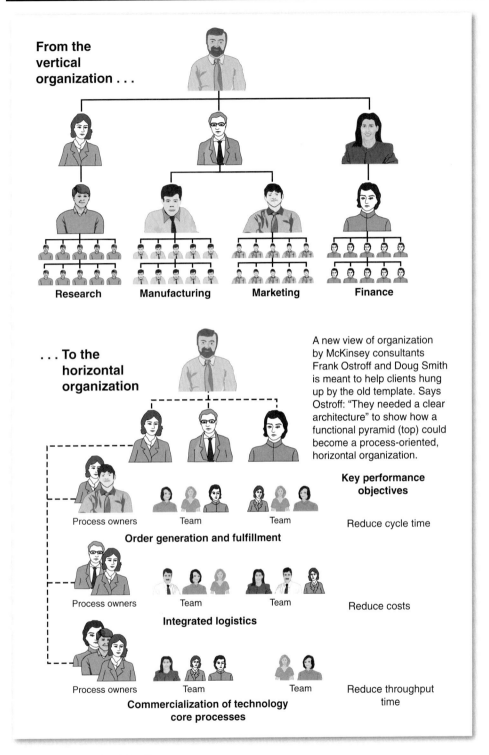

From the vertical organization . . .

Research   Manufacturing   Marketing   Finance

. . . To the horizontal organization

A new view of organization by McKinsey consultants Frank Ostroff and Doug Smith is meant to help clients hung up by the old template. Says Ostroff: "They needed a clear architecture" to show how a functional pyramid (top) could become a process-oriented, horizontal organization.

Key performance objectives

Process owners   Team   Team
Order generation and fulfillment

Reduce cycle time

Process owners   Team   Team
Integrated logistics

Reduce costs

Process owners   Team   Team
Commercialization of technology core processes

Reduce throughput time

Source: Tony Mikolajczyk for *Fortune.*

areas of the plant, so that each group has representatives from both upstream and downstream operations. An adviser sits in the back of the room and speaks up only if the team needs help.

What vaults Bayamón into the next century is the way it teaches its workers. Says Harvard professor Shoshanna Zuboff, author of *In the Age of the Smart Machine:* "The 21st-century company has to promote and nurture the capacity to improve and to innovate. That idea has radical implications. It means learning becomes the axial principle of organizations. It replaces control as the fundamental job of management."

Bayamón is a perpetual-learning machine. Hourly workers change jobs every six months, rotating through the factory's four main work areas. In six months they'll begin their second circuit of the plant, and everyone on the floor will know his job and how it affects the next person in line. The reward for learning is a triple-scoop compensation plan that pays for skill, knowledge, and business performance. The first time around, workers get a 25-cent-an-hour pay raise at each rotation; thereafter they can nearly double their pay by "declaring a major," so to speak, and learning a skill like machine maintenance or quality control. More pay comes from passing courses in English, business practices, and other subjects. Toss in bonuses—$225 a quarter or more—for meeting plantwide performance goals and having perfect attendance. Promotions and layoffs will be decided by skill level, not seniority. In just a year the work force became 20% more productive than its nearest company equivalent on the mainland, and Jarrosiak predicts productivity will rise 20% more by the end of 1993.

For years plants like Bayamón existed barely connected to the organizations of which they are a part. Some Procter & Gamble factories were worker run as long ago as 1968, a fact concealed from competitors—and sometimes from headquarters. The Gaines pet food plant in Topeka, Kansas, just celebrated 20 years of self-management. For two decades, under three owners—Anderson Clayton, General Foods, and Quaker Oats—Topeka has always placed first when its labor productivity was compared with that of other pet food plants within its company. According to Herman Simon, plant manager for 17 years, higher-ups who saw the numbers vowed never to mess with the plant. But they rarely went away determined to make their other factories over in its image.

Says a frustrated William Buehler, senior vice president at Xerox: "You can see a high-performance factory or office, but it just doesn't spread. I don't know why." One reason is that nervous executives experiment where failure won't be fatal, and thereby contain the gains too. Says Jarrosiak: "I hate pilot programs off in a corner of a plant. You need commitment."

You also need to be able to envision how such operations fit into a large-scale enterprise. Says McKinsey's Ostroff: "Executives know what teams can do. But they need a picture that links the high-performance team to the whole organization and multiplies the gains." It's relatively easy to oversee one of these operations when it's confined within one function, like manufacturing. For self-directed management to spread, a company must lay goals, responsibilities, and measurements *across* functions. Ostroff argues: "Senior managers need to be able to say 'empowerment' and 'accountability' in the same sentence."

Business processes—almost sure to become a term you will hear lots of—can form the link between high-performance work teams and the corporation at large. Organizing around processes, as opposed to functions, permits greater self-management and allows companies to dismantle unneeded supervisory structures.

It's a management axiom that crab grass grows in the cracks between departments. Purchasing buys parts cheap, but manufacturing needs them strong. Shipping moves goods in bulk, but sales promised them fast. "I call it Palermo's law," says Richard Palermo, a vice president for quality and transition at Xerox. "If a problem has been bothering your company and your customers for years and won't yield, that problem is the result of a cross-functional dispute, where nobody has total control of the whole process." And here's Palermo's corollary: People who work in different functions hate each other.

Upon this fratricidal scene, enter the process doctor. Depending on which consulting firm he's coming from, he may describe his work as "reengineering" or "core process redesign" or "process innovation." Michael Hammer, a consultant in Cambridge, Massachusetts, defines, though not exactly lyrically, what the doctor is up to: "Reengineering is the fundamental analysis and radical redesign of business processes to achieve dramatic improvements in critical measures of performance."

Process management differs from managing a function in three ways. First, it uses external objectives. Old-line manufacturing departments, for example, tend to be measured on unit costs, an intradepartmental number that can lead to overlong production runs and stacks of unsold goods. By contrast, an integrated manufacturing and shipping process might be rated by how often it turns over its inventory—a process-wide measurement that reveals how all are working together to keep costs down. Second, in process management employees with different skills are grouped to accomplish a complete piece of work. Mortgage loan officer, title searcher, and credit checker sit and work together, not in series. Third, information moves straight to where it's needed, unfiltered by a hierarchy. If you have a problem with people upstream from you, you deal with them directly, rather than asking your boss to talk to theirs.

Reengineered processes have been in place at Kodak for more than two years. The 1,500 employees who make black and white film—inevitably called Zebras—work not in departments but in what's called "the flow." (Black and white is big business: about $2 billion a year from sales of 7,000 products used in printing, X-rays, even spy satellites.) Headed by Richard Malloy, a 25-member leadership team watches the flow. They measure it with end-of-process tallies like productivity. Within the flow are streams defined by "customers"—Kodak business units—and scored on customer satisfaction measures such as on-time delivery. One stream, for example, is charged with making hundreds of types of film for the Health Sciences Division and works closely with it to schedule production and to develop new products, a Zebra specialty. In the streams most employees work in self-directed teams. A few functions—accounting and human resources—remain outside the streams.

When the flow began in 1989, the black and white film operation was running 15% over budgeted cost, took up to 42 days to fill an order, was late a third of the time, and scored worst in Kodak's morale surveys. Last year the group came in 15% under budgeted cost, had cut response time in half, was late one time out of 20, and wore the biggest smiles in Rochester, New York. Why? Says Zebra Robert Brookhouse: "When you create a flow and a flow chart, you find where you're wasting time, doing things twice. And because we own our entire process, we can change it."

Organizing around a process seems to yield sterling results as consistently as high-involvement factories do. Privately held Hallmark (1991 sales: $2.9 billion) expects big gains now that Steven Stanton of CSC Index, a Cambridge, Massachusetts, consulting firm, has helped the company reengineer its new-product process. The greeting-card maker lives or dies on new stuff—some 40,000 cards and other items a year, the work of 700 writers, artists, and designers on what Hallmark boasts is the world's largest creative staff. The process of developing a new card had become grotesque; it took two years—longer than the road from Gettysburg to Appomattox Court House. The company was choking on sketches, approvals, cost estimates, and proofs. Says Hallmark's Don Fletcher: "We needed a lot of people just to check items in and out of departments."

Fletcher's title, vice president for business process redesign, pretty much tells what happened. Starting this spring, about half the staff will be put to work on cards for particular holidays like Valentine's Day or Christmas. The birthday and get-well card folks will follow. A team of artists, writers, lithographers, merchandisers, bean counters, and so on will be assigned to each holiday. Team members are moving from all over a two-million-square-foot office building in Kansas City so they can sit together. Like a canoe on a lake, a card will flow directly from one part of the process to the next within, say, the Mother's Day team; before, it had to be portaged from one vast department to the next. This should cut cycle time in half, which will not only save money but will also make the company more responsive to changing tastes.

Hallmark hasn't eradicated departments. There will be "centers of excellence" to which workers will return between projects for training and brief, special stints, a bit like homerooms in high school. For now, department heads remain the senior managers of the business. But the head of graphic arts, which makes separations and proofs, has told Fletcher that he hopes the department infrastructure will eventually dissolve in the flow.

McKINSEY'S PLAN

It's hot stuff at McKinsey & Co. these days: a ten-point blueprint for a horizontal company prepared by Frank Ostroff and Doug Smith, consultants in the firm's organization-performance group.

1. *Organize primarily around process, not task.* Base performance objectives on customer needs, such as low cost or fast service. Identify the processes that meet (or don't meet) those needs—order generation and fulfillment, say, or new-product development. These processes—not departments, such as sales or manufacturing—become the company's main components.

2. *Flatten the hierarchy by minimizing subdivision of processes.* It's better to arrange teams in parallel, with each doing lots of steps in a process, than to have a series of teams, each doing fewer steps.

3. *Give senior leaders charge of processes and process performance.*

4. *Link performance objectives and evaluation of all activities to customer satisfaction.*

5. *Make teams, not individuals, the focus of organization performance and design.* Individuals acting alone don't have the capacity to continuously improve work flows.

6. *Combine managerial and non-managerial activities as often as possible.* Let workers' teams take on hiring, evaluating, and scheduling.

7. *Emphasize that each employee should develop several competencies.* You need only a few specialists.

8. *Inform and train people on a just-in-time, need-to-perform basis.* Raw numbers go straight to those who need them in their jobs, with no managerial spin, because you have trained front-line workers—salesmen, machinists—how to use them.

9. *Maximize supplier and customer contact with everyone in the organization.* That means field trips and slots on joint problem-solving teams for all employees all the time.

10. *Reward individual skill development and team performance instead of individual performance alone.*

That's the right idea, say hard-core process managers. If you reengineer a process, pocket a one-time gain, and return to your desk, says McKinsey's Smith, "the barnacles you scrape off will just grow back." The way to keep them off, says Hammer, is to obliterate the functions: "In the future, executive positions will not be defined in terms of collections of people, like head of the sales department, but in terms of process, like senior-VP-of-getting-stuff-to-customers, which is sales, shipping, billing. You'll no longer have a box on an organization chart. You'll own part of a process map."

Can a whole company literally lie on its side and organize horizontally, by process? You got it, says Allied-Signal's Bossidy: "Every business has maybe six basic processes. We'll organize around them. The people who run them will be the leaders of the business."

An industrial company might select processes like new-product development, flow of materials (purchasing, receiving, manufacturing), and the order-delivery billing cycle. Into these process flows will go management teams to tend subprocesses and teams of workers to carry out tasks. Whoever is needed will be there: The materials-flow group might have finance folks but no marketers—but the marketers will be plentiful in the new-product process. There are no departments in Bossidy's 21st-century corporation: "You might have a CFO, but he won't have many people who report to him."

If metallurgists and actuaries are taken out of departments and clumped around processes, what happens to their specialized skills? A minor problem, argues James Champy, CEO of CSC Index: "State-of-the-art knowledge comes from a small group of people. Most people in a function don't *contribute* expertise. They execute." Put the innovators in a stafflike or lablike group. Create a house Yellow Pages so functional expertise is easy to find even though dispersed. Link experts in a real or electronic network where they can keep each other up to date and can get training and career development help.

"That's okay," says Bossidy. "The engineers can have a club. But they can't work in the same room, and they can't sit at the same table at the company banquet." His vision is somewhat radical, he admits, understating the case. "So corporations will first try to make the matrix work. Boy, that will drive employees and managers nuts."

One trouble with breaking down the walls: In most companies functional and hierarchical walls are load bearing. Remove them and the roof caves in. A big burden they bear is to collect, evaluate, and pass on information. Another is to determine employees' career paths—to define ambition, reward, and sycophancy. In a flat shop of teams and processes, both information flow and careers will have to be different.

Walk around futuristic companies and you see odd sights: suppliers who work in their customers' offices; widely available, easy-to-read charts tracking scrap, on-time delivery, and other data that rivals would kill for; hourly workers logged onto PCs, reading their e-mail. They're all part of an effort to put information where it can be used at the moment it's needed. Says Delta Consulting's David Nadler: "In the organization of the future, information technology will be a load-bearing material—as hierarchy is now. You can't have self-management without it." That is, computer networks and the information they carry will help define your corporate structure. Let information flow wherever it's needed, and a horizontal self-managed company is not only possible, it's inescapable.

Building computer highways that can transport cost and other data sideways within a process, as well as vertically to top management, is a step in this direction. Other steps include training that teaches workers how their actions affect overall business performance and measurements that direct tasks at optimum outcomes, such as rewarding salespeople for gross margin, not gross sales.

You have to transport power as well as knowledge. In a hierarchy, rank defines authority: A manager can okay deals up to $50,000, his boss to $100,000, her boss to $250,000 . . . That's obsolete, in Harvard business school professor Quinn Mills's view. The question isn't how high the money gets; it's how high your customer's blood pressure gets. "Does he need an answer immediately? Do you have to be able to be flexible? If so, you have to empower the person who talks to the customer." If you can't entrust such matters to the folks in the field, maybe you should switch places with them. They can have your desk, where the decisions, obviously, are less important.

What happens to the career ladder? CSC Index Chief Executive Champy suggests that law firms, with only three levels of hierarchy—associate, partner, and senior partner—might provide the very model of a modern career path. Says Champy: "A lawyer's career is a progression to more complex work—tougher cases, more important clients. Titles don't change, but everyone knows who has the highest status."

The oldest art in organization design—carving out strategic business units—will still matter in this new world. The goal, as Nadler sees it, is to create "enterprises with clear customers, markets, and measures, and few internal boundaries." That means letting sets of customers or customer needs define business units, and grouping into businesses the people and processes necessary to serve them.

That's how Xerox designed its new horizontal organization. Till this year, Xerox was set up in the usual functions—R&D, manufacturing, sales, and the like. The new design creates nine businesses aimed at markets such as small businesses and individuals, office document systems, and engineering systems. Each business will have an income statement and a balance sheet, and an identifiable set of competitors. New manufacturing layouts will permit so-called focused factories dedicated to specific businesses.

Most of the businesses will sell through a new Customer Operations Group, a mingling of sales, shipping, installation, service, and billing, created so customers can keep just one phone number on their Rolodexes. In fact, the businesses will sell *to* Customer Operations—that is, negotiate contracts—so that market forces extend deeply into the company. Teams lead the businesses, whose building blocks are what CEO Paul Allaire calls "microenterprise units": complete work processes or subprocesses. Says Allaire, "We've given everyone in the company a direct line of sight to the customer."

In a functional hierarchy, job descriptions, career paths, and information flow are all geared toward control—of work, workers, and knowledge. Compare that with the evolving 21st-century company, where work is lined up with customers, not toward bosses. Senior executives have charge of the handful of processes that are critical to satisfying customers.

Self-directed, the work force does most of the hiring, scheduling, and other managerial tasks that once ate up kazillions in indirect labor costs. The few people left between the executives and the work teams spend their time trying to change the organization, not to control it: They are reaching out to grab a new technology or a new customer, or to respond to a new demand from an old one. Jobs, careers, and knowledge shift constantly.

The boundaries of the company will be fluid too. The growing number of strategic alliances suggests as much. So do the actions of companies like Wal-Mart stores and Procter & Gamble, which have inter-woven their order-and-fulfillment process so that the bells of Wal-Mart's cash registers in effect ring in P&G warehouses, telling them to ship a new box of Tide to replace the one you just bought.

In the view of Harvard economist Robert Reich, the boundaries will become so fluid that corporations will become temporary arrangements among entrepreneurial cadres. Except for high-volume, capital-intensive work, says Reich, "every big company will be a confederation of small ones. All small organizations will be constantly in the process of linking up into big ones."

That may be more fluidity than most people can accept, at least as long as mortgage applications ask, "How long have you been with your current employer?" But the new flexible organization will be a powerful competitor. Smith finds a metaphor in *Terminator II,* the movie where Arnold Schwarzenegger faces a metal monster that liquefies, then hardens again in a new shape—now a man, now a machine, now a knife. Says Smith: "I call it the *Terminator II* company." How'd you like to have to compete with one of those?

WHAT A ZOO CAN TEACH YOU

The Zoological Society of San Diego has done more than most businesses to transform itself into a 21st-century organization. It deserves to be seen for its management as well as for its spectacular collection of beasts and birds.

With 1,200 year-round employees, $75 million in revenues, and five million visitors a year, the San Diego Zoo and its Wild Animal Park make a sizable outfit whose competitors—among them Walt Disney and Anheuser-Busch, owner of nearby Sea World—are real gorillas. Also, as a world-renowned scientific and conservation organization, the zoo must maintain high technical standards and a Caesar's-wife purity on environmental and other issues.

The zoo is steadily remodeling to show its animals by bioclimatic zone (an African rain forest called Gorilla Tropics, or Tiger River, an Asian jungle environment) rather than by taxonomy (pachyderms, primates). As displays open—three out of ten are finished—they're fundamentally altering the way the zoo is run.

The old zoo was managed through its 50 departments—animal keeping, horticulture, maintenance, food service, fund raising, education, and others. It had all the traits of functional management, says David Glines, head of employee development. Glines started out as a groundsman, responsible for keeping paths clear of trash. If he was tired or rushed, Glines remembers, "sometimes I'd sweep a cigarette butt under a bush. Then it was the gardener's problem, not mine."

The departments are invisible in the redesigned parts of the zoo. Tiger River, for instance, is run by a team of mammal and bird specialists, horticulturists, and maintenance and construction workers. The four-year-old team, led by keeper John Turner, tracks its own budget on a PC that isn't hooked up to the zoo's mainframe. Members are jointly responsible for the display, and it's hard to tell who comes from which department. When the path in front of an aviary needed fixing last autumn, the horticulturist and the construction man did it.

Seven people run Tiger River; when it started there were 11, but as team members learned one another's skills, they decided they didn't need to replace workers who left. (P.S.: They're all Teamsters union members.) Freed from managerial chores now handled by teams, executives can go out and drum up more interest in the zoo.

Any effect on business? Southern California tourism took some hits in 1991—first from the Gulf war, then from the recession—but the San Diego Zoo enjoyed a 20% increase in attendance. Part of the reason is price: At $12 it costs less than half as much to enter the zoo gates as it does to get into Disneyland.

Zoo director Douglas Myers credits employees' sense of ownership. Says he: "I told them recession is coming; we're going to target our marketing on the local area alone, and we're going to ask all our visitors to come back five times—so each time they'd better have more fun than the time before. The employees came through."

39 | ORGANIZING FOR MODERN TECHNOLOGY AND INNOVATION: A REVIEW AND SYNTHESIS

William E. Souder

Professor of Industrial Engineering and Director of the Technology Management Studies Group, University of Pittsburgh, Pittsburgh, PA 15261 (U.S.A.)

ABSTRACT

Classical and modern organization designs are reviewed and evaluated in terms of their capabilities for handling radical or major innovations. The choice of an effective organization design is shown to be related to the nature of the technological and market environments. Only Type IV organization designs, the modern-integrative organization designs, are shown to have the necessary qualities for handling all the phases in the life cycle of a major innovation. Though difficult to implement and maintain, Type IV organization designs are shown to be a potent tool for those modern managers who fully understand how to use them.

INTRODUCTION

Product and process innovations have shaped much of today's quality of life. The innovation process has been responsible for numerous new products, technologies, industries, jobs and favorable balances of trace.

However, this happy picture of an ever-expanding economy, buoyed along by the innovation process, has begun to pale in recent years [2, 10, 13]. The thesis of this paper is that the vehicle for innovation—the organization of the firm—has not kept pace with the demands of modern technologies and the needs of today's societies. Many companies are attempting to manage space-age technologies and to serve modern societal needs with handicraft-vintage organizations. The innovation process will continue to be hampered as long as this mismatch continues.

REQUIREMENTS FOR INNOVATION

Characteristics of Innovations

The "innovation process" consists of a series of organized activities which transform technical ideas into profitable products. Many different descriptions of this process have been developed (e.g., see [59], pp. 52–104). Basically, the innovation process may

Souder, William E., "Organizing for Modern Technology and Innovation: A Review and Synthesis," *Technovation*, (Netherlands), 2 (February), 27–44.

be conceptualized as consisting of two major stages of activities: initiation and implementation. The initiation stage includes idea generation and development—the usual functions of R&D and engineering departments. The implementation stage includes the commitment of other organizational resources to the idea to commercialize it—the usual functions of production, marketing and sales departments.

Characteristically, radical or major innovations entail relatively heavy R&D costs. They may also involve heavy commercialization costs, especially if the markets are not immediately receptive to the innovation. Socio-behavioral costs (the disruption to established organizational behaviors) may also be high. Major innovations are also likely to carry high risks of failure to the innovating firm. In addition, there may be great uncertainties about the risks involved and the future value of the innovation to the firm even if it does succeed.

Most innovations have a quality of urgency and timeliness about them. They can fail if they emerge either too early or too late in the marketplace. Most innovations involve a combination of several technologies. Thus, they require interdisciplinary talents and "know-how." Major innovations also seem to require time for incubation and gestation. Unlike other efforts, they cannot be rushed or greatly accelerated.

Qualities of Innovative Organizations

The left side of Table 39-1 summarizes some important characteristics of innovations. The right side of Table 39-1 summarizes the qualities of successful innovative organizations. Each of the qualities listed in Table 39-1 is required in order to handle the corresponding characteristics of innovations. For instance, the willingness and readiness of the performing organizations to accept change is fundamental to successful innovative efforts [59, 5, 8, 9, 14, 25, 37, 53, 3]. An innovation, by its very nature, introduces change into an organization. The development and introduction of a new product often involves changes in the established authority patterns, decision-making behaviors, information needs, physical facilities, service operations and distribution channels.

TABLE 39-1 Characteristics of Major Innovations and the Corresponding Required Qualities of Innovative Organizations

Characteristics of Major Innovations	Required Qualities of Innovative Organizations
1. High socio-behavioral costs	Readiness to accept change, altered behaviors and organizational disruptions
2. High research, development and commercialization costs	Long-term commitment to technology
3. Time for idea germination and gestation	Some "slack" and autonomy of members to pursue their own ideas; patience coupled with decisiveness in permitting ideas to gestate and in allocating resources to those with greatest commercial prospects
4. High risk and uncertainty	Willingness to face uncertainties and take balanced risks
5. Urgency and timeliness	Timeliness in sensing environmental changes and responding to them; open channels of communication with the external environment
6. Involvement of various combinations of several technologies that may exist within and outside the firm	Openness of internal, cross-functional communication; diversity of internal talents and cultures; many external contacts and information sources
7. Cross-specialized talents of individuals and interdisciplinary "know-how"	A climate that fosters the natural confrontation and resolution of interdepartmental rivalries and conflicts; a network of many reciprocally dependent role-persons whose domain spans the usual departmental structures of organizations
8. High potential profit	Growth orientation

In short, the innovation process involves the implementation of new ideas and the learning of new ways, which may usher in many new social and behavioral patterns. The organization that is unwilling to accommodate itself to these new patterns may be unable to innovate.

The ability of the organization to accurately sense its threats and opportunities in a timely fashion has been found to relate to success in handling innovations [59, 53, 7, 56, 26, 51, 2]. In general, this kind of alertness goes hand-in-hand with a top management that is committed to environmental scanning, market research and competitive analysis. The most successful innovators have a constant awareness of where they stand vis-a-vis their environments, and an appreciation of the performance gap between the organization's current and potential achievements [10, 30]. In general, open "all-channel" communication patterns, and a diversity of subcultures often characterize innovative organizations [7, 48, 50]. These qualities permit these organizations to move quickly into various roles and situations and to be highly responsive and adaptable to changing market needs.

Another requirement for successful innovation is an organizational climate that fosters long-term commitments to technology [59, 14, 56, 13]. The most innovative firms exhibit a quality of fatherly, guiding patience in permitting ideas to germinate and gestate. But this patience must not be a "hands-off" approach. It must be accompanied by a decisiveness in allocating resources. At the end of the gestation period, preferential treatment must be accorded to those ideas which show the greatest promise of contributing to the firm's long range goals. This decisiveness eliminates an "on-again/off-again" climate that often prevails at less-innovative firms. An "on-again/off-again" climate not only disrupts current efforts, but it also shuts off the future flow of ideas [48, 34, 1, 36].

Willingness to take calculated risks and face uncertainties is another salient characteristic [56, 48, 36, 50, 4, 55]. This does not mean that successful innovators actually gamble more than non-innovators. Rather, innovative firms are more willing to look long and hard at risky opportunities, to face them, and to include them in a balanced portfolio of high and low risk proposals. They are also able to assess more accurately the level of risk and not be frightened away by "imaginary" risks.

Interdepartmental conflict can be a severe barrier to innovation, especially at the implementation stage. Goal conflicts, problems of reciprocal communication and a lack of openness commonly characterize the relationship between marketing and R&D departments [41, 12, 42]. Yet, a complete lack of conflict does not seem to make an organization more innovative. It appears that the presence of some conflict is desirable, though the results here are mixed [47, 42]. However, it is clear that the fashion in which conflict is handled *is* highly important. Sweeping conflict under the rug does not work [46, 47, 44]. Rather, a willingness to confront and resolve conflicts is a salient climate for many innovative organizations [46, 38]. In fact, the most successful organizations seem to be constantly in search of interdepartmental conflicts. They seek out undetected discontent and constructive frustrations which can be creatively resolved. The process of resolving these conflicts often leads to new ideas, innovations and a more receptive organizational climate [43, 46, 42].

The external orientation of an organization also influences its ability to innovate successfully. Studies show that open channels of communication and contacts with outside sources are very important [56, 23]. Contacts with scientists, customers and others outside the innovating organizations can be a fertile source of critical information and "know-how" [16, 35].

"Slack," freedom or autonomy are generally believed to be related to innovativeness because they foster the development of creative potentials among organization members [48, 50, 45]. Steiner [50], for example, states the case against tight control, centralization of power and bureaucracy. "This climate is characterized by high productivity and efficiency, but low innovative capacity . . . A monocratic social structure, a production-oriented ideology, a detailed allocation of resources, an extrinsic reward system based on status and power and a control system designed to suppress conflict— all are characteristics of the bureaucratic form. In general, a bureaucracy tends to reduce the potential for innovative behavior. For innovative behavior, the required characteristics are: uncommitted resources, a diversity of inputs, structural looseness, freedom from unusual external pressures, . . . decentralization, freer communications, . . . rotation of assignments, greater reliance on group processes. . . ." [p. 36].

In monolithic organization structures, the higher the person's position the more capacity he has to be a successful innovator, and the more radical the development he will be able to introduce. Small companies that dominate their markets may be able to function well and innovate using this "top man down" concept, if the top man is a creative-idea person. But in the larger companies, multiple-role persons will be needed. For instance, studies show that the most successful innovative companies have individuals who play various reciprocal roles. There are persons who generate creative ideas. There are several other individuals who champion these ideas. And still other individuals help to implement, "fit" or link the ideas to the existing organizational goals and needs [54, 55, 57, 17, 39, 40]. Hence, organization structures and climates that foster the autonomous development of these collaborative roles and teamwork activities will foster innovation.

MANAGEMENT'S DESIGN FUNCTION

It is management's responsibility to see that the seven qualities listed in Table 39-1 are fully developed and maintained. For the modern manager, the successful performance of this design function may be more important than his other traditional functions of planning, organizing, directing and controlling. If the organization structure is not properly designed to cope with modern technological imperatives and environmental forces, then no amount of planning, organizing, directing and controlling efforts can compensate for it.

Basically, two kinds of design tools are available to the manager. One is management philosophy. The other is the organization structure.

MANAGEMENT PHILOSOPHIES FOR INNOVATION

An individual's philosophy is a rather abstract and intangible quality. We are often inclined to feel that philosophies are elusive and theoretical—of little practical relevance in real day-to-day management activities. Nothing could be further from the truth. A person's philosophy guides his general perceptions, beliefs and actions. Management philosophies pervade management behaviors, and ultimately impact many other persons.

Classical Management Philosophies

In the extreme, only two management philosophies are available: classical and modern. The classical concepts of management date from the writing of Fayol, Taylor, Gantt and others in the early 1900s [18, 52, 15]. Within the classical concepts, management's functions are to plan, organize, direct and control the work of others. "Optimum" solutions to problems are sought, based on short-term economic criteria. Authority is vested in a single person, who sits at the top of the organization. A rigid chain of command flows from the top to the bottom of the organization, which is pyramidal in its physical appearance. The organization is structured into functionally specialized units, e.g., production, finance, etc. The classical philosophy holds that organizational efficiency is maximized and conflicts are minimized if these functions are kept independent and non-overlapping. This idea is also extended to subdividing individual jobs and functions into their simplest elements, e.g., one person drills the hole in a sheet metal panel, another inserts a bolt, a third person puts a nut on the bolt, etc. The line (directing) and staff (technical support service) functions are kept rigidly separate and non-overlapping. Close personal control and scrutiny of others is practiced. There are many rules and policies. Rewards are based on technical proficiency and individual outputs vis-à-vis the established quotas.

Thus, the classical ideas emphasize rigidly specialized behavior patterns, rational economic decision making, and well-defined goals. There is little or no latitude for individual initiative or deviation from the prescribed roles and norms. The emphasis is on the one "best" way to routinely perform repetitive tasks—at the minimum cost and with the maximum efficiency.

Modern Management Philosophies

Modern management concepts date from the research and writings of March and Simon, Mayo, Barnard and the systems theorists [18, 28, 29, 9, 54, 4, 27]. In contrast to the classical concepts, the major managerial functions are considered to be harmonizing, providing for change, and adapting the organization to evolving needs. Satisfactory (as opposed to "optimal") solutions to problems are sought, in terms of achieving an equitable balance between all concerned parties. Authority is decentralized, participation is the mode, and the organization is viewed as having many sources of ideas, power and influence. Cross-departmental teams, autonomous groups, project teams and "matrix" forms of organizations are commonly used [9, 49, 9, 6]. The modern concepts recognize that there is often a natural overlap between jobs and functions. This overlap is valued as a potential source of synergism and creative outputs. It is often carefully preserved by assigning shared responsibilities, e.g., making *both* marketing *and* research jointly responsible for new products [44, 4, 48, 47, 42].

In the modern approach, there are few prescribed rules, policies and behaviors. Horizontal, colleague-based relationships are stressed. This is in contrast to the vertical boss-employee relationships of the classical approach. In the modern approach, interpersonal relationships are generated to meet the needs of the situation. Rewards are based on group effort and contribution. Unique solutions to problems are sought. Variety, diversity, flexibility and adaptability are emphasized. The modern philosophy seeks the creation of new forms, products and processes to meet the needs and demands of a changing environment [6, 24]. Goals are a moving target and not clearly definable.

Table 39-2 lists the salient attributes of the classical and modern management philosophies. Note the considerable differences in how these two philosophies view the human element, as expressed in items 4, 5, 7, and 9 in Table 39-2. The classical philosophy views the employee as simply another resource—to be managed in whatever way best achieves the organization's goals. This philosophy constrains innovative employee behaviors. The modern philosophy views the employee as a wealth of creative talent which, if given the proper environment, can benefit all parties. This philosophy encourages innovative employee behaviors.

ORGANIZATION STRUCTURES FOR INNOVATION

Organization structures influence behaviors and the interactions of the people within them. Thus, though having the "right" organization structure may not by itself be sufficient to achieve innovation, it is a necessary prerequisite.

Most organization structures are a variant of the four basic structural types portrayed in Figure 39-1. The Type I and II structures correspond to the classical management philosophy. The Type III and IV structures correspond to the modern management philosophy.

The Type I Structure

The Type I structure has a high steady state efficiency. This type of structure has a superior capability for handling routine, repetitive problems. Decisions are centralized, lines of communication are short, and the specific departmental functions of selling, producing, etc. are clearly defined. This is an ideal structure for handling non-complex or routine problems. It is the most efficient structure for handling a well-known technology. It is also the appropriate structure for coping with stable business environments. These

TABLE 39-2 Classical vs. Modern Management Philosophies	
Classical	*Modern*
1. Tasks are sub-divided into their smallest units, which are rigidly defined	There is adjustment and continued redefinition of tasks through the interactions of the organizational members
2. There is a specific definition of responsibility that is attached to the individual's functional role	There is a broader acceptance of responsibility and a commitment to the organization that goes beyond the individual's functional role
3. There is a strict hierarchy of control and authority	There is a much lower degree of hierarchy of control and authority; sanctions derive more from a presumed community of interest
4. Communication is mainly vertical, between superiors and subordinates	Communication is lateral, between people of different ranks, and it resembles consultation rather than command
5. The communications consist largely of instructions and decisions issued by superiors	The content of the communication is information and advice, and it flows in all directions
6. Loyalty and obedience to the organization and to superiors are highly valued	Commitments to the achievement of tasks and the expansion of the firm are highly valued
7. An individual's importance and prestige are judged by his loyalty to the organization	An individual's importance and prestige are judged by his affiliations and his expertise in larger environments
8. Economic efficiency is the goal	Balance, equilibrium and creativity are sought
9. Conflict is suppressed by dividing up and separating potential conflictful persons and functions	Conflict and its resolution is valued for its potential creative output; love-hate job relationships are considered natural and joint responsibilities are often assigned
10. Single-dimension objectives are common and optimal solutions are sought with respect to this one objective	Multiple objectives and constraints exist, and satisfactory solutions are sought which result in an equitable distribution to all parties
11. Top-down vertical, authority-centered management is the mode; line management methods are used	Horizontal, expertise-centered management is the mode; teams, taskforces and project management methods are used
12. Goals are clearly defined at all levels, with one visible pathway to each goal	There are multiple goals, not as clearly defined, with multiple paths to reach these objectives

environments are characterized by low product evolution rates, and stable, well-defined market needs.

The Type II Structure

If diverse market needs and ill-defined technologies characterize the business, then Type I organizations will not be able to respond to these demands. The Type II organization is much more appropriate. Type II structures have much greater potential for responding to local diversities and variations. In Type II organizations, division managers have the resources and power to engage in product line expansions and incremental innovations within their existing businesses. Moreover, new divisions may be added as a result of the activities of the long range planning group (LRPG).

However, Type II structures lack strategic adaptability and strategic reponsiveness. There is no explicit provision for new ideas that do not fit into current divisional product lines. A Type II structure will eventually find itself limited by the cult of short-term profit and loss. There will be an overpowering need to meet stringent return on investment

FIGURE 39-1 Organization Structure Types.

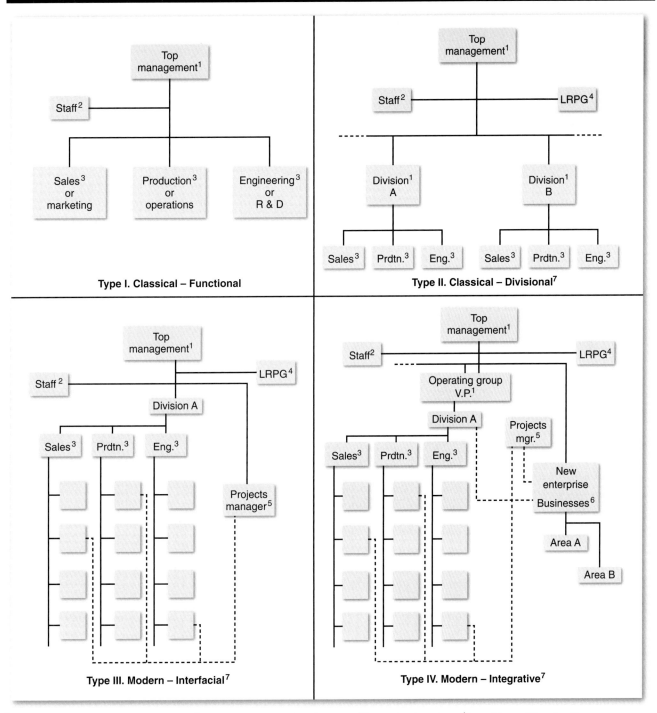

Type I. Classical – Functional

Type II. Classical – Divisional[7]

Type III. Modern – Interfacial[7]

Type IV. Modern – Integrative[7]

[1]Strategic and administrative functions; [2]Purchasing, accounting, law, etc.; [3]Operating functions; [4]Long Range Planning Group: senses new opportunities, awakens the organization to new needs, market intelligence, diversification plans, etc.; [5]Administration of longer range, cross-functional projects; [6]Strategic, administrative and operating functions; [7]The organization can be further expanded by adding more divisions.

criteria. And there will be ever-present pressures to maintain current products, and to stay within the current lines of business represented by the divisions. Moreover, when a Type II structure diversifies by adding new divisions, the older divisions are unlikely to die off. This compounds the problems of internal control and coordination.

The Type III Structure

Type I and II organizations generally lack the capability to effectively carry a new technical idea from its embryonic beginnings to the new product stage. The Type III structure attempts to solve this problem by the use of project efforts and project management systems. Theoretically, Type III structures are responsive, flexible and adaptable—ideally suited to handling the initiation stage of the innovation process. The number of projects undertaken by the projects manager can increase or decrease in response to changing diversification strategies, and in response to competitive needs for new or improved products. A variety of interdisciplinary personnel needs can be drawn from across the functional areas and assembled into a project team under the projects manager. When the project is completed the personnel can be returned to their functional areas or transferred to other projects.

In real life, however, Type III structures often create many problems. The diversion of manpower from the functional areas runs the potential risk of hurting the company's "bread-and-butter" operations. Thus, top management must constantly make difficult choices between the short-range functional needs of the organization and the long range project efforts. On the other hand, there is the opposing danger that project efforts will become on-and-off activities, as the occasional fire-fighting needs of the divisions take manpower away from the projects. These needs will create constant conflicts in authority between the projects managers and the divisional managers. It may be noted that numerous variants of the project manager system have been used, e.g., see [49, 9, 6]. However, all require enormous talents in leadership, conflict management, human relations management and personnel administration abilities [9, 32].

Perhaps the most serious failure of the Type III structure is its inability to handle the implementation stage of the innovation process. There is no structural provision for commercializing the new products that come from completed projects. What happens to them? Operating divisions do not want them unless they are fully developed, well-established in their markets, highly profitable and relatively riskless—a monumental feat for newly developed innovations! Thus, given the necessary managerial talents, Type III structures may be excellent vehicles for initiating innovations and transforming technical ideas into products. But Type III organizations make no contribution in the step from a potentially good product to a market success.

It is interesting to note the dramatic rise in popularity of the Type III structure during the past 20 years [1, 9, 6, 11, 24]. Yet, the number of commercially successful innovations, as a proportion of the technical ideas generated, has not shown a similar increase. In fact, surveys show that although the technical success rate (the transformation rate of ideas into technical products) may have risen, the commercial success rate apparently has not [38, 42, 44, 26, 56, 10, 16]. Transforming technical successes from the lab into commercial successes for the firm remains a major problem [44, 46, 38]. Type III structures make no contribution to the solution of these problems.

The Type IV Structure

The Type IV structure is an integrative form that combines the better qualities of all the other types. Currently profitable products and established product lines are housed in business groups. To facilitate efficiency, each major product line within each group is housed within its own division. This portion of the organization thus resembles the Type II structure. New product and new market ventures that have not yet achieved a break-even level of profits are temporarily housed in a new enterprise group until they become profitable. A project manager system serves as a source of new ideas projects and ventures for this new enterprise group. This portion of the organization resembles the Type III structure.

Thus, the Type IV structure harmonizes both the innovative and steady state needs of the firm. Additionally, Type IV structures explicitly provide linkages between the organization and its environment. Environments' changes (shifts in markets, competition, etc.) are quickly sensed and reported to the organization through the LRPG. Type II and III structures also have the LRPG sensing and reporting function, but these structures lack the explicit linking and implementation qualities of Type IV structure. Depending on the nature of the environmental changes, a Type IV organization can respond by assembling a new product development project, by increasing the resources devoted to its new enterprise group, or by engaging in cost reducing activities within its functional departments.

Type IV structures have high capabilities for implementation and linking. The LRPG has the responsibility for continuously supplying information to the new enterprise manager. The new enterprise manager is responsible for coordinating and linking the new product activities with the operating divisions, the projects area and the LRPG. Because of these linkages, it is natural for the division manager, the projects manager and the new enterprise manager to meet periodically as a new products committee. New technical ideas thus receive a complete hearing from the divisional, the project and the new enterprise management, with top management, resolving any conflicts. Completed projects have a new enterprise "safe home" to go to once they are completed. They can remain in their safe home until they become profitable (at which time an operating division may be more eager to sponsor them), or they may become a division on their own, if warranted.

Type IV structures also provide a necessary separation between current profit concerns and concerns for the long range future. The current-product group vice presidents are devoted to optimizing the steady-state efficiency of current products. Top management is thereby freed to concentrate on strategic matters and concerns for long range growth and balance.

The Type IV structure is no panacea. It requires great managerial talent. There will be problems and conflicts because of the authority overlaps. Difficulties in generating teamwork and collaboration will arise. But firms that have committed themselves to Type IV structures have been able to make them work [24, 11, 44]. A variety of Type IV structures have been employed [44, 50, 31]. In some cases, the project managers borrowed functional personnel as needed. In others, the project managers had a permanent cadre of people. Many variations have been used with respect to steering committees, linking arrangements and joint responsibilities [38, 42]. Many variations in the characteristics of the LRPG and new enterprise groups have also been used. These variations reflected differences in the nature of the technologies, the states-of-the-art, the dynamic nature of the markets, and the personalities of the managements at these firms [42, 44, 47].

IMPLEMENTING THE DESIGNS

Matching Structures with Technologies and Environments

In an extensive survey of successful firms in several industries, Woodward [58] found that the most effective organization structures and management control systems varied systematically with the nature of the production technology. The classical management philosophy was the most successful in those firms with continuous production technologies. The modern philosophy was the most successful under unit production technologies. Woodward concluded that a relatively higher level of job knowledge was required to handle unit technologies. Under such conditions, employees are more likely to perform effectively when they are given more freedom on the job and more participation in decisions which relate to them. The successful firms recognized this, and delegated greater authority to the lower levels of the organization.

Burns and Stalker [4] arrived at similar conclusions in their survey. They found that the classical management philosophy could be successfully used when the technical and market environment of the firm was well-understood and stable. Confectionary

TABLE 39-3   Contingent Conditions and the "Best" Organization Structures

		Market and Technological Environments	
		Stable	Dynamic
Need for Innovation	Low	Type I Structures Classical Philosophy	Type III Structures Modern Philosophy
	High	Type II Structures Classical Philosophy	Type IV Structures Modern Philosophy

and insurance firms typified this category. By contrast, the modern management philosophy was successfully used by pharmaceutical and electronics firms, who characteristically faced dynamic markets and less-understood technologies. These ideas have been further reinforced by the results from more recent studies [27, 47, 42, 44, 38]. For instance, successful plastics firms used modern organization structures to effectively cope with their more dynamic markets and uncertain technologies. Successful containers and board-box firms used classical structures [27].

Thus, as illustrated by Table 39-3, stable environments are generally characterized by low needs for innovation, an emphasis on standardization and efficiency, close cost control, stable organization behaviors and routine operations. Type I structures and the classical philosophies are the most appropriate for firms operating under these conditions. However, even in relatively stable environments some product and process evolutions are needed from time to time. Thus, a Type II structure may be more appropriate.

Where the environment is dynamic, the needs for major technological innovation, creativity and non-standard behaviors are relatively greater. As noted in Table 39-3, Type III structures and the modern management philosophy are capable of handling this need for periodic or episodic innovations and new products. Firms that do not want to be or cannot be the innovative leaders in their industries, firms that are reactive rather than proactive, firms that take a defensive rather than an offensive posture—all will find Type III structures adequate.

But, when the need for innovation is continuous, and when the environment is dynamic, as Table 39-3 shows, Type IV structures are more appropriate. Under these circumstances, technical ideas must continuously stream from R&D into the business side of the organization, and these ideas must constantly be nurtured and pushed along to commercial reality. A blend of individual behaviors and specialized activities is required. But, because they are reciprocally dependent, these activities must be linked together and integrated into a harmonious system. The Type IV structure is the only one capable of handling this demanding need for linking and integration in an effective fashion.

Table 39-3 may leave one with the incorrect impression that the choice of the "best" organization structure can be reduced to a few simple rules. The precise determination of whether an environment is stable or dynamic can be a difficult task. Some environments are obviously dynamic: new products evolve rapidly, the customer wants change quickly, supply markets are volatile, the technological state-of-the-art is constantly changing, and the technical and market uncertainties are relatively high. In those environments, one must literally innovate to stay alive. Type IV structures are clearly indicated. But, in other cases the indicators may be less clear. The choice of the "best" structure then becomes a matter of experienced management judgment [44, 46, 47, 42, 33].

Handling Life Cycle Needs: Some Examples

Recent studies [20, 37, 44, 31] indicate that the choice of an appropriate organization structure and management philosophy should be consistent with the life cycle phase of the innovation. The first phase in the innovation process involves idea generation and idea development. Here, low degrees of formalization, bureaucracy and centralization appear necessary. Scientific personnel need individualized personal freedom, available resources, and "seed" money to test their ideas. These conditions suggest the need for either a Type III or IV structure and the modern management philosophy. This first phase of activities could thus be carried out in either the project manager's area or the new enterprise area.

Once an idea is initiated and formalized, a second phase begins. Here, the interdisciplinary talents of a team of individuals is required to more fully develop the idea into a product. The emphasis is on accomplishing known tasks. But high degrees of inventiveness and ingenuity are needed regarding *how* they are accomplished. High degrees of inter-departmental collaboration and cooperation are also needed during this phase. Hence, either a Type III structure or a Type IV structure is appropriate for this second phase of activities.

The third phase of the innovation process involves product finalizing, production start-up and commercialization. Here, close control and monitoring are important. There is little room for creativity, and efficiency is the major criterion. This phase usually involves the achievement of tightly controlled, specialized tasks. Thus, Type I or Type II structures are indicated.

The history of the DuPont company provides an illustration of this concept of a gradual metamorphosis in organization structure types as a company grows and diversifies. During the 1920s and 1930s, DuPont used the classical philosophy and a Type II structure to manage its old-line explosives products. As the company diversified into synthetics, it found it necessary to move to Type III and IV structures [48, 11]. The history of the Dow Corning Company provides another illustration [21, 22]. As it began to diversify, the Dow Corning Company encountered many internal problems in communication between its production, marketing and financial departments. Stiff competition, a lack of long range corporate planning and a lack of communication between the divisions combined to threaten its future growth. Thus, the company reorganized from a Type I to a Type II structure. This structure stimulated improved inter-divisional and inter-departmental collaboration, and enabled the company to develop many new products and processes. But it was soon found that this structure did not provide the capability to effectively manage the new products once they were placed on the market. Thus, the company went to a Type IV structure. Decision making was pushed as far down into the organization as possible. A guiding body, the Corporate Business Board, maintained the overall corporate balance and prevented the potential splinter-effect of several semi-autonomous businesses. Functional and business managers were jointly responsible for periodic performance reviews. A Product Management Group was set up and charged with the long range planning of product families.

This discussion reveals a picture of an evolving organization form, which metamorphoses in parallel with its maturation. Greiner [20] presents a picture which implies that successful organizations must constantly metamorphose in even more complex ways than the above discussions imply. He distinguishes five environmentally-induced phases of growth. Each phase requires an organization structure change, in order for the firm to be able to cope with the new demands placed on it. Thus, life cycle considerations suggest that a chameleon-like quality characterizes organizations that are successful innovators. However, two primary abilities seem to be required: an ability to sense what form is needed, and an ability to quickly move into that form. Type IV organizations seem to contain within them all the structural variations that might be needed over a typical life cycle.

SUMMARY AND CONCLUSIONS

A new era of management challenge is upon us. Today's business climate is marked by a slow-down in the rate of new product introductions, greater market uncertainty, increased pressures from government and competition, rapidly evolving technologies, rising costs, and a generally non-expanding business environment. New organizations and managerial philosophies are needed to cope with these challenges. Type I and II organization structures, which functioned well in earlier eras, are woefully inadequate to handle today's conditions. Similarly, classical management philosophies are incapable of meeting today's human and non-human needs. Type III and IV organization structures and modern management philosophies are required, in order to effectively manage the innovation processes which vitalize our economy. Only Type IV structures have the integrative qualities needed for handling all phases of the innovation process. And only Type IV structures have the flexibility and adaptability for handling a diversity of changing technologies and environments. Moreover, only Type IV structures have the capability of evolving to meet the changing life cycle needs which arise as a firm matures and grows.

Type IV structures require great managerial talents in coordination and people-management. They are not especially easy to implement and maintain. Their successful use requires that management fully understand the nature of the firm's technology and the firm's market environments. Usually, an ongoing program of well-planned organization development activities is also needed [19]. But modern managers who learn how to effectively use Type IV structures as a vehicle for coordinating human and non-human resources will be able to meet tomorrow's challenges. The evidence indicates that those who do not learn to use Type IV structures may not survive the prevailing challenges and demands.

Acknowledgements

Portions of this study were funded by a grant from the Carl Foundation and by NSF grants 75-17195 and 79-12927.

References

1. Allen, T.J., 1977. Managing the Flow of Technology. MIT Press, Cambridge.
2. Behrman, J.N. and Fisher, W.A., 1980. Science and Technology for Development. Oelgeschlager, Gunn and Hain, Cambridge.
3. Bisio, Attilio and Gastwirt, L., 1979. Turning Research Development Into Profits. AMACON Division of the American Management Association, New York.
4. Burns, T. and Stalker, G., 1961. The Management of Innovation. Tavistock Publications, London.
5. Caroll, J., 1967. A note on departmental autonomy and innovation in medical schools. Journal of Business, (October), 4: 531–534.
6. Changing the company organization chart. Management Record, (November, 1969): 10–15.
7. Clark, T.N., 1968. Institutionalization of innovations in higher education. Administrative Science Quarterly, 13: 1–25.
8. Clarke, T.E., 1981. R&D budgeting—the Canadian experience. Research Management, 24, (3) (May): 32–37.
9. Cleland, D.I. and King, W.R., 1975. Systems Analysis and Project Management. McGraw-Hill, New York.
10. Cooper, R.G., 1980. Project Newprod: What Makes a New Product a Winner? Quebec Industrial Innovation Center, Montreal.
11. Corey, E.R. and Star, S.H., 1971 Organization Strategy. Harvard University Press, Cambridge.
12. Corwin, R.G., 1969. Patterns of organizational conflict. Administrative Science Quarterly, 14, (4) (December): 507–520.
13. Dean, B.V. and Goldhar, J.L. (Eds.), 1980. Management of Research and Innovation. Studies in the Management Sciences. Vol. 15. North-Holland, New York.
14. Evan, W. and Black, G., 1967. Innovation in business organization: some factors associated with success or failure of staffproposals. Journal of Business, 40: 519–530.
15. Fayol, H., 1949. General and Industrial Management. Trans. by Constance Storrs. Sir Isacc Pitman and Sons, London.
16. Ford, D. and Ryan, C., 1981. Taking technology to market. Harvard Business Review, (March–April): 117–126.
17. Frohman, A.L., 1976. Critical mid-management functions for innovation Research Management, 19, (4) (July): 7–14.
18. George, C., 1955. History of Management Thought. Prentice-Hall, Englewood.
19. Gibson, J.L., Ivancevich, J.M. and Donnelly, J.H., 1976. Organizations: Behavior, Structure and Process. Irwin-Dorsey, Dallas, pp. 403–428.
20. Greiner, L.E., 1972. Evaluation and revolution as organizations grow. Business Review, 50 (July): 37–46.
21. Grubber, W.H. and Niles, J.S., 1972. Put innovation in the organization structure. California Management Review, 14 (Summer): 29–35.
22. Goggin, W.C., 1974. How the multidimensional structure looks at Dow Corning. Harvard Business Review, 52 (January–February): 54–65.
23. Hage, J. and Aiken, M., 1970. Social Change in Complex Organizations. Random House, New York.
24. Jasinski, F.J., 1959. Adopting organizations to new technology. Harvard Business Review, 46 (January–February): 79–86.

25. Knight, K.E., 1967. A descriptive model of the intra-firm innovation process. The Journal of Business, 40: 478–496.

26. Lin, N. and Zaltman, G., 1973. Dimensions of Innovations: Process and Phenomena of Social Change. Wiley Interscience, New York.

27. Lawrence, P.R. and Lorsch, J.W., 1967. Organization and Environment: Managing Differentiation and Integration. Harvard University Press, Boston.

28. March, J.G. and Simon, H.A., 1958. Organizations. Wiley, New York.

29. McGuire, J.W., 1964. Theories of Business Behavior. Prentice-Hall, Englewood Cliffs, New Jersey.

30. Midgley, D.F., 1977. Innovation and New Product Marketing. Croom Helm, London.

31. Mintzberg, H., 1981. Organization design: fashion or fit. Harvard Business Review (January–February): 103–116.

32. Pesham, J., 1970. Matrix management: a tough game to play. Dun's Review (August): 31–34.

33. Rowe, L.A. and Boise, W.B., 1974. Organizational innovation: Current research and evolving concepts. Public Administration Review, 34: 284–93.

34. Sahal, D., 1980. Research, Development and Technological Innovation. Lexington Books, D.C. Heath & Co., Mass.

35. Schnee, J., 1978. International shifts in innovative activity: the case pharmaceuticals. Columbia Journal of World Business, (Spring): 12–22.

36. Science and technology: getting business and research on the same track. The Economist, (May 16, 1981): 105–106.

37. Shepard, H.A., 1967. Innovation resisting and innovation producing organisations Journal of Business, 40: 470–477.

38. Souder, Wm.E. and Chakrabarti, A.K., 1978. The R&D marketing interface: Results from an empirical study of innovation projects. IEEE Trans, on Eng. Mgt. (4) (October): 88–93.

39. Souder, Wm.E and Zeigler, R.W., 1977. A review of creativity and problem solving techniques. Research Management, 20, (4) (July): 34–42.

40. Souder, Wm.E. and O'Keefe, W.F., 1979. Fourteen useful techniques for problem solving and creative thinking. Administrative Review, 14, (4) 39–64.

41. Souder, Wm.E., 1975. A review of organizational conflict and integration. Technology Management Studies Group paper (August 30).

42. Souder, Wm.E., 1981. Disharmony between R&D and marketing. Industrial Marketing Management, 10, (1) (Jan–Feb): 67–73.

43. Souder, Wm.E., 1977. Effectiveness of nominal and interacting group decisions processes for integrating R&D and marketing. Management Science, 23 (6) (Feb) 595–605.

44. Souder, Wm.E., 1978. Effectiveness of product development methods. Industrial Marketing Management, 7, (5) (October): 299–307.

45. Souder, Wm.E., 1981. Effects of release-time on R&D outputs and scientist gratification. IEEE Trans. on Eng. Mgt., EM–28, (1) (February): 8–12.

46. Souder, Wm.E., 1981. Encouraging entrepreneurship in large corporations. Research Management, 24, (3) (May): 18–22.

47. Souder, Wm.E., 1980. Promoting an effective R&D/ marketing interface. Research Management, 23, (4) (July): 10–15.

48. Steele, L.W., 1975. Innovation in Big Business. American Elsevier, New York.

49. Steiner, G.A. and Ryan, W.G., 1968. Industrial Project Management. Collier-Macmillan Canada, Toronto.

50. Steiner, S.A., 1965. The Creative Organization. The University of Chicago Press, Chicago.

51. Stober, G.J. and Schumacher, D. (Eds.), 1973. Technology Assessment and Quality of Life. Elsevier Scientific, New York.

52. Taylor, F.W., 1911. The Principles of Scientific Management. Harper and Brothers, New York.

53. Thompson, V.A., 1965. Bureaucracy and Innovation. Administrative Science Quarterly, 10: 1–20.

54. Tushman, M.L. and Scanlan, T.J., 1981. Boundary spanning individuals: their role in information transfer and their antecedents. Academy of Management Journal, 24, (2): 289–305.

55. Twiss, B., 1974. Managing Technological Innovation. Longman, London.

56. Utterback, J.M., 1971. The process of technological innovation within the firm Academy of Management Journal, 14: 75–88.

57. Wilson, J.Q., 1966. Innovation in organization: notes toward a theory. In James D. Thompson (Ed.), Approaches to Organization Design. University of Pittsburgh Press.

58. Woodward, J., 1965. Industrial Organization: Theory and Practice. Oxford University Press, London.

59. Zaltman, G., Duncan, R. and Holbek, J., 1973. Innovations and Organizations. Wiley, New York.

40

A DUAL-CORE MODEL OF ORGANIZATIONAL INNOVATION[1]

Richard L. Daft

Queen's University

This paper examines the role of administrators and technical employees in the process leading to innovation adoption. A marked division of labor is found. The evidence indicates that two distinct innovation processes—bottom-up and top-down—can exist in organizations. The findings are used to propose a dual-core model of organizational innovation.

There is growing evidence that organization leaders have an impact on organizational innovation. Hage and Dewar (1973) recently reported that elite values toward change are a better predictor of new program adoption by health and welfare agencies than the structural characteristics of the agencies. Becker (1970) and Carlson (1964, 1965) linked innovation adoption to the status and sociometric centrality of organization top administrators. Other studies have found frequency of innovation associated with the cosmopolitan orientation of top administrators (Kaluzny, Veney & Gentry, 1972) and with administrator motivation to innovate (Mohr, 1969).

But the precise role of organization leaders in the innovation process is not clear. One explanation for the above findings is that leaders are active in the innovation process. Top administrators serve as a bridge between the organization and the technological environment. Top administrators' exposure, status and rank place them in a position to introduce change into the organization. They are exposed to new ideas, and their ideas count. Organization leaders can also be active in other ways, as Hage and Dewar (1973) suggest, such as searching for funds to implement new programs.

Another explanation for the findings is that top administrators influence organizational innovation without actually introducing innovations. A major function of top administrators is to set goals and priorities (Selznick, 1957). If a goal of innovation is established, innovation initiation may originate with lower organization members. Studies that report positive associations between innovation adoption and member exposure (Aiken & Hage, 1971), member education and training (Sapolsky, 1967;

ACADEMY OF MANAGEMENT JOURNAL by RICHARD L. DAFT. Copyright 1978 by ACADEMY OF MANAGEMENT (NY). Reproduced with permission of ACADEMY OF MANAGEMENT (NY) in the format Textbook via Copyright Clearance Center.

Richard L. Daft is Assistant Professor, School of Business, Queen's University, Kingston, Ontario.

[1]This research was supported by the School of Graduate Studies, Queen's University. Don Nightingale made several helpful comments on an earlier draft of this paper. A special thanks to Lou Pondy for suggesting the dual-core idea.

Palumbo, 1969; Evan & Black, 1967), and decentralization (Hage & Aiken, 1967) all support the explanation that top administrators are not themselves active innovators. Freedom and exposure of employees at lower organization levels enable innovative ideas to enter the organization and be proposed. The leader role is to set innovation goals, encourage innovation initiatives from lower members, and approve or disapprove innovation proposals.

Thus the research evidence can be used to support different explanations for the relationship between leader behavior and innovation. Leaders may actively initiate innovations, or they may not. Much of the evidence bearing on this issue is from studies that have correlated administrator or organization attributes with innovation adoption. We have learned a great deal about the correlates of innovation adoption from these studies. But we have learned little about the activity leading to adoption. We don't know where ideas enter the organization, who proposes them or why.

The innovation studies are characteristic of other organization research. Obtaining data across multiple organizations for correlational analysis makes it difficult to obtain the specific evidence needed to support or refute alternative theoretical explanations about underlying processes (Argyris, 1972; Child, 1972; Weick, 1974). Most researchers make conjectures about process on the basis of correlation studies, as well they should. But many of our explanations remain at the level of conjecture.

One of the challenges facing organization researchers is to design studies that provide insight into underlying organization processes. In the case of organizational innovation, this kind of insight would have at least two benefits. First, obviously, is the knowledge gained from finding new explanations or identifying the correct explanation among several feasible alternatives. The second benefit is a practical one. Fundamental knowledge about the innovation process, especially its early stages—where ideas originate and who proposes them—will suggest how organizations should be designed (Pondy, 1972) to facilitate or inhibit the flow of ideas that lead to innovation adoption.

The purpose of this paper is to report the results of one attempt to gather evidence that will explain more fully the innovation process in organizations. The behavior of administrators vis-à-vis lower employees as innovation initiators is examined for a sample of school organizations. The findings are related to the professionalism of organization members, organization size, and frequency of innovation adoption.

THE INNOVATION PROCESS

The process of innovation is frequently described as consisting of four essential steps, starting with the conception of an idea, which is proposed, then a decision is made to adopt, and finally the innovation is implemented. The focus of this paper is on the innovation proposal and the decision to adopt, with special attention given to proposals. There has been little research on this part of the innovation process.

Who proposes innovation ideas for adoption? Most new ideas probably originate with organization members who span the boundary between organizations and technological environments. William Evan (1966) has theorized that administrators and lower employees both initiate innovations, depending upon the type of innovation to be proposed. Evan argues that organizations can maximize adoptions by having innovative ideas originate at both ends of the organizational hierarchy: Administrative ideas would originate near the top of the hierarchy and trickle down; technical innovations would originate near the bottom of the hierarchy and trickle up. Innovative ideas follow different paths from conception to approval and implementation.

The notion of two distinct innovation proposal patterns is intriguing. Innovative ideas may be moving through the hierarchy in different directions, and the direction taken may affect chances for adoption. The point at which new ideas originate is probably a function of task differentiation. Organization members who work within a functional area will tend to be the local experts in that area. They will be the most knowledgeable people in the organization regarding problems, new ideas, and the suitability of ideas for use in their task domain.

A new idea thus will be brought into the organization by organization experts who are interested in and aware of that particular kind of development. Experts in the technical aspect of an organization will tend to be those people working on or near the core technology (Thompson, 1967). These people will be aware of technical problems, they can tell whether a new idea will fit into their current technology, and they have the expertise to implement the innovation. Technical ideas proposed by administrators and others outside the technical domain will tend to be out of synchronization with perceived needs and are less likely to be acceptable. Hence, new ideas that relate to the production process will tend to originate below the administrative level.

Top managers are the experts with regard to administrative arrangements. They are concerned with administrative problems and will be tuned to new developments that apply to these problems. Lower level managers and workers are less likely to see the big picture administratively, so their proposals are not likely to be appropriate. Board members may also propose administrative innovations. These innovations will tend to be proposed and approved near the top of the hierarchy and implemented downward. Administrators have a definite role initiating innovations, but it is probably limited to administrative ideas.

The hypothesized task specialization regarding innovation initiation will depend to a great extent upon the professionalism of the employees in the technical core and organization size. Core employees will tend to be the largest group in the organization and will constitute the largest interface with the technological environment. The professionalism of this group will be associated with member education and training, participation in professional activities, exposure to new ideas, autonomy, and the desire for recognition from peers rather than from the formal hierarchy. Many innovations are adopted because current techniques are perceived as unsatisfactory—when a performance gap exists (March & Simon, 1958). Professionals tend to see problems because of high aspirations and performance standards. As the professional level of the technical group increases, involvement with the initiation of technical innovations will increase. Technical core employees can be expected to learn about and propose nearly all technical innovations adopted in the organization. The administrator role in technical innovation will be minimized.

When the professional level of core members is low, the core members will tend to be less active as innovation initiators. If the organization is to be innovative, administrators will have to initiate a larger share of the technical innovations. Innovation specialization will be reduced. Administrator initiatives will probably meet with some success because employees who are not attached to a professional ideology are less resistant to changes initiated by top managers (Zald & Denton, 1963).

Another strategy available to administrators is collaboration with core members on technical proposals. If an administrator and employee work together on an innovation proposal, resistance to management's initiative will be reduced. Collaboration will engage core employees in the innovation process. Collaboration is essentially an implementation strategy, and is similar to the "mutual understanding" strategy for implementing scientific research (Churchman & Scheinblatt, 1965). The present study is not concerned with techniques of implementation, except as implementation strategies are reflected in proposal initiation. Collaboration is a realistic proposal strategy for administrators. But collaboration is not expected to be needed or used when core members are highly professional.

Organization size probably will have consequences for the initiation of innovation proposals that are similar to the consequences of employee professionalism. Large organizations are characterized by greater division of labor. Technical employees in large organizations will be specialized and concerned with innovations in their task domain. Administrators also will be specialized and employed full-time on administrative activities. There will also tend to be greater formalization and less contact between technicians and administrators in large organizations. Thus there should be fewer collaborations.

The discussion thus far has been concerned with the source of innovation proposals. Employee professionalism and organization size are also expected to influence the absolute number of innovation proposals and adoptions. Wilson (1966) and Zaltman, Duncan and Holbeck (1973) argue that employee professionalism and organization complexity are associated with a greater number of innovation proposals. However, they also argue that these same characteristics inhibit adoption. Autonomous employee specialists will propose ideas relevant to themselves, but will resist proposals by others. Likewise, the division of labor in large, complex organizations leads to increased proposals, but the coordination and compliance necessary for adoption is more difficult to achieve. If innovation proposals generally result in adoption, then factors such as professionalism and size should be associated with greater proposals and adoptions. However, if Wilson (1966) and Zaltman et al. (1973) are correct, then these variables may have opposing effects upon adoptions. The number of final adoptions cannot be predicted on the basis of proposals alone.

In summary, then, administrators and technical core employees are expected to play important but different roles in the innovation process: (1) Each group is expected to initiate innovations pertaining to their own organization task; (2) this division of labor is expected to heighten as employee professionalism and organization size increase; (3) the absolute number of proposals initiated by each group is also expected to increase as professionalism and size increase; but (4) the greater number of proposals may not lead to greater adoptions because professionalism and size may be associated with greater resistance to adoption.

RESEARCH METHOD

Organizational innovation is usually defined as the adoption of a new idea or behavior by an organization. But new compared to what? Becker and Whisler define innovation as something new in relation to the organization's technological environment. They suggest that innovation is "the first or early use of an idea by one of a set of organizations with similar goals" (Becker and Whisler, 1967, p. 463). Innovation has also been defined as the adoption of an idea or behavior that is new to the organization adopting it (Mohr, 1969; Aiken & Hage, 1971). The idea can be old with regard to other organizations so long as the idea has not previously been used by the adopting organizations.

The definition adopted for this research is the definition provided by Becker and Whisler (1967). The internal organizational process may be similar for the adoption of innovations by either of the above definitions. But the focus of this research is on the adoption of innovations from the developing pool of new ideas in the organization's technological environment.

The definition of technical versus administrative innovation is taken from Evan (1966). A technical innovation is an idea for a new product, process or service. An administrative innovation pertains to the policies of recruitment, allocation of resources, and the structuring of tasks, authority and reward. Technical innovations usually will be related to technology, and administrative innovations will be related to the social structure of the organization.

The Sample

The sample of organizations for this study consists of 13 suburban high school districts in Cook County, Illinois. Each school district is engaged in a similar function, with similar goals and ownership, and they use the same technology. The districts range in size from approximately 3,600 to 14,600 students.

Each district has a seven-member school board elected by district residents. The school board is the top policy and decision body in the district. The superintendent is the top operating manager in the district, reporting directly to the school board. A principal is assigned to each school, and he/she is the line officer. The usual line of authority goes from the school board to the superintendent to the principal and then to the teacher.

It should be emphasized that the organizational unit under study is the school district, not the individual high school. The district is the legal organizational entity in

Illinois. The school board, superintendent, assistant superintendents and other district-level staff administer the entire district. Most of the data stored in state educational agencies are for the district rather than individual high schools. Typical schools have 2,000–2,500 students. Hence, large districts tend to have more schools than small districts. If the presence of multiple schools influences the innovation process, this effect will be partially captured by the measure of district size.

The Data

The school districts were surveyed during 1972 to learn which innovations had been adopted during the prior several years. Professional educators and books on education were also consulted to learn about new developments in the field of high school education. The reported innovations were assembled into a master innovation checklist of about 150 items. The checklist was taken to each district, and through interviews with curriculum coordinators and senior administrators it was determined whether each innovation was ever proposed or seriously considered for adoption, which innovations were actually adopted in the district, the year adopted, and where the idea originated (e.g., teacher, principal, et cetera).

The eight-year period from 1964–72 was chosen as the criterion of innovation newness. Such a time period is long enough to include the diffusion of major developments in the recent past, but districts do not receive credit for adopting techniques which were available in the technological environment for a long period of time. An analysis of the dates of innovation adoption revealed that many reported innovations were not new to the technological environment. Two innovations had been adopted as early as 1952 by one or two districts. Sixty-eight of the items on the master checklist met the time period criterion. They represent educational and administrative developments that became available to this set of organizations during the 1964–72 period.

An independent measure of the adoption of innovations was available to validate the memories of the informants and the data collection procedure. A survey of new programs in Cook County high schools was conducted in 1965 by the Cook County Superintendent of Schools. A few of the programs included in the Cook County survey also appeared on the master checklist for this study. For the common programs, the number of adoptions reported for each district in the Cook County survey and on the checklists for this study were compared. The number of adoptions reported by each source are correlated .63 across the districts, which suggests that both surveys are measuring the same phenomenon. The .63 correlation is only for adoptions during 1965 and earlier. It is reasonable to expect that the informants would be just as accurate and probably more so for adoptions after 1965, which are the majority of innovations for this study.

Fifty of the 68 innovations are classified as technical because they represent changes in educational content or method. Most of the technical innovations are new courses, new curricula, and new teaching techniques. Examples of curricular innovations include Harvard Project Physics, Oceanography and the substitution of numerous optional short courses for the traditional required English courses. New teaching techniques include individually paced coursework and dial-access retrieval systems.

The 18 administrative innovations represent changes in the structure or process of the organization itself. Examples of administrative innovations are such things as the scheduling of students, the structure of high school organizations, the location of classes, and program budgeting. These innovations do not directly affect classroom method or content.

Five hierarchical levels were coded as initiating innovative ideas: student, teacher, principal, superintendent, school board. The teachers are the line workers and most directly involved in the production process. Principals are administrators at a middle management level. The superintendent is the top administrator.

Teacher professionalism is measured as the percentage of district certified staff who have completed a masters degree. The educational level in the district is a surrogate for the cluster of traits associated with employee professionalism, such as autonomy, expertise, education and training, and professional affiliations. The data on educational levels were provided by the Illinois Office of the Superintendent of Public

Instruction. The school districts in the sample ranged from 37 percent of teachers with masters degrees to 77 percent.

The educational level of district superintendents was also measured, but did not provide any useful variance across districts that could be used in the analysis. Ten of the 13 superintendents had doctorates. The other three had work beyond the masters degree. Two of the nondoctorates were in the two districts with the lowest average teacher education. The other nondoctorate was in the district with the fifth lowest level of teacher education. Teacher education and administrator education tend to be strongly associated in these school districts.

Unexpected Finding

One idea to be explored in this study was the notion that organizational variables simultaneously generate innovation proposals and inhibit decisions to adopt. For the hundreds of innovation adoptions reported by the districts for the 1964–72 period, only about half a dozen instances occurred where the innovation was proposed but not adopted. What could this mean? It could mean that the organizational memory for unadopted proposals is short. However, the informants seemed certain that a given innovation had never been proposed for adoption. Perhaps informal processes are at work whereby innovations that have a high probability of adoption are the ones that tend to be proposed. This finding may also mean simply that most serious proposals are adopted in these organizations. It might be unusual to reject serious proposals. This would mean that getting the innovation proposed is the most important step in the innovation process. This possibility will be examined in more detail after the other data are analyzed.

Analysis

The sameness of proposals and adoptions has consequences for the data analysis. Only one dependent variable—number of adoptions—will be used in the analysis. It is not possible to discriminate between the number of proposals and the number of adoptions.

For the analysis described in the next section, any adoption of the 68 innovations by any of the 13 districts is counted as a separate observation. The strategy of analyzing separate innovation decisions has been recommended by Downs and Mohr (1976). This strategy enables a clear test of the hypothesis that administrative and technical innovations originate with different groups in the organization. The school districts are then divided into subgroups according to district professionalism, size, and number of adoptions. Comparing these subgroups reveals how these variables influence the internal innovation process. A total of 414 adoptions occurred across these 13 districts from the pool of 68 innovations. It was not possible to trace 26 adoptions to the point of initiation. Thus, the analysis in the next section is based upon 388 innovation adoptions.

THE FINDINGS

The data in Table 40-1 show that teachers are by far the major source of technical ideas (70 percent). The principal and superintendent levels are about equally active as sources of technical ideas (8 percent and 9 percent respectively), but both levels are much less active than teachers. For administrative ideas, activity increases with hierarchial level. Teachers initiate only 13 percent of administrative innovations, principals initiate 22 percent and superintendents initiate 45 percent. Collaborations between administrators and teachers account for a similar proportion (12 and 15 percent) of each innovation type.

Very few innovative ideas originate with students or school boards. There is little reason to expect students to be the source of innovations. Students are recipients of educational services, and they have little expertise and little exposure to new ideas. The small number of ideas from the school board is a little bit surprising. Board members are laymen and apparently leave the responsibility for initiating innovations to the experts within the organizations. If the board is to influence innovation adoption it

TABLE 40-1 Innovation Type and Where Initiated[a]

	Innovation Type			
	Technical		Administrative	
Where Initiated	Percent	n	Percent	n
Students	1	(4)	4	(4)
Teachers	70	(210)	13	(11)
Principals	8	(24)	22	(19)
Superintendents	9	(26)	45	(40)
School Board	.3	(1)	1	(1)
Collaborations	12	(35)	15	(13)
	100	(300)	100	(88)

[a]$X^2 = 108.7$ with 5 *df*, $p < .001$.

TABLE 40-2 Employee Professionalism and Where Initiated, by Innovation Type

	Technical Innovations[a]						Administrative Innovations[b]					
	Professionalism						Professionalism					
	High		Medium		Low		High		Medium		Low	
Where Initiated	%	$(\bar{x})$[c]	%	$(\bar{x})$	%	$(\bar{x})$	%	$(\bar{x})$	%	$(\bar{x})$	%	$(\bar{x})$
Teachers	93	(24.0)	66	(14.8)	53	(11.0)	47	(2.0)	10	(0.8)	0	(0.0)
Administrators	7	(1.8)	15	(3.3)	29	(6.0)	47	(2.0)	56	(4.5)	97	(6.6)
Collaborations	0	(0.0)	19	(4.3)	17	(3.6)	6	(0.3)	34	(2.8)	3	(0.2)
	100	(25.8)	100	(22.3)	100	(20.6)	100	(4.3)	100	(8.0)	100	(6.8)
Number of adoptions	103		89		103		17		32		34	

[a]$X^2 = 46.3$ with 4 *df*, $p < .001$.
[b]$X^2 = 36.8$ with 4 *df*, $p < .001$.
[c]$\bar{x}$ = the average number of adoptions per district.

may be by helping establish a favorable climate for innovation and by approving proposals by others, rather than by being the source of new ideas. The small number of ideas from students and school board member supports the notion that innovation ideas originate with task experts within the organization.

Students and school board members are dropped from the remaining analysis because they account for so few innovations. Principals and superintendents are combined into an administrator category. There is a strong relationship between innovation type and where the innovation is initiated when principals and superintendents are combined. Seventy percent of technical innovations originate with teachers alone, and 67 percent of administrative innovations originate with administrators.

In Table 40-2 the school districts are divided into categories according to educational level of the teachers. Districts which have 64 percent or more teachers with masters degrees are in the high professional category; districts with from 47 to 63 percent of teachers with masters degrees are in the medium professional category; and districts with less than 47 percent of teachers with masters degrees are in the low professional category.

The Table 40-2 data indicate that teacher professionalism has considerable bearing on where ideas originate in the school district. In districts with highly professional teachers, the teachers propose 93 percent of the technical innovations. This drops off to 66 percent and 53 percent in the medium and low professional districts. The proportion of technical innovations initiated by administrators behaves just the opposite: Administrators propose only 7 percent of the technical innovations in the high professional districts, and this increases to 29 percent in the low professional districts. Collaboration between administrators and teachers is also more important in the medium and low professional districts.

There may be some question about who initiates collaborations. From discussions with the superintendents in the sample about the innovation process, it seems that nearly all collaborations are initiated by administrators. The superintendents said that teachers have little reason to seek a collaboration with an administrator because teachers have to work with technical innovations, and when teachers really want a technical innovation they can usually have it. This is consistent with the earlier finding that most proposals are adopted. But when administrators want the teachers to adopt a technical innovation it is a different matter. If the teachers don't want an innovation, they frequently can resist administrator influence. One way to combat this is for the administrator to collaborate with one or more teachers in proposing the innovations for adoption.

The Table 40-2 data suggest that some sort of a power balance model also may influence collaborations. The percentage of collaborations is higher in the medium professional districts for both technical and administrative innovations. Collaboration is especially infrequent for technical innovations in the high professional districts where teachers may have exclusive influence in the educational domain.

The average number of adoptions per school district $(\overline{x})$ is included in Table 40-2 and subsequent tables. In the high professional districts, teachers account for more than twice as many technical innovation adoptions per district (24 versus 11) as in the low professional districts. The increased activity of administrators in the low professional districts (6.0 versus 1.8) is partly successful in overcoming the lack of teacher activity, but the high professional districts still adopt somewhat more innovations than the others (25.8 versus 20.6).

A similar pattern of activity is observed on the right side of Table 40-2 for administrative innovations. Teachers propose nearly half (47 percent) of the administrative innovations in the high professional districts and none in the low professional districts. Administrators initiate a larger percentage of administrative innovations only as teacher education decreases. Highly educated teachers appear to generate an idea "push" from the bottom of the organization. The professional push even intrudes into which might be considered administrator territory—ideas for administrative innovations. When teachers are less professional and less active, administrators take on a larger share of the idea load.

The districts where administrators propose the largest percentage of administrative ideas also adopt a larger number of administrative innovations. Teacher involvement in administrative innovations does not lead to a large number of adoptions. Organizations appear to only adopt a larger number of innovations of either type when individuals in the relevant task domain actively initiate them. The involvement of teachers in administrative innovations or administrators in technical innovations is associated with fewer total adoptions of each innovation type.

The data in Table 40-2 suggest that organizations are characterized by different innovation processes depending upon employee professionalism. In the high professional districts, the process tends to be bottom-up. Teachers apparently see problems, want to solve them, know about innovations, and hence propose most innovations that are adopted in the district. The administrators can be involved in activities other than innovation initiation. The consequence of this bottom-up process is a large number of technical innovation adoptions. The low professional organizations are characterized by more of a top-down innovation process. The administrators take a greater role in the initiation phase of innovation. Administrators initiate more technical innovations, which partly offsets the smaller number of technical innovations initiated by teachers. The top-down districts also adopt somewhat more administrative innovations.

The influence of organization size is less striking on the innovation process. In Table 40-3 the organizations are divided into three groups according to number of students: small = 3,600 to 4,600 students; medium = 4,700 to 7,000 students; and large = 7,200 to 14,600 students. Large districts are characterized by a slightly greater percentage of technical innovation proposals by teachers, and somewhat fewer collaborations. The reason is probably that large organizations have greater differentiation between

TABLE 40-3 Organization Size and Where Initiated, by Innovation Type

	Technical Innovations[a]						Administrative Innovations[b]					
	Size						Size					
	Large		Medium		Small		Large		Medium		Small	
Where Initiated	%	$(\bar{x})$[c]	%	$(\bar{x})$	%	$(\bar{x})$	%	$(\bar{x})$	%	$(\bar{x})$	%	$(\bar{x})$
Teachers	77	(19.7)	69	(17.0)	69	(13.2)	12	(1.0)	20	(1.2)	7	(0.4)
Administrators	17	(4.3)	23	(5.6)	10	(1.8)	64	(5.3)	77	(4.8)	70	(3.8)
Collaborations	6	(1.7)	8	(2.0)	21	(4.0)	24	(2.0)	3	(0.2)	22	(1.2)
	100	(25.3)	100	(24.6)	100	(19.0)	100	(8.3)	100	(6.2)	100	(5.4)
Number of adoptions	77		123		95		25		31		27	

[a]$X^2 = 16.1$ with 4 $df, p < .005$.
[b]$X^2 = 6.9$ with 4 $df, p < .10$.
[c]$\bar{x}$ = the average number of adoptions per district.

TABLE 40-4 Number of Adoptions and Where Initiated, by Innovation Type

	Technical Innovations[a]						Administrative Innovations[b]					
	Number of Adoptions						Number of Adoptions					
	High		Medium		Low		High		Medium		Low	
Where Initiated	%	$(\bar{x})$[c]	%	$(\bar{x})$	%	$(\bar{x})$	%	$(\bar{x})$	%	$(\bar{x})$	%	$(\bar{x})$
Teachers	77	(22.2)	71	(15.4)	54	(7.3)	16	(1.4)	6	(0.4)	40	(0.7)
Administrators	16	(4.6)	19	(4.2)	14	(2.0)	75	(6.4)	68	(4.8)	60	(1.0)
Collaborators	7	(2.2)	10	(2.2)	32	(4.3)	9	(0.8)	26	(1.8)	0	(0.0)
	100	(29.0)	100	(21.8)	100	(13.6)	100	(8.6)	100	(7.0)	100	(1.7)
Number of adoptions	145		109		41		43		35		5	

[a]$X^2 = 19.1$ with 4 $df, p < .001$.
[b]$X^2 = 8.8$ with 4 $df, p < .10$.
[c]$\bar{x}$ = the average number of adoptions per district.

teachers and administrators and more highly professional teachers and administrators. When an individual in either group wants a technical innovation, he/she is more likely to initiate it alone. In the small districts, the administrators are probably closer to the teachers and are better able to collaborate to get innovations adopted.

Size has virtually no effect on the process of administrative innovation. The source of innovations is not significantly different across the three size categories. Size is apparently associated with frequency of innovation, however. More innovations of each type are initiated and adopted in large districts. For administrative innovations this is probably due to the greater number of ideas and the greater need for innovation experienced in large organizations. For technical innovations the greater frequency of innovation is probably due to the greater range of services required by a diverse student population and somewhat greater professionalism of teachers. The adoption of more innovations by large school districts is congruent with other research (Baldridge & Burnham, 1975).

The final part of the analysis compares districts that adopt many innovations to districts that adopt few (Table 40-4). It seems from Table 40-4 that districts which adopt many technical innovations do so because of teacher activity. Teachers alone propose 77 percent of the technical innovations in the highly innovative districts for an average of 22 adoptions per district. In the low innovation districts, teachers alone propose only 54 percent of technical innovations, which is 7.3 innovations per district. The proportion of technical innovations proposed by administrator's is similar across the districts, suggesting that administrative initiative is not a major factor in technical innovation. The proportion of innovations initiated via collaboration increases as district innovativeness decreases (7 percent versus 32 percent). Collaboration is probably a response by administrators to lower innovation activity. In the high innovative districts there is little need for administrators to cross over and collaborate with teachers. The pattern of technical innovation in Table 40-4 is similar to the pattern in Table 40-2, which suggests that one reason for district innovativeness is the level of teacher professionalism.

The data on the right side of Table 40-4 indicate that the proportion of administrative innovations proposed by administrators is moderately related to the frequency of adoption. In districts which adopt the most administrative innovations, 75 percent are proposed by administrators alone compared to only 60 percent in low innovation districts. Across all districts in the sample, the key to the adoption of administrative innovations clearly rests with administrators. The data do not tell us exactly why administrators are more active in some districts, but it is probably because they are in larger organizations and in organizations characterized by a centralized, top-down administrative process.

DISCUSSION: A DUAL-CORE MODEL OF ORGANIZATIONAL INNOVATION

The purpose of this study was to explore the early stages in the innovation process to learn something about where innovative ideas are proposed and why. The findings have to be treated as tentative, because they are based upon a small number of organizations and a single type of organization. Within these school organizations, however, the observed relationships were quite strong. At one level of interpretation, the findings support Evan's trickle-up, trickle-down theory and a contingency approach to innovation. The process of innovation appears to be contingent upon both the type of innovation and the professional level of employees. Innovations tend to be brought into an organization and proposed by individuals who are the experts in a particular task domain and who will use the innovation. A further interpretation of the findings—and one which goes beyond the data—is that they suggest a fundamental reinterpretation of certain ideas about organizational innovation.

Consider the following possibility: School organizations, and perhaps other organizations, have dual cores—the technical core described by Thompson (1967) and an administrative core. Each core has its own participants, its own goals, problems, activities, technology and environmental domain. Each core is essential to total organization functioning. The technical and administrative cores may have their own buffers, and in fact serve to buffer one another—each taking responsibility for certain sectors of the external environment. Innovation can take place in either core.

The administrative core is above the technical core in the hierarchy, and the domain of the administrative core includes the organization itself. Under certain circumstances the two cores are loosely coupled, i.e., attachments between them are weak and each retains identity and separateness (Weick, 1976). In school organizations, employee professionalism is important to coupling and innovation. When teachers are highly professional, the technical core will be only loosely coupled to the administrative core. When teacher professionalism is low, the administrative core will be some-what more dominant, and the technical core will be tightly coupled to it. As professionalism increases within the "host" core relative to the other, responsibility for innovation within the core increases. Moreover, as professionalism increases, "host" core participants are more likely to initiate innovations into the other core.

In other types of organizations, the amount of innovation and the degree of coupling between the two cores may be a function of technology, rate of change, and uncertainty in the environmental domain as well as employee professionalism. Administrative innovation and tight coupling will tend to occur when an organization must be poised to adapt to changes in goals, policies, strategies, structure, control systems, and personnel, all of which are in the administrative domain. The technical core becomes relatively more innovative, and loosely coupled, when changes in core technology are of primary importance.

Explaining the adoption of innovation as a function of two organizational cores is a departure from the current theorizing. There are two findings in the data which point toward this new interpretation. First is the importance of innovation type. Innovation action takes place in two different areas of the organization—the technical core and the administrative core—and innovations serve the respective groups. Technical ideas percolate from within the technical core and administrative ideas originate within the administrative core. Past empirical research has displayed only casual regard for innovation type. Technical and administrative innovations have been combined in unknown ways, so that the explanatory power of innovation type and the importance of two separate innovation centers has been obscured.

The second finding concerns the relative innovation balance between the two cores. In some organizations, such as in the high professional districts studied here, nearly all innovations originate within the technical core, and nearly all innovations adopted by the organization are technical in nature. The organizational focus is upon technical innovation. The technical core appears to act independently (loose coupling), and administrators play a secondary role, routinely approving most proposals. In other organizations, the administrative component is relatively more important. The organization adopts greater numbers of administrative innovations. A substantial portion of technical innovations originate within the administrative core. The technical core appears to be subordinate and tightly coupled to an active and influential administrative core.

With these ideas in mind, that organizations have dual cores and that organizations vary in the relative innovativeness and degree of coupling between these cores, it becomes possible to explain and reinterpret extant innovative ideas.

In a discussion of innovation research, Aiken and Hage (1971) concluded that organic organizations have characteristics that facilitate innovations. Among these characteristics are involvement in professional associations and a high intensity of communication within organization groups. The high professional districts in this sample might be characterized as similar to the organic model described by Aiken and Hage. They also tend to be most innovative, *but only for innovations within the technical core.* This relationship does not hold for innovations in the administrative core. Low professional districts, which have tighter coupling and a dominant administrative core, tend to adopt more administrative innovations.

Zaltman, Duncan, and Holbeck (1973) argue that organizations typically need one type of organization structure (low formalization, decentralization, high complexity) to generate innovation proposals and the opposite structure (high formalization, centralization, low complexity) to facilitate adoption and implementation. Yet the unexpected finding reported earlier in this paper indicates that proposals tend to be adopted; whatever circumstances engendered proposals in these districts did not inhibit adoption. The reason the Zaltman et al. argument is not supported becomes clear when one considers that innovation activity takes place in two separate cores. It seems likely that low formalization, decentralization, and high complexity (professionalism) are suited to both *initiation and adoption* of innovations within the technical core. The opposite structural conditions facilitate innovation in the administrative core. High formalization, centralization, low complexity (professionalism) and tight coupling fit the initiation and adoption of innovations which pertain to the organization itself. These innovations often are pushed onto the technical core. For both types of innovations, proposals tend to be approved and implemented because the people who are involved with the innovations, the local experts, are within the respective cores and typically have a hand in initiating the changes.

The notion of dual organizational cores also helps integrate disparate findings in the innovation literature. Several studies have attributed successful innovation to the professionalism of organization members (Sapolsky, 1967; Evan & Black, 1967; Hage & Aiken, 1967). Zald and Denton (1963) and Corwin (1972), however, did not find a positive relationship between professionalism and innovation. The studies which reported positive associations between professionalism and innovation typically dealt with new programs and other innovations which were pertinent to the technical core. Technical innovations are more likely to be pushed for adoption by professional employees. Zald and Denton, however, were studying the introduction of new organizational goals in the YMCA, which takes place within the administrative core and is a top-down process. This innovation is most likely to be successful when employees are low professionals and tightly coupled to administrators. In the study by Corwin, innovations were introduced by Teacher Corps interns who were assigned to schools to act as a catalyst and influence teachers to adopt innovations. This influence is not likely to be particularly effective in loosely coupled organizations where teachers are already well exposed and will initiate their own innovations.

Finally, the dual-core conceptualization of organizational innovation has implications for the management of innovation. The dual-core concept helps answer the question raised at the beginning of this paper—what is the role of top administrators in the innovation process? When innovation and adaptation within the technical core is desired, the advice is relatively straightforward: Acquire highly professional employees for the technical core, and let *them* handle innovation. Professional employees are aware of problems in their work, they are versed in the state of the art of their technology, and they should have the freedom (loose coupling) to innovate as they see fit. Approval of their proposals should be relatively routine. Acquisition of highly professional employees is not always possible, of course, because of financial constraints. In this case, administrators may have to be more active, which may mean tighter coupling and greater innovation activity from within the administrative core.

For administrative innovations, the administrators are the experts. It is their responsibility to scan the environment for suitable ideas and initiate them in the administrative core. Administrative innovations often affect the technical core. Hence, this type of innovation activity will be most successful when the technical core is tightly coupled to the administrative core and when authority is centralized with administrators.

In conclusion, the exploration into the origin of innovation proposals has yielded substantial insight about the process of innovation. The conceptualization of organizations as having two major centers—dual cores—in which innovation and change occur, seems to explain the research findings. An important consideration for future research is that innovation processes are differentiated and complex. Organizational and environmental variables may be associated with innovation activity in one core but not with activity in the other core. Future investigators must distinguish innovation types and the location of innovation activities to achieve valid results. The focus of this paper has been on the source of innovation proposals and the effects of organization size and professionalism. Perhaps future research can integrate additional organization and environmental variables with the dual-core processes described here.

References

1. Aiken, M., and J. Hage. "The Organic Organization and Innovation," *Sociology,* Vol. 5 (1971), 63–82.
2. Argyris, C. *The Applicability of Organizational Sociology* (Cambridge: Cambridge University Press, 1972).
3. Baldridge, J. V., and R. A. Burnham. "Organizational Innovation: Individual, Organizational, and Environmental Impacts," *Administrative Science Quarterly,* Vol. 20 (1975), 165–176.
4. Becker, M. H. "Sociometric Location and Innovativeness: Reformulation and Extension of the Diffusion Model," *American Sociological Review,* Vol. 35 (1970), 267–282.
5. Becker, S. W., and T. L. Whisler. "The Innovative Organization: A Selective View of Current Theory and Research," *Journal of Business,* Vol. 40 (1967), 462–469.
6. Carlson, R. O. "School Superintendents and the Adoption of Modern Math: A Social Structure Profile," in Mathew G. Miles (Ed.), *Innovation in Education* (New York: Bureau of Publications, Teacher's College, Columbia University, 1964).
7. Carlson, R. O. *Adoption of Educational Innovations* (Eugene: Center for the Advanced Study of Educational Administration, University of Oregon, 1965).
8. Child, J. "Organizational Structure, Environment and Performance: The Role of Strategic Choice," *Sociology,* Vol. 6 (1972), 1–22.
9. Churchman, C. W., and A. H. Scheinblatt. "The Researcher and the Manager: A Dialectic of Implementation," *Management Science,* Vol. 11 (1965), B69–B87.
10. Corwin, R. G. "Strategies for Organizational Innovation: An Empirical Comparison," *American Sociological Review,* Vol. 37 (1972), 441–454.
11. Downs, G. W. Jr., and L. B. Mohr. "Conceptual Issues in the Study of Innovation," *Administrative Science Quarterly,* Vol. 21 (1976), 700–713.
12. Evan, W. M. "Organizational Lag." *Human Organization,* Vol. 25 (1966), 51–53.
13. Evan, W. M., and R. Black. "Innovation in Business Organizations: Some Factors Associated with Success or

Failure of Staff Proposals," *Journal of Business,* Vol. 40 (1967), 519–30.

14. Hage, J., and M. Aiken. "Program Change and Organizational Properties," *American, Journal of Sociology,* Vol. 72 (1967), 503–519.

15. Hage, J., and R. Dewar. "Elite Values Versus Organizational Structure in Predicting Innovation," *Administrative Science Quarterly,* Vol. 18 (1973), 279–290.

16. Kaluzny, A. D., J. E. Veney, and J. T. Gentry. "Innovation of Health Services: A Comparative Study of Hospitals and Health Departments," (Paper presented at the University of North Carolina Health Services Research Center Symposium on Innovation in Health Care Organizations, Chapel Hill, N.C., May 18–19, 1972).

17. March, J., and H. Simon. *Organizations* (New York: Wiley, 1958).

18. Mohr, L. B. "Determinants of Innovation in Organizations," *American Political Science Review,* Vol. 63 (1969), 111–126.

19. Palumbo, D. J. "Power and Role Specificity in Organization Theory," *Public Administration Review,* Vol. 29 (1969), 237–248.

20. Pondy, L. R. "Letter to the Editor," *Administrative Science Quarterly,* Vol. 17 (1972), 408–409.

21. Sapolsky, H. M. "Organization Structure and Innovation," *Journal of Business,* Vol. 40 (1967), 497–519.

22. Selznick, P. *Leadership in Administration* (New York: Harper and Row, 1957).

23. Thompson, J. O. *Organizations in Action* (New York: McGraw-Hill, 1967).

24. Weick, K. E. "Amendments to Organizational Theorizing," *Academy of Management Journal,* Vol. 17 (1974), 487–502.

25. Weick, K. E. "Educational Organizations as Loosely Coupled Systems," *Administrative Science Quarterly,* Vol. 21 (1976), 1–19.

26. Zald, M. N., and P. Denton. "From Evangelism to General Service: The Transformation of the YMCA," *Administrative Science Quarterly,* Vol. 7 (1963), 214–234.

27. Zaltman, G., R. Duncan and J. Holbeck. *Innovations and Organizations* (New York: Wiley, 1973).

41

INNOVATION IN CONSERVATIVE AND ENTREPRENEURIAL FIRMS: TWO MODELS OF STRATEGIC MOMENTUM

Danny Miller

Ecole des Hautes Etudes Commerciales, Montreal, Canada and McGill University, Montreal, Canada

Peter H. Friesen

McGill University, Montreal, Canada

SUMMARY

Two very different models of product innovation are postulated and tested. The *conservative* model assumes that innovation is performed reluctantly, mainly in response to serious challenges. It therefore predicts that innovation will correlate positively with environmental, information processing, structural and decision making variables that represent, or help to recognize and cope with these challenges. In contrast, the *entrepreneurial* model supposes that innovation is always aggressively pursued and will be very high unless decision makers are warned to slow down. Thus negative correlations are predicted between innovation and the variables that can provide such warning. Correlational and curvilinear regression analyses revealed that each model was supported by conservative and entrepreneurial subsamples, respectively, in a diverse sample of 52 Canadian firms.

INTRODUCTION

There is much controversy in the literature on organizational innovation. According to Downs and Mohr (1976: 700):

> Perhaps the most alarming characteristic of the body of empirical study of innovation is the extreme variance among its findings, what we call instability. Factors found to be important for innovation in one study are found to be considerably less important, not important at all, or even inversely important in another study. This phenomenon occurs with relentless regularity . . . In spite of the large amount of energy expended, the results have not been cumulative.

Of the 38 propositions bearing directly on the act of innovation cited by Rogers and Shoemaker (1971: 350–376), 34 were supported in some studies and found to receive

Miller, Danny and Peter H. Friesen. (1982), "Innovation in Conservative and Entrepreneurial Firms: Two Models of Strategic Momentum," *Strategic Management Journal*, 3 (January–March), 1–25.

no support in others. The four consistently predictive propositions were treated in very few studies.

We believe that in studies of product innovation, many of the conflicts in the literature have been caused by the failure of researchers to take into account the nature of the innovative strategy of the firm, something that is often determined by executives on the basis of their goals and temperaments. Some executives decide that regular and extensive innovation in product lines or services and product designs should be a vital element of strategy. Their 'entrepreneurial' firms may try to obtain a competitive advantage by routinely making dramatic innovations and taking the concomitant risks. Other organizations are run by more conservative managers who may view innovation as costly and disruptive to production efficiency. Such 'conservative' firms will innovate only when they are very seriously challenged by competitors or by shifting customer wants. The thesis of this paper is that the impact upon product innovation of environmental, information processing, structural and decision making variables will vary significantly and systematically among entrepreneurial and conservative firms; that future research on the determinants of innovation must consider organizational strategy.

Based on previous empirical research, the paper develops distinct arguments concerning the determinants of innovation in conservative and entrepreneurial firms. It then presents data from a diverse sample of 52 Canadian business firms which show how different are the correlates of product innovation for both kinds of firms. The scope of the paper is limited to innovations in product lines, product designs, and services offered. It does not extend to technological or administrative innovations. Only business firms are studied. Our arguments or findings may not hold for other types of organizations. Finally, although we sometimes talk about the 'determinants' of innovation, the direction of causality is always in doubt, and, strictly speaking, we should refer only to 'correlates' of innovation.

MOMENTUM AND INNOVATION

Miller and Friesen (1980) have shown that momentum is a pervasive force in organizations; that past practices, trends and strategies tend to keep evolving in the same direction, perhaps eventually reaching dysfunctional extremes. For example, the implementation of bureaucratic controls may be followed by more of the same until the organization begins to take on a very mechanistic mantle. Centralization of authority often continues until the organization becomes an autocracy, while decentralization can lead to the proliferation of uncoordinated departmental fiefdoms. Miller and Friesen (1980) found that the same might be true of innovation. Firms with a propensity to innovate become still more innovative, sometimes passing the point of dramatically diminished returns. Conservative firms on the other hand sometimes drift towards complete stagnation.

It is reasonable to believe that momentum and its resultant excesses will be attenuated by influences that warn of the dangers of conservative and entrepreneurial extremes. There may be a number of such mitigating influences. First, they may take the form of information processing devices such as scanning and control systems that bring information about the environment and operating efficiency to decision makers. Second, they may include structural integration devices that inform decision makers of the consequences of innovation. Finally, they may comprise decision making methods such as the amount of analysis, planning and consideration of overall strategy, which describe how carefully information is being processed. Dangerous momentum-induced extremes of too much or too little innovation are expected to be reduced by these warning devices.

If this is true, the determinants of innovation must vary as a function of the type or direction of innovation invoked by a firm's innovation strategy. In samples of innovative firms where the danger is reaching too high a level of innovation, mitigating factors such as the use of information processing and decision making devices will correlate negatively with innovation. That is, firms with good warning systems will be less innovative than firms that lack such systems. In contrast, for samples of firms pursuing conservative 'low innovation' strategies, the operative danger is most likely to be strategic stagnation. Here the mitigating factors will correlate positively with innovation as effective warning systems serve as an incentive for innovation. In other words, the existence of momentum implies that we need at least two models to predict innovation, the first applicable in conservative firms, the second, in bold entrepreneurial firms. We shall present and test these models in an attempt to resolve some of the conflicts in the literature on innovation.

THE CONSERVATIVE MODEL OF INNOVATION

The literature on product innovation, although fraught with conflict, seems to point preponderantly to a conservative model of innovation. Basically, the model implies that innovation is not a natural state of affairs, that it must be encouraged by challenges and threats, and that it requires a particular type of structure and an effective information processing system to make conservative managers aware of the need for change. We contend that the conservative model will apply to firms that perform very little innovation or risk taking. These are roughly reminiscent of the reactors of Miles and Snow (1978), the stagnating firms of Miller and Friesen (1978), and the adapters of Mintzberg (1973). Here, innovation is performed infrequently, and, perhaps, because of its disruptive nature, reluctantly. The conservative model suggests that innovation will only take place when there are felt pressures. It postulates four types of prerequisites, or at least strong facilitators, of innovation. First, there must be environmental *challenges* before innovation occurs. For example, because they create a need for innovation, factors such as environmental dynamism and hostility would be expected to correlate positively with innovation. Second, there must be *information* about these challenges brought to key decision makers by effective scanning and control systems. Third, there must be an *ability* to innovate, that is created by adequate resources, skilled technocrats, and structural devices. And finally, there must be decision making methods appropriate for innovation projects. For example, the extent to which key decision makers analyse innovation-related information and use it for planning and strategy development is expected to correlate positively with innovation. As we shall see, many of the findings in the literature seem to support our conservative model. What follows are some specific predictions implied by this model.

Environmental Variables

Myers and Marquis (1969) found that 53 per cent of the product and technological innovations in their sample came in response to market, competitive, or other external environmental influences. The more *dynamic* and *hostile* (i.e. competitive) the environment, the greater the need for innovation and the more likely it is that firms will be innovative. When competitors' products change rapidly or when customer needs fluctuate, the conservative model hypothesizes that innovation will be common. In stable environments this is less likely to be true (Burns and Stalker, 1961). Another environmental dimension may also be germane: namely, that of *heterogeneity*. Firms operating in many different markets are likely to learn from their broad experience with competitors and customers. They will tend to borrow ideas from one market and apply them in another. According to Wilson (1966), the greater the diversity of the organization, the greater the probability that innovations will be proposed, and the greater the probability that organization members will conceive major innovations. Of course diversity in organization personnel, operating procedures, technologies and administrative practices increases with environmental heterogeneity (Peters, 1969).

Information Processing Variables

Burns and Stalker (1961) have argued that mechanistic structures impede innovation while organic structures facilitate it, in part because the former have much less information processing capacity. Subsequent literature has shown that there are at least two types of information processing categories that can influence innovation. Aguilar (1967),

Baker, Siegman and Rubenstein (1967), Utterback (1971), Keller and Holland (1975) and Tushman (1977) have called attention to the role of *scanning* the environment, claiming that a primary limitation on a firm's innovativeness is its ability to recognize the needs and demands of its external environment. Perceived market needs accounted for 75 per cent of the ideas for innovation (Baker *et al.*, 1967). This is confirmed by the work of Carter and Williams (1957), Myers and Marquis (1969) and Mueller (1962), and the survey of Rogers and Shoemaker (1971: 372–373). *Controls* also are said to facilitate innovation. Controls that monitor task performance and financial results are said to identify areas of weakness and to prompt remedially oriented innovations (Rosner, 1968; Downs, 1966: 191).

Structural Variables

One important structural variable that has been demonstrated to be associated with innovation is *centralization* (or concentration) of authority for decision making. According to Thompson (1969: 25):

> . . . dispersal of power is important because concentrated power often prevents imaginative solutions of problems. When power meets power, problem solving is necessarily called into play . . . Dispersed power, paradoxically, can make resources more readily available to support innovative projects, because it makes possible a larger number and variety of subcoalitions. It expands the number and kinds of possible supporters and sponsors.

Hage and Aiken (1970) seem to concur, but Normann (1971) disagrees, claiming that the major innovations, which he calls 'reorientations,' were made in companies which were either family owned or otherwise had a strong concentration of power. Only a powerful leader is able to overcome resistance to change and to make bold innovations. Rogers and Shoemaker's (1971: 384) review indicates that Normann's (1971) position is the one most strongly supported by previous studies.

Technocrats and professionals such as scientists and engineers possess the knowledge and training that often make them most capable and motivated to discover new products and processes. Professional employees may best be able to recognize the need for change (Hage and Aiken, 1970: 33) and therefore firms that have a high percentage of influential technocrats will tend to be the most innovative.

Mohr (1969) has emphasized the need for organizational *resources* in prompting innovation. Most major innovations are too costly to be undertaken by organizations that are short of financial capital. Abundant material, capital equipment, and human resources are also necessary. For example, some kinds of innovation require laboratories, scientists, and financial slack resources that are not needed for day-to-day operations. New product introductions often require much expenditure for R&D, test-marketing and changes in production facilities.

The final structural dimensions that we shall consider have been introduced by Lawrence and Lorsch (1967). They are *differentiation* and *integration,* respectively. For our purposes, the first will refer to the extent to which an organization's products require different marketing and production methods and procedures (our indicants of this scale will differ from Lawrence and Lorsch (1967)). Hage and Aiken (1970) have argued that the existence of very different groups in the firm will make available more varied sources of information for developing new programmes. Complex innovations require a diversity and richness of inputs which are most likely to be available only in differentiated organizations (Wilson, 1966; Thompson, 1969). But differentiation causes conflicts among sub-units and departments unless there are *integrative* devices used to ensure effective collaboration. It is necessary to keep departmental parochialism to a minimum. In carrying out complex new product innovations it may be necessary for members of the R&D, marketing, finance, and production departments to work together intensively. Unless there are integrative devices such as task forces, interdepartmental committees, integrative personnel, or matrix structures, collaboration is difficult and conflicts and mistakes result (Lawrence and Lorsch, 1967; Galbraith, 1973).

Decision Making Variables

The final set of variables that can stimulate innovation in conservative firms describes the way executives use and process information in decision making. Given that the organization gathers the appropriate information about the environment and about organizational performance through its scanning and control systems, and given that this information is communicated to appropriate decision makers, it is still necessary for this information to be *used* and evaluated by executives charged with making key decisions. For example, if conservative executives ignore relevant information that signals the need to innovate, then innovation will not take place. Some important decision making style variables are degree of analysis of information, amount of planning, and the amount of explicit conceptualization of strategies. The more *analysis* is performed by key decision makers, that is, the greater the tendency to search deeper for the roots of problems and to generate the best possible solution alternatives, the more likely it is for innovation opportunities to be discovered and actualized. Managers who make seat-of-the-pants decisions are unlikely to spend the time and effort required to recognize the need for innovations. This may be true, for example, of Cyert and March's (1963) satisficing and uncertainty avoiding firms, and of Lindblom's (1968) remedially focused organizations.

Planning horizons (or *futurity,* as we shall call the variable) are also very likely to influence organizational innovation. Executives who are concerned with putting out fires will be too preoccupied with such matters of the moment to be able to assess the long-term adequacy of their product lines and product designs. They will fail to perceive the need for innovation. The more future-oriented the firm, the greater the concern with change and therefore with innovation (Ansoff, 1965; Andrews, 1980).

Our final variable is the consciousness of strategy and concerns the degree to which strategies have been explicitly considered and deliberately conceptualized. Executives whose attention is devoted exclusively to non-strategic matters tend to muddle through and are much less likely to engage in product innovation (Mintzberg, 1973; Miles and Snow, 1978; Miller and Friesen, 1978), but where there is a concerted attempt to decide upon the product–market orientation of the firm, there is a greater likelihood that target markets will be defined more broadly. Consideration is given to goals and opportunities, and therefore to programmers of innovation.

THE ENTREPRENEURIAL MODEL OF INNOVATION

In sharp contrast to the conservative model, we now outline the entrepreneurial model which applies to firms that innovate boldly and regularly while taking considerable risks in their product–market strategies. The entrepreneurial strategy might be followed, for example, by Collins and Moore's (1970) and Mintzburg's (1973) entrepreneurial firms, Miles and Snow's (1978) prospectors, and Miller and Friesen's (1978) adaptive, innovative, and impulsive firms. According to the entrepreneurial model, innovation is seen as good in itself, as a vital and central part of strategy. The entrepreneurial model postulates that firms will engage in much innovation unless there are certain key obstacles acting to stop it. First, innovation will be very high unless good scanning or control systems reveal it to be too expensive or wasteful, that is, there will be negative correlations of scanning and controls with innovation. Second, effective analysis of decisions, futurity, and explicit and conscious considerations of strategy will also guard against the natural tendency towards innovative excess. Here again we expect to find negative correlations. Third, because strategy is expected to be the main driving force behind innovation, the role of environment as an innovation incentive will be reduced. However, because innovation can itself induce environmental dynamism and heterogeneity, there still should be positive correlations between innovation and environment. Finally, the frequently observed positive covariance between innovation and structural factors such as technocratization, and differentiation should prevail, but at a lower level of significance than for conservative firms. This is again because goals and strategy, not structure or environment, are claimed to be the prime causes of innovation in entrepreneurial firms. Now we can derive some predictions that follow from the entrepreneurial model.

Environmental Variables

For entrepreneurial as for conservative firms, environmental variables are expected to relate positively to innovation. Entrepreneurial firms are often found in *dynamic* and *hostile* environments because their venturesome managers prefer rapidly growing and opportuneful settings; settings which may have high risks as well as high rewards. Such firms may even be partly responsible for making the environment dynamic by contributing challenging product innovations (Peterson and Berger, 1971). Because innovation prompts imitation, the more innovative the firms, the more dynamic and competitive (hostile) their environments can become. Innovation is also likely to be positively correlated with *heterogeneity* because firms that innovate are more likely to come up with products and services that can be exploited in different markets (Chandler, 1962). Notice that in entrepreneurial firms, unlike conservative firms, innovation may *cause* dynamism, hostility, or heterogeneity, rather than the other way around. If so, the greater latitude for strategic choice (e.g. to innovate in stable environments) will cause correlations between innovation and environment to be lower in entrepreneurial samples than in conservative samples.

Information Processing Variables

Traditionally, the impact of information processing variables upon innovation has not been clear. Although there have been numerous empirical studies, these often conflict. For example, Rogers and Shoemaker (1971: 373–374) found 46 studies that showed early adopters of innovations to have greater exposure to information channels than later adopters, while 14 studies did not support this finding. They also found that 12 studies showed that earlier adopters scan or seek information about innovations more than later adopters, while two studies contradicted this. We believe that for studies of business firms, this conflict can be resolved by examining the role of strategy. While we postulated that samples of conservative firms would demonstrate correlations between innovation and information processing, an opposite relationship might be obtained in entrepreneurial samples. Some entrepreneurial firms may have a tendency to innovate too much. A proclivity towards taking risks, and an innovation-embracing ideology can cause firms to squander resources in the pursuit of superfluous novelty. An effective *control* framework can flag the need to reduce the scope and expense of projects and to slow down an overly rapid pace of innovation. *Scanning* the environment to monitor the more parsimonious strategies of competitors is also expected to have a dampening effect upon innovation as opportunities for resource savings are discovered.

Structural Variables

For much the same reasons as those presented in the corresponding section of the discussion of the conservative firms, most structural variables are predicted to have a positive correlation with innovation in entrepreneurial firms. The only qualifier we must add is that, in general, the positive relationships between structure and innovation should be weaker in the entrepreneurial sample. This is because the innovativeness of entrepreneurial firms is believed to be determined more by the strategy of the firm and the aims of its venturesome top managers than by structure. It would not be surprising to find some entrepreneurial firms that have a tendency to innovate a great deal even though their structures are less than ideal for this, according to the literature supporting the conservative model.

The *integration* variable should be negatively correlated with innovation in entrepreneurial samples. Integrative devices such as committees, task forces, and integrative personnel bring important facts to bear upon decisions. The innovation proposals of enthusiastic but reckless executives are likely to be pared down by departments whose aim it is to ensure effective resource management and efficiency.

Decision Making Variables

The variables called *analysis, futurity,* and *consciousness of strategy* are expected to correlate negatively with the degree of product innovation. Essentially the same rationale applies to substantiate these predictions as was presented in the section on information processing variables. Analysis, planning, and the deliberate attempt explicitly to formulate strategies will provide the firm with a better knowledge of its opportunities and excesses. Any tendency to overindulge in product innovation may be curbed by these activities.

METHODOLOGY

The Variables and Questionnaires

In order to test the predictions derived in the last section we employed a lengthy questionnaire to gather information on variables of environment, information processing, organization structure, decision making style, product innovation, and risk taking. Appendix 1 presents the questionnaire. All scale items were averaged for each variable to obtain the variable scores. Table 41-1 presents the construct reliability measure of each of our variables. In every instance, the Cronbach alpha measure (which averaged 0.74 for all variables) well exceeded the guidelines set up by Van de Ven and Ferry (1980: 78–82) for measuring organizational attributes. Construct reliability therefore appeared to be very acceptable.

TABLE 41-1   Means, Standard Deviations and Cronbach Alphas

Variables	Conservative Sample N = 29 Mean	S.D.	Entrepreneurial Sample N = 18 Mean	S.D.	Total Sample N = 52 Mean	S.D.	Cronbach Alpha
Environment							
Dynamism	3.7	1.3	4.4	1.6	3.9	1.4	0.74
Heterogeneity	3.5*	1.6	4.7*	1.4	4.1	1.6	0.84
Hostility	3.9†	1.1	4.7†	1.0	4.2	1.1	0.55
Information processing							
Scanning	4.6	1.3	4.8	1.4	4.7	1.4	0.74
Controls	4.3	1.5	4.6	1.9	4.4	1.7	0.69
Structure							
Centralization	5.2	1.0	4.9	1.5	5.1	1.2	0.79
Technocratization	3.4†	1.3	4.9†	1.7	4.0	1.7	0.69
Resources	4.4	1.4	4.2	1.2	4.3	1.3	0.68
Differentiation	2.8†	1.7	4.6†	1.4	3.5	1.7	0.88
Integration	4.8	1.2	4.9	1.0	4.8	1.2	0.71
Decision making							
Analysis	3.9	1.0	4.3	1.5	4.0	1.3	0.62
Futurity	3.8	1.4	4.5	1.4	4.1	1.5	0.83
Consciousness of strategy	3.4*	1.6	4.5*	1.4	3.9	1.6	N/A‡
Product innovation	2.3†	0.8	5.3†	0.8	3.5	1.6	0.77
Risk taking	3.0†	1.0	4.7†	0.8	3.6	1.2	0.91

*and †signify that the sample means differ significantly at the 0.05 and 0.01 levels of significance using a two-tailed *t*-test.
‡ Only one scale was used to measure this variable.

Data Sample

Our data sample consists of 52 business firms that range in size from sales of less than $2,000,000 to those of over $1 billion. Mean sales are $237 million and the standard deviation is $649 million. The average number of employees is 2,270. Firms are in industries as varied as retailing, furniture manufacturing, broadcasting, pulp and paper, food, plastics, electronics, chemicals, meatpacking, publishing, construction, and transportation. No industry represents more than 10 per cent of the sample. Still, we cannot pretend here to have a random sample since its geographic area is restricted to the Montreal region, and because firms were chosen by teams of second year MBA students according to their personal interests. However, because of the broad representation of types and sizes of businesses, and because no one type of firm dominates the sample, these exploratory findings should have a high degree of generality.

All responses to the questionnaire were obtained by interviews. This ensured that executives could have any vague items explained to them and it removed any problem of missing data. While it is difficult to estimate a response rate, most interviewing teams were able to obtain cooperation from the first company they contacted. About 30 per cent of the teams approached two or three firms before they were able to gain admission to the firm to carry out their field study.

All respondents used in the analysis had the rank of divisional vice president or higher. In 67 per cent of the cases, more than one respondent per firm completed the questionnaire. In such a case, the ratings of the highest ranking respondents were used. Where responses differed by more than two points on the scales among the respondents, responses were averaged. This happened for 8 per cent of all the scores. In 73 per cent of the cases, the data was supplied by the chief executive. Inter-rater reliability was adequate across all of the variables. The scores of the raters were significantly correlated at beyond the 0.01 level of significance for *all* of the variables. In cases of diversified and divisionalized companies, each division was treated as a separate entity to ensure that questions could be answered unambiguously. Thus, five of the 'firms' in the sample were really 'divisions' rather than autonomous organizations. In every case the divisions represented profit centres and were controlled on the basis of their financial performance.

To carry out our analysis, we had to split the sample into two groups which were unambiguously conservative and entrepreneurial. Two dimensions were used to achieve this: innovation and risk taking. Firms whose scores on innovation and risk taking averaged less than or equal to 3.5 on the 7 point scales were classified as conservative (innovation and risk taking were positively correlated with a product moment correlation of 0.51 and an *N* of 52). Such firms tended to be risk averse and engaged in relatively little product innovation. Firms whose score on innovation and risk taking averaged greater than or equal to 4.5 on the 7 point scales were classified as entrepreneurial. Firms with average scores of greater than 3.5 and less than 4.5 tended to be in a grey area. They manifested high risk taking and low innovation, or vice versa, and therefore were deleted from the *sub-sample* analysis because they could not be unambiguously classified.

FINDINGS: DISTINCTIONS BETWEEN CONSERVATIVE AND ENTREPRENEURIAL FIRMS

We called our sub-samples 'conservative' and 'entrepreneurial' and must now justify these appellations. We cannot from our data directly determine the underlying management philosophies or motives of the firms in these groups. However, it is possible to determine whether the partitioning of the sample based upon risk taking and innovation produced other intergroup differences among the variables, differences that are consistent with the themes of conservatism and entrepreneurialism.

Our characterization of entrepreneurial firms was loosely based upon Miller and Friesen's (1978) innovators and entrepreneurs, Miles and Snow's (1978) prospectors, and Mintzberg's (1973) entrepreneurial organizations.[1] We would thus expect the entrepreneurial sample to display many of the collateral characteristics proposed for their firms by these authors. From Table 41-1, we can see that this expectation is fulfilled. Most notable are the significantly higher degrees (than for conservatives) of environmental hostility and organizational differentiation (c.f. Miller and Friesen, 1978), heterogeneity and technocratization (Miles and Snow, 1978), and consciousness of strategy (Mintzberg, 1973). The rate of growth in sales for the entrepreneurial firms from which we could obtain data averaged 14.7 per cent per annum for the last three years of operation. This is significantly higher (at the 0.10 level) than the 8.2 per cent rate of growth for conservatives, and this finding is again consistent with the characterizations in the literature.

It is not hard to surmise possible reasons for the sub-group differences. For example, perhaps entrepreneurial firms operate in more heterogeneous markets and become more differentiated as a consequence of their innovativeness. Innovations can lead them into new and different markets. Also, a high level of technocratization might be necessary to help such firms innovate and cope with their more hostile and diverse environments. Finally, consciousness of product-strategy and futurity may be high because major innovations force firms to consider where they have been and where they wish to be.

Turning to the conservative firms, we can again see that the figures in Table 41-1 are consistent with characterizations in the literature. The attributes of low differentiation, market homogeneity, and unconscious strategies, are in line with features of the types that served as a conceptual genesis for our conservatives, namely, Miles and Snow's (1978) defenders, Miller and Friesen's (1978) stagnating firms, and Mintzberg's (1973) adapters. The conservatives' collateral attributes make sense in the light of the low levels of risk taking and innovation. Low innovation forces firms to operate in environments that are not very hostile or challenging. It requires very few scientists, engineers, or other innovation-facilitating technocrats. Also, firms can be relatively undifferentiated because environments are simple and unthreatening. Finally, the tendency to adhere to past products and practices makes rare the need consciously to reconceptualize strategy or to have high levels of futurity.

We were concerned that the observed differences in the sub-samples might derive from sources having nothing to do with the strategies implied by our models, sources such as environmental dynamism, information processing and decision making characteristics, resource availability, industry, and firm size. Perhaps all firms receiving and analysing the same information about their environments and having the same resources would be equally innovative. Or perhaps, instead of being related to strategy, innovation is solely a function of industry differences, firm size, or environmental dynamism. Fortunately, these alternatives could be ruled out. Table 41-1 reveals no significant differences in the levels of dynamism, scanning, controls, analysis or resources between the samples. Also, firms do not differ significantly in size (number of employees averaged 1,830 for entrepreneurs and 2,480 for conservatives—these figures were not significantly different at the 0.10 level). Finally, we could detect no systematic differences in the industry composition of the samples. For instance, both conservative and entrepreneurial firms were found in industries such as retailing, food, banking, telecommunications, transportation, meatpacking, electronics, furniture manufacturing, aircraft parts, and chemicals. Thus overlap was considerable. Some industries that were unique to conservatives were drugs, distilling, apparel manufacturing, automotive parts and computer services, while industries unique to entrepreneurial firms included boat-building, plastics, and pollution control. It is reasonable to believe that both entrepreneurial and conservative firms could be found in all of these industries.

To conclude, we seem, roughly speaking, to have effected a categorization that manifests both discriminant and convergent validity. However, a word a caution is in order. We have shown that so far our sub-sample statistics are consistent with our models of conservative and entrepreneurial behaviour. We are therefore tentatively justified in applying the interpretations and predictions derived from these models to the respective sub-samples. This does not mean, however, that there are no interpretations inconsistent with our models that can also be used to explain the figures of Table 41-1 or the correlational and regression results that we shall be discussing. This is always the case, but particularly here. Our models were couched in dynamic terms and relate to managerial motives and cognitions, but the data are cross-sectional and do not measure motives or cognitions directly. Thus, while our interpretations are and will be consistent with our data, they will be by no means uniquely determined by them. Subsequent longitudinal research will be necessary further to explore the findings and inferences of this exploratory study.

CORRELATIONAL ANALYSIS

We can now begin to test the predictions that were implied by the conservative and entrepreneurial models of innovation. Some of the relevant data are to be found in Table 41-2, which presents the product-moment correlations between product innovation and all other variables for conservative and entrepreneurial sub-samples and for the total sample. It shows rather strong confirmation of many of the predictions of the respective models. We shall discuss the findings for each class of variables in turn.

Environmental Variables

Our discussion predicted that there would be significant positive correlations between environmental variables and innovation for both types of firms, but that strategic choice rather than environmental pressures would play a greater role in promoting innovation in entrepreneurial firms. The opposite was postulated for conservative firms.

TABLE 41-2 Product–Moment Correlations with Innovation

Variables	Conservative Sample N = 29	Entrepreneurial Sample N = 18	Total Sample N = 52	Significance Levels of Differences in rs between Samples (Fisher Transform)§
Environment				
Dynamism	0.32†	0.36*	0.36‡	NS
Heterogeneity	0.36†	0.28	0.49‡	NS
Hostility	0.33†	0.25	0.43‡	NS
Information processing				
Scanning	0.27*	−0.36*	0.08	0.05
Controls	0.38†	−0.41†	0.07	0.005
Structure				
Centralization	0.15	0.25	−0.03	NS
Technocratization	0.18	0.15	0.44‡	NS
Resources	0.13	−0.30	−0.05	0.09
Differentiation	0.26*	−0.09	0.48‡	NS
Integration	0.11	−0.33*	−0.03	0.09
Decision making				
Analysis	0.13	−0.39†	0.09	0.05
Futurity (planning)	0.41‡	−0.67‡	0.20*	0.001
Consciousness of strategy	0.47‡	−0.47†	0.33‡	0.001

*, †, ‡respectively, indicate that the correlation coefficient is significant at the 0.10, 0.05, and 0.01 level of significance.

§We wished to determine if the correlation coefficients of both sub-samples represented populations having the same true correlation p. We tested the hypothesis using the ratio

$$\frac{Z_1 - Z_2}{\sigma_{(Z_1 - Z_2)}}$$

where Z_1 represents the Fisher transformed value of the correlation coefficients r_{xy} such that,

$$Z = \tfrac{1}{2}\log_e\left(\frac{1 + r_{xy}}{1 - r_{xy}}\right)$$

and

$$\sigma_{(Z_1 - Z_2)} = \sqrt{\left(\frac{1}{N_1 - 3} + \frac{1}{N_2 - 3}\right)}.$$

The implication was that environment–innovation correlations would therefore be higher for conservatives. While our results were consistent with this conjecture they cannot be unambiguously interpreted. Although all correlations are significant at or beyond the 0.05 level in the conservative sample, only one correlation is significant at beyond the 0.10 level in the entrepreneurial sample. Unfortunately, we cannot make too much of these differences, since none are statistically significant using Fisher's Z statistic. What is more, the differences in the significance levels may be due mainly to the fact that the entrepreneurial sample is smaller than the conservative one. Thus we have achieved only very weak support for our hypothesis.

While environment seems to be importantly related to innovation for the total sample, our initial sense that the relationship would be more strongly determined in conservative sub-samples must await further testing. Longitudinal studies should help to decide whether environment prompts innovation in conservative firms and if the reverse direction of causality obtains in entrepreneurial firms. As it stands, it is just as credible from the correlational analysis that one simple linear model can explain the relationship between environment and innovation. The more dynamic, hostile, or heterogeneous the environment, the higher the level of innovation. This result should be held in abeyance however pending the examination of our multiple regression models.

Information Processing Variables

Both of the information processing variables show the predicted statistically significant differences between the conservative and entrepreneurial samples of firms. *Scanning* serves to bolster innovation in firms that are classified as conservative. Attempts to gather information from the environment may make managers aware of the disadvantages of their own product lines and the superiority of the product lines of competitors. Scanning also can point out changing customer desires and buying patterns. In other words, scanning demonstrates the need for innovation to conservative managers. It tells them that it is time to change products and product lines. The conservative nature of these firms ensures that unless this occurs there will be very little innovation.

The entrepreneurial firms show an opposite relationship between scanning and innovation. A significantly *negative* correlation is manifested. Perhaps this finding is caused by information that induces highly innovative and risk embracing executives to slow down. Scanning may reveal that competitors succeed without introducing many new products, that they cut costs by taking advantage of long production runs, product standardization, and the 'economies of stability.' Market research may show that customers favour established brands, or pay attention to factors of price and quality more than variety and novelty. The effect of such information might be to reduce superfluous and expensive product-innovation.

The same duality in the findings occurs when we examine the relationship between the use of organizational controls and innovation. Controls indicate the need for innovations in conservative firms while pointing to the need to curb innovative excesses in entrepreneurial firms. It is interesting that the relationship between *controls* and innovation is greater than that between scanning and innovation. Controls provide concrete financial information that is harder to explain away or to rationalize. Controls may indicate to entrepreneurial executives that a great deal of money has been spent on innovation and that very little return has been forthcoming. They may show that reserves of capital have been badly depleted, that productivity and efficiency has fallen, or that scrap rates have escalated because of too much product line diversity or change. In conservative firms controls may reveal significant declines in market share, a dramatic reduction in the sales of older, more obsolete products, and declining profitability.

Structural Variables

Modest support has been found for the predictions of Normann (1971) and Rogers and Shoemaker (1971: 384) who postulated that *centralization* is positively correlated with innovation. The reasons for this prediction were given earlier. However, we hesitate to place much reliance on the finding since none of our coefficients is significant at the 0.10 level, and the negative sample-wide correlation coefficient appears to confuse things. Perhaps in some types of organizations, centralization boosts innovation, while in others it serves to obstruct it. Miller (1979) found that this relationship varied in magnitude and direction according to the developmental or evolutionary path being followed by the firm. The confusion in the literature surrounding this relationship may be due to a failure to distinguish carefully among different organizational types. Unfortunately, our findings are not very enlightening on this point.

Technocratization is positively correlated with innovation in both of the sub-samples as well as in the total sample. This is in line with most of the predictions in the literature (c.f. Hage and Aiken, 1970; Zaltman, Duncan and Holbek, 1973). It is interesting that the sample-wide correlation is much more significant than the correlations of the conservative and entrepreneurial sub-samples. This may be because the conservative firms are less technocratized *and* less innovative than the entrepreneurial firms. When the sub-samples are combined, a very positive correlation results. Unfortunately, this result too contributes little new information since it merely supports the consensus in the literature.

The finding on *resource availability* surprised us at first. We predicted a positive correlation with innovation for both sub-samples, but got a negative one for the entrepreneurial firms. Perhaps this is because among very high innovators, resources are depleted by too much expenditure on new designs and new products. Among the more restrained innovators in the entrepreneurial sample, resources are less likely to be squandered. This confirms the notion that many entrepreneurial firms tend to over-spend on innovation and that scanning and control devices are required to inform managers of the hazards of this practice. Collectively, the results so far seem to be telling a story that is consistent with our models.

We predicted that *differentiation* and *integration* would both correlate positively with innovation, but more so in the conservative than in the entrepreneurial sample. This is what we found. Differentiation is significantly correlated with innovation in the conservative sample. Perhaps high levels of differentiation may help conservative firms to innovate because they generate a greater variety of new product ideas (Lawrence and Lorsch, 1967). The existence of diverse groups of specialists and practical managers may create an appropriate environment for creativity (Wilson, 1966). This does not, however, seem to be the case in the entrepreneurial sample, where there is actually a slightly negative correlation between innovation and differentiation. We predicted that innovation in entrepreneurial firms might be a function of the personality and goals of top executives rather than the nature of the organization's structure. The findings are consistent with this. So is the relatively high correlation between centralization and innovation in the entrepreneurial firms. Powerful top executives are unencumbered by other more risk-averse managers. They are therefore free to innovate more boldly and intensively. The amount of innovation may thus be more a function of the personal predilections of the executives in entrepreneurial firms than of the degree of differentiation. Indeed, in extremely differentiated firms, it is more difficult for a chief executive to hoard power, and his impact on innovation will decline correspondingly. It is possible that this may be the cause of the negative correlation between innovation and differentiation in entrepreneurial firms.

We also found that integration may facilitate innovation somewhat in the conservative firms and restrain it in the entrepreneurial firms. The first relationship is not surprising. It has been widely predicted in the literature (Lawrence and Lorsch, 1967: Galbraith, 1973). Innovation requires the collaboration of various departments and groups of specialists in order to generate ideas for new products, and to plan and actualize their design, production, and marketing. However, the relatively low correlation coefficient for innovation and integration in the conservative sample seems to indicate that integration is not a very key factor in innovation. Perhaps some conservative firms wait so long to innovate that they are finally forced into it. They must eventually come up with new products even if they do not have adequate integrative mechanisms to do so effectively. Thus the integration–innovation relationship will be weak. Also, the availability of integrative mechanisms will not serve as a very great inducement to innovate to conservatives who are reluctant to recognize that their product lines need updating. Perhaps then, for conservatives, integration may be a better predictor of innovative success or effectiveness than of the *amount* of innovation.

As we hypothesized, in entrepreneurial firms, integration seems to behave like an information processing device. It can serve to warn executives of the dangers or costs of excessive innovation. This might happen as, say, cross-functional committees allow production managers to resist pressures from marketing or R&D departments to introduce new products. There is a freer exchange of information so departments that must bear the brunt of too much innovation will be capable of communicating the nature of their difficulties to other departments. This makes it likely that remedial action will be taken more quickly. Hence the negative correlation between innovation and integration in the sample of entrepreneurial firms.

Decision Making Variables

We hypothesized that the decision making variables would behave very much like the information processing variables; they would tend to boost innovation in conservative firms and to curb excessive innovation in entrepreneurial firms. Again, the findings strongly support the prediction. *Analysis, futurity* and *consciousness of strategy* formulation correlate positively with innovation in conservative firms and negatively in entrepreneurial firms. The activity of analysing decisions, carefully weighing alternative courses of action, planning future activities, and explicitly formulating strategy causes there to be a greater awareness of the problems and opportunities facing the firm. In sluggish reactive firms, this may tend to boost innovation, while in overly innovative firms it can reduce innovation.

MULTIPLE REGRESSION ANALYSIS

In order to test the models further, multiple regressions were run on the conservative and entrepreneurial sub-samples. The results confirmed the correlational findings and explained a very high percentage of the variance in our dependent variable of innovation. Stepwise regression procedures were used to obtain the best models with our variables. A partial F statistic of 1.0 was used as the cutoff point to ensure that only the most predictive variables would be used. For the conservative sample, the best equation was:

$$\text{INNOVATION} = -1.74 + 0.25 \text{ DYNAMISM} + 0.26 \text{ HOSTILITY} \\ + 0.11 \text{ SCANNING} + 0.26 \text{ FUTURITY} \\ + 0.16 \text{ CONSC.STRATEGY}$$

Partial F ratios for the variables were 12.4, 9.5, 2.6, 13.3, and 5.7, respectively, with 1, 27 degrees of freedom; all but the third were significant at beyond the 0.05 level. The R^2 was 0.678, the multiple R was 0.823, and the adjusted R^2 was 0.608. The overall F statistic was 9.67 which is significant at beyond the 0.01 level with 5, 23 degrees of freedom.

Essentially then, the conservative model was strongly supported. Environmental, information processing, and decision making variables were significantly and positively related to innovation in samples of conservative firms.

For the entrepreneurial sample, we obtained the following regression equation:

$$\text{INNOVATION} = 3.74 - 0.17 \text{ SCANNING} - 0.14 \text{ CONTROLS} \\ + 0.20 \text{ CENTRALIZATION} + 0.27 \text{ TECHNOCRATIZATION} \\ + 0.30 \text{ DIFFERENTIATION} - 0.31 \text{ FUTURITY} \\ - 0.15 \text{ RESOURCES}$$

Partial F ratios for the variables were 2.1, 3.1, 4.9, 9.8, 7.2, 7.7, and 1.6, respectively, with 1, 16 degrees of freedom. All but the first and last were significant at beyond the 0.10 level. The R^2 was 0.785, the multiple R was 0.886, and the adjusted R^2 was 0.634. The overall F statistic was 5.21, which is significant at beyond the 0.01 level with 7, 10 degrees of freedom.

The entrepreneurial model is strongly supported. It is notable that while environmental dynamism and hostility were prominent in the conservative regression model, no environmental variables approached significance in the entrepreneurial model. Perhaps then, as predicted, strategic goals and top executive motivations are more important than environment in promoting innovation in entrepreneurial firms. This is consistent with the significant relationship between centralization and innovation. Powerful entrepreneurial top executives can more easily implement bold innovations than can those who must share their power with more conservative counterparts. The observed levels of significance for variables of technocratization and differentiation probably result from the tendency for innovation to require experts and more complex structures, or, perhaps, vice versa (Burns and Stalker, 1961; Lawrence and Lorsch, 1967). Finally, the negative regression coefficients that were expected for information processing and decision making variables also were found.

CURVILINEAR REGRESSION ANALYSIS OF THE COMBINED SAMPLE

The correlational and regression results suggest that there might be a curvilinear relationship between information processing and decision making variables and the level of product innovation. At low levels of innovation there should be a positive correlation between innovation and information processing or decision making variables, while at high levels of innovation a negative relationship would be manifested. An inverted U-shaped curve such as the one in Figure 41-1 is expected to result.

The regression equation that would reflect this relationship is: $Y = \alpha + \beta_1 X_1 - \beta_2 X_2^2$, where the dependent variables would be scanning, controls, analysis, futurity and consciousness of strategy, while the independent variables would be innovation and innovation-squared. The results of the analyses are given in Table 41-3. They are based upon data from all 52 firms in the sample.

In all but one regression, the additional variance explained by the X^2 term is statistically significant at beyond the 0.05 level. This is shown by the second partial F statistic for each equation. The appropriateness of the curvilinear function appears to be unquestionable. The inverted U shape of the curve is indicated by the negative beta coefficients for all of the second order independent variables.

An examination of the information processing variables of Equations 1 and 2 of Table 41-3 reveals that the total F statistics are only significant at about the 0.10 level. This may indicate that there is some substitutability among the variables of scanning and controls in influencing innovation. In some cases, controls may flag the need to boost or curtail innovation, while in other cases, scanning may serve this purpose. If so, we should expect that when we perform regression using an information processing composite variable that is formed by taking an average of scanning and control scores, the significance of the results will be boosted. Equation 6 shows that this is exactly what happens.

FIGURE 41-1   Innovation, Information Processing, and Decision Making

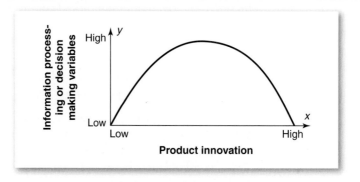

TABLE 41-3 Results of Curvilinear Regression Analysis

General Form: $Y = \alpha + \beta_1$ (Innovation) $+ \beta_2$ (Innovation)^2

1. Scanning $= 2.61 + 1.15I - 0.16I^2$

    $F^* = \qquad\qquad 4.3^{\ddagger} \qquad 4.0^{\ddagger}$ Total $F = 2.2$ $R^2 = 0.08$

2. Controls $= 1.85 + 1.57I - 0.20I^2$

    $F = \qquad\qquad 4.8^{\ddagger} \qquad 4.5^{\ddagger}$ Total $F = 2.4^{\dagger}$ $R^2 = 0.09$

3. Analysis $= 2.60 + 0.85I - 0.10I^2$

    $F = \qquad\qquad 2.4 \qquad 2.1$ Total $F = 1.3$ $R^2 = 0.05$

4. Futurity $= 0.97 + 1.81I - 0.22I^2$

    $F = \qquad\qquad 9.3^{\S} \qquad 7.9^{\S}$ Total $F = 5.2^{\S}$ $R^2 = 0.17$

5. Con. Str. $= -0.09 + 2.20I - 0.25I^2$

    $F = \qquad\qquad 12.8^{\S} \qquad 9.6^{\S}$ Total $F = 8.5^{\S}$ $R^2 = 0.26$

6. I. P. Comp. $= 2.23 + 1.41I - 0.18I^2$

    $F = \qquad\qquad 7.2^{\S} \qquad 6.7^{\ddagger}$ Total $F = 3.6^{\ddagger}$ $R^2 = 0.13$

7. D. Mkg. Comp. $= 1.16 + 1.62I - 0.19I^2$

    $F = \qquad\qquad 11.9^{\S} \qquad 9.6^{\S}$ Total $F = 7.0^{\S}$ $R^2 = 0.22$

8. Total Comp. $= 1.59 + 1.54I - 0.19I^2$

    $F = \qquad\qquad 12.1^{\S} \qquad 10.3^{\S}$ Total $F = 6.6^{\S}$ $R^2 = 0.21$

[*] In all cases the partial F statistic is given for the 'innovation' and 'innovation squared' independent variables, with 1, 49 degrees of freedom. The total F applies to the whole regression analysis and has 2, 49 degrees of freedom.

[†, ‡, §] indicate the statistical significance of an F-test at the 0.10, 0.05 and 0.01 levels, respectively.

Though the R^2 statistics are small, this is not a serious problem since we are not using the regressions to predict the scores along the dependent variables. We merely wished to show that the relationship between innovation and intelligence variables is of the inverse-U type.

The decision making variables of futurity and consciousness of strategy manifest very significant curvilinear relationships with innovation (see Equations 4 and 5). The analysis variable does not, perhaps because it displayed only a very modest positive correlation with innovation in the conservative sample. Nonetheless, the overall finding for the decision making composite variable (formed by taking the mean score of analysis, futurity, and consciousness of strategy) shown in Equation 7 is highly significant. Again, it is possible that there exists some substitutability among the variables.

Finally, we decided to take a total composite of all five variable relating to information processing and decision making. Again the curvilinear relationship between the composite and innovation variables is highly significant, as we can see from Equation 8. In all except Equation 3, our predictions were well supported.

CONCLUSION

Two very different models of innovation were proposed and tested. Each seemed to be substantially borne out in different sub-samples of firms. The 'conservative' model views product innovation as something done in response to challenges, occurring only when very necessary. The model predicts that innovation will not take place *unless:* (a) there are serious challenges, threats, or instabilities in the environment; (b) these are brought to the attention of managers and consciously analysed by them, and (c) structural, technocratic, and financial resources are adequate for innovation. In short, positive and significant correlations are expected of innovation with environmental, information processing, decision making, and structural variables. The predictions of the conservative model were borne out for our sub-sample of conservative firms.

A very different 'entrepreneurial' model was also proposed. This model predicts that innovation is a natural state of affairs; that it will be boldly engaged in unless there is clear evidence that resources are being squandered in the pursuit of superfluous novelty. The model postulates that innovation will tend to be excessive and extremely *high* unless: (a) information processing (scanning and control) systems warn executives of the dangers of too much innovation, and (b) analytical and strategic planning processes and structural integration devices do the same. In other words, negative correlations of innovation with information processing, decision making, and structural integration devices are expected. The entrepreneurial model also predicts low order positive correlations of innovation with environment and more significant positive correlations with structural devices. Goals and strategies rather than environment or structure are seen to be the key impetuses to innovation. Most of the predictions derived from the entrepreneurial model were borne out by our sub-sample of entrepreneurial firms.

A central message that emanates from this research is that the determinants of product innovation in firms are to a very great extent a function of the strategy that is being pursued. The impact of structural, information processing, decision making, and even, to a lesser degree, some environmental and structural devices appears to be a function of whether firms have adopted a conservative or an entrepreneurial strategy. Many of the conflicts in the innovation literature that have been highlighted by Rogers and Shoemaker (1971), Downs and Mohr (1976), and Zaltman *et al.* (1973) show promise of being resolved when we begin to look at strategy as a mediating influence in the relationships between innovation and its context. Indeed, one must take very seriously John Child's (1972) suggestion that we view organizations in a less deterministic light and pay more attention to the role of strategic choice. To understand the relationships among innovation, structure and environment, it may be necessary to study managerial motives, ideologies, and goals.

On a somewhat more practical plane, the research suggests that in addition to making remedial efforts to stimulate innovation in stagnating firms, it might also be useful to take care that innovation does not become an end in itself. It is necessary to ensure that the rate of innovation does not outstrip its utility or the organization's ability to pay. If Miller and Friesen (1980) are correct, there may be a tendency for any organizational trend to have momentum, that is, to feed upon itself, perhaps being protracted past the point of usefulness. This might be true of the drift towards excessive conservatism *or* excessive entrepreneurialism. Practitioners should begin to focus upon the second danger as well as the first.

We shall close with a note of caution. Our findings suggested the applicability of two distinct models of innovation in different contexts, but these models are probably not the only ones consistent with our data and indeed go beyond the data in the explanations that are offered. Further longitudinal research into the impact of managerial motives and goals upon innovation, and their relationships to environment and structure would at this time be most useful to help provide a more solid basis for our conclusions.

APPENDIX 1: QUESTIONNAIRE

Please answer the following questions for the industry that accounts for the largest % of your sales (in other words, your principal industry). Always answer by *circling* the correct digit unless otherwise noted. How *rapid* or *intense* is each of the following in your main industry? Please *circle* the number in each scale that best approximates the actual conditions in it.

Environmental dynamism (V. 1)

1. Our firm must rarely change its marketing practices to keep up with the market and competitors.

Our firm must change its marketing practices extremely frequently (e.g. semiannually).

2. The rate at which products/ services are getting obsolete in the industry is very slow (e.g. basic metal like copper).

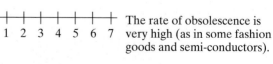

The rate of obsolescence is very high (as in some fashion goods and semi-conductors).

3. Actions of competitors are quite easy to predict (as in some primary industries).

1 2 3 4 5 6 7

Actions of competitors are unpredictable.

4. Demand and consumer tastes are fairly easy to forecast (e.g. for milk companies). | 1 2 3 4 5 6 7 | Demand and tastes are almost unpredictable (e.g. high fashion goods).

5. The production/service technology is not subject to very much change and is well established (e.g. in steel production). | 1 2 3 4 5 6 7 | The modes of production/service change often and in a major way (e.g. advanced electronic components).

Environmental heterogeneity (V. 2)

6. We are a very undiversified firm and cater to the same buyers (e.g. local beer firms). | 1 2 3 4 5 6 7 | We are a highly diversified conglomerate and operate in unrelated industries (e.g. Litton, Gulf and Western).

Are there great differences amongst the products/services you offer, with regard to:

	About the same for all our products	*Varies a great deal from one line to another*
7. customers' buying habits		1 2 3 4 5 6 7
8. the nature of the competition		1 2 3 4 5 6 7
9. market dynamism and uncertainty		1 2 3 4 5 6 7

Environmental hostility (V. 3)

10. The environment causes a great deal of threat to the survival of our firm. | 1 2 3 4 5 6 7 | There is very little threat to survival.

How severe are the following challenges:

	This is not a great threat	*This is a very substantial threat*
11. tough price competition		1 2 3 4 5 6 7
12. competition in product quality or novelty		1 2 3 4 5 6 7
13. dwindling markets for products		1 2 3 4 5 6 7
14. scarce supply of labour/material		1 2 3 4 5 6 7
15. government interference		1 2 3 4 5 6 7

Scanning (V. 4)

Rate the extent to which the following scanning devices are used by your firm to gather information about its environment:

	Not ever used	*Used extremely frequently*
16. routine gathering of opinions from clients		1 2 3 4 5 6 7
17. explicit tracking of the policies and tactics of competitors		1 2 3 4 5 6 7
18. forecasting sales, customer preferences, technology, etc.		1 2 3 4 5 6 7
19. special market research studies		1 2 3 4 5 6 7

Controls (V. 5)

Rate the extent to which the following control devices are used to gather information about the performance of your firm:

	Used rarely or for small part of operations						*Used frequently or throughout the firm*

20. a comprehensive management control and information system

   1   2   3   4   5   6   7

21. use of cost centres for cost control

   1   2   3   4   5   6   7

22. use of profit centres and profit targets

   1   2   3   4   5   6   7

23. quality control of operations by using sampling and other techniques

   1   2   3   4   5   6   7

24. cost control by fixing standard costs and analysing variations

   1   2   3   4   5   6   7

25. formal appraisal of personnel

   1   2   3   4   5   6   7

Centralization (V. 6)

Which levels of management are usually responsible for making decisions of the following types?

	Middle managers	*Functional top executives if divisional structure*	*Divisional top executives or functional ones if no divisional structure*	*Topmost levels of management*
Capital budgeting	1	3	5	7
		(Scales 26, 32, and 38)		
New production introduction	1	3	5	7
		(Scales 27, 33, and 39)		
Acquisitions of firms	1	3	5	7
		(Scales 28, 34, and 40)		
Pricing of major product lines	1	3	5	7
		(Scales 29, 35, and 41)		
Entry into major new markets	1	3	5	7
		(Scales 30, 36, and 42)		
Hiring and firing senior personnel	1	3	5	7
		(Scales 31, 37, and 43)		

Score scales 32 to 37 to indicate which levels of management are responsible for *initiating* each of the above decisions (use √'s), and scales 38 to 43 to indicate which levels *approve* them.

Technocratization (V. 7)

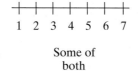

44. In decision making, there is great reliance on personnel with experience and common sense.

   1   2   3   4   5   6   7

    Some of both

In decision making, there is great reliance on specialized technically trained line and staff personnel.

45. In your operations, what is the required level of formal technical competence of your first line supervisors?

No training beyond at most high school (e.g. super-markets).

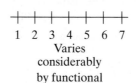

   1   2   3   4   5   6   7

    Varies considerably by functional area

A minimum of a bachelor's degree with specialization (e.g. consulting, engineering firms, etc.).

46. The firm employs very few professionals such as engineers, scientists, and accountants (less than 1 per cent of people other than first line production workers).

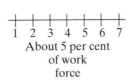
1 2 3 4 5 6 7
About 5 per cent of work force

The firm employs many such personnel (over 20 per cent of people other than first line production workers).

Resource availability (V. 8)

Rate the abundance of the following resources for your firm:

| | *This resource is very scarce and/or prohibitively expensive* | | | | | | *This resource is quite plentiful* |

47. Capital
1 2 3 4 5 6 7

48. Skilled labour
1 2 3 4 5 6 7

49. Material supplies
1 2 3 4 5 6 7

50. Managerial talent
1 2 3 4 5 6 7

Differentiation (V. 9)

How many distinctly different (i.e. unrelated) product lines or services does your firm market?

51. Only one.
1 2 3 4 5 6 7
More than 10 (e.g. conglomerate firm).

How similar are these product lines or services in terms of (i) the technology used to produce them and (ii) their markets?

52. Technology: very similar technologies (e.g. all produced with similar equipment).
1 2 3 4 5 6 7
Very dissimilar (e.g. customized production for one, mass production for another).

53. Markets: very similar in terms of required marketing strategy, types of customers, pricing, etc. (e.g. one product, one market).
1 2 3 4 5 6 7
Very dissimilar markets in terms of required marketing strategy (if selling both boxed cereals and industrial cement).

Integration (V. 10)

In assuring the compatibility amongst decisions in one area (e.g. marketing) with those in other areas (e.g. production), to what extent are the following 'integrative mechanisms' used?

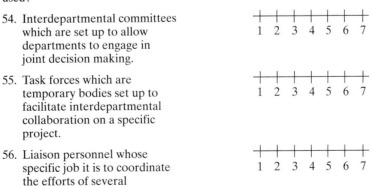

54. Interdepartmental committees which are set up to allow departments to engage in joint decision making.
1 2 3 4 5 6 7

55. Task forces which are temporary bodies set up to facilitate interdepartmental collaboration on a specific project.
1 2 3 4 5 6 7

56. Liaison personnel whose specific job it is to coordinate the efforts of several departments for purposes of a specific project.
1 2 3 4 5 6 7

To what extent is decision making at top levels in your firm characterized by participative, cross-functional discussions in which different departments, functions, or divisions get together to decide the following classes of decisions?

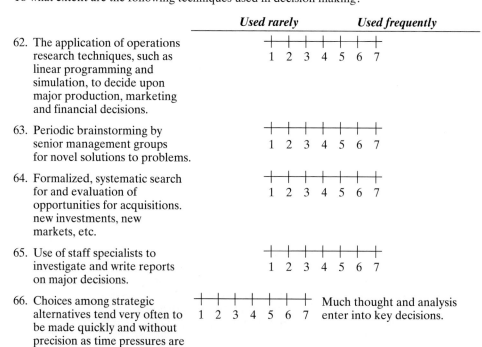

	Rare use of committees or infrequent informal collaboration						*Frequent use of committees and/or informal interdepartmental collaboration*

57. Product or service related decisions concerning production, marketing, and R&D strategies.

1 2 3 4 5 6 7

58. Capital budget decisions—the selection and financing of long term investments.

1 2 3 4 5 6 7

59. Long term strategies (of growth diversification, etc.) and decisions related to changes in the firm's operating philosophy.

1 2 3 4 5 6 7

60. Each department makes decisions more or less on its own, without regard to other departments.

1 2 3 4 5 6 7   There is a great deal of departmental interaction on most decisions.

61. Often there is a lack of complementarity between decisions made in one department and those in another.

1 2 3 4 5 6 7   Decisions of the different departments tend to be mutually reinforcing.

Decisions of the difficult departments neither help or hinder each other.

Analysis (V. 11)

To what extent are the following techniques used in decision making?

	Used rarely		*Used frequently*

62. The application of operations research techniques, such as linear programming and simulation, to decide upon major production, marketing and financial decisions.

1 2 3 4 5 6 7

63. Periodic brainstorming by senior management groups for novel solutions to problems.

1 2 3 4 5 6 7

64. Formalized, systematic search for and evaluation of opportunities for acquisitions. new investments, new markets, etc.

1 2 3 4 5 6 7

65. Use of staff specialists to investigate and write reports on major decisions.

1 2 3 4 5 6 7

66. Choices among strategic alternatives tend very often to be made quickly and without precision as time pressures are often substantial.

1 2 3 4 5 6 7   Much thought and analysis enter into key decisions.

Futurity (V. 12)

67. Decisions aimed at the resolution of crisis are most common.

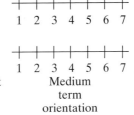

1 2 3 4 5 6 7

Decisions aimed at exploiting opportunities in the environment are most common.

68. There is a bird-in-the-hand emphasis on the immediate future in making management decisions.

1 2 3 4 5 6 7
Medium
term
orientation

Long term (over 5 years) goals and strategies are emphasized.

To what extent are the following activities carried out?

Very rarely/or haphazardly —— *Very frequently and intensively*

69. Long term forecasting of sales, profits and the nature of markets.

1 2 3 4 5 6 7

70. Long term forecasting of the technology relevant to products and services offered by firms.

1 2 3 4 5 6 7

71. Planning of long-term investments.

1 2 3 4 5 6 7

Consciousness of strategies (V. 13)

72. Administrative and product/ market strategies have not been explicitly conceptualized.

1 2 3 4 5 6 7

Strategies are well and precisely conceptualized and guide the *modus operandi* and decisions.

Product innovation (V. 14)

73. There is a strong emphasis on the marketing of true and tried products or services.

1 2 3 4 5 6 7

There exists a very strong emphasis on R&D, technological leadership, and innovations.

How many new lines of products or services has your firm marketed in the past 5 years? Please exclude mere minor variations.

74. No new lines of product or services in past 5 years.

1 2 3 4 5 6 7

Hundreds of new lines of products or services in past 5 years.

75. Changes in product lines have been mostly of a minor nature (e.g. putting in towel with the soap).

1 2 3 4 5 6 7

Changes in product lines have usually been dramatic (e.g. changing from mechanical to electric calculators).

Risk taking (V. 15)

76. There is a strong proclivity to low risk projects (with normal and certain rates of return).

1 2 3 4 5 6 7

The firm has a strong proclivity for high risk projects (with chances of very high return).

77. Owing to the nature of the environment it is best to explore it gradually via timid, incremental behaviour.

1 2 3 4 5 6 7

Bold, wide-ranging acts are viewed as useful and common practice.

References

Aguilar, Francis. *Scanning the Business Environment,* Macmillan, New York, 1967.

Andrews, Kenneth. *The Concept of Corporate Strategy,* Irwin, Homewood, Ill., 1980.

Ansoff, H. Igor. *Corporate Strategy,* McGraw-Hill, New York, 1965.

Baker, Norman, James Siegman, and Albert Rubenstein. 'Effects of perceived needs on the generation of ideas in R&D labs,' *IEEE Transactions on Engineering Management,* **EM-14,** 1967, pp. 156–163.

Burns, Tom and G. M. Stalker. *The Management of Innovation,* Tavistock, London, 1961.

Carter, Charles and Bruce Williams. *Industry and Technical Progress,* Oxford, London, 1957.

Chandler, Alfred D. *Strategy and Structure,* MIT Press, Cambridge, Mass., 1962.

Child, John. 'Organizational structure, environment, and performance: The role of strategic choice', *Sociology,* **6,** 1972, pp. 2–22.

Collins, Orvis and David G. Moore. *The Organization Makers,* Appleton, Century, Crofts, New York, 1970.

Cyert, Richard M. and James G. March. *A Behavioral Theory of the Firm,* Prentice-Hall, Englewood Cliffs, N.J., 1963.

Downs, Anthony. *Inside Bureaucracy,* Little, Brown, Boston, 1966.

Downs, George W. and Lawrence B. Mohr. 'Conceptual issues in the study of innovation,' *Administrative Science Quarterly,* **21,** 1976, pp. 700–714.

Galbraith, Jay. *Designing Complex Organizations,* Addison-Wesley, Reading, Mass., 1973.

Hage, Jerald and Michael Aiken. *Social Change in Complex Organizations,* Random House, New York, 1970.

Keller, Robert and Winford Holland. 'Boundary spanning roles in an R&D organization,' *Academy of Management Journal,* **18,** 1975, pp. 388–393.

Lawrence, Paul R., and Jay Lorsch. *Organization and Environment,* Harvard, Boston, 1967.

Lindblom, Charles. *The Policy-making Process,* Prentice-Hall, Englewood Cliffs, N.J., 1968.

Miles, Raymond E. and Charles C. Snow. *Organizational Strategy, Structure and Process,* McGraw-Hill, New York, 1978.

Miller, Danny. 'Strategy, structure and environment: Context influences upon some bivariate associations,' *Journal of Management Studies,* **16,** 1979, pp. 294–316.

Miller, Danny and Peter H. Friesen. 'Archetypes of strategy formulation,' *Management Science,* **24,** 1978, pp. 921–933.

Miller, Danny and Peter H. Friesen. 'Momentum and revolution in organizational adaptation,' *Academy of Management Journal,* **23,** 1980, pp. 591–614.

Mintzberg, Henry. 'Strategy making in three modes,' *California Management Review,* **16,** 1973, pp. 44–53.

Mohr, Lawrence B. 'Determinants of innovation in organizations,' *American Political Science Review,* **63,** 1969, pp. 111–126.

Mueller, W. F. 'The origins of the basic inventions underlying DuPont's major product and process innovations, 1920–1950,' in R. R. Nelson (ed.), *The Rate and Direction of Inventive Activity,* Princeton University, Princeton, 1962, pp. 323–360.

Myers, Summer and Donald G. Marquis. *Successful Industrial Innovation,* National Science Foundation, Washington D.C., 1969.

Normann, Richard. 'Organizational innovativeness: Product variation and reorientation,' *Administrative Science Quarterly,* **16,** 1971, pp. 203–215.

Peters, Donald H. 'Commercial innovation from university faculty: A study of the invention and exploitation of ideas,' *Sloan School of Management Working Paper,* No. 406–69, M.I.T., Cambridge, Mass., 1969.

Peterson, R. and D. Berger. 'Entrepreneurship in organizations,' *Administrative Science Quarterly,* **16,** 1971, pp. 97–106.

Rogers, Everett M. and F. Floyd Shoemaker. *Communication of Innovations: A Cultural Approach,* Free Press, New York, 1971.

Rosner, Martin M. 'Administrative controls and innovation,' *Behavioral Science,* **13,** 1968, pp. 36–43.

Thompson, Victor A. *Bureaucracy and Innovation,* University of Alabama Press, Alabama, 1969.

Tushman, Michael L. 'Special boundary roles in the innovation process,' *Administrative Science Quarterly,* **22,** 1977, pp. 587–605.

Utterback, James M. 'The process of technological innovation within the firm,' *Academy of Management Journal,* **14,** 1971, pp. 75–88.

Van de Ven, Andrew and Diane Ferry. *Measuring and Assessing Organizations,* Wiley, New York, 1980.

Wilson, James Q. 'Innovation in organization: Notes toward a theory,' in James D. Thompson (ed.), *Approaches to Organizational Design,* University of Pittsburgh, Pittsburgh, 1966, pp. 193–218.

Zaltman, Gerald, Robert Duncan, and Jonny Holbek. *Innovations and Organizations,* Wiley, New York, 1973.

Endnote

1. It is important to note that the term 'entrepreneurial' is used here in its broadest sense, namely to refer to bold risk taking and high levels of innovation, and *not* to owner-managed or small, centralized companies.

42 | ORGANIZING AND LEADING "HEAVYWEIGHT" DEVELOPMENT TEAMS

Kim B. Clark

Steven C. Wheelwright

Effective product and process development requires the integration of specialized capabilities. Integrating is difficult in most circumstances, but is particularly challenging in large, mature firms with strong functional groups, extensive specialization, large numbers of people, and multiple, ongoing operating pressures. In such firms, development projects are the exception rather than the primary focus of attention. Even for people working on development projects, years of experience and the established systems—covering everything from career paths to performance evaluation, and from reporting relationships to breadth of job definitions—create both physical and organizational distance from other people in the organization. The functions themselves are organized in a way that creates further complications: the marketing organization is based on product families and market segments; engineering around functional disciplines and technical focus; and manufacturing on a mix between functional and product market structures. The result is that in large, mature firms, organizing and leading an effective development effort is a major undertaking. This is especially true for organizations whose traditionally stable markets and competitive environments are threatened by new entrants, new technologies, and rapidly changing customer demands.

This article zeros in on one type of team structure—"heavyweight" project teams—that seems particularly promising in today's fast-paced world yet is strikingly absent in many mature companies. Our research shows that when managed effectively, heavyweight teams offer improved communication, stronger identification with and commitment to a project, and a focus on cross-functional problem solving. Our research also reveals, however, that these teams are not so easily managed and contain unique issues and challenges.

Heavyweight project teams are one of four types of team structures. We begin by describing each of them briefly. We then explore heavyweight teams in detail, compare them with the alternative forms, and point out specific challenges and their solutions in managing the heavyweight team organization. We conclude with an example of the changes necessary in individual behavior for heavyweight teams to be effective. Although heavyweight teams are a different way of organizing, they are more than a new structure; they represent a fundamentally different way of working. To the extent that both the team members and the surrounding organization recognize that phenomenon, the heavyweight team begins to realize its full potential.

TYPES OF DEVELOPMENT PROJECT TEAMS

Figure 42-1 illustrates the four dominant team structures we have observed in our studies of development projects: functional, lightweight, heavyweight, and autonomous (or tiger). These forms are described below, along with their associated project leadership roles, strengths, and weaknesses. Heavyweight teams are examined in detail in the subsequent section.

Functional Team Structure

In the traditional functional organization found in larger, more mature firms, people are grouped principally by discipline, each working under the direction of a specialized subfunction manager and a senior functional manager. The different subfunctions and functions coordinate ideas through detailed specifications all parties agree to at the outset, and through occasional meetings where issues that cut across groups are discussed. Over time, primary responsibility for the project passes sequentially—although

FIGURE 42-1   Types of Development Teams

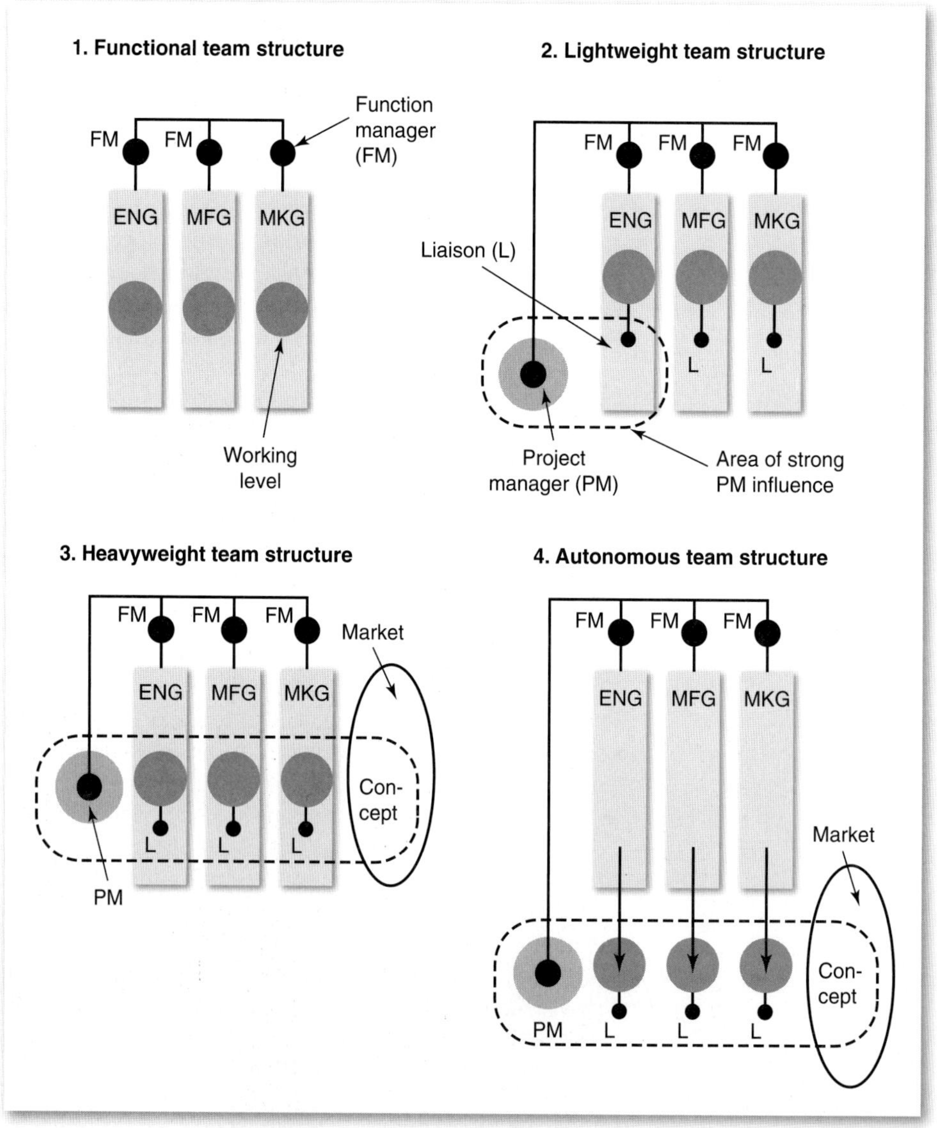

often not smoothly—from one function to the next, a transfer frequently termed "throwing it over the wall."

The functional team structure has several advantages, and associated disadvantages. One strength is that those managers who control the project's resources also control task performance in their functional area; thus, responsibility and authority are usually aligned. However, tasks must be subdivided at the project's outset, i.e., the entire development process is decomposed into separable, somewhat independent activities. But on most development efforts, not all required tasks are known at the outset, nor can they all be easily and realistically subdivided. Coordination and integration can suffer as a result.

Another major strength of this approach is that, because most career paths are functional in nature until a general management level is reached, the work done on a project is judged, evaluated, and rewarded by the same subfunction and functional managers who make the decisions about career paths. The associated disadvantage is that individual contributions to a development project tend to be judged largely independently of overall project success. The traditional tenet cited is that individuals cannot be evaluated fairly on outcomes over which they have little or no control. But as a practical matter, that often means that no one directly involved in the details of the project is responsible for the results finally achieved.

Finally, the functional project organization brings specialized expertise to bear on the key technical issues. The same person or small group of people may be responsible for the design of a particular component or subsystem over a wide range of development efforts. Thus the functions and subfunctions capture the benefits of prior experience and become the keepers of the organization's depth of knowledge while ensuring that it is systematically applied over time and across projects. The disadvantage is that every development project differs in its objectives and performance requirements, and it is unlikely that specialists developing a single component will do so very differently on one project than on another. The "best" component or subsystem is defined by technical parameters in the areas of their expertise rather than by overall system characteristics or specific customer requirements dictated by the unique market the development effort aims for.

Lightweight Team Structure

Like the functional structure, those assigned to the lightweight team reside physically in their functional areas, but each functional organization designates a liaison person to "represent" it on a project coordinating committee. These liaison representatives work with a "lightweight project manager," usually a design engineer or product marketing manager, who coordinates different functions' activities. This approach usually figures as an add-on to a traditional functional organization, with the functional liaison person having that role added to his or her other duties. The overall coordination assignment of lightweight project manager, however, tends not to be present in the traditional functional team structure.

The project manager is a "lightweight" in two important respects. First, he or she is generally a middle- or junior-level person who, despite considerable expertise, usually has little status or influence in the organization. Such people have spent a handful of years in a function, and this assignment is seen as a "broadening experience," a chance for them to move out of that function. Second, although they are responsible for informing and coordinating the activities of the functional organizations, the key resources (including engineers on the project) remain under the control of their respective functional managers. The lightweight project manager does not have power to reassign people or reallocate resources, and instead confirms schedules, updates time lines, and expedites across groups. Typically, such project leaders spend no more than 25% of their time on a single project.

The primary strengths and weaknesses of the lightweight project team are those of the functional project structure. But now at least one person over the course of the project looks across functions and seeks to ensure that individual tasks—especially those on the critical path—get done in a timely fashion, and that everyone is kept aware of potential cross-functional issues and what is going on elsewhere on this particular project.

Thus, improved communication and coordination are what an organization expects when moving from a functional to a lightweight team structure. Yet, because power still resides with the subfunction and functional managers, hopes for improved efficiency, speed, and project quality are seldom realized. Moreover, lightweight project leaders find themselves tolerated at best, and often ignored and even preempted. This can easily become a "no-win" situation for the individual thus assigned.

Heavyweight Team Structure

In contrast to the lightweight set-up, the heavyweight project manager has direct access to and responsibility for the work of all those involved in the project. Such leaders are "heavyweights" in two respects. First, they are senior managers within the organization; they may even outrank the functional managers. Hence, in addition to having expertise and experience, they also wield significant organizational clout. Second, heavyweight leaders have primary influence over the people working on the development effort and supervise their work directly through key functional people on the core teams. Often, the core group of people are dedicated and physically co-located with the heavyweight project leader. However, the longer-term career development of individual contributors continues to rest not with the project leader—although that heavyweight leader makes significant input to individual performance evaluations—but with the functional manager, because members are not assigned to a project team on a permanent basis.

The heavyweight team structure has a number of advantages and strengths, along with associated weaknesses. Because this team structure is observed much less frequently in practice and yet seems to have tremendous potential for a wide range of organizations, it will be discussed in detail in the next section.

Autonomous Team Structure

With the autonomous team structure, often called the "tiger team," individuals from the different functional areas are formally assigned, dedicated, and co-located to the project team. The project leader, a "heavyweight" in the organization, is given full control over the resources contributed by the different functional groups. Furthermore, that project leader becomes the sole evaluator of the contribution made by individual team members.

In essence, the autonomous team is given a "clean sheet of paper"; it is not required to follow existing organizational practices and procedures, but allowed to create its own. This includes establishing incentives and rewards as well as norms for behavior. However, the team will be held fully accountable for the final results of the project: success or failure is its responsibility and no one else's.

The fundamental strength of the autonomous team structure is focus. Everything the individual team members and the team leader do is concentrated on making the project successful. Thus, tiger teams can excel at rapid, efficient new product and new process development. They handle cross-functional integration in a particularly effective manner, possibly because they attract and select team participants much more freely than the other project structures.

Tiger teams, however, take little or nothing as "given"; they are likely to expand the bounds of their project definition and tackle redesign of the entire product, its components, and subassemblies, rather than looking for opportunities to utilize existing materials, designs, and organizational relationships. Their solution may be unique, making it more difficult to fold the resulting product and process—and, in many cases, the team members themselves—back into the traditional organization upon project completion. As a consequence, tiger teams often become the birthplace of new business units or they experience unusually high turnover following project completion.

Senior managers often become nervous at the prospects of a tiger team because they are asked to delegate much more responsibility and control to the team and its project leader than under any of the other organization structures. Unless clear guidelines have been established in advance, it is extremely difficult during the project for senior managers to make mid-course corrections or exercise substantial influence without destroying the team. More than one team has "gotten away" from senior management and created major problems.

THE HEAVYWEIGHT TEAM STRUCTURE

The best way to begin understanding the potential of heavyweight teams is to consider an example of their success, in this case, Motorola's experience in developing its Bandit line of pagers.

The Bandit Pager Heavyweight Team

This development team within the Motorola Communications Sector was given a project charter to develop an automated, on-shore, profitable production operation for its high-volume Bravo pager line. (This is the belt-worn pager that Motorola sold from the mid-1980s into the early 1990s.) The core team consisted of a heavyweight project leader and a handful of dedicated and co-located individuals, who represented industrial engineering, robotics, process engineering, procurement, and product design/CIM. The need for these functions was dictated by the Bandit platform automation project and its focus on manufacturing technology with a minimal change in product technology. In addition, human resource and accounting/finance representatives were part of the core team. The human resource person was particularly active early on as subteam positions were defined and jobs posted throughout Motorola's Communications Sector, and played an important subsequent role in training and development of operating support people. The accounting/finance person was invaluable in "costing out" different options and performing detailed analyses of options and choices identified during the course of the project.

An eighth member of the core team was a Hewlett Packard employee. Hewlett Packard was chosen as the vendor for the "software backplane," providing an HP 3000 computer and the integrated software communication network that linked individual automated workstations, downloaded controls and instructions during production operations, and captured quality and other operating performance data. Because HP support was vital to the project's success, it was felt essential they be represented on the core team.

The core team was housed in a corner of the Motorola Telecommunications engineering/manufacturing facility. The team chose to enclose in glass the area where the automated production line was to be set up so that others in the factory could track the progress, offer suggestions, and adopt the lessons learned from it in their own production and engineering environments. The team called their project Bandit to indicate a willingness to "take" ideas from literally anywhere.

The heavyweight project leader, Scott Shamlin, who was described by team members as "a crusader," "a renegade," and "a workaholic," became the champion for the Bandit effort. A hands-on manager who played a major role in stimulating and facilitating communication across functions, he helped to articulate a vision of the Bandit line, and to infuse it into the detailed work of the project team. His goal was to make sure the new manufacturing process worked for the pager line, but would provide real insight for many other production lines in Motorola's Communications Sector.

The Bandit core team started by creating a contract book that established the blueprint and work plan for the team's efforts and its performance expectations; all core team members and senior management signed on to the document. Initially, the team's executive sponsor—although not formally identified as such—was George Fisher, the Sector Executive. He made the original investment proposal to the Board of Directors and was an early champion and supporter, as well as direct supervisor in selecting the project leader and helping get the team underway. Subsequently, the vice president and general manager of the Paging Products division filled the role of executive sponsor.

Throughout the project, the heavyweight team took responsibility for the substance of its work, the means by which it was accomplished, and its results. The project was completed in 18 months as per the contract book, which represented about half the time of a normal project of such magnitude. Further, the automated production operation was up and running with process tolerances of five sigma (i.e., the degree of precision achieved by the manufacturing processes) at the end of 18 months. Ongoing production verified that the cost objectives (substantially reduced direct costs and improved profit margins) had indeed been met, and product reliability was even higher than the standards already achieved on the off-shore versions of the Bravo product. Finally, a variety of lessons were successfully transferred to other parts of the Sector's operations, and additional heavyweight teams have proven the viability and robustness of the approach in Motorola's business and further refined its effectiveness throughout the corporation.

The Challenge of Heavyweight Teams

Motorola's experience underscores heavyweight teams' potential power, but it also makes clear that creating an effective heavyweight team capability is more than merely selecting a leader and forming a team. By their very nature—being product (or process) focused, and needing strong, independent leadership, broad skills and cross-functional perspective, and clear missions—heavyweight teams may conflict with the functional organization and raise questions about senior management's influence and control. And even the advantages of the team approach bring with them potential disadvantages that may hurt development performance if not recognized and averted.

Take, for example, the advantages of ownership and commitment, one of the most striking advantages of the heavyweight team. Identifying with the product and creating a sense of esprit de corps motivate core team members to extend themselves and do what needs to be done to help the team succeed. But such teams sometimes expand the definition of their role and the scope of the project, and they get carried away with themselves and their abilities. We have seen heavyweight teams turn into autonomous tiger teams and go off on a tangent because senior executives gave insufficient direction and the bounds of the team were only vaguely specified at the outset. And even if the team stays focused, the rest of the organization may see themselves as "second class." Although the core team may not make that distinction explicit, it happens because the team has responsibilities and authority beyond those commonly given to functional team members. Thus, such projects inadvertently can become the "haves" and other, smaller projects the "have-nots" with regard to key resources and management attention.

Support activities are particularly vulnerable to an excess of ownership and commitment. Often the heavyweight team will want the same control over secondary support activities as it has over the primary tasks performed by dedicated team members. When waiting for prototypes to be constructed, analytical tests to be performed, or quality assurance procedures to be conducted, the team's natural response is to "demand" top priority from the support organization or to be allowed to go outside and subcontract to independent groups. While these may sometimes be the appropriate choices, senior management should establish make-buy guidelines and clear priorities applicable to all projects—perhaps changing service levels provided by support groups (rather than maintaining the traditional emphasis on resource utilization)—or have support groups provide capacity and advisory technical services but let team members do more of the actual task work in those support areas. Whatever actions the organization takes, the challenge is to achieve a balance between the needs of the individual project and the needs of the broader organization.

Another advantage the heavyweight team brings is the integration and integrity it provides through a system solution to a set of customer needs. Getting all of the components and subsystems to complement one another and to address effectively the fundamental requirements of the core customer segment can result in a winning platform product and/or process. The team achieves an effective system design by using generalist skills applied by broadly trained team members, with fewer specialists and, on occasion, less depth in individual component solutions and technical problem solving.

The extent of these implications is aptly illustrated by the nature of the teams Clark and Fujimoto studied in the auto industry.[1] They found that for U.S. auto firms in the mid-1980s, typical platform projects—organized under a traditional functional or lightweight team structure—entailed full-time work for several months by approximately 1,500 engineers. In contrast, a handful of Japanese platform projects—carried out by heavyweight teams—utilized only 250 engineers working full-time for several months. The implications of 250 versus 1,500 full-time equivalents (FTEs) with regard to breadth of tasks, degree of specialization, and need for coordination are significant and help explain the differences in project results as measured by product integrity, development cycle time, and engineering resource utilization.

But that lack of depth may disclose a disadvantage. Some individual components or subassemblies may not attain the same level of technical excellence they would under a more traditional functional team structure. For instance, generalists may develop a windshield wiper system that is complementary with and integrated into the total car system and its core concept. But they also may embed in their design some potential weaknesses or flaws that might have been caught by a functional team of specialists who had designed a long series of windshield wipers. To counter this potential disadvantage, many organizations order more testing of completed units to discover such possible flaws and have components and subassemblies reviewed by expert specialists. In some cases, the quality assurance function has expanded its role to make sure sufficient technical specialists review designs at appropriate points so that such weaknesses can be minimized.

Managing the Challenges of Heavyweight Teams

Problems with depth in technical solutions and allocations of support resources suggest the tension that exists between heavyweight teams and the functional groups where much of the work gets done. The problem with the teams exceeding their bounds reflects in part how teams manage themselves, in part, how boundaries are set, and in part the ongoing relationship between the team and senior management. Dealing with these issues requires mechanisms and practices that reinforce the team's basic thrust—ownership, focus, system architecture, integrity—and yet improve its ability to take advantage of the strengths of the supporting functional organization—technical depth, consistency across projects, senior management direction. We have grouped the mechanisms and problems into six categories of management action: the project charter, the contract, staffing, leadership, team responsibility, and the executive sponsor.

The Project Charter

A heavyweight project team needs a clear mission. A way to capture that mission concisely is in an explicit, measurable project charter that sets broad performance objectives and usually is articulated even before the core team is selected. Thus, joining the core team includes accepting the charter established by senior management. A typical charter for a heavyweight project would be the following:

> The resulting product will be selected and ramped by Company X during Quarter 4 of calendar year 1991, at a minimum of a 20% gross margin.

This charter is representative of an industrial products firm whose product goes into a system sold by its customers. Company X is the leading customer for a certain family of products, and this project is dedicated to developing the next generation platform offering in that family. If the heavyweight program results in that platform product being chosen by the leading customer in the segment by a certain date and at a certain gross margin, it will have demonstrated that the next generation platform is not only viable, but likely to be very successful over the next three to five years. Industries and settings where such a charter might be found would include a microprocessor being developed for a new computer system, a diesel engine for the heavy equipment industry, or a certain type of slitting and folding piece of equipment for the newspaper printing press industry. Even in a medical diagnostics business with hundreds of customers, a goal of "capturing 30% of market purchases in the second 12 months during which the product is offered" sets a clear charter for the team.

FIGURE 42-2   Heavyweight Team, Contract Book—Major Sections

- Executive Summary
- Business Plan and Purposes
- Development Plan
  —Schedule
  —Materials
  —Resources
- Product Design Plan
- Quality Plan
- Manufacturing Plan
- Project Deliverables
- Performance Measurement and Incentives

The Contract Book

Whereas a charter lays out the mission in broad terms, the contract book defines, in detail, the basic plan to achieve the stated goal. A contract book is created as soon as the core team and heavyweight project leader have been designated and given the charter by senior management. Basically, the team develops its own detailed work plan for conducting the project, estimates the resources required, and outlines the results to be achieved and against which it is willing to be evaluated. (The table of contents of a typical heavyweight team contract book are shown in Figure 42-2.) Such documents range from 25 to 100 pages, depending on the complexity of the project and level of detail desired by the team and senior management before proceeding. A common practice following negotiation and acceptance of this contract is for the individuals from the team and senior management to sign the contract book as an indication of their commitment to honor the plan and achieve those results.

The core team may take anywhere from a long week to a few months to create and complete the contract book; Motorola, for example, after several years of experience, has decided that a maximum of seven days should be allowed for this activity. Having watched other heavyweight teams—particularly in organizations with no prior experience in using such a structure—take up to several months, we can appreciate why Motorola has nicknamed this the "blitz phase" and decided that the time allowed should be kept to a minimum.

Staffing

As suggested in Figure 42-1, a heavyweight team includes a group of core cross-functional team members who are dedicated (and usually physically co-located) for the duration of the development effort. Typically there is one core team member from each primary function of the organization; for instance, in several electronics firms we have observed core teams consisting of six functional participants—design engineering, marketing, quality assurance, manufacturing, finance, and human resources. (Occasionally, design will be represented by two core team members, one each for hardware and software engineering.) Individually, core team members represent their functions and provide leadership for their function's inputs to the project. Collectively, they constitute a management team that works under the direction of the heavyweight project manager and takes responsibility for managing the overall development effort.

While other participants—especially from design engineering early on and manufacturing later on—may frequently be dedicated to a heavyweight team for several months, they usually are not made part of the core team though they may well be co-located and, over time, develop the same level of ownership and commitment to the project as core team members. The primary difference is that the core team manages the total project and the coordination and integration of individual functional efforts, whereas other dedicated team members work primarily within a single function or subfunction.

Whether these temporarily dedicated team members are actually part of the core team is an issue firms handle in different ways, but those with considerable experience tend to distinguish between core and other dedicated (and often co-located) team members. The difference is one of management responsibility for the core group that is not shared equally by the others. Also, it is primarily the half a dozen members of the core group who will be dedicated throughout the project, with other contributors having a portion of their time reassigned before this heavyweight project is completed.

Whether physical colocation is essential is likewise questioned in such teams. We have seen it work both ways. Given the complexity of development projects, and especially the uncertainty and ambiguity often associated with those assigned to heavyweight teams, physical colocation is preferable to even the best of on-line communication approaches. Problems that arise in real time are much more likely to be addressed effectively with all of the functions represented and present than when they are separate and must either wait for a periodic meeting or use remote communication links to open up cross-functional discussions.

A final issue is whether an individual can be a core team member on more than one heavyweight team simultaneously. If the rule for a core team member is that 70% or more of their time must be spent on the heavyweight project, then the answer to this question is no. Frequently, however, a choice must be made between someone being on two core teams—for example, from the finance or human resource function—or putting a different individual on one of those teams who has neither the experience nor stature to be a full peer with the other core team members. Most experienced organizations we have seen opt to put the same person on two teams to ensure the peer relationship and level of contribution required, even though it means having one person on two teams and with two desks. They then work diligently to develop other people in the function so that multiple team assignments will not be necessary in the future.

Sometimes multiple assignments will also be justified on the basis that a function such as finance does not need a full-time person on a project. In most instances, however, a variety of potential value-adding tasks exist that are broader than finance's traditional contribution. A person largely dedicated to the core team will search for those opportunities and the project will be better because of it. The risk of allowing core team members to be assigned to multiple projects is that they are neither available when their inputs are most needed nor as committed to project success as their peers. They become secondary core team members, and the full potential of the heavyweight team structure fails to be realized.

Project Leadership

Heavyweight teams require a distinctive style of leadership. A number of differences between lightweight and heavyweight project managers are highlighted in Figure 42-3.

FIGURE 42-3 Project Manager Profile	*Lightweight* (*limited*)	*Heavyweight* (*extensive*)
Span of coordination responsibilities	├───────────────────┤	
Duration of responsibilities	├───────────────────┤	
Responsible for specs, cost, layout, components	├───────────────────┤	
Working level contact with engineers	├───────────────────┤	
Direct contact with customers	├───────────────────┤	
Multilingual/multi-disciplined skills	├───────────────────┤	
Role in conflict resolution	├───────────────────┤	
Marketing imagination/concept champion	├───────────────────┤	
Influence in: engineering	├───────────────────┤	
marketing	├───────────────────┤	
manufacturing	├───────────────────┤	

Three of those are particularly distinctive. First, a heavyweight leader manages, leads, and evaluates other members of the core team, and is also the person to whom the core team reports throughout the project's duration. Another characteristic is that rather than being either neutral or a facilitator with regard to problem solving and conflict resolution, these leaders see themselves as championing the basic concept around which the platform product and/or process is being shaped. They make sure that those who work on subtasks of the project understand that concept. Thus they play a central role in ensuring the system integrity of the final product and/or process.

Finally, the heavyweight project manager carries out his or her role in a very different fashion than the lightweight project manager. Most lightweights spend the bulk of their time working at a desk, with paper. They revise schedules, get frequent updates, and encourage people to meet previously agreed upon deadlines. The heavyweight project manager spends little time at a desk, is out talking to project contributors, and makes sure that decisions are made and implemented whenever and wherever needed. Some of the ways in which the heavyweight project manager achieves project results are highlighted by the five roles illustrated in Figure 42-4 for a heavyweight project manager on a platform development project in the auto industry.

The *first role* of the heavyweight project manager is to provide for the team a direct interpretation of the market and customer needs. This involves gathering market data directly from customers, dealers, and industry shows, as well as through systematic study and contact with the firm's marketing organization. A *second role* is to become a multilingual translator, not just taking marketing information to the various functions involved in the project, but being fluent in the language of each of those functions and making sure the translation and communication going on among the functions—particularly between customer needs and product specifications—are done effectively.

A *third role* is the direct engineering manager, orchestrating, directing, and coordinating the various engineering subfunctions. Given the size of many development programs and the number of types of engineering disciplines involved, the project manager must be able to work directly with each engineering subfunction on a day-to-day basis and ensure that their work will indeed integrate and support that of others, so the chosen product concept can be effectively executed.

A *fourth role* is best described as staying in motion: out of the office conducting face-to-face sessions, and highlighting and resolving potential conflicts as soon as possible. Part of this role entails energizing and pacing the overall effort and its key subparts. A *final role* is that of concept champion. Here the heavyweight project manager

FIGURE 42-4	The Heavyweight Project Manager
Role	***Description***
Direct Market Interpreter	First hand information, dealer visits, auto shows, has own marketing budget, market study team, direct contact and discussions with customers
Multilingual Translator	Fluency in language of customers, engineers, marketers, stylists; translator between customer experience/requirements and engineering specifications
"Direct" Engineering Manager	Direct contact, orchestra conductor, evangelist of conceptual integrity and coordinator of component development; direct eye-to-eye discussions with working level engineers; shows up in drafting room, looks over engineers' shoulders
Program Manager "in Motion"	Out of the office, not too many meetings, not too much paperwork, face-to-face communication, conflict resolution manager
Concept Infuser	Concept guardian, confronts conflict, not only reacts but implements own philosophy, ultimate decision maker, coordination of details and creation of harmony

becomes the guardian of the concept and not only reacts and responds to the interests of others, but also sees that the choices made are consistent and in harmony with the basic concept. This requires a careful blend of communication and teaching skills so that individual contributors and their groups understand the core concept, and sufficient conflict resolution skills to ensure that any tough issues are addressed in a timely fashion.

It should be apparent from this description that heavyweight project managers earn the respect and right to carry out these roles based on prior experience, carefully developed skills, and status earned over time, rather than simply being designated "leader" by senior management. A qualified heavyweight project manager is a prerequisite to an effective heavyweight team structure.

Team Member Responsibilities

Heavyweight team members have responsibilities beyond their usual functional assignment. As illustrated in Figure 42-5, these are of two primary types. Functional hat responsibilities are those accepted by the individual core team member as a representative of his or her function. For example, the core team member from marketing is responsible for ensuring that appropriate marketing expertise is brought to the project, that a marketing perspective is provided on all key issues, that project sub-objectives dependent on the marketing function are met in a timely fashion, and that marketing issues that impact other functions are raised proactively within the team.

But each core team member also wears a team hat. In addition to representing a function, each member shares responsibility with the heavyweight project manager for the procedures followed by the team, and for the overall results that those procedures deliver. The core team is accountable for the success of the project, and it can blame no one but itself if it fails to manage the project, execute the tasks, and deliver the performance agreed upon at the outset.

Finally, beyond being accountable for tasks in their own function, core team members are responsible for how those tasks are subdivided, organized, and accomplished. Unlike the traditional functional development structure, which takes as given the subdivision of tasks and the means by which those tasks will be conducted and completed, the core heavyweight team is given the power and responsibility to change the substance of those tasks to improve the performance of the project. Since this is a role that core team members do not play under a lightweight or functional team structure, it is often the most difficult for them to accept fully and learn to apply. It is essential, however, if the heavyweight team is to realize its full potential.

FIGURE 42-5 Responsibilities of Heavyweight Core Team Members

Functional Hat Accountabilities
- Ensuring functional expertise on the project
- Representing the functional perspective on the project
- Ensuring that subobjectives are met that depend on their function
- Ensuring that functional issues impacting the team are raised pro-actively within the team

Team Hat Accountabilities
- Sharing responsibility for team results
- Reconstituting tasks and content
- Establishing reporting and other organizational relationships
- Participating in monitoring and improving team performance
- Sharing responsibility for ensuring effective team processes
- Examining issues from an executive point of view (Answering the question, "Is this the appropriate business a response for the company?")
- Understanding, recognizing, and responsibly challenging the boundaries of the project and team process

The Executive Sponsor

With so much more accountability delegated to the project team, establishing effective relationships with senior management requires special mechanisms. Senior management needs to retain the ability to guide the project and its leader while empowering the team to lead and act, a responsibility usually taken by an executive sponsor—typically the vice president of engineering, marketing, or manufacturing for the business unit. This sponsor becomes the coach and mentor for the heavyweight project leader and core team, and seeks to maintain close, ongoing contact with the team's efforts. In addition, the executive sponsor serves as a liaison. If other members of senior management—including the functional heads—have concerns or inputs to voice, or need current information on project status, these are communicated through the executive sponsor. This reduces the number of mixed signals received by the team and clarifies for the organization the reporting and evaluation relationship between the team and senior management. It also encourages the executive sponsor to set appropriate limits and bounds on the team so that organizational surprises are avoided.

Often the executive sponsor and core team identify those areas where the team clearly has decision-making power and control, and they distinguish them from areas requiring review. An electronics firm that has used heavyweight teams for some time dedicates one meeting early on between the executive sponsor and the core team to generating a list of areas where the executive sponsor expects to provide oversight and be consulted; these areas are of great concern to the entire executive staff and team actions may well raise policy issues for the larger organization. In this firm, the executive staff wants to maintain some control over:

- resource commitment—head count, fixed costs, and major expenses outside the approved contract book plan;
- pricing for major customers and major accounts;
- potential slips in major milestone dates (the executive sponsor wants early warning and recovery plans);
- plans for transitioning from development project to operating status;
- thorough reviews at major milestones or every three months, whichever occurs sooner;
- review of incentive rewards that have company-wide implications for consistency and equity; and
- cross-project issues such as resource optimization, prioritization, and balance.

Identifying such areas at the outset can help the executive sponsor and the core team better carry out their assigned responsibilities. It also helps other executives feel more comfortable working through the executive sponsor, since they know these "boundary issues" have been articulated and are jointly understood.

THE NECESSITY OF FUNDAMENTAL CHANGE

Compared to a traditional functional organization, creating a team that is "heavy"—one with effective leadership, strong problem-solving skills and the ability to integrate across functions—requires basic changes in the way development works. But it also requires change in the fundamental behavior of engineers, designers, manufacturers, and marketers in their day-to-day work. An episode in a computer company with no previous experience with heavyweight teams illustrates the depth of change required to realize fully these teams' power.[2]

Two teams, A and B, were charged with development of a small computer system and had market introduction targets within the next twelve months. While each core team was co-located and held regular meetings, there was one overlapping core team member (from finance/accounting). Each team was charged with developing a new computer system for their individual target markets but by chance, both products were to use an identical, custom-designed microprocessor chip in addition to other unique and standard chips.

The challenge of changing behavior in creating an effective heavyweight team structure was highlighted when each team sent this identical, custom-designed chip—the "supercontroller"—to the vendor for pilot production. The vendor quoted a 20-week turnaround to both teams. At that time, the supercontroller chip was already on the critical path for Team B, with a planned turnaround of 11 weeks. Thus, every week saved on that chip would save one week in the overall project schedule, and Team B already suspected that it would be late in meeting its initial market introduction target date. When the 20-week vendor lead time issue first came up in a Team B meeting, Jim, the core team member from engineering, responded very much as he had on prior, functionally structured development efforts: because initial prototypes were engineering's responsibility, he reported that they were working on accelerating the delivery date, but that the vendor was a large company, with whom the computer manufacturer did substantial business, and known for its slowness. Suggestions from other core team members on how to accelerate the delivery were politely rebuffed, including one to have a senior executive contact their counterpart at the vendor. Jim knew the traditional approach to such issues and did not perceive a need, responsibility, or authority to alter it significantly.

For Team A, the original quote of 20-week turnaround still left a little slack, and thus initially the supercontroller chip was not on the critical path. Within a couple of weeks, however, it was, given other changes in the activities and schedule, and the issue was immediately raised at the team's weekly meeting. Fred, the core team member from manufacturing (who historically would not have been involved in an early engineering prototype), stated that he thought the turnaround time quoted was too long and that he would try to reduce it. At the next meeting, Fred brought some good news: through discussions with the vendor, he had been able to get a commitment that pulled in the delivery of the supercontroller chip by 11 weeks! Furthermore, Fred thought that the quote might be reduced even further by a phone call from one of the computer manufacturer's senior executives to a contact of his at the vendor.

Two days later, at a regular Team B meeting, the supercontroller chip again came up during the status review, and no change from the original schedule was identified. Since the finance person, Ann, served on both teams and had been present at Team A's meeting, she described Team A's success in reducing the cycle time. Jim responded that he was aware that Team A had made such efforts, but that the information was not correct, and the original 20-week delivery date still held. Furthermore, Jim indicated that Fred's efforts (from Team A) had caused some uncertainty and disruption internally, and in the future it was important that Team A not take such initiatives before coordinating with Team B. Jim stated that this was particularly true when an outside vendor was involved, and he closed the topic by saying that a meeting to clear up the situation would be held that afternoon with Fred from Team A and Team B's engineering and purchasing people.

The next afternoon, at his Team A meeting, Fred confirmed the accelerated delivery schedule for the supercontroller chip. Eleven weeks had indeed been clipped out of the schedule to the benefit of both Teams A and B. Subsequently, Jim confirmed the revised schedule would apply to his team as well, although he was displeased that Fred had abrogated "standard operating procedure" to achieve it. Curious about the differences in perspective, Ann decided to learn more about why Team A had identified an obstacle and removed it from its path, yet Team B had identified an identical obstacle and failed to move it at all.

As Fred pointed out, Jim was the engineering manager responsible for development of the supercontroller chip; he knew the chip's technical requirements, but had little experience dealing with chip vendors and their production processes. (He had long been a specialist.) Without that experience, he had a hard time pushing back against the vendor's "standard line." But Fred's manufacturing experience with several chip vendors enabled him to calibrate the vendor's dates against his best-case experience and understand what the vendor needed to do to meet a substantially earlier commitment.

Moreover, because Fred had bought into a clear team charter, whose path the delayed chip would block, and because he had relevant experience, it did not make sense to live with the vendor's initial commitment, and thus he sought to change it. In contrast, Jim—who had worked in the traditional functional organization for many years—saw vendor relations on a pilot build as part of his functional job, but did not believe that contravening standard practices to get the vendor to shorten the cycle time was his responsibility, within the range of his authority, or even in the best long-term interest of his function. He was more concerned with avoiding conflict and not roiling the water than with achieving the overarching goal of the team.

It is interesting to note that in Team B, engineering raised the issue, and, while unwilling to take aggressive steps to resolve it, also blocked others' attempts. In Team A, however, while the issue came up initially through engineering, Fred in manufacturing proactively went after it. In the case of Team B, getting a prototype chip returned from a vendor was still being treated as an "engineering responsibility," whereas in the case of Team A, it was treated as a "team responsibility." Since Fred was the person best qualified to attack that issue, he did so.

Both Team A and Team B had a charter, a contract, a co-located core team staffed with generalists, a project leader, articulated responsibilities, and an executive sponsor. Yet Jim's and Fred's understanding of what these things meant for them personally and for the team at the detailed, working level was quite different. While the teams had been through similar training and team startup processes, Jim apparently saw the new approach as a different organizational framework within which work would get done as before. In contrast, Fred seemed to see it as an opportunity to work in a different way—to take responsibility for reconfiguring tasks, drawing on new skills, and reallocating resources, where required, for getting the job done in the best way possible.

Although both teams were "heavyweight" in theory, Fred's team was much "heavier" in its operation and impact. Our research suggests that heaviness is not just a matter of structure and mechanism, but of attitudes and behavior. Firms that try to create heavyweight teams without making the deep changes needed to realize the power in the team's structure will find this team approach problematic. Those intent on using teams for platform projects and willing to make the basic changes we have discussed here, can enjoy substantial advantages of focus, integration, and effectiveness.

Endnotes

1. See Kim B. Clark and Takahiro Fujimoto, *Product Development Performance* (Boston, MA: Harvard Business School Press, 1991).

2. Adapted from a description provided by Dr. Christopher Meyer, Strategic Alignment Group, Los Altos, CA.

SECTION VIII

ACCELERATING INNOVATION

Introduction

It has been said that new product development (NPD) and product innovation are exceedingly complex and chaotic processes that are necessary for the survival of every firm and industry. Some researchers have suggested that NPD acceleration be employed as a prominent tool to gain a competitive advantage. The articles selected for this section address this issue head-on in an attempt to not only understand how to make this important process less chaotic and more successful, but also to accelerate such a process at the same time. The four articles in this section offer the reader suggestions for NPD acceleration methodologies, caveats associated with many of the suggested methods, models for decreasing the NPD cycle time, and warnings concerning the hastening of the NPD process.

Murray R. Millson, S. P. Raj, and David Wilemon suggest five major NPD acceleration approaches that can be employed by new product developing firms. From a review of existing literature in marketing, business, strategy, manufacturing, and organization management associated with the topic of how to make processes operate faster, these authors have synthesized five basic NPD acceleration approaches. They note that the five approaches may be employed alone or in combination and potentially offer the greatest acceleration potential when used in conjunction with one another. The five approaches derived from their research are simplify, eliminate delays, eliminate steps, parallel process, and speed up operations. Occasionally, the first step, simplify, poses comprehension difficulties and, therefore, we define it as any action undertaken to make the process of developing new products easier. For example, a reduction in the number of component suppliers typically makes purchasing and the NPD process simpler. The other four approaches are usually thought of as unrelated processes, but the authors suggest that there is an order to their effective implementation. They submit that the five approaches are most effective when processes are simplified first; then it often becomes apparent which steps are unnecessary and can be eliminated altogether. The third approach to accelerate the development of new products is to parallel process non-dependent processes that lead to a parallel series of activities that can be reviewed so as to eliminate delays within and between the discrete activities of each parallel path in the overall process. Finally, if the process is not progressing as quickly as necessary, it can then, and only then, be sped up or pushed ahead. The authors note that there needs to be an understanding of the NPD process as it is currently performed to ascertain whether the trade-offs between the opportunity costs associated with process slowness and the risks of acceleration are warranted. Management needs to be cognizant of these issues prior to any adjustment of their NPD process.

In the second article, Christopher Meyer and Ronald E. Purser present six steps that can be taken to shorten the cycle time of a firm's NPD process. First, the authors define fast cycle time (FCT) as "... the ongoing ability to identify, satisfy, and be paid for meeting customer needs faster than anyone else." They point out that although one-shot cycle time reductions might be useful, they do not provide long-term competitive advantages. Moreover, they note that FCTs are the responsibility of all organizational functions and that quality cannot be traded off against developmental cycle reductions. These authors make another interesting observation in that the slowest sub-cycle limits the overall cycle time and, therefore, even the process of selling products and delivering them to customers needs to be evaluated as part of an overall NPD cycle analysis. A final admonition of these authors is to meet customer expectations and needs, because a fast cycle that does not end with satisfied customers is unsuccessful. With these definitions stated, the authors explain each of their six steps for cycle time reduction. The first step is to reflect on what customers regard as added value associated with every NPD activity and level of an organization. Second, ensure that the entire organization is focused on activities that provide value to customers. Third, organizations need to be redesigned to become flatter, to reduce bureaucratic roadblocks, to facilitate the deployment of multifunctional teams, and to provide greater ease of information flow between departments and the external environment. Fourth, process development and enhancement should be pursued with as much enthusiasm as product development and modification. Fifth, the authors suggest that "stretch" goals need to be set and progress against those goals needs to be openly evaluated. Such a process provides intense motivation for those performing NPD activities. The sixth and final step in their process is to create an environment that stimulates and rewards continuous learning. These authors conclude their article by noting that cycle time reductions entail work which is often not an easy task. They also note that if cycle times can be reduced and world-class quality can be maintained, a competitive advantage can be attained.

Preston G. Smith and Donald G. Reinertsen, in the third article, focus on informing readers of new techniques for accelerating their NPD processes. These authors warn that using development techniques that are widespread may not offer competitive advantages. They present ten techniques that can assist R&D managers in their efforts to reduce NPD cycle times. They suggest that managers have varying developmental systems that suit diverse new product objectives; managers apply appropriate developmental processes that agree with financial assessments that relate to a balance of cost overruns and project delays; managers are wary of designs and changes that increase project complexity; managers enter new areas of technology in an evolutionary manner; managers should be frugal with engineering time during the early NPD stages; managers staff NPD teams in an effort to complete particular projects more quickly than others and, therefore, have fewer projects in process at any one time; managers should hire more engineering generalists while using specialists only where absolutely required; managers should let the development team manage itself so that problem-solving occurs at the lowest possible level; managers must teach new product developers to weigh technical and market risks to strike a balance between the analysis of project requirements and the testing of particular solutions to project requirements; and managers should not commit all of their resources to immediate projects, because important projects arise continually and important new projects may have to be ignored. These authors conclude that all of their suggestions need to be simultaneously implemented. But if all techniques cannot be simultaneously implemented, then as many as possible should be implemented because they tend to have a synergistic impact on the reduction of NPD cycle times.

C. Merle Crawford, in the final article of this important section, warns the reader to be conscious of potential "hidden" costs that are often associated with the process of developing new products in an accelerated fashion. Crawford points out that, although he is an advocate of accelerated NPD processes, implementers of such time- and cost-saving techniques should be wary of and assess the "price" associated with the pursuit of accelerated product development. The author notes that "hidden" costs can be categorized into five groups. The first group of costs is based on an assessment of the type of innovations that are most often selected due to acceleration principles. Many projects are chosen so that they can be completed quickly. These projects often represent incremental innovations that are selected at the expense of more radical innovations that are many times more profitable in the long term and provide greater benefit to society. A second category of hidden costs associated with accelerated product development come in the form of NPD steps that are often eliminated to derive faster cycle times. Frequently steps that are eliminated are those that involve gathering information, and do not directly impact the development of the physical product. Crawford notes that the elimination of these steps is the basis for the high failure rates of many products that meet their financial demise due to no market need for them, the market need was not fully met, or the product was not marketed properly to reach the proper target market. The third hidden cost of accelerated product development is associated with the formation of small teams that theoretically can make rapid decisions and are flexible enough to maneuver through the maze of bureaucratic red tape to finish development more quickly than teams employing alternative methods. This important technique can lead to elite sub-organizations that either shun others or can fail to gain support of other groups when needed. Moreover, the creation of such small groups can manifest severe problems for both leaders and members when the members return to their "home" organizational groups from either successful or unsuccessful experiences in the world of NPD. The fourth hidden cost area associated with accelerated product development is made up of the unexpected inefficiencies that occur during the development of new products in existing environments that were created for previously developed products. These situations exist because there is often no time to generate the proper infrastructure for the engineering, production, and marketing of new products that do not fit a firm's current product development "mold." The final area of hidden costs that Crawford discusses includes costs associated with the impact that accelerated product development has on employees, suppliers, and customers who are forced to bend and, perhaps, break to implement reduced cycle times.

References

Crawford, C. Merle. 1992. The hidden costs of accelerated product development. *Journal of Product Innovation Management* 9: 188–199.

Meyer, Christopher and Ronald E. Purser. 1993. Six steps to becoming a fast-cycle-time competitor. *Research Technology Management* 36(5): 41–48.

Millson, Murray R., S. P. Raj, and David Wilemon. 1992. A survey of major approaches for accelerating new product development. *Journal of Product Innovation Management* 9(1): 53–69.

Smith, Preston G. and Donald G. Reinertsen. 1992. Shortening the product development cycle. *Research Technology Management* 35(3): 44–49.

43

A SURVEY OF MAJOR APPROACHES FOR ACCELERATING NEW PRODUCT DEVELOPMENT

*Murray R. Millson, S. P. Raj
and David Wilemon*

Product life-cycles are becoming shorter, leading firms to reduce the time to bring new products to market. Being early can provide a significant competitive advantage, making the acceleration of new product development (NPD) an important area for research and inquiry. Based on their review of a wide range of literatures in business strategy, marketing, new product development, manufacturing and organization management, Murray Millson, S. P. Raj and David Wilemon report a general set of techniques for reducing the developmental cycle time for new products. The article develops a hierarchy of available NPD acceleration approaches and discusses potential benefits, limitations and significant challenges to successful implementation.

INTRODUCTION

The current state of business in the United States and in the world is one of rapid change. Product life-cycles, markets, competitors, suppliers, customers, technologies, and products themselves are just a few of the important variables that affect organizations. The fact that these variables change is not as much of a surprise as is the rate of change. Observers note that tomorrow's products will have life-cycles that are much shorter than those experienced by products of the past [22, 42]. Ohmae [52] points out that short life-cycles make technology markets akin to the fashion industry. He notes, for example, that the model life for audio components is about 6 months and for the early facsimile machines it was a mere 4 months! Although these products typically undergo multiple incremental development phases, Gomory and Schmitt [29] note that repeated rapid developments cumulate to major product changes that leave competitors behind if they lack a quick-response capability.

A similar result also is seen with more radical innovations. Here, most of the cycle shortening is generated by changing technology in the firm's environment. The vacuum tube, the mechanical calculator, and carbon paper are classic examples of products that have their life-cycles cut short by superior, new technologies. Mechanical typewriters had a 30 year life-cycle; electromechanical typewriters had a 10 year life-cycle, and

Address correspondence to David Wilemon, Director, Innovations Management Program, Syracuse University, School of Management, Syracuse, NY 13244–2130.

Millson, Murray R., S. P. Raj, and David Wilemon, (1992), "A Survey of Major Approaches for Accelerating New Product Development," *Journal of Product Innovation Management,* vol. 9, no. 1, pp. 53–69.

electronic typewriters have quickly been replaced by word processors and personal computers. Shorter product life-cycles demand even shorter new product development (NPD) cycles. Some firms are meeting the acceleration challenge successfully as the following examples indicate:

> Honda turns out new models in less than 4 years from drawing board to show-room, compared with 5 years for most domestic manufacturers [40];
> AT&T now takes 1 year to design a new phone; down from its previous 2 years [15];
> HP took 22 months for its new DeskJet printer, down from its old 4 ½ years [15];
> Xerox cut its development time from 6 years down to 3 [57]; and
> Honeywell, which used to take 4 years to design and build a new thermostat, now takes only 12 months [8].

How did they do it? Can others do the same? We focus on answers to these questions in this article. We attempt to point out the trade-offs necessary to bring innovative products to rapidly-changing markets in the shortest time. A typical NPD cycle involves a series of steps such as idea generation, product screening, product development, and commercialization. A firm's functional departments including marketing, research, engineering, and manufacturing usually participate in only a few of these steps. When each task is complete, the NPD responsibility is passed along to the next set of participants. Takeuchi and Nonaka [69] indicate that the serial nature of NPD steps is like a relay race. They warn that in the new corporate relay race there are many more "runners" than in a conventional relay race and the potential for "baton dropping" is far greater, leading to costly delays. A number of authors in the NPD and marketing literatures have emphasized the importance of integration between functions such as marketing, R&D, and manufacturing [11, 31, 36, 38, 66], the need for continuous interaction between these departments, and an appreciation of each other's roles. In this article we investigate how these functional areas can work together to accelerate NPD.

In addition to operating within a changing technological and competitive environment, there are other important reasons for shortening the NPD process. Any company that wishes to be proactive must master accelerated product development. First, the market share advantages that go to "pioneer" firms have been explored by Urban et al. [73], Gold [26], and others, and emphasized by Day and Wensley [13] in terms of the pioneer's opportunity to create the rules for subsequent competition so that they favor their position. In a highly competitive environment, to be first in the market demands short NPD. Even to be a successful later entrant requires relatively fast NPD capabilities to meet customer needs before they change. An important exception involves late market entrants that are well known, have exceptional product quality, excellent service, and persistent industry "staying" power. IBM's introduction of their "PC" is an excellent example. Second, important cost benefits can be achieved by firms that learn to manage the acceleration of NPD. Significant advantages accrue because resources are utilized more creatively and efficiently, costs are reduced, and work-in-process bottlenecks are minimized.

Speed in new product development also pays off as demonstrated by a McKinsey Company economic model, which shows that high technology products that come out 6 months late but on budget will earn 33% less profit over a 5-year period, whereas being on time and even as high as 50% over budget only shaves off 4% in profitability [15]. One source of such profitability is the higher price that an early entrant can charge. Ohmae [52] illustrates the rates of price changes for computer memory chips and personal computers in Japan: 64k chips introduced in 1981 dropped the same amount in price in 6 months as 4k chips introduced in 1974 dropped in about 7 years. A personal computer model introduced in Japan in 1983 dropped in price at a rate of 3.7% a month compared with a 0.9% price rate decrease for a computer introduced in 1981. Consequently, a late entrant may never see profitability during a model cycle. This sense of urgency is contrasted between Japanese and American firms in a recent study by Mansfield [46]. He concludes that Japanese firms seem willing to devote twice as many resources as American companies do in pursuit of speed. As it is difficult to build speed without trust and open communication there is an intangible but valuable boost to organizational loyalty [57] in addition to the morale that comes from working for a company that is a leader.

SOURCES OF INFORMATION

Information for this article was obtained from two sources. First, published research involving NPD cycle acceleration is meager but growing [32, 59, 60, 61]. Much of the research that has been published has focused on the manufacturing step, and to a lesser degree the product design step [18, 62, 64, 65]. The other NPD areas and the NPD process as a whole provide fertile research opportunities. The current NPD literature typically proposes specific tactics such as the elimination of approvals, that may be used by firms to reduce their NPD times. These specific tactics, while valuable in themselves, may not be applicable to all firms. We surveyed the literature to identify tactics many firms take and then grouped them into a few approaches that most firms can use to speed up their NPD process. These approaches can be used in all phases of NPD. We illustrate their use by the R&D, marketing, and manufacturing functions.

Second, we provide some empirical support for our NPD acceleration approaches based on discussions with two industrial groups. One group comprised 30 new product development managers who were attending a university-sponsored seminar, while the second group involved 12 R&D directors from large technology- and industrial-based companies. The information provided by the new product development managers and R&D directors comprising our sample is employed in conjunction with examples from the literature to support the description and application of our NPD approaches. Our sampling of NPD professionals helps provide a fuller context regarding the benefits and limitations of our NPD acceleration approaches.

NPD ACCELERATION APPROACHES

Our analysis of the new product literature revealed many NPD acceleration tactics. We formed five generic NPD acceleration approaches by clustering similar tactics. All five approaches are focused on the reduction of the time required to complete the overall NPD cycle. These are common principles, but each company may differ in the choice of specific approaches to adopt and implement. All along the new product development path a product development group can utilize the following five basic approaches alone or in combination: (1) simplify, (2) eliminate delays, (3) eliminate steps, (4) speed up operations, and (5) parallel process. Figure 43-1 highlights their interrelatedness. Due to the scope and complexity of these approaches we also note that these acceleration modes overlap. The concept of a supportive corporate culture is shown as the context encompassing the five NPD acceleration approaches.

Figure 43-2 provides several examples that illustrate the applicability of our NPD acceleration approaches to major new product development phases. These examples, in addition to others from specific firms, are discussed in this article. We use these examples to demonstrate each approach's applicability to manufacturing, marketing, and R&D. We employ Figure 43-2 as a focus and orienting framework to guide us through the application of our five acceleration approaches to the various facets of NPD.

SIMPLIFY

Making operations simpler is the first basic approach that can accelerate NPD. As our other four approaches also may result in simplifying NPD, we specifically define NPD simplification as any action that makes processes, communications, and interfaces easier to perform and manage. Therefore, simplifying can provide greater focus and definition to designs as well as organizations.

New product development is complex and the standard paradigm for dealing with complexity is to break down the overall task into individual parts for specialists to

FIGURE 43-1   Major Approaches for Accelerating NPD Projects.

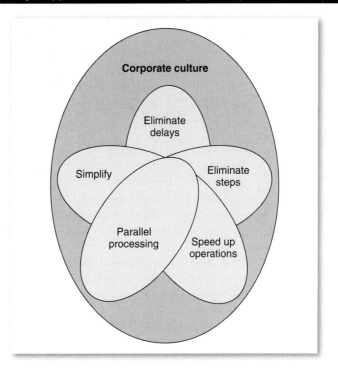

FIGURE 43-2   Applications of NPD Acceleration Approaches.

Acceleration Methods	Major New Product Development Phases		
	Research and Development	*Manufacturing*	*Marketing*
Simplify	Generate explicit R&D goals and link with other groups	Reduce number of vendors and simplify documentation	Focus product requirements and minimize user education requirements
Eliminate Delays	Link R&D goals and Mfg. capabilities and provide early product training	Reduce work-in-process and maintain equipment	Reduce marketing plan delays and reduce launch delays
Eliminate Steps	Utilize "lead user" ideas and reduce number of parts	Reduce assembly steps and create more reliable products	Minimize formal market testing and reduce marketing approvals
Speed Up	Use small groups to generate ideas and initiate Computer Aided Design	Install on-line product testing and Computer Aided Manufacturing	Reduce test market time and create customer alliances
Parallel Processing	Institute mutually exclusive research and parallel known applied sciences	Provide collateral and/or contingency facilities	Concurrent marketing and plan customer service early

master. While this appears to simplify the original tasks in R&D, marketing, and manufacturing, quite the reverse may happen. As time progresses, the separate parts become more and more isolated with the result that the original reason for complexity, namely the interrelatedness of tasks, is forgotten. What should have been an iterative process with feedback is now linearized and sequentialized resulting in disjointed efforts. As Van de Ven [76, p. 598] states, ". . . the whole often turns out to be less than or a meaningless sum of the parts. . . ." In a similar vein Heany and Vinson [37, p. 22] add, "It is anything but easy to integrate the contributions of a large group of specialists."

We suggest that NPD simplification in human systems may be achieved, not so much by finely separating all possible tasks, but by integrating tasks into more meaningful groups. We call this process "NPD task clustering," which can be achieved through appropriate job design. This notion is supported by Hackman et al. [33] when they point out that "Task Identity," (grouping activities so that they can be identified as a "whole"), is a dimension that leads to meaningful work. Meaningful work is a psychological state that can result in personal and work outcomes such as higher quality work performance, higher motivation, and greater job satisfaction. In addition, Champoux [9], whose sample included white and blue collar employees, found a positive attitude towards reasonable increases in job scope. More recently, Gardner [25] studied "activation theory," which describes the relationship between performance and/or satisfaction and an individual's level of stimulation towards a task. He determined that low levels of activation or stimulation created by low task complexity results in much lower performance and satisfaction than moderately complex activities. Therefore, we suggest that an appropriate clustering of NPD activities can create the personal excitement and commitment required to accelerate the NPD process.

Many other management theorists [12, 37, 39, 64] emphasize that jobs can be made more flexible. Cusumano [12, p. 37] notes that productivity in manufacturing will be increased if ". . . the number of job categories [are reduced] to only a few, so that they [management] could move workers to different positions easily and expand worker job routines. . . ." Overall simplification is achieved when workers are trained to perform and take responsibility for a group of tasks. Likewise, at higher organizational levels such as product planning, a team approach ensures constant flow of information across functions and minimizes the problem of ignoring interdependencies at the boundaries [2, 51, 71]. Even within functions, perhaps the deliberate overlapping of responsibilities can help ensure adequate contact and understanding among personnel.

In addition to manufacturing, R&D is another candidate for acceleration by simplification. R&D can have far-reaching effects on the remainder of the NPD process and, therefore, should be thoroughly scrutinized [63]. The research portion of R&D is the more challenging part to simplify because of its emphasis on the "creation" of new methods and products. Research may be simplified by employing explicit objectives, which can help focus the research process. In its drive to develop complex digital switches, Northern Telecom broke its immensely complex development program into a series of manageable tasks with recognized market demand for each; in effect, it employed "planned incrementalism." Using this step-by-step approach it first introduced a PBX and then other intermediate products before achieving the final design of the DMS 100, a major development [43]. As researchers often strive for elegant solutions, increasing the emphasis on less sophisticated, workable solutions can simplify and thus shorten the research activity. Ignoring, rather than rewarding, a not-invented-here (NIH) attitude is a giant step in simplifying the research process. Extinction of NIH can be achieved by rewarding researchers for creatively using existing data, information, and ideas.

Schrage [65] argues that process R&D is as important as new product R&D. Therefore, there needs to be a link between the two activities so that there is a bidirectional flow of information between product design and process design. He notes that IBM has special teams that link researchers with developers. Instead of producing pieces of technology, they create coherent wholes. The concept of an integrated R&D function, comprising both new products and new processes, can provide better coordination of the total design process and facilitate the acceleration of NPD. By designing for manufacturability, development avoids creating a complex product with little regard for the intricacies of manufacturing [29]. By monitoring the simplicity of the product and process design in a holistic manner, manufacturing processes are simplified and costs are reduced with enhanced quality. Increased information flow can make process personnel more aware of product features and the product personnel more aware of process capabilities.

Linking groups simplifies the flow of information. "The building of such linkages between marketing, engineering, and manufacturing decisions during new product development fosters teamwork" [37, p. 28]. Effective teamwork among the different functional groups can simplify documentation requirements, information flows, and formal procedures. In an attempt to simplify information flow, Yoshiro Maruta (president, KAO Corporation, 1989) notes that in his company information is fed directly to those concerned through a computerized information network. Thus, long complex hierarchical communication paths are simplified.

Manufacturing processes may be simplified by incorporating new fabrication and assembly techniques, such as robotic and laser technologies. These technologies have an even greater impact when the product has already been simplified. For example, products that have fewer components will have shorter assembly and fabrication processes and be more adaptable to the implementation of robotic assembly.

Another way to simplify manufacturing activities is by creating products with standard components and assemblies that may be shared among various products. The elimination of parts can also simplify the NPD steps. Ettlie [19] notes that Chrysler has shortened its list of options from 60 to 25, which reduced the number of parts most plants must handle from about 8,000 to fewer than 5,000. IBM's new Selectric typewriter has only 1/50th the number of parts its old Selectric model had, and its Pro Printer is made of snap on parts with no screws or bolts [7]. Such programs can have significant "payback" in other areas such as material purchasing, product design, drafting, product assembly, and testing.

The simplification of a firm's products can have important implications for marketing. Marketing plays a key role in helping to focus product definition, which best serves customer needs. By carefully assessing important customer needs a simpler product definition may result rather than one that is complicated by trying to meet peripheral needs. IBM provides one such example of a simplified design program. Main [45] notes that IBM's redesign of its medium-sized computers, the 9370 and AS/400, reduced the number of cabinets required to 3 as opposed to the 15 different "boxes" previously required. Incremental product changes such as these help address customer requirements such as reduced floor space availability.

New product marketing can benefit from part reduction programs in ways such as simplifying customer part replacement requests and product warranty servicing that can be easily facilitated. Improved customer service can result in increased customer satisfaction. A product design that calls for a reduced number of parts may be perceived as a positive attribute by customers. Moreover, enhanced product reliability can be promoted as a powerful product feature.

Another example of NPD simplification that involves marketing entails reducing the number of suppliers a firm uses. This can eliminate some of the benefits of pure competitive bidding, but with increased inter-firm cooperation and agreements that encourage trust, parts and raw material can be obtained faster, with less cost and better quality [18]. One example of a company that has implemented this form of simplification is Xerox. Ettlie [19] notes that Xerox has adopted a posture more like the Japanese by dealing with fewer suppliers. Xerox has reduced the number of their suppliers from 5,000 to 300. Also, more recent trends in accelerating NPD call for using suppliers who can provide quality subassemblies by working with company design engineers rather than merely supplying components. Companies can also benefit from supplier-initiated innovations such as the balance shaft developed for General Motors by Simpson Industries, Inc. and molded plastic parts designed by D. J. Inc. of Louisville, Kentucky for General Electric [6].

Organizations are prime candidates for simplification. The 12 R&D directors we questioned noted that the simplify approach can be used to produce flatter organizations and, therefore, reduced levels of reporting and time. Functions may need to be realigned for the most efficient utilization of research effort, information, and plant and equipment. Such realignment requires discovering the complexities within the operation and moving to a more informal, flexible structure. Kanter [39] notes that an ideal entrepreneurial corporation is characterized by an integrative culture and structure that removes barriers to communication and minimizes hard-and-fast rules. In a similar vein, Morgan [48] notes that organizational hierarchy stifles debate and therefore constructive conflict. He advocates smaller, flatter organization structures that are communication-intensive. Speeding up operations requires giving employees more responsibility and flexibility. AT&T, for example, provided high degrees of autonomy to its development teams in deciding on a phone's design, manufacture, and cost with very favorable results [15]. Carefully evaluating how information flows and how decisions are made can help identify the areas where simplification can yield "added value."

ELIMINATE DELAYS

A second approach for accelerating NPD involves eliminating delays. To eliminate delays, all tasks can be reviewed for unused time or slack between and within activities. Bottlenecks can be identified and backlogs can be eliminated so that material, ideas, and information can steadily move through the NPD process. There is a caveat, however. Research has shown that slack is a source of innovation and creativity [41] and is used as a buffer by firms confronted by uncertain environments [24]. Operational slack provides workers with the opportunity to review their jobs, to learn to perform them more creatively and efficiently, and to obtain higher-quality results. This notion highlights a potential tradeoff between high product quality and the speed of production.

The Just-In-Time (JIT) manufacturing process originated as a production scheduling method to minimize costly delays and inventory [12, 64]. When a manufacturing firm uses the JIT scheduling philosophy, the organization transits from the traditional "push" system, such as Material Requirements Planning (MRP), to a "pull" concept of production and development scheduling. A push system pushes products through each portion of the NPD cycle so that inventories build up between operations when ensuing operations are not prepared to receive work-in-process. However, in a pull system work is timed and does not leave one station until requested by the next.

The JIT concept can be applied to other functions in the firm as well. For example, the prototype creation group might "pull" the next design from design engineering. The design group could take longer to make sure that the design is "right," up to the point the prototyping group requests the next design.

The advantages of JIT in all functions are found primarily in the reduced cost and time associated with work-in-process inventory, which makes it a useful technique to apply to the development of innovative products. In some areas the work-in-process inventory is comprised of ideas, plans, and procedures as opposed to material and assemblies. Schmenner [64] indicates that excess capacity is much more desirable than excess inventory. Excess capacity allows the firm to become more flexible so that the firm can produce to the specific needs of the market [64]. Cost is reduced by not having material in inventory and by not having to rework as many defective "products" when a systematic error is discovered. Any delay caused by waiting to perform the pull process will be much more than compensated for by the reduced time and cost attributable to "the costs associated with inspection and reinspection, handling, warehousing, inventory, scrap, and rework" [23, p. 64].

An article in *The Economist* [17] describes how Benetton, the clothing manufacturer, uses the eliminate delays NPD acceleration approach to meet customer demand and reduce the time to market. Benetton, which operates in an environment of volatile fashion, makes many of its garments in a neutral color and then dyes them at the last minute to meet fashion trends. This approach helps Benetton eliminate fabrication delays and accelerate new color fashions to market.

The JIT principle clearly can be applied to the development and launch of new products. Marketing needs to be concerned with the elimination of NPD delays that occur beyond the boundaries of the firm. Specifically, coordination needs to be maintained between the firm and its channel members relative to initial new product launch information, the availability of product documentation and, most importantly, the availability of the product itself. The manufacturing firm and its channel members need to work together to facilitate adequate information and product coordination, which ensures customer satisfaction. Developing new product literature and advertising can be planned early in the NPD process to eliminate delays in commercialization. This is especially beneficial as difficulties that create unanticipated delays will be less significant if they are handled earlier in the NPD process.

The concept of "throughput time reduction" is discussed primarily in the manufacturing literature [64]. Throughput time is the length of time between the arrival of raw materials at the factory and the shipment of the finished product. Schmenner [64] notes that the reduction of throughput time is the single most important determinant of improved factory productivity because it forces management to focus on critical elements such as inventory reduction, factory layout, engineering change minimization, and production schedule stabilization.

The throughput time concept holds equally well for the NPD process. Raw material for various NPD processes may include the ideas, models, and procedures used to generate design packages or marketing plans. Engineering designs and marketing plans that are moved methodically through the NPD process will produce products faster than designs that are rushed through their creation processes but spend much of their transit time waiting in queues to have "value added."

Frequently, rushed designs contain errors. NPD delays are encountered while these errors are corrected, in addition to the delays caused by the products, processes, and launches that may have to be reworked or scrapped due to manufacturing or marketing errors. Research objectives and designs that do not consider the available production equipment and tools also can create delays. This calls for design reviews that not only scrutinize the design for faults, but also evaluate the design for producibility. Delays may be avoided by training personnel who will be involved with a new product after the design phase. The sales and customer service personnel will be better able to perform their functions if they receive timely new product design instruction.

Because throughput is a measure of productivity (i.e., products per time), the throughput of designs or plans as well as products can be increased by decreasing the time or increasing the number of "good" designs, plans, or products produced. Schmenner [64, p. 13, parenthetical words added] states, "The tortoise-type factory (firm) can actually make things faster, not because its equipment (personnel) runs at higher speeds, but because materials (designs/plans) keep moving, slowly but surely (steadily), through each process step." The "tortoise-type" factory or firm is driven by processes like JIT, which pull ideas and products through the NPD process at a constant, steady pace. In contrast to the "tortoise" approach, Putnam [54] describes the "hare" approach when he notes an observation made by one manager, "We don't have time to do it right, but we have time to do it over and over." Stated in another way, a continuous, well planned NPD process will produce higher quality results faster than a "hurry-up-and-wait" process.

Delay elimination also applies to interpersonal interactions. The managers and R&D directors in our small samples pointed out that delay elimination was enhanced by teamwork, employee empowerment, and management support for NPD activities. They also noted that "early buy-in" and "sign-up" generate the energy and motivation to succeed.

ELIMINATE STEPS

A third NPD acceleration approach involves eliminating unnecessary activities. The objective here is to shorten or completely eliminate unnecessary NPD operations. This activity may initially be viewed as removing the "nice to do" tasks while retaining the "must do" tasks.

Bower and Hout [5] state that the firm's primary focus should always remain creating value for the customer. Therefore, tasks can be evaluated by the "added value" each task contributes to customer satisfaction. The identification of customer values is a critical function that helps crystallize the "must do" tasks and helps develop an NPD priority system. The reduced cost of products attributable to eliminated tasks can lower the price to the final consumer. The overall reduction in the NPD cycle can launch new technologies and designs more quickly.

Any steps, tasks, or interfaces that are removed from the NPD process can save the time and costs required to perform those tasks. Ernst's [18] study of IBM, for example, indicated that in addition to reducing the number of their suppliers, IBM placed rigid quality requirements on them and then eliminated receiving inspections. An additional benefit of having a few, highly-trusted suppliers is that Just-In-Time scheduling can be implemented much easier.

Ernst [18] notes that both IBM and Xerox have created a strategy of reducing the parts count in their products. Such a reduction in parts implies that an associated number of tasks or assembly operations can be eliminated. Ernst [18] also states that Ford and Xerox have cut the number of parts in some of their products by 79% and 50%, respectively. Part reduction has many other implications and benefits related to task elimination such as fewer component drawings and associated drawing inspections and approvals. Moreover, less inventory is required and supplier interfaces are minimized. Products with fewer parts can be designed for easier maintenance thereby reducing the number of tasks related to the repair of products found defective during product test and inspection.

The elimination of steps approach is important and may be applied to many facets of NPD activity. As in the manufacturing function, the elimination of approvals in marketing and R&D that are determined unnecessary assists NPD acceleration. Our sample of R&D and new product development managers noted that many approval procedures are very cumbersome, and we add that they may be required solely to support particular individual's power needs. Potential areas for approval elimination include new product sales promotions, advertising, quantity discounts, return policy, and pricing processes. Marketing is also in a good position to obtain the information needed to determine the steps in the NPD process that do not add product value for the customer. The elimination of test marketing activities is a decision that requires careful attention. A computer market simulation may be used as a substitute for a field test market as the duration of a test market may cause the firm to lose its market opportunity to an "accelerating" competitor. Another alternative to time-consuming test marketing is the sequential roll-out of successive product models. In addition, new product ideas and concepts derived from lead users may not require test markets.

Capital budgeting also provides an unlikely, but fertile area for identifying activities to accelerate the NPD process [27, 64]. A climate of trust can reduce the number of times finance departments and other groups request the NPD team to justify its estimates. The elimination of budget and appropriation interactions was high on the list of activities to be eliminated by the NPD managers and R&D directors sampled during our research. Further, if a typical budget process takes 6 months, any time savings here would be important. Recent developments in expert systems can help to eliminate steps in cost approximation as well as in establishing break-even points for particular designs based on production volumes [77]. Advanced material, labor, and estimated competitive demand information can be used to generate a portfolio of prices and returns that may be refined as the NPD process progresses. This information can provide early substantiation of project revenue to help eliminate iterations in the budgeting process.

Urban and von Hippel [75] have recognized another way to eliminate steps. They indicate that in fields of rapid change, firms should look to lead users for new product concepts. Lead users comprise a firm's most important customers. A lead user of a firm's products may design a new product or adapt a firm's product to more closely fit their own needs. Marketing, through the firm's sales force, is in a good position to monitor customer activities that involve the use of its firm's products. An example of this situation is an electronics firm that designs a piece of test equipment for its own use. The design may be obtained from this particular electronics firm by a test equipment manufacturer. The test equipment manufacturer might then provide this piece of test equipment to both the electronics firm and the electronics industry. The ready design and initial market accelerates the test equipment manufacturer's new product development process and product launch by eliminating the research phase and minimizing the design phase of the NPD cycle. In a similar vein Cookson [10] and Gomory and Schmitt [29] cite one view of how Japanese companies minimize the use of extensive market research studies by quickly getting the product to lead users, obtaining their reactions, and making refinements to the technology.

SPEED-UP OPERATIONS

"Speed-up" is the fourth and the most common NPD acceleration approach. As Dumaine [15, p. 55] points out, however, "Practically everyone agrees that the worst way to speed up a company is by trying to make it do things just as it does, only faster." Even with this warning, some processes exist that can be made to operate at a faster pace especially with help from technological advances. Accelerating operations essentially requires that certain activities be performed more rapidly. Process acceleration can apply to every task from idea generation to product distribution.

In addition to product concept acceleration processes, several well-known advanced manufacturing and design automation processes may be employed to accelerate the NPD cycle. Much has been written about the need to automate—a technological term for speeding up. Importantly, however, both Teresko [70] and Ernst [18] indicate that firms need to simplify their operations prior to automation. Ernst [18] points out that a reduction in the number of parts in a product eases the automation of its assembly and increases productivity. In addition, he states that without first simplifying, ". . . the result can be an automated disaster" (p. 32). This implies that the elimination of delays and operations should precede the automation (speed-up) of a firm's processes.

Workers, for example, who are given new tools and applicable training can perform NPD functions far faster. Computer Aided Design/Computer Aided Manufacturing (CAD/CAM) systems are examples of engineering tools that can speed new product design. Computer simulation tools applied to models developed in CAD systems allow designs to be tested earlier in the NPD cycle. Machine-controlled processes, especially in manufacturing, can be made to operate faster. Our sample of NPD managers and R&D directors noted that the efficiency of new technology is not the only criterion for its implementation. The implementation of new speed-up technologies must be accompanied by personnel training and the allocation of resources to make these technologies effective and efficient.

A marketing example of our speed-up approach is demonstrated by the Limited's distribution channel. Main [45, p. 50] notes that, "The Limited rushes new fashions off the design board and into its 3,200 stores in less than 60 days, while most competitors still order Christmas apparel the previous May." He also points out that consumer preferences are closely tracked by point-of-sale computers. Small, highly motivated, informed groups involved in NPD processes, such as those performing the idea generation process or the screening of new product ideas, may reach consensus and complete assignments faster than larger, more cumbersome groups. Communicating information accurately can impact the time required to develop new products. Locating such functions as engineering and manufacturing engineering or engineering and marketing together or adjacently can enhance and quicken the NPD process [31]. Further, new communication technologies such as electronic and voice mail can facilitate the speeding up of communication.

There are, of course, important caveats associated with technologically-driven speed-up methods. One involves the generation of scrap by pushing automated processes beyond their limits. In addition, hostility can result when workers are pushed beyond their capabilities. As a consequence, attempts to accelerate NPD may be sabotaged. A second caveat involves group processes. Small groups may generate ideas faster than large groups but they may not generate the breadth of valuable ideas. A third caveat involves automated product testing. Tests run at rates faster than a new product's normal operating cycle may not properly emulate the product's end use and can therefore possess latent defects that may be discovered by customers.

PARALLEL PROCESSING

Paralleling specific activities can provide exciting possibilities for accelerating NPD. The objective of simultaneous, concurrent, or overlapping NPD operations involves performing at least two tasks at the same time. Parallel processing is depicted by Critical Path Methodologies (CPM), such as Program Evaluation and Review Technique

(PERT). Although PERT and CPM are not dependent on parallel processing, these techniques provide the user with a tool to increase the number of tasks that can be performed simultaneously. These tools also provide users the ability to review and modify the NPD process.

When PERT is used a project's tasks can be reviewed for dependency. Each task whose starting point is dependent on another task's completion point is sequentially linked with it. All other tasks are reviewed for dependencies and are oriented in paths parallel to the original path. The CPM analyzes the project's longest projected time to completion.

Once the CPM procedure has been applied to NPD, it is time to consider whether the NPD process can be shortened. This is accomplished by removing delays, in addition to minimizing dependencies, so that more NPD tasks can be located in parallel paths. This process involves repeatedly "testing assumptions" about what tasks are required in the NPD critical path.

Batson [3] indicates that critical path methods are most often used after a program enters preliminary design. This implies that the degree of uncertainty in the earlier NPD stages, such as R&D (research especially), can be great, and therefore parallel processing at these very early stages can involve considerable risk. A major feature of the NPD–CPM method is its careful and comprehensive review of critical path tasks as candidates for additional simplification, elimination, and paralleling.

An illustration of parallel processing is presented by Steinberg [68] in his discussion of large-scale technological projects. His most revealing research discovery was that the projects in which parallel processing failed were those that started parallel development before the probability of failure and the overall project risk had been significantly reduced. This implies that the failed projects he researched, such as the Nuclear Airplane, had begun parallel R&D efforts prior to having basic scientific and engineering problems resolved. Resources were wasted because parallel operations were started prematurely. As pointed out by the NPD managers in one of our samples, very crucial NPD programs may be implemented by operating two or more NPD teams in parallel, each pursuing different approaches and technologies but each sharing information with the other(s).

The projects that Steinberg [68] notes as successes, the Manhattan and the Apollo projects, had static objectives in addition to low probability of failure and overall project risk. Technologies used to implement these projects already had been developed. This factor was a major contributor to the low probability of failure and the reduced overall project risk.

Parallel processing may be implemented all along the NPD process. A British Aerospace Corporation study showed that 85% of a product's cost was locked in by the engineering design phase [77]. Additionally, Putnam [54] notes that serial product development processes result in only the most serious errors being caught early in the NPD process. Very often, designs are being reworked when they should be in manufacturing. This results in increased costs and delays. Dean and Susman [14] argue that the "old," sequential method of design engineering, "throwing the product design over the wall" into manufacturing's domain is no longer acceptable. They note that in some cases companies have to implement many engineering changes long after the products have been introduced because the original product design was too costly to produce with the company's existing manufacturing resources. Another example of parallel processing involves the design review process. GM's Chevrolet-Pontiac-Canada group shortened its development time by about 14 weeks by requiring the finance and engineering departments to review designs in parallel [8].

Another useful concept relating to the NPD design function involves the focus on "design for parallel design and manufacture." For example, systems engineering could be performed with consideration for parallel lower level hardware and software design phases. In addition, these lower level design phases can be developed so that product fabrication and assembly are performed in parallel in manufacturing.

While Schrage [65] argues for the linking of process and new product R&D, Dean and Susman [14] advocate the paralleling of the design engineering and manufacturing engineering processes. The NPD managers and R&D directors in our sample also pointed out that in addition to linking product and process engineering through "simplified" communications these two functions can also be overlapped. This is a good example of the usefulness of the interdisciplinary teamwork that can be achieved early in the NPD process. By paralleling these two efforts information can be shared and more producible designs can result. Beginning process development early in the product development cycle provides the opportunity to obtain a better fit between product and process technologies. This approach allows product design engineering to iron out design flaws prior to manufacturing. Chrysler, for example was able to save 25%–40% in program costs, usually incurred because of mid-stream changes, by including manufacturing early on [8]. Process development (in-depth specification and manufacturing engineering after working prototype development) takes almost as long as several earlier stages [58]. Mansfield [46] found that American firms, when compared with Japanese firms, were slower in the manufacturing/commercialization of new products. Therefore, this appears to be a prime area for parallel processing.

Other NPD activities may also be overlapped; for example, test engineering may use early design information to assure that new products are tested and inspected in a systematic manner. Purchasing may be able to order long lead time items in advance of the formal issue of engineering documents. By involving suppliers early in the design stage, Navistar, a truck manufacturer, incorporated a key suggestion from a supplier in the initial design rather than have the idea come to light much later and cause retooling and delays [15].

Rapidly moving new products to market is no advantage if products that consumers don't want are the result [43]. This condition becomes more likely to occur when market information is uncertain. Due to the high levels of uncertainty and risk associated with new product development, marketing can obtain important information by early target market determination and by maintaining close contact with the target market in parallel with other early tasks in the new product development process. Therefore, early links with customers help accelerate the NPD process. For example, Boeing reviewed different concepts with customers' design engineers to help establish desirable product features [43]. By pushing lead users into the process early, and continuing to work with them in parallel, it is possible to avoid the pitfalls that are based on a one-shot market research project at the conceptual stage [4]. Additionally, marketing can provide product pricing information, set up distribution channel arrangements and dealer training, sales force deployment, and advertising decisions in parallel with product development and manufacturing tasks [16]. Dusenbury [16] relates an actual case where the CPM method was adopted and an NPD project was completed in 36 weeks instead of the 76 weeks that the more standard approach would have taken.

In all of these examples functions that traditionally occur later in the NPD process benefit from information generated by much earlier activities. When development cycles are short, opportunities to introduce new ideas also are brief. By parallel processing, many of the functional areas can be involved earlier in the NPD process.

IMPLICATIONS AND SUMMARY

Implications for Management

Our survey of NPD acceleration approaches has important implications for management. First, much has been said about the lack of quality in American products and services. NPD speed that create quantity without quality should not be the objective of these acceleration approaches. Firms that do not attend to their customers' needs in today's highly competitive environment will not survive. Because most customers are concerned about the quality of their purchases, these acceleration approaches need to be focused on the development of quality products. Such strategies as simplify and eliminate steps lend themselves to this end. The simplify and eliminate steps approaches can also assist in product part reduction programs. Such activities tend to make products more reliable and easier to repair. Customers increasingly demand these attributes.

We have noted that the speed-up approach is probably the least effective of our five potential NPD acceleration approaches. This is especially true when related to labor-intensive activities. Tasks are often divided into very small increments so that they may be performed quickly, many individuals can learn the tasks, and worker replacement is expedient. Speed-up may also entail the constant badgering of employees to ensure that speed is maintained. Thus, the speed-up of employees can have detrimental effects. Employees may react to the pressure to speed up in many ways other than faster performance.

An additional pitfall that may occur when attempting to speed up NPD processes involves the use of simulations. Test markets may be replaced with computer simulations that can save time and cost, and maintain NPD secrecy. A potential fault with this technique lies in the inability of the model builders to design a simulation that accurately portrays market conditions. Many problems can arise during the development of a simulation model such as an inaccurate design of the consumer's decision-making process, unforeseen competitive responses, and changes in consumers' perceptions of the new product.

Implementing new product development *acceleration takes time.* Management should not expect to implement these approaches instantly and obtain immediate results. In many situations a firm's NPD process has become so bogged down in bureaucracy that the organizational changes alone required to speed up an NPD process may take months to implement. This should not deter management from taking the first step towards "acceleration." The question is not whether or not to accelerate NPD, it's how to best get an NPD acceleration plan implemented.

The implementation of our NPD acceleration approaches clearly presents challenges. These approaches should be implemented in a logical, purposeful, and incremental manner [12]. Such an implementation process can dull the shock of such extensive changes within an organization. Successful implementation is critical if the full benefits of these acceleration approaches are to be realized. Implementation requires continuous, open, and timely communication among all members of a firm.

To obtain the greatest effectiveness, all of the NPD acceleration approaches should be implemented. They do not necessarily have to be implemented simultaneously but a plan for full implementation should be created. We attempt to rank our five approaches to NPD acceleration. Our suggested order of implementation is illustrated in Figure 43-3. The conceptual basis for our hierarchy stems from an effort to

FIGURE 43-3   Hierarchy of NPD Acceleration Approach Implementation.

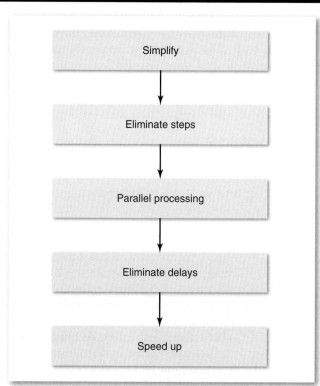

define the sequence that would provide the greatest ease of implementation and the least amount of wasted effort at later stages. We consider simplification to be the most important NPD acceleration approach. Many times products, tasks, and organizations can be easily simplified as long as interfaces with other products, tasks, and organizational elements are considered. Product parts simplification, as noted earlier, has many positive effects such as cost reduction, fewer suppliers, and greater product reliability.

Next in our implementation sequence is eliminate steps. This approach is a natural by-product of product and process simplification. Product simplification can lead directly to the elimination of NPD process steps. More importantly, it can be wasteful to parallel or speed up activities that are to be subsequently deleted.

The next NPD acceleration approach in our hierarchy is parallel processing. This approach, although potentially effective in accelerating NPD, is difficult to implement before nonessential tasks are removed. Effective parallel processing depends on having the required NPD tasks identified.

The fourth NPD acceleration approach is to eliminate delays. Delay elimination is more easily accomplished when the set of tasks to be performed is well known and integrated in a "simple" manner. This implies that the NPD tasks should be scrutinized and unneeded ones eliminated before delays are addressed. Each path in a parallel arrangement can now be scrutinized for dysfunctional delays.

The last of our five NPD acceleration approaches to be implemented should be speed-up. As noted earlier, speeding up systems without simplifying the tasks, eliminating unneeded tasks, parallel processing, and eliminating delays can lead to an accelerated disaster.

From our review of the literature it appears that simplify and speed-up are implemented most frequently. We would agree that simplify is the proper approach to initiate an NPD acceleration project as it provides a significant basis for other approaches. Speeding up is often perceived as one of the most useful approaches to implement especially in labor-intensive NPD operations. However, unless speeding up results from technology, as we have noted, this may not be the most prudent alternative.

Finally, we have summarized some of the potential positive and negative ramifications of implementing each acceleration approach. This information is based on data obtained from our survey of the literature and evaluations of our NPD acceleration approaches provided by the 30 new product development managers and the 12 R&D directors referred to earlier. These results are summarized in Figure 43-4.

Summary

Five major approaches for accelerating the NPD process have been presented. The approaches include simplifying operations, eliminating delays, eliminating steps, speeding up operations, and paralleling processes. These approaches may be incorporated alone or in combination and, we emphasize, they may be applied to "all" of the firm's departments and "all" of the NPD functions. While many of these techniques are used in manufacturing environments, they have important applications in other functions such as marketing and R&D. To achieve a holistic approach to NPD acceleration, these suggested approaches need to be applied to the entire NPD process. As Krubasik [43] has discussed, managers must actively consider the trade-offs between opportunity costs (associated with slowness) and development risks (developing technology and understanding market needs). That is, speed must be seen in the larger context of a firm's strategic objectives.

The implementation of our NPD acceleration approaches may put considerable strain on an organization. Although we have suggested that all of our approaches be implemented, we believe that the implementation hierarchy offered provides a logical sequence that can minimize problems. We posit that any stress presented by the introduction of these approaches will be more than compensated for by the time and cost reductions achieved in the modification of the NPD process.

As demonstrated by the examples presented, some firms have already implemented individual pieces of this concept. The companies that have begun to implement some

FIGURE 43-4   Potential Benefits and Limitations of Major NPD Acceleration Modes.

Approaches	Potential Benefits	Potential Limitations
Simplify	• Makes technology and design more understandable • Applies to external, human corporate relationships • Streamlines reports, documents, and controls • Understandability fosters trust • Flatter organizations	• Re-entry problems of "project dedicated" team members back into their functional groups at project completion • Not meeting customer requirements • Higher costs if external vendors are used to augment NPD process • Not meeting product design requirements • Lack of project status detail • Lack detail if reporting/controls not adequate • Use of trust to simplify NPD process can lead to inadequate critical thinking, e.g., group think
Eliminate Delays	• Fosters clearer "up front" thinking—vision • Encourages early technology investigation of long-lead items	• Hurried acceptance of the NPD vision • Early captial appropriations/alternate technologies may result in poor estimates • Early launch may lead to inadequate product documentation
Eliminate Steps	• Forces build/buy decisions—may increase quality and speed • Authorizing signature elimination moves authority down the organizational hierarchy • Eliminates redundant incoming tests and inspections • Helps eliminate "Not Invented Here" attitude	• If external vendors are used, cost, quality, proprietary advantages may be lost • Senior management may be reluctant to decentralize NPD decision-making • Requires vendors supplying component parts to adopt high quality standards to minimize "in-house" testing
Speed Up	• Forces use of new technologies, (i.e., for communication—FAX, electronic mail) • "Smarter" and "shorter" testing algorithms • Switch from matrix to project organization structure increases focus on NPD	• Higher stress • Danger of inadequate NPD project documentation • Higher risk may occur if some phases are shortened, e.g., testing
Parallel Processing	• Simultaneous engineering, testing, and market research • Increased knowledge of other functions • Fosters teamwork activities	• Potential for confusion • Higher stress levels • NPD participants must work with greater uncertainty • More frequent communication required • More resources required • Need for teamwork training

specific acceleration approaches often report that they have shortened their NPD time considerably. Therefore, the initial success of these specific and often piecemeal NPD acceleration approaches stands as testimony to the promise of full implementation. We suggest that if the five NPD acceleration approaches explored here are employed in a thoughtful manner, a firm's time to develop important new products can be significantly reduced.

This approach to new product development acceleration is viable and essential for firms in the 1990s and beyond. We believe that NPD acceleration is much more than just an interesting concept.

Biographical Sketches

Murray R. Millson is a doctoral candidate at Syracuse University in the School of Management. He has a B.S. in Electrical Engineering and an M.S. in Industrial Management from Clarkson University and an M.B.A. from Syracuse University. Mr. Millson is a Registered Professional Engineer in Quality Engineering in the state of California. His business career includes 20 years with the General Electric Company in various engineering and management assignments. His current research interests include new product development, business partnering, business and marketing strategy, and consumer behavior related to new product introductions.

S. P. Raj is Distinguished Professor of Marketing and Associate Dean for Academic Affairs in the School of Management at Syracuse University. He earned a bachelor's degree in Electrical Engineering from the Indian Institute of Technology, Madras, India, in 1975 and master's and Ph.D. degrees from Carnegie Mellon University in 1977 and 1980, respectively. He received the John D. C. Little Best Paper Award from the Institute for Management Sciences on Marketing in 1988. He is faculty coordinator of the Marketing Program for the Incubation Center in the New York State Center for Advanced Technology in Computer Applications and Software Engineering (CASE). His research has been published in such journals as *Marketing Science, Journal of Marketing, Journal of Marketing Research, Journal of Consumer Research, Transactions on Engineering Management,* and *Journal of Product Innovation Management.*

David Wilemon is Professor of Marketing and Director of Syracuse University's Innovation Management Program. He is a member of the American Marketing Association, Engineering Management Society, Academy of Management, and the Institute of Management Science. He received his doctorate from Michigan State University. His professional and research interests focus on new corporate ventures, high-performing technical teamwork, R&D management, and innovation management. His research appears in such journals as *Academy of Management Journal, Journal of Marketing, Organizational Dynamics, California Management Review, Journal of Product Innovation Management, Columbia Journal of World Business,* and *Transactions on Engineering Management.* He has been an advisor to several technology-based organizations including Apple Computer, Bell Laboratories, IBM, Data General, DEC, GE, Bechtel, UpJohn, United Technologies, ICI Pharmaceuticals, Schlumberger, 3M, NASA, and the European Space Agency.

The authors would like to thank Peter and Anne Klein for their generous support of the Syracuse University Innovation Management Program. In addition, we thank Professor Al Bean and the Center for Innovation Management Studies (CIMS) at Lehigh University for ongoing support of our Research Program on New Product Development Acceleration.

References

1. Altier, W. J. Task forces: An effective management tool. *Management Review* 52–57 (February 1987).

2. Ancona, D. G. and Caldwell, D. Improving the performance of new product teams. *Research-Technology Management* 33(2):25–29 (March–April 1990).

3. Batson, R. G. Critical path acceleration and simulation in aircraft technology planning. *IEEE Transactions on Engineering Management* EM-34(4):244–251 (November 1987).

4. Bonnet, E. B. Nature of the R&D/marketing cooperation. *R&D Management* 16(2):117–126 (1986).

5. Bower, J. L. and Hout, T. M. Fast cycle capability for competitive power. *Harvard Business Review* 110–118 (November/December 1988).

6. Burt, D. N. Managing suppliers up to speed. *Harvard Business Review* 127–135 (July–August 1989).

7. Innovation. *Business Week* Special issue. (1989).

8. Bussey, J. and Sease, D. R. Speeding up. *Wall Street Journal* (February 23, 1988).

9. Champoux, J. E. A three sample test of some extensions to the job characteristics model of work motivation. *Academy of Management Journal* 23(3):466–478 (1980).

10. Cookson, C. Creativity in reverse. *Across the Board* Conference Board, 50–51 (November 1988).

11. Crawford, C. M. Defining the charter for product innovation. *Sloan Management Review* 22(1):3–12 (Fall 1980).

12. Cusumano, M. A. Manufacturing innovation: Lessons from the Japanese auto industry. *Sloan Management Review* 29–39 (Fall 1988).

13. Day, G. S. and Wensley, R. Assessing advantage: A framework for diagnosing competitive superiority. *Journal of Marketing* 52–53 (1988).

14. Dean, J. W., Jr. and Susman, G. I. Organizing for manufacturable design. *Harvard Business Review* 28–32 (January–February 1989).

15. Dumaine, B. How managers can succeed through speed. *Fortune* 53–59 (February 13, 1989).

16. Dusenbury, W. CPM for new product introductions. *Harvard Business Review* 124–136 (July–August 1967).

17. Another day, another bright idea. *Economist* 307(7546):82–88 (April 16, 1988).

18. Ernst, R. G. How to streamline operations. *The Journal of Business Strategy* 8:32–36 (Fall 1987).

19. Ettlie, J. E. *Taking Charge of Manufacturing.* San Francisco, CA: Jossey-Bass Publishers, 1988.

20. Feldman, S. P. How organizational culture can affect innovation. *Organizational Dynamics* 57–68 (Summer 1988).

21. Filley, R. D. Roundtable participants discuss systems integration trends, strategies, champions. *Industrial Engineering* 18:26–33 (August 1986).

22. Foster, R. N. *Innovation: The Attacker's Advantage.* McKinsey & Co., Inc., Summit Books, 1986.

23. Frazier, G. L., Spekman, R. E. and O'Neal, C. R. Just-in-time exchange relationships in industrial markets. *Journal of Marketing* 52:52–67 (October 1988).

24. Galbraith, J. R. Organization design: An information processing view. *Interfaces* 4(2):28–36 (May 1974).

25. Gardner, D. G. Task complexity effects on non-task-related movements: A test of activation theory. *Organizational Behavior and Human Decision Processes* 45(2):209–231 (1990).

26. Gold, B. Approaches to accelerating product and process development. *Journal of Product Innovation Management* 1(4):81–88 (1987).

27. Gold, B. Charting a course to superior technology evaluation. *Sloan Management Review* 19–27 (Fall 1988).

28. Gomory, R. E. Turning ideas into products. *The Bridge* 18(1):11–14 (Spring 1988).

29. Gomory, R. E. and Schmitt, R. W. Step-by-step innovation. *Across the Board* Conference board, 52–56 (November 1988).

30. Gummer, B. So what's new?: Organizational innovation and entrepreneurship. *Administration in Social Work* 10(2):91–105 (Summer 1986).

31. Gupta, A. K., Raj, S. P. and Wilemon, D. A model for studying R&D-marketing interface in the product innovation process. *Journal of Marketing* 50:7–17 (April 1986).

32. Gupta, A. K. and Wilemon, D. Accelerating the development of technology-based new products. *California Management Review* 24–67 (Winter 1990).

33. Hackman, J. R., Oldham, G., Jamson, R. and Purdy, K. A new strategy for job enhancement. *California Management Review* 17(4):57–70 (1975).

34. Hage, J. Responding to technological and competitive change: Organizational and industry factors. In: *Managing Technological Innovation,* Donald D. Davis and Associates, (eds.). San Francisco, CA: Jossey-Bass Publishers, 1986, pp. 44–71.

35. Hall, J. Managing for group effectiveness. In: *Models for Management: The Structure of Competence,* John A. Shtogren (ed.). The Woodlands, TX: Teleometrics Publisher, 1980, pp. 308–331.

36. Hauser, J. R. and Clausing, D. The house of quality. *Harvard Business Review* 63–73 (May–June 1988).

37. Heany, D. F. and Vinson, W. D. A fresh look at new product development. *The Journal of Business Strategy* 5:22–28 (Fall 1984).

38. Hise, R. T., O'Neal, L., Parasuraman, A. and McNeal, J. U. Marketing/R&D interaction in new product development: Implications for new product success rate. *Journal of Product Innovation Management* 7(2):142–155 (1990).

39. Kanter, R. M. Supporting innovation and venture development in established companies. *Journal of Business Venturing* 1:47–70 (1985).

40. Kiley, D. Can VW survive? *Adweek's Marketing Week* 1:18–22 (May 1989).

41. Knight, K. E. A descriptive model of the intra-firm innovation process. *Journal of Business* 40:478–496 (1967).

42. Kotler, P. *Marketing Management—Analysis Planning, Implementation and Control.* Englewood Cliffs, NJ: Prentice-Hall, 1988.

43. Krubasik, E. G. Customize your product development. *Harvard Business Review* 46–50 (November–December 1988).

44. Lambkin, M. Order of market entry and performance: The experience of start-up ventures. *PIMSLETTER* 41, The Strategic Planning Institute, Cambridge, MA. 1987.

45. Main, J. The winning organization. *Fortune* 50–54 (September 26, 1988).

46. Mansfield, E. Speed and cost of industrial innovation in Japan and the United States: External versus internal technology. *Management Science* 34(10):1157–1168 (October 1988).

47. Maruta, Y. Business management in response to the advanced information age. *Management Japan* 22(1) (Spring 1989).

48. Morgan, G. *Riding the Waves of Change.* San Francisco, CA: Jossey-Bass Publishers, 1988.

49. Morgan, G. and Ramirez, R. Action learning: A holographic metaphor for guiding social change. *Human Relations* 37(1):1–26 (1983).

50. Moriarity, R. T. and Swartz, G. S. Automation to boost sales and marketing. *Harvard Business Review* 100–109 (January–February 1989).

51. Mower, J. C. and Wilemon, D. Rewarding technical teamwork. *Research—Technology Management* 32:24–29 (September–October 1989).

52. Ohmae, K. Managing innovation and new products in key Japanese industries. *Research Management* 28(4): 11–18 (July–August 1985).

53. Peters, T. *Thriving on Chaos: Handbook for a Management Revolution.* New York, NY: Alfred A. Knopf, 1987.

54. Putnam, A. O. A redesign for engineering. *Harvard Business Review* 139–144 (May–June 1985).

55. Rabino, S. and Moskowitz, H. R. Optimizing the product development process: Strategical implications for new entrants. *Sloan Management Review* 45–51 (Spring 1980).

56. Reich, R. B. Entrepreneurship reconsidered: The team as hero. *Harvard Business Review* 65(3):77–83 (May–June 1987).

57. Reiner, G. Cutting your competitor to the quick. *The Wall Street Journal* p. A16 (November 21, 1988).

58. Roberts, E. B. Managing invention and innovation. *Research-Technology Management* 31(1):11–29 (January–February 1988).

59. Rohan, T. M. World-class manufacturing: In search of speed. *Industry Week* 239(17):78–83 (September 3, 1990).

60. Rosenau, M. D., Jr. *Faster New Product Development: Getting the Right Product to Market Quickly.* New York, NY: American Management Association, ANACOM, 1990.

61. Rosenau, M. D., Jr. From experience faster new product development. *Journal of Product Innovation Management* 5(2): 150–153 (1988a).

62. Rosenau, M. D., Jr. Speeding your new product to market. *The Journal of Consumer Marketing* 5(2):23–26 (1988b).

63. Rydz, J. S. *Managing Innovation.* Cambridge, MA: Ballinger Publishing Company, 1986.

64. Schmenner, R. W. The merit of making things fast. *Sloan Management Review* 11–17 (Fall 1988).

65. Schrage, M. R&D just ain't what it used to be. *The Wall Street Journal* p. A10 (October 10, 1988).
66. Shrivastava, P. and Souder, W. The strategic management of technological innovations: A review and a model. *Journal of Management Studies* 24(1):25–41 (1987).
67. Souder, W. E. Managing relations between R&D and marketing in new product development projects. *Journal of Product Innovation Management* 5:6–19 (1988).
68. Steinberg, G. M. Comparing technological risks in large-scale national projects. *Policy Sciences* 18:79–93 (1985).
69. Takeuchi, H. and Nonaka, I. The new product development game. *Harvard Business Review* 137–146 (January–February 1986).
70. Teresko, J. Making it simpler. *Industry Week* 67–68 (April 18, 1988).
71. Thamhain, H. J. Managing technologically innovative team efforts toward new product success. *Journal of Product Innovation Management* 7(1):5–18 (1990).
72. Tushman, M. and Nadler, D. Organizing for innovation. *California Management Review* 28(3):74–92 (Spring 1986).
73. Urban, G. L., Carter, T., Gaskins, S. and Mucha, Z. Market share rewards to pioneering brands: An empirical analysis and strategic implications. *Management Science* 32(6):645–649 (1986).
74. Urban, G. L., Hauser, J. R. and Dholakia, N. *Essentials Of New Product Management.* Englewood Cliffs, NJ: Prentice Hall, Inc., 1987.
75. Urban, G. L. and von Hippel, E. Lead user analyses for the development of new industrial products. *Management Science* 34(5):569–582 (May 1988).
76. Van de Ven, A. H. Central problems in the management of innovation. *Management Science* 32(5):590–607 (May 1986).
77. Villers, P. Introducing MCAE: Expert tools for engineering. *Computers in Mechanical Engineering* 6(3):37–52 (November–December 1987).
78. Wind, Y. and Mahajan, V. PERSPECTIVE New product development process: A perspective for reexamination. *Journal of Product Innovation Management* 5:304–310 (1988).

44

SIX STEPS TO BECOMING A FAST-CYCLE-TIME COMPETITOR

Reducing Product Development Cycle Time Requires a Systematic Strategy That Begins by Focusing on What Adds Value to Your End Customer

Christopher Meyer and Ronald E. Purser

OVERVIEW

In order to compete in the global marketplace, operating and organizing to achieve fast cycle time (FCT) is increasingly becoming a cardinal concern for research and technology managers. Reducing product development cycle time requires a systematic strategy that can align the organization's work activities so that they add value to the end customer. Aligning the organization around a clear value proposition, however, first requires an in-depth assessment of the critical work processes and understanding of the entire value delivery system. Following this step, redesigning the organization into multi-functional teams with challenging cycle time goals and publicly measurable indicators allows them to pursue process improvements and increases organizational learning.

Reducing product development cycle time is emerging as a cardinal concern for the nineties. The infectious demand for producing new products faster will require more companies to adopt a fast-cycle-time (FCT) strategy.

We define FCT as the ongoing ability to identify, satisfy and be paid for meeting customer needs faster than anyone else. There are several key words in this definition. The first is *ongoing*. Although useful, single-shot cycle time reductions do not provide a sustainable competitive advantage. In a competitive environment, the race is never over. Competitors who improve continuously will pass those who pause to relax.

The next key word is *identify*. FCT is the responsibility of all organizational functions—from the start of the business cycle through the end. Some incorrectly consider cycle time to be only a manufacturing or engineering issue. However, the firm that identifies the customer's need first has a head start in filling that need.

Satisfy means that one cannot sacrifice quality for time. The old rule was that if you required a product quickly, it could cost more and the quality couldn't be guaranteed.

Meyer, Christopher and Ronald E. Purser. 1993. Six steps to becoming a fast-cycle-time competitor. *Research Technology Management* 36 (5): 41–48.

That thinking is dead. World-class competitors such as Toyota have clearly demonstrated that speed does not have to sacrifice quality or cost.

Paid refers to the attention FCT companies place on completing the business cycle. For example, while Toyota was able to reduce its manufacturing cycle time to 2 days, it still took 17 days to sell and deliver its cars. FCT companies view their organizations as value delivery systems. As a system, the slowest sub-cycle limits the overall system's total cycle time.

Meeting customer needs declares that products or services that do not meet customer needs are not acceptable.

And last, *faster than anyone else* reflects the reality of increasing competition. If there is a foreign or domestic competitor who is faster, it is only a matter of time before they will dominate that market. Detroit and the semiconductor industry have both learned the hard lesson of ignoring international competition.

Reducing product development cycle time requires a systematic strategy. This article defines the six key steps to becoming a FCT competitor and outlines how to implement them.

Step 1: Understand what your end customer regards as added value, and reflect that in every job and level within the organization.

An FCT strategy focuses the entire organization on work that adds value to the end customer while concurrently trying to eliminate anything that does not. Thus, product development managers in FCT companies structure and manage their organizations as value delivery systems focused on adding value for their customers. In order to do this, all employees must know who the end customers are and what is added value to them. Only people who *pay* for the product are end customers.

There may be more than one end customer. For example, consumer products have several end customers along the distribution chain, starting with the distributor and ending at the consumer. To distributors, packaging may be a value added component of the product, whereas for the consumer, packaging adds little value. The main lesson here is to understand what is value added for each customer you serve.

This end customer view contrasts with the notion of internal customers popularized by quality programs. The internal customer concept suggests that each job has an upstream supplier and a downstream customer. For example, manufacturing is the customer of engineering's designs. While this approach improves understanding of mutual dependencies, calling internal groups customers can cause people to incorrectly equate internal definitions of value added with those of the end customer. The difference is critical: End customers generate revenue while internal customers generate cost. For example, internal customers create 99 percent of the paperwork in organizations. Paperwork rarely adds value to end customers. Using the end customer's definition of value added exposes non-value added time and activities. Motorola, for example, no longer encourages the internal customer perspective.

After defining the end customer, one has to define what is value added in their eyes. A rule of thumb for determining value added is whether or not the end customer is willing to pay for the product, service or feature. If they are not willing to pay for it, then it is probably not value added. The information to make this determination comes from one place: the customer.

Traditionally, we have relied on sales and marketing to channel the customer's definition of value added into the organization. While efficient in the use of people, this approach limits the direct contact other functions have with the customer. It is increasingly evident that expanding the breadth of organizational contact with the end customer sharpens all employees' understanding of what is value added, as well as their motivation to deliver it.

For example, a leading manufacturer of electronic test equipment conducted a focus group in which customers compared their equipment to a competitor's. Invited to the focus group were several young engineers from the development team. Standing behind a one-way mirror, the engineers saw that most of the customers were attracted to their company's product before it was turned on. But after it was turned on, the customers drifted en masse to the competitor's product. Why? Simply because the display on the competitor's product was easier to read. Because display readability was not an issue for the engineers' young eyes, they had dismissed customer complaints. Seeing their competitor's "inferior" product surrounded by customers quickly changed their minds.

In another example, it was a Du Pont development technicians' visit to Reebok that generated a competitive response to Nike's "air cushion" heel. The technicians

All employees must know who the end customers are and what is added value to them.

were there for another purpose; yet when they heard of this problem, they devised a solution involving implanted rubber tubes—made, of course, by Du Pont. These examples illustrate that making customer needs visible to those who have traditionally been isolated or removed from the end customer can quickly reorient functional activities toward outcomes that are truly value added.

While end customers are the ultimate source of defining what is or is not value added, top management is responsible for defining the organization's value added focus and allocating resources accordingly. It does this by defining a *value proposition* for the organization. The value proposition is unique to each organization and defines that organization's value adding strategy.

A well defined value proposition that is aligned with customer needs is critical for ensuring competitive advantage. For example, prior to 1989 Quantum Corporation, a computer disk manufacturer, had a value proposition that stressed quality and performance. Quantum's position in the marketplace grew accordingly. In contrast, a new competitor, Conner Peripherals, had an explicit value proposition to be first to market with their products. Conner's philosophy of "sell, design, build" focused on being first to market with products designed specifically for their customers' needs. In contrast, Quantum had been designing disk drives to meet market standards rather than a specific customer's needs. By carefully picking leading computer manufacturers as its customers, Conner was able to leverage the initial sales and development effort into a broader market opportunity. This was most graphically seen in Conner's relationship with Compaq Computer. Compaq was one of the initial investors in Conner as well as being the initial customer. Compaq's success in the PC market established a presence for Conner's drives.

As Conner's success grew, Quantum reexamined its value proposition of quality and performance relative to Conner's focus on custom designs done fast. Quantum determined that product performance was important, but availability of new products was even more so. In short, quality and performance value were insufficient without time to market. Even though many of Conner's customers complained about the quality of early models, one should not forget that these complainers were purchasing their drives from Conner, not Quantum. This is not to suggest that quality should be ignored in favor of developing products faster, but, rather, that a fanatical devotion to technical elegance can often undermine a company's ability to compete against those who can deliver their products faster. In sum, the value proposition focuses behavior and resources.

A good value proposition clarifies what is value added from what is not. As simple as this may appear, many organizations have value propositions that are not clearly stated. Management often assumes the value proposition is obvious and understood by all. Therefore, it concentrates on managing operations. Each element of the organization may have its own operating definition of the value proposition and act accordingly. The net result is that value adding efforts do not build on, but actually subvert one another. Ultimately, the customer becomes confused.

An organization must be aligned around its value proposition. When it is not, people may be working hard but the net force of their collective efforts will be significantly less. Alignment is more than a function of common understanding. Structural elements such as reward systems, policies, cultural norms, and organization design must be in alignment as well.

To foster alignment, management should continuously communicate and test whether the value proposition is incorporated into each job. Like management, each employee has his or her own mental model of how they should add value for the customer. Without ongoing education efforts, employees may use outdated or conflicting models. Educational efforts minimally include exposing all employees to the corporate mission and value proposition on a regular basis. Additional methods may include:

- One-way briefings such as corporate video newscasts, "all hands" meetings, annual reports, and internal newsletters.
- Staff meetings where senior managers explicitly employ the value proposition as a criterion for decisions.
- Special meetings to describe *and* test the value proposition with key constituencies, including project reviews, new employee orientation, buzz groups, brown bag lunches, etc.
- Company symbols and giveaways such as desk accessories, T-shirts and coffee cups.

Step 2: Focus the entire organization on work that adds value to the end customer.

As we have stated, there are two types of work: value added and non-value added, the former being work for which the customer is willing to pay. For example, painting a car a specific color is value added work, whereas testing the paint for durability is not something a customer is willing to pay for. Surprised? Many might argue that untested paint could fade quickly, thus upsetting the customer. No question about that, but consider your reaction to a car's price sticker that showed below the $699 for optional leather seats a $45 charge for paint testing!

Non-value added practices such as testing are required because we do not fully trust the process being tested. This may be because the process is not well understood or developed or it may be due to poor operating practices. In either case, testing is a stop gap measure until the process is made stable. In the language of quality experts, testing quality into the product is inferior to designing it in. While one may argue as to when a process is stable enough to eliminate testing, the goal of doing so should always be present.

The only way to identify which work adds value is to study the organization's value delivery system. Constructing a high-level map can provide a macro view of the entire organization's value delivery system. Figure 44-1 is a generic example of such a map.

FIGURE 44-1 Understanding Work Flow Begins with Construction of a High-Level Map of the Organization's Value Delivery System.

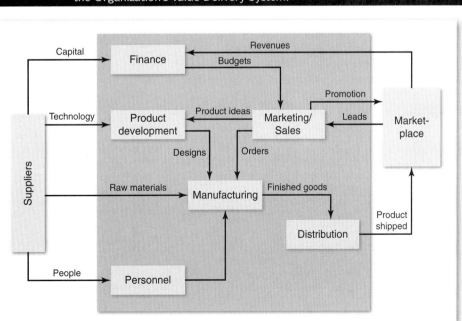

By limiting the amount of detail, it is easier to identify which steps are the most important value adding processes. For some, it may be steps in the process engineering or development process, while for others it could be the testing or prototype stages. Once identified, critical processes can be exploded in greater detail by flow charting and tracing the multi-functional processes and interdependencies, as illustrated in Figure 44-2. At the least, this process map should identify the critical players, key tasks and the time required to complete them. In addition, it is also useful to specify the inputs and outputs of critical steps.

The map should accurately reflect how the process works today. During the mapping exercise, there is a strong urge to incorporate how the process ought to look or be changed. It is important to resist this urge and to defer these discussions until the map is completed. Until there is agreement on how the work flows are currently conducted, such discussions can become irrelevant. However, reaching agreement is not necessarily easy. Everyone has their own model of how the value delivery system works. Defined by personal experience, these models differ for each individual.

Similarly, senior management's models are frequently built on past experience that may no longer be valid. For example, a high technology company wanted to reduce new product development time and therefore mapped the entire development process. Management was shocked to discover that the product definition phase often took as long as 12 months. Its mental model was based on experience gained when the company was much smaller and products were simpler. Management had lost contact with the impact of many small process changes made over time.

The mapping process does not require everyone to agree on each and every step. Rather, strive for general agreement that the map accurately reflects the most critical

FIGURE 44-2   Differentiating Value Added from Non-Value Added Work Requires a More Detailed Map of the Work and Information Flows Between Functions and Departments.

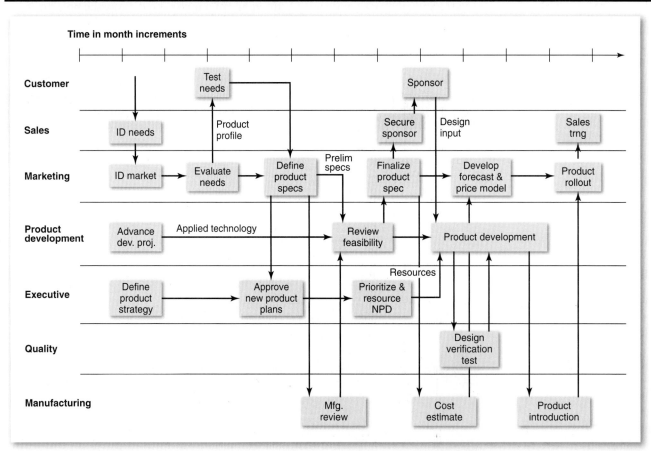

process steps. Once this is achieved, review the map and identify value added and non-value added steps. Test each non-value added task to eliminate or compress it. First efforts typically result in a "shrinkage" of the current process. A shrinkage has the same basic structure as the current process with many non-value activities removed. Shrinkages will often cut cycle time by 50 percent or more. But one should not stop here. Shrinkages are the results of picking the low-hanging fruit. These are efficiency improvements which do not fundamentally restructure the value delivery process or yield a *substantial* competitive advantage. Major breakthroughs come from insights that fundamentally restructure the core elements of the value delivery process. Clearly understanding the current delivery process, combined with seriously questioning and entertaining creative alternatives, generates such insights.

To become an FCT competitor, one must understand the value delivery process sufficiently to define and focus everyone's attention on value added work. It is curious that American business leaders love to invoke sports metaphors as competitive models yet rarely include the attention sports professionals pay toward process analysis and improvement. Specifically, world champions such as the San Francisco 49ers spend 100 hours off the field for every hour played. They use non-game time to analyze films about their value delivery process or for training. Yet in an informal survey that we conducted during a series of California Institute of Technology FCT seminars, we never found more than two executives per class who spend more than one day a month examining their organizations' work processes. One cannot expect dramatic breakthroughs without putting in more time.

Step 3: Redesign your organization so that it is flat and based on multi-functional teams, with blurred boundaries—inside and out.

By definition, large, hierarchical organizations can never be quick. The multi-functional, team-based organization is an alternative. Composed of people from different functional disciplines, the teams have responsibility for the core value-added work processes of the business. Rather than operating as a coordinating body on top of the existing functional organization, the team focuses on delivering the organization's value proposition, and is allocated resources accordingly. Teams are typically organized around major product or market groupings.

Business teams are different from a classic matrix organization primarily in the breadth and scope of their responsibility. Theoretically, a matrix divides the power equally between project and functional bosses. In practice, the functional bosses wield more than 50 percent of the power. Because the core value adding process is within the team, the team-based organization keeps at least 51 percent of the power in the team.

Overly simplified, the teams become the line organization and the functions become staff. In contrast to the team itself, the team-based organization resists easy depiction. The supporting cast and connections to other teams are in constant flux. Teams are nodes in an organic network that continually adjusts itself in response to new customer demands. The role of the functions is to support the teams in the value-adding processes as defined by the teams.

Placing the core value delivery process into teams requires a fundamental shift in the organization's power structure. If management allows functional dominance to continue, employees will accurately perceive the teams as nice but not essential. The success of a multi-functional, team-based organization depends on creating a new organization *architecture*. The worst thing one could do would be to throw a group of people from engineering, operations and marketing together and call them a multi-functional team. They would find themselves struggling to define their role as they simultaneously tried to shift the organization's functional orientation. Well-designed team-based structures define the roles and responsibilities for those off the team as well as those on the team. Issues to be considered in the architecture include:

- Initial definition of team goals.
- Team charter.

- Team member responsibilities.
- Boundary conditions/limits of the teams.
- Linkages to other teams, functions and management.
- Team and personal rewards.
- Team support requirements from functions.

To work effectively, senior management must make certain that clear goals and chartered responsibilities are part of the team's design (1). This is management's control mechanism. Within these defined parameters, teams have the power to take whatever actions are necessary to serve customers. Because the team contains the functional expertise required, there are few cracks for issues to fall into.

In the same way that multi-functional teams blur boundaries within the organization, FCT competitors attempt to do the same thing between suppliers and customers. FCT companies consider suppliers and customers as partners in the value delivery effort. The fewer boundaries that exist in space or time, the more effective the value delivery process can be.

We never found more than two executives per class who spend more than one day a month examining their organizations' work processes.

For example, Quantum Corporation designs application-specific integrated circuits (ASIC) for chip vendor manufacturers. Quantum now includes FCT in its vendor selection criteria. The net result is that a recent supplier placed two engineers plus their own engineering workstations at Quantum to speed the design of an ASIC. The cost to Quantum: nothing.

At the other end of the spectrum, customers are being included in the design phase of the value delivery process. For example, Conner Peripherals begins a product development effort only after they have a customer commitment for that product. Their senior technologist spends much of his time on the road meeting *and selling* customers.

The message is clear: to become fast, redesign your organization for speed. Just as one should not try to turn an oil tanker into a ski boat, one should not try to speed up a large, hierarchical organization. Overcoming the inherent structural limitations of centralized control and specialization is not possible. Flat, multi-functional, team-based organizations provide the architecture that enables locally informed and quick decision making.

Step 4: Pursue process development as avidly as product or service development.

Process improvements can provide tremendous leverage. A single improvement can ripple across the product delivery system. For example, one of the major dilemmas in developing and manufacturing technology-intensive products is the ability to test them for functionality, reliability and quality. Frequently in their zeal to develop the product, development engineers do not focus on test development until late in the development process. In order to improve and innovate testing, the product development process must be changed. In short, test development must come earlier.

At Quantum, for example, managers realized that the bottlenecks that occurred downstream during testing were a significant impediment to rapid introduction of new products. Typically, drives were tested at the back end of the process using specially designed test equipment. The test hardware and software was developed after the product was well along in development. Early prototypes were typically tested by engineering and did not utilize any production test equipment because it was not readily available. In addition, there was always the issue of keeping the test equipment that was used up to date. Frequently, new drives would fail tests not because the drive was bad but because the test software was often a revision or two older than the drive it was testing.

Another factor that contributed to delays was the cost and number of testers. Testers represent one of the largest capital outlays required in drive development and manufacturing. For example, the more volume produced, the more testers that are required. Thus, testers came to be viewed as a significant bottleneck. And, when orders dropped, testers represented a very expensive and underutilized investment.

Quantum's approach to this problem was to incorporate "self-test" procedures within the drive itself. This required development engineers to design the test procedure into the product. It was an elegant approach. A more conventional approach would have been to persuade development engineers to pay more attention to test development earlier in the product development process. However, this approach has no real hook that grabs the development engineer. In contrast, development engineers had no choice but to focus their creative energies on process development when they were faced with the challenge that the product needed to be delivered without having to go through testing in downstream stages.

Why don't more organizations pay attention to process development? Three reasons stand out:

1. Because significant process improvements take time to design and implement, instant results are rare. In addition, it may take time for employees to learn and familiarize themselves with new work processes.
2. The second reason is embodied in the old development axiom that what you measure is what people pay attention to. The vast majority of organization performance measures are end results. While these measures tell us what we have accomplished, they provide little insight into how we did it. Because we don't measure the process itself, people don't pay much attention to improving it.
3. The third reason is closely related: We focus whatever measures we *do* use on those items that are easiest to measure. The dilemma created is similar to the drunk who looks for his keys only under the lamp post because that is where the light shines. Most organizations limit their process measures to the tangible, linear work processes such as those found in manufacturing. Those processes are much easier to measure precisely than the non-linear work process found in design engineering, R&D, marketing, or sales. Non-linear work process measures are not as precise, nor do they need to be. What is most important is to develop measures that aid cycle time improvement efforts. Relative measures that compare current cycle time to past are sufficient.

Process improvement begins with allocating time to it in conjunction with the establishment of performance measures. Simple as this sounds, focusing on the "what" is so familiar that it takes effort to shift attention to the "how." Making process improvement routine requires improvement goals, dedicated time, appropriate rewards, forums for process improvement work, and skills to do it. This starts with top management since people take their cues from them.

Because people don't measure the process itself, they don't pay much attention to improving it.

An excellent starting point for the top team is to develop the macro map of the value delivery system that we described earlier. For each critical process, select a process champion from the top team. The champion is responsible for ensuring the continuous improvement of that process. This includes developing improvement goals and performance measures. Incorporating these goals into each executive's personal objectives and performance review makes process improvement very real.

Process champions do not work alone. They must involve those intimately familiar with the process in the diagnostic and improvement effort. A favorite tactic uses this enlarged group to create two additional maps. The first is the detailed map of the targeted process (Figure 44-1) and the second proposes a new process architecture. The new architecture map becomes the foundation of the process improvement plan.

The mapping process creates a forum where people can engage in a dialogue around process improvements. Some firms find it useful to continue to segregate process improvement work from the mainstream in order to gain momentum. Others devote time to process improvement within their existing meetings. The point is that one must create, communicate and use clear forums for such process improvement dialogues.

Step 5: Set "stretch" cycle time goals and measure progress publicly.

Initial FCT goals should seek a minimum 50 percent improvement in cycle time. Setting goals lower than this does not achieve the cycle time reduction available or required to compete. Merely working harder within the existing process can reduce cycle time by 20–30 percent. When management sets a more aggressive goal, it signals the organization that everyone must consider new ways of working. This challenge in turn stimulates learning.

In the past, cycle time reductions were confined to manufacturing and were viewed in terms of incremental cost or efficiency improvements rather than as a competitive strategy. Knowledge work has received little attention, yet this is where the greatest leverage is (2). For example, the average design cycle of U.S. auto makers has been six years while production cycle time is less than a day. Until international competition in the auto industry made it clear that U.S. development cycles were double the Japanese, managers didn't realize that breakthroughs in excess of 50–200 percent were achievable. The reality is such improvements are now the minimum required merely to catch up!

When communicating stretch goals, expect people to respond with skepticism. Their response is entirely rational since they are being asked to make dramatic improvements without knowing exactly how they will do it. For this reason, it is essential that management have a strong FCT improvement vision that they agree to. Hewlett-Packard's CEO John Young asked all employees to cut in half the time it takes to break even on a new product. This vision provides a picture of the future to sustain people along the hard journey of getting there. Since the vision in only as effective as management's belief and enthusiasm in it, people will test it for holes as soon as it is communicated.

Defining the beginning and end of the cycle and sub-cycles is the first step in developing measures. This can be more difficult than it appears, since defining when a customer's need first exists is not easy or precise. Recognize that beginning and end points are inherently arbitrary choices. One can always mount a rational argument for other points. Select points that make sense for your industry and organization. If there are any sub-cycles that you will be focusing on, such as new product development, define that cycle as well. Once completed, establish the organization's initial FCT goal by benchmarking total current cycle time against your best competitor worldwide. Recognize that their current capability is the *minimum* target you can set since they won't be standing still. Only if the gap between you and them is enormous should an interim goal be selected.

Hewlett-Packard starts the new product development cycle when applicable technology exists within H-P Labs. The end of the cycle is when the profits from the product equal the total investment in the product. They call this break-even time (BET). The primary reason for using break-even time (BET). The primary reason for using break-even time is to discourage quick introduction of products that fail to meet customer's needs. Quantum begins its new product development cycle with the first approved specification and ends at the passage of a process maturity test. Pick what works for your business.

Defining the cycle and sub-cycles permits internal comparison to past efforts and external comparison to competitors. For example, pick the last three products in a given area and see how long they took to develop. In doing so, it is quite easy to examine what contributed to FCT and what impeded it. This can also occur with key components required to build those products. Quantum has analyzed the time it has taken to develop firmware on every disk drive the company has made. The beauty of this approach is that it quickly moves the FCT conversation to the operating level and stimulates quality improvement discussions.

It is highly advantageous to distribute and display cycle time measures. A lack of feedback regarding results limits the possibility for initiating improvements. Research demonstrates that major breakthroughs frequently come from people who are less

Initial FCT goals should seek a minimum 50 percent improvement in cycle time.

familiar with the process. As functions and teams develop their own FCT goals, display them. Graphics are far superior to tables and words.

One cannot understate the importance of aggressive FCT goals and publicly displayed measurements. Perhaps a colleague of mine describes this best using what he calls Management's Apparent Interest Index. Employees throughout an organization take action based on what they believe interests management. If management frequently discusses FCT, sets clear goals and consistently updates public measures, employees will recognize and act on management's attention. Without these factors, management's apparent interest will not be visible.

Step 6: Create an environment that stimulates and rewards continuous learning and action.

Increasing the rate of organizational learning is the heart of an FCT competitive strategy. As a relatively new area, organizational learning deserves special attention. Learning in organizations is a reiterative process by which individual insights and discoveries are converted into organizational knowledge (3). Thus, organizational learning involves the building of a knowledge base that can be made accessible to others, shared, evaluated, and codified—rendering the knowledge independent of the inventor or person who originally generated the insight. Moreover, access to a shared knowledge base in organizations is critical; a lack of knowledge can result in major product errors and delays (4).

By reducing the time it takes to learn, fast-cycle organizations internally benefit from a parallel reduction in the time it takes them to detect and correct errors in the product development process. Many development efforts have been delayed, or have failed, because errors in the early stages of development were either ignored or went undetected.

Failure to detect errors in product development is costly, since problems are usually not seen until prototypes have been scaled up or advanced into manufacturing—usually with disastrous results (5). Similarly, product development efforts are thwarted when problems take too long to fix. Knowing what caused a problem (error detection) is useful only when someone acts to prevent its recurrence (error correction). Hence, the ability to correct errors in a timely manner once they have been detected is also critical to organizational effectiveness. Fast cycle companies are intent on increasing the rate of organizational learning.

Organizational learning is an organizational *process*, as opposed to merely the collection or summation of individual insights. Further, there are two critical differences between organizational and individual learning. First, organizations have a collective purpose, and to be useful, learning in an organization must be in line with that purpose. Second, organizations are social systems. While individual learning can be entirely personal, organizational learning requires that employees at large have access to the learning process and understand the new knowledge created.

Learning in public presents major dilemmas, however. Consider the following: Organizations reward technical competence, which drives people to speak out only when they know the right answer. According to this definition, learning is equated with competence. Thus, if the behavioral norms of the organization reward people who demonstrate competence, it would be wise to be quiet if one didn't know something. *Yet, if people cannot be public about what they don't know, how can we expect them to learn?* The logic of this model is as frightening as it is clear. FCT organizations and leaders begin by rewarding the right questions as much as they do the right answers.

A further dilemma is that the knowledge we have gained to date blocks the path to organizational learning. These established mental models are deeply entrenched and act as walls: they support what we are doing today *and* they act as barriers to thinking and doing differently (6). The older our organization is, the more we must "unlearn" in order to learn. The process of learning requires letting go of existing beliefs about current organizational practices, technologies and existing power relationships.

The first wall to destroy is the belief that learning is not work. Shoshana Zuboff describes this new order best:

> Learning is no longer a separate activity that occurs either before one enters the workplace or in remote classroom settings. Nor is it an activity preserved for a managerial group. The behaviors that define learning and the behaviors that define productivity are one and the same. Learning is not something that requires time out from being engaged in productive activity, learning is the heart of productive activity. To put it simply, learning is the new form of labor (7).

To become an FCT competitor, it is essential that senior management embrace organizational learning as a strategic objective. The executive's job is to define a *strategy and system architecture* that increases the speed of learning throughout the firm. Because organizational learning is a social activity, it requires an architecture that creates forums where ideas and experience can be exchanged. The multi-functional team creates such a forum for task-related interactions between people of diverse background and experience. When combined with a clear team goal and rewards, individuals enthusiastically engage in both dialogue and discussions of differences that functional organizations usually evade or ignore. Insights that could not have been attained by individuals acting alone inevitably result from these interactions. In sum, team members gain invaluable experience by being actively engaged in the process of organizational learning.

> *To become an FCT competitor, it is essential that senior management embrace organizational learning as a strategic objective.*

While organizational learning is a new area of strategic focus for corporations, there are no hard and fast templates to follow. Leading FCT competitors are writing the rules right now by defining both a strategy and an architecture that supports learning in their organizations.

CARDIAC STRESS TEST?

Developing an FCT capability does not come easily. FCT requires *a systemic integration of new values, structures and rewards into the core work process.* One cannot simply accelerate the work pace without negative impact. First, people will make the same mistakes they always have, only quicker. Second, management will rapidly burn out the organization's most important resource: people. An image employees often have when they first hear about reduced cycle time is a cardiac stress test. They equate reducing cycle time to speeding up the organizational treadmill. Regrettably, they are often correct.

The shift to a process-sensitive, learning organization requires time and effort. New values and structures take hold only as old ones are retired. FCT yields a sustainable competitive advantage because it is woven into the cultural fabric of the entire organization's value delivery process.

World-class quality has become the "ante" required to be a global competitor, but it does not ensure leadership. Any organization that couples world-class quality with an FCT capability will have a competitive edge.

About the Authors

Christopher Meyer is managing director of the Strategic Alignment Group, Inc., in Portola Valley, California. He is a recognized expert in designing and implementing cycle-time-reduction strategies, specializing in knowledge work such as new product development. He has served as vice president of human resources for Silicon Graphics Computer Systems and organizational effectiveness advisor for Exxon Chemicals and the Zialog Corporation. He received his Ph.D. and Masters from the University of Southern California in organizational behavior, and currently teaches the California Institute of Technology "Faster Cycle Time" executive seminar. His recent book, *Fast Cycle Time: How To Align Purpose, Strategy and Structure for Speed,* is published by the Free Press.

Ronald Purser has been an assistant professor in the Center for Organization Development at Loyola University in Chicago since 1990. He has served as a consultant to such companies as Polaroid, General Electric, Storage Technology, Arthur Anderson, Exxon Chemicals, and Procter & Gamble on large-scale improvement projects involving the redesign of knowledge-based work systems. He received his Ph.D. in organizational behavior from Case Western Reserve University, and has published many articles in academic journals on engineering and technology management.

References

1. Wolff, Michael. "Teams Speed Commercialization of R&D Projects." *Research. Technology Management* September–October (1988): 8–10.
2. Nonaka, Ikujiro. "The Knowledge-Creating Company." *Harvard Business Review*, November–December (1992): 96–104.
3. Shrivastava, Paul. "A Typology of Organizational Learning Systems." *Journal of Management Studies* 20, No. 1 (1983): 9–25.
4. Purser, Ronald, Pasmore, William, and Tenkasi, Ramkrishnan. "The influence of deliberations on learning in new product development teams." *Journal of Engineering and Technology Management* 9 (1992): 1–28.
5. Purser, Ronald. "Redesigning the Knowledge-Based Product Development Organization: A Case Study in Sociotechnical Systems Change." *Technovation* 11 No. 7 (1991): 403–416.
6. Senge, Peter. *The Fifth Discipline: The Art and Practice of Organizational Learning.* New York: Doubleday, 1990.
7. Zuboff, Shoshana. *In the Age of the Smart Machine.* New York: Basic Books, 1988.

45

SHORTENING THE PRODUCT DEVELOPMENT CYCLE

Here Are 10 Areas in Which R&D Managers Can Help to Shorten the Cycle Time for New Products and Projects

Preston G. Smith
and Donald G. Reinertsen

OVERVIEW

As techniques like cross-functional development teams and concurrent engineering become widespread, these approaches to shortening development cycles lose their competitive edge. Decisive advantage is likely to come from the techniques competitors are not using. The authors explain that there are other untapped sources of cycle time reduction for R&D managers to exploit. These include opportunities to accelerate the "fuzzy front end," in which half of a typical development cycle vanishes before the team even starts work. The authors caution against structuring a development process around a company's largest projects because this can excessively delay smaller ones. They also question the use of phased development systems, which often cause delays in their attempts to standardize control of projects.

The demands on product developers have never been greater. Product life cycles have shortened and continue to shrink. Product technologies, particularly in the electronics and materials areas, are changing faster than ever. As a consequence, the pressure is on to shorten product development cycles.

Frequently, the R&D manager becomes the focal point of efforts to cut development time. To deal effectively with this challenge, the technical manager must look beyond popular but limited solutions to see the breadth of the problem. Such techniques and tools as quality function deployment (QFD), simultaneous engineering, and computer-aided design (CAD) still leave many time-saving opportunities untouched (1).

Great reductions in cycle time are obtainable by applying various techniques blended to suit a particular company's needs. Fortunately, the R&D manager is in a strong position to initiate and foster many time-saving approaches. This article covers 10 such approaches in which such managers play a particularly important role.

Smith, Preston G. and Donald G. Reinertsen. 1992. Shortening the product development cycle. *Research Technology Management* 35(3): 44–49.

1. BE FLEXIBLE ABOUT PROCESS

There are many sound approaches to managing R&D projects. Each method has its advantages and shortcomings. The correct approach can only be selected when one has a clear vision of which advantages are critical in a particular situation. For example, consider the tradeoff between managing development time and technical risk. Most product development systems, such as phased systems (see box, pp. 623–624), are designed to monitor and control technical risk. Such systems are effective and appropriate where reducing technical risk is the paramount concern. Yet managing technical risk is not always the prime objective. Speed can be more important when trying to head off an emerging competitor, and cost can dominate our concerns in a mature market.

The most effective organizations have different development systems available and tuned to suit these distinct objectives. Without alternative processes, all projects tend to get sent through the same process, a common denominator that suits no objective well. In practice it usually errs on the side of minimizing technical risk at the expense of speed. This one-size-fits-all mentality usually creates a system tailored to the largest, most complex projects to the detriment of simpler ones. If the R&D manager is successful in minimizing product complexity, simpler systems can be used.

2. LET ECONOMICS BE YOUR GUIDE

You need a yardstick to decide which development goal to stress for a particular project, and in business the time-tested yardstick is marked in dollars. It is both simple and valuable to develop financial yardsticks for the development process. Such yardsticks tell you the relative financial impact of project delay versus a product cost overrun. They guide you toward choosing the most productive development goal and applying a development process that facilitates this goal.

In addition to these strategic decisions, there are countless daily tactical decisions where yardsticks help to make accurate, fast, low-level decisions on tradeoff issues. For example, is it worth spending $100 on air freight to get a sample into a customer's hands for evaluation two days sooner? How about buying an extra microscope for $2000 if it will cut a week off of the schedule? Or $50,000 for temporary tooling that will allow you to start production two months early while permanent tooling is being made? Without sound decision rules these decisions are likely to be made both incorrectly and slowly.

The financial model that provides the yardsticks is not hard to build (2), but it requires cross-functional effort. The finance department may have the greatest expertise in financial model building, and marketing has important data. But R&D should probably initiate this activity because it will obtain the greatest benefit from the model. For instance, it is not unusual to discover that the product's development expense has far less impact on its life cycle profitability than development delay. When this is the case, R&D managers who spend much of their time massaging the budget are concentrating on a low-leverage area.

3. WATCH OUT FOR COMPLEXITY

The degree of complexity in a project determines the effort needed and thus the length of the development cycle. Although this is not surprising, product development people are frequently startled to discover how quickly complexity mounts.

For example, consider the experience of a company that makes industrial process controls. They made ambitious plans to use a microprocessor in their product for the first time, figuring that this is hardly a new technology anymore. To make full use of the new capability, they tapped a new market they had been unable to serve previously, and they added new product features that had been unavailable to them before. In retrospect, they realized that complexity had multiplied on them. Microprocessors may have been familiar components to others, but this firm had to learn how to procure them, design for them, test and assemble them—everything. In addition, they had to master the new features and establish the new market. This project was slow and fraught with other difficulties.

Complexity is insidious because it multiplies quickly and its effects are indirect and often not apparent. It increases the risk—both technical and market (discussed later). It increases workloads because many more interactions among elements must be considered. It tends to draw in more people, often specialists, which complicates communication and decision making. All of this necessitates a more complicated—thus slower—management process.

The way to get new products out quickly is to minimize complexity by moving in short, simple steps, sampling customer response along the way by selling intermediate models (2). This incremental innovation strategy involves two roles for the R&D manager. First, as manager of technical people who generally enjoy experimenting with new technologies, the R&D manager needs to temper others' desires to put the latest technologies into new products by applying his or her accumulated wisdom. In particular, stress the use of carryover parts and standard components, such as fasteners and connectors. Emphasize inelegant but clean architectures (2). Rechannel the technical brainpower toward solving those problems that will provide more substantial benefit for the customer.

These days the Japanese are often held up as innovation leaders, particularly companies like Honda. In fact, these companies control their pace of innovation carefully. Even their "all new" products are often far from all new. For instance, the initial Acura automobile models which made their debut in 1986 were advertised as "new automobiles . . . designed and engineered from the driver out." However, inspection of the Acura Integra revealed that the skin was indeed new, but many functional components—the most highly engineered ones like the engine, brakes, door latches, and panel instruments—were carryovers from Honda Civics and Accords.

Complexity is insidious because it multiplies quickly and its effects are indirect and often not apparent.

4. MANAGE THE INVENTION PIPELINE

Complexity is minimized by moving into new areas in a planned and evolutionary way, as just covered. This does not mean that newness is avoided. Quite the contrary, newness and invention must be embraced and managed.

Invention presents a dilemma to rapid product development. On the one hand, invention is essential to innovation: continual repackaging is a dead-end strategy. On the other hand, invention is a notoriously unpredictable activity. It cannot be scheduled into a normal project, much less an accelerated one. Any attempt to schedule this wild card into a project just adds uncertainty to the schedule, and in some markets schedule uncertainty is more detrimental than a longer but certain schedule.

Resolving this dilemma falls to the R&D manager. The solution is to invent offline in a separately scheduled program that is tightly integrated with your market and product plans. Companies like Canon, Honda and Sony are innovation leaders because they devote considerable resources to maintaining a storehouse of developing technologies basic to their businesses. Both the invention track and the product development track are market driven, and both are given resources adequate to keep projects moving swiftly. The difference is that the former is loosely scheduled while the latter is tightly scheduled. When a technology reaches the point that much of its schedule uncertainty is eliminated, it switches tracks.

Consider the two types of failures that occur when this type of system is short-circuited. Many companies try to avoid the invention track by integrating it with the product development track. Then, schedule uncertainty is high in development projects, which ultimately causes both employees and customers to have little regard for development schedules. Every project proceeds at its own pace, unable to be accelerated.

The other failure is even worse. In this case a company simply does not invent. Its development schedules are predictable, but so is its demise.

BEWARE OF PHASED DEVELOPMENT

The concept of dividing a project into phases and funding each phase only if its satisfies certain prerequisites would appear to be a good management tool. Yet, as consultants, we see an oil-and-water relationship between phased systems and accelerated development.

Developed by NASA as the PPP (phased project planning) process, phased development systems are designed to control technical risk. But when speed is important, market risk becomes more critical: even if the product is designed according to spec, there is a significant possibility for market failure if it is introduced late. When technical risk must be balanced with market risk, a monolithic PPP-type system is no longer the clear choice. Adaptation and balance are needed in the project management system, and the balance shifts toward empowering the people and away from depending on formal control systems.

The question is really where the balance should lie. We advise some companies, usually fast-growing small ones, to formalize their review systems because with the product line and the staff growing rapidly, more formal management checks are needed to avoid technical failures. Yet in the majority of cases we see phased control systems that are overly cumbersome for a firm's needs. Sometimes a company will just adopt another's phase process, as we once observed when a 100-person instrument manufacturer adopted Hewlett-Packard's phase process, figuring that HP was also an instrument producer—a very good one indeed. But HP's process, fine-tuned for a large company with dozens of divisions, was excess baggage for this small firm.

FUNDAMENTAL LIMITATIONS

Phased systems have a number of fundamental limitations that restrict the ability to shorten development cycles. They often preclude employing one of the most fundamental time-shrinking tools: overlapping activities. Often a particular stream of activities could be overlapped to advantage, but a phase review breaks the chain by requiring that all activities be finished up for review before the next phase can start.

Moreover, the very act of discovering overlapping opportunities requires a new attitude for an organization long indoctrinated in a sequential phased review process. It is that much more difficult to get people thinking creatively about overlapping dissimilar activities when their mindset is built around established phase gates.

Overlapping is enabled by employing partial, fragmentary information that evolves in a stream (2).

Phased systems fight against partial information, providing credit and passage to the next phase only when the information package is complete. Here again, the time-saving opportunities must be discovered in a particular circumstance by thinking creatively about inching forward with the information at hand. A tidy phase framework discourages these discoveries.

Exploiting system architecture opportunities is another means of compressing development cycles (2). By dividing a product into subsystem modules with relatively clean interfaces and ample performance margins, these modules can be developed concurrently by different teams. For example, a transceiver might be divided into a power supply, a transmitter, a receiver, and an audio amplifier. There is no reason to believe that these four modules will have the same timing. One module might require more conceptual design or technology exploration, while another might need a great deal of prototype testing. Putting all modules in a lockstep phase review process stretches the overall cycle.

Moreover, a phased system encourages queues. Queue reduction is a huge and inexpensive opportunity to shorten cycles simply because most development projects spend the majority of their time sitting in queue somewhere. With phases, queues build up in preparation for a review. (Remember that only a complete package is acceptable for a review, so some items wait while the package is completed.) Then, when the review is complete, a flood is released into the next stage of the system, swamping it.

For example, upon final approval of the design, purchasing may be faced with simultaneously ordering a million dollars of capital equipment from a dozen suppliers. Or in one case we observed, the chief engineer signed and released into manufacturing nearly 500 drawings in a single day when his project passed a milestone. You could actually observe the glut passing through the manufacturing transition process.

A phased process also causes problems when, as is often the case in practice, "the product" is really a line of products in different sizes, materials or colors. Then, forcing all variants into synchronization for convenience in review creates both pre-review delays and post-review gluts unnecessarily.

RESPONSIBILITY BELONGS TO PEOPLE

In short, phased approaches are attempts to build judgment into the process rather than into the people. It is reactive, it is slow, and it removes the responsibility from the people doing the work, where the responsibility belongs.

(continued)

Shifting away from a phased process is difficult. There is a great deal of management comfort involved in taking a thorough, formal look at a project periodically and making an explicit decision whether or not to proceed. Unfortunately, the cost can be high when time is at stake. A balance must be struck between comfort and speed, and all too often, comfort wins out even when speed is the key competitive factor.

Some rapid product development specialists suggest that the phased approach should remain the foundation but that the phases should be compressed and "dead time" between phases should be eliminated (5). Our observations of how development projects actually proceed in industry suggests that the greatest opportunities for improvement lie in eliminating the delays associated with synchronization and queueing. This requires a fundamental departure from the phased approach, not fine-tuning it.—**D.R. and P.S.**

5. AVOID THE "THINKING STAGE" TRAP

Other departments are often quick to blame R&D for slow product development, but the fact is that half of the typical product development cycle has vanished before development is even authorized (2). What we call the fuzzy front end is frequently one of the largest and cheapest opportunities to shorten the development cycle.

The front end of a development project starts when the need for a new product is first apparent, whether the company acts on it or not. Product need could be mandated by the enactment of a new government regulation, the emergence of a new technology, or certainly, the appearance of a competing product. The front end terminates when the firm commits significant human resources to development of the product.

We are not suggesting that the front end is unimportant; it is more like the heavens—mostly empty. Some crucial decisions are made during this period regarding the size of the market opportunity, the target customer, alignment with corporate strategy, and availability of key technologies and resources. In fact, research on the market success of new products suggests that products fail because companies don't do enough of this "homework" (3). Nonetheless, front-end time is still mostly a vacuum, largely because managers who haven't calculated the dollar value of development delay believe that time is free until people are assigned to the project.

As an R&D manager, your role in this phase is to be hard-nosed about using your people on product concepts. Resist the attempts of marketing or general management to have one of your people "look at" an idea in their "spare time." Remind them that delay erodes product profitability, and offer to assign one of your people immediately at full- or half-time to reach a certain decision by a definite date. If you aren't this serious about using your resources, then the company isn't serious about the product concept.

6. STAFF TEAMS ADEQUATELY

Our experience, and that of many others, suggests that product development proceeds most quickly and effectively with a team of six to ten full-time members. Although some products, like automobiles, computers or aircraft, require more effort than this, far more common is the development project that seems too small to justify this level of commitment. It receives perhaps a full-time person, a couple of part-timers, and a flock of bit-part participants. Given the heavy load of projects underway at a typical company, this appears to be the best that can be done. No single project has enough importance to command adequate resources.

The solution to this situation is simple in principle. If each project requires a certain number of person-years of effort, consider doubling the staff on half of the projects and complete them in half the time. Then do the other half of the projects similarly. Fewer projects will be underway at any point in time, but the same number will be completed each year.

Half of the typical product development cycle has vanished before development is even authorized.

Although the annual output is the same, the shorter, more intense project option has several benefits. The projects started first get to market sooner, giving them a competitive advantage and a longer sales life. The ones started later are completed no later than before, but they enjoy the advantages of a late start, such as better market information and more recent technologies. Both the early starts and the late starts reap the advantages of a short cycle: fewer opportunities for the market or the project objectives to shift, which means less redesign.

The shorter, more intense option is a valid model if project pacing is primarily dependent on labor availability, that is, project tasks typically sit waiting for people to work on them. In our experience, this is a frequent occurrence. Occasionally, project pacing depends primarily on outside events, like tooling lead time or prototype testing time, in which case it may not be possible to save appreciable time through heavier staffing.

A common objection here is that a more intense effort suggests large teams and thus a greater communication burden, which negates part of the anticipated benefit. However, we can obtain the extra effort without extra people by staffing teams with full-timers rather than part-timers.

Although it is possible to overstaff a team, our experience suggests that American development teams suffer much more from fragmented understaffing than from overstaffing.

7. STAFF WITH GENERALISTS

Often teams are fragmented, having many part-time members, because people are viewed too narrowly, and they in turn often mold themselves as narrow specialists. Some people indeed must be highly trained in a specific technical area in order to advance the state of the art, but the need for such skills is limited in most product development, which instead stresses application and integration. Having a narrow person on a development team causes the R&D manager three problems:

- First, it is difficult to keep such people fully occupied on the project. They tend to split their time commitment among one or more other projects. They drift in and out of a project as their particular skills are needed or as they have the time. They may shift to another project when the going gets tough on a particular project. Consequently, the team leader is consumed by simply keeping the team together and communicating with the part-timers, not on the primary task of developing the product.
- The second difficulty with specialization on the team is that good products require balance to provide value to the customer. This balance is achieved most quickly and with the least communication burden if everyone involved has a solid appreciation of the customer, the economics, the various technologies involved, and the manufacturing methods.
- Third, a high degree of specialization inhibits the manager's ability to redeploy people within a development team to match the workload, which leads to queues and delay.

There are a couple of implications for the R&D manager. First, staff teams with generalists or those willing to become generalists. This will give the team a more comprehensive view, which will allow them to move quickly and precisely. It will also strengthen the team if team members can shift to various secondary team jobs rather than dropping off of the team for a while.

Second, encourage and develop generalists. We recently saw a manufacturing engineer take on the company's cost accounting system when the manufacturing costs for his product weren't coming out to his liking. He didn't overhaul the corporate system, but he did negotiate a more equitable way of costing his product, a more creative one than a cost accountant was likely to have proposed. He learned a lot about cost accounting in the process, and he is now more valuable to his organization.

Deliberately expose people to new areas, either by transferring them to new departments or through outside training. Send your engineer to an accounting course or your draftsperson to a production machine programming course; encourage a marketing person to enroll in a microwave fundamentals course. Just by staying on a development team from start to finish, people will broaden, but this process can be accelerated through deliberate training.

8. LET THE TEAM MANAGE THE TEAM

Product development is just a succession of problems to be solved, so development speed depends on the speed of the problem-solving process, which in turn depends on how tightly problem-solving loops are connected. Every time the team has to go outside of itself to obtain a decision, additional delay is incurred. The farther it has to go, geographically or organizationally, the greater the delay is likely to be.

Product development proceeds most quickly and effectively with a team of 6–10 full-time members.

A Boston-area computer peripherals firm attacked the problem-solving-loop issue directly. The vice president observed that their development team was wasting time because designers weren't getting good enough guidance at their weekly meetings. They would design what they thought was desired, only to find out a week later that they were off track and most of the week had been wasted. So the vice president organized short, daily team meetings at the ten o'clock coffee break. Not only was there less waste of design talent, but everybody moved faster and more surefootedly because progress was now measured on a daily basis.

Just as important as the fivefold shortening of the loop is the vice president's role in this process. He recognized the problem, got the group to meet daily, and even attended many of the meetings. But he didn't run the meetings or participate in their content. He only made sure the group got together daily and left each meeting with a clear idea of what they would be doing next. The team ran the team, and if the company had had a team leader, the vice president's involvement would have been unnecessary.

Getting the team to run itself involves a couple of difficult organizational challenges. In typical organizations, managers of R&D and other functions typically control pieces of development projects, which are completed as these managers coordinate their efforts—often slowly. These roles must shift as the team assumes control of the project. The functional managers now act as advisors and coaches, assisting their colleagues on the team but not using the colleagues as conduits to carry information back to the functional manager for a decision. If this occurs, the organization has just installed a group of puppets as an additional level in the decision-making process. The R&D manager will still have plenty to manage, but his or her role changes with respect to a fast development team.

Frequently the team is also uncomfortable with its new role of making final decisions. If it tries to toss the decision back to management, management must simply toss it back to the team. Before long the team will rely on management as a source of decision-making information, not as a source of decisions.

9. MANAGE BOTH TECHNICAL AND MARKET RISK

Risk management has always been a large part of the technical manager's job. As cycle length shrinks, this job becomes even more essential. Faster projects employ a greater amount of task overlapping, which creates loose ends and, in turn, more opportunities for key steps to be omitted accidentally (2). If the team is managing itself, as just suggested, there is less formal opportunity for the management hierarchy to apply its considerable experience to averting past mistakes. Finally, there is less time available in a compressed schedule to recover from problems.

Fortunately, there is a great deal the R&D manager can do to manage risk in an accelerated project. Sensitivity to risk comes in part from years of experience, which managers are more likely to possess than are the members of the team. Through frequent informal interactions with the team, management can see potential pitfalls and inject insight to cope with them, all without infringing on the team's charter to make its own decisions.

One area where the manager's experience is most valuable is in balancing testing and analysis. Many technical people are prone to analyze an issue profusely before building something and testing it. Just making a model seems like an unprofessional expedient, but expedients are often just what we are looking for as we try to shrink tasks. Others, who may lack the analytical skills or discipline, do the opposite. They build and test repeatedly before thinking much about what the underlying issues may be, so they waste time in resolving risk, too.

The trick is in knowing when to test and when analysis would get the answer faster, or better yet, how test and analysis can be blended to get the best of both. The R&D manager's accumulated wisdom can be invaluable in raising and helping to resolve these issues. The manager also must make sure that analytical and testing resources, such as an open lab, are easily available to the team for this hands-on work.

Risk is of two types: technical risk, which is the inability to satisfy the product specification, and market risk, which is the inability to sell the product assuming it meets specifications. We tend to concentrate on technical risk, ignoring market risk, because we have better techniques for resolving technical risk, it is easier to identify and measure, and its symptoms usually appear sooner.

The R&D manager's job here is to teach the rest of the organization that market risk is just as real as technical risk and that the same general risk management techniques apply to it, although the two should be managed independently (2).

10. DEVELOP A RESERVE

We have saved the toughest topic until last. As suggested in **6,** above, development projects are slow largely because they spend most of their lives waiting to be worked on. Projects are abundant but resources are tight. One reason for this predicament is that we use the popular development funnel concept where it doesn't apply.

For some products, often chemical products, the concept of a development funnel does make sense. The failure rate in the initial feasibility stages of a project is high, and the cost of these stages is low. So we start lots of projects at the top of the funnel, and a few winners flow from the bottom through a natural selection process.

Ironically, the development funnel doesn't work well for many products because the failure rate isn't high enough. Such projects are more likely to succumb to market causes either before or after development than to fail on technical grounds during development. Nevertheless, companies load the funnel with plenty of new-product ideas, and marketing is in fact encouraged to overstock the funnel (2). Because few projects actually fail, projects languish in the funnel awaiting resources. R&D managers must discourage application of the development funnel mentality where it does not apply. Applying it under low failure-rate circumstances generates a glut and demoralizes technical people whose perfectly acceptable projects get shelved in midstream for lack of resources.

American development teams suffer much more from fragmented understaffing than from overstaffing.

However, eliminating just the glut is not going far enough. There actually has to be some slack because unplanned new product ideas will arise unexpectedly. The time-competitive firm needs some reserve development capacity to respond to these customer needs quickly, just as they retain reserve manufacturing capacity to fill unanticipated production orders responsively.

This presents a difficult challenge for the R&D manager. At planning time, don't accept a full load and then a bit more to cover fallout. Instead, leave some unused capacity for the really new projects.

This completes our tour of 10 areas where the R&D manager can shorten development time dramatically. You obtain the greatest benefit by making all of these improvements, because they all reinforce one another. But this is a long-term goal because no company we know of does all of these things well yet. So get started with some of them, perhaps by using a pilot rapid development project to initiate several of the changes immediately (2). Finally, get the non-R&D parts of the company involved compressing development time too. Even those apparently removed from the process, like corporate planners, have essential parts to play (4).

About the Authors

Preston Smith and Donald Reinertsen are coauthors of *Developing Products in Half the Time,* (Van Nostrand Reinhold, 1991). They are management consultants based in West Hartford, Connecticut, and Redondo Beach, California, respectively. Both have concentrated for several years on rapid product development techniques, Smith initially as staff consultant with Emhart Corporation and Reinertsen initially with McKinsey & Company. Smith received his Ph.D. in engineering from Stanford University; Reinertsen has a B.S. in electrical engineering from Cornell and an M.B.A. from Harvard.

References

1. Reinertsen, Donald (1991); "Outrunning the Pack in Faster Product Development," *Electronic Design*, 39, 1, pp. 111–118.
2. Smith, Preston, G., and Donald G. Reinertsen (1991); *Developing Products in Half the Time* (New York: Van Nostrand Reinhold).
3. Cooper, Robert G. (1988); *Winning at New Projects* (Reading, Mass: Addison-Wesley).
4. Reinertsen, Donald G., and Preston G. Smith (1991); "The Strategist's Role in Shortening Product Development Cycles," *The Journal of Business Strategy,* July/Aug. pp. 18–22.
5. Rosenau, Jr., Milton D. (1990); *Faster New Product Development* (New York: AMACOM).

46

THE HIDDEN COSTS OF ACCELERATED PRODUCT DEVELOPMENT

C. Merle Crawford

Rarely has a strategic management option captured American industry as has the thrust of accelerated product development. When accompanied by the goals of lowered cost and increased new product quality, it seems almost unstoppable. However, industry may have been swept up in the enthusiasm. Any strategic option so tempting (with long lists of advantages and no suggested limitations) needs to be viewed critically. Merle Crawford reveals several "hidden costs" of accelerated development. He does not oppose the new strategy, and indeed endorses it highly, but urges that it be considered carefully before application. His analysis suggests that acceleration is far more widely applied than is good for any industrialized economic system.

Over the past 5 years we have seen widespread trial and adoption of what is called *accelerated product development* (APD). The focus is the entire process of product innovation, not just the R&D/design/engineering/manufacturing phases that are sometimes equated with the term *development*. (See Figure 46-1 for an explanation of what APD is coming to mean.)

Though not yet subjected to serious critique by the academic researchers, word through the business press is exciting. Reductions of development time from 36 months to 18 months are common. Who can fault that? Users of the approach imply that they are extending the techniques of acceleration to many other projects.[1] Specific benefits are summarized by a member of the Boston Consulting Group staff as higher prices, opportunity to incorporate the latest technology, more accurate forecasts of customer needs and increased market share [37]. All of us who work on product innovation welcome new ideas for the development process, and most of what we've heard about APD makes sense. Much of it will find a permanent home in our tool kits, partly because we are already familiar with the techniques in selective settings. People in the fast-paced food industry yawned when Digital shocked its managers by giving a team *only* 12 months to develop a lower-cost mouse. Now might be a good time to drop the other shoe. Accelerated product development has a price tag, a much larger one than most of its eager (and very busy) practitioners talk about. The purpose of this article is to take a hard look at that price tag.

Address correspondence to Professor C. Merle Crawford, Graduate School of Business Administration. University of Michigan. Ann Arbor, MI 48109.

Crawford, C. Merle. 1992. The hidden costs of accelerated product development. *Journal of Product Innovation Management* 9: 188–199.

FIGURE 46-1 What Is Accelerated Product Development?

We lack a good definition of APD because each firm seems to be creating its own methods of accelerating the new product process, but the threads are three. First, the *strategic* view is changing to include seeking more incremental innovation, scheduling planned obsolescence (replacing products more frequently than demanded by the market), dividing technology development into engineer-dominated and science-dominated (the latter, especially on major products, is difficult to accelerate), stressing product quality at all points, reducing capital investments as much as possible and demanding quick response to changes in the marketplace.

Second, *administrative* support systems are being overhauled to allow faster approvals, an overall corporate culture based on speed in everything, an organization that is lean and flat but that stresses training and giving workers motivation and reward systems that include equity positions if possible, less structure in the operation, new ways of "selling" R&D capability throughout the firm and the establishment of firm deadlines on everything.

Third, *new methods* are vigorously sought. One well-publicized tool is the *team,* or *venture team,* involving a strong leader, little formality and structure and the full range of functions, especially manufacturing, engineering, marketing, distribution and purchasing. A second category of new methods stresses *going outside* for all resources possible—R&D consortiums of several types, alliances with vendors, customers and third parties and use of new product development consultants and suppliers. A third category of new methods involves *technology*— new software such as computer-aided engineering, stereolithography, artificial intelligence and integrated information systems, plus visual communication devices to increase quality and quantity of communication.

In a nutshell, APD asks us to focus on product innovation (sometimes only the incremental portion) and, if necessary, build an entirely new way of running it, from a far-off vendor through our internal resources and to the customer. No policy or practice is sacred, creativity is expected, management is in support, and there are excellent rewards for meeting new and tough performance standards.

An awareness of the costs, especially the hidden ones, will help direct the acceleration to its proper applications. Otherwise, the innocent and uncritical acceptance of speed will lead to misuse, frustrated team players and a reduction in other types of product development that also are badly needed.

THE SOURCES OF HIDDEN COSTS

The hidden costs of speeded-up development are of five types:

1. Low-profit, trivial innovation tends to drive out the more profitable breakthrough types. Gresham's law about "bad money driving out the good" works on innovation.
2. Many mistakes happen when skipping steps sacrifices necessary information [10].
3. A surprisingly negative and disruptive side to new styles of small-team management sometimes appears. It can boost people costs.
4. Unexpected inefficiencies result when the process of innovation warps under pressure; the various steps don't respond evenly to cuts in the time budget.
5. A firm's complex set of support resources can get chewed up by pressure from players on speeded-up teams.

After looking at the costs, we will see what steps managers can take to capitalize on the new approach without being overcome by those costs.

Hidden Cost #1: Low-Profit, Trivial Innovation Tends to Drive Out the More Profitable Breakthrough Types. Gresham's Law About "Bad Money Driving Out the Good" Works on Innovation.

Managers are usually skeptical of strategic myopia—the commitment to one strategy above all others.[2] Unfortunately, APD seems to fit only incremental innovation and actually may threaten other types. A research report from Arthur D. Little [34, p. 16], a leading consultant on technological innovation, said "One of the critical choices in innovation strategy is whether to seek major breakthroughs or smaller, incremental innovations. Our answer is that in most cases, if you know roughly where you want to go, incremental innovation is faster and cheaper." *Incremental innovation* is that which advances a product or product line in little steps—small changes, made often. *Breakthrough* (pioneering) *innovation* creates entirely new products, and new markets as well. Most firms need both (and a middle ground too), and spend their money in an effort to get them. The relative emphasis may, of course, shift across various businesses within these firms. In the process there is healthy, built-in competition for resources.

We should be careful to note that incremental and breakthrough innovation can both be consistent with today's emphasis on core technologies. DuPont, Merck and others certainly have breakthrough products within their core technologies. Generic copiers in the same pharmaceutical industry have minuscule incremental innovation, often totally outside any core technology restrictions.[3]

Ralph E. Gomory, former technical head at IBM, and Roland W. Schmitt, his counterpart at GE, have recently argued that we have historically weighted the scales toward breakthrough, innovation but need to push now for more incremental innovation. They favor speeding up the process [20].

Gresham's Law about bad money is relevant here. Economist Gresham noted many years ago that if a monetary system contains a mix of sound and unsound paper, the bad money will always tend to drive out the good. It's not appropriate to use the terms *good* and *bad* for new products, but many people feel that emphasis on incremental projects will inevitably lead to less emphasis on the breakthrough type. There is only so much "emphasis" to spread across the portfolio, just as when a laser concentrates light it leaves surrounding areas in the dark. Resources devoted to incrementalism may be more highly protected in the short run, leaving breakthrough projects to lag.

Edwin Land, founder of Polaroid, insisted that any R&D project had to be almost impossible, or he would not allocate money to it. APD would probably have been anathema to him, though some suggest that his later years with the firm would have been more productive had there been more incremental work to balance his blockbusters. This might suggest that APD is a better strategy for larger, established firms than for younger, growing ones.

Even APD users say one sometimes has to decide what the firm wants to deemphasize. Several recent articles suggest that Xerox may have so concentrated on copiers that it hurt its work *beyond* copiers [24, 47, 48]. Xerox's stated mission now emphasizes document handling.

Some firms tell us their first criterion in screening a new product concept is: How long will it take? One example, from many, is Honeywell's Building Controls Division, where managers stopped the tracking of costs on new product projects and implemented a milestones system [18]. They apparently felt that it was more valuable to control time than money within the context of their overall approach to development. If slow, screening is insensitive to sales potential. Apparently there is little consideration given to opportunity costs, and strong efforts are made to achieve a company-wide commitment to speed.

It seems that by the very nature of the process, APD works best on incremental projects, in practice, even if not in theory. It may not be a coincidence that several recent articles on APD have mentioned cars, textiles, software, an improved air grinder, a new thermostat, a desktop microfilming machine, later versions of workstations, motorcycles, mid-size and small computers, toilet fixtures, hand tools and small kitchen appliances. These are rather clearly markets that are in, or nearing, their mature phase, a time when incremental product development takes over from the more innovative and expansive phases. We occasionally hear promoters of APD warning managers to "avoid technological leaps" [2].

APD also takes sides in the struggle between strategies of technology and of market. Which side to depend on doesn't seem to matter; there is usually one ready to go, and the other is left to scurry along in a necessarily minor role. As many people now think that *dual* drive (a solid market opportunity *and* an available technology) is best, speed may tempt managers to make the weaker choice of a single drive [14].

Critical here, of course, is risk and the company attitude toward it. To some managers, doing nothing is less risky than doing something later shown to be clearly wrong, so the mindset favors small changes. The breakthrough project is not only delayed but often destroyed (the scientist leaves the firm, the technology is sold, a competitor discovers it).

Is there any evidence that APD is reducing major innovations? Here's a list.

1. Expenditures on R&D have had trouble holding their own lately [27]. In spite of annual predictions of increasing spending, actual expenditures have been disappointing. Moreover, expectations are that spending on *basic* research will actually fall, as funds go to "new business projects."

2. As stated above, some proponents of speed have gone so far as to argue that speed is the only game. As one division general manager put it, "A speed-based system doesn't work if you're tracking it by the amount of money spent."[4] Under these conditions, managers may find it difficult to defend spending money (and time) on projects whose finish dates fall off the tracking system. Such a strategy, of course, may not be appropriate for other operating units within the same company.

3. Arguments for faster new product development include lower product cost and improved manufacturability, descriptors that clearly are associated with incrementalism. With exceptions, of course, cost and manufacturability contribute mainly to current market competitiveness; breakthrough projects (more likely offering significant *product* differentiation) offer cost and manufacturing advantages only as a by-product.

4. Integrated manufacturing systems (especially Just-in-Time arrangements) are high on managements' agendas today, and such systems are noted for using process innovations that work against product innovation (e.g., supplier plants located next door, long-term supply and/or sales contracts, volume accounts, major process capital investments). Suppliers locked up in integrated manufacturing systems may degenerate into external workbenches, expensive new equipment (beyond a point) becomes inflexible, and the locking of arms may be good for insiders but keeps out some firms (especially smaller ones) that may have new product contributions to make. Japanese firms are apparently rethinking the immobility of capital brought about by supplier plants "next door" [1, 16, 23].

5. To gain speed it is necessary to avoid projects that require lots of learning. APDers must stick to what they know well. Some people find they can have it both ways by designing *families* of products; later members of the family may be imperfectly understood at the beginning when the APD effort is initiated.[5] This, of course, puts some pressure on the later stages, especially marketing. Arthur D. Little reported a similar variation from their research: Sony (and others) have found that by breaking their R&D into small projects and opting for a high frequency of product introductions, each new product can incorporate just a few technological innovations. If a promising innovation has to be deferred, it is no matter; there is another new product coming down the line soon [34]. These modifications show that there are ways for a firm to have its (speed) cake and good bites of innovation too, but managers have to accept the need to be creative. The key is that speed is achieved within the constraints of an overriding vision of innovation.

6. Many honored innovators have extolled the value of product champions, but champions are unwanted (and said to be unnecessary) in APD. They tend to fight the rejection of their product/technology, and people on a tight timetable have no need for troublemakers. The enthusiasm of a whole team presumably makes a single champion redundant, but some people forget that champions are not needed just for radical innovations; they are needed anytime there is internal opposition to a new program, and such opposition may come from manufacturing, purchasing or sales, even if the new product is at best a modest product improvement. A project that needs no champion is virtually certain to be bringing about very little institutional change.

7. We often hear about how the use of small teams lets the product innovation work proceed without the "interference" of top managements. Such interference is apparently helpful in avoiding the slow-downs associated with brining management up to date, but it is widely recognized that top managements play a major role in product innovation. This suggests that much APD is focused on projects whose product innovation charters call for risks low enough that top managements can stay hands-off.

8. It might be no coincidence that top managements are adopting APD during the same period when they are slashing middle managements. I've seen no research on the subject, but it would seem likely that skeleton crews and wide spans of control are associated with lesser innovativeness.

9. Lastly, the food industry has used speeded-up product innovation for many years. New product failure rates there are very high (some reports show 90%, versus an all-industry rate of around 35%), and true innovation is rare [13].

Hidden Cost #2: Many Mistakes Happen When Skipping Steps Sacrifices Necessary Information.

The key steps omitted in APD seem to be ones that involve the acquisition of information. There is less technical R&D/engineering, no basic market studies, a bare minimum of concept testing and other pretechnical work, most product requirements written from current staff knowledge and experience and little if any product use testing or market testing [4]. There is no attempt to study options at decision points. Even if each of five information rejections has an 80% chance of being right, the probability of being right on all five is 33%. Information rejection, defendable when done once, becomes very risky when repeated as policy down the line.

Research shows there are three major causes of new product failure: no need for the item, a need wasn't met or the item was not marketed wisely [5, 8, 25]. All three causes can be overcome by widely accepted market research during development, but with APD there is rarely time. Some are now asking whether skipping testing may actually *add* time to the project, given the iterations otherwise required later [2]. What this amounts to is false economy of time.

Many firms do something comparable to what is called Beta testing in the computer industry—give a few customers some of the product and see if it "works." It takes just a few weeks, but it doesn't settle a key issue: does the new item actually meet the customer's *need?* That takes longer, and APD doesn't have longer.

Frito-Lay had an interesting experience when, upon acquiring a new CEO, a well-established and successful new products program came under the stopwatch. Launches were speeded up, and key information-gathering steps were skipped or misused. In just a few years there was evidence that product failures helped cause the ousting of the new CEO, and replacement leadership said there would be a "return to the basics" [17].

A similar story with another very large consumer packaged-goods firm involved a management that threw out their formal new product process in the late 1970s and promptly lost $1.5 billion on new products. Current (1990) thinking in the firm was to get back to basics by reintroducing the new product process [9].

Lest this article give the impression that skipping field market research is a weakness only of packaged-goods firms, recall that General Electric also had a product quality problem on a new compressor for refrigerators. This product failure may well cost GE a half billion dollars before all the dust settles [33, 35]. Amdahl had a similar experience in marketing an incompletely tested new mainframe computer that just didn't work; their next venture, 3 years later, was with a thoroughly field-tested model that succeeded very well [3].

These examples suggest the dangers of skipping steps in the product innovation process, action that usually results in loss of key information. Though these examples are anecdotal, research data support them.[6]

During the entire product development process decisions are calculated risks. We lack certainty in everything. Risks by definition are occasionally costly, yet proponents of APD claim speed is associated with *lower* costs. Speeding up must be used only in those cases where experience permits *reduction* of risk.

We went through the same thing early in the life of Critical Path Scheduling, where parallel processing was used to squeeze the time dimension; but we only overlapped steps when we were quite sure there would not be a problem (or where there was no interdependence between the steps and thus shouldn't have been sequenced in the first place). This means information already in hand.

APD requires that at many steps in the process the natural desire for additional information must be squashed, even if that one piece of information is customer acceptance. So one critical hidden cost is the cost of failure; and it will be there, unless the projects are so safe there is no risk.

Hidden Cost #3: A Surprisingly Negative and Disruptive Side to New Styles of Small-Team Management Sometimes Appears. It Can Boost People Costs.

Accelerated product development apparently demands interfunctional teams as the mechanism by which traditional bureaucratic encumbrances are overridden; but a team system can be tricky. For example, teams are used to gain added flexibility (outside the bureaucracy) yet teams also may be very *in*flexible. The team's assignment has to be unidirectional, and we know a strongly commissioned team will indeed market a new product, whether ready or not. After all, that was its assignment, and promotions and salary increases will come accordingly. Team members with fire in their bellies don't dally.

This is myopia within flexibility, the same as discussed earlier in connection with integrated manufacturing systems. One technique that aids APD is the early elimination of options—reducing the number of alternatives kept open in the development process. This increases one's vulnerability to the moves and countermoves of competitive firms, thus weakening the accuracy of demand forecasts.

APD teams are necessarily small if they are to move fast. The operating style is that fringe people are invited into the clubhouse from time to time, but mainly it is team members who make forays outside the clubhouse when they need some specific help. Thus it is not surprising that small teams sometimes report rejection and non cooperation by support groups. Smallness also leads to elitism, especially on venture teams. What is the effect on the attitudes and work habits of people just not quite on the team? What do they think when the team members get the big rewards—the ones associated with successful APD projects?

Teams also have leaders, and we're seeing impressive new methods of team leadership—healthy, positive, dynamic, indirect. Yet when published accounts of team actions part the curtains, we often see the shadow of a dictator. When push comes to shove, democracy is weak. That Frito-Lay CEO (above) was described by one of his staff: "When he stepped things up he didn't care who he stepped *on*." What are the hidden costs of 14-hour days? Many readers, for example, will recall the vivid and devastating personal pains disclosed in *The Soul of a New Machine,* the story of a new minicomputer development at Data General [28]. Some team members suspect *speeding*-up is the old-time assembly line *speed*-up in a new costume. It will be interesting as researchers get into this new type of team and find out what participants really think, and more important, what personal risks and added efforts they are willing to put out, and for how long. Sustainability is suspect.

Some team leaders have already had multiple success stories and eagerly seek new team assignments. Others can't wait to get off the team. How many 12-month projects can the average manager survive? Assuming that the damage is mental, how can it be assessed? Isn't there burnout, and if so, isn't the manager under pressure not to show it, especially if the rewards go to the hare, not the tortoise? Such practice is questionably cost-effective. Too, we are entering an era of limited supply of skilled workers; is this the best way to use them?

Even where team leaders want to avoid excessive pressure, and know full well how to generate positive teamwork, there are costs that managements may object to.

Digital Equipment Corporation, for example, appointed an experienced leader for their computer-mouse project (mentioned above) who immediately asked for a 30 day orientation period; team members would get acquainted, socialize and prepare to work together. He got his wish, and the project was more than successful, but how many managements would cut normal time from 2 years to 1, and then allow the first month to be spent in backyard barbecues and hikes in the woods?

Of no less significance, and still hidden, are the *indirect* costs of teams—such as people being pulled off other work, special handling by top management, reintegrating team members back into the regular organization upon failure or completion of the team's assignment and forcing the solo players to live a loner's life in a team world. Steve Sakoman, Apple hardware developer, indicated the problems such people may face when he said that today's rugby players (on fast teams) should not be the "stereo-typical engineer who sits off in a corner, never goes home and sleeps on a mat" [47].

Hidden Cost #4: Unexpected Inefficiencies Result When the Process of Innovation Warps Under Pressure; the Various Steps Don't Respond Evenly to Cuts in the Time Budget.

In recent years we have seen great progress in creating an effective and efficient product innovation process.[7] That process is still evolving, and needs experimentation; it can be warped and distorted under pressure. When pushed, we tend to make do with what we have, rather than developing the right tools and other resources. The new product may call for a special sales force, distributed field service capability, a stand-by plan if anticipated problems come up during launch and so on. These are obstacles to be overcome, and any one may kill chances to hit the deadline. When so, it is difficult to resist the temptation to proceed as though these needs do not exist.

Even ideation can suffer. Active, purposeful ideation is at the heart of successful innovation. Nothing, absolutely nothing, beats having an important customer problem to deal with—new products people want to market solutions to problems, not solutions looking for problems or solutions that aren't quite solutions. Teams in a hurry tend to work from suggestions already on the table (from the sales force, product management, engineering or wherever).

Innovation is a process of defining an objective (performance, feature, customer saving or the like) and then evolving something that will achieve the objective. The process is *focused creativity,* not shooting in the dark. A push for speed early in a project tends to diffuse our picture of the objective—if we don't take the time to make it clear, requirements will change constantly under pressure, and scientists and engineers have to shoot at moving targets. Thus almost all people offering advice on APD urge that time be spent at the beginning to make sure the target is clear and achievable. To save time, we either have to make the target very simple (incremental innovation) or accept partial innovation. Some call this *continuing compromise* (e.g., dropping from three forms of the new item to just one, with the others to follow "soon"). Unless the followers are well into development when the first one is launched, this is not a valid process [12].

Hidden Cost #5: A Firm's Complex Set of Support Resources Can Get Chewed Up by Pressure From Players on Speeded-Up Teams.

Teams make use of many other people and systems. Even within a team, there will occasionally be scientists who are forced to cave in or get out. There are others for whom there isn't adequate training and orientation time, and others whose inability to handle risk makes them a psychological mismatch. Teams also require people who are good communicators and effective teammates, but there is a worldwide shortage of such people. What does intense team participation do to people who are simply not good team people?

Even if there are no basic attitude changes by the participants, we can certainly expect behavioral ones. Players will learn how to survive; messengers who carry bad news do indeed get shot. Where, for example, were the top executives at Frito-Lay who felt they had no recourse but to let the new CEO overhaul a well-functioning product innovation system? We don't know the internal dynamics, of course, and perhaps they tried, but given threatening environments, some managers with good potential find those places in the firm where there is less pressure, or they begin giving management and the team what it wants, hiding the real costs as necessary.

Once an operation really commits to acceleration, would it be "bad news" that an exciting longer-term discovery was made in the lab, and would this information have to be squelched? Managers may opt against becoming a champion for it—indeed, may purposely distance themselves from it.

Then we have the people who work in staff service departments (packaging, legal, government, human resources, quality and so on) who find it difficult to charge off the "costs" of speed. For example, we really don't know what behavioral changes rapid introduction of incremental products brings about in a sales force.

What has just been said is speculative. We lack good research in this area, but the nature of the speeded-up system is such that many of the human costs will for a long time be hidden.

Perhaps more obvious, but also costly, are the negative effects on suppliers, who often must cooperate closely in these accelerated programs.[8] Must they write off the added costs associated with speeding up by giving less service and assistance to other lines and developments and by coming up with fewer improvements on their own initiative? One answer is that the APD supplier must in turn seek more innovativeness in *its* suppliers, but that assumption is fraught with many questions.

Lastly, we cannot forget the customer, where effects can be similar to those on suppliers. Resellers are wary of joining manufacturers' systems, and often are strong enough to force adaptation the other way (Wal-Mart recently made Procter & Gamble bend its logistics system to meet that of the chain). End-users may be happy with short-term incremental innovation, but unwilling to commit to a supplier whose contributions are primarily line extensions. They may want true innovation to help them solve their bigger problems and also to avoid the substantial switching costs associated with this steady "stream of improved products" (such as with office computer systems).

SOME OF THE ARGUMENTS FOR ACCELERATED PRODUCT DEVELOPMENT ARE VERY WEAK

The opening sections of this article cited the very real and valid reasons for APD. However, much of the talk surrounding this topic verges on hype. Here are four arguments that are very weak indeed.

1. *APD must be good; the Japanese use it.* Auto industry executives and engineers have heard this so much they must have dreams in which their 5's (for years) are magically converted into Honda-Toyota 3's. Most of the Japanese projects done using intensive APD appear to be incremental, but, of course, one person's incrementalism is another person's breakthrough. The developments of the Japanese auto companies demonstrate well the strategic interest many managements put on core technologies [36]. Second, the Japanese gain time by freezing specs early, and then *immediately* beginning a follow-on project for the improvements delayed by the freezing. They don't reject options, only when they are to be used.

2. *APD must be good; look how XYZ Company did it.* The fact that XYZ did something is worthwhile to know, and many such examples are given in this article, but we need to look at their total experience. For example, reports from firms active in APD often are laced with phrases like "be realistic," "don't be overly ambitious," "don't try to make advances in too many areas at once" and "our worst disasters have come when we rushed out with a product in time to hit the show." All of these suggest rather major cost problems just below the surface. Further, there is no evidence that anyone has bothered to look at what

was postponed or dropped in order that the favored project could be rushed to market, and it is impossible to assess the long-term consequences (good or bad).

3. *APD must be good; look at the close teamwork, the customer involvement and so on.* In this reasoning, APD writers tend to take credit for any innovations in the innovation process. For example, we now hear that R&D directors are asking their staffs of scientists to scout out around their firms and find applications for their new technologies. This is fine; there are many ways of "selling" R&D, and there will be more, but they should be used regardless of the speed dimensions of particular projects.

Another example concerns involvement of the customer: proponents of APD claim that faster development equals higher quality, but along the way they have the teams work closely with the customer. It is a pity that speed has to be the lever to get us to do what we should be doing all the time, on all of our projects—that is, building new products on the solving of customer problems.

Other APD programs have included selling all participants on the importance of the project and getting top management to personally order cooperation by all parties. These efforts will almost guarantee a launch, but pulling out all stops means overriding budgets and other programs. The costs become hidden only because we don't calculate them; and we sometimes don't look too closely at the failure rates of such "top-down" products.

4. *APD must be good; order-of-market-entry data show it pays to be first.* There are no such data, except those that assume the second and third entries have comparable products. Given second tier *adaptive* innovation (which second and third entries should always have) shares are determined by the quality of those improvements. The literature is full of testimony to this.[9] Moreover, don't confuse order-of-entry with speed. Order-of-entry studies imply that to be first, one must be fast, but this isn't necessarily true. Speed is probably most essential to early followers, as they jockey for shares and try to overtake the pioneer. We talk a lot about famous pioneers (3Ms Post-it Notes, Birdseye frozen vegetables, and Federal Express overnight delivery), but we forget such winning non-pioneers as IBM computers, Texas Instrument transistors and hand calculators, Matsushita VCRs, Kimberly Clark Huggies, Bartles & James wine coolers and hundreds more. The picture is a mix: who would have thought that Anheuser Busch couldn't overtake Miller Lite; who would have expected RCA to lose its pioneering position in color TV [22]?

Research data here yield little truth, given the vagaries of business conditions, regulation, competitive product differentiation, price ploys and the like.

APD success stories from industry have almost all concerned early attempts. They are very encouraging, and so were the experiments at Western Electric's Hawthorn plant 65 years ago. The "Hawthorn effect" is widely documented, so we should be sure the 5th, 10th, and 20th APD projects work out before we jump to conclusions. There may be added costs of keeping teams dedicated after the novelty and attention have worn off. Also, what works on a limited scale can fail badly when applied on a larger scale. We should be careful not to evaluate strategically what is essentially a tactical tool.

Recently we have been reading McKinsey & Co. data which show that to be late, but on budget, loses more money than to come in on time and over budget.[10] What we read are *citations* of the original publication and they are incomplete. The author of the report, Donald Reinertsen, a McKinsey Associate, actually used his findings to warn the reader: "The new product race does not always go to the swift. Speed is sometimes secondary and, if unduly emphasized, can lead to disaster."

The commonly cited data about lateness costing more profits than being over budget and on time applies only to "high-growth markets and short product life-cycles." For example, in slower-growth markets, a 9% product-cost overrun "resulted in a devastating 45% decrease in [life-cycle] profits." In addition, Reinertsen warned,

"A company that stresses speed above all else indeed can manage to achieve early profit gains, but the crash program inevitably results in high product costs, [and] early profits dissolve as margins are squeezed by high costs and rapidly dropping prices." The data were apparently derived in one particular product setting, and with one particular accounting, and the "costs" of being on time included only the amount the project was over budget; researchers excluded the costs sunk in other projects that had to be dumped or permanently delayed while the subject one was being rushed to market. The study also excluded most of the costs discussed in this article.

My point is this: so far we have seen too much specious reasoning and hoopla and not enough hard data from experience over time. It is interesting that Reinertsen is now a leader in urging *responsible* accelerated product development [44].

SOME ACTIONS THAT WILL LET A MANAGEMENT CAPITALIZE ON A WORTHY NEW CONCEPT YET AT THE SAME TIME HELP HOLD DOWN THE HIDDEN COSTS

First, spell out new products strategy clearly, and get understanding and agreement on it. If primarily incremental innovation is desired, say so, but otherwise, what mix of incremental, expansion and breakthrough projects is desired? Should the mix vary by market, by company profitability level and so on? Under the stress of day-to-day business the APD projects carry big sticks—other projects need firm management support to stay on their course. APD fits especially well with lines that have short life-cycles, low switching costs, ease of customer understanding on new features and reduced barriers to entry.

Second, review constantly to see if the innovation mix desired is being achieved. Study progress reports, time schedules, and people's feelings. There may be more hidden "bad news" than realized, especially if the organization has given a lot of publicity to its adoption of accelerated product development. Changes in the firm's accounting system may be necessary [32].

Third, select two typical APD projects that have run their course and hold postmortems. Postmortem is an unfortunate term, as technically it applies to products that fail, but there may be "failure" even in what appears to be a winner, so the process is the same. In addition to the most important issue of method, check specifically for burnout, repressions and dictators. This may be tough to do, given the pressurized environment of APD, but it is relevant information.

Fourth, keep asking for evidence that APD projects offer genuine benefits to the customer. Does the customer *agree* there is usable value added? This protects against the tendency for speeded-up projects to compromise on key benefits.

Fifth, pick one project and have an independent party try to assess the true hidden costs. This effort will defy the accounting system, but judgments can be made if the proper investigator can be found.

Sixth, taking into consideration the hidden costs discussed in this article, manage the APD program in a way to avoid the biggest problems. This means (1) keep one eye clearly on the slower-moving breakthrough programs and ask about their problems, (2) keep asking for evidence that key speeded-up decisions are information-based, (3) have someone on staff who understands product innovation and is independent of the time pressures faced by the teams and (4) check to see that suppliers are not being asked to pay too high a price to play on your teams.

Seventh, if contemplating putting an accelerated program into action, be sure the overall product innovation system to be changed is itself a good one. Several recent research studies indicate that more time may be saved by having a good overall system than by trying to fine-tune a defective system [10, 21, 42]. As one report put it, "The most common mistake made in product development programs is failing to execute all the steps." The report added that skipping steps and doing them in illogical order will "produce a large percentage of false starts, program delays, budget overruns, late product introductions and program cancellations" [42].

CONCLUSION

This article has taken as given that accelerated product development is virtually a revolution in product innovation management. We have seen the practice spread, and the reports are generally encouraging. Taking unnecessary time out of a development project strengthens the overall competitiveness of an organization. Product innovativeness offers a long list of advantages.

Unfortunately, the APD revolution is spreading too fast. Adherents are overlooking research reports that warn about its limitations. One bundle of limitations relates to what are here called *hidden costs*. These are sometimes just hidden in an accounting sense (data on them are not usually available), sometimes they are indirect and sometimes they are opportunity costs.

The potential payoff for speeding up the product innovation process is too great to have success riding on what so far has been mainly anecdotal evidence and on management's hope that there are no significant hidden costs. This article has attempted to spell out the various types of hidden costs that exist, and proposes some actions managements can take to reduce the chances of a major blind siding.

Biographical Sketch

C. Merle Crawford is Professor of Marketing in the University of Michigan Business School. He holds a Ph.D. in Business from the University of Illinois. Professor Crawford was on the faculty at the University of Florida. From there he joined the marketing department at Mead Johnson & Co. (now a Bristol-Myers Squibb division), first as Director of Marketing Research, then as Director of Product Management, then as Marketing Director. He joined the Michigan faculty in 1965. He has been on the University's and the School's Executive Committees, and was founding president of the Product Development & Management Association. Most recently he has been serving on the PDMA Board and as Abstracts Editor for this journal.

The author thanks the following people who participated in the very helpful review process: Robert G. Cooper, Thomas D. Kuczmarski, Milton D. Rosenau, Robert R. Rothberg, David Wilemon, and two unnamed reviewers. None of these individuals agreed with everything in the draft and in fact made many suggestions (some strongly worded). They have not seen the final manuscript.

References

1. Arnold, Ulli and Barnard, Kenneth N. Just-In-Time: Some marketing issues raised by a popular concept in production and distribution. *Technovation* 9(5):401–431 (1989).

2. Barr, Vilma. Six steps to smoother product design. *Mechanical Engineering* 48–51 (January 1990).

3. Beauchamp, Mark. Learning from disaster. *Forbes* 96–97 (October 19, 1987).

4. Bertrand, Kate. New product success starts with homework. *Business Marketing* 36–38 (August 1988).

5. Booz-Allen and Hamilton. *New Product Management for the 1980s.* New York, NY: 1982.

6. Bower Joseph L. and Hout, Thomas M. Fast-cycle capability for competitive power. *Harvard Business Review* 66(6):110–118 (November–December 1988).

7. Bylinsky, Gene. Turning R&D into real products. *Fortune* 72–77 (July 2, 1990).

8. Cooper, R. G. New product success in industrial firms. *Industrial Marketing Management* 11:215–223 (1982).

9. Cooper, R. G. Stage-gate systems: A new tool for managing products. *Business Horizons* 33(3):44–54 (May–June 1990).

10. Cooper, Robert G. and Kleinschmidt, E. J. An investigation into the new product process: Steps, deficiencies, and impact. *Journal of Product Innovation Management* 3(2):71–85 (June 1986).

11. Cooper, R. G. and Kleinschmidt, E. J. Resource allocation in the new product process. *Industrial Marketing Management* 17(3):261–262 (August 1988).

12. Crawford, C. Merle. How product innovators can foreclose the options of adaptive followers. *Journal of Consumer Marketing* 5(4):17–24 (Fall 1988).

13. Crawford, C. Merle. New product failure rates: A reprise *Research* Technology Management 30(4):20–24 (July–August 1987).

14. Crawford, C. Merle. The dual drive concept of product innovation *Business Horizons* 34(3):32–37 (May–June 1991).

15. Dumaine, Brian. How managers succeed through speed. *Fortune:* 54–59 (February 13, 1989).

16. Emshwiller, John R. Suppliers struggle as big firms slash their vendor rolls. *The Wall Street Journal* B1 (August 16, 1991).

17. Fannin, Rebecca. Frito-Lay: The binge is over. *Marketing & Media Decisions* 54–60 (April 1987).

18. Gerber, Beverly. Speed: Where the people fit in. *Training* 27 (August 1989).

19. Gold, Bela. Approaches to accelerating product and process development. *Journal of Product Innovation Management* 4(2):81–88 (June 1987).

20. Gomory, Ralph E. and Schmitt, Roland W. Step-by-step innovation. *Across the Board* 52–56 (November 1988).

21. Gupta, Ashok and Wilemon, David L. Accelerating the development of technology-based new products. *California Management Review* 33(2):24–44 (Winter 1990).

22. Haines, Daniel W., Chandran, Rajan and Parkhe, Arvinde. Winning by being the first to market . . . or second? *Journal of Consumer Marketing* 6(1):63–69 (Winter 1989).

23. Hall, Ernest H. Jr. Just-in-time management: A critical assessment. *The Academy of Management Executive* 3(4):315–317 (November 1989).

24. Hooper, Laurence. Xerox tries to shed its has-been image with big new machine. *The Wall Street Journal* A1 (September 20, 1990).

25. Hopkins D. S. *New Product Winners and Losers.* New York. NY: The Conference Board. 1980.

26. IBM extending its reach. *Software Magazine* 21–23 (March 1988).

27. Industrial Research Institute's Annual R&D Trends Survey. *Research* Technology Management* 34(1):12–14 (January–February 1991).

28. Kidder, John Tracy. *The Soul of a New Machine.* Boston. MA: Little Brown, 1981.

29. Kleinfield, N. R. How "Strykeforce" beat the clock. *The New York Times* Section 3, 1 (March 25, 1990).

30. Krubasik, Edward G. Customize your product development. *Harvard Business Review* 66(6):46–52 (November–December 1988).

31. Lilien, Gary L. and Yoon. Eunsang. The timing of competitive market entry: An exploratory study of new industrial products. *Management Science* 36(5):568–584 (May 1990).

32. Main, Jeremy. The winning organization. *Fortune* 50–60 (September 26, 1988).

33. Naj, Amal Kumar. GE's latest invention: A way to move ideas from lab to market. *The Wall Street Journal* A1 (June 19, 1990).

34. Nayak, P. Ranganath. Planning speeds technological development. *Planning Review* 18(6):14–19 (November–December 1990).

35. O'Boyle, Thomas F. GE refrigerator woes illustrate the hazards in changing a product; firm pushed development of compressor too fast, failed to test adequately. *The Wall Street Journal* A1 (May 7, 1990).

36. Prahalad, C. K. and Hamel, Gary. The core competence of the corporation. *Harvard Business Review* 68(3):79–91 (May–June 1990).

37. Reiner, Gary. Winning the race for new product development. *Management Review* 78(8):52–53 (August 1989).

38. Reinertsen, Donald G. Whodunit? The search for new product killers. *Electronic Business* 62–66 (July 1983).

39. Robinson, William T. Product innovation and start-up business market share performance. *Management Science* 36(10):1279–1289 (October 1990).

40. Rosenau, Milton D. Jr. Faster new product development. *Journal of Product Innovation Management* 5(2):150–153. (June 1988).

41. Rosenau, Milton D. Jr. *Faster New Product Development.* New York, NY: AMACOM, 1990.

42. Rudolph, Stephen E. and Lee, W. David. Lessons from the Field. *R&D Magazine* 119+ (October 1990).

43. Smith, Preston G. Winning the new products rat race. *Machine Design* 95–98 (May 12, 1988).

44. Smith, Preston G. and Reinertsen, Donald G. *Developing Products in Half the Time.* New York, NY: Van Nostrand Reinhold, 1991.

45. Souder, William E. and Nassar. Suheil. Choosing an R&D consortium. *Research* Technology Management* 33(2):35–41 (March–April 1990).

46. Stalk, George Jr. and Hout, Thomas M. Competing against time. *Research* Technology Management* 33(2):19–24 (March–April 1990).

47. Uttal, Bro. Speeding new ideas to market *Fortune* 62–66 (March 2, 1987).

48. Vogel, Todd. At Xerox they're shouting "once more into the breach." *Business Week* 62+ (July 23, 1990).

Endnotes

1. The better reports on recent activities in this field are given in the References section: [6,7,19,21,29,32,40–42,44,46].

2. For good reason. McKinsey & Company's Krubasik made clear the need for a mix of strategic options—based on a matrix of opportunity costs and entry risk [30].

3. For more on core technologies, see Prahalad and Hamel [36].

4. John Bailey, Honeywell Building Controls, see Gerber [18].

5. From personal correspondence with Milton D. Rosenau, Jr.

6. Cooper and Kleinschmidt [11]. Cooper, in personal correspondence, says his research proves that the best way to save time is to do the job right the first time.

7. Several such studies have already been cited. One in particular involves the concept of stage-gate [9].

8. This includes suppliers of R&D, as well as of materials and parts. See Souder and Nassar [45]. IBM seeks finished software this way [26].

9. Two of the better articles on this subject are Lilien and Yoon [31] and Robinson [39]. The latter article has an excellent bibliography. Readers should note that definitions in this area of study permit seemingly conflicting interpretations of the data.

10. The original report on this study was by Reinertsen [38], but more recent sources are Dumaine [15] and Smith [43].

SECTION IX

MANAGERIAL PRACTICES AND INNOVATION STRATEGIES

Introduction

This section offers the reader a collection of managerial practices and strategies. These tools provide managers with an assortment of practical techniques and useful processes that can be employed to address innovation-related issues involving human interactions in addition to organizational structures. The employment and management of concepts such as mission, power, trust, partnering, communications, and the innovation process are discussed in the following articles. Whereas many of the foregoing sections have presented articles that involved empirical works, this section offers theoretically developed articles that embody knowledge and principles that can be transferred directly to daily practice. In most instances, the articles selected for this section depict strategies and techniques that can be applied in commercial as well as not-for-profit organizations. Moreover, a theme that becomes apparent is the degree to which leaders and managers of organizations need to undertake the daunting task of balancing the necessity to simultaneously *stay on course* and redirect the efforts of their organizations. Although the topics most often deal with complex issues including the management of disruptive technologies, the creation of complex strategic integration initiatives, and the processes surrounding the successful identification, management, and remuneration of innovation champions, the examples and information described in the following articles can be judiciously employed by our readers in diverse operating organizations.

In our first selection, Lori A. Fidler and J. David Johnson offer an article that sheds light on innovation management issues surrounding the effects of risk, innovation complexity, communication cost, and the role of power in innovation implementation. This article represents another view of how and why many firms are successful in the process of adopting and implementing innovations. They assert that one function of the process of organizing is the removal of variability through the reduction of uncertainty. They postulate that organizations that effectively adopt and implement innovations are those that have effective communication channels available to overcome resistance to innovations. However, they note that the success of any product or process adoption or implementation is a function of the complexity of the innovation in question. These authors state that successful innovation implementation is not solely the decision to adopt but involves the routinization, incorporation, and stabilization of an innovation into ongoing business activities. They conclude that the higher the risk of innovating, the greater the complexity of the innovation, the greater the costs of innovation communication, and, therefore, communication networks with greater capacity and "bandwidth" are required. In addition, they also point out that the greater the innovation complexity and the greater the innovation risk, more personal communication channels need to be employed in conjunction with more intensive persuasive power strategies.

The second article, by David Cawood, offers a military model for managing innovation in business. The author cites the similarity between guerrilla warfare and managing innovation as proof that military tactics can be applicable to business. Cawood points to six concepts that one can follow to implement his military model in an area of business innovation, especially from an organizational and management perspective. These concepts are mission, focus, flexibility, commitment, trust, and communication. The mission of the business needs to be stated succinctly and transcend anyone's ego. There also needs to exist a vision and a single-mindedness about winning the battle for business. Focus indicates that there is a unified effort and that a business must sustain an intense sense of purpose until its objectives are achieved. Flexibility specifies that even though focus is vital to success, there are numerous ways of getting from A to B. Therefore, firms need to focus on their objectives and goals, and determine the best methods for achieving them with special provisions for tactical changes if necessary. Commitment is the fourth of Cawood's elements. He points out that a half-hearted effort is never victorious. Trust is the fifth element in Cawood's arms arsenal. Trust is necessary because innovation is continually destroying the "old" and increasing risk levels. The final element is communication, which supports the other five because it makes the mission known, it reinforces trust, and it allows the "players" to understand the focus.

Andre L. Delbecq and Peter K. Mills provide the third selection in Section IX. In their research, they investigate and compare the processes employed by high and low innovation organizations in an effort to understand the basic characteristics of such organizations. Delbecq and Mills note that innovation is what enables organizations to respond to changing environments. But, they, like Downs and Mohr before them, point out early in their work that there has yet to be devised a reliable model for such an important process. Their investigation views the innovation process as a four-step process that includes idea generation, preliminary analysis, a decision to adopt or reject, and implementation. They also add that the process of innovation depends upon three variables: the motivation to innovate, the obstacles to innovation, and the resources available to overcome innovation obstacles. They examine the process and the results of each of the four steps in their innovation process relative to high and low innovation organizations. They conclude that successful innovation depends on an organization's willingness to commit the necessary time, money, and leadership to research and development. Moreover, they point out that successfully innovative organizations are especially adept at perseverance and "follow-through" to support new ideas.

Murray R. Millson, S. P. Raj, and David Wilemon offer the fourth article in this section, which involves the pursuit of new product development (NPD) and product innovation through the employment of strategic alliances. In this article, the authors define new product alliances as any formal or informal "cooperative" arrangement that supports the joint development and commercialization of new products. These researchers point out that NPD is becoming increasingly expensive and risky. They suggest that several forms of cooperative NPD strategies can be advantageous to innovative organizations. It is noted that NPD is not a discrete event but a maturation process that involves several stages that occur over time. The authors suggest a four-stage maturation process, including *awareness* of the need for an alliance and the search for potential alliance partners; *exploration* of a potential partner's needs, alliance structures, potential partners' organizational sizes, and the investigation of day-to-day alliance management issues; the consummating of an alliance contract that occurs in the *commitment* stage; and the eventual, amicable *dissolution* of the alliance after what is hopefully a successful NPD project. These authors conclude that the alliance formation process they describe in conjunction with the warnings they offer can lead to win-win NPD situations for all partners and provide an alternative to the traditional in-house, do-it-all-alone NPD process.

For this section's fifth selection, we present a book chapter by David J. Teece, which poses a framework within which the profits that accrue from innovation can be analyzed. The purpose of his model is to answer the general question: what are the circumstances under which the recognized technological progressiveness of a firm or nation may not be sufficient to capture the benefits stemming from its scientific and technological capabilities? To address this question, Teece focuses on units of analysis at both the firm and international levels. He notes that his framework can assist in explaining the share of profits that accrue to innovating firms compared to those firms that imitate or follow such leaders. He points out that this framework demonstrates that the distribution of innovation profits can be profoundly influenced by important strategic variables such as the structures of firms and their boundaries in concert with national policies.

In the next article, Robert A. Burgelman and Yves L. Doz address the concept of strategic integration. They define *complex strategic integration* (CSI) as bringing together scarce resources in a multibusiness environment to pursue opportunities that can lead organizations to greater prosperity by taking full advantage of all of the capabilities of the multibusiness organization. The authors note that creating complex strategic integration is often a balance between the concepts of scope and reach. *Scope-driven* strategic integration reinforces and builds on an organization's core businesses and competencies, whereas *reach-driven* strategic integration attempts to redirect the efforts of an organization into new businesses and novel competencies. The authors suggest that the balancing effect of complex strategic integration can maximize the profitable growth of organizations. To achieve this end, the authors recommend that senior management needs to focus on three major initiatives. The first is organizational structuring that provides a framework for assessing organizational interdependencies. The second initiative involves managerial control systems that provide four critical functions, including system diagnostics, belief systems that encourage cooperation, boundary-setting systems to keep *reach integration* in check, and interactive control systems that provide reminders and a focus on *complex strategic integration* for senior executives. And, the third initiative encompasses managerial incentives that focus managerial attention on the integration of strategic issues. To complete their discussion of complex strategic integration, the authors delineate the components of a skill set that top managers need to possess. The three major elements of this skill set include cognitive, political, and entrepreneurial skills.

In the seventh article, Joseph L. Bower and Clayton M. Christensen discuss important issues surrounding the development and commercialization of sustaining and especially disruptive technologies. The authors point out that there is a significantly high failure rate for organizations that pursue the development of disruptive technologies without understanding the important associations between disruptive technologies and an organization's current technologies and lines of business. First, they stress that it is important to be able to differentiate disruptive from sustaining technologies. The authors also suggest that organizations need to understand the "S" curves depicting the performance trajectories of current as well as new technological innovations. If these two types of technologies have similar performance attributes, they are more than likely sustaining innovations. However, if the performance attributes of new technologies differ from current technologies, the new technologies can be considered disruptive. The authors note that it is not sufficient for the trajectories of the performance attributes of new technologies to surpass current technologies because the attributes of new technologies may be better suited to new markets with customers who value the new attribute sets. Next, Bower and Christensen note that managers of successful businesses supported by thriving technologies can make a number of fatal mistakes when they consider potentially disruptive technologies being developed by competitors or contemplated by internal R&D. These mistakes include asking questions of current customers. If the technologies are disruptive, the innovation's attributes may not match the product attributes that current customers are looking for or are familiar with. Additionally, if the technologies are disruptive, the organization may not receive the support from marketing and sales that is necessary due to marketing's focus on current, successful technologies. Emerging technologies need to have market expectations that are in line with those of startups rather than current technologies that have earned large market shares. Finally, disruptive technologies need to have independent organizations within which to grow. Sustaining technologies may be able to be folded back into mainstream organizations, however, when disruptive technologies are integrated into mainstream organizations, they often do not flourish.

Jane M. Howell, in the eighth article in this section, defines the concept of champions of innovation and investigates the major characteristics of innovation champions. In her work, she suggests significant differences between effective and ineffective innovation champions by analyzing two case studies. She attempts to understand how innovation champions identify potential innovations to advance as well as locate sponsors' or stakeholders' support for their innovation processes. Finally, she proposes a sequence of steps that managers can take to cultivate innovation champions in their organizations. Howell specifically points to three personal characteristics of effective innovation champions that include having and embracing contextual and relationship knowledge and skill, exhibiting an internal self-control orientation that is grounded in their passion for projects and a "can do" attitude, and a high degree of self-monitoring that provides the basis for being able to frame and articulate ideas and concepts in a variety of ways to significantly different audiences. The author concludes with seven actions that executives, business leaders, or, as Howell notes, "champion breeders" can take to influence and nurture innovation champions:

1. Intentionally recruit and select innovation champions.
2. Actively coach the selected innovation champions.
3. Demonstrate concern for the career paths of innovation champions.
4. Provide instances for innovation champions to volunteer for projects as opposed to making assignments.
5. Recognize and honor the achievements of innovation champions.
6. Create a learning environment by using failures for educational purposes as opposed to icons for punishment.
7. Increase the stature of innovation champions through positive internal and external visibility relative to their organizations.

The next article selected for this section aligns well with the previous one in that the authors, Jenssen and Jørgensen, provide an extensive literature review related to innovation championship as well as suggesting a model to explain the behavior of innovation champions. The authors proceed from a resource-based theoretical approach to support their model, which has *performance* as its dependent variable. It can be noted from the model that *performance* can be interpreted as both the performance of the innovating organization as well as the performance of a particular innovation or technology. In concert with the major thesis of the authors, it is the variable of *resource acquisitions strategies* that directly impacts performance and it is the *human and social* capital amassed by the innovation champion that directly influences the resources acquired and the strategies employed to obtain them. The authors discuss three dimensions of human and social capital: personal characteristics of innovation champions, the work and social experience of such champions, and the innovation champion's position in business and social networks. In addition to their discussion of the human and social capital characteristics of innovation champions, three specific methods for resource acquisition are presented that comprise a series of *rational* strategies that include negotiating, team building, and motivating; a participation process of resource acquisition involving opinion leaders and others within an organization; as well as *bootlegging*, which involves clandestine methods by which innovation champions acquire necessary resources. Jenssen and Jørgensen note that support from top management considerably reduces the need for illegitimate resource-gathering methods. In conclusion, the authors suggest several questions for future research surrounding topics such as the need for multiple innovation champions to support complex innovations and the impact of organizational structures on innovation champions and their resource acquisition capabilities.

Our tenth article, devoted to practical innovation issues, is authored by Robert A. Burgelman and Liisa Välikangas. The authors suggest that *internal corporate venturing* (ICV) is a cyclical phenomenon and, therefore, can be likened to seasonal changes that we all experience. They go on to suggest that there are four important results of the interaction between the current viability of corporations' mainstream businesses and the immediate availability of uncommitted or slack resources. The four consequences of this interaction include: (1) ICV orphans, which are the result of a combination of uncommitted funds and businesses that generate capital sufficient to meet corporate profitability objectives; (2) all-out ICV drive, which is manifest when resources are available but mainstream businesses are not expected to meet profitability objectives; (3) ICV irrelevance, which is derived from a combination of a lack of venturing funds and promising mainstream business endeavors; and (4) desperately seeking ICV, which emanates from a mixture of a lack of uncommitted resources merged with mainstream businesses that possess inadequate growth potential. In the context of these four ICV cyclical stages, the authors describe implications for the strategic management of ICV. A few of the major points that they make include ICV being a much too important organizational activity to be dictated by short-term strategic pressures and a firm's changing financial conditions, the warning that competitors may very well be working on similar innovations as those that in-house innovators are interested in, and ICV should be recognized as an integrated, ongoing component of an organization's strategy-making process. The authors conclude with the caveat that ICV cyclicality will not disappear in the short-term and, therefore, top managers need to understand how to manage ICV and its potential cycles.

Next, we focus on an article by Clayton M. Christensen, Matt Verlinden, and George Westerman that presents a model suggesting a causal sequence found in organizations and markets as they are created and evolve. Their model indicates a causal path that organizations take as transaction costs decrease; technological advance outstrips consumer needs, products progress from specialty items to products in which modularity and customization is of primary concern, and where product and technological knowledge migrates from unstructured technical dialog to industry standards. Such a causal path describes the trajectory that organizations take from completely integrated organizations to flat disintegrated organizations. The authors point out that, although they recognize this causal path, there can be several tiers within a market for which products of varying functionality are appropriate. Therefore, with regard to markets that are over-served with product functionality, we are more likely to find that organizations are more integrated, develop disruptive technologies, and provide products with increasing customization and modularity. Whereas in markets that are under-served with regard to product functionality, we should find organizations that are more stratified (disintegrated), develop sustaining technologies, push the current state-of-the-art, and attempt to offer current customers increased product performance. The authors investigated the mortgage banking industry in their research to demonstrate that their model explains equally well the progress of organizational structural changes in service organizations as well as organizations of goods manufacturers. Their model also provides for the direction of an organization's progression to change from a disintegrated to an integrated organizational state once again. The authors note that such evolutionary paths are created by resurgence in marketplaces around product performance "gaps" that are identified by consumers, especially at lower market levels. The authors also point out that the downside of the progression from integration to modularity comes with a decreased ability to differentiate one's products from competitor's products through superior design. With regard to the profitability of various organizations in a supply chain, the authors show that there can be important differences in the degree of integration between various levels in supply chains. The reason for this is the degree of interdependence or modularity of products produced that is paced by whether the market at that supply chain level is being over- or under-served in terms of product functionality.

Our concluding article in this section by Jonathon Linton describes his research regarding the forecasting of demand, supply, and pricing of disruptive process technologies in emerging markets. The author presents a number of forecasting methods: "S" curve techniques, linear methods, and the Delphi and scenario approaches to market forecasting. Linton describes a process for developing measures for demand, supply, and the demand/supply gap in addition to exploring the potential effects of excess supply or demand and increases and decreases of demand and supply in his selected markets. Due to the exceptionally uncertain environments faced by emerging, disruptive process technologies, the author suggests employing a bootstrapping or Monte Carlo simulation technique to create numerous random forecasts, to assure that one of those created will portray the future. He then suggests creating probability ranges for the resulting forecasts to provide a confidence range of forecasts that includes the most probable forecasts. To demonstrate his forecasting process, the author employs data that relates to microelectromechanical systems (MEMS). He concludes with implications for both government policy and corporate strategic decision makers responsible for demand and supply forecasting in uncertain environments.

References

Bower, Joseph L. and Clayton M. Christensen. 1995. Disruptive technologies: Catching the wave. *Harvard Business Review* (January/February): 43–53.

Burgelman, Robert A. and Yves L. Doz. 2001. The power of strategic integration. *MIT Sloan Management Review* (Spring): 28–38.

Burgelman, Robert A. and Liisa Välikangas. 2005. Managing internal corporate venturing cycles. *MIT Sloan Management Review* 46(4): 26–34.

Cawood, David. 1994. Managing innovation: Military strategy in business. *Business Horizons* 27(November/December): 62–66.

Christensen, Clayton M., Matt Verlinden, and George Westerman. 2002. Disruption, disintegration, and dissipation if differentiability. *Industrial and Corporate Change* 11(5): 955–993.

Delbecq, Andre L. and Peter K. Mills. 1986. Managerial practices that enhance innovation. *Organizational Dynamics* 14(Summer): 24–34.

Fidler, Lori A. and J. David Johnson. 1994. Communication and innovation implementation. *Academy of Management Review* 8(4): 704–711.

Howell, Jane M. 2005. The right stuff: Identifying and developing effective champions of innovation. *Academy of Management Executive* 19(2): 108–119.

Jenssen, Jan Inge and Geir Jørgensen. 2004. How do corporate champions promote innovations? *International Journal of Innovation Management* 8(1): 63–86.

Linton, Jonathan D. 2003. Determining demand, supply, and pricing for emerging markets based on disruptive process technologies. *Technological Forecasting and Social Change* 71(1/2): 105–120.

Millson, Murray R., S. P. Raj, and David Wilemon. 1996. Strategic partnering for developing new products. *Technology Management* 39(2): 41–49.

Teece, David J. 1988. Capturing value from technological innovation: Integration, strategic partnering, and licensing decisions. *Interfaces* 18(3): 46–61.

47

COMMUNICATION AND INNOVATION IMPLEMENTATION

Lori A. Fidler

University of Wisconsin-Milwaukee

J. David Johnson

Arizona State University

The capacity of a decision unit to induce innovation implementation within an adoption unit is crucial to organizational success. Risk and complexity are characteristics of innovations that can lead to resistance within organizational adoption units. Communication costs, types of power, and communication channels are structural characteristics that can be used by a decision unit to overcome this resistance. The interaction of these factors can determine the degree of successful innovation implementation within organizations.

Modern organizations must constantly adapt to survive in today's rapidly changing environment. As a result the implementation of innovations is crucial to organizational success in terms of both the redirection and the integration of the organization as a system (Wager, 1962) and for organizational effectiveness generally (Rogers & Agarwala-Rogers, 1976). A number of factors can potentially mediate the success of implementation, including the interdependence of components of the system, their diversity, goal agreement, the nature of the formal management system, external conditions (Galbraith, 1973), and the general organizational cultural norms towards innovation (Deal & Kennedy, 1982). Although all of these factors can impact innovation implementation, the acceptance of an innovation often rests on the extent to which communication can act to reduce uncertainty by ameliorating such factors as risk and complexity and thus permitting the assimilation of the new practice or technology into the constraints of the ongoing organizational system, which these mediating factors reflect.

Indeed, more generally, some view the primary purpose of organizing as the reduction of variability through the overcoming of uncertainty (Weick, 1969). Because this reduction of uncertainty occurs primarily through communication, there can be little separation between processes of communication and change within organizations. An organization that cannot change, adopting innovation to meet changing environmental conditions while matching intraorganizational constraints, eventually will find itself no longer competitive in an increasingly complex and technologically sophisticated economy.

Because of its central role, an increased understanding of the part communication plays in innovation implementation has important pragmatic implications for management and potential heuristic value for future research in this area. The nature of information transmitted concerning an innovation can be grouped into three general categories: (1) information concerning the innovation; (2) influence and power information related to innovation; and (3) information concerning the operationalizing of the innovation (Schramm & Roberts, 1971). This paper is an attempt to specify the manner in which characteristics of the innovation transmitted in communication messages and structural aspects of organizations related to communication determine the ultimate implementation of innovations in organizations.

Innovations can take several forms: innovation in (1) a product or service; (2) a production process; (3) organizational structure; (4) people; and (5) policy (Zaltman, Duncan, & Holbek, 1973). Whatever its form, a unique feature of innovation in an organizational setting, which serves to distinguish it from innovation in the society at large, is that a unit of higher status and authority can decide to adopt an innovation that another segment of the organization must implement. In organizations the former unit has been termed the decision unit and the latter has been termed the adoption unit, and the process as a whole has been described as an authority-innovation decision (Rogers & Shoemaker, 1971). The separation of these two organizational functions, innovation and operations, has been viewed as a critical design feature that leads to increased innovations on the part of can organization (Galbraith, 1982). Successful implementation of an innovation can be conceived of as the routinization, incorporation, and stabilization of the innovation into ongoing work activity of organizational units. For organizations, "the bottom line is implementation (including its institutionalization), and not just the adoption *decision*" (Rogers & Adhikayra, 1979, p. 79).

Advocating change necessarily results in increased uncertainty, which can lead to resistance to innovations by adoption units (Coch & French, 1948; Katz and Kahn, 1978). Communication plays a key role in overcoming resistance to innovations and in the reduction of uncertainty. For successful communication to occur, the message transmitted by a decision unit must evoke similar symbol-referent relationships for both parties. The very existence of these commonly shared symbol systems reduces uncertainty by making interactions more predictable (Farace, Monge, & Russell, 1977).

Uncertainty is conceived of as a function of the number of alternatives and the probability of each alternative occurring (Farace et al., 1977). Complexity and risk are elements of uncertainty crucial to the ultimate implementation of innovations. Complexity relates to the number of potential alternatives perceived in an innovation adoption. Risk is the perceived consequences to the adoption unit associated with the implementation of an innovation adoption (Lowrance, 1980).

Overcoming the perceptions of risk and complexity held by the adoption unit is crucial to inducing the involvement needed for successful implementation (Bennis, 1965). Because implementation requires some modification in actual practice, the active involvement of the adoption unit often is essential for successful implementation (Rogers & Adhikayra, 1979). For the purposes here, involvement can be considered to be an attitudinal acceptance of the decision unit's message, which results in behavioral activities beyond those associated with routine compliance with organizational directives. Both risk and complexity also relate directly to the capacity of communication messages to reduce uncertainty in the adoption unit; hence they relate to the capacity of the decision unit to send effective communication messages—messages that bring the receiver into greater compliance with the source (Farace, Taylor, & Stewart, 1978).

The reduction of uncertainty inherent in communication can decrease resistance to innovations, but usually decision units also must exert some degree of power and influence to facilitate innovation implementation. In fact, the various types of power and the communication channels available to transmit influence and information concerning innovations are the primary structural characteristics of organizations that affect the ultimate implementation of an innovation. The commonly used types of power in organizational settings have different communication costs associated with them.

These communication costs are determined by the amount of resources expended in the transmission of a message (Farace et al., 1978).

Some combinations of power, complexity, and risk can overload available channels, creating an upper limit to the capacity of an organization to implement certain innovations successfully. It is argued that an organization's success in overcoming complexity and risk associated with innovations will be determined in large part by the amount of resources it devotes to structural characteristics related to organizational communication.

RISK

For an organizational adoption unit, the key element in its response to an innovation is the perceived consequences of engaging in the new behavior advocated in the communication message from the decision unit, because implementation of an innovation implies action and attendant consequences (Kivlin & Fliegel, 1967). The presence of risk in an innovation can lead to greater resistance than is present in normal organization operations; the very novelty of the innovation entails more risk for the adoption unit and for the organization as a whole (Rogers & Adhikayra, 1979). In fact, the greater the uncertainty of outcome regarding an innovation, the greater the degree of perceived risk toward implementing the innovation.

Innovations involve new situations such that the chances of loss are formally unpredictable (Strassman, 1959), and advocated changes offer a potential threat to organizational members that will increase with increases in the degree of advocated change (Huse, 1975; Zaltman & Duncan, 1977). The more successful a decision unit in decreasing the adoption unit's perception of risk, the less the resistance to innovation implementation.

P1: The more risk perceived in an advocated innovation, the less the likelihood of successful innovation implementation by an adoption unit.

COMPLEXITY

Complexity refers to the number of dimensions along which an innovation can be evaluated by a potential receiver; thus it is an inherent characteristic of messages concerning an innovation. As Bohlen has noted: "Other factors equated, the more complex an idea is, the more slowly it tends to be adopted" (1971, p. 807). The greater the complexity related to using an innovation or in merely understanding the innovation cognitively, the greater the resistance to an innovation in organizations (Zaltman & Duncan, 1977). Accordingly:

P2: Generally, the greater the complexity of an innovation advocated by an organizational decision unit, the less the likelihood of successful innovation implementation.

The complexity of an innovation is related to its uncertainty because with greater complexity more dimensions (or alternatives) must be considered. Thus there is an increased number of factors to evaluate; and with more dimensions to consider, fewer can be known with any certainty. Thus, complexity increases the perceived risks associated with an advocated innovation, and these two factors together can interact to increase resistance to an innovation.

POWER AND COMMUNICATIONS COSTS

The various types of power used to overcome resistance on the part of the adoption unit become crucial in determining innovation implementation; implementation of an innovation behaviorally within an organization can be hindered through both passive and active resistance (Zaltman et al., 1973). The types of power used by the decision unit to induce the adoption unit to implement an innovation have important consequences for the costs of communication incurred in innovation implementation. These types of power also induce differing levels of involvement with the innovation, a factor that usually is crucial to the successful adoption of any innovation.

Communication Costs

Generally, three main types of power, or the capacity or potential to determine the actions of the adoption unit, can be used by the decision unit: sanction, authority, and influence. Sanction refers to the ability to control the adoption unit's action through the active manipulation of resources under the decision unit's control.

Reward and coercion are two separate manifestations of sanction power (French & Raven, 1959). Both rest on the belief of the adoption unit that the decision unit controls material and psychological resources that are important to it. Although both of these types of power can be effective, their use incurs considerable costs to the decision unit. First, they require the continuous expenditure of resources, some of which may result in satiation, or the satisfaction of related needs, so that rewards no longer motivate. Second, both require constant monitoring of the adoption unit to ensure that it is acting in a manner that is consonant with either continued reward or punishment. Thus there are heavy communication costs (see Figure 47-1) to the decision unit in terms of both determining what may reward or punish the adoption unit at any particular time and also reviewing the adoption unit's activities.

Authority, or legitimate power in French and Raven's (1959) taxonomy, rests on the belief of the adopting unit (resulting from an internalized norm or value) that the decision unit has the right to dictate innovations. The use of this type of power has several advantages over the use of sanctions: (1) it does not require constant monitoring; (2) legitimate power derives from previous rewards and punishments associated with socialization and thus does not require specific sanctions for every innovation; (3) satiation is less of a problem because the satisfaction of specific needs is not the motivating force; and (4) communication costs are associated primarily with transmission of information concerning the innovation through formal channels.

> *P3: Legitimate power results in less communication costs to the decision unit than the use of sanctions in securing eventual innovation implementation.*

Influence rests on the capacity of the decision unit to cause changes in the adopting unit's behavior by the use of more subtle, informal, and often cognitively oriented means than those associated with sanction or authority. The adoption unit consciously chooses to commit itself to the innovation as a result of these cognitive processes. There are three primary types of influence: referent, expert, and persuasion.

FIGURE 47-1 Communication Costs and Levels of Involvement Associated with Various Types of Power

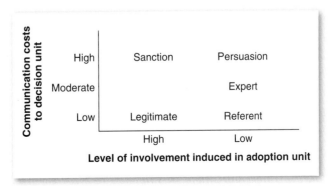

Referent power is based on the adoption unit's identification with the decision unit (French & Raven, 1959). Indeed, the greater the prestige of the decision unit, the more likely it is to influence the adoption of an innovation (Huse, 1975). In the case of referent power, the adopting unit institutes an innovation merely because the decision unit has done so; the decision unit may not even be aware of its influence. The communication costs associated with this type of power are almost exclusively associated with the transmission of information concerning the nature of innovation and are borne primarily by the adoption unit.

More central to the problem addressed here is the use of influence based on expert power, or the adoption unit's perception that the decision unit has greater knowledge in the salient area of the innovation, and thus its judgment of the innovation's utility should be accepted. The communications costs associated with the use of this type of power will vary with the complexity of the innovation. In the case of a simple innovation, the costs may be very low, approaching the level of the use of legitimate power. However, for complex innovations the use of this type of power can result in high communication costs associated with the mere transmission of information concerning implementation of the innovation.

In utilizing persuasion, the decision unit communicates evidence, arguments, and a rationale advocating implementation of the innovation by the adopting unit. In essence, pervasive efforts attempt to convince the adopting unit that it should change its behavior voluntarily. The communication costs associated with the use of this type of power are high initially; and, at least in the case of counterpersuasion attempts, they may be continuous.

> *P4: Communication costs related to the use of influence in securing eventual innovation implementation generally will be highest for persuasion, followed by expert power, with referent power requiring the lowest communication costs to the organizational decision unit.*

Level of Involvement Induced

Each of the foregoing types of power can result in changes in behavior, and in some instances they may be used simultaneously to even greater effect, but they each induce differential levels of involvement in the adopting unit. High levels of involvement usually play a crucial role in the ultimate implementation of innovations. Figure 47-1 graphically reveals the relationship among the five types of power discussed in the previous section and their position on the dimensions of communication costs and involvement.

Use of sanction power typically results in a relatively low level of involvement. In the case of rewards, the resulting involvement can be characterized as calculative and of low intensity (Etzioni, 1961). In this instance, adoption units will perform in the minimally acceptable manner for as long as the reward is present. Use of coercive power, on the other hand, results in an alienative involvement, with intensely negative attitudinal orientations (Etzioni, 1961). The use of legitimate power usually dampens the creativity of workers and impairs their willingness to suggest modifications, because they are not active participants in the decision making process. Typically, when legitimate power is used, the adoption unit will engage in routine, mechanical operationalizing of an innovation that is identified with the decision unit. However, in actual practice successful innovation implementation requires some modification based on the experience of users.

Influence power results in more active involvement on the part of the adoption unit because these methods usually entail an attitude change that is positive to the required behavioral change (Kelman, 1961). In both expert and referent power there is voluntary acceptance of the innovation resulting from perceived characteristics of the decision unit. Because effective persuasion results in greater participation in the implementation of innovations, it usually results in less resistance to technological change (Kelman, 1961). Because of the voluntary, spontaneous acceptance associated with successful persuasion, this type of power is associated most clearly with ensuring the active involvement needed for implementation of an innovation (Bennis, 1965). Indeed, especially in the case of high levels of identification, attitudinal acceptance may result in an intensely positive or normative conversion to the position advocated by the decision unit (Etzioni, 1961).

> *P5: As a result of the active involvement it induces, generally the use of influence will be more effective in organizational innovation implementation than either sanction or legitimate power.*

Effects of Risk and Complexity

The complexity and perceived risk inherent in innovations interact with the types of power to determine the communication costs associated with the implementation of particular innovations. Indeed, the perception of risk often is a result of a lack of knowledge concerning the implications of an innovation (Strassman, 1959), which necessitates additional information transfer to reduce uncertainty. The more risky the adoption of an innovation, the more likely it is that the adoption unit will be resistant, requiring more rewards or influence attempts before acquiescing in the implementation of an innovation (Zaltman & Duncan, 1977).

> *P6: Generally the greater the perceived risk, the greater the exercise of power by the organizational decision unit needed to implement an innovation.*

Complexity also affects the types of power that will be used to promote innovation implementation. For example, the more facets to an innovation, the more actions that have to be rewarded and somewhat relatedly, the greater the volume of information related to persuasion. Thus the high communication costs of persuasion and sanction—and also, in this case, expert power—increase almost exponentially with greater complexity; however, the communication costs of other types of power, legitimate and referent, increase more linearly because the invocation of these types of power is inherent in the messages concerning the innovation.

> *P7: In effectively implementing an innovation, there is a linear increase in the communication costs of legitimate or referent power with increasing complexity.*
> *P8: In effectively implementing an innovation, there is a multiplicative increase in communication costs associated with persuasion, sanction, and expert power with increasing complexity.*

These hypotheses suggest that the effectiveness of various types of power in overcoming resistance is limited because of uncertainties resulting from increasing risk and complexity. For example, the use of expert power usually is insufficient by itself when a high degree of uncertainty exists (Zaltman & Duncan, 1977); it explains the innovation at a cognitive level, but the threat of risk may not be mediated. With an increase in risk and complexity, the decision unit is limited in its use of legitimate power; it probably would need to exercise authority beyond accepted parameters. When authority is used to excess, there is a constant danger that the decision unit's authority over the adoption unit may actually decrease (French & Raven, 1959).

Generally, persuasive strategies have been found to be the most effective means of ensuring the successful implementation of a highly risky and complex innovation within organizations (Bennis, 1965; Zaltman & Duncan, 1977). Effective persuasion can best overcome resistance attributable both to lack of understanding and to fear; in addition, its use results in a higher level of involvement (Bennis, 1965). Of course, when persuasion is ineffective, a decision unit may still involve sanction and legitimate power as last resorts. Although persuasion generally is the most effective strategy, it also is the most costly. It is so costly, in fact, that there may be increasingly diminishing utility to the organization in the implementation of highly risky and complex innovations.

COMMUNICATION CHANNEL EFFICACY

One of the primary structural features associated with the diffusion of innovations within systems is the number and arrangement of recurring communication channels. These channels have differing capacities for handling particular types of information, and their combined capacities limit the raw volume of information in any system. Communication channel efficacy within organizations refers to the ratio of resources expended to the utility of a transmission event (Farace et al., 1978). The efficacy of a channel is important. It determines in part the ultimate cost effectiveness of the process of innovation implementation. Two types of information that flow along these channels are of special concern: information relating to the innovation itself and power-related information, which serves to secure compliance within the adoption unit.

Generally, two channels have been focused on in innovation research: interpersonal, involving primarily face to face modalities; and mediated channels (often referred to as mass media), which typically are interposed in some way between source and receiver (Rogers & Shoemaker, 1971). Often the capacity of interpersonal channels to provide social support and enhanced confidence in the outcomes of the innovation can be crucial in innovation implementation (Katz, 1957, 1961). Typically interpersonal channels are more likely to meet the specific needs and questions of the adoption unit as a result of their immediacy of feedback and the situation specificity of their communication (Schramm, 1973). As a result, they act to reduce uncertainty by imparting information that leads to increased understanding of the innovation.

Mediated channels, such as written ones, tend to provide information of a fairly general nature, but such information often is not specific enough to overcome perceptions of risk (Cartwright, 1949; Rogers, 1976). However, when risk is not a major factor, the use of mediated channels becomes more efficacious, especially when considering their speed to larger audiences and their multiplicative power (Picot, Klingenberg, & Kranzle, 1982; Schramm, 1973).

> *P9: For increasingly risky innovations, interpersonal channels will become increasingly effective in innovation implementation; conversely, with decreases in perceived risk, mediated channels become more efficacious in innovation implementation.*

The more complex the innovation, the greater the resulting work-related uncertainty, and hence the greater the communication costs associated with its implementation (Katz & Tushman, 1979). Interpersonal channels generally have been found to be more useful in transmitting highly complex subject matter (Chapanis, 1971; Conrath, Buckingham, Dunn, & Swanson, 1975; Picot et al., 1982; Tushman, 1978). These channels generally are more flexible than mediated ones, and they can activate more senses and can be more attuned to the specific problems of receivers (Picot et al., 1982; Rogers & Shoemaker, 1971; Tushman, 1978). Interpersonal channels also are able to carry more information through a variety of codes; as a result of this "richness" of channel, they are in a better position to reduce the uncertainty caused by complexity in organizational settings (Holland, Stead, & Leibrock, 1976; Picot et al., 1982). However, the communication costs associated with the use of interpersonal channels generally are quite high. In situations of low complexity a minimum of activity is necessary to relate dimensions to the experience world of the adoption unit. Thus mediated channels can widely distribute the essential information concerning the innovation with a minimun of effort (Picot et al., 1982; Rogers & Shoemaker, 1971).

> *P10: For increasingly complex innovations, interpersonal channels will become increasingly effective in innovation implementation; conversely, with decreases in complexity, mediated channels will become more efficacious in innovation implementation.*

In organizational literature, power-related information flowing along communication channels typically has been discussed in terms of its formality, with interpersonal channels usually related to informal influence and mediated channels associated with the formal authority structure (Dahle, 1954; Tompkins, 1967). Legitimate and sanction power typically are tied to this formal authority structure, and messages concerning them typically flow along mediated channels. Conversely, messages from the decision to the adoption unit regarding innovation implementation involving influence typically flow along more interpersonal channels. For innovations for which a minimum degree of resistance is expected, typically mediated channels will be used. However, when risk and complexity act to increase resistance to innovations, interpersonal channels became more effective in implementing innovations (Picot et al., 1982).

Particularly important in the implementation of risky and complex innovations are subformal channels. These channels are primarily interpersonal and reflect the informal authority structure of an organization (Downs, 1967). Indeed, interpersonal influence processes often are viewed as playing a determinant role in the implementation of innovations within organizations (Holland et al., 1976; Picot et al., 1982; Rice & Rogers, 1981), and subformal channels are the primary conduits of this type of influence.

P11: With increasing risk and complexity, the greater the access of the decision unit to the adoption unit via subformal channels, the greater the likelihood of successful innovation implementation.

CONCLUSION

The propositions developed here suggest specific strategies that can be utilized in successful innovation implementation within organizations. The introduction of the notion of channel efficacy, however, also suggests some potential problems. The general techniques involved in successful innovation implementation have been known in broad detail for a long period of time, but units within organizations have still proved remarkably resistant to innovation. An examination of the interaction among the various factors that contribute to successful implementation can provide an explanation for this state of affairs.

Figure 47-2 details the interactive effects of risk, complexity, and the communication costs of power on communication channel load. For simplicity, these factors, which can be presumed to vary in intensity, are divided into two conditions, either high or low. A cursory examination of the resulting eight conditions reveals some substantial barriers to innovation implementation in specific situations. When all of the factors are high, the volume of communication needed to overcome resistance may be too

FIGURE 47-2 Relationship Between Risk, Complexity, and Communication Costs of Power and Channel Load

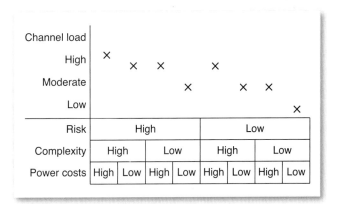

great, potentially overloading available channels (both interpersonal and mediated) or making the costs of implementing the innovation greater than its potential benefits. The remaining seven conditions have more moderate loads, although still high in some instances. The lowest level at which risk, complexity, and the communication costs of influence are all low represents the optimal situation for using mediated channels.

There appears to be a direct inverse relationship between the amount of information load associated with particular conditions and the presumption of the relative success of implementation. Certainly with a highly risky and complex innovation that requires high volumes of communication to effect, the chances of successful implementation become problematical.

An organization in an ideal world could choose to expend the effort to implement an innovation in these conditions, but, especially for the all high condition, there may not be the channel capacity to effect it, especially if the normal operational level of organizational information load is maintained. Thus these contingent situations suggest that there is a practical upper bound to implementing innovations within organizations.

References

Bennis, W. G. Theory and method in applying behavioral science to planned organizational change. *Applied Behavioral Science,* 1965, 1, 337–360.

Bohlen, J. M. Research needed on adoption models. In W. S. Schramm & D. F. Roberts (Eds.), *The process and effects of mass communication.* Urbana, Ill.: University of Illinois Press, 1971, 798–815.

Cartwright, D. Some principles of mass persuasion: Selected findings of research on the sale of U.S. war bonds. *Human Relations,* 1949, 2, 253–267.

Chapanis, A. Prelude to 2001: Explorations in human communication. *American Psychologist,* 1971, 26, 940–961.

Coch, L., & French, J. R. Overcoming resistance to change. *Human Relations,* 1948, 1, 512–532.

Conrath, D. W., Buckingham, P., Dunn, E., & Swanson, J. N. An experimental evaluation of alternative communication systems as used for medical diagnosis. *Behavioral Science,* 1975, 20, 296–305.

Dahle, T. L. An objective and comparative study of five methods of transmitting information to business and industrial employees. *Speech Monographs,* 1954, 27, 21–28.

Deal, T. E., & Kennedy, A. A. *Corporate cultures: The rites and rituals of corporate life.* Reading, Mass.: Addison-Wesley, 1982.

Downs, A. *Inside bureaucracy.* Boston: Little, Brown, 1967.

Etzioni, A. *A comparative analysis of complex organizations: On power involvement and their correlates.* New York: Free Press, 1961.

Farace, R. V., Monge, P. R., & Russell, H. *Communicating and organizing.* Reading, Mass.: Addison-Wesley, 1977.

Farace, R. V., Taylor, J. A., & Stewart, J. P. Criteria for the evaluation of organizational effectiveness: Review and synthesis. In B. Ruben (Ed.), *Communication yearbook 2.* New Brunswick, N.J.: Transaction Books, 1978, 271–292.

French, J. R. P., Jr., & Raven, B. The bases of social power. In D. Cartwright (Ed.), *Studies in social power.* Ann Arbor, Mich.: Institute for Social Research, 1959, 150–167.

Galbraith, J. R. *Designing complex organizations.* Reading, Mass.: Addison-Wesley, 1973.

Galbraith, J. R. Designing the innovating organization. *Organizational Dynamics,* 1982, 11(3), 5–25.

48

MANAGING INNOVATION: MILITARY STRATEGY IN BUSINESS

David Cawood

"How in God's name do you think you lead . . . ? By the strength of your arm only?
No. But by your brain . . . And by magic."

—from *Tai-Pan* by James Clavell

Militaristic analogies to organizational life have been around for a long time. From Machiavelli to *The Book of Five Rings,* enthusiastic quotes justify the use of harsh tactics as part of any strategy. The critics of this kind of thinking have been quick to point out that modern organizational life is far too complex for simplistic models based on "shoot first" techniques. Contemporary writers such as Karl Weick attack the military metaphor in terms of its rigidity and lack of subtlety. Yet some of the less publicized aspects of military innovativeness are particularly relevant in the realm of corporate strategy, and, I believe, will become even more so in the next decade. As executives struggle to make sense out of these new business management practices, more parallels are emerging between the challenges they face and those encountered by military strategists.

In recent history, traditional armies have been undermined by the shock tactics of guerilla forces: the enemy changed the rules, and old strategies were suddenly irrelevant and ineffective. Long-standing assumptions were challenged and rejected. In this century, the English were the first to be introduced to these harsh realities by the Boers in South Africa. The Irish Republican Army benefited considerably from observing this conflict, as did Gandhi, who was actually a noncombatant participant. By the time of World War II, the British and others had learned a great deal. They had evolved elite corps of professional *counterterrorists,* the Green Berets and the Israelis at Entebbe being only a few of these new masters of military innovation.

In much the same way, as modern organizations become increasingly undermined by the impact of economic and technological changes, they will need to master new skills. The concept of managing innovation deals with continual challenges to the status quo by devising counter tactics and encouraging even more challenges.

What can be learned from the military professionals who have been forced to successfully manage unpredictability and turbulence? Are there lessons to be drawn from

Cawood, David, (1994), "Managing Innovation: Military Strategy in Business," *Business Horizons,* 27, Nov.–Dec., 62–66.

their experiences that could apply to modern managers? Drawing on my early experience as a draftee officer in a counterterrorist unit, and after fifteen years as a teacher and international consultant, I am convinced that the parallels between these two groups grow stronger by the day. By this I do not mean to advocate a simplistic military model, or to suggest that organization life should be a battlefield. But we all know that it is a minefield, and that careful, well-chosen measures are needed to cope with the realities of the times.

MISSION

The concept of managing innovation can best be understood when broken down into six key concepts. At the core of these is the mission, the first and highest order concept, because it refers to the chosen overall direction of the organization. It suggests both the tangible direction and the less tangible but vital sense of a guiding vision, both of which are essential to organizational strategy. Managing innovation begins with the mission; the second through sixth concepts deal with the specifics of making the mission become a reality.

Effective counterterrorist units have a very clear idea of their overall purpose or mission, and each individual within a unit finds a personal meaning in that mission. This is a point of crucial importance. Corporate goals must transcend any one ego, they must be communicable, and communicated, to every person, and they must have potential personal meaning at all levels. This is a tall order. Few company presidents recognize that this orchestration of the "grand image" is the essence of organization culture, and even fewer see it as part of their job. A lucky few inherit an image with which they can be personally congruent, but most continue with the quarterly reviews, because there is nothing in their training that deals with image formation, nurturing, or communication. One book that illustrates this concept better than any business text is James Clavell's *Tai-Pan,* which illustrates the intuitive, visionary element of the mission that gives individuals the capability and determination to ensure its realization. In *Tai-Pan* this unifying vision was the grand image of Hong Kong. The "magic" Clavell refers to in the opening quotation of this article is missing from too many organizations.

A corporation's strategic direction must, of course, be shared with the key decision makers. In counterterrorist units, anyone with a personal ideology that differs from the central ideology is dealt with quickly and effectively at the most senior level. But too many organizations soldier on with one, two, or more vice-presidents openly criticizing the chosen strategy. These dissenters often have built a support team of key subordinates over the years, and few senior executives fully understand the real costs of the resulting "them versus us" antagonism.

This situation is further complicated by the staggering interrelatedness of problems caused by the inherent complexity of modern organizational life itself. In what have been aptly described as "wicked" problem situations, any action one takes in this environment will undoubtedly have an effect on someone else, or indeed, on many others. Samuel Culbert and John McDonough in *The Invisible War* describe the resulting dilemma of the decision makers as "fragmenting."

"Thus we [managers] boggle at answering the simplest questions. We're in the ridiculous position of figuring out an ingenious response, one that responds to five or six interests at once, to a question which may pose us with an impossible personal predicament while others view our answers as simplistic and representative of a stereotypical thinker."

As these problems will only become more interrelated, it is critical for the senior corporate level or "dominant coalition" to be clear on its direction, and to have the courage to deal with any destructive dissent that threatens the organization's mission.

The second and third key components of strategy are actually twin concepts and although we will examine them one after the other, the reader is asked to bear their duality in mind. The two concepts, *focus* and *flexibility,* will be linked together shortly.

FOCUS

Counterterrorists are very clear on the need for focus. Literally a single shot is all one may get before betraying his position. It can take months of planning and days of calculating split-second timing to set up the "hit"—the one shot. Parallels with organizations of the 1980s and 90s can be clearly drawn. In the field of marketing, for example, this concept is evidenced by the demise of the mass marketing blitz. Each shot must now be targeted for a stratified and defined segment of the marketplace.

The idea of focusing on or returning to one's fundamental areas of strength is certainly widespread, and in turbulent times, the need to manage and understand the basics of one's business is even more crucial. Any reading of current business literature offers numerous examples of this "consolidation" type of thinking. We can predict much heavier competition in more basic businesses as people start to focus on squeezing out extra margins, while pressure on productivity factors will increase. The race will go to those who can squeeze the hardest and still retain morale among their people over the long haul.

The concept of focusing is derived from the physical act of bending dispersed rays onto a single, central area. A magnifying glass concentrates the power of the sun over a small area. Similarly, the concept of organizational power goes beyond merely having access to resources; it means strengthening or intensifying one's position through effectively concentrating available resources into a single unified effort. Organizational power comes from the ability to harness resources around a single theme and "go for it" in ways which will produce desired and meaningful results.

Focusing is a pivotal and exciting aspect of working in corporate turnaround situations. A frequent and valid object of attack in these situations is "slack." A few years back I moved in on a slack-filled, failing organization. Within three months it was leaner, meaner, and starting to hum again. An entire regional head office was removed, and the regional operation was controlled directly from the corporate head office. One year later a survey of executives removed in the turnaround revealed that they were unanimously positive about the situation. As a result, they too had been forced to focus, and felt better for it despite their difficulties at the time. Focus, though, in order to work, has to be executed with a feel for timing and place, or with *flexibility*.

FLEXIBILITY

Counterterrorists know the virtue of flexibility on a minute-to-minute basis. I have found these people far more aware than many managers of the idea that there are numerous ways of getting from A to B, and that the longest road on one set of criteria may be the shortest on another. Flexibility applied to strategy and its implementation is the ability to take the most intelligent and advantageous option available to achieve one's strategic goals. It encompasses the ability to be prepared at all times, and on all levels, to switch gears, regroup, and reroute if a route appears that is simply better than the original. It also involves the ability to let the mission, rather than tradition, guide. It may be necessary to break a mold or two in order to achieve a goal.

Flexibility can also be built into the organization by encouraging and training generalist skills and attitudes. A true generalist is one who, within a given field or industry, possesses real, usable skills in each major function of that field. The classic "old" Chrysler versus Mazda reaction to the energy crisis provides a good illustration of this point. Chrysler laid off workers and left a limited number of specialists to design the Omni, a product that was plagued with problems, while at Mazda, everyone took a cut in pay and joint management/worker teams who were completely generalist-trained designed the GLC, which performed and sold superbly.

The Japanese could not have accomplished this without already having flexibility at all levels, or without having a generalist framework. In the simplest terms, this means that marketing people and accountants literally know how to use a welding torch. Chrysler was limited by individuals who were not trained to be flexible, and who therefore created an inflexible organization. Thorough generalist training provides an enormous opportunity for regrouping and adapting to reality.

North Americans often replace the true generalist concept with the "business school" interpretation of a generalist: a few courses in marketing, a few in production management. My MBA equipped me only with the ability to be a dangerous menace to a good production manager. Jay Galbraith's recent work on innovation stresses the need for generalists. But where will they come from? MBA programs do not provide a sufficient level of depth in most subject areas. My own experience, and that of the major international companies with whom I work, reflects a rising groundswell of criticism of the fundamental training of MBAs. They are simply not equipped to be truly flexible, because flexibility implies depth as well as breadth.

On another structural level, flexibility implies having an integrated network of divisions that offer the diversification necessary to accommodate external changes. The undisciplined pursuit of too much of this type of flexibility, however, led to the great conglomerate race of the 1960s and to the subsequent and continuing problems of managing corporate/divisional relationships. I believe that these developments have indirectly accounted for the majority of consultant interventions ever since.

In the context of strategy there are trade-offs involved with focus and flexibility. There is increasing pressure on organizations to focus, and limited tolerance of flexibility, because it is perceived on the surface level as random. Striking a working balance between the two is crucial to innovative organizations; in fact, it is absolutely fundamental to developing strategy. Organizations must continuously monitor themselves so that they avoid the dangers of over-emphasis on one or the other.

COMMITMENT

Commitment is a wide-ranging concept that must be evident on each level of an organization. Here, we will look at a few of these situations, but it should be recognized that half-hearted commitment is counterproductive at any level. In terms of commitment counterterrorists, once launched of a paratroop mission, are luckier than executives facing an equally hair-raising mission. At least, when the rip cord is pulled, that's it. The adrenalin from knowing there is no turning back helps performance enormously. Turning back, or even thinking about it, wastes energy and blocks wholehearted commitment.

The fact that people pursue self-interests at work is well known, but the challenge of harnessing those interests into an organizationally relevant, committed force requires real magic. What special force was Delta Airlines able to harness so that more than 70 percent of their 37,000 employees pledged part of their salaries to present the company with a $30 million plane? The seventy-two pounds of velvet ribbon tied around the plane as gift wrapping conveyed some of the power of the grand image that motivated each one of those talented people. How to put that image into a tangible format which has the power to move people, and at more than only an intellectual level, poses a challenge to all corporate leaders. *Emotions* must be invoked to achieve true commitment. Simplistic motivational "rah rahs" are not enough. Images must be genuine and non-manipulative to survive increasingly sophisticated employee scrutiny, while leader commitment at the personal level is also vital. Involvement with the troops to show personal caring has been the hallmark of most counterterrorist leaders.

Commitment can be found at the root of just about every evidence of genius. John Hayes and several other researchers have done in-depth studies of many famous professionals including artists, composers, chess champions and sports stars. Without exception, all of the virtuosos studied had worked at their professions for years. One researcher points to the discipline needed to attain the automaticity which frees one up to see perceptual patterns. Clearly, the master is beyond needing to consciously remember the fundamentals. Hayes quotes French writer Andre Gide as saying that art is a collaboration between God and the artist, and the less the artist does the better.

Hayes disagrees: "I've found that God does not apparently want to collaborate with anyone who hasn't worked hard for ten years." Commitment is a necessity. However, among a group of personally committed individuals, trust is not guaranteed. Personal commitment without trust in other team members is the source of many vicious power struggles within organizations. *Trust* is the fifth essential component of the successful implementation of strategy.

TRUST

Trust is an abused word—it is still being expected of us. But if it is not put into a framework of specific activities, the request for trust becomes manipulative. An effective formula, which my clients find very useful, illustrates the specific action components of trust:

$$\text{TRUST} = \frac{\begin{array}{l}\text{Opportunity to} \\ \text{assess others'} \\ \text{competence}\end{array} \times \begin{array}{l}\text{Ability to disclose} \\ \text{relevant facts}\end{array} \times \begin{array}{l}\text{Skills in conflict} \\ \text{management, and} \\ \text{feedback-seeking}\end{array} \times \text{Respect}}{\text{Risk}}$$

Before taking a closer look at these components, one should note the implications of their multiplicative relationship. Any one high, or low, element will rapidly strengthen, or weaken, trust, and a zero in any element in the numerator will reduce the whole to zero. In other words, trust needs skills to be developed—and can be easily destroyed.

The first element of the formula is the opportunity to assess competence. Today, task forces are increasingly popular organization-integrating vehicles which provide excellent opportunities for this assessment. Task forces, can, however, be more damaging than just about any other form of life—let alone the more complex matrix structures. In a case study involving eight people who were on a task force, discussions of the study resulted in each one of the eight names being suggested as the "person most to blame" for the problems. When task forces go wrong, everyone begins to look like an idiot, or worse, like a manipulative idiot. Task forces have a huge built-in structural instability because they demand that people establish new temporary lateral relationships and abandon years of behavioral training developed since early childhood. To accomplish this people need new training, and they need it before the job, not on the job. Many breakdowns of trust are both predictable and preventable. I no longer encourage consulting projects to incorporate task forces without a commitment from the client to ensure prior training of all participants.

Counterterrorists know this. On the beaches at San Diego, the naval trainees practice rock launches of dinghies, a classic example of providing the opportunity to assess others' competence *before* the heat is really on. Debriefing sessions are then used to deal with the next elements of the formula.

The ability to disclose relevant facts and feelings is so fundamental to trust that it is often ignored. Yet this is a key variable that we look for unconsciously in salespeople, friends, and family. A prime ingredient of successful negotiations is the mutual disclosure of relevant interests. Not only does this provide a greater pool of potential benefits for both parties, but it builds trust. It is not, however, without its problems. We tend to trust people less if they disclose inappropriately sensitive material early in a relationship. This can be a very subtle form of dependency-generating behavior, especially if it comes from a subordinate.

When something goes wrong in a group, as it always does, then conflict skills are necessary. The management of conflict requires some very clearly identifiable skills which can be learned. This package of essential skills includes assertiveness, or saying what one means in non-aggressive or non-defensive ways, and contracting and problem-solving, which involves finding mutual interests rather than mutual antagonisms. Without these skills we tend to fall back into our old, counterproductive ways of handling stress. The last element in the numerator is respect. The formula originally referred to "liking," but that is not really necessary—respect is the minimum necessary requirement. Trust can grow in an environment of professional respect that may be followed by personal respect, and finally by liking.

The entire formula rests on the risk in the denominator. Innovators destroy organizations; by its nature, innovation increases perceived risk. The true "idea generator" is a destroyer of the old organization, and is constantly raising risk levels. Effective managers of innovation need to work on the upper elements of the formula if trust is not to be eroded by an escalating, and accurate, perception of risk. Just as the beaches of California provide a low risk environment for months of daily naval training, the investment of time in lower risk team building allows for more experimentation with, and learning of the items in, the numerator of the trust formula.

COMMUNICATION

The sixth and final concept, communication, is in danger of becoming perhaps the greatest cliche of all. It is well known from the work of Henry Mintzberg and others that managers spend proportionately more of their time involved in pure communication as they rise in the organization. The problem here is that as they rise, the degree of organizational sheltering decreases, and these managers become increasingly exposed to the multitude of "stakeholders," those who have or who feel they have an interest in the organization, with whom they must now communicate. It is at this point that they are victims of the "wicked" problems discussed earlier, ones which are so heavily interconnected and complex that the communicator can be rendered ineffective. Thus, it is critical that key decision makers become managers of meaning. The manager must keep the grand image clearly in focus while communicating with the stakeholders. This means using all of the resources and vehicles of communication available to get the message—the strategy—across in a language the listener will understand. Counterterrorists understand well that communication must be in the language of one's own people, but not in the language of the competitors. Piet Hein's famous "Grooks" were produced as innocent poems to foil World War II occupation forces—they contained secret messages of optimism and subversion to those who could understand them.

The decision makers at Sperry Rand have focused on "listening skills" in an extensive long-range advertising campaign reflecting an important part of their overall strategic focus. To communicate this message they use dramatic graphics and implement it internally through in-house training. But they have created a double-edged sword. Heaven help a Sperry Rand manager who turns a customer off through not listening. Once the focus has been placed on communicating, the message had better be congruent and accurate all the way down the line.

The president of an engineering group in Eastern Canada was surprised when I criticized the new permanent lobby motif—a map of the world showing its extensive international experience. I had just worked through a strategy exercise with them where it was agreed they would be far more selective in future international work and would focus on Canadian resource-servicing. The real reason behind the display was that the vice-president of marketing enjoys travel and has a host of excellent "war stories" about overseas work that are inevitably triggered by the display. The problem was that key managers and clients were getting a mixed message. Regionalism was the strategy, but internationalism was in the lobby.

Rigid structures are threatened by change, and they do crumble. Although superficial militaristic analogies are not uncommon, I believe that the models presented by counter-terrorists offer a deeper pool of tested experience to corporate decision makers. For the first time in history, management will now have to focus on the formalized questioning and deliberate undermining of "smooth" operations. For the first time, assumptions about strategy long held by most decision makers will have to be challenged intelligently and systematically by the decision makers themselves before that challenge comes from their stakeholders and sabotages their organizations.

People are becoming more committed to the search for personal meaning. This is good news on a universal level, but it poses serious challenges as organizations become increasingly complex, more tied to their environments, and face mounting pressures to induce innovation resulting in further destabilization. Certainly there is no quick solution. But the six interlocking concepts outlined here do present some systematic and proven guiding fundamentals that can assist organizations in remaining relevant and effective in the face of these inevitable changes.

About the Author

David Cawood is the Director of the Mackenzie Institute, and Head of its Consulting Services Group. He is also a part-time professor in the Executive Programs Division of the University of British Columbia, Vancouver, Canada.

49

MANAGERIAL PRACTICES THAT ENHANCE INNOVATION

Andre L. Delbecq
Peter K. Mills

This article offers insight into how innovation is successfully accomplished by comparing the treatment of new ideas in high- and low-innovation organizations.

Innovation is widely held to be a vital component of a healthy organization. After all, it is innovation that enables an organization to respond to changing markets and thus retain its competitiveness.

The nature of innovation has been the focus of many studies during the past two decades, yet a reliable model for successful innovation has not emerged. This is due in part to the highly individual nature of the subject: Every innovation is by definition unique. For example, on the individual level, "cosmopolitans" (those with an orientation that goes beyond their organizations) and "locals" are early adopters of different kinds of innovations, according to Marshall Becker. Interestingly, Thomas Robertson and Yuram Wind found that those business units in which cosmopolitans and locals jointly make decisions are most likely to adopt innovations. Moreover, Walter Adams and Joel Dirlam found that relatively unsuccessful firms have been leaders with respect to some innovations. Michael Tushman noted that some effective innovating teams rely on "boundary spanners" to keep the other members informed, but other studies by Tushman and Robert Katz also found that teams relying on boundary spanners were less effective than when members kept themselves up-to-date and performed their own boundary-spanning activity. Finally, even the size of the organization, in studies done by Edwin Mansfield, could not be correlated with successful innovation.

In the midst of this theoretical confusion, useful lessons for the practicing manager are often lost. The purpose of this article is to offer insight into some basic characteristics of both high- and low-innovation organizations.

Over the past three years we have tested selected theses regarding innovation-enhancing practices with several hundred managers in high-technology firms and health-services organizations. At this point we have come to a reasonable consensus regarding some practical processes that managers can put into place in most organizations. These processes are the focus of this article.

We make no pretense that these processes are all a manager needs to know about innovation or that they serve as sole predictors of success or failure in innovation. They are, simply, actions that the managers in our sample of high-technology product-producing

Delbecq, Andre L. and Peter K. Mills, (1986), "Managerial Practices That Enhance Innovation," *Organizational Dynamics*, 14 (Summer), 24–34.

and service-providing organizations believe are within the capability of most managers to implement and that in both theory and practice help increase rates of successful innovation.

Before we begin, let us briefly define our terms. Innovation is a significant change within the organization or its line of services or products that (a) requires a substantial adjustment in functions and/or structures, and (b) is successfully introduced, decided upon, and incorporated into the organization. As such it differs from "incremental change" (involving minimal disruption, usually within current tradition) and "invention" (which might not become institutionalized).

PROCESS PHASES

The process of innovation in organizations is dependent on the interaction among three variables: the motivation to innovate, the obstacles against innovation, and the number of resources available to overcome or neutralize such obstacles. To make sense out of the innovation process, it is helpful to divide "innovation" into a sequence of phases based on Herbert Simon's model of decision making. Successful innovation usually follows a sequence such as the following:

- *Idea generation.* A preliminary concept of an innovation is developed by an advocate within the organization.
- *Preliminary analysis.* A preliminary feasibility study is undertaken to see whether the innovation is desirable, achievable, and advantageous for the organization.
- *Decision to adopt.* A formal decision is reached to commit resources to the innovation.
- *Implementation.* Over time, the innovation is institutionalized as a permanent change in the organization and/or its outputs.

This sequence of events varies in success stories. However, our purpose here is to be prescriptive, and since this outline is the "preferred" sequence in high-innovation organizations, we will follow it in presenting norms for structure and process. We will do so by describing how low-innovation and high-innovation organizations manage each phase; in the process we will present prescriptive norms for successful innovation.

During the past three years we asked several hundred managers to tell us a "success story," an innovation that they succeeded in incorporating into their organization, or a "failure story," an innovation they still felt was technically correct but that was not successfully introduced. Following their descriptions of successes and failures, we analyzed the processes that either were present and explained part of the success, or were absent but could have been implemented to prevent or mitigate failures. Thus the norms evolved out of dialogue, and while they are consistent with many research findings, they represent summary judgments rather than conventional data and have been generalized further for the purposes of this article.

PROCESS PHASE ONE: IDEA GENERATION AND INITIAL MANDATE

The ways in which ideas were acted upon in low- and high-innovation organizations were markedly different and reflected two very different structural contexts.

Low-Innovation Organizations

The process of idea generation and the manner in which the idea for innovation was initially pursued in low-innovation organizations are revealed in this typical failure story:

A professional or technical member of the organization sees an opportunity to combine a problem that clients or customers often complain about with a technical answer that he or she believes the organization could provide as a product or service. He or she presents the idea to the immediate supervisor, who is vaguely encouraging. Emotionally the employee feels the superior is supportive but cautious because of competing demands for resources. No special funds are available for innovation, but "maybe" a small amount of money can be scrimped together from the line budget. "Let me talk to the top brass," the supervisor says. Later, very modest funding is made available, but top-management support regarding the project is still vague. Because of the limited funds, the advocate and one or two colleagues attempt to develop the innovation largely by working overtime. Meanwhile, the advocate feels some anger when a pet idea of another colleague—perceived by the advocate as a closer friend of the manager—receives greater support. Further, he or she notices that management also finds line-budget funds for another recommendation—made by a powerful clique—that is less controversial and closer to company tradition.

In the eyes of the advocate, changing market conditions and customer requirements could have validated the legitimacy of the suggested innovation if he or she had received sufficient support. However, starved for resources and obliged to work on the innovation largely as "overload," he or she becomes discouraged and either lets the project fade for lack of attention, leaves the organization and develops the project as an entrepreneur, or joins a competitive organization in which the innovation is more likely to be favorably received.

The "failure stories" are filled with themes of ambivalent support, inadequate resources during the fragile, initial periods of development, constant efforts to "sell" and "justify" increased need for resources (with concomitant personal risk), infighting over resources, and decisions based on "political" connections as opposed to "unbiased" assessment of alternative recommendations for innovation. While belief and enthusiasm carry the advocate forward for a period of time, frustration, a sense of betrayal, and lack of sufficient funds will often lead to one of the withdrawal scenarios already described. Technical inadequacy is seldom the explanation given for project failure.

In summary, in low-innovation organizations:

- Sponsorship is obtained by seeking resources through line managers primarily responsible for supporting existing activities.
- Risks are assumed solely by the advocate; he or she must often accept under-resourcing, since permission and support depend on the patronage of managers who may see the request as "outside" normal budgets, or even as a nuisance.
- The degree of organizational support assigned to a project generally is perceived as based on the values and interests of a dominant coalition rather than on the objective merit of the project.
- Insufficient startup funds are allocated by squeezing token resources from line budgets and thus make innovation directly competitive with existing activities.
- Decisions on startups of innovations occur randomly as individuals "get ideas," whether or not the decision fits in with a planning cycle or the project is advantageous relative to other potential innovations.

[I]nnovation in organizations is dependent on the interaction among three variables: the motivation to innovate, the obstacles against innovation, and the number of resources available . . .

Incredible as it seems, this is the "managerial" context described by the majority of respondents to whom we talked about innovation in the average, complex organization.

High-Innovation Organizations

The stories in high-innovation organizations show the innovation advocates operating in an entirely different structural context. Individuals in these organizations indicated that special funds are set aside specifically to support innovation. Sometimes the fund is formally labeled "venture capital" or "research and development." Sometimes it is simply a discretionary fund. But money *is* available that is intended solely for the purpose of stimulating new activities. The money cannot be folded into line budgets. Further, the fund is earmarked for real *innovation*; changes *within tradition* are expected to be funded by line budgets.

In these organizations line managers are not the decision makers with whom the advocate deals. A special committee reviews proposals for innovations at regular intervals. The majority of these decision makers are individuals *not* responsible for current operations; they often are outside advisors and consultants. Sometimes innovation is relegated to a subcommittee of an external advisory group or board of directors. At other times, those in charge of innovation simply are a collection of organization "wise men." While line management is usually represented on the committee by one or two individuals, the dominant membership is not "vested," since they are not managers of existing operations.

The review group often spends considerable time doing its own environmental surveillance, and is particularly sensitive to new developments in the economy and the market, among competitors, and in new technological developments. The review body sees its mandate as the expenditure of venture funds in a manner responsive to new challenges in the aggregate environment, not only in support of proposals that strengthen existing operations. Its decisions are not perceived as token largesse to pay off creative individuals. Rather, the review group funds feasibility studies as "strategic decisions" signaling an organizational commitment to respond to changes in the environment. The review body does not pay for the self-serving projects of "prima donnas." By assigning one of its own members to work with the advocate and his or her project group in designing and carrying out a feasibility study, the committee guarantees that the study is an *organization* project—as opposed to Engineer Smith's or Dr. Jones's project.

The stories of managers from high-innovation organizations include references to "R&D" funds, venture capital, comparative proposal review, shared organizational sponsorship, and adequate funds for feasibility studies, as well as describe a clear point at which the feasibility-study group must report back to obtain a formal decision to implement.

In summary, the managerial process of high-innovation organizations in early stages of idea generation and approval is characterized by:

- Separate funds for innovation.
- Periodic reviews of informal proposals by a committee separate from line management.
- Clearly mandated feasibility studies with adequate funds.
- Project groups to undertake the feasibility studies that are enlarged to include one or more opinion leaders other than the advocate.

Not radical medicine, yet these practices are still absent from many contemporary organizations.

None of the above practices diminish the importance of the original advocate or his or her belief, motivation, or energy. Without the advocate—the primary ingredient—innovation seldom succeeds. But what these practices provide is adequate support and sponsorship so that a realistic feasibility study is possible without excessive overload, impoverished support, inadequate sponsorship, or excessive political sniping. These practices don't afford lavish support, but they do help achieve the support and sponsorship necessary to move creativity toward innovation.

Implementation of most of the above practices was within the power of the CEOs and division managers with whom we talked. In most organizations in which they were not in force, managers felt that these practices could be successfully introduced; that their absence was due simply to oversight rather than intrinsic organizational barriers. Most managers felt they could persuade their organizations to begin such practices if evidence of their value was available.

Finally, a word of caution. Innovation-enhancing practices in phase one should be kept relatively informal. Research, such as the work of Thomas Allen and Herbert Menzel, shows that informal interpersonal communication is a primary means of disseminating innovations and other important new ideas. The best proposals are four- to six-page "concept documents." The most effective processes are distinctly nonbureaucratic. Dialogue and shared judgment are at the core. Paperwork is minimal.

PROCESS PHASE TWO: FEASIBILITY STUDY TO DEFINE THE MARKET NEED AND EXPLORE POTENTIAL SOLUTIONS

The scope of a feasibility study makes all the difference in determining real customer needs and how those needs most adequately can be met.

Low-Innovation Organizations

The essential error made by low-innovation organizations when preparing a feasibility study is parochialism. For example, often the advocate—with one or two colleagues—will determine the demand for a new idea by speculating among themselves and adding only selective data that support their concept of the market. In effect, their feasibility study is largely an intellectual simulation, conducted behind closed doors and utilizing limited data.

Not surprisingly, the result of such feasibility studies often include these classic errors:

- Overestimation of demand, so that revenue expectations are entirely unrealistic.
- Underestimation of differences within the market, so that flexible designs with differentiated modifications desired by different consumers are not considered.
- Overly complex designs, attractive to the engineering sophisticate but intimidating to the uninitiated.
- Inadequate consideration of the orientation and training (and little or no consideration of the marketing) required to introduce the product to all but a small number of early adopters.

In effect, technical adequacy (if not superiority) is substituted for market analysis and client sensitivity.

High-Innovation Organizations

In high-innovation organizations, closeness to the average potential user is the key. In fact, the entire feasibility-study team lives with a sample of potential customers by making use of a variety of involvement techniques: field visits, focus groups, in-depth interviews, and so forth. Further, a large number of organizational "boundary spanners" not formally a part of the feasibility-study group (sales, technical service, management) are also queried in the product-definition phase. Almost all innovation success stories include radical redefinition of the product or service as a result of taking into account the "real world" of the average potential customer. Making the product or service the customer *really* wants (rather than the product or service the engineer *thinks* the customer wants) often calls for substantial conceptual reorientation by the feasibility-study team.

Similarly, cosmopolitanism is brought to bear on the "solution" contained in the proposed product or service. Since the innovation is "new" to the organization, successful feasibility-study teams reach deeply for ideas from noncompetitive companies in related fields, study previous design successes and failures, and talk with a broad sample of creative thinkers, both within and outside their own company, who are not part of the feasibility-study team. In a word, "search behavior," as Herbert Simon would label it, substitutes for creative speculation. Transferable lessons are less costly than reinventing the wheel.

In summary, feasibility studies in high-innovation organizations include:

- Extensive and intensive interaction with clients and organizational boundary spanners, which often result in a reconceptualization of the product or service.
- Contacts within and outside the firm that help the study team incorporate a flexible core design that can (over time) permit variable models to appeal to

variable client groupings, and realistically approximate production costs based on the experience of others who produced related products or services.

All of this might seem to be a simple extrapolation of a basic marketing orientation. One must remember, however, that the individuals involved in product development are often not from marketing. The key is to structure a feasibility study that brings the design team as close to market realities as a key marketing person might be. Successful managers of innovation guide the feasibility study group through a "real world" exposure and sensitization process, which inevitably results in a reconceptualization of both the product and real customer wants and the design and manufacturing requirements—based on the insight and experience of individuals outside the design team.

PROCESS PHASE THREE: DECISION TO ADOPT

It would seem that this third phase is the simplest. The group completing the feasibility study presents a proposal to management based on the study and gets a "go" or "no go" decision. In fact, this phase is subject to the greatest number of stumbling blocks.

Low-Innovation Organizations

Below is a list of just some of the adoption problems found in low-innovation organizations:

- The advocate is isolated from the feasibility-study group and is forced to negotiate one-on-one with a single superior. This creates a situation in which power and personality rather than the data from the feasibility study, determine the resources allocated to the project.
- The advocate receives no formal commitment from the organization. Tentative permission to proceed is given, with equally tentative resource allocations that may be withdrawn later as new resource or political pressures emerge. Normally the advocate leaves the organization under these conditions.
- The go-ahead is given without clearance of the necessary resources. The project withers from insufficient support.
- The advocate is inflexible in negotiation, insisting on the "rightness" of the feasibility study. Since no modifications are negotiated, the project is vetoed even though most people feel the core idea is correct.
- A powerful critic becomes an outspoken "gunslinger," and management backs off support, even though the critic does not represent a majority opinion among reviewers.
- The proposal stalls in committee until people lose interest or the window of opportunity closes.

High-Innovation Organizations

In high-innovation organizations, the results of the feasibility study are first reviewed informally but always are followed up with a formal decision. Thus an opportunity exists for early dialogue, with time and support for building modifications into the proposal to increase potential for organizational acceptance. This interactive review process is neither a one-shot, "go" or "no go" review of a final proposal nor an endless review process. It is normally a one- to three-meeting sequence.

The reviewers' role is to help make proposals more feasible and not an opportunity to play critic. Reviewers have an obligation to see to fruition a number of proposals so that the overall innovation effort is not stultified.

Since consensus is rare, some formal voting mechanism (such as ratings, rankings, or gradings) is used to aggregate the review committee's judgment. No single reviewer, as a minority critic, can veto any project. He or she, however, can simply register a dissenting—but not necessarily overriding—opinion.

Advocates from the feasibility-study group expect to incorporate modifications and do not demand that the "purity" of the original proposal be maintained. Mutual adjustment rather than hard bargaining among study group members is the norm. These adjustment decisions are arrived at through group dialogue (both the reviewer group and advocate group are involved) to avoid petty personality conflicts and power games.

Projects that need more than minimum resources to be done well are not put on "starvation diets" that doom them to a slow death. A critical mass of human and financial support is essential to success. Projects are reviewed periodically within a common time frame to allow for quality comparisons.

The decision to adopt moves the proposal forward with a clear organizational commitment to the implementation design and makes the risk an organizational one. The advocate does not carry the entire burden of possible failure on his or her shoulders. Should the results of implementation be disappointing, the advocate is not used as a scapegoat. The project was, after all, a shared organizational judgment. Indeed, in excellent companies good humor and reassignment with full dignity follow the failure of risky projects.

PROCESS PHASE FOUR: IMPLEMENTATION

One might think that at this stage implementation is automatic. After all, hasn't the feasibility study and design provided an action plan ready to be carried out? Of course, it is not that simple.

Low-Innovation Organizations

Two reasons cited for failure in the stories from low-innovation organizations are under-resourcing (which we have already addressed) and its opposite: trying an immediate, large-scale, direct implementation.

Projects that need more than minimum resources to be done well are not put on "starvation diets" that doom them to a slow death. A critical mass of human and financial support is essential to success.

This error is not organizational hesitance. Rather, it is a delusion of grandeur: "Let's implement directly, immediately, and on a large scale. Let's commit a great amount of resources to assure success." Unfortunately, the assumption of predictability upon which a direct implementation is based is almost always a fantasy. When the inevitable glitches occur, or when performance is unfavorable, the error is compounded as the organization throws more money at the problem to save face, even in light of negative evaluation feedback.

This tendency to rush in prematurely with direct, large-scale implementation efforts seems to be the result of a strong psychological urge to remove the cognitive dissonance associated with risk taking. It turns out to be exactly the wrong strategy most of the time and doubles the tendency for later scapegoating, since a great amount of resources were squandered before adequate feasibility data were obtained.

High-Innovation Organizations

High-innovation organizations, by contrast, begin with a small, controlled pilot study conducted by early adopters. The enthusiasm of early adopters (who often are advocates) allows them to be patient with glitches and to contribute to as well as support the necessary product modifications and organizational adaptation needed for new innovations. In the worst possible scenario—a test that proves to be a failure—a small pilot study permits the organization to withdraw the innovation with little loss of either face or resources, since commitment is limited in a pilot. In other words, pilot studies help maintain the attitude that the initial implementation is clearly experimental and the results will require further modifications before direct, large-scale implementation can occur.

Even where the results are favorable, considerable qualification must occur during the pilot as a prelude to later large-scale implementation. For example, in a small-scale pilot:

- The product or service is "debugged" in the supportive atmosphere of early adoptors who want the innovation to succeed, are patient with trial-and-error learning, and assist in problem solving to work out glitches.
- The types of training materials, support services, instructional manuals, and so forth, that will be needed become clear. Time is available to develop these materials for customers. Further, service manuals can be prepared to specify practices necessary to deal with weaker or more eccentric aspects of even a good first-generation product or service. Modifications are made to make the product or service more "user friendly."
- Experimentation leads to variations in design that can be offered in later product generations and will enlarge the range of options available to different users, thus enlarging the potential market.
- Estimates of service and assistance requirements develop so that maintenance and service cost estimates will be realistic.

The pilot allows for organizational adaptation and market research, which support later technological transfer and broadscale marketing. It is always difficult to find the golden mean between adequate testing time and organizational adaptation and lost market opportunity. However, only one change is given to make a first impression; rushing in with a poorly performing product and inadequate support for customer orientation, maintenance, and service may prove deadly.

SUMMARY

In high-innovation organizations, special funds earmarked for research and development are used to support experimental activities. A special committee accepts or rejects an innovator's proposal and undertakes a feasibility study. The feasibility-study team uses a marketing orientation to determine if a real customer need exists and how it may best be met. By the time a proposal reaches the adoption stage, the advocate's original idea has been modified by input from study-group members. The project is given an adequate funding level and is monitored and audited on a regular basis. Finally, implementation takes place first on a small scale so that, in the event of failure, a minimum amount of resources will be lost.

Essentially, successful innovation depends on a company's willingness to commit the necessary time, money, and leadership to research and development. In the simplest terms, the difference between high- and low-innovation organizations is that the latter are willing to follow up and follow through on behalf of new ideas.

About the Authors

Andre L. Delbecq is dean of the Leavey School of Business and Administration at the University of Santa Clara, in California. He received his B.B.A. cum laude from the University of Toledo and earned his M.B.A. and doctorate from Indiana University.

For a number of years his research has focused on three topics: managerial decision-making techniques for strategic planning, the development of new products and technologies, and organizational design for facilitating innovation. He is the author of the Nominal Group Technique and the Program Planning Model, both of which have been widely adopted for facilitating decision making and planning.

Delbecq is currently involved in studies of innovation in the high-technology industries in Silicon Valley. He sits on several corporate boards and is chairman of the board of directors of Nutech, a nuclear engineering services company in San Jose. He has served on the Board of Governors and as chairman of the Public Management Division and the Organization and Management Theory Division of the Academy of Management and currently chairs the Managerial Consultation Division. He has been elected fellow of the Academy in recognition of his outstanding contributions in research, scholarship, and service.

Peter K. Mills is an assistant professor in the Leavey School of Business and Administration at the University of Santa Clara, in California. He received his doctorate from the University of California at Irvine.

Mills' research interests are the design of service organizations, the pricing of power in organizations, and innovation.

Selected Bibliography

Two classics deal with innovation as a process. The first is the major work by Everett Rogers titled *Diffusion of Innovations* (Free Press at Glencoe, 1962). Two decades have passed since its publication, but this book still offers the most lucid portrayal of innovation as a phased change that occurs over time. On the organizational side, Gerald Zaltman et al.'s book titled *Innovations in Organizations* (John Wiley & Sons, 1973) gives particular attention to the relationship between management structure and the change process. This is our favorite source book for understanding the interplay between structure and process—or phases in innovation.

The following sources deal with organizational factors in innovation: "Innovation, Integration, and Marginality: A Survey of Physicians" (*American Sociological Review,* October 1960), by Herbert Menzel; "The Speed of Response of Firms to New Techniques," (*Quarterly Journal of Economics,* May 1963), by Edwin Mansfield; and "Big Steel, Invention, and Innovation" (*Quarterly Journal of Economics,* May 1966), by Walter Adams and Joel Dirlam.

Examples of studies that have further explored the idea of cosmopolitanism in innovation are "Sociometric Location and Innovativeness: Reformulation and Extension of the Diffusion Model" (*American Sociological Review,* April 1970), by Marshall Becker; "Hospital Adoption of Innovation: The Role of Integration into External Informational Environments" (*Journal of Health and Social Behavior,* April 1978), by John Kimberly; "Organizational Cosmopolitanism and Innovativeness" (*Academy of Management Journal,* June 1983), by Thomas Robertson and Yuram Wind; and "A Contingent Approach to Strategy and Tactics in Project Planning" (*American Planning Association Journal,* April 1979), by John Bryson and Andre Delbecq.

Two important studies on information processing and innovation are "External Communication and Project Performance: An Investigation into the Role of Gatekeepers" (*Management Science,* November 1980), by Michael Tushman and Robert Katz; "Communication Across Organizational Boundaries: Special Boundary Roles in the Innovation Process" (*Administrative Science Quarterly,* December 1977), by Michael Tushman; and *Managing the Flow of Technology* (MIT Press, 1977), by Thomas Allen.

Finally, *The New Science of Management Decision* (Harper & Row, 1960), by Herbert Simon and "Determinants of Innovation in Organizations" (*American Political Science Review,* March 1969), by Lawrence Mohr are pertinent works on decision making and innovation.

50

STRATEGIC PARTNERING FOR DEVELOPING NEW PRODUCTS

A Four-Stage Process Can Help Management Answer the Questions It Must Answer When Forming Partnerships to Develop New Products

Murray R. Millson, S. P. Raj and David Wilemon

OVERVIEW

New product development (NPD) is becoming increasingly complex and costly. One consequence of this is that more companies are using various partnering arrangements to accomplish their innovative goals. This article presents a process that can impact the important decisions relating to the successful development of new products by partners. NPD partnering is not a discrete event but a maturation process involving several stages including awareness, exploration, commitment, and dissolution. Issues that require consideration during this partnering process include identifying both the originating firm's needs and the partner's needs, understanding the likely consequences of the relative size and capabilities of partners, and selecting the appropriate alliance strategy.

The study of new product development (NPD) typically focuses on activities *within* a single firm. Important exceptions include the work done by Urban and von Hippel in which they discuss employing new product ideas developed by customers as "lead users" (1) and the examination of large-scale R&D projects performed by consortia (2). In the last few years there has been a proliferation of various kinds of cooperative arrangements which has generated a heightened interest in partnering by managers and scholars (3,4). Many terms are used to describe cooperative activity between two or more firms, but we use the general term "NPD alliance" to indicate any form of formal or informal cooperative arrangement related to the joint development and commercialization of new products.

Millson, Murray R., S. P. Raj, and David Wilemon, "Strategic Partnering for Developing New Products," *Research Technology Management*, vol. 39, no. 2, 1996, pp. 41–49.

The literature identifies several pressing NPD problems (5,6,7). Among the most important ones: 1) many firms lack the resources to develop needed new products; 2) the increased reliance on corporate mergers and acquisitions to obtain growth via new products often creates problems of "fit"; 3) many firms neglect or perform important NPD activities poorly; and 4) even though innovative new products are identified by customers, suppliers and other outside organizations, such new product information is not heeded. We contend that these and other NPD problems are often amenable to partnering solutions.

With innovation so important to most firms' survival (8), why don't some firms pursue new product development more actively? One explanation is that these firms lack the resources or personnel to carry out NPD activities. Although firms in this situation understand that they have significant NPD deficiencies, they may lack either the knowledge, capabilities and/or the desire to pursue corrective measures.

Another problem relates to those firms that recognize they have NPD deficiencies and attempt to "buy" their way into a new product arena. Such firms appear to either desire a great deal of control over their NPD efforts or do not recognize alternative NPD options (e.g., partnering). Therefore, to enter a market with a new product, these companies choose either to merge with other organizations that are developing new products or to acquire other companies that have recently launched new products. These actions can solve NPD problems but they often create additional, more severe, challenges related to integrating new personnel, handling financial burdens, and redundant functional departments.

A third NPD problem relates to firms that develop new products internally but ignore or poorly perform particular activities in their nominally sophisticated NPD processes. These firms either do not possess the requisite skills to achieve a high level of proficiency in certain NPD tasks or else they are rushed by competitive pressures to speed up their NPD processes. In either case, these firms jeopardize their new product's success because "a more complete new product process appears to make a difference" (6).

An additional NPD problem is that many firms either do not develop new products or develop them poorly because they do not utilize important information and resources offered by external organizations such as customers and suppliers. These firms may not be aware that customers, suppliers and other firms are potential partners that can contribute to their NPD goals.

We suggest that these four NPD challenges can be either fully or partially resolved by implementing NPD alliances.

A MATURATION PROCESS FOR NPD PARTNERING

As noted by Slowinski et al, NPD partnering is a process and not a discrete event (9). This section presents a methodology which can be followed to develop NPD partnering relationships. The development of new products with partners is modeled as a relationship creation process. Building on the earlier work of Dwyer, Schurr and Oh we depict in Figure 50-1 a partnering process consisting of four major stages: awareness, exploration, commitment, and dissolution (10). We posit that developing successful new products with partners usually follows such a maturation process.

First, new product developers often become aware of other firms' competencies as they identify their own weaknesses in relation to their strengths. Management closely and objectively scrutinizes in-house NPD capabilities during the *awareness* stage. For example, firms may have a technology competence but lack market access for new product or process technologies. This awareness can create a desire for additional information. First interested in developing new products are actively searching for complementary resources during this stage; e.g., technology, market access, capital, manufacturing, etc.

Second, awareness of a potential partner's competencies is a by-product of an accurate understanding of one's own limitations. Questions that can be asked

FIGURE 50-1 A New Product Development (NPD) Alliance Formation Process Can Be Used as the Basis for Determining Answers to Important Partnering Questions.

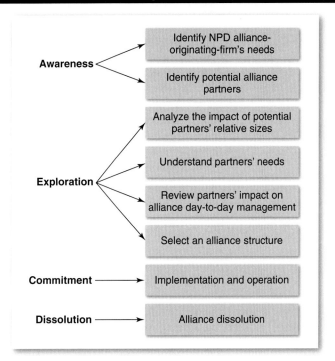

include: Can another firm's competence provide an important advantage? Are another firm's capabilities applicable to the proposed product line or markets? Advertising in trade publications, exhibits at trade shows, and word-of-mouth information in the industry all provide useful insights into a potential partner's resources. Firms desiring to form NPD partnerships can obtain additional information indirectly from a potential partner's suppliers, customers and competitors or by contacting the firm directly.

As the potential NPD partners begin to examine their potential fit, the process enters the *exploration* stage. It is here that critical issues such as power, control and trust are initially confronted. Also, each partner begins to determine whether the prospective bond will foster a "win-win" outcome for both firms. At this time, partnering firms also create the internal and mutual justifications and the plans required to move joint NPD programs forward.

Dwyer et al portray trust as ". . . an important concept in understanding expectations for cooperation and planning . . . " (10, p. 18). They imply that uncertainty is the major source of concern in these situations. In situations where trust is poised against risk, it is often difficult to provide a suitable environment for partnerships. Dealing with uncertainty and promoting trust requires careful, mindful negotiation. A degree of faith may be required if no information is available on which to base trust, since trust builds on fulfilled expectations. We suggest that NPD partners move through the exploratory stage slowly, while sharing ideas, removing uncertainty and gaining trust through observed behavior.

Exploration also is the stage in which considerable testing and evaluation of potential partners occurs. This stage provides time for additional information gathering and evaluation as the firms become more familiar with the resources each is willing to provide to an NPD program.

An initial new product development project proposal is presented to a potential partner as the final step of the exploration stage. As a rule, trust is building and uncertainty and risk are decreasing during this stage. Partners can reap important NPD benefits from the information obtained during this stage, even if the initial set of potential partners scrutinized does not fulfill the needs identified during the awareness stage.

The third stage in the NPD relationship development process is *commitment*. Here two or more firms become contractual partners. This stage also entails the operation and management of an alliance. The NPD process can accelerate considerably at this time. With much of the relationship uncertainty removed, and each firm's technical competence assessed, there is enough information to develop a contract. At this stage, the partners continue to search for additional ways to utilize each other's resources, in addition to assessing their partner's behavior. An important difference between this stage and the exploration stage in a healthy alliance is the increased degree of trust and confidence based on fulfilled expectations. Improved trust can provide the basis for further and more extensive risk-taking, which can benefit both partners (10).

It is during the commitment stage that partners reach a degree of satisfaction with the performance of their relationship that virtually excludes other partners that could have provided similar resources. The immense cost of switching partners encourages partners to remain in the relationship. In other words, it would take an extremely "good deal" for one member to dissolve the partnership to obtain equivalent rewards.

Dissolution is the final stage in this NPD partnering process. Much has been written concerning the rapidly changing environments of most companies (11). This suggests that many unforeseen circumstances can arise to radically change the requirements and plans of the most well-intentioned partnering firms. Without clear, well-planned, documented agreements, unanticipated consequences can be devastating—especially for the weaker alliance member.

> **NPD partnering is a process and not a discrete event.**

Some firms may pursue their individual goals so rapidly that a trusting relationship is never realized. Other firms may move too fast in entering a partner's market, or some firms may push too hard to incorporate another's technology. The urgency with which firms pursue their individual goals (opportunism) can limit the degree of trust that is developed. A lack of communication or distorted communication between partners also can hinder the development of trust.

We advocate careful deliberation and in-depth NPD process understanding during the early NPD stages. During these initial stages, partners can agree on a well-thought-out, documented plan that embraces each partner's goals and methods for mutual new product development. Such a plan can be made for a reasonable length of time and then renewed, contingent upon the level of trust and progress toward the goals of the partnership (12). Although Borys and Jemison point out that contracts are more inflexible and less encompassing than purely "trusting" relationships (13), the NPD process governance contract does eliminate some uncertainty in addition to its potential speed and ease of implementation.

Written agreements can provide clear direction for NPD programs and describe such factors as: the needs of the participating firms, the alliance structure, ongoing alliance management practices, and the conditions and process for alliance dissolution. Often the most difficult part of a written agreement is stipulating how and when such partnerships will be dissolved. Like a marriage, "the couple" does not typically want to consider "breaking up" when they are on the threshold of a potentially exciting beginning and are attempting to build trust and commitment. In fact, the termination of a partnership may be likened to a divorce and can represent a powerful and emotional situation even when the dissolution is planned (10).

The dissolution of an NPD partnership is more than likely to be initiated by one of the firms in the partnership whereas it took two (or more) firms to create the partnership. Depending upon contract stipulations, dissolution can be short or long and can be painful for all partners. Unplanned and unilaterally driven partnership dissolutions are more likely to be "lose-lose" situations. Even the opportunistic partner that desires to dissolve the partnership in order to pursue other opportunities can encounter misfortune. When a firm dissolves an NPD relationship unilaterally, the dissolution may be perceived by a new partner as evidence of untrustworthy behavior. Firms that plan for the long term and initially develop NPD relationships cautiously are more likely to avoid such devastating situations.

QUESTIONS TO BE ADDRESSED

Several questions need to be addressed during the awareness and exploration stages and *prior* to formal negotiations. The central question a firm needs to answer is: What benefits will we gain from partnering with another firm? Other questions that require attention are:

- What are the needs of NPD alliance partners?
- What are the benefits and costs of an alliance involving new product technology or new market access?
- What types of alliances will yield both the flexibility and control needed to facilitate the development of desired new products?
- What are the important issues that need to be documented and verified when developing new products, markets or technologies, especially as they relate to the eventual dissolution of alliance arrangements?
- What would be the relative size (power) of the allied firms? What are the implications of these relative sizes to alliances created to engage in NPD efforts?

Figure 50-2 presents several factors that impact NPD success through alliances (14,6). The classification displayed in Figure 50-3 identifies a range of the most likely alliance partners. Some NPD needs can be better fulfilled by one type of partner than another. The outcome of this decision depends on the resources sought by a firm from NPD partners and the deficiencies it has with its own NPD process.

FIGURE 50-2 Among the Many Factors That Influence the Success of NPD Alliances, the Most Important Involves the Explicit Definition of the Benefits an NPD Partnering Firm Will Obtain from an Alliance.

FIGURE 50-3 The Selection of NPD Alliance Partners Is an Important Step in the New Product Alliance Formation Process. Particular Types of Partners can Complement a Firm's Major NPD Capabilities.

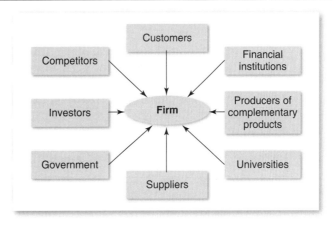

ASCERTAINING THE "NEED" TO ALIGN

NPD alliance objectives need to be congruent with a firm's mission, strategies and innovation objectives. A clear definition of need is the single most important activity that senior management undertakes during the formation of an NPD alliance. This definition provides clear roles for the partners and clarifies the purpose of a new product program. This can minimize destructive conflicts between partners and provide a means for measuring a new product's success. Such "needs" definition requires more communication and integration than NPD processes within most individual organizations.

A firm should have an NPD need or problem and be searching for a solution (which may be an alliance with another firm) rather than have a solution (a business alliance) searching for a need or a "problem" with the NPD process. One reason alliances fail is the lack of careful, mindful analysis of the ramifications of partnering *before* an alliance is formed (15). Moreover, as Kanter warns:

> . . . select only those relationships that are sufficiently important that they
> will be entered into with full commitment and with the willingness to invest
> the resources and make the internal changes that successful external
> partnerships entail—the sharing of information, the linking of systems, and
> the establishment of agreements for governing the partnership. (16, p. 349)

Anderson and Narus point out that firms contemplating cooperative relationships should segment potential partners into groups (17). NPD partners can be segmented by the value of the resources or skills that can fulfill a new product developing firm's need(s). These needs can involve material supply, distribution channel development, cost reduction, image enhancement, process technology, and various other innovation needs.

In addition, firms should focus primarily on NPD alliances that support their primary field(s) of expertise. This assures that a firm will enter an alliance with an identifiable strength, not solely attempting to overcome a weakness. Such a warning coincides with the emphasis that many firms are placing on their core businesses (18). This message is particularly important for firms that tend to generate and pursue ideas or innovations outside the bounds of their core expertise.

Firms that form alliances to fulfill common goals are more likely to succeed. When a successful new product represents a joint goal, neither alliance partner "wins" unless the *overall* NPD process is successful. Alliances based on complementary needs can be particularly successful because each firm knows that the other offers something of value. For example, a firm that controls distribution channels can move a partner's newly developed product to market more rapidly than the firm that developed the new product but has no distribution network. The superordinate goal of successful new product commercialization can provide a powerful focus for such an alliance.

IDENTIFYING POTENTIAL PARTNERS

An NPD partner can be selected after the new product-developing firm clearly determines its specific needs. As partners with different expertise can fulfill particular NPD requirements better than others, firms planning NPD alliances need to be keenly aware of prospective partners' resources, motives, competencies, and weaknesses. Managers considering NPD partnerships also should assess such attributes of potential partners as: the relative size of the firms in terms of physical factors (capital, employees, geography, physical assets); technological factors (product lines, process capabilities, patents, R&D); marketing factors (distribution, customer knowledge, and image); existing alliances (with competitors, customers, or suppliers or raw materials, ideas, or capital); and similarities and differences in corporate cultures. Brockhoff notes that a partner's experience in cooperative relationships can reduce transaction costs in an alliance and that reduced transaction costs are highly correlated with success (19).

Three important resources usually sought by firms during new product development are capital, technology, and/or market access. In general, organizations represented by the classifications depicted in Figure 50-3 do not have equal access to these resources. Financial institutions, investors and government agencies are typically sources of capital, although in some instances customers, suppliers or the providers of complementary products may be motivated to invest in particular NPD projects.

> *A clear definition of need is the single most important activity that senior management undertakes during NPD alliance formation.*

Sources of technology are typically universities, suppliers, channel members, and even competitors. In addition, Urban and von Hippel encourage firms to look to certain "lead" customers for new ideas and technologies (1). An unlikely source of new technology can be a firm's competitors, as in the alliances involving Texas Instruments and Hitachi (20) and General Motors and Toyota (21). Interestingly, firms that compete in one market may become vibrant partners in non-competitive arenas. Competitors, for example, can provide technologies that are required for NPD efforts but are unrelated to other product categories that form the basis for competition between the two firms.

A third important need that encourages firms to engage in NPD alliances is market access. Partners that typically fulfill this need are customers, suppliers, channel members, firms producing complementary products, and competitors. A potential choice in this situation is a member of a currently functioning marketing channel.

Here is an example of an alliance in which the firms had their needs and core businesses well in focus and fulfilled their objectives through a joint venture: General Electric and Ford worked together to produce an improved generation of automotive lighting devices. Both companies gained from their investment in this endeavor. GE received a new product, the arc discharge automotive lamp, while Ford obtained vehicles with greater fuel economy. This benefit was based upon the increased aerodynamic designs attained from the compactness and the reduced heat generation of the new lighting design (22).

An activity closely associated with needs definition is "needs communication." If the management of one firm identifies needs but does not communicate them to an alliance partner, expectations are missed and problems occur. These problems can be exaggerated when the sizes of the firms are asymmetric.

ANALYZING THE IMPACT OF RELATIVE SIZE

Schwadel describes a new product joint venture involving IBM and Sears that experienced many difficulties early in their NPD process due to "glitches" in the software that controlled a video communications process (23). If one of these firms had been small, it might have been unable to withstand such difficulties or the financial pressures involved. Schwadel points out, "The venture is a high-risk proposition, even for companies with pockets as deep as IBM's and Sears's" (p. B4). This example demonstrates an alliance in which both partners worked through difficult times largely due to their financial staying power. This illustration also suggests that alliances formed between firms of approximately equal size, especially when both are large, are more likely to succeed. When firms are asymmetric, a larger firm can typically take greater risks than a smaller firm can afford. Needs definition and contractual agreements involving alliances between asymmetrically-sized firms are, therefore, even more important than in cases involving symmetrically-sized firms.

UNDERSTANDING POTENTIAL PARTNERS' NEEDS

The determination of the specific needs of partners is one of the most difficult alliance formation challenges. Success in ascertaining these needs is predicated on: (1) senior management's diligence; (2) interfirm openness; and (3) realistic needs definition. In spite of such difficulties, it is important to recognize a potential partner's needs *prior* to creating an NPD alliance. Full recognition and understanding can foster early planning activities and alleviate tension throughout the relationship. As Anderson and Narus state, ". . . collaborative relations prosper as long as the supplier firm and customer firm each have significant and roughly the same dependence upon the relationship" (17).

As an example, many alliances between Japanese companies and small American firms during the last decade were formed in response to Japan's need to access U.S. markets and avoid U.S. protectionist measures. The American firms participating in these ventures also had needs, including financing and foreign market access, that made these relationships viable (24).

Some firms that are "technology-rich" but lack market access often trade their technology for access to channels of distribution, only to find that technology is transferred more rapidly than market capability. This is exemplified by cases in which American firms offered technology and Japanese firms offered market access. Often, Japanese firms achieved technological competence before American firms gained competence with the Japanese channel structure. Situations such as these also can occur between technology-rich and market-rich firms within the U.S. These examples point out that technology-based firms need to construct their alliances judiciously so that they are assured equitable returns on their alliance investment.

Firms that form alliances to fulfill common goals are more likely to succeed.

For the firm seeking to accurately understand a partner, the following suggestions are offered.

1. Liaison personnel assigned to integrate the partner and its management must "listen" closely to ascertain the partner's real needs and intent. Rather than making assumptions, it is necessary to probe for understanding when communication is not clear.
2. Demonstrate the behavior desired from a partner. Refrain from testing one's partner, which can lead to suspicion and loss of trust. It is also important to be explicit regarding what can and cannot be discussed, e.g., proprietary product or process technology.
3. Make intentions known before acting. Fulfilled expectations lead to greater trust and openness.
4. Finally, create goals that encompass and integrate the objectives of all partners. Such behavior provides the "glue" that holds an alliance together.

REVIEWING IMPACT ON ALLIANCE MANAGEMENT

Implementation of an NPD project that results from alliance planning is very important (25). There are a number of issues that can have a significant impact on the success of an NPD alliance that are difficult, if not impossible, to stipulate in contracts or to scrutinize during needs analysis. Some of the more important ones involve integrating managerial and technology-based systems, accommodating different business cultures, developing conflict management processes, and managing dysfunctional political activities.

Specific interpersonal issues are difficult to forecast during the early NPD alliance planning stages; partnering firms need to foster mutual trust so that dysfunctional events can be managed without jeopardizing the success of the alliance. Investigating, negotiating and problem-solving are important personal skills required of liaison and management personnel involved in forming NPD alliances. Investigation skills are necessary primarily during the awareness and exploration stages to ascertain an alliance-originating firm's needs, identify potential partners with appropriate skills and resources, and determine the probable needs of partners. Negotiating, which requires effective listening and speaking, is particularly important during the exploration stage prior to formal commitment. But negotiating is also needed during the commitment stage to ensure a win-win outcome when differences and conflicts occur that were not anticipated during the operation and management of the partnership. Finally, problem-solving skills are especially useful during the commitment stage. And problem solving can be a focal skill during dissolution if the division of non-contractual and intellectual property becomes an issue.

SELECTING AN ALLIANCE STRUCTURE

Figure 50-4 identifies end points of a spectrum of partnership forms and is based on the amount of equity invested by the partners in the NPD alliance (26,27,16). As one partner's equity increases, that partner's control over alliance operations typically increases while the structural flexibility of the alliance is likely to decrease.

To further illuminate the major characteristics of NPD alliances, we now describe four major alliance strategies:

1. *Mergers and Acquisitions.* —Full equity ownership is an organizational construct accomplished through such actions as mergers and acquisitions to acquire promising new technologies, new product developments or market access. The result is organizations that are wholly-owned entities and are not typically employed solely to develop new products (13). Therefore, we do not consider mergers and acquisitions as belonging to our NPD partnering typology.

2. *Joint Ventures.* —The alliance organizational structure that Harrigan describes as partial equity ownership includes joint ventures (26,4,27). Schillaci defines a joint venture as follows:

> In the broadest sense, a joint venture is a cooperative business agreement between two or more firms that want to achieve similar objectives. This agreement usually involves the creation of a new corporate entity to satisfy the mutual needs of all parties involved (15, p. 60).

The creation of a third firm to implement the joint venture plan is usually a major difference between NPD joint ventures and other alliance structures (26,27). Joint NPD ventures are typically entered into in order to foster long-term business relationships. This type of alliance is more like a marriage in that there is a building and accumulating of community property.

Harrigan indicates, however, that the NPD joint venture is often an unstable organizational form (26,27). These hybrid organizations tend to be unstable because even though partners initially desire long-term relationships, one partner is likely to buy out the interests of the other partner(s). Killing points out that 30 to 40 percent of all joint ventures fail (28). He notes that many of these failures are due to a lack of trust among personnel provided by the initiating firms to staff the NPD joint venture.

Kanter also likens joint ventures to opportunistic alliances and states that, ". . . partners get from each other a competence that will allow them to move more

FIGURE 50-4 Partners Selecting a Structure for an NPD Alliance Can Benefit by Investigating the Amount of Control, Organizational Flexibility, and Equity Investment Required by Each Partner.

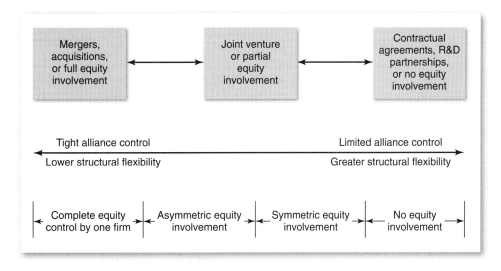

quickly toward their own business goals" (2, p. 185). She warns that, ". . . once one of the partners has gained experience with the competence of the other, the alliance is vulnerable to dissolution . . ." (p. 185). Her warning suggests that potential partners should be mindful of the competencies they offer in NPD alliances. On a more positive note, Harrigan's analyses indicate that joint ventures can indeed be beneficial to those firms willing to invest the time and effort in their operation (26,27). Thus, it is important for managers to clearly understand how joint ventures can help their firms fulfill mutual NPD needs.

We have noted that joint venture alliances can be beneficial to firms that invest time and effort in their operation; but NPD joint ventures that stimulate the creation of a third firm may be more likely to fail, due to the dilution of effort between new product development and new firm formation. The creation of a new organizational structure, business strategy and administrative procedures, in addition to the development of a new product, can be a considerable, even overwhelming, challenge for some firms.

Refrain from testing one's partner, which can lead to suspicion and loss of trust.

Because a joint venture entails the formation of a third firm, it can be a viable alternative in many NPD situations. We suggest that most firms interested in new product development initially begin their joint venture relationships with a no-equity arrangement. Such an arrangement can allow partnering firms to move slowly while gaining trust since low joint investment implies reduced financial risks.

3. *Consortia.* —The consortium organizational structure is more often used in large, complex, multidisciplinary research programs such as the MIT–AT&T–IBM superconductor consortium (29), the Microelectronics and Computer Technology Corporation (30), Bellcore (31), and Sematech (32), than in the traditional development of new products. These research programs typically focus on the development of significant new product and/or process technologies. The longevity of consortia alliances typically is based on the duration of a particular research program. When such a program concludes, the technological benefits derived are retained and employed by the individual participants in the consortia.

Consortia are typically formed when substantial monetary investments need to be made and inordinate risks must be taken (2). The consortium alliance structure is often used to minimize the risk of any one participant, to accumulate needed capital, and to acquire human, technological and physical resources. Due to the somewhat temporary nature of consortia, there usually is little mutual buildup of, or investment in, community assets to be used in the actual production of new products compared to joint ventures. Additionally, there may be a limited resource commitment by member firms. The Microelectronics and Computer Technology Corporation initially intended to staff the consortium with employees from the constituent firms (33), yet after six years of operation, only 15 percent of the employees were "on loan" from member firms. With the loosening of U.S. antitrust laws and the potential for mutual production projects, consortia may be designed to have greater longevity and become more common (34).

Another example of a research consortium was U.S. Memories, composed of several U.S. companies led by IBM (35). Texas Instruments and Motorola were conspicuously absent from the group. While the participants wanted to learn about the design technology required to reestablish the U.S. as a major producer of dynamic random access memory (DRAM) chips, Texas Instruments and Motorola elected to obtain direct access to Japan's chip process technologies. Such actions reemphasize our contention that each potential alliance member needs to determine what is needed, who can supply it, and what is the best way to realize its objectives. A consortium may not provide sufficient rewards for all potential partners and, therefore, may generate limited incentives to participate (32). In this example, Texas Instruments and Motorola decided that they could obtain more valuable information from Japanese firms than from alliances with U.S. firms, which were for the most part less knowledgeable than themselves.

The Japanese have formed many consortia involving large banks, the Ministry of International Trade and Industry, and technology firms. Japan has had success with these cooperative research projects, but many Japanese consortia also have failed to achieve their goals (29). Chipello suggests that some consortia members engage in behavior that hinders commitment and goal achievement (36). A member firm may, for example, hold back its top scientists; disagree regarding common research programs and practices; become bogged down in consortium administrative processes; or attempt to block how the research will be used and which firms should receive it.

Global consortia activity appears to be one way by which large, complex projects will be undertaken in the future (37). This trend is defining larger competing entities that may continue to function in new and different areas if successful in their current endeavors. With increased competition from the European Economic Community, there will likely be more consortia formed in Europe as well as in Asia.

4. *Partnerships.* —The partnership NPD alliance structure is one of the most common and useful, due to its fairly unstructured form. When a firm needs to reposition its competitive posture, partnerships can often be a faster approach to NPD than internal development, and often less costly, less irreversible and more feasible than mergers (38). Unlike the joint venture, the NPD partnership does not form a third firm; unlike consortia, partnerships usually involve only two firms. In addition, the partnership structure does not create the inflexibility or expense of mergers and acquisitions. Kanter points out that partnerships represent a strategy entailing far more than a handshake (2). She notes that partners need allies, not manipulated adversaries. This alliance structure, which has been called by such names as "cooperative agreements" or "R&D partnerships," can be particularly effective for firms developing new products.

Moreover, the partnership alliance structure is related to the futuristic organizational form suggested by Miles and Snow (39). They postulate that firms in the 21st century will be temporary in the sense that they will be composed of many firms brought together by an entrepreneur and maintained in a functioning network through various contractual relationships. Such a model can provide a high viable approach for NPD in an increasingly turbulent and global environment.

There are many advantages to becoming partners, such as helping smaller firms compete with larger firms, structural flexibility, and speedier access to product development capabilities (2). Technology and market access are other important competitive advantages that can be acquired through partnerships. Although occasionally conceived as temporary organizations, these relationships can be long term and need to be evaluated thoroughly prior to implementation.

IN CONCLUSION

NPD alliances can create effective win-win situations. A positive attitude toward an alliance partner can do much to overcome such concerns as lack of trust, different managerial and cultural styles, conflict management, and control of new organizational entities.

Ohmae states, "Alliances are not tools of convenience" (40, p. 144). Yet, NPD alliances can be highly important instruments for serving customers in a global marketplace. Therefore, senior management needs to treat a proposal to form an alliance as potentially important to the business that the alliance involves. Understanding the issues presented here can make the alliance evaluation process more meaningful and can help partnering firms avoid many of the problems common to poorly conceived NPD alliances.

Of the many questions surrounding new product development, three fundamental questions remain that focus on the subject of new product success. Are NPD processes based on partnering arrangements more successful than those that are not? What performance factors are associated with successful new products developed by partners? Are these factors similar to those related to successful new products produced by individual firms? Answers to these questions can assist new product development managers in their quest to develop the most successful new products possible.

About the Authors

Murray Millson is a visiting professor at the Graduate School of Management, University of Western Australia, Nedlands. His business career includes 20 years with the General Electric Company in various engineering and management assignments. He is a Registered Professional Engineer in quality engineering in the state of California. His current research includes new product development, business partnering, business and marketing strategy, and consumer behavior related to new product introductions. He earned a B.S. in electrical engineering and an M.S. in industrial management from Clarkson University and M.B.A. and Ph.D. degrees from Syracuse University.

S. P. Raj is distinguished professor of marketing and associate dean for academic affairs in the School of Management at Syracuse University (New York). He earned a bachelor's degree in electrical engineering from the Indian Institute of Technology, Madras, and master's and Ph.D. degrees from Carnegie Mellon University. He received the John D. C. Little Best Paper Award from the Institute for Management Sciences on marketing in 1988. He is faculty coordinator of the marketing program for the Incubation Center in the New York State Center for Advanced Technology in Computer Applications and Software Engineering (CASE).

David Wilemon is professor of marketing and director of Syracuse University's Innovation Management Program. He received his doctorate from Michigan State University. His professional and research interests focus on new corporate ventures, high-performing technical teamwork, R&D management, and innovation management. He has been an advisor to technology-based organizations including Apple Computer, Bell Laboratories, IBM, Data General, DEC, GE, Bechtel, Upjohn, United Technologies, ICI Pharmaceuticals, Schlumberger, 3M, NASA, and the European Space Agency.

References

1. Urban, Glen L. and Eric von Hippel. "Lead User Analysis for the Development of New Industrial Products." *Management Science,* vol. 34, no. 5, May 1988, pp. 569–582.

2. Kanter, Rosabeth Moss. "Becoming PALs: Pooling, Allying, and Linking Across Companies." *Academy of Management Executive,* vol. III, no. 3, 1989, pp. 183–193.

3. Contractor, F. J. and P. Lorange. "Competition vs. Cooperation: A Benefit/Cost Framework for Choosing Between Fully-owned Investments and Cooperative Relationships." *Management International Review,* Special Issue 1988, pp. 5–18.

4. Harrigan, K. R. "Strategic Alliances and Partner Asymmetries." *Management International Review,* Special Issue, 1988, pp. 53–72.

5. Wind, Yoram and Vijay Mahajan. "New Product Development Process: A Perspective for Reexamination." *Journal of Product Innovation Management,* vol. 5, 1988, pp. 304–310.

6. Cooper, R. G. and E. J. Kleinschmidt. "An Investigation into the New Product Process: Steps, Deficiencies, and Impact." *Journal of Product Innovation Management,* vol. 3, no. 2, 1986, pp. 71–85.

7. Lawton, Leigh and A. Parasuraman. "So You Want Your New Product Planning To Be Productive." *Business Horizons,* vol. 23, no. 6, 1980, pp. 29–34.

8. Cooper, R. G. and E. J. Kleinschmidt. "New Product Processes at Leading Industrial Firms." *Industrial Marketing Management,* vol. 20, 1991, pp. 137–147.

9. Slowinski, Gene, George F. Farris, and David Jones. "Strategic Partnering: Process Instead of Event." *Research Technology Management,* May–June, 1993, pp. 22–25.

10. Dwyer, F. Robert, Paul H. Schurr and Sejo Oh. "Developing Buyer-Seller Relationships," *Journal of Marketing,* vol. 51, April 1987, pp. 11–27.

11. Morgan, Gareth. *Creative Organization Theory.* Sage Publications, Newbury Park, 1989.

12. Devlin, Godfrey and Mark Bleackley. "Strategic Alliances—Guidelines for Success." *Long Range Planning,* vol. 21, no. 5, 1988, pp. 18–23.

13. Borys, Bryan and David Jamison. "Hybrid Arrangements as Strategic Alliances: Theoretical Issues in Organizational Combinations." *Academy of Management Review,* vol. 14, no. 2, 1989, pp. 234–249.

14. Zirger, Billie Jo and Modesto Maidique. "A Model of New Product Development: An Empirical Test." *Management Science,* vol. 36, no. 7, 1990, pp. 867–883.

15. Schillaci, Carmela Elita. "Designing Successful Joint Ventures." *The Journal of Business Strategy,* vol. 8, no. 2, Fall 1987, pp. 59–63.

16. Kanter, Rosabeth Moss. *When Giants Learn To Dance.* Simon and Schuster, New York, 1989.

17. Anderson, James C. and James A. Narus. "Partnering as a Focused Market Strategy." *California Management Review,* vol. 33, no. 3, 1991, pp. 95–113.

18. Saddler, Jeanne. "Specialized Firms Stick to the Straight and Very Narrow." *The Wall Street Journal,* May 19, 1989, p. B2.

19. Brockhoff, Klaus. "R&D Cooperation between Firms: A Perceived Transaction Cost Perspective." *Management Science,* vol. 18, no. 4, 1992, pp. 514–524.

20. Kraar, Louis. "Your Rivals Can Be Your Allies." *Fortune,* vol. 119, no. 7, March 27, 1989. pp. 66–76.

21. Brown, Clair and Michael Reich. "When Does Union–Management Cooperation Work? A Look at NUMMI

and GM–Van Nuys." *California Management Review,* vol. 31, no. 4, Summer 1989, pp. 26–44.

22. Sharkey, Joe. "GE, Ford Enter Joint Venture on Auto Lights." *The Wall Street Journal,* June 23, 1989, p. B2.

23. Schwadel, Francine. "IBM–Sears Venture In Videotex Is Hit By Service Outage." *The Wall Street Journal,* May 11, 1989, p. B4.

24. Tyebjee, Tyzoon T. "A Typology of Joint Ventures: Japanese Strategies in the United States." *California Management Review,* vol. 31, no. 1, Fall 1988, pp. 75–86.

25. Voss, C. A. "Implementation: A Key Issue in Manufacturing Technology: The Need for a Field of Study." *Research Policy,* vol. 17, no. 2, April 1988, pp. 55–63.

26. Harrigan, K. R. "Joint Ventures and Competitive Strategy." *Strategic Management Journal,* vol. 9, no. 2, 1988, pp. 141–158.

27. Harrigan, K. R. *Strategies for Joint Ventures,* Lexington Books, Lexington, Mass., 1985.

28. Killing, J. P. *Strategies for Joint Venture Success.* Praeger, New York, 1983.

29. Chipello, Christopher J. "MIT, AT&T, IBM Form a Consortium In Superconductors." *The Wall Street Journal,* May 24, 1989, pp. B2.

30. Peck, Merton. "Joint R&D: The Case of Microelectronics and Computer Technology Corporation." *Research Policy,* vol. 15, 1986, pp. 219–231.

31. Gover, James E. "Analysis of U.S. Semiconductor Collaboration." *IEEE Transactions on*

Engineering Management, vol. 40, no. 2, May 1993, pp. 104–113.

32. Smith, Lee. "Can Consortiums Defeat Japan?" *Fortune,* vol. 119, no. 12, June 5, 1989, pp. 245–254.

33. Buyers, Kathleen and David Palmer. "The Microelectronics and Computer Technology Corporation." *Administration and Society,* vol. 21, May 1989, pp. 101–127.

34. Guterl, Fred. "MCC: The Dilemma of Joint Research." *Business Month,* vol. 129, no. 3, March 1987, pp. 49–51.

35. Schlesinger, Jacob M. "Two U.S. Makers of Chips Develop Closer Japan Ties." *The Wall Street Journal,* July 21, 1989, p. B2.

36. Chipello, Christopher J. "More Competitors Turn To Cooperation." *The Wall Street Journal,* June 23, 1989, p. B1.

37. Ouchi, William, and Michele Bolton. "The Logic of Joint Research and Development." *California Management Review,* vol. 30, no. 3, Spring 1988, pp. 9–33.

38. Porter, M. and M. B. Fuller. "Coalitions and Global Strategy." in M. Porter (ed.), *Competition in Global Industries,* Boston, Mass., Harvard Business School Press, 1987, pp. 315–344.

39. Miles, Raymond E. and Charles C. Snow. "Fit, Failure, and the Hall of Fame." *California Management Review,* vol. 26, no. 3, 1984, pp. 10–28.

40. Ohmae, Kenichi. "The Global Logic of Strategic Alliances." *Harvard Business Review,* March–April, 1989, pp. 143–154.

51

CAPTURING VALUE FROM TECHNOLOGICAL INNOVATION: INTEGRATION, STRATEGIC PARTNERING, AND LICENSING DECISIONS

David J. Teece

School of Business Administration
University of California
Berkeley, California 94720

The competitive potential embedded in new technology is not always captured by the innovator. Follower firms, customers, and suppliers are often the principal beneficiaries. When innovating firms lose to followers or imitators, the reason is often the failure of the innovator to build or access competitive capacity in activities, such as manufacturing, which are complementary to the innovation. This paper analyzes the make-or-buy decision with respect to these capacities in different competitive environments, including that of rapid technological change and easy imitation. Often it is pointless for firms to invest in R&D unless they are also willing to invest in the development of certain complementary capacities, at home or abroad.

It is commonly recognized that firms responsible for technological breakthroughs and for technological enhancement of existing products and processes are often unable to commercialize the product so that the product concept ultimately fails. Myriads of would-be innovators have discovered that technical success is necessary but not sufficient for establishing economic utility and commercial acceptance. A less commonly recognized but equally important phenomenon is the firm that is first to commercialize a new product concept but fails to extract economic value from the innovation, even though it is of great value to consumers and is the source of economic rents (profits) to competitors. The phenomenon unquestionably exists and has obvious significance for the dynamic efficiency of the economy as well as for the distribution of income, domestically and internationally. In the international context, it has important ramifications for economic relations, for commercial policy, and for corporate strategy.

I offer a framework that may shed light on the factors that determine who wins from innovation: the firm that is first to market or those that follow. The follower firms may or may not be imitators. The framework seems useful for explaining the share of the profits from innovation accruing to the innovator compared to the followers (Figure 51-1), and for explaining a variety of interfirm activities such as joint ventures, coproduction agreements, cross distribution arrangements, and technological licensing.

Teece, David J. 1988. "Capturing value from technological innovation: Integration, strategic partnering, and licensing decisions." *Interfaces* 18(3): 46–61. Courtesy of The Institute of Operations Research and the Management Sciences (INFORMS), 7240 Parkway Drive, Suite 310, Hanover, MD 21076 USA.

FIGURE 51-1   The Benefits from Innovation, Sometimes Referred to as Economic Rents, Are Divided Among Innovator, Imitators, Suppliers, and Customers. A Normative Framework Developed in This Paper Can Guide Innovating Firms to Capture a Large Portion of the Rents in Environments Where Imitation Is Easy.

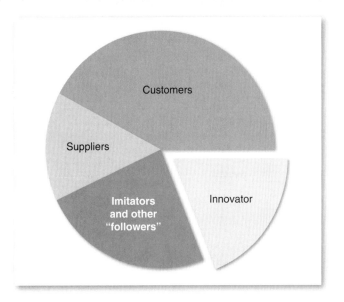

THE PHENOMENON

The EMI Scanner is a classic case of a losing innovation [Martin 1984]. By the early '70s, the UK firm, Electrical Musical Industries (EMI) Ltd., was producing a variety of products including phonographic records, movies, and advanced electronics. EMI had developed high resolution TVs in the '30s, pioneered airborne radar during World War II, and developed the UK's first all solid-state computers in 1952.

In the late '60s Godfrey Houndsfield, an EMI senior research engineer, engaged in research on pattern recognition, which resulted in his displaying a scan of a pig's brain. Subsequent clinical work established that computerized axial tomography (CAT) was viable for generating cross-sectional "views" of the human body; this was the greatest advance in radiology since the discovery of X-rays in 1895.

The US was the major market for the product. However, EMI was UK based and lacked a marketing capability or presence in medical electronics in the United States. Because the scanner was a complex product, it required an organization that had service and training capacity as well as marketing ability. EMI's competitors, such as Siemens and GE, had these assets.

A market for CAT scanners rapidly emerged after EMI displayed advanced prototypes in Chicago in November 1972. By 1975, EMI had an order backlog of £55 million. Expectations of £100 million a year in scanner sales by EMI were projected by investors, and stock analysts began to think of EMI as shaping up for a success of the magnitude of Xerox's in the previous decade.

By the mid-'70s imitators had emerged, most notably GE with faster scanners tailored more closely to the needs of the medical profession and supported in the field by experienced marketing and service personnel. Simultaneously, health care regulations in the United States imposed a requirement that hospitals obtain certificates of need before purchasing high priced items like scanners. EMI was forced to sell its scanner business and in April of 1980 announced a sale to GE. At that time EMI indicated that it had lost £26 million on the business. Meanwhile, GE's operations were believed to be quite profitable. Subsequently, GE and Johnson & Johnson each paid EMI $100 million in damages for patent infringement.

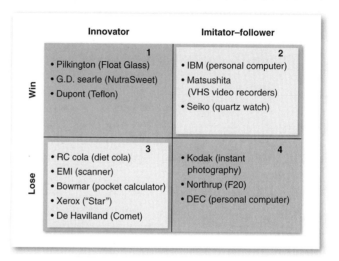

FIGURE 51-2 There Is Lore, but Little Analytics, to Explain When and Why Innovators Lose Out to Imitators and Followers. Xerox, for Instance, Has Been First to Commercialize Key Computer Technologies Developed in Its Parc Facility; However, in Several Instances It Has Failed to Recover Its Investment, while Competitors, such as Apple, Have Done Fabulously Well with Derivative Technology.

Other examples of losing innovators are RC Cola, Bowmar, Xerox, and de Havilland. RC Cola, a small beverage company, was the first to introduce cola in a can and the first to introduce diet cola. Both Coca Cola and Pepsi followed almost immediately, depriving RC of any significant advantage from its innovation. Bowmar, which introduced the pocket calculator, was not able to withstand competition from Texas Instruments, Hewlett Packard, and others and went out of business. Xerox failed to succeed with its entry into the office computer business, even though Apple succeeded with the MacIntosh, which contained many of Xerox's key product ideas, such as the mouse and icons. The de Havilland Comet saga has some of the same features. The Comet I jet was introduced into the commercial airline business two years or so before Boeing introduced the 707, but through an unfortunate series of events, de Havilland failed to capitalize on its substantial early advantage.

CAPTURING THE RENT STREAM FROM INNOVATION: BASIC BUILDING BLOCKS

In order to develop a coherent framework within which to explain the distribution of outcomes illustrated in Figure 51-2, three fundamental building blocks must first be described: the appropriability regime, complementary assets, and the dominant design paradigm.

REGIMES OF APPROPRIABILITY

The term *regime of appropriability* refers to aspects of the commercial environment, excluding firm and market structure, that govern an innovator's ability to capture the rents associated with innovation. The most important dimensions of such a regime are the nature of the technology and the efficacy of legal mechanisms of protection such as patents, copyrights, and trade secrets.

It has long been known that patents do not work in practice as they do in theory. Rarely, if ever, do patents confer perfect appropriability, although they do afford considerable protection on new chemical products and on some mechanical inventions. Many patents can be "invented around" at modest costs. They are especially ineffective at protecting process innovations. Often patents provide little protection because the legal requirements for upholding their validity or for proving their infringement are high.

In some industries, particularly where the innovation is embedded in processes, trade secrets are a viable alternative to patents. Trade secret protection is possible, however, only if a firm can put its product before the public and still keep the underlying technology secret. Usually only chemical formulas and industrial-commercial processes (for example, cosmetics and recipes) can be protected as trade secrets after the products are "out."

The degree to which knowledge is tacit or codified also affects the ease with which it can be imitated. Codified knowledge is easy to transmit and receive and is more exposed to industrial espionage and the like. Tacit knowledge by definition is difficult to articulate, and so its transfer is difficult unless those with the know-how can demonstrate it to others [Teece 1981].

Empirical research by Levin, Klevorick, Nelson, and Winter [1984] demonstrates that patents and trade secrets often do not afford significant protection. Their results show considerable collinearity among certain mechanisms of appropriability. They conclude that "at the expense of some oversimplification, the data suggest that the mechanism of appropriation may reduce to two dimensions: one associated with the use of patents, the other with lead time and learning-curve advantages. For process innovations, secrecy is closely connected with exploiting lead time and learning advan-

Who wins from innovation?

tages. For product innovation, sales and service efforts are part of the package" [p. 18]. These findings are tentative and must be interpreted with care. They do, however, indicate that methods of appropriability vary markedly across industries and probably within industries as well.

The property rights environment within which a firm operates can thus be classified according to the nature of the technology and the efficacy of the legal system to assign and protect intellectual property. While a gross simplification, a dichotomy can be drawn between products for which the appropriability regime is "tight" (technology is relatively easy to protect) and those for which it is "weak" (technology is almost impossible to protect). An example of the former is the formula for Coca Cola syrup; an example of the latter is the Simplex algorithm in linear programming.

THE DOMINANT DESIGN PARADIGM

Thomas Kuhn's seminal work [1970] describes the history and social psychology of science on the basis of the notion of a paradigm. The concept of a paradigm as applied to scientific development is broader than that of a theory. In fact, a paradigm is a Gestalt that embodies a set of scientific assumptions and beliefs about certain classes of phenomenon. Kuhn suggests that there are two stages in the evolutionary development of a given branch of a science: the preparadigmatic stage, when there is no single generally accepted conceptual treatment of the phenomenon in a field of study, and the paradigmatic stage, which begins when a body of theory appears to have passed the canons of scientific acceptability. The emergence of a dominant paradigm signals scientific maturity, and the acceptance of agreed upon standards by which what Kuhn calls "normal" scientific research can proceed. These standards remain in force unless or until the paradigm is overturned. Revolutionary science is what overturns normal science, as when the Copernicus theories of astronomy overturned Ptolemy's in the 17th century.

Abernathy and Utterback [1978] and Dosi [1982] have provided a treatment of the technological evolution of an industry which appears to parallel Kuhnian notions of scientific evolution. In the early stages of industry development, product designs are fluid, manufacturing processes are loosely and adaptively organized, and generalized capital is used in production. Competition among firms manifests itself in competition among designs, which are markedly different from each other. This might be called the preparadigmatic stage of an industry.

At some point after considerable trial and error in the marketplace, one design or a narrow class of designs begins to emerge as the more promising. Such a design must be able to meet a whole set of user needs in a relatively complete fashion. The Model

Expectations of £100 million a year in scanner sales by EMI were projected.

T Ford, the IBM 360, and the Douglas DC-3 are examples of dominant designs in the automobile, computer, and aircraft industries.

Once a dominant design emerges, competition shifts to price and away from design. Competitive success then shifts to a whole new set of variables. Scale and learning become much more important, and specialized capital is deployed as competing firms seek to lower unit costs by exploiting economies of scale and learning. Reduced uncertainty over product design provides an opportunity to amortize specialized long-lived investments.

Innovation is not necessarily halted once the dominant design emerges; as Clarke [1985] points out, it can occur lower down in the design hierarchy. For instance, a "V" cylinder configuration emerged in automobile engine blocks during the 1930s with the emergence of the Ford V-8 engine. Niches were quickly found for it. Moreover, once the product design stabilizes, there is likely to be a surge of process innovation as producers attempt to lower production costs for the new product (Figure 51-3).

The Abernathy-Utterback framework does not characterize all industries. It seems more suited to mass markets where consumer tastes are relatively homogeneous. It appears less characteristic of small niche markets where the absence of scale and learning economies attaches much less of a penalty to multiple designs. In these instances, generalized equipment will be employed in production.

The existence of a dominant design watershed is of great significance to the distribution of rents between innovator and follower. The innovator may have been responsible for the fundamental scientific breakthroughs as well as the basic design of the new product. However, if imitation is relatively easy, imitators may enter the fray, modifying the product in important ways, yet relying on the fundamental designs pioneered by the innovator. When the game of musical chairs stops, and a dominant design emerges, the innovator might well end up at a disadvantage. Hence, when imitation is possible, and when it occurs coupled with design modification before a dominant design emerges, a follower's modified product has a good chance of being anointed as the industry standard.

FIGURE 51-3   When New Technologies Are Commercialized, Process Innovation often Follows Product Innovation. As the Rate of Product Innovation Slows, Designs in the Marketplace Tend to Become More Standardized, Providing the Opportunity for Large-Scale Production and the Deployment of Specialized Assets. The Nature of Competition and the Requirements for Marketplace Success Shift Dramatically as the Market Evolves from its Early Preparadigmatic Phase (with Competition based On Features and Product Performance) to Its Post Paradigmatic Phase (with Competition Based More on Price).

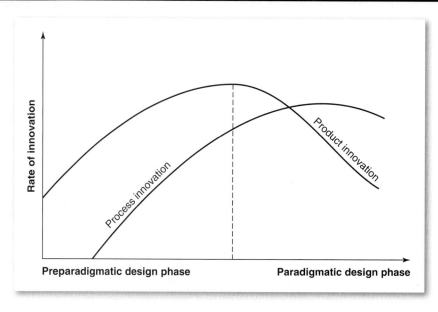

COMPLEMENTARY ASSETS

Let the unit of analysis be innovation. An innovation consists of certain technical knowledge about how to do things better. Assume that the know-how in question is partly codified and partly tacit. In order for such know-how to generate a rent stream, it must be sold or used in the market.

In almost all cases, the successful commercialization of an innovation requires that the know-how in question be utilized in conjunction with such services as marketing, competitive manufacturing, and after-sales support. These services are often obtained from complementary assets that are specialized. For example, the commercialization of a new drug is likely to require the dissemination of information over a specialized information channel. In some cases, as when the innovation is systemic, the complementary assets may be other parts of a system. For instance, computer hardware typically requires the development of specialized software, both for the operating system and for applications. Even when an innovation is autonomous, the services of certain complementary assets will be needed for successful commercialization (Figure 51-4).

Whether the assets required for least cost production and distribution are specialized to the innovation turns out to be important in the development presented below. Complementary assets can be generic, specialized, or cospecialized.

Generic assets are general purpose assets that do not need to be tailored to the innovation. Specialized assets are those on which the innovation depends, tailored to that innovation. Cospecialized assets are those for which there is a bilateral dependence. For instance, specialized repair facilities are needed to support Mazda's rotary engine. These assets are cospecialized because of the mutual dependence of the innovation and the repair facility. Container shipping required a similar deployment of cospecialized assets in specially designed ships and terminals. However, the dependence of trucking on containerized shipping was less than that of containerized shipping on trucking: trucks can convert from containers to flat beds at low cost. An example of a generic asset would be the manufacturing facilities needed to make running shoes. Generalized equipment can be used except for the mold for the sole.

FIGURE 51-4 In Order to Innovate, Firms Need Complementary Assets and Technologies to Support the Commercialization of Some Core Technology. These Assets Typically Include Manufacturing, Distribution, and Sales and Service. They May Already Reside In-House. If Not, They Are Conceivably Available Through Merger, Acquisition, or Contract. The Key Consideration Is the Terms Upon Which They Are Available to the Innovator.

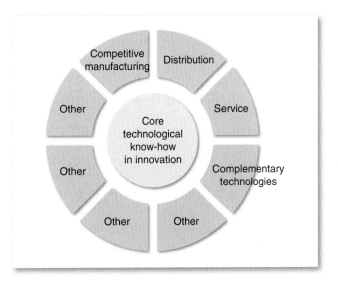

IMPLICATIONS FOR PROFITABILITY

These three concepts can now be related in a way that will shed light on the imitation process and the distribution of rents between innovator and follower. In those few instances where the innovator has ironclad patent or copyright protection, or where trade secrets effectively deny imitators access to the product, the innovator is almost assured of capturing the lion's share of available profits for some period of time. Even if the innovator does not have the desirable complementary assets, ironclad protection of intellectual property will afford it time to obtain them. If these assets are generic, a contractual relationship may suffice; the innovator may simply license its technology. Specialized R&D firms are viable in such an environment. Universal Oil Products, an R&D firm developing refining processes for the petroleum industry, was such an innovator. If, however, the needed complementary assets are specialized or cospecialized, contractual relationships are exposed to hazards, because one or both parties will have to commit capital to certain irreversible investments, which will be valueless if the relationship between innovator and licensee breaks down. Accordingly, the innovator may want to integrate by owning the specialized and cospecialized assets. Fortunately, the factors which make for difficult imitation will enable the innovator to build or acquire those complementary assets without competing with innovators for their control.

Competition from imitators is thus muted in tight appropriability regimes, which sometimes characterizes the petrochemical industry. In this industry, the protection offered by patents is fairly easily enforced. A factor that helps the licensor is that most petrochemical processes are designed around a specific variety of catalysts that can be kept proprietary. An agreement not to analyze the catalyst can be extracted from licensees, affording extra protection. Even if such requirements are violated by licensees, the innovator is still well positioned: the most important properties of a catalyst are related to its physical structure, and the process for generating this structure cannot be deduced from structural analysis alone. Every reaction technology a company acquires is thus accompanied by an ongoing dependence on the innovating company for the catalyst appropriate to the plant design. Failure to comply with the licensing contract can result in a cutoff in the supply of the catalyst and possibly in facility closure.

RC Cola was the first to introduce cola in a can and the first to introduce diet cola.

Similarly, if an innovator comes to market in the preparadigmatic phase with a sound product concept but the wrong design, a tight appropriability regime will afford it the time needed to get the design right. The best initial design concepts often turn out to be hopelessly wrong, but if the innovator possesses an impenetrable thicket of patents, or simply has technology that is difficult to copy, then the market may well afford the innovator the time necessary to find the right design.

However, tight appropriability is the exception rather than the rule. Most innovators must formulate and implement complex business strategies to keep imitators at bay. The nature of the strategic challenge will vary according to whether the industry is in the paradigmatic or preparadigmatic phase.

In the preparadigmatic phase, the innovator, with little or no intellectual property protection available for its technology, must be careful to let the basic design float until the design seems likely to become the industry standard. In some industries this may be difficult as little opportunity exists for product modification. In microelectronics, for example, designs become locked in when the circuitry is chosen. Product modification is limited to debugging and software changes. An innovator must begin the design process anew if the product does not fit the market well. To some extent, new designs are dictated by the need to meet certain compatibility standards so that the new hardware can interface with existing applications software. In one sense, therefore, design for the microprocessor industry today is relatively straightforward: deliver greater power and speed while meeting the industry standards of the existing software base. However, from time to time windows of opportunity allow the introduction of entirely new families of microprocessors that will define a new industry and software standard. Then basic design parameters are less defined and can float until market acceptance is apparent.

The early history of the automobile industry—an industry characterized by a weak appropriability regime—exemplifies the importance of selecting the right design in the preparadigmatic stages. None of the early steam cars survived when the closed-body, internal combustion engine automobile emerged as the dominant design. The steam car, nevertheless, had virtues, such as reliability, that the internal combustion engine autos of that time did not.

The British fiasco with the Comet I is also instructive. De Havilland had picked an early design with significant flaws. By racing on to production, the innovator suffered an irreversible loss of reputation that seemed to prevent it from converting to what subsequently became the dominant design.

In general, innovators in weak appropriability regimes need to be intimately connected with the market so that designs are based on user needs. When multiple parallel and sequential prototyping is feasible, it has clear advantages. Usually, it is too costly. Development costs for a large commercial aircraft can exceed one billion dollars; variations on one theme are all that is possible.

Hence, the probability that the first firm to commercialize a new product design will enter the paradigmatic phase with the dominant design is problematic. The probabilities will be higher the lower the cost of prototyping and the more tightly coupled the firm is to the market. The firm's relationship to the market is a function of organizational design and can be influenced by managerial choices. The cost of prototyping is embedded in the technology and cannot be greatly influenced by managerial decisions. Hence, in industries with large developmental and prototyping costs—where choices are irreversible and where innovation of the product concept is easy—the innovator would be unlikely to emerge as a winner at the end of the preparadigmatic stage if the appropriability regime is weak.

In the preparadigmatic phase, complementary assets do not loom large. Rivalry is focused on trying to identify the design that will dominate the industry. Production volumes are low, and little can be gained from deploying specialized assets since scale economies are unavailable and price is not a principle competitive factor. However, as the leading design or designs are revealed by the market, volumes increase and firms gear up for mass production by acquiring specialized tooling and equipment, and possibly specialized distribution as well. Since these investments are irreversible, they are likely to proceed with caution. Islands of asset specificity will thus begin to form in a sea of generalized assets.

However, as the terms of competition begin to change and prices become increasingly unimportant, complementary assets become critical. Since the core technology is easy to imitate, commercial success depends on the terms under which the required complementary assets can be accessed.

At this point, specialized and cospecialized assets become critically important. Generalized assets, almost by definition, are always available in an industry, and even if they are not, they do not involve significant irreversibilities. Even if there is insufficient capacity, additional capacity can be put in place with little risk. Specialized assets, on the other hand, involve significant irreversibilities and cannot be easily accessed by contract. Recontracting hazards abound when dedicated assets that do not have alternative uses are supported entirely by contractual arrangement [Williamson 1975, 1981, 1985, Teece 1980, 1982, 1985]. Owners of cospecialized assets, such as distribution channels or specialized manufacturing capacity, are clearly advantageously positioned relative to an innovator. Indeed, when they hold an airtight monopoly over specialized assets, and the innovator is in a regime of weak appropriability, they could command all of the rents to the innovation. Even without a monopoly, specialized assets are often not as easy to replicate as the technology. For instance, the technology in cardiac pacemakers was easy to imitate; competitive success was determined by who controlled the specialized marketing. A similar situation exists in the US for personal computers:

There are a huge number of computer manufacturers, companies that make peripherals (e.g., printers, hard disk drives, floppy disk drives), and software companies. They are all trying to get marketing distributors because they cannot afford to call on all of the US companies directly. They need to go through retail distribution channels, such as Business-land, in order to reach the marketplace. The problem today, however, is that many of these companies are not able to get shelf space and thus are having a very difficult time marketing their products. The point of distribution is where the profit and the power are in the marketplace today [Norman 1986, p. 438].

CHANNEL SELECTION ISSUES

Access to complementary assets is critical if the innovator is to avoid handing over the lion's share of the profits to imitators or to the owners of specialized and cospecialized complementary assets. What controls should the imitator establish over these critical assets?

Many channels can be employed. At one extreme, the innovator could integrate into all of the necessary complementary assets, an option that is probably unnecessary and prohibitively expensive. The assets and competencies needed may be numerous, even for quite simple technologies. To produce a personal computer, for instance, a company needs expertise in semiconductor technology, display technology, disk-drive technology, networking technology, keyboard technology, and several others. No company, not even IBM, has kept pace in all of these areas by itself.

Patents do not work in practice as they do in theory.

At the other extreme, from handling all technologies internally the innovator could attempt to access these assets through contractual relationships (for example, component supply contracts, fabrication contracts, and distribution contracts). In many instances, contracts may suffice, although they expose the innovator to various hazards and dependencies that it may want to avoid. In between these two extremes are a myriad of intermediate forms and channels. I will analyze the properties of two extremes and also describe a mixture.

CONTRACTUAL MODES

The advantages of a contractual solution—whereby the innovator contracts with independent suppliers, manufacturers or distributors—are obvious. The innovator will not have to make the capital expenditures needed to build or buy the assets. This reduces risks as well as cash requirements. Also, contractual relationships can bring added credibility to the innovator, especially if the innovator is unknown and the contractual partner is established and viable. Indeed, arms-length contracting which embodies more than a simple buy-sell agreement is becoming so common and is so multifaceted that the term strategic partnering has been devised to describe it. Even large companies such as IBM are now engaging in it. For IBM, partnering buys access to new technologies enabling the company to learn things they couldn't have learned without many years of trial and error. IBM's arrangement to use Microsoft's MSDOS operating system software on the IBM PC facilitated the timely introduction of IBM's personal computer into the market. Had IBM developed its own operating system, it would probably have missed the market window.

Smaller, less integrated companies are often eager to sign on with established companies because of the name recognition and reputation spillovers. For instance, Cipher Data Products contracted with IBM to develop a low-priced version of IBM's 3480 0.5 inch streaming cartridge drive, which is likely to become the industry standard. Cipher management recognizes that one of the biggest advantages to dealing with IBM is that, once you've created a product that meets the high quality standards necessary to sell into the IBM world, you can sell into any arena. Similarly, IBM's contract with Microsoft meant instant credibility to Microsoft [McKenna 1985, p. 94].

It is important to recognize that strategic partnering, which is currently very fashionable, exposes the innovator to certain hazards, particularly when the innovator is trying to use contracts to access special capabilities. First, it may be difficult to induce suppliers to make costly irreversible commitments which depend for their success on the success of the innovation. To expect suppliers, manufacturers, and distributors to do so is to expect them to take risks along with the innovator. For the innovator, this poses problems similar to those associated with attracting venture capital. The innovator must persuade its prospective partner that the risk is a good one. The situation is open to opportunistic abuses on both sides. The innovator has incentives to overstate the value of the innovation, while the supplier has incentives to "run with the technology" should the innovation be a success.

Instances of both parties making irreversible capital commitments nevertheless exist. Apple's Laserwriter—a high resolution laser printer which produces near typeset quality text graphics—is a case in point. Apple persuaded Canon to participate in the development of the Laserwriter; Canon provided subsystems from its copiers, but only after Apple contracted to pay for a certain number of copier engines and cases. In short, Apple accepted a good deal of the financial risk in order to induce Canon to assist in the development and production of the Laserwriter. The arrangement appears to have been prudent, yet there were clearly hazards for both sides. It is difficult to write, execute, and enforce complex development contracts, particularly when the design of the new product is still floating, which it often is, even after commercialization. Apple was exposed to the risk that its co-innovator Canon would fail to deliver, and Canon was exposed to the risk that the Apple design and marketing effort would not succeed. Still, Apple's alternatives may have been rather limited, in that it did not have the technology to go it alone.

The current euphoria over strategic partnering may be partially misplaced. Its advantages are being stressed (for example, by McKenna [1985]) without a balanced presentation of costs and risks. These have been described by Williamson [1975, 1985]. Briefly, there is the risk that the partner will not perform according to the innovator's perception of what the contract requires; there is the added danger that the partner may imitate the innovator's technology and attempt to compete with the innovator. The danger is particularly acute if the provider of the complementary asset is uniquely situated with respect to that asset and also can absorb and imitate the technology. Contractual or partnering strategies are unambiguously preferred, however, where the complementary assets are generic and in competitive supply. Because alternatives exist, failure of the partner to perform according to the contract is not particularly damaging on the innovator.

INTEGRATION MODES

An alternative organizational arrangement is for the firm to provide the necessary complementary assets internally. This in-house approach facilitates greater control, but it is costly in terms of managerial and financial resources.

There are clear advantages to integration when assets are in fixed supply over the relevant time period. To avoid a speculative price run-up, the assets in question must be acquired by the innovator before their connection with the innovation is public knowledge. If the value of the complementary asset to the innovator leaks out, the owner of a critical complementary could extract a portion of the rent stream that the innovation was expected to generate. Such bottleneck situations are not uncommon, particularly in distribution.

However, an innovator may not have the time or the money to acquire or build the complementary assets it would like to control. Particularly when imitation is easy, timing becomes critical. Innovators, therefore, need to rank complementary assets as to their importance. If the complementary assets are critical, ownership is warranted, although if the firm is cash constrained, a minority equity position may well be a sensible trade-off. If the complementary asset in question is technology, this calculus needs to be revised in terms of the desired equity position. This is because ownership of complementary enterprises appears to be fraught with hazards, as integration tends to destroy incentives and cultures, particularly when a deep hierarchy is involved.

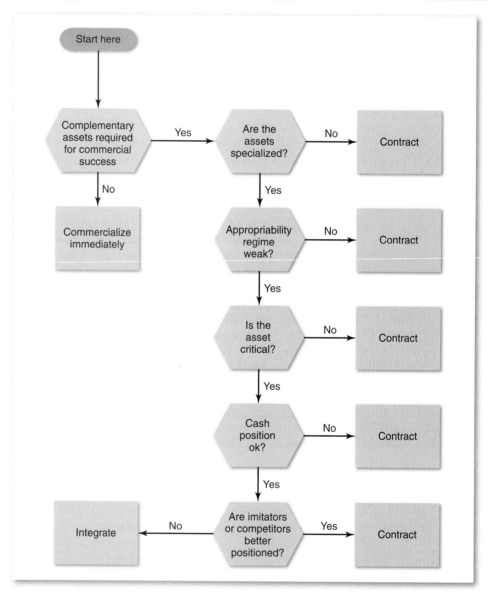

FIGURE 51-5 When Making R&D and Commercialization Decisions, Managers Must Identify, Preferably Ahead of Time, the Complementary Assets the Innovation Will Need for Successful Commercialization. Contractual Alternatives Will Make Strategic Sense if the Complementary Assets Are Not Specialized, or if the Innovators' Position Regarding Its Intellectual Property Is Ironclad, or for Assets which Are Not Critical, or for Assets in which the Innovator Does Not Have or Cannot Obtain the Necessary Financial Resources, or for Assets in which Imitators Are in any Case Already Irrevocably Better Positioned. Otherwise, the Integration (In-House) Alternative Ought to be Preferred.

When imitation is easy, building or buying specialized complementary assets must be considered in light of the moves of competitors. Building loses its point if one's imitators can do it faster. Figure 51-5 summarizes the factors to be considered in deciding between contracting and building or buying (mixed modes and intermediate solutions are ignored in order to simplify the analysis.)

If the innovator is a large enterprise that controls many of the relevant complementary assets, integration is not likely to be the issue it might be for a smaller company. However, in industries experiencing rapid technological change, no single company is likely to have the full range of expertise needed to bring advanced products to market in a timely and cost-effective fashion. In such industries, integration is an issue for large as well as small firms.

MIXED MODES

Organizational reality rarely affords the possibility of choice among pure forms of economic organization. Integration and contract are, accordingly, rarely seen without some accommodation to each other. The reality of business is that mixed modes—involving the blending of elements of integration and contract—are rather common. Still, in examining such intermediate forms, it is instructive to bear in mind the simple economics of pure forms.

Sometimes mixed modes represent transitional phases. For instance, because computer and telecommunication technologies are converging, firms in each industry are discovering that they need the technical capabilities of the other. This interdependence requires the collaboration of those who design different parts of the system; intense cross-boundary coordination and information flows must be supported. When separate companies collaborate, the parties must often agree on complex protocol issues. Contractual difficulties can be anticipated since the selection of common technical protocols among the parties will often be followed by investments in specialized hardware and software. There is little doubt that this was a key part of IBM's motivation in purchasing 15 percent of PBX manufacturer Rolm in 1983 and expanding that position to 100 percent in 1984. IBM's stake in Intel, which began with a 12 percent purchase in 1982, is most probably not a transitional phase leading to 100 percent purchase, because both companies realized that the two corporate cultures are not very compatible.

An example of how profoundly changing technology can affect the boundaries of the firm—and the identity of the firm at the nexus of contracts needed to develop and manufacture complex products—can be found in the jet fighter business. Avionics now constitutes about one third of the cost of a fighter, up from about 15 percent a decade ago (Figure 51-6). Avionics is expected to be even more important in the future, both in terms of cost and in terms of performance. Given the fairly widespread diffusion of airframe and propulsion technology, the superiority of fighters today and in the future will depend primarily upon the sophistication and capability of the aircraft's electronics. Indeed, in the future, computer manufacturers like AT&T and IBM may become prime contractors for advanced weapons systems, including fighters. In a related way, VHSIC technology is regarded as a key factor in reestablishing what the US sees as a

FIGURE 51-6 The Trend in Fighter Plane Subsystem Costs Has Been Away from Air Vehicle and Propulsion and Toward Avionics, and This Trend Is Likely to Continue. An Implication Is That Companies in the Electronics Industry, Like IBM and AT&T, May Be Prime Contractors for Future Generations of Aircraft.

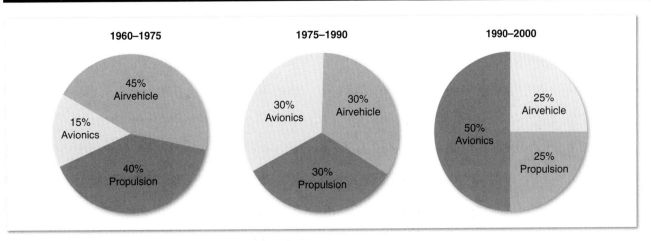

necessary degree of operational supremacy for its forces against the numerical superiority of the Soviet Union and the Warsaw Pact. It will be an essential ingredient of new aircraft programs such as the USAF's ATF advanced tactical fighter, the US Navy's VFMX air superiority fighter, and the US Army's LHX light battlefield helicopter, not to mention extensive upgrading of current equipment such as the F-15 and F-16 fighters and AH-64 helicopter [*Jane's All the World's Aircraft* 1983–84, p. 24].

Of particular relevance here is the USAF's advanced tactical fighter (ATF). While it is still too early to discuss electronics definitively, according to *Jane's* (1983–84, p. 26], a number of technological areas can be identified that will be required in the ATF, including the integration of flight and propulsion control systems, fly-by-wire, and integration of cockpit displays, probably with a voice command system to enhance the HOTAS (hands on throttle and stick). Advanced heads-up display and VHSIC technology will also be critical.

In order to compete in the advanced fighter market in the future, prime contractors will have to be on the leading edge with respect to avionics technology. A manufacturer that fails to develop or acquire such technology must expect to be shut out of a growing portion of the market.

Airframe companies without considerable in-house electronics capability will probably not be able to contract with electronics companies for the requisite subsystems. Because avionics is becoming the core technology that dictates other elements of design, it will not be enough for airframe companies to contract with both avionics and propulsion companies. Indeed, the leading fighter manufacturers—such as General Dynamics and McDonnell Douglas—have developed in-house avionics capabilities. Were these companies to fail to build a substantial in-house capability, it might be impossible, in the future, for them to design competitive fighter planes using avionics subcontractors.

The reason is that complex trade-offs often exist between avionics and air-vehicle design—trade-offs that are much more complex and dynamic than between air vehicle and propulsion. Moreover, much of the avionics of a fighter plane is specific to that aircraft. In the absence of in-house avionics capabilities, jet fighter manufacturers would be unable, without extremely close collaboration with avionics' subcontractors, to formulate and implement new fighter plane concepts. Moreover, the kind of collaboration required would require deep dependence of a kind very likely to lead to contractual vulnerabilities.

CONCLUSION

Clearly, the boundaries of an innovating firm are an important strategic variable, particularly when intellectual property protection is weak, as with microelectronics. The control of complementary assets, particularly when they are specialized or cospecialized, helps establish who wins and who loses from innovation. Imitators can do better than innovators if they are better positioned on cost and quality with respect to critical complementary assets, such as manufacturing.

There are important implications for corporate strategy. Except in unusual circumstances, innovating firms must emphasize the development of cost-competitive capabilities in the activities downstream from R&D if they are to profit from investment in R&D. Being first to market is no longer a guarantee of commercial success, particularly if to achieve early market entry the innovating firm engages in risky contracts with manufacturers, distributors, and developers of complementary technologies.

For public policy, a related set of implications follow. Government policy which equates policies to assist innovation with policies to assist R&D is increasingly wide of the mark. Except in special circumstances, national prowess in research and development is neither necessary nor sufficient to ensure that the innovator (rather than followers) captures the greater share of the profits available from innovation. Public policy towards science and technology must recognize how important the technological infrastructure (particularly education at all levels and manufacturing) is to the ability of domestically-based firms to build the requisite competitive capacities needed to capture value from innovation.

Acknowledgments

I thank Raphael Amit, Harvey Brooks, Therese Flaherty, Richard Gilbert, Heather Haveman, Mel Horwitch, Gary Pisano, Richard Rumelt, Raymond Vernon, and Sidney Winter for helpful discussions relating to the subject matter of this paper. A related treatment of the issues in this paper was published in *Research Policy* 1986, Vol. 15, No. 6.

References

Abernathy, W. J. and Utterback, J. M. 1978, "Patterns of industrial innovation," *Technology Review,* Vol. 80, No. 7 (January/July), pp. 40–47.

Clarke, Kim B. 1985, "The interaction of design hierarchies and market concepts in technological evolution," *Research Policy,* Vol. 14, No. 5 (October), pp. 235–251.

Dosi, G. 1982, "Technological paradigms and technological trajectories," *Research Policy,* Vol. 11, No. 3 (June), pp. 147–162.

Jane's All the World's Aircraft 1983–84, McGraw-Hill, New York.

Kuhn, T. 1970, *The Structure of Scientific Revolutions,* University of Chicago Press, Chicago, Illinois.

Levin, R.; Klevorick, A.; Nelson, N.; and Winter, S. 1984, "Survey research on R&D appropriability and technological opportunity," unpublished manuscript, Yale University.

Martin, Michael 1984, *Managing Technological Innovation and Enterpreneurship*, Reston Publishing Company, Reston, Virginia.

McKenna, R. 1985, "Market positioning in high technology," *California Management Review,* Vol. 27, No. 3 (Spring), pp. 82–108.

Norman, D. A. 1986, "Impact of entrepreneurship and innovations on the distribution of personal computers," in *The Positive Sum Strategy,* eds. R. Landau and N. Rosenberg, National Academy Press, Washington, DC, pp. 437–439.

Teece, D. J. 1980, "Economics of scope and the scope of the enterprise," *Journal of Economic Behavior and Organization,* Vol. 1, No. 3, pp. 223–247.

Teece, D. J. 1981, "The market for know-how and the efficient international transfer of technology," *Annals of the American Academy of Political and Social Science,* Vol. 458 (November), pp. 81–96.

Teece, D. J. 1982, "Towards an economic theory of the multiproduct firm," *Journal of Economic Behavior and Organization,* Vol. 3, No. 1, pp. 39–63.

Teece, D. J. 1985, "Multinational enterprise, internal governance, and industrial organization," *American Economic Review,* Vol. 75, No. 2 (May), pp. 233–238.

Williamson, O. E. 1975, *Markets and Hierarchies,* The Free Press, New York.

Williamson, O. E. 1981, "The modern corporation: Origins, evolution, attributes," *Journal of Economic Literature,* Vol. 19, No. 4 (December), pp. 1537–1568.

Williamson, O. E. 1985, *The Economic Institutions of Capitalism,* The Free Press, New York.

52 | THE POWER OF STRATEGIC INTEGRATION

Robert A. Burgelman and Yves L. Doz

How can multibusiness corporations exploit the opportunities that take full advantage of their capabilities and their potential to pursue new strategies?

All multibusiness corporations face the strategic imperative imposed by the stock market: maximizing the profitable growth of their businesses. Long-term success in meeting that imperative requires developing new strategy-making capabilities. During the early 1990s, many multibusiness companies focused on improving profitability through operational integration. They reengineered, focusing on the capabilities that would improve speed, quality and efficiency—and pruning business activities that no longer fit the value-creation logic of the corporate strategy. Then, starting in the late 1990s, senior managers began to focus on integrating strategies to add to revenue growth. Strategic integration involves more fully exploiting growth potential by combining resources and competencies from business units and directing those units toward new business opportunities that extend the existing corporate strategy.[1]

Today leaders of multibusiness corporations are learning to identify the *maximum-strategic-opportunity set*—those opportunities that can let companies take the fullest advantage of their capabilities and their potential to pursue new strategies. But to exploit those opportunities, managers need to become accomplished at what we call *complex strategic integration* (CSI). (See "About the Research.")

FIVE FORMS OF STRATEGIC INTEGRATION

Perceiving the maximum-strategic-opportunity set and tackling complex strategic integration are difficult responsibilities. Senior managers must be able to see potential business opportunities that do not yet exist—as well as the unarticulated strategies that are at the frontier of what a company is capable of doing. To help with those tasks, we propose a conceptual framework that features two dimensions (*scope* and *reach*) affecting the five forms of strategic integration (*overambitious, minimal, scope-driven, reach-driven* and *complex*). (See "Strategic Integration in the Multibusiness Corporation.")

A location on the scope dimension indicates the extent to which pursuing a new business opportunity requires the collaboration of existing business units within the corporate strategy. Intel's chipset and motherboard businesses, for example, need to collaborate on developing demand for new products for the company's core microprocessor business.

Burgelman, Robert A. and Yves L. Doz. 2001. "The power of strategic integration." *MIT Sloan Management Review* (Spring): 28–38.

A location on the reach dimension indicates the extent to which developing a new business opportunity does require changing the existing corporate strategy—perhaps by transforming a business unit or creating a new one. To cite Intel again, in 1999 the company extended its corporate strategy beyond its traditional focus on personal computers and pursued business opportunities in appliances by forming a Home Products Group within its Intel Architecture Business Group.[2]

Among the five forms of strategic integration, overambitious strategic integration and minimal strategic integration are the two that value-minded companies should avoid. Overambitious strategic integration corresponds to the opportunity set defined by maximum scope and reach; it assumes that a company's available capabilities do not impose trade-offs between scope and reach. Jim Robinson's effort to turn American Express into a "financial supermarket" during the late 1980s and early 1990s is one

---

STRATEGIC INTEGRATION IN THE MULTIBUSINESS CORPORATION

There are five forms of strategic integration: overambitious, minimal, scope-driven, reach-driven and complex. Complex strategic integration (CSI) is the one that multibusiness corporations should seek. Although each form offers a set of opportunities, the maximum strategic opportunities flow from CSI. Complex strategic integration has the maximum scope and reach that is consistent with the realities of both external and internal constraints. Scope relates to the core strategy; reach refers to new strategies.

Overambitious strategic integration assumes that a company's available capabilities do not impose trade-offs between scope and reach. Companies that use minimal strategic integration have opportunities defined by the perceived limits on scope and reach. Scope-driven strategic integration corresponds to the opportunities defined by maximum scope and company perceptions about the limits of reach. Reach-driven strategic integration corresponds to the opportunity set defined by maximum reach and the perceived limit on scope.

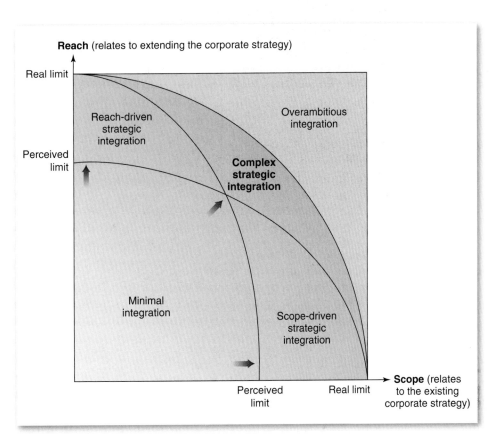

example of that type of strategic integration.[3] Minimal strategic integration corresponds to the opportunity set defined by perceived limits on scope and reach. Traditional strategy-making approaches based on capital-investment and portfolio-planning decisions are typical. Two other forms, scope-driven strategic integration and reach-driven strategic integration, are productive but fail to maximize the company's growth potential.

The fifth form, complex strategic integration, corresponds to the maximum-strategic-opportunity set. The maximum-strategic-opportunity set features as much scope and reach as is consistent with the trade-offs that the real world imposes. It is neither overambitious nor overly cautious. Companies achieving complex strategic integration take into account external constraints such as regulatory, technological and market forces plus internal limitations on competencies, capabilities and resources.[4] Complex strategic integration involves the discovery and creation of new business opportunities that combine resources from multiple units within the company (each with its particular perspective and vested interests) in order to extend the corporate strategy in new directions. It sometimes includes integrating contributions from external partners.[5]

Few multibusiness companies are currently proficient in exploiting the maximum-strategic-opportunity set, but some of the new high-technology giants—in particular Cisco Systems, Intel, Hewlett-Packard and STMicroelectronics—are trying to develop the capability. (See "Hewlett-Packard's Transformation.") Cisco has pursued a corporate strategy that depends on the company's ability to achieve complex strategic integration. Cisco continues to be able to extend the frontier of the maximum-strategic-opportunity set. It does so by quickly identifying, acquiring and integrating the winning companies in the technological-innovation races in newly emerging industry segments that are important for Cisco's strategy of serving corporate customers' networking needs. The stock market's perception that Cisco is succeeding in its efforts sustains the high share price that enables it to buy the winners in the first place, even at hefty premiums. STMicroelectronics offers another example of a company with a focus on improving complex strategic integration. (See "Complex Strategic Integration at STMicroelectronics.")

TWO COMPLEX-STRATEGIC-INTEGRATION CHALLENGES

Developing a complex-strategic-integration capability involves two important challenges for executives: first, managing the evolving tension between reinforcing the company's core business and redirecting strategy; second, managing the sharing and transferring of resources among business units.

The Tension Between Reinforcing the Core and Redirecting Strategy

Complex strategic integration depends on finding the right balance over time between reinforcing the core and redirecting strategy. Whereas reinforcement enables moving forcefully and rapidly along a given strategic trajectory, redirection helps a company shift its strategic trajectory, often in anticipation of or in response to major discontinuities. Finding a balance is hard for multibusiness companies used to pursuing more limited forms of strategic integration. In practice, complex strategic integration may start as pure reinforcement or redirection and then evolve toward a more balanced approach.[6]

Scope-Driven Strategic Integration Reinforces the Core

Strongly centralized companies that have emphasized the interdependencies among their various businesses tend to be scope-driven. Intel (during Andy Grove's tenure as CEO) and Disney (under Michael Eisner) are examples of companies that have been most comfortable finding opportunities by extending their scope.[7] Scope-driven strategic integration contributes to the reinforcement of the strategic thrust of the company's core business. It strives to capitalize on deepening competence and capturing market

HEWLETT-PACKARD'S TRANSFORMATION

Hewlett-Packard is one of the world's most adaptive large, established companies. For decades, the HP Way provided guidance for transforming the company through organic growth and metamorphosis. Although occasionally succumbing to pressures to centralize, HP always reverted back to an organizational form containing distinct business units serving distinct markets with technology-based product-leadership strategies. By 1999, HP had 83 businesses, each with its own resources and profit-and-loss responsibility. However, as one top executive observed, "We weren't articulating a corporate strategy." Another said, "We talked about portfolio management, but we didn't do much."

Between 1996 and 1999, HP's profitable-growth performance disappointed the stock market. During that period, the company came to the conclusion that its measurement and instruments businesses no longer fit the corporate strategy and needed to be spun off. The current CEO was reaching retirement age, and HP's board of directors hired Carly Fiorina to replace him. The new CEO represented three firsts for HP: She was an outsider, she did not have a technical background, and she was a woman. Fiorina brought HP's senior executives together at an offsite meeting in August 1999 to, as she put it, "introduce them to their company. They had concentrated so much on their own businesses that they did not see that HP was unfocused and wide and shallow."

Fiorina went in search of what the founders had intended with the HP Way and reformulated the belief system, which she embodied in the "Rules of the Garage." The Rules of the Garage capture HP's traditional emphasis on inventiveness, product leadership, trust, collaboration, customer focus, abhorrence of bureaucracy, and the desire to make a contribution. The Rules of the Garage were designed to help change senior executives' attitudes and behavior, which Fiorina believed had become caricatures of what the founders had intended.

During the first nine months of her tenure, Fiorina made several changes to HP's structure to increase its strategic-integration capabilities. She quickly learned that customers found HP's fragmentation a hindrance to doing business. In early October 1999, she announced a new organizational structure. The new structure featured four worldwide regions cutting across 16 businesses in which the "back-end," or "product-facing," computer and printer groups would interact closely with the "front end," or "customer-facing," organizations serving the business-to-business and business-to-consumer market segments. The purpose of the reorganization was to ensure a cohesive and coherent customer experience across all business units.

To increase interdependence at the top-management level, Fiorina also changed the way the executive council operated. And she altered the incentive structure, making top executives' variable compensation dependent on the overall performance of the corporation. One hundred top-level executives were placed on the scheme initially, with more targeted to join later.

Looking forward, HP's senior executives face three major strategic challenges. One is to continue to win in each of the core businesses against very strong competitors: Canon and Lexmark in printers, Sun Microsystems and IBM in high-end servers, Dell and Compaq in desktop systems. The second challenge is to exploit existing synergies across HP's business units through scope-driven strategic integration. The third is to identify and exploit new business opportunities on the basis of HP's unique combination of assets: In short, complex strategic integration. It remains to be seen how Fiorina's efforts to increase CSI capability will work out over the next few years. But her efforts are on the frontier of multibusiness strategic leadership.

---

share through the continuous concerted action of multiple business units. Reinforcing the core requires rapidly mobilizing resources across multiple business units, scaling up to selectively pursue major opportunities and dropping opportunities that could stretch resources too thin.

Whereas reinforcement enables moving forcefully and rapidly along a given strategic trajectory, redirection helps a company shift its strategic trajectory, often in anticipation of or in response to major discontinuities.

If companies traditionally have emphasized scope and reinforcement, it may be hard for them to become comfortable with reach-driven strategic integration and redirection. Because redirection requires figuring out the strategic context for a new business, it is more risky and difficult than reinforcement. Only by increasing the quality of strategic decision making can companies improve the odds of making the right decisions in unfamiliar areas. That may require breaking major corporate decisions into sequences of learning and commitment, with risks contained and reassessed at each stage and at each management level involved in the decision-making process.

COMPLEX STRATEGIC INTEGRATION AT STMICROELECTRONICS

STMicroelectronics resulted from the merger of Italy's SGS Microelettronica and France's Thomson Semiconducteurs. The merger brought together power, signal, analog and digital capabilities in one company. ST developed its complex-strategic-integration capability while responding to the needs of a major customer, Seagate, which needed a smaller, simpler, highly reliable disk-drive controller (and read-write system). ST integrated the various required capabilities, which resided in different divisions and in locations as dispersed as Grenoble, Milan, Ireland and Phoenix, Arizona. During the 1990s the approach pioneered for Seagate became a tried and tested CSI capability within ST, leading to the creation of new opportunities. The Seagate experience gave rise not only to a strategy but to a process that fostered lateral collaboration for creating and pursuing new opportunities.

ST's distinctive strategy is to develop "systems on a chip": to integrate into a single chip the functions normally performed by different integrated circuits assembled on a board. That strategy addresses a fast-growing market segment that lies between custom-made, application-specific integrated circuits (ASICs) and mass-produced general-purpose microprocessors. Often the system-on-a-chip strategy relies on customers who specify which capabilities they need to integrate from the various ST subunits. The customer becomes a strategic-integration hub for ST units.

Although seemingly random and often quite informal, complex strategic integration at ST is supported by managerial skills and increasingly well-honed tools (structure, control systems, incentives and behavioral norms). In addition to the regular operating units, ST created a "headquarters region," which it uses deliberately to explore CSI opportunities. Following a period in the early 1990s when efforts to achieve complex strategic integration sometimes stumbled on transfer pricing and sales-credit issues, a see-through management control system was put in place to enable recognition of business-unit contributions to CSI projects. Measurement and reward systems encourage the pursuit of joint opportunities among business units.

Most ST managers have spent their whole career with the company, know one another well, and understand the perspectives and interests of others. ST is seen as a family in which individual motives are fairly transparent. Thus there is a high level of mutual understanding and trust. In addition, ST's managers come from more than a dozen countries, many of whom permanently reside in the United States but have maintained their ties to Europe. The pool of cosmopolitan managers has the necessary skills to integrate across national and cultural boundaries.

Customer needs are viewed as sources of CSI initiatives. At ST, a project requiring complex strategic integration becomes real as soon as it has a customer. Among the projects, some are considered of strategic importance for the company's future. Those are dubbed "Golden Projects," and top management gives them priority access to resources.

Intel's networking venture provides an example of the difficulties of achieving redirection. Intel had entered the networking business in the late 1980s as a result of internal entrepreneurship, and it garnered several hundred million dollars in sales by the mid-1990s. Yet the general manager was not able to get Intel's highly focused top management to view the networking business as strategic. As a result, it received only limited internal resources. In the face of the rapid growth of the networking industry during the mid-1990s, Intel remained a second-tier player. Only in 1997, when then-COO Craig Barrett raised concerns about Intel's ability to develop new businesses, was a new general manager able to get top management to view networking as strategic for the company.

Reach-Driven Strategic Integration Supports Redirection

Strongly decentralized companies that traditionally have emphasized corporate entrepreneurship and organic diversification around core competencies tend to be reach-driven. Johnson & Johnson, 3M and Hewlett-Packard (before the arrival of CEO Carly Fiorina) are classic examples. Reach-driven strategic integration helps companies achieve profitable growth through redirecting the strategy. Often discontinuities make previously peripheral competencies more central to the evolution of the company and lead to opportunities to leverage those competencies.

The technical or market signals associated with the discontinuities, however, are often difficult for corporate managers, who are removed from the front line, to detect. Redirection therefore requires the involvement of middle and senior managers. Dick Hackborn's successful effort to drive Hewlett-Packard toward a leading strategic position in digital printing during the early 1980s is illustrative.[8] Internal entrepreneurs also have redirected Johnson & Johnson's and 3M's evolution.

Becoming comfortable with scope-driven strategic integration and reinforcement is the key integration challenge for companies traditionally emphasizing reach and redirection. Pursuing scope-driven strategic integration often requires strong top-management intervention. That was the case at 3M and Johnson & Johnson during the early 1990s, when the CEOs sought to increase cross-business collaboration in their entrepreneurial, strategically fragmented companies.[9]

Only top management can create a corporate context that makes complex strategic integration an ongoing institutionalized process rather than an infrequent occurrence relying on ad hoc championing efforts of some highly dedicated managers.

Johnson & Johnson's effort to create a Hospital Services Group (HSG) during the 1980s provides a prime example of the difficulties of achieving reinforcement in companies that traditionally emphasize reach and redirection.[10] HSG was a response to hospitals' demands for greater efficiency. HSG wanted to provide a unified interface with hospital customers for ordering, billing and logistics. It took many years, however, for Johnson & Johnson to secure the collaboration of its fiercely independent product divisions for creating such a cross-business group.

Managing Resource Scarcity and Mobility

The second top-management challenge involves managing resource scarcity and mobility. Complex strategic integration requires sharing and transferring resources among business units. Tangible resources—such as money, capital equipment, raw materials, types of labor and management time—must be allocated among different business units. The scarcity of such resources creates a zero-sum game: What one unit gets, the others cannot. By contrast, some intangible resources—such as corporate brands, patents, know-how, technology and competencies (unless embodied in specific people)—are more like public goods: Their use in one part of the organization to pursue one set of opportunities does not prevent their use elsewhere. Although the sequence of specific projects may still occasionally pit managers against one another in competing for some resources, the availability of free resources creates a positive-sum game, in which self-interested but forthright cooperation pays off.[11]

Another important consideration is that some resources are more mobile than others. Corporate image, for example, is a resource that is highly mobile and applicable across multiple opportunities at no extra cost and without requiring managers to actively share. Some resources are less mobile because they require the sharing of information to create an information advantage (as the various business units of American Express did in trying to leverage data on consumers' spending patterns). Tapping other resources may require setting up and managing interdependent joint projects across units. That would be true for HP or Motorola to make automotive electronics. Again, top-level leadership can help. GE management, for example, helped overcome the inherent difficulties of moving resources when it established General Electric Credit Corp. to assist GE's industrial businesses in winning major customer contracts.

BUILDING A COMPLEX-STRATEGIC-INTEGRATION CAPABILITY

Like most other key corporate capabilities, building CSI capability is a task for the highest level of management. Only top management can create a corporate context that makes complex strategic integration an ongoing institutionalized process rather than an infrequent occurrence relying on ad hoc championing efforts of some highly dedicated managers. Top management needs to ensure that all high-level managers develop the skills necessary to effectively pursue CSI opportunities.[12]

CSI Context

To develop a corporate context that encourages complex strategic integration, top management should focus on organizational structure, managerial control systems and managerial incentives. Each makes a distinct contribution to CSI, and each needs to reinforce the others.

Organizational Structure

For effective collaboration, a company's organizational structure must be able to accommodate the real and evolving interdependencies among new and existing businesses. Companies need a framework for assessing the interdependencies that complex-strategic-integration initiatives create—and a repertoire of organizational-design options to augment the company's entrepreneurial capability.[13] Intel, Nokia and Lucent, for instance, have created new-venture groups—a first step in using structure to facilitate CSI. As evolving CSI efforts generate new information, previous assessments must be re-evaluated and existing structural arrangements reconsidered.

Another structural approach might involve setting up integrators—senior executives or a corporate staff unit whose role is to stimulate operational units to pursue complex strategic integration. For instance, Bob Pittman played a key business-integrator role after the merger of Time Inc. and Warner Communications. Another structural approach is to redistribute the complex-strategic-integration task by giving senior executives dual responsibilities: being in charge of major functional or business activities while also being responsible for new-business development based on complex strategic integration. That is essentially the approach adopted by HP's Fiorina.[14]

Managerial Control Systems

Managerial control systems can encourage CSI, too. One scholar has identified four types.[15] First are diagnostic control systems, which can foster cooperation if they register cross-unit contributions. However, most focus on individual business-unit performance and may deter business-unit managers from strategic-integration activities. For instance, ABB was initially successful in developing business-area strategies that required fairly intense cross-business collaboration.[16] However, ABB's Abacus diagnostic control system, which closely monitored the performance of the company's thousands of investment and profit centers, concentrated on individual unit performance and impeded strategic integration. By 1996, top management felt that ABB had become too fragmented. The result was "over-individualistic behaviors by the rulers of smaller kingdoms," as one observer noted. The problem is not uncommon. Collaboration requires a level of sophistication and self-confidence that may elude managers used to operating under control systems that emphasize individual unit performance.

Second are belief systems, which help define behavioral norms that support cooperation and reciprocity. Cooperation and reciprocity are probably easiest to develop in companies such as investment banks, which engage in multiple deals involving the same networks of people. In such companies, reciprocity norms govern repeated interactions. Cooperation and reciprocity are less easy to develop in situations involving the infrequent, large, one-time commitments that complex strategic integration may call for. They usually emerge gradually over time as part of a culture of trust and support among managers. For instance, at 3M, the business units own products, but not technologies. People really believe that technologies are freely available to anyone at 3M who wants to use them for new-business development.

Third are boundary-setting control systems. They are useful in identifying major risks, in particular those that lead companies to pursue overambitious strategic integration. Intel's New Business Group sets boundaries. It aims, as much as possible, to avoid entering new areas in direct competition with existing customers. However, boundaries need to be sufficiently dynamic that they can accommodate serendipity in complex strategic integration.

Finally, interactive control systems help top management signal the importance of CSI. With interactive control systems, complex strategic integration stays on the table in all high-level discussions about corporate strategy. Thus when Intel's Craig Barrett

ABOUT THE RESEARCH

When the authors decided to start exploratory field research focused on complex strategic integration in multibusiness companies, systematic research on the subject was virtually nonexistent. They carried out some of the field research jointly during spring 1998, interviewing senior and top executives at several European companies. In parallel with those interviews. Yves Doz and his colleagues José Santos and Peter Williamson carried out detailed field studies at several European and Asian multinational companies, scrutinizing strategic integration among business units, geographic subunits and partners. The research also explored how small entrepreneurial ventures (such as flat-screen developer PixTech) and new venture groups in established companies such as Nokia could mobilize competencies from longer, better-established partners, and achieve complex strategic integration (CSI) in multipartner value-creating webs.

Robert Burgelman's longitudinal research of Intel Corp.'s strategy-making process highlighted the difficulty of reach-driven strategic integration in a highly focused company. And his field study of Hewlett-Packard highlighted the difficulty of scope-driven strategic integration in a highly fragmented company. The study of the first nine months of Carly Fiorina's tenure as HP's new CEO (July 1999 to April 2000) focused on her efforts to create a CSI capability. The research involved interviews with all the members of HP's newly formed executive council and with several senior and midlevel general managers. Other parts of the research involved case writing about companies such as Intel, Disney, USA Networks, America Online and Time Warner—companies trying to cope with the convergence of several industry segments in the information-processing industry and struggling to develop some CSI capability to capitalize on that convergence.

started involving several hundred senior executives in discussions about how to increase the company's new-business-development capability, he was able to spur the 1999 creation of the New Business Group.

Managerial Incentives

A major responsibility for the top management of multibusiness corporations is developing and maintaining incentives that encourage the most promising managers to pursue complex-strategic-integration initiatives—without losing their focus on the competitive reality their individual businesses face.[17] Incentives must be consistent with structural arrangements and control systems.[18] Unfortunately, business-unit managers often face conflicting incentives. And although managers of business units confronted by slowing growth may be motivated to seek cross-business cooperation, managers of profitable and growing business may not.

The challenge is one of imagination, intellectual grasp and capacity for recognizing good strategies. Executive development can play an important role by putting managers into positions where they can learn by doing.

In addition, business-unit managers may perceive incentives for cooperation as blurring their accountability and diffusing responsibilities in dysfunctional ways. A senior executive at a European high-technology company observed that managers' ability to look beyond the borders of their own business and to think creatively always had been one of the most important criteria for ascending to higher levels in his company. He felt that job rotation and international assignments used for that purpose had led executives to focus on the scope dimension, which "in some cases perhaps led to weaker performance in terms of reach." The same executive added that the current preoccupation with single-business-unit performance was threatening to weaken the incentives for managers to focus on strategic integration.

CSI Skills

In addition to creating a corporate context that encourages complex strategic integration, top management needs to ensure that the corporation nurtures and develops three mutually supportive senior-executive skill sets. Cognitive, political and entrepreneurial skills can be developed through education and job assignments.

Cognitive Skills

Part of the required CSI skill set is cognitive. Complex strategic integration requires senior executives to think up new strategies that bring together activities and projects located in different parts of the corporation. The challenge is one of imagination, intellectual grasp and capacity for recognizing good strategies. Different managers undoubtedly have different aptitude. But executive development can play an important role by putting managers into positions where they can learn by doing. Sometimes, however, high-level managers try too hard, taking their dreams for reality until, as American Express did with its financial-supermarket strategy, they find themselves in the overambitious set. One of the skills needed is the ability to decide when to exit businesses and abandon dreams as Hewlett-Packard did when it divested its test-and-measurement businesses to focus more on its computer and printer businesses.

Political Skills

Complex strategic integration involves reconfiguring the flow of company resources through cross-unit projects. Unit boundaries get redefined, and often individual business-unit charters do, too.[19] It is primarily top management that needs to build a consistent corporate context to foster and encourage cooperation among units.[20] But other high-level managers lobbying for changes in the structural and strategic contexts of the company play a key role. They need strong political skills to gain support from top management and peers for their complex-strategic-integration initiatives. They need to execute partnerships with peers, to create common ground and shared vision, and to manage conflicts between business units. They need to be able to define solutions that serve the interests of various business units (while serving the corporation) and to entice other business-unit managers and top management to cooperate. The skills match those of good politicians, successful coalition builders and diplomats in complex alliances.

Entrepreneurial Skills

Complex strategic integration also requires entrepreneurial skill: the ability to perceive profitable business opportunities and to attract the necessary corporate resources. CSI calls for transforming a project from a small venture to an opportunity for major corporate renewal. Senior executives must master such activities as strategic building and organizational championing so that they can determine the strategic context for major initiatives and convince top management to pour in resources.[21]

THE UNIQUE ROLE OF TOP MANAGEMENT

Top management's task is to develop a strategy-making process that can balance the challenges associated with exploiting existing and new opportunities simultaneously. In multibusiness corporations, that means developing a CSI capability. Corporate leaders must make an explicit commitment to articulating a corporate strategy that facilitates exploring and exploiting the maximum feasible strategic opportunities. Understanding the importance of both reach and scope, they must make sure that managers understand that their chances for increasingly senior positions depend on their demonstrated ability to bring complex-strategic-integration initiatives to successful completion. Promoting executives on the basis of their demonstrated CSI results speaks louder than statements about the need to create shareholder value. Top management will have to work on developing a CSI corporate context and CSI skills. Mistakes will be made, but the key is to spot them quickly and correct them. The relative importance of CSI initiatives and individual businesses may vary over time as the company evolves through different life cycles and industry transitions. But the leaders of multibusiness corporations should never vacillate in their support for complex strategic integration and its critical role in the company's future.

Additional Resources

Little has been written about the management process involved in complex strategic integration. However, research on integration after acquisitions provides some insight on getting different organizational entities to work together. Interested readers will appreciate P.C. Haspeslagh and D.B. Jemison's 1991 Free Press book, "Managing Acquisitions: Creating Value Through Corporate Renewal." For research on strategic integration in companies operating in the global economy, we recommend Y. Doz, J. Santos and P. Williamson's "From Global to Metanational: Competing in the Global Knowledge Economy," which is scheduled for release this year.

About the Authors

Robert A. Burgelman is a professor of management at Stanford University's Graduate School of Business in Stanford, California. Yves L. Doz is dean of executive education and a professor of global technology and innovation at INSEAD in Fontainebleau, France. Contact the authors at burgelman_robert@gsb.stanford.edu and yves.doz@insead.fr.

References

1. WPP, a holding company of independent marketing-services companies created by Martin Sorrell in 1985, is a good example. WPP seeks to create superior value for customers, employees and shareholders by getting its highly independent businesses to collaborate. See J.L. Bower and S. Ellingson-Hout, "WPP: Integrating Icons," Harvard Business School case no. 9-396-249 (Boston: Harvard Business School Publishing Corp., 1996).

2. R.A. Burgelman, D.L. Carter and R.S. Bamford, "Intel Corporation: The Evolution of an Adaptive Organization," Stanford Business School case no. SM-65 (Stanford, California: Stanford Business School, 1999).

3. D.A. Garvin, "Harvey Golub: Recharging American Express," Harvard Business School case no. 9-396-212 (Boston: Harvard Business School Publishing Corp., 1996).

4. The opportunities identified in the strategic-integration framework are different from the growth vectors in Ansoff's product-market framework. For instance, the scope-driven opportunity set could involve product development (new products developed by two or more business units together for their existing markets) or market development (new markets developed by two or more business units with their combined existing products) or both. Ansoff's framework also does not consider trade-offs among the various growth vectors as a result of resource constraints nor the strategic-integration issues across business units possibly involved in the various growth vectors. On the other hand, the business opportunities generated in the context of each form of strategic integration can be fruitfully interpreted in terms of Ansoff's typology. The two frameworks are thus complementary. See H.I. Ansoff, "Corporate Strategy: An Analytic Approach to Business Policy for Growth and Expansion" (New York: McGraw-Hill, 1965). The assessments involved in establishing the different opportunity sets may vary across different parts of a company. A high degree of participation, negotiation and flexibility will be necessary in the process of establishing the maximum strategic-opportunity set in order to get companywide support. And significant external and/or internal changes may affect the frontier over time. Sometimes, such changes force companies to disengage from a major profitable opportunity when it does not fit any more with the corporate value-creation logic. Hewlett-Packard's 1999 exit from test and measurement businesses is an example.

5. Y.L. Doz and G. Hamel, "Alliance Advantage" (Boston: Harvard Business School Press, 1998).

6. Robert Burgelman thanks Pekka Ala-Pietila, president of Nokia Corp., for that insight (personal communication).

7. R.A. Burgelman, "Strategy Is Destiny: How Strategy Making Shapes a Company's Future" (New York: The Free Press, in press): and J. Kolotouros, J. Maggioncalda and R.A. Burgelman, "Disney in a Digital World," Stanford Business School case no. SM-29 (Stanford, California: Stanford Business School, 1996); and J. Kolotouros and R. Burgelman, "Disney in a Digital World (B)," Stanford Business School case no. SM-29B (Stanford, California: Stanford Business School, 1998).

8. S.K. Yoder, "How HP Used Tactics of the Japanese To Beat Them at Their Game," The Wall Street Journal, Sept. 8, 1994, A1.

9. J.M. Hurstak and A.E. Pearson, "Johnson & Johnson in the 1990s," Harvard Business School case no. 9-393-001 (Boston: Harvard Business School Publishing Corp., 1993); and C.A. Bartlett and A. Mohammed, "3M: Profile of an Innovating Company," Harvard Business School case no. 0-384-054 (Boston: Harvard Business School Publishing Corp., 1995).

10. F. Aguilar, "Johnson & Johnson (B): Hospital Services," Harvard Business School case no. 9-384-054 (Boston: Harvard Business School Publishing Corp., 1983).

11. For early work on resource sharing among business units, see A. Gupta and V. Govindarajan, "Resource Sharing Among SBU's: Antecedents and Administrative Implications," Academy of Management Journal 29 (1986): 695–714. Also, top management can use various approaches to foster resource sharing. Bob Pittman, co-COO of AOL Time Warner, is renowned for his ability to get independent business-unit leaders to collaborate. He does so by convincing them that they'll will win bigger by cooperating and also makes sure to give them the

credit for successful cooperation. See C. Yang, R. Grover and A.T. Palmer, "Show Time for AOL Time Warner," Business Week, Jan. 15, 2001, 56–64.

12. The contextual factors and skills proposed for building a company's CSI capability can be related to McKinsey & Co.'s 7-S framework, which encompasses strategy, structure, systems, skills, style, staffing and shared values. The 7-S framework also emphasizes the importance of configuration and the balancing of each in harmonious ways. The contextual factors we propose touch on structure, systems and shared values. The proposed cognitive, political and entrepreneurial skills have obvious bearing on skills but also touch on style and staffing. Identifying the maximum strategic-opportunity set speaks directly to the strategy component in the 7-S framework. Examining what changes are needed in a company's existing 7-S configuration in order to build a company's CSI capability is an important task for top management.

13. R.A. Burgelman, "Designs for Corporate Entrepreneurship in Established Firms," California Management Review 26 (spring 1984): 154–166.

14. R.A. Burgelman and P. Meza, "The New HP Way," Stanford Business School case no. SM-7 (Stanford, California: Stanford Business School, 2000).

15. R. Simons, "Levers of Control: How Managers Use Innovative Control Systems To Drive Strategic Renewal" (Boston: Harvard Business School Press, 1994).

16. C.A. Bartlett and S. Ghoshal, "Beyond the M-Form: Toward a Managerial Theory of the Firm," Strategic Management Journal 14 (1993): 23–46.

17. The difficulties associated with aligning incentives in multibusiness companies lead economists to emphasize the benefits of narrow (single) business strategies. See J.J. Rotemberg and G. Saloner, "Benefits of Narrow Business Strategies," American Economic Review 84 (1994): 1330–1349.

18. For an analytical approach to designing the relationships among incentives and strategy and structure in complex corporations using multiple dimensions in their structure (for example, function, product, geography), see D.P. Baron and D. Besanko, "Strategy, Organization and Incentives: Global Corporate Banking at Citibank," Research Paper Series no. 1488. Stanford University Graduate School of Business, Stanford, California, 1998.

19. D.C. Galunic, "Recreating Divisional Domains: Coevolution and the Multibusiness Firm" (Ph.D. diss., Department of Industrial Engineering and Engineering Management, Stanford University, 1994).

20. T.R. Eisenmann and J.L. Bower, "The Entrepreneurial M-Form: Strategic Integration in Global Media Firms." Organization Science (May–June 2000): 348–355.

21. For a discussion of the key entrepreneurial activities, see R.A. Burgelman, "Managing the Internal Corporate Venturing Process," Sloan Management Review 25 (winter 1984). On a smaller scale, "patching"—which involves adding, splitting, transferring or combining chunks of businesses—is also a potentially useful entrepreneurial skill. See K.M. Eisenhardt and S.L. Brown, "Patching: Restitching Business Portfolios in Dynamic Markets," Harvard Business Review (May–June 1999): 72–85.

53

DISRUPTIVE TECHNOLOGIES: CATCHING THE WAVE

Joseph L. Bower and Clayton M. Christensen

One of the most consistent patterns in business is the failure of leading companies to stay at the top of their industries when technologies or markets change. Goodyear and Firestone entered the radial-tire market quite late. Xerox let Canon create the small-copier market. Bucyrus-Erie allowed Caterpillar and Deere to take over the mechanical excavator market. Sears gave way to Wal-Mart.

The pattern of failure has been especially striking in the computer industry. IBM dominated the mainframe market but missed by years the emergence of minicomputers, which were technologically much simpler than mainframes. Digital Equipment dominated the minicomputer market with innovations like its VAX architecture but missed the personal-computer market almost completely. Apple Computer led the world of personal computing and established the standard for user-friendly computing but lagged five years behind the leaders in bringing its portable computer to market.

Why is it that companies like these invest aggressively—and successfully—in the technologies necessary to retain their current customers but then fail to make certain other technological investments that customers of the future will demand? Undoubtedly, bureaucracy, arrogance, tired executive blood, poor planning, and short-term investment horizons have all played a role. But a more fundamental reason lies at the heart of the paradox: leading companies succumb to one of the most popular, and valuable, management dogmas. They stay close to their customers.

Although most managers like to think they are in control, customers wield extraordinary power in directing a company's investments. Before managers decide to launch a technology, develop a product, build a plant, or establish new channels of distribution, they must look to their customers first: Do their customers want it? How big will the market be? Will the investment be profitable? The more astutely managers ask and answer these questions, the more completely their investments will he aligned with the needs of their customers.

This is the way a well-managed company should operate. Right? But what happens when customers reject a new technology, product concept, or way of doing business because it does *not* address their needs as effectively as a company's current approach? The large photocopying centers that represented the core of Xerox's customer base at first had no use for small, slow tabletop copiers. The excavation contractors that had relied on Bucyrus-Erie's big-bucket steam- and diesel-powered cable shovels didn't want hydraulic excavators because initially they were small and weak.

Bower, Joseph L. and Clayton M. Christensen. 1995. "Disruptive technologies: Catching the wave."
Harvard Business Review (January/February): 43–53.

IBM's large commercial, government, and industrial customers saw no immediate use for minicomputers. In each instance, companies listened to their customers, gave them the product performance they were looking for, and, in the end, were hurt by the very technologies their customers led them to ignore.

We have seen this pattern repeatedly in an ongoing study of leading companies in a variety of industries that have confronted technological change. The research shows

> *Managers must beware of ignoring new technologies that don't initially meet the needs of their mainstream customers.*

that most well-managed, established companies are consistently ahead of their industries in developing and commercializing new technologies— from incremental improvements to radically new approaches—as long as those technologies address the next-generation performance needs of their customers. However, these same companies are rarely in the forefront of commercializing new technologies that don't initially meet the needs of mainstream customers and appeal only to small or emerging markets.

Using the rational, analytical investment processes that most well-managed companies have developed, it is nearly impossible to build a cogent case for diverting resources from known customer needs in established markets to markets and customers that seem insignificant or do not yet exist. After all, meeting the needs of established customers and fending off competitors takes all the resources a company has, and then some. In well-managed companies, the processes used to identify customers' needs, forecast technological trends, assess profitability, allocate resources across competing proposals for investment, and take new products to market are focused—for all the right reasons—on current customers and markets. These processes are designed to weed out proposed products and technologies that do *not* address customers' needs.

In fact, the processes and incentives that companies use to keep focused on their main customers work so well that they blind those companies to important new technologies in emerging markets. Many companies have learned the hard way the perils of ignoring new technologies that do not initially meet the needs of mainstream customers. For example, although personal computers did not meet the requirements of mainstream minicomputer users in the early 1980s, the computing power of the desktop machines improved at a much faster rate than minicomputer users' *demands* for computing power did. As a result, personal computers caught up with the computing needs of many of the customers of Wang, Prime, Nixdorf, Data General, and Digital Equipment. Today they are performance-competitive with minicomputers in many applications. For the minicomputer makers, keeping close to mainstream customers and ignoring what were initially low-performance desktop technologies used by seemingly insignificant customers in emerging markets was a rational decision—but one that proved disastrous.

The technological changes that damage established companies are usually not radically new or difficult from a *technological* point of view. They do, however, have two important characteristics: First, they typically present a different package of performance attributes—ones that, at least at the outset, are not valued by existing customers. Second, the performance attributes that existing customers do value improve at such a rapid rare that the new technology can later invade those established markets. Only at this point will mainstream customers want the technology. Unfortunately for the established suppliers, by then it is often too late: the pioneers of the new technology dominate the market.

If follows, then, that senior executives must first be able to spot the technologies that seem to fall into this category. Next, to commercialize and develop the new technologies, managers must protect them from the processes and incentives that are geared to serving established customers. And the only way to protect them is to create organizations that are completely independent from the mainstream business.

No industry demonstrates the danger of staying too close to customers more dramatically than the hard-disk-drive industry. Between 1976 and 1992, disk-drive performance improved at a stunning rate: the physical size of a 100-megabyte (MB) system shrank from 5,400 to 8 cubic inches, and the cost per MB fell from $560 to $5. Technological change, of course, drove these breathtaking achievements. About half of the improvement came from a host of radical advances that were critical to continued improvements in disk-drive performance; the other half came from incremental advances.

The pattern in the disk-drive industry has been repeated in many other industries: the leading, established companies have consistently led the industry in developing and adopting new technologies that their customers demanded—even when those technologies required completely different technological competencies and manufacturing capabilities from the ones the companies had. In spite of this aggressive technological posture, no single disk-drive manufacturer has been able to dominate the industry for more than a few years. A series of companies have entered the business and risen to prominence, only to be toppled by newcomers who pursued technologies that at first did not meet the needs of mainstream customers. As a result, not one of the independent disk-drive companies that existed in 1976 survives today.

To explain the differences in the impact of certain kinds of technological innovations on a given industry, the concept of *performance trajectories*—the rate at which the performance of a product has improved, and is expected to improve, over time—can be helpful. Almost every industry has a critical performance trajectory. In mechanical excavators, the critical trajectory is the annual improvement in cubic yards of earth moved per minute. In photo-copiers, an important performance trajectory is improvement in number of copies per minute. In disk drives, one crucial measure of performance is storage capacity, which has advanced 50% each year on average for a given size of drive.

Different types of technological innovations affect performance trajectories in different ways. On the one hand, *sustaining* technologies tend to maintain a rate of improvement; that is, they give customers something more or better in the attributes they already value. For example, thin-film components in disk drives, which replaced conventional ferrite heads and oxide disks between 1982 and 1990, enabled information to be recorded more densely on disks. Engineers had been pushing the limits of the performance they could wring from ferrite heads and oxide disks, but the drives employing these technologies seemed to have reached the natural limits of an *S* curve. At that point, new thin-film technologies emerged that restored—or sustained—the historical trajectory of performance improvement.

On the other hand, *disruptive* technologies introduce a very different package of attributes from the one mainstream customers historically value, and they often perform far worse along one or two dimensions that are particularly important to those customers. As a rule, mainstream customers are unwilling to use a disruptive product in applications they know and understand. At first, then, disruptive technologies tend to be used and valued only in new markets or new applications; in fact, they generally make possible the emergence of new markets. For example, Sony's early transistor radios sacrificed sound fidelity but created a market for portable radios by offering a new and different package of attributes—small size, light weight, and portability.

In the history of the hard-disk-drive industry, the leaders stumbled at each point of disruptive technological change: when the diameter of disk drives shrank from the original 14 inches to 8 inches, then to 5.25 inches, and finally to 3.5 inches. Each of these new architectures initially offered the market substantially less storage capacity than the typical user in the established market required. For example, the 8-inch drive offered 20 MB when it was introduced, while the primary market for disk drives at that time—mainframes—required 200 MB on average. Not surprisingly, the leading computer manufacturers rejected the 8-inch architecture at first. As a result, their suppliers, whose mainstream products consisted of 14-inch drives with more than 200 MB of capacity, did not pursue the disruptive products aggressively. The pattern was repeated When the 5.25-inch and 3.5-inch drives emerged: established computer makers rejected the drives as inadequate, and, in turn, their disk-drive suppliers ignored them as well.

But while they offered less storage capacity, the disruptive architectures created other important attributes—internal power supplies and smaller size (8-inch drives); still smaller size and low-cost stepper motors (5.25-inch drives); and ruggedness, light weight, and low-power consumption (3.5-inch drives). From the late 1970s to the mid-1980s, the availability of the three drives made possible the development of new markets for minicomputers, desktop PCs, and portable computers, respectively.

Although the smaller drives represented disruptive technological change, each was technologically straightforward. In fact, there were engineers at many leading companies who championed the new technologies and built working prototypes with bootlegged

FIGURE 53-1 How Disk-Drive Performance Met Market Needs

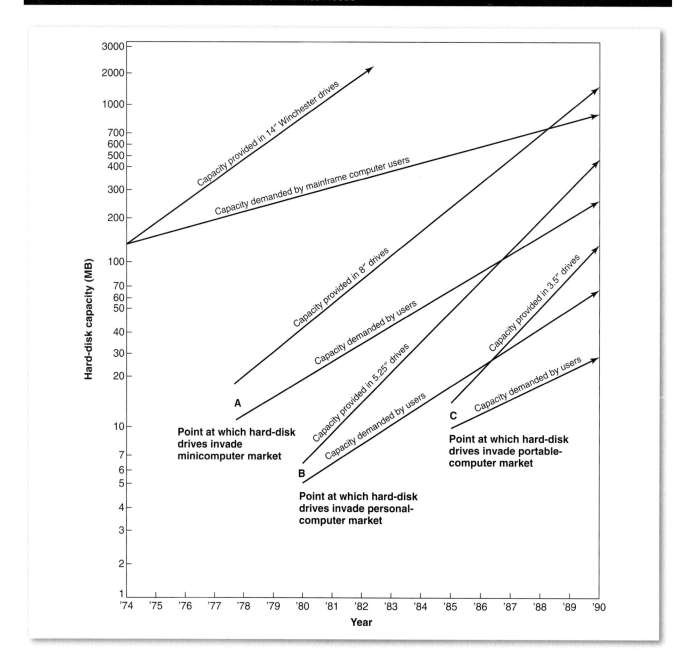

resources before management gave a formal go-ahead. Still, the leading companies could not move the products through their organizations and into the market in a timely way. Each time a disruptive technology emerged, between one-half and two-thirds of the established manufacturers failed to introduce models employing the new architecture—in stark contrast to their timely launches of critical sustaining technologies. Those companies that finally did launch new models typically lagged behind entrant companies by two years—eons in an industry whose products' life cycles are often two years. Three waves of entrant companies led these revolutions; they first captured the new markets and then dethroned the leading companies in the mainstream markets.

How could technologies that were initially inferior and useful only to new markets eventually threaten leading companies in established markets? Once the disruptive architectures became established in their new markets, sustaining innovations raised each architecture's performance

None of the established leaders in the disk-drive industry learned from the experiences of those that fell before them.

along steep trajectories—so steep that the performance available from each architecture soon satisfied the needs of customers in the established markets. For example, the 5.25-inch drive, whose initial 5 MB of capacity in 1980 was only a fraction of the capacity that the minicomputer market needed, became fully performance-competitive in the minicomputer market by 1986 and in the mainframe market by 1991. (See Figure 53-1.)

A company's revenue and cost structures play a critical role in the way it evaluates proposed technological innovations. Generally, disruptive technologies look financially unattractive to established companies. The potential revenues from the discernible markets are small, and it is often difficult to project how big the markets for the technology will be over the long term. As a result, managers typically conclude that the technology cannot make a meaningful contribution to corporate growth and, therefore, that it is not worth the management effort required to develop it. In addition, established companies have often installed higher cost structures to serve sustaining technologies than those required by disruptive technologies. As a result, managers typically see themselves as having two choices when deciding whether to pursue disruptive technologies. One is to go *downmarket* and accept the lower profit margins of the emerging markets that the disruptive technologies will initially serve. The other is to go *upmarket* with sustaining technologies and enter market segments whose profit margins are alluringly high. (For example, the margins of IBM's mainframes are still higher than those of PCs). Any rational resource-allocation process in companies serving established markets will choose going upmarket rather than going down.

Managers of companies that have championed disruptive technologies in emerging markets look at the world quite differently. Without the high cost structures of their established counterparts, these companies find the emerging markets appealing. Once the companies have secured a foothold in the markets and improved the performance of their technologies, the established markets above them, served by high-cost suppliers, look appetizing. When they do attack, the entrant companies find the established players to be easy and unprepared opponents because the opponents have been looking upmarket themselves, discounting the threat from below.

It is tempting to stop at this point and conclude that a valuable lesson has been learned: managers can avoid missing the next wave by paying careful attention to potentially disruptive technologies that do *not* meet current customers' needs. But recognizing the pattern and figuring out how to break it are two different things. Although entrants invaded established markets with new technologies three times in succession, none of the established leaders in the disk-drive industry seemed to learn from the experiences of those that fell before them. Management myopia or lack of foresight cannot explain these failures. The problem is that managers keep doing what has worked in the past: serving the rapidly growing needs of their current customers. The processes that successful, well-managed companies have developed to allocate resources among proposed investments are *incapable* of funneling resources into programs that current customers explicitly don't want and whose profit margins seem unattractive.

Managing the development of new technology is tightly linked to a company's investment processes. Most strategic proposals—to add capacity or to develop new products or processes—take shape at the lower levels of organizations in engineering groups or project teams. Companies then use analytical planning and budgeting systems to select from among the candidates competing for funds. Proposals to create new businesses in emerging markets are particularly challenging to assess because they depend on notoriously unreliable estimates of market size. Because managers are evaluated on their ability to place the right bets, it is not surprising that in well-managed companies, mid and top-level managers back projects in which the market seems assured. By staying close to lead customers, as they have been trained to do, managers focus resources on fulfilling the requirements of those reliable customers that can be served profitably. Risk is reduced—and careers are safeguarded—by giving known customers what they want.

Seagate Technology's experience illustrates the consequences of relying on such resource-allocation processes to evaluate disruptive technologies. By almost any measure, Seagate, based in Scotts Valley, California, was one of the most successful and aggressively managed companies in the history of the microelectronics industry: from its inception in 1980, Seagate's revenues had grown to more than $700 million by 1986. It had pioneered 5.25-inch hard-disk drives and was the main supplier of them to IBM and IBM-compatible personal-computer manufacturers. The company was the leading manufacturer of 5.25-inch drives at the time the disruptive 3.5-inch drives emerged in the mid-1980s.

Engineers at Seagate were the second in the industry to develop working prototypes of 3.5-inch drives. By early 1985, they had made more than 80 such models with a low level of company funding. The engineers forwarded the new models to key marketing executives, and the trade press reported that Seagate was actively developing 3.5-inch drives. But Seagate's principal customers—IBM and other manufacturers of AT-class personal computers—showed no interest in the new drives. They wanted to incorporate 40-MB and 60-MB drives in their next-generation models, and Seagate's early 3.5-inch prototypes packed only 10 MB. In response, Seagate's marketing executives lowered their sales forecasts for the new disk drives.

Seagate paid the price for allowing start-ups to lead the way into emerging markets.

Manufacturing and financial executives at the company pointed out another drawback to the 3.5-inch drives. According to their analysis, the new drives would never be competitive with the 5.25-inch architecture on a cost-per-megabyte basis—an important metric that Seagate's customers used to evaluate disk drives. Given Seagate's cost structure, margins on the higher-capacity 5.25-inch models therefore promised to be much higher than those on the smaller products.

Senior managers quite rationally decided that the 3.5-inch drive would not provide the sales volume and profit margins that Seagate needed from a new product. A former Seagate marketing executive recalled, "We needed a new model that could become the next ST412 [a 5.25-inch drive generating more than $300 million in annual sales, which was nearing the end of its life cycle]. At the time, the entire market for 3.5 inch drives was less than $50 million. The 3.5-inch drive just didn't fit the bill—for sales or profits."

The shelving of the 3.5-inch drive was *not* a signal that Seagate was complacent about innovation. Seagate subsequently introduced new models of 5.25-inch drives at an accelerated rate and, in so doing, introduced and impressive array of sustaining technological improvements, even though introducing them rendered a significant portion of its manufacturing capacity obsolete.

While Seagate's attention was glued to the personal-computer market, former employees of Seagate and other 5.25-inch drive makers, who had become frustrated by their employers' delays in launching 3.5-inch drives, founded a new company, Conner Peripherals. Conner focused on selling its 3.5-inch drives to companies in emerging markets for portable computers and small-footprint desktop products (PCs that take up a smaller amount of space on a desk). Conner's primary customer was Compaq Computer, a customer that Seagate had never served. Seagate's own prosperity, coupled with Conner's focus on customers who valued different disk-drive attributes (ruggedness, physical volume, and weight), minimized the threat Seagate saw in Conner and its 3.5-inch drives.

From its beachhead in the emerging market for portable computers, however, Conner improved the storage capacity of its drives by 50% per year. By the end of 1987, 3.5-inch drives packed the capacity demanded in the mainstream personal-computer market. At this point, Seagate executives took their company's 3.5-inch drive off the shelf, introducing it to the market as a *defensive* response to the attack of entrant companies like Conner and Quantum Corporation, the other pioneer of 3.5-inch drives. But it was too late.

By then, Seagate faced strong competition. For a while, the company was able to defend its existing market by selling 3.5-inch drives to its established customer base—manufacturers and resellers of full-size personal computers. In fact, a large proportion of its 3.5-inch products continued to be shipped in frames that enabled its customers to mount the drives in computers designed to accommodate 5.25-inch drives. But, in the end, Seagate could only struggle to become a second-tier supplier in the new portable-computer market.

In contrast, Conner and Quantum built a dominant position in the new portable-computer market and then used their scale and experience base in designing and manufacturing 3.5-inch products to drive Seagate from the personal-computer market. In their 1994 fiscal years, the combined revenues of Conner and Quantum exceeded $5 billion.

Seagate's poor timing typifies the responses of many established companies to the emergence of disruptive technologies. Seagate was willing to enter the market for 3.5-inch drives only when it had become large enough to satisfy the company's financial requirements—that is, only when existing customers wanted the new technology. Seagate has survived through its savvy acquisition of Control Data Corporation's disk-drive business in 1990. With CDC's technology base and Seagate's volume-manufacturing expertise, the company has become a powerful player in the business of supplying large-capacity drives for high-end computers. Nonetheless, Seagate has been reduced to a shadow of its former self in the personal-computer market.

It should come as no surprise that few companies, when confronted with disruptive technologies, have been able to overcome the handicaps of size or success. But it can be done. There is a method to spotting and cultivating disruptive technologies.

DETERMINE WHETHER THE TECHNOLOGY IS DISRUPTIVE OR SUSTAINING

The first step is to decide which of the myriad technologies on the horizon are disruptive and, of those, which are real threats. Most companies have well-conceived processes for identifying and tracking the progress of potentially sustaining technologies, because they are important to serving and protecting current customers. But few have systematic processes in place to identify and track potentially disruptive technologies.

One approach to identifying disruptive technologies is to examine internal disagreements over the development of new products or technologies. Who supports the project and who doesn't? Marketing and financial managers, because of their managerial and financial incentives, will rarely support a disruptive technology. On the other hand, technical personnel with outstanding track records will often persist in arguing that a new market for the technology will emerge—even in the face of opposition from key customers and marketing and financial staff. Disagreement between the two groups often signals a disruptive technology that top-level managers should explore.

DEFINE THE STRATEGIC SIGNIFICANCE OF THE DISRUPTIVE TECHNOLOGY

The next step is to ask the right people the right questions about the strategic importance of the disruptive technology. Disruptive technologies tend to stall early in strategic reviews because managers either ask the wrong questions or ask the wrong people the right questions. For example, established companies have regular procedures for asking mainstream customers—especially the important accounts where new ideas are actually tested—to assess the value of innovative products. Generally, these customers are selected because they are the ones striving the hardest to stay ahead of *their* competitors in pushing the performance of *their* products. Hence these customers are most likely to demand the highest performance from their suppliers. For this reason, lead customers are reliably accurate when it comes to assessing the potential of sustaining technologies, but they are reliably *in*accurate when it comes to assessing the potential of disruptive technologies. They are the wrong people to ask.

A simple graph plotting product performance as it is defined in mainstream markets on the vertical axis and time on the horizontal axis can help managers identify both the right questions and the right people to ask. First, draw a line depicting the level of performance and the trajectory of performance improvement that customers have historically enjoyed and are likely to expect in the future. Then locate the estimated initial performance level of the new technology. If the technology is disruptive, the point will lie far below the performance demanded by current customers. (See Figure 53-2.)

FIGURE 53-2   How to Assess Disruptive Technologies

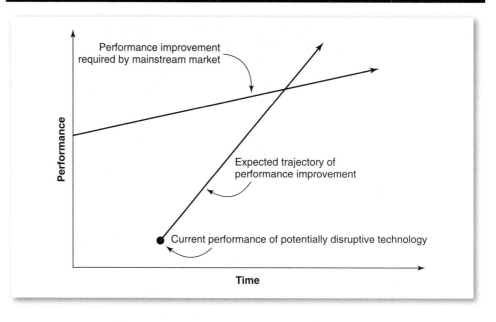

What is the likely slope of performance improvement of the disruptive technology compared with the slope of performance improvement demanded by existing markets? If knowledgeable technologists believe the new technology might progress faster than the market's demand for performance improvement, then that technology, which does not meet customers' needs today, may very well address them tomorrow. The new technology, therefore, is strategically critical.

Instead of taking this approach, most managers ask the wrong questions. They compare the anticipated rate of performance improvement of the new technology with that of the established technology. If the new technology has the potential to surpass the established one, the reasoning goes, they should get busy developing it.

Pretty simple. But this sort of comparison, while valid for sustaining technologies, misses the central strategic issue in assessing potentially disruptive technologies. Many of the disruptive technologies we studied *never* surpassed the capability of the old technology. It is the trajectory of the disruptive technology compared with that of the *market* that is significant. For example, the reason the mainframe-computer market is shrinking is not that personal computers outperform mainframes but because personal computers networked with a file server meet the computing and data-storage needs of many organizations effectively. Main-frame-computer makers are reeling not because the performance of personal-computing technology surpassed the performance of mainframe *technology* but because it intersected with the performance demanded by the established *market.*

Consider the graph again. If technologists believe that the new technology will progress at the same rate as the market's demand for performance improvement, the disruptive technology may be slower to invade established markets. Recall that Seagate had targeted personal computing, where demand for hard-disk capacity per computer was growing at 30% per year. Because the capacity of 3.5-inch drives improved at a much faster rate, leading 3.5-inch-drive makers were able to force Seagate out of the market. However, two other 5.25-inch-drive makers, Maxtor and Micropolis, had targeted the engineering-workstation market, in which demand for hard-disk capacity was insatiable. In that market, the trajectory of capacity demanded was essentially parallel to the trajectory of capacity improvement that technologists could supply in the 3.5-inch architecture. As a result, entering the 3.5-inch-drive business was strategically less critical for those companies than it was for Seagate.

Small, hungry organizations are good at agilely changing product and market strategies.

LOCATE THE INITIAL MARKET FOR THE DISRUPTIVE TECHNOLOGY

Once managers have determined that a new technology is disruptive and strategically critical, the next step is to locate the initial markets for that technology. Market research, the tool that managers have traditionally relied on, is seldom helpful: at the point a company needs to make a strategic commitment to a disruptive technology, no concrete market exists. When Edwin Land asked Polaroid's market researchers to assess the potential sales of his new camera, they concluded that Polaroid would sell a mere 100,000 cameras over the product's lifetime; few people they interviewed could imagine the uses of instant photography.

Because disruptive technologies frequently signal the emergence of new markets or market segments, managers must *create* information about such markets—who the customers will be, which dimensions of product performance will matter most to which customers, what the right price points will be. Managers can create this kind of information only by experimenting rapidly, iteratively, and inexpensively with both the product and the market.

For established companies to undertake such experiments is very difficult. The resource allocation processes that are critical to profitability and competitiveness will not—and should not—direct resources to markets in which sales will be relatively small. How, then, can an established company probe a market for a disruptive technology? Let start-ups—either ones the company funds or others with no connection to the company—conduct the experiments. Small, hungry organizations are good at placing economical bets, rolling with the punches, and agilely changing product and market strategies in response to feedback from initial forays into the market.

Consider Apple Computer in its start-up days. The company's original product, the Apple I, was a flop when it was launched in 1977. But Apple had not placed a huge bet on the product and had gotten at least *something* into the hands of early users quickly. The company learned a lot from the Apple I about the new technology and about what customers wanted and did not want. Just as important, a group of *customers* learned about what they did and did not want from personal computers. Armed with this information, Apple launched the Apple II quite successfully.

Many companies could have learned the same valuable lessons by watching Apple closely. In fact, some companies pursue an explicit strategy of being *second to invent*— allowing small pioneers to lead the way into uncharted market territory. For instance, IBM let Apple, Commodore, and Tandy define the personal computer. It then aggressively entered the market and built a considerable personal-computer business.

Every company that has tried to manage mainstream and disruptive businesses within a single organization failed.

But IBM's relative success in entering a new market late is the exception, not the rule. All too often, successful companies hold the performance of small-market pioneers to the financial standards they apply to their own performance. In an attempt to ensure that they are using their resources well, companies explicitly or implicitly set relatively high thresholds for the size of the markets they should consider entering. This approach sentences them to making late entries into markets already filled with powerful players.

For example, when the 3.5-inch drive emerged, Seagate needed a $300-million-a-year product to replace its mature flagship 5.25-inch model, the ST412, and the 3.5-inch market wasn't large enough. Over the next two years, when the trade press asked when Seagate would introduce its 3.5-inch drive, company executives consistently responded that there was no market yet. There actually *was* a market, and it was growing rapidly. The signals that Seagate was picking up about the market, influenced as they were by customers who didn't want 3.5-inch drives, were misleading. When Seagate finally introduced its 3.5-inch drive in 1987, more than $750 million in 3.5-inch drives had already been sold. Information about the market's size had been widely available throughout the industry. But it wasn't compelling enough to shift the focus of Seagate's managers. They continued to look at the new market through the eyes of their current customers and in the context of their current financial structure.

The posture of today's leading disk-drive makers toward the newest disruptive technology, 1.8-inch drives, is eerily familiar. Each of the industry leaders has designed one or more models of the tiny drives, and the models are sitting on shelves. Their capacity is too low to be used in notebook computers, and no one yet knows where the initial market for 1.8-inch drives will be. Fax machines, printers, and automobile dashboard mapping systems are all candidates. "There just isn't a market," complained one industry executive. "We've got the product, and the sales force can take orders for it. But there are no orders because nobody needs it. It just sits there." This executive has not considered the fact that his sales force has no incentive to sell the 1.8-inch drives instead of the higher-margin products it sells to higher-volume customers. And while the 1.8-inch drive is sitting on the shelf at his company and others, last year more than $50 million worth of 1.8-inch drives were sold, almost all by start-ups. This year, the market will be an estimated $150 million.

To avoid allowing small, pioneering companies to dominate new markets, executives must personally monitor the available intelligence on the progress of pioneering companies through monthly meetings with technologists, academics, venture capitalists, and other nontraditional sources of information. They *cannot* rely on the company's traditional channels for gauging markets because those channels were not designed for that purpose.

PLACE RESPONSIBILITY FOR BUILDING A DISRUPTIVE-TECHNOLOGY BUSINESS IN AN INDEPENDENT ORGANIZATION

The strategy of forming small teams into skunk-works projects to isolate them from the stifling demands of mainstream organizations is widely known but poorly understood. For example, isolating a team of engineers so that it can develop a radically new sustaining technology just because that technology is radically different is a fundamental misapplication of the skunk-works approach. Managing out of context is also unnecessary in the unusual event that a disruptive technology is more financially attractive than existing products. Consider Intel's transition from dynamic random access memory (DRAM) chips to microprocessors. Intel's early microprocessor business had a higher gross margin than that of its DRAM business, in other words, Intel's normal resource-allocation process naturally provided the new business with the resources it needed.

Creating a separate organization is necessary only when the disruptive technology has a lower profit margin than the mainstream business and must serve the unique needs of a new set of customers. CDC, for example, successfully created a remote organization to commercialize its 5.25-inch drive. Through 1980, CDC was the dominant independent disk-drive supplier due to its expertise in making 14-inch drives for mainframe-computer makers. When the 8-inch drive emerged, CDC launched a late development effort, but its engineers were repeatedly pulled off the project to solve problems for the more profitable, higher-priority 14-inch projects targeted at the company's most important customers. As a result, CDC was three years late in launching its first 8-inch product and never captured more than 5% of that market.

When the 5.25-inch generation arrived, CDC decided that it would face the new challenge more strategically. The company assigned a small group of engineers and marketers in Oklahoma City, Oklahoma, far from the mainstream organization's customers, the task of developing and commercializing a competitive 5.25-inch product. "We needed to launch it in an environment in which everybody got excited about a $50,000 order," one executive recalled." In Minneapolis, you needed a $1 million order to turn anyone's head." CDC never regained the 70% share it had once enjoyed in the market for mainframe disk drives, but its Oklahoma City operation secured a profitable 20% of the high performance 5.25-inch market.

Had Apple created a similar organization to develop its Newton personal digital assistant (PDA), those who have pronounced it a flop might have deemed it a success. In launching the product, Apple made the mistake of acting as if it were dealing with an established market. Apple managers went into the PDA project assuming that it had to make a significant contribution to corporate growth. Accordingly, they researched customer desires exhaustively and then bet huge sums launching the Newton.

In order that it may live, a corporation must be willing to see business units die.

Had Apple made a more modest technological and financial bet and entrusted the Newton to an organization the size that Apple itself was when it launched the Apple I, the outcome might have been different. The Newton might have been seen more broadly as a solid step forward in the quest to discover what customers really want. In fact, many more Newtons than Apple I models were sold within a year of their introduction.

KEEP THE DISRUPTIVE ORGANIZATION INDEPENDENT

Established companies can only dominate emerging markets by creating small organizations of the sort CDC created in Oklahoma City. But what should they do when the emerging market becomes large and established?

Most managers assume that once a spin-off has become commercially viable in a new market, it should be integrated into the mainstream organization. They reason that the fixed costs associated with engineering, manufacturing, sales, and distribution activities can be shared across a broader group of customers and products.

This approach might work with sustaining technologies, however, with disruptive technologies, folding the spin-off into the mainstream organization can be disastrous. When the independent and mainstream organizations are folded together in order to share resources, debilitating arguments inevitably arise over which groups get what resources and whether or when to cannibalize established products. In the history of the disk-drive industry, *every* company that has tried to manage mainstream and disruptive businesses within a single organization failed.

No matter the industry, a corporation consists of business units with finite life spans: the technological and market bases of any business will eventually disappear. Disruptive technologies are part of that cycle. Companies that understand this process can create new businesses to replace the ones that must inevitably die. To do so, companies must give managers of disruptive innovation free rein to realize the technology's full potential—even if it means ultimately killing the mainstream business. For the corporation to live, it must be willing to see business units die. If the corporation doesn't kill them off itself, competitors will.

The key to prospering at points of disruptive change is not simply to take more risks, invest for the long term, or fight bureaucracy. The key is to manage strategically important disruptive technologies in an organizational context where small orders create energy, where fast low-cost forays into ill-defined markets are possible, and where overhead is low enough to permit profit even in emerging markets.

Managers of established companies can master disruptive technologies with extraordinary success. But when they seek to develop and launch a disruptive technology that is rejected by important customers within the context of the mainstream business's financial demands, they fail—not because they make the wrong decisions, but because they make the right decisions for circumstances that are about to become history.

About the Authors

Joseph L. Bower is the Donald Kirk David Professor of Business Administration at the Harvard Business School in Boston, Massachusetts.

Clayton M. Christensen, an assistant professor at the Harvard Business School, specializes in managing the commercialization of advanced technology.

Endnote

1. Robert A. Eurgelman, "Eading Memories: A Process Theory of Strategic Business Exit in Dynamic Environ- ments," *Administrative Science Quarterly* 39 (1994), pp. 24–36.

54

THE RIGHT STUFF: IDENTIFYING AND DEVELOPING EFFECTIVE CHAMPIONS OF INNOVATION

Jane M. Howell

EXECUTIVE OVERVIEW

To overcome organizational inertia or fierce opposition and move new product ideas from small to large project endeavors, market launch, and ultimate market success requires champions. Yet we do not know much about what makes some champions effective while others fail to deliver the goods. What I discovered by studying 72 innovations in 38 companies is that effective champions differ from ineffective ones in their personal characteristics and behaviors, how they identify the innovations to back, and how they promote them to gain the support they need to bring ideas to realization as new products or services. Effective champions are distinguished by three behaviors: conveying confidence and enthusiasm about the innovation; enlisting the support and involvement of key stakeholders; and persisting in the face of adversity. Relying on their personal networks inside and outside of the organization, they scout widely for new ideas and opportunities to pursue. Effective champions build support for the innovation by astutely analyzing key stakeholders' interests and tailoring their selling strategies to be maximally persuasive, and by tying the innovation to positive organization outcomes such as profitability, enhanced reputation, or strategic advantage. I conclude with seven action steps that enterprise leaders can take to breed, rather than block, potential champions in their organizations.

"The toughest sales job for anyone is to sell their own company on new ideas and new opportunities."

—A champion for the development of a new product line for an industrial filter company

Research shows that when looking at the full range of a new product development project's progress from raw idea to market success, 90 percent of raw ideas actually never advance beyond the idea generator's desktop. Of the remaining 10 percent of ideas that succeed in advancing beyond the drawing board to the small project stage, only 3 percent obtain the backing to develop into significant projects, less than 2 percent become major development efforts, less than 1 percent are ever launched commercially, and only .3 percent achieve commercial success. So approximately 3,000 raw innovative ideas are required to yield one commercially successful new product.[1]

Why do thousands of these innovative ideas die? One answer is that new product development efforts depend, in part, on champions to initially recognize potential winners among the myriad of raw new product ideas generated by innovators, and then to persistently work at gathering the support and resources needed to advance those ideas through the various project stages to successful commercial launch. Champions are individuals who informally emerge to promote the idea with conviction, persistence, and energy, and willingly risk their position and reputation to ensure the innovation's success.[2] "Without dedicated champions, ideas for product innovations may remain dormant for future development and implementation."[3]

Champions are widely acknowledged as pivotal to innovation speed and success. Some champions are extraordinarily successful in promoting innovations that reap profitable growth for the company, whereas others fail miserably in their promotion attempts and innovations are shelved. I was curious about what might account for this difference. For example, what behaviors distinguish effective from ineffective champions? How do effective champions identify potential innovation ideas, present and promote these ideas to obtain backing from influential stakeholders, and maneuver them through the organizational minefields to introduce product innovations? And what are the personal characteristics that distinguish more from less successful champions?

To learn more about the personal characteristics and behaviors of champions and how they identify and promote ideas, a ten-year research program was launched that studied 72 champions of technology or product innovations in 38 companies.[4] In contrast to project managers who are formally appointed to lead the project and have responsibility for its overall progress and profitability, champions are self-appointed volunteers for the project; it is not within their job mandate to seek out and promote innovations. All innovations were new technologies that represented a significant financial investment for the company. In-depth interviews with champions and executives were conducted, and champions, executives and innovation team members were surveyed. A complete description of this research program's objectives, the innovations, and the method used to identify champions and examine their personal characteristics, behaviors, and activities are described in the Appendix.

In this article I begin with two case studies that distinguish the behaviors of an effective and an ineffective champion. Next, I dissect the process of championship by describing how champions identify potential innovations and then obtain stakeholders' support and commitment to them. Finally, I highlight what champions really want in their work lives, and detail seven action steps that enterprise leaders can take to cultivate potential champions in their organizations.

IDENTIFYING CHAMPION BEHAVIORS

A new idea needs someone who will exercise the required social and political effort to galvanize support for the business concept among key stakeholders, create internal acceptance of the new idea, and represent the venture to resource allocators to ensure sufficient resources are released for development. Some champions can do this very well, others fail. So what are the key differences in behavior between effective and ineffective champions?

Below are two cases showing what the effective champion did, and what the ineffective one failed to do. Both champions were involved in the development of transportation safety-related products in their companies; however one was viewed as highly effective whereas the other was seen as ineffective by their respective executive and innovation team members.

A Case Example of an Effective Champion

Working for a multinational semiconductor company, Robert Vincent championed the development of an airbag accelerometer, an electronic device that measures acceleration and deceleration and triggers airbag deployment when readings fall beyond a specified range. Even before he knew exactly what product the innovation team would develop using the sensor technology, Vincent displayed unusual confidence in its ability to deliver what the customer wanted. By a process he called "selling vapor ware," Vincent took a catalog of imagined products that the innovation team "might be able to build if someone was interested" to potential customers.

Fired by two different division managers, Vincent showed exceptional tenacity by convincing the president and the chairman of the board twice to reinstate him to continue with the project. He described himself as the "recruiter and resource procurer, doing all the things that nobody else knew how to do or that needed to be done, identifying all the gaps, and finding the right people or obtaining the needed resources." He was very creative in obtaining funding for the project. When funding was unavailable, he pushed to complete a $10 million contract in half the time so that he could use the balance of $5 million to support the new product's development.

Vincent adapted his selling approach to suit different audiences. He claimed that the most effective way to get people on board when promoting an innovation was to "understand what people need to hear and give them the information in the form that they can process in a way that is useful for them." For example, "You tell the president of the company who has a marketing background that there are 50 million cars, each with an airbag, currently using a $75 dollar solution and we have a $5 solution. You tell the guy who is running manufacturing that he won't have to buy any capital equipment to do this job."

A Case Example of an Ineffective Champion

Mike Ellis, who worked for a leading aerospace company, championed a flight safety system that integrated deployable flight data recorder, cockpit voice recorder, and emergency locator beacon technology for use on helicopters. To gain support for the project, Ellis actively lobbied the air-worthiness authorities to make it illegal for potential customers not to use the product. He also sold the idea by "using the TWA disaster to prove the usefulness of a product such as ours that floats." Eventually, an opportunity to develop the technology was identified with Phoenix Helicopter International, a major European helicopter assembler.

As the project evolved, Ellis grew very close to his engineering counterparts at Phoenix. He viewed the project as his "baby" and readily accommodated customer requests to keep the project alive and moving forward, despite questions from his own company about whether the project made sense from a business perspective. Ellis did succeed in having resources allocated to the project, but only by a step-by-step process that involved "spoon feeding the company a little bit at a time and getting them more and more involved." Throughout the project, Ellis continued to focus on the customer's needs around systems design, to the exclusion of promoting the project inside his own company and keeping the project manager and top management team informed of his activities, despite repeated requests for progress reports.

The project was shut down twice. The first time, Ellis "quietly kept up correspondence with the customer." The second shut down occurred after Ellis and the project manager gave a presentation to the top management team outlining that the budget was close to being spent, production had not started, and there were no allowances for contingencies such as delays in materials procurement. Neither Ellis nor the project manager or any of the innovation team members were able to explain the reasons for the potential cost overrun of nearly $1 million, a fact that was more alarming to the top management team than the actual overrun.

After an investigation assessing the viability of the project and the cost and schedule to complete it, the leadership changed from the project manager to a team of four people to get the project back on track. Ellis was told to withdraw from the project and focus on his own job responsibilities. According to one team member, "I think the project had enough of a reputation for not communicating. We had become so isolated that people thought it was time to intervene. I think Mike really did a number on himself by not communicating."

What's the Difference?

Analysis of these two cases reveals that while both Vincent and Ellis were considered champions, differences in their behaviors affected both innovation success as judged by company executives, and how effective they were perceived to be as champions by innovation team members. The differences lie in the frequency with which they conveyed confidence and enthusiasm in the innovation, enlisted the support and involvement of key stakeholders, and persisted in the face of adversity.

Vincent confidently committed to selling a product to customers that had yet to be developed and showed enthusiastic zeal for the potential of the airbag accelerometer in his discussions with key stakeholders. He reached across different levels and functions in the company, from the president to the director of manufacturing, to sound out his idea and increase receptivity and commitment to it. Vincent also showed tenacity when on two occasions he convinced the President and the Chairman of the Board to reinstate him after being fired by different divisional managers in order to keep the innovation moving forward. When no resources were available to support the airbag accelerometer innovation, he completed another project in record time and used the savings to fund the development of the innovation.

In contrast, Ellis's enthusiasm about the flight safety system project was directed towards the customer Phoenix Helicopter; he did little to build the confidence and enthusiasm of the hands-off project manager or top management team. He focused his energies on designing the product with the customer and the innovation team, leaving top management in the dark about the project's progress. While top management repeatedly asked Ellis and the project manager for project updates, their requests were ignored. Ellis showed persistence in continuing to communicate with Phoenix Helicopter when the project was shut down and in securing resources step-by-step along the way. However, he isolated himself, ignored business realities, and did little to work through internal challenges, such as dealing with budget overruns, the feasibility of manufacturing the product, and potential difficulties in procuring materials, with key stakeholders.

Champion behaviors focus on *what* champions do to promote innovation in organizations. I also wanted to understand *how* champions identify potential ideas for development and then promote them to obtain resources and support, ultimately leading to innovation success.

HOW CHAMPIONS OPERATE

How effective versus ineffective champions actually operate to identify new ideas and promote them is not well understood. The champions' role in the innovation process has typically focused on their involvement in idea promotion, yet it also seems that champions' participation in identifying new ideas would have several pay-offs.[5] In their search for and discovery of new ideas, champions can provide encouragement to idea generators, as well as gain early exposure to and knowledge of the project that could lend more credibility to their subsequent promotion efforts. Two research questions were investigated:

1. How do effective champions identify potential innovation ideas?
2. How do effective champions promote innovation ideas to gain much-needed support from key stakeholders?

IDENTIFYING INNOVATION IDEAS

We discovered that champions provide enthusiastic support for creative ideas by sheltering new ideas from premature evaluation, advocating new ideas, and recognizing the production of new ideas. Specifically, to discover new ideas and opportunities generated by others, champions engaged in scouting activities. We also learned that two personal characteristics distinguished champions who actively engaged in scouting activities: breadth of interest and flexible role orientation.

Scouting for New Ideas

More effective champions were scouts who continually scanned their environment for ideas and information in order to identify promising opportunities.[6] They initiated contacts with customers or users to gain awareness of their needs, and directly applied technical and market oriented knowledge to the innovation. In fact, champions who used their well developed networks inside and outside the organization to source new ideas were associated with more successful innovations than champions who relied on written materials exclusively. Returning to the case example of an effective champion, Vincent continually looked for new ideas from "every source known to man." He cited journals, magazines, television news programs, universities, colleagues, customers and suppliers as his most frequent information sources. "I sort of keep my mind going around like a lighthouse beacon searching for new ideas," declared Vincent. "You have to be open minded. Ideas will come from places that you never thought possible."

According to another effective champion, "The role that I played was looking for those sorts of opportunities, which meant being involved in things that were not directly related to this project, then you get more of a renaissance view. A renaissance person is someone who is an expert in a lot of different fields as opposed to a single field. As that relates to communications, I participated in a lot of research forums inside and outside the company, publishing activities, conferences, and meetings with customers, just to bring a lot of diverse input into the project. The more diversity the better."

By having their finger on the pulse of internal and external trends, developments, and events, especially through personal contacts, effective champions sourced new ideas that others may not have considered. Ultimately, building political awareness, relationships, and information networks with a broad range of individuals and groups enables champions to persuade their constituents to support the innovation. Since champions often assume high risks by advocating innovations, their accurate assessment of environmental resources and constraints is important in planning strategies and actions leading to successful product innovations.

Breadth of Interest and Flexible Role Orientation

I learned that champions who actively scout for new ideas have two hallmark personal characteristics: breadth of interest and flexible role orientation. Champions have broad general knowledge, experience in a wide range of domains, and diverse interests that prompted them to seek information from different sources.[7] They are well versed in emerging technologies, products, processes, and markets and distill the implications for their organizations.

Champions also have a flexible role orientation: they have a broad vision of their role, going above and beyond their prescribed responsibilities to engage in creative and innovative activities. A flexible role orientation includes keeping one's own knowledge and skills up-to-date, developing and making recommendations concerning issues affecting the organization, and keeping well informed about issues where their opinion might be useful.[8]

Champions' wide ranging interests and flexible role orientation prompt them to immerse themselves in business units outside of their own unit, and seek problems to work on from their network of relationships. Obtaining information from different sources is critical for them to discover new ideas.

PROMOTING INNOVATION IDEAS

Once new ideas are identified, champions prompt enterprise leaders and other key stakeholders to appreciate, pay attention to, and support new product opportunities by packaging and selling product innovation ideas in unique ways. But how do effective champions differ from ineffective ones in their idea promotion efforts? Here I describe two strategies used by effective champions to influence key stakeholders to value and support the new initiative: framing the innovation as an opportunity and using informal

TABLE 54-1 Effective versus Ineffective Champions: What Are the Differences?

	Effective Champions	*Ineffective Champions*
Idea Generation		
Scouting for New Ideas	Scout widely for new ideas and information. Rely on personal networks.	Use few sources for new ideas and information. Rely on written information.
Breadth of Interest	Wide general knowledge, breadth of experience, diverse interests.	Narrower range of general knowledge, depth of experience, focused interests.
Flexible Role Orientation	View role broadly, well informed about issues that affect the organization.	See role as more limited, less knowledge about issues affecting the organization.
Idea Promotion		
Framing the New Idea	Frame idea as an opportunity. Tie idea to positive organizational outcomes such as profitability, enhanced reputation, or strategic advantage.	Frame idea as a threat. Tie idea to negative organizational outcomes such as loss of business, tarnished reputation, or legal liability.
Selling Channels	Use both formal and informal selling channels.	Use formal selling channels only.
Control Orientation	Internal control: belief that events can be influenced by them.	External control: belief that events are beyond their control.
Self-monitoring	High self-monitors: analyze potential reactions of influence targets and tailor their selling strategies to be maximally persuasive.	Low self-monitors: unable or unwilling to accurately perceive reactions of others and use the same selling strategies in different situations.
Contextual Knowledge	Extensive strategic and relational knowledge.	Little strategic and relational knowledge.

selling channels. Underlying these strategies for framing and selling innovation ideas are three personal characteristics: internal control orientation, self-monitoring, and contextual knowledge. Table 54-1 summarizes the key differences between effective and ineffective champions in generating and promoting new initiatives.

Framing the Innovation as an Opportunity versus a Threat

A striking difference between effective and less effective champions is whether they present the product innovation idea to key stakeholders as an opportunity or as a threat. I discovered that more effective champions frame innovation ideas as opportunities, where there is high potential for gain and success is likely.[9] They tie the innovation to positive organizational outcomes including profitability, market share, customer expectations, strategic advantage, and organizational reputation. When champions label innovative ideas as opportunities, people are attracted to the cause and are actively involved and committed to contribute positively to the innovation.

Although he could have framed the airbag accelerometer innovation negatively in terms of avoiding potential lawsuits due to serious injuries in traffic accidents, Vincent chose instead to focus on its market viability and potential profitability. Not once during the interview did Vincent mention the role of the product in the context of an automobile accident. Another effective champion advocated that, "This new product will generate both revenues and publicity, and also increase our reputation of expertise and success."

Less effective champions present ideas as threats that imply a negative situation in which loss is likely and over which one has relatively little control.[10] Since threats are personally offensive, people are repelled from joining and participating in an innovation which offers few prospects for success. Utilizing threats to draw attention to the innovation also diminishes champions' perceived influence and erodes their credibility. For example, Ellis drew on an airline disaster to prove the usefulness of the flight safety system and lobbied to make it illegal for potential customers not to use it. Another ineffective champion stated, "If we are not successful, we can kiss that OE [original equipment] business good-bye for a long time. A lot of people are watching including the competition we took the job from. They would love us to fail. It's extremely important to us."

Managers are often advised to think of a new idea as an opportunity as if it were a magic potion guaranteeing that people will embrace and support a product innovation. As we can see in this study of champions, perhaps the power of the advice derives from the visions of success and personal gain it elicits—visions that raise motivation levels, build support for the fledgling innovation effort, and create momentum for change.

Informal Selling Channels

Beyond framing the innovation in appealing ways, idea promotion involves conscious choices about the formality of the selling channels used.[11] Selling channels can be formal (e.g., report writing, weekly staff meetings, quarterly reviews, formal presentations to groups) or informal (e.g., hallway conversations, one-on-one appeals to boss or peers, private meetings with relevant individuals). I discovered that both effective and ineffective champions used formal organizational channels to promote the innovation. But effective champions' unique contribution to promotional efforts stems from their more frequent and adept use of informal selling processes.

One effective champion explained how he built support and sponsorship among powerful insiders through informal selling channels: "At the very high executive level, we would have a five or ten minute hallway conversation between walking from their offices to come over here for an update. And that was usually quite effective. Letting them know here is a five-minute summary of where we are, here is where we are going to need your help so that when you get into the meeting it is not a shock. Or this would be the opportunity for him to say, 'Don't ask me that when we are in public because I can't commit to anything.'" Another successful champion remarked, "And of course the key is to talk it up, communicate, talk to people, create excitement, every group meeting give an update. Every time you see the president give him an update. You see the president walking across the parking lot as you are going to your car, try to cut him off because you know he is going to ask you about the program."

Effective champions consulted widely, involving and informing key stakeholders to garner support. As one champion observed, "You need to motivate the personnel working on it and the people involved with it. All the way down to the people who assemble the prototype units. Getting them involved, explaining to them what is happening, how their contributions are going to affect the overall program, trying to motivate them."

The alignment of the innovation with the company's vision and strategy guided effective champions' influence approach. In cases where the innovation diverged significantly from the enterprise leaders' vision and strategy, champions sheltered the idea from scrutiny. They recognized that early and active promotion of the project itself could lead to its premature demise. Under these circumstances, effective champions created awareness among enterprise leaders about a looming challenge, but did not immediately propose a solution. Instead, they built a groundswell of support among insiders through informal influence tactics, unofficially demonstrated feasibility of the idea through bootlegged funds and positive results, and then enticed enterprise leaders with the prospect that the innovation represented a solution to a pressing problem.

By comparison, in cases where the innovation was aligned with enterprise leaders' strategic priorities, effective champions actively built support and consensus among all stakeholders for the innovation through informal persuasive tactics. Then they presented the opportunity and its solution to the executive committee using rational and strategic arguments to justify resources to support the initiative.

In contrast to effective champions who adapted their informal selling efforts based on the match between the innovation idea and strategic dispositions of enterprise leaders, ineffective champions seeking executive support for a new product idea often pushed too hard, too soon, without sufficiently building desire for the innovation among stakeholders. They fervently proposed a solution to a challenge without considering top management dispositions or the strategic context. They failed to read the signals about how to effectively gain support for the innovation.

Furthermore, whereas effective champions proactively maintained a free flow of information to and from the innovation team and represented the innovation favorably to influential stakeholders, less effective champions isolated the innovation team by creating impenetrable boundaries and controlling the release of information.[12] Guarding the release of information was evident in the case study of Mike Ellis, who purposely kept the top management team in the dark about the budget and schedule shortfalls on the flight safety system project. In his mind, Ellis personally owned the project and failed to see the need to manage the impressions of outsiders, build alliances, and seek enterprise leaders' support.

Contextual Knowledge, Control Orientation, and Self-Monitoring

Three personal characteristics enabled champions to promote innovations successfully: contextual knowledge, control orientation, and self-monitoring. In-depth contextual knowledge of the organization's strategy and key stakeholders in the innovation process helps champions promote innovative ideas more effectively. Strategic knowledge concerns champions' understanding of the goals, objectives, plans and strategies of the organization, including the market and the competition. Relational knowledge refers to the extent to which champions are aware of the presence and role of key actors in the innovation process.[13] I discovered that more effective champions had a deep understanding of both the strategic and relational context of their organization that enabled them to effectively package their ideas and customize their promotional attempts.

Individuals with an internal control orientation believe they have the ability to influence the direction of events, whereas those with an external control orientation believe events are beyond their control.[14] More effective champions had an internal orientation, expressing confidence in their ability to influence persuasively people's attitudes. In the words of one champion, "What's different about champions is their can do attitude. For me, I can't stand to lose. What sets me apart is an idea, a love, a passion for my project. A desire to leave a footprint and make it happen. I'm not afraid to take a step forward and fail. I don't think about failing; I assume I'll succeed." Another champion commented, "I don't believe there is anything you can't do. That is just a personality thing. The guy right next to me isn't any less smart, he just doesn't have that confidence."

Self-monitoring is the ability to monitor and control one's expressive behavior.[15] High self-monitors are able to analyze the situation for clues about how their selling efforts will be received by their targets of influence and adjust their selling strategies to be maximally persuasive. Low self-monitors are unable or unwilling to accurately perceive the thoughts and reactions of others and use the same arguments and communication style in different situations.[16]

More effective champions were high self-monitors who displayed flexibility in framing ideas in ways that were most appropriate for their audience. For example, Vincent approached the company president who had a marketing background by emphasizing the market opportunity and financial gain that could accrue from pursuing the innovation. For the manufacturing manager, he focused on ease of manufacturing and the fact that existing capital equipment could be used to produce the product. As another effective champion stated, "You just have to really read people and see what is the best way to getting them to buy into it and if it doesn't work, then you have to try something else with them."

In contrast, Mike Ellis was a low self-monitor who used a "one size fits all" approach in continually relying on his knowledge of the innovation and the customer to influence others to accept his viewpoint. He failed to change his message to fit with the targets he was trying to influence. Consequently, his message was ignored.

A cautionary note is needed here. In the extreme, some champions who persuasively tailor their arguments to sway their audience may use manipulative tactics to try to get their way. For example, they might oversell the merits of their idea, understate the risks, or present an unrealistic picture of the budget and schedule. Senior executives may readily be swept away by the persuasiveness of the champion's arguments for the innovation, and must be vigilant in their assessment of both the innovation and the integrity of its proponent.

LEADERS' ACTIONS TO CULTIVATE CHAMPIONS

Given the importance of champions for innovation success, what actions can enterprise leaders take to encourage the emergence and effectiveness of potential champions? In my view, making the match between potential champions' expectations and enterprise leaders' actions is required for champions and innovation to flourish.

What Potential Champions Really Want

So what matters most to potential champions, those individuals who aspire to identify and promote a new idea when the opportunity arises? As summarized in Table 54-2, I identified six things that potential champions want, and do not want. First of all, given their wide-ranging interests, flexible view of their role, innovative orientation, and desire to influence the direction of events, they want to work in a company that grows through innovation, seizes new product or market opportunities, and operates flexibly. Willingness to experiment with new ideas, an orientation towards creativity and innovative change, open communication of information and ideas, and access to resources sends clear signals that the organizational culture supports innovation efforts.[17] What potential champions do *not* want is to be working in company that efficiently produces a limited set of products for narrow market segments where the demand for innovation is low.[18] Hierarchy and bureaucracy that smothers innovation and discourages creative thinking is the death knell for cultivating a cohort of potential champions of innovations. In this case, potential champions will be stifled, and undoubtedly fight an uphill battle to promote new initiatives.

Second, potential champions want to be surrounded by other innovators who challenge their thinking, thrive on change, and continually seek different ways to do things. Working with people who believe in the status quo, have a "don't rock the boat mentality," and shoot down any new idea is extremely frustrating for potential champions. Third, potential champions want to be constantly challenged and to learn; being stuck in a routine role with little opportunity to learn saps champions' motivation to discover any new initiative. Fourth, potential champions wanted to be connected, not isolated, internally and externally. Forging wide ranging relationships inside and outside the organization is the lifeblood for champions as they source creative ideas.

Fifth, recognizing potential champions' contributions spurs even greater efforts from them to discover and promote new ideas; ignoring potential champions' accomplishments substantially diminishes their enthusiasm to undertake the arduous innovation journey. Finally, potential champions want to work for champion "breeders" not "blockers." Table 54-3 outlines seven actions that champion breeders take to cultivate potential champions and blockers take to thwart them.

Champion Breeders versus Champion Blockers

Action #1. Champion breeders recruit and select potential champions even if they are difficult to manage.

TABLE 54-2 Understanding Champions	
What Potential Champions Want	*What Potential Champions Do NOT Want*
To work in an organization that grows through innovation, operates flexibly and exploits new product and market opportunities	To work in an organization with a stable environment that efficiently produces limited number of products for narrow market segments, and demand for innovation is low
To work with other innovators in the organization	To work with others who value the status quo
To be constantly challenged and to learn	To be stuck in a routine role with little chance to learn
To be connected internally and externally	To be isolated internally and externally
To be recognized	To be ignored or managed on a "routine"
To work for breeders of champions	To work for blockers of champions

TABLE 54-3 Champion Breeders versus Champion Blockers	
Champion Breeders	*Champion Blockers*
Recruit and select potential champions even if they are difficult to manage	Recruit and select easy to manage people
Coach for skill development	Don't coach effectively
Mentor for career development	Fit champions into roles that are inside their comfort zone
Let champions volunteer for assignments that they crave	Appoint champions to lead innovations
Recognize innovation achievements	Do not recognize innovation accomplishments
View failure as a learning opportunity and help champions learn from failure	Blame champions for failures
Raise the profile of champions	Keep champions' light under a barrel

Champions question the status quo, voice contrary views, and push enterprise leaders to think and do things differently. Blockers view aspiring champions as challenging their authority, disruptive, or just plain annoying, resulting in their unwillingness to hire such high maintenance candidates. Conversely, breeders strategically recruit and select individuals with initiative, creativity, and enterprising qualities. They are open to constructive dissent and view questioning as a valuable way to provide them with a source of new perspectives and ideas and help them avoid mistakes and problems. They hire champions in quantity and cultivate them.

To recruit and select those who thrive in innovative environments, breeders focus more broadly on the dispositional attributes of potential candidates and consider applicants in terms of "who they are, not just what they can do."[19] During the selection process, making the match between individual values and interests, and the organization's core values, vision, and strategy, will help produce the type of proactive, creative individuals breeders desire.[20]

There are three indicators enterprise leaders can use to assess individuals' champion potential:

1. Personal characteristics associated with champion behavior such as self-monitoring, an internal control orientation, flexible role orientation, breadth of knowledge, and wide communication networks can be evaluated.
2. The champion behavior questionnaire measures how frequently individuals persist when facing obstacles, get others involved in the initiative, and show confidence and enthusiasm about the initiative.
3. Behavioral event interviews assist in identifying promising candidates to lead change. Have they persevered in tackling a challenging initiative? Do they express strong conviction and enthusiasm about a new venture they have started? Are they adept at managing relations with others?

And getting champions within your own company to do the hiring increases the probability of attracting and selecting the right candidates!

Action #2. Coach for skill development.

While recruiting and selecting potential champions with the requisite personal characteristics, behaviors, and values to join the company substantially increases the probability that innovation will occur, to boost that probability even higher, breeders actively coach people who aspire to be champions from the first day on the job. They coach prospective champions about how to frame ideas as opportunities in a compelling way and to link them to valued organizational outcomes, and offer constructive feedback and feedforward to them about how to present their ideas with greater audience impact and field tough questions. Equipping possible champions with framing and informal influence skills can help them avoid pitfalls, such as a poor first impression or failure to generate enthusiasm for ideas, and contribute to their ultimate success.

By comparison, blockers fail to coach champions effectively. They manage-by-exception, pointing out champions' mistakes without offering any developmental advice. At best, champions are led by benign neglect.

Action # 3. Mentor for career development.

Breeders connect aspiring champions to other influential people in the company so they can gain a different perspective on the business, learn about different career opportunities, and have another sounding board about their ideas and aspirations. They challenge potential champions with stretch opportunities that they really, really desire, such as supplying them to different business units to face new challenges or assigning them to work on an important strategic initiative, to develop their leadership capabilities. On the other hand, blockers fit champions into roles that are inside their comfort zone.

Beyond career development, breeders invest their personal credibility and reputation in aspiring champions. They run interference for champions when they hit roadblocks, offer champions support when their ideas are thwarted or fall on deaf ears, and protect champions from political infighting to sustain the innovation's momentum. With these privileges come obligations. The quid pro quo for breeders' support is that champions act in the interest of the company, not themselves, in promoting a new initiative, and manage their relationships with others respectfully and astutely. Breeders need to recognize and manage quickly any signs that champions are developing an "entitlement mentality" or arrogance about their status, which undermines both the champions' and enterprise leaders' credibility.

Action #4. Let champions volunteer for stretch assignments that they crave.

Breeders recognize that champions who volunteer to spearhead innovations will demonstrate unwavering commitment to the idea and be seen as more genuine in their promotional efforts since they chose to put themselves on the line in order to sell the idea. Blockers formally appoint individuals to lead an innovation by giving them some form of legitimate authority that in reality undermines their credibility in the selling process by bringing their motives into question.

Action #5. Recognize innovation achievements.

Breeders recognize champions' achievements in a variety of creative ways, such as offering champions the opportunity to take a paid sabbatical to research a potential idea, to lead an exciting new initiative, to work with a leader who recognizes and develops creative talent, or to network with other champions in different business units. Breeders invent celebratory mechanisms and recognition awards for innovative change to honor champions' accomplishments and enable them to do their work through their personal support. Blockers ignore champions' innovation attempts entirely.

Action #6. View failure as a learning opportunity, and help champions learn from failure.

Rather than blame champions for failures as blockers do, breeders see failures as learning in action. Failures are viewed as an investment in education. When a project derails, breeders insist that the champion act as a pathologist and conduct a formal autopsy on what went wrong. The failure is documented and the reasons why the innovation didn't work are candidly discussed. This is a visible way of extracting the learning, creating a store of knowledge around innovation successes and failures, and reinforcing the importance of inquiry and understanding of any initiative.

Action #7. Raise the profile of champions.

Blockers keep champions' light under a barrel and take credit for any innovation. In contrast, breeders "champion the champions" by promoting their competencies and accomplishments to other enterprise leaders in a variety of ways—asking them to present their project idea to the Board of Directors, inviting them to a "breakfast of champions" to meet with the CEO once a month for an informal dialogue, or featuring them in company videos or newsletters that celebrate best practices. Breeders follow the creed "whoever does the work gets the recognition."

Champions as the Key to Innovation

Product innovation is critical to organizational productivity and competitiveness. Company survival will continue to depend, in part, on a stream of creative product advances such as those nurtured by champions. How champions are supported and made a conscious part of the innovation process is probably an organization's single most important area of leverage for maintaining and improving effective innovation. Without strategic recruitment, selection, and support by enterprise leaders, at best championship will be an episodic activity that relies on a combination of chance and extraordinary individual effort to push creative ideas forward. At worst, potential champions will give up and leave the company with the innovative idea in hand to promote elsewhere.

In order to bring innovative ideas to life, enterprise leaders need to create the context in which championing innovation becomes embedded in the fabric of the organization. It is incumbent on leaders to strategically recruit, select, develop, and recognize potential champions, to provide opportunities for them to build internal and external networks of relationships and go beyond their prescribed role to spark new ideas, and to create a culture where innovation is encouraged and appreciated. Without these actions, innovation will remain a random event.

APPENDIX

In our ten-year research program investigating champions we collected data on 72 technology or product innovations in 38 companies. This program was conducted in three phases, and the objectives, sample and method for each phase is described.

Phase 1

In Phase 1 we studied the personality characteristics, leadership behaviors and influence tactics of champions of technological innovations. An innovation was defined as the adoption of a new product or process related to the application of information technology. Technological innovations were selected using three criteria: 1) the innovation was designed for use by managers and/or professionals; 2) the innovation represented a significant financial investment for the company according to executives; and 3) the innovation was implemented within the 18 months prior to the study. Based on survey responses from 88 out of 350 chief executive officers of large Canadian corporations, and follow-up interviews with 56 of these executives, 25 technological innovations met the selection criteria.

In order to identify champions, company executives named the individuals who had played a key role in the introduction and implementation of the innovation. They were then given a description of five roles (technical innovator, business innovator, chief executive, project champion, and user champion) and asked to identify the individual who filled this role in the innovation.[21] A project champion was defined as the individual who informally emerged and made a decisive contribution to the innovation by actively and enthusiastically promoting its progress through critical stages of the innovation.[22]

Key individuals identified by the executives were then interviewed, and often identified other key players, who were also interviewed. All interviews were conducted using a structured protocol developed by the researchers that focused on the champion's influence tactics, leadership behaviors, career experience and so on, and were tape recorded. In total, 153 individuals were interviewed for 1.5 hours on average.

Twenty-five project champions were identified based on complete (100 percent) agreement among key individuals. A comparison group of 25 "non-champions" was created based on two criteria: 1) both champions and non-champions were involved in the same innovation, volunteered for the project, matched on demographic variables (e.g., functional area, position level), and were from the same organization; and 2) non-champions played an active informal role in the innovation process, but were not identified by their peers as fitting one of the five roles described above.

The transcripts of the champion and non-champion interviews were content analyzed for themes relating to leadership behavior and influence tactics based on the literature. Questionnaire measures were completed by champions to assess their personality characteristics and by key individuals to rate champions' leadership behavior. To test the hypotheses related to differences between champions and non-champions on personality, leadership, and influence variables, a MANOVA and regression analysis were conducted. Further interview data were gathered from this sample to understand the role champions and non-champions play in the identification and promotion of ideas in the innovation process, and hypotheses were tested using paired sample t-tests and Partial Least Squares (PLS) analysis.

Phase 2

In Phase 2 of our research program we defined, developed, and tested a measure of champion behavior. First, we interviewed via telephone 73 executives and middle managers who were asked to identify a comprehensive list of champion behaviors, that is, what champions actually do to promote innovations in organizations. They identified 105 behaviors undertaken by champions. Next we surveyed a different group of 194 middle managers and executives to assess which of the 105 behaviors were most representative of champions. Twenty-nine behaviors were deemed to represent the core of the domain of championship. Results from a principal components analysis followed by a confirmatory factor analysis indicated that of the 29 champion behaviors, 14 met the selection criteria for retention. The champion behavior measure was composed of three factors: 1) persisting under adversity; 2) expressing enthusiasm and confidence about the success of the innovation; and 3) getting the right people involved. Analyses of the psychometric properties of this 14-item measure indicated acceptable reliability based on Cronbach's alpha coefficient, as well as acceptable convergent and discriminant validity using correlation analysis. Sample statements from the champion behavior measure include "points out the reasons why the innovation will succeed" and "knocks down barriers to the innovation."

Phase 3

In order to shed light on how champions contribute to innovation success, we conducted a longitudinal study of 47 product innovations. We defined a product innovation as a new technology or a combination of technologies introduced commercially to meet either an external user's or a market's need. Product innovations were selected using three criteria: 1) the innovation originated internally and was new to the company on the dimensions of products, markets, and technologies; 2) the product had a development cycle of 1.5 to 3 years; and 3) the innovation required significant investment of company resources according to company executives.

Companies were identified through a survey of 250 Chief Executive Officers of the largest North American firms in the automotive, aerospace, and electronics industries, in terms of sales. Using the same method as Phase 1, company executives were asked to identify a product innovation and the key people involved in the project. Based on these interviews, 47 product innovations and 47 champions were identified that clearly met the established criteria. Thirteen organizations agreed to participate in the study with an average of four projects each.

We conducted tape recorded interviews with the identified champions about the projects, and surveyed 47 divisional general managers and 237 innovation team members to understand the impact of champion behavior on innovation success over time. Innovation success was measured by several indicators such as the project's technical quality, budget and cost performance, and meeting assigned schedules. Questionnaire measures were completed by team members to assess champions' behavior using the measure described above. Divisional managers rated innovation success during the implementation phase of the innovation, and then again one year later. We tested hypotheses at the project level of analysis using PLS.

We also studied how champions identify potential product innovation ideas and how they present these ideas to gain support from key stakeholders. Interview transcripts were content analyzed for themes related to champions' framing the innovation as a threat or opportunity. Survey data were also obtained from champions on their personal characteristics and activities and were analyzed using PLS.

Acknowledgements

I appreciate the constructive and helpful feedback on earlier versions of this paper that I have received from my colleagues Paul Beamish and Jeffrey Gandz, as well as two anonymous reviewers. I am also grateful to my three colleagues who have been involved in this research program with me: Kathleen Boies, Christopher Higgins, and Christine Shea.

About the Author

Jane M. Howell holds the Taylor/Mingay Chair in Management and is Professor of Organizational Behavior at the Ivey Business School, The University of Western Ontario. She received her Ph.D. in Business Administration from The University of British Columbia. Her research interests include champions of innovation, leadership, and followership. Contact: jhowell@ivey.uwo.ca.

Endnotes

1. Stevens, G.A., & Burley, J. 1997. 3000 raw ideas = 1 commercial success! *Research Technology Management*, 40: 16–28.

2. The definition of a champion is derived from Achilladelis, B., Jervis, P., & Robertson, A. 1971. *A study of success and failure in industrial innovation*. Sussex, England: University of Sussex Press. The informal emergence of champions in organizations is highlighted in two articles: Schon, D.A. 1963. Champions for radical new inventions. *Harvard Business Review*, 41(2): 77–86; Tushman, M.L., & Nadler, D. 1986. Organizing for innovation. *California Management Review*, 28(3): 74–92.

3. Frost, P. J., & Egri, C. P. 1991. The political process of innovation. In B.M. Staw & L.L. Cummings (Eds.), *Research in organizational behavior*: 229–295. Greenwich, CT: JAI Press.

4. This research program is reported in the following published studies: Howell, J.M., & Higgins, C.A. 1990. Champions of technological innovation. *Administrative Science Quarterly*, 35: 317–341; Howell, J.M., & Higgins, C.A. 1990. Leadership behaviors, influence tactics, and career experiences of champions of technological innovation. *Leadership Quarterly*, 1: 249–264; Howell, J.M., & Higgins, C.A. 1990. Champions of change: Identifying, understanding, and supporting champions of technological innovations. *Organizational Dynamics*, 19: 40–55; Howell, J.M., & Shea, C.M. 2001. Individual differences, environmental scanning, innovation framing and champion behavior: Key predictors of project performance. *Journal of Product Innovation Management*, 18(1): 15–27; Howell, J.M., & Boies, K., 2004. Champions of technological innovation: The influence of contextual knowledge, role orientation, idea generation and idea promotion on champion emergence. *Leadership Quarterly*, 15: 123–143; Howell, J.M., Shea, C.M., & Higgins, C.A. Champions of product innovations: Defining, developing and validating a measure of champion behavior. *Journal of Business Venturing*, in press; Howell, J.M. & Shea, C.M. 2004. The

impact of external communication activities, champion behavior, and team potency on predicting project performance. *Group & Organization Management*, in press.

5. Research on champions of innovation has typically focused on their involvement in idea promotion. See, for example, Burgelman, R.A. 1983. A process model of internal corporate venturing in the diversified major firm. *Administrative Science Quarterly*, 28(2): 223–244; Howell & Higgins, 1990; Galbraith, J.R. 1982. Designing the innovating organization. *Organizational Dynamics*, 10: 5–25; Venkataraman, S., MacMillan, I., & McGrath, R. 1992. Progress in research on corporate venturing. In D. Sexton (Ed.), *State of the art in entrepreneurship*: 487–519. New York: Kent Publishing.

6. For research on the external communication strategies used by new product development teams see Ancona, D.G., & Caldwell, D.F. 1992. Bridging the boundary: External activity and performance in organizational teams. *Administrative Science Quarterly*, 37: 634–665.

7. Theory and research suggest that individuals who promote innovation tend to be characterized by broad general knowledge and experience in a wide range of domains. See Amabile, T.M. 1988. A model of creativity and innovation in organizations. In B.M. Staw & L.L. Cummings (Eds.), *Research in Organizational Behavior*: 123–167. Greenwich, CT: JAI Press; Keller, R.T. & Holland, W.E. 1975. Boundary spanning roles in a research and development organization: An empirical investigation. *Academy of Management Journal*, 18: 388–393.

8. Parker, S.K., Wall, T.D., & Jackson, P.R. 1997. "That's not my job": Developing flexible employee work orientations. *Academy of Management Journal*, 40: 899–929.

9. Dutton, J.E., & Jackson, S.B. 1987. Categorizing strategic issues: Links to organizational action. *Academy of Management Review*, 12: 76–90; Jackson, S.B., & Dutton, J.E. 1988. Discerning threats and opportunities. *Administrative Science Quarterly*, 33: 370–87.

10. Ibid.
11. Dutton, J.E., Ashford, S.J., O'Neill, R.M., & Lawrence, K.A. 2001. Moves that matter: Issue selling and organizational change. *Academy of Management Journal,* 44: 716–736; Dutton, J.E., & Ashford, S.J. 1993. Selling issues to top management. *Academy of Management Review,* 18: 397–428.
12. Ancona & Caldwell, 1992.
13. Dutton, et al., 1993.
14. Gurin, P., Gurin G., Morrison, B.M. 1978. Personal and ideological aspects of internal and external control. *Social Psychology,* 41: 275–96; Mirels, H.L. 1970. Dimensions of internal and external locus of control. *Journal of Consulting and Clinical Psychology,* 34: 226–228.
15. Snyder, M. 1974. Self-monitoring of expressive behavior. *Journal of Personality and Social Psychology,* 30: 526–537; Lennox, R., & Wolfe, R. 1984. Revision of the self-monitoring scale. *Journal of Personality and Social Psychology,* 46: 1349–1364.
16. Snyder, 1974.
17. Amabile, T.M., Conti, R., Coon, H., Lazenby, J., & Herron M. 1996. Assessing the work environment for creativity. *Academy of Management Journal,* 39: 1154–1184.
18. Campbell, D.J. 2000. The proactive employee: Managing workplace initiative. *Academy of Management Executive,* 14: 52–66; Floyd, S.W., & Wooldridge, B. 1992. Middle management involvement in strategy and its association with strategic type: A research note. *Strategic Management Journal,* 13: 153–167.
19. Campbell, 2000, p. 62.
20. Ibid.
21. Achilladelis et al., 1971.
22. Ibid.

HOW DO CORPORATE CHAMPIONS PROMOTE INNOVATIONS?

Jan Inge Jenssen

Agder University College and Agder Research, Norway
jan.i.jenssen@hia.no

Geir Jørgensen

Agder University College and Agder Research, Norway
geir.jorgensen@agderforskning.no

The aim of this paper is to discuss which factors influence the impact of innovation champions on organisations. This is done by means of a systematic review of existing research. Many of the studies do not have a solid theoretical base. However, we find that resource dependency theory provides a theoretical framework in which innovation champions can be understood. We also show explicitly how other theories such as network theory, agency theory, and personal trait theory are needed in order to explain certain elements of the champions' behaviour. We propose an overall model, discuss theoretical and managerial implications of previous research, and suggest areas for future research.

KEYWORDS
Champion; innovation; change; review; resource dependency.

INTRODUCTION

Background

Increased turbulence, complexity and global competition in organisation environments have made identification, development, evaluation and adoption of innovations the decisive factors for the growth, productivity, competitiveness, survival, and profitability of organisations (Morgan, 1988; Delbecq and Mills, 1985; Bigoness and Perreault, 1981; Zaltman *et al.*, 1973). Organisations of all kinds must be able to generate and utilise innovations (Ekvall, 1988). The word innovation stems from the Latin word "innovare," which means to renew. In this context innovation is defined as ideas, formulas, programmes or technologies, which the organisation in question regards as new (Evan, 1993; Beatty and Gordon, 1991; Marcus, 1988).

The significant impact of innovation champions on innovation success has been revealed in several research projects (Beath, 1991; Beatty and Gordon, 1991; Holbek, 1990; Howell and Higgins, 1990b; Littler and Sweeting, 1985). Schön identified the role

Jenssen, Jan Inge and Geir Jørgensen. 2004. "How do corporate champions promote innovations?" *International Journal of Innovation Management* 8(1): 63–86.

of the champion in the innovation process in 1963. According to Schön (1963, p. 84) "the new idea either finds a champion or dies." From this perspective the champion is viewed as a representative for new technology converting potential users to actual users. An essential question is what factors affect the champion's impact in the organisation. For this reason this paper brings the following question into focus: *What are the human and social capital characteristics of innovation champions, and what resource acquisition strategies influence their endeavours?* We seek to answer this question through a systematic review of existing research.

Despite their important innovative role in organisations, champions have received little systematic attention (Lawless and Price, 1992) and much of the research has been carried out without a clear theoretical base. The reason for this might be related to the fact that no single theory provides a foundation for a comprehensive understanding of such a role. It is necessary to draw on several theoretical perspectives and the study of champions is necessarily eclectic. However, we will argue that resource-based theory provides the most comprehensive theoretical foundation framework in which champions may be interpreted. We view the champion process as a resource acquisition process. Champions do not own or control resources (Stevenson and Gumpert, 1985). They must decide what combination of resources to acquire (Van de Ven, 1993) and engage in the struggle of gaining control over these resources. Champions enter into a process where one resource is leveraged to obtain another (Green *et al.*, 1999). In a discussion of entrepreneurship and resource-based theory Alvarez and Busenitz (2001) extend the boundaries of the theory to also include the "individual-specific resources that facilitate" the assembling of resources (p. 775). In our contexts this implies that the human and social capital of the champion should be looked upon as resources for the innovation championship.

Definition and Model

Several definitions of champions are proposed in the literature. Roure (2001) provides an overview of different definitions. These definitions include five elements:

- *Character*: willing to take risks (Maidique, 1980; Markham, 1998; Schön, 1963), an early idea adopter (Maidique, 1980), positive behavioural support (Markham *et al.*, 1991), diplomatic talent (Markham, 1998; Chakrabarti and Hauschildt, 1989)
- *Willingness to contribute*: a strong advocate (Ettlie *et al.*, 1984), enthusiastically promoting (Roure, 2001; Schön, 1963), actively and vigorously promoting (Beath, 1991; Howell and Higgins, 1990b), inordinate interest (Markham, 1998), pushing the project (Beath, 1991), a decisive contribution (Roure, 2001; Howell and Higgins, 1990b; Rothwell, 1974), advocates . . . beyond the job requirement (Markham, 1998), overcoming opposition (Markham, 1998), leading a coalition (Markham, 1998), obtains resources (Roure, 2001)
- *The means applied*: advocate (Ettlie *et al.*, 1984; Markham, 1998; Markham *et al.*, 1991), linkage (Chakrabarti and Hauschildt, 1989), selling ideas (Chakrabarti and Hauschildt, 1989; Smith *et al.*, 1984; Schön, 1963), informal sales (Schön, 1963), getting the management's interest/approval (Roure, 2001; Roberts and Fusfeld, 1982; Chakrabarti, 1974), translate the technical language of the innovation (Chakrabarti and Hauschildt, 1989), plan action (Chakrabarti and Hauschildt, 1989), navigate the socio-political environment (Day, 1994), build support (Markham, 1998; Howell and Higgins, 1990b)
- *The goals*: successful innovation implementation (Maidique, 1980), promoting innovation (Shane, 1994), ensuring that innovation is implemented (Howell and Higgins, 1990b)
- *The context*: inside the corporation (Day, 1994), in a situation without the control of necessary resources (Stevenson and Jarillo, 1990)

We suggest a definition including elements from all these five categories: *A champion is an individual that is willing to take risks by enthusiastically promoting the development and/or implementation of an innovation inside a corporation through a resource*

FIGURE 55-1 A Model.

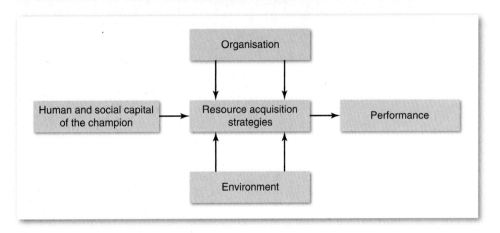

acquisition process without regard to the resources currently controlled. The last part of such a definition excludes individuals in leadership positions with the necessary authority and resources available (Krackhardt, 1995; Stevens and Jarillo, 1990). Our definition also emphasises the resource acquisition process. We recognise the fact that groups of individuals may promote innovations (Hauschildt and Kirchmann, 2001). However, there are few studies in this area and we will not focus on group championship.

The literature review shows that there are human and social capital characteristics of the champion that initiate actions. Human capital includes all aspects of the personality, experience and competence available to the champion (Jenssen and Havnes, 2002). Social capital is "the information, trust, and norms of reciprocity inhering in one's social networks" (Woolcock, 1998).

According to Westlund and Bolton (2001), human capital cannot accumulate without a basis of social capital. Also, the champions apply a variety of strategies in order to acquire the necessary set of resources. The success of innovation initiatives is also contingent with environmental factors outside the control of the champion (such as the size of external funds) and of the organisational factors such as leadership support and organisational culture. Based on this line of reasoning we have developed a model (Figure 55-1).

In this paper we focus on human and social characteristics of champions and resource acquisition strategies. Two organisation-related factors that are assumed to have a direct influence on the resource acquisition strategies are also discussed. In the model these factors are also assumed to interact with the resource acquisition strategies on performance. We believe that there is the same type of impact from the environment as there is from organisational factors on resource acquisition strategies and performance. However, we will not focus on these relationships in this paper.

HUMAN AND SOCIAL CAPITAL OF CHAMPIONS

Personal Characteristics

As pointed out, from a resource-based perspective the issue in this and the two following sections is the individual-specific resources of innovation champions. For instance, the innovation literature describes them as risk takers (Beatty and Gordon, 1991; Cox, 1976; Schön, 1963), who are socially independent (Cox, 1976) and politically clever (Beath, 1991; Dean, 1987; Burgelman, 1983; Schön, 1963). They also have charisma which refers to the ability to articulate a catchy and fascinating vision, inspire and encourage other organisation members to greater effort, and to the ability to gain respect, loyalty and trust. In addition, champions have great confidence in their own capability and mission. They are motivated by a confidence in and an enthusiastic attitude towards the new technology and what it can do for the company (Howell and Higgins, 1990a).

One of champions' major challenges is to convince those who are sceptical towards or dismissive of the innovation in the beginning. In the literature emphasis has been given to the champion's capacity to inspire others and gain binding support for the innovation from other organisation members (Dean, 1987; Burgelman, 1983; Maidique, 1980). Schön (1963, s. 84) has described champions as follows: "it is characteristic of champions . . . that they identify with the idea as their own, and with its promotion as a cause, to a degree that goes far beyond the requirements of their job." The abilities to inspire, to stimulate intellectually, and to assess individuals are characteristics of champions (Beath, 1991; Howell and Higgins, 1990b). Inspiration involves emotional appeal and communicative strength. Intellectual stimulation expresses the ability to suggest creative ideas that challenge and change organisation members' understanding of the problems the organisation faces and the solution to these problems. Individual assessment refers to the ability to develop an individual approach to the various organisation members.

Howell and Higgins (1990a) claim that great self-confidence, go-ahead spirit, energy and risk-taking are the most important characteristics of champions. An aspect of the champions' self-confidence is the ability to hold onto their ideas and continue to promote the ideas in spite of many obstacles. Through actively asserting their opinion, often by repeating the same arguments, the champions overcome resistance. In this manner great energy and drive constitute an important quality of champions. Beatty and Gordon (1991) also maintain that champions must promote innovation with patience and aggressiveness, often over a long period of time.

Due to the fact that a series of authors have drawn parallels between champions and entrepreneurs, this literature can probably be used to identify important quality traits in the champion personality (Beatty and Gordon, 1991; Pinchot, 1985; Maidique, 1980; Collins and Moore, 1970). McClelland (1967) found in a study of entrepreneurs that they had a great need for achieving something, were willing to take personal responsibility for decisions, preferred decisions that involved a moderate degree of risk, were interested in factual knowledge about the outcome of the decisions and disliked routine work. Roberts (1968) and Wainer and Rubin (1969) found that the companies with the highest output were led by entrepreneurs with a great need to achieve something and a moderate need for power.

According to Ekvall (1988) entrepreneurs are often flexible individuals who seek freedom. They detest rules and regulations, long decision-making processes and having to take into consideration aspects that are not directly linked to the actual problem solution. Based on interviews and life history analyses, Kets de Vries (1977) found that entrepreneurs are innovative and have the ability to start over again if they encounter adversity and are disappointed. Howell and Higgins' (1990b) findings suggest that there are certain personality traits that dispose some individuals to come forward as champions. If such individual differences are ignored, an important human resource in the organisation may be missed. In addition, the two authors maintain that personality characteristics have the greatest importance when the situation is marked by surrounding or technological changes.

Other important qualities of a champion include technical know-how and analytical skills (Beatty and Gordon, 1991). Professional skills can be decisive when it comes to ensuring that the champion has the necessary authority within the organisation. If organisation members regard the champion as one of the leading experts in the organisation in the area of current interest, the champion's chances of breakthrough are considerably strengthened. Analytical skills are also regarded as essential for innovations where budgeting, planning and control are central tasks. More generally this implies that leadership and managerial skills of the champion are of consequence especially when it comes to achieving an innovation breakthrough in the organisation (Beatty and Gordon, 1991; Conger and Kanungo, 1987; Oberg, 1972). The champion takes an active part in management and this implies that the champion must personally have an influence on the conduct and actions of other actors in the organisation (Holbek, 1990). In particular, it is the ability inherent in the champion's role to spark off commitment that is emphasised in the literature.

This is supported by Chakrabarti (1974) who has specified what he thinks are quality traits in those individuals who meet the champion role in an efficient way. He stresses that the champion needs to have an understanding of the technological aspects of the innovation, its advantages and limitations, as well as knowledge of the organisation so that the innovation's relevance can be assessed. This will give the champion knowledge about who will use the innovation and how it should be marketed internally. Chakrabarti (1974) emphasises the necessity of push and endurance in order to avoid resistance hampering the process during its course. Having a "good nose" and diplomatic skills are also important since the champion must communicate with, connect and integrate different individuals and groups, both inside and outside the organisation.

Rothwell *et al.* (1974) point out as well that power and status play an important part in the champion's effort to convince. Power, respect and status give greater "force" in the champion role. A high-ranking job, a good education, experience and competence will together give grounds for such a position (Holbek, 1990). Organisation members are more easily persuaded to do things in a new way when the champion is knowledgeable and has authority.

Champion Experience

Even though personality characteristics are assumed to be essential for the champion's power to persuade, his or her experience is of value as well. In Howell and Higgins' (1990a) study the objects of the study were champions who had been employed by the companies they represented during a period of 18 years on average. Long organisational experience may have several effects. First, champions with a long time of service in the organisation will probably have experienced previous innovation projects, either as a champion or as an ordinary organisation member. In this way an experienced champion may often be familiar with the risk, uncertainty and resistance associated with innovations.

Another effect of long company experience is the fact that the champion has considerable knowledge of the trade in which the organisation operates. Quite often he or she is able to identify an idea, technology or process, which is well suited for the company. Knowledge of the trade is often the basis for innovations (Pearson, 1988). In addition, the champion may use knowledge of the trade and organisational experience to put forward an argumentation that has great validity both within the management and among the subordinate staff. By catering for the needs and attitudes that exist in the organisation, as well as for the company's competitive position, the champion is more likely to succeed in implementing an innovation.

Champions with long experience in the same company have often worked in different departments or within different areas of the organisation. Such a broad background gives the champion the advantage of knowing various parts of the organisation at the same time as he or she gains a broader perspective.

Perhaps the most important effect of long-term experience is the champion's possibilities when it comes to building information and communication networks (Howell and Higgins, 1990a). Networks like these may be decisive in the champion's efforts to spread information and convince the remaining actors in the organisation of the innovation's excellence. By appealing to and making the most of his or her personal connections the champion may succeed in spreading the information to the various parts of the organisation. Experience from different parts of the organisation strengthens the champion's network and enables him to accumulate information and support (Beath, 1991). An important factor in relationships is trust. Long-lasting organisational experience makes it possible to build up trust. In addition, the champion will often obtain trust and authority in innovation issues as a result of lengthy company and trade-specific experience.

Network Position

The types of relations the champion has with the other organisation members are assumed by Beatty and Gordon (1991) to provide the champion with the power to convince. A network perspective on the champion process may help us to understand relationships and their effects on the development and implementation of innovations. The champion's initial network may influence the resource acquisition strategies and the success of the effort (Krackhardt, 1995). However, networking is also, as will be discussed, a part of the resource acquisition strategy itself.

There are different types of networks and ties among the players inside and outside an organisation. Granovetter (1973) has suggested that weak ties are often more vital than strong ties when it comes to understanding certain network phenomena. He argues that strong ties are likely to unite similar layers in knots. The type of information available through such networks is often redundant. Weak ties often form bridges or connections to other parts of the social system, which one would normally have no access to. The strength of a tie is brought about by the amount of time, emotional intensity, intimacy and return that characterise the relationship.

Even if weak ties provide access to non-redundant information, the actors who experience change and uncertainty will usually concentrate on developing strong relationships in order to reduce the uncertainty. People often resist change and they dislike uncertainty. Strong ties can form a basis for trust and provide support in situations with great uncertainty. Thus Krackhardt (1992) maintains that change cannot be brought about by weak ties, but by strong friendship relations (philos-relations). Job mobility and long organisational experience make it possible to establish such relationships (Howell and Higgins, 1990a). This is supported by Schön (1963) who maintains that champions actively put forward their ideas through informal processes. Beatty and Gordon (1991) emphasise that informal communication channels are the main source of information about the innovation.

The emotional component in friendship relations is essential in order to understand the dynamics involved in organisation crises and changes. In situations where great changes threaten the status quo there is often considerable resistance among organisation members. If the champion is to achieve a breakthrough for the innovation in such a situation, it is not sufficient to provide information only. The critical resource necessary to overcome this resistance is often the confidence which organisation members have in the person who occupies the champion role (Krackhardt and Stern, 1988). The champion's chances of gaining support for his or her arguments rely on long-lasting strong and emotional ties. Big changes do not require information only, but also confidence. This kind of confidence is found in close relationships between friends (Krackhardt, 1992).

In order to succeed the champions should, according to this line of arguments, maximise their strong and "weak" ties in the organisation. However, the structural position in the champion's network may also influence the ability to promote innovations. Based on Burt (1992; 1997), Krackhardt (1995) argues that the opportunity to promote an innovation is a function of "structural holes" in the person's network inside the organisation. If the champion has a relationship with two persons inside the organisation who are not connected to each other, this is a structural hole and the champion has a base of power to utilise the information from the two persons. This implies that an individual connected to many people that are not connected to each other has a better chance of obtaining the necessary set of resources than he or she would have in other network positions.

RESOURCE ACQUISITION STRATEGIES

A Broad Repertoire of Influence Tactics

To our knowledge, a resource-based perspective has been applied in very few empirical investigations of innovation champions. However, there are several studies in the field of entrepreneurship where such a perspective is applied. For instance, Alvarez and Busenitz (2001) use resource-based theory to show "how entrepreneurship generally involves the founder's unique awareness of opportunities, the ability to acquire the resources needed to exploit the opportunity, and the organisational ability to recombine homogeneous inputs into heterogeneous output" (p. 771). From such a perspective the entrepreneurial problem is to acquire the appropriate and innovative set of resources and ensure that resources are combined and used in such a way that they generate profit. In the same way this study applies a resource-based approach which implies that innovation champions use their human and social capital and apply different resource acquisition strategies. In order to gain access to the resources that will create a vital heterogeneity of output the champions have to apply a number of creative acquisition strategies. For instance, if the champions want to convince various interest groups they need to make frequent efforts and they have to have the ability to vary influence tactics (Beatty and Gordon, 1991; Howell and Higgins, 1990a). Schön (1963, p. 84) argues that champions are "capable of using any and every means of informal sales and pressure in order to succeed." Also, several case studies show that champions use a broad variety of influence tactics (Beath, 1991; Dean, 1987; Burgelman, 1983; Kipnis *et al.*, 1980).

Rational Strategies

Personal characteristics of the person one wants to influence determine the choice of influence strategy (Howell and Shea, 2001; Kipnis *et al.*, 1980; Mowday, 1979). The champion faces several challenges in the innovation struggle. Carrying out everyday business tasks, controlling performance, detecting problems and ensuring a reasonable profit are essential in organisations. To a great extent, this is how it should be. However, structures, processes and organisation members in charge of daily operations may very well block new ideas and implementation of important changes (Pearson, 1988). Therefore, special attention is drawn to the champion's efforts to turn "resistance to change" into "commitment to change." Also, the champion has to obtain the necessary resources for the change that is initiated. Communication strategies and influence tactics applied by the champion should be adapted to the sub-cultures in the organisation.

Several researchers report that the probability of a breakthrough for planned changes in the organisation was strongest when one stated the reason for change and made a plan which illustrated how performance could be improved (Beatty and Gordon, 1991; Howell and Higgins, 1990b; Nutt, 1986). The rational presentation of ideas and informal exchange of information are connected to the influence of management, whereas one-sided argumentation and sanctions are typical when influencing organisation members on lower levels (Howell and Higgins, 1990b; Kipnis *et al.*, 1980). Certain factors in the specific champion's situation are also of importance when it comes to choosing influence tactics (Kipnis et al., 1980). For instance, research has shown that champions operate in different ways dependent on the innovation support available in the organisation (Howell and Higgins, 1990a).

An essential responsibility of the champion is to draw attention to new ideas, needs and possibilities and to try to make organisation members appreciate them (Van de Ven, 1986). A much used influence tactic is the traditional rational process in which the champion presents a solid business idea in order to gain top management support and subsequently tries to sell the idea to the users (Beath, 1991; Howell and Higgins, 1990a). This corresponds to Burgelman's (1983) findings that champions actively attempted to influence the management attitude towards the innovation. In order to gain management support it is often required that the champion puts forward a thoroughly prepared idea with documentation concerning benefits and financial consequences. If the management is convinced, they can contribute to selling the idea among potential users in the organisation. If the management shares the champion's vision and understands the innovation potential, the champion will meet less resistance. It is far more difficult for the champion who intends to sell new ideas in organisations where the management considers any proposal that challenges the status quo as undesirable (Howell and Higgins, 1990a).

The various rational approaches used in order to obtain management support are often dependent on the existing attitudes in the organisation. Some situations require a purely financial approach in which the expected profit and "pay-back" period are estimated. This kind of tactics is often used when the champion faces a bureaucracy which has a negative attitude towards the innovation. A related method is to strengthen the financial analysis with strategic arguments. This is sometimes necessary for champions who operate in a conservative organisation culture and when it is difficult to estimate the costs and benefits of an innovation. If there is financial ambiguity, a clearly stated strategic argument may be applied. A strategic argument alone may only be sufficient in organisations marked by a positive outlook as regards the innovation (Howell and Higgins, 1990a).

After having obtained management approval the champion builds a coalition of supporters in order to implement the change. The champion will gather support at the lower levels in the organisation by "selling" the change (Beatty and Gordon, 1991). He or she may inspire the organisation members by sharing the vision of the innovation potential (Beatty and Gordon, 1991; Howell and Higgins, 1990a). Enthusiasm and commitment about an innovation may provide a sense of purpose and meaning for the organisation members. In this way the motivator role becomes an important part of the champion's field of action. Through conversations, encouragement and active co-ordination the champion can motivate other organisation members to innovative behaviour and contribute to removing some of the social and structural barriers that prevent such innovation. (Holbek, 1990). In the motivator role the champion may also recognise and develop the potential of other members of the organisation in order to realise the innovation purpose (Beath, 1991; Howell and Higgins, 1990b). In the effort of building a coalition of supporters the champion has an integrating and co-ordinating role involving negotiation and bargaining (Holbek, 1990). It is important to integrate the interested parties inside and outside the project group during both planning and implementation.

In order to maintain management commitment, support and involvement in the organisation it is essential that the champion provides information concerning the progress of the project. By using a rational influence process, which is the most common approach to innovations, the champion operates within the organisation's rules and regulations.

A Participating Process

Another influence tactic is a participating process, which is identified by Howell and Higgins (1990a). Dependent upon the situation such a process could be an integrated part of a rational process. The emphasis is placed on communication, collaboration and evaluation. From such a perspective the organisation members are involved in the innovation before the final implementation decision is made. After an idea has been generated, information concerning the idea's potential costs and benefits is gathered. This information is then spread out to the organisation members and used to gather support for the innovation idea. In this period the champion tries to build up supporting coalitions at various organisation levels using motivational methods and negotiation as described in the previous section. Generally, the champion will make an attempt to gather support from colleagues who enjoy confidence in the organisation (opinion leaders). These colleagues will then sell the innovation to the rest of the organisation by stressing its advantages and importance.

Broad innovation support is assumed to increase the possibilities of wholehearted support by the management of the organisation (Howell and Higgins, 1990a). When management approval of the innovation is followed by a broad participation at the lower levels in the organisation early in the process, the resistance against the innovation from the employees working on these levels may be reduced. The champion, who is using a participating process, operates in line with cultural values that give weight to broad participation and support in the organisation before the management must make the implementation decision.

Bootlegging

The third influence tactic has the following pattern: The champion generates and implements ideas without getting permission and approval from the individuals that have the formal authority to make decisions in the organisation. Rules are put aside and ignored. It is a process with strong parallels to what Augsdorfer (1994, p. 91) calls bootlegging. It includes activities "without explicit approval from the responsible manager" and it "incorporates a dimension of secrecy." The champions applying such a strategy are similar to what Meyerson (2001, p. 93) calls "tempered radicals." "If they speak out too loudly, resentment builds toward them; if they play by the rules and remain silent, resentment builds inside them." Such individuals often "work quietly to challenge prevailing wisdom and gently provoke their organisational culture."

This influence tactic is used when the rest of the organisation does not share the champion's personal vision and it is typical in organisation cultures marked by considerable change resistance. Actors with power in the organisation are often unwilling to risk their reputation by supporting something that breaks with the established organisational norms.

Under such conditions the champion may choose to continue without support. The champion bypasses the organisation's bureaucracy and saves time this way (Beath, 1991) because he or she believes that the good idea will not survive if it has to work its way through a hierarchy of decision-makers (Ekvall, 1988). The champion applies several tactics in the innovation process such as disrupting others' expectations as a protest or demonstration of one's own values, taking a force coming towards one and redirecting it in the way preferred (verbal jujitsu), looking for and capitalising on change opportunities, and building alliances, etc. (Meyerson, 2001).

Champions also assume that the innovation will sell itself at a later stage of the innovation development and they continue the innovation process without approval from the proper decision makers. Gradually the champion will seek to demonstrate and sell the new idea, technology or process to the remaining organisation members whenever possible. As soon as the innovation is implemented the champion will try to attract attention to the innovation. After having gained informal support for the innovation, the champion may seek approval through the formal and authorised channels in the organisation.

This illegitimate resource acquisition strategy is probably used in many companies. Augsdorfer (1994) even argues that sophisticated leaders, who understand the chaotic nature of decision-making processes, accept the fishy activity and they also acknowledge the benefits of it to the company while less sophisticated leaders with a simple linear model of decision-making are unable to accept the method.

The Influence of Management and Culture on Resource Acquisition Strategies

As shown, much of the literature discusses how the champion applies different resource acquisition strategies in order to overcome resistance to change in the organisation. This may require both rational resource acquisition strategies and bootlegging. However, the literature also discusses how management may support the champion (e.g. Pearson, 1988; Littler and Sweeting, 1985). Management may see how the champions' insights, thinking, and decisions represent a source of competitive advantage. If their way of thinking is similar to entrepreneurs, champions are rare and difficult to imitate. This is partly because their ability is socially complex and their knowledge is tacit and cannot be articulated easily (Alvarez and Busenitz, 2001). When their ideas are exploited they may lead to original products or processes that are difficult to copy by competitors. In other words the management may see the champions as a resource that is important to cultivate within the organisation in order to uphold the competitiveness over time.

Assistance from persons with power and authority that support and legitimise the innovation and innovation supportive measures can be of vital importance for a successful innovation (Holbek 1990). From a resource dependency perspective, management support may be seen as vital for gaining political support, material resources, information resources (Beath, 1991), and/or slack resources (Nam and Tatum, 1997). In other words, management support may stimulate positively champions' acquisition of the necessary variety of resources. It is also probable that it may reduce the need to apply non-legitimate resource acquisition strategies. However, the last argument has not yet, as far as we know, been investigated in any study.

Management may themselves have seen the necessity of supporting the champion in order to change or the management may have seen that a certain innovation supports and promotes the vision of the organisation (Pearson, 1988; Littler and Sweeting, 1985). However, a situation where the management is not initially supportive and where the innovation is resource-demanding requires a resource acquisition strategy conducive to gaining support from management.

The type of management support might have a different effect on champions' resource acquisition. Management commitment in writing may be helpful, but it is, according to Littler and Sweeting (1985), often not enough. Management that follows up its commitment through action increases the chance for success. Successful champions may also be dependent upon the organisation's willingness to place the necessary time, capital and management at champions' disposal. Support from the professional expertise to the staff (Kanter, 1983), willingness to follow up and carry out the new ideas (Beatty and Gordon, 1991; Delbecq and Mills, 1985), and a management that acts as a sponsor and contributes with the necessary capital for planning and implementation of the innovation (Holbek, 1990) are assumed to support the champion and simplify the resource acquisition process.

Management support also legitimises the resource acquisition of the champion (Beath, 1991) and it will probably reduce the necessity of using too much force and too many non-legitimate resource acquisition strategies. Also, by clearly recognising creative ideas and signalling that management appreciates change, leaders can motivate the champion to make extra efforts and encourage other actors in the organisation to accept the innovation (Howell and Higgins, 1990a). Only support from management is always enough. Also support from the majority in the organisation is often required in order to proceed with new and potentially risky ideas (Schön, 1963). If innovative work is to bear fruit, it takes more freedom, quicker decision-making, more time, greater failure tolerance and more flexibility than what is adequate in day-to-day operations (Ekvall, 1988).

Many projects have failed as a consequence of a power struggle in the organisation, resistance by interest groups which will protect their own position, as well as narrow-mindedness or conflicts when it comes to budgeting. By protecting the champion from such negative impact, the management can encourage the champion in the resource acquisition effort (Beatty and Gordon, 1991; Howell and Higgins, 1990a). The champion can thus use the energy to convince the ordinary organisation members and overcome the resistance that often prevails on lower levels of the organisation.

Some studies have found that national culture influences organisational culture and the preferred resource acquisition strategies of the champion (Roure, 2001; Shane *et al.*, 1995; Shane, 1995, 1994b, 1994c,). For instance in a culture where leaders can be approached easily, the champion does not need to be on a high hierarchical level and close to top management. The opposite is true in other cultures (Roure, 2001). Also, the more power distance there is in a society, the more organisation members prefer champions to gain management support for their efforts to overcome resistance to innovative ideas (Shane *et al.*, 1995).

Several researchers have examined the problem where a dominating organisational culture blocks innovations (Strebel, 1987; Kanter, 1986; Burgelman, 1983; Lawrence and Dyer, 1983). Since organisation members are "programmed" to focus on and protect existing practice (Van de Ven, 1986), they will often resist the introduction of new procedures, routines or technology (Leonard-Barton and Kraus, 1985;

Sturdivant *et al.*, 1985). The resulting tension may be referred to as the conflict between stability, control and predictability on the one hand and the risk and uncertainty on the other (Ekvall, 1988). Topalian (2000) argues that innovation leaders should promote, develop and sustain an innovation-friendly culture.

DISCUSSION, IMPLICATIONS AND FUTURE RESEARCH

Resource Dependency Perspective and Research Methodology

Organisations tend to be bureaucratic and have a reward system that favours administrative rather than innovative skills. However, innovations are of vital importance for organisations' productivity, competitive strength and survival. The presence of innovation champions can be an essential prerequisite for successful innovations and for companies' competitiveness. We argue in this paper that it may be fruitful to study corporate innovation champion processes from a resource dependency perspective as a resource acquisition process. The champion uses his or her human and social capital (personal traits, experience, network position) and applies a broad repertoire of strategies (networking, communication, etc.) in order to acquire the necessary resources for his or her endeavour. The research on championship from a resource dependence perspective is, however, limited. We believe that there should be more attention paid to the study of how resource dependency theory can enhance our understanding of the champion process. As indicated the resource dependency perspective seems to provide an overall theoretical framework from which the whole champion process can be explored. The other theories applied in the literature reviewed (personal trait theory, network theory, and agency theory) seem to be necessary because they match the need to understand limited parts of the champion process.

Also, most studies on championship are case studies or traditional surveys. However, the effort made by champions is a time-consuming process including a broad range of activities. Longitudinal studies are therefore necessary in order to gain more insight into this complex process. Also, there has been little attention paid to the relationships between environment factors and championship. How important is external support for champions? How do external sources influence the resource acquisition methods and the interest of champions?

The Factors and Their Relative Importance

The research reviewed has a very applied and normative profile. It is full of advice on what factors champions and managers should apply in order to develop and implement innovations. The content and style of the review reflect this fact. Therefore, we will provide an overview of the most important factors influencing the resource acquisition process discussed in this paper. As pointed out, research recognises champions' human and social capital, resource acquisition strategies, and organisation/leadership characteristics as important for successful innovations. The literature review reveals that most focus is put on (1) the innovation champions' human and social capital and (2) their resource acquisition strategies. The factors discussed in these two areas are shown in Table 55-1. In accordance with the literature, these factors should be used in practice. However, the overview also reveals some weaknesses in the champion research that it is necessary to mention in this concluding section.

As the table shows, a high number of human and social capital factors and resource acquisition strategies are assumed to influence the champion process. However, the research does not say much about the relative importance of the factors and in which environment the different champion characteristics and resource acquisition strategies are most important and effective. These issues should be addressed in future research.

Networks and Resource Acquisitions

Network position and networking are, as discussed in this paper, important for the efficiency of champions' resource acquisition process. Therefore, the social network perspective provides a valuable set of concepts in which factors influencing the

TABLE 55-1 Champion Characteristics and Resource Acquisition Strategies.

Champion Characteristics	*Resource Acquisition Strategies*
Personal characteristics	*Rational strategies*
• socially independent	• rational presentation of vision, strategies, financial analysis and pay-back estimates
• politically clever	• solid business plan
• self-confidence	• selling of ideas first to top management then to other employees
• risk taker	
• charisma	• give recognition and develop others' potential
• energetic and enthusiastic	• building coalitions
• the ability to inspire, to stimulate intellectually, and to assess individuals	• apply different negotiate and bargain methods
• persistent	• using different sanction methods
• flexible	*Participating process*
• socially, professionally and managerial skilled	• communication, collaboration evaluation
	• involvement of employees
Experience	*Bootlegging*
• long and varied experience in the same company	• rules are set aside
• knowledge of the particular trade	• bypassing of the bureaucracy
• high-ranking job	• disrupting others' expectations
Position in network	• redirecting forces coming towards you in the way you prefer
• many weak and strong ties	• looking creatively on change opportunities
• bridging structural holes	• building alliances

resource acquisition process such as the size and structure of networks and champions' position in networks may be explored. However, the research on networks and innovation championship is limited and our understanding of how champions build and maintain their network and how the networks are structured is therefore incomplete. Particularly our knowledge about organisation-external relationships is limited. Questions that should be answered in future research are what is the optimal size of the champions' network, how diverse should the network be, and what is the optimal structure of networks of innovation champions (e.g. density and redundancy)?

The entrepreneurship literature might provide a basis for further research on champions' networks. We believe, however, that contextual differences between corporate champions and independent entrepreneurs might create dissimilarities in the resource types that are needed and in the resource acquisition process (Green *et al.*, 1999). These differences imply that we cannot uncritically apply the conclusions from the entrepreneurship research in order to understand corporate championship. Therefore, the disparity between independent entrepreneurs and champions should be investigated.

Selecting and Managing Champions

The literature review apparently reveals a contradiction. *On the one hand* the champion applies resource acquisition strategies that in some cases are legitimate and that in some cases are aimed at introducing innovations against the will of management and/or subordinates. It seems that the champion always acts unselfishly and in the best interest of the organisation but the organisation and its leadership do not understand this and resist changes. From such a perspective, for example, the formal appointment of champions will not be of current interest (Howell and Higgins, 1990b). *On the other hand* support of champions from the management is considered as vital by several researchers and formal appointment should be considered (McCorkle *et al.*, 2001). This raises the question whether the organisation can cultivate and manage champions in any way.

Research has not given sufficient answers to this question. However, a view recognising that management and other organisation members are positive to innovation champions and wish to support and manage them does not exclude bootlegging in some situations or in some departments or level of organisation. In fact Lawless and Price (1992) argue that it is necessary to study the organisation members (the users) as proactive technology consumers rather than opponents of change. They also point out that there has not been any attempt to investigate incentives in influencing the actions of champions. In other words Lawless and Price (1992) believe that champions can be identified and managed. However, they recognise the difficulty of such a job because the members of organisations often are at a great disadvantage with regard to information, compared to champions. In such a situation champions may act out of self-interest which organisation should protect themselves against. This is a typical agency problem.

There are fundamentally two main methods for rewarding performance. If the contribution to the organisational goal is easy to observe, the rewards should be behaviour-based. If it is difficult to observe how activities and outcome relate and the results are easily measured, then outcome-based rewards should be preferred. However, there are problems related to applying both behaviour and outcome rewards to control innovation champions. The champion is a unique source with few substitutes and there is much uncertainty related to the innovation, which creates considerable information asymmetry between the champion and the users. In such a situation it is difficult to apply traditional incentives. Lawless and Price (1992) argue that the organisation has to rely on the champion's reputation and second opinions to evaluate the innovation champions. However, the effectiveness of these devices and their manner of application are not very well known. Therefore, the researchers emphasise the necessity for further investigation of these two devices. We believe that it is not only necessary to investigate the devices, but it is also essential to study the relationship between the innovation champions and the organisation generally. In what way are innovation champions acting out of self interest and what is the effect of such behaviour on the best interest of the organisation? Will it stimulate the resources acquisition process to identify and appoint innovation champions and how will this identification affect their motivation? Should the organisation try to manage and control champions? If so, how can management manage and control the champion? These questions have not yet been answered satisfactorily.

Organisational Structure, Group Championship and Resource Acquisition

In the proposed model (Figure 55-1) we assume that organisational factors influence the resource acquisition process of innovation champions. We also briefly discussed how management and organisational culture may impact the resource acquisition process. However, structural factors may also influence the emergence of champions and the acquisition methods applied. There has been very little research into this issue except that it is argued that organic organisations probably enhance the expression of individual behaviour and therefore increase the likelihood of champions in emergence (House, 1991; Howell and Higgins, 1990b). We believe that this issue creates great opportunities for future research. Examples of research questions are: What kind of organisational structure stimulates champions? Do different structures have an impact on the choice of resource acquisition strategies and on the organisational benefits of innovation champions?

This paper also shows that the research is focused on individual champions. One person is often assumed to fight for the development and implementation of a certain innovation. However, innovations that require comprehensive changes may necessitate more effort than one individual can provide. This issue has not been focused on much in research, except for Hauschildt and Kirchmann (2001) who have pointed to the need for more than one champion in complex innovations. We therefore argue that issues related to team championship should be investigated closely. Examples of research questions are: What are the extra effects of more than one champion and how are acquisition strategies changed when there is more than one champion? Answers to such questions might be essential for champions and managers in their effort to change organisations.

Acknowledgement

We would like to thank the research programmes ED 2000, VC 2010, the project Innovation in small high tech companies (sponsored by the Research Council of Norway) and Agder Maritime Research Foundation for their support in this research project.

References

Alvarez, SA and LW Busenitz (2001). The entrepreneurship of resource-based theory. *Journal of Management,* 27, 755–775.

Augsdorfer, P (1994). The manager as pirate: An inspection of the gentle art of bootlegging. *Creativity and Innovation Management,* 3, 91–95.

Beath, CM (1991). Supporting the information technology champion. *MIS Quarterly,* 15, 355–372.

Beatty, CA and J Gordon (1991). Preaching the gospel: The evangelist of new technology. *California Management Review,* 33, 73–94.

Bigoness, WJ and WD Perreault (1981). A conceptual paradigm and approach for the study of innovators. *Academy of Management Journal,* 24, 68–82.

Burgelman, RA (1983). Managing the internal corporate venturing process. *Sloan Management Review,* 25, 33–48.

Burt, R (1992). *Structural Holes. The Social Structure of Competition.* Massachusetts: Harvard University Press.

Burt, R (1997). The contingent value of social capital. *Administrative Science Quarterly,* 42, 339–365.

Chakrabarti, AK (1974). The role of the champion in product innovation. *California Management Review,* 17, 58–62.

Chakrabarti, AK and J Hauschildt (1989). The division of labour in innovation management. *RandD Management,* 19, 161–171.

Collins, O and DG Moore (1970). *The Organisation Makers.* New York: Appleton-Century-Croft.

Conger, JA and RN Kanungo (1987). Toward a behavioral theory of charismatic leadership in organisational settings. *Academy of Management Review,* 12, 637–647.

Cox, LA (1976). Industrial innovation: The role of the people and cost factors. *Research Management,* 19, 29–32.

Day, DL (1994). Raising radicals: Different processes for championing innovative corporate ventures. *Organisation Science,* 5, 148–172.

Dean, JW (1987). Building the future: The justification process for new technology. In *New Technology as Organisational Innovation: The Development and Diffusion of Microelectronics,* J Pennings and A Buitendam (eds.), pp. 35–58. Massachusetts: Ballinger Publication.

Delbecq, AL and PK Mills (1985). Managerial practices that enhance innovation. *Organisational Dynamics,* 14, 24–34.

Ekvall, G (1988). *Förnyelse och Friktion. Om Organisation, Kreativitet og Innovation.* Borås: Centraltryckeriet AB.

Ettlie, JE, WP Bridges and RD O'Keefe (1984). Organisational strategy and structural differences for radical versus incremental innovation. *Management Science,* 30, 682–695.

Evan, EM (1993). *Organisation Theory: Research and Design.* New York: Macmillan Publishing Company.

Granovetter, M (1973). The strength of weak ties. *American Journal of Sociology,* 78, 1360–1380.

Green, PG, CG Brush and MM Hart (1999). The corporate venture champion: A resource-based approach to role and process. *Entrepreneurship: Theory and Practice,* 23, 103–122.

Hauschildt, J and E Kirchmann (2001). Teamwork for innovation—The "troika" of promotors. *R&D Management,* 31, 41–49.

Holbek, J (1990). Lokale innovasjonstiltak: Pådrivers plass som ildsjel og integrator. In *Ledelse og Innovasjon i Kommunene,* H. Baldersheim (ed.), pp. 142–167. Oslo: Tano.

House, RJ (1991). The distribution and exercise of power in complex organisations. A MESO theory. *Leadership Quarterly,* 2, 23–58.

Howell, JM and CA Higgins (1990a). Champions of change: Identifying, understanding, and supporting champions of technological innovations. *Organisational Dynamics,* Summer, 40–57.

Howell, JM and CA Higgins (1990b). Champions of technological innovation. *Administrative Science Quarterly,* 35, 317–341.

Howell, JM and CM Shea (2001). Individual differences, environmental scanning, innovation framing, and champion behavior: Key predictors of project performance. *The Journal of Product Innovation Management,* 18, 15–27.

Jenssen, JI and PA Havnes (2002). Public intervention in the entrepreneurial process. A study based on three Norwegian cases. *International Journal of Entrepreneurial Behaviour and Research,* 8, 173–188.

Kanter, RM (1983). *The Change Masters: Innovation and Entrepreneurship in the American Corporation,* New York: Simon and Schuster.

Kanter, RM (1986). When a Thousand Flowers Bloom: Structural, Collective, and Social Conditions for Innovation in Organisations. Unpublished manuscript, Massachusetts: Harvard Business School.

Kets de Vries, MFR (1977). The entrepreneurial personality: A person at the cross-roads. *Journal of Management Studies,* 14, 34–37.

Kipnis, D, SM Schmidt and I Wilkinson (1980). Intraorganisational influence tactics: Exploration in getting one's way. *Journal of Applied Psychology,* 65, 440–452.

Krackhardt, D (1992). The strength of strong ties: The importance of philos in organisations. In *Networks and Organisations. Structure, Form and Action,* N Nohria and RG Eccles (eds.), pp. 216–239. Massachusetts: Harvard Business School.

Krackhardt, D (1995). Entrepreneurial opportunities in an entrepreneurial firm: A structural approach. *Entrepreneurship: Theory and Practice,* 19, 53–69.

Krackhardt, D and R Stem (1988). Informal networks and organisational crisis: An experimental simulation. *Social Psychology Quarterly*, 51, 123–140.

Lawless, MW and LL Price (1992). An agency perspective on new technology champions. *Organisation Science*, 3, 342–355.

Lawrence, PR and D Dyer (1983). *Renewing American Industry*. New York: Free Press.

Leonard-Barton, D and WA Kraus (1985). Implementing new technology. *Harvard Business Review*, 63, 102–110.

Littler, DA and RC Sweeting (1985). Radical innovation in the mature company. *European Journal of Marketing*, 19(4), 33–53.

Maidique, MA (1980). Entrepreneurs, champions, and technological innovation. *Sloan Management Review*, 21, 59–76.

Marcus, AA (1988). Implementing externally induced innovations: A comparison of rulebound and autonomous approaches. *Academy of Management Journal*, 31, 235–256.

Markham, SK (1998). A logitudinal study of how champions influence others to support their projects. *Journal of Product Innovation Management*, 15, 490–504.

Markham, SK, SG Green and B Raja (1991). Champions and antagonists: Relationships with R&D project characteristics and management. *Journal of Engineering and Technology Management*, 8, 217–242.

McClelland, DC (1967). *The Achieving Society*. New York: Free Press.

McCorkle, DE, JF Alexander and J Reardon (2001). Integrating business technology and marketing education: Enhancing the diffusion process through technology champions. *Journal of Marketing Education*, 23, 16–27.

Meyerson, DE (2001). Radical change, the quiet way. *Harvard Business Review*, 79, 92–101.

Morgan, G (1988). *Riding the Waves of Change*. San Francisco: Jossey-Bass.

Mowday, RT (1979). Leader characteristics, self-confidence, and methods of upward influence in organisational decision situations. *Academy of Management Journal*, 22, 709–725.

Nam, CH and CB Tatum (1997). Leaders and champions for construction innovation. *Construction Management Economies*, 15, 259–270.

Nutt, PC (1986). Tactics of implementation. *Academy of Management Journal*, 29, 230–261.

Oberg, W (1972). Charisma, commitment, and contemporary organisation theory. *M. S. U. Business Topics*, 20, 18–22.

Pearson, AE (1988). Tough-minded ways to get innovative. *Harvard Business Review*, 66, 99–106.

Pinchot, G (1985). *Intrapreneuring: Why You Don't Have to Leave the Corporation to Become an Entrepreneur*. New York: Harper and Row.

Roberts, EB (1968). A basic study of innovators: How to keep and capitalize on their talents. *Research Management*, 11, 249–266.

Roberts, EB and AR Fusfeld (1982). Critical functions: Needed roles in the innovation process. In *Career issues in human resource management*, R Katz (ed.), pp. 182–207. New Jersey: Prentice-Hall.

Rothwell, REA (1974). SAPPHO updated—Project SAPPHO phase II. *Research Policy*, 3, 258–291.

Roure, L (2001). Product champion characteristics in France and Germany. *Human Relations*, 54, 663–682.

Schön, DA (1963). Champions of radical new inventions. *Harward Business Review*, 41, 77–86.

Shane, S (1994a). Are champions different from non-champions? *Journal of Business Venturing*, 9, 394–421.

Shane, S (1994b). Championing innovation in the global corporation. *Research Technology Management*, 37, 29–36.

Shane, S (1994c). Cultural values and the championing process, *Entrepreneurship: Theory and Practice*, 18, 25–42.

Shane, S (1995). Uncertainty avoidance and the preference for innovation champion role. *Journal of International Business Studies*, 26, 47–68.

Shane, S, S Venkataraman and I MacMillan (1995). Cultural differences in innovation championing strategies. *Journal of Management*, 21, 931–952.

Smith, JJ, JE McKeon, KL Hoy, RL Boysen, L Shechter and EB Roberts (1984). Lessons from 10 case studies in innovation. *Research Management*, 27, 23–27.

Stevenson, HH. and DE Gumpert (1985). The heart of entrepreneurship. *Harvard Business Review*, 63, 85–94.

Stevenson, HH and JC Jarillo (1990). A paradigm of entrepreneurship: Entrepreneurial management. *Strategic Management Journal*, 11, 17–27.

Strebel, P (1987). Organizing for innovation over an industry cycle. *Strategic Management Journal*, 8, 117–124.

Sturdivant, F, J Ginter and A Sawyer (1985). Manager's conservatism and corporate performance. *Strategic Management Journal*, 6, 17–38.

Topalian, A (2000). The role of innovation leaders in developing long-term products. *International Journal of Innovation Management*, 4, 149–171.

Van de Ven, AH (1986). Central problems in the management of innovation. *Management Science*, 32, 590–607.

Van de Ven, AH (1993). The development of an infrastructure for entrepreneurship. *Journal of Business Venturing*, 8, 211–230.

Wainer, HA and IA Rubin (1969). Motivation of research and development entrepreneurs: Determinants of company success. *Journal of Applied Psychology*, 53, 590–607.

Westlund, H and R Bolton (2001). *Local Social Capital and Entrepreneurship*. Proceedings of the Western Regional Science Association, Palm Springs, CA, USA.

Woolcock, M (1998). Social capital and economic development: Toward a theoretical synthesis. *Theory and Society*, 27, 151–208.

Zaltman, G, R Duncan and J Holbek (1973). *Innovation and Organisations*. New York: John Wiley and Sons.

56

MANAGING INTERNAL CORPORATE VENTURING CYCLES

Robert A. Burgelman and Liisa Välikangas

Companies too often vacillate in their commitment to internal corporate venturing activities, leading to less than optimal outcomes. Executives need to better understand—and manage—the factors that drive cyclicality in internal corporate venturing.

Thirty years of systematic study of internal corporate venturing has revealed that many major corporations experience a strange cyclicality in their ICV activity. (See "About the Research," p. 28.) Periods of intense ICV activity are followed by periods when such programs are shut down, only to be followed by new ICV initiatives a few years later. Like seasons, internal corporate venturing programs begin and end in a seemingly endless cycle.

Consider Lucent Technologies' New Ventures Group, which was set up to reap commercial value from Bell Labs technology. In January 2000, the group was acclaimed as exemplifying best practice for a new-ventures division.[1] Yet Lucent, in the aftermath of the telecom downturn, in 2002 sold 80% of its interest in the New Ventures Group to Coller Capital, a British private-capital management company.

Other ICV programs have substantially changed their character or mission. In its first three years of existence, Baxter International Inc.'s nontraditional-innovation program, for example, transformed its mission from the pursuit of new technologies in new markets to the exploration of business opportunities closer to the core business.[2] (A new CEO has recently revived a broader search for new growth areas.) A few years ago, Shell GameChanger, the radical innovation program at Royal Dutch/Shell Group of Companies, might have solicited ideas ranging from carpooling to waste reclamation to sandwich sales to urbanites. However, in today's innovation climate, such ideas are too radical.[3]

Xerox Corp. offers still another example. After ad hoc efforts to manage its technology ventures, Xerox established an innovation board in the 1980s to aid decision making. The administrative board soon gave way in 1989 to an internal venture-capital group called Xerox Technology Ventures, to invest in Xerox technologies that showed market potential but were outside Xerox's core business interests. XTV was terminated in the mid-1990s, and yet another structure, called Xerox New Enterprise, became its replacement. XNE took more aggressive ownership of the ventures yet sought to infuse them with entrepreneurship. XNE, in turn, was terminated in the late 1990s.[4]

Burgelman, Robert A. and Liisa Välikangas. 2005. "Managing internal corporate venturing cycles."
MIT Sloan Management Review 46(4): 26–34.

These examples should not come as a surprise. Earlier research found that in many companies, ICV programs manifest significant cyclicality.[5] Chesbrough describes the ICV cycle as follows: "The general pattern is a cycle that starts with enthusiasm, continues into implementation, then encounters significant difficulties, and ends with eventual termination of the initiative. Yet within a few years, another generation of businesses undertakes the effort anew, and the cycle occurs again."[6] This recurring phenomenon seems wasteful of a company's financial and human resources. ICV programs are usually closed before investment pays off, and careers are often damaged. Also, potentially important learning from a previous program often does not inform the next one.

Interestingly, as our recent examples indicate, ICV cyclicality continues several decades after researchers first observed the phenomenon. That suggests that companies have not yet learned to use some of the research findings about ICV in their strategic-management approaches. It also underscores the fact that managing ICV is quite difficult. It is so difficult that one scholar, Andrew Campbell, has argued in a recent debate in *European Business Forum* against even trying to develop a strategic leadership discipline for dealing with internal corporate venturing as a dynamic internal force.[7] Instead, Campbell recommends adopting a tight, top-driven approach to project selection that leaves very little room for new-business experimentation. He and others basically advocate giving up on what they call "new leg" venturing: efforts to develop entirely new businesses for the corporation.[8]

The fact that ICV activities have persisted over decades, however, suggests that the management issues associated with ICV cyclicality are not likely to go away.[9] Historical evidence from the last three decades suggests that the perceived importance of ICV may fade away for a while, but ICV predictably comes back with a vengeance and will likely continue to be a nagging strategic leadership challenge for top management.

WHY INTERNAL CORPORATE VENTURING CYCLES PERSIST

Early research efforts suggested that the interplay between the prospects of a company's mainstream businesses and the availability of uncommitted financial resources created a strong force driving ICV cyclicality.[10] There are four common situations that can result from that interplay. (See Figure 56-1.)

FIGURE 56-1 What Drives Internal Corporate Venturing Cycles?

Unless executives understand and manage the factors that cause cyclicality in internal corporate venturing, a company's ICV strategy is apt to fluctuate over time, varying with the growth prospects of the main business and the availability of uncommitted financial resources.

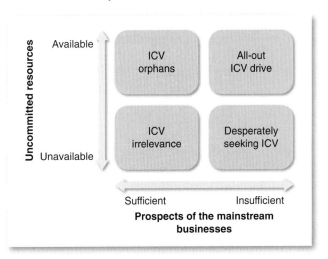

Source: Adapted from R.A. Burgelman, "Corporate Entrepreneurship and Strategic Management: Insights From a Process Study," Management Science 29, no. 12 (December 1983): 1349–1365, and R.A. Burgelman, "Strategy Is Destiny: How Strategy-Making Shapes a Company's Future" (New York: Free Press, 2002).

Situation 1: "ICV Orphans" If a company has uncommitted financial resources, it can afford to support internal-venturing projects. If, however, the prospects of the main-stream businesses are sufficient to meet the company's profitable growth objectives, there is little motivation to support ICV actively, and top management is more likely to pay lip service to it. A number of entrepreneurial projects that nevertheless have managed to get started in the nooks and crannies of various business units are likely to drift along as "orphan" projects. In this case, the ICV cycle has started, even though top management is not actively managing it.

Situation 2: "All-Out ICV Drive" If the company has financial resources available but the prospects of the mainstream business are expected to be insufficient for meeting corporate objectives for profitable growth, top management is motivated to support ICV projects actively. In this situation, top management is likely to form a new-venture division or new-business group. Such a structural arrangement then becomes the home for all existing ICV orphan projects and also serves as the implementation tool for starting an ambitious top-driven ICV program.

Situation 3: "ICV Irrelevance" If there are few uncommitted financial resources available, but the prospects of the mainstream businesses at the moment look sufficiently promising, top management is likely to consider ICV largely irrelevant. All attention is to be focused on exploiting opportunities in the core businesses.

Situation 4: "Desperately Seeking ICV" A lack of uncommitted financial resources combined with a mainstream business with inadequate growth prospects is likely to lead top managers to latch on desperately to the first reasonable-looking ICV project that comes their way. Given the limited choice of ICV projects that executives face in this situation and the substantial uncertainty associated with any ICV project, the likelihood of failure is high.

FORCES DETERMINING THE LENGTH OF THE ICV CYCLE

To some extent, corporate venturing may follow the ups and downs of the economy. When cash is readily available, corporations invest in new-venture programs; when cash becomes short, the programs are terminated. However, the macroeconomic explanation for ICV cyclicality is probably partial at best. Corporate strategic and administrative factors likely have greater bearing on the length of the venturing cycle.

Estimates of the length of the ICV cycle vary. Block and MacMillan assess the cycle to be 10 years.[11] Fast, however, notes that the corporate venturing programs started by many Fortune 500 companies in the late 1960s and early 1970s were disbanded during the late 1970s.[12] Burgelman's in-depth study of a new-venture division in a large diversified company during the mid-to-late 1970s also found a somewhat shorter cycle.[13]

Annual budgeting and three-year rolling budgets may contribute to the ICV cycle by establishing a one- to three-year time horizon in which top management expectations must be met or a venture program risks being deemed ineffective. This time-line puts perverse pressures on ventures to "grow big fast" and potentially leads to dysfunctional managerial behavior, such as neglecting to develop the organizational infrastructure of a venture in order to secure continued and timely new-product development.[14]

Biggadike has shown that, on average, it takes 10 to 12 years before the return on investment for new ventures equals that of mature businesses.[15] That is much longer than the average time fast-track executives are expected to stay in the same job in most large companies. This creates at least three potential problems. First, executives who do stay that long in a venture-manager position may be running severe career risks, especially if the venture eventually is unsuccessful.[16] Second, unless the company's human resources function has developed clear executive career paths that require

ABOUT THE RESEARCH

The foundation of this paper is a mix of field research conducted over a 30-year period, examples from our current field research, analysis of other scholars' research, and examples derived from past and recent business press. Burgelman has studied internal corporate venturing in a number of companies in different industries since the mid-1970s. His most recent research on ICV has been at Intel Corp. in the context of a comprehensive study of the role of strategy making in corporate evolution, and he is currently collaborating with Monitor Ventures, part of the consulting firm Monitor Group to develop a strategic-leadership discipline for sustained ICV management. Välikangas has worked with a number of leading companies to develop their internal innovation capabilities in pursuit of strategic resilience, and this paper draws on that work. In her work at the Woodside Institute, she is currently exploring innovative practices in core management processes such as strategic planning and internal venturing.

experience in venture positions and has ensured that capable managers are available to take over from those who are due to rotate out of a venture position, either some executives will end up staying in the position too long or the venture program will experience disruptive management changes.[17] A recent case study of a product innovation in a technology company, for example, showed that frequent changes in the executive sponsor were detrimental to the commercial success of a disruptive innovation.[18] Third, unless a process is in place to measure managerial performance in new ventures in terms of clearly established milestones, executives may engage in rational but narrowly opportunistic behavior; they may focus on achieving short-term results at the expense of building the necessary infrastructure for long-term venture development.[19] They do so because they anticipate that, given the normal rotation of executives to different positions, someone else will be in charge by the time the innovation can be fully harvested.

FORCES DRIVING THE END OF AN ICV CYCLE

The simplest driver for ending ICV programs is their failure to deliver. But if corporate venturing programs are typically closed before they have had a chance to prove themselves, other reasons than mere performance must be involved. Recent studies of various forms of corporate venturing shed interesting new light on the role of performance in ending an ICV cycle.[20] In particular, some ICV programs have been terminated despite their apparent success. In general, these findings suggest that both top management and the executives involved in the ICV program fail to appreciate the role of ICV in a company's corporate strategy.

One important case involves Xerox Technology Ventures in the mid-1990s. This program is credited with *too much success* in that "success might have made the [Xerox's] internal units look bad by comparison."[21] There was the added fear that such success might have come at the expense of Xerox shareholders, as the startups funded by XTV may have competed for business with Xerox.[22]

In another case, a group of scientists at AT&T Corp. started a campaign called Opportunity Discovery Department in 1995 and sought to revitalize Bell Labs research and its links to the corporate strategy.[23] ODD developed innovative strategies, worked with business units to think of future scenarios, networked with many external experts, and ignited a grassroots movement of some 400 people. The ODD initiative came to an end, however, in 1998 as the group was judged by standard performance metrics to have failed to produce enough patents. A more important reason was that management found it difficult to accept that the group was taking credit for strategy making, something that was considered a top-management responsibility and privilege. Those who saw setting strategy as their prerogative perceived ODD as a threat, and the group's highly innovative approach only added to the discomfort.

Administrative factors can also end an ICV cycle. Companies often reorganize to meet changing environmental demands or to keep things fluid. An ICV program may create interference with the new organizational structure. A newly appointed executive to the ICV program may not be committed to the course of action taken by the prior manager and may want to leave a mark by making changes. In addition, ICV programs are usually easy targets for incoming CEOs to end.

The combination of such administrative issues with a general lack of understanding of the role of ICV programs in long-term corporate-development strategy may lead to what game theorists call "weakness of will."[24] Weakness of will is about the inability to sustain commitment. Investing in innovation is a long-term commitment and sometimes involves difficult trade-offs with short-term pressures. As Machiavelli observed, the benefits to the innovator are uncertain, but the costs to those affected by the changes involved are not.[25] That is one reason resistance to innovation is likely to be stronger within an established organization than support for it.

IMPLICATIONS FOR STRATEGIC MANAGEMENT OF ICV

After a recent downsizing of corporate ventures, one CEO lamented privately that the extent of the cuts had eliminated future growth options. As that lament illustrates, the bad news stemming from our analysis is that ICV cyclicality is a nagging strategic leadership challenge facing top management of established companies. The good news is that the cyclicality of ICV is primarily the result of executives failing to master the forces that cause fluctuations in long-term support for ICV—a failure that can be remedied.

Too often, there is either too much or too little venturing going on at any point in established corporations, and top management allows support for ICV to oscillate among the four scenarios described earlier. ICV, however, is too important for a company's long-term success to be dictated by fluctuating financial fortunes, short-term strategic pressures, perverse administrative routines or fickle management fads. Research shows that achieving growth through diversifying acquisitions is fraught with expensive failure.[26] Thus internal corporate venturing remains a key capability for established companies seeking to achieve strategic renewal and avoid stalled growth.[27] It is a strategic leadership imperative for top management to learn to better manage the ICV cycle. Specifically, several important implications for the discipline of ICV strategic management emerge from our analysis.[28]

Even when not needed to support profitable growth objectives, ICV activity can be an important indicator of where the company's employees think future opportunities lie.

There is always ICV going on, so manage it. There may not be a dedicated internal-venturing unit in a company, yet it is likely that some employees are exploring new-business opportunities that are outside the scope of the corporate strategy at the time that the initiatives originate. Internal-venturing activity may very well be an irrepressible force in all established companies.[29] Realizing that ICV activity is actually hard to stamp out completely may increase top management's motivation to manage it better.

However, without management encouragement, much of the autonomous, employee-driven ICV activity will cease, either because the employees involved grow frustrated by an eventual lack of traction or because they leave the company to pursue the opportunity in a startup. This is often the case in companies in Situation 1, in which orphan ICV initiatives find it difficult to get senior management support, and even sometimes in Situation 3, where the ICV initiatives that are likely to emerge are considered irrelevant.

To better capitalize on the company's natural source of ICV activity, top management needs to put in place a process that makes entrepreneurial employees comfortable coming forward with their ideas and mobilizes senior management to begin determining the new opportunities' "strategic context," a process that involves evaluating innovations and championing promising ones that the company can then embrace and fully support.[30] Such a process needs to superimpose *strategic* discussions on top of financial analyses such as net present value calculations, in order to better ascertain what the potential impact of an innovation may be on the company's future.

An old but striking example of the hazards of evaluating innovations by strictly financial measures is the emergence of electronic fuel injection.[31] Today, Robert Bosch GmbH, based in Stuttgart, Germany, is a leading supplier of electronic fuel-injection systems. However, Bendix, an American company, invented electronic fuel injection. At Bendix, net present value calculations, together with anticipated near-term reactions from original equipment manufacturers in the United States, did not suggest that electronic fuel injection would be an economically viable new product. When Volkswagen AG decided to work with Bosch to bring a mass-produced car with electronic fuel injection to market during the late 1960s, Bendix opted to license its technology to Bosch. By the time Bendix realized that electronic fuel injection would be a big opportunity and rushed to pursue it, it was too late, given the time remaining on its patents, to establish a position of market leadership.

By now, the concept of "disruptive technology" has begun to raise top management's awareness of the need to adopt a more strategic approach to innovation.[32] But the link between disruptive technology and ICV, which is often its source, remains undermanaged. Eastman Kodak Co. is a case in point. One of the great industrial and commercial success stories of the 20th century, Kodak had a somewhat checkered history in pursuing ICV during the 1970s and 1980s.[33] During the late 1990s, however, the company was still seeking to migrate from film—a source of a "breathtaking" decline in earnings—to invest $3 billion in digital photography, a major disruptive force.[34] Ironically, Kodak had been making investments in digital photography since 1972. However, by 2003, film still accounted for about 50% of Kodak's profits.[35]

View ICV as a source of insights that can inform strategic direction. Even when not needed to support profitable growth objectives at a particular moment in time, ICV activity can be an important indicator of where the company's employees think future opportunities lie. Indeed, self-organizing, emergent ICV activity can be an important source of strategic foresight. Smart top executives recognize that ICV is a discovery process that should be evaluated first and foremost in terms of the information that it generates and not viewed only in terms of dollars added to the revenue line.[36] Rather than seeking to quash ICV or direct it too heavily, top management should view it as a source of strategic insight into the future. Senior executives should be interested in the ideas and related autonomous strategic initiatives that entrepreneurial employees may be working on in their spare time. Management should try to understand what is so motivating and promising that people are willing to work on it, often after regular working hours or on weekends. If a company's employees are working on such innovations, competitors and startups may also be. Companies can capitalize on grassroots innovation by their employees. For example, during the last five years, Whirlpool Corp. has systematically tapped employee ideas, ending up with a pipeline of product innovations including dishwashers for single-person households, ovens that freeze and heat, and garage appliances for men.[37]

An "all-out ICV drive" biases the process and often engenders costly mistakes. Such top-driven initiatives tend to warp the ICV process because many employees then perceive the ICV career route as the most attractive one simply because of management's forcefully expressed interests. As a result, the mainstream business runs the risk of losing top talent, to the great frustration and resentment of those still generating all of the company's profits. Intel Corp.'s all-out drive in the late 1990s to develop new businesses, for example, had executives in the microprocessor business complaining that they could not hold on to key employees who wanted to join the more exciting new ventures supported by top management. Top-driven ICV may also result in big losses, because top management may prematurely invest significantly to try to fully exploit and accelerate new growth opportunities. For example, by the time Iridium LLC, a satellite-telephone service, filed for Chapter 11 bankruptcy in August 1999, Motorola Inc. had invested $3.5 billion in the venture.

If ICV is desperately needed, it may be almost too late. When desperately seeking ICV, a company is faced with the dire prospect of a decaying core business. Such decay is often caused by disruptive technologies, which the company may very well have dabbled in early on but given up or failed to capitalize on. To avoid ending up in this situation, it is imperative that top management remains actively involved in a corporate ICV strategy on a continuous basis even when the mainstream business is prospering. If top management waits until new business opportunities are desperately needed, it is usually already very late in the game.

LESSONS FROM INTEL

Research on Intel Corp. illustrates factors that drive ICV cyclicality and also illustrates that by recognizing the ongoing strategic importance of ICV, companies can mitigate some of the cyclicality. Between 1987 and 1997, Intel essentially operated in Situation 1 (ICV Orphans) as its core microprocessors for the personal-computer market segment propelled it from about $3 billion in revenue in 1988 to about $27 billion by 1997, accompanied by extraordinary profitability. Toward the end of 1997, however, the PC market segment seemed to be slowing down significantly, which put Intel in Situation 2 (All-Out ICV Drive). Top management engaged in something of a crash effort to turbocharge its new-business development efforts, creating a New Business Group in 1998 to do so. Many orphan projects were transferred to the NBG. At the same time, top management initiated some very large new ventures. In part hampered by the downturn of the economy and the Internet bust, most of these ventures did not succeed.

Nevertheless, the emphasis on new-business development led Intel to embrace more forcefully new initiatives in the wireless-communications and networking-communications markets, thereby significantly expanding the scope of its corporate strategy. By 2001, however, Intel top management faced competing needs: continuing to invest in new ventures, raising the investment stakes in the core businesses to stay ahead of the competition in technology and manufacturing, and continuing to nurture the money-losing but promising new businesses in networking and wireless communications. Predictably, the perceived relevance of ICV diminished significantly, and the new business group was scaled back. The ICV activity was merged with Intel Capital, Intel's corporate venture-capital arm, in late 2002. Subsequently, Les Vadasz, president of Intel Capital, and John Miner, vice president and general manager of the New Business Group, were jointly managing the merged group.

From this point on, Intel Capital's charter included not only external but also internal investments in areas that were potentially important for Intel's future businesses. The New Business Group was renamed New Business Incubation Group and became a corporate "greenhouse" where companies and technologies that were too new to be easily placed within Intel were nurtured and protected from the demands of the established groups. John Miner says that "after reorganizing the New Business Group, we completely refocused on activities that benefit from being part of Intel. All our ventures build products that can be done on a wafer. We have activities in hand-held wireless, display and pixel-processing technologies, wireless and nonwireless broadband, and photonic components. We focus on the early technology-capture process to develop new business applications and look for commercialization opportunities."

Miner also says, "We always look for two-way linkages with other parts of Intel. Two business opportunities came directly from the [company's] Wireless Computing and Communications Group; they will go back there. On the other hand, we also have two for which it is not yet clear where they will go." With regard to NBI, Miner believes that "a key challenge is how to maintain corporate-level interest. We continuously try to develop strategic value for the company, and we want to pay our own way doing it. The biggest challenge is lateral, how to work with peers in other parts of the company and look farther out for strategic gaps they may need to fill—without necessarily having agreement on the strategy. We think that doing new businesses internally and organically makes them easier to assimilate, and less costly. But sometimes we do it in parallel, both through incubation and through small acquisitions."

BUILDING LEADERSHIP CAPABILITY TO MANAGE THE ICV CYCLE

How can companies develop the necessary strategic leadership to avoid getting trapped in any of the four common situations associated with the ICV cycle? To avoid the pitfalls of unmanaged cyclicality, ICV should be viewed as an integrated and continuous part of the company's strategy-making process, rather than as an insurance policy whose appeal varies according to the prospects of the company's mainstream businesses. Effectively integrating ICV into the strategy-making process requires recognition on the part of top management that internal corporate venturing involves a distinct strategic leadership discipline—a discovery process based on experimentation and selection[38]—that informs executives about emerging opportunities and facilitates nuanced adjustments to the company's strategic direction.[39] Treating ICV this way consistently over time is likely to raise important questions that will help shape corporate strategy. For instance, which new opportunities consistent with the core strengths of the company does ICV open up? Which new leverage points in competition might ICV provide? How does ICV inform us about the potentially unmet needs of our customers and new market segments? What does ICV tell us about the blind spots in our current competitive strategy, especially in relation to potentially disruptive technologies?

UPM-Kymmene Corp., a leading Finland-based forest and paper-products company that is listed on the Helsinki and New York stock exchanges, has experienced benefits from its venturing activities, in part because the activities both challenge and broaden

> *UPM-Kymmene Corp., a leading Finland-based forest and paper-products company, has venturing activities that both challenge and broaden the interpretation of corporate strategy.*

the interpretation of corporate strategy. UPM has a history of new business creation beyond paper, partly through one of its predecessor companies, Yhtyneet Paperitehtaat. The company's newest venture, UPM Rafsec, was founded in 1997 to mass-produce radio-frequency identification tags for global markets. Currently, through its New Ventures organization, UPM is dedicated to exploring new areas in which the company has materials and manufacturing know-how, such as printed electronics, nanotechnology, smart labels and chemical indicators. But New Ventures also helps facilitate innovation more broadly inside UPM's core businesses. It has developed forums for innovators across focal areas—called "clusters"—that represent core technologies and significant future opportunity for existing UPM divisions. These clusters and their activities offer vehicles for cross-divisional collaboration, bringing innovation processes and tools that New Ventures has developed from the venturing periphery to the core. For instance, New Ventures has helped introduce product-development tools, such as prototyping, that make innovation less risky and more efficient. The return on investment for UPM's small 13-person New Ventures group is so far perceived to be high and exemplary.

When companies recognize the importance of ICV to strategy, they are less likely to try to do away with ICV entirely. Intel's decision in 2001 to scale back rather than end its efforts to develop new ventures offers an example of a leading corporation attempting to better manage the ICV cycle. (See "Lessons From Intel," p. 31.) Intel is persisting as the company tries to make its commitment to venturing pay off in the long run.[40]

Taking control of the ICV cycle allows executives to rationalize resource allocation. This will reduce the tendency to flood ICV with resources in good times, which takes away entrepreneurial hunger, and to starve it in bad times, which aborts potential successes. Rationalizing resource allocation implies careful early experimenting with small amounts of resources to gain insight into radically new opportunities that inherently involve high technological and market uncertainties. It also implies consistent nurturing of new businesses that pass strategic and financial milestone reviews, with carefully calibrated resource commitments increasing over extended periods.[41] It is important to maintain some predictability in resource allocation so that, once milestones have been met, further funding will result independently of the business cycle.

Another key aspect of managing internal corporate venturing cyclicality is making ICV a responsibility of all senior executives. If senior executives in the mainstream businesses do not feel that they share responsibility for ICV, do not feel that ICV efforts are central and lasting, or do not feel that the executives running ICV are equally able peers, the forces driving ICV cyclicality are likely to prevail. In order to make a new venture a corporate success, executives involved in ICV need to be able to sponsor and guide the new venture and to start the process of determining its strategic context within the corporation. Determining a new venture's strategic context involves working diligently to explore its links to the corporate strategy and to persuade top management to make the venture part of the corporate business portfolio. But that process depends on getting support from at least some of the senior executives from the mainstream businesses, so that top management can be assured that the rest of the organization will embrace the new venture. As a result, a climate of mutual respect on the part of all the senior executives involved is critical. Intel achieved this by assigning highly respected senior executives to head up its ventures organization. Nokia Corp., too, achieved this, in part through the development of a ventures board of directors on which all the senior executives serve. And, equally importantly, the president of Nokia was put in charge of all the company's corporate venturing efforts.[42]

ICV cyclicality is probably here to stay because of the powerful forces that create it. Learning to better manage the ICV cycle, however, is important for large, established companies because other profitable growth avenues may not be promising. Major, portfolio-diversifying acquisitions are costly and often do not create shareholder value. Smaller and midsize acquisitions can play an important role, but eventually smallish acquisitions may not remain sufficient to reach corporate growth objectives. Developing an effective ICV capability thus seems an unavoidable strategic imperative for top management of large companies.[43] We should perhaps not be surprised that few companies have been successful in developing such a capability because the strategic leadership skills that are required to effectively explore and develop ill-defined and uncertain new-venture opportunities are different from those required to exploit well-defined and incremental core-business opportunities. Our analysis suggests, however, that top management can learn to better manage the forces that drive ICV cyclicality—and avoid being driven by them.

Acknowledgments

The authors thank Julian Birkinshaw of the London Business School and Bill McKelvey of the University of California, Los Angeles, for helpful comments and queries.

About the Authors

Robert A. Burgelman is the Edmund W. Littlefield Professor of Management at Stanford University Graduate School of Business, where he is also director of the Stanford Executive Program.

Liisa Välikangas is the managing director of the Woodside Institute and an adjunct professor at Helsinki School of Economics. Contact the authors at burgelman_robert@gsb.stanford.edu and lvalikangas@woodsideinstitute.org.

Endnotes

1. Corporate Strategy Board, Executive Inquiry, "The New Venture Division, Attributes of an Effective New Business Incubation Structure" (January 2000): 14.
2. A. Hunt, vice president of innovation, Baxter International Inc., interview with L. Välikangas, fall 2004.
3. L. Välikangas, "Shell GameChanger: Mastering the Corporate Innovation Game," working paper, Woodside Institute, Woodside, California, 2004.
4. H. Chesbrough, "Graceful Exits and Missed Opportunities: Xerox Management of its Technology Spin-off Organizations," Business History Review 76, no. 4 (2002): 803–837.
5. The literature on ICV is broad if somewhat fragmented, reflecting sustained interest on the part of scholars and practitioners over many decades. It is true that the phenomenon of ICV cyclicality has been "in the air" for a long time. See, for example, N.D. Fast, "The Rise and Fall of Corporate New Venture Divisions" (Ann Arbor, Michigan: UMI Research Press, 1978); R.A. Burgelman, "Corporate Entrepreneurship and Strategic Management: Insights From a Process Study," Management Science 29, issue 12 (December 1983): 1349–1365; R.A. Burgelman, "Managing the New Venture Division: Research Findings and Implications for Strategic Management," Strategic Management Journal 6, no. 1 (March 1985): 39–55. However, it has seldom been the main focus of attention in the ICV literature, and there has been little systematic discussion of what generates

the start, duration and ending of the ICV cycle. For a fairly recent textbook-style overview of the broad ICV literature, see M. Morris and D. Kuratko, "Corporate Entrepreneurship: Entrepreneurial Development Within Organizations" (Fort Worth: Harcourt College Publishers, 2002). For a recent anthology of various entrepreneurship-related perspectives, see M.A. Hitt, R.D. Ireland, S.M. Camp and D.L. Sexton, eds., "Strategic Entrepreneurship: Creating a New Mindset" (Oxford: Blackwell Publishers, 2002).

6. H. Chesbrough, "Designing Corporate Ventures in the Shadow of Private Venture Capital," California Management Review 42, no. 3 (2000): 31–49.

7. A. Campbell and R.A. Burgelman, "EBF Debate: Should Companies Be Cautious Entrepreneurs . . . or Should They Embrace a Dynamic Force?" European Business Forum, no. 15 (fall 2003): 12–15; and A. Campbell and R.A. Burgelman, "EBF Debate: 'Wait and Watch' versus 'Practice and Get Luckier,' European Business Forum, no. 16 (winter 2003–2004): 36–39. For an effort to integrate Campbell's and Burgelman's perspectives in the debate, see R.M. Kanter "Exploring the Innovation Pyramid," European Business Forum, no. 16 (winter 2003–2004): 40–42. For a complete statement of Campbell's position, see A. Campbell and R. Park, "The Growth Gamble" (London: Nicholas Brealey, 2005).

8. See also A. Campbell, J. Birkinshaw, A. Morrison, R. van Basten Batenburg, "The Future of Corporate Venturing," MIT Sloan Management Review 45, no. 1 (fall 2003): 30–37. For another view advocating a limited role for ICV, see C. Zook with J. Allen, "Profit From the Core: Growth Strategy in an Era of Turbulence" (Boston: Harvard Business School Press, 2001).

9. Such persistence may be attributed partly to internal entrepreneurship being a dynamic force that is an important motivator at work. Corporate venturing offers many employees a chance to follow their interests and passion, often in addition to their regular tasks. D. Duarte and N. Snyder, in "Strategic Innovation: Embedding Innovation as a Core Competency in Your Organization" (New York: Jossey-Bass, 2003), describe how Whirlpool Corp. was able to tap the ideas and passions of many of its employees by making innovation a corporatewide privilege and capability.

10. Burgelman, "Corporate Entrepreneurship and Strategic Management," 1349–1365.

11. Z. Block and I.C. MacMillan, "Corporate Venturing: Creating New Businesses Within the Firm" (Boston: Harvard Business School Press, 1993).

12. Fast, "The Rise and Fall of Corporate New Venture Divisions." For more recent commentary on the short life spans of new venture divisions, see D.A. Garvin, "A Note on Corporate Venturing and New Business Creation," research note, Harvard Business School Press (March 2001): 1–21.

13. R.A. Burgelman, "Managing Innovating Systems: A Study of the Process of Internal Corporate Venturing" (Ph.D. diss., Columbia University, 1980).

14. R.A. Burgelman, "A Process Model of Internal Corporate Venturing in the Diversified Major Firm," Administrative Science Quarterly 28, no. 2 (June 1983): 223–245. See also R.A. Burgelman and L.R. Sayles, "Inside Corporate Innovation: Strategy, Structure and Managerial Skills" (New York: Free Press, 1986).

15. R. Biggadike, "The Risky Business of Corporate Diversification," Harvard Business Review 56 (May–June 1979): 103–111.

16. See, for example, F.J. Aguilar, "Bard Medsystems Division: Intrapreneurial Showcase," Harvard Business School case no. 1-387-183 (Boston: Harvard Business School Publishing, 1987). which narrates the career hazards of an entrepreneurial division manager who stays more than eight years in a struggling new venture.

17. Burgelman, "Managing Innovating Systems."

18. J. Moldenhauer-Salazar and L. Välikangas, "Radical Innovation Through the Looking Glass" (presentation at Strategic Management Annual Conference, Baltimore, Nov. 9–12, 2003).

19. Burgelman, "A Process Model of Internal Corporate Venturing in the Diversified Major Firm." For similar behavior in the strategic capital-investment process, see J. Bower, "Managing the Resource Allocation Process" (Boston: Harvard Business School Press, 1970). For a more theoretical examination of opportunistic behavior, see, for instance, O.E. Williamson, "Markets and Hierarchies: Analysis and Antitrust Implications" (New York: Free Press, 1975).

20. P. Gompers and J. Lerner, "The Determinants of Corporate Venture Capital Success: Organizational Structure, Incentives and Complementarities," chap. 1.1 in "Concentrated Corporate Ownership," ed. R. Morck (Chicago: University of Chicago Press, 2000).

21. H. Chesbrough, "Making Sense of Corporate Venture Capital," Harvard Business Review 80, no. 3 (March 2002): 90–99.

22. Chesbrough, "Graceful Exits and Missed Opportunities," 803–837.

23. A. Muller and L. Välikangas, "An ODD Reaction to Strategy Failure in America's Once Largest Telco," European Management Journal 21, no. 1 (2003): 109–118.

24. S. Postrel and R.P. Rumelt, "Incentives, Routines and Self-Command," Industrial and Corporate Change 1, no. 3 (1992): 397–425.

25. N. Machiavelli, "The Prince" (London: Penguin Books, reissued 2003).

26. See, for example, M. Hayward and D.C. Hambrick, "Explaining the Premium Paid for Large Acquisitions: Evidence of CEO Hubris," Administrative Science Quarterly 42, no. 1 (1997): 103–129; and M.E. Porter, "From Competitive Advantage to Corporate Strategy," Harvard Business Review 65, no. 3 (May–June 1987): 43–59.

27. J. Mackey and L. Välikangas, "The Myth of Unbounded Growth," MIT Sloan Management Review 45, no. 2 (winter 2004): 89–92.

28. Burgelman has presented evidence that exploring and exploiting new-business opportunities outside the scope of the corporate strategy requires a different leadership discipline than the discipline necessary to exploit existing opportunities, but requires a discipline nevertheless. See R.A. Burgelman, "Strategy Is Destiny: How Strategy-Making Shapes a Company's Future" (New York: Free Press, 2002). See also R.A. Burgelman, "Strategy as

Vector and the Inertia of Coevolutionary Lock-in," *Administrative Science Quarterly* 47, no. 2 (2002): 325–357.

29. For a discussion of ICV initiatives as a natural dynamic force in organizations, see R.A. Burgelman, "Corporate Entrepreneurship and Strategic Management," and R.A. Burgelman, "EBF Debate: Must We All Be Entrepreneurs Now?" *European Business Forum* 15 (fall 2003): 13–15. Van de Ven and Garud, who found evidence that internal entrepreneurs tend to persist in their behavior under conditions of ambiguity and slack despite negative feedback, provide some evidence for the irrepressible entrepreneurial spirit. See A. Van de Ven and R. Garud, "An Empirical Evaluation of the Internal Corporate Venturing Process," *Strategic Management Journal* 13, no. 8 (summer 2002): 93–110. Alva Taylor found that initiators of new products outside the scope of the existing corporate strategy did so in part because they anticipated that if their initiative was not embraced by the company, they would be able to find a new job related to their initiative in another company in the industry. See A.H. Taylor, "A Process Study of the Influence of Competition Between New Product Initiatives on Innovation and Organizational Learning" (Ph.D. diss., Stanford University, 2000).

30. "Strategic context determination refers to the political process through which middle-level managers attempt to convince top management that the current concept of strategy needs to be changed so as to accommodate successful new ventures." See Burgelman, "A Process Model of Internal Corporate Venturing in the Diversified Major Firm," 237–238, and R.A. Burgelman, "Managing the Internal Corporate Venturing Process," *Sloan Management Review* 25, no. 2 (winter 1984): 33–48. Strategic context determination critically depends on "organizational championing" by executives. This is the most difficult and least understood part of the ICV process, and the part that is most likely to break down.

31. M.E. Porter and S.J. Roth, "Bendix Corporation," *Harvard Business School* case no. 9-387-257 (Boston: Harvard Business School Publishing, 1985).

32. C.M. Christensen, "The Innovator's Dilemma" (Cambridge: Harvard Business School Press, 1997).

33. See N. Nohria, "Internal Corporate Venturing at Eastman Kodak: A New Chapter in the Rise and Fall of the New Venture Division," working paper, Harvard Business School, Boston, 1992.

34. "Kodak Cuts Dividend by 72% to Finance Digital Transition," *Wall Street Journal*, Sept. 26, 2003.

35. "Kodak Aims to Become a Model of Reinvention," *Financial Times*, Sept. 27, 2003.

36. Burgelman and Sayles, "Inside Corporate Innovation." This insight suggests the need for caution in too quickly adopting the distinction made by Campbell and others between "new leg venturing" and "innovation venturing." If ICV is indeed a discovery process, it may be clear only after the fact whether some initiative was important for the core business or truly a diversifying activity.

37. N. Snyder and D. Duarte, "Strategic Innovation" (New York: Jossey-Bass, 2003).

38. Burgelman, "Corporate Entrepreneurship and Strategic Management" and Burgelman, "Strategy Is Destiny." McGrath and MacMillan provide a practical tool for planning for a new venture that takes into account how the process differs from planning for mainstream businesses. See R.G. McGrath and I.C. MacMillan, "Discovery-Driven Planning," *Harvard Business Review* 73, no. 4 (July–August 1995): 44–53.

39. G. Hamel and C.K. Prahalad, "Competing for the Future" (Boston: Harvard Business School Press, 1994).

40. R.A. Burgelman and P. Meza, "Intel Beyond 2003: Looking for Its Third Act," Stanford Business School case SM-106 (Stanford: Stanford Business School, 2003).

41. This is an area where the advice of Campbell and Harris to exert caution in supporting ICV is valuable. While we strongly argue for continued support of ICV efforts, we also argue for a more deliberate and controlled resource-allocation management to help dampen ICV cyclicality. See A. Campbell and R. Harris, "The Growth Gamble."

42. Pekka Ala-Pietilä, president of Nokia Corp., communication with R.A. Burgelman, fall 2000.

43. In fact, new ventures pursued in the ICV mode often need to be augmented with relatively small to midsize acquisitions in order to scale up within a limited time horizon to a size that makes the venture relevant from the corporate point of view. But such "strategic building" activities will benefit from already having some business initiative going that offers insight into what might be the right acquisition in the first place. In that sense, ICV can potentially play an important role in a more broadly conceived idea of the "absorptive capacity" of the corporation. On strategic building, see Burgelman, "Managing the Internal Corporate Venturing Process," 33–49. On absorptive capacity, see W.M. Cohen and D.A. Levinthal, "Absorptive Capacity: A New Perspective on Learning and Innovation," *Administrative Science Quarterly* 35, no. 1 (March 1990): 128–134.

57

DISRUPTION, DISINTEGRATION AND THE DISSIPATION OF DIFFERENTIABILITY

Clayton M. Christensen, Matt Verlinden, and George Westerman

This paper proposes a deductively derived model to help managers who preside over decisions to integrate or outsource to assess *ex ante* whether, when and why it might be strategically and competitively important to develop internal capabilities to perform certain activities in-house, and when it would be sensible and safe to outsource elements of value-added. Among the paper's conclusions are that the competitive advantage from vertical integration is strongest in tiers of the market where customers are under-served by the functionality or performance available from products in the market. Vertical integration tends to be a disadvantage when customers are over-served by the functionality available from products in the market. Vertically integrated firms will therefore often dominate in the most demanding tiers of markets that have grown to substantial size, while a horizontally stratified, or disintegrated, industry structure will often be the dominant business model in the tiers of the market that are less demanding of functionality.

INTRODUCTION

Whether to become or remain vertically integrated is a question of vast strategic importance in many industries. In recent years, firms such as Alcoa, Lucent and General Motors, for whom vertical control over most steps in their value chains had historically constituted an important basis of competitive advantage, have sold upstream businesses that produced components or intermediate materials, in order to focus on the portions of their value chains that they consider to be core to their business. Others, like IBM, continue to own but are de-coupling upstream from downstream operations, tasking the former to sell components openly in the market, and the latter to procure components from external suppliers when necessary to maintain competitiveness. In contrast, Microsoft is aggressively integrating downstream from its initial operating system products into a variety of applications software markets; Intel has integrated into chipsets and motherboards using its microprocessors; and telecommunications and entertainment companies have integrated together in bewildering ways.

Some business experts have praised these actions, while other reputable observers have reacted with skepticism. For example, IBM's management have been criticized for having outsourced the microprocessor and operating system of their personal computer from Intel and Microsoft, choosing to participate primarily in the design and assembly stages of value-added in their product. While history has proven the decision to have been unfortunate for IBM, at the time the decision was made it was judged by many as the right thing to do.[1] It has indeed been difficult to predict, a priori, which of these moves toward or away from vertical integration would be judged in retrospect as having been managerially astute, and which would be viewed as strategically flawed. Too often for decisions as important as these, their wisdom can only be judged with the benefit of history.

This paper proposes a deductively derived model to help managers who preside over decisions to integrate or outsource to assess *ex ante* whether, when and why it might be strategically and competitively important to develop internal capabilities to perform certain activities in-house, and when it will be sensible and safe to outsource elements of value-added. Our conclusions are that:

1. The competitive advantage from vertical integration is strongest in tiers of the market where customers are under-served by the functionality or performance available from products in the market. Vertical integration tends to be a disadvantage when customers are over-served by the functionality available from products in the market.

2. As a result of (1), vertically integrated firms will often dominate in the most demanding tiers of markets that have grown to substantial size, while a horizontally stratified, or disintegrated, industry structure will often be the dominant business model in the tiers of the market that are less demanding of functionality.

3. The tendencies listed in (1) and (2) occur in end-use markets for complete product systems, such as automobiles and computers. But they also can occur in the markets for subsystems and components, which themselves comprise multiple constituent parts and materials.

4. Most often, vertically integrated firms tend to dominate many markets at the outset. Because of the patterns observed in our earlier studies, however—in which the pace of technological progress proceeds at a faster rate than customers in any given tier of the market can utilize that progress—the dominant business model in any given tier of the market will tend to shift over time from vertically integrated firms to a horizontally stratified population of specialized firms.

5. The generalization in (4) can be reversed, however, when performance gaps emerge in markets due to discontinuous shifts in the functionality demanded by customers. When this occurs, the pendulum of competitive advantage is likely to swing back toward vertically integrated firms, as companies seek to compete with each other on the basis of superior product functionality again.

6. When the dominant business model in a tier of the market shifts from vertical integration to horizontal stratification, the ability to achieve above-average profitability tends to transfer from the firms that design and assemble end-use products that historically had not been good enough, to those that build those subsystems which limit performance of the end-use system, and which therefore are not good enough.

These conclusions began to take their initial shape in studies of the patterns of vertical integration and disintegration in the disk drive industry, in which the pendulum of competitive advantage swung repeatedly between integrated and non-integrated firms, in various tiers of the market (Christensen, 1993, 1994; Chesbrough and Kusunoki, 2001). This paper's conclusions have not been built inductively from empirical analysis, however. They have been derived deductively by combining the results of the disk drive studies with other scholars' examinations of technological modularity (Ulrich, 1995; Sanchez and Mahoney, 1996; Baldwin and Clark, 1997), and with concepts of the drivers of change in the basis of competition (Christensen, 1996; Adner and Levinthal, 2001). In this paper we provide some preliminary but promising empirical evidence supporting the model, and use the model to examine briefly the histories of the computer, automobile, software, photonics, financial services and microprocessor industries, to suggest that the model might be more broadly useful. Our primary purpose in offering this paper is to invite other scholars to test empirically these hypotheses, and thereby continue to build deeper understanding of the circumstances under which we might expect integration and non-integration to confer competitive advantage or disadvantage.

RELATIONSHIP TO PRIOR STUDIES OF VERTICAL INTEGRATION

The model presented in this paper does not address every rationale for vertical integration and disintegration. We believe, however, that it builds upon and extends the foundations laid by several important scholars who have studied the causal drivers behind integration. Stigler's (1951) causal model, echoing Adam Smith's (1776) original analysis of the specialization of labor, asserted that a driver of specialization was market size. He observed that many industries begin as vertically integrated ones due to their small size. They then increasingly become populated by specialist firms as they grow. Stigler posited that later in the life cycle, when demand begins to contract, industries consequently tend to reintegrate. Although we agree that scale is a factor, our model views scale often as an outcome of other factors that drive specialization, rather than as a fundamental causal driver of it.

Coase (1937) and Williamson (1985) introduced the role of transaction costs as the causal driver of the optimal boundaries of the organization. There are many types of transaction costs, including threat of intellectual property appropriation (Teece, 1986), lock-in (Williamson, 1979), asset specificity (Williamson, 1979; Klein *et al.,* 1978) and the challenges of coordinating interdependent investments (Chandler, 1977). Demsetz (1988) characterized transactions costs as the costs of search and maintenance, showing how these vary across the industrial life cycle. A stream of subsequent scholars within the transactions cost paradigm, including Teece (1986), Langlois (1994), Becker and Murphy (1992), Sanchez and Mahoney (1996), and Chesbrough and Teece (1996), have identified a specific type of transactions cost—the challenge of coordination amongst diverse specialists—as a driver of managerial integration across such interfaces. Monteverde's (1995) construct of "unstructured technological dialogue" describes the management challenge when an interface between stages of value-added is interdependent and not well specified. Our model builds most directly upon Monteverde's concept.

Scholars working in a parallel stream have studied in engineering terms the concepts of architectural modularity, in order to define more precisely the conditions under which suppliers and customers of products and services might need to engage in structured versus unstructured technological dialogue (e.g. Henderson and Clark, 1990; Clark and Fujimoto, 1991; Christensen, 1994; Ulrich, 1995; Ulrich and Eppinger, 1995; Chesbrough and Kusunoki, 2001; and Baldwin and Clark, 2000).

The contribution we hope to make to the work of these scholars is to define the underlying factors that cause dialogue between customers and suppliers to be unstructured (which can entail high transactions costs if the dialogue transcends the boundaries of firms) or structured (which lowers transactions costs between firms). We also describe underlying mechanisms that may cause structured dialogue to become unstructured, and vice versa. In addition, our model helps explain why the power to earn attractive profits resides at specific locations in a value-added chain, but not at others (Porter, 1985). It also specifies the factors that can cause the power to earn attractive profit to shift to other stages of value-added.

DEFINITIONS

The key unit of analysis in our model is the *interface* at which a supplier of value-added and a customer of that value-added interact—whether that interface is within or between organizations. It is at this interface that structured or unstructured dialogue occurs. The specific terms that scholars, such as those noted above, use to describe this dialogue vary (Billington and Fleming, 1998; Fixson, 2000). For our purposes, we assert that for structured dialog to occur across an interface between stages or elements of value-added, three conditions must be met.

1. The customer that procures or uses a piece of value-added must understand and be able to specify to its supplier which attributes or parameters of the product or service must be provided, and to what tolerances.
2. Metrics for those attributes must exist, and the technology to measure those attributes must be available, reliable and unambiguous; and
3. The procuring company must understand the interactions or interdependencies between the attributes of what is provided and the performance of the system in which the procurer will use it. If there is any variation in what is provided, the procurer needs to understand how, when and why it will affect the performance of the system (Taguchi and Clausing, 1990).

If these three conditions are met, then the interface between a provider of an element of value-added and its user can be termed a *modular* interface, across which structured technical dialogue can occur. At modular interfaces, the necessary information exists for a market to function efficiently. Modular interfaces can occur across the boundaries of companies and across boundaries of functional groups within a company (such as between product design and manufacturing). They can also occur between groups within a project team; and they can exist between individuals. Such interfaces occur in products, services and systems of use. Henceforth in this paper, when we use the term *product,* we intend for it to apply to a service as well.

When these three conditions are not met at an interface, then we term it an *interdependent* interface,[2] across which *unstructured* technical dialogue must occur. At interdependent interfaces, the necessary information required for an efficiently functioning market does not exist. Management and integration, rather than markets, constitutes the most efficient coordinating mechanism across interdependent interfaces.[3]

Few products, services or systems would be composed exclusively of modular or interdependent interfaces—suggesting that architectures that are entirely modular or entirely interdependent would be rare extremes at opposite ends of a spectrum. This also suggests that we could rarely characterize an entire industry as being dominated by integrated or specialized firms—because this is likely to vary at the interfaces of different pieces of value-added. It will also vary, as shown below, by tier of the market.[4]

The use of these definitions in the model presented below yields results that are consistent with the findings of scholars such as Sanchez and Mahoney (1996) and Chesbrough and Teece (1996). We assert that if these three conditions of modularity—specifiability, measurability and predictability—exist at any interface, it improves the potential for an efficiently functioning market to emerge at that interface. Markets are more effective coordinating mechanisms across modular interfaces than is managerial coordination. On the other hand, management will trump market coordination in cases where an interface is interdependent.

THE CAUSES OF SWINGS BETWEEN VERTICAL INTEGRATION AND STRATIFICATION

Many companies today are striving to outsource those elements of value-added that do not build upon their strengths and can therefore be procured more cost-effectively from suppliers. History has shown, however, that many industries pass through repeated cycles in which competitive advantage rests alternately with integrated and nonintegrated business models (Christensen, 1994; Fine, 1998)—suggesting that decisions to integrate or disintegrate that make sense in one context can create disadvantages when things change.

Our studies of how disruptive innovations can cause well-managed companies to fail can shed some light on the drivers behind this cyclical pattern. Because this work has been reported elsewhere, it will only be briefly summarized here.[5] There are two elements to this model, as depicted in Figure 57-1. The first asserts that in most markets there is a trajectory of performance improvement that customers can actually absorb or

FIGURE 57-1   The Intersecting Trajectories of Improvements That Customers Can Utilize Versus Those That Innovators Provide.

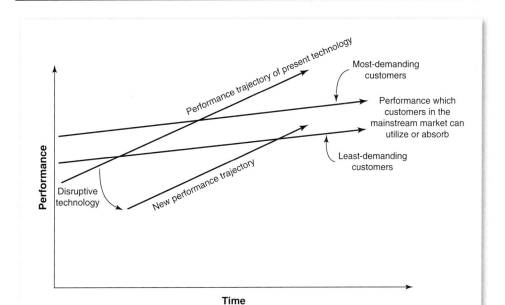

utilize over time, represented by the gently sloped lines. Secondly, as depicted by the steeply sloped lines, there is a distinctly different trajectory of performance improvement that the innovators in an industry provide to their market, as they introduce new and improved products. Our studies have shown that the trajectory of technological progress almost always outstrips the abilities of customers to utilize the improvement.

This means that companies whose product functionality is closely tuned to what customers in a tier of a market may need at one point in time typically improve products at such a rate that they overshoot what those same customers actually can utilize in later years. In other words, the functionality of a product can over-satisfy what less-demanding customers in lower tiers of the market need, even while customers in more demanding tiers of the market continue to need more functionality than even the best available products offer. It also means that "disruptive technologies"—simpler, more convenient products that initially do not perform well enough to be used in mainstream markets—can take root in undemanding tiers of the market and then improve at such a rapid rate that they can squarely address mainstream market needs in the future.

This model has been used to describe how minicomputers displaced mainframes, and how personal computers displaced minicomputers. It illustrates how hydraulic excavator manufacturers overthrew makers of cable shovel makers; and how the Japanese automakers assaulted western car markets. It describes the mechanism through which steel minimills have been displacing integrated mills; by which the packet-switched telecommunications infrastructure is disrupting the circuit-switched network; and many others. The model has been expanded and refined, using very different research methods, by Adner and his colleagues (Adner, 1999; Adner and Levinthal, 2001; Adner and Zemsky, 2001), among others.

During the early years of many industries, in the left-most regions of Figure 57-1, product functionality is not good enough to satisfy the needs of customers in most tiers of the market. Competition during this era therefore focuses predominantly on product functionality: designing and producing higher-performing products is a fundamental mechanism by which companies strive to get ahead of each other (Christensen, 1996, 1997; Adner and Levinthal, 2001; Adner and Zemsky, 2001). These competitive pressures compel engineers to fit the pieces of their product together in new and untested ways in each successive product generation, as they work to wring as much performance as possible from the technology that is available. As a result, product designs tend to be interdependent, rather than modular, during this era: the design of each part tends to be contingent upon the design of other parts, and upon the way they interact within the overall system architecture. There are often powerful interdependencies between design and manufacturing during this era that are similarly based in the competitive need to stretch functionality to the frontiers of what is possible.[6]

There are two reasons why interdependent architectures predominate during eras when product functionality is not yet good enough for what customers need. The first was articulated by Ulrich (1995), who showed that creating a modular architecture—especially one that is defined by industry standards—forces designers to compromise or back away from the frontier of what is technologically possible. At the left side of Figure 57-1, backing off is not competitively feasible. The second reason is that new technologies are often employed in the stages and tiers of an industry where competitors are stretching toward the frontier of functionality. It is when new technologies are used to do things that have never been done before that engineers most often encounter interdependent interfaces: they do not know what to specify, cannot accurately measure important attributes and do not yet understand how variation in one subsystem will impact overall system performance. Unstructured technical dialogue is therefore the language required to compete successfully when a product's functionality is not good enough to address targeted customers' needs.

In early mainframe computers, for example, the logic circuitry could not be designed until the operating system was designed; the operating system could not be designed until the core memory was designed; and the core memory could not be designed until the logic circuitry had been designed. Manufacturing methods powerfully affected whether the system performed as it was designed to do. Everything depended upon everything else. A company could not have existed in that industry as an independent supplier of logic circuitry or operating systems, or as a contract manufacturer, because clear, modular interfaces had not yet been established to define how the parts would fit together. This implies that integrated companies can be expected to dominate at the interfaces between pieces of value-added where functionality is not good enough. The dominance of IBM in mainframe computers, Digital Equipment in minicomputers, General Motors and Ford in the automobile market, Alcoa in aluminum, Standard Oil in oil, and Xerox in photocopying are all examples of firms whose vertical integration conferred competitive advantage during an era when performance was not good enough.

Because these conditions often typify an industry during its early years, scholars such as Stigler (1951) and Chandler (1977) have observed that integrated firms generally comprise the predominant business model as most industries grow towards substantive mass. Certainly industries must achieve a certain critical mass in order to support specialized competitors. We assert, however, that the fundamental causality of integrated firms being dominant at the outset and then displaced by specialized ones is not the passage of time or a general evolution towards "maturity" or large scale *per se*. Rather, it is this causal sequence:

1. When functionality is not good enough to address what customers in a given tier of the market can utilize, firms compete by making better products.
2. In order to make the best possible products with the technology that is available, product architects tend to employ interdependent, proprietary architectures, because building a modular system around industry standards forces them to back away from the frontier of what is technologically possible. In tiers of the market where product functionality is not good enough, competitive conditions penalize companies that attempt to do this. New technologies are often employed in these conditions.
3. Because this entails unstructured technical dialogue, transactions costs are minimized through integration. Integration constitutes an important competitive advantage in managing the interdependencies in design, manufacturing, sales, service and procurement during this period.[7]

When the functionality of available products surpasses what customers in a tier of a market can utilize, however, competition changes. Customers experience diminishing marginal utility from further improvements, and consequently are less willing to reward further improvements with higher prices. Innovators therefore need to find other ways to compete profitably for the business of customers in tiers of the market who are over-served by functionality. Our research suggests that very often, speed to market becomes a critical dimension of competition in the lower-right regions of Figure 57-1. Similarly, the ability to conveniently customize the features and functions of products to the specific needs of customers in ever-smaller market niches becomes a critical trajectory of innovation that enables firms to get ahead of their competition and maintain profit margins (Pine, 1992; Christensen, 1996, 1997; Adner and Levinthal, 2001).

The efforts of disruptive competitors to be fast and flexible in this era of overshoot at the right side of Figure 57-1 forces them to create modular product designs in order to be competitive—because modularity creates many more options for speed, cost reduction and customization (Baldwin and Clark, 2000). When available functionality more than satisfies what customers can utilize, designers have the slack to back away from the frontier of what is technologically possible, in order to define modular architectures (Ulrich, 1995). Modularity often begins to take form in companies' proprietary interface specifications, which enable them to outsource components and subsystems at arm's length from other organizations (Sanchez and Mahoney, 1996). When one company's modular interface specifications become accepted by multiple competitors, they can become industry standards. Industry standard modularity enables firms that design and assemble products to introduce new and customized products even more rapidly than they could when interfaces were modular but proprietary, as designers and assemblers can mix and match the most effective components from the best suppliers.

Over time, the lower overheads and scale economics that focused component suppliers enjoy, coupled with the speed-to-market and flexibility advantages enjoyed by non-integrated assemblers, enables a population of horizontally stratified firms to displace vertically integrated firms (Grove, 1996; Fine, 1998; Baldwin and Clark, 2000). Modular specifications constitute sufficient information for an efficient market to work; and market-based coordination (structured technical dialogue) trumps managerial coordination across modular interfaces (Sanchez and Mahoney, 1996).

In summary, the chain of causality that shifts competitive advantage in a given tier of a market from integrated firms is this:

1. When the functionality of available products outstrips the ability of customers in a tier of the market to utilize further improvements, companies must compete differently to win the business of customers who are over-served by functionality. Innovations that facilitate speed to market, and the ability to customize features and functions in response to the needs of customers in ever-smaller market niches, become the trajectories of improvement that customers reward with premium prices.
2. Efforts to compete along these dimensions of speed, flexibility and customization cause product architectures to evolve toward modularity. This facilitates speed and flexibility.
3. Modularity then enables independent, focused providers of individual pieces of value-added to thrive, because transactions cost-minimizing structured technical dialogue can occur. As a result, an industry which at one point was dominated by integrated firms becomes dominated by a population of specialized, non-integrated firms.

Figure 57-2 summarizes the conditions in which we would expect an industry to be characterized by functionality-based competition amongst integrated firms employing interdependent architectures (Region A) versus those in which the industry would be characterized by speed- and convenience-based competition within a population of specialized competitors who interact within modular architectures (Region B).[8]

A significant body of scholarship (e.g. Teece, 1986) has focused on the appropriability of knowledge as a critical factor affecting decisions to integrate or disintegrate. We

FIGURE 57-2 Overshooting the Functionality That Customers Can Utilize Triggers Change in the Way Companies Must Compete.

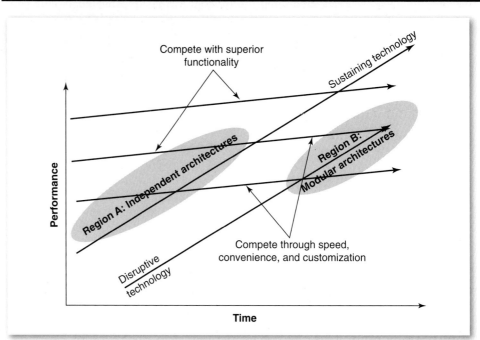

hope that our model casts additional insight on this phenomenon as well. It implies that when the functionality of a product is not good enough to address customers' needs, the language of successful competition must be unstructured technical dialogue. The interactions through which this dialogue occurs are the "locations" where the organization's capabilities to design and manufacture better products reside. This tacit knowledge or capability cannot be appropriated by competitors. When overshooting has occurred and competitive forces drive architectures toward modularity, however, then the capability for fitting the pieces of the product together which had resided in unstructured technical dialogue becomes embodied in the interface standards—structured technical dialogue—that define how the modules fit and work together. This enables competitors to appropriate what had been proprietary capability and know-how.

Case Evidence Supporting the Disintegration Model

The model presented above was deductively derived through a synthesis of various scholars' work. In this section we offer preliminary empirical evidence—some of it in the form of numerical analysis, some in the form of narrative history—that is consistent with the chain of causality in this model. In case studies of industries as diverse as disk drives, computers, financial services and microprocessors, we observe a process similar to the one outlined above that transferred competitive advantage from integration towards non-integration. We summarize these observations in the following.

Evidence from the Disk Drive Industry

Our earlier research described how the performance of disk drives improved at a more rapid pace than the ability of customers in any given tier of the market could absorb those improvements. Over and over, this enabled disruptive innovators piercing into the market's underbelly to displace the industry's leaders (Christensen and Rosenbloom, 1995; Christensen and Bower, 1996).

This continuous process of up-market migration implies (in the language of this paper) that architectural modularity is likely to occur in the least-demanding tiers of the market first; and that at any point in time we should expect the most demanding tiers of the market, which are the most under-served by the functionality of available products, to be populated by more technologically interdependent products. Consequently, we would expect integrated firms' market positions to be strongest in the most demanding tiers of the market, and the market shares of non-integrated firms to be strongest in the least-demanding, most over-served tiers of the market.

In our study of the disk drive industry, we devised a method to measure the degree to which the architecture of a drive was modular or interdependent. It is an indirect measure, but seems to support the notion that modularity appears first in the least-demanding tiers of the market, where the phenomenon of overshooting first occurs. The analysis suggests that modular architectures then migrate toward more demanding tiers of the market, as this ongoing process of overshooting successively more demanding tiers of the market continues.

To do this analysis, we built a database of every model of disk drive introduced by any company in the world between 1975 and 1998—4334 models in all. This constitutes a complete product census for the industry in these years.[9] For each of these models, we had data on the types of components that were used in the drive—including hardware components, and the types of firmware and software coding that were employed. We then estimated regression equations, in which the dependent variable was the recording density of the drive.[10] The independent variables were the year in which the drive was introduced, the size of the drive[11] and the components that were used in the drive—represented by dummy variables for each type or generation of component technology. Where interviews with engineers suggested that interactions amongst components might affect the recording density achieved in a product, interaction terms were included in the analysis. The equation was estimated in the following form:

$$\ln(\text{Recording Density}) = B_1 + B_2(\text{Year}) + B_3(\ln \text{Disk Diameter}) + B_4(\text{Component Dummy 1}) + \ldots + B_n(\text{Component Dummy } n)$$

The coefficients that were estimated for each of the component dummy variables measured the extent to which the use of various component technologies added to or detracted from the recording density of the product. The coefficient of the year variable measured the annual improvement in recording density that resulted from general, incremental advances that could not be linked to the use of particular new architectural, component, software or firmware technology. Detailed results from this analysis are reported in Appendix 1. The adjusted R^2 was 0.95, indicating that the variables accounted for most of the variation in density across products in the sample.

This equation allowed us to estimate the expected recording density of each drive, given its size, the components that were used and the year in which it was designed. We could then compare the expected density with the density that its engineers actually achieved. We called the ratio of the actual recording density to the expected density the *architectural efficiency* of the drive, and calculated this ratio for every disk drive model in the database.[12] An architectural efficiency ratio of 1.0 indicates that the engineers achieved exactly the expected density. Ratios above 1.0 indicate that, through clever product design, the engineers were able to wring more recording density out of the same set of components than the average engineer would have done. A ratio of less than 1.0 suggests that the drive's engineers got less-than-expected performance, given the components that they used.

If the interface standards amongst the components were so completely defined that engineers had no degrees of freedom in designing how they would fit the components together in the drive's architecture—i.e. if the design were completely modular—then we would expect the architectural efficiency of the population of drives to be 1.0 and the standard deviation of architectural efficiency to be 0. The larger the standard deviation in the architectural efficiency of the product models in this population, the greater the scope for differentiated techniques for integrating components. In other words, the greater the standard deviation, the greater the degree of architectural interdependency in product designs. And the lower the standard deviation, the greater the degree of architectural modularity in the drive.

Figure 57-3 maps on its vertical axis the standard deviation of the architectural efficiency of drives sold into the desktop computer market between 1980 and 1995,

FIGURE 57-3   The Progress of Modular Architectures Through Progressively Demanding Tiers of the Disk Drive Market.

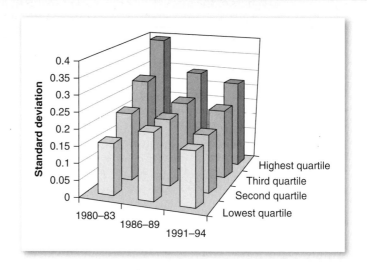

by tier of the market—ranging from the drives in the lowest-capacity quartile at the front to those of the highest-capacity quartile in the back.[13] Fleming and Sorenson (2001) used very different methods to arrive at a similar conclusion.

Note that the standard deviation increases from front to back—from the lowest quartile to the highest quartile in each of the periods—suggesting that the degree of interdependency was always greater in the most-demanding tiers of the market. While the degree of interdependence/modularity seems to have been stable over time in the lowest quartile of products, in the second, third and fourth product quartiles the degree of interdependency decreased monotonically over time, as the ongoing process of over-shooting and increased modularity progressed upward through tiers of the market. This suggests that the scope for product differentiation was always most limited in the lowest tiers of the market in which customers were most over-served and greatest in the most demanding tiers, where customers' thirst for improved performance still required more interdependent architectures. The stable standard deviation in the lowest tier of the market supports the notion that few products are entirely modular at every interface.[14]

As shown below, the industry's vertically integrated firms—particularly IBM—have dominated the most-demanding tiers of the market, while non-integrated manufacturers such as Quantum and Western Digital held the largest shares in the least-demanding end of the market.[15]

The Computer Industry

We do not have a similar set of detailed, component-level data for the computer industry as for disk drives, but it appears that a similar pattern holds in this industry as well. Products in the most performance-demanding tiers of the market are architecturally interdependent and proprietary, and are supplied by integrated companies. The architectures of products targeted at progressively less performance-intensive tiers of the market are progressively more modular, and are supplied by progressively less-integrated companies.

In the early years of digital computing, when the functionality of available products fell short of what the mainstream markets needed, the computer industry was dominated by integrated players such as IBM. Even today, the most demanding tiers of the mission-critical enterprise server business continue to be dominated by integrated companies such as Hewlett Packard, IBM and Silicon Graphics. Their products are technologically interdependent, built around proprietary reduced instruction set computer (RISC) microprocessors and proprietary UNIX operating systems whose key properties are interdependently designed and manufactured, largely in house. The performance of their products has overshot what is utilized in all but the most demanding tiers of the market—where unit volumes are so small, in fact, that Silicon Graphics' once-spectacular growth trajectory has sputtered.

Products in the next-lower tiers of the server business are more modular in character. Sun Microsystems' Solaris operating system, for example, is rapidly becoming a standard. Predictably, this market tier is dominated by less-integrated manufacturers. Sun, for example, continues to design its own microprocessor and operating system, but licenses them to competitors and outsources fabrication. Sun is aggressively pushing up-market to disrupt Hewlett Packard, IBM and Silicon Graphics, carrying its more modular architecture with it in the process.[16]

The less-demanding tiers comprising the business computing market are dominated by suppliers such as Compaq, Dell and Gateway, whose products are consummately modular. These firms are not integrated; most components in their products are supplied by specialist companies. Manufacturing and the in-bound and outbound logistics are often managed by contractors such as Solectron, and even the design of some products is being out-sourced. Dell, in particular, leverages its status as a non-integrated assembler of modular products to conveniently customize its computers to the specifications of individual customers, and deliver the machines to their doorsteps within 48 hours. These firms began their histories squarely in the personal computer space, and have aggressively carried modularity and disintegration up-market, disruptively stealing market share in the workstation and server space from Sun. As components get more capable, the non-integrated companies carry their modular architecture up-market—hence, disintegration is occurring in progressively more demanding tiers of the market.

Mortgage Banking

The mortgage banking industry has historically been dominated by integrated institutions such as savings banks and savings and loans institutions, which collected and serviced deposits, originated loans, evaluated borrowers' credit worthiness, assessed property values, closed loans and serviced them. In terms of the definition of modularity noted above, there were no standard ways to measure the riskiness of a loan made to any borrower, and as a result, markets could not emerge at the interface of these stages of value-added.

Asset securitization and credit scoring systems that originated in the credit card industry essentially replaced bank officers' judgement with simple metrics—they brought modularity. With credit scoring came knowledge of which attributes of the borrower needed to be specified, and technology for measuring those attributes became known. Likewise, asset securitization transformed loans from non-standard assets with uncertain risks and returns, to standardized units with easily measured risk and return. Credit scoring and securitization took root in the 1960s in the lowest tier of the lending market—credit cards of retailers such as Sears. These then migrated up-market, usurping open credit cards, auto loans, mortgage loans and, most recently, small business loans. In each of these market tiers, integrated commercial and savings banks have been replaced by a horizontally stratified population of specialist firms such as MBNA, GMAC, GE Capital, Countrywide and FNMA. Integrated banks' share of the mortgage market, for example, has eroded from over 90% in the 1960s to 39% by 1999. A population of specialized firms now originate most mortgages, perform credit checks, value collateral, close loans and service them (Hodes and Hall, 1999).

Disintegration of the Microprocessor Industry

Our final case is the microprocessor industry. Although the microprocessor is a component within a modular personal computer, the microprocessor itself is a complex, technologically interdependent system. Projects to develop next-generation microprocessor platforms consume time and resources of a magnitude similar to those that were required to design new mainframe computers. Intel is an integrated company, designing for itself each element of the microprocessor in an interdependent, iterative process. Its "copy exactly" method of transferring designs into volume production is a testament to the complex and poorly understood interdependencies between design and manufacturing.

While the speed of complex instruction set (CISC) microprocessors has gotten fast enough that Intel and AMD are disrupting RISC microprocessor-based machines in the higher tiers of the market, their products have overshot the speed that typically is utilized in mainstream business applications. In fact, Monroe (1999) has shown that the Moore's Law pace at which transistors are being made available per area of silicon is outstripping the ability of circuit designers to utilize transistors by 40% each year. As a consequence, in the less performance-demanding tiers of the market, the architecture of microprocessors, such as the Intel Celeron processor, is becoming more modular (interview with Mr. Randy Steck, Intel Architecture Labs, July 1999). And at the lowest end, for those chips in hand-held wireless digital appliances, companies like Tensilica have begun to offer web-based tools that enable applications developers to assemble from modular components custom-designed microprocessors and systems-on-a-chip whose features and functionality are tuned exactly to the requirements of the application. Design cycles for these modular microprocessors are measured in weeks, rather than years (Bass and Christensen, 2002).

The findings of Macher (2001) support these assertions. He has shown that integrated semiconductor manufacturers perform better than non-integrated ones in the most performance-demanding tiers of the market, whereas the opposite is the case in less-demanding tiers. Furthermore, with clearer design-for-manufacturing rules as an interface, chips positioned away from the leading edge are increasingly being fabricated in independent silicon foundries, which he shows are able to bring products to market much more rapidly than integrated firms.

Synthesis Across These Cases

Table 57-1 summarizes the patterns revealed in this set of cases. It lists down the leftmost column the causal chain in the model we are proposing. For each of the industries we have studied, an X in the cells of the table indicates where that phenomenon was observed.

Case Studies in Reintegration

The trajectory maps in Figures 57-1 and 57-2 suggest that the predominant business model in many industries generally will evolve from integrated firms toward non-integrated, specialized business models. But on occasion the trend has reversed itself, back towards integration. Other financial reasons for reintegration are considered in Section 5. The factor that seems to have driven the re-ascendance of integration as a source of competitive advantage, however, was the occurrence of a "performance gap"—an upward shift in the functionality that customers needed. In terms of Figures 57-1 and 57-2, this involves an upward shifting of the dotted, gently sloping lines to a new height. The emergence of these performance gaps can throw an industry back into a "Region A" situation, as depicted in Figure 57-2. When this happens, it demands again true managerial and technological reintegration, as innovators through unstructured technical dialogue are again forced to piece the components of their products together in unconventional and untested ways, in order to push performance as close as possible to what customers have begun to demand. The following sections describe in some detail why and how this happened in disk drives, and then recount a similar pattern in the software industry as well.

Reintegration in Disk Drives

Through most of the 1990s the 3.5-inch drive market was largely in Region B of Figure 57-2. These drives were used primarily in desktop personal computers, and their capacity—as big as 60 GB—had substantially overshot what customers actually were able to utilize in the mainstream tiers of that market. As shown above, the architecture of drives sold into this market was increasingly modular, especially in its less-demanding tiers. This meant that components from a variety of suppliers could be mixed and matched with predictable results in new product designs. This market, consequently, was dominated by less integrated companies—Seagate, Quantum, Western

TABLE 57-1 Supporting Evidence in Case Studies for Key Elements of the Model				
	Disk Drives	*Computers*	*Financial Services*	*Micro-Processors*
1. At the outset, when available functionality is insufficient to meet customer needs in mainstream tiers of the market, product architectures are interdependent.	X	X	X	X
2. The industry is dominated at this time by vertically integrated firms.	X	X	X	X
3. The functionality provided by the leading integrated firms overshoots what customers in lower tiers of the market can utilize and are willing to pay for.	X	X		X
4. The basis of competition in those tiers of the market that are over-served in functionality changes. Speed to market, and the ability to conveniently customize features and functions become competitively important.	X	X		X
5. Product architectures become modular to facilitate competition on new dimensions.	X	X	X	X
6. Modularity enables non-integrated firms to compete. In those tiers of the market in which overshooting and modularity have occurred, the industry tends to disintegrate; a horizontally stratified population of specialist firms displaces integrated ones.	X	X	X	X
7. Because the pace of technological progress proceeds faster than the ability of customers in given tiers of the market to absorb it, the sequence of events in steps 1–6 above recurs, in each progressively more demanding tier of the market.	X	X	X	X

Digital and Maxtor. IBM, the most extensively integrated competitor, was barely been able to sustain a foothold in that market.[17]

The 2.5-inch disk drive market, in contrast, was in Region A. Even though they emerged chronologically after the 3.5-inch drive, the functionality of 2.5-inch drives used in notebook computers was not yet good enough. The reason? Computer users attempted to use notebook computers for essentially the same applications as they used desktop computers. Because the 2.5-inch drives in notebooks have one-sixth the surface area for recording than their 3.5-inch desktop siblings,[18] for most of the 1990s notebook computer users were largely dissatisfied with the capacity, weight and power consumption of 2.5-inch drives. As a result, 2.5-inch drives were built around MR heads and PRML error detection codes—complex, non-standard technologies that required interdependent, iterative design processes in order to wring as much performance as possible out of these new technologies.[19]

The 2.5-inch drive market was dominated by the industry's most technologically integrated companies—IBM, Toshiba, Hitachi and Fujitsu. Although this market had been served for a few years at its outset by non-integrated firms, as the character of customers' needs became clear, the non-integrated players with their modular product architectures were completely driven from that market. Their share fell from 96% in 1990 to 13% in 1996 and 3% in 1998, as the integrated firms learned to focus their diverse technological capabilities on the customers' needs for maximum recording density. Evidence of the re-ascendance of the integrated business model is summarized in Table 57-2.

There is now some evidence that the capacity trajectory of 2.5-inch drives has begun to intersect with the capacity demanded in the notebook computer marketplace. This portends another pendulum swing towards modular architectures, shifting competitive advantage back toward non-integrated competitors in this particular market.

TABLE 57-2 Contrast in 1998 Market Shares Held by Non-Integrated Versus Integrated Companies in the Over-Satisfied 3.5-Inch Market and the Under-Satisfied 2.5-Inch Market

Market Shares in the 3.5-Inch Market (%)		Market Shares in the 2.5-Inch Market (%)	
Integrated firms	8	Integrated firms	97
IBM	4	IBM	67
Toshiba	1	Toshiba	21
Hitachi	2	Hitachi	5
Fujitsu	1	Fujitsu	4
Less-Integrated Firms	87	Less-Integrated Firms	1
Seagate/Conner	33	Seagate/Conner	0
Quantum	23	Quantum	0
Western Digital	23	Western Digital	0
Maxtor	8	Maxtor	1
Others	5	Others	2
Total	100	Total	100

Source: Disk/Trend Report, 1999.

Chesbrough and Kusunoki (2001) describe the difficulties that non-integrated firms have escaping the "modularity trap" when an industry passes through a "technology phase shift," suggesting that if they consciously and capably manage the swings between interdependence and modularity, integrated firms ought to have long-term performance advantages over non-integrated firms. Our work supports their finding, and perhaps adds a bit more specificity about the causes of "technology phase shifts," the "double helix" pattern that Fine (1999) observed and the "architectural reconfigurations" that Henderson and Clark (1990) examined.

Personal Computer Software

Just like the 2.5-inch disk drive market, the personal computer software market when it coalesced was populated by non-integrated companies. Microsoft's DOS constituted a standard interface into which non-integrated software vendors such as WordPerfect, Borland, Lotus and Harvard Graphics could "plug" their modules. But within a few years, as customers came to understand what they wanted, a "performance gap" emerged—PC users began demanding the ability to transport portions of graphics, spreadsheets and word processing files into other types of file. This performance gap demanded integration, and Microsoft responded by creating non-standard, interdependent connections amongst its Windows operating system and its suite of office applications—and later its Internet Explorer. Almost overnight, Microsoft's non-integrated competitors vaporized.[20]

Today, however, the pendulum seems to be swinging in the other direction. The functionality and number of features in most of Microsoft's products have dramatically overshot what most of its customers actually are able to use. Non-integrated software firms writing to disruptive internet protocols and the Java programming language, with their modular architectures, are capturing a dominant share of internet-oriented applications, in a classic disruptive technology fashion. Linux, an operating system whose modular architecture enables open-source devotees independently to maintain and improve elements of the system, is beginning to disintegrate certain tiers of the market as well.

These cases of reintegration constitute what Yin (1984) calls *theoretical* replications of the model proposed in this paper. The model suggests that overshooting the functionality required in a tier of the market precipitates a change in the basis of competition, which in turn causes product or service architectures to evolve from interdependency toward modularity. This in turn causes industry structures to evolve from vertical integration towards specialized stratification. In the cases described immediately above, the emergence of functionality gaps, or "under-shooting," caused this process to reverse itself towards integration.

SHIFTS IN THE LOCUS OF PROFITS

Our research also suggests that the stages of value-added in which attractive profits can be made tend to differ from the left to the right sides of the disruptive technologies map. During eras characterized by Region A in Figure 57-2, the largest vertically integrated firms, which engage in designing and assembling architecturally interdependent end-use products whose performance is not yet good enough, tend to capture a disproportionate share of their industry's profits. During the eras of horizontal stratification described as Region B, in contrast, the firms engaged in those same stages of value-added—where more-than-good-enough modular products are designed and assembled—typically find it very difficult to earn more than subsistence profits. Whereas component suppliers tend to struggle to be profitable in Region A, in Region B the firms that supply technologically interdependent subsystems to the assemblers make the lion's share of profit.

The reason why the ability to earn attractive profits flips is that two factors that drive the ability to earn unusual profits—steep scale economics and the ability to create differentiated products—favor designers/assemblers in Region A and subsystem suppliers in Region B. In the next section we will recount in some detail how and why this happened in the disk drive industry, and then suggest how the same phenomenon seems to be occurring in the computer, telecommunications and automobile industries as well.

The Narrowing Scope for Differentiation

Modularity brings benefits of speed, lower cost and technological flexibility, as Baldwin and Clark (2000) have described. Indeed, adopting modular product architectures is critical to survival in a world where, as suggested in Figure 57-2, the basis of competition centers upon speed to market and the ability to conveniently customize features and functions to the needs of specific sets of customers. Without modular architectures and disintegrated business models, firms in Region B simply could not compete effectively.

The downside of modularity is that it seems also to narrow the ability of competitors to differentiate their products through superior design. This was demonstrated in the analysis summarized in Figure 57-3, which described how the variability in the architectural efficiency of disk drives dropped as product architectures became more modular. In addition to losing the ability to differentiate products on the basis of performance, the designers and assemblers of modular products also lose their ability to differentiate on the basis of cost. The cost structure of non-integrated design/assembly firms tends to be dominated by variable, rather than fixed, costs. Because it is high fixed costs that give rise to steep scale economics, assemblers of modular products compete on relatively flat scale curves, meaning that small competitors can enjoy similar costs as larger ones.

In an attempt to illustratively measure the flattening of scale economics in a modular world, we collected data on the unit volumes, total costs and product line complexity for each disk drive manufacturer and built a regression model that allowed us to estimate each manufacturer's cost, during each year, to produce a drive of a given capacity. The equation takes the form

$$\ln(\text{Product Cost}) = B_0 + B_1 \ln(\text{Drive Capacity}) + B_2 \ln(\text{Total Units Produced}) + B_3 \ln(\text{Product Line Complexity})$$

The variables are defined as follows: *Product Cost* is calculated by dividing the total operating costs in the company, exclusive of interest and taxes, by the number of disk drive units produced. Hence, we call this measure *fully allocated product cost*. *Drive Capacity* is the weighted average capacity of the disk drive units shipped each year by the company. This is an important variable, because higher-capacity drives are more costly to produce. We expected the coefficient of this variable to be positive. *Total Units Produced* is the total number of disk drives shipped during the year. We expected the coefficient of this variable to be negative, positing that as scale increased, unit costs would fall. *Product Line Complexity* is the number of product families produced by the company in the year. We expected the coefficients of this variable to be positive—overhead costs per unit would increase as increasing complexity of the product line would demand higher management overheads.

All of the data required for this calculation were taken from *Disk/Trend Report*. The equation for the early 1980s, when modular architectures were just beginning to penetrate the industry, was

$$\ln(\text{cost/unit}) = 296.39 - 0.146(\text{year}) - 0.370 \ln(\text{unit volume}) + 0.126 \ln(\text{no. of families}) + 0.511 \ln(\text{weighted mean MB/unit})$$

t-statistics: (-3.44) (-4.70) (1.68) (6.23) $R^2 = 0.88$

The equation for the early 1990s, when modular architectures had become pervasive, was

$$\ln(\text{cost/unit}) = 322.22 - 0.160(\text{year}) - 0.15 \ln(\text{unit volume}) + 0.014 \ln(\text{no. of families}) + 0.544 \ln(\text{weighted mean MB/unit})$$

t-statistics: (3.41) (-0.52) (0.12) (4.20) $R^2 = 0.88$

Note how the scale coefficient fell and became statistically insignificant, as did the complexity coefficient (no. of families). We would expect both in a regime of modularity.

We estimated this equation for each year. The coefficient B_2 constituted a measure of the steepness of the scale economics in disk drive manufacturing at each point in the industry's history. Using this equation, we could then estimate what it would cost each manufacturer to make a drive of a given capacity, given the scale at which it produced in any year, and the complexity of its product line, measured by the number of product families. The scale curve as it looked in the late 1980s is shown in Figure 57-4, which charts the fully allocated costs on the vertical axis and each firm's production volumes on the horizontal axis for a typical modular 100 MB 3.5-inch drive. It shows that the scale economics in design and assembly of modular disk drive designs were flat—small competitors could add this value almost as cost-effectively as the largest firms—because the cost structure was dominated by variable rather than fixed costs.

For the makers of modular disk drives, competition in the absence of performance and cost differentiability has been difficult and unrewarding. It is the users of disk drives, not the manufacturers, who have reaped the benefits of lower cost, more flexibility and greater speed in product development that result from modularity. Typical gross margins for high-volume drives used in desktop personal computing fell from 35% in 1984 to become mired in the 10–15% range in the last years of that decade.

The Profitability of Component Manufacture

While the business of design and assembly of modular drives was a wearying race on an accelerating treadmill in Region B of Figure 57-2, the business of making heads

FIGURE 57-4   Scale Economics in the Design and Assembly of Modular 3.5-Inch Drives in the Late 1980s.

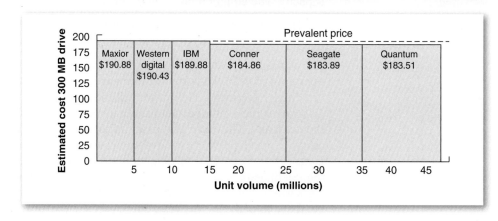

and disks during this same period shifted progressively to Region A of Figure 57-2. In order to force the cost of disk drives ever-lower, designers could never be satisfied with the functionality (recording density achievable) of heads and disks—because the higher the recording density, the fewer the number of disk platters and heads required in the drive. As a consequence, over this period heads and disks themselves become more technologically interdependent assemblies of materials, creating substantial scope for product differentiation. The high fixed costs of designing and manufacturing thin film disks and MR heads steepened the scale economics in this slice of value-added as well. Figure 57-5 shows, for example, that Komag, the largest independent disk manufacturer (which also made the highest-performance disks in the industry),[21] had substantially lower costs than its competitors. Because products were differentiable and scale economics were steep, the leading independent component makers were highly profitable. In contrast to the 11% annual rate of return that the shareholders of non-integrated disk drive assemblers received between 1988 and 1994, the leading component makers, Komag and Read-Rite, returned 38% annually to their shareholders.

In response to this shift in the stage of value-added in which attractive profits could be earned, some leading assemblers of drives began producing their own components. Figure 57-5 makes it easy to see why. Although their costs of production were higher than Komag's, the price at which assemblers were buying disks from Komag was determined where the supply and demand curves intersected—at the cost of the *marginal* supplier in the market—Akashic. As long as their scale enabled them to produce at greater volumes than the marginal supplier, and as long as the scale curve sloped steeply enough, these companies found disk-making to be a more attractive slice of value-added in which to participate than was design and assembly (see footnote 21). Hence, one of the leading non-integrated assemblers, Conner Peripherals, built an independent business to manufacture disks; and another, Seagate, developed businesses to make both disks and heads, which involved even steeper scale economics. These firms initially made components for internal consumption only, but ultimately found it compelling to sell to competing assemblers as well.[22] A number of analysts, in fact, reported that for many years in the 1990s over 100% of these firms' profits could be attributed to the value they captured in component manufacturing operations (meaning that they lost money in design and assembly). IBM subsequently has followed suit in selling components into the market as well.

It is important to note that while economists might call these firms' migration into making components "vertical integration," it would be more accurate to say that they

FIGURE 57-5 Supply Curve for the Thin Film Disk Industry, 1994.

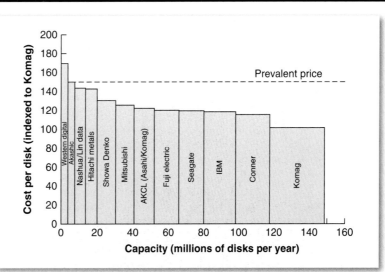

established managerially and technologically independent business positions in the component-manufacturing stage of value-added. This stemmed from a very different motivation and entailed a very different management structure than did the requirement to create new, interdependent product architectures, built through unstructured technical dialogue in response to the performance gaps described above.

Our conclusion, in essence, is that attractive profits tend to be earned where performance is not yet adequate relative to the needs of user in the next stage of value-added; and where, therefore, product architectures are likely to be proprietary and interdependent in character. Because the pace of performance improvement typically outstrips the ability of customers to utilize that improvement, the places in the value chain that presently enjoy attractive profitability are likely to lose their ability to continue those levels of profitability, and vice versa. In the following, we will summarize how this same shift in the ability of designers/assemblers versus component suppliers to capture attractive profits occurred in computers, and is beginning to happen in the automobile industry.

Shift in the Locus of Profitability in the Computer Industry

The largest firms that designed and assembled computers in the technologically interdependent era—particularly IBM and Digital Equipment—captured extraordinary profits because of the differentiability of their products and the high fixed costs (and consequently steep scale economics) in design and manufacturing. They wielded such power that most of their parts suppliers survived at subsistence levels of profitability. But, as personal computers with modular architectures came to dominate mainstream markets, the tables turned. How does a designer of a modular personal computer in a firm such as Compaq create a better product than competitors such as Dell, Gateway, Hewlett Packard or IBM? Incorporate a faster microprocessor? A higher capacity hard drive? More megabytes of DRAM? In a consummately modular product there are so few degrees of design freedom that the only way to offer a better product is to offer higher-performance components, which competitors can also offer. When most costs are variable, the scale curve flattens substantially: it becomes difficult to assemble at lower costs too. As speed to market and the ability to mass-customize become the only dimensions along which assemblers of modular products can compete, firms in this stage of value-added can find competition to be an unrewarding race on an accelerating treadmill.[23]

The impact on the profitability of design and assembly in the computer value-added chain has been predictable. "In 1986, companies that built and sold computer systems captured about 80% of the total profits being generated in the computer industry. By 1991, however, systems makers were getting just 20%. The market reallocated profits to the component makers" ("Deconstructing the Computer Industry," *Business Week,* 23 November 1992: 90–96). Indeed, in the modular era it has been interdependent subsystem makers such as Intel, Microsoft and Applied Materials—whose products themselves are technologically interdependent, involve high fixed costs and consequently enjoy steep scale economics—that have captured a disproportionate share of industry profits.

Strategists often use a "five forces" framework to describe where in the value chain competitive advantage and attractive profits can be built. We believe that the mechanism described here may define the dynamic, causal mechanisms behind the somewhat static characterizations of market power described in Porter's (1980, 1985) work.

This implies, of course, that through ongoing processes of overshooting and disruption, we are likely to see yet further shifts in the locus of power to earn profit in this industry. For example, as the functionality of operating systems, microprocessors and MR heads becomes more than good enough, and as disruptive hand-held wireless computing/communication devices emerge (which are not yet good enough), it is very possible that the power to earn attractive profits will migrate away from the "back-end" locations where it has resided to the stage of value-added where the end-use product is designed and assembled. We would welcome any efforts by other scholars to evaluate this hypothesis.[24]

The World Automotive Industry

Our final "case study" is not historical, but is predictive: we will use the model to project how the structure of the world auto industry might evolve in response to the tendencies we have chronicled here. We hope that this case study will help other scholars visualize better the implications of the mechanisms described above, and assess how they might play out in other industries that presently are dominated by large integrated firms. Theory can only be built cumulatively if scholars' explanations of cause and effect can be falsified, when used to predict what we are likely to see under various circumstances (Kuhn, 1962; Kaplan, 1986). We hope that future scholars, looking through the lenses of our model, can see anomalous phenomena as the auto industry evolves, and bring better theory to the academy.

The performance of automobiles has overshot the ability of most customers to utilize it, on several dimensions. Autos today routinely go 150,000 miles and more. They often go out of fashion before they wear out. Many car owners simply cannot utilize even longer-lasting cars. While technology enables comfortably-sized cars to travel 30 and more miles per gallon of fuel (some new hybrid gas–electric vehicles get 80 m.p.g.), consumers' rush toward less efficient sport-utility vehicles suggests that the car makers have overshot on this dimension of performance as well. Although autos are capable of cruising at speeds exceeding 90 miles per hour, traffic laws will not allow it. The list could go on.

The major disruptive innovators in the world automotive industry in the last 30 years have been Japanese firms, such as Toyota, which entered North American and European markets with low-priced offerings, and subsequently moved up-market in a classic disruptive fashion. Analysts have noted that a key tool used by these disruptive innovators to control costs and accelerate their product design cycle has been their use of a tiered supplier system (Dyer, 1996). Rather than designing and manufacturing their own components and performing all system design and assembly in-house, as General Motors and Ford traditionally had done, the disruptive Japanese innovators procured subsystems from a limited number of "Tier 1" suppliers, such as Nippon Denso. Their more modular product architectures, and the supplier infrastructure that mirrored them, helped the Japanese disruptors bring new designs to market much more rapidly than their American and European competitors.

Just as in computers, the basis of competition in the mainstream tiers of the automobile market is changing as the functionality of cars has overshot what is actually utilized by customers. Speed to market is increasingly important (Stalk and Hout, 1990; Clark and Fujimoto, 1991). Design cycles, which often took 6 years in the "Region A" era of the industry's history, have been shortened to 2 years today and are converging on 18 months. The ability to conveniently customize the features of each car for specific customers is emerging as a critical differentiator. For example, Toyota recently announced that its customers could custom-order cars for delivery within 5 days (Simison, 1999). The acceleration in time-to-market and improving ability to customize conveniently is being enabled by a steady modularization of the architecture.

To stay abreast of the frenetic pace of product development in the industry, General Motors has disintegrated by bundling its component-making companies into Delphi Corporation and spinning it off. Ford followed suit by spinning off Visteon.

To date, the industry seems to have evolved in a way that is quite consistent with the early steps in our model. If it continues to evolve along the path predicted by the model, we might expect the following developments in the coming years.

Ever-more-modular automobiles, comprised of increasingly standardized subsystems provided by Tier 1 suppliers, will likely take root initially at the lowest tiers of the market, amongst disruptive auto makers whose only hope for gaining a competitive edge is to introduce models faster than the competition, and who want to flatten the scale curve.[25] These are firms that will want to be able to design and assemble autos with the lowest ratio of fixed to variable costs possible.[26] We would expect auto makers in the more sophisticated tiers of the market to remain more vertically integrated, longer into the future, than would auto makers at the low end.

As the Tier 1 module suppliers experience the freedom to make trade-offs within the subsystem in order to minimize cost and optimize performance, subject to the interface constraints specified by the car companies, the internal architecture of the subsystem will become progressively more interdependent. The Tier 1 suppliers will begin to see interactions amongst the components that they were unable to see when they were fragmented suppliers of individual parts. Hence, the performance of subsystems from different suppliers is likely to become more differentiated.

At the outset, the subsystems from which the modular autos will be built are unlikely to interface with each other according to industry standards—the interface specifications will continue to be detailed by the car designers. But there will likely come a point when cars come to be designed around the interface specifications that Tier 1 suppliers articulate.

The number of suppliers of subsystems in the world industry is then likely to drop, as a result of steepening scale economics in design and manufacturing of those interdependent products. In contrast, the scale economics in the design and manufacture of cars are likely to flatten, as the job of designing and assembling modular cars becomes ever simpler. In fact, it will become increasingly possible to design and accurately simulate the performance of cars on a computer. The number of auto brands, therefore, is likely to maintain steady or even increase, as barriers to entry erode.

Ironically, even though the functionality of cars has overshot what consumers can actually utilize, car makers will continue to strive to offer products that are better than the competition. Customers will be reluctant to pay for the superfluous functionality, but, given the choice between equally priced autos, consumers will always accept the one with better performance, even though they will pay little for it. This means that car makers that refuse to keep racing up-market will lose share and profits. Because the designs are modular, however, the only way for car companies to differentiate the performance of their products from those of competitors will be to offer the best subsystems. This means that, by definition, suppliers of subsystems will be in Region A, even as their customers, the car makers, are in Region B. Hence, the internal architecture of the subsystems will increasingly become interdependent. It will therefore be difficult for focused firms that make only one or a few of the components comprising the subsystem to survive.

As the automobile becomes progressively more modular and the subsystems more interdependent, the ability to capture a disproportionate share of the industry's profits will migrate from the car makers to the Tier 1 subsystem suppliers. This probably will not be the case with all subsystems in the automobile, however. Extraordinary profits will accrue to those suppliers whose subsystems are in Region A, which forces their designs toward the interdependent end of the architectural spectrum. Subsystems which themselves perform beyond what the car makers need, and are therefore architecturally modular, are unlikely to generate abnormally attractive profits. Hence, the strategies that integrated manufacturers such as General Motors and Ford have followed in spinning off their components operations in order to be more cost- and speed-competitive in the stage of value-added where attractive profits formerly were made, mirror almost exactly IBM's decision to out-source the microprocessor and operating system to Intel and Microsoft, so that it could continue to design and assemble personal computers.

Implications for Integration and Outsourcing Strategies

We hope this model can add insights to two pieces of prevailing wisdom about industry structure and outsourcing. The first is about the general trend seen in most industries, where dominant, integrated firms over time give way to a horizontally stratified population of specialized firms (Chesbrough and Teece, 1996; Grove, 1996). Our contribution is that the causal mechanism that precipitates the vertical disintegration of industries may be the overshooting of the functionality that actually is utilized in certain tiers of the market. Overshooting precipitates a change in the basis of competition towards speed to market and the ability to conveniently customize features and functions. This, in turn, requires the modularization of product architectures which, finally, enables industry disintegration or deconstruction (Langlois and Robertson, 1992). This means that we would expect integrated firms to remain strong in tiers of the market that are under-served by the functionality of prevailing products, and that industries will trend toward reintegration when shifts in what customers demand cause performance gaps to emerge.

The second insight relates to the simple rule that managers and consultants use in making outsourcing decisions—that firms should outsource components or services if it is not their core competence, or if somebody else can do it at lower cost. This logic almost always makes compelling sense on the surface. But this research suggests that this logic can lead a firm to outsource those pieces of value-added in which most of the industry's profit will be made in the future—and to retain activities in which it is difficult to create enduring, differentiable advantages versus competitors. Although these hypotheses require further study, it appears that the assemblers of modular items at any stage of the value chain—whether they be end-use products, subsystems or components—are likely to struggle to achieve competitive advantage and to earn attractive profits. Attractive profitability seems to flow from the point of customer contact back through the product system to the point at which unsatisfied demand for functionality, and therefore technological interdependency, exists. Hence, these dynamics can cause the point of attractive profitability to shift from the system provider to the subsystem or component providers—from the front end to the back end to the front end again—as these dynamics work through an industry.

Address for Correspondence

Clayton M. Christensen, Harvard Business School.

APPENDIX 1: NOTES ON THE CALCULATION OF ARCHITECTURAL EFFICIENCY

To measure the abilities of different companies to extract performance from any given set of components, we conducted a multivariate regression analysis of the components used in 4,334 disk drives introduced in the industry between 1979 and 1997. The equation estimated in this analysis measured the extent to which the year in which a product was introduced, and the different components (represented by dummy variables) that were used, contributed to the differences in areal recording density (megabits per square inch of disk surface) of different disk drive models. Essentially, the equation derived from this analysis allowed us to estimate, on average for the entire industry, what recording density could be achieved at a given point in time with any set of components. Likewise, the coefficients in this equation measured the improvement in recording density that we would expect the average engineer in the industry to have achieved by using each new component technology.

This equation was used to estimate the areal density that each disk drive manufacturer should have been able to achieve at the time each of its models was introduced, given the set of components used in that model. The ratio of the actual recording density of the product to the predicted density was termed the *architectural efficiency* of the drive. A ratio of 1.2 meant that the company's engineers got 20% greater density out of a given set of components than was average for the industry, whereas one of 0.8 meant that the company succeeded in only getting 80% of the recording density that would have been average for the industry, given the components that were used.

Iansiti (1997) introduced the concept of "technological yield." This is a measure of the differences in product performance that stem from clever product design, rather than from use of superior components.

Table 57A-1 presents the coefficients of variables in the equations that were estimated. The dependent variable in each case was the log of areal density. Following

TABLE 57A-1

	Coefficient	t-Statistic	*Original Technology to which the New Technology's Performance is Compared*
Constant	−0.913	−3.04	
Year of introduction	0.199	57.80	NA: this is a continuous, not dummy variable
Disk diameter	−0.00154	−9.69	none; continuous variable, in centimeters
New head and disk technologies			
MIG head	0.047	2.00	ferrite head
Thin film head	0.251	13.50	ferrite head
MR head	0.838	22.70	ferrite head
Thin film disk	0.188	9.45	particulate oxide disk
Interaction of thin film head and thin film disk	−0.295	−3.35	
Actuator technologies			
Stepper motor	−0.428	−18.30	voice coil motor
Torque motor	−0.157	−4.93	voice coil motor
Rotary actuator design	0.063	3.55	linear actuator design
Optical positioning system	−0.380	−3.75	stepper positioning
Dedicated surface servo	0.020	−1.27	stepper positioning
Embedded servo	0.169	8.67	stepper positioning
Recording/error correction codes			
2,7 RLL recording code	0.207	9.23	modified frequency modulation (MFM) code
1,7 or 8,9 RLL recording code	0.439	14.40	MFM code
0,4,4 PRML recording code	0.585	11.90	MFM code
0,6,6 PRML recording code	0.775	13.00	MFM code
Interfaces			
PC/AT	0.073	2.64	ST412 interface
SCSI	0.099	3.83	ST412 interface
SCSI2	0.197	6.43	ST412 interface
SCSI3	0.324	2.80	ST412 interface
SMD	0.356	11.80	ST412 interface
ESDI	0.214	6.96	ST412 interface
ANSI	0.226	2.53	ST412 interface
IBM	0.287	6.55	ST412 interface
Proprietary interfaces	0.113	3.54	ST412 interface
Other interfaces	0.314	10.30	ST412 interface
Other technologies			
Zone-specific bit recording rate	0.127	6.35	uniform rate regardless of distance from center
Ramp loaded heads	0.106	1.61	heads rise from surface of the disk
Number of observations	4334		
Adjusted R^2	0.951		

Christensen (1992 a,b), the reference components were those in common use in 1979. In the database, the use of new-technology components was indicated with a system of dummy variables. The table below lists only those component, software and architectural variables with *t*-statistics during at least one period of >2.00. In addition, a few variables for unusual interfaces were not reproduced in this table, for the sake of brevity. Note that the adjusted R^2 of 0.951 suggests that these variables account for much of the variation in observed areal density among the models of disk drives designed over this period.

APPENDIX 2: NOTES ON THE CALCULATION OF THE INDUSTRY SUPPLY OR SCALE CURVE IN FIGURE 57-4

The purpose of this regression analysis was to calculate the steepness of scale economics in the stage of value-added involving the design and assembly of disk drives at various points in time over the industry's history. The companies whose data were used for these calculations were disk drive companies that were only engaged in design and assembly. Firms that not only designed and assembled, but also manufactured some or all of the components they used could not be included in the study, because reported costs could not be allocated accurately to the various stages of value-added. The data was drawn from *Disk/Trend Report,* as well as from the financial statements of the companies, for the years 1981–1989. The analysis could not be extended beyond 1989 because there were too few surviving firms engaged solely in the business of designing and assembling disk drives. Firms had either exited the industry, integrated into making disk drive components or integrated into making other products.

The equation that was estimated was of the form

$$\ln(\text{cost/unit}) = B_0 + B_1(\text{year}) + B_2 \ln(\text{unit volume}) + B_3 \ln(\text{no. of product line complexity}) + B_4 \ln(\text{drive capacity})$$

The choice of these variables as the ones most likely to impact total cost was grounded in research conducted by the first author that has been synthesized in the Harvard Business School teaching case, "Michigan Manufacturing Corporation" (HBS case no. 9-694-051).

The variables were defined as follows: *cost/unit* was calculated by dividing the total operating costs in the company, exclusive of interest and taxes, by the number of disk drive units produced. Hence, this measure is the *fully allocated product cost* for each company, for each year. *Drive capacity* is the weighted average capacity of the disk drive units shipped each year by the company. This is an important control variable, because each company's product mix was differently distributed across tiers of the market, and higher-capacity drives are more costly to produce. We expected the coefficient of this variable to be positive. *Unit volume* is the total number of disk drives shipped during the year. We expected the coefficient of this variable to be negative, positing that firms with larger production scale would enjoy lower costs, and that as any firm's production scale increased, its unit costs would fall. *Product line complexity* is the number of product families produced by the company in the year. We expected the coefficients of this variable to be positive—overhead costs per unit would increase as increasing complexity of the product line would demand higher management overheads. The definition of a product family was that used in Christensen (1992b).

We estimated coefficients for the equation for panels of years: 1981–1984 and 1986–1989. An alternative approach, to include a dummy variable for each year during this period, was not feasible because in some years there were fewer than thirty observations. The equation for the years 1981–1984, when modular architectures were just beginning to penetrate the industry, was

$$\ln(\text{cost/unit}) = 296.39 - 0.146(\text{year}) - 0.370 \ln(\text{unit volume}) + 0.126 \ln(\text{no. of families}) + 0.511 \ln(\text{weighted mean MB/unit})$$

t-statistics: $(-3.44)\ (-4.70)\ (1.68)\ (6.23)\ R^2 = 0.88$

The equation for the years 1986–1989, when modular architectures had become much more pervasive in 3.5-inch drives used in desktop computers, was

$$\ln(\text{cost/unit}) = 322.22 - 0.160(\text{year}) - 0.15 \ln(\text{unit volume}) + 0.014 \ln(\text{no. of families}) + 0.544 \ln(\text{weighted mean MB/unit})$$

t-statistics: $(3.41)\ (-0.52)\ (0.12)\ (4.20)\ R^2 = 0.88$

Several comparisons between these measurements merit mention. First, the year term is essentially a "catch-all," whose coefficient represents the year-to-year reduction in cost attributable to engineering and product technology improvements. The relative stability of the coefficients measured in the two time panels suggests that the variables in the equations vary independently, and that probably no other important explanatory variables are missing from these estimations, which have interactions with the variables shown. The coefficient of the "weighted average megabytes per unit" variable was similarly stable, as we would expect: adding an extra megabyte of capacity to a drive ought to result in a predictable increment to cost.

Note how the coefficient of the unit volume variable was negative and statistically significantly different from zero, suggesting rather steep scale economics in the 1981–1984 period. The coefficient was statistically insignificant in the later period, suggesting that scale economics were not a significant driver of cost: the scale curve seems to have flattened. Similarly, the product line complexity variable, which was modestly significant during the era of architectural interdependency, was insignificant when modular architectures were more pervasive—reflecting the fact that modularity facilitates increased product variety without the significant cost penalties incurred when architectures are interdependent.

One reviewer of this paper noted that because of the large standard error of the coefficient of the scale variable in the second period, we actually cannot reject, based upon statistical analysis along, the null hypothesis that scale economics might still have been steep during this period. Nonetheless, industry executives who have reviewed the work uniformly felt that there were almost no differences in cost across the five largest firms. We take this statistical analysis, therefore, to be consistent with the theory (a high proportion of variable to fixed costs flattens the scale curve), as well as consistent with the perceptions of industry executives.

References

Abernathy, W. and J. Utterback (1978), "Patterns of industrial innovation," *Technology Review,* **50** (June–July), 40–47.

Adner, R. (1999), "A demand-based view of the emergence of competition: demand structure and technology displacement," working paper, Insead.

Adner, R. and D. Levinthal (2001), "Demand heterogeneity and technology evolution: implications for product and process innovation," *Management Science, 47,* 611–628.

Adner, R. and P. Zemsky (2001), "Disruptive technologies and the emergence of competition," working paper, Insead.

Baldwin, C. Y. and K. B. Clark (1997), "Managing in an age of modularity," *Harvard Business Review,* **75** (September–October), 84–93.

Baldwin, C. Y. and K. B. Clark (2000), *Design Rules: The Power of Modularity.* MIT Press: Cambridge, MA.

Bass, M. J. and C. M. Christensen (2002), "The future of the microprocessor business," *IEEE Spectrum,* **39** (April), 34–39.

Becker, G. S. and K. M. Murphy (1992), "The division of labor, coordination cost, and knowledge," *Quarterly Journal of Economics, 107,* 1137–1160.

Billington, C. and L. Fleming (1998), "Technological evolution, standard interfaces, and new market opportunities," *POMS Series in Technology and Operations Management,* 30–41.

Bower, J. L. and C. M. Christensen (1995), "Disruptive technologies: catching the wave," *Harvard Business Review,* January–February.

Chandler, A. D. (1977), *The Visible Hand.* The Belknap Press of Harvard University Press: Cambridge, MA.

Chesbrough, H. W. and K. Kusunoki (2001), "The modularity trap: innovation, technology phase shifts and the resulting limits of virtual organizations," in I. Nonaka and D. J. Teece (eds), *Managing Industrial Knowledge.* Sage: London, ch. 10.

Chesbrough, H. W. and D. J. Teece (1996), "When is virtual virtuous?" *Harvard Business Review,* **74** (January–February), 65–74.

Christensen, C. (1992a), "Exploring the limits of the technology S-curve (parts 1 and 2)," *Production and Operations Management,* **1,** 334–366.

Christensen, C. M. (1992b), "The innovator's challenge," unpublished DBA thesis, Harvard Business School.

Christensen, C. M. (1993), "The rigid disk drive industry: a history of commercial and technological turbulence," *Business History Review,* **67,** 531–588.

Christensen, C. M. (1994), "The drivers of vertical disintegration," Harvard Business School working paper.

Christensen, C. M. (1996), "Patterns in the evolution of product competition," *European Management Journal,* **15,** 117–127.

Christensen, C. M. (1997), *The Innovator's Dilemma: When New Technologies Cause Great Firms to Fail.* Harvard Business School Press: Boston, MA.

Christensen, C. M. (2001), "The law of conservation of modularity," working paper, Harvard Business School.

Christensen, C. M. and E. Armstrong (1998), "Disruptive technologies: a credible threat to leading programs in continuing medical education?" *The Journal of Continuing Education in the Health Professions,* **18,** 69–80.

Christensen, C. M. and J. L. Bower (1996), "Customer power, strategic investment, and the failure of leading firms," *Strategic Management Journal*, **17**, 197–218.

Christensen, C. M. and R. S. Rosenbloom (1995), "Explaining the attacker's advantage: technological paradigms, organizational dynamics, and the value network," *Research Policy*, **24**, 233–257.

Christensen, C. M. and R. S. Tedlow (2000), "Patterns of disruption in retailing," *Harvard Business Review*, **78** (January–February), 42–45.

Christensen, C. M. and M. Verlinden (1999), "Hewlett Packard's Merced decision," Harvard Business School case study #9-699-011.

Christensen, C. M., F. Suarez and J. Utterback (1998), "Strategies for survival in fast-changing industries," *Management Science*, **44**, S207–S220.

Christensen, C. M., R. Bohmer and J. Kenagy (2000), "Will disruptive innovations cure health care?" *Harvard Business Review*, **78**(September–October), 102–111.

Christensen, C. M., T. Craig and S. Hart (2001), "The great disruption," *Foreign Affairs*, **80**, 80–95.

Clark, K. B. and T. Fujimoto (1991), *Product Development Performance*. Harvard Business School Press: Boston, MA.

Coase, R. H. (1937), "The nature of the firm," *Economica*, **4**, 386–405.

Demsetz, H. (1988), "The theory of the firm revisited," *Journal of Law, Economics and Organization*, **4**, 141–161.

Disk/Trend Report (1999), Disk/Trend Inc.: Mountain View, CA.

Dyer, J. (1996), "How Chrysler created an American keiretsu," *Harvard Business Review*, **74**(July–August), 42–56.

Fine, C. (1998), *Clockspeed*. Perseus Press: New York.

Fixson, S. (2000), "A taxonomy development: mapping different product architectures," working paper, Technology, Management and Policy Program, Massachusetts Institute of Technology.

Fleming, L. and O. Sorenson (2001), "Technology as a complex adaptive system: evidence from patent data," *Research Policy*, **130**, 1019–1039.

Grove, A. S. (1996), *Only the Paranoid Survive*. Doubleday: New York.

Henderson, R. and K. B. Clark (1990), "Architectural innovation: the reconfiguration of existing product technologies and the failure of established firms," *Administrative Science Quarterly*, **35**, 9–30.

Hodes, M. S. and G. W. Hall (1999), "Home run: taking a closer look at internet mortgage finance," Goldman Sachs Investment Research.

Iansiti, M. (1997), *Technology Integration*. Harvard Business School Press: Boston, MA.

Kaplan, R. (1986), "The role for empirical research in management accounting," *Accounting, Organizations and Society*, **11**, 429–452.

Klein, B., R. Crawford and A. Alchian (1978), "Vertical integration, appropriable rents, and the competitive contracting process," *Journal of Law and Economics*, **21**, 297–326.

Kuhn, T. (1962), *The Structure of Scientific Revolutions*. The University of Chicago Press: Chicago, IL.

Langlois, R. N. (1994), "Capabilities and vertical disintegration in process technology: the case of semiconductor fabrication equipment," working paper, CCC.

Langlois, R. N. and P. L. Robertson (1992), "Networks and innovation in a modular system: lessons from the microcomputer and stereo component industries," *Research Policy*, **21**, 297–313.

Macher, J. T. (2001), "Vertical disintegration and process innovation in semiconductor manufacturing: foundries vs. integrated producers," working paper, Robert E. McDonough School of Business, Georgetown University.

Maynard, M. (1998), "GM considers switch to modular assembly," *USA Today*, December 16, 2B.

Monroe, D. (1999), "The end of scaling: disruption from below," in S. Luryi, J. Xu and A. Zaslavsky (eds), *Future Trends in Microelectronics: Beyond the Beaten Path*. Wiley: New York.

Monteverde, K. (1995), "Technical dialog as an incentive for vertical integration in the semiconductor industry," *Management Science*, **41**, 1624–1638.

Pine, B. J. (1992), *Mass Customization: The New Frontier in Business Competition*. Harvard Business School Press: Boston, MA.

Porter, M. (1980), *Competitive Strategy*. The Free Press: New York.

Porter, M. (1985), *Competitive Advantage*. The Free Press: New York.

Porter, M. (1996), "What is Strategy?," *Harvard Business Review*, **74** (November–December), 61.

Rosenbloom, R. S. and C. M. Christensen (1995), "Technological discontinuities, organizational capabilities, and strategic commitments," *Industrial and Corporate Change*, **3**, 655–685.

Sanchez, R. and J. T. Mahoney (1996), "Modularity, flexibility and knowledge management in product and organization design," *Strategic Management Journal*, **17** (Winter special issue), 63–76.

Simison, R. L. (1999), "Toyota develops a way to make a car within 5 days of a custom order," *Wall Street Journal*, 6 August, A4.

Smith, A. (1776), *The Wealth of Nations* [Modern Library: New York, 1994].

Stalk, G. (1993), "Japan's dark side of time," *Harvard Business Review*, **71**(July–August).

Stalk, G. and T. Hout (1990), *Competing Against Time*. The Free Press: New York.

Stigler, J. (1951), "The division of labor is limited by the extent of the market," *Journal of Political Economy*, **59**, 185–193.

Stuckey, J. and D. White (1993), "When and when not to vertically integrate," *McKinsey Quarterly*, no. **3**, 3–27.

Taguchi, G. and D. Clausing (1990), "Robust quality," *Harvard Business Review*, **68**(January–February), 65–75.

Teece, D. (1986), "Profiting from technological innovation: implications for integration, collaboration, licensing and public policy," *Research Policy*, **15**, 285–305.

Ulrich, K. (1995), "The role of product architecture in the manufacturing firm," *Research Policy,* **24,** 419–440.

Ulrich, K. and S. Eppinger (1995), *Product Design and Development.* McGraw-Hill: New York.

Waid, D. (1989), *Rigid Disk Drive Magnetic Head/Media Market and Technology Report.* Peripheral Research Corporation: Santa Barbara, CA.

Williamson, O. (1979), "Transactions cost economics: the governance of contractual relations," *Journal of Law and Economics,* **23,** 233–261.

Williamson, O. (1985), *The Economic Institutions of Capitalism.* Prentice-Hall: Englewood Cliffs, NJ.

Yin, R. (1984), *Case Study Research: Design and Methods.* Sage: Beverly Hills, CA.

Endnotes

1. See, for example, the discussion of IBM's outsourcing decisions in *Fortune,* 14 April 1997.

2. Ulrich (1995) and others use the term "integral" to refer to interfaces where these conditions are not met, and Chesbrough and Teece (1996) use the term "systemic." We have chosen the term "interdependent" because it seems more descriptive of the situation. The other terms connote enough other meanings that we have chosen to employ this new term.

3. This assertion mirrors Monteverde's conclusion that "Roughly speaking (since other things also matter), firm boundaries . . . should congeal around transactions rich in such technically necessary, unstructured dialog" (Monteverde, 1995: 1629).

4. In earlier papers about these phenomena (Christensen and Rosenbloom, 1995; Christensen, 1997: ch. 2), we describe the existence of a "value network"—a nested ecosystem of suppliers and customers whose constituent companies share similar business models and process rhythms, which tend to move up-market and get disrupted as a group. The evidence in Section 5 of this paper suggests that all companies within a particular value network are not likely to uniformly employ modular or interdependent architectures. Elsewhere, Christensen suggests the existence of a "Law of Conservation of Modularity"—a generalization asserting that interfaces across sequential elements in a value-added chain are likely to be alternately interdependent and modular (Christensen, 2001).

5. The initial findings that the pace of technological progress can outstrip the abilities of customers to utilize that progress were detailed in Christensen (1992a, b). Having assembled a complete census of data on every disk drive model introduced by each company in the world disk drive industry between 1970 and 1990, Christensen measured through regression analysis the trajectory of improvement in the storage capacity of each form factor of disk drives during this period. Then, using data on disk drive capacity actually used in various classes of computers, he measured through regression analysis the trajectory of improvement utilized by customers in various tiers of the market. These results were described in Christensen (1993), Christensen and Rosenbloom (1995), Bower and Christensen (1995), Rosenbloom and Christensen (1995) and Christensen and Bower (1996). Similar econometric analysis was used in Christensen (1997) to measure the trajectories of improvement in functionality that manufacturers of excavating equipment provided, in contrast to the trajectory of performance improvement that various types of contractors were able to utilize. The "disruptive technologies model" was inductively derived from these empirical analyses. Dan Monroe of Bell Laboratories (Monroe, 1999) and Mick Bass of Hewlett Packard (Bass, 2000) subsequently have empirically measured the same phenomena in semiconductor products. Christensen (1997) also uses the model in a deductive mode, comparing the predictions of the model to qualitative data about the histories of established and entrant companies in the computer, steel, retailing, motor controls, motorcycle and accounting software industries. Subsequent studies have found the same phenomenon in medical education (Christensen and Armstrong, 1998), retailing (Christensen and Tedlow, 2000), healthcare (Christensen *et al.,* 2000), macroeconomic growth (Christensen *et al.,* 2001) and semiconductor products (Bass and Christensen, 2002). Professor Ron Adner and his colleagues (Adner, 1999; Adner and Levinthal, 2001; Adner and Zemsky, 2001) have recently examined the same phenomenon using deductive, modeling methods.

6. Stuckey and White (1993) assert that industries will remain vertically integrated when there is *asset specificity* (a fixed asset is geographically so restricted that it is *de facto* tied to another asset), *technical specificity* (two pieces of equipment can work only with each other, and will not easily work with others) and *human capital specificity* (people whose skills are of value only within a particular working relationship). In the parlance of this paper, each of these situations is architecturally *interdependent.*

7. Stigler's (1951) observation that industries tend to reintegrate and consolidate as they became mature in their later stages also may not result from shrinking scale *per se.* We have written elsewhere that after the dimensions of innovation in functionality, reliability and convenience are exhausted, price-based competition becomes predominant. It is possible that costs can be minimized most effectively from within an interdependent product architecture and integrated business model. For example, our conversations with some of Dell Computer's competitors have surfaced the possibility that Dell is over-serving the market in terms of convenience and customization—and that there are real overhead costs associated with its business model and product architecture. If an integrated supplier like IBM now offered to the market a single one-size-fits-all personal computer with more-than-enough microprocessor speed, display pixels and memory capacity, it might possible be able to steal substantial share at the low end from Dell. It is possible, therefore, that the causality of what Stigler observed is the mechanism that we discuss here.

8. The advent of a modular architecture in many cases seems associated with the emergence of a dominant design (Abernathy and Utterback, 1978; Christensen *et al.*, 1978). This association is not yet clear enough in our minds to say more than this. The possibility of this linkage, however, is something that we invite other scholars to study with us.

9. The data were obtained as a generous gift from Mr. James Porter, Editor of *Disk/Trend Report*. We have entered the data in a huge Excel spreadsheet, and would be happy to share the data with colleagues who wish to analyze it further (available on request from C.M.C). Although *Disk/Trend Report* recently ceased publication, the San Jose Public Library holds past copies of the reports.

10. Recording density is measured as the number of megabits of information that can be stored on a square inch of disk area.

11. The diameter of the disk actually has a strong effect on the recording density that is feasible, because the inertial problems of precisely positioning larger components over a particular track of data are much greater in large drives than small drives.

12. Professor Marco Iansiti (Iansiti, 1997) used different methods to develop an analogous measure in his study of product design processes in the computer workstation industry. He labeled his measure "technological yield." We prefer to use the term "architectural efficiency," to be consistent with earlier publications that employed this measure (Christensen, 1992a, b) and because it is more descriptive of the phenomenon we are trying to measure. Whereas Iansiti compared what was theoretically achievable versus what was actually achieved, we have measured the average of all engineers' work versus the work of the individual product design teams that developed each of the products.

13. There is a common problem in analyses of this sort, as one of the reviewers of this paper pointed out. Quoting from the review letter, "[If] you plot the size of the residual at different levels of the dependent variable, [you often] find that the residual is larger on the larger end of the distribution of the dependent variable, and smaller at the smaller end of the distribution of the dependent variable. It would be very surprising to have found any other pattern, [because] is common for errors to be heteroscedastic in proportion of the to the dependent variable." He or she is correct. It is for this reason that our measure of architectural efficiency we have used in these studies is the ratio of actual to expected recording density, rather than the absolute magnitude of the residual. Using the ratio normalizes for the effect of the absolute magnitude. Indeed, had we not normalized in this way, the plot would have been extraordinarily misleading because recording densities have increased dramatically over the period.

14. The only deviation from the trend towards increased modularity seems to have occurred in the late 1980s, when the drive makers in all tiers of the market began to use thin film heads. As Waid (1989) notes, thin film heads constituted a fundamentally interdependent technological challenge during the earliest years of their use, because many elements of the drive's design were inter-

dependent with elements of the thin film head design. This supports the point suggested above that when new technologies are used their interactions with other elements in the system design are not well understood.

15. Some readers of earlier drafts of this paper have wondered whether, in the lower tiers of truly commoditized product markets, architectures might become interdependent again. If everybody in a significant portion of a market wanted exactly the same features and functions, and their desires were stable over time, the flexibility and options value of modularity might have little value (Baldwin and Clark, 2000). It then might be possible that a single interdependent product design might indeed be a lowest-cost solution.

16. The pattern in which these waves of disruptive technologies are sweeping through the tiers of the computing market is described in greater detail in Christensen and Verlinden (1999).

17. We have deliberately used the term "less integrated" rather than "non-integrated" here because, by this point in the industry's history, all of these firms were integrated to some extent, positioned at various points along the spectrum. Seagate (especially after having acquired Conner Peripherals) had a thriving disk-making operation, and had a magneto-resistive (MR) head operation that was beginning to bear fruit. It had deep expertise in thin film head-making. Quantum designed its controller circuitry but outsourced everything else, including manufacturing. It had attempted to begin making MR heads by purchasing Digital Equipment's disk drive business, but stumbled badly. By 1998 it had essentially passed the MR head hot potato to Matsushita Kotobuki Electric (MKE), its manufacturing partner, and MKE was laboring to learn how to make and integrate the heads. Western Digital and Maxtor were the least integrated. IBM was by far the most extensively integrated—especially in the linkages between its components, its research activities that supported advanced-technology components and its read—write channel design activities. The main differences in integration between IBM and Seagate are in IBM's extensive research activities, and in the manner in which IBM's engineers seem to be able to integrate their pieces of value-added—especially at the partial response, maximum likelihood (PRML)—MR head interface.

18. Each 2.5-inch disk has half the recording area of a 3.5-inch disk, but because the 2.5-inch form factor is used in notebook computers, it must be much thinner, allowing fewer disks to be stacked on a spindle than in the 3.5-inch architecture.

19. Evidence that the architecture of 2.5-inch disk drives is interdependent rather than modular comes from many sources. This first was a set of twenty-four interviews conducted with engineering managers at IBM, the industry's most integrated company; Seagate, a partially integrated firm; Quantum, a non-integrated assembler of drives, and Read-Rite and Komag, which were non-integrated suppliers of heads and disks, respectively. In every case, they noted that in using PRML codes and MR heads (defined below) to maximize the density of 2.5-inch drives, they could not work with suppliers because they could not specify what suppliers had to deliver, and could not measure whatever attributes of the heads were most critical

for maximizing performance. They all attributed IBM's success in this market to its ability to conduct all of the required design and manufacturing in house, in integrated teams. We also conducted statistical analyses of the phenomena, showing how the statistical significance of interaction terms between components in the regression equations described in the appendix varied across 3.5-inch and 2.5-inch drives. We have not included those results in this paper because of length constraints, but they point to the same conclusion. Drives whose functionality is nearer to the frontier of feasibility have more interdependence in their architectures. The interdependency between these technologies occurs in what engineers in the industry call "the channel." MR heads offer a completely different, and much more sensitive, method for detecting changes in the flux field on a disk than prior inductive head technology—enabling much smaller magnetic domains to be created on disks. PRML software algorithms detect when errors in reading data might have occurred and, based upon patterns in other data, estimate what the missing or erroneous data are. The ability to maximize recording density by using the most advanced MR heads depends upon the ability of PRML coders to identify and correct error patterns, which arise because of the way the heads are designed. Both pieces of technology must be done interdependently. This is not the case with the technologies that are used away from the frontier of possibility, such as inductive thin-film heads and run-length limited (RLL) error-correction codes. Both can be procured and used off the shelf from third parties.

20. It seems that the foresight of Microsoft's management team is a common interpretation of why Microsoft made this move toward interdependent architectures, whereas firms that were managed by less aggressive or competent teams, such as WordPerfect, Novell and Lotus, missed this opportunity. To provoke discussion, we are specifically proposing that there is a more fundamental causality behind what happened: the performance gap forced integration, and Microsoft was in the best position to respond.

21. The sources of these data were *Trend/Focus,* an annual market research report on the industry supplying components to the disk drive assemblers, and the engineering staff at Komag. Figure 57-5 was constructed with an economic model built in conjunction with the engineering staff at Komag, which estimated the cost of producing a disk of a given quality at various volumes. By inserting *Trend/Focus* data into the model, we developed estimates of the production costs of various competitors.

22. By the late 1990s, Komag's profits had plummeted. But in an odd way, its collapse supports the thesis of this section. So many disk drive assemblers had been enticed into making their own disks because of the profitability of disk-making relative to final product assembly, that little merchant-market volume was available to Komag by the late 1990a. Its costs consequently rose and its profitability was decimated. But it was the profits that attracted the assemblers into disks, and not the requirement for technological and managerial coordination that drove this move to vertical integration. A similar fate befell Read-Rite, at least temporarily. Especially with the advent of magneto-resistive heads in the mid-1990s—an immature technology with steep scale economics—the design/assembly firms that could afford it brought as much head-making capacity in-house as possible.

23. The first firms to identify how the basis of competition amongst assemblers of modular products in over-served tiers of the market shifts to speed and customization can, in fact, do well for a time. This was certainly the case with Dell Computer and Chrysler, for example. The operations-based abilities to compete in these terms against other assemblers, however, can be replicated, as Porter (1996) notes. One of the foremost prophets of time-based competition, George Stalk, recognized the same unattractive end-game for modular assemblers (Stalk and Hout, 1990; Stalk, 1993).

24. We have an additional hypothesis. Assemblers of modular products, such as Compaq Computer, increasingly outsource more and more value-added to contract manufacturers. Firms such as Solectron, Celestica and Flextronics, for example, began as circuit board assemblers. They then integrated forward into assembling computer motherboards. They then advanced into assembling the entire computer; then into managing inbound and outbound supply chain logistics; and most recently, into the design of the products themselves. Why would the contract manufacturers find it attractive to integrate *into* the very stages of value-added that the computer companies found it attractive to get *out* of? The computer makers need to keep improving return on assets. When the assemblers of modular products cannot differentiate in performance or cost, the cannot improve the numerator of the return-on-assets ratio (ROA). They only have leverage over the denominator—they improve ROA—and they do this by outsourcing asset-intensive stages of value-added. This accentuates the "modularity trap" that Chesbrough and Kusunoki (2001) describe.

25. Maynard (1998) points out that even General Motors is seriously considering implementing modular designs and assembly lines at the *low* end of its product line.

26. Chrysler's recent entry into the Brazilian automobile market is an example of this. Because Chrysler was the thirteenth company to enter the Brazilian market, it could not justify the typical investment (usually hundreds of millions of dollars) required to build a traditional assembly facility, given the initial market share it could reasonably expect to capture. In order to achieve profitability at low volumes, Chrysler's strategy has been to modularize both the vehicle design and the assembly process. A few suppliers design and build major subsystems in their own plants. They deliver these major modules to the Chrysler line, where the modules fit together in far fewer steps, with far less capital investment, than typically required (White, 1998).

58

DETERMINING DEMAND, SUPPLY, AND PRICING FOR EMERGING MARKETS BASED ON DISRUPTIVE PROCESS TECHNOLOGIES

Jonathan D. Linton

Lally School of Management and Technology, Rensselaer Polytechnic Institute, 110 8th Street, Troy, NY 12180, USA

ABSTRACT

A model for forecasting the likely market size and demand for an early-stage emerging process technology is considered. This method takes into account markets, supply, demand, supply/demand gap, pricing, implications to government policy, corporate strategy, and value of intellectual property. For the purpose of illustration, forecasting of microsystems is considered.

KEYWORDS

Disruptive; Shortage; Emerging markets; Pricing

INTRODUCTION

The purpose of this paper is to develop a forecasting model for profitability of innovations based on disruptive process technologies. A model for forecasting the likely market size and demand for an early-stage emerging technology is developed. This method considers the market for an emerging technology in terms of supply, demand, supply/demand gap, pricing, as well as implication to government policy, corporate strategy, and value of intellectual property. For the purpose of illustration, forecasting of microelectromechanical systems (MEMS) is considered. The paper begins by reviewing the relevant literature. Next, the model is developed. The application of the model to MEMS is considered. Finally, implications and conclusions are offered.

The role of "creative destruction" [1], the long waves of technological change [2] and technological discontinuities as substantial sources of corporate and the national competitive advantage are well known [3–5]. These concepts are, however, weakly linked to microeconomic topics, such as supply, demand, and price, that are introductory

E-mail address: linton@rpi.edu (J.D. Linton).

Linton, Jonathan D. 2003. "Determining demand, supply, and pricing for emerging markets based on disruptive process technologies." *Technological Forecasting and Social Change* 71(1/2): 105–120.

topics in college economics [6]. This lack of connection is due to the breach of the critical microeconomic assumption of *all other things being equal.* With emerging technologies, there is instability [7] in both supply and demand so "all other things" are not equal. Basic microeconomics is useful in many situations but does not address technological change [8]. This is critical since microeconomic theory cannot account for the creative destruction of new product innovation that is discussed by Schumpeter [1], let alone the tremendous economic disruption resulting from the long waves described by Kondratieff [2]. This is a concern, since these disruptions to equilibrium markets are the basis of tremendous economic growth for nations [9] and opportunities for profit for both entrepreneurs and firms [1, 4, 10].

If one could apply microeconomic theory to emerging technologies and markets, useful insights into such issues as supply, demand, and price and how they relate to the competitive advantage of firms [8], as well as nations [9], would be obtained. Yet, forecasting an emerging technology at best involves tremendous corporate and personnel risk. The vast majority of forecasting processes has been developed for sustaining technologies or technologies that are currently the industry-standard technology/product paradigm [11, 12]. Since there are few tools that assist us in forecasting emerging technologies, and this activity is essential for decision making, this shortfall must be addressed. This paper does so by offering a method for considering possible scenarios of the uncertain future and the outcome of these scenarios to gaps between supply and demand, pricing and profitability, value of intellectual property, and the effects of possible corporate strategies and government policies. Scenario analysis has been used in the past by corporations and governments to consider competitive intelligence, risk in large complex projects, technological uncertainty, and the ongoing management of highly uncertain environments [13–20]. Thus, in the face of uncertainty, we can consider the different possible scenarios and their relative likelihood, assuming current beliefs regarding the future are valid. Although such an assumption of validity is risky, forecasting emerging technologies is essential and of value to government, industry, and the financial community. Consequently, forecasts will be conducted regardless of the validity of the forecasts [21–23]. Under such circumstances, developing a "better," but still flawed method, is worthwhile.

FORECASTING PRACTICE

The most commonly used methods in forecasting assume that the past is indicative of the future [24, 25]. The linear assumption, common with these methods, is replaced by one of a number of different models for technology forecasting. A variety of S-shape models have been proposed to take into consideration the expansion and eventual decline of the technology, either in terms of market or performance improvements, under consideration in the forecast [11, 12, 26]. The S-curve models, although attractive, have suffered from instability just prior to and after periods of logistic growth [7, 27, 28]. This apparently chaotic behavior further complicates forecasting. However, having provided this caveat, S-curves will be considered further.

The most commonly used S-curve models are those of Bass [29], Fisher–Pry [30–33], and Gompertz [12, 34–37]. Forecasting has been extended further by applying the Lotka–Volterra model to technology forecasting by considering the alternative technologies as "predator" and "prey" [38–40]. For many purposes, these methods are suitable. However, they offer little guidance for forecasting either demand or supply in markets that may not yet exist [3, 41, 42].

To consider cases where these mathematical approaches do not provide satisfactory insights, past practice is to conduct foresight exercises, scenario analysis, and the use of system dynamics. Foresight projects commonly use consultation with experts via the Delphi method to determine the likely future development of the technology [22, 43–48]. Scenario analysis considers the effects of certain situation on an organization, industry, or country [13, 15, 19, 49].

The scenarios considered might be the result of a foresight exercise. Alternatively, these scenarios might be obtained using a model to simulate possible future states.

System dynamics is used to develop scenarios of future states [11, 50–53]. Past assessments using these system dynamic models that tended to describe a small number of possible trajectories were usually incorrect, for example, Schnaars et al. [23]. The most notable example of model error is probably the Club of Rome Report's [54] false characterization of the impending peril that our planet faced. False alarms such as this have discredited and undoubtedly discouraged other attempts at forecasting based on system dynamics. Here, the use of multiple methods is proposed. Mackay and Metcalfe [55] have advocated such an approach for discontinuous innovation, which is a term that describes most disruptive process technologies. By combining the use of expert opinions, simulation, and system dynamics with the computational power that is now available, it is possible to efficiently generate thousands of scenarios that are more likely to describe the future and the range of possibilities that exist in the future. Consequently, forecasting to assist in "road mapping" is now more useful. Having briefly considered the techniques used for technological forecasting, microeconomics is briefly considered.

MICROECONOMICS

Important questions regarding disruptive process technologies, such as MEMS or nanotechnologies, focus on (1) sufficient capability to fulfill supply requirements to protect national interests (such as security) and (2) to determine which markets are most likely to be profitable. To consider either of these questions, it is necessary to understand the relative balance between supply and demand. A limited capability to produce products based on a disruptive process technology, such as MEMS, could result in a threat to a country—for example, an inability to produce sufficient quantities of vaccine or detectors to warn of biological or chemical threats. From a firm perspective, product scarcity due to supply constraints allows the manufacturer(s) to behave as either a monopolist or oligopolist. Under conditions of monopoly or oligopoly, it is possible for firms to obtain much greater profits than under conditions of product surplus and price-based competition [56–61]. From the perspective of a country, it is important to ensure that sufficient supply is available for national interests and to recognize that policies that encourage excess capacity may not result in the maximum economic growth benefits offered by the technology. From the perspective of a firm, the markets worth pursuing are those with the greatest likelihood of scarcity, since this offers the possibility that the firm may behave as a monopolist or oligopolist and obtain the associated profits. Consequently, a firm must protect a design or process with patents. Alternatively, a firm must have a set of production-related skills and assets that are difficult to duplicate. Having reviewed the relevant forecasting and economics literature, the model for considering supply/demand gaps for disruptive process technologies is now taken up.

DEFINING A MODEL TO CONSIDER SUPPLY AND DEMAND UNCERTAINTY

To consider the market structure for an emerging technology, one must consider possible markets, supply, demand, and the gap between supply and demand. *Possible markets* are the separate markets that either exist or are expected to exist for products based on a disruptive process technology. The *supply* of product is the current capacity for the manufacture of the product and the ability and rate of suppliers to add additional capacity if it is required by the market. The *demand* for product are predictions—in the face of uncertainty—of how much product is purchased, assuming sufficient supply is available at a given time. The *gap between supply and demand* is whether there is an excess in either demand or supply. If there is an excess in supply, a surplus exists and pricing will tend to be based on a set margin above the cost of manufacture. Under this scenario, price will tend to be a function of two variables: the rate of decline of cost and the magnitude of the excess of supply. If there is an excess in demand, a shortage will exist and pricing will tend to be a function of the value that the product *offers* in each particular market application. Possible markets with the highest product value-added will be satisfied first. The price is expected to be some proportion of the value-added of the application. Possible markets with lower value-added will only be partially supplied or not supplied at all. If one or more possible markets are not supplied, a shortage, additional supply will become available at later periods as manufacturers increase capacity to supply the unsatisfied demand for product. Depending on the degree of the gap between supply and demand, the supply or capacity will increase at either the maximum rate possible or the proportion of the maximum rate required to satisfy future predictions of needs (demand). A shortage will continue for multiple periods if either predictions or assumptions of the demand of the possible market underestimate the actual demand. Alternatively, a shortage may exist for multiple periods because future demand exceeds the ability to bring new capacity for satisfying demand on-line. Shortages in capacity allow firms to behave as monopolists or oligopolists and to obtain excess profits.

In many cases in the past, growth industries have been supply constrained. A lack of supply allows for oligopolistic behavior by manufacturers. During this time, the firms in the industry generate greater than normal profit, since the price of product is linked to customer perception of the value-added that is provided by the product, as opposed to the cost of manufacture. In response to these attractive market conditions, capacity tends to expand unless certain barriers to entry, such as intellectual property, prevent capacity expansion. Eventually, producers collectively overpredict demand resulting in the availability of greater capacity or potential supply than is required by market demand. At this point, the market-pricing regime changes from an oligopolistic pricing model to perfect competition. That is, price is now based on the cost of production as different suppliers lower their prices to ensure that they are able to use the productive capacity that they have invested in. In microeconomics, the price-taker model describes this scenario. For further details on the price-taker model, the reader is referred to the microeconomic pricing literature [6].

It is important to note that growth industries that are supply constrained are not always profitable. If a policy of forward pricing is adopted, firms will sell products at or below production cost to build market share; the result is a financial loss. The underlying logic is that profitability will increase as production volume increases, since the cost of production will decline rapidly due to learning curve effects [62–65]. Forward pricing can discourage entry of new firms by providing a financial barrier to entry. Such an approach favors customers in the short term, since the customers benefit from lower prices. However, in the long term, suppliers are more likely to be in a position of monopoly or oligopoly and may profit accordingly. Whereas, benefit or value-based pricing favors manufacturers, in the short-run, since the manufacturers are able to capture more of the value that the product offers the customers.

The overall gap between supply and demand, however, does not provide insight into the pricing and relative profitability of all suppliers. Generally, an emerging process technology results in separate products for a number of different markets. Suppliers are unlikely to be able to produce products for all markets, since different clusters of capital plant and production or technical skills are required for satisfaction of the needs of different markets [66, 67]. Consequently, one must consider the current and future availability of supply for specific markets, since most suppliers are expected to be limited in which markets they are capable of supplying. One consequence is that the capacity to supply may exceed customer demand for the process technology overall (a surplus), but that certain product markets with specific technical or performance characteristics may be supply constrained (demand exceeds supply—a shortage). This is critical since knowledge of differences in specifications or performance characteristics that are likely to be in short supply offers insights into which manufacturers are most likely to produce products that are perceived as valuable and are supply constrained (an important consideration for both national security and investment).

Identification of performance characteristics or properties in which a shortage of production capacity is likely offers insight into which technological challenges need to be overcome and intellectual property needs to be controlled to expand or constrict supply for a specific market [68, 69]. From the perspective of the supplier, a better understanding of which intellectual property needs to be controlled may result in higher prices and profits in a certain *market*. Alternatively, knowledge of which intellectual property or technical problems prevent rapid expansion of production is a question of great importance to governments if a lack of productive capacity impacts national security. In summary, the consideration of knowledge, intellectual property, and technical problems that constrict the ability to satisfy market demand for specific products can be identified. Since it is possible to identify the knowledge that restricts capacity, it is worth considering the implications and assessment of the duration and degree of the capacity restrictions.

There are many implications of the differences in supply and demand and insights into pricing and the value of intellectual property offered through this type of analysis. Prior to considering these implications to corporate strategy and government policy, how supply/demand gaps are identified through the operationalization of supply and demand forecasts is considered.

FORECASTING SUPPLY AND DEMAND GAPS

To determine the likely supply/demand gaps, we must first model the supply and demand for the different potential markets. Supply and demand for potential markets are highly uncertain. In the face of uncertainty, simulation is typically used to identify different possible scenarios [70–72]. Consequently, we must first determine the distribution of possible outcomes and then generate a large number of random scenarios to consider different possible future states and the likelihood of these occurring (based on current existing assumptions regarding the future). The process of randomly generating a large number of future outcomes, based on the distribution of possible outcomes, is referred to as bootstrapping or Monte Carlo simulation. Bootstrapping has been used to offer insight into a variety of questions that involve high levels of uncertainty [73–77]. Since the uncertainty is such a crucial issue, three examples are briefly considered to illustrate the determination of a distribution of possible outcomes.

1. IBM initially misestimated the size of the computer market—management believed it would be very small. Fortunately for IBM, their management introduced products that would dominate a market orders-of-magnitude larger than initial estimates. IBM's early market estimate was a single point, based on a set of assumptions that proved to be wrong. Other organizations and people produced estimates based on different sets of assumptions. The result of the differences in assumptions in some cases will lead to a forecast of larger or smaller forecasts than was the case with IBM. If the population of forecasts or estimates is taken, the *correct* forecast will be among this group. In addition, some forecasts will prove to be overly optimistic and others overly pessimistic.

2. The result of the competition between sales of Beta versus VHS format videocassette recorders is surprising to most. The Beta format was technically superior to VHS. Consequently, many people expected that this format would eventually dominate or capture the entire market. However, the proponents of VHS managed to overcome their product's technological inferiority, further details can be found in Ref. [78]. Many predicted that the Beta format would eventually dominate this market. Consequently, we would expect a distribution of forecasts to be heavily skewed towards high sales of Beta-based videocassette recorders. However, some manufacturers, movie distributors, video rental storeowners, and consumers saw that VHS offers advantages. These proponents of VHS technology clearly predicted sales of VCRs skewed towards the VHS format. Because if they did not consider this outcome to be possible, they would not have invested in the VHS-based technology. Consequently, the full distribution of possible outcomes includes the possibility of dominance for either technology, as well as both technologies capturing different shares of the market.

3. Finally, there is tremendous disagreement currently regarding the size of the cellular telephone market. Some suggest that the market for cellular telephones is at most one per person. However, optimists have suggested that the market may be as large as each person, each household, each vehicle, each pet, and each appliance. The actual outcome is likely to be contained in the distribution of possible outcomes. It is not possible to determine which of the possible future states is correct, but it is possible to determine the range of possible future states and the proportion of future states that fall in between or above specified limits that are deemed of interest to the forecaster.

The general steps for the determination and assessment of opportunities/threats associated with supply/demand gaps for emerging technologies are as follows:

1. forecast demand,
2. forecast supply,
3. determine gaps between supply and demand,
4. interpret implications of the gaps.

To determine the demand for product, it is necessary to identify the markets that will be served by the technology, determine the model for forecasting the size of each market as a function of time, and then utilize simulation and bootstrapping to determine a confidence range for each market at each time period under consideration.

Markets

The first task is to determine how many different potential markets there are for the technology. These markets may offer substantial historic data (over 10 years), a few years of historic data or may involve markets for products that have not yet been launched. Depending on the age of the market, different methods for forecasting market growth can be used (see Linton and Walsh [79] for further discussion of this).

Demand Forecasting

It is likely that different techniques will be used for forecasting different markets, since some markets may be 10 years old, whereas other products may not be introduced until a few years after the date that the forecast model is defined. Once forecasting methods and parameters are selected for each of the different markets, the markets are simulated using bootstrapping. The results are collected in such a manner that they can be considered in terms of a confidence range. (A confidence range being the likelihood in which a forecast will fall between specified values.)

Supply

Having collected forecast demand data for the product markets, we now consider the capacity or ability to supply to meet demand requirements. The current productive capacity must be determined. In addition, the following information is required:

1. increases in capacity due to learning curve effects—a range of estimates must be made to define the likely distribution of learning curve effects (see Yelle [64]),
2. decreases in capacity due to equipment wear and tear and plans for retirement of existing capacity,
3. plans to increase capacity and the timing of these capacity increases (also need to factor in Points 1 and 2 to these calculations),
4. the rate at which capacity can be added and estimates of the cost of increasing productive capacity at different rates (this indicates the potential for supplier to respond to short falls in productive capacity).

Forecasting Excess Supply or Demand

The supply can be determined based on the current productive capacity, and the decisions regarding additional capacity can be based on the demand for product in each market. The difference between the capacity to supply a particular market and market demand can now be determined. If supply exceeds demand, then all customers are likely to have their orders for product filled. Since there is additional capacity (excess supply), it is likely that suppliers will compete on a price basis to ensure that their plant is used at as high a capacity as possible. Consequently, the price of product will be based on the cost of manufacture plus some margin to cover other expenses and a reasonable profit (perfect competition). Alternatively, if only a few suppliers are expected in the market, the firm's strategy may involve implicit price collusion. Either way, the firm can expect some decline in profit margin.

If demand exceeds supply, we expect productive capacity to be added rapidly and the price of the product to reflect the value that customers extract from its application (monopoly or oligopoly product rents). Premiums may be charged, since customers will be willing to pay up to the value the product contributes to their specific application. For some customers, that value of the product is lower than the current price of the product, in which case, they will wait until capacity increases or overall demand declines so they can purchase the product at a price that is equal or below the value they perceive the product to have for their application. The speed of product adoption by a specific potential customer is positively related to the difference between the value of the product in the application under consideration and the asking price for the product. Consequently, opportunities exist where product value can exceed initial price by an order of magnitude; such value–price differences are often the justification for investment in a portfolio of start-ups by venture capital firms. Through modeling of supply and demand data, it is possible to eliminate ventures that do not meet these criteria and identify a smaller group of manufacturing and/or design firms that do meet these criteria under certain circumstances. Furthermore, one can identify what those circumstances are. To demonstrate this method of modeling supply and demand, MEMS are used as an illustration.

AN APPLICATION OF THE FORECAST: MEMS

MEMS are tiny physical structures manufactured using processes that are similar to those used by the microelectronics industry to produce electronic devices. MEMS can be used to sense, process, and respond to stimuli in their environment. MEMS have been applied as a substitute in markets where a reduction in size and weight is advantageous. For example, in aerospace applications, traditional micromechanical sensors have been replaced by MEMS due to the tremendous savings in fuel requirements resulting from the low weight of MEMS sensors. MEMS are also used for applications where miniaturization allows applications that were not possible before. An example of this is the Chemical-lab-on-a-chip. Miniaturization allows for the mass production of low-cost small chemistry tests that can detect neurotoxins or biohazards that can be incorporated into the garments of soldiers, rescue workers, or other people that are at a high risk of being exposed to dangerous chemicals or organisms.

To analyze supply and demand gaps in the MEMS industry, we first must determine the different markets that are relevant to this technology. Many markets and applications already exist. Other markets are expected to be established and grow in the short to medium term. Based on the Tschulena's [80] study, 26 markets were identified for this process technology (see Table 58-1). Half of these markets currently exist, the remaining 13 markets are expected to become established and grow in the near to medium term.

Having identified the markets in Table 58-1, the next step is to forecast demand in the face of uncertainty. Due to the relative youth of even most of the existing markets, market data on recent sales are either nonexistent or of questionable accuracy. Since there is substantial uncertainty, our forecast must reflect this. As discussed earlier, forecasting under uncertainty can be achieved using the Monte Carlo method (bootstrapping) from a distribution of possible outcomes. In the case of MEMS, this is achieved by collecting information from different sources on market size and anticipated market size. Some of these forecasts are exceedingly positive. Whereas other forecasts that are offered are rather pessimistic. These forecast values are treated as a

TABLE 58-1 Summary of Existing and Emerging Markets in Microsystems and Preferred Production Technologies for Their Manufacture

Current Applications	Emerging Applications
Print heads—HARM or bulk	Drug delivery systems—HARM or SSM
Pacemakers—HARM or SSM	Optical switches—any
In vitro diagnostics—HARM	Lab on a chip—HARM
Hearing aids—any	Magneto optical heads—HARM
Pressure sensors—bulk	Projection valves—any
Chemical sensors—bulk or HARM	Coil on chips—any
Infrared images—HARM or SSM	Micro relays—any
Accelerometers—HARM or SSM	Micromotors—HARM
Gyroscopes—HARM or SSM	Inclinometers—bulk or SSM
Magnetoresistive sensors—HARM	Injection nozzles—HARM
Microspectrometers—HARM or SSM	Anticollision sensors—HARM or SSM
Optical displays—HARM or SSM	Electric noses—any
Hard disk drive heads—bulk or HARM	RF devices—HARM or SSM

uniform distribution with equal weights given to each market size forecast. In this case, the highest and lowest values of each forecast are treated as minima and maxima. Intermediate points are used to indicate changes in the steepness of the slope (for an example, see Figure 58-1).

This process is repeated for each of the markets using published values or expert opinions for the future dates of interest. Once the distributions for demand forecasts for all possible markets are considered, the possible outcomes are obtained for each market using bootstrapping (see Table 58-2 for an example). The number of bootstrap values to be resampled to obtain stable confidence ranges is a subject of some debate. For example, Booth and Sarkar [81] and Hall [82] disagree, stating that as few as 10 samples are required or as many as 800 samples might be needed. Consequently, we suggest that resampling should be conducted at least 1,000 times for each application or market under consideration.

Forecasting Supply

For forecasts of supply, one must identify which markets can be supplied by the same set of physical capital and production and technical skills. In MEMS manufacturing,

FIGURE 58-1 Depiction of the Distribution for the Market Size of a Market Based on Different Opinions of Market Size

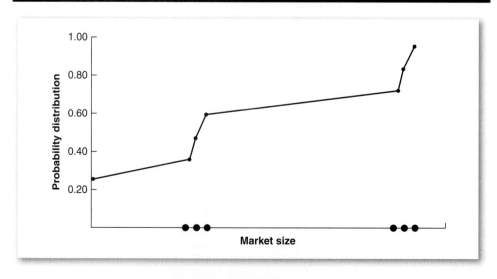

TABLE 58-2 Depiction of the Determination of a Forecast Value Based on the Generation of a Random Value

Market	Distribution	Example of Distribution in Parentheses and Randomly Generated Value	Example of Assigned Value Based on Randomly Generated Number
A	standard normal	(50,10)−1	40
B	uniform	(3,6) 0.2	3.6
C	expert opinion	(5,7,10) 0.75	8.5

there are three types of production technology—surface micromachining (SSM), bulk micromachining, and high-aspect-ratio MEMS (HARM). Certain MEMS-based products can only be made with specific technologies (see Table 58-1). Consequently, one must:

1. identify which of these technologies can produce which products.
2. identify what special capabilities, if any, are required to manufacture a product with a given technology.

For MEMS, the most critical production ability and product characteristics are the ability to integrate with electronics, feature size, precision required, product volume desired, and differences in requirements for base materials by the application. Having determined the characteristics necessary for a manufacturer to be able to supply the market for a specific product, the question of interest are the following:

1. What are the current capabilities for production in the world?
2. What rate will these facilities be able to add on additional capacity (and at what cost)?
3. What rate can new entrants add capacity to this market (what are the barriers to setting up green-field production sites)?

Using the information on possible demand, current capacity, and the rate at which capacity can be added in the future, it is possible to determine the future potential capacity to supply. These information requirements may seem daunting. However, most of this information is available from Industry Associations [83]. In MANCEF's recent study of production foundries, 17 production-proven foundries exist. Of these foundries, 14 can produce products made with bulk micromachining, 9 can produce products made with SSM, and 2 can produce products made with HARM. It has also been determined that production capacity in HARM or bulk micromachining can be added in under a year. However, additional production capacity based on SSM requires up to 2 years before product is manufactured. Consequently, products that can be manufactured only with SSM processes are the only products that are likely to be in short supply. In the case of products based on the other two-production technologies, ownership and protection of product design are likely to be the basis of monopoly or oligopoly profits.

Given the different possible markets for MEMS and distribution of beliefs of market demand, one can generate a population of possible values for MEMS sales. Given information on the current availability to produce MEMS-based products of different types and the likely range of capabilities to meet demand in the future, one can generate a population of predictions indicating the likelihood of demand being met or exceeded by supply. If demand is met or exceeded by supply, either pricing will be based on margin or manufacturers will switch production capacity to satisfy unmet demand for another product, thereby assuring that multiple markets are under the more profitable "value pricing" regime, then the customer preferred less profitable "margin pricing" regime.

Having briefly considered the MEMS industry, we have determined that due to the ability to rapidly add manufacturing capacity for either HARM or bulk micromachining, production competence in either of these manufacturing technologies is unlikely to lead to sustained competitive advantage. However, in the short-run surface, micromachining facilities may be exceedingly profitable since the delay in ability to add on additional capacity may result in product shortages allowing firms with SSM capabilities to behave like oligopolists and extract higher than typical profits. Alternatively, excess profits will result from the ownership of appropriable product designs (not from the ability to manufacture the products specified by the designs). Having considered forecasting supply and demand and imbalances between supply and demand for emerging process technologies generally and MEMS more specifically, the implications of these forecasts to government policy and corporate strategy are considered.

IMPLICATIONS FOR GOVERNMENT POLICY AND CORPORATE STRATEGY

There are a variety of implications of the results of a model of supply and demand in the face of uncertainty to both corporations and government [73, 84]. In the case of government, it can be determined whether there are sufficient supply capabilities to meet both national security needs and economic interests. By considering current supply capabilities and the ability to add on additional supply, one may assess which parts of the potential future markets can be supplied and which markets are likely to be supply constrained. If it is apparent that possible markets of interest are supply constrained, then the government can take action to support or encourage activities that will eliminate the knowledge and production gaps that exist—if a constrained supply is considered undesirable. More generally, the model offers insights into the size of the market and the degree of likely competition and profitability of participating firms. Such information is of assistance in developing national policy of whether or not to target a specific technology or sector. Once decisions are made about what type of support or encouragement the government may offer, simulations can be run to determine the different likely effects that these new policies may have on the earlier model. In addition to the implications for policy makers and government that have just been reviewed, there are also important implications for corporations.

Supply and demand forecasting of emerging process technologies offers benefits to corporations. Using these forecasts, corporations can determine whether a potential market(s) is likely to be oversupplied or undersupplied. In cases of undersupply, investment in or maintenance of existing production capacity increases is attractive. Similarly, the value of intellectual property protection can be determined by considering the effect different types of intellectual property will have on different potential markets and the gap between supply and demand. If the intellectual property has a high value-added for a specific application or market and is appropriable, through, for example, patenting, then the intellectual property has a high value. In fact, the value of such a design can be calculated using real options [85]—through consideration of the magnitude of the value-added, the proportion of the value-added obtainable as part of the sales price and the likely number of units sold. Furthermore, companies can determine what the value is of additional capacity and any premium associated with capacity that is flexible enough to produce products in more than one market. In summary, the supply/demand model under uncertainty can assist corporations in determining whether to invest in production capacity, the value of flexible manufacturing capacity and the value of protecting, purchasing, and selling intellectual property.

Having considered how to forecast supply/demand gaps and their implications to both governments and corporations, conclusions are offered.

CONCLUSIONS

A method is offered to calculate supply and demand in emerging markets under uncertainty. This is an important advance, since it allows for uncertainty to be taken into consideration for forecasting, which, although realistic, was often missing in the past. By taking uncertainty into account and calculation of a population of possible customer demands and supper production, the degree of shortage or surplus is identified. This offers insights into the pricing and profitability of these markets. Furthermore, it can be used for assessing the value of flexibility in manufacturing and the value of specific intellectual property.

To better benefit this method, consideration of technological trajectories and substitution effects for competing technologies must be considered. Furthermore, learning curve effects for existing players and new entrants must be clearly defined—either as a value or a range of values.

Acknowledgements
The author would like to thank Hal Linstone, Steven Walsh, and two anonymous reviewers for their valuable input that has notably improved this paper.

About the Author
Jonathan Linton is an assistant professor of the Lally School of Management and Technology at Rensselaer Polytechnic University. He holds a PhD in Management Science and an MBA from York University, Toronto. He also holds a BESc (Materials) and a BSc (Biology) from the University of Western Ontario, London. Dr. Linton is a registered professional engineer. His work considers issues at the intersection of operations management and emerging technologies. He has published in a variety of journals including *IEEE Transactions on Engineering Management, R&D Management, Interfaces, and Technological Forecasting and Social Change.*

References

1. J.A. Schumpeter, Capitalism, Socialism, and Democracy, Harvard School Press, Cambridge, MA, 1939.
2. N.D. Kondratieff, The Long Wave Cycle, Richardson and Snyder, New York, 1984.
3. J.D. Linton, Forecasting the marketing diffusion of disruptive and discontinuous innovation, IEEE Trans. Eng. Manage. 49 (4) (2002) 365–374.
4. G. Moore, Crossing the Chasm, Harper Business Press, New York, 1991.
5. J. Bower, C. Christensen, Disruptive technologies, catching the wave, Harvard Bus. Rev. 73 (1) (1995) 43–53.
6. P.A. Samuelson, W.D. Nordhaus, Economics, McGraw-Hill, New York, 1997.
7. H.A. Linstone, Complexity science: implications for forecasting, Technol. Forecast. Soc. Change 62 (1999) 79–90.
8. M. Porter, Competitive Advantage, Harvard Business School Press, Boston, 1980.
9. M. Porter, Competitive Advantage of Nations, Free Press, New York, 1990.
10. S. Walsh, B. Kirchhoff, Entrepreneurs opportunities in technology-based markets, in: P. Phan (Ed.), Technological Entrepreneurship, Information Age Publishing, Greenwich, CT, 2002, pp. 17–31.
11. J.P. Martino, Technological Forecasting for Decision Making, American Elsevier Publishing, New York, 1972.
12. A.L. Porter, A.T. Roper, T.W. Mason, F.A. Rossini, J. Banks, Forecasting of Management and Technology, Wiley, New York, 1991.
13. S.H. Kim, T.H. Kim, Y. Kim, I.G. Na, Korean energy demand in the new millennium: outlook and policy implications 2000–2005, Energy Policy 29 (11) (2001) 899–999.
14. S.E. Krentz, R.S. Gish, Using scenario analysis to determine managed care strategy, Healthc. Financ. Manage. 54 (9) (2000) 41–43.

15. A.L. Gilbert, Using multiple scenario analysis to map the competitive futurescape: a practice-based perspective, Compet. Intell. Rev. 11 (2) (2000) 12–33.
16. S. Baker, D. Ponniah, S. Smith, Techniques for the analysis of risks in major projects, J. Oper. Res. Soc. 49 (6) (1998) 567–572.
17. J.A. Bers, G.S. Lynn, C.L. Spurling, A venerable tool for a new application: using scenario analysis for formulating strategies for emerging technologies in emerging markets, Eng. Manag. J. 9 (2) (1997) 33–40.
18. A. Sheel, Monte Carlo simulations and scenario analysis—decision-making tools for hoteliers, Cornell Hotel Restaur. Adm. Q. 36 (5) (1995) 18–26.
19. Y. Matsuoka, M. Kainuma, T. Morita, Scenario analysis of global warming using the Asian Pacific Integrated Model (AIM), Energy Policy 23 (4–5) (1995) 357–370.
20. T.K. Moulik, B.H. Dholakia, R.H. Dholakia, K.V. Ramani, P. Shukla, Energy planning in India: the relevance of regional planning for national policy, Energy Policy 20 (9) (1992) 836–846.
21. B.J.C. Yuan, P.C. Chang, A study forecasting the development tendency of the textile industry in Taiwan, Int. J. Technol. Manag. 24 (2,3) (2002) 296–313.
22. S. Breiner, K. Cuhls, H. Grupp, Technology foresight using a Delphi approach: a Japanese–German study, R&D Manag. 24 (2) (1994) 141–153.
23. S.P. Schnaars, S.L. Chia, C.M. Maloles, Five modern lessons from a 55-year-old technological forecast, J. Prod. Innov. Manag. 10 (1993) 66–74.
24. J.E. Hanke, A.G. Reitsch, Business Forecasting, 6th ed., Prentice Hall, Upper Saddle River, NJ, 1986.
25. J.H. Wilson, B. Keating, Business Forecasting, 2nd ed., Irwin, Chicago, 1994.
26. R.N. Foster, Innovation: the Attacker's Advantage, McKinsey & Company, New York, 1986.

27. T. Modis, Fractal aspects of natural growth, Technol. Forecast. Soc. Change 47 (1) (1994) 63–73.

28. T. Modis, A. DeBecker, Chaoslike states can be expected before and after logistic growth, Technol. Forecast. Soc. Change 41 (2) (1992) 111–120.

29. F.M. Bass, A new product growth model for consumer durables, Manag. Sci. 15 (5) (1969) 215–227.

30. P.J. Palmer, D.J. Williams, An analysis of technology trends within the electronics industry, Microelectron. Int. 17 (1) (2000) 13–27.

31. K. Hatten, M.L. Piccoli, An evaluation of a technological forecasting method by computer-based simulation, Acad. Manage. J. 8 (1973) 60–83.

32. J.C. Fisher, R.H. Pry, A simple substitution model of technological change, Technol. Forecast. Soc. Change 3 (1971) 5–88.

33. R.C. Lenz, Rates of adoption/substitution in technological change, Technology Futures, Austin, TX, 1985.

34. T. Islam, D.G. Fiebig, N. Meade, Modelling multinational telecommunications demand with limited data, Int. J. Forecast. 18 (4) (2002) 605–627.

35. J. Morrison, How to use diffusion models in new product forecasting, J. Bus. Forecast. Methods Syst. 15 (2) (1996) 6–9.

36. C.L. Lackman, Logit forecasting of high tech products, Ind. Manag. 35 (2) (1993) 20–21.

37. J.C. Lee, K.W. Lu, S.C. Horng, Crystal technological forecasting with nonlinear models, J. Forecast. 11 (3) (1992) 195–206.

38. S.A. Morris, D. Pratt, Analysis of the Lotka–Volterra competition equations as a technological substitution model, Technol. Forecast. Soc. Change 70 (2) (2003) 103–133.

39. C. Marchetti, N. Nakicenovic, The Dynamic of Energy Systems and the Logistic Substitution Model (Report RR-79-13), International Institute for Applied Systems Analysis, Laxenburg, Austria, 1979.

40. C. Marchetti, Darwin and the future of ISDN, in: M. Bonatti, M. Decina (Eds.), Traffic Engineering for ISDN Design and Planning, North-Holland, New York, 1988, pp. 77–96.

41. M.N. Sharif, C. Kabir, A generalized model for forecasting technological substitution, Technol. Forecast. Soc. Change 8 (4) (1976) 353–364.

42. J.R. Bright, Practical Technology Forecasting: Concepts and Exercises, Pemaquid Press, Austin, TX, 1978.

43. P. McGeehin, UK Technology foresight-sensors strategy for 2015, Sens. Rev. 22 (4) (2002) 303–319.

44. G. Reger, Technology foresight in companies: from an indicator to a network and process perspective, Technol. Anal. Strateg. Manag. 13 (4) (2001) 533–559.

45. S. Hanney, M. Henkel, D. von Walden Laing, Making and implementing foresight policy to engage the academic community: health and life scientists' involvement in, and response to, development of the UK's technology foresight programme, Res. Policy 30 (8) (2001) 1203–1227.

46. L. Sanz-Menendez, C. Cabello, Understanding technology foresight: the relevance of its S&T policy context, Int. J. Technol. Manag. 21 (7,8) (2001) 661–667.

47. E. Massod, The changing culture of British science, Nature 393 (6680) (1998) 8.

48. L. Georghiou, The UK technology foresight programme, Futures 28 (4) (1996) 359–377.

49. F. Tessun, Scenario analysis and early warning systems at Daimler-Benz Aerospace, Compet. Intell. Rev. 8 (4) (1997) 30–40.

50. M.D. Ferguson, Forecasting as a learning tool, J. Bus. Forecast. Methods Syst. 11 (3) (1992) 27–41.

51. J.W. Forrester, Economic conditions ahead: understanding the Kondratieff wave, Futurist 19 (3) (1985) 16–20.

52. J.W. Forrester, Global modelling revisited, Futures 14 (2) (1982) 95–110.

53. C. Kabir, M.N. Sharif, P. Adulbhan, System dynamics modeling for forecasting technological substitution, Comput. Ind. Eng. 5 (1) (1981) 7–21.

54. D.L. Meadows, The Limits to Growth: a Report for the Club of Rome's Project on the Predicament of Mankind, Universe Books, New York, 1972.

55. M.M. Mackay, M. Metcalfe, Multiple method forecasts for discontinuous innovations, Technol. Forecast. Soc. Change 69 (3) (2002) 221–232.

56. T. Nagle, Economic foundations for pricing, J. Bus. 57 (1) (1984) S3–S26.

57. H. Demsetz, Barriers to entry, Am. Econ. Rev. 72 (1982) 47–57; Disruptive innovation, in: D.F. Kocaoglu, T.R. Anderson (Eds.), Technology Management in the Knowledge Era, Portland State University, Portland, 2001, pp. 391–399.

58. G. Loomes, Why oligopoly prices don't stick, J. Econ. Stud. 8 (1) (1981) 37–46.

59. F.M. Scherer, Industrial Market Structure and Economic Performance, 2nd ed., Rand McNally & Company, Chicago, 1980.

60. K.S. Palda, Pricing Decisions and Marketing Policy, Prentice Hall, Englewood Cliffs, NJ, 1971.

61. J. Robinson, The Economics of Imperfect Competition, Macmillan, London, 1933.

62. R.S. Blancett, Learning from productivity learning curves, Res. Technol. Manag. 3 (2002) 54–58.

63. L. Argote, D. Epple, Learning curves in manufacturing, Science 247 (4945) (1990) 920–924.

64. L.E. Yelle, The learning curve: historical review and comprehensive survey, Decis. Sci. 10 (2) (1979) 302–328.

65. T.P. Wright, Factors effecting the cost of airplanes, J. Aeronaut. Sci. 3 (4) (1936) 122–128.

66. C.K. Prahalad, G. Hamel, Competing for the Future, Harvard Business School Press, Boston, 1994.

67. S. Walsh, J.D. Linton, The competence pyramid: a framework for identifying and analyzing firm and industry competence, Technol. Anal. Strateg. Manag. 13 (2) (2001) 165–177.

68. R.J. Van Wyk, Management of technology: new frameworks, Technovation 7 (1992) 341–351.

69. R.J. Van Wyk, Panoramic scanning and the technological environment, Technovation 2 (2) (1984) 100–120.

70. A. Law, W. Kelton, Simulation Modeling and Analysis, 3rd ed., Irwin/McGraw-Hill, Burr Ridge, IL, 2000.

71. J. Evans, D. Olson, Introduction to Simulation and Risk Analysis, Prentice Hall, Upper Saddle River, NJ, 1998.

72. B. Khoshnevis, Discrete Systems Simulation, McGraw-Hill, New York, 1994.

73. J.D. Linton, J.S. Yeomans, The role of forecasting in sustainability, Technol. Forecast. Soc. Change 70 (1) (2002) 21–38.

74. A.C. Davison, D.V. Hinckley, Bootstrap Methods and their Applications, Cambridge Univ. Press, New York, 1997.

75. B. Efron, R. Tibshirani, An Introduction to the Bootstrap, Chapman & Hall, New York, 1993.

76. J.H. Bookbinder, A.E. Lordahl, Estimation of inventory re-order levels using the bootstrap statistical procedure, IIE Trans. 21 (4) (1989) 302–312.

77. S.C. Peters, D.A. Freedman, Using the bootstrap to evaluate forecasting equations, J. Forecast. 4 (1985) 251–265.

78. M. Cusumano, Y. Mylonadis, R.S. Rosenbloom, Strategic maneuvering and mass-market dynamics: the triumph of VHS over Beta, Bus. Hist. Rev. 66 (1) (1992) 51–94.

79. J.D. Linton, S. Walsh, Forecasting micro electro mechanical systems: a disruptive innovation, in: D.F. Kocaoglu, T.R. Anderson (Eds.), Technology Management in the Knowledge Era, Portland State University, Portland, 2001, pp. 391–399.

80. G. Tschulena, MST markets and products, Proceedings of the Commercialization of Microsystems '96, Semiconductor Equipment and Materials International (SEMI), Mountain View, CA, 1996, pp. 69–76.

81. J.G. Booth, S. Sarkar, Monte Carlo approximation of bootstrap variances, Am. Stat. 52 (1998) 354–363.

82. P. Hall, On the number of bootstrap simulations required to construct a confidence interval, Ann. Stat. 14 (1986) 1453–1462.

83. MANCEF, International Microsystems Roadmap, SEMI, San Jose, CA, 2002.

84. S. Walsh, J.D. Linton, Infrastructure and emerging markets: implications for strategy and policy makers, Eng. Manag. J. 12 (2) (2000) 23–31.

85. L. Trigeorgis, Real Options. Managerial Flexibility and Strategy in Resource Allocation, MIT Press, Cambridge, MA, 1996.

SECTION

X

THE FUTURE OF INNOVATION AND ITS MANAGEMENT

Introduction

As we begin our final section, we want to take a moment to reflect on the previous sections, the enormity of the discipline of innovation, and what the future might hold for innovation progress. First, we hope that we have compiled and provided important insights into the history and the legacy of the innovation researchers who are a part of the innovation discipline. Through various authors and researchers, we have provided the reasons for innovation, we have presented authors who have offered insights into how innovation in organizations progresses over time, and we have provided a snapshot of innovation and inventive thought from early in the twentieth century. Moreover, we focused on the creation, adoption, diffusion, and implementation of important areas for innovation such as product, process, and organizational innovation. We also included a special section presenting insights into service innovations that we view as a major research area for the twenty-first century. We conclude this book with a section addressing the practical and sometimes sticky issues of innovation management, especially as they relate to the risk that managers and consumers take on a daily basis. We offer our thoughts as a platform for future innovation thought and research.

Second, we provide a balanced assortment of innovation thought that has been generated over the past century. More than likely, we have neglected some articles, book chapters, and monographs that surely merit inclusion and we apologize for those oversights. We have, however, addressed the primary areas of innovation and, although it is our intent that the selected research be biased toward more current studies, we hope that we have also represented the tenor of the research that forms the groundwork of the discipline of innovation that was performed since 1929. As was stated at an innovation symposium not so long ago, the arena of innovation research is enormous; however, it is incumbent on current-day researchers and students of innovation to become familiar with all aspects of the discipline including its history to increase their understanding and better perform their current research.

Third, a major purpose of our effort here is to consolidate but also to commemorate the many researchers who have worked tirelessly in an effort to provide the world with information that we hope will be used not only to populate academic journals, but to develop new goods, services, and organizations that will benefit society and people worldwide. As can be noted by the statements of many of the authors included herein, the battle and opportunity to understand and describe the many issues surrounding innovation in its multitude of forms is far from won. In this final section, we offer eight articles that provide us with a peek at the potential of innovation research and new product development (NPD).

In the first selection David Wilemon and Murray Millson offer a glimpse into what they see as the future of an NPD process. Because no one can view something that has never existed, this article attempts to use the current state of NPD to provide a stepping stone to the future. The authors perceive that this is a good vantage point because many new product developers are currently progressing in this direction. The traditional NPD process is first described step by step and then analyzed in this article. Next, the authors describe the flaws contained within what they refer to as the current NPD paradigm. The current NPD paradigm encompasses the seven steps of the NPD process as depicted in most of the current literature. The seven steps include new product strategy development, idea generation, concept screening and evaluation, business analysis, product development, test marketing, and commercialization. Flaws such as the process' linearity and the growing imperative for global NPD are thought to be two important paradigm shift indicators. These indicators present conditions under which the current NPD paradigm cannot successfully operate. In terms of Thomas Kuhn, these indicators demonstrate that the current paradigm may not be able to solve the kinds of problems that remain in the innovation and NPD arena. The authors then present a concept of a *new* new product development paradigm that is grounded in both innovation and organizational theory. This new paradigm includes features such as a non-linear process that makes it applicable to a sequence of NPD projects as opposed to a single project, the inclusion of both a consumer and an R&D knowledge-base as a stepping-off point for new projects, and relationships based on the concepts of empowerment, involvement, and customer satisfaction to provide links to the human and market elements associated with the development of new products. The authors conclude this article with implications for managers that include admonitions to encourage organizational learning, to emphasize innovation and quality, to develop a prospector culture (Miles & Snow), to develop specific product technologies and core competencies, to create an NPD acceleration capability, to develop an innovation infrastructure, and to foster a holistic NPD perspective.

The second article, by Michael A. Mische and Warren Bennis, examines the process of reinventing an organization through reengineering. They point out that they are in no way implying that the process of reinventing an organization is a simple, Band-Aid procedure. They indicate that the intent of this reinvention process is to renew leadership and optimize an enterprise's competitive position. They emphasize that today's environment and defining values differ greatly from those of much of the twentieth century, but also that the organizational theories developed by the classical theorists such as Frederick Taylor and Abraham Maslow continue to form the cornerstone of operations for both American and Global organizations. The focus here is on the transformation of corporate cultures and processes to obtain a significant competitive position that, as the authors point out, requires radical and dramatic operational and organizational changes. Mische and Bennis note that traditional doctrines, management practices, business activities, and organizational paradigms must be challenged. No *sacred cows* should be left unquestioned nor stones unturned. This reengineering process results in the radical redeployment of enterprisewide resources as well as human capital into cross-functional processes and structures to optimize shareholder wealth, competitive positioning, and societal contributions. The authors list many tenets of reinvention, some of which are: increased throughput through productivity, achieving quantum results, and eliminating low-value work and hierarchical organizations. The crux of this reinvention process can be recognized by noting that the majority of an organization's transformation is cultural, occurring as managers and employees move from hierarchical structures and classical command behaviors to flat structures and empowered work groups.

For the third selection in this final section, we offer the research of Shona L. Brown and Kathleen M. Eisenhardt, in which they attack the NPD literature and divide it into three streams: that which views NPD as a rational plan, that which views it as a communications web, and that which recognizes NPD as a problem-solving process. They then synthesize the results of these three streams of literature and compose a model of factors that are associated with the success of newly developed products. They proceed to specify potential paths for further investigations into the area of NPD success by reviewing their model for concepts and links that are not well-defined or appear to be missing. The authors based the construction of their integrative model of product development on the observation that the current literature has a large number of overlapping and complementary sets of constructs. For example, they note that the rational plan perspective provides a sweeping view of NPD that gets ever narrower as the researcher moves to the problem-solving perspective and then to the communications web perspective. Even so, there are many constructs, such as the development team and new product success measures, that are employed in the rational plan that are also employed in the communications web and problem-solving perspectives. Moreover, the authors demonstrate that the three NPD literature streams have complementary theoretical approaches. They summarize the discussion of their integrative model by reiterating that the innovation literature is fragmented and varied, and that the three streams of literature that they have identified provide a superb basis for an integrative model of NPD such as that described in their research. Finally, they suggest that there are vast arenas to be probed in the discipline of NPD and that their model can assist in these investigations.

Cornelius Herstatt and Eric von Hippel present a case study based on von Hippel's concept of "lead user" methods. In this selection, the authors report on a successful field application of the lead user method in a low-tech environment to determine concepts necessary for the development of new industrial products. These researchers investigated a firm that produced construction products and materials. It is evident from the results achieved by these researchers that the lead user method continues to hold great promise for industrial product developers. The traditional market research process is described in conjunction with the lead user process. It is noted that, whereas the traditional market research process employs large samples of potential new product users, the lead user approach uses only a small sample of potential users. Additionally, the traditional market research process tends to investigate potential users from an arms-length perspective. The lead user process attempts to bring potential users into a joint development process of new products. Such joint development is often possible because lead users are defined as firms that face specific, identified needs that the general market will face in the future, but lead users will face those needs much sooner, and expect to significantly gain from obtaining solutions to identified problems and needs. There are four steps in the process of lead user market research. First, identify characteristics, trends, and other indicators that separate lead users from other potential users in the market. Second, identify a couple of lead users by employing the characteristics isolated in the first step. Third, a small group of potential lead users is brought together with the engineering and marketing departments of the research firm to develop a product concept that both solves the lead user's problems and is responsive to the design and manufacturing concerns of the researching firm. The final step in the lead user approach is to test the product concept with other firms in the industry to understand whether or not those firms might have a need for such a product currently or some time in the future. In conclusion, the authors note that the lead user method proved to be less costly, identified promising new product concepts much faster, and provided better outcomes for the participating firm in this case study than other methods of market research have done.

In the fifth article, Edward Roberts reviews the years from approximately 1921 through 1988 with a focus on where invention and innovation research has been and where it is heading. He begins with his definition of innovation, equating it to the sum of invention plus exploitation. He then describes a model of the management of technology and describes the model's associated process as creating new knowledge, generating new ideas focused on new and enhanced products, developing those new ideas into operating prototypes, and transferring those prototypes to manufacturing, distribution, and use. Roberts notes two key generalizations regarding the management of technology. First, technological innovation is a multistage process that has significant variations in its primary tasks as well as the managerial issues and effective management practices that occur during these stages. Second, innovation occurs through efforts carried out primarily within organizational contexts involving frequent interaction with external technological and marketing environments. Roberts then focuses his discussion on three major concepts associated with the management of technology: staffing, structure, and strategy. The author concludes his paper by pointing to a few important axioms, such as:

1. group diversity has a major influence on technical performance,
2. competitive product profiling is a useful method for initiating technical planning, and
3. "market pull" far more often leads to successful innovations than does "technology push."

Luke Pittaway and associates present an in-depth analysis of the existing literature surrounding the relationship between an organization's capacity to innovate and its networking propensity and knowledge. The authors performed an extensive review of various literature databases to establish their information sources and have provided a detailed perspective of their analytic and qualitative approaches to this process. A few interesting findings of this literature review process, as described by the authors are: The preponderance of innovation networking research has been performed in the United Kingdom and the United States with fewer studies being carried out in European or Asian countries; the academic disciplines performing research in the areas of innovation and networking include economic and regional policy, organizational behavior, sociology, operations management, political economy, entrepreneurship and small business, technology management, marketing, and strategic management; and the primary journals that had published this type of research at the time of the writing of this paper included *Research Policy, Journal of Business Venturing, Regional Studies, Technovation,* and *International Journal of Technology Management.* Their literature review indicated that the major benefits to be obtained through networking include risk sharing, market access, accelerating new products to market, combining complementary skills, safeguarding intellectual property rights (IPR), and accessing *external* knowledge. With the benefits of networking for innovation in mind, there appears to be no consensus as to the network configuration that is *best* in all situations. Therefore, different organizational strategies can dictate various network structures and governance approaches. Luke Pittaway and associates additionally analyze the impact that networking with suppliers, customers, third parties, science partners, finance partners, and institutional entities such as incubators, science parks, and clusters of firms, as well as network governance and management, have on the relationship between innovation and organizational networking. They conclude with summarizing thoughts regarding network failure and limitations of innovation networks relative to organizational innovativeness.

The seventh article in our concluding section focuses on the future of innovation and especially radical innovations within large, dominant organizations. Chandy and associates posit that beliefs associated with radical innovativeness or *managerial expectations* regarding the potential consequences of investment in radical innovations that innovation managers in large, dominant firms hold, can play a crucial role in explaining the discrepancy in research findings relative to the relationship between the dominance (greater investments, greater market share, and greater resources than competitors) of large firms and their propensity to adopt or develop radical innovations. Such radical innovations require substantially different technological and marketing skills than are typically associated with existing products and technologies. The authors employ a variety of research tools, including experimental techniques based on a business "gaming" software platform, survey research, and in-depth interviews as well as field studies to demonstrate the relationships among organizational dominance, managerial expectations, and radical innovation in addition to positioning these associations in commercial contexts. The focus of analysis in their field study is the association between Internet banking, as a radical innovation, and the managerial expectations and responses of brick-and-mortar bank managers to this potentially disruptive technology. In the experimental portion of their study, they manipulated their treatment groups by proposing to one treatment group that a new technology would make their existing banking technology obsolete. Their proposition for the second treatment group was that a new banking technology would complement their existing banking technology. The study results suggest that dominant organizations invest more heavily in radical innovation than less dominant organizations. Also, informing study *treatment managers* of dominant organizations that new technologies will make their existing technologies obsolete is significantly related to radical innovation investment. However, informing study *treatment managers* of dominant organizations that new technologies will *complement* (provide ancillary products) their existing technologies provided mixed results when a comparison of experimental and field findings was performed.

In the final article, Henry Chesbrough provides another glimpse of the future of innovation in his description of *open innovation* and issues surrounding the management of intellectual property in the twenty-first century and beyond. Chesbrough points out that the current paradigm in innovation proposes that innovating organizations need to be entirely self-reliant in that they should perform processes such as idea generation, product development, product distribution, development financing, product servicing, and customer support without the assistance of other organizations. He suggests that this process be entitled *closed innovation.* The major reasons for managers behaving in this manner are based on the assumptions that one cannot be certain of the quality, availability, and capability of external organizations. He notes a number of assumptions that organizations hold about the "right way" to innovate, that have led to the mindset of a closed innovation paradigm. It can be seen that the closed innovation paradigm closely resembles the perspective of an organization that is focused on the products that it produces rather than the customers that it serves. One of the primary potential fallacies that supports Chesbrough's open innovation model is an organization's assumption that the internal control of NPD, R&D, and the development process will lead to a *first to market position* that will accordingly be followed by increased profits, market share, and R&D funding for further investment. Chesbrough points to several environmental changes that have precipitated a shift in the manner by which organizations enter innovation processes. Some of these changes include the mobility of people and knowledge, the acceleration of the NPD process by small, agile organizations, and an increasing availability of capital. He points out that these changes significantly interfere with the extant innovation paradigm. His examination of the *closed innovation* model leads to an emergent model of *open innovation* (external and internal ideas can progress through internal and external paths to market) in which he explores the concepts of the *locus of innovation,* the link between intellectual property value and business models, and the model of open innovation in detail.

References

Brown, Shona L. and Kathleen M. Eisenhardt. 1995. Product Development: Past Research, Present Findings, and Future Directions. *Academy of Management Review* 20(2): 343–378.

Chandy, Rajesh, Jaideep C. Prahu, and Kersi D. Antia. 2003. What Will the Future Bring? Dominance, Technology Expectations, and Radical Innovation. *Journal of Marketing* 67(3): 1–18.

Chesbrough, Henry. 2003. The Logic of Open Innovation: Managing Intellectual Property. *California Management Review* 45(3): 33–58.

Herstatt, Cornelius and Eric von Hippel. 1992. From Experience: Developing New Product Concepts Via the Lead User Method: A Case Study in a 'Low-Tech' Field. *Journal of Product Innovation Management* 9: 213–221.

Mische, Michael A. and Warren Bennis. 1996. Reinventing Through Reengineering: A Methodology for Enterprisewide Transformation. *Information Systems Management* 13 (Summer): 58–65.

Pittaway, Luke, Maxime Robertson, Kaamal Munir, David Denyer, and Andy Neely, 2004. Networking and Innovation: A Systematic review of the Evidence. *International Journal of Management Reviews* 5/6 (3/4): 137–168.

Roberts, Edward. 1988. Managing Invention and Innovation: What We've Learned. *Research–Technology Management* 31 (January/February): 11–29.

Wilemon, David and Murray Millson. 1994. The Emerging Paradigm of New Technology Development. in *Managing New Technology Development,* editors William Souder and J. Daniel Sherman, New York: McGraw-Hill, Inc.

59

THE EMERGING PARADIGM OF NEW TECHNOLOGY DEVELOPMENT

David Wilemon
Murray Millson
Syracuse University

This chapter summarizes all the steps in the new technology development process discussed in Chaps. 2 through 7. The reader will also note that this chapter includes some discussion of the product R&D step. The focus of this chapter is on contrasting the traditional paradigm with the newly emerging paradigm for new product development. The authors make a case for the necessity of an entirely new paradigm. What is wrong with the old paradigm? How will the new paradigm be an improvement? What are the implications for managers? How can traditional organizations and traditional managers participate effectively in the new paradigm? These are some of the important questions answered in this chapter.

Wm. E. Souder and J. Daniel Sherman

INTRODUCTION

This chapter addresses and integrates four important new product development (NPD) topics. First the traditional NPD process is described. This discussion will provide a platform from which to describe a shift that is taking place in the manner by which new products are developed. The "old" NPD process is a prescriptive model for the development of new products. While many firms develop new products, fewer companies are following the rigid, linear NPD path so frequently depicted in the literature.

Second, in addition to a description of the traditional NPD process, this chapter examines several problems and limitations associated with its application. It is noted that these problems can hinder new product success even when the traditional NPD process is explicitly followed. Many of these problems have been identified previously (Wind and Mahajan, 1988). This chapter summarizes them to demonstrate how they are fueling what is described as a "paradigmatic shift."

Third, a detailed assessment of an emerging NPD paradigm is presented. This chapter discusses the current state of NPD paradigm change and characterizes the attributes of a new paradigm, along with developing a perspective on its future evolution

TABLE 59-1 Transition from the Traditional to the Emerging NPD Paradigm

Traditional	*Paradigmatic shift indicators*	*Emerging*
Linear	Changes in organizational structures	Iterative; overlapping
Functional separateness	Globalization of new product development	Functional integration
Intermittent projects	Accelerated new product development	Continuous innovation
Efficiency/cost focus	Heightened concern for product quality	Effectiveness & efficiency
R&D driven	Enhanced communication for information technologies	Customer solution driven
Single-loop learning		Double-loop learning
Single firm development		Network of firms
Domestic perspective		Global perspective
Quality is expensive		Quality reduces cost
Short-term sales & profits used to measure success		Long-term customer satisfaction used to measure success

and growth. Attributes of the traditional NPD paradigm, an emerging NPD paradigm, and paradigmatic shift indicators are displayed in Table 59-1.

Finally, what firms can do to employ this new process is described and implications relative to the actions management must take to participate in this emerging process are suggested. This chapter describes how to achieve "new product successes" in and through the use of the emerging NPD processes. This discussion is summarized by presenting an integration of the traditional NPD process, NPD process shift indicators, the emerging NPD paradigm, and dimensions and elements of firm participation in the NPD arena of the future.

TRADITIONAL NEW PRODUCT DEVELOPMENT

The traditional NPD process depicted in Figure 59-1 (Crawford, 1991; Cooper, 1992; Cooper and Kleinschmidt, 1991; Booz, Allen and Hamilton, 1982) is now seen as the standard, normative process employed to develop new products. It is a process typically performed by a single business organization for new product development. Figure 59-1 represents an aggregate version of the traditional NPD process. Each step in the figure can be envisioned as a synthesis of many microelements which better depict all of the NPD activities. The NPD process has been described by only a very few steps such as the two steps (stage 1: creation and development and stage 2: adoption and implementation) of Knight (1967) or the four steps (idea conception, idea proposal, adoption decision, and implementation) of Daft (1978). Such depictions have evolved into many more steps as researchers and practitioners have more precisely defined the activities that take place within the overall process and in each step.

The process portrayed in Figure 59-1 represents a paradigm of NPD. It implies certain "rules" that are accepted by many who study and participate in the NPD process. As such, this figure prescribes what is to be done to develop new products. These steps are described in the following sections.

New Product Strategy Development

A first broad step in the traditional NPD paradigm is the generation of "a strategy" to guide the creation of new products. "Strategy" also can describe the parameters within which the NPD process is to operate. Crawford (1991) depicts NPD strategy as a Product Innovation Charter (PIC). PICs perform two important functions. They integrate corporate strategy with plans for proposed new products and they delineate guidelines for new product planning. PIC-based guidelines include such details as the product class within which a new product(s) will fit, customers for whom new products will be developed, and process or product technologies through which new products are created. Strategy formation and PIC development provide the foundation for the

FIGURE 59-1 The Traditional New Product Development Process.

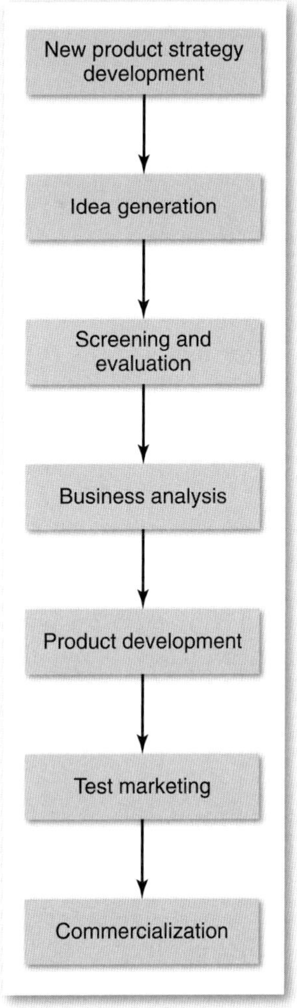

remainder of the NPD process by providing a structure and context within which additional NPD decisions can be made.

Idea Generation

Idea generation is the second step of the NPD paradigm. During this step new product ideas and concepts are discovered and created. Typically, large numbers of ideas and concepts are generated. Firms attempt to obtain ideas from many sources such as customers, sales personnel, marketing, and R&D. Moreover, firms employ many methods or approaches to obtain new product ideas from these sources. Idea-gathering approaches encompass activities such as eliciting new product suggestions from customers and others and brainstorming sessions and other creativity practices that can assist new product producers.

Screening and Evaluation

The third step of the traditional NPD paradigm involves screening and evaluating product ideas and concepts. This step acts as a filter or choice-making process for the many ideas and concepts gathered. Firms can employ several procedures to screen and evaluate new product ideas and concepts: rudimentary design and producibility studies can be made; preliminary customer reaction tests can be performed; and standardized checklists that scrutinize such factors as product idea fit with (1) the sales force, (2) desired new product lines, and (3) the type of customers the firm wants to serve.

Some firms perform extensive customer concept testing during this step. This entails developing a new product idea to the point that its attributes are clear and its product technology (how the product delivers customer benefits) is defined. Concept testing usually is only performed on those new product ideas that have passed more rudimentary filters like a demonstrated fit with the firm's new product strategy. It is important to screen out poor new product ideas through evaluation because as soon as customer evaluations, business potential assessments, and prototype construction begin, costs rapidly increase.

Business Analysis

The next step in the traditional NPD paradigm is business analysis. During this step much effort is applied to ascertain a new product's financial viability. A product's sales potential is assessed in both the current period and some time into the future. Product concepts that demonstrate the potential to become financial successes are allowed to progress beyond this point. Marketing plans are developed. Costs and prices are also estimated. The opportunity to perform an in-depth assessment of the process technology (how the product is to be fabricated and assembled) is pursued, along with an analysis of the resources required to design various versions of the new product under scrutiny.

Product Research and Development (R&D)

Product R&D follows the successful completion of business analysis. During this step, the investment made relative to each product concept significantly increases. The product concept evolves into a tangible product during this step. The manufacturing equipment needed to fabricate and assemble a new product must be constructed or purchased. Equipment obtained early in the product R&D step is used to make the first prototypes of a product concept. Later in this step, additional equipment is obtained to establish processes for generating larger quantities of the product (pilot runs). Pilot runs provide insight into the eventual full-scale production operation necessary to commercialize new products.

As in other earlier steps, all functional groups need to work together. It is highly important that design, development, manufacturing, and marketing closely coordinate their activities during product development (Hise et al., 1990) because, as the prototype takes form and pilot runs are planned, important customer-desired attributes can be overlooked.

Test Marketing

Test marketing is next in the traditional NPD process. For consumer goods, this traditionally implies a bona fide test market in which products are sold through typical channels of distribution, promotions are employed that have been created for the new product, and "everyday or expected" prices are sought. Alternative forms of market testing that firms employ include computer simulation of customer preferences and simulated test markets. Computer product test simulations offer advantages such as reduced test time and lower costs than traditional test marketing efforts. Another alternative is simulated test marketing. Unlike computer simulations, simulated test marketing employs actual customers and, therefore, mitigates one problem associated with computer simulations. For technology-based products "test marketing" may be implemented by placing a new product with a few important and trusted customers.

Commercialization

The final step of the traditional NPD process involves new product commercialization. The ability to commercialize arises from an integration of product and market capabilities and activities. During this step the product can be launched or offered to all parts of a national or world market simultaneously or it can be rolled out regionally. A roll-out strategy allows firms to be more conservative in their marketing approach, but it also allows the competition time to imitate.

TABLE 59-2   Traditional NPD Paradigm Limitations
Linear and fragmented
R&D as driver/limited marketing and customer involvement
Time crunch during final steps
High probability for total redesign/compounding of errors
Tendency to develop me-too products
Low transfer of learning between new product projects

TRADITIONAL NPD PARADIGM LIMITATIONS

Although the traditional NPD model noted in Figure 59-1 represents the current NPD paradigm for most firms, it has received significant criticism. As noted in Table 59-2, a number of limitations exist that preclude this paradigm from fulfilling the need for greater success in the development of new products. Wind and Mahajan (1988) note:

> . . . most new product entries are "me too," slightly modified products, or line extensions. There are relatively few truly innovative new products, and, most disturbing, the success rate of new-product entry is still abysmal (p. 304).

The first significant limitation to be found with the traditional NPD process is embedded in its linearity and the isolation of its steps. Linearity projects a simple picture onto a very complex process. It implies, for instance, that later steps cannot begin until prior steps are completed. Additionally, the sequential character of this paradigm suggests noniteration—the notion that earlier steps cannot be repeated once later steps have begun.

The traditional NPD paradigm gives the appearance that some functions or organizational groups could successfully perform the tasks of each process step without integration with other functions. One might think, for example, that senior management would be responsible for new product strategy, engineering for product development, finance for business analysis, and marketing for commercialization. Such paradigmatic implications are far from the truth. Not only does interfunctional integration need to occur during each step of NPD but multifunctional approaches are necessary to bridge gaps between steps, which the traditional NPD paradigm fails to address. In addition, with judicious planning, NPD steps can be overlapped to complete the entire process faster, which represents another process aspect that is not adequately addressed by the traditional NPD paradigm.

The traditional NPD paradigm appears to relate most closely to organizations that are engineering driven or technology-push oriented. These firms have a strong R&D team and a management philosophy that supports the development of new products through internal engineering "breakthroughs." Marketing is likely to have limited influence on NPD. Consequently, customer desires may not be incorporated into new products. Such companies rely on engineering to make the best product choices for customers. This results in an NPD process that is heavily biased toward new technology-driven products. The results of such a process or paradigm may not be acceptable to a firm's customers and, hence, denote meaningful limits to the usefulness of such an approach.

In addition to applying or translating limited marketing input, early NPD steps of the traditional NPD paradigm tend not to be well performed. Especially in engineering-driven firms, product idea screening with customers and customer concept testing tends to be minimized. The portion of the NPD process that is most familiar to engineering and with which engineering has the most interest typically is product R&D. Therefore, it is not surprising that engineering or technology-push firms employing the traditional NPD paradigm tend to excel at product development but falter during other critical NPD steps. Even in technology-driven firms, product development steps based on the traditional NPD paradigm can be problematic. The most technically proficient products may be created, but they might not sell if customer needs are not met.

In addition to early steps of the NPD process being rather improperly performed, the steps at the end of the NPD process also do not receive their rightful share of attention in traditional NPD paradigm analysis and enactment. Later NPD steps are often shortened to meet scheduled launch dates, and product test marketing of any kind can be seriously compromised. Also, since the traditional NPD paradigm can be viewed as a series of steps requiring functional specialization, steps in which the firm has little or no expertise may be inadvertently omitted or be ineffectively performed. A final problem with the traditional NPD paradigm involves product or design faults found late in the process. In the traditional paradigm there is little provision for looking ahead. Therefore, when a design or marketing problem is required. Such major schedule slippages can cause market windows to close before products are launched.

An emerging NPD paradigm can offer solutions to these limitations in the form of paradigmatic changes such as overlapping steps, intelligent up-front planning, and continuous new product innovation. The next section presents an examination of such an emerging NPD paradigm.

AN EMERGING NPD PARADIGM

Due to the limitations associated with the traditional NPD paradigm, the complexity of the NPD process itself, the structural changes taking place in many firms, and the complex environments in which new products are developed, the paradigm for the development of new products is evolving. As a paradigm, the traditional NPD process represents the way firms have produced new products. Because this paradigm is viewed as the standard approach to develop new products, rules have been created to support this approach. These rules have become the pillars upon which the traditional NPD paradigm rests. Given the view that the traditional NPD paradigm is "the right way," new-product-developing firms typically attempt to follow this methodology.

Many firms realize their NPD opportunities within the boundaries of these existing rules and their associated organizational structures. Even when difficulties like performing the linear NPD process faster or fusing better connections among the serial steps of the NPD process are discovered, firms often attempt to solve those problems within their known paradigmatic rules. Attempts to realize new opportunities through traditional NPD processes have not produced solutions that fulfill current NPD challenges. Consequently, the major objective—to increase the rate of new product success—also is unmet.

Since many problems are not solved within the traditional NPD paradigm, more and more firms are "breaking the rules" to find new solutions. There are some very compelling reasons to break the rules. These include the abysmally low new product marketplace success rate, the high cost of new product failure combined with rapidly changing consumer tastes, and the knowledge many managers have that NPD skills comprise an important strategic advantage in a fast-developing global economy.

Firms that break the rules of the traditional NPD paradigm are creating a new paradigm, a revolution, or a "paradigmatic shift." As Kuhn (1970) notes:

> The decision to reject one paradigm is always simultaneously the decision to accept another, and the judgment leading to that decision involves the comparison of both paradigms with natural *and* with each other (p. 77).

In addition, he points out that:

> Political revolutions are inaugurated by a growing sense . . . that existing institutions have ceased adequately to met the problems posed by an environment that they have in part created . . . scientific revolutions are inaugurated by a growing sense . . . that an existing paradigm has ceased to function adequately in the exploration of an aspect of nature to which the paradigm itself had previously led the way (p. 92).

Paradigmatic shifts can be likened to earthquakes. Sometimes they are slow and rumble along and other times they are swift and cataclysmic. In the case of the NPD process, the paradigmatic shift appears to be more of a slow, yet steady rumble. Both the slow and the fast processes have important implications for new product developers. It may appear that a slow change process is better for firms so that they can remain abreast of the situation and adjust accordingly. However, a slow paradigmatic shift may be more disastrous than a sudden one. An analogy that depicts this situation is the timeless anecdote about boiling the frog. A frog is more likely to jump out of water that is rapidly heated, whereas a frog may feel confident of adapting to water that is heated slowly. Either way, the frog is in trouble. The only difference is that in the former case the end comes more quickly and perhaps more mercifully. In the case of NPD paradigm changes, the situation is similar. The firm that notices a rapid change in the way new products are developed may "jump" onto new methods. When the process changes slowly, firms may be reluctant to change or not notice the change until the competition has "boiled them." A description of an emerging NPD paradigm and an exploration of the indicators that a paradigmatic shift is actually under way is presented next.

A New Model for NPD

Figure 59-2 portrays the model of a new NPD paradigm. It not only depicts the core processes, as Figure 59-2 does for the traditional NPD paradigm, but it includes the

FIGURE 59-2   An Emerging NPD Paradigm.

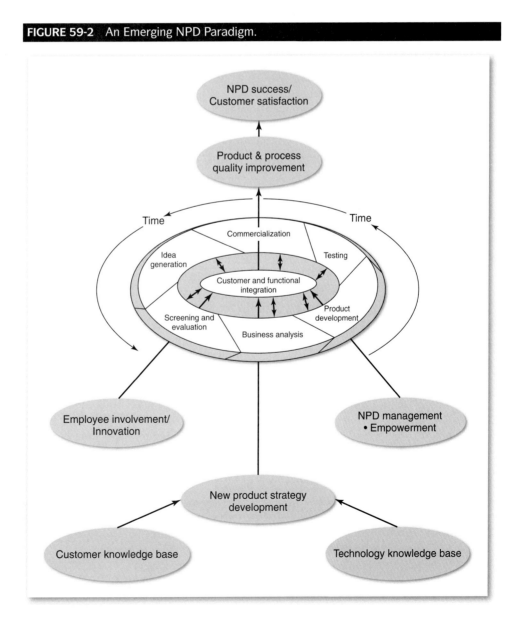

support concepts without which the NPD process cannot successfully function. This model implies that successful NPD must be driven from a sound customer and technical knowledge base. This means that for a product-developing firm to be successful it must be both market and technology driven. Figure 59-2 points out that a firm's new product strategy is a synergy of its customer orientation, technical know-how, and vision of the future.

A conscientiously crafted new product strategy is implemented through simultaneous employee empowerment and concomitant involvement and innovation of the workforce. This synergistic process typically has been described as involving members within a particular function and only for the duration of that function's NPD task. This new model suggests that the "players" are management, an NPD team, the workforce, customers, and perhaps other organizations such as suppliers or partners. Moreover, this model implies that synergy or integration must occur for the duration of the NPD process.

Another important aspect of this model is that it portrays the traditionally linear NPD process as a circle with its center supported by the integration of the internal and external organizations required to implement an NPD strategy. The circle of NPD tasks indicates continuous innovation linking the iterations of the development of a new product to one another and one NPD project to another. Moreover, the model suggests all of the integrated NPD personnel may have an input into each task of the NPD process. A final difference between this emerging model and the traditional model is that the tasks of this process can be overlapped. This is indicated, for example, by business analysis beginning before screening and evaluation has been completed.

The output of the model for the emerging NPD paradigm is improved product and process quality, which translate into increased customer satisfaction and NPD success. Thus, this emerging NPD paradigm can help fulfill a primary objective of new product development—market success. The following describes organizational and environmental activity that foretells the emergence of a new NPD paradigm.

Paradigmatic Shift Indicators

If NPD process change is depicted as a slowly evolving paradigmatic shift, how can management recognize that a shift is occurring and that this condition is not simply a trend within the traditional NPD paradigm? First, managers need to be able to distinguish between trends which are continuations of activities that are controlled by the rules of the traditional paradigm and activities that appear to be controlled by forces that break the traditional paradigm's operating tenets. Minor discontinuities in trends also must not be mistaken for paradigmatic shifts.

Trends are outcomes of decisions that are derived from the interaction of behaviors of many actors in the NPD process, such as the firm itself, the competition, and the state of the economy in general. Paradigms embrace the rules guiding the behaviors of those actors. Managers must be able to trace their way backward to the causes of the behaviors and separate those behaviors that are generated by actors who change their governing rules intentionally or unintentionally. They must also do this with those behaviors that are created within the scope of the traditional paradigm's rules but have interacted in such a way as to cause a change in an outcome trend. Five organizational and environmental factors that are indicative of an NPD paradigmatic shift are proposed. They are itemized in Table 59-3. The five factors include organizational restructuring, new product development globalization, NPD acceleration, concern for product quality, and the advent of new communication and information transfer technologies.

TABLE 59-3 Paradigmatic Shift Indicators

Changes in organizational structures
Globalization of new product development
Accelerated new product development
Heightened concern for product quality
Enhanced communication and information technologies

ORGANIZATION STRUCTURE CHANGES AND ORGANIZATIONAL RESTRUCTURING

This section presents two general types of business restructurings that are indicative of a paradigmatic shift. The first is the development of new products by firms with flatter organizational structures caused by fewer people than previously, especially managerial personnel. The second is the development of new products by multiple firms.

Flatter Organizations

Growth in profits has often been associated with growth in firm size, especially in terms of assets and personnel. It can be said that a correlation between profit and personnel growth has been a "rule" of the traditional NPD paradigm. Managers typically would not consider the development of a new product or product line without a considerable increase in personnel. Increasingly, organizations are creating and developing superior new products without adding to their workforces.

Since a paradigm involves rules, it is somewhat like a very high-level strategy or plan. If the strategy or traditional paradigmatic rule of "large organizations are needed to generate large profits by developing significant new products" is changed to "smaller organizations can develop significant new products and generate equally large profits," firms that have flatter, smaller organizations will operate under new paradigmatic rules. Currently many companies develop new products in organizations restructured to "do more with less." From this perspective firms have become flatter and the span of control of many mangers has far exceeded that recommended by classical organization theorists. The flattening of new-product-developing organizations has made way for a greater delegation of responsibility to people at lower levels in organizations. Moreover, managers now responsible for many more personnel do not have time for detailed instructional sessions with each employee—therefore, people within organizations increasingly are empowered to make and implement important NPD decisions.

Multiple-Firm NPD

A second indication that the NPD paradigm is shifting vis-à-vis organizational structure is the use of networks to develop new products. Under the rules of the traditional NPD paradigm, firms typically choose to "go it alone." Under the rules of the traditional paradigm, managers are unwilling to share the profits of new product success with other, external new-product-developing organizations. It has been common for firms to build up large R&D departments to search for ideas and develop new products. Today it is common for firms to share the profits and risks of new product ventures with partners who employ their expertise to compensate for weaknesses within other NPD organizations.

Network-type organizations can be fashioned in many ways. Joint ventures in which a third firm is created to develop and market new products have been very common, especially with firms doing business crossing national boundaries (Harrigan, 1985). Another approach is strategic partnering. In this environment, the participating firms retain their own identity, typically creating contracts that stipulate the degree and type of interaction desired between or among partnering firms.

Whereas NPD under the traditional paradigm typically was based on a high degree of secrecy, NPD under the rules of this emerging paradigm is based on information sharing by partnering firms. New product information sharing causes organizational boundaries to blur. Such blurring is due to the sharing of people and resources needed to develop new products that are successful in the marketplace. Although sharing NPD information is critical to this emerging NPD paradigm, it is important to note that *not everything* can be shared. Each firm's critical core expertise needs to be protected to secure each firm's competitiveness and place in the network structure.

Global New Product Development

In the traditional NPD paradigm, it is believed that large markets, especially those of economically developed nations, should be targets for newly developed products.

Therefore, firms should design, manufacture, and market their products close to such markets. In this emerging NPD paradigm, firms are actively seeking personnel, funds, other resources, and customers from all parts of the globe. This shift is occurring because foreign firms with high-quality products and the ability to obtain low-cost labor and materials have stretched beyond their borders to gain market access. Many firms that previously operated under the rules of the traditional NPD paradigm are now taking a "global" NPD perspective.

In this emerging NPD paradigm, new product developers are increasingly becoming firms without countries; they place their operations in whatever part of the world they believe is the best from cost, customer, and competitive perspectives. Such firms develop new products for any customer that needs their products, manufacture in parts of the world that offer economical labor and materials, and perform research and development activities where there are high concentrations of scientific and technical skills.

New Product Development Acceleration

Another sign that a new NPD paradigm is emerging involves the interest of firms in the speed with which they develop and market new products. Many firms are finding that the traditional, serial NPD process does not allow them to become product pioneers in their chosen marketplaces. The rules of the traditional NPD paradigm indicate that NPD steps should progress in sequence (e.g., one step should not begin until a prior step is completed).

Firms previously took several years to conceptualize, design, manufacture, and market new products. Today many firms have less than 1 year to develop a new product, and some companies are even striving for new product launches in as little as 6 months. The shortening of the NPD process allows firms to more precisely time their new product introductions. For example, Honda, AT&T, Hewlett Packard, and Xerox have taken steps to reduce the duration of their NPD processes for new automobiles, telephones, printers, and copiers, respectively. They are thereby entering markets earlier and satisfying customers' needs sooner.

This emerging NPD paradigm recognizes that products need to be developed in a timely manner. In order to do so, firms are simplifying products and production processes, eliminating unneeded process activities and delays, paralleling and overlapping process operations, and speeding up NPD tasks to accelerate their NPD processes (Millson, Raj, and Wilemon, 1992). The traditional NPD process simply takes too long. When firms had less competition and product life cycles were much longer, the traditional NPD process was adequate. Today, competition can arise from many points around the world. This makes it far more difficult to assess the length of new product life cycles.

New-product-developing firms have become very proactive in the replacement of their current products with new offerings—this is in response to concerns about accelerating NPD to meet launch windows and preempt competitive efforts. Firms have become particularly challenged by the need to replace their own product offerings when customers want new product solutions to their problems and for meeting business opportunities.

Product Quality

In addition to accelerating the NPD process, firms must assure the design and manufacture of high-quality products. More than ever, customers expect new products to meet high quality standards. In the traditional NPD paradigm, product quality was sought by each organizational function that performed a step along the linear NPD process. "Quality" typically was measured by a product's conformance to engineering standards and specifications. These measurements usually did not occur until the new product had reached the product development step.

In this emerging NPD paradigm, process and product quality standards are developed from customer wants and needs. Product quality is measured by customer satisfaction throughout the NPD process. Again, important differences can be noted between the operating rules of the traditional and emerging NPD paradigms.

One program that is changing the shape of new-product-developing firms is Total Quality Management (TQM). TQM is associated with many important management functions and attributes such as education, communication, performance effectiveness and efficiency, and management style. TQM requires firms to "break down" communication barriers, develop measurable goals for individuals and teams, and focus on continuous quality improvement in all areas. The implementation of TQM typically necessitates dramatic social change within organizations. Many times the achievement of such major social change requires organizations to modify their organizational cultures (Scurr, 1991).

TQM also requires a firm to take a holistic view of itself and its environment. The TQM process demands that all activities be performed in a high-quality manner. The emphasis of TQM is on the total organization; management communicates a basic premise to all employees which states that employees have "customers" for their product efforts "within" the organization, in addition to the "external" customers of the firm. Each customer's needs must be clearly understood. The supplier—an individual employee or the firm as a whole—must put forth every effort to satisfy customers' needs and desires. Quality Function Deployment (QFD), a more narrowly defined process, is a disciplined system for incorporating customer wants and needs into new products. A major objective of QFD is to incorporate customer requirements into new products at the most rudimentary level of the manufacturing process. QFD accomplishes the incorporation of customer needs in product designs by first understanding those needs and wants. The QFD process involves the creation of matrices that relate engineering solutions to customer needs. The correlation between engineering solutions and customer requirements is monitored to ascertain when and where trade-offs are required. When trade-offs are necessary, customer needs are reviewed to determine how to provide the highest customer satisfaction.

TQM addresses the social, educational, and communication aspects of the NPD process while QFD can coordinate the screening, evaluation, and product development steps of the NPD process. Companies who participate in this NPD paradigm need to study both processes and determine where each supports their NPD needs.

Communication and Information Technologies

A final paradigmatic shift indicator is the increased use of state-of-the-art communication and information technologies in NPD. Even relatively small firms are employing sophisticated communication technologies to develop new product offerings.

Some of the new devices that are speeding and easing the NPD process include the use of personal and laptop computers, facsimile machines, computer workstations, and networks and their associated software by new product designers, manufacturers, and commercializers. In some instances, these devices are eliminating the need for drafting personnel because the design process has been automated to permit the input and continual reprocessing of design information directly into NPD databases. These databases are also remotely accessible by manufacturing engineers and purchasing agents, thereby speeding the development of production equipment and the early procurement of production materials and capital equipment. Databases also are accessible to field personnel, such as sales and new-product-developing partners. This rapid access to new product information helps firms satisfy customer needs before their competitors do (Kalashian, 1990).

Travel costs and NPD partner remoteness have prompted increased reliance on sophisticated communication and information equipment. Devices such as video conferencing and Electronic Data Interchange (EDI) have assisted in both timely new product decision making and receipt of raw materials. NPD partners can now interactively create and screen new product ideas where they previously shared pictures and concepts by mail or personal transport.

Communication and information storage and transmission devices are speeding the NPD process by allowing partners to form NPD network organizations. These developments violate the rules of traditional NPD because they allow steps to overlap and multiple firms to efficiently work together on NPD projects. We can anticipate that these developments in information and communication technology will increase the rate at which a revolutionary NPD paradigm emerges.

Summary of Paradigmatic Shift Indicators

Employment of network organizational structures to develop new products and the implementation of product quality-enhancing processes are paradigmatic shift indicators. Such choices allow firms to change their new product development rules. The NPD success associated with flatter, smaller structures indicates that large organizations are no longer seen as necessary for achieving profitable new products. The globalization of the NPD process implies that firms no longer view the development of products solely within the confines of a single firm as necessary, nor does management believe that new products should always be designed, manufactured, and launched in a domestic market alone. Firms that accelerate their NPD processes are relying on a nonlinear view of NPD as a way to recognize and meet the demands of new product launch windows. TQM and QFD are complementary processes that can be employed to attain new and better products faster. The implementation of these processes requires a new perspective of the NPD process in that customers both external and internal to the organization become the focus of the NPD effort. Use of high-technology communication and information storage and transmission devices also is accelerating the transition to an emerging NPD paradigm. The development, adoption, and rapid diffusion of user-friendly software, electronic hardware, and more computer-literate personnel indicate that many firms are concomitantly creating a holistic NPD perspective—a radically different approach to NPD than that prescribed by the traditional NPD paradigm.

NEW PARADIGM PARTICIPATION

This section describes how firms can perceive the emergence of a new paradigm for NPD, "learn" its attributes, and participate in it. Firms that are willing and able to participate must be prepared to make difficult, sometimes radical modifications in their organizations and operating philosophies in order to move from their "old" NPD ways to new behaviors and ways of thinking. Table 59-4 presents recommendations for firms that wish to participate in this emerging NPD paradigm: (1) encourage organizational learning, (2) emphasize continuous innovation and quality improvement, (3) develop a prospector culture, (4) develop specific product technologies, (5) create an NPD acceleration capability, (6) create an innovation infrastructure, and (7) foster a holistic NPD perspective.

Encourage Organizational Learning

There are three major methods by which learning occurs in organizations. The first level of learning can be described as the process of detecting "and correcting" errors (Argyris, 1977) or incremental innovation (McKee, 1992). The second level can be viewed as "double-loop" learning (Argyris, 1977) or discontinuous innovation (McKee, 1992). And the third and highest level of learning can be envisioned as "deutero" learning (Bateson, 1972) or organizational learning (McKee, 1992).

TABLE 59-4 NPD Paradigm Participation Recommendations

Encourage organizational learning
Emphasize continuous innovation/quality
Develop a prospector culture
Develop specific product technologies
Create an NPD acceleration capability
Develop an innovation infrastructure
Foster a holistic NPD perspective

Organizational learning can help management understand the differences between the traditional and emerging NPD paradigms, provide information transfer between NPD projects and supporting organizational functions, assist in making sound NPD decisions, reinforce the importance of new organizational cultures, and enlighten people in their effort to create successful new products (Wheelwright and Clark, 1992).

The first product innovation learning method described by McKee (1992) may be the most common and easiest to undertake. This incremental learning model is a simple "closed-loop" system and can be likened to a temperature control system containing a thermostat as a control mechanism (Staudt, Taylor, and Bowersox, 1976). To operate this type of mechanism the thermostat is first set to a desired temperature. When the ambient temperature varies above or below acceptable limits, either a heater or an air conditioner turns on to "correct the error," which returns the area environment to the preset temperature. The error information comprising a temperature that is outside prescribed limits is the knowledge that actuates the system and inhibits further learning to take place in regard to the environment at temperatures outside the preset control limits. In this sense, the system has only learned to be in control by returning the temperature to the preset condition. Single-loop learning assumes the "correct" NPD process is known, and after an initial condition is set and a difference is detected, the learning process returns the system to the known condition, and the cycle begins again.

The second product innovation learning process described by McKee (1992) is much less common and far more difficult to employ. The description of this process, for example, begins much like the first one in that a temperature control system also can be used as the basis of the learning system. In this scenario the thermostat is set for a particular temperature, as in the previous example, and acceptable limits are set to allow the temperature control system to return the environment to the preset temperature when either the high or low limit is exceeded. Therefore, a single-loop learning system is the core of this process. In addition to the core single-loop learning system, this second learning methodology employs another control loop that embraces the entire single-loop system. This second loop system operates by occasionally asking the "operator" of the temperature control system whether the preset temperature is appropriate. Therefore, this system has the ability to learn about "errors" or "temperature settings" that are outside the single-loop control limits if the "operator" chooses to do so.

An example of such learning systems can be derived from the oil crisis of the early 1980s. Many people traditionally kept their homes near 80°F. Therefore, their thermostats were set near 80° and their temperature control systems would return their living areas to 80° when temperature deviations occurred. This is an example of a single-loop learning system in which no one questioned the validity of the preset temperature of 80° because it was a "normal" house temperature. With the oil crisis of the 1980s came much higher oil prices and higher energy bills. Those home owners who questioned the validity of operating their houses at 80°F were employing double-loop learning. Many of these home owners found that they did not need to have their homes at 80° to feel comfortable and that there were other ways to attain comfort at other ambient temperatures.

Another perspective of these learning systems can be found by analyzing the concepts of "doing things right" and "doing the right things." People are typically rewarded for doing things right and occasionally punished for doing things wrong. Moreover, errors are often associated with doing things wrong. At an early age, we are taught to do things right and not make mistakes. We are often reprimanded for behaviors that are deviations from the "normal" ways things should be done and occasionally rewarded for complying with others' wishes and desires. Therefore, "doing things right" is analogous to single-loop learning or incremental product innovation in which we are given limits regarding our new product methods and are rewarded for remaining within the limits of preset behavior or punished for deviating from that behavior. It is interesting to note that in such systems any deviation from the norm for any reason is regarded as an error. Obviously, this is a very confining system although simple and fairly easy to understand and operate.

On the other hand doing the right things requires a more complex control system. To do the right things, we must first find out what the right things are and then create and implement them efficiently. This form of new product learning is analogous to discontinuous innovation (McKee, 1992). A process that questions the activities that are being performed before attempting to perform them is double-loop learning. It is this system of learning that forms part of the basis for participation in this emerging NPD paradigm. The behaviors associated with double-loop learning lead to effective performance because the right things are being done. A note of caution must be made here. We also must perform the core, single-loop learning process because to be efficient we must do the right things right.

The third and highest level of learning in new-product-developing organizations is organizational (McKee, 1992) or deutero learning (Bateson, 1972). The organizational level of learning is concerned with institutionalizing NPD learning experiences to improve the effectiveness of future new product developments. This is the type of learning which firms that wish to fully participate in this emerging NPD paradigm must achieve.

This level of learning is not focused on the incremental enhancements of a single product or product line as in single-loop learning. Nor is this level of learning only associated with the development of a new-to-the-world product via discontinuous innovation. The organizational level of learning provides the learning that is necessary to carry a firm through the development of many new products whether they are incremental or discontinuous. This level of learning provides the "glue" that links NPD programs together in a continuous NPD effort.

To engage in organizational or deutero learning, McKee (1992) notes that "unlearning" may need to occur. To accomplish this firms can foster cultures that accept and learn from errors. In some instances firms may need to remove people to "unlearn." Firms need to provide individuals with error-learning skills to engage in single-loop learning to enhance their personal performance. Firms also need to reward the communication and the shared learning derived from this process. To move beyond single-loop learning, firms need to refrain from punishing failure and reward the "learning" that occurs when NPD tasks fail. These learnings need to be shared. The freedom to take risks and to learn from failure allows people to expand their limits; it can also lead to highly effective double-loop learning. The unconditional sharing of both successes and failures supported by an organizational culture committed to innovation can provide the basis for a learning organization (McKee, 1992).

Emphasize Continuous Innovation and Quality Improvement

The process of continuous innovation can be seen as a cultural attribute supported by a nurturing management philosophy. Continuous innovation connotes an ongoing renewal and quality improvement of products, processes, and organizations. The emerging NPD paradigm embraces the notion of increased customer satisfaction through product solutions that are more closely aligned with the changing needs of customers. Such new product-customer need alignment can only stem from the continuous development and timely introduction of new products, including the knowledge about products and their servicing.

Continuous innovation and development of high-quality, customer-satisfying products are important facets of this emerging NPD paradigm. Continuous NPD is important because it is easier to manage, fosters less hostility within organizations, is less disruptive, serves customers' needs better, provides continuous interaction with customers, and is a process that is synergistic with organizational learning and the strategy of prospecting.

In an environment of continuous change, it is vitally important for firms to create and communicate clear and compelling organizational directions. Such communication, based on serving customers well, can provide the context and structure for constant improvement and innovation. Within such a context the development of new products can become less stressful. The management of the development of new products is a challenging experience at best. To marshal the financial and personnel resources each time a new product is planned can be difficult. Continuous product innovation represents a way to start from a base or vision that provides the necessary explanations and justifications for NPD and a core of personnel from which to move from one product to another. Continuous product innovation can reduce the resentment that comes from selecting only a few personnel to be a part of a periodic NPD effort upon which a firm's survival rests. Moreover, continuous product innovation reduces the potential "we-they" attitudes that are often created when collateral organizations, elite groups, and "skunk works" are formed to develop new products.

Continuous product innovation can reduce the disruption that comes with intermittently removing people from their "regular" positions to be part of a segregated NPD effort. Continuous processes also mitigate situations in which "extra" or "undone" work from NPD personnel falls on others to either "clean up" or simply implement. If most personnel (some individuals will not want to participate in NPD) are selected from time to time to participate in the development of the next product iteration, the people left behind will not perceive themselves as the employees that get the "leftover" jobs.

To continuously innovate, firms must foster ongoing, highly productive interactions with their customers. This means organizational members must be in contact with customers before, during, and after product development and launch. Increased customer interaction provides firms with more in-depth understanding of customer wants and needs in addition to the increased trust that can be formed by customers who perceive employees to be genuinely interested in their problems. An important aspect of continuous product innovation and quality improvement—or operations—is that customers are served better. Customer service involves increased understanding of the problems customers want solved.

In these turbulent times, firms need to be doing all they can to stimulate customers and employees. Continuous innovation at all of the three previously mentioned learning levels is desirable. New, incremental changes and product enhancements can be made to current products and manufacturing processes to keep customers interested and costs decreasing. In addition, new product solutions to new and current customer problems need to be addressed. This entails employing discontinuous learning and major innovation. Continuous product renewal and development by different or overlapping groups moves the firm to the third, or organizational, level of new product learning. To facilitate this process, senior management needs to be committed to continuous innovation, give individuals and groups rewards that support continuous innovation, and develop a climate of intelligent risk taking where failures lead to learning and eventual success, not punishment.

Develop a Prospector Culture

Miles and Snow (1978) note four types of strategies that organizations employ to adapt to their environments. They point out that firms behave as either *prospectors, defenders, analyzers,* or *reactors*. Firms that select a prospecting strategy continuously search for market opportunities and create the change and uncertainty to which their competitors must respond. These firms "experiment" with new products, new markets, and new ways of thinking and behaving as their standard mode of operation. Due to such a constant state of flux, however, prospecting may not be the most efficient strategy.

A defender, on the other hand, typically has a limited product market (a specific product or product line targeted toward a particular market) and is an expert in this narrow market domain. The focus of such firms is on developing process adjustments to increase the efficiency of their processes, typically to reduce manufacturing costs. Miles and Snow (1978) describe analyzers as firms that develop some attributes of both the prospector and the defender. These firms are not as aggressive in the marketplace as prospectors and tend to create me-too products. Additionally, analyzers are not as introverted as defenders and, therefore, tend to be somewhat less focused on process development. The firms that comprise the fourth typology, reactors, are typified by inconsistent and unstable adjustments to changes in their environments. Therefore, these organizations are typically less successful than the other three types of firms.

The contrasting adaptation processes of the prospectors and the defenders can be seen as learning systems (McKee, 1992). The defender continually develops the process technology for its current product market. In this respect it develops limits relative to the quality of its product and creates and enhances process technologies to improve its cost position while attempting to hold its product quality constant. The defender's approach toward growth comes from its cost leadership position and a desire to gain greater market penetration and share. The defender is less likely to investigate developments outside its primary product market domain. The best defenders have well-developed single-loop learning systems to keep costs low and efficiency high. These firms have the capability to perform double-loop learning but are likely to find it more difficult. This difficulty comes from the defender's lack of market and environmental scanning. This lack of scanning lowers the potential for defenders to become compelled to question their governing policies and regulations. In other words, when a defender employs its NPD process, it is likely to be the traditional paradigm because defenders are less likely to detect shifts in the need to do things differently.

The prospector, on the other hand, is primarily interested in growth from the development of new products and the creation of new markets. This environmental adaptation strategy requires the continuous monitoring of the environment in domains remote from a prospector's current area of interest. Prospectors also are dedicated to finding new customers and new problems to solve for current customers. The implementation of this strategy is more likely to promote the questioning perspective required by the double-loop learning system and, therefore, detect and foster paradigmatic shifts. Such detection is important to prospectors and defenders alike, but prospectors appear to have an advantage. Therefore, in terms of the previous discussion, prospectors are more likely to do the right things and be more effective, whereas defenders are more likely to do things right and be more efficient.

It appears as though the business environment will be increasingly turbulent. Firms from all points on the globe will soon be competing in many markets as countries develop. The prospector that does the right thing and does the right thing right may be a new breed. This combination of a prospector with defender efficiencies is not an analyzer that brings forth me-too products at an acceptable cost. This new breed of firm brings forth innovative customer solutions and understands how to transport product innovation and learning to manufacturing processes and administrative systems to offer differentiated products in a highly efficient manner. Therefore, firms need to be prospectors first and defenders second.

A caveat is important here. It must be remembered that these two strategies are mechanisms employed to adapt to the environment. If the environment is stable and certain, a defender's perspective can be adequate. But, if the environment is uncertain and turbulent, a prospector's perspective can be more beneficial. In addition, a prospector can create and disturb an environment in ways that are incompatible with a defender's strategy. In recent years most organizational environments have become turbulent, uncertain arenas. This environmental phenomenon can be considered to be a force behind the NPD paradigmatic shift. Therefore, a prospector's NPD paradigm will more likely shift toward this emerging NPD paradigm before firms following other environmental adaptation strategies, such as defenders.

Develop Specific Product Technologies

In order to innovate continuously, a firm needs to develop specific new product and process technologies. A product technology strategy can be defined as a particular way of providing customer benefits through the firm's product offerings. For example, some running shoe firms provide a more comfortable shoe by producing a wedge insert to support the runner's heel, whereas other firms have incorporated an air bag design to provide running comfort for their customers. The development of specific product technology strategies requires the choice of the best product solutions for customer problems and an organizational focus on those solutions. Therefore, the creation of specific product-technology strategies requires integrated inputs from all organizational functions. Organizational integration becomes a major factor in the development of specific product technologies and participation in this emerging NPD paradigm.

Process technologies can provide significant competitive advantages, deal primarily with the production of the product, and typically only affect activities internal to the organization. Product technologies also provide significant competitive advantages but extend beyond the organization to include how customer problems are solved and how information external to the organization can assist in the higher integration of organizational functions. Process technologies are primarily the domain of manufacturing, while product technologies fit and fulfill customer needs, mesh with marketing skill and expertise, and are supported by engineering's knowledge and aptitude. Moreover, product technology more than process technology requires that firms become prospectors. Therefore, for a firm to develop an effective product technology it needs a prospector's close customer contacts, an understanding of customer needs and problems, and alternative solutions for those problems. In addition, such firms need to possess a process capability that can be associated with the product solution which incorporates the chosen product technology.

Proprietary process technologies have given defenders competitive cost advantages. Such proprietary technologies were thought to have offered even more security than patents. Proprietary process technologies may no longer offer the competitive advantages they once did because of the unintended "technology transfer" of "process secrets" via layoffs and the increased mobility of personnel. Firms that develop specific product technologies and enter markets early with advanced solutions to customer problems can obtain competitive advantages in the 1990s.

Specific product technology strategies and their communication are important to a firm's participation in this emerging NPD paradigm because customers desire high-quality products *and* services. In addition to durability and reliability, product performance is a critical aspect of product quality (Garvin, 1984). Since product performance depends on the means by which the product solves customer problems and provides customer benefits, product and process technologies together become an important factor in the ability of a firm to participate in this new NPD paradigm.

Create an NPD Acceleration Capability

Another factor that must be considered by potential participants in this emerging NPD paradigm is the creation of a product acceleration capability. To participate in this emerging NPD paradigm, a capacity needs to be developed that provides firms with the ability to accelerate the activities of their NPD processes in order to take advantage of fast-closing customer-related new product launch windows.

There are few hard and fast rules to rely on to determine which new products need accelerating. Nor is it always economical to do so (Rosenau, 1988). It also is evident that not all new products require accelerating. It appears that each new product needs to be analyzed from a customer's need perspective, taking into account proposed and existing products and competitive positions. Firms that are continuously innovating, developing entirely new products, and iterating relatively new products are close to their customers and can ascertain which new product programs need acceleration.

The determination of strategic new product launch windows helps firms understand which new products need acceleration. A constant scrutinization of both the customers' needs and competitors' activities can be used to develop a product acceleration priority list. As a practical matter, NPD acceleration should become less important as firms develop cultures of continuous NPD and quality improvement. The reduced need for NPD acceleration should occur because firms will be continually focused on customers' needs.

In some cases, however, firms will need to accelerate the development of new products. To do this, five major acceleration techniques are recommended (Millson, Raj, and Wilemon, 1992). First, firms may be able to simplify products, the organizations associated with the development of new products, and the processes required for new product development. This can be achieved by reducing the number of parts and vendors used, creating effective linkages between NPD organizations, and assigning meaningful tasks to people. Second, firms need to eliminate all unnecessary activities associated with the development of new products, such as shortening the typically long list of approval signatures. Third, firms can minimize unnecessary delays between NPD activities and within major NPD tasks. This means that the personnel involved in succeeding steps of the NPD process should be informed when their efforts are required and materials and information need to be scheduled to eliminate delays in the NPD process. A fourth action that can be taken to accelerate the development of new products involves the paralleling and overlapping of NPD steps. This requires a review of the necessary NPD activities to determine which activities can be started before others are complete. This acceleration activity also requires risk taking, especially when the early steps of the NPD process are paralleled or overlapped. This technique requires that firms accept the risk that new product assumptions will not change significantly during the NPD process. The fifth action firms can take to accelerate the development of new products is to speed up NPD activities. This requires increased employee motivation and an investment in equipment to automate NPD processes.

Create an Innovation Infrastructure

This section addresses the often forgotten administrative actions, procedures, and systems required to support the development of new products, especially a process of continuous new product innovation. Examples of these administrative systems include firms' accounting processes, purchasing systems, training procedures, and human resource management (HRM) organizations.

First, managers need to understand how these traditional support structures operate and the information that they provide. Without this understanding, rational changes or additions to such administrative systems cannot be instituted. Second, managers need to understand what information they need in order to make effective decisions. Needless changes to existing systems only serve to aggravate individuals who operate them and reduce the trust of managers responsible for important system changes. Third, managers need to understand how their reward systems support or inhibit continuous product innovation. Well-intentioned reward systems can inhibit behaviors necessary to the functioning of continuous product innovation and product quality improvement. For example, rewarding personnel involved in the launch of a new product but not the people who made the critical changes to the accounting system (who provide the information needed to assess each separate iteration of a new product's development) is not enough to assure continued support during succeeding product iterations.

A final area to evaluate for its impact on continuous NPD is represented by the systems that support the hiring and training of employees. The interaction between new product managers and human resources managers can be highly beneficial to the development of new products. In situations where products are continuously developed and many personnel are employed during the development process, training is important. In organizations where new products are continuously developed, the transfer of information and learning experiences from one product iteration to the next is crucial for the acceleration of succeeding iterations and new product success.

Foster a Holistic NPD Perspective

It is essential for managers to combine the foregoing concepts into an integrated package. The "winners" in the new NPD paradigm will eventually implement all of the previous suggestions. It is the "fit" among these elements that allows firms to become effective participants in this emerging NPD paradigm. Holistic implies that the process of developing new products is only as strong as its weakest link. Some of the links include the ability of personnel and organizations to learn and to transfer information among themselves and their markets through continuous innovation. Moreover, the environmental adaptation strategy of prospecting as a process fits well with a well-developed organizational learning environment. Developing specific product technologies which require close ties to customers also meshes well with the process of prospecting and learning and enables firms to better understand and serve their customers. Additionally, all of these concepts apply to the development of a culture of continuous product innovation and iterative product development which needs to be supported by a management philosophy that empowers people to do the right things. Morgan (1986) notes:

> Where corporate culture is strong and robust, a distinctive ethos pervades the whole organization: empowering employees to exude the characteristics that define the mission or ethos of the whole; e.g., outstanding commitment to service, perseverance against the odds, a commitment to innovation . . . (p. 139).

A holistic perspective of continuous NPD needs to involve all of the NPD support functions and the NPD team, not just from a necessity point of view but from a total organizational team perspective. Including these support functions provides management with a better idea of how NPD information and learning flows through and is used by firms.

IMPLICATIONS FOR INNOVATION MANAGERS

NPD managers need to become keenly aware of the factors associated with this emerging NPD paradigm. This new paradigm will undoubtedly influence NPD throughout the 1990s and beyond. Further, it has the potential to produce many of the answers that the traditional NPD paradigm has been unable to provide. A commitment to create a vision of the future that employs this NPD paradigm others many important implications for managers. These implications stem from the performance of the activities associated with participation in this emerging NPD paradigm. They include "learning to learn," slowing down to speed up, doing more with less, focusing on customer-defined product quality, developing a global NPD perspective, and effectively managing, storing, communicating, and using strategic information. The implications related to the performance of the behaviors required by this emerging NPD paradigm are summarized in Table 59-5.

Change Culture: Recognize and Acknowledge Errors

Perhaps the most critical personal task managers have before them while attempting to participate in this emerging NPD paradigm is the struggle involving the process of relearning how to learn. Learning to learn implies that NPD managers and other

TABLE 59-5 Implications of Emerging NPD Paradigm Participation

New Paradigm Behaviors	*Implications and Requirements*
Encourage organizational learning	Change culture; recognize and acknowledge errors
Develop a prospector culture	
Create an NPD acceleration capability	Plan, focus, and commit before speeding ahead
Develop specific product technologies	Focus to maximize resources
Emphasize continuous innovation/quality	Think like a customer, not a producer
Create an innovation infrastructure	Information is precious
Foster a holistic NPD perspective	Think globally

personnel must be able to recognize and admit their mistakes. As children, people are given the inquisitiveness that is required to start them off in the world. Basically children are given "blank slates" with which to work. Children start to write on their slates as soon as they have experiences. Fortunately, they also are given another important tool: good erasers. When new experiences appear to conflict with the information children have detailed on their slates, they look for guidance and can readily make adjustments or delete the text altogether. At this time in their lives they don't know that they aren't supposed to make mistakes; they feel free to start over without external or internal impugnation. As children grow older, they unfortunately lose that precious quality of being able to start over, their erasers wear out, and they are often stuck with what is written on their slates.

The implication here is that someone else's eraser may be required to make adjustments and carry on. This change of culture and personal point of view can be difficult. But it is a basic premise of this emerging NPD paradigm. Change can occur. Old perspectives are not cast in concrete. Progress can be made.

Plan, Focus, and Commit Before Speeding Ahead

The idea here is slow down to speed up. This apparent oxymoron is offered to point out that "speed" is not required all of the time. Stopping to smell the roses is an often-cited recommendation. This message should not be discarded. This emerging NPD paradigm implies that a new view of NPD should be taken. Tough decisions need to be made and risks need to be taken. And most of all, minds need to be opened to allow plans for the future to be made. Such plans will provide the capability to accelerate the development of new products. Anything short of a solid planning effort will typically result in progressing through the NPD process very fast, only to result in failure or an iteration of at least a portion of an errant process.

Focus to Maximize Resources

Focus to maximize resources implies doing more with less. The caption "do more with less" is very well used, but it does have importance in the context of this emerging NPD paradigm. In terms of the development of new products, doing more with less implies that management should strive for excellence in carefully selected new product categories. This means that firms need to focus their product markets and therefore their NPD efforts. This type of product-market concentration significantly helps perform the screening and evaluating activities described in the traditional NPD process, in addition to streamlining the firm's supporting infrastructure. Such a focus keeps the firm from wasting resources on developing concepts and products that detract energy from core businesses. A firm may continue to have multiple businesses and employ this emerging NPD paradigm. But each business must generate a sense of focus and commitment to its own product markets. The new product strategy step of the traditional NPD paradigm provides such a product-market focus.

A caveat regarding the focusing of effort in the NPD process and strategy formulation process needs explanation. Idea generation requires both focused and unfocused approaches. This means that during this particular task the participants need to be encouraged to wander as far and wide in their thinking as possible. This is another area where the child's clean slate metaphor applies. The idea generators for new products must have no restraints until they are required to determine what to do with the new product ideas they have generated. An idea far afield may eventually be associated with a very profitable product at a later date. And product ideas that are not applicable now may become viable future alternatives.

Think Like a Customer—Not a Producer

Management needs to understand its customers' perspective of quality. This statement has implications for new product developers and involves many aspects of this emerging NPD paradigm. Three important NPD aspects that are associated with the customers' view of product quality include the concepts of a specific product technology, continuous product innovation, and customer satisfaction or product redesign after launch.

First, to become a leader in a product category, firms must be able to develop distinctive product technologies that solve customer problems better than competitors. This means that new product developers need to intimately understand customer problems in order to be able to develop new product solutions perceived as providing highquality answers to those problems. Second, the culture and process of continuous product innovation instructs firms to "get close" to their customers' problems, offer tailored solutions, and rapidly enhance those solutions to move even closer to the "target" product. Continuous product innovation also requires that firms remain close to their customers "after" new products are launched. Third, customer satisfaction needs to be monitored to ascertain which product benefits need to be left intact, which ones need to be changed, and which ones are so far off that customers actually make product changes themselves. Such customer redesigns need to be understood and assimilated into the new product technology.

Information Is Precious

Becoming a good prospector, creating tailored new product technologies, and developing a learning organizational culture implies that management operating in this emerging NPD paradigm must manage, store, and use information effectively and efficiently. Information is the glue that links the various parts of this emerging NPD paradigm together to form the holistic picture required for NPD success.

Critical decisions associated with strategic information involve important choices about what information to manage, store, and use. These are not easy questions to answer and the answers can differ for each product category and firm. In general, firms need to consider two important factors related to new product information. These factors involve (1) understanding what information is important for developing successful new products and (2) training personnel to use that information.

There are two primary sources of NPD information. Much of the information that is important to new product developers comes from customers and represents the first source of NPD information. The second source of important NPD information comes from product and process technology specialists working on technologies that can support the products and production processes associated with both the ideas and concepts derived early in the NPD process. Given this information, management must instruct its new product development personnel in information use. It is most important that such information be readily available and easy to use. If a firm's important information is hidden and unwieldy, there will be much time wasted and many developers will cease to use it in favor of "personal databases" and "seat-of-the-pants" experience. This type of subjective information should always play a part in the making of good decisions, but the use of personal information makes it difficult to quickly obtain decisions with shared meanings. These problems can be solved through the implementation of shared databases and instruction for all new product developers relative to its use. Information access needs to be controlled but not to the extent that makes it difficult for developers. Data input and modification should be more stringently controlled. But even these processes need to be accessible to some so the NPD process is not unjustifiably slowed.

Think Globally

The final implication for managers participating in this emerging NPD paradigm is to create a global new product perspective. NPD managers need to develop a world view to be aware of new markets, competitive forces in both foreign and domestic markets, and new, more economical resources such as materials, technology, and personnel. This can be achieved by developing first-rate environmental scanning capabilities.

Holistic structures make internal what is all too often perceived and managed as external in centralized hierarchies, namely new markets that provide firms with additional outlets for new and existing products. These new markets also can provide additional customer and product information. Moreover, foreign countries can provide test markets for new products and the ability to experiment with various marketing plan configurations.

A second dimension of corporate activity typically perceived to be "external" becomes "internal" when corporations recognize that becoming aware of global competitive forces is more important than ever before. Even if a firm does not participate in global markets, it must ascertain the ability of competitors operating in those markets to attack its domestic markets. A firm cannot assume that its lack of interest in foreign markets will prevent foreign competitors from entering domestic markets, no matter how small. Circumstances in foreign "home" marketplaces may be such that they give foreign competitors incentives to attack even small markets in different parts of the world.

A final point concerning the creation of both a global and holistic perspective involves an assessment of the most economical manner to develop new products over the long term. The economical development of new products can entail the employment of resources from many different parts of the globe. A critical issue related to the employment of global resources involves the interface between the personnel that perform the steps of the NPD process. The ease of NPD task performance may be hindered by the incorporation of very economical material resources from other geographic locations because the providers of the material may not be perceived as team players by the employees operating in the "home" office. Such hindrances can have devastating effects on the overall results of the NPD process. This implies that a holistic NPD perspective is not only required but needs to be a deliberate undertaking.

SUMMARY

This chapter has described an emerging NPD paradigm. An NPD paradigm is described and the implications of a paradigmatic shift are presented. An NPD paradigm represents the "right way" to develop new products by many new product developers. Therefore, an NPD paradigmatic shift is a change from the traditional NPD paradigm to a new paradigm. The traditional NPD paradigm was described and a variety of limitations associated with it were presented, including its linearity, lack of customer focus and involvement, the inconsistency with which it is implemented by new product developers, and its inability to offer consistently successful results. It was also noted how these problems might be solved by following the rules of this emerging NPD paradigm.

Changes in organizational phenomena were offered as evidence of the presence of an emergent NPD paradigm. Moreover, those indicators were closely linked to the solutions of problems that the traditional NPD paradigm has not been able to solve. Indicators such as flatter new-product-developing organizations, organizations with global perspectives, and organizations that incorporate NPD acceleration techniques into their NPD processes were pointed to as indicative of the emergence of a revolutionary NPD paradigm.

The requirements for firms to successfully participate in this emerging NPD paradigm were presented. Concepts such as double-loop and organizational learning were presented and the necessity of continuous innovation also was emphasized. Participating firms are expected to become learning organizations with an internal culture of continuous product development and product quality improvement and an operations flow involving the creation and communication of specific process and product technology strategies. To accomplish these actions, firms need to develop holistic NPD perspectives which represent the final requirement for participating in this new NPD paradigm.

Finally, implications were offered for managers who decide to invest their resources and behave as prescribed by this emerging NPD paradigm. These behaviors include the need to change the firm's organizational culture, intelligently plan before accelerating NPD, obtain a comprehensive technology focus and operation, think like a customer to develop a sound product quality perspective, discover what information to employ in NPD, and develop a holistic, global NPD perspective.

References

Argyris, Chris. "Double Loop Learning in Organizations," *Harvard Business Review,* 55, 1977, 115–125.

Bateson, Gregory. *Steps to an Ecology of Mind,* NewYork: Ballantine, 1972.

Booz, Allen and Hamilton. *New Products Management for the 1980s,* New York: Booz, Allen and Hamilton, 1982.

Cooper, Robert G. "The NewProd. System: The Industry Experience," *Journal of Product Innovation Management,* 9, 1992, 113–127.

—— and Kleinschmidt, Elko J. "New Product Processes at Leading Industrial Firms," *Industrial Marketing Management,* 20, 1991, 137–147.

Crawford, C. Merle. *New Products Management,* Homewood, Ill.: Richard D. Irwin, Inc., 1991.

Daft, Richard L. "A Dual-Core Mode of Organizational Innovation," *Academy of Management Journal,* 21, 1978, 193–210.

Garvin, David A. "What Does 'Product Quality' Really Mean?" *Sloan Management Review,* Fall 1984, 25–43.

Harrigan, Katherine R. *Strategies for Joint Ventures,* Lexington, Mass.: Lexington Books, 1985.

Hise, Richard T., O'Neal, Larry, Parasuraman, A., and McNeal, James U. "Marketing/R&D Interaction in New Product Development: Implications for New Product Success Rates," *Journal of Product Innovation Management,* 7, 1990, 142–155.

Kalashian, Michael. "EDI: A Critical Link in Customer Responsiveness," *Manufacturing Systems,* 8, 1990, 20–26.

Knight, Kenneth E. "A Descriptive Model of the Intra-Firm Innovation Process," *Journal of Business,* 40, 1967, 478–496.

Kuhn, Thomas, *The Structure of Scientific Revolutions,* Chicago: The University of Chicago Press, 1970.

McKee, Daryl. "An Organizational Learning Approach to Product Innovation," *Journal of Product Innovation Management,* 9, 1992, 232–245.

Miles, Raymond E., and Snow, Charles C. *Organizational Strategy, Structure, and Process,* New York: McGraw-Hill, 1978.

Millson, Murray, Raj, S. P. and Wilemon, David. "A Survey of Major Approaches for Accelerating New Product Development," *Journal of Product Innovation Management,* 9, 1992, 53–69.

Morgan, Gareth. *Images of Organization,* Newbury Park: Sage Publications, 1986.

Rosenau, Milton D. "From Experience Faster New Product Development," *Journal of Product Innovation Management,* 5, 1988, 150–153.

Scurr, Colin. "Total Quality Management and Productivity," *Management Services,* 35, Oct. 1991, 28–30.

Staudt, T. A., Taylor, D. A., and Bowersox, D., *A Managerial Introduction to Marketing,* Englewood Cliffs, N.J.: Prentice-Hall, 1976, 49–52.

Wheelwright, Steven, and Clark, Kim. *Revolutionizing Product Development,* New York: The Free Press, 1992.

Wind, Yoram, and Mahajan, Vijay. "New Product Development Process: A Perspective for Reexamination," *Journal of Product Innovation Management,* 5, 1988, 304–310.

60

REINVENTING THROUGH REENGINEERING

A Methodology for Enterprisewide Transformation

Michael A. Mische and Warren Bennis

Reinventing through reengineering targets traditional business practices to renew leadership and optimize an enterprise's competitive position and shareholder value. This article dispels the myths that have led to unsuccessful reengineering efforts, discusses the elevated role of information technology in the reengineering process, and presents a comprehensive reengineering work plan for achieving a true enterprisewide transformation.

The closing decade of the twentieth century is experiencing changes of historical proportions in economic dynamics, consumer expectations, spending patterns, individual career aspirations, life-style choices, and working patterns. These changes—which are permanent, systemic, and without precedent—are part of the transformation to a world economy. The combination of societal changes, process and technology innovations, a conscious melding of diversity, and the development of a highly intertwined global economy is transforming the organization and the way it does business.

Although today's environment and defining values differ greatly from those of much of the twentieth century, many organizations are still ruled by the same old management practices, processes, and organizational theories developed long ago by such management luminaries as Frederic Taylor, Alfred Sloan, Henry Ford, Luther Gulick, and Abraham Maslow. These doctrines of yesteryear compromise the ability of organizations to compete. Straddled with rigid policies and procedures, stoic organizational structures, and a preoccupation with historical preservation of yesterday's management practices, the cultures and structures of these organizations simply do not allow them to be agile and adaptive in a real-time world. At the threshold of the twenty-first century, such organizations find themselves grappling to improve their competitive position.

It is no longer sufficient for managers merely to react to customer needs or to rely on traditional methods of leadership and organizational techniques to build markets and increase earnings. At issue today are the basic premises and theories of how organizations are structured, operated, and compete in a new and dynamic world

Mische, Michael A. and Warren Bennis. 1996. Reinventing Through Reengineering: A Methodology for Enterprisewide Transformation. *Information Systems Management* 13 (Summer): 58–65.

order. The essence of the competitive problem for many managers, and its long-term solution, lies neither in the economy, in traditional prescriptions, nor in trendy situational management methods such as total quality management (TQM), activity value assessment, business process improvement, continued process improvement, or self-managed work teams. Rather, it lies in the most fundamental theory and structure of the organization and its leadership practices.

Several of today's organizations are leading a renaissance that cannot be attributed to quality improvements, improved economies, or technology alone. The changes and results achieved are far too dramatic to be completely related to better products and services. Something much more fundamental and pervasive is going on—something called reinvention through reengineering.

WHAT IS REINVENTION?

Reengineering has been around for a long time. When global manufacturers rushed to material requirements planning (MRP) systems in the 1960s and 1970s, they in effect reengineered their manufacturing and scheduling practices. The use of electronic data interchange (EDI) substantially reengineered the administrative, buying, shipping, and receiving practices of many retailers, carriers, manufacturers, and distributors. So historically, organizations actually performed reengineering without ever calling their efforts reengineering. In this sense, reengineering is not new; however, the context and arena in which reengineering is applied is very new. This is reinvention.

Those few businesses that have purposely reinvented themselves through reengineering their cultures and processes have achieved nothing less than astonishing results. For example, in the late 1980s when Chrysler began to again falter, its leadership adopted a cross-functional approach to management and product development that integrated accounting, sales, marketing, engineering, parts, and manufacturing into a team that ultimately launched the LHS car. For the last two years, the Chrysler Concorde, LHS, Cirrus, Eagle Vision, and Dodge Intrepid automobiles have helped Chrylser achieve record earnings and sales figures in North America.

Another much heralded but overly sensationalized example of reengineering occurred in the Ford Motor Co. This well-known story involves Ford's accounts payable department. With more than 500 people in a clerical function, Ford learned that there was a tremendous disparity between its staffing and those of Mazda, which staffed its accounts payable department with five clerks. Ford's long-standing business practices created many organizational disconnections and work fragmentation that forced the need for many people. When Ford finally redefined its work flows, it reportedly reduced its staffing by some 75%. Although it is not easy to understand the justification for 500 accounts payable clerks in the first place, Ford nonetheless reinvented its processes.

With mounting pressures and the potential for tremendous return on effort, it is little wonder that organizations are flocking to reinvention and reengineering.

DEFINING BUSINESS PROCESS REENGINEERING

Business process reengineering is the avant-garde term of 1990s. Reengineering is highly touted, often doubted, and overused. Unfortunately, reengineering has come to mean many different things, and it is this inconsistency that has contributed to the misuse and misunderstanding by management, consultants, and the public alike. Nonetheless, there is a growing phenomenon of organizations stampeding headlong, sometimes blindly, into something called reengineering.

What is business process reengineering? Is reengineering a new management concept, a trendy consulting gimmick, or another panacea for chronically ill and mismanaged organizations? What does it mean to reengineer a process? These may be the billion-dollar questions of the nineties.

Ten Great Myths of Reengineering

We begin our definition of reengineering by stating what reengineering is not. Following are the Ten Great Myths of Reengineering.

Myth 1: Reengineering assumes that an organization has done all the wrong things, all along; it should obliterate everything and start over. Reality: Reengineering recognizes that an organization has been successful and has done a number of things correctly, but maybe not perfectly. Reengineering cultivates the great things an organization has done by challenging it to do them better and, most important, differently. Innovation is the key to competitive advantage and reengineering.

Myth 2: Reengineering is information technology, systems integration, applications development, client/server, and the migration away from mainframes. Reality: Reengineering recognizes that information technology is an enabling agent of change and is essential to any reengineering effort. However, in and by itself, reengineering is not simply about information technology.

Myth 3: Reengineering requires downsizing and personnel reductions. Reality: Nothing could be further from the truth. Reinventing the enterprise through reengineering is about doing things differently and more effectively, with or without existing resource levels.

Myth 4: Reengineering means doing more work with less resources. Reality: Reengineering means creating greater leverage and efficiencies through process innovation, seamless and harmonious work flows, and more agile organizational structures.

Myth 5: Reengineering can fix any problem and any issue. Reality: Reengineering is not a short-term, quick-fix management tool. Reengineering is systemic and facilitates tremendous cultural and institutional changes.

Myth 6: Reengineering can be performed and managed by anyone. Reality: Reinventing the organization through reengineering requires mature business judgment, extensive and broad-based experience, a bold vision, and a refined methodology.

Myth 7: Reengineering can be sponsored by anyone in the organization. Reality: Reengineering is about reinventing the organization; success therefore depends on its being sponsored by the highest levels of leadership in the organization.

> **Reengineering is systemic and facilitates tremendous cultural and institutional changes.**

Myth 8: Reengineering can occur without significant organizational change and transformation. Reality: Reinvention through reengineering is transformation. Reengineering creates a new organization, different organizational structures, and a new leadership mentality.

Myth 9: Reengineering creates chaos and anxieties and can be disruptive and detrimental to the organization. Reality: Reengineering causes change, and change for most organizations and their managers can be excruciatingly difficult. If reengineering is not managed and performed properly, chaos and lasting scars will result.

Myth 10: Reengineering is scientific. Reality: Reengineering is not a physical or natural science. Scientific concepts and techniques could very well find their way into a reengineering process, but they are not reinvention through reengineering.

Some consulting organizations and companies that profess to practice reengineering approach it as incremental improvement to existing practices. The rationale is to identify incremental improvements to fundamental business processes that can generate savings, mostly within the existing framework and structure of the organization. That is, do it faster and even better, but do it essentially under the prevailing structures and doctrines. The savings self-fund the next phase of the reengineering project.

In no way is this approach even remotely related to reengineering. Why? Because incremental approaches are not reinvention and do not lead to cultural transformation and quantum benefits; they are not designed to do so. Incremental approaches are limited in scope and usually satisfy an immediate need or remedy a specific problem.

REINVENTION DEFINED

Reinventing the enterprise through reengineering requires radical and dramatic operational and organizational transformation. Reengineering is about understanding and organizing around outcomes about how work should be performed, and about how the organization should be aligned, managed, and led. Reengineering is about listening to customers, changing the established rules and tradition-bound culture, creating tangible value in work, generating, learning and ideas, sharing knowledge, and reinventing processes and management practices.

Our definition of reengineering lies at the end of spectrum among definitions that suggest organizational transformation and reinvention. It is as follows:

- Reengineering is the process of reinventing the enterprise and cultural transformation through aggressively challenging traditional doctrines, management practices, business activities, and organizational paradigms; and the reinventing and redeployment of enterprisewide capital and human resources into cross-functional processes and structures to optimize competitive position, shareholder value, and societal contribution.

Tenets of Reinvention

Five tenets guide all reinvention and reengineering efforts:

- *Increasing throughput and productivity.* Reengineering seeks to optimize organizational practices through the creation of seamless and harmonious processes that have an uninterrupted, natural flow and velocity.
- *Enhancing quality and shareholder value.* Reengineering optimizes shareholder value and creates competitive advantage through innovation.
- *Achieving quantum results.* Reengineering is mandated with a mission and passion to achieve quantum results and strategic advantage through innovation and the radical transformation of the enterprise.
- *Compressing time and consolidating functionality.* Reengineering is designed to create processes and organizations that are leaner, flatter, and more adaptive. Agility and the ability to anticipate and rapidly assimilate market trends, customer needs, and competitor initiatives are trademarks of the reinvented enterprise.
- *Eliminating low-value work and hierarchical organizations.* Reengineering constructively interrogates work and organizations to assess value, purpose, and content. Work of seemingly low shareholder and competitive value, as well as responsible organizations, are repositioned to provide greater contribution or eliminated.

The technology may be state-of-the art, but the organization's use of it is not.

Rather than concentrating on specific tasks performed within the rigid boundaries of a department and blindly accepting long-standing cultural doctrines and organizational rules, reinventing through reengineering boldly challenges the traditional paradigm and historical notions of leadership and organizational structures. Reengineering asks five questions of the organization and its operational processes:

- Why does the organization perform a process a certain way?
- What value is produced for the customers and shareholders by performing the process this way?

- What better ways can the process be done that will enhance value?
- What breakthrough results can the organization achieve?
- What cross-organizational talents and resources are required?

Results of Reinvention

The results of successful reinvention are measured in a stepwise progression rather than in the traditional incremental curves associated with classical methods such as business process and productivity improvement, organizational effectiveness, and industrial engineering. The results of a successful reinvention and transformation process can be significant: productivity improvements of from 40% to more than 80%; staff reductions of 25% to more than 75%; inventory reductions of 40% to 50%; cycle-time improvements of 50% to 300%; and direct cost reductions of 25% to more than 60%. These percentages are not the traditional 5%, 10%, and 15% gains that many organizations are quite content to achieve. In addition to the quantitative benefits, reinvention results in:

- Increased employee interest in and appreciation of the enterprise—its leadership, products, and customers.
- Improved organizational cooperation, teamwork, understanding of needs and performance measures, and communication.
- Increased employee knowledge of the organization's identity and direction, role in the marketplace, and competitors.
- Improved alignment of personnel and a better matching of skills and empowerment to new responsibilities and reinvented processes.
- New individual performance measures and performance evaluation methods.

Reinventing the enterprise through reengineering is thus a distinct and permanent change in the principles of business leadership, management, operations, and organization.

ITS ROLE IN REENGINEERING

Information technology is fundamental to the competitive posture of the enterprise and essential to any reengineering process. Information technology is the enabling agent that provides the necessary infrastructure that links the organization together and supports process innovation, organizational integration, and cross-functionalization. Without enabling technology solutions, process innovation and quantum results cannot be achieved.

Unfortunately, the majority of systems used by many organizations reflect their historical processes and hierarchical structures. Many systems and their supporting technologies are overly complex, not integrated, and dependent on traditional mainframe and proprietary technologies. Rather than enabling cross-functional processes, the typical application used in many organizations merely automates the obvious and accelerates the existing without interrogating the rationale and methods. In short, the technology may be state-of-the-art, but the organization's use of it is not.

The implications for many organizations are excruciatingly obvious: expenditures for technology continue to increase; investment return and end-user productivity

Many organizations find that before they can significantly change their business practices through reengineering, they must first reengineer their IT organizations.

remain low; and there is a growing disconnection between information technology—its applications and support structures—and the strategic and competitive needs of the enterprise. As a result, many organizations find themselves in a dual reengineering situation; before they can significantly change their business processes and practices through reengineering, they must first reengineer their information technology organizations.

In reinventing the enterprise, the role of information technology is elevated to a new level of unprecedented importance. Virtually every major business practice and administrative process is affected by reengineering and its enabling technology at some point. Five principles are associated with the role of information technology in the reinvention process:

- Information technology will replace manual processes, paper, forms, and traditionally structured operations.
- Information technology will consolidate and eliminate many traditional tasks, human resources, and associated costs.
- Information technology will enable transnational expansion and virtual enterprises and employees.
- Information technology will enable the consolidation of functionality and creation of cross-functional organizations and integrated processes.
- Information technology will create and support a common standard and framework for managing shareholder resources for enhanced competitiveness, not greater management control.

Because reinventing the enterprise results in a very different organization, it is little wonder that the information technology resources of these organizations must also be reinvented. In the reengineered enterprise, the reinvented information technology has six differentiating characteristics:

1. Applications and computing platforms that are demassed, decoupled, and scalable to specific business needs and their constituents.
2. Applications and data that are cross-platform functional.
3. Data that is accessible, rationalized, and consolidated in warehouses.
4. Applications that are built to common standards using a variety of productivity tools.
5. Applications and platforms that are portable and shared among various process constituencies and organizations.
6. Technology resources that are logically consolidated and physically distributed.

The concepts of logical consolidation and physical distribution are essential to the realization of the reinvented enterprise. Logical consolidation refers to the development and implementation of common enterprisewide policies, processes, performance measures, standards, and leadership for the effective deployment and use of IT resources and personnel, irrespective of location. The physical distribution of information technology includes both human and technical resources. Under logical consolidation, technology resources and capabilities are located with their respective processes and functions under a common, logical, enterprisewide organization and management structure. In short, technology resources coreside with their constituents but are managed according to a common set of measurements and under a uniform management structure.

THE PROCESS OF REENGINEERING: A PRACTICAL FRAMEWORK FOR SUCCESS

Initiating a reinvention journey is relatively easy and is done almost daily. However, as many organizations have learned, successful reinvention and transformation of the enterprise through reengineering is quite a different matter. In fact, only 30% to 40% of true reinvention efforts ever achieve their stated objectives.

With a growing number of organizations launching reengineering efforts and spending tens, and in some cases hundreds, of millions of dollars, there is a very real need for a realistic and responsive methodology to guide leaders through the process of innovation, organizational transformation, and competitive repositioning. The comprehensive reengineering work plan (CRW) does just that through its five phases:

- Creation of a vision and setting of objectives.
- Evaluative baselining and benchmarking.
- Process innovation and reengineering.
- Organizational transformation.
- Continuous calibration and improvement.

FIGURE 60-1   The Five Phases of Reengineering

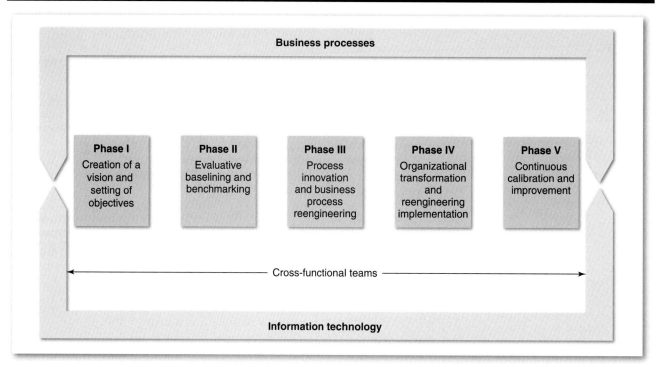

Figure 60-1 illustrates our five-phase approach for reinventing the organization through reengineering. It is based on a unique concept called process clusters, which is used to organize the work and flow of the reinvention journey. The methodology contains 23 process clusters representing more than 700 individual work steps. Specialized data collection and analytical instruments are used to support the reinvention through reengineering process. A description of each of the five phases follows.

Phase I: Creating a Vision and Setting Objectives

The starting point for all reengineering projects is the creation of a vision. A vision is necessary to establish the parameters of the effort, the direction and scope of the project, and the specific targets and objectives of the process. Visions are important because people can aspire to them and align their efforts with them. Visions are also integral to effective communication.

From the vision, specific and well-defined objectives are developed. The objectives form the milestones and targets for the reinvention process.

Phase II: Evaluative Baselining and Benchmarking

During this phase, organizational responsibilities, personnel assignments, reports, work volumes, and value created are documented and analyzed. This baselining is necessary for developing the appropriate benchmarks and comparisons and for identifying potential candidates for reengineering that will best support the vision and objectives developed in phase I.

The baselining and benchmarking step involves a validation of information that provides a comparison of internal performance measurements to peer or external benchmarks and best practices. This comparison process provides key information and insights into how existing processes perform, why they behave a certain way, what the cycle times and costs of the process are, how the organization is supporting the process, the rationale and management practices of the organization for the process, and a host of other important information required for reinventing through reengineering.

Extreme care must be exercised in using benchmarks, however, because they often are superficially interpreted. In using benchmarks it is not as important to have a comparative number as it is to understand how the benchmark was developed, how the data was defined and analyzed, and whether the benchmark is appropriate for the specific circumstances. Generalized benchmarks, such as those that may be bought or added on to an existing group, are interesting, but they can easily be misinterpreted and corrupted.

Phase III: Process Innovation and Reengineering

The third phase of the reengineering journey involves the essence of reengineering: process innovation and functional consolidation. The main challenge in this phase is identifying and understanding that a series of individual tasks, which transverse organizational boundaries, can aggregate to a seamless business process. This process was always present; however, it was obscured among many tasks (most of which were unnecessary), departments, organizational layers, and responsibility centers.

Fundamental to reinventing and reengineering is the identification of core processes and the development of new "to-be" business processes. Process innovation and organizational consolidation are achieved by interrogating and reducing the traditional practices to their essence and establishing a new value chain of the activities that create a seamless and harmonious process.

In reinventing and reengineering processes, effort is concentrated on identifying break-through opportunities and designing new work steps and organizations that will create quantum gains and competitive advantage. The effort involves visualizing work as concurrent and natural activities, not traditional or linear processes. The reengineering team must be free to explore, test, modify, and resequence everything related to the process without regard for organizational resistance and individual agendas. This openness and constant challenging of existing processes promotes creative synergy and ultimately produces quantum results.

Phase IV: Organizational Transformation and Reengineering Implementation

The fourth phase of the reinvention journey is the most challenging and demanding: the actual transformation to the reinvented enterprise. Once traditional business practices have been reengineered into business processes, they must be implemented and successfully integrated into the organization. This integration involves employee education, leadership, organizational change, and structural realignment and redeployment of technical and human resources. The majority of transformation is cultural, occurring as managers and employees move from hierarchical structures, classic command-and-control behavioral patterns, and job-specific tasks and measurements to empowered work groups, process teams, and value-chain decision making.

Figure 60-2 contrasts the reengineered organization and the traditional organization. In the reinvented enterprise, knowledge of the process and the value contribution created by work drive new measures for both performance and compensation. Organizational advancement and performance measurement are directed away from the traditional criteria of knowing a set of internal procedures, job-specific tasks, and the number of people managed to having a broad understanding of the process and how that process links and integrates with other processes and areas of the organization. Individual creativity, collective problem solving, and the ability to work without inordinate levels of supervision and organizational checks and balances are trademarks of the reinvented enterprise. Contributing to a network of knowledge workers, working as an effective team member, possessing event-driven leadership skills, creating collective ownership and responsibilities, and the ability to forge synergistic organizational linkages are coveted personal attributes in the reinvented organization.

Phase V: Continuous Calibration and Improvement

The fifth phase of reengineering is one of continuous commitment to the process of reengineering and improving shareholder value and competitive position. During this

FIGURE 60-2   A Comparison of Organizational Functioning in the Traditional and Reengineered Enterprises

Traditional Paradigm—The Hierarchical Orientation Based on "Boxes and Lines"	*Reengineering Paradigm—Cross-Functional Horizontal Orientation Based on "Diamonds and Circles"*
Hierarchical organization, work groups, committees, and task forces.	Networked working teams, leaner structures, flatter organization.
Independent function that passes off work to successor function.	Integrated and seamless functions that perform value-added work.
Creates its own performance metrics, measurement standards, and information.	Uses common measures and information.
Departmentally focused, mission-specific, and silo structure.	Cross-functional process.
Task-specific, work fragmentation.	Process-driven, seamless integration.
Concentrated spans of control and separation of duties.	Open empowerment; cross-functional duties and knowledge.
Reactive to needs.	Innovative and proactive.
Driven by a top-down mandate.	Enabled by a top-down vision.
Cost-driven; performs to budget.	ROI and value-driven.
High command and control.	Compressed decision making at the process and customer levels.
Maximizes task efficiency.	Maximizes effectiveness and value to customer and shareholder.
Standardizes all products; has homogenous processes but with many exceptions.	Tailored to market, channel, and customer; private label.
Linear and sequential work steps.	Concurrent and natural work flow.
Designs procedures, identifies the exceptions, and designs more procedures.	Understands exceptions and uses many processes.
Reconciles, audits, reconciles again; creates reports and enters them into personal computers.	Doesn't waste time on administrative make-work.
Transaction-oriented.	Harmonious and seamless flow.

perpetual phase, reengineered processes and transformed operations and organizations are constantly evaluated and calibrated to the vision and goals established in phase I and the current environment of the organization to ensure that desired results are achieved. This phase also involves reaching out to customers, business partners, and potential business alliance members to create new processes designed to achieve greater integration among processes and organizations.

CONCLUSION

Today, business leaders are confronted with enormous pressures and opportunities. Some are superimposed, others are self-inflicted, and some evolve through the dynamics of societal and technological change. In this global world of borderless customers, real-time service, and instantaneous transactions, it is no longer sufficient to manage organizations using traditional structures and measures. The issues and needs are too complex, the opportunities are fleeting, and the stakes are far too high.

Organizations that successfully navigate the difficulties of reengineering achieve renewed leadership and quantum results. Those that do not will simply run on their own inertia until the markets and competitors eclipse them and shareholders mandate a change. The choice is clear: reinvent the organization through reengineering and flourish—or perish.

About the Authors
Michael A. Mische a management consultant with the Synergy Consulting Group, Inc., in Boalsburg PA. Warren Bennis is Distinguished Professor of Business Administration and founder of the Leadership Institute at the University of Southern California in Los Angeles. This article is adapted from the authors' book, The 21st Century Organization: Reinventing Through Reengineering (San Diego: Pfeiffer & Co., 1995).

61

PRODUCT DEVELOPMENT: PAST RESEARCH, PRESENT FINDINGS, AND FUTURE DIRECTIONS

Shona L. Brown and Kathleen M. Eisenhardt

Stanford University

The literature on product development continues to grow. This research is varied and vibrant, yet large and fragmented. In this article we first organize the burgeoning product-development literature into three streams of research: product development as rational plan, communication web, and disciplined problem solving. Second, we synthesize research findings into a model of factors affecting the success of product development. This model highlights the distinction between process performance and product effectiveness and the importance of agents, including team members, project leaders, senior management, customers, and suppliers, whose behavior affects these outcomes. Third, we indicate potential paths for future research based on the concepts and links that are missing or not well defined in the model.

Innovation research splits into two broad areas of inquiry (Adler, 1989). The first, an economics-oriented tradition, examines differences in the patterns of innovation across countries and industrial sectors, the evolution of particular technologies over time, and intrasector differences in the propensity of firms to innovate (e.g., David, 1985; Dosi, 1988; Nelson & Winter, 1977; Urabe, Child, & Kagono, 1988). The second, an organizations-oriented tradition, focuses at a microlevel regarding how specific new products are developed (e.g., Ancona & Caldwell, 1992b; Clark & Fujimoto, 1991; Zirger & Maidique, 1990). Here, the interest is in the structures and processes by which individuals create products. In this article, we focus on this latter area of the broader innovation literature.

Product development is critical because new products are becoming the nexus of competition for many firms (e.g., Clark & Fujimoto, 1991). In industries ranging from software to cars, firms whose employees quickly develop exciting products that people are anxious to buy are likely to win. In contrast, firms introducing "off-the-mark" products are likely to lose. Product development is thus a potential source of competitive advantage for many firms (Brown & Eisenhardt, 1995). Product development is also important because, probably more than acquisition and merger, it is a critical means by which members of organizations diversify, adapt, and even reinvent their firms to match evolving market and technical conditions (e.g., Schoonhoven, Eisenhardt, & Lyman, 1990). Thus, product development is among the essential processes for success, survival, and renewal of organizations, particularly for firms in either fast-paced or competitive markets.

During the past 10 years, the pace of product-development research has quickened as numerous academic scholars have probed the secrets of product-development prowess (e.g., Ancona & Caldwell, 1990; Clark & Fujimoto, 1991; Dougherty, 1990; Zirger & Maidique, 1990). Interest in product development plus preachings about the importance of proficient product development have reverberated in the popular press (*Business Week*, 1992; Dumaine, 1991; Schendler, 1992). The underlying rationale appears to be that, although technical and market changes can never be fully controlled, proactive product development can influence the competitive success, adaptation, and renewal of organizations. However, because this large and fragmented literature has not been tied together to create cogent understanding, it is difficult to grasp what is actually known. Thus, the purpose of this article is to improve the understanding of product development.

We begin by organizing the empirical literature on product development into three streams: product development as *rational plan, communication web,* and *disciplined problem solving.* By the empirical literature on product development, we mean articles published in major English-language organizations-oriented North American and European journals where this work is likely to appear[1] and a few, unpublished studies. We specifically focus on normative empirical studies of product development in which the development project is the unit of analysis. Even with these constraints, it is still impossible to cover all studies in one review article. As we built the literature review, we selected studies based on the rigor of their empirical methods and the degree to which they were cited by others. We allowed the network of studies to grow forward and backward in time with no constraints. As a cross-check against the burgeoning network of citations, we iteratively returned to the journals. Through this process, the three distinct networks of research that we describe and the temporal boundaries between 1969 and the present emerged.

Second, we synthesize these research findings into a model of factors affecting the success of product development (see Figure 61-1). This model integrates the common findings of the research streams and blends in complementary ones. In addition, the model attempts to build a theoretical framework for the findings in these streams.

Third, we indicate potential paths for future research. These paths are centered on the effects that the development process and product concept have on product success, patterns of organizing product-development work, strategic management, and customer/supplier involvement. Overall, the intent of the article is to contribute an understanding of the past literature, a model of current thinking, and a sense of future directions.

LITERATURE REVIEW

The product-development literature is vast, ranging from broad-brush explorations to in-depth case studies and across many types of products, firms, and industries. In this section, we create an organizing template for this work. Although several templates are possible, we have organized this one around three emergent research streams: rational plan, communication web, and disciplined problem solving. The three streams are summarized along key dimensions in Table 61-1.

We shaped our review around these streams because each involves a pattern of cumulative citations evolving from one or two pioneering studies. The rational stream builds on the Myers and Marquis (1969) and SAPPHO studies (Rothwell, 1972; Rothwell et al., 1974); the communication stream, on the early work of Allen at the Massachusetts Institute of Technology (MIT) (1971, 1977); and the problem-solving stream, on Imai and colleagues' (1985) study of successful Japanese products. Each stream's focus reflects an evolution based on the constructs highlighted in the pioneering works. The result has been three relatively coherent and distinct bodies of research.

Further, although there are overlaps in focus across the streams (e.g., all streams investigate how different players, processes, and structures affect performance),

FIGURE 61-1 Factors Affecting the Success of Product-Development Projects[a]

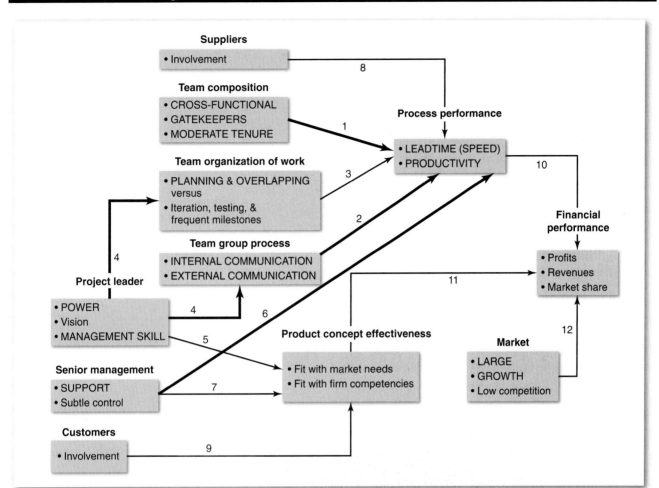

[a]**Capital letters and thickened lines indicate robust findings.**

research within each stream centers on particular aspects of product development. The rational plan research focuses on a very broad range of determinants of *financial performance* of the product, whereas the communication web work concerns the narrow effects of *communication* on project performance. Disciplined problem solving centers on the effects of product—a development team, its suppliers, and leaders on the actual *product-development process*.

Moreover, the research within each stream is theoretically and methodologically similar. The rational plan perspective is primarily exploratory and atheoretical and, thus, helps to broadly define the relevant factors for product-development research. The communication web stream complements this atheoretical view by relying on information-processing and resource dependence theoretical perspectives in the context of traditional research studies. The disciplined problem-solving stream takes the theoretical perspective of information processing one step further to problem-solving strategies, using a progression from inductive to deductive research and an emphasis on global industry studies.

Overall, these three streams seem, to us, to capture best the cumulative patterns of product-development research. In this section, we outline these streams, including their key concepts, critical findings, underlying theory, methods, strengths, and weaknesses. However, as noted, although these streams are coherent bodies of work, they also complement and somewhat overlap one another. So, in the subsequent section, we emphasize these overlaps and complementarities by blending them into an integrative model of product development.

TABLE 61-1 Comparison of Three Research Streams

Concepts	Rational Plan	Communication Web	Disciplined Problem Solving
Key idea	Success via superior product, attractive market, rational organization	Success via internal and external communication	Success via problem solving with discipline
Theory	Mostly atheoretical	Information and resource dependence	Information including problem solving
Methods	Bivariate analysis; single informant; many independent variables	Deductive and inductive; multivariate; multiple informants	Progression from inductive to deductive; multiple informants; single industry, global studies
Product	Product advantage—cost, quality, uniqueness, fit with core competence	—	Product integrity—product vision that fits with customers and firm
Market	Size, growth, competition	—	—
Senior management	Support	—	Subtle control
Project team	X-functional, skilled	—	X-functional
Communication	High cross-functional	High internal, high external—various types and means	High internal
Organization of work	Planning and "effective" execution	—	Overlapped phases, testing, iterations, and planning
Project leaders	—	Politician and small group manager	Heavyweight leader
Customers	Early involvement	—	—
Suppliers	Early involvement	—	High involvement
Performance (dependent variable)	Financial success (profits, sales, market share)	Perceptual success (team and management ratings)	Operational success (speed, productivity)

Product Development as Rational Plan

This rational plan perspective emphasizes that successful product development is the result of (a) careful planning of a superior product for an attractive market and (b) the execution of that plan by a competent and well-coordinated cross-functional team that operates with (c) the blessings of senior management. Simply put, a product that is well planned, implemented, and appropriately supported will be a success.

The focus in this stream is on discovering which of many independent variables are correlated with the financial success of a product-development project. The studies often are exploratory, and their perspective is broad. Typically, researchers gather questionnaires or possibly interview responses from well-placed, single informants. Informants usually are asked to explain why a product succeeded or failed, using a wide spectrum of internal and external factors. However, because results are often empirically observed correlations with success, the theoretical understanding of relationships usually is quite limited, and nonsignificant findings often are not reported. Selected studies in this stream are summarized in Table 61-2, and a model is presented in Figure 61-2.

TABLE 61-2 Rational Plan Perspective: Selected Studies

Study	Sample	Context	Performance Measure (Dependent Variables)	Key Results (Independent Variables)
Myers & Marquis (1969)	567 successful product & process developments	121 U.K. construction, railroad, & computer firms	Product revenue or savings in production costs	Market: Market pull most important Communication: X-functional
SAPPHO (Rothwell, 1972; Rothwell et al., 1974)	43 success/failure product pairs	UK chemical & instrument firms[a]	Profitability & market share of product	Market: Understand user needs Senior Management: Involved
New Product (Cooper, 1979)	102 successful & 93 failed products	103 Canadian industrial firms	Profitability of product	Product: Unique or superior in customer's eyes Market: High growth, not competitive, unsatisfied customers Communication: Have synergy across different functions
Cooper & Kleinschmidt (1987)	123 successful & 80 failed products	125 Canadian manufacturing firms	11 financial measures, including profitability, market share, relative revenues	Product: Clear concept, better because of cost or quality or uniqueness Market: Attractive in size and growth potential Communication: Have synergy across different functions Senior management: Supportive Organization of work: Predevelopment planning
Stanford Innovation Project (Maidique & Zirger, 1984, 1985; Zirger & Maidique, 1990)	86 success/failure product pairs	86 U.S. *Fortune* 1,000 electronics firms	Profitability of product	Product: Synergy with competencies, better because of cost or quality or uniqueness Market: Large and growing Communication: High internal communication in X-functional teams Senior management: Supportive

[a]Number of firms was not reported.

847

FIGURE 61-2   Rational Plan Model of Product Development

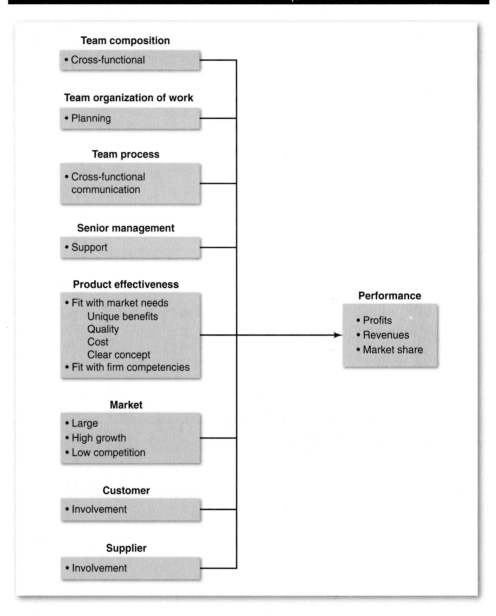

The earliest work in this stream emphasized the importance of market issues over purely technical ones for successful product development. For example, Myers and Marquis (1969) studied the development of 567 successful products and processes in over 100 firms and 5 industries. Their principal result was that market pull (i.e., identifying and understanding users' needs) was substantially more important to the success of the products than technology push, and thus a cross-functional view was a key component of product success.

Later studies added failures to the mix (e.g., Rothwell, 1972; Rubenstein, Chakrabarti, O'Keefe, Souder, & Young, 1976). The SAPPHO studies (e.g., Rothwell, 1972; Rothwell et al., 1974) were conducted using 43 success and failure pairs among chemical and instruments firms within the United Kingdom. The authors found that 41 factors, including understanding users' needs, attention to the market, efficient development, and senior leadership, were significantly related to successful product development. Although the large number of factors makes it difficult to hone precise managerial and theoretical implications, this breadth of findings yields a comprehensive view of the important issues within product development. The SAPPHO studies were then followed by similar studies in other countries such as Finland (Kulvik, 1977), Hungary (Szakasits, 1974), and West Germany (Gerstenfeld, 1976).

Subsequent research sharpened the emergent emphases on *product* advantages, *market* attractiveness, and *internal organization*. Particularly important were two studies by Cooper (1979; Cooper & Kleinschmidt, 1987). The first, the NewProd study (Cooper, 1979), examined 102 successful and 93 failed products within 103 industrial firms in Canada. A subsequent study by Cooper and Kleinschmidt (1987) examined hypotheses from the NewProd and other studies using 203 products in 125 manufacturing firms, including 123 successes and 80 failures. Data were gathered from either the most knowledgeable manager or managers using a structured interview questionnaire. Success and failure were measured by 11 mostly financial measures, including profitability, payback, sales, and market share.

The authors observed that the most important determinant of product success was product advantage. The intrinsic value of the product, including unique benefits to customers, high quality, attractive cost, and innovative features, was the critical success factor. Such products were seen as superior to competing products and solved problems that customers faced.

Internal organization also was critical to product success. Particularly important was predevelopment planning. This included developing a well-defined target market, product specifications, clear product concept, and extensive preliminary market and technical assessments. Other internal organization factors also were important, including cross-functional skills and their synergies with existing firm competencies. Top management support also was important, but less so than these other factors.

Finally, market conditions also affected product success. Cooper and Kleinschmidt (1987) found that products that entered large and growing markets were more likely to be successful. In addition, products introduced into markets with low overall intensity of competition were more successful. However, they also noted that market characteristics were less important to commercial success than were product and internal organization factors such as product advantage, clear product concept, and predevelopment planning.

More recently, Cooper and Kleinschmidt (1993) conducted another NewProd study of product development in the North American and European chemical industries. The authors replicated some of their earlier findings. Most notably, they once again found that product advantage was most strongly associated with financially successful products. Contrary to their earlier study, the authors found in this case that market competitiveness had no relationship with product success. These results suggest that the effect of market competitiveness on project outcomes needs further investigation.

The Stanford Innovation Project also emphasized product advantages, market attractiveness, and internal organization. Seventy product success/failure pairs initially were surveyed and, from these, 21 case studies were subsequently conducted (Maidique & Zirger, 1984, 1985). The third study expanded the first two by examining 86 success/failure product pairs (Zirger & Maidique, 1990). The data were gathered using a questionnaire that asked respondents to compare a product success with a product failure within their firms. Twenty-three items were examined using factor analysis and then 2-group discriminant analysis (Zirger & Maidique, 1990). The respondents were senior executives in the electronics industry who were attending an executive education program. Success was measured by whether executives considered the product to be a financial loss or a profit contributor. All hypotheses were supported.

The authors' conclusions read like a blueprint for a rationally planned product-development effort. First, excellent internal organization was important (i.e., smooth execution of all phases of the development process by well-coordinated functional groups). For example, the authors wrote, "Products are more likely to be successful if they are planned and implemented well" (Zirger & Maidique, 1990: 879). Products that had top management commitment and were built on existing corporate strengths were also likely to be successful. In addition, product factors were critical. Successful products provided superior customer value through enhanced technical performance, low cost, reliability, quality, or uniqueness. Finally, market factors also affected product success. Early entry into large, growing markets was more likely to lead to success.

More recently, other authors have identified specific aspects of rational planning, such as predevelopment planning (Dwyer & Mellor, 1991) and a focus on marketing and R&D involvement (Hise, O'Neal, Parsuraman, & McNeal, 1990), that correlate with product success. Another trend is to focus not on financial success but rather specifically on the speed of product development (e.g., Cordero, 1991; Mabert, Muth, & Schmenner, 1992). For example, Gupta and Wilemon (1990) focused on accelerating product-development pace. These authors polled 80 executives concerning factors that slowed or accelerated the development processes. Their suggestions for fast product development emphasized internal organization, including the importance of early cross-functional, customer, and supplier involvement in the process and visible top management support, more resources, and better teamwork (Gupta & Wilemon, 1990).

Overall, according to this stream of research, successful product development is the result of rational planning and execution. That is, successful products are more likely when the *product* has marketplace advantages, is targeted at an attractive *market,* and is well executed through excellent *internal organization.* Specifically, internal organization is conceptualized as carefully planned predevelopment activities, execution by competent and well-coordinated cross-functional teams playing on the synergies of the firm, and significant support from top management.

This broad-brush approach leads to an excellent and a comprehensive overview of the product-development process, which emphasizes features of the product, internal organization, and the market. This same breadth, however, also somewhat undermines the contributions of the stream. To use a colloquialism, it is often difficult to observe the "new product development" forest amid myriad "results" trees. The findings of many studies read like a "fishing expedition"—too many variables and too much factor analysis. In this research stream, it is not uncommon for a study to report 10 to 20 to even 40 or 50 important findings (e.g., Hise et al., 1990; Rubenstein et al., 1976). Further, extensive bivariate analysis is commonplace, and this blurs possible multivariate relationships.

Second, the research stream relies heavily on retrospective sense making of complex past processes, usually by single informants. Individuals often are asked to quantify subjective judgments surrounding long lists of success and failure factors. The frequent use of single informants simply exacerbates these methodological problems. Thus, the research results are likely to suffer from a host of attributional and other biases, memory lapses, and myopia, which are associated with subjective, retrospective sense-making tasks.

Most important, the research in this stream often presents results without relying on well-defined constructs. Thus, is it surprising that better products are more likely to be successful or that well-executed processes are likely to produce more successful products? Rather, the next step is figuring out just what is a "better" product or just how do people go about the "effective" execution to develop such a product. Research in this stream is largely atheoretical as well, and so it fails to take the next theory-building step. For example, Zirger and Maidique (1990) found that entry into large, growing markets improves a project's performance. However, this result is not theoretically integrated with existing research that warns of first-mover disadvantages (Lieberman & Montgomery, 1988) or describes the power of imitation strategy (Bolton, 1993). Moreover, given their often exploratory nature, studies in this stream often do not report nonsignificant findings, which further inhibits theory building. Nonetheless, despite these shortcomings, this research stream has been enormously important, particularly in creating an early and a broad understanding of which factors are essential for successful product development and for emphasizing the role of the market in what is often conceived of as a purely technical or organizational task.

Product Development as Communication Web

A second stream of product-development research centers on communication. This research stream has evolved from the pioneering work of Allen at MIT (1971, 1977). The underlying premise is that communication among project team members and with outsiders stimulates the performance of development teams. Thus, the better that members are connected with each other and with key outsiders, the more successful the development process will be.

In contrast to the first perspective, this stream is narrowly focused on one independent variable—communication. Thus, these studies emphasize *depth,* not breadth as in the rational plan, by looking inside the "black box" of the development team. They complement the rational lens by including political and information-processing aspects of product development. The result is excellent theoretical understanding of a narrow segment of the phenomenon. In this case, there also is greater methodological sophistication (e.g., multiple informants, multivariate analysis) than in the first stream. Selected studies in this stream are highlighted in Table 61-3, and a model is presented in Figure 61-3.

Some of the earliest empirical research along these lines was focused on the flow of information in R&D groups (e.g., Allen, 1971, 1977). Often the approach used was to have professionals keep track of their communications for some period of time. For example, Katz and Tushman (1981) studied the performance of project groups in the R&D facility of a large corporation. In 60 project groups, a total of 345 professionals kept track of their communications for a randomly chosen day each week for 15 weeks.

The results of these early studies highlight the importance of *external communication* to success. Specifically, these studies observed the presence of "gatekeepers"— (i.e., high-performing individuals who also communicated more often overall and with people outside their specialty) (Allen, 1971). These gatekeepers brought information into the organization and dispersed it to fellow team members. The authors noted that gatekeepers not only gathered and translated external information, but they also facilitated the external communication of their fellow team members (Katz & Tushman, 1981). Further, members of development projects with gatekeepers performed better than those without, even after accounting for the direct effect of the gatekeeper's high, personal performance. Teams with gatekeepers communicated more externally, leading to improved project performance (Katz & Tushman, 1981). Finally, Von Hippel (1986) noted how important communication with key customers was regarding better product designs.

Other authors have built on this early work by Allen and colleagues. For example, the content of external communication has been examined closely by Ancona and Caldwell (1990, 1992a,b). These authors collected questionnaires from 409 members of 45 new product-development teams in 5 companies on communication and success patterns. Success was measured by subjective team and management ratings of performance. The authors found that team members communicated more with outsiders who had similar functional backgrounds. Thus, when there were more functions represented on the team, there was more external communication by the team as a whole and better management-rated performance (Ancona & Caldwell, 1992a).

More important, the authors (Ancona & Caldwell, 1990) developed a typology of external communication or "boundary-spanning" behaviors. Ambassador activities consisted of political activities such as lobbying for support and resources as well as buffering the team from outside pressure and engaging in impression management. Task coordination involved coordination of technical or design issues. Scouting consisted of general scanning for useful information, whereas guard activities were those intended to avoid the external release of proprietary information.

Ancona and Caldwell (1992b) subsequently identified group-level strategies employed by the 45 product-development teams in their sample. One of this study's most interesting findings was that the frequency of external communications was *not* a significant predictor of team performance. Rather, communication strategy was germane. The most successful product-development teams engaged in a comprehensive external communication strategy, combining ambassador and task-coordination behaviors that helped these teams to secure resources, gain task-related information, and so enhance success. In contrast, less successful product-development teams used strategies involving fewer types of external communication activities and less overall external

TABLE 61-3 Communication Web Perspective Selected Studies

Study	Sample	Context	Performance Measure (Dependent Variables)	Key Results (Independent Variables)
Allen (1971, 1977) Katz & Tushman (1981)	R&D professionals i.e., 345 professionals in 60 projects (Katz & Tushman)	large U.S. R&D laboratories	Management rated overall technical performance of project	Communication: Technology gatekeeper, frequent external communication; Project Leader: As politician
Katz (1982)	50 R&D project groups	1 large U.S. R&D laboratory	Team and management rated performance for overall team performance	Communication: Curvilinear relationship with group longevity, mediated by external communication
Katz & Allen (1985)	86 R&D project teams	9 technology-based major U.S. firms	Senior management rated team performance	Project Leader: Project manager as powerful small-group manager; functional manager as inward- & technology-focused leader
Keller (1986)	32 R&D project groups	1 large U.S. R&D organization	Team & management rated performance for quality, budget, schedule	Communication: Internal communication as group cohesiveness
Ancona & Caldwell (1990, 1992a, 1992b)	45 product-development teams	5 large high-tech firms[a]	Team and management rated performance for innovation, schedule, efficiency, budgets, and conflict	Communication: External communication combining ambassadorial and task coordination; internal communication as defined goals, workable plans, and prioritized work
Dougherty (1990, 1992) Dougherty & Corse	40 product-development projects	15 large high-tech firms (chemicals & computers/communication)[a]	Failure (cancellation) & success as rated by management	Communication: Overcome "thought world" barriers through interactive and iterative communication, concrete experiences, and violating organizational routines

[a]Geographic location of firms was not reported.

FIGURE 61-3   Communication Web Model of Product Development

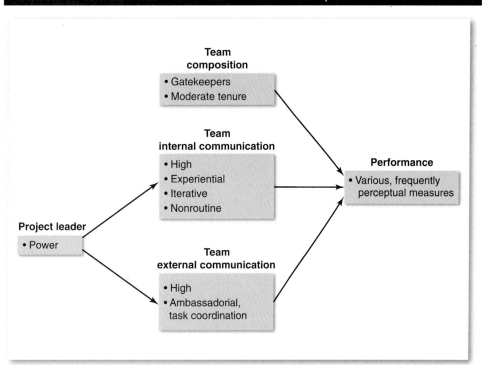

communication. Thus, more effective teams engaged in both political and task-oriented external communications, suggesting that product-development teams must attend not only to the frequency of external communication, but also to the nature of that interaction (Ancona & Caldwell, 1992b). Work by Benjamin (1993) has led to similar conclusions regarding the importance of external political communication and impression management.

There also has been interest in *internal communication* among team members. For example, in his study of 32 project groups, Keller (1986) found that internal group cohesion helped performance. Similarly, Ancona and Caldwell (1992a) found that teams with more thorough internal communication (e.g., they defined goals better, developed workable plans, and prioritized work) had superior performance. Also, Joyce (1986) observed that powerful project leaders in matrix organizations often enhanced the quantity of internal communication but decreased its quality.

The critical cross-functional issues of internal communication have been explored by Dougherty (1990, 1992; Dougherty & Corse). This research consisted of a multiple case, inductive study of the barriers that hinder cross-functional communication. The study examined 18 new product-development efforts in 5 firms. Failed products were those that were canceled after introduction. Successful products were those that were meeting or exceeding expectations after introduction. Later research (Dougherty & Corse) extended the sample to 40 projects, 134 people, and 15 firms. A key feature is emphasis on innovative product development in large, established firms.

Dougherty (1990) demonstrated that various functional departments were tantamount to "thought worlds," each with its own "fund of knowledge"—what members know—and "system of meaning"—how members know (Dougherty, 1992). Not surprisingly, individuals from different departments understood different aspects of product development, and they understood these aspects in different ways. This difference led to varying interpretations, even of the same information. Interestingly, what distinguished successful projects was not the absence or presence of these barriers, but rather how they were overcome. For successful products, cross-functional personnel combined their perspectives in a highly interactive, iterative fashion (Dougherty, 1990). This type of internal communication appeared to increase information content. In contrast, failed products were characterized by sequential attention by functional groups such that each departmental view dominated a particular phase of the project.

Project teams also overcame cross-functional communication barriers when team members participated in concrete tasks together and violated routines such as usual relationships and divisions of tasks (e.g., Dougherty, 1992; Dougherty & Corse). These tactics for organizing internal communication appeared to increase the information flow during the communication process. Dougherty (1992) described, for example, how one team met with customers directly in focus groups to achieve a common team understanding of who the customer was. This common experience improved the information content of the communication as team members developed a common understanding of the customer while working together.

Finally, researchers also have been interested in how communication affects the performance of teams over time. For example, Katz (1982) explored the relationship among the mean tenure of a team, the degree of external communication, and performance. In his study of 50 product-development teams in a large American corporation, he found that initially group performance increased with increasing mean tenure of the group, but this relationship reversed and performance dropped off after five years. The decline in performance was significantly correlated with a decline in external communication.

In summary, the results indicate that *external communication* is critical to successful product development. However, this stream goes beyond this rather intuitive result to illustrate how teams increase their external communication and what types of communication are important. Specifically, successful product-development teams include gatekeepers, who encourage team communication outside of their groups, and powerful project managers, who communicate externally to ensure resources for the group. In addition, such teams also engage in extensive political and task-oriented external communication. The underlying rationale is that politically oriented external communication increases the resources of the team, whereas task-oriented external communication increases the amount and variety of information. These types of communication, in turn, aid the development-process performance.

Similarly, *internal communication* improves development-team performance. For example, managers who are inwardly focused on the technical issues of the project will enhance internal communication and improve team performance. Cross-functional teams that structure their internal communication around concrete tasks, novel routines, and fluid job descriptions also have been associated with improved internal communication and successful products. These observations on how to break down cross-functional barriers are particularly critical insights. Thus, high internal communication increases the amount and variety of internal information flow and, so, improves development-process performance.

Overall, two theoretical themes emerge in the literature. One, an information-processing view, emphasizes that frequent and appropriately structured task communication (both internal and external) leads to more comprehensive and varied information flow to team members and, thus, to higher performing development processes. The second, a resource dependence view, emphasizes that frequent political communication (typically external) leads to higher performing development processes by increasing the resources (e.g., budget, personnel, equipment) available to the team.

In contrast, the principal shortcoming of this perspective is that it is so focused on communication by project team members that other factors (e.g., organization of the work, product attributes, market attractiveness) are neglected. There are also other problems. For example, although this research is more methodologically sophisticated than the first stream (e.g., multiple informants, multivariate analysis, tighter constructs), performance measures frequently are very subjective, and so it is difficult to know whether the results would replicate for more objective measures of performance, such as product profitability. In addition, the research in this stream does not distinguish between different types of products, such as incremental versus breakthrough versus platform products. However, as Katz (1982) observed, such distinctions may affect appropriate types of communication.

Despite these problems, this research stream has been influential, particularly in highlighting the political and information-processing dynamics underlying the communication processes of successful product-development teams. Thus, the in-depth focus of the communication web complements the sweeping perspective of the rational plan.

Product Development as Disciplined Problem Solving

A third stream of research is what we have termed the *disciplined problem-solving* perspective. This stream evolved from studies of Japanese product-development practices in the mid-1980s (e.g., Imai et al., 1985; Quinn, 1985). In this case, successful product development is seen as a balancing act between relatively autonomous problem solving by the project team and the discipline of a heavyweight leader, strong top management, and an overarching product vision. The result is a fast, productive development process and a high-quality product concept. Selected studies are summarized in Table 61-4, and a corresponding model appears in Figure 61-4.

Case-based research (Imai et al., 1985; Quinn, 1985; Takeuchi & Nonaka, 1986) laid the groundwork for this stream of research. For example, Imai and colleagues (1985) studied seven successful product-development efforts in five different Japanese companies across several industries. The seven products included Fuji-Xerox's FX-3500 copier, the City box-car by Honda, and the Canon Auto Boy (Sure Shot) camera. Performance was defined in terms of speed and flexibility of development.

The authors found several management practices that were particularly effective for fast, efficient product development. One was the extensive use of supplier networks. The researchers observed that strong formal ties to suppliers and R&D networks were very important to the product-development process. In such networks, suppliers can acquire a very high level of technical skill in a specialized area, which allows them to fulfill sudden or unusual requests quickly and effectively.

Imai and colleagues (1985) also observed a problem-solving strategy involving cross-functional development teams that aided effective product development. When the development team was composed of members with varied functional specializations, team members had access to more diverse information. In addition, cross-functional teams permitted the overlap of development phases, which also quickened the pace of product development. Furthermore, the authors observed that product development was accelerated by overlapping of development phases and cross-functional teams only if supported by continuous communication among project members. This communication increased the information flow among team members, making it easier for team members to understand each other's specialties and to coordinate overlapped development phases. The creation of redundant information (Nonaka, 1990) and an emphasis on extensive multifunctional training (Imai et al., 1985) also were related to this style of problem solving.

Finally, Imai and colleagues (1985) noted that rather than playing just a supportive role, as suggested by the rational plan studies (e.g., Cooper & Kleinschmidt, 1987; Gupta & Wilemon, 1990; Zirger & Maidique, 1990), senior management should engage in "subtle control." The key idea behind subtle control is that members of successful project teams maintain a balance between allowing ambiguity, such that creative problem solving can flourish at the project team level, and exercising sufficient control, such that the resulting product fits with overall corporate competencies and strategy. The authors found that, for the best performance results, senior management engaged in subtle control by communicating a clear vision of objectives to their teams while simultaneously giving team members the freedom to work autonomously within the discipline of that vision.

Later research replicated and extended this early work. For example, several Harvard researchers studied the management of product-development projects in the auto industry (Clark et al., 1987; Clark & Fujimoto, 1991; Hayes, Wheelwright, & Clark, 1988). These very impressive data consist of in-depth case studies of 29 major car-development projects across 20 companies—3 American, 8 Japanese, and 9 European.

TABLE 61-4 Disciplined Problem Solving: Selected Studies

Study	Sample	Context	Performance Measure (Dependent Variables)	Key Results (Independent Variables)	
Imai et al. (1985) Takeuchi & Nonaka (1986)	7 successful development projects	5 Japanese companies	Speed, flexibility	Senior management: Communication:	Subtle control High internal team communication, multilevel learning
				Organization of work:	Cross-functional teams, overlapping phases
				Suppliers:	High involvement
Harvard Auto Study (Clark, Chew, & Fujimoto, 1987; Clark & Fujimoto, 1991; Hayes et al., 1988)	29 development projects	20 firms in the auto industry—U.S., Japan, and Europe	Quality, speed, productivity	Product: Communication:	Product integrity High internal team communication
				Organization of work:	Cross-functional teams, overlapping phases, predevelopment planning
				Project leader:	Heavyweight project manager
				Supplier:	High involvement
MIT Auto Study (Womack et al., 1990)	Same as Harvard study plus consolidated data from other sources	Same as Harvard study	Operational variables, including quality, speed, productivity	Communication:	High internal team communication
				Organization of work:	Cross-functional teams, overlapping phases, predevelopment planning
Iansiti (1992, 1993)	27 development projects	Firms in mainframe computer industry—U.S., Europe, Japan[a]	Speed, productivity	Product: Organization of work:	Product integrity Predevelopment planning
Eisenhardt & Tabrizi	72 development projects	36 Asian, U.S., & European computer firms	Speed	Organization of work:	Cross-functional teams, iterative prototype and test process, limited planning and use of CAD, don't reward for schedule

[a]Number of firms was not reported.

FIGURE 61-4   Disciplined Problem-Solving Model of Product Development

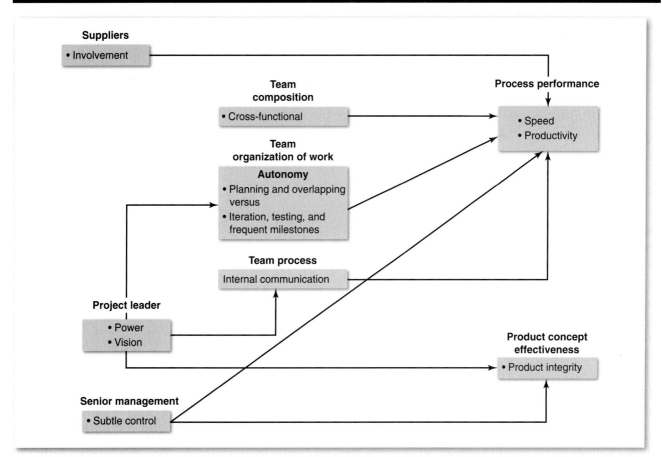

Similar to the aforementioned study by Imai and his colleagues, this research examined new models of established products, not breakthrough products. This auto industry data measured the performance of the product-development process along three dimensions: total product quality, lead time, and productivity.

The authors (e.g., Clark et al., 1987; Clark & Fujimoto, 1991) replicated earlier findings. They reported that extensive supplier networks coupled with overlapping product-development phases, communication, and cross-functional groups (what they term *integrated problem solving*) improved the performance of development teams. The authors also introduced two central concepts: heavyweight team leaders and product integrity. These two concepts help to clarify the meaning of subtle control.

"Heavyweight" team leaders are powerful "linking pins" who, on the one hand, coordinate the activities of a product-development team and, on the other hand, work with senior management to create an overarching product concept. Thus, senior management can exercise subtle control through the use of such leaders who manage their teams in the context of a product vision. The findings indicate that these team leaders are able to gain resources, command respect, and break down traditional functional allegiances while simultaneously building a strong product vision (Clark et al., 1987; Clark & Fujimoto, 1991; Hayes et al., 1988).

"Product integrity" (Clark & Fujimoto, 1991), unlike the dimensions of product attractiveness in the rational plan perspective such as low price, describes the notion of a product's being consistent with the corporate image. Product integrity implies a clear vision of the product's intended image, performance, and fit with corporate competencies and customers. By focusing on establishing product integrity, senior management can ensure that an overall vision for the product is communicated to the project team and, thus, balance the autonomy gained through heavyweight leadership.

Finally, this study also added an emphasis on predevelopment activities. Hayes and others (1988) described how bringing conflicts to the surface early in the development process was an important factor in successful development projects. By resolving conflicts through mutual accommodation at low levels in the organizational hierarchy, a clear project vision was established early on, which subsequently sped up the development process.

A study related to the Harvard auto industry research, the MIT International Motor Vehicle Program, examined lean versus mass production in the auto industry. This study (Womack, Jones, & Roos, 1990) presented Clark and Fujimoto's (1991) data along with some consolidated data from secondary sources. Not surprisingly, many of their conclusions, such as the importance of powerful leaders, overlapping development phases, predevelopment activity, and internal communication to product development, replicated those of the Harvard study (Clark et al., 1987; Clark & Fujimoto, 1991; Hayes et al., 1988).

More recent research in this stream emphasized industries with less domination by Japanese competitors and more scientific content. For example, Iansiti (1992, 1993) deductively examined the mainframe computer industry. His data consisted of 27 in-depth studies that represent all the major products developed by the 12 chief competitors in the mainframe computer industry (from Japan, the United States, and Europe) during the 1980s. The author focused on the development of technologies associated with the packaging and interconnect system of the mainframe processor.

The primary result is that a high system focus (i.e., a combination of technical integration, exposure to systems integration, and accumulation of interaction knowledge) predicted both lead time and productivity. Similar to product integrity, system focus implied concern for how technology choices for a given component fit with the product as a whole. Like predevelopment activities, system focus also involved early planning for the integration of new technology, product expectations, and manufacturing systems into the problem-solving process. Thus, this result strengthened earlier findings that predevelopment planning and product integrity enhanced the performance of product-development teams.

A study by Eisenhardt and Tabrizi examined the computer industry in Japan, Europe, and the United States. This deductive study considered 72 products in 36 firms, including the personal, workstation, mainframe, and peripherals segments of the industry. Thus, the average product life cycle was substantially shorter than in the mainframe computer or automobile industry studies. The data were collected on site using research teams who helped firm personnel gather data. The focus was on speed of development as the performance measure. Specifically, the authors compared a compression model of fast product development with an experiential approach.

The unique insight of this study is that fast product development was associated with the experiential approach (Eisenhardt & Tabrizi, in press). Product teams who engaged in more experiential or improvisational product design through frequent iterations, more testing, frequent milestones, and powerful leadership developed products more quickly. In contrast, attempts simply to compress the product-development cycle through the use of computer-aided design (CAD), rewards for schedule attainment, supplier involvement, overlapping development stages, or extensive planning not only did not accelerate pace, but, in fact, often slowed it. The exception was the mainframe segment in which the use of CAD, supplier involvement, and overlap effectively accelerated the pace. Thus, these results suggest that there are two relevant problem-solving models for organizing product development. One focuses on factors such as planning and overlap that are relevant for more stable products in mature settings (e.g., Clark & Fujimoto, 1991; Iansiti, 1992), and the other focuses on experiential product design that is relevant for less predictable products in uncertain settings, such as personal computers, work-stations, and peripherals. Finally, as in the previous research, cross-functional teams sped up development for all industry segments.

In summary, this stream of research envisions successful product development as disciplined problem solving. That is, successful product development involves relatively autonomous *problem solving* by cross-functional teams with high communication and the organization of work according to the demands of the development task. This perspective also highlights the role of project leaders and senior management in giving problem solving a *discipline*—a product vision. There is an emphasis on both project and senior management, on the one hand, to provide a vision or discipline to the development efforts and yet, on the other hand, to provide autonomy to the team. Thus, this stream portrays product development as a *balancing act* between product vision developed at the executive level and problem solving found at the project level.

In contrast to the rational plan stream, this stream is more specific about the effective organization of work and is more focused on the development process and product concept than on the financial success of the product. In contrast to the communication web perspective, this stream has a broader scope and considers the role of suppliers and senior management in addition to project leaders and teams. Methodologically, the data are much richer and more detailed than the single-informant information that underlies much of the rational stream. Theoretically, this perspective extends the information-processing view of the communication web research by emphasizing not only the amount and variety of information, but also its organization into problem-solving strategies.

However, the stream suffers from several shortcomings. One is that there is a lack of political and psychological realism. In comparison with the communication web, there is naive understanding of the political realities of product development, such as the dependence of project teams on external actors for resources. From a psychological standpoint, there is little appreciation of the problems of actually motivating people and making cross-functional teams, high communication, and overlapping work. Moreover, the heavyweight leaders seem almost "superhuman" in their skills and duties.

Second, some of the constructs are challenging to comprehend. For example, subtle control, product vision, and system focus are vague concepts. Even with attempts at clarification (e.g., Clark & Fujimoto, 1990; Clark & Wheelwright, 1992), product integrity and heavyweight project leader concepts also remain hazy. Although this lack of clarity may reflect the complexity of the subject (or perhaps the often non-Western origin of the ideas), it also impairs the usefulness of the perspective.

Finally, there is an extensive reliance on a Japanese viewpoint. Even though Japanese comparisons have been critical to improving thinking, Japanese industrial dominance sometimes makes it unclear which features are important to product development and which are simply Japanese. This concern seems particularly relevant to the supplier network findings (e.g., Clark & Fujimoto, 1991; Imai et al., 1985), which are dependent on the specifics of the Japanese industrial infrastructure. Nonetheless, the image of product development as disciplined problem solving is a powerful and sophisticated metaphor for successful product development.

TOWARD AN INTEGRATIVE MODEL OF PRODUCT DEVELOPMENT

In the previous section, we described three streams of product-development research. These streams evolved from different sources and focused on somewhat different aspects of product development. However, as we observed previously, they also offer complementary and sometimes overlapping insights into product development. In this section, we rely on these insights to provide the basis of an integrative model.

Key to developing this model is the observation that the three streams focus on both overlapping and complementary sets of constructs. The rational plan perspective contributes a sweeping view of product development, including team, senior management, market, and product characteristics to predict financial success. In contrast, the problem-solving perspective has a more deeply focused view on the actual development process (i.e., those project team and management factors that contribute to a better product-development process and a more effective product concept). The concepts are more elaborated than in the rational plan perspective so that, for example, the "effective execution" of the rational plan is given more concrete and detailed development in the problem-solving perspective. The communication web perspective is narrower still. This research centers on a very specific, although important, aspect of product development, namely on internal and external communication by project team members.

Also key to developing an integrative model is the observation that the streams have complementary theoretical approaches. The rational plan perspective is largely atheoretical, consisting of collections of associations. In contrast, the product-solving perspective has a cognitive theoretical orientation, which links ideas about information and its organization to effective problem solving. Finally, the communication perspective relies on a simpler but consistent theoretical view of information (i.e., the amount and variety of information) and a complementary political perspective, which emphasizes the need for resources.

These overlapping and complementary focal interests as well as the theoretical complementarities suggest that the streams are ready for synthesis into an integrative model. In this section, we craft such an integrated conceptual perspective that summarizes key findings within the literature and provides a departure point for future studies of product development. The resulting model is depicted in Figure 61-1.

Model Overview

The organizing idea behind the model in Figure 61-1 is that there are multiple players whose actions influence product performance. Specifically, we argue that (a) the project team, leader, senior management, and suppliers affect *process performance* (i.e., speed and productivity of product development), (b) the project leader, customers, and senior management affect *product effectiveness* (i.e., the fit of the product with firm competencies and market needs), and (c) the combination of an efficient process, effective product, and munificent market shapes the *financial success* of the product (i.e., revenue, profitability, and market share).

Underlying these relationships are the theoretical underpinnings that we have identified from the combined research streams. Thus, process performance is driven by the amount, variety, and problem-solving organization of information and by the resources available to the team. Product effectiveness is driven by the input of leaders, senior management, and customers into the formation of a clear product vision (a less well-understood process). Both product effectiveness and process performance influence the financial success of the product. We turn now to a description of the model, arranged according to the key players.

Project Team

The heart of the product-development process and the focus of much research is the project team. Project team members are the people who actually do the work of product development. They are the people who transform vague ideas, concepts, and product specifications into the design of new products. Not surprisingly, then, the project team is central to our model of product development. Specifically, we argue that the *composition, group process,* and *work organization* of the project team affect the information, resources, and problem-solving style of the team. These, in turn, ultimately influence process performance (i.e., speed and productivity of the process) (Figure 61-1).

Regarding composition, consistent with all three streams, *cross-functional teams* are critical to process performance (e.g., Clark & Fujimoto, 1991; Dougherty, 1992; Zirger & Maidique, 1990). We define *cross-functional teams* as those project groups with members from more than one functional area such as engineering, manufacturing, or marketing. The underlying reasoning is that the functional diversity of these teams increases the amount and variety of information available to design products. This increased information helps project team members to understand the design process more quickly and fully from a variety of perspectives, and thus it improves design process performance. Moreover, the increased information helps the team to catch downstream problems such as manufacturing difficulties or market mismatches before they happen, when these problems are generally smaller and easier to fix. Thus, consistent with the empirical support in all three research streams, cross-functional teams are associated with high-performing processes. Moreover, this link (1) in the model is among the most important and empirically robust (e.g., Clark & Fujimoto, 1991; Dougherty, 1992; Zirger & Maidique, 1990).

Gatekeepers are another important facet of project team composition. Gatekeepers are individuals who frequently obtain information external to the group and then share it within the project team. Similar to cross-functional teams, they affect process performance by increasing the amount and variety of information available in the design process. Gatekeepers expose the project team members to more and diverse information such as new technical developments occurring outside the group. Although gatekeepers are probably less important in cross-functional teams because the members of such teams have natural outside contacts in their functional homes, gatekeepers clearly increase the external information reaching the project team (link 1 in the model) (Allen, 1971, 1977; Katz & Tushman, 1981).

Finally, *team tenure* is a third composition factor that plays a role in influencing process performance. Teams with a short history together tend to lack effective patterns of information sharing and working together (Katz, 1982). Thus, the amount and variety of information that can be communicated among project team members is limited by this unfamiliarity. In contrast, teams with a long tenure together tend to become inward focused and neglect external communication (Katz, 1982). This tendency restricts the information and resources from outside the team that the team members receive. Because neither of these situations is desirable, process performance is highest when team tenure is at moderate levels. At this level of tenure, team members are most likely to engage in both extensive internal and external communication and, therefore, to receive maximum benefit. As Katz found (1982), this leads to higher project performance (link 1 in the model).

Another important factor affecting process performance is group process, especially communication. Results from all three research streams indicate that effective group processes, particularly those related to communication, increase information and so are essential for high-performing development processes (e.g., Imai et al., 1985; Katz, 1982; Zirger & Maidique, 1990). In the case of *internal communication* (e.g., Dougherty, 1990; Keller, 1986), frequent communication increases the amount of information directly in that more communication usually yields more information. More subtly, frequent communication also builds team cohesion, which then breaks down barriers to communication and so increases the amount of information as well (Keller, 1986). Moreover, especially when this communication is effectively structured (e.g., includes concrete communication surrounding shared group experiences and non-routine rule breaking [Dougherty, 1992]), it cuts misunderstandings and barriers to interchange so that the amount of information conveyed is increased. This, in turn, improves the speed and productivity of the entire development process (Dougherty, 1992).

In the case of *external communication,* frequent communication with outsiders such as customers, suppliers, and other organizational personnel opens the project team up to new information (e.g., Clark & Fujimoto, 1991; Imai et al., 1985; Katz, 1982; Katz & Tushman, 1981). When this external communication is task oriented, team members gain information from diverse viewpoints beyond those of the team. Further, when the communication is frequent, project teams are likely to develop an absorptive capacity such that they become more efficient in gaining and using the information being conveyed. Both of these factors should improve the productivity and pace of the development process. Also important is external communication in the form of political activities such as lobbying for resources, engaging in impression management, and seeking senior management support for the project (Ancona & Caldwell, 1992b). Taken together and consistent with previous research, internal and external communication both increase the amount and variety of information and the resources available to the project team. These, in turn, improve process performance. These links (link 2 in the model) are also among the most empirically robust (e.g., Ancona & Caldwell, 1992b; Clark & Fujimoto, 1991; Imai et al., 1985; Katz, 1982; Katz & Allen, 1985; Katz & Tushman, 1981).

The third team feature of the model is the problem-solving strategy by which team members organize their work. As described in the problem-solving stream, several empirical findings suggest a contingent set of problem-solving strategies that are appropriate for different types of tasks (Eisenhardt & Tabrizi). Each strategy represents a different structuring of information. For stable and relatively mature products such as automobiles (Hayes et al., 1988; Womack et al., 1990) and mainframe computers (Eisenhardt & Tabrizi, Iansiti, 1992), product development is a complex task for which tactics such as *extensive planning* and *overlapped development stages* are appropriate. These tactics assume a certain but often complex problem-solving task that can be rationalized. For example, consistent with the rational and problem-solving perspectives, planning (e.g., Cooper & Kleinschmidt, 1987; Hayes et al., 1988; Iansiti, 1992; Zirger & Maidique, 1990) improves the speed and productivity of the development process by eliminating extra work, rationalizing and properly ordering the steps of the process, and avoiding errors. Similarly, overlapped development stages improve process performance (Clark & Fujimoto, 1991; Imai et al., 1985) by allowing at least partially simultaneous execution of development steps such as design and test, which often are viewed as sequential. In effect, the development process is squeezed together (e.g., Clark & Fujimoto, 1991).

In contrast, when there is more uncertainty in the design process, such as in rapidly changing industries (e.g., microcomputers), more experiential tactics, including *frequent iterations* of product designs, *extensive testing* of those designs, and *short milestones* (i.e., short time between successive milestones) improve process performance (e.g., Eisenhardt & Tabrizi). The underlying idea is that under conditions of uncertainty it is not helpful to plan. Rather, maintaining flexibility and learning quickly through improvisation and experience yield effective process performance (e.g., Eisenhardt & Tabrizi, Miner & Moorman, 1993; Weick, 1993). However, although these ideas may be attractive, they have not been examined extensively, and the contingencies between these factors and the previously mentioned factors of overlap and planning have not been well explored empirically (link 3 in the model). As we will discuss, further elaboration and testing of this part of the model are prime opportunities for future research.

Project Leader

Even though the cross-functional team is the heart of efficient product development, the project leader is the pivotal figure in the development process. Consistent with the communication and problem-solving perspectives, the project leader is the linking pin or bridge between the project team and senior management. Therefore, as indicated in Figure 61-1 the project leader critically affects both the process performance (i.e., speed and productivity of the development process) and the effectiveness of the product (e.g., Clark & Fujimoto, 1991; Joyce, 1986; Katz & Allen, 1985). Several characteristics of the project team leader are particularly germane.

One central characteristic is the *power* of the project leader. By powerful leaders we mean those project leaders with significant decision-making responsibility, organizationwide authority, and high hierarchical level. Such leaders are particularly able to improve process performance. The underlying rationale is that such leaders are highly effective in obtaining resources such as more personnel and larger budgets for the project team. As Ancona and Caldwell (1992b) observed, powerful project leaders are particularly effective politicians in lobbying for resources, protecting the group from outside interference, and managing the impressions of outsiders. In contrast, less powerful project leaders are likely to be less successful in gaining needed talent and financial support and in shielding the team from outside interference. In addition, powerful leaders also may command greater respect and, thus, may be able to attract better project team members to the group and to keep groups focused and motivated (Clark & Fujimoto, 1991). These qualities, in turn, create a faster and more productive development process. Moreover, because the importance of a powerful leader has been demonstrated in both the communication and problem-solving streams (e.g., Clark & Fujimoto, 1991; Katz & Allen, 1985) (link 4 in the model), it is a robust link.

A second, important characteristic of the project leader is *vision*. Vision involves the cognitive ability to mesh a variety of factors together to create an effective, holistic view and to communicate it to others. Specifically, in the case of product development, this means meshing together firm competencies (e.g., particular technical, marketing, or other skills) and strategies with the needs of the market (e.g., consumer preferences for style and cost) to create an effective product concept. As described in the problem-solving perspective, this is a critical characteristic of project leaders because they often are central to the creation of the product concept. Project leaders, together with senior management, frequently shape the overall product concept and communicate it to project team members (Clark & Fujimoto, 1991). However, even though this aspect of project leadership is, we think, compelling, our understanding of exactly what vision is, what an effective product is, and the theoretical links between the two is very weak (link 5 in the model). As we discuss further in our suggestions for future research, understanding this creative task is an important research direction.

Finally, project team leaders also are small-group managers of their project teams. Surprisingly, however, there is very little research about appropriate internal *management skill* for project leaders beyond studies of matrix communication and leadership (Joyce, 1986; Katz & Allen, 1985). Perhaps, simply, the general research on leadership of small groups applies here.

Senior Management

Although the team and project leader are critical in the product-development process, senior management is important as well. Consistent with studies in the rational stream, senior management *support* is critical to successful product-development processes (e.g., Cooper & Kleinschmidt, 1987; Gupta & Wilemon, 1990; Rothwell, 1972; Zirger & Maidique, 1990). By support we mean the provision of resources to the project team, including both financial and political resources. The underlying reasoning is that this support is essential for obtaining the resources necessary to attract team members to the project, to gain project approval to go ahead, and to provide the funding necessary to foster the development effort. Thus, as shown in Figure 61-1, senior management support is essential for fast and productive product development. This link (6 in the model) is well supported in the literature (e.g., Cooper & Kleinschmidt, 1987; Gupta & Wilemon, 1990; Katz & Allen, 1985; Zirger & Maidique, 1990).

Second, as described by Imai and colleagues (1985) in the problem-solving perspective, the ability of senior management to provide what they term *subtle control* also is important to both superior process performance and effective products. Much like the vision of project leaders, subtle control involves having the vision necessary to develop and communicate a distinctive, coherent product concept. As we described previously, senior management and project leaders often work together to develop such a product concept. At the same time, subtle control also involves delegation by senior management to project teams such that they have enough autonomy to be motivated and creative. We argue that such creativity and motivation are likely to yield a better development process. However, as in the case of project leader vision, the subtle control and product effectiveness concepts and their theoretical links are blurred and lack rigorous empirical examination (link 7 in the model). We will discuss this lack of clarity in our suggestions for future research.

Suppliers and Customers

The final key players in the model are suppliers and customers. Previous research has associated a faster development process with early (Gupta & Wilemon, 1990) and extensive (Clark & Fujimoto, 1991; Imai et al., 1985) supplier involvement. As explained in the problem-solving stream, extensive supplier involvement in product design can cut the complexity of the design project, which in turn creates a faster and more productive product-development process. Such involvement also can alert the project team to potential downstream problems early on, at a point when they are easier and faster to fix. Customer involvement also has been shown to improve the effectiveness of the product concept in the rational plan stream (e.g., Cooper & Kleinschmidt, 1987; Zirger & Maidique, 1990). However, it is not clear exactly how or when suppliers and customers are appropriately involved in the development process, and the evidence is not unaminous (e.g., Eisenhardt & Tabrizi, in press). Thus, even though the participation of these outside constituents is probably important, the empirical literature is imprecise (links 8 and 9 in the model). Again, we address this in our discussion of future research.

Financial Success

The previous discussion linked the key players in product development to process performance and product effectiveness. The final portion of the model combines these two factors with characteristics of the market to predict the financial performance of the product.

The underlying rationale for the link (10 in the model) between *process performance* and *financial success* of the product is twofold. A productive process means lower costs and thus, lower prices, which, in turn, should lead to greater product success. Second, a faster process creates strategic flexibility and less time to product launch, both of which may lead to financially successful products. The second predictor of the financial success of the product is *product effectiveness* (link 11 in the model). As shown in the rational plan literature (e.g., Cooper & Klein-Schmidt, 1987; Zirger & Maidique, 1990), product characteristics such as low-cost and unique benefits and fit-with-firm competencies create financially successful products. Presumably, such products are more attractive to consumers.

Finally, consistent with research in the rational stream (Cooper & Kleinschmidt, 1987; Zirger & Maidique, 1990), the third link (12 in the model) ties a *munificent market* to financial success. Specifically, we define a munificent market as one that is large and growing and has low competition. The reasoning is that such markets offer the possibility of large sales and, in the case of growing markets, competitive instability that may favor new products.

Overall, the argument is that a strong product-development process, an attractive product, and a munificent market should lead to a financially successful product. However, although these links have some substantiation in the rational plan literature and seem plausible, they have received little rigorous testing and rely on limited theoretical logic. As we will discuss, this portion of the model presents another excellent opportunity for future research.

AGENDA FOR FUTURE RESEARCH

As noted in the previous section, many of the concepts and theoretical links presented in the model in Figure 61-1 have been well studied. However, some concepts are less sharply defined, and some theoretical links are not well tested. These shortcomings present research opportunities.

One research opportunity is to examine the primary links of the model—that is, the links among process performance, effective product, market factors, and financial performance. As was noted, these links have been primarily empirically examined in the rational plan research stream. However, because the methodology in this research stream so often involves subjective, retrospective responses by single informants and bivariate analysis, the validity of these links is tenuous. Thus, a test of these fundamental theoretical links would be useful. A related research opportunity is determining the relative importance of these factors. For example, although Cooper and Kleinschmidt (1987, 1993) found that the market was not as relevant as other variables in predicting product success, it would be useful to examine the robustness of this claim.

Another related opportunity is to examine whether process performance, product effectiveness, and munificent markets are actually independent variables. For example, market factors may moderate the relationship of process performance and product effectiveness to financial success.[2] It may well be that process performance and product effectiveness are important predictors of financial success only in poor markets, whereas most products will be successful in munificent markets. This reasoning reemphasizes the need to garner a better understanding of the relative importance that these factors have in driving financial performance.

A second area of research is the organization of work. As was noted, two models have emerged to describe alternative organizations of work. One is the fairly well-studied model that includes extensive planning and overlapped development stages (e.g., Hayes et al., 1988; Iansiti, 1993) that was developed in the context of complex products in mature markets. A more recent model, related to improvisational thinking, emphasizes experiential product development such as frequent iterations, testing, and milestones (Eisenhardt & Tabrizi, in press), yet this second model has received only limited empirical examination. Indeed, other research suggests that our understanding is incomplete. For example, Tyre and Hauptman (1992) argued that the degree of system-level change is another contingency factor in the organization of work. In addition, a provocative study by Benghozi (1990) of a massive, long-term innovation project in the French telecommunication industry sketches a third model. For huge and lengthy projects, Benghozi (1990) suggested that *innovation routines,* which include dynamic planning, monitoring, and scheduling projects over time as the environment changes, are needed. Overall, the point is that exploring contingent models for the organization of work is an important path for future research.

Third, our understanding of how senior managers affect development is incomplete. They are consistently found to be important contributors to project success (e.g., Clark & Fujimoto, 1991; Cooper & Kleinschmidt, 1987; Zirger & Maidique, 1990). However, the management-related concepts in Figure 61-1 such as vision, subtle control, and even support are vague. There is also little understanding of the links between product effectiveness and the creative processes by which senior managers and others match firm competencies with market needs to create an effective product concept. This process has been virtually unexplored. In addition, previous research (and thus our model) is vague regarding how the responsibilities of senior management are distinct from the responsibilities of project leaders. For example, should senior managers or project leaders be responsible for ensuring that products are synergistic with the core competencies of the firm (Leonard-Barton, 1992)? Most important, the model echoes the product-development literature in conceptualizing only two levels of management: a project leader and senior management, yet in reality, frequently there are several levels of management with presumably different responsibilities. How do these levels interact? How do these members of different levels of management affect technology strategies and the management of multiple product-development projects for which they are responsible? Thus, the concepts surrounding senior management and its link to product effectiveness offer prime opportunities for future research.

CONCLUSION

We began this paper by noting that product development is the nexus of competition for many firms as well as the central organizational process for adaptation and renewal. Simply put, product development is critical to the viability of firms and an important core competence, yet it is challenging to understand the findings of the related empirical research because this literature is so fragmented and varied.

The article has three conclusions. One is that the product-development literature can be organized into three streams of research: product development as rational plan, communication web, and disciplined problem solving. We have highlighted these three streams of research as well as their key findings, strengths, and weaknesses. Second, we conclude that these streams can be synthesized into a model of factors affecting product-development success. Given the complementary nature of past research, we were able to craft an integrated conceptual perspective that combines many of the empirical findings. Third, we conclude that there are research implications for the future based on the mixture of support for various findings in the model. We developed a brief outline of potential research paths based on constructs and theoretical links that are fuzzy or less explored in our model and the literature as a whole. Overall, this article attempts to contribute an understanding of past literature, a model of current thinking, and a vision for future research.

We end by looping back to the wider innovation literature. As we noted at the outset, there are two broad areas of inquiry (e.g., Adler, 1989) that complement one another. The economics-oriented branch offers an understanding of innovation across industries and the evolution of technologies that provides a useful context for thinking about product development. However, even in more organizational-level work in this branch (e.g., Nelson & Winter, 1982), the actual process of product development is still largely a "black box." At best, this work simply describes the evolution of idiosyncratic innovation routines within organizations (Nelson & Winter, 1982). More often, there are no organizational effects at all. Complementary to this branch of innovation research, the product-development literature opens up that black box by providing depth and rich understanding of how actual products are developed within firms, a critical core capability for many firms. This research indicates the organizational structures, roles, and processes that are related to enhanced product development. Although much remains to be explored, the product-development branch remains essential for a complete picture of innovation.

Acknowledgments
The writing of this article was generously supported by funding from the Alfred P. Sloan Foundation to the Stanford University Computer Industry Project. Kathleen M. Eisenhardt also was generously supported as the Finmeccanica Faculty Scholar. The authors thank Deborah Dougherty, D. Charles Galunic, Rebecca Henderson, Neil Kane, Laura Kopczak, Dorothy Leonard-Barton, and Mark Zbaracki for their helpful comments. In addition, they thank Susan E. Jackson and the anonymous reviewers at *AMR* for their insightful suggestions.

About the Authors
Shona L. Brown received her Ph.D. from Stanford University. She is a postdoctoral research associate in the School of Engineering at Stanford. Her research interests include the formation of strategic capabilities, learning within and across firms, and product innovation.

Kathleen M. Eisenhardt received her Ph.D from Stanford University. She is an associate professor of strategy and organization in the School of Engineering at Stanford. Her research interests center on the management of high-technology firms, including evolutionary change, product innovation, strategic decision making, and entrepreneurship.

References

Adler, P. 1989. Technology strategy: A guide to the literatures. In R. Rosenbloom & R. Burgelman (Eds.), *Research on technological innovation, management, and policy*, vol. 4: 25–151. Greenwich, CT: JAI Press.

Allen, T. J. 1971. Communications, technology transfer, and the role of technical gatekeeper. *R&D Management*, 1: 14–21.

Allen, T. J. 1977. *Managing the flow of technology*. Cambridge, MA: MIT Press.

Ancona, D. G., & Caldwell, D. F. 1990. Beyond boundary spanning: Managing external dependence in product development teams. *Journal of High Technology Management Research*, 1: 119–135.

Ancona, D. G., & Caldwell, D. F. 1992a. Demography and design: Predictors of new product team performance. *Organization Science*, 3: 321–341.

Ancona, D. G., & Caldwell, D. F. 1992b. Bridging the boundary: External process and performance in organizational teams. *Administrative Science Quarterly*, 37: 634–665.

Benghozi, P. 1990. French telecom. *Organization Studies*, 4: 531–554.

Benjamin, B. 1993. *Understanding the political dynamics of developing new products*. Working paper, Stanford University Graduate School of Business, Stanford, CA.

Bolton, M. K. 1993. Imitation versus innovation: Lessons to be learned from the Japanese. *Organizational Dynamics* (3): 30–45.

Brown, S. L., & Eisenhardt, K. M. 1995. *Core competence in product innovation: The art of managing in time*. Working paper, Department of Industrial Engineering and Engineering Management, Stanford University, Stanford, CA.

Burgelman, R., & Sayles, L. 1986. *Inside corporate innovation*, New York: Free Press.

Business Week. 1992. Inside Intel. June 1: 86–90, 92, 94.

Clark, K. B., Chew, W. B., & Fujimoto, T. 1987. Product development in the world auto industry. *Brookings Papers on Economic Activity,* 3: 729–781.

Clark, K. B., & Fujimoto, T. 1990. The power of product integrity. *Harvard Business Review,* 68(6): 107–118.

Clark, K. B., & Fujimoto, T. 1991. *Product development performance.* Boston: Harvard Business School Press.

Clark, K. B., & Wheelwright, S. C. 1992. Organizing and leading "heavyweight" development teams. *California Management Review,* 34(3): 9–28.

Cooper, R. G. 1979. The dimensions of industrial new product success and failure. *Journal of Marketing,* 43: 93–103.

Cooper, R. G., & Kleinschmidt, E. J. 1987. New products: What separates winners from losers? *Journal of Product Innovation Management,* 4: 169–184.

Cooper, R. G., & Kleinschmidt, E. J. 1993. Major new products: What distinguishes the winners in the chemical industry? *Journal of Product Innovation Management,* 10: 90–111.

Cordero, R. 1991. Managing for speed to avoid product obsolescence: A survey of techniques. *Journal of Product Innovation Management,* 8: 283–294.

David, P. 1985. Clio and the economics of QWERTY. *American Economic Review,* 75: 332–337.

Dosi, G. 1988. Sources, procedures, and microeconomic effects of innovation. *Journal of Economic Literature,* 26: 1120–1171.

Dougherty, D. 1990. Understanding new markets for new products. *Strategic Management Journal,* 11: 59–78.

Dougherty, D. 1992. Interpretive barriers to successful product innovation in large firms. *Organization Science,* 3: 179–202.

Dougherty, D., & Corse, S. M. When it comes to product innovation, what is so "bad" about "bureaucracy?" *Journal of High Technology Management Research.*

Dumaine, B. 1991. Closing the innovation gap. *Fortune,* December 2: 56–59, 62.

Dwyer, L., & Mellor, R. 1991. Organizational environment, New product process activities, and project outcomes. *Journal of Product Innovation & Management,* 8: 39–48.

Eisenhardt, K. M., & Tabrizi, B. Accelerating adaptive processes: Product innovation in the global computer industry. *Administrative Science Quarterly.*

Gerstenfeld, A. 1976. A study of successful projects, unsuccessful projects and projects in process in West Germany. *IEEE Transactions in Engineering Management,* 23: 116–123.

Gupta, A. K., & Wilemon, D. L. 1990. Accelerating the development of technology-based new products. *California Management Review,* 32(2): 24–44.

Hargadon, A. B., & Sutton, R. I. 1994. *Exploiting exploration: The routinization of innovation in the product-development process.* Working paper, Department of Industrial Engineering and Engineering Management, Stanford University, Stanford, CA.

Hayes, R. H., Wheelwright, S. C., & Clark, K. 1988. *Dynamic manufacturing.* New York: Free Press.

Hise, R. T., O'Neal, L., Parasuraman, A., & McNeal, J. U. 1990. Marketing/R&D interaction in new product development: Implications for new product success rates. *Journal of Product Innovation Management,* 7: 142–155.

Iansiti, M. 1992. *Science-based product development: An empirical study of the mainframe computer industry.* Working paper, Harvard Business School, Cambridge, MA.

Iansiti, M. 1993. Real-world R&D: Jumping the product generation gap. *Harvard Business Review,* 71(3): 138–147.

Imai, K., Ikujiro, N., & Takeuchi, H. 1985. Managing the new product development process: How Japanese companies learn and unlearn. In R. H. Hayes, K. Clark, & Lorenz (Eds.), *The uneasy alliance: Managing the productivity-technology dilemma:* 337–375. Boston: Harvard Business School Press.

Joyce, W. F. 1986. Matrix organizations: A social experiment. *Academy of Management Journal,* 3: 536–561.

Katz, R. 1982. The effects of group longevity on project communication and performance. *Administrative Science Quarterly,* 27: 81–104.

Katz, R., & Allen, T. J. 1985. Project performance and the locus of influence in the R&D matrix. *Academy of Management Journal,* 28: 67–87.

Katz, R., & Tushman, M. L. 1981. An investigation into the managerial roles and career paths of gatekeepers and project supervisors in a major R&D facility. *R&D Management,* 11: 103–110.

Keller, R. T. 1986. Predictors of the performance of project groups in R&D organizations. *Academy of Management Journal,* 29: 715–726.

Kulvik, H. 1977. *Factors underlying the success and failure of new products.* (Report No. 29). Helsinki, Finland: University of Technology.

Lieberman, M., & Montgomery, D. 1988. First-mover advantages. *Strategic Management Journal,* 9: 41–58.

Leonard-Barton, D. 1992. Core capabilities and core rigidities: A paradox in managing new product development. *Strategic Management Journal,* 3: 111–125.

Mabert, V. A., Muth, J. F., & Schmenner, R. W. 1992. Collapsing new product development times: Six case studies. *Journal of Product Innovation Management,* 9: 200–212.

Maidique, M. A., & Zirger, B. J. 1984. A study of success and failure in product innovation: The case of the U.S. electronics industry. *IEEE Transactions in Engineering Management,* 4: 192–203.

Maidique, M. A., & Zirger, B. J. 1985. The new product learning cycle. *Research Policy,* 14: 299–313.

Miner, A. S., & Moorman, C. 1993. *Organizational improvisation in new product development and introduction,* Proposal for research, School of Business, University of Wisconsin, Madison.

Myers, S., & Marquis, D. G. 1969. *Successful industrial innovations.* (NSF 69-17). Washington, DC: National Science Foundation.

Nelson, R., & Winter, S. 1977. *An evolutionary theory of economic change.* Cambridge, England: Belknap Press.

Nonaka, I. 1990. Redundant, overlapping organization: A Japanese approach to managing the innovation process. *California Management Review,* 32(3): 27–38.

Quinn, J. B. 1985. Managing innovation: Controlled chaos. *Harvard Business Review,* 63(3): 73–84.

Rothwell, R. 1972. *Factors for success in industrial innovations from project SAPPHO—A comparative study of success and failure in industrial innovation.* Brighton, Sussex, England: S.P.R.U.

Rothwell, R., Freeman, C., Horsley, A., Jervis, V. T. P., Robertson, A., & Townsend, J. 1974. SAPPHO updated—Project Sappho phase II. *Research Policy,* 3: 258–291.

Rubenstein, A. H., Chakrabarti, A. K., O'Keefe, R. D., Souder, W. E., & Young, H. C. 1976. Factors influencing success at the project level. *Research Management,* 16: 15–20.

Schoohoven, C. B., Eisenhardt, K. M., & Lyman, K. 1990. Speeding products to market: Waiting time to first product introduction in new firms. *Administrative Science Quarterly,* 35: 177– 207.

Schlender, B. R. 1992. How Sony keeps the magic going. *Fortune,* February 24: 76–79, 82, 84.

Szakasits, G. G. 1974. The adoption of the SAPPHO method in the Hungarian electronics industry. *Research Policy,* 3: 18–28.

Takeuchi, H., & Nonaka, I. 1986. The new new product development game. *Harvard Business Review,* 64(1): 137–146.

Tyre, M., & Hauptman, O. 1992. Effectiveness of organizational responses to technological change in the production process. *Organization Science,* 3: 301–320.

Urabe, K., Child, J., & Kagono, T. 1988. *Innovation and management: International comparisons.* Berlin: de Gruyter.

Weick, K. E. 1993. The collapse of sensemaking in organizations: The Mann Gulch disaster. *Administrative Science Quarterly,* 38: 628–652.

Womack, J. P., Jones, D. T., & Roos, D. 1990. *The machine that changed the world.* New York: HarperCollins.

Zirger, B. J., & Maidique, M. 1990. A model of new product development: An empirical test. *Management Science,* 36: 867–883.

Endnotes

1. We included *Administrative Science Quarterly, Academy of Management Review, Organization Science, Organizational Studies, Journal of Management Studies, Harvard Business Review, California Management Review, Research Policy,* and *Journal of Product Innovation Management.*

2. We thank an anonymous *AMR* reviewer for this insightful suggestion.

62

FROM EXPERIENCE: DEVELOPING NEW PRODUCT CONCEPTS VIA THE LEAD USER METHOD: A CASE STUDY IN A "LOW-TECH" FIELD

Cornelius Herstatt and Eric von Hippel

Conventional market research methods do not work well in the instance of many industrial goods and services, and yet, accurate understanding of user need is essential for successful product innovation. Cornelius Herstatt and Eric von Hippel report on a successful field application of a "lead user" method for developing concepts for needed new products. This method is built around the idea that the richest understanding of needed new products is held by just a few users. It is possible to identify these "lead users" and then draw them into a process of *joint* development of new product concepts with manufacturer personnel. In the application described, the lead user method was found to be much faster than traditional ways of identifying promising new product concepts as well as less costly. It also was judged to provide better outcomes by the firm participating in the case. The article includes practical detail on the steps that were used to implement the method at Hilti AG, a leading manufacturer of products and materials used in construction.

INTRODUCTION

In a recent study of the market research preferences and practices of Swiss machinery manufacturers, Herstatt found that the firms viewed joint product development with users to be the most effective way to accurately understand user needs. At the same time, he found that the firms seldom employed this form of "market research," because they regarded it as being very complex, costly and difficult to implement.

Herstatt found no convincing reason *why* this form of market research would be inherently more complex or expensive than other, less-preferred methods, and so decided to conduct a "lead user" market research case study as a form of anecdotal research into the matter. In this article, we report on the procedures he used and the outcomes he obtained. As the reader will see, the method, which involves joint user–manufacturer development of new product concepts, was successfully applied in

Address correspondence to Professor Eric von Hipple. MIT Sloan School of Management. Room E52–556. Cambridge. MA 02139.

Herstatt, Cornelius and Eric von Hippel. 1992. From Experience: Developing New Product Concepts Via the Lead User Method: A Case Study in a 'Low-Tech' Field. *Journal of Product Innovation Management* 9: 213–221.

869

this case study. Further, anecdotal information provided by the firm participating in the case indicates that concept development with lead users was twice as fast as and half the cost of methods previously used.

WHAT IS "LEAD USER" MARKET RESEARCH?

Traditional market research methods are designed to sample the needs of a relatively large group of users, analyze the data obtained and then present the findings to product developers. In many fields, however, the richest understanding of needed new products and services is held by just a few users. Von Hippel [4,5] developed a method that exploits this fact by prescribing that firms interested in identifying needs for new products and services begin by identifying a small sample of "lead users." These especially sophisticated users are drawn into a process of *joint* development of new product or service concepts with manufacturer personnel. Then, the likely commercial appeal of the concepts developed with lead users is tested against a population of more ordinary users.

"Lead users" of a novel or enhanced product, process or service have been defined by von Hippel as those who display *both* of two characteristics with respect to it:

1. They face needs that will be general in a marketplace—but face them months or years before the bulk of that marketplace encounters them.
2. They expect to benefit significantly by obtaining a solution to those needs.

Thus, a manufacturing firm with a current strong need for a process innovation that many manufacturers will need in 2 years' time would fit the definition of lead user with respect to that process.

Each of the two lead user characteristics specified above provides an independent and valuable contribution to the type of new product need and solution data lead users possess. The first is valuable because, as empirical studies in problem-solving have shown, users who have real-world experience with a need are in the best position to provide accurate data regarding it. When new product needs are evolving rapidly, as in many high-technology product categories, only users at the "front of the trend" will presently have the real-world experience that manufacturers must analyze if they are to understand accurately the needs that the bulk of the market will soon face.

The utility of the second lead user characteristic is that users who expect high benefit from a solution to a need can provide the richest need and solution data to inquiring market researchers. This is because, as has been shown by studies of industrial product and process innovations [2], the greater the benefit a given user expects to obtain from a needed novel product or process, the greater will be his or her investment in obtaining a solution.

In sum, lead users are users whose present strong needs will become general in a marketplace months or years in the future. Because lead users are familiar with conditions that lie in the future for most others, the lead user market research method can help manufacturers acquire need and solution information that will be useful in the development of "next generation" concepts for new products and services.

FOUR STEPS IN A LEAD USER STUDY

A lead user market research study involves four major steps, which are described in detail in articles by von Hippel [4] and Urban and von Hippel [3]. In brief summary, these are as follows. Step 1 involves specifying the characteristics lead users will have in the product/market segment of interest. That is, one must identify the trend(s) on which they lead the market, and also must specify indicators that show that they expect relatively high benefit from obtaining a solution to their trend-related needs. (One frequently useful proxy for expectations of high benefit is evidence of product development or product modification by users. As noted earlier, user investment in innovation, and user expectations of related benefit, have been found to be correlated.)

The second step is to identify a sample of lead users who meet both of the lead user criteria established in step 1. Such a group will be both at the leading edge of the trend being studied and will display correlates of high expected benefit from solutions to related needs. The third step is to bring the sample of lead users together with company engineering and marketing personnel to engage in group problem-solving sessions. The outcome of these sessions is one or more "lead user" product or service concepts judged by session participants to be both responsive to lead user needs and responsive to manufacturer concerns regarding producibility, etc.

Finally, as the needs of today's lead users are not necessarily the same as the needs of the users who will make up a major share of tomorrow's predicted market, the fourth and final step in the lead user market research method is to test whether concepts found valuable by lead users also will be valued by the more typical users in the target market.

THE CASE STUDY

The company participating in this study was Hilti AG, a leading European manufacturer of components, equipment and materials used in construction. Hilti has major production facilities in Europe, the United States and Japan, and sells worldwide.

The product line we elected to concentrate on in our lead user case study was "pipe hangers"—a relatively "low-tech" type of fastening system often used in commercial and industrial buildings. Pipe hangers are assemblages of steel supports and pipe clamps and other hardware components used to securely fasten pipes to the walls and/or ceilings of buildings. Sometimes pipe hangers can be quite simple and support only a single pipe. Frequently, however, they are relatively complicated structures that simultaneously support and align a number of pipes of different sizes and types (Figure 62-1).

In the paragraphs that follow, we will describe how each of the four steps in a lead user study was carried out in this case.

STEP 1: SPECIFICATION OF LEAD USER INDICATORS

Recall that lead users of a product, process or service are defined as those who display two characteristics with respect to it: they have needs that are advanced with respect to an important marketplace trend(s) and they expect to benefit significantly by obtaining a solution to those needs. To identify lead users of pipe-hanging hardware, a first step was to identify important trends and users with relatively high benefit expectations related to these.

Identification of Trends

Identification of important trends in the evolution of user needs in pipe-hanging hardware began with a survey of experts. A brief analysis of the target market showed that people with expert knowledge in the relevant field would be found among "layout engineers," the specialists in charge of planning complex pipe networks in commercial and industrial buildings (layout engineers also are key decision makers with respect to determining which components will be bought and used for the pipe networks they design).

Expert advisors for this study were found in construction departments of technical universities, professional engineering organizations and municipal departments responsible for approving the design of pipe networks. Some of these were already known to the Hilti R&D department; others were identified via recommendations. Ultimately, the panel of experts who provided information for this study consisted of eight leading layout engineers in Switzerland, Germany and Austria; two researchers from the construction departments of the Swiss Federal Institute of Technology and the University of Darmstadt; one engineer from a professional organization in Bonn; and one engineer each from the municipal building departments in Bern and Berlin.

FIGURE 62-1   A Conventional Pipe Hanger Configured to Support Several Pipes.

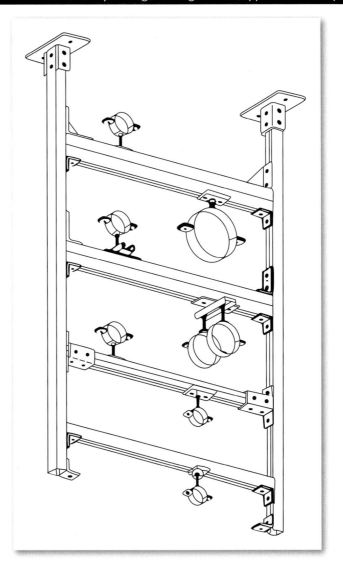

The trends identified as most important by the experts surveyed regarding pipe-hanger systems were as follows:

Trend 1: There is an increasing need for pipe-hanger systems that are extremely easy to put together—so easy that instruction booklets will not be needed. Such systems should have significantly fewer components than at present. They should adapt to a wide range of application conditions, and should be based on a simple, consistent construction principle.

Reason for trend: Education levels among installers are going down in many countries.

Trend 2: There is a need for rapidly actuated, positive, interlocking fasteners to connect pipe hanger elements together securely and to attach the completed hangers securely to building walls and ceilings.

Reason for trend: Safety standards in many countries are getting more stringent. Some of the multiple screws and bolts now used to assemble hangers (see Figure 62-1) may be inadvertently overlooked by installers—with consequent risk of field failure.

Trend 3: There is a need for pipe hangers made from lighter, noncorrodible materials. Pipe hangers should therefore increasingly be made of plastics rather than of the steel elements that are used almost exclusively today.

Reason for trend: Pipe-hanging systems made of steel are heavy and therefore difficult and dangerous to hang under some field conditions. In addition, steel is subject to corrosion and failure in wet environments or environments where chemicals are present.

Solutions that offered improvements with respect to these (somewhat overlapping) trends were expected to result in significant benefits for the users of pipe hangers. The skills required of installers would be reduced; fewer components would have to be stocked by users; the speed and safety of installation would be greatly increased; and the risk of field failures would be reduced.

Identification of High-Benefit Expectations

Expectations of innovation-related benefit on the part of users can be identified by survey, and this approach has been successfully applied elsewhere [3,4]. However, as mentioned earlier, innovation-related *activity* by users also can serve as a proxy for expectations of benefit, and this is the approach used here.

Users showing innovation activity were identified by conducting telephone interviews with a sample of 74 interviewees. Because, as will be described in the next section, the same sample was screened to simultaneously identify users having *both* lead user characteristics (ahead with respect to identified trends and having high expected benefit), we will defer a detailed discussion of methods and findings with respect to user innovation activity until we describe how step 2 was carried out in this study.

Here, we simply note that users engaged in innovating were determined by questions such as "Do you/did you ever build and install pipe-hanger hardware of your own design? Do you/did you ever modify commercially available pipe-hanger hardware to better suit your needs?" We also note that a high fraction of users interviewed (36%) were in fact found to display this characteristic.

STEP 2: IDENTIFICATION OF LEAD USERS

Once the trends and the user benefit characteristics were specified that would be used to identify lead users, the next step was to identify a lead user sample. This was begun by identifying, in cooperation with Hilti, a random sample of firms that buy and use pipe hangers. This sample was then screened to identify a subset of lead users within it.

The firms that install pipe-hanging systems are specialists in installing pipe networks in commercial and industrial buildings—for example, industrial plumbing firms. Installation of pipe hangers is a subtask in the larger task of pipe installation. The tradesmen who actually install pipe hangers comprised the group in which lead users would be identified. (Installers of pipe hangers have only a moderate-level technical education. In the countries from which our user sample was drawn—Switzerland, Germany and Austria—these installers complete 8 years of general schooling, and then take a 2- or 3-year vocational training program in their particular trade. Finally, they pass a municipal examination and receive a license to practice.)

Hilti has a number of geographically based sales divisions with close and frequent customer contacts. The German, Austrian and Swiss sales divisions (selected because of their geographical accessibility) were asked to provide the names of firms they thought were buyers of pipe-hanger systems made either by Hilti or its competitors. In this request no mention was made of either customer innovativeness or customer size. The three sales divisions eventually responded with the names of 120 firms they thought met the criteria.

Next, attempts were made to contact all 120 user firms for a telephone survey. Ultimately, 74 of these were in fact successfully contacted and judged suitable for and willing to undertake more detailed interviews (20 of the 120 were excluded because

TABLE 62-1 Percent of Sample Found to Have Lead User Characteristics in Two Studies

	Sample of Pipe-Hanger Users	*Sample of PC-CAD Users*[a]
Users at front of selected trend(s):	30% (22)	28% (38)
Users who built own prototype products:	36% (27)	25% (34)

[a]Data source: Urban and von Hippel [3].

they could not be reached after five telephone calls; 16 were excluded because they were found to be not currently using the product type at issue and ten were not included simply because they were not willing to participate in an interview).

In the instance of the 74 firms who were willing to participate in a telephone interview, interviewers sought to identify the most expert person on the products under investigation. To do this, the first contact at each firm was asked: "Whom do you regard the most expert person on pipe-hanger systems in your company, and can we talk to that person?" The interviewers were referred to expert "fitters"—employees who actually install pipe-hanging systems in the field—in 64 of the 74 instances. In the remaining ten cases they were referred to direct supervisors of fitters, all of whom had moved into supervisory positions only after extensive experience in the field.

Interviews were next conducted with all 74 individuals. The interviews were aimed at identifying a subset of users in the total user sample who had both of the two lead user characteristics (being ahead on the trends identified by the experts and expecting high benefit from innovations along these dimensions).

The proxy used for "ahead on identified trends" was simply: (1) did the interviewees agree that advances along the trends that had been specified by the expert panel were in fact needed and important and (2) could the interviewees describe at least some technically interesting ideas regarding these trends? As we noted in our discussion of step 1 in a lead user study, the proxy used for "user innovation benefit expectations" was: had the users developed or modified pipe hangers in ways that they felt represented improvements with respect to the identified trends?

As a result of the interviews just described, a significant number of lead users of pipe-hanging hardware [22] were identified. Table 62-1 summarizes the findings on this matter and, as a matter of interest, compares these with data drawn from the Urban and von Hippel [3] study of PC-CAD (PC-computer-aided design) users. In both studies, there was a high overlap where users displayed the two lead user characteristics.

It is interesting to note that, as is shown in Table 62-1, 27 (36%) of our random sample of users of pipe-hanging systems had designed, built and installed hangers of their own devising in one or more cases. This compares very favorably with the 25% of innovating users found in the technically sophisticated field of PC-CAD.

STEP 3: LEAD USER PRODUCT CONCEPT DEVELOPMENT

A group of 22 lead users of pipe hangers had now been identified. The next task was to determine whether some of these lead users could be joined with expert Hilti personnel to produce novel product concepts that would be judged by Hilti marketing researchers and by routine users to be the basis of valuable commercial products, and that would be judged to be practicably manufacturable by Hilti engineers.

Selection of Lead User Concept Group

Recall that, in the method step described just above, a group of 22 lead users had been identified among a total user sample of 74 users. Two more tests were next applied to this sample to identify those few lead users who seemed to be most appropriate to invite to join with Hilti engineers and other experts in a 3-day concept generation workshop. These additional tests were intended to select the users most likely to be effective in such a workshop, and consisted simply of the judgment of the person who had interviewed the user on two matters: Did the interviewer judge that the user could describe his experiences and ideas clearly? Did the user seem to have a strong personal interest in the development of improved pipe-hanger systems? Fourteen of the 22 lead users met these additional tests and were invited to join the workshop.

Twelve of the 14 lead users contacted—ten pipe fitters plus two supervisors of fitters—agreed to join the product concept development workshop. Interestingly, the two that did not were users who had patented their own pipe-hanger system designs. These two were not willing to present their ideas in a workshop, most probably because they were concerned about the diffusion of their proprietary-technical know-how.

All users who joined the workshop formally agreed that any inventions or ideas developed during the sessions would be the property of Hilti. As compensation, every participant was offered a small honorarium. Interestingly, most of the participants did not accept this; they felt sufficiently rewarded by simply attending and contributing to the planned workshop.

Three-Day Product Concept Generation Workshop

The goal of the product concept generation workshop sponsored by Hilti was to develop the conceptual basis for a novel pipe-hanger system with characteristics identified in the technical trend analysis described earlier. To most effectively meet this goal and to efficiently transfer the workshop findings to Hilti, the lead users at the workshop were joined by two of the expert layout engineers who had participated in the trend analysis segment of our study. Invitees from Hilti consisted of the marketing manager, the product manager and three engineers who worked on the design of pipe-fastening systems.

The workshop was carried out over a 3-day period, and was organized as follows:

Day 1. The entire group conducted a review of important trends and problems in pipe-hanging systems. Next, five relatively independent problem areas were defined by the group, and a subgroup was established to work on each. The five subgroup topics were (1) methods of attaching pipe hangers to ceilings or walls; (2) design of support elements extending between the wall attachment and pipe clamp itself; (3) design of the pipe clamps; (4) design of the methods of attaching various system components to each other in the field and (5) methods of conveniently adjusting length of supporting members at the field site. Membership in the subgroups was at the option of workshop participants, and shifts in membership were made from time to time to avoid the possible danger of premature fixation on individual problem-solving ideas championed by individual users. Each of the subgroups was assisted by technicians from Hilti or external layout engineers.

Day 2. The five subgroups worked on their problem areas in the morning, and in the afternoon all took a break from the specific problems at hand and participated in some general problem-solving and creativity exercises such as role-playing and team-building exercises. The purpose of these was both to lessen pressure on participants and to make them more comfortable with each other. After a short while, the workshop was in fact characterized by very strong group cohesion and intensive, cordial interaction.

Day 3. The subgroup ideas were presented to the entire group for evaluation and suggestions. As an aid to this evaluation effort, each of the subgroup ideas was evaluated on the three criteria of originality (how revolutionary and novel is the solution from a technical point of view?), feasibility (how quickly can the solution be realized employing currently available technology?) and comprehensiveness of solution (does the idea represent a single solution or does it resolve several user problems simultaneously?). Next, membership in the subgroups was changed, work on the most promising concepts was continued and informal engineering drawings were produced by participants. Finally, these were critiqued and modified by the entire group and merged into one joint concept.

Results of Product Concept Generation Workshop

At the conclusion of the workshop, the single pipe-hanger system design was selected by the total group as incorporating the best of all the elements discussed in the sub-groups, and this was the system recommended to Hilti.

After the workshop, the technical and economic feasibility of the new product concept proposed by the lead users was evaluated further by Hilti personnel. At the conclusion of this work, it was decided that the lead users had indeed developed a very valuable new pipe-hanger system. In the judgment of company experts it was well in advance of the offerings of competitors. Hilti, based in Lichtenstein, is a leading European manufacturer of components, equipment and materials used in construction. The firm's products range from fastening systems to drilling and cutting equipment to specialty chemicals. It has major production facilities in Europe, the United States and Japan, and sells worldwide. In 1990 the worldwide sales of Hilti were approximately 2 billion Swiss francs.

STEP 4: TESTING WHETHER LEAD USER CONCEPTS APPEAL TO ORDINARY USERS

The fourth and final step in the lead user market research method involves testing whether typical users in a marketplace find the product or service concept developed by lead users to be attractive. Because Hilti's internal evaluation showed the potential commercial value of the lead user concept to be very high, they were not willing to present it to a random sample of ordinary users for evaluation but instead decided to simply test the lead user product concept on a sample of 12 "routine" users.

The companies selected for this "routine user" sample were drawn from the sample of 74 interviewed companies. The selection criteria were that the telephone interview data showed them *not* to be lead users, and also that they must have had a long, close relationship with Hilti. (The latter requirement was added because the company wished to have confidence that these users would be willing to honor a request to keep the details of the new system secret.) The interviewees selected were buyers as well as users. They had the dominant role in the purchasing decisions of their own companies with respect to pipe hangers.

The 12 user–evaluators were asked to review the proposed pipe-hanger system in detail, noting particular strengths and weaknesses. Their response was very positive. Ten of the 12 preferred the lead user product concept over existing, commercially available solutions. All except one of the ten expressed willingness to buy such a pipe-hanger system when it became available, and estimated that they would be willing to pay a 20% higher price for it relative to existing systems.

COMPARISON OF LEAD USER METHOD WITH METHOD ORDINARILY USED BY HILTI

The case study was, as reported above, very successful. Interestingly, Hilti personnel informally judged that the lead user method, beginning with a technological trend identification and ending with a novel product concept, was significantly faster and cheaper than the more conventional marketing research methods they normally used. Unfortunately, data needed to test this judgment carefully did not exist in the firm. However, it was possible to compare the time and costs expended in this first lead user study by Hilti with the time and costs expended on a project that they had recently conducted, and judged to be of very similar scope and complexity (Table 62-2).

The process Hilti conventionally used took a total (elapsed time) of 16 months from start to final agreement on the specifications of the product to be developed, and cost $100,000. The work began with marketing personnel collecting and evaluating data on needs and problems from customers (5 months; $56,000); then marketing explained to engineering what it had found, and these two groups jointly developed tentative product specifications (2 months; $5,000). Next, engineering went off on its own to develop technical approaches to meeting the agreed-upon specifications (4 months; $23,000). Then,

TABLE 62-2	Anecdotal Time and Cost Comparison Between Two Product Concept Generation Efforts at Hilti	
Concept Generation Method Employed	*Time and Cost Expenditure for Concept Generation, Evaluation and Acceptance by Hilti*	
Lead user method	9	$51,000
Conventional method	16	$100,000

engineering got together with marketing to evaluate and adjust these (3 months; $10,000). Finally, both engineering and marketing wrote up a formal product specification and submitted it to management for formal approval (2 months; $5,000).

In contrast, the lead user method took a total (elapsed time) of 9 months and cost $51,000 from the start of work to final agreement on the specifications of the product to be developed. In this instance, the major steps were all conducted by a project group headed by the manager of the pipe-hanger product line. The group membership consisted of two development engineers and two market specialists. One of the latter was responsible for pipe hangers specifically, and one was a market research methods expert from Hilti's central market research group. The steps carried out by this group (and described in detail earlier in the article) were survey of experts (2 months; $9,000); telephone survey (2 weeks; $8,000); Lead User Workshop (3 days; $24,000); internal evaluation of lead user concept (3 months; $4,000); concept test on routine user group (2 months; $4,000); writing of formal product specification submission to management for formal approval (2 months; $2,400).

In sum, the lead user method consumed only 56% of the time used for the project put forward by Hilti as comparable. In our estimation and that of Hilti personnel, the reason for the time saving appeared to lie mainly in the systematic, parallel involvement of engineers, marketing people and highly qualified users, as opposed to the serial involvement of these groups used in the earlier method. Because of this, time-consuming feedback loops or reconsiderations, often produced by misinterpretations or information-filtering in the serial method, were avoided.

The cost of the lead user process also was found to be significantly lower than market research methods previously used by Hilti (approximately 50%). An informal evaluation of the reasons for this, conducted with Hilti personnel, suggests that the cost saving had two principal causes. First, the costs for customer surveys were smaller in the lead user method (in the lead user project, only 12 selected users were involved in joint, face-to-face discussions; in the conventional project, approximately 130 interviews with a randomly selected group of users, each involving face-to-face visits by manufacturer personnel, were carried out in three different countries). Second, the solutions provided by the lead user group required less work on the part of Hilti technical departments than did the ideas provided by marketing researchers in the conventional method (in the lead user project, people from Hilti's technical departments had direct user contact and had been involved in concept development from the start; they therefore had richer data regarding user needs in the lead user project than they did in the conventional project).

DISCUSSION

In this case study, the lead user method worked well in a relatively "low-tech" product category whose users were not characterized by advanced technical training. A significant fraction of all users sampled was found to have lead user characteristics. A group selected from among these proved very effective in working with company personnel on new product concept development. They did in fact develop a new system judged to be very valuable by both the manufacturer and a group of nonlead users. Also and importantly, study participants found participation to be both useful and enjoyable.

Bailetti and Guild [1] report on a study that explicitly measured the responses of design engineers to visits with lead users. They also found that participants judged this experience to be very valuable.

An additional, unanticipated result of the lead user method was an observed improvement of teamwork within Hilti, manifested in a significant improvement in the level of cooperation between the technical and marketing groups in the company. One reason for this was apparently that the teamwork built into the lead user method had a carry-over effect. Also, as product and performance requirements of innovative users were immediately translated into language meaningful to *both* engineers and marketing people, a shared language was created that made further cooperation easier.

Although the lead user method worked well in this case study, the reader should note that it is still a very new method. Details of method application will appropriately differ from study to study—and we are all still learning.

About the Authors
Dr. Cornelius Herstatt (M.B.A. and Ph.D., University of Zurich, Switzerland) is a consultant at Arthur D. Little, International. Dr. Herstatt concentrates his consulting work on corporate strategy and management of technology issues. One of his special interests is the implementation and further development of lead user methods for the rapid identification of new product and service opportunities. He has published a number of articles on topics in the areas of management of technology and innovation management.

Professor Eric A. von Hippel (B.A., Harvard College: M.S., MIT: Ph.D., Carnegie-Mellon University) is Professor of Management of Technology at the MIT Sloan School. Dr. von Hippel's research is focused on topics related to the management of innovation. Recently, he has developed a "lead user" method for use in new product development, which has proven very effective when applied by major manufacturers of consumer and industrial products and services. In cooperation with MIT, he has just produced a video course on industrial applications of the lead user method, *Learning from Lead Users* (MIT, 1991). He also has recently published a book entitled *The Sources of Innovation* (Oxford University Press, 1988).

References

1. Bailetti, Antonio J. and Guild, Paul D. Designers' impressions of direct contact between product designers and champions of innovation. *Journal of Product Innovation Management* 8(2):91–103 (June 1991).
2. Mansfield, Edwin. *Industrial Research and Technological Innovation: An Econometric Analysis.* New York, NY: W.W. Norton & Company, 1968.
3. Urban, G. and von Hippel, E. Lead user analyses for the development of new industrial products. *Management Science* 34(5):569–582 (May 1988).
4. von Hippel, E. Lead users: A source of novel product concepts. *Management Science* 32(7):791–805 (July 1986).
5. von Hippel, Eric. *The Sources of Innovation,* New York, NY: Oxford University Press, 1988.

Related Readings

Biegel, U. *Kooperation zwischen Anwender und Hersteller im Forschungs- und Entwicklungsbereich.* Frankfurt/New York/Paris: 1987.

Foxall, G. User initiated product innovations. *Industrial Marketing Management* 18(2):95–104 (May 1989).

Gemünden, H. G. *Investitionsguetermarketing, Interaktionsbeziehungen zwischen Hersteller und Verwender Innovativer Investitionsgueter.* Tübingen, 1981.

Geschka, H. Erkenntnisse der Innovationsforschung— Konsequenzen für die Praxis. *VD-Berichte* 724, Neue Produkte-Anstösse, Wege, Realisierte Strategien, Dusseldorf, 1989.

Shaw, B. The role of the interaction between the user and the manufacturer in medical equipment innovation. *R&D Management* 15(4):283–92 (October 1985).

Voss, C. The role of users in the development of applications software. *Journal of Product Innovation Management* 2(2): 113–21 (June 1985).

63

MANAGING INVENTION AND INNOVATION: WHAT WE'VE LEARNED

Edward B. Roberts

Technological innovation can alter the competitive status of firms and nations but its purposeful management is complex, involving the effective integration of people, organizational processes and plans.

When the Industrial Research Institute was founded in 1938, industrial research in the United States had experienced 20 years of dramatic growth, despite the shock of the Depression, and was poised on the brink of World War II expansion that gave it the form and scope we see today. MIT historian Howard Bartlett reported that from 1921 to 1938 the number of U.S. companies with research staffs of more than 50 persons grew from 15 to 120 (1).

Despite continued rapid increases in industrial R&D involvement and resource commitment over the following 25 years, in 1962, when we founded the MIT Sloan School of Management's Research Program on the Management of Science and Technology, we encountered an academic tradition that for the most part had paid little attention to the organization and management of large-scale technology-based programs. Indeed it was for the purpose of bringing academic research-based insights to bear on such technological enterprises that James Webb, the visionary administrator of the National Aeronautics and Space Administration, urged us with exhortation and funds to begin our research program.

Prior to our start, academics had concentrated largely on two themes: historical romanticism about the lives and activities of great "creative inventors," like Edison and Bell, and psychological research into the "creativity process." While those writings made interesting reading, in my judgment neither track contributed much useable knowledge for managers of technical organizations. Indeed with such rare exceptions as Jewkes et al. (2), the few university researchers who were focusing at that early time upon issues of R&D management were not paying much attention to organizational variables or to innovation as a multi-stage, multi-person, complex process. Perhaps not surprisingly, industry in the early 1960s appeared rather unenthusiastic about social science attempts to probe the underpinnings of effective research, development and technology-based innovation. In contrast, I sense broad acceptance in the 1980s of the

Roberts, Edward. 1988. Managing Invention and Innovation: What We've Learned. *Research–Technology Management* 31 (January/February): 11–29.

results of many academic studies of RD&E, with the Industrial Research Institute especially noteworthy in its efforts to advance collaboration in the field of management of technological innovation.

INVENTION AND INNOVATION

Roundtable discussions at the 1970 annual IRI spring meeting provide a useful starting point for this review—a set of definitions of the invention and innovation process:

Innovation is composed of two parts: (1) the generation of an idea or invention, and (2) the conversion of that invention into a business or other useful application ... Using the generally accepted (broad) definition of innovation—all of the stages from the technical invention to final commercialization—the technical contribution does not have a dominant position (3).

This leads me to a simple definition of my own, but nonetheless one that I feel is critical to emphasize: *Innovation = Invention + Exploitation.*

The invention process covers all efforts aimed at creating new ideas and getting them to work. The exploitation process includes all stages of commercial development, application and transfer, including the focusing of ideas or inventions toward specific objectives, evaluating those objectives, downstream transfer of research and/or development results, and the eventual broad-based utilization, dissemination and diffusion of the technology-based outcomes.

The overall management of technological innovation thus includes the organization and direction of human and capital resources toward effectively: (1) creating new knowledge; (2) generating technical ideas aimed at new and enhanced products, manufacturing processes and services; (3) developing those ideas into working prototypes; and (4) transferring them into manufacturing, distribution and use.

Technologically innovative outcomes come in many forms: incremental or radical in degree; modifications of existing entities or entirely new entities; embodied in products, processes or services; oriented toward consumer, industrial or governmental use; based on various single or multiple technologies. Whereas invention is marked by discovery or a state of new existence, usually at the lab or bench, innovation is marked by first use, in manufacturing or in a market.

Most organized scientific and engineering activity, certainly within the corporation, is beyond the idea generating stage and produces not radical breakthroughs but rather a broad base of incremental technological advance, sometimes leading cumulatively over time to major technical change. Academic research in the area of technology management has focused primarily on incremental product innovations oriented toward industrial markets. (Interestingly academic marketing research has focused primarily on incremental product innovations aimed at consumer markets.) Neither the less frequently arising areas of radical innovation nor process innovation has received much systematic attention from academia, unfortunately.

One of my favorite visual aids is Figure 63-1, portraying a process view of how technological innovation occurs, and emphasizing two key generalizations. First, technological innovation is a multi-stage process, with significant variations in the primary task as well as in the managerial issues and effective management practice occurring among these stages. Figure 63-1 presents six stages, but the precise number and their division are somewhat arbitrary. What is key is that each phase of activity is dominated by the search for answers to different managerial questions.

At the outset, for example, emphasis is on finding a motivating idea, a notion of possible direction for technical endeavor. Coming up with one or more technical and/or market goals that stimulate initiating a research, development and/or engineering (RD&E) project is the task undertaken during Stage 1. The relevant managerial question for this stage is how do more and better targets get generated? Which people, which structures, which strategies can be employed toward more effective idea generation for these objectives? Good managerial practice at this stage frequently involves loose control, "letting many flowers bloom," pursuing parallel and diverse approaches,

FIGURE 63-1 The Process of Technological Innovation Can Take as Long as 20–30 Years, According to Some Studies, but for Most Industrial Product Innovations the Duration from Initial Idea to Market Is More Likely to Be Three to Eight Years.

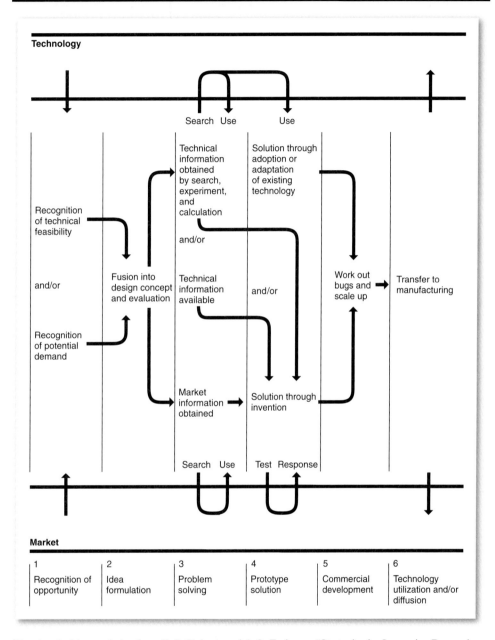

(Reprinted with permission from E. B. Roberts and A. L. Frohman, "Strategies for Improving Research Utilization," *Technology Review*, vol. 80, no. 5, March/April 1978.)

fostering conflict or at least contentiousness, stimulating a variety of inputs. Critical at this early stage is ready access to small amounts of R&D financing, free of heavy and discouraging evaluative procedures. A major mistake is to set up stringent formal processes for approval of the small sums needed to try out an idea. Distributing small "pots of gold" for first or second level R&D supervisors to dispense at their discretion, akin to Texas Instruments' heralded "$25,000 money," makes good sense.

Later, the Stage 5 commercial development for example, the task involves in-depth specification and manufacturing engineering of ideas that have by now already been reduced to an acceptable working prototype. The managerial issues in this stage involve coordinating a number of engineers of different disciplinary backgrounds toward achieving, within previously estimated development budget and schedule, a predefined technical output ready for manufacture in large volume, reliably, and at competitive production costs. Effective managerial practice in this stage might well involve tight control, elimination of duplication, strong financial criteria for resource use accompanied by formal evaluation, single-minded even somewhat rigid adherence to plan, especially in regard to those resources—in many ways the opposite of what is encountered in Stage 1!

The next generalization embodied in Figure 63-1 is that innovation occurs through technical efforts carried out primarily within an internal organizational context, but involving heavy interaction with the external technological as well as market environment. Proactive search for technical and market inputs, as well as receptivity to information sensed from external sources, are critical aspects of technology-based innovation. All studies of effective innovations have shown significant contributions of external technology and have found success heavily dependent upon awareness of customer needs and competitor activity. Indeed one of the most important trends in industrial innovation activity during the 1980s is the continuing increase in the use of external sources of technology as critical supplements to internal R&D efforts.

The details of Figure 63-1 specify a set of key flows and decision points that occur during the process of innovating. A number of major managerial elements that are embodied in those details will be treated in the remainder of this article. Two aspects of the diagram, however, are potentially misleading and deserve immediate mention. First, for ease of presentation all stages are shown at equidistant intervals, inappropriately suggesting perhaps the similarity of these phases from a time duration and/or resource consumption perspective. This is by no means true. In particular, while each technical field is characterized by quite different schedule and resource requirements, Stage 5, commercial development, usually takes as long as the several earlier stages combined and requires more resources than most of the other stages together. That is the reason for tight financial standards being properly applied immediately prior to a project's entry to this stage.

> *A major mistake is to set up stringent formal processes for approval of the small sums needed to try out an idea.*

Second, for simplicity sake no feedbacks are pictured in Figure 63-1 from later stages back to earlier ones. Yet, inevitably, these feedbacks exist and cause reiteration to occur among the stages. For example, involvement in the problem-solving process, Stage 3, generates new insights as to alternative idea formulations, Stage 2; and efforts at transfer into manufacturing as part of technology utilization, Stage 6, often create new requirements for problem-solving, Stage 3. Indeed a recent article by Kline (4) argues that the multiple feedback loops are the essence of the innovation process. Thus the real process of technical innovation involves flows back and forth over time among differing primary activities, internal and external to the dominant innovating organization, with major variations arising throughout the process in regard to specific tasks, managerial issues and managerial answers.

Beyond my descriptive perspective on how innovation occurs is Peter Drucker's (5) prescriptive advocacy as to how it ought to happen: "Systematic innovation . . . consists in the purposeful and organized search for changes, and in the systematic analysis of the opportunities such changes might offer for economic or social innovation." Drucker identifies seven sources for innovative opportunity, listed in Table 63-1.

TABLE 63-1 Seven Sources for Innovative Opportunity

The unexpected
The incongruity
Process need
Changes in Industry or market structure
Demographics
Changes in perception, mood, and meaning
New knowledge, both scientific and nonscientific

From P. F. Drucker, *Innovation and Entrepreneurship: Practice and Principles.* New York: Harper & Row, Publishers, 1985.

Most challenging to those of us committed to the development and use of new science and technology is Drucker's assertion that "contrary to almost universal belief, new knowledge—and especially new scientific knowledge—is not the most reliable or most predictable source of successful innovations." As with most Drucker "truths," this one is intuitively attractive, as well as unverified in any systematic manner. Whether or not new science is a critical "source" of successful innovations no doubt depends on how you define both "science" as well as "source." But there is no doubt that advances in science and technology are instrumental to the development and implementation of almost all successful product and process innovations. It is the rare case that a success stems from merely a repackaging of previously existing science and technology.

Rather than focusing at this point on the claimed sources from which innovations arise, the remainder of this article concentrates on three dimensions—staffing, structure and strategy—each subject to managerial influence and/or control. (I will discuss innovation sources much more in the section on Structure.) A fourth dimension, systems support, will be treated in depth in another article in this Golden Anniversary series. Taken together, improved management of these dimensions contributes critically to achieving successful institutionalized innovation. Throughout the article I shall be seeking to blend the findings from academic research on the management of invention and innovation with the experiences and observations of successful industrial and government technology managers.

STAFFING CONSIDERATIONS

Two primary issues arise in regard to staffing the technological organization: what kinds of people need to be involved for effective technical development, and what managerial actions can be taken to maximize their overall productivity. In regard to people requirements, as explained by Roberts and Fusfeld (6), a number of "critical behavioral roles," not just technical skills, must be practiced by the people involved in a technical development. By combining the management of technological innovation literature with our own consulting experiences we identified five key roles for achieving successful innovation, which we have been able to use to enhance RD&E organizational performance. Following us others have since added to this list, generating as many as 12 key roles needing separate monitoring and support.

Critical Innovation Roles

First are *idea generators*, the creative contributors of new insights that both initiate projects and contribute to problem solutions throughout technical projects (7,8). Ideas can be drawn from the "market pull" of sensing real or potential customer needs or demands, or from the "technological push" of envisioning the possible extension of technological performance of a material, component or system. Ideas include not just those which lead to project initiation, but also the many throughout an innovation-seeking endeavor which contribute importantly toward invention or innovation outcomes. Thus idea generators for technical projects may be scientists or engineers, sales or marketing persons, or even managers! The rare but valuable idea generators are those who come up with multiple ground-breaking ideas over their careers, such as S. D. Stookey at Corning Glass Works who among other successes came up with key ideas for photosensitive glass and Pyroceram (9). Individual differences that are either innate or developed over long periods no doubt account for many of the distinctive characteristics of effective idea-generators. But many sources of heightened idea creativity arise from managerial influences, for example from the internal organizational climate or environment and especially from supervisory practices. These are discussed in greater detail in my later section on Individual and Organizational Productivity.

There are, however, significant differences between "idea-havers" and "idea-exploiters"—those who come up with ideas and those who do something with the ideas they have generated (10, 11). This holds true whether the ideas are born in universities, government labs or in industry. The generally low rate of energetic pursuit of newly created RD&E ideas mandates the requirement for the second key role in technical innovation-seeking activities, that of the *entrepreneur* or *product champion*. Entrepreneurs advocate and push for change and innovation; they take ideas, whether their own or others', and attempt to get them supported and adopted. Most major studies of factors affecting product success have found the active presence of a product champion to be a necessary condition for project success (12). For example, in recent years the late Ken Estridge gained widespread repute as the product champion behind IBM's successful development and launch of its personal computer. Law Lehr rose to the presidency of 3M as an eventual outgrowth of his own championing of 3M's health products business (13). And despite not being a family member of the closely-held Pilkington Glass company, Alistair Pilkington became "process champion" for the revolutionary float-glass process which dramatically changed the company and the industry and again, not incidentally, led this "champion" into the chairmanship of the firm.

As I reported in my first *Research Management* article, the entrepreneurial "role" is the same, whether carried out internally in existing organizations or "externally" in their own newly founded companies (14). But the mode of behavior and what is needed for "internal" vs. "external" entrepreneurial success may well be different, as expanded by Maidique (15). My own studies of "internal entrepreneurs" found that they needed

The active presence of a product champion is a necessary condition for success.

to be sensitive to company politics and the latest corporate "buzzwords" in order to gain internal support, and as indicated below required a high level "sponsor" to lead them through the corporate jungle. Lehr (13) argues that strong entrepreneurial efforts are needed even within companies that have long traditions of fostering entrepreneurship, in order to overcome inevitable managerial resistance.

A third required role in effective innovative activities is the *program manager or leader,* sometimes strangely called the "business innovator," supplying the support functions of planning, scheduling, monitoring and control, technical work supervision, business and financial coordination relating to the R&D project (16,17). This is the one "role" which is also usually an assigned job in the organization, the other roles being incidental to an individual's specific work assignment.

Gatekeepers, or special communicators, are the fourth critical role identified, the link-pins who frequently bring information messages from sources outside of a project group into that group (18). These human bridges join technical, market and manufacturing sources of information to the potential technical users of that information. Gatekeepers may bridge one technical group to another within the same company, or may link university research activities to a corporate advanced technology center, or may tie customer concerns into a supplier's design team.

Tom Allen's pioneering empirical studies of the functioning of the technical gatekeeper have been extended by many other academics and broadly accepted and applied throughout industry and government. For example, a study of so-called "bridge scientists" at Stanford Research Institute found that such individuals are rare but easily identified (19). Effective "bridgers" were found to be interpersonally able (e.g., good listeners), have depth in at least one discipline, have a wide range of interests, and be oriented toward problem solving. As I have argued repeatedly (6) a vital extension of the concept is the recognition that some gatekeepers can "bridge" to market or manufacturing inputs, rather than just technical information, often bringing in raw or processed information, or points of view, that are otherwise lacking within the R&D organization itself.

The final key role is that of the *sponsor* or *coach,* performed usually by a more senior person who is neither carrying out the R&D itself nor is directly and personally aggressively championing the change. The role is one of providing encouragement, psychic support, facilitation to the more junior people involved in the task implementation, often including important help in "bootlegging" the resources needed by those trying to move technological advances forward in an organization (14). My research data affirmed the logical—the higher up in an organization a sponsor was located, the higher the probability of success of internal efforts to generate new product lines. Sponsors are often needed for idea generators, project managers, and especially for

AN INVENTOR CONSIDERS THE PROCESS

I think the processes of invention are like creativity in the arts. The artist does not start with a blank piece of paper. He may have a blank piece of paper in front of him, but he starts with his prior training, his culture, and a bag of tricks based on his own past experience. A poet uses the words he has learned, the words of his language, and no other. His appreciation of beauty is the result of his training and culture. He is driven by ambition, ego, or desire for glory and reward.

This is identical to the drives and mechanisms of the inventor. The inventor also starts with a blank piece of paper, but he uses his training, experience, and intuition not only to create a solution, but often to invent a problem. The invention of a problem is a far greater achievement than inventing a solution. Great inventions are the mothers of necessity and not the other way around.

An inventor may recognize a need before the rest of the world does, or he may create the need because he recognizes that his invention could make life richer, easier, or in some other way, better. He uses his technology as an artist uses his. Technology is only a means to an end. The elegance and beauty of a simple solution to a complicated problem and the appreciation of this elegance, beauty, and simplicity is as much a form of art as putting together notes, words, or colors by an artist.

The question has often been raised as to whether public or even private incentives, drives, and promotional schemes can increase the output of inventions. I have no doubt that the answer is a resounding "yes." A climate of good music for an appreciable time would produce great musicians and composers. There is a great deal of potential talent of all kinds in the genes of the human race. If one wants to produce great soccer players, one has to encourage the playing of soccer, and now and then a great Pele does result. If you teach a great many young people how to play the violin, you would get a few great violinists; if you teach them how to sing, you will get some great singers. Similarly, you can encourage inventions.

This requires creation of glory, rewards, "hoopla" in the media, and all the things that encourage people to pursue any field of activity.

—**Jacob Rabinow,** holder of more than 200 patents including the magnetic particle clutch, the automatic clock regulator and, most recently, a pickproof lock; writing in *Chemtech,* March 1980, p. 145.

entrepreneurs. A good example of the effectiveness of the "ultimate sponsor," the corporate chief executive officer, is Chapman's sponsorship of Gorman's work on "available light motion pictures" at Eastman Kodak (20). But CEOs as project sponsors can be organizationally dangerous too! Who is to turn off the CEO's pet project when it runs amok?

These several critical roles are all needed within or in close contact with each internal working group in order for it to achieve successfully the goals of an innovative outcome. But in addition, the effective development and maintenance of a technical organization requires recognition of these differentiated roles in order to create and implement appropriate people management processes, including recruiting, job assignment, personnel development and training, performance measurement and rewards.

Individual and Organizational Productivity

Beyond the people and role behaviors needed for effective staffing are the principal managerial acts that can affect staff creativity, inventiveness and productivity. The 30 years of *Research Management* reveal plentiful discussions of approaches for stimulating creative idea-generating among scientists and engineers, including such techniques as brainstorming, Synectics, and morphological analysis. (See 21 and 22 for extensive reviews.) Despite the enthusiastic testimony in the various articles, I remain unconvinced that systematic evidence supports the use of these methods, which frankly I view as mainly gimmicks. As documented below, effective individual and group supervision, including proper maintenance of group diversity and task challenge, seem to me more likely to produce useable ideas.

Stages of a scientist's or engineer's career, and the composition of his/her immediate work group are primary influences upon technical productivity (or creativity or inventiveness, if you prefer). This generalization rests upon a broad foundation of research into the performance of technical people and project groups. Katz (23) has demonstrated that technical professionals evolve through three career stages which he labels socialization, innovation and stabilization. As with the different stages of a project cycle, each stage of an individual's career provides a new set of managerial challenges for maximizing personal productivity. The setting of work norms, providing task direction, and joining new employees into the internal technical communications network are managerial issues confronted during the socialization or job "break-in" stage. In contrast, maintaining the employee's earlier motivation and renewing technical skills are among the very different sort of questions needing treatment in the stabilization or job maturity phase.

But personal and group productivity are not just influenced by the individual's job cycle. The nature of the immediate work group, its composition and supervision, matter greatly. In general what Kuhn (24) called "creative tensions," a mix between comfort-reinforcing stability and conflicting challenge, seems desirable. For example, multi-dimensional diversity among technical colleagues in a project team heightens technical performance (7). Variations in age, technical background, even personal values, correlate with enhanced group productivity. This need for internal challenge is further reflected in the findings that the average years a group has worked together significantly impacts upon that group's technical productivity (25). The long-term stable technical group apparently becomes too self-secure, diminishes its outside technical contacts, and decreases its performance. Supervisory intervention at the technical group or RD&E project level seems able to affect this performance, however. For example, technical skills of the first-level group leader, and not human relations skills, enhance a group's effectiveness (26). And even the stable technical team can be moved to high-performing status with proper leadership, in this case requiring strong direction and control by the project manager (17). Thamhain and Wilemon (27) support the importance of the project manager's technical expertise and reliance upon work challenge as major sources of effective technical performance.

ORGANIZATION STRUCTURE

The design of organization structures that will enhance technological innovation requires focusing on both the organization's inputs and its outputs.

Effective RD&E organizations need appropriate technical and market information inputs; and their outputs need to be integrated toward mission objectives and transferred downstream toward their ultimate users.

Market Inputs

Managerial research has repeatedly demonstrated that 60 to 80 percent of successful technical innovations seem to have been initiated by activities responsive to "market pull," i.e. forces reflecting orientation to perceived need or demand (28–30). Of particular note is the recent IRI study of basic research in industry (31), which among many other interesting conclusions produced the unsought finding that "most innovations come about as a result of the recognition of a market need or opportunity. While the push of new technology is also important, it plays a distinctly secondary role." These studies less frequently indicate how technical organizations uncover these needs. Sometimes one person's personal "hobby-horse" forces "market" consciousness to initiate and sustain a technical program, especially when coupled with that individual's entrepreneurial drive and skills, as in Peter Goldmark's successful pursuit of the long-playing record. As Goldmark exclaimed, "My initial interest in the long-playing record (LP) arose out of my sincere hatred of the phonograph . . . it seemed to violate what I thought the quality of music should be" (32).

In organizations less dominated by one key figure, "market gatekeepers" or customer liaison personnel frequently aid the technical organization to better understand its customers' requirements, priorities or preferences. For example, Corning Glass supposedly discovered the need for optical waveguides as a result of one of its staff visiting the British Post Office. Organizing to gain meaningful market inputs for

Stages of a scientist's or engineer's career and composition of his/her immediate work group are primary influences upon technical productivity.

research and engineering use may depend upon explicit assignments of such responsibilities to cooperating marketing staff or to RD&E people themselves. The product development cycle should be organized, as suggested in Figure 63-1, to bring market inputs into design repeatedly, during the early product specification stage, and again during prototyping through active involvement of selected customers. As a sharp contrast to desirable practice, in one consulting project for a major chemical company I found the sales organization prohibiting R&D people from visiting "their" customers, lest the R&D people agree with customer complaints!

A special prospective customer for innovations, often overlooked when R&D does occasionally seek market inputs, is the company's own manufacturing activity. Yet depending on the company and industry, the manufacturing organization turns out to be the eventual "customer" of anywhere from one to two thirds of the company's technological developments. Manufacturing, similar to an outside unrelated potential product customer, has to decide whether or not it wants to "buy" an internally developed improvement in materials, components, manufacturing equipment or overall production process, for its own internal "consumption." That prospective in-house manufacturing "customer" deserves at least the same degree of involvement with the design and development process as does an outside firm or individual. If R&D's "market-oriented" ties to its own manufacturing group can be improved, the potential for significantly impacting company performance is high, especially given the recent IRI study results that show R&D aimed at process innovation as far more likely to succeed than that targeted toward new and improved products (33). But I am convinced that overcoming the gap between the central lab and a major plant installation usually needs special efforts and sometimes creative organizational designs, in particular when important process changes are contemplated.

Rather than seeking collaboration to provide market information to the RD&E process, many companies have ill-advisedly substituted marketing-oriented control of RD&E. Organizational subordination of research and engineering to "product managers" (inevitably marketing or sales people) or tight budgetary control of RD&E by these units may force market-based criteria to dominate technical project selection. But this is usually accompanied by a short-term quick-fix orientation, erosion of technical capability, and gradual destruction of product/process competitiveness. Analyses by Souder (34) have demonstrated that strong and positive relations between R&D and marketing organizations significantly improve the track record on new product introductions. In my experience this is best achieved by welding partnerships among equals, rather than by extracting compliance from subordinates. Good examples of such R&D/marketing partnerships are evident in the team structures used by both Hewlett-Packard and 3M in their new product pursuits.

Market research techniques have long been used to help define consumer preferences in new product designs (35). These methods have been less helpful for developing industrial goods. Recently von Hippel (36) has demonstrated that potential industrial customers whose needs place them at the leading edge of technological demands can be used to specify detailed desired performance characteristics and features for as yet nonexisting products. Military or space research requirements are frequent sources of such "leading edge" requirements. Fusfeld (37) has long used this insight in developing forecasts of the rate of market penetration of new technologies. The problem however is to distinguish a customer demand that is truly in the vanguard of future broader market needs from the "cry for help" from what amounts to the "lunatic fringe" that exists in almost every technical field. That fringe also has needs that are real and extraordinary, but unfortunately not representative of future growth opportunities.

Technical Inputs

Despite the presumed dominant role of "market pull" as a source of innovative projects, "technology push," i.e. undertaking projects for advancing the technical state-of-the-art in an area without anticipation of the specific commercial benefits to be derived, is also the critical source of many significant product and process successes.

The many studies cited earlier still show these technology-push successes to be in the minority, but unfortunately do not clearly indicate the relative worth of the two approaches. One confusion leading to arguments is to assert that if market pull is the key, then market research should be more effective than it has proven to be! Collier (38) for example quotes Barnes' listing of "Neoprene, nylon, polyethylene, silicones, penicillin, Teflon, transistors, xerography, and the Polaroid Land camera" as not resulting from "a market research study of what people *said* they wanted." While market research is not the only or even the primary indicator of "market pull," many research directors especially sympathize with Collier's point of view. Guy Suits (39), long-time leader of General Electric's research efforts, cites Langmuir's work on hydrogen dissociation, leading to a new type of welding, as a good example of technology push. Indeed Casey (40) goes further, arguing that misleading market research was a contributor to the long period required for commercial development of high fructose corn syrup. More logs are heaped on this fire when one cites the supposed market research studies (often claimed to have come from the same large consulting organization!) that demonstrated no meaningful market prospects for computers, instant photography or the dry copier.

When technical advancement is the goal, managers have long understood that professional depth in an organization is achieved by grouping people together in their own area of specialization, with work assigned and performance supervised by a more accomplished person of the same specialization (41). This approach is called functional or discipline-based or specialty-oriented organization. It is the traditional organization structure of the craft guild and of the university. Multiple specialists working together interact comfortably, using the same general knowledge base, analytic skills and tools, and vocabulary. When technical people are organized in functional arrays, their natural interplay brings depth of specialized capabilities to bear on technical problems. Indeed, Marquis and Straight found that technical groups organized in functional forms have the highest technical excellence (42).

But in any nontrivial technical field the vast majority of applicable technical know how exists outside of a performing technical organization. For technical effectiveness even a strong functional team needs to draw upon the pre-existing technical knowledge that is in the outside world, whether in the technical literature, in already developed products and processes, or especially in the minds of other technical professionals. For example, as illustrated in Table 63-2 several studies point out that for innovations eventually developed within a firm, about 60 percent of the sources of the initial technical ideas had outside origins (28). Allen (43) has demonstrated the relative differences among channels for technical information input to an organization, distinguishing what is readily accessed from what is used most effectively in coming up with high-rated problem solutions. His work as well as that of others (44, 45) indicates the minor role played by the literature, especially in contributions to engineering and development, in contrast with personal contacts, experience and training.

One factor that inadvertently has significant effect on technical inputs to RD&E groups is the architectural layout of their work space. Early observations by Jack Morton, then vice president of semiconductor research at Bell Laboratories, led to his concern for the physical separation between technical organizations that were intended

TABLE 63-2   Sources of Ideas for Innovations Developed within the Firm

Author	*Study*	*N*	*% from Outside the Firm*
Langrish et al.	Queen's Awards	51	65
Mueller	Du Pont	25	56
Myers/Marquis	5 Industries	157	62
Utterback	Instruments	32	66

From data contained in J. M. Utterback, "Innovation in Industry and the Diffusion of Technology," *Science 183,* February 15, 1974.

to relate to each other (46). Research at MIT by Muller-Thym in the early 1960s empirically established spatial effects on the frequency of communication among engineers and scientists in the same laboratory. These concepts have been well-developed by Allen (18) into careful findings on specific design elements of RD&E architecture. The distance between two potential communicators, vertical separation, walls and other architectural features importantly influence technology flows.

Thusfar I have addressed what affects technical inputs in support of an organization's internal invention activities, the first element of the two-step innovation process I defined initially. What about technical inputs not aimed at invention but rather at innovation directly? Clearly technological solutions (inventions) already exist elsewhere, and an innovating organization might merely adopt or adapt them by slight modification for a new purpose. This would permit skipping the first stage of invention and going directly to the exploitation stage. An early U.S. study determined that 22 percent of key successful innovations had been adopted or adapted (44) while comparable U.K. data indicated a 33 percent adoption rate (45). Japanese data on license fee payments for foreign technology show a long-established pattern of heavy use of outside technology. A small study of Taiwanese innovations found adoptions to have accounted for the bulk of successes (47). While specific percentages no doubt have changed in recent years, adoption or adaptation of prior outside inventions is a major source of innovation worldwide, but apparently still substantially underutilized by U.S. firms. In recent years the growth of research consortia, effective or not, and the rapidly growing number of "strategic alliances" between large corporations and new firms in areas of emerging technologies indicate that more looking to the outside for technology is taking place, even by U.S. companies. I will discuss this development further in the section on Strategy.

Many companies have ill-advisedly substituted marketing-oriented control of RD&E.

One unique source of potential adoptions is the user. von Hippel (48) has shown that users frequently create and implement innovations for their own use, followed later by manufacturer adoptions of those innovations for large-scale production and distribution. His research on scientific instruments and several areas of manufacturing equipment demonstrated that heavy percentages of new products had been user-developed.

Technical organizations need to be designed to facilitate accessing these several different sources of technical information inputs, whether as contributions toward internal inventions or as sources for adoption more directly as innovations. A variety of approaches are suggested, ranging from such simple considerations as ensuring that at least some salespeople have technical skills and/or incentives so that they bring back a customer's ideas in addition to his orders. Much more ambitious are the IBM marketing department's several "applied science centers" across the United States, established adjacent to concentrations of innovative users to learn about new software and hardware developments and transfer that technical information back into IBM's product development groups. IBM's Cambridge operation in Technology Square, working closely with MIT's pioneering Project MAC, thus became the source of IBM's first commercial computer time-sharing system, a field adaptation of an innovative user's development. As one approach to overcome biases against outside sources of technology, increasingly corporations are establishing the position of Chief Technical Officer or Vice President of Technology, with broad responsibility for both internal technology development as well as external technology acquisition. Organizational experiments to enhance both technical and market information inputs are underway across a broad front.

Output-Focused Organization

Just as the functional organization structure maximizes technical inputs, the project, program, mission or product organization is intended to integrate all inputs toward well-defined outputs. By placing in the same group, under a single leader, all the contributors toward a given objective, the project organization maximizes coordination and control toward achieving output goals. The Marquis and Straight study (42) cited earlier supports these findings. But project structures have a fundamental flaw that seriously affects many technical organizations. The project form tends to remove technical people from organizational groups in which they interact with colleagues of their own scientific or engineering discipline. Furthermore, the project manager may be technically expert, but inevitably in only one of the disciplines of his or her subordinates, not all of them. If the project has long duration, especially when the technology base is rapidly changing, the technical skills of the project members erode over time due to lack of stimulating technical reinforcement and supervision.

This dilemma has led to the creation of an organization that is intended to be a "compromise"—the "matrix" structure in which technical performers are supposed to maintain active membership in two organizations, their original discipline-based functional group as well as the focused project group. In theory the "matrixed" person thus has two bosses, one functional and one project, each of whom will extract his appropriate "due," thereby attempting simultaneously to maintain the technical skills and performance of the individual, more or less, while orienting his loyalty and contributions toward the project's output goals, more or less! However, most technical "matrix" organizations are only "paper" matrices, not "real" matrices—they appear to be matrices on organization charts but do not strongly pull the engineer between two conflicting masters.

If one wanted to obtain truly matrixed individuals, the influences that push a technologist's time and attention toward competing sets of objectives (e.g., functional excellence vs. project schedule demands) would have to be roughly balanced between those objectives. A technical contributor's priorities are influenced by: (a) who is responsible for his/her performance evaluation and reward distribution; (b) who makes the individual's specific task assignments; (c) where is the individual physically located relative to the two "competing" managers; (d) what is the longer-term career relevance of the competing groups; and (e) what is the relative persuasiveness (whether based on personality or power) of the two managers. Achieving even a rough balance among these influences would only be practicable by dominance of the functional manager on some of these dimensions, dominance of the project manager on others, and perhaps rough equivalence of the two managers on still other influences upon matrixed persons. The absence of reasonable balance in most "paper matrixed" cases leads the actual situation to its "default" condition, with the achieved results reflecting the characteristics of the dominant organization form, either functional or project but seldom both. Recent studies suggest that certain patterns of dominance among these contending influence sources achieve better performance of matrix organizations (25).

Output Transfers

But in addition to generating outputs, the technical organization needs to be designed to enhance output transfer downstream toward eventual customers and users. Downstream is where innovation takes place and where benefits are realized! A consulting survey of prestigious major corporate research laboratories has indicated high degree of dissatisfaction with the extent and effectiveness of transfer of results to potential recipient groups (49, 50). Three different clusters of bridging approaches were found helpful in increasing transfer in those labs—procedural, human and organizational. Most organizations used a variety of these approaches, often several simultaneously. My findings have been reaffirmed by recent comparative case studies by an internal task force at IBM (51) and by a consulting project at Union Carbide (52), among others.

Procedural methods include: joint planning of RD&E programs by the performing group and the organization that is expected to be the receiver, often resisted by R&D as an "invasion" of its turf; joint staffing of projects, especially pre- and post-transfer downstream; and joint project appraisal after project completion, done cautiously if at all after failures in order to avoid destructive fingerpointing.

Human bridges are the most effective transfer mechanisms, especially the upstream and downstream transfers of people. Movement of people upstream: (a) brings with them information on the context of intended project use; (b) establishes direct person-to-person contacts that will be helpful in later post-transfer troubleshooting;

Most technical "matrix" organizations are only "paper" matrices, not "real" matrices.

and (c) creates the image that the project eventually being transferred has involved prior ownership and priority inputs from the receiving unit. Later movement of people downstream: (a) carries expertise for post-transfer problem-solving; and (b) not unimportant, conveys the risk-reducing impression that the receiving unit will not be stuck with solving post-transfer problems by itself. Other human bridges that are widely used include rotation programs, market gatekeepers, joint problem-solving sessions, and other formal and informal meetings.

Organizational techniques for enhancing transfer are usually more complicated to design and implement than procedural or human bridge approaches. "Integrators," sometimes named "transfer managers," or integrating departments are frequently appointed to tie together the sending and receiving organizations. This person or unit is given the responsibility for moving the project from the sender into operating condition in the receiver organization, either lacking authority in one or the other organization or being matrixed between both.

More ambitious organizational approaches include dedicated transfer teams, established solely for the period during which technical results are being transferred to their "customers," done especially for moving purchased process technology. Venture teams, discussed further below, are also employed to reduce functional organizational transfer issues, shifting leadership responsibility among the many-disciplined team members as the primary phase of the project shifts from research to engineering to manufacturing to sales.

STRATEGY

Strategic management of technology includes both strategic planning and strategic implementation aspects at either of two levels: (a) overall, for the entire technology-dependent firm, government agency, division or product line; or (b) more focused, for just the technology development/acquisition process/department/laboratory of the entire organization. As recently as ten years ago neither of these levels of strategy was the subject of much serious scholarship, or even management consulting practice. Few researchers carefully studied the overall management of the technology-intensive company. And fewer still addressed the questions of how to incorporate technological considerations into overall business strategy.

Strategic planning focuses upon the formulation of an organization's goals and objectives, and upon developing the policies needed to achieve those objectives, including identification of the organization's primary resources and priorities. But developing corporate strategy with such a global perspective, including technological dimensions, is quite new. Indeed the evolution of corporate strategic planning as a field of practice is divisible more-or-less into three decades: the 1960s, during which multi-year budget projections became the earliest forms of financial planning, sometimes mislabelled "long-range planning"; the 1970s, when market growth/share matrices and market attractiveness considerations added a new dimension to strategic analysis; and the 1980s, during which technology as a strategic factor became so widely acknowledged as to cause firms and even countries to realize that financial, marketing, and technological considerations needed to be integrated in overall strategy development (53).

Strategic Thinking and Planning

Horwitch and Prahalad (54) provided an early set of perspectives at the overall strategic level, differentiating the key issues of technology-oriented strategic management among three modes: the small, usually single-product, high-tech firm; the large, multi-market, multi-product corporation; and the multi-organization, even multi-sector societal program. For each of these, Horwitch and Prahalad find a primarily nonoverlapping set of strategic issues and priorities. More recent writing has focused upon similarities between the first two "modes," the entrepreneurial smaller firm and the successfully innovative larger corporation (55–58; see also 14). Maidique and Hayes conclude that to be innovative the large corporation needs to manage the "paradox" of chaos versus continuity, similar to the "creative tensions" required for the innovative technical person (7, 24).

In moving from strategic thinking toward strategic planning we need principles for developing more detailed technology strategies. But what are the underpinnings of technological change, especially as it relates to the corporation, upon which overall technology strategy should be based? Three general observations seem critical here, all linked to the dynamics of technological innovation processes: (1) there are characteristic patterns over the life cycle of a technology in how frequently product versus process innovations occur; (2) each stage of a technology has differing critical implications for innovation, including type, cost, degree of invention, and source; and (3) an organization's efforts to generate technological innovation create almost inevitable internal dynamics in the allocation of R&D efforts, generating multiple management problems. Each of these is discussed more fully below, with suggestions of related technology planning and strategy development approaches.

Utterback and Abernathy (59) demonstrated that a technology tends to evolve in three stages. Most technologies move from an early "fluid stage," dominated by frequent product innovations, through a "transition stage," characterized by significant process innovation and the emergence of a dominant product design, into a "specific stage," featuring lower rate of and more minor product and process innovations. While variations in this pattern of course occur, some of which are already well understood (60, 61), this generalization becomes one important basis for developing a company's or a product line's technology strategy.

One of the most significant findings from this research has been the reaffirmed role of the smaller firm as the dominant source of innovation during the earliest emerging stage of a technology, with the locus of innovation shifting toward larger companies in the transitional and more mature stages of a technology (59). Most studies that have sought to find differences in R&D productivity as a function of company size have not made this critical distinction as to the stage of technology or type of innovation. Consequently, the findings of these economic analyses have varied unconvincingly all over the lot, from some that have asserted the large company is most productive of innovations to others that have claimed the exact opposite, to still other studies that have found nonlinear ties between size and R&D results.

The potential stability or predictability in patterns of technology evolution is the rationale for attempting to use technological forecasting techniques as part of technology planning and strategy development. Most technology forecasting methods are simple, often inadequate for the task (62, 63). Indeed despite recent "rediscovery" by some consultants of technology S-curves for forecasting and planning (64), the intellectual development of the technology forecasting field more or less stopped over a decade ago (65, 66). Yet some corporations have benefited enormously from thoughtful application of technology forecasting methods to their strategic analyses. Tracy O'Rourke, the chief executive officer of Allen-Bradley, for example, cites a comprehensive technology forecast as the basis for planning his company's successful transition from electromechanical to solid state electronic devices (67).

Each stage of a technology is associated with different strategic implications. The earliest stage in a technology's life cycle tends to feature frequent major product innovations, heavily contributed by small entrepreneurial organizations, often closely tied to lead user needs. The development of frozen orange juice concentrate by the National Research Corporation and its spinoff companies is one such example (68). The present rash of biotechnology discoveries are coming primarily from university laboratories directly or from young small enterprises, leading irresistably to the explosion of biotech alliances between large companies and the new startups. The same alliance pattern has evolved in the areas of machine vision and artificial intelligence.

The intermediate stage of a technology's life cycle may include major process innovation, with continuing but lessened product variation occurring, with increasing numbers of competitors, both large and small. To achieve the dominant product-process design during this stage, large corporations sometimes undertake long-term

TABLE 63-3 Cost-Reducing Innovation in Du Pont Rayon Plants

Plan	*Contribution of* **Minor** *Technical Change to %* *of Net Reduction in Unit Costs Due to Technical Change*
Spruance II-A	83
Spruance I	80
Old Hickory	79
Spruance III	46
Spruance I	100

From data in S. Hollander, *The Sources of Increased Efficiency.* Cambridge: MIT Press, 1965.

development programs that combine many elements of applied research and engineering. For example, General Motors' successful efforts in developing its two-cycle diesel engine included more than ten major developments needed for the final system (69).

The late stage of a technology features less frequent minor product and process innovations, contributed primarily by large corporations, motivated mostly by cost reduction and quality improvement operational objectives. As illustrated by Hollander's (70) careful analysis of Du Pont rayon innovations, shown in Table 63-3, these numerous minor innovations can produce dramatic cumulative impact upon costs. In fact the so-called "learning curve," i.e. decreasing unit manufacturing cost as cumulative production increases, results primarily not from the volume itself but rather from the usual continuing allocation of engineering efforts to incremental cost reduction projects as a product line's volume increases. Management of the technical investment is the primary source of the so-called "learning curve" competitive advantage, not the share of market.

These key dimensions of a technology described above should strongly influence choices made by a firm or government agency in developing its technological strategy. A company's detailing of its "product innovation charter" (71), or its application of project selection principles or techniques (72) as part of technology planning, ought to reflect at least general consideration of the current stages of its principal technologies. In particular, the late stage of one technology usually corresponds to earlier stages of other potentially threatening technologies. Most corporations fail to anticipate or even appropriately respond to these technological threats (64, 73).

Technology life cycles occur in an industry as a whole, thus providing an "environmental" set of influences upon a single organization's strategy. A different kind of cycle, however, is produced within a firm by its own attempts to develop and commercially exploit technology. As a major project moves downstream through a multi-stage research-design-development-production engineering-field trouble shooting technical organization, decisions on acquisition and allocation of technical resources can cause major instability in overall performance, including in the rate and character of new product releases and resulting sales and profits (74, 75). For many small firms the resulting "boom then bust" often spells disaster. Similar though less evident problems arise at the product line level of large corporations and government agencies. Self-induced cycles of primarily discovery followed then by primarily exploitation seem to have plagued the growth years of Polaroid Corporation, for example, contributing to its financial crises of the late 1970s.

Japanese R&D strategy may be in transition toward what has been a dominant U.S. approach.

Large-scale and realistic computer simulation models have been developed and increasingly employed in recent years for helping to cope with this aspect of technology and overall organizational strategy development (65, 74–76). While these computer modeling methods are primarily strategic support tools, the technological forecasting and project selection techniques that were mentioned principally enhance tactical and operational aspects of technology planning and management. Other approaches to technology planning have been developed and successfully applied at both the tactical and strategic levels. For example, Crawford (71) has conceptualized a "product innovation charter" that contains five major areas for inclusion in a formal strategy statement, with each of the five subdivided into finer categories. Crawford argues for taking into account explicitly the company's: target business arenas; objectives of product innovation; specific program of activities; the degree of innovation sought; and any special conditions or restrictions on the strategy.

Another most impressive technique for technology planning is "competitive product profiling," in which an organization's product line is compared to its key competitors in terms of seven technology-based measures: functional performance; acquisition cost; ease-of-use; operating cost; reliability; serviceability; and system compatibility (77). IBM adds "availability" to this list of competitive measures, making "reliability, availability, serviceability" (RAS) a critical element of its internal technology planning. Extending this approach to analysis of competitive manufacturing processes has been attempted, but with less success due to relative lack of competitor data. Fusfeld (77) has tried to overcome this limitation and bring technology planning to the level of assessment of overall organizational capability. He uses in his analytical framework the "technology planning unit," the level of generic technology in the organization as it is being applied to a particular market opportunity, and tries to evaluate relative technical strength. Further developments of technology planning approaches, especially at the strategic level, are needed and can be expected during the coming decade (78).

Strategic Implementation

But beyond strategic planning must come strategic implementation. Tactics and operations are the means of implementation of strategy. Not much has yet been written about specific implementations of technology strategies. At the national level, Johnson (79) has concluded that, relative to American firms, Japanese industry has more heavily invested in applied rather than basic research, adopting and improving on preexisting products and technologies, in already well-developed market areas. He cites government policies in regard to patents, subsidies and tax incentives as important in both countries. In his recent survey studies while at MIT, Hirota (80) has developed strong empirical evidence on U.S.-Japanese technology strategy differences, supporting but going beyond Johnson's observations. However, recent Japanese pioneering efforts in such areas as compact-disk technology and more advanced semiconductor memories suggest that Japanese R&D strategy may be in transition toward what has been a dominant U.S. approach (81).

Although now also of increasing interest to nontechnical industries, the so-called "venture approaches" have been a unique means for implementing overall strategies seeking accelerated technology-based new business development for growth and/or diversification. These venture approaches involve larger organizations in attempts to emulate or couple with smaller entrepreneurial units. The spectrum of possible strategic and organizational alternatives includes: venture capital investments in young "emerging technology" companies; sponsored spin-offs of new product development-commercialization groups; "new style joint ventures" that feature alliances between large and small companies; internal ventures; and integrated venture strategies (82). Collaborative undertakings among U.S. firms are growing dramatically, involving new linkages with universities and especially new investment/development/commercialization ties with young high technology companies (83, 84).

A subject of active study and industrial practice off and on since the early 1960s, venture approaches have recently become increasingly attempted by companies and even countries as part of their strategies for intensifying their technological industrial base. Venture strategies require long-term persistence for effective implementation and dramatic differences in management style and policies from traditional mainstream approaches. These demands for "managerial innovation" are seldom adequately met, producing high failure rate among corporate venturers (85, 86). Yet the occasional dramatic success, such as Texas Instruments' entry into the semiconductor business (87) or IBM's Personal Computer venture or 3M's "Post-Its" offer sufficient upside attraction to keep companies making new venture attempts.

The variety of venture alternative for entering new businesses has raised issues as to means for selecting among them. Roberts and Berry (88) have devised a research-based matrix reflecting primarily the organization's "familiarity" with the market and

SUMMING UP

- Technological innovation is a multi-sage process. with major differences need for effective management of each stage of activity.

- To achieve effective innovation, an organization requires that "critical role-players" collaborate in a formal or informal team relationship. These critical roles include the idea generator, the entrepreneur, the program manager, several types of gatekeepers, and the sponsor.

- Group diversity is a major influence upon technical performance. A group that stabilizes its membership for too long not only decreases its productivity but tends to become insular and to evidence "Not Invented Here" behavior.

- Highest product development success rates are produced when marketing and R&D organizations work in close collaboration.

- "Market pull" far more frequently leads to successful innovations than does "technology push," although both sources of initiating projects account for success and failure alike.

- Users not only furnish critical "market needs" input data to designers, but in some industries supply the actual innovations that manufacturers later adapt, improve and commercialize.

- Downstream transfer of RD&E results can be improved through use of multiple procedural, human, and organizational "bridges." Human bridges are the most effective transfer mechanism, and people movements, rotations, and face-to-face meetings should be used routinely and frequently.

- Most technologies move through evolutionary stages: an early one dominated by frequent product innovations; a transition characterized by increased process innovation and the emergence of a dominant product design; and a mature stage featuring much lower rate and more minor degree of both product and process innovation. A firm's innovation strategy and technological resource allocations should differ markedly depending upon the stage of its primary technology.

- "Competitive product profiling" is a useful method for initiating technical planning in a company, comparing the key technical performance characteristics of a product line with competitors' related products.

- Recent growth of venture capital and alliance methods reflects increasing recognition of the need to link external technologies with internal capabilities.

- Top management commitment is essential to assure success of broad-based programs aimed at institutionalizing the development of effective product and process innovations.

FOR FURTHER READING

The list of references for this article can provide a career-time of study and thought for the innovation-seeking manager. Some direction to priorities among that list, and some additional items, may help the reader to enhance both learning and performance in regard to managing invention and innovation. For those with general interests I suggest three alternative beginnings. The most used "reference" book is the compilation of readings by Tushman and Moore (editors), *Readings in the Management of Innovation* (Pitman, 1982). We use it as the text for our introductory courses in managing technology at the MIT Sloan School of Management. Just emerged from the printers is my own assemblage of articles from the *Sloan Management Review*—E. B. Roberts (editor), *Generating Technological Innovation* (Oxford University Press, 1987), which follows the organization of this article in its sectioning the discussions of innovation into considerations of staffing, structure, and strategy. Another interesting new general book is Fred Betz's, *Managing*

Technology (1987). All three of the above provide the breadth of multiple authors' viewpoints on lots of issues on the management of technological innovation. An additional report on the same subject, especially useful for those thinking about setting up internal company management programs or university courses, is the National Research Council's *Management of Technology: The Hidden Competitive Advantage* (National Academy Press, 1987).

For those with more specific interests, the most important people-oriented readings include two "classics": Pelz and Andrews, *Scientists in Organizations* (U. of Michigan Press, 1976), which has a comprehensive and well-organized presentation of factors affecting individual and team performance in R&D settings; and Tom Allen's *Managing the Flow of Technology* (MIT Press, 1977), which uniquely treats how engineers and scientists acquire and use technical information, including exploration of such influences as organization form, laboratory architecture, and

(Continued)

FOR FURTHER READING (*Continued*)

personal characteristics. Immodestly I also suggest further reading of my recent work, Roberts and Fusfeld. "Staffing the innovative technology-based organization," *Sloan Management Review,* spring 1981, which proposes a view of people management that stresses the different key roles needed for achieving effective innovation.

In regard to structural perspectives, I suggest (but suspect it will be hard to find) Jack Morton's fascinating insights based on his Bell System experiences: Morton, *Organizing for Innovation* (McGraw-Hill, 1971). A new release by Eric von Hippel, *Sources of Innovation* (Oxford University Press, 1988), focuses upon the user's role as innovator, as well as the economic influences on innovations from suppliers and others. Later this year, my colleague Mel Horwitch's new book, *Post-Modern Management* (Free Press, 1988), will deserve your attention, as it probes corporate technology strategy issues with special emphasis upon the new organizational structures being developed and implemented by innovation-seeking companies.

On the dimension of innovation strategy, a few works deserve further assessment. William

Abernathy's pathfinding *The Productivity Dilemma* (Johns Hopkins, 1978) points out the problems of innovating in a mature industry and the consequences of failing to innovate. Good evidence of how general is the problem of non-response to technological innovation can be found in Richard Foster's *Innovation: The Attacker's Advantage* (Summit, 1986), but frankly I find a bit overdone the emphasis upon comparing Scurves as an indicator of the need and timing for change. Later this year James Utterback promises his book from Ballinger Publishing, tentatively called *The Dynamics of Industrial Innovation.* Jim's manuscript provides deep insights into the relative roles of product versus process innovation within a technological life cycle. My biased interest in corporate venture strategies for new business development causes me to end this list by recommending further reading of my "New Ventures for Corporate Growth," *Harvard Business Review,* July-August 1980, as well as my article with Charles Berry, "Entering New Businesses: Selecting Strategies for Success." *Sloan Management Review,* Spring 1985.—**E. B. R.**

---

technology aspects of the new business. The Roberts/Berry framework, supported by a field test in a large diversified U.S. firm, concludes essentially that the further the new area is from the firm's base "familiar" business, the less resource-intense the venture approach to be taken. An unpublished Japanese analysis of corporate venture success and failure and a host of studies performed by members of my mid-career MIT Management of Technology Program have strengthened the data support for "familiarity" as a powerful determinant of business development. Further reaffirming this emphasis upon "familiarity" as a key variable for eliciting strategic direction are the recent findings by Meyer and Roberts (89) that the more successful small high-technology companies pursue product development strategies that are focused upon moderate degrees of technological and market change. Much more research is needed to test she applicability of these results in other industries and with larger companies.

With the exception of its brief mention above in regard to U.S. and Japanese R&D investments, the role of government policies and actions in affecting technology strategy has been ignored thusfar. Yet government regulatory activities in regard especially to health and safety have had significant positive and negative influences on technological innovation (90–92). But, as pointed out by Abernathy and Chakravarthy (93), government's strategic role has also included actions to create technologies directly (via the Horwitch/Prahalad Mode III, for example, 54) as well as indirectly through market modifications (94). In a sense the variety of alternatives facing governments for influencing technological change are equivalent to the corporate venture alternatives described previously.

IN CONCLUSION

Recent work by Gobeli and Rudelius (95) provides a fitting basis for finishing this article. In their integrative comparative analysis of five firms in the technology-intensive cardiac-pacemaker industry they observe the differing competitive impacts that have come from the multiple stages of the innovation process. Managing at the creativity phase is not enough, nor even is managing manufactured quality sufficient, nor is managing that is focused primarily upon any other single aspect of innovation. They reaffirm the importance of key innovation-supporting people roles. Gobeli/Rudelius describe the importance of market-technology linkages, effective program management, government intervention, and appropriate goal-setting, planning and risk-taking for firms in this medical electronics industry.

Technological innovation can provide the potential for altering the competitive status of firms and nations. It can contribute to increased corporate sales and profits, as well as individual and national security and well-being. But its purposeful management is complex, involving the effective integration of people, organizational processes and plans. Only recently have some companies undertaken bold and broad action steps to try to institutionalize an effective product and process innovation program. Two firms in particular, long known for effective innovation, have publicized ambitious multi-faceted endeavors. 3M has based its attempts heavily upon a so-called "intrapreneurship" approach, while Corning Glass has developed a more broad-based effort, including redesigning organization structures, changing incentive programs, and undertaking widespread management involvement and educational change activities. In both cases leadership for these multi-year institutional change programs came from the CEO's office. Other companies would be wise to consider whether top-down company-wide commitments to accelerate and enhance effective innovation might not also apply to them.

This article has argued a host of generalizations about managing the process of invention and technological innovation, each supported by literature, empirical research, and practitioner experience. Some of these generalizations have already been widely diffused into practice, such as recognition of the gatekeeper's importance to information flow and nearly everyone's efforts to stimulate internal entrepreneurship. Some of my other contentions may still be subject to debate, modification and even rejection as we learn more.

Both academics and technology managers need to join in this continuing search for clearer managerial insights about technological invention and innovation and more effective organizational performance. The National Research Council's recent report, *Management of Technology: The Hidden Competitive Advantage,* summed up the goals: "Effective work in the field of Management of Technology can play a crucial role in devising the strategies and imparting the skills and attitudes to U.S. engineers and managers that they will need in the future technology-dominated economy" (96). It listed eight challenges of critical importance to industrial competitiveness: How to integrate technology into the overall strategic objectives of the firm; How to get into and out of technologies faster and more efficiently; How to assess/evaluate technology more effectively; How best to accomplish technology transfer; How to reduce new product development time; How to manage large, complex, and interdisciplinary or interorganizational projects/systems; How to manage the organization's internal use of technology; How to leverage the effectiveness of technical professionals. Hopefully more light will be shed on these key industrial needs prior to the IRI's Diamond Jubilee!

About the Author

Edward B. Roberts has been a leader for 25 years in research and education on the management of technological innovation and its practical application to management. With prior engineering and management degrees from MIT, Roberts completed his MIT Ph.D. in economics in 1962 with a dissertation on the dynamics of R&D projects. That same year he joined Donald G. Marquis in establishing MIT's Research Program on the Management of Technology, which he has directed since Marquis' death in 1973. His research focused early on the formation and growth of technology-based companies and evolved into broad studies of entrepreneurship in both large and small organizations. His other research interests have included project management, R&D commercialization, technical innovation processes, university-industry technology transfer, and corporate technology strategy. In 1980 he and Herbert Hollomon co-founded the mid-career MIT Program In the Management of Technology, a 12-month Master's Degree program for experienced scientists and engineers seeking increasing responsibilities in industry and government.

As co-founder and president of the consulting firm of Pugh-Roberts Associates, Inc. since 1963, Roberts has developed its dual focus upon corporate strategic analysis and technology management and organization, transferring research findings from MIT into industrial practice. Roberts' interests in technological entrepreneurship have involved him in the co-founding of a number of companies, including Medical Information Technology, Inc. (MEDITECH) and the Zero Stage Capital group of venture capital investment firms, as well as in serving on the boards of directors of numerous high-technology firms.

References

1. H. R. Bartlett. *The Development of Industrial research in the United States.* Washington: National Research Council, 1941.

2. J. Jewkes, D. Sawers, and R. Stillerman. *The Sources of Innovation.* London: Macmillan, 1958.

3. *Research Management.* "Top Research Managers Speak Out on Innovation," November 1970.

4. S. J. Kline. "Innovation is Not a Linear Process." *Research Management,* 1985.

5. P. F. Drucker. *Innovation and Entrepreneurship: Practice and Principles.* New York: Harper & Row, 1985, 35–36.

6. E. B. Roberts and A. R. Fusfeld. "Staffing the Innovative Technology-Based Organization," *Sloan Management Review,* vol. 22, no. 3, Spring 1981.

7. D. Pelz and F. M. Andrews. *Scientists in Organizations,* Revised Edition. Ann Arbor, Michigan: University of Michigan Press, 1976.

8. F. M. Andrews. "Innovation in R&D Organizations: Some Relevant Concepts and Empirical Results," in E. B. Roberts et al., editors. *Biomedical Innovation.* Cambridge: MIT Press, 1981.

9. S. D. Stookey. "History of the Development of Pyroceram," *Research Management,* Autumn 1958.

10. D. Peters and E. B. Roberts. "Unutilized Ideas in University Laboratories," *Academy of Management Journal,* vol. 12, no. 2, June 1969.

11. E. B. Roberts and D. Peters. "Commercial Innovation from University Faculty," *Research Policy,* vol. 10, no. 2, April 1981.

12. A. H. Rubenstein, A. K. Chakrabarti, R. D. O'Keefe, W. E. Souder, and H. C. Young. "Factors Influencing Innovation Success at the Project Level." *Research Management,* May 1976.

13. L. W. Lehr. "Stimulating Technological Innovation: The Role of Top Management," *Research Management,* November 1979.

14. E. B. Roberts. "Entrepreneurship and Technology: A Basic Study of Innovators," *Research Management,* vol. 11, no. 4, July 1968.

15. M. A. Maidique. "Entrepreneurs, Champions, and Technological Innovation," *Sloan Management Review,* vol. 21, no. 2, Winter 1980.

16. D. G. Marquis and I. M. Rubin. "Management Factors in Project Performance." MIT Sloan School of Management Working Paper, 1966.

17. R. Katz and T. J. Allen. "Project Performance and the Locus of Influence in the R&D Matrix," *Academy of Management Journal,* vol. 26, 1985.

18. T. J. Allen. *Managing the Flow of Technology.* Cambridge: MIT Press, 1977.

19. J. Gartner and C. S. Naiman. "Overcoming the Barriers to Technology Transfer," *Research Management,* March 1976.

20. L. J. Thomas. "Available Light Movies—An Individual Inventor Made it Happen," *Research Management,* November 1980.

21. W. E. Souder and R. W. Ziegler. "A Review of Creativity and Problem Solving Techniques," *Research Management,* July 1977.

22. H. Geschka. "Introduction and Use of Idea-Generating Methods," *Research Management May 1978.*

23. R. Katz. "Managing Careers: The Influence of Job and Group Longevities," in R. Katz, editor. *Career Issues in Human Resource Management.* Englewood Cliffs, NJ.: Prentice-Hall, 1982.

24. T. S. Kuhn. *The Structure of Scientific Revolutions.* Chicago: University of Chicago Press, 1963.

25. R. Katz and T. J. Allen. "Investigating the Not Invented Here (NIH) syndrome: A Look at the Performance, Tenure, and Communication Patterns of 50 R&D Project Groups," *R&D Management,* vol. 12, no. 1, 1982.

26. G. F. Ferris. "The Technical Supervisor: Beyond the Peter Principle," *Technology Review,* 1973.

27. H. J. Thamhain and D. L. Wilemon. "Leadership, Conflict, and Program Management Effectiveness," *Sloan Management Review,* vol. 19, no. 1, Fall 1977.

28. J. M. Utterback. "Innovation and the Diffusion of Technology," *Science,* vol. 183, no. 4125, 15 February 1974.

29. A. Gerstenfeld. "A Study of Successful Projects, Unsuccessful Projects, and Projects in Process in West Germany," *IEEE Transactions on Engineering Management,* vol. EM-23, no. 3, 1976.

30. R. Rothwell, C. Freeman, A. Horsley, V. T. P. Jervis, A. B. Robertson, and J. Townsend. "SAPPHO, updated-project SAPPHO phase II." *Research Policy,* vol. 3, 1974.

31. W. C. Fernelius and W. H. Waldo. "Role of Basic Research in Industrial Innovation," *Research Management,* July 1980.

32. P. C. Goldmark. "How the LP Record was Developed—Or the Case of the Missing Fuzz," *Research Management,* July, 1974.

33. N. R. Baker, S. G. Green, and A. S. Bean. "The Need for Strategic Balance in R&D Project Portfolios," *Research Management,* March-April 1986.

34. W. E. Souder. "Effectiveness of Product Development Methods," *Industrial Marketing Management,* vol. 7, 1978.

35. G. L. Urban and J. R. Hauser. *Design and Marketing of New Products.* Englewood Cliffs, NJ.: Prentice-Hall, 1980.

36. E. A. von Hippel. "Lead Users: A Source of Novel Product Concepts," *Management Science,* July 1986.

37. A. R. Fusfeld. "How Not to Fall on Your Face in Technological Forecasting." *Inside R&D,* vol. 7, no. 2, January 1978.

38. D. W. Collier. "More Effective Research for Large Corporations," *Research Management,* vol. 12, no. 3, May 1969.

39. C. G. Suits. "Selectivity and Timing in Research," *Research Management,* vol. 5, no. 6, 1962.

40. J. P. Casey. "High Fructose Corn Syrup—A Case History of Innovation," *Research Management,* September 1976.

41. P. R. Lawrence and J. W. Lorsch. *Organization and Environments.* Boston: Harvard Business School, 1967.

42. D. G. Marquis and D. L. Straight. "Organizational Factors in Project Performance." MIT Sloan School of Management Working Paper #133–65, 1965.

43. T. J. Allen. "Performance of Information Channels in the Transfer of Technology," *Industrial Management Review,* vol. 8, no. 1, Fall 1966.

44. S. Myers and D. G. Marquis. *Successful Industrial Innovation,* Washington: National Science Foundation, 1969.

45. J. Langrish, M. Gibbons, W. G. Evans, and F. R. Jevons. *Wealth from Knowledge.* London: Macmillan, 1972.

46. J. A. Morton. *Organizing for Innovation.* New York: McGraw-Hill, 1971.

47. A. Gerstenfeld and L. H. Wortzel. "Strategies for Innovation in Developing Countries," *Sloan Management Review,* vol. 19, no. 1, 1977.

48. E. A. von Hippel. "Has a Customer Already Developed Your Next Product?" *Sloan Management Review,* vol. 18, no. 2, Winter 1977.

49. E. B. Roberts. "Stimulating Technological Innovation: Organizational Approaches," *Research Management,* vol. 22, no. 6, November 1979.

50. E. B. Roberts and A. Frohman. "Strategies for Improving Research Utilization," *Technology Review,* vol. 80, no. 5, March/April 1978.

51. H. Cohen, S. Keller, and D. Streeter. "The Transfer of Technology from Research to Development," *Research Management,* May 1979.

52. J. J. Smith, J. E. McKeon, K. L. Hoy, R. L. Boysen, L. Shechter, and E. B. Roberts. "Lessons from 10 Case Studies in Innovation," *Research Management,* vol. 27, no. 5, September–October 1984.

53. E. B. Roberts. "Strategic Management of Technology," in *Global Technological Change: Symposium Proceedings.* Cambridge: MIT Industrial Liaison Program, June 1983.

54. M. Horwitch and C. K. Prahalad. "Managing Technological Innovation—Three Ideal Modes," *Sloan Management Review,* vol. 17, no. 2, Winter 1976.

55. J. B. Quinn. "Technological Innovation, Entrepreneurship, and Strategy," *Sloan Management Review,* vol. 20, no. 3, Spring 1979.

56. T. J. Peters and R. H. Waterman. *In Search of Excellence.* New York: Harper & Row, 1982.

57. M. A. Maidique and R. H. Hayes. "The Art of High-Technology Management," *Sloan Management Review,* vol. 25, no. 2, Winter 1984.

58. J. Friar and M. Horwitch. "The emergence of technology strategy: a new dimension of strategic management," *Technology in Society,* vol. 7, nos. 2 and 3, Winter 1985/1986.

59. J. M. Utterback and W. J. Abernathy. "A Dynamic Model of Product and Process Innovation," *Omega,* vol. 3, no. 6, 1975.

60. J. M. Utterback. "Systems of Innovation: Macro/Micro," in W. N. Smith and C. F. Larson, editors. *Innovation and U.S. Research.* Washington: American Chemical Society, 1980.

61. J. M. Utterback and L. Kim. "Invasion of a Stable Business by Radical Innovation," in P. R. Kleindorfer, editor. *The Management of Productivity and Technology in Manufacturing.* New York: Plenum Press, 1986.

62. E. B. Roberts. "Exploratory and Normative Technological Forecasting: A Critical Appraisal," *Technological Forecasting,* vol. 1, no. 2, Fall 1969.

63. A. R. Fusfeld and F. C. Spital. "Technology Forecasting and Planning in the Corporate Environment: Survey and Comment," in B. V. Dean and J. L. Goldhar, editors. *Management of Research and Innovation.* TIMS Studies in the Management Sciences, vol. 15, North-Holland Publishing Co., 1980.

64. R. N. Foster. *Innovation: The Attacker's Advantage.* New York: Summit Books, 1986.

65. E. B. Roberts. *The Dynamics of Research and Development.* New York: Harper & Row, 1964.

66. J. P Martino. *Technological Forecasting for Decision Making.* New York: Elsevier, 1972.

67. T. O'Rourke. Presentation at Pugh-Roberts Associates, Inc., Workshop on Critical Issues in Technology Management, April 15, 1986.

68. D. H. Peters, "The Development of Frozen Orange Juice Concentrate," *Research Management,* vol. 11, no. 1, January 1968.

69. K. A. Richardson. "Research Toward Specific Goals: Development of the Light-Weight, Two-Cycle Diesel," *Research Management,* Summer 1958.

70. S. Hollander, *The Sources of Increased Efficiency,* Cambridge: MIT Press, 1965.

71. C. M. Crawford, "Defining the Charter for Product Innovation," *Sloan Management Review,* vol. 22, no. 1, Fall 1980.

72. M. R. Baker and W. H. Pound, "Project Selection: Where We Stand," *IEEE Transactions on Engineering Management,* vol. EM-11, no. 4, December 1964.

73. A. C. Cooper and D. Schendel. "Strategic Responses to Technological Threats," *Business Horizons,* vol. 19, no. 1, February 1976.

74. E. B. Roberts. "Research and Development System Dynamics," in E. B. Roberts, editor. *Managerial Applications of System Dynamics,* Cambridge: MIT Press, 1978.

75. H. B. Weil, T. A. Bergan, and E. B. Roberts. "The Dynamics of R&D Strategy," in E. B. Roberts, editor. *Managerial Applications of System Dynamics,* Cambridge: MIT Press, 1978.

76. K. G. Cooper. "Naval Ship Production: A Claim Settled and a Framework Built," *Interfaces,* vol. 10, no. 6, December 1980.

77. A. R. Fusfeld. "How to Put Technology into Corporate Planning," *Technology Review,* vol. 80, May 1978.

78. M. E. Porter. *Competitive Advantage: Creating and Sustaining Superior Performance,* New York: The Free Press, 1985.

79. S. B. Johnson. "Comparing R&D Strategies of Japanese and U.S. Firms," *Sloan Management Review,* vol. 25, no. 3, Spring 1984.

80. T. Hirota. "Environment and Technology Strategy of Japanese Companies," MIT Sloan School of Management Working Paper #1671-85, June 1985.

81. M. A. Cusumano. "Diversity and Innovation in Japanese Technology Management," in R. S. Rosenbloom, editor. *Research on Technological Innovation, Management, and Policy.* Greenwich, CT; JAI Press, 1986.

82. E. B. Roberts. "New Ventures for Corporate Growth," *Harvard Business Review,* vol. 59, no. 4, July–August 1980.

83. D. Dimanescu and J. W. Botkin. *The New Alliances: America's R&D Consortia.* Cambridge: Ballinger Publishing, 1986.

84. *Business Week. Strategic Alliances: New Competitive Muscle.* New York: October 6–7, 1986.

85. E. B. Roberts and A. Frohman. "Internal Entrepreneurship: Strategy for Growth," *The Business Quarterly,* vol. 37, no. 1, Spring 1972.

86. N. Fast. "A Visit to the New Venture Graveyard," *Research Management,* March 1979.

87. P. E. Haggerty. "Strategy, Tactics, and Research," *Research Management,* vol. 9, no. 3, 1966.

88. E. B. Roberts and C. A. Berry. "Entering New Businesses: Selecting Strategies for Success," *Sloan Management Review,* vol. 26, no. 3, Spring 1985.

89. M. H. Meyer and E. B. Roberts. "New Product Strategy in Small Technology-Based Firms: A Pilot Study," *Management Science,* vol. 32, no. 7, July 1986.

90. W. M. Capron, editor. *Technological Change in Regulated Industries.* Washington: The Brookings Institution, 1971.

91. T. J. Allen, J. M. Utterback, M. S. Sirbu, N. A. Ashford, and J. H. Hollomon. "Government Influence on the Process of Innovation in Europe and Japan," *Research Policy,* vol. 7, no. 2, April 1978.

92. O. Hauptman and E. B. Roberts. "FDA Regulation of Product Risk and its Impact Upon Young Biomedical Firms," *Journal of Product Innovation Management,* vol. 4, No. 2, June 1987.

93. W. J. Abernathy and B. S. Chakravarthy. "Government Intervention and Innovation in Industry: A Policy Framework," *Sloan Management Review,* vol. 20, no. 3, Spring 1979.

94. J. M. Utterback and A. E. Murray. "The Influence of Defense Procurement and Sponsorship of Research and Development on the Development of the Civilian Electronics Industry." MIT Center for Policy Analysis Working Paper CPA-77-2, June 1977.

95. D. H. Gobeli and W. Rudelius. "Management Innovation: Lessons from the Cardiac-Pacing Industry," *Sloan Management Review,* vol. 26, no. 4, Summer 1985.

96. National Research Council. *Management of Technology: The Hidden Competitive Advantage.* Washington: National Academy Press, 1987.

64

NETWORKING AND INNOVATION: A SYSTEMATIC REVIEW OF THE EVIDENCE

Luke Pittaway, Maxine Robertson, Kamal Munir, David Denyer, and Andy Neely

Recent work on competitiveness has emphasized the importance of business networking for innovativeness. Until recently, insights into the dynamics of this relationship have been fragmented. This paper presents a systematic review of research linking the networking behaviour of firms with their innovative capacity. We find that the principal benefits of networking as identified in the literature include: risk sharing; obtaining access to new markets and technologies; speeding products to market; pooling complementary skills; safeguarding property rights when complete or contingent contracts are not possible; and acting as a key vehicle for obtaining access to external knowledge. The evidence also illustrates that those firms which do not co-operate and which do not formally or informally exchange knowledge limit their knowledge base long term and ultimately reduce their ability to enter into exchange relationships. At an institutional level, national systems of innovation play an important role in the diffusion of innovations in terms of the way in which they shape networking activity. The paper provides evidence suggesting that network relationships with suppliers, customers and intermediaries such as professional and trade associations are important factors affecting innovation performance and productivity. Where networks fail, it is due to inter-firm conflict, displacement, lack of scale, external disruption and lack of infrastructure. The review identifies several gaps in the literature that need to be filled. For instance, there is a need for further exploration of the relationship between networking and different forms of innovation, such as process and organisational innovation. Similarly, we need better understanding of network dynamics and network configurations, as well as the role of third parties such as professional and trade associations. Our study highlights the need for interdisciplinary research in these areas.

INTRODUCTION

The systematic review from which the findings in this paper are presented is motivated by a quest to establish the extent to which UK companies are engaged in networking activities when seeking to develop their innovative capacity. Specifically, the objectives of the review are to:

1. establish the nature of the relationship between networking and innovation

Pittaway, Luke, Maxine Robertson, Kaamal Munir, David Denyer, and Andy Neely, 2004. Networking and Innovation: A Systematic review of the Evidence. *International Journal of Management Reviews* 5/6 (3/4): 137–168.

2. compare the degree and impact of networking behaviour in the UK with that of businesses in competing countries
3. explore examples and literature on the failure of business-to-business networks
4. generate insights informing policies aimed at fostering business-to-business networking leading to greater innovative capacity and
5. identify areas for future research for the Economic and Social Research Council's (ESRC) research priorities board.

The Porter Report (Porter and Ketels 2003) establishes that inter-organizational networking is critical for the development of innovative ability in firms. The extent to which UK firms are involved in networking and how this activity translates into innovative outcomes is, however, less clear in the report. For instance, Porter's study concludes that the UK under-performs key competitors in this area but provides little in the way of evidence to justify the claim. The purpose of the review is therefore systematically to explore the evidence in view of the Department of Trade and Industry (DTI) mandate: *Are UK businesses effective in external networking with other businesses in support of innovation?* Following consultation, it was agreed that the review should concentrate on *business-to-business networking; the extent to which networking translates into innovative outcomes* and should include *some reference to examples of failure in the construction and maintenance of networks*. In this paper, the authors present a sub-set of the findings from the systematic review and consider the *general* evidence base that has explored the relationship between innovation and networking across countries and sectors. In the following section, we outline the specific methodology we adopt to conduct this particular review.

METHODOLOGY

Despite the significant number of studies that have been conducted in this general area since the 1980s, little attempt has been made to translate these findings systematically into a comprehensive review of current knowledge. Further, there have been few attempts to link such knowledge with policy decision-making. The complexity of the issues involved requires a systematic review exploring all aspects of the existing literature and empirical evidence. The study aims to fill this gap, thereby enhancing our understanding of the relationship between networking and innovation (Pittaway *et al.* 2004).

A number of themes are pursued. First, the study seeks to understand how formal institutional mechanisms aimed at promoting business to business networking activity may operate, for example: mediated by professional associations; incubators; clusters etc. Secondly, it aims to explore the relationship between informal networking and innovation (for example, communities of practice, mentoring schemes, knowledge brokerage, and entrepreneurial networks etc.). Thirdly, it explores how networking behaviour can be successfully translated into tangible outcomes specifically related to innovation. Finally, the study looks for examples of network failure and inertia militating against innovation occurring.

The review strategy has a number of stages designed to provide a systematic and explicit method for the review as outlined in the Introduction to this special issue of the Journal. The following steps are taken in this particular study (with these steps guided both by the general methodology as previously outlined and by the need to adapt to the particular requirements of the subject of study):

1. The review team identified keywords on the subject based on their prior experience. These words were identified using a form of brainstorming. They included, for example, innovation, networking, diffusion, collaboration, actor network theory and brokers, among others.
2. The keywords were constructed into search strings. For example, the search string [Network* AND innovat* OR effect* OR collapse OR dysfunction OR disintegrate] was used as a secondary method for finding citations on the failure of innovation networks.

3. An initial search of ABI Proquest was undertaken using the basic search string innovat? AND network? The results were analysed in Procite and used to identify further keywords for the main search. For example, additional words, such as complexity, embeddedness, social capital, co-operation, alliance and proximity were found to be important during this secondary analysis.

4. The basic search string innovat? AND network? was used in seven search engines to identify three key citation indexes for the review. These were chosen based on the volume of citations relevant to the basic search string. The search engines reviewed include ABI Proquest (1294), Business Source Premier (1088), Science Direct (1473), Web of Science—Social Science Citation Index (1543), EBSCO (390), PsycINFO (560) and Emerald (904);

5. The citation databases (ABI Proquest, Science Direct and Web of Science) chosen were reviewed using the search strings identified in steps (2) and (3). These search strings were progressively analysed from the most basic to the most complex. For example, the basic search string 'Innovat* AND network'* added 'AND ties OR dynamic* OR isomorphism OR knowledge (w) spill'* when the review wanted to identify articles relevant to the dynamics of network relationships. A full protocol for the use of these search strings was devised and followed in the review process.

6. The citations identified were reviewed according to the inclusion and exclusion criteria (Appendixes 1 and 2). Two stages were undertaken to reduce the number of citations. The first analysed the titles of articles according to the exclusion criteria, and the second analysed the abstracts according to the inclusion criteria.

7. The reviewers cross-checked the reference sections of the included articles to assess the search strategy.

8. Using the inclusion and exclusion criteria the articles were separated into A, B and C lists. The A list represented articles of particular relevance that had interesting empirical approaches. The B list represented articles of some relevance where there may have been some question over the value of the empirical work. The C list represented articles that were either of little relevance or which were predominately conceptual.

9. The AIM Fellows were invited to assess the A list of articles and further articles were added according to their professional recommendation, further cross-checking the veracity of the A list identified by the systematic review.

10. The existing citation abstracts were reviewed according to the quality criteria (Appendix 3). After steps (1)–(7), 174 citations remained in the A list.

11. The A-list articles were selected, and their abstracts were imported from Proquest to Nvivo. The abstracts were coded according to their content and a report structure was identified based on the coding of abstracts.

12. Articles were reviewed according to their relevant subject theme as identified in the narrative coding in step (8).

13. Sections were written as the articles relevant to particular themes were reviewed.

METHODOLOGICAL CHALLENGES

The subject of networking has been studied widely in a number of disciplines using a range of meta-theoretical assumptions and methodologies. In this review, the researchers focused specifically on business-to-business networks and how they impact on innovation. Consequently, there were inherent complexities that the team needed to overcome and some limitations of the approach used:

1. The terms networking and innovation are inherently ambiguous, presenting definitional issues. The initial definition for innovation used was the DTI's (2003) as outlined in the next section. This was operationalized in the systematic review by using the keywords; innovat,* diffusion, knowledge (w) spill,* product

(w) development, invent,* process (w) change and research (w) development. Networking was defined initially as: "*a firm's set of relationships with other organizations*" (Perez Perez and Sanchez 2002). In the review, networks were operationalized by using the keywords; network,* mentors, knowledge (w) brokers, communities (w) practice, collaborat,* ties, relation,* co-operation, agglomeration, alliance,* proximity, intermediary and interaction. These root words were found using two strategies. First, a brainstorming exercise involving the research panel and, secondly, an initial search of ABI Proquest using the root term innovat* AND network,* which examined the keywords of over 1000 research papers to identify other appropriate search terms (e.g. the terms research (w) development, agglomeration and proximity were found using the second strategy). The review technique consequently found articles that examined many forms of innovation and networking;

2. Another major challenge was to synthesize data from a range of disciplines. The study conducted was interested in empirical findings not conceptual or theoretical studies. Typically, forms of data range extensively in this subject domain. In economic geography, detailed statistical studies of patents and patent citations are used to explore links between firms while, in other subjects, empirical approaches use ethnographic or interpretive methodologies. The challenge for the researchers was to assess quality and synthesize findings without preference for particular forms of knowledge, while producing a meta-analysis. The researchers, therefore, did not seek a meta-analysis in the form traditionally associated with medical sciences and, instead, adapted quality assessments according to the form of methodology used in particular studies. In the findings that follow, one can uncover the conclusions from good ethnographic studies alongside complex statistical studies and, in Appendix 3, the generalizability criteria were not applied; instead, an additional assessment of "contribution" was introduced.

3. One limitation that has emerged following this systematic review is linked to the publishing preferences of particular disciplines. To some extent the findings highlighted do overlook some important contributions from sociology and business history. This occurs because systematic reviews undertake detailed searches in citation databases. Where the preference in a discipline is to publish books and book chapters (as in sociology), there is a danger that a systematic review may overlook these contributions. The current databases available do not allow this problem to be easily overcome.

4. The volume of papers on the subject presented interesting challenges. In the first stage, we identified 628 papers that were relevant to the subject being investigated. Following more detailed analysis of abstracts, 332 papers were identified as relevant. The research team adapted the methodology by analysing in detail the abstracts, applying the relevance criteria in Appendix 2 and scoring each paper according to contribution and degree of likely relevance. The researchers were consequently able to separate the papers into A (179), B (76) and C (77) lists. All these papers were deemed to be relevant, but some more so than others, and the A list was ranked more highly in terms of likely relevance. Clearly, one potential limitation here is a relevant article could fail to make the A list because of a poorly written abstract.

5. The A list of 179 continued to present a large volume of papers. In order to provide a structured approach to the review, the researchers imported the citations and abstracts into NVIVO and used emergent coding to code each abstract. The approach had many advantages when dealing with a large systematic review. First, it allowed the key themes to emerge from the data (in this case the abstracts). Secondly, the researchers were able to gain a holistic understanding of the evidence base, as described in the next section. Finally, the coding themes helped the researchers identify which papers would contribute to which themes, reducing the need to read each article in its entirety and allowing a larger data set to be represented in the study.

Stage	Name	Included	Excluded	Duplicates
TABLE 64-1	Number of Relevant Citations Found During Each Stage of Review			
v	DATABASE ANALYSIS	628	—	—
vi(a)	TITLE ANALYSIS	375	157	96
vi(b)	ABSTRACT ANALYSIS	332	43	—
vii	A ranked	179	—	—
	B ranked	—	76	—
	C ranked	—	77	—
viii	POST ABSTRACT CODING	174	—	5
x	NARRATIVE INCLUSIONS	20	—	—

THE EVIDENCE BASE

In this paper, a sub-set of the systematic review evidence is presented exploring the relationship between networking and firms' propensity to innovate. Here, we explain the precise nature of the total evidence base used for the study. The systematic review was carried out according to the methodology presented. In the first stage of the review, 628 papers were found by searching ABI Proquest, Science Direct and Web of Science citation indexes using the search strings developed. Table 64-1 highlights the number of citations relevant to the subject found according to stage of the review.

The results show that networking and innovation are studied in a number of fields within social science. These include economic and regional geography, organizational behaviour, sociology, operations management, political economy, entrepreneurship and small business, technology management, marketing and strategic management. The key journals contributing to the review illustrate the fields of study that have most to say about the subject. The top five journals in terms of their coverage of this topic in the review were *Research Policy, Journal of Business Venturing, Regional Studies, Technovation* and *International Journal of Technology Management.* In addition to these journals, the review sourced articles from another 47 journals. It is interesting to note that from 325 papers on the subject found before the articles were ranked, mainstream US management journals were under-represented. For example, the *American Journal of Management* had only one paper, the *American Management Review* had one and the *Administrative Science Quarterly* had only two. Speculating why this occurs is probably unwise. One rationale is that the majority of studies in management have been within organizational behaviour, entrepreneurship or supply chain management, and this could explain the under-representation. For example, the mainstream *British Journal of Management* has only one paper, while *Organization Studies* has nine, the *Journal of Business Venturing* has 33 and *Management Science* has five.

Undertaking a keyword analysis illustrates the nature of the papers reviewed for this study. The top ten keywords (in order of importance) in the review are Innovations, Research and Development, Small Business, Alliances, Regions, Technology Change, Statistical Analysis, Business Networking, Organization Theory and Product Development. The industrial focus of the papers included is presented in Table 64-2.

Table 64-2 highlights the industries studied and the number of papers relevant to each. The sample of papers in the review is consequently balanced toward the high-technology and manufacturing industries. It is clear that some caution should therefore be applied when seeking to generalize the conclusions from this study to primary or service industries, as they only represent 5.7% and 2.9% of the sample, respectively.

The papers reviewed are also analysed according to the countries that feature within studies. This analysis shows that 36 papers have empirical data based on the UK, 35 on the USA, 42 on other European Countries (Germany, with 14 studies, is the highest other European country included in the review), 11 are on Asian countries (Japan 11) and three are on other countries (Australia, Brazil and Israel). The number of studies focusing on the UK is quite high, illustrating that UK academics have made an above average contribution to the subject. It should be noted, however, that the

TABLE 64-2 Industrial Analysis of Papers Reviewed

Industry	No. of Papers (A List)	% of Sample
Primary Industries	4	5.7
Energy Industry	1	
Agriculture	1	
Oil and Gas	2	
Manufacturing Industries	12	17.1
Automobile Component Industry	3	
Ceramics Industry	1	
Mechanical Engineering Industry	2	
Medical Equipment Industry	3	
Clothing Industry	2	
Packaging Machine Industry	1	
Service Industries	2	2.9
Food Industry	1	
Financial Services Industry	1	
High-Technology Industries	52	74.3
Chemicals Industry	6	8.6
Plastics	1	
Petrochemicals	1	
Enzymes	1	
Defence Industries	3	4.3
Electronics (and related)	23	32.9
Software	3	
Semiconductors	7	
Robotics	2	
Home Automation	1	
Telecommunications	3	
Pharmaceutical Industries	20	28.6
Biotechnology	11	
Embryonic	1	

overall total of papers focusing on the UK, although filtered to a smaller number using quality criteria, remains relatively low in terms of total numbers (36 out of 127 papers).

Following the analysis of the A-list citations using NVIVO (stage 8) a thematic analysis was developed. The results of the thematic analysis are presented in Table 64-3.

The thematic review illustrates that a large proportion of the articles reviewed focused on the firm level (micro) factors exploring how networks are managed and work in practice (57.7%). A smaller proportion of the evidence examines the macro or networking infrastructure that can support networking activity (42.3%). When the year of publication is considered, it becomes clear that this subject of study and the evidence base is relatively recent. For example, from 1999 to 2003, our search located 93 papers on the subject while, from 1981 to 1986, only four papers were found. The analysis of the citations on networking and innovation also shows an upward trend between 1981 and 2003. The low number of articles for the period 1981–1986 may be due to poor coverage in the citation databases. The data may also illustrate, however, that it is a relatively new area of investigation, and published work during this period is therefore quite limited.

In summary, with regard to the overall sample of evidence used in this paper a number of key points can be made. First, the evidence base used in this study is somewhat dominated by a focus on technology and new technology industries. Secondly, the evidence is mainly focused on the UK, USA and Germany, with some bias toward the period 1995–2003. Finally, the research to date lacks some depth in terms of the very limited number of studies that have been carried out. The research is also fragmented as it is spread across a large number of authors, journals and disciplines in social science.

TABLE 64-3 Thematic Analysis of Papers Reviewed

Coding	Theme	Description	No. of Papers	% of Themes
1	Network Formation	Studies that focus on how networks form and what factors inhibit or assist their formation	8	4.9
2	Diversity of Partners	These papers focus on the importance of diverse partners in networks	5	3.1
2.2	Suppliers	Articles which focus on the importance of supply networks within the innovation process	12	7.4
2.3	Institutional Factors	Research which explores the value and contribution of institutional mechanisms for promoting networking	6	3.7
2.4	Customers	Studies which explore the important role of customer business-to-business networks in the innovation process	4	2.5
2.5	Third Parties	These papers focus on the role of third party networks, e.g. professional and trade associations and consultants	11	6.8
2.6	Science Partners	Research papers focusing on science partners as network brokers within business networks	14	8.6
2.7	Finance Partners	Focusing on studies which explain the important role of equity finance networks in the innovation process	9	5.5
3.1	Network Behaviour	How different behaviours within networks lead to different forms of benefits	27	16.6
3.2	Network Governance	Papers that explore the role of governance within networks	13	8.0
3.3	Network Management	Studies which look at the effective management of networks by firms	37	22.7
3.4	Network Configuration	Research examining the make-up of networks and how these can be formed to benefit strategic goals	17	10.4

The main conclusion drawn from the sample used in this systematic literature review is that the subject area may require some prioritization by a "critical mass" of academics over a prolonged period if the evidence base is to be improved and expanded.

What follows is our analysis of the general relationship between innovation and networking based on a sub-set of the empirical evidence that was derived from the systematic literature review. The following section provides an overview of this relationship. We then present a schematic which illustrates this relationship. This schematic serves to structure the analysis that follows, where we consider the role of the parties that constitute the networking interface and infrastructure. We finish our analysis by considering evidence on the limitations of networks in innovation processes and network failure. To conclude the paper, we consider important areas for future research and briefly highlight policy implications derived from the existing evidence base.

OVERVIEW OF THE RELATIONSHIP BETWEEN INNOVATION AND NETWORKING

The work in this study is cognizant of the DTI's emphasis that innovation is the *successful* exploitation of new ideas. The successful exploitation of a new idea relates to different forms of innovation—product, process or organizational innovations. The study, therefore, adopts the DTI's broad definition:

> Innovation is the successful exploitation of ideas, into new products, processes, services or business practices, and is a critical process for achieving the two complementary business goals of performance and growth, which in turn will help to close the productivity gap. (DTI's Innovation Report 2003, 8)

The study consequently assumes that innovation is about both the generation *and* the exploitation of new products, processes, services and business practices. As products become increasingly modular and knowledge is distributed across organizations (Baldwin and Clark 2000), firms recognize an increasing requirement to collaborate with other firms both formally and informally (Fischer and Varga 2002). Indeed, the locus of innovation is no longer the individual or the firm but, increasingly, the network in which a firm is embedded (Powell *et al.* 1996). Many scientific and technological breakthroughs result from numerous contributions of many actors working in networks (Bougrain and Haudeville 2002), and the standards necessary for a technology to function across different markets depend increasingly on networks of firms (Munir 2003).

A UK sector that exemplifies the positive relationship between networking activity and innovation is the biotechnology sector (Baum *et al.* 2000). The value of collaboration for innovation is widely documented as a key feature of the biotechnology industry (Baum *et al.* 2000; Oliver and Liebeskind 1997; Staropoli 1998). A rapidly evolving, complex knowledge base underpins the industry, and the competencies and capabilities needed to take a scientific breakthrough in biotechnology to the market are scattered across a host of different organizations both large and small (Riccaboni and Pammolli 2003). While the biotech industry illustrates the importance of networking for innovation, the review high lights the need to network when seeking to innovate as a prerequisite across the majority of sectors (Elg and Johansson 1997; Hyun 1994; Nieuwenhuis 2002; Streb 2003). Networking behaviour is identified as significantly boosting the innovation output and competitiveness of firms in a diverse range of industries (Ahuja 2000; Powell *et al.* 1996). Industries where networking has had an identifiable impact on innovation include service industries[1] (Elg and Johansson 1997; Knights *et al.* 1993), primary industries[2] (Jacquier-Roux and Bourgeois 2002; Nieuwenhuis 2002), manufacturing industries[3] (Biemans 1991; Grotz and Braun 1997; Hyun 1994; Izushi 1997; Shaw 1993) and high-tech industries[4] (Coles *et al.* 2003; Frenken 2000; Reed and Walsh 2002; Romijn and Albaladejo 2002; Streb 2003).

Gemser *et al.* (1996), for example, demonstrate the impact of networking in the global pharmaceutical industry, the US computer industry and the Italian furniture industry. They demonstrate that the annual growth rate of 18% in the pharmaceutical industry was largely linked to networked research and development. Likewise, the development of clusters in the US computer industry was based on networking and proximity, which led to an increase in innovation and assisted rejuvenation of the industry during the 1980s (Almeida and Kogut 1999; Gemser *et al.* 1996). In the Italian furniture industry, the international competitiveness of the industry is largely down to continuous improvements and product differentiation, which has been supported by the presence of industrial districts consisting of a network of small, loosely organized (family) firms which are geographically clustered (Gemser *et al.* 1996). Using the examples of Concorde and Airbus, Frenken's (2000) analysis of the history of the aircraft industry also shows the key role of transnational networks in the development of innovative aircraft (Frenken 2000; Reed and Walsh 2002). He explains how the recombination of national strengths/competencies via networks and projects can play an important role in the identification of new opportunities (Frenken 2000).

Gemünden *et al.*'s (1996) study also examines the networking effects of innovation in six high-tech industries. This study demonstrates that firms using particular forms of networking categorized by their relationship with specific parties were likely to have nearly 20% more product improvements than firms that did not network. Likewise, the development of new products is 7–10% higher in these firms. The degree of innovation success in the study also illustrates a much greater chance of the innovation's being technically successful and more economically relevant where firms used networks (Gemünden *et al.* 1992, 1996).

The innovation benefits of networking identified by the literature include: (1) risk sharing (Grandori 1997); (2) obtaining access to new markets and technologies (Grandori and Soda 1995); (3) speeding products to market (Almeida and Kogut 1999); (4) pooling complementary skills (Eisenhardt and Schoonhoven 1996; Hagedoorn and Duysters 2002); (5) safeguarding property rights when complete or contingent contracts are not possible (Liebeskind *et al.* 1996); and (6) acting as a key vehicle for obtaining access to external knowledge (Cooke 1996; Powell *et al.* 1996). The evidence from the literature review also illustrates that those firms which do not co-operate and which do not formally or informally exchange knowledge limit their knowledge base on a long-term basis and ultimately reduce their ability to enter into exchange relationships (Shaw 1993, 1998).

It is also important to recognize that, while networks play a crucial role promoting the development of innovations within and across firms, they also play a key role in the diffusion of innovations across and within sectors (Almeida and Kogut 1999; Baptista 1999; Erickson and Jacoby 2003; Furtado 1997; Newell and Clark 1990; Nooteboom 2000; Swan *et al.* 1999; Verspagen 1999). For example, at an institutional level, national systems of innovation do play an important role in the diffusion of innovations in terms of the way in which they shape networking activity (Furtado 1997; Nooteboom 2000). Nooteboom's study (2000), for example, characterizes the UK innovation system as one that promotes the diffusion of more radical innovations which demand entrepreneurial activity cutting across sectors, rather than promoting the diffusion of innovation within sectors. This clearly has networking implications. At an organizational level, the involvement of managers and lower-level employees in professional, industry and cross-industry networks has been found to promote the diffusion of innovations (Erickson and Jacoby 2003; Robertson *et al.* 1996). The more involvement individuals have in these forums, the more likely it is that the firms in which they are employed will adopt new innovations (Newell and Clark 1990; Swan *et al.* 1999).

Networks are critical not only for accessing knowledge to create in-house innovations, or for the diffusion of technological innovation, but they are equally important for learning about innovative work practices that other organizations have developed or adopted (Biemans 1991; Erickson and Jacoby 2003). They influence this in a number of ways. First, by enhancing access to knowledge—promoting awareness and early adoption of innovations—and, secondly, by promoting social interaction, generating trust and reciprocity that is conducive to knowledge transfer (Almeida and Kogut 1999).

To summarize, with regard to the relationship between networking and the diffusion of innovations, the majority of research highlights the role of individuals and, more specifically, the importance of interpersonal and informal networking for the diffusion of innovations (Conway 1995; Robertson *et al.* 1996). More generally, however, while the utility of networks for enhancing the development of innovations and innovation diffusion is well established, there appears to be a need for more focused research on the impact of networking on the development and diffusion of different forms of innovation (e.g. product, process and organizational).

OVERVIEW OF NETWORK FORMATION AND CONFIGURATION

The literature provides two major reasons to explain why business-to-business networks form. The first focuses on the resource requirements of firms where they are *induced* to form network relationships with other firms as a way of obtaining access to technical and/or commercial resources they lack (Ahuja 2000; D'Cruz and Rugman 1994; Staropoli 1998). From this perspective, the availability of opportunities to form relationships tends not to be viewed as a constraint. The second argues that *opportunities* to form links tend to reflect prior patterns of inter-firm relationships (Ahuja 2000). A firm's ability to develop network relationships with other firms is consequently based on its existing relationships and network capability (Cooke 1996; Granovetter 1985; Kash and Rycroft 2000).

Research conducted in the global chemical industry between 1979 and 1991 (Ahuja 2000) highlights that firms were most keen to form linkages with other firms where those firms had a high level of commercial competence. There exist at least two barriers to network formation, however. First, firms with high levels of technical and commercial competence are less likely to see the value of forming network relationships with other firms (Gales and Boynton 1992; Kitching and Blackburn 1999). Secondly, businesses with few existing relationships often lack the technical and commercial competences required when trying to attract partners (Ahuja 2000; Erickson and Jacoby 2003). A study of the UK/US defence industry, for example, highlights that, while dependency in relationships occurs because of the breadth of links between partners, such dependency and breadth often lead to the emergence of more complex networks (Coles *et al.* 2003; Grandori and Soda 1995).

The relative ease with which business-to-business networks form is also found to be influenced by social institutions (Nooteboom 2000). In the empirical evidence, these institutions can shape the cultural conditions and infrastructure for networking, as well as acting as brokers and intermediaries in network formation (Bolton *et al.* 1994). Institutions such as the legal system, the banking and finance system, and the structure of labour markets, the education system and the political system (Grandori and Soda 1995) all shape the development of the infrastructure that is required to assist the formation of business-to-business networks (Nooteboom 2000).

In terms of what types of firm engage in networking activity, networking is not only found to be valuable for established businesses but is also beneficial for entrepreneurs (Larson 1991; Leonard-Barton 1984; Liao and Welsch 2003). Through networking, the success rate of entrepreneurial initiatives can be enhanced (Baum *et al.* 2000) because interpersonal and inter-organizational relationships enable actors to gain access to a variety of resources held by other actors (Ostgaard and Birley 1996). For example, network relations provide emotional support for entrepreneurial risk taking, and this, in turn, is thought to enhance the desire to remain in business (Hoang and Antoncic 2003).

A number of other studies also show that successful entrepreneurs consistently use networks to get ideas and gather information and advice (Birley 1985, 1987; Smeltzer *et al.* 1991). Ties to venture capitalists and professional service organizations are other means for tapping into key talent and market information (Bower 1993; Bygrave 1987, 1988; Freeman 1999). Alliances enable firms to gain access to resources, particularly when time is of the essence (Baum *et al.* 2000; Carayannis *et al.* 2000; Teece 1986). Networks enable small business owners to link into R&D that is contracted out by larger firms, to engage in joint R&D ventures, and to set up marketing and manufacturing relationships (Rothwell 1991; Rothwell and Dodgson 1991). As Baum *et al.* (2000) find, start-ups can enhance their early performance at the time of their founding through establishing an alliance network (Carayannis *et al.* 2000), by configuring the network to provide efficient access to diverse information and capabilities (Teece 1986), and by allying with potential rivals that provide more opportunity for learning and less risk of intra-alliance rivalry (Baum *et al.* 2000; Bower 1993).

The literature on network formation and networking activity therefore clearly demonstrates that, while firms collaborate in networks for many different reasons, the most common reason for doing so is to gain access to new or complementary competencies, technologies and markets (Coles *et al.* 2003). The question of how firms should position themselves within networks, or what kinds of network configurations facilitate innovation, however, remains ambiguous (Gemünden *et al.* 1996; Riccaboni and Pammolli 2003). The literature highlights the important role that trust plays in developing and sustaining successful networking activities in terms of the creation, flow and integration of knowledge (Bolton *et al.* 1994; Coles *et al.* 2003; Cooke 1996) but, importantly, what constitutes successful network structures is debated widely in the literature (Ahuja 2000; Bower *et al.* 1997; Gemser *et al.* 1996). For example, Shan *et al.* (1994) suggest that the number of collaborative relationships that a firm is involved in is positively related to innovation output while, conversely, closed networks have been found to foster innovation more than open ones (Coleman 1988). In further disagreement, Burt (1992) finds that, rather than maximizing the number of ties, firms should strive to position themselves strategically in gaps between different nodes, so as to become intermediaries. Contrary to this perspective, Brass and Burkhardt (1992) propose that the best position is one where all firms are tied only to the focal actor. Ahuja's (2000) empirical findings suggest that the benefits of increasing trust, developing and improving collaboration and reducing opportunism shapes network structures, creating cohesive interconnected partners.

These studies consequently highlight that there is no consensus as to the optimal networking configuration. The nature of networks encountered in this review illustrate that the optimal design for a network is contingent on the actions that the structure seeks to facilitate (Gemser *et al.* 1996). For example, a network composed of relationships with partners with few ties to others would enable control for the principle partner. Such a network might be the objective for a firm seeking power over its buyers or suppliers (Bruce and Rodgus 1991; Hyun 1994; Lincoln *et al.* 1998; Reed and Walsh 2002). A network composed of partners with many interlocking and redundant ties would facilitate the development of trust and co-operation. Such a network may be useful when all partners are faced with common problems, for example, adverse legislative actions or new technological opportunities (Almeida and Kogut 1997; Conway 1995; Knights *et al.* 1993). A network of many non-overlapping ties would provide information benefits. Such a network would be ideal for an organization whose primary business entails the brokerage of information or technology (Arndt and Sternberg 2000; Bee 2003).

The evidence on network configuration shows that the nature of a network is dependent on its industrial context and on what a firm is seeking to use its network for (Kaufmann and Tödtling 2000; Nooteboom 2000). The evidence on network configuration presented in Table 64-4 shows a number of key points:

1. The nature of network configuration and its utility for innovation and competitiveness depends on the strategic requirements of individual firms (Birley 1985; Koch 2003; Ostgaard and Birley 1994).
2. Firms will use networks in different ways and will reconfigure them if necessary (Kash and Rycroft 2002; Larson 1991).

TABLE 64-4 Network Configuration

Authors	Date	Summary
Koch	2003	Intensive field studies in two constellations of enterprises were carried out. One is a segment-collaboration between a few manufacturing companies and a software house, the other a complex and extensive innovation network. These studies show how negotiations, shifting positions of players, mobilizing stable elements of the network when developing new ones, and interplays between internal and external collaboration are integral and inevitable in the product development process.
Kash and Rycroft	2002	Case studies of the innovation pathways traced by six complex technologies indicate that innovations can be grouped into three quite distinct patterns. Transformation: the launching of a new trajectory by a new network and technology. Normal: the evolution of an established network and technology along an established trajectory. Transition: the movement to a new trajectory by an established network and technology.
Baum *et al.*	2000	New firm alliance networks are studied to investigate the impact of variation in start-ups' alliance network composition on their early performance. An analysis of Canadian biotech start-ups' performance shows how variation in the alliance networks start-ups configure at the time of their founding produces significant differences in their early performance.
Gemünden *et al.*	1996	Based on the assumption that intensity and structure are the most important dimensions of a firm's technological network the study identifies seven different types of technology-oriented network configurations. Drawing upon a database of 321 high-tech companies, it is shown that innovation success is significantly correlated with a firm's technological network. Product and process innovations are shown to demand different types of network configurations.
Ostgaard and Birley	1994	Shows that entrepreneurs use networks differently depending on the strategic orientation of their business.
Burt	1992	Illustrates that an actor's informational advantage will be maximized when network ties are diverse and loosely interconnected. Participating in closed networks increases reliability of information, while participating in many is consistent with an information searching strategy.
Larson	1991	This paper examines the conditions under which successful partnership networks were formed by four entrepreneurial companies. This research suggests that a network organizational form can be cultivated by smaller companies and the data gathered indicate that these alliances do not form by chance. They are patterned, predictable exchange structures that can be replicated and used to improve a firm's competitive position.
Coleman	1988	Illustrates that information diffusion is enhanced when a network is tightly inter-connected and closed. Closure ensures that those who do not observe reciprocity norms or who transmit faulty information will be ostracized.

3. Network configuration often differs between different forms of innovation required by actors; networks for product innovation are quite different from networks for process innovations (Bower 1993; Bower and Keogh 1996; Bruce and Moger 1999; Gemünden *et al.* 1996).

4. The nature of a firm's alliance network during business formation can have important ramifications for future business performance (Baum *et al.* 2000; Birley 1987; Carayannis *et al.* 2000).

5. All types of network configuration constantly change and adapt, depending on the requirements of partners and the context within which the network operates (Kash and Rycroft 2002; Koch 2003; Larson 1991).

The evidence reviewed shows that network configurations are dynamic and principally guided by the choices of partners and their network management capabilities and are beyond the direct influence of policy intervention (Rychen and Zimmermann 2002; Saxenian 1990). The evidence also suggests that network infrastructures can have an indirect positive or negative impact on network configurations and can consequently encourage or hinder the development of certain forms of network relationships (Boter and Holmquist 1996; Momma and Sharp 1999; Walcott 1999).

To summarize regarding networking formation and network configurations for innovation, a number of points can be established from the empirical data. Networking can have a positive impact on innovation in all organizational contexts (i.e. within established large organizations, small businesses and new entrepreneurial start-ups). Network forms are, however, complex, and research has not yet clearly demonstrated which configurations most affect innovation in particular contexts. Furthermore, there are a range of identifiable factors promoting and preventing the establishment of business networks. Following this initial analysis of the evidence on the relationship between networking and innovation, network formation and network configuration, a schematic was developed to structure the more detailed analysis presented in the next sections of the paper. Figure 64-1 presents this schematic.

FIGURE 64-1   Networking and Innovation: A Schematic.

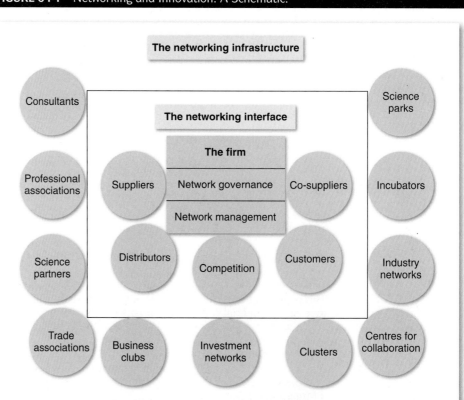

In the following sections, detailed empirical evidence from the systematic literature review is provided to explore more fully: (1) the parties involved and the inter-relationships between the networking infrastructure and networking interface; and (2) the importance of network management and network governance to network activity and relations as presented in Figure 64-1.

INTER-RELATIONSHIPS BETWEEN THE NETWORKING INFRASTRUCTURE AND NETWORKING INTERFACE

The Importance of Partner Diversity

Research on "innovation systems" has recently illustrated that innovation occurs more effectively where there is exchange of knowledge between systems (for example, between different industries, between regions or between science and industry) (Kaufmann and Tödtling 2000, 2001; Ritter and Gemünden 2003). Based on this work, the importance of diversity of relationships in networks has been shown to have an impact on innovativeness (Kaufmann and Tödtling 2000, 2001; Rothwell 1991). The value of diverse partners for innovation is demonstrated in Kaufmann and Tödtling's (2001) empirical research, and the conclusions drawn in this study are also supported by Perez Perez and Sanchez's (2002) work on technology networks in the Spanish automobile industry and Romijn and Albu's (2002) work on small high-technology firms in the UK. These studies show that innovation is influenced by many actors both inside and outside the firm, and that the most important partners are from the business sector—customers first (33.5% of firms), and suppliers second (21.9% of firms) (Kaufmann and Tödtling 2000, 2001). Studies on partnering also show that the willingness of firms to co-operate outside these "direct" relationships is rather limited. For example, co-operation with universities occurs for only 8.9% of firms in Kaufmann and Tödtling's work. In contrast, however, research in Germany highlights significant national differences with respect to involvement with research institutes and universities, and illustrates the importance of scientific partners in some industry sectors (Gemünden *et al.* 1992, 1996; Ritter and Gemünden 2003).

The type of partner firms engaged in networking appears to be related to the type of innovation occurring (Freel 2003; Kash and Rycroft 2000, 2002). For example, incremental innovators rely more frequently on their customers as innovation partners (Biemans 1991), whereas firms that have products new to a market are more likely to collaborate with suppliers and consultants (Baiman *et al.* 2002; Ragatz *et al.* 1997). More advanced innovators, and the development of more radical innovations, demand more interaction with universities (Hausler *et al.* 1994; Liyanage 1995). For example, the conclusion of Gemünden *et al.*'s (1992) detailed survey of 4,564 firms in the Lake Constance region (on the border between Austria, Germany and Switzerland) makes the point well, based on sound empirical evidence examining interactions between firms, customers, suppliers and university interactions:

> Firms which do not supplement their internal resources and competence with complementary external resources and knowledge show a lower capability for realizing innovations. (Gemünden *et al.* 1992, 373)

In conclusion, the evidence shows that the innovation process, particularly complex and radical innovation processes, benefits from engagement with a diverse range of partners which allows for the integration of different knowledge bases, behaviours and habits of thought. Formal and informal communication between people with different information, skills and values increases the chance of unforeseen novel combinations of knowledge, which can lead to radical discoveries. More risk-averse firms, however, tend to link their innovation activities and networking relationships to customers, because knowledge of clients' demands reduces the risk of failure for the innovating firm. Innovation is no less valuable but is more incremental, and productivity gains are more modest. This suggests a direct relationship between type of networking activity and innovation type (e.g. radical or incremental). All the studies highlighted in this section also show that firms that do not network possess much lower levels of competence in innovation (e.g. Gemünden *et al.* 1992; Ritter and Gemünden 2003).

The Role of Suppliers

The integration of suppliers in the innovation process has been highlighted as one of the factors leading to frame-breaking innovation (Kaufmann and Tödtling 2001; Perez Perez and Sanchez 2002; Romijn and Albu 2002). The value of including suppliers in new product development innovation has been widely documented in the supply chain literature (Hyun 1994; Lincoln *et al.* 1998; Ragatz *et al.* 1997). For example, firms having strong supplier networks report higher levels of productivity than those reporting weak alliances over time (Perez Perez and Sanchez 2002). Within the evidence reviewed, it is found that the effective integration of suppliers in new product development processes can

1. have a significant impact on cost, quality, technology, speed and responsiveness of buying companies (Ragatz *et al.* 1997; Ritter and Gemünden 2003)
2. help manufacturers identify improvements that are necessary for them to remain competitive (Lincoln *et al.* 1998; Perez Perez and Sanchez 2002)
3. enable firms to bring to bear wider expertise during the development process (Romijn and Albaladejo 2002; Romijn and Albu 2002)
4. help reduce concept-to-customer cycle time, costs and reduce quality problems (Ragatz *et al.* 1997)
5. lead to higher levels of productivity and quality (Perez Perez and Sanchez 2002)
6. assist with improvements in the overall design effort (Conway 1995)
7. lead to closer, more open supplier relationships (Conway 1995; Hyun 1994)
8. create easier access to supplier knowledge and expertise in the longer-term (Conway 1995; Lorenzoni and Lipparini 1999)
9. provide clearer focus on the projects that require joint development (Ragatz *et al.* 1997)
10. lead to improved communication between the partners (Reed and Walsh 2002; Ritter and Gemünden 2003).

Consequently, the supply chain literature has illustrated the value of supplier interaction in innovation and has sought to explain how these interactions can be most effectively managed (e.g. Lamming *et al.* 2002). Table 64-5 summarizes the identified improvements for effective supplier integration in Ragatz's *et al.* (1997) study.

When examining management practices, including suppliers in the buyer's development team is the largest single differentiator between the least and most successful innovation efforts (Ragatz *et al.* 1977). The degree of involvement of suppliers tends to depend on the nature of projects (Harryson 1997). Open and direct communication between companies, however, is identified as the critical success factor during supplier interactions in new product development processes (Harryson 1997; Lincoln *et al.* 1998; Perez Perez and Sanchez 2002; Ragatz *et al.* 1997). Interestingly, it is also noted that companies that network effectively with suppliers also invest more in research and development, because they require an infrastructure in which to frame collaborative behaviour (Perez Perez and Sanchez 2002).

TABLE 64-5 Degree of Innovation Improvement Resulting from Supplier Integration (Adapted from Ragatz *et al.* 1997)

	Most Successful Cases of Integration	Least Successful Cases of Integration
Purchased material cost relative to historical costs	15.0%+	(5.0%)
Purchased material quality relative to historical quality	40.0%+	(7.5%)
Development cycle time	25.0%+	(30.0%)

In summary, the supply chain literature on networking behaviour and innovation shows that supply relationships are one of the most important networking arrangements affecting innovation performance and productivity (e.g. Lincoln *et al.* 1998). Such relationships can be managed if firms are committed to collaboration, skilled in managing network relationships and are prepared to invest in research and development (Lamming *et al.* 2002). Although much of the evidence points toward the important role of suppliers, co-suppliers and distributors in the innovation process, it is to customers that businesses most often turn when seeking network relationships on issues associated with innovation (Kaufmann and Tödtling 2000, 2001; Ragatz *et al.* 1997).

The Role of Customers

Von Hippel (1978) was one of the first researchers to highlight the pivotal role of customers or users in innovation processes. He highlights two forms of approach to innovation and networks, and argues that customer focused approaches are the most effective as opposed to product focused ones. Customers should play an active role in the innovation process and are capable of identifying novel ideas for development (Von Hippel 1978). A systematic study of practices leading to commercial success in innovation also illustrates the important role of understanding users' needs and engaging them in the innovation process (Freeman 1982). Ragatz *et al.* (1997) shows that customers are considered to be the most important partners during incremental innovation (as do Biemans 1991; Bruce and Rodgus 1991).

Other studies highlight that the linking of marketing and technical activities early in the innovation process enables products to be developed with full awareness of the customer's needs (Biemans 1991; Bruce and Rodgus 1991). Moreover, too much emphasis on technical excellence or marketing can lead to innovations that are too highly priced or over-engineered (Walsh *et al.* 1988). Such network relationships with customers are viewed to be important because

1. dialogue between key business customers and suppliers not only allows firms to learn of existing needs but also lead to the discovery of new needs in advance of the competition (Bruce and Rodgus 1991)
2. customers who are actively engaged in the early stages of product innovation will assist the development of ideas (Biemans 1991)
3. customer involvement reduces the risks of innovation (Gemünden *et al.* 1992; Ragatz *et al.* 1997)
4. the innovator learns from the customer the likely market potential of the product idea (Gemünden *et al.* 1992).

In Gemünden *et al.* (1992), for example, 75% of companies engage customers in the innovation process, and nearly 50% identified it as a precondition for innovation success. Conway (1995), in his study of 35 successful innovations, finds that customers are crucially important at the idea generation stage of the innovation process. Companies that state they received essential information from customers are more successful with technological innovation and have greater commercial success (Conway 1995). Despite this evidence of the value of business customers in the innovation process, more detailed empirical study shows that customer involvement tends to be useful at the beginning, in terms of idea generation, but is less so during the developmental process where the manufacturer tends to lead (Biemans 1991; Bruce and Rodgus 1991; Conway 1995; Gemünden *et al.* 1992).

In summary, the importance of networking with business customers is confirmed and is shown to offer many benefits. The nature of the value of networks with key customers needs to be treated with some caution. Such networking relationships appear to be ideal for promoting incremental innovation and customers can usefully help innovators identify market opportunities. The extent to which customers actively contribute to the innovation process is less clear, as the evidence points to this being driven by the innovating firm balancing market awareness with technical feasibility. Table 64-6 shows a sample of the evidence on the "Networking Interface."

TABLE 64-6   Impact of Business-to-Business Networks on Innovation in the Market Interface (A Sample of the Evidence)

Author	Data Used in Study	Dates	Location of Study	Summary of Empirical Findings
Ritter and Germünden	Survey of 308 mechanical and electrical engineering companies	2003	Germany	Study focuses on medium-sized companies. Data were analysed using LISREL 8 using a polychoric correlation matrix. They show important statistical links between network competence and innovation success. Managing key partners in the network interface is crucial for innovation.
Perez Perez and Sanchez	Postal survey of 58 automotive suppliers	2002	North Eastern Spain	Reasons for suppliers to engage in enterprise networks. Exchange of know-how and access to technologies (93%); strengthening client–supplier relationships (79%); use of comparative advantages (80%); access to new markets (80%); benchmarking (90%). Used bivariate correlations. Firms co-operating with customers (68%); with suppliers (50%); with universities and research institutes (35%).
Romijn and Albu	Interviews with small electronics firms (17 software and 16 electronics firms)	2002	South-east of England	Used Spearman correlation coefficients to explore forms of innovation output with key partners in networks. Shows that firms interact with some partners for more radical innovation—suppliers 0.343,* and universities 0.353* while they work with other firms for more incremental forms of innovation—customers 0.437** (**0.01 level of significance; *0.05 level of significance).
Kaufmann and Tödtling	Postal survey of firms in the REGIS project	2000	Styria, Wales, Tampere and the Basque Country	The distribution of innovation forms differs by region. Of 93 firms in Styria, 98 firms in Wales, 138 in Tampere and 54 in the Basque Country, the majority of network relationships were with customers (~90% of firms) and with suppliers (~70%). Relationships with other partners were typically lower (e.g. universities 30%). A more detailed analysis of means illustrates that customers were perceived to be the most important contributors in innovation networks.
Conway	Empirical case studies of 35 commercially successful innovations. Winners of the Queens Award for Technological Achievement and the Best Design Award	1995	UK	Suggests that prior research shows that networking contributes to between 34% and 65% of inputs to the development of successful product innovation. 23% of the innovations studied required critical informal networks for the key innovative solution. 54% employed inputs from external sources, and a further 46% of the firms received useful inputs from informal sources. Even where these relationships were between suppliers or customers, friendships were one of the most important aspects for informal inputs.

As outlined, networks in the market interface are the key relationships between a firm and its direct business associates. These networks typically include suppliers, co-suppliers, distributors, customers and firms offering business services (e.g. accountants and legal firms). The following section of the paper will consider the broader networking infrastructure by examining the role of third parties within innovation networks.

The Role of Third Parties

In general, the role of third parties, such as professional associations, trade associations and publicly funded bodies specifically aimed at promoting innovation (such as technology transfer centres) have a positive impact on the development of inter-organizational networks and innovation (Conway 1995; Grotz and Braun 1997; Hanna and Walsh 2002). There are a number of characteristics of third party involvement, however, that need to be considered (see Table 64-7).

TABLE 64-7 Role of Third Parties

Authors	Date	Summary
Hanna and Walsh	2002	Research comparing small firm networking facilitated by publicly funded bodies in Italy, Denmark and the US highlighted the need for third parties to remain "*neutral*" in the facilitation process. Rather than encouraging the development of particular network relationships or innovations, publicly funded bodies should provide information and expertise but, more importantly, focus on promoting the development of trust and confidence among network members.
Grotz and Braun	1997	Research across 155 SMEs in Germany highlighted that formalized technology transfer does not have an impact on regional economies unless it is organized as an interconnected system with many entry points. Technology transfer centres cannot promote networking unless the skills, know-how and finance are already in place and a socio-cultural infrastructure exists. Again professional associations were found to be useful forums promoting the development of socio-cultural infrastructures.
Robertson *et al.*	1996	It is important to note that professional associations are not necessarily neutral conduits in the diffusion process. Research in the UK automotive sector highlighted that some professional associations have a pro-innovation bias and promote particular versions of "best practice" that are not necessarily appropriate across all firms in a sector.
Conway	1995	Research across a sample of 35 UK innovations highlights the reliance on *informal* (in some cases *ad hoc*) third-party involvement for successful innovation, particularly during the crucial idea generation phase. This can lead to over-dependence on key individuals who actually play no formal role in the process.

Third parties have a dual role in promoting innovation. They ideally act as neutral knowledge brokers (though see Robertson *et al.* 1996) but also act as important conduits for the development of *informal relationships* (personal relations between individuals), which are the basis for the development of network relationships, particularly between small firms (Cooke 1996; Hanna and Walsh 2002). Although professional associations, trade associations and consultants make some important contributions to the network infrastructure, they are one of many network mechanisms that improve regional infrastructures[5] (Janne 2002). Science partners (categorized as universities, technical colleges, research institutes, applied science consultancies and independent research and design laboratories) also all play an important role within the network infrastructure (Verspagen 1999).

The Role of Science Partners

While the review focuses principally on business-to-business networks, science partners do play an important role as independent network brokers and intermediaries within business networks, and this is explored by the study. The important role of informal personal relationships in networks outside the market interface is also evident in the wider evidence on science partners (Kaufmann and Todtling 2001; Verspagen 1999). As well as direct benefits of interaction between science and industry, science partners provide an important role as intermediaries within networks (Bougrain and Haudeville 2002).

The evidence on science partners shows that they contribute to innovation networks, usually through informal-personal networks (Bower and Keogh 1996) and that their contribution is important in enabling firms to develop thinking that steps outside their particular business system (Liyanage 1995). Science partners also act as brokers or intermediaries within networks, enabling different business systems to communicate by generating trust between different parties in their common role as neutral agents (Hausler *et al.* 1994). The evidence demonstrates that science partners tend to be most important where the innovation is relatively radical in orientation (Ebadi and Utterback 1984; Fritsch 2001; Verspagen 1999).

The Role of Venture Finance Partners

The importance of appropriate venture finance and loan finance for innovation has been widely documented (Harding 2000). The importance of finance networks, however, has received less attention, but is arguably of equal importance. The evidence base on venture capital networks and innovation shows a number of key issues. Co-investment between venture capital firms in entrepreneurial businesses has been shown to be beneficial for venture capitalists and provides better quality and larger funds for entrepreneurial businesses (Bygrave 1987, 1988). The quality of links between venture capital firms therefore provides an important networking infrastructure for the commercialization of innovation (Florida and Kenney 1988a).

The establishment of venture capital firms locally in established technology centres (e.g. Cambridge in the UK) enables firms to prosper via the higher concentration of good deals (Keeble *et al.* 1998, 1999). Such finance networks, when well developed, attract further start-up activity, creating a self-reinforcing cycle (Florida and Kenney 1988b). Venture capital firms can and do act as key brokers within technology and innovation networks, introducing key partners to prospective and current firms with whom they have invested (Bygrave 1987, 1988).

The evidence on informal investment networks (business angel networks) highlights similar issues. Haar *et al.* (1988) show that informal investment networks are particularly important during a firm's pre-start-up, start-up and early growth stages of development, and that most referral networks for informal finance are composed of family and friends (Haar *et al.* 1988). Other studies show, similar to formal investment, that syndicated investments have a greater chance of success, and often lead to higher investment levels in entrepreneurial firms (Harrison and Mason 1992, 1996). The ways in which investments are made within the informal market are perceived to be less sophisticated and more inefficient than the formal venture capital market (Wetzel 1987).

Examining the evidence on finance networks shows that they are important within the networking infrastructure and that co-operative investment appears to be beneficial for both investing firms and entrepreneurial businesses. The evidence supports this point in both the formal and informal marketplace for venture capital funds.

The Role of Institutional Mechanisms

Institutional mechanisms designed specifically to create and facilitate networks come in many forms. The most common forms are clusters, incubators and centres for co-operation (Hendry *et al.* 2000; Holbrook 1995). The evidence in this study examining networking and innovation and the role of institutional mechanisms is considered insufficient to draw any useful conclusions. It is possible that the lack of coverage occurs owing to the nature of the methodology employed. Based on the systematic nature of the approach, however, this area clearly presents a priority for future research. Despite this insufficiency of the evidence, it is possible that innovation policies and regional infrastructures can assist networking activities leading to innovation—how they do so, and their degree of effectiveness in doing so, is unclear (Staber 2001). The detailed evidence in the review focusing on how institutional mechanisms can support and assist the development of business-to-business networks is shown in Table 64-8.

The evidence found in this review shows that clusters do not always contribute to business-to-business networking (Hendry *et al.* 2000). Where clusters exist, but networking does not happen, there is evidence that innovation occurs less often and is less successful (Staber 2001). The extent to which Science Parks promote business-to-business networks appears to be mixed, with some evidence for and against their capacity to promote networking (Phillimore 1999). Detailed evidence on how Science Parks might promote such networks also appears to be lacking (Phillimore 1999).

The evidence on incubation tends not to focus specifically on the networking advantages of firms operating within incubators. It does illustrate, however, some general benefits where networking is cited (Smilor 1987a,b). Again the detailed evidence on incubators' role in creating and supporting business networks is inconsequential. Likewise, although National and Regional Centres for collaboration are cited in the Porter report (Porter and Ketels 2003) as valuable for networking (as highlighted in the Australian Wine Cluster), and good examples have been found by this study in the

TABLE 64-8 Role of Institutional Mechanisms

Authors	Date	Institutional Mechanism	Summary
Rothschild and Darr	2003	Incubators	The study focuses on the construction and maintenance of informal networks of innovation in a technological incubator affiliated with a leading Israeli university. A wide array of exchange relationships (formal and informal), ranging from the use of library and laboratory services to an extensive and ongoing barter exchange of knowledge, know-how and even shared practice is found and shown to impact on innovation.
Staber	2001	Clusters	Proportional hazard estimates show that location in clusters of firms in the same industry increased business failure rates and did not necessarily contribute to networking behaviour.
Phillimore	1999	Science Parks	The Western Australian Technology Park networks between WATP companies and universities were examined. It was found that there was more interaction than might be estimated and several different categories of company which existed at the Park are identified in terms of their interactive behaviour. An overview of the literature suggests that Science Parks do not assist networking a great deal, but Phillimore's results disagree.
Smilor	1987b	Incubators	The study sought to understand how the incubator concept works in practice. In addition to a national survey, the research incorporated on-site review, case-study analysis and in-depth interviews with incubator managers and directors. Ten factors were identified as important to the effective management of the incubator system: (1) on-site business expertise, (2) access to financing and capitalization, (3) in-kind financial support, (4) community support, (5) entrepreneurial network, (6) entrepreneurial education, (7) perception of success, (8) selection process for tenants, (9) tie to a university, and (10) concise program milestones with clear policies and procedures.
Smilor	1987a	Incubators	In 1985, a national survey of new business incubators was conducted, and responses were received from 50 of 117 incubators. Extensive on-site analysis and in-depth interviews with incubator managers and directors were performed. Incubators were found to provide four benefits to tenants: (1) development of credibility, (2) shortening of the learning curve, (3) quicker solution of problems, and (4) access to an entrepreneurial network.

UK (Grabher 2001), none of the evidence directly addresses their value in terms of networking and innovation. There is clearly some scope for these initiatives and anecdotal evidence supporting their formation, but limited current evidence explaining their value. One finding from this study, therefore, is an urgent need to examine in more detail the available evidence on institutional mechanisms and their usefulness when promoting innovation networks.

NETWORK GOVERNANCE AND MANAGEMENT

In general, network ties have been found to be much more conducive to the exchange of information and knowledge across partners than market mechanisms (Gales and Boynton 1992; Lipparini and Sobrero 1994). The characteristics of network ties, however, are significantly shaped by modes of network governance and network management (Bolton *et al.* 1994). In principle, the socialization that starts to occur through networks that develop from weak to strong over time engenders trust, which makes network ties a superior conduit for information flow (Coles *et al.* 2003; Larson 1991). Owing to its positive impact on information flows, trust-based behaviour, characterized by implicit open-ended contracts, is cited as a crucial factor in enhancing innovation through inter-firm collaboration (Hausler *et al.* 1994; Hoang and Antoncic 2003) and an integral reason for longevity for inter-firm networks (Lipparini and Sobrero 1994).

Inclinations towards trust, opportunism, legal contracting and self-interest are all shaped by the institutional context in which firms operate (Cooke and Wills 1999; Keeble *et al.* 1998, 1999). Distinctions have been made between the US/UK and Japanese/German systems of innovation, highlighting more reliance on legal contractual arrangements in network relationships in the UK, and a system of innovation more conducive to the development of radical innovations (Janne 2002; Nooteboom 2000). Research in the biotechnology and semiconductor industries in the US, UK, Germany and Japan also support this view (Bolton *et al.* 1994).

The type of interdependence characterizing the network relationships between firms is found to be an important mediating variable in terms of establishing the appropriate governance mechanisms that will promote innovation (Grandori 1997; Grandori and Soda 1995). Grandori's review highlights that firms clearly need to establish what type of interdependence exists between themselves and other firms in the network in order to ascertain the appropriate form of governance. Under- and over-formalization of the network are both recognized as being detrimental to innovation (Nooteboom 2000). Consequently, how networks are governed plays an important role in their effectiveness and their capacity to assist the innovation process (Coles *et al.* 2003).

Network management is also considered crucial for successful innovation, and firms need to become good at it (Ferrary 2003; Gemser *et al.* 1996). Not all firms are able to create and manage their collaborations to maximum advantage (Hanna and Walsh 2002; Pammolli and Riccaboni 2002). Some of the research reviewed points out that both experience and ability to absorb knowledge embodied in new technologies and ideas (Cohen and Levinthal 1990) are critical skills a firm requires when exploiting relationships. The research has shown the importance of network management generally (Coles *et al.* 2003; Ritter and Gemünden 2003) and, specifically, the role of product champions and gatekeepers (Shaw 1998), the nature of networking practices (Biemans 1991) and decision-making behaviour on network activity (Ebadi and Utterback 1984). The evidence on the management of networks shows that managing informal and formal agreements, while establishing trust, means that the management of network relationships is inherently difficult (Biemans 1991). Those responsible for managing network relationships need to learn core network competencies over time (Coles *et al.* 2003). For example, they need to be able to identify when an agreement needs a contract or should be based on good faith, what role should friendship or reputation play in the identification of partners, and what kinds of milestones or interventions are needed to ensure a project stays on course (Shaw 1998).

Knowledge of how to collaborate accumulates over time through experience, reflection and interpretation (Lorenzoni and Lipparini 1999). Learning from collaboration is found in the empirical work to be a function of a firm's access to knowledge and its possession of the capabilities for utilizing the relationships and knowledge established (DeSanctis *et al.* 2002). The evidence found in the review shows that a firm's competence of managing networks can differ substantially, and networks can be shaped and deliberately designed to meet the firm's innovation needs. The evidence reported links a firm's networking competence and management with its innovative capacity. The degree to which firms learn about new opportunities is a function of the extent of their existing participation in networks (Powell *et al.* 1996).

To conclude our analysis of the empirical evidence on the relationship between networking and innovation, the next section focuses on the evidence relating to network failure and the limitations of networks in innovation processes.

NETWORK FAILURE AND NETWORK LIMITATIONS

The vast majority of the evidence analysed is overall extremely positive about the value of business-to-business networks and their impact on the innovation process. No systematic review on this subject would be complete, however, without some focus on why networks fail or the factors that prevent the effective operation of networking behaviour. Networks appear to encounter problems for a variety of reasons. For example, these problems could arise as a consequence of displacement, or be due to inter-firm conflict, lack of scale, external disruption and lack of infrastructure (Bower *et al.* 1997; Hobday 1994; Izushi 1997).

Networks can endure and evolve over many years. As a consequence, they go through periods of conflict between partners, and such conflicts can and do lead to the failure of the network (Coles *et al.* 2003). Although networks can go through internal strife, they also encounter displacement and conflict with other alternative networks. Izushi (1997), for example, examines the technological adaptation by small and medium-sized firms in a Japanese district of traditional ceramics manufacturing, which has moved into high-technology applications. He explains how external ties to networks prevailing in new Japanese industries have endangered the existence of innovative networks in an old industrial region.

All networks have rules of engagement which constrain the partners' behaviour (Boter and Holmquist 1996). These rules are governed by the network's governance mechanisms and the infrastructure (particularly industrial culture) within which the network is embedded (Rychen and Zimmermann 2002). For example, the pharmaceutical industry has an industrial culture that has encouraged more open and networked innovation, while the defence sector, owing to the sensitivities surrounding the technologies, has tended towards narrower and more focused networks (Bower 1993; Frenken 2000). Although the impact of networking on innovation performance seems conclusive, some studies show that innovation can occur more effectively within large organizations. Hobday (1994) shows that failure in Silicon Valley is linked to networks of small firms being unable to capitalize on the profits that can be made during the maturity stage of innovations (Hobday 1994). Once the initial innovation has been developed, networks of small firms are shown to be unable to access sufficient resources and scale to commercialize the innovation appropriately. Consequently, they are unable to maximize profits from the opportunity (Hobday 1994). Walcott (1999), studying high-technology firms in the deep south of the US, shows that the clustering of related industries is fostered by a shortage of appropriately configured laboratory and office space at the intermediate stage of the business growth, which encourages information sharing and co-operative behaviour by necessity. The lack of key networking mediating organizations critically retarded the development of the firms in the study.

A number of other studies reviewed show that events outside an industry, particularly government policy, can have a disproportionate effect leading to network failure (Bower *et al.* 1997). These failures, however, tend to be of existing networks, and sometimes can lead to more innovative solutions not less. For example, changes in government policy towards contracting customs in the North Sea oil and gas related industries led to the reduction of R&D in larger contractors and new innovative solutions from groups of small firms (Bower *et al.* 1997). Sectoral patterns associated with technological change can also create disruption by displacing previously accepted boundaries between industries (Furtado 1997). For example, Glasmeier (1991) shows, in a study of the Swiss watch industry, that the emphasis on technological innovation realized through co-operation lacked a detailed appreciation of historic networks. While networks can and do promote innovation within an existing technological framework, they are subject to disorganization and disintegration during periods of technological change.

A study by Rychen and Zimmermann (2002) on the microelectronics cluster in the Marseilles area of France also highlights that decisions guided by national policy that seek to implant clusters or networks into areas which do not take into consideration local conditions are likely to fail. They show that localized (regional) policy is more appropriate for the formation of infrastructures that tend to depend somewhat on existing networks in a locality. This evidence is supported by a study of 85 semiconductor firms in Silicon Valley, which shows how the existence of dense social networks led to industrial collaboration and reciprocal innovation. In turn, this led to the establishment of formal institutions for collaboration (Saxenian 1990).

The evidence on weak ties shows that networks can exist but not work effectively because of weak relationships between partners, or because firms are unable to extract value from their networks (Gales and Boynton 1992). In a qualitative study of eight space research innovation projects, Gales and Boynton (1992) show that increasing uncertainty in the network's role or conditions can lead to the development of only weak ties. In their study, projects with the greatest uncertainty have the smallest networks. Ahuja (2000), using a longitudinal study of the chemicals industry, shows that "structural holes," where important partners are missing within networks, also have a negative effect on innovation. As previously discussed, however, Burt's (1992) research demonstrates contrary findings.

The evidence on finance networks shows that they are important for ensuring coinvestment. Such investment enables risk to be spread, and usually leads to better quality investments and larger levels of investment for individual firms. If the investment infrastructure (venture finance networks) is weak, it appears that it can lead to the failure of new technologies or practices to enter markets, and the premature failure of entrepreneurial firms (Bygrave 1987, 1988; Harrison and Mason 1996).

Although networks have been shown to contribute to innovation and competitiveness, they can also inhibit innovation by encouraging anti-competitive behaviour (Knights *et al.* 1993). Ultimately, the value of a network depends on what it is used for. The use of networking has also been shown to be against the strategic interests of particular companies at certain times (Love and Roper 2001; Tomas and Arias 1995). From the review of the evidence, a number of other limitations of networking are demonstrated.

1. Love and Roper (2001), when modelling UK, German and Irish investment in research and development in manufacturing, find no link between external networking and innovation performance. Instead, they find that innovation is more dependent on internal organizational networks. This is also supported by Fischer and Varga (2002) in their study of manufacturing firms in Vienna. As most of the evidence in this review concentrates on high-technology industries it is possible that these studies show a different need for external business networks in the manufacturing sector.
2. Harris *et al.* (2000) find that inter-firm networking can *facilitate* the innovation process, but it will not necessarily lead to innovation success.
3. Meyer-Stamer (1995) suggests caution when applying the idea of inter-firm networks in developing nations. The study of network infrastructures in Brazil concludes that, even after improvements in the network infrastructure had led to better competitive performance, a large competitiveness gap remained. This indicates that networking may be an important facilitator in the innovation process, but other things are more fundamental (e.g. skill base of labour markets and regulation) and drive innovation and competitiveness more generally.
4. Tomas and Arias (1995) also point out that closely connected networks also entail drawbacks (for example, increasing the complexity of the innovation process, losing ownership control of the innovation and information lopsidedness) where partners have very different understandings about the nature of agreements.

CONCLUSIONS

This review of the evidence base concerning the relationship between networking and innovation highlights a number of areas in need of future research. The first obvious gap in the literature concerns the relationship between networking and different forms of innovation (e.g. process and organizational innovation). To date, the focus of research across disciplines has been primarily on product innovations. While process and organizational innovation may be, by their very nature, more difficult to study, the types of networking activity occurring in the development, diffusion and implementation of process and organizational innovation warrant serious attention. It may then be possible to compare networking activities and configurations across these different types of innovation and derive useful conclusions about the differences.

More generally, perhaps the most significant area for future research is in the area of network dynamics and network configurations. The evidence suggests that there is considerable ambiguity and debate within the literature regarding appropriate network configurations for successful innovation. While networking configurations are clearly contingent upon such factors as sector, type of innovation (radical versus incremental; product versus process), far more detailed research needs to be conducted in this area. By recognizing that networks are inherently dynamic, research could benefit from adopting a longitudinal approach.

Related to this, it is clear that, while considerable research has been conducted on the networking activities that occur between suppliers, customers and firms (operating within the networking interface), and this has been demonstrated to provide clear benefits, far more research is needed to explore and understand the ways in which diversity of partners facilitates innovation. In addition, the role of third parties operating within the networking infrastructure, such as professional and trade associations, is under-researched. The evidence base suggests that third parties are important for the development of informal relationships, but the processes through which informal networking relationships develop and subsequently affect innovation clearly needs to be investigated further.

A key feature of informal networking is the transfer of tacit knowledge promoting learning—such informal networking provides significant benefits for innovation. Although this has been highlighted throughout much of the literature, the mechanisms through which this occurs are an important area for future understanding.

What is surprising from this review is the very limited published research found on institutional mechanisms for facilitating networking and their impact on innovation. What evidence exists is also mixed in terms of their impact. Given the policy implications, it is an area requiring urgent attention.

The review also highlights that study on innovation and networking attracts interest across many disciplines, and it is useful to suggest here that funding be provided for more interdisciplinary research in the areas that are highlighted above. Different disciplines, for example, may have very different approaches to conducting research on the role of informal networking activity in innovation versus formal networking activity. If funding were made available across disciplines in this one particular area, it might be possible to develop a substantive evidence base relatively quickly.

Some broad policy implications can also be derived from this literature review. First, current research supports the view that networking significantly boosts innovation output and the competitiveness of firms in a diverse range of industries and, importantly, networking activities do require an appropriate infrastructure. Likewise, firms that do not co-operate have access to a limited knowledge base over the longer term. Consequently, governments should focus considerable attention on the development of strategies for assisting the development of networking infrastructures.

Managerial networking across contexts impacts on the adoption of good practice. Policies promoting management networking (e.g. seed funding for business clubs, venture networks and industry conventions) should, in principle, promote diffusion. Such networks range in focus, but diffusion of practices may occur more effectively where networks are cross-functional, engaging actors from a diverse range of contexts. The review also highlights that networks do impact on long-term innovation (Gemünden *et al.* 1992). Where close collaboration already exists, incentive policies can promote the continuance of long-term relationships (Fritsch 2001). Finally, access to networks for prospective entrepreneurs is essential because they allow access to resources and provide both emotional and business support (Baum *et al.* 2000).

Appendix 1. Inclusion Criteria

No.	Criteria	Reason for Inclusion
1	Theoretical papers—internal/ external validity	Provide the working assumptions to be used in the report
2	Working papers	Ensure coverage the most current research
3	All sectors	Examine how networking activities differ between sectors in the UK
4	US/Scandinavia/France/Germany/ UK/Japan	Ensure cross country comparisons
5	Quantitative and qualitative empirical studies	Capture all empirical evidence
6	Business to business networks	Focus on relationships between private sector organizations. Public sector will be included where they act as brokers in business to business networks

Appendix 2. Exclusion Criteria

No.	Criteria	Reason for Exclusion
1	Pre-1980	With very few exceptions, contributions to networking theory started to be published after 1980
2	Neural networks	These are not inter-organizational networks
3	Network externalities	These are not inter-organizational networks
4	Network effects	These are not inter-organizational networks
5	Information systems	Exclude many articles on networking that focus on how IT systems are linked together
6	Information technology	Exclude many articles on networking that focus on how IT systems are linked together
7	Compatibility	Exclude many articles on networking that focus on how IT systems are linked together

Exclusion Terms

AND NOT information technology
AND NOT information technology OR information systems
AND NOT information technology OR information systems OR neural networks
AND NOT information technology OR information systems OR neural networks OR Internet
AND NOT information technology OR information systems OR neural networks OR Internet
Innovat? AND network? AND fail? OR collapse OR dysfunction OR disintegrate
Innovat? AND network? AND incubat? OR cluster?
Innovat? AND mentor? OR knowledge brokers OR communities (w) practice

Appendix 3. Quality Criteria

Quality Assessment Criteria

Element	Level				
	0 Absence	*1 Low*	*2 Medium*	*3 High*	*Not Applicable*
1. Theory robustness	The article does not provide enough information to assess this criterion	Poor awareness of existing literature and debates. Under- or over-referenced. Low validity of theory	Basic understanding of the issues around the topic being discussed. The theory weakly is related to data	Deep and broad knowledge of relevant literature and theory relevant for addressing the research. Good relation theory-data	This element is not applicable to the document or study
2. Implication for practice	The article does not provide enough information to assess this criterion	Very difficult to implement the concepts and ideas presented. Not relevant for practitioners or professionals	There is a potential for implementing the proposed ideas, with minor revisions or adjustments	Significant benefit may be obtained if the ideas being discussed are put into practice	This element is not applicable to the document or study
3. Methodology, data supporting arguments	The article does not provide enough information to assess this criterion	Data inaccuracy and not related to theory. Flawed research design	Data are related to the arguments, though there are some gaps. Research design may be improved	Data strongly supports arguments. Besides, the research design is robust: sampling, data gathering, data analysis is rigorous	This element is not applicable to the document or study
4. Generalizability	The article does not provide enough information to assess this criterion	Only to the population studied	Generalizable to organizations of similar characteristics	High level of generalizability	This element is not applicable to the document or study
5. Contribution plus a short statement summarizing the article's contribution	The article does not provide enough information to assess this criterion	Does not make an important contribution. It is not clear the advances it makes	Although using others' ideas, builds upon the existing theory	Further develops existing knowledge, expanding the way the issue was explained so far	This element is not applicable to the document

925

About the Authors
Luke Pittaway is from the Institute for Entrepreneurship and Enterprise Development, Lancaster University Management School, Lancaster LA1 4YX, UK. Maxine Robertson is from IKON Research Centre, Warwick Business School, University of Warwick, Coventry CV4 7AL, UK. Kamal Munir is from the University of Cambridge, Judge Institute of Management, Cambridge CB2 1AG, UK. David Denyer is from the Cranfield School of Management, Cranfield University, Cranfield, Bedford MK43 0AL, UK. Andy Neely is from the Advanced Institute of Management Research, 6 Huntsworth Mews, London Business School, London NW1 6DD, UK.

References

Ahuja, G. (2000). The duality of collaboration: inducements and opportunities in the formation of interfirm linkages. *Strategic Management Journal,* 21, 317–343.

Almeida, P. and Kogut, B. (1999). Localization and knowledge and the mobility of engineers in regional networks. *Management Science,* 45, 905–917.

Arndt, O. and Sternberg, R. (2000). Do manufacturing firms profit from intraregional innovation linkages? An empirical based answer. *European Planning Studies,* 8, 465–485.

Baiman, S., Rajan, M.V. and Kanodia, C. (2002). The role of information and opportunism in the choice of buyer–supplier relationships/discussion. *Journal of Accounting Research,* 40, 247–278.

Baldwin and Clark (2000). *Design Rules,* Vol. 1, *The Power of Modularity.* Cambridge, MA: MIT Press.

Baptista, R. (1999). The diffusion of process innovations: a selective review. *International Journal of the Economics of Business,* 6(1), 107–129.

Baum, J., Calabrese, T. and Silverman, B. (2000). Don't go it alone: alliance network composition and start-ups performance in Canadian biotechnology. *Strategic Management Journal,* 21, 267–294.

Bee, E. (2003). Knowledge networks and technical invention in America's metropolitan areas: a paradigm for high-technology economic development. *Economic Development Quarterly,* 17(2), 115–131.

Biemans, W. (1991). User and third-party involvement in developing medical equipment innovations. *Technovation,* 11, 163–182.

Birley, S. (1985). The role of networks in the entrepreneurial process. *Journal of Business Venturing,* 1, 107–117.

Birley, S. (1987). New ventures and employment growth. *Journal of Business Venturing,* 2, 155–165.

Bolton, M., Malmrose, R. and Ouchi, W. (1994). The organization of innovation in the United States and Japan: Neoclassical and relational contracting. *Journal of Management Studies,* 31, 653–679.

Boter, H. and Holmquist, C. (1996). Industry characteristics and internationalization processes in small firms. *Journal of Business Venturing,* 11, 471–487.

Bougrain, F. and Haudeville, B. (2002). Innovation, collaboration and SMEs internal research capacities. *Research Policy,* 31, 735–747.

Bower, D.J. (1993). New product development in the pharmaceutical industry: pooling network resources. *Journal of Product Innovation Management,* 10, 367.

Bower, D. and Keogh, W. (1996). Changing patterns of innovation in a process-dominated industry. *International Journal of Technology Management,* 12, 209–220.

Bower, D., Crabtree, E. and Keogh, W. (1997). Rhetorics and realities in new product development in the subsea oil industry. *International Journal of Project Management,* 15, 345–350.

Brass, D. and Burkhardt, M. (1992). Centrality and power in organizations. In Nohria, N. and Eccles, R. (eds), *Networks and Organizations.* Boston: Harvard University Press, 191.

Bruce, M. and Moger, S.T. (1999). Dangerous liaisons: an application of supply chain modelling for studying innovation within the UK clothing industry. *Technology Analysis & Strategic Management,* 11, 113–125.

Bruce, M. and Rodgus, G. (1991). Innovation strategies in the enzyme industry. *R&D Management,* 21, 319.

Burt, R. (1992). *Structural Holes: The Social Structure of Competition.* Cambridge, MA: Harvard University Press.

Bygrave, W. (1987). Syndicated investments by venture capital firms: a networking perspective. *Journal of Business Venturing,* 2, 139–154.

Bygrave, W. (1988). The structure of investment networks of venture capital firms. *Journal of Business Venturing,* 3, 137–157.

Carayannis, E.G., Kassicieh, S.K. and Radosevich, R. (2000). Strategic alliances as a source of early-stage seed capital in new technology-based firms. *Technovation,* 20, 603–615.

Cohen, B. and Levinthal, D. (1990). Absorptive capacity: a new perspective on learning and innovation. *Administrative Science Quarterly,* 35, 128.

Coleman, J. (1988). Social capital in the creation of human capital. *American Journal of Sociology,* 94, 95–120.

Coles, A., Harris, L. and Dickson, K. (2003). Testing goodwill: conflict and cooperation in new product development networks. *International Journal of Technology Management,* 25, 51–64.

Cooke, P. (1996). The new wave of regional innovation networks: analysis, characteristics and strategy. *Small Business Economics,* 8, 159–171.

Cooke, P. and Wills, D. (1999). Small firms, social capital and the enhancement of business performance through innovation programmes. *Small Business Economics,* 13, 219–234.

Conway, S. (1995). Informal boundary-spanning communication in the innovation process: an empirical study. *Technology Analysis & Strategic Management,* 7, 327–342.

D'Cruz, J.R. and Rugman, A.M. (1994). Business network theory and the Canadian telecommunications industry. *International Business Review*, 3, 275–288.

DeSanctis, G., Glass, J. and Ensing, I. (2002). Organizational designs for R&D. *Academy of Management Executive*, 16(3), 55–66.

DTI (2003). *Innovation Report—"Competing in the Global Economy: the Innovation Challenge,"* http://www.dti.gov.uk/innovationreport/index.him

Ebadi, Y.M. and Utterback, J. (1984). The effects of communication on technological innovation. *Management Science*, 30, 572–586.

Elg, U. and Johansson, U. (1997). Decision making in inter-firm networks as a political process. *Organization Studies*, 18, 361–384.

Eisenhardt, K. and Schoonhoven, C. (1996). Resource-based view of strategic alliance formation: strategic and social effects in entrepreneurial firms. *Organization Science*, 7, 136–150.

Erickson, C. and Jacoby, S. (2003). The effects of employer networks on workplace innovation and training. *Industrial and Labor Relations Review*, 56, 203–223.

Ferrary, M. (2003). Managing disruptive technologies life cycle by externalising the research: social network and corporate venturing in the Silicon Valley. *International Journal of Technology Management*, 25, 165–180.

Fischer, M. and Varga, A. (2002). Technological innovation and interfirm cooperation: an exploratory analysis using survey data from manufacturing firms in the metropolitan region of Vienna. *International Journal of Technology Management*, 24, 724–742.

Florida, R. and Kenney, M. (1988a). Venture capital and high technology entrepreneurship. *Journal of Business Venturing*, 3, 301–319.

Florida, R. and Kenney, M. (1988b). Venture capital-financed innovation and technological change in the USA. *Research Policy*, 17, 119–137.

Freel, M.S. (2003). Sectoral patterns of small firm innovation, networking and proximity. *Research Policy*, 32, 751–770.

Freeman, C. (1982). *The Economics of Industrial Innovation*, Cambridge, MA: MIT Press.

Freeman, J. (1999). Venture capital as an economy of time. In Leenders, R. and Gabbay, S. (eds), *Corporate Social Capital and Liability*. Boston: Kluwer Academic, 460.

Frenken, K. (2000). A complexity approach to innovation networks. The case of the aircraft industry (1909–1997). *Research Policy*, 29, 257–272.

Fritsch, M. (2001). Co-operation in regional innovation systems. *Regional Studies*, 35, 297–307.

Furtado, A. (1997). The French system of innovation in the oil industry some lessons about the role of public policies and sectoral patterns of technological change in innovation networking. *Research Policy*, 25, 1243–1259.

Gales, L. and Boynton, A. (1992). Information ties and innovation management: a qualitative assessment of information processing and the strength of weak ties. *Journal of High Technology Management Research*, 3, 169–188.

Gemser, G., Leenders, M. and Wijnberg, N. (1996). The dynamics of inter-firm networks in the course of the industrial life cycle: the role of appropriability. *Technology Analysis and Strategic Management*, 8, 439–453.

Gemünden, H., Heydebreck, P. and Herden, R. (1992). Technological interweavement: a means of achieving innovation success. *R&D Management*, 22, 359–376.

Gemünden, H.G., Ritter, T. and Heydebreck, P. (1996). Network configuration and innovation success: an empirical analysis in German high-tech industries. *International Journal of Research in Marketing*, 13, 449–462.

Glasmeier, A. (1991). Technological discontinuities and flexible production networks: the case of Switzerland and the world watch industry. *Research Policy*, 20, 469–485.

Grabher, G. (2001). Ecologies of creativity: the village, the group, and the heterarchic organisation of the British advertising industry. *Environment and Planning A*, 33, 351–374.

Grandori, A. (1997). An organizational assessment of interfirm coordination modes. *Organization Studies*, 18, 897–925.

Grandori, A. and Soda, G. (1995). Inter-firm networks: antecedents, mechanisms and forms. *Organization Studies*, 16, 183–214.

Granovetter, M. (1985). Economic action and social structure: the problem of embeddedness. *American Journal of Sociology*, 91, 481–510.

Grotz, R. and Braun, B. (1997). Territorial or trans-territorial networking: spatial aspects of technology-oriented co-operation within the German mechanical engineering industry. *Regional Studies*, 31, 545–557.

Haar, N., Starr, J. and MacMillan, I. (1988). Informal risk capital investors: investment patterns on the East Coast of the U.S.A. *Journal of Business Venturing*, 3, 11–29.

Hagedoorn, J. and Duysters, G. (2002). External sources of innovative capabilities: the preference for strategic alliances or mergers and acquisitions. *Journal of Management Studies*, 39, 167–188.

Hanna, V. and Walsh, K. (2002). Small firm networks: a successful approach to innovation? *R&D Management*, 32, 201–207.

Harding, R. (2000). Venture capital and regional development: towards a venture capital system. *Venture Capital*, 2(4), 287–311.

Harris, L., Coles, A. and Dickson, K. (2000). Building innovation networks: issues of strategy and expertise. *Technology Analysis & Strategic Management*, 12, 229–241.

Harrison, R. and Mason, C. (1992). International perspectives on the supply of informal venture capital. *Journal of Business Venturing*, 7, 459–475.

Harrison, R. and Mason, C. (1996). Developments in the promotion of informal venture capital in the UK. *International Journal of Entrepreneurial Behaviour & Research*, 2(2), 6–33.

Harryson, S. (1997). How Canon and Sony drive product innovation through networking and application-focused R&D. *Journal of Product Innovation Management*, 14, 288–295.

Hausler, J., Hohn, H. and Lutz, S. (1994). Contingencies of innovative networks: a case study of successful R&D collaboration. *Research Policy*, 23, 47–66.

Hendry, C., Brown, J. and Defillippi, R. (2000). Regional clustering of high technology-based firms: opto-electronics in three countries. *Regional Studies*, 34, 129–144.

Hoang, H. and Antoncic, B. (2003). Network-based research in entrepreneurship: a critical review. *Journal of Business Venturing*, 18, 165–187.

Hobday, M. (1994). The limits of Silicon Valley: a critique of network theory. *Technology Analysis & Strategic Management*, 6, 231–243.

Holbrook, D. (1995). Government support of the semiconductor industry: diverse approaches and information flows. *Business and Economic History*, 24(2), 133.

Hyun, J.H. (1994). Buyer supplier relations in the European automobile component industry. *Long Range Planning*, 27(2), 66–75.

Izushi, H. (1997). Conflict between two industrial networks: technological adaptation and inter-firm relationships in the ceramics industry in Seto, Japan. *Regional Studies*, 31, 117–129.

Jacquier-Roux, V. and Bourgeois, B. (2002). New networks of technological creation in energy industries: reassessment of the roles of equipment suppliers and operators. *Technology Analysis and Strategic Management*, 14, 399–417.

Janne, O.E.M. (2002). The emergence of corporate integrated innovation systems across regions: the case of the chemical and pharmaceutical industry in Germany, the UK and Belgium. *Journal of International Management*, 8(1), 97–119.

Kash, D.E. and Rycroft, R.W. (2000). Patterns of innovating complex technologies: a framework for adaptive network strategies. *Research Policy*, 29, 819–831.

Kash, D.E. and Rycroft, R. (2002). Emerging patterns of complex technological innovation. *Technological Forecasting and Social Change*, 69, 581–606.

Kaufmann, A. and Tödtling, F. (2000). System of innovation in traditional industrial regions: the case of Styria in a comparative perspective. *Regional Studies*, 34, 29.

Kaufmann, A. and Tödtling, F. (2001). Science–industry interaction in the process of innovation: the importance of boundary-crossing between systems. *Research Policy*, 30, 791–804.

Keeble, D., Lawson, C., Moore, B. and Wilkinson, F. (1999). Collective learning processes, networking and "institutional thickness" in the Cambridge region. *Regional Studies*, 33, 319–332.

Keeble, D., Lawson, C., Lawton-Smith, H., Moore, B. and Wilkinson, F. (1998). Internationalisation processes, networking and local embeddedness in technology-intensive small firms. *Small Business Economics*, 11, 327–342.

Kitching, J. and Blackburn, R. (1999). Management training and networking in small and medium-sized enterprises in three European regions: implications for business support. *Environment and Planning C—Government and Policy*, 17, 621–635.

Knights, D., Murray, F. and Willmont, H. (1993). Networking as knowledge work. A study of strategic interorganizational development in the financial services industry. *Journal of Management Studies*, 30, 975–996.

Koch, C. (2003). Innovation networking between stability and political dynamics. *Technovation*, 24, 729–739.

Lamming, R., Hajee, D., Horrill, M., Kay, G. and Staniforth, J. (2002). Lessons from co-development of a single vessel processor: methodologies for managing innovation in customer–supplier networks. *International Journal of Technology Management*, 23, 21–39.

Larson, A. (1991). Partner networks: leveraging external ties to improve entrepreneurial performance. *Journal of Business Venturing*, 6, 173–188.

Leonard-Barton, D. (1984). Interpersonal communication patterns among Swedish and Boston-area entrepreneurs. *Research Policy*, 13, 101–114.

Liao, J. and Welsch, H. (2003). Social capital and entrepreneurial growth aspiration: a comparison of technology- and non-technology-based nascent entrepreneurs. *Journal of High Technology Management Research*, 14, 149–170.

Liebeskind, J., Porter, O., Zucker, L. and Brewer, M. (1996). Social networks learning and flexibility: sourcing scientific knowledge in new biotechnology firms. *Organization Science*, 7, 428–443.

Lincoln, J., Ahmadjian, C. and Mason, E. (1998). Organizational learning and purchase-supply relations in Japan: Hitachi, Matsushita and Toyota compared. *California Management Review*, 40, 241.

Lipparini, A. and Sobrero, M. (1994). The glue and the pieces: entrepreneurship and innovation in small-firm networks. *Journal of Business Venturing*, 9, 125–140.

Liyanage, S. (1995). Breeding innovation clusters through collaborative research networks. *Technovation*, 15, 553–567.

Lorenzoni, G. and Lipparini, A. (1999). The leveraging of interfirm relationships as a distinctive organizational capability: a longitudinal study. *Strategic Management Journal*, 20, 317–338.

Love, J. and Roper, S. (2001). Location and network effects on innovation success: evidence for UK, German and Irish manufacturing plants. *Research Policy*, 30, 643–661.

Meyer-Stamer, J. (1995). Micro-level innovations and competitiveness. *World Development*, 23(1), 143–148.

Momma, S. and Sharp, M. (1999). Developments in new biotechnology firms in Germany. *Technovation*, 19, 267–282.

Munir, K. (2003). Competitive dynamics in face of technological discontinuity: a framework for action. *Journal of High Technology Management Research*, 14, 93–109.

Newell, S. and Clark, P. (1990). The importance of extraorganizational networks in the diffusion and appropriation of new technologies—the role of professional-associations in the United-States and Britain. *Knowledge-Creation Diffusion Utilization*, 12(2), 199–212.

Nieuwenhuis, L.F.M. (2002). Innovation and learning in agriculture. *Journal of European Industrial Training*, 26(6,7), 283.

Nooteboom, B. (2000). Institutions and forms of coordination in innovation systems. *Organization Studies*, 21, 915–939.

Oliver, A.L. and Liebeskind, J. (1997). Three levels of networking for sourcing intellectual capital in biotechnology: implications for studying interorganizational networks.

International Studies of Management and Organization, 27(4), 76–103.

Ostgaard, T.A. and Birley, S. (1994). Personal networks and firm competitive strategy—a strategic or coincidental match. *Journal of Business Venturing,* 9, 281–305.

Ostgaard, T.A. and Birley, S. (1996). New venture growth and personal networks. *Journal of Product Innovation Management,* 13, 557–558.

Pammolli, F. and Riccaboni, M. (2002). Technological regimes and the growth of networks: an empirical analysis. *Small Business Economics,* 19, 205–215.

Perez Perez, M. and Sanchez, A. (2002). Lean production and technology networks in the Spanish automotive supplier industry. *Management International Review,* 42(3), 261.

Phillimore, J. (1999). Beyond the linear view of innovation in science park evaluation—an analysis of Western Australian Technology Park. *Technovation,* 19, 673–680.

Pittaway, L., Robertson, M., Munir, K., Denyer, D. and Neely, A. (2004). Networking and innovation: a systematic review of the literature. Advanced Institute of Management Research, London, http://www.aimresearch.org/ aimforum.shtml

Porter, M. and Ketels, C.H.M. (2003). *UK Competitiveness: Moving to the Next Stage.* Management Research Forum, Summary Report 6. London: Advanced Institute of Management Research, London, http://www.aimresearch. org/AIM

Powell, W.W., Koput, K.W. and Smith-Doerr, L. (1996). Interorganizational collaboration and the locus of innovation: networks of learning in biotechnology. *Administrative Science Quarterly,* 41(1), 116–145.

Ragatz, G., Handfield, R. and Scannell, T. (1997). Success factors for integrating suppliers into new product development. *Journal of Product Innovation Management,* 14, 190–202.

Reed, F.M. and Walsh, K. (2002). Enhancing technological capability through supplier development: a study of the UK aerospace industry. *IEEE Transactions on Engineering Management,* 49(3), 231.

Riccaboni, M. and Pammolli, F. (2003). Technological regimes and the evolution of networks of innovators. Lessons from biotechnology and pharmaceuticals. *International Journal of Technology Management,* 25, 334–349.

Ritter, T. and Gemünden, H.G. (2003). Network competence: its impact on innovation success and its antecedents. *Journal of Business Research,* 56, 745–755.

Robertson M., Swan, J. and Newell S. (1996). The role of networks in the diffusion of technological innovation. *Journal of Management Studies,* 33, 333–360.

Romijn, H. and Albaladejo, M. (2002). Determinants of innovation capability in small electronics and software firms in southeast England. *Research Policy,* 31, 1053–1067.

Romijn, H. and Albu, M. (2002). Innovation, networking and proximity: lessons from small high technology firms in the UK. *Regional Studies,* 36, 81–86.

Rothwell, R. (1991). External networking and innovation in small and medium-sized manufacturing firms in Europe. *Technovation,* 11, 93–112.

Rothwell, R. and Dodgson, M. (1991). External linkages and innovation in small and medium-sized enterprises. *R&D Management,* 21, 125–137.

Rychen, F. and Zimmermann, J. (2002). Birth of a cluster: the microelectronics industry in the Marseilles metropolitan area. *International Journal of Technology Management,* 27, 792.

Saxenian, A. (1990). Regional networks and the resurgence of Silicon Valley. *California Management Review,* 33, 89–112.

Shan, W., Walker, G. and Kogut, B. (1994). Interfirm cooperation and startup innovation in the biotechnology industry. *Strategic Management journal,* 15, 387–394.

Shaw, B. (1993). Formal and informal networks in the UK medical equipment industry. *Technovation,* 13, 349–365.

Shaw, B. (1998). Innovation and new product development in the UK medical equipment industry. *International Journal of Technology Management,* 15, 433.

Smeltzer, L., Van Hook, B. and Hutt, R. (1991). Analysis and use of advisors as information sources in venture startups. *Journal of Small Business Management,* 29(3), 10–20.

Smilor, R. (1987a). Commercializing technology through new business incubators. *Research Management,* 31(5), 36.

Smilor, R. (1987b). Managing the incubator system: Critical success factors to accelerate new company development. *IEEE Transactions and Engineering Management,* 34(3), 146–156.

Staber, U. (2001). Spatial proximity and firm survival in a declining industrial district: the case of knitwear firms in Baden-Wurttemberg. *Regional Studies,* 35, 329–341.

Staropoli, C. (1998). Cooperation in R&D through a network, and "organizational gamble"? An empirical analysis of Rhone Poulenc Rorer-Gencell. *Technology Analysis and Strategic Management,* 10, 511–527.

Streb, J. (2003). Shaping the national system of inter-industry knowledge exchange: vertical integration, licensing and repeated knowledge transfer in the German plastics industry. *Research Policy,* 32, 1125–1140.

Swan, J., Newell, S. and Robertson, M. (1999). National differences in the diffusion and design of technological innovation: the role of inter-organizational networks. *British Journal of Management,* 10, 45.

Teece, D. (1986). Profiting from technological innovation: implications for integration, collaboration, licensing and public policy. *Research Policy,* 15, 285–305.

Tomas, J. and Arias, G. (1995). Do networks really foster innovation? *Management Decision,* 33(9), 52–56.

Verspagen, B. (1999). Large firms and knowledge flows in the Dutch R&D system: a case study of Philips Electronics. *Technology Analysis & Strategic Management,* 11, 211–233.

von Hippel, E. (1978). Successful industrial products from customer ideas: a paradigm, evidence and implications. *Journal of Marketing,* 42(1), 39–49.

Walcott, S. (1999). High tech in the Deep South: biomedical firm clusters in metropolitan Atlanta. *Growth and Change,* 30(1), 48–74.

Walsh, V., Roy, R. and Bruce, M. (1988). Competitive by design. *Journal of Marketing Management,* 4(2), 201–216.

Wetzel, W.E. Jr (1987). The informal venture capital market: aspects of scale and market efficiency. *Journal of Business Venturing,* 2, 299–313.

Notes

1. Financial services and food.
2. Agriculture; energy; oil and gas.
3. Automobile components; ceramics manufacturing; clothing; mechanical engineering; packaging machine industry.
4. Aerospace and defense; biotechnology; electronics; embryonics; enzymes; home automation; petro- chemicals; plastics; robotics; semiconductors; software; telecommunications.
5. A regional infrastructure is defined here as a political, economic and geographical region, as represented by the English regions covered by UK Regional Development Agencies (e.g. North West England).

65

WHAT WILL THE FUTURE BRING? DOMINANCE, TECHNOLOGY EXPECTATIONS, AND RADICAL INNOVATION

Rajesh K. Chandy, Jaideep C. Prabhu, and Kersi D. Antia

Are dominant firms laggards or leaders at innovation? The answers to this question are conflicting and controversial. In an attempt to resolve conflicting answers to this question, the authors argue that dominance is a multifaceted construct in which individual facets result in differing (and countervailing) propensities to innovate. To identify the overall effects of dominance, it is necessary to consider the effects of these facets taken together. The authors also study a hitherto ignored yet important driver of innovation, technology expectations, and show that managers have widely divergent expectations of the same new technology. Furthermore, even when their expectations are the same, managers of dominant firms display investment behavior at odds with their counterparts at nondominant firms. The authors use a triangulation of research methods and combine insights from lab studies with those from field interviews, archival data, and a survey of bricks-and-mortar banks' responses to Internet banking.

The relationship between dominance and innovation is one of enduring (and renewed) interest to scholars in marketing, corporate strategy, economics, and sociology, among other fields (Cooper and Schendel 1976; Henderson 1993; Miller 1990; Scherer 1992; Schumpeter 1942). The prognosis from this research has mostly been gloomy, albeit with a hint of hope. First, the gloomy part: Many scholars note that as firms become more dominant, they become more wedded to the status quo and reluctant to embrace radically new products (e.g., Cooper and Schendel 1976; Henderson 1993; Schumpeter 1942). Incremental improvements become firms' preferred mode of action, and dominant firms either spurn radical innovations or, at best, leave them to collect dust on laboratory shelves (e.g., Utterback 1994). As the technological environment turns on the dominant firms, their reluctance to pursue radically new products eventually leads to their weakening and downfall. Dominant firms' very success sows the seeds of their failure. For this reason, some scholars have compared dominant firms to Icarus, the tragic figure from Greek mythology whose success at flying to great

Chandy, Rajesh, Jaideep C. Prahu, and Kersi D. Antia. 2003. What Will the Future Bring? Dominance, Technology Expectations, and Radical Innovation. *Journal of Marketing* 67(3): 1–18.

heights led to his death when the sun melted his wings and he plunged into the sea (Miller 1990).

However, reality does not always adhere to the plot of a Greek tragedy; there are some reasons for hope. As Cohen and Levin (1989, p. 1078) state in an extensive review of the literature, the results linking dominance and innovation "are perhaps most accurately described as fragile." Followers of a more recent school of thought note that dominant firms do enjoy some important advantages. For example, dominant firms have greater access to resources, which is a key advantage in trying to build and sustain radically new technologies and markets. Some recent research suggests that large and incumbent firms are often some of the most aggressive radical innovators (e.g., Chandy and Tellis 2000; Zucker and Darby 1997). A casual glance at business periodicals reveals that many dominant firms actively pursue such new technologies and are relatively successful in doing so. What explains this performance? Little is known about why some dominant firms pursue radical innovations aggressively and others do not.

We attempt to reconcile the opposing views on the relationship between dominance and radical innovation. We consider dominance a composite of several facets, each with different and countervailing behavioral effects on firms' propensity to innovate. This viewpoint is in contrast to existing research, which (1) has typically equated dominance with related though conceptually distinct proxies, such as firm size and incumbency, and (2) has rarely integrated the different facets of dominance to assess its overall effect on radical innovation. By examining the behavioral consequences of each facet of dominance and the combined effects of these facets taken together, we attempt to provide a clearer understanding of the relationship between dominance and innovation, something that researchers in the field have repeatedly called for (e.g., Scherer 1992).

We argue that there is another, hitherto overlooked, reason some dominant firms invest aggressively in radical innovation and others do not: managerial expectations. When a radically new technology is nascent, managers confronting the same technology may hold differing expectations about the technology's likely effect on existing products. Specifically, managers may hold at least three differing expectations about the technology's likely effect on existing products:

1. The new technology will enhance the effectiveness of existing products, just as electric motors made dishwashers and laundry machines more powerful.
2. The new technology will make existing products obsolete, just as integrated circuit technology made slide rules obsolete.
3. The new technology will have little or no effect on existing products, just as microwave heating technology hardly affected conventional oven sales.

We argue that these expectations result in significantly different levels of investment in radical innovation. Moreover, managers who have the same technology expectations may exhibit different investment behavior, depending on their level of dominance in the existing product generation. Studying expectations and their interaction with firms' overall dominance provides a more complete explanation for the empirical disconnect between the pessimistic predictions of much of the literature on dominance and radical innovation and the aggressively innovative behavior of some dominant firms.

In addition, studying expectations helps us understand the dynamics of investment in radical new technology before the actual effects of the technology are evident. Although emerging research focuses on the effects of radically new technologies on existing products (e.g., Anderson and Tushman 1990; Cooper and Schendel 1976), most of this research examines the impact of new technologies in a historical context, after the impact is already evident. It is possible to categorize specific technologies post hoc as having helped, hindered, or had no effect on the existing product category (Utterback 1994), but managers make investment decisions before the effects have taken place. Key decisions are made while the technology is still nascent, when its eventual effect on existing products is far from certain. Yet little research has examined decision making by managers in this "pre-paradigmatic" stage of radical innovation (Dosi 1982).

Moreover, many authors note the importance of a "vision" for the future in promoting radical innovation (see Ohmae 1984). By introducing managers' expectations into the analysis, we present a view of managers as active agents who employ their imaginations in making decisions and who, to a certain extent at least, are instrumental in creating their own futures. We show that "paranoid" firms (e.g., Grove 1996) are the most aggressive innovators.

Finally, we use experimental techniques to investigate the causal relationships among dominance, expectations, and radical innovation, and we use field studies to provide real-world context and insight. Few studies of innovation employ time-series experimentation to examine causality (Poole et al. 2000; Weick 1967). Our field study enables us to study real-world firms in an industry facing the effects of a radically new technology; specifically, we study how managers of bricks-and-mortar banks responded to the advent of Internet banking. We employ multiple methods—in-depth interviews, survey data, and archival data—to study the impact of dominance and expectations at a unique point in the evolution of Internet banking. The triangulation of research methods yields a rich payoff in terms of empirical insight, a balance of internal and external validity, and robust findings.

THEORY

Definitions

The term *dominance* refers to the extent of market power that firms enjoy (Bain 1968; Scherer 1980). A *radical innovation* is a product that requires substantially different technology and marketing skills compared with existing products in the industry (Chandy and Tellis 1998; see also Garcia and Calantone 2002). The greater a firm's emphasis on a radically new product, the more aggressive it is in radical innovation. We define *technology expectations* as managers' beliefs about the likely impact (obsolescence, enhancement, or no effect) of the new technology on existing products.

Conceptual Overview

Investment in a radical innovation is a function of a firm's motivation and ability to do so. Firms with the motivation and ability to invest are likely most aggressive in pursuing the radical innovation. Firms' dominance affects their motivation and ability to invest. Dominant firms are prone to inertia and escalation of commitment, both of which reduce motivation to invest. As a result, dominant firms may show a preference for the status quo; that is, they may continue with the existing product generation. However, dominant firms are also wealthier than nondominant firms and therefore have greater ability to invest in the radical innovation.

Technology expectations have a critical role in driving investment in radical innovation. Specifically, they alter the manner in which managers frame an investment and, by doing so, amplify (or diminish) managers' motivation to pursue radical innovation. The effect of expectations on the motivation to pursue radical innovation results in a corresponding change in firms' investment aggressiveness.

Study Scope and Assumptions

For conceptual and empirical clarity, we restrict our scope to incumbent firms. Thus, we do not attempt to explain the behavior of firms that have no presence in the existing product generation. This approach is in line with previous research, which also focuses on incumbent firms (e.g., Chandy and Tellis 1998; Hannan and Freeman 1989; Scherer 1992). All incumbent firms have a stake in the status quo because they have some investments in the current product generation.

We assume the impact of the new technology on existing products to be an exogenous shock: Individual firms, even powerful ones, have little control (at least in the long run) over whether the new technology enhances, makes obsolete, or has no effect on current products (see Anderson and Tushman 1990; Solow 1956). Although some dominant firms might appear all-powerful and invincible at one point, over the long run few firms control the fates of technologies and industries.

We also assume that managers (even those of wealthy firms) have capital constraints. One consequence of capital constraints is that investing in a new product implies less investment in existing products; that is, there is a trade-off between existing products and new products. Investing in the new product likely makes a firm less competitive in the existing product generation (e.g., Blundell, Griffith, and Van Reenen 1999). The default course of action is therefore to continue investing in the existing product generation; the alternate course of action is to invest in the new product.

HYPOTHESES

Are dominant firms more or less likely than nondominant firms to invest aggressively in a radical innovation? Schumpeter (1942) first highlighted the role of market power in innovation, arguing that dominance favors radical innovation. Many researchers have since steadily attempted to test Schumpeter's hypothesis empirically (see Cohen 1995; Scherer 1992), yet few researchers provide a behavioral rationale for dominant firms' radical innovation behavior (Scherer 1992). Indeed, prominent researchers have criticized the atheoretical nature of work in the field (Cohen 1995). We highlight the multifaceted nature of dominance and provide behavioral explanations of how each facet affects dominant firms' investment in innovation. We also consider how these facets taken together influence the overall impact of dominance on investment in radical innovation.

The Many Faces of Dominance

Consider Microsoft or Intel today. Both firms are well entrenched and thus have larger investments in their current markets than do other firms. They also have greater market shares than do other firms. Finally, both firms are wealthier and have greater access to resources than do other firms. These three facets—greater investments, greater market shares, and greater resources—define dominance (see Bain 1968; Borenstein 1990, 1991). These three facets may also have different impacts on dominant firms' motivation and ability to pursue radical innovation. Although there is a substantial literature on some behavioral effects, such as escalation of commitment and inertia, previous research has not linked these effects to the three facets of dominance or brought together these effects to understand the overall influence of dominance on radical innovation (see Cohen 1995; Scherer 1992). By doing so, we hope to clarify the conflicting views in the literature on dominance and radical innovation.

Escalation of Commitment: The Effect of Investments

The theory of escalation of commitment attempts to explain why people continue to pursue courses of action even after it is irrational to do so (Boulding, Morgan, and Staelin 1997; Staw 1981). According to this theory, managers frame the decision to invest in a new product relative to continuing with the initial commitment to the old product. The more committed managers are to the old course of action, the greater the loss they perceive in the decision to switch to the new course of action (Bazerman 1994). Loss aversion (Kahneman and Tversky 1979) therefore causes managers to be unlikely to switch from the old course of action (Brockner and Rubin 1985) and to place less emphasis on the new compared with the old course of action. By definition, all incumbents have some investment in (and therefore some commitment to) the existing product generation (see Brockner and Rubin 1985; Staw 1981). However, because dominant firms have more investments in the existing product than do other firms, they are especially prone to escalate their commitment to the existing product compared with the radical innovation. Thus,

> H_{1a}: The larger a firm's investments in the existing product generation, the less aggressively its managers invest in the radical innovation relative to the existing product generation.

Inertia: The Effect of Market Success

Incumbent managers' susceptibility to inertia, and their resulting preference for the status quo, is well documented in prior research (Hannan and Freeman 1989; Nelson and Winter 1982). All incumbents are prone to inertia, but as with escalation of commitment, dominant incumbents may be especially susceptible to it. A major source of inertia in a firm is its perceived success in its current course of action (see Leonard-Barton 1992; Nelson and Winter 1982). The more successful the firm perceives its current course of action, the more it reinforces its commitment to that course of action. A strong market position signals the validity of the firm's decision-making procedures; it legitimizes precedents and causes them to become normative standards for the future (Hannan and Freeman 1989; Nelson and Winter 1982). The firm subsequently makes decisions about the future simply based on inertia from the past. According to this argument, the stronger a firm's market position, the greater are the inertial constraints it faces. Dominant firms therefore are less motivated to switch from the status quo, and they likely invest less aggressively in radical innovation than do nondominant firms. Therefore,

> H_{1b}: The stronger a firm's market position in the existing product generation, the less aggressively its managers invest in the radical innovation relative to the existing product generation.

The Wealth Effect

The escalation of commitment and inertia arguments do not, however, account for dominant firms' having more resources than other firms. The greater wealth of dominant firms provides them with greater ability to invest in radical innovation. Greater wealth also cushions dominant firms from the risk of failure inherent in radical innovation (Nohria and Gulati 1996); thus, dominant firms have the means to experiment extensively in research and development, which could result in dominant firms investing more in a new product. Managers of dominant firms may also invest heavily in radically new products rather than existing products because they might stand a greater chance of making the new idea a marketplace success than would firms with few financial and marketing resources. For example, dominant firms likely have larger sales forces, which enables them to ensure greater distribution of a fledgling product (Chandy and Tellis 2000). Thus,

> H_{1c}: The greater a firm's wealth, the more aggressively its managers invest in the radical innovation relative to the existing product generation.

Taken together, what are the overall effects of dominance on managers' investment aggressiveness in radical product innovation? Recent evidence suggests that, overall, dominant firms are likely more aggressive in their investments in a radically new product than are other firms. Radical innovations are resource intensive and could become increasingly so over time (e.g., Chandy and Tellis 2000; Jelinek and Schoonhoven 1990). In addition, the innovation ethic is now more widespread among managers, including those of dominant firms. This awareness of the need for innovation is partly a result of a significant recent literature on the (beneficial and destructive) effects of innovation (e.g., Christensen 1997; Hamel 1999), combined with the many consulting and education activities by the authors and followers of this literature (e.g., Hamel 2001; Mack 1999). The implication of these arguments is that any increased inertia and escalation of commitment that comes with dominance might be outweighed by the benefits of greater wealth. In light of these findings, we propose the following:

> H_{1d}: Overall, managers of dominant firms invest more aggressively in the radical innovation relative to the existing product generation than do managers of nondominant firms.

Expectations and Radical Innovation

In the subsequent paragraphs, we develop hypotheses on the role of technology expectations in radical innovation decisions in general. We then consider how these expectations influence dominant and nondominant firms. Throughout the section, we compare the condition in which managers expect the new technology to enhance the existing technology or to make it obsolete with the case in which they expect the new technology to have no impact on existing technology. Thus, the no-effects expectation is the benchmark against which we compare the other two types of expectations: obsolescence and enhancement.

Obsolescence Versus No-Effect Expectations

Expectations of obsolescence cause managers to be less secure about their current course of action (e.g., Jassawala and Shashittal 1998). In this case, the new technology has a negative effect on the success of the current course of action, based as it is on the old, soon-to-be-obsolete technology. Managers who expect obsolescence therefore perceive that continuing with the existing technology will lead to a major loss in market position. Conversely, managers who expect the new technology to have no effect on existing products perceive no such loss (and, therefore, no effect on the success of the current course of action) (see Clark and Montgomery 1996; Grove 1996). Thus,

> H₂: Managers who expect the radical innovation to make existing products obsolete invest more aggressively in the radical innovation relative to the existing product generation than do those who expect the new technology to have no effect on existing products.

Enhancement Versus No-Effect Expectations

What if managers expect that investing in the new technology is likely to enhance the performance of existing products? We argue that these managers invest less aggressively in the new technology than do managers who expect the technology to have no effect. The rationale for this hypothesis rests on the absence of a compelling incentive to switch emphasis from an existing technological base that is expected to be only enhanced by the new technology. Specifically, managers who expect enhancement do not frame investing in the new technology and continuing with the old technology as competing courses of action. Moreover, they perceive that the existing technology plays a significant, enhanced role in the market (e.g., Jassawala and Shashittal 1998). They therefore expect the new technology to have a positive effect on the success of the current course of action. Because the new technology is an exogenous shock, this positive outcome occurs regardless of a firm's own investments in the new technology (Solow 1956). The managers' perceptions of greater success by maintaining the current course of action feeds their inertia (Henderson 1993; Nelson and Winter 1982) and reinforces their commitment to the existing technology. Managers who expect no effect, however, experience less inertia and escalation of commitment, because they receive no such reinforcement. Thus,

> H₃: Managers who expect the radical innovation to enhance existing products invest less aggressively in the radical innovation relative to the existing product generation than do those who expect the new technology to have no effects on existing products.

Interaction of Dominance and Expectations

As we noted previously, there is considerable empirical evidence that some dominant firms invest aggressively in radical new technologies and others do not. What explains this variation in dominant firms' investment in radical innovation? In an attempt to address this question, we examine the interaction effects of firm dominance and managers' technology expectations on the level of investment in radical innovation.

Under expectations of obsolescence, managers of all firms, dominant and nondominant, perceive that maintaining the current course of action will cause a loss in market position. However, dominant firms have more to lose from obsolescence than do their nondominant competitors. Specifically, dominant firms risk losing their strong market position because their success is based on the old technology. Thus, managers of dominant firms perceive the new technology to be a greater threat to their market position than do managers of nondominant firms. Therefore, managers of dominant firms are even more motivated than are those of nondominant firms to break out of their inertia, reduce their commitment to the existing product generation, and invest aggressively in radical innovation. Thus,

> H_4: Dominant firm managers who expect the radical innovation to make existing products obsolete invest more aggressively in the radical innovation relative to the existing product generation than do nondominant firm managers with the same expectations.

We noted previously that when managers expect the new technology to enhance the performance of the existing technology, managers of both dominant and nondominant firms might invest less aggressively than they would otherwise. However, dominant firms expect to gain more than nondominant firms would from the positive influence of the new technology. Specifically, given dominant firms' stronger market position, any positive influence from the new technology on existing products is magnified. Managers of dominant firms therefore expect to be even more successful by maintaining the existing course of action. This perception of renewed (enhanced) success causes dominant firms to be less motivated and more wedded to the status quo when they expect enhancement. Therefore, they invest even less aggressively in radical innovation under this condition. Thus,

> H_5: Dominant firm managers who expect the radical innovation to enhance the performance of existing products invest less aggressively in the radical innovation relative to the existing product generation than do nondominant firm managers with the same expectations.

METHOD

We used two empirical approaches: (1) time-series, cross-sectional analysis in a controlled setting and (2) structured interview–informed survey research combined with archival data in a field setting. The time-series, cross-sectional analysis tests causal links among the key variables being studied. In-depth interviews enabled us to obtain direct, firsthand insights into the actual dynamics of technology expectations and radical innovation. Archival data, together with our survey of managers in an industry confronting radical innovation (i.e., retail banking and the Internet), provide evidence of the applicability of our arguments to a real-world context. By employing multiple methodologies to investigate radical product innovation in a programmatic fashion, we can better ensure the internal and external validity of the research (e.g., Winer 1999). As Jick (1979) notes, multiple and independent methods, such as the ones proposed here, do not share the same weaknesses or potential for bias. Triangulation is particularly appropriate for initial research in an area, because it provides "thick descriptions" of phenomena and facilitates their interpretation.

LAB STUDIES

Research Context

We used the MARKSTRAT2 simulation (Larreche and Gatignon 1990) to test our hypotheses in a controlled setting. MARKSTRAT provides an excellent environment for this research for several reasons, which we outline in Appendix A. We tested our hypotheses over two separate studies. Study 1 tests H_1, which describes competing arguments on the role of dominance in decisions on radical innovation. Study 2 tests hypotheses H_2–H_5, which incorporate the effects of technology expectations on radical innovation. The subsequent sections provide the details of each study and descriptions of the results.

STUDY 1

Subjects and Procedure

In Study 1, we used data from eight MARKSTRAT2 runs (each run involved the creation of one industry), conducted with MBA students at a large public university in California. For each run, we randomly assigned participants to teams of three to four members each and then randomly assigned the teams to 1 of 5 possible firms per industry (in MARKSTRAT there are 5 firms per industry). All participants played the run over seven periods in six of the runs and over ten periods in the other two. Overall, therefore, we gathered data from 40 firms competing across eight runs (industries) over seven to ten periods for a total of 310 observations.

We collected data on each firm's expenditures, market shares, and budgets in each period in the Sonite (existing technology) and Vodite (new technology) markets.[1] We used these variables to test for the relative strength of escalation of commitment, inertia, and wealth, respectively, and the overall effect of dominance on firms' relative expenditure on new technology (H_{1a}–H_{1d}).

Measures

Consistent with our definition, we measured investment aggressiveness in a relative sense: each firm's expenditure in the Vodite market divided by its combined expenditures in the Sonite and Vodite markets. These expenditures include research and development and advertising expenses that are specific to the Sonite and Vodite products.[2] This measure of investment in radical innovation thus measures the firm's emphasis on Vodite investments relative to its overall product investments.[3] We also measured investment in absolute terms: the firm's total investments in the Vodite market.

Recall that the escalation of commitment effect is based on the firm's level of past investments. To test the escalation of commitment effect, we calculated the average cumulative expenditures by the firm in the existing (Sonite) technology until the previous period. The inertia effect is based on the firm's market position. To test the inertia effect, we used the firm's average market share (in MARKSTRAT dollar sales) in the existing technology until the previous period. The wealth effect is based on the firm's financial resources. To test the wealth effect, we used the average cumulative budget available to the firm until the current period.[4] (In MARKSTRAT, a firm's budget is a linear function of its net marketing contribution or profit.) We obtained all this data from the output that MARKSTRAT2 provides to the game administrator. MARKSTRAT2 also provides each team with information on its market share, profits, and several other variables each period.

We also tested the overall effect of dominance on investment in the radically new technology. To do so, we first conducted a principal component factor analysis of the previous three variables (past investment, market share, and budget). We used the factor score from this factor analysis as a consolidated measure of firm dominance (Bollen and Lennox 1991).

Model Formulation

To test our hypotheses, we use a fixed-effects model with a Prais-Winsten regression estimator that accounts for AR(1) serial correlation and computes panel-corrected standard errors (Greene 2000). The fixed-effects specification listed subsequently also enables us to account for unobserved heterogeneity due to team-, firm-, and industry-specific effects. We estimate the following two equations to test hypotheses H_{1a}–H_{1d}, which pertain to the effect of dominance on investment in radically new technology. Equation 1 decomposes the effects of dominance into the escalation of commitment, inertia, and wealth effects. Equation 2 represents the overall effects of dominance (measured with the factor score from the factor analysis described previously) on radical innovation.

(1) $\text{Investment}_{it} = \alpha_0 + \alpha_1$ (average cumulative expenditures in existing technology)$_{i,\,t-1}$

$\qquad + \alpha_2$ (average market share in existing technology)$_{i,t-1}$

$\qquad + \alpha_3$ (average cumulative budget)$_{i,\,t}$

$\qquad + \phi$ (industry average expenditure)

$\qquad + \kappa$ (firm) $+ \nu_i + \varepsilon_{it}.$

(2) $\text{Investment}_{it} = \beta_0 + \beta_1$ (dominance)$_{i,\,t-1} + \lambda$ (industry average expenditure) $+ \gamma$ (firm) $+ \nu_i + \varepsilon_{it},$

where

$\quad$ investment = (new technology expenditure)/(total expenditure in new and existing technology) for relative measure of investment and new technology expenditure for absolute measure of investment,

$\quad$ industry average expenditure = a variable that controls for industry-specific effects,

$\qquad$ firm = a matrix of dummies that control for firm-specific fixed effects,

$\qquad \varepsilon_{it} = \rho\varepsilon_{i,\,t-1} + \eta_{it}, |\rho| < 1, \eta_{it} \sim \text{IIN}(0, \sigma_\eta^2),$ and

$\qquad \nu_i$ = team-specific errors.

Results

Table 65-1 presents the estimation results for Study 1. All reported coefficients reflect standardized values (Kim and Ferree 1981). For this and all subsequent analyses, we also computed the White (1980) general test statistic; the tests indicate that heteroskedasticity is not a problem. We use the terms α_{iR} and β_{iR} to refer to the coefficients based on the relative measure, and we use α_{iA} and β_{iA} to refer to the coefficients based on the absolute measure of investment in radical innovation. We account for industry-specific effects by including an industry-level variable that measures the average total expenditure in each period across all firms in the industry. The firm variable controls for heterogeneity due to firm assignment (e.g., differences in starting positions for Firms 1–5). We only include statistically significant fixed effects in the final regression equation.

The escalation of commitment effect (H_{1a}) implies that a firm with many investments in an existing product generation invests less aggressively in the radical innovation. We found a significant, negative effect of past Sonite expenditures on the

TABLE 65-1 Dominance and Its Facets (Study 1)

Independent Variables	Process	Hypothesized Effect	Relative Vodite Investment		Absolute Vodite Investment	
			Model 1	Model 2	Model 1	Model 2
Expenditures in existing technology	Escalation of commitment	−	−.08*		−.18***	
Market share in existing technology	Inertia	−	−.20**		−.17**	
Budget	Wealth	+	.40***		.24***	
Dominance		+		.40***		.15*
Industry average expenditure			.24***	.22***	.68***	.57***
Firm 2			.32***	.26***		
Firm 3			−.27***		−.79***	
R^2			.38	.28	.42	.31

*$p < .10$.

**$p < .05$.

***$p < .01$.

Note: Models 1 and 2 present the estimation results of Equations 1 and 2, respectively.

aggressiveness with which firms invest in the radical innovation ($\alpha_{1R} = -.08$, $p < .10$; $\alpha_{1A} = -.18$, $p < .01$). The inertia effect (H_{1b}) argues that, other things being equal, managers with strong market positions likely continue with the existing product generation at the expense of the radical innovation. We found that firms with high lagged market shares invest less aggressively in new Vodite products than do other firms ($\alpha_{2R} = -.20$, $p < .05$; $\alpha_{2A} = -.17$, $p < .05$). The wealth effect (H_{1c}) suggests that high profits endow dominant firms with resources that enable them to be more aggressive in their investments in radical innovation than are other firms. The results indicate a positive, significant effect of firms' budgets on investment in radical innovation ($\alpha_{3R} = .40$, $p < .01$; $\alpha_{3A} = .24$, $p < .01$).

We further test the overall effect of dominance (H_{1d}) by estimating Equation 2. The factor score from the factor analysis of the past investment, market share, and wealth variables has a positive coefficient that is significantly different from zero ($\beta_{1R} = .40$, $p < .01$; $\beta_{1A} = .15$, $p < .10$).

Discussion

The Study 1 results suggest that the three facets of dominance—market share, investments, and wealth—affect innovation behavior differently; therefore it is important to account for these differing effects. Overall, dominance has a positive effect on the aggressiveness with which managers pursue radical innovation, but managers might hold different expectations about the likely effects of the new technology on existing products. We manipulate participants' expectations about the effects of the new technology in Study 2.

STUDY 2: EXPERIMENT

In Study 2, we attempt to answer the question, How do expectations about new technology influence managers' product development decisions in dominant and nondominant firms? We used time-series, cross-sectional data to test our causal relationships in a controlled setting.

Subjects and Procedure

Similar to Study 1, we used the MARKSTRAT2 simulation to test the hypotheses.[5] Participants in the simulation were graduate students in business at a public university in Europe. We conducted the study over one semester and used data from six concurrent runs (industries) of the simulation. We randomly assigned participants to teams of three to four members each. We then randomly assigned these teams to firms in one of the six industries. All participants played the game over eight periods. Therefore, we gathered data from 30 firms competing in six industries over eight periods for a total of 240 observations.

We experimentally manipulated (at the industry level) participants' expectations about the radically new technology.[6] We assigned ten teams each (two industries each consisting of five firms) to the enhancement and obsolescence conditions. We assigned the teams in the remaining two industries to the no-effect and control conditions, respectively.

H_2–H_5, which we test in this study, pertain to the role of technology expectations and their interaction with dominance. Because our interaction hypotheses apply only to overall dominance, we did not decompose the overall measure of dominance in this analysis. We did, however, replicate our test of hypotheses H_{1a}–H_{1c} by reestimating Equation 1 with Study 2 data. We also surveyed each team in each period on its perceived dominance (see Appendix B). The correlation between this measure and our archival measure of dominance is high ($r = .84$, $p < .01$), which indicates that our measure of dominance reflects participants' own views of their relative market position.

We introduced the technology expectation manipulations at the end of the fourth period, by which point clear patterns of dominance had emerged in each industry.

Specifically, by the end of the fourth period, the cumulative marketing contribution of firms across industries ranged from $26 million to $486 million. None of the participants had made any investments in the new product generation before this time, and they did not have any market research data on the new product generation for much of the time until we introduced the manipulations. Thus, participants made decisions on the new product after we introduced the technology expectation manipulations.

Manipulations

At the end of the fourth decision period, we provided participants with a memo that contained information on prospects for the radically new technology (see Appendix C). We told firms in the enhancement (obsolescence) conditions that the new technology was likely to make products based on the existing technology more effective (obsolete). We instructed firms in the no-effect (no specific expectations) conditions that the new technology was likely to have no effect (unclear effects) on products based on the existing technology.

As we noted previously, the MARKSTRAT student manual actually suggests that there are no interactions between the existing and the new technologies. To allow for varying expectations about the effects of the new technology, the simulation administrator instructed participants at the start of the simulation to ignore this sentence in the student manual. As part of the cover story for the experiment, the administrator told participants that the game parameters had been modified at the start and that the effects of the new technology were unclear. The administrator also noted that a memo with information about the likely effects of the new technology was forthcoming. Manipulation checks indicate that the cover story worked as intended.

Manipulation Checks

To further understand the process underlying participants' investment decisions in each condition, we also surveyed each team on its perceptions of the potential for gains or losses in the industry in the next period (the two items for this perceived loss scale are provided in Appendix B). We collected this perceptual data for each period after the fourth period, when we distributed the memo. The differences in covariance-adjusted means of perceived loss across conditions are as expected. Specifically, the difference between obsolescence and no effect (1.82, $p < .05$) and enhancement and no effect (-6.38, $p < .05$) is statistically significant and in the right direction. The difference between the no-effect and no-specific-expectations conditions is not statistically significant at $p < .05$. These data provided additional evidence for our manipulations.

Model Specification

To test hypotheses H_2–H_5, we again used the Prais-Winsten regression estimator to estimate the following fixed-effects model with AR(1) errors.

$$
\begin{aligned}
(3) \quad \text{Investment}_{it} = {} & \beta_0 + \beta_1 (\text{dominance})_{i, t-1} + \beta_2 (\text{enhancement})_i \\
& + \beta_3 (\text{obsolescence})_i \\
& + \beta_4 (\text{dominance}_{i, t-1} \times \text{enhancement})_i \\
& + \beta_5 (\text{dominance}_{i, t-1} \times \text{obsolescence})_i \\
& + \gamma (\text{loan})_{i, t-1} \\
& + \lambda (\text{industry average expenditure}) \\
& + \tau (\text{firm}) + v_i + \varepsilon_{it}.
\end{aligned}
$$

Enhancement and obsolescence are represented as dummy variables. Participants in the no-specific-expectations and no-effect conditions behaved similarly on key variables of interest. Therefore, we pooled these two groups into one no-effects condition. The coefficients for the enhancement and obsolescence conditions are therefore estimated relative to this control condition. The loan amount (if any) is represented by the

TABLE 65-2 Facets of Dominance (Study 2 Control Condition)

Independent Variables	Hypothesized Effect	Relative Vodite Investment	Absolute Vodite Investment
Expenditures in existing technology	−	−.17*	.06
Market share in existing technology	−	−1.04***	−.75**
Budget	+	1.24 ***	.96***
Industry average expenditure		1.13*	.56
Firm 3			.76***
Loan		.45**	.38*
R^2		.41	.60

*$p < .10$.

**$p < .05$.

***$p < .01$.

TABLE 65-3 Dominance and Expectations (Study 2)

Independent Variables	Hypothesized Effect	Relative Vodite Investment	Absolute Vodite Investment
Dominance	+	.18**	.55**
Obsolescence	+	.24**	.24*
Enhancement	−	−.52**	−.41*
Dominance × obsolescence	+	.21*	.34*
Dominance × enhancement	−	.06	.01
Industry average expenditure		.62**	.43*
Firm 3		.35**	.37**
Firm 5		.37**	.22*
Loan		−.04	.36**
R^2		.57	.42

*$p < .05$.

**$p < .01$.

loan variable; other variables are as defined previously. Because the objective of this study is to test the effects of technology expectations on investment behavior, we only used data collected after the period in which the memo with the experimental manipulation had been administered (n = 120).

Results

Replication Tests of H_{1a}–H_{1c}

Because hypotheses H_{1a}–H_{1c} apply to investment behavior in the absence of obsolescence or enhancement expectations, we estimated Equation 1 only for those teams that fell into the control condition. This analysis is a conceptual replication of the corresponding analysis in Study 1. The results in Table 65-2 are consistent with our hypotheses (with the exception of the escalation of commitment effect on absolute investment) and provide further support for hypotheses H_{1a}–H_{1c}.

Main Effects of Expectations

H_2 suggests that managers who expect a new technology to make existing products obsolete invest more aggressively in radical innovation than do managers who expect the new technology to have no effect on existing products. The results support this hypothesis (see Table 65-3). Specifically, obsolescence has a positive, statistically significant main effect on investment in radical innovation ($\beta_{3R} = .24, p < .01; \beta_{3A} = .24, p < .05$).

For the enhancement versus no-expectation condition, H_3 proposes that managers invest less aggressively in a radical innovation than do managers who expect no effect. In support of H_3, the coefficient of enhancement is negative and statistically significant ($\beta_{2R} = -.52, p < .01; \beta_{2A} = -.41, p < .05$).

Interactions of Dominance and Expectations

H_4 predicts that, given expectations of obsolescence, managers of dominant firms likely invest more aggressively in radical innovation than do managers of nondominant firms. As predicted, the coefficient for the interaction of dominance and obsolescence is positive and significant ($\beta_{5R} = .21, p < .05; \beta_{5A} = .34, p < .05$), in support of H_3.

H_5 predicts that, given expectations of enhancement, managers of dominant firms likely invest less aggressively in the new technology than do managers of nondominant firms. This hypothesis is not supported: The coefficient for the interaction of dominance and enhancement is not significantly different from zero ($\beta_{4R} = .06, p = .26$; $\beta_{4A} = .01, p = .28$).

Main Effect of Dominance

The results in Table 65-3 indicate that the main effect of dominance is positive and significant ($\beta_{1R} = .18, p < .01; \beta_{1A} = .55, p < .01$). The results support H_{1d}: Managers of dominant firms tend to invest more aggressively in radical innovation than do managers of non-dominant firms.[7]

Discussion

Overall, the results indicate that technology expectations play a complex role in driving investments in radical innovations. An expectation of obsolescence causes both dominant and nondominant firms to invest significantly greater proportions of their resources toward radical innovations than do firms in industries in which expectations of no effect are prevalent. The situation is different in an industry in which the enhancement expectation is prevalent. Both dominant and nondominant firms invest significantly lower proportions toward radical innovation in such industries, compared with industries facing expectations of obsolescence or no effect. Moreover, regardless of whether the expectation is one of obsolescence or enhancement, expectations have a greater effect on investment behavior for dominant firms than for nondominant firms.

Given its longitudinal and experimental design, the MARKSTRAT-based study helps ensure internal validity. Study 3 presents insights from a real industry and practicing managers involved in making actual financial decisions.

STUDY 3: FIELD STUDY OF RETAIL BANKING

The U.S. retail banking industry during 1999 and 2000 proved an excellent setting for our field study (see Schotema 2001). We provide details in Appendix D. The following sections describe the full-scale field study, in which we attempt to quantify the effects of expectations and dominance on bricks-and-mortar banks' investments in Internet banking. (Additional details on the methodological aspects of the study are available in Chandy, Prabhu, and Antia's [2003] work.)

Unit of Analysis and Sampling

Our unit of analysis is the U.S. retail banking division for each bank (the key informant was the officer in charge of U.S. retail banking or the equivalent). We used a frequently updated and detailed database published by Thomson/Polk to construct our sample frame, which consisted of 550 U.S. retail banks, chosen randomly from the population of U.S. retail banks. Our data collection efforts yielded a total of 189 usable questionnaires, representing a 39.4% response rate. The mean number of employees at responding institutions was 428 (standard deviation = 2933) and the mean number of bricks-and-mortar branches was 27 (standard deviation = 147). Of the 189 usable questionnaire responses, 129 were from publicly held retail banks. We also checked for nonresponse bias; results indicate that such bias is unlikely.[8]

Measures

The final measures for each construct appear in Appendix B. Table 65-4 reports the correlation matrix and descriptive statistics for these measures.[9] The scale of relative

TABLE 65-4 Descriptive Statistics and Correlation Matrix (Field Survey)

	Mean	Standard Deviation	Relative Internet Investment	Absolute Internet Investment	Dominance	Enhancement	Obsolescence	No Effect	Willingness to Cannibalize
Relative Internet investment	12.09	5.84							
Absolute Internet investment	13.49	5.85	.84***						
Dominance	0	1	.12*	.11*					
Enhancement	.58	.49	−.01	.00	.06				
Obsolescence	.10	.29	.07	.08	−.03	−.38***			
No effect	.32	.46	−.04	−.06	−.04	−.81***	−.22***		
Willingness to cannibalize	12.42	3.41	.24***	.22***	−.08	.00	−.04	.02	
Public ownership	1.66	.47	−.23***	−.22***	−.15**	−.11*	.10*	.07	−.08

*p < .10.

**p < .05.

***p < .01.

investment comprises three items with an α of .88, and the scale of absolute investment comprises four items with an α of .86. To further test the convergent validity of our measure, we also included a third, nonperceptual measure of investment in the survey (see Appendix B). The correlations between this measure and our dependent measures of relative and absolute investment are .67 ($p < .01$) and .63 ($p < .01$), respectively.

We measured expectations (obsolescence, enhancement, and no effect) by asking respondents to allocate 100 points to reflect their beliefs about the likely impact of the Internet on bricks-and-mortar banking, both in the short term (next two years) and in the long term (next ten years). Recall that our hypotheses compare the behavior of firms that expect obsolescence and enhancement with that of firms that expect no effect. To ensure consistency with our hypotheses and comparability between the experimental and the field studies, we averaged the short- and long-term variables and created two dummy variables (enhancement and obsolescence) to represent the three conditions. We categorize a firm as expecting enhancement (or obsolescence) if it allocates more points to that condition relative to the median number of points allocated to that condition across all firms.[10]

Consistent with the in-depth interviews we conducted and the measure of dominance adopted in Studies 1 and 2, we measured dominance as a composite of three accounting variables. We used the average dollar value of bricks-and-mortar assets (net of depreciation) as a measure of investment in the existing product, average dollar value of deposits as a measure of market share,[11] and average net equity (total equity capital net of preferred and common stock, surplus, and undivided profits from bricks-and-mortar operations) as a measure of cumulative earnings. These averages are over a six-year period before the survey (using five- and four-year averages produces consistent results). To minimize common method bias, we collected archival data on the preceding variables from the Federal Deposit Insurance Corporation. We controlled for individual firms' willingness to cannibalize with a three-item, seven-point scale adapted from Chandy and Tellis (1998). In addition, we controlled for banks' ownership with a dummy variable coded as 1 for publicly owned banks and as 0 otherwise.

Analysis

We regressed firms' investments on the hypothesized explanatory variables, including the moderators and control variables, as depicted in Equation 4. We used Lance's (1988) residual centering approach to reduce multicollinearity in the interaction terms.

$$(4) \; \text{Investment} = \beta_0 + \beta_1 (\text{dominance}) + \beta_2 (\text{obsolescence})$$
$$+ \beta_3 (\text{enhancement})$$
$$+ \beta_4 (\text{dominance} \times \text{obsolescence})$$
$$+ \beta_5 (\text{dominance} \times \text{enhancement})$$
$$+ \beta_6 (\text{willingness to cannibalize})$$
$$+ \beta_7 (\text{public ownership}) + \varepsilon.$$

Results

Table 65-5 presents regression coefficients for Equation 4. The models are statistically significant ($F = 11.74, p < .01$; $F = 26.62, p < .01$, for relative and absolute measures, respectively) and explain a significant percentage of variation in Internet banking investments ($R^2 = .14$ and .12, respectively).

In support of H_{1d}, the results suggest that, in general, managers of dominant firms invest more aggressively in radical innovation than do managers of nondominant firms ($\beta_{1R} = .12, p < .01$; $\beta_{1A} = .11, p < .01$). We also find significant support for H_2 ($\beta_{2R} = .12, p < .05$; $\beta_{2A} = .13, p < .05$). However, we do not find support for H_3, which involves the main effect of expectations of enhancement ($\beta_{3R} = -.00$; $\beta_{3A} = .02$).

H_4 is supported ($\beta_{4R} = .07, p < .01$; $\beta_{4A} = .04, p < .05$), indicating that dominant firm managers who expect the new technology to make existing products obsolete invest more aggressively in radical innovation than do managers of nondominant firms

TABLE 65-5   Dominance and Expectations (Field Survey)

Independent Variables	Hypothesized Effect	Relative Internet Investment	Absolute Internet Investment
Dominance	+	.12**	.11**
Obsolescence	+	.12*	.13*
Enhancement	–	–.00	.02
Dominance × obsolescence	+	.07**	.04*
Dominance × enhancement	–	–.09*	–.07*
Willingness to cannibalize		.24**	.21**
Public ownership		–.19**	–.19**
R^2		.14	.12

*$p < .05$.

**$p < .01$.

TABLE 65-6   Facets of Dominance (Field Survey, Control Condition)

Independent Variables	Hypothesized Effect	Relative Investment	Absolute Investment
Assets in existing technology	–	–3.37**	–3.01**
Deposits in existing technology	–	3.38**	2.95**
Net equity	+	.22*	.26*
Willingness to cannibalize		.29*	.27*
Public ownership		–.13	–.10
R^2		.19	.16

*$p < .05$.

**$p < .01$.

with the same expectations. We also find support for H_5, which posits that dominant firm managers who expect the new technology to enhance the performance of existing products invest less aggressively in radical innovation than do managers of nondominant firms with the same expectations ($\beta_{5R} = -.09, p < .05; \beta_{5A} = -.07, p < .05$). As we expected, banks with greater willingness to cannibalize ($\beta_{6R} = .24, p < .01; \beta_{6A} = .21, p < .01$) invest more in radical innovation, though public banks invest less in Internet banking ($\beta_{7R} = -.19, p < .01; \beta_{7A} = -.19, p < .01$).

Finally, Table 65-6 presents the parameter estimates for the replication tests of hypotheses H_{1a}–H_{1c} using Equation 1. These results suffer from multicollinearity and should be interpreted with caution. The results in Table 65-6 are mostly consistent with our hypotheses (with the exception of the effect of deposits on investment, which is positive instead of negative). Thus, we find some additional support for H_{1a} and H_{1c} in the Internet banking context.

DISCUSSION

Contributions to Research

This article makes three main contributions to the research on radical innovation (for a summary of results across measures and contexts, see Tables 65-7 and 65-8). First, we reconcile the opposing views in the literature on the relationship between dominance and radical innovation. Existing research typically equates dominance with related though conceptually distinct proxies, such as firm size, and rarely integrates the three facets of dominance to assess its overall effects on radical innovation. We show that relying solely on individual proxies leads only to an incomplete picture and, more significant, to misleading conclusions. Dominance is a rich composite of all three facets. Only when these facets are examined in a composite manner can the overall effects of dominance on radical innovation be properly identified.

TABLE 65-7 Summary of Hypotheses and Results on Facets of Dominance

			Studies and Measures of Radical Innovation					
			Study 1		Study 2		Study 3	
Independent Variables	Hypothesis	Predicted Effect	Relative Investment	Absolute Investment	Relative Investment	Absolute Investment	Relative Investment	Absolute Investment
Expenditures in existing technology	H_{1a}	−	Supported	Supported	Supported	Not supported	Supported	Supported
Market share in existing technology	H_{1b}	−	Supported	Supported	Supported	Supported	Not supported	Not supported
Wealth	H_{1c}	+	Supported	Supported	Supported	Supported	Supported	Supported
Dominance	H_{1d}	+	Supported	Supported	Supported	Supported	Supported	Supported

TABLE 65-8 Summary of Hypotheses and Results on Expectations and Dominance

			Studies and Measures of Radical Innovation			
			Study 2		Study 3	
Independent Variables	Hypothesis	Predicted Effect	Relative Investment	Absolute Investment	Relative Investment	Absolute Investment
Obsolescence	H_2	+	Supported	Supported	Supported	Supported
Enhancement	H_3	−	Supported	Supported	Not supported	Not supported
Dominance × obsolescence	H_4	+	Supported	Supported	Supported	Supported
Dominance × enhancement	H_5	−	Not supported	Not supported	Supported	Supported

Second, we help explain why some dominant firms invest aggressively in radical innovation and others do not. We examine the role of expectations; in particular, we examine how different expectations increase or decrease managers' motivation to maintain the status quo rather than invest in radical innovation. Research so far has not accounted for the effect of expectations on investment in radical innovation. Most research has instead focused on evaluating the impact of the new technology in hindsight, that is, after it has been introduced. Yet, as we argue and show, managers form expectations and make investments in radical innovation before the eventual effects are evident. Managers' a priori expectations strongly affect their investment decisions. To the best of our knowledge, our study is the first to incorporate the important role such expectations play. Our findings suggest that the fear of obsolescence is a greater incentive to invest in new technologies than is the lure of enhancement. Our findings also suggest that current research is overly pessimistic in portraying dominant firms as laggards in pursuing radically new technologies.

Contributions to Practice

Our results have implications for managers of both dominant and nondominant firms. For dominant firms, the results suggest that they have less to worry about than some of the existing research might lead them to believe. Although some aspects of dominance—greater investments and stronger market position in the existing product generation—reduce dominant firms' motivation to invest in radical innovation, dominant firms' greater wealth compensates for this reduction. Across three studies—two in the lab and one in the real-world context of Internet banking—dominance, as an overall composite of its various facets, has a positive impact on investment in radical innovation.

Our findings also point to an important way that dominant firms can overcome the negative effects of inertia and escalation of commitment. When managers of dominant firms believe that the new technology is likely to make the existing products obsolete, their behavior hardly suggests sloth or inertia. This finding may partly explain the energetically innovative behavior of firms such as Intel and Microsoft, where such fear of obsolescence is a strong part of the corporate mind-set (Gates, Myrvhold, and Rinearson 1995; Grove 1996). The results suggest that such "paranoia" causes firms to pursue investments aggressively in radically new technologies.

Our results also show that dominant firm managers who believe that the new technology is likely to increase sales of their existing products actually invest less aggressively in the new technology than do managers who believe otherwise. Consequently, the fear of loss as a result of obsolescence appears to be a much stronger motivator of investments in radical innovation among such firms than is the lure of gains from enhancement. This result has important implications for product champions and change agents trying to steer a dominant firm toward a new technology. Such persons should use obsolescence rather than enhancement as the rallying cry for their troops.

APPENDIX A: SUITABILITY OF MARKSTRAT CONTEXT

First, decisions on new technology are intrinsic in the MARKSTRAT decision environment. Participants make decisions about the adoption of a new technology and develop radically new products (Vodite) even as they manage portfolios of products based on an existing technology (Sonite). More specifically, the Vodite fits our definition of a radical innovation as a product that involves technology and marketing skills that are new to the industry (see Garcia and Calantone 2002). For example, the MARKSTRAT2 student's manual describes Vodites as products that come from "a basic technological breakthrough" and that "satisfy an entirely different need than that of the Sonites" (Larreche and Gatignon 1990). Second, managers and academics alike consider MARKSTRAT a realistic simulation of the real world (Glazer and Weiss 1993; Kinnear and Klammer 1987). Third, researchers have frequently used the simulation to study how managers make decisions (e.g., Glazer, Steckel, and Winer 1992; Glazer and Weiss 1993). Therefore, MARKSTRAT provides a well-tested research environment. Fourth, participants make decisions on various business issues, including targeting and positioning, advertising, sales force, pricing, and distribution (Larreche and Gatignon 1990) in addition to technology investment decisions. Because decision makers' attention is not focused on technology and new product decisions, MARKSTRAT provides a relatively conservative means of testing our research hypotheses. Fifth, the MARKSTRAT context enables us to collect data on (1) the decision-making processes used by participants over time and (2) the actual decisions they made during this period. This longitudinal information is extremely difficult to obtain in the field.

APPENDIX B: MEASURES

Items marked with an asterisk are reverse coded. All Likert-type items are seven-item, "strongly agree" to "strongly disagree," and have Cronbach's alpha and item parameter values for the factor structure matrix reported.

Measures of Constructs Used in Study 2

Perceived Dominance

1. Our performance so far has been better than that of everyone else in our industry.
2. We have had few serious threats to our position as industry leaders so far.
3. We have led the market from the start.

Perceived Loss

How would you characterize the situation you face in the MARKSTRAT industry in the next period?

a)   1   2   3   4   5   6   7
    Potential   Potential
    for loss   for gain*

b)   1   2   3   4   5   6   7
    Positive   Negative
    Situation   situation

Measures of Constructs Used in Study 3

Investment in Internet Banking

Listed below are statements regarding your Internet-related investments:

(A) in general
(B) relative to bricks-and-mortar operations
(C) relative to total development expenditures

Please indicate the extent to which you agree or disagree with the following statements.

Measure of Absolute Investments in Internet Banking ($\alpha = .86$)
(A) Our Internet related investments in general:

1. We have done very little with respect to Internet banking at our bank.*   .92
2. Our bank has only a token Web presence.*   .74
3. We haven't done much yet to develop our Internet banking capabilities.*   .93
4. Most of our development expenditures are targeted toward Internet banking efforts.   .57

Measure of Relative Investments in Internet Banking ($\alpha = .88$)
(B) Relative to our bricks-and-mortar operations:

1. We have not invested aggressively in Internet banking.*   .96
2. Our bank is yet to make significant investments in Internet banking.*   .94
3. We have earmarked few managerial resources to Internet banking in the short term.*   .71

Nonperceptual Measure of Investments in Internet Banking
(C) Relative to total development expenditures:
Please indicate the percentage of your bank's development expenditures on Internet banking in the last year, relative to total development expenditures: _____%

Willingness to Cannibalize ($\alpha = .70$)

1. Our bank's investments in bricks-and-mortar branches make switching to Internet banking difficult.* .74
2. We rely too much on our bricks-and-mortar branches to switch focus to Internet banking.* .78
3. We are reluctant to cannibalize our investments in bricks-and-mortar branches.* .63

Technology Expectations

Please indicate your expectations about the likely effects of the Internet on bricks-and-mortar banking IN GENERAL (i.e., across all retail banks), by allocating 100 points across the following three alternative scenarios.

For example, if you strongly believe that Internet banking is very likely to have **no effect** on bricks-and-mortar banking in the next two years, you could allocate the 100 points above as follows: (a) 0 points, (b) 0 points, and (c) 100 points. If you believe all three scenarios are equally likely, you could allocate the 100 points above as follows: (a) 33.3 points, (b) 33.3 points, and (c) 33.3 points.

	Points Awarded	
Scenario	In the Next Two Years	In the Next Ten Years
1. Internet banking is likely to make bricks-and-mortar banking *obsolete.*		
2. Internet banking is likely to *enhance* bricks-and-mortar banking.		
3. Internet banking is likely to have *no effect* on bricks-and-mortar banking.		

APPENDIX C: EXPERIMENTAL MANIPULATIONS

To: XXX Industry Participants
From: Technology Marketing Consultants, Inc.
CC: MARKTSTRAT Administrator
Date: XX/XX/XX
Subject: How will Vodite technology affect the Sonite industry?

Per your request, we conducted an extensive study of the likely effects of the Vodite technology on the Sonite industry. This study involved analysis of multiple sources of data, including the following:

- In-depth interviews with 78 leading technology and market experts
- A survey of 2132 likely Vodite buyers
- An observational study of product usage patterns in 165 selected households in a representative test market
- Historical data on sales and adoption patterns of other (comparable) consumer durable goods

Obsolescence Manipulation, Emphases in Original

Based on the results of this analysis, it is our opinion that products based on the Vodite technology are *quite likely* to make Sonite products *obsolete.* Vodites fulfill similar needs relative to Sonites and serve similar customers. Yet the performance of Vodite-based products is likely to be superior to Sonite products. For example, the introduction of tape recorders decreased the sales of gramophones. The Vodite technology is also projected to offer greater opportunities for performance improvement relative to the Sonite product category. Thus, our analysis indicates that Sonite sales will probably drop substantially as the Vodite technology is developed and introduced to the market.

Enhancement Manipulation, Emphases in Original

Based on the results of this analysis, it is our opinion that products based on the Vodite technology are *quite likely* to make Sonite products *more effective* than before. Vodites fulfill similar needs relative to Sonites and serve similar customers. Moreover, their performance characteristics are likely to *complement* those of the Sonite products. For example, the introduction of camcorders led to an increase in the sale of videocassette recorders. The Vodite technology is also projected to offer greater opportunities for performance improvement in the Sonite product category. Thus, our analysis indicates that Sonite sales will probably increase substantially as the Vodite technology is developed and introduced to the market.

No-Effect Manipulation, Emphases in Original

Based on the results of this analysis, it is our opinion that products based on the Vodite technology are *quite likely* to have *no effect* on Sonite products. Vodites fulfill somewhat different needs relative to Sonites. The performance characteristics of Vodite-based products are likely to be *different* from Sonite products. For example, the introduction of microwave ovens had no effect on the sales of conventional ovens. Performance improvement in the Vodite technology is also projected to be independent of any improvements in the Sonite product category. Thus, our analysis indicates that Sonite sales will probably be unaffected as the Vodite technology is developed and introduced to the market.

Control Condition

Our analysis indicates little consensus among experts and consumers on how the Vodite technology will affect Sonite products. Three different scenarios are possible.

- The Vodite technology may make Sonite products obsolete, leading to a decrease in Sonite sales. For example the introduction of tape recorders decreased the sales of gramophones.
- The Vodite technology may make Sonite products more effective, leading to an increase in Sonite sales. For example, the introduction of camcorders led to an increase in the sale of videocassette recorders.
- The Vodite technology may have no effect on Sonite products. For example, the introduction of microwave ovens had no effect on the sales of conventional ovens.

Given the uncertainty in the market at the present time, we are unable to provide any definitive forecasts on which of these three scenarios is most likely to come true.

APPENDIX D: SUITABILITY OF INTERNET BANKING CONTEXT

First, Internet banking fits our definition of radical innovation. In the banking context, the World Wide Web is widely considered an innovation that caused discontinuities both in the technology embedded in new products that employed it and in the marketing skills needed to market the products (Schotema 2001; for a more general discussion of the World Wide Web and radical innovation, see also Garcia and Calantone 2002). Internet banking was, especially at the time of the study, salient in the minds of banking executives (Fraser 1996). Yet only a handful of banks had achieved the ability to conduct transactions over the Internet during 1999 and 2000. Specifically, according to data from the Online Banking Report, only 319 (3.12%) of the 10,239 banks operating in the United States in 1999 had Internet transaction capability by the end of that year, and only 462 (4.62%) of the 10,006 banks operating in the United States in 2000 had Internet transaction capability by the end of that year. The banks' actions with respect to Internet banking were considered likely to have considerable impact on their competitive positions going forward. Second, our research also revealed considerable variance in opinions about the likely effects of the Internet on bricks-and-mortar banking. Third, U.S. banking firms vary considerably in market positions, assets, and resources, which thereby enabled us to test the effects of dominance on innovation.

Structured interviews with 14 industry executives with diverse designations (chief information officer, chief technology officer, e-commerce director, head of retail banking, president) provided further confirmation of the suitability of the Internet banking context for our research on radical innovation. From the interviews, it became clear that some managers expected Internet banking to make bricks-and-mortar banking obsolete in the not-too-distant future, but others expected Internet banking to enhance bricks-and-mortar banking. These two expectations closely fit the two key conditions that are of theoretical interest to us: obsolescence and enhancement.

About the Authors

Rajesh K. Chandy is Assistant Professor of Marketing, Carlson School of Management, University of Minnesota. Jaideep C. Prabhu is Assistant Professor of Marketing, Judge Institute of Management, University of Cambridge. Kersi D. Antia is Assistant Professor of Marketing and Earl H. Orser/London Life Faculty Fellow, Richard Ivey School of Business, University of Western Ontario. This research was supported by a grant from the Marketing Science Institute. The authors thank Raul Rivadeneyra, Bharat Sud, and Pratik Sharma for help with data collection; Kathy Jocz for help in securing access to managers; and Don Barclay, Mark Bergen, Ed Blair, Niraj Dawar, Raj Echambadi, Robert Fisher, Yany Gregoire, Brigitte Hopstaken, Mike Houston, George John, Eli Jones, Akshay Rao, Gerry Tellis, Mark Vandenbosch, Eden Yin, and participants at seminars at University of Houston, University of Central Florida, and University of Minnesota for their valuable input.

References

Anderson, Philip and Michael L. Tushman (1990), "Technological Discontinuities and Dominant Designs: A Cyclical Model of Technological Change," *Administrative Science Quarterly,* 35 (December), 604–633.

Armstrong, J. Scott and Terry S. Overton (1977), "Estimating Non-response Bias in Mail Surveys," *Journal of Marketing Research,* 14 (August), 396–402.

Bain, J. (1968), *Industrial Organization.* New York: John Wiley & Sons.

Bazerman, Max (1994), *Judgment in Managerial Decision Making,* 3rd ed. New York: John Wiley & Sons.

Blundell, Richard, Rachel Griffith, and John Van Reenen (1999), "Market Share, Market Value, and Innovation in a Panel of British Manufacturing Firms," *Review of Economic Studies,* 66 (July), 529–54.

Bollen, Kenneth and Richard Lennox (1991), "Conventional Wisdom on Measurement: A Structural Equation Perspective," *Psychological Bulletin,* 110 (September), 305–314.

Borenstein, Severin (1990), "Airline Mergers, Airport Dominance, and Market Power," *American Economic Review Papers and Proceedings,* 80 (2), 400–404.

——— (1991), "The Dominant-Firm Advantage in Multi-Product Industries: Evidence from the U.S. Airlines," *Quarterly Journal of Economics,* 106 (4), 1237–66.

Boulding, William, Ruskin Morgan, and Richard Staelin (1997), "Pulling the Plug to Stop the New Product Drain," *Journal of Marketing Research,* 34 (February), 164–76.

Brockner, Joel and Jeffrey Z. Rubin (1985), *Entrapment in Escalating Conflicts: A Social Psychological Analysis.* New York: Springer-Verlag.

Chandy, Rajesh, Jaideep C. Prabhu, and Kersi D. Antia (2003), "What Will the Future Bring? Technology Expectations, Dominance, and Radical Product Innovation," Working Paper #02-122. Cambridge, MA: Marketing Science Institute.

——— and Gerard Tellis (1998), "Organizing for Radical Product Innovation: The Overlooked Role of Willingness to Cannibalize," *Journal of Marketing Research,* 35 (November), 474–87.

——— and ——— (2000), "The Incumbent's Curse? Incumbency, Size, and Radical Product Innovation," *Journal of Marketing,* 64 (July), 1–17.

Christensen, Clayton (1997), *The Innovator's Dilemma: When New Technologies Cause Great Firms to Fail.* Boston: Harvard Business School Press.

Clark, Bruce H. and David B. Montgomery (1996), "Perceiving Competitive Reactions: The Value of Accuracy (and Paranoia)," *Marketing Letters,* 7 (March), 115–29.

Cohen, Wesley M. (1995), "Empirical Studies of Innovative Activity," in *Handbook of the Economics of Innovation and Technological Change,* Paul Stoneman, ed. Cambridge, MA: Blackwell, 1059–1107.

——— and Richard C. Levin (1989), "Empirical Studies of Innovation and Market Structure," in *Handbook of Industrial Organization,* Vol. 2, R. Schmalensee and R.D.

Willig, eds. New York: Elsevier Science Publishers, 182–264.

Cooper, Arnold C. and Dan Schendel (1976), "Strategic Responses to Technological Threats," *Business Horizons,* 19 (1), 61–69.

Dosi, G. (1982), "Technological Paradigms and Technological Trajectories," *Research Policy,* 11 (3), 147–62.

Ettlie, J.E. and A. Rubenstein (1987), "Firm Size and Product Innovation," *Journal of Product Innovation Management,* 4 (June), 89–108.

Fraser, Jill (1996), "Will Banking Go Virtual?" *Inc. Technology,* 18 (13), 49.

Garcia, Rosanna and Roger Calantone (2002), "A Critical Look at Technological Innovation Typology and Innovativeness Terminology: A Literature Review," *Journal of Product Innovation Management,* 19 (February), 110–32.

Gates, Bill, Nathan Myrvhold, and Peter Rinearson (1995), *The Road Ahead.* New York: Viking.

Glazer, Rashi, Joel Steckel, and Russell Winer (1992), "Locally Rational Decision Making: The Distracting Effect of Information on Managerial Performance," *Management Science,* 38 (February), 212–26.

——— and Allen Weiss (1993), "Marketing in Turbulent Environments: Decision Processes and the Time-Sensitivity of Information," *Journal of Marketing Research,* 30 (November), 509–521.

Greene, William (2000), *Econometric Analysis.* Upper Saddle River, NJ: Prentice Hall.

Grove, Andrew (1996), *Only the Paranoid Survive.* New York: Currency Doubleday.

Hamel, Gary (1999), "Bringing Silicon Valley Inside," *Harvard Business Review,* 77 (September–October), 71–84.

——— (2001), "Innovation's New Math," *Fortune,* 144 (July 9), 130–33.

Hannan, M.T. and J. Freeman (1989), *Organizational Ecology.* Cambridge, MA: Harvard University Press.

Henderson, R. (1993), "Underinvestment and Incompetence As Responses to Radical Innovation: Evidence from the Photolithographic Alignment Equipment Industry," *RAND Journal of Economics,* 24 (2), 248–71.

Jassawala, Awan R. and Hemant C. Shashittal (1998), "Accelerating Technology Transfer: Thinking About Organizational Pronoia," *Journal of Engineering and Technology Management,* 15 (June), 153–57.

Jelinek, Mariann and Claudia Schoonhoven (1990), *The Innovation Marathon: Lessons from High Technology Firms.* Cambridge, MA: Blackwell.

Jick, Todd D. (1979), "Mixing Qualitative and Quantitative Methods: Triangulation in Action," *Administrative Science Quarterly,* 24 (December), 602–611.

Kahneman, Daniel and Amos Tversky (1979), "Prospect Theory: An Analysis of Decisions Under Risk," *Econometrica,* 47 (2), 263–91.

Kim, Jae-On and G. Donald Ferree Jr. (1981), "Standardization in Causal Analysis," in *Linear Models in Social Research,* Peter V. Marsden, ed. Beverly Hills, CA: Sage Publications, 22–43.

Kinnear, Thomas C. and Sharon K. Klammer (1987), "Management Perspectives on MARKSTRAT: The GE Experience and Beyond," *Journal of Business Research,* 15 (November), 491–502.

Lance, Charles E. (1988), "Residual Centering, Exploratory and Confirmatory Moderator Analysis, and Decomposition of Effects in Path Models Containing Interactions," *Applied Psychological Measurement,* 12 (June), 163–75.

Larreche, Jean-Claude and Hubert Gatignon (1990), *MARKSTRAT 2.* Palo Alto, CA: Scientific Press.

Leonard-Barton, D. (1992), "Core Capabilities and Core Rigidity: A Paradox in Managing New Product Development," *Strategic Management Journal,* 13 (March–April), 111–25.

Mack, Toni (1999), "Gentle Giant," *Forbes,* 163 (January 25), 93.

Miller, Danny (1990), *The Icarus Paradox: How Exceptional Companies Bring About Their Own Downfall: New Lessons in the Dynamics of Corporate Success, Decline, and Renewal.* New York: HarperBusiness.

Nelson, R. and S. Winter (1982), *An Evolutionary Theory of Economic Change.* Cambridge, MA: Belknap.

Neter, J., W. Wasserman, and M. Kutner (1985), *Applied Linear Statistical Models.* Homewood, IL: Richard D. Irwin.

Nohria, Nitin and Ranjay Gulati (1996), "Is Slack Good or Bad for Innovation," *Academy of Management Journal,* 39 (5), 1245–65.

Ohmae, K. (1984), *The Mind of the Strategist: Business Planning for Competitive Advantage.* New York: McGraw-Hill.

Poole, Marshall S., Andrew Van de Ven, Kevin Dooley, and Michael Holmes (2000), *Organizational Change and Innovation Processes: Theory and Methods for Research.* New York: Oxford University Press.

Scherer, F.M. (1992), "Schumpeter and Plausible Capitalism," *Journal of Economic Literature,* 30 (September), 1416–33.

Schotema, Robert (2001), *Electronic Banking: The Ultimate Guide to Business and Technology of Online Banking.* Veenendaal, Netherlands: SCN Education BV.

Schumpeter, J.A. (1942), *Capitalism, Socialism, and Democracy.* New York: Harper.

Solow, Robert M. (1956), "A Contribution to the Theory of Economic Growth," *Quarterly Journal of Economics,* 70 (February), 65–94.

Speier, Cherie and Viswanath Venkatesh (2002), "The Hidden Minefields in the Adoption of Sales Force Automation Technologies," *Journal of Marketing,* 66 (July), 98–111.

Staw, Barry M. (1981), "The Escalation of Commitment to a Course of Action," *Academy of Management Review,* 6 (October), 577–87.

Utterback, J.M. (1994), *Mastering the Dynamics of Innovation.* Boston: Harvard Business School Press.

Weick, Karl E. (1967), "Organizations in the Laboratory," in *Methods of Organizational Research,* Victor H. Vroom, ed. Pittsburgh: University of Pittsburgh Press.

White, H. (1980), "A Heteroskedasticity-Consistent Covariance Matrix Estimator and a Direct Test for Heteroskedasticity," *Econometrica,* 48 (5), 817–38.

Winer, Russell S. (1999), "Experimentation in the 21st Century: The Importance of External Validity," *Journal of the Academy of Marketing Science,* 27 (Summer), 349–58.

Zucker, Lynne and Michael Darby (1997), "Present at the Biotechnological Revolution: The Transformation of Technological Identity for a Large Incumbent Pharmaceutical Firm," *Research Policy,* 26 (December), 429–58.

Endnotes

1. The MARKSTRAT manual instructs participants that the existing and new technologies are independent of each other; that is, the growth of the new technology has no effect on the existing technology. As a result, all participants in this study have the same expectation of no effects. We thus control for the effect of expectations on investment behavior.

2. In MARKSTRAT2, expenses related to sales force and distribution are not specific to a particular technology. Consequently, we do not expect these expenses to have a systematic impact on the firm's expenses in the new technology relative to the existing technology. Although firms spend money to purchase Sonite and Vodite specific market research, the costs of the market research are low compared with the other expenses. They are also relatively constant across all teams (see, e.g., Glazer and Weiss 1993, p. 516). Consequently, we do not include sales force and market research expenses in calculating technology expenditures. On average, market research expenditures are 5% of total expenditures (standard deviation = 3, range = 0%–18%). To check for robustness, we also estimated Equation 3 using a measure of investment that included market research expenditures. The effects remain robust to this change.

3. Use of the relative measure results in a dependent variable that lies between zero and one. To avoid the problem of predictions outside this range, we used a logistic transformation, $y = \ln[p/(1 - p)]$; this also provides a unit of measurement that is related more linearly to the independent variables (Neter, Wasserman, and Kutner 1985). Our use of generalized least squares estimation for each operationalization of the dependent variable enables us to report R^2 measures. To facilitate the logistic transformation, we replaced data points with zero values with a small fraction (.01) and those with values of 1 with .99.

4. In this study, and in Studies 2 and 3, we also used single-period measures of each of these components of dominance. The effects remain robust to these alternate formulations.

5. All aspects of the game were identical to those in Study 1, with one exception. In Study 2, we made interest-free loans available, subject to a formal application process. We did so because the positive overall effect of dominance in Study 1 could potentially have been due to a MARKSTRAT-specific bias in favor of initially wealthy firms. We wished to rule out this possibility in Study 2. We made the availability of interest-free loans known to all participants in the first period and reminded them of it in every period. Some firms sought and received loans, and others did not. We control for the loan amount in our models.

6. We chose not to manipulate dominance because Study 1 suggests that this factor varies naturally within the simulation from period to period. Even if we had ensured starting positions that place some firms in a better position than others, this superiority would have washed out because of subjects' use of individual strategies. Therefore, we measured dominance as a continuous function of firms' average cumulative budgets, past investments, and market share by using a factor analysis procedure identical to Study 1.

7. Some scholars (e.g., Ettlie and Rubenstein 1987) have suggested a nonlinear (U-shaped or inverted U-shaped) relationship between dominance and innovation. To test for possible nonlinearity in the effects of dominance, we also tested an alternate model that included a squared dominance term in Equation 1. The coefficient for this term was not significantly different from zero; therefore, we do not include the results in Table 65-3.

8. The first wave of responses included 139 of the 189 usable responses. We first tested for differences between early and late respondents (Armstrong and Overton 1977), using the focal variables of the study as dependent variables. The analysis of variance yielded no significant differences on any of the variables ($F = 04$; $p = .52$). We further compared the two groups on the mean number of employees, assets, deposits, net equity, and ownership pattern. We did not find any significant differences between the two groups on any of these measures.

9. The overall fit of the mixed-measurement model consisting of the three reflective scales and the composite index of dominance is high ($\chi^2_{70} = 104.7$, $p = .005$; Cmin/degrees of freedom = 1.49; root mean square error of approximation = .05; Akaike information criterion = 202.71; comparative fit index = .99; normed fit index = .98; and Tucker-Lewis index = .99), suggesting unidimensionality of the reflective scales. All items loaded on their prespecified constructs and had t-values significant at .05, which provides evidence of convergent validity. Appendix B presents the item parameter values for the factor structure matrix and Cronbach's alpha estimates for all reflective scales. All reliability estimates exceed .70. An alternate model with cross-loadings specified failed to converge, which supports the discriminant validity of the constructs. Discriminant validity of the scales is further supported by the Lagrange-multiplier tests: None of the possible cross-loadings exceeds the critical value of the χ^2 with one degree of freedom (Speier and Venkatesh 2002).

10. In 14 cases, the previous procedure assigns firms to more than one condition. In these cases, to maintain the mutually exclusive nature of the dummy variables, we assigned the firm to the condition with the higher average score. The parameter estimates remain robust to dropping these 14 cases.

11. The market share for any firm is simply that firm's sales divided by industry sales. In our case, the denominator term (industry sales) is constant across all firms because our data comes from a single industry. As such, a firm sales measure is equivalent to a market share measure.

66

THE LOGIC OF OPEN INNOVATION: MANAGING INTELLECTUAL PROPERTY

Henry Chesbrough

What accounts for the apparent decline in the innovation capabilities of so many leading companies, at a time when so many promising ideas abound? My research suggests that the way we innovate new ideas and bring them to market is undergoing a fundamental change. In the words of the historian of science Thomas Kuhn, I believe that we are witnessing a "paradigm shift" in how companies commercialize industrial knowledge.[1] I call the old paradigm Closed Innovation. It is a view that *says successful innovation requires control.* Companies must generate their own ideas and then develop them, build them, market them, distribute them, service them, finance them, and support them on their own. This paradigm counsels firms to be strongly self-reliant, because one cannot be sure of the quality, availability, and capability of others' ideas: "If you want something done right, you've got to do it yourself."

The logic that informed Closed Innovation thinking was an internally focused logic. This logic wasn't necessarily written down in any single place, but it was tacitly held to be self-evident as the "right way" to innovate. Here are some of the implicit rules of Closed Innovation:

- We should hire the best and the brightest people, so that the smartest people in our industry work for us.
- In order to bring new products and services to the market, we must discover and develop them ourselves.
- If we discover it ourselves, we will get it to market first.
- The company that gets an innovation to market first will usually win.
- If we lead the Industry in making investments in R&D, we will discover the best and the most ideas and will come to lead the market as well.
- We should control our intellectual property, so that our competitors don't profit from our ideas.

The logic of Closed Innovation created a virtuous circle (Figure 66-1).Companies invested in internal R&D, which led to many breakthrough discoveries. These discoveries enabled those companies to bring new products and services to market, to realize more sales and higher margins because of these products, and then to reinvest in more internal R&D, which led to further breakthroughs. And because the intellectual property (IP) that arises from this internal R&D is closely guarded, others could not exploit these ideas for their own profit.

Chesbrough, Henry. 2003. The Logic of Open Innovation: Managing Intellectual Property. *California Management Review* 45(3): 33–58.

FIGURE 66-1   The Virtuous Circle

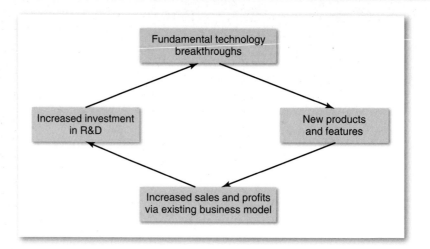

For most of the twentieth century, this paradigm worked, and worked well. The German chemicals industry created the central research laboratory, which it used to identify and commercialize a tremendous variety of new products. Thomas Edison created a U.S. version of this laboratory, used it to develop and perfect a number of important break-throughs, and founded General Electric's famed laboratory. Bell Laboratories discovered amazing physical phenomena and harnessed its discoveries to create the transistor, among its many important achievements. Moreover, the U.S. government created an ad hoc central research laboratory to conduct a crash project on nuclear fission, which led to the development of the atomic bomb.

Figure 66-2 depicts this Closed Innovation paradigm for managing R&D. The heavy solid lines show the boundary of the firm. Ideas flow into the firm on the left and flow out to the market on the right. They are screened and filtered during the research process, and the surviving ideas are transferred into development and then taken to market.

In Figure 66-2, the linkage between research and development is tightly coupled and internally focused. Our extant theories of managing R&D are built on this conception. Examples of this thinking are the stage gate process, the chain link model, and the product development funnel or pipeline found in most texts on managing R&D.[2] Projects enter on the left at the beginning, and proceed within the firm until they

Chesbrough is an Assistant Professor and Class of 1961 Fellow at Harvard Business <hchesbrough@hbs.edu>

FIGURE 66-2   The Closed Paradigm for Managing Industrial R&D

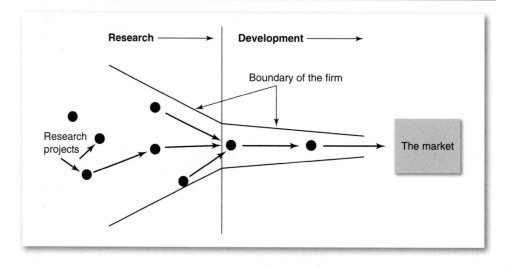

are shipped to customers on the right of the figure. The process is designed to weed out false positives, projects that look initially appealing, but later turn out to be disappointing. The surviving projects, having survived a series of internal screens, hopefully have a greater chance of success in the market.

EROSION FACTORS THAT UNDERMINED THE LOGIC OF CLOSED INNOVATION

In the last years of the twentieth century, though, several factors combined to erode the underpinnings of Closed Innovation. One factor was the growing mobility of highly experienced and skilled people. When people left a company after working there for many years, they took a good deal of that hard-won knowledge with them to their new employer. (The new employer, though, neglected to pay any compensation to the previous employer for that training.) A related erosion factor was the burgeoning amount of college and post-college training that many people obtained. The growing number of such people allowed knowledge to spill out of the knowledge silos of corporate central research labs to companies of all sizes in many industries. A further factor was the growing presence of private venture capital (VC), which specialized in creating new firms that commercialized external research and converting these firms into growing, valuable companies. Often, these highly capable start-up firms became formidable competitors for the large, established firms that had formerly financed most of the R&D in the industry—the very ideas these new companies fed off of as they competed for industry leadership.

The logic of Closed Innovation was further challenged by the increasingly fast time to market for many products and services, making the shelf life of a particular technology ever shorter. Moreover, increasingly knowledgeable customers and suppliers further challenged the firm's ability to profit from their knowledge silos. And non-U.S. firms became more and more effective competitors as well.

When these erosion factors have impacted an industry, the assumptions and logic that once made Closed Innovation an effective approach no longer applied (Figure 66-3). When fundamental technology breakthroughs occurred, the scientists and engineers who made these breakthroughs were aware of an outside option that they formerly lacked. If the company that funded these discoveries didn't pursue them in a timely fashion, the scientists and engineers could pursue these breakthroughs on their own—in a new start-up firm. The start-up company would commercialize the breakthroughs. Most often, the company failed (shown in Figure 66-3 as Rest in Peace [RIP]). But if it became successful, it might achieve an initial public offering (IPO) or

FIGURE 66-3 The Virtuous Circle Broken

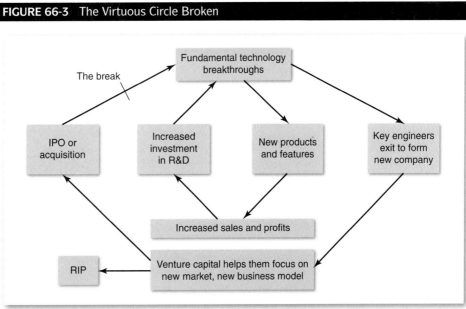

be acquired at an attractive price. The successful start-up would generally *not* reinvest in new fundamental discoveries. Like Cisco, it would instead look outside for another external technology to commercialize.

The presence of this outside path broke the virtuous circle. The company that originally funded the breakthrough did not profit from its investment in the R&D that led to the breakthrough. And the company that did profit from the breakthrough generally did not reinvest its proceeds to finance the next generation of discovery-oriented research. This severed link between research and development meant that there would not be another round of investment in basic research to fuel another round of advances.

In situations in which these erosion factors have taken root, Closed Innovation is no longer sustainable. For these situations, a new approach, which I call Open Innovation, is emerging in place of Closed Innovation. Open Innovation is a paradigm that assumes that firms can and should use external ideas as well as internal ideas, and internal and external paths to market, as the firms look to advance their technology. Open Innovation combines internal and external ideas into architectures and systems whose requirements are defined by a business model. The business model utilizes both external and internal ideas to create value, while defining internal mechanisms to claim some portion of that value. Open Innovation assumes that internal ideas can also be taken to market through external channels, outside the current businesses of the firm, to generate additional value. Figure 66-4 illustrates this Open Innovation process.

In Figure 66-4, ideas can still originate from inside the firm's research process, but some of those ideas may seep out of the firm, either in the research stage or later in the development stage. A leading vehicle for this leakage is a start-up company, often staffed with some of the company's own personnel. Other leakage mechanisms include external licensing and departing employees. Ideas can also start outside the firm's own labs and can move inside. As Figure 65-4 shows, there are a great many potential ideas outside the firm. In Figure 65-2, the solid lines of the funnel represented the boundary of the firm. In Figure 65-4, the same lines are now dotted, reflecting the more porous boundary of the firm, the interface between what is done inside the firm and what is accessed from outside the firm.

Although the Open Innovation process still weeds out false positives (now from external as well as internal sources), it also enables the recovery of false negatives, that is, projects that initially seem almost worthless, but turn out to be surprisingly valuable. Often these projects find value in a new market, rather than in the current market. Or they may be worthwhile if they can be combined with other projects. These opportunities were frequently overlooked by the earlier Closed Innovation process.

FIGURE 66-4   The Open Innovation Paradigm for Managing Industrial R&D

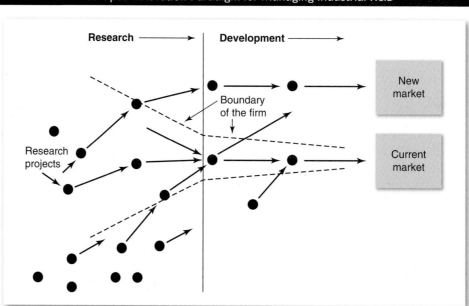

TABLE 66-1 Contrasting Principles of Closed and Open Innovation

Closed Innovation Principles	*Open Innovation Principles*
The smart people in our field work for us.	Not all the smart people work for us. We need to work with smart people inside and outside our company.
To profit from R&D, we must discover it, develop it and ship it ourselves.	External R&D can create significant value; internal R&D is needed to claim some portion of that value.
If we discover it ourselves, we will get it to market first.	We don't have to originate the research to profit from it.
The company that gets an innovation to market first will win.	Building a better business model is better than getting to market first.
If we create the most and the best ideas in the industry, we will win.	If we make the best use of internal and external ideas, we will win.
We should control our IP, so that our competitors don't profit from our ideas.	We should profit from others' use of our IP, and we should but others' IP whenever it advances our own business model.

At root, the logic of Open Innovation is based on a landscape of abundant knowledge, which must be used readily if it is to provide value to the company that created it. The knowledge that a company uncovers in its research cannot be restricted to its internal pathways to market. Similarly, its internal pathways to market cannot necessarily be restricted to using the company's internal knowledge. This perspective suggests some very different organizing principles for research and for innovation.

Table 66-1 shows some of the principles of this new paradigm and contrasts them with the earlier logic of the Closed Innovation approach.

ASSESSING THE PREVALENCE OF OPEN INNOVATION

This is not to argue that all industries now operate in an Open Innovation regime. Some industries have not been severely impacted by the erosion factors noted previously, and they continue to operate in a Closed Innovation regime. Nuclear reactors and aircraft engines are two industries in which reliance on one's own ideas, and internal commercialization paths to market, appear to remain the dominant innovation mode. (The innovation process of designing and assembling aircraft using those engines, however, is undergoing important changes.)

Other industries have been in an Open Innovation mode for many years: The Hollywood film industry, for example, has innovated for decades through a network of partnerships and alliances between production studios, directors, talent agencies, actors, scriptwriters, specialized subcontractors (e.g., suppliers of special effects), and independent producers. Modern-day investment banking has been using external ideas for its innovations for many years as well. Newly minted Ph.D.s and even university finance professors develop new, exotic varieties of investment instruments to hedge against risks that could not have been financed a generation ago.

These different industries can be located on a continuum, one end of which includes industries in which entirely Closed Innovation conditions prevail, the other end containing industries with fully Open Innovation conditions:[3]

Closed Innovation	*Open Innovation*
• Examples of industries: nuclear reactors, mainframe computers	• Examples of industries: PCs, movies
• Largely internal ideas	• Many external ideas
• Low labor mobility	• High labor mobility
• Little VC	• Active VC
• Few, weak start-ups	• Numerous start-ups
• Universities unimportant	• Universities important

Many industries are in transition between the two paradigms: Automotive, biotechnology, pharmaceuticals, health care, computers, software, communications, banking, insurance, consumer packaged goods, and even military weapons and communications systems are examples. It is within these transition areas that the book's concepts will be the most important. In these industries, many critically important innovations have emerged from what seemed like unlikely places. The locus of innovation in these industries is moving beyond the confines of the central R&D laboratories of the largest companies and is spreading to start-ups, to universities, and to other outsiders.

BUSINESS MODELS AND MANAGING INTELLECTUAL PROPERTY

Licensing technology is an important part of managing intellectual property (IP). How companies manage IP depends critically on whether they operate in a Closed Innovation paradigm or an Open Innovation paradigm. The Closed Innovation paradigm assumes that you must "make" your ideas and monetize them through your own products. A company manages IP to create and maintain control over its ideas and to exclude others from using them. The Open Innovation paradigm assumes that there is a bountiful supply of potentially useful ideas outside the firm and that the firm should be an active buyer and seller of IP. A company manages IP not only to leverage its own business, but also to profit from others' use of the company's ideas.

The link between IP and a company's business model is overlooked by many proponents of managing IP. Consider the following claim: "[C]orporate America is wasting a staggering $1 trillion in underutilized patent assets. Given the pressures on companies these days to maximize shareholder return, this underutilization of technology assets represents either a stinging myopia regarding intellectual property or the greatest opportunity to be handed to chief financial officers in a generation."[4]

This claim is typical of many made by enthusiasts of IP. They claim that IP has enormous potential value, if only companies would pay proper attention to managing it. These proponents have half a point. There is indeed latent economic value in companies' IP, and some of that value has not been realized. Yet as I will discuss on the following pages, most patents are worth very little, and it is hard to know in advance which patents are valuable and which are not. Moreover, the claim as it stands is incomplete, because it assumes that technology assets have some inherent value, independent of any business model used to employ them. Technology by itself has no inherent value; that value only arises when it is commercialized through a business model. As with xerography and some other PARC spin-off technologies, the same technology commercialized through two different business models will yield two different economic outcomes. An awareness of the business-dependent value of technology is a crucial insight here, because much of the work on managing IP *assumes that there is some objective value* for a technology, separate from how it is commercialized.[5] As a result, the enthusiasm for more proactive IP management, such as that noted in the preceding quote, misses some key issues—and opportunities—in managing IP.

We will start by exploring the market for ideas in general and then will discuss how a company's business model can motivate the company to be a seller as well as a buyer in this market. Once we understand the overall market for ideas, we will discuss how companies can manage IP in this environment. A great deal of the conventional wisdom on this topic fits with the logic of control and exclusion that characterized the Closed Innovation paradigm. Using the logic of Open Innovation, we will sketch out a very different approach to managing IP. To create value from a technology, companies must create a business model for it, or else allow someone else's business model to govern the value realizable from the innovation. Alternatively, a company's business model might dictate that the company would be better served by publishing its knowledge, whereas at other times, a company would be better off protecting it instead.

The Market for Intellectual Property

We need to start by defining our terms and clarifying what IP is and is not. Not all ideas are protectable as IP, and many ideas that might be protectable are not protected

FIGURE 66-5 Ideas and Intellectual Property

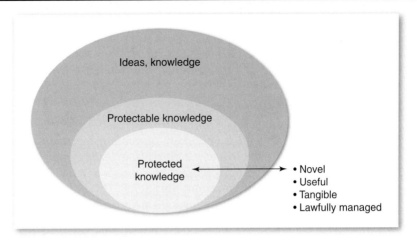

(Figure 66-5). Intellectual property refers to the subset of ideas that are novel, are useful, have been reduced to practice in a tangible form, and have been managed according to the law.[6] Although IP encompasses patents, copyrights, trade secrets, and trademarks, this article focuses primarily on patents. Patents are the leading source of trade in IP, and many of the issues in managing patents will also apply to the management of other types of IP.

By some measures, the market for patents and licenses is enormous. The dominant players in the worldwide patent and licensing markets, the United States, Japan, and the European Union (EU), accounted for more than 90 percent of the $142 billion global royalty receipts in 2000, according to the Bureau of Economic Analysis in the U.S. Department of Commerce.[7] The United States was the largest net exporter of royalties, with royalties and fees received from foreign firms in 1998 amounting to $36 billion, which was three times the $11.3 billion spent by U.S. firms on offshore technology. This surplus was driven by trade with Asia, where Japan, the single largest consumer of U.S. IP, accounted for 45 percent of all royalties and licenses, with South Korea, in second place, making up 18 percent.[8]

While the overall market for this exchange is huge, the majority of exchange occurs between affiliates of the same firm operating in different countries, rather than in the open market. In the United States, 73 percent of all international licensing volume in 1998 was due to these transactions between affiliated firms.[9] This exchange is driven by many considerations outside the scope of this article, such as tax rates and where firms wish to take profits in their activities.

Nonetheless, the amount of arm's-length transactions in patents and licenses is also substantial and growing. The estimated $66 billion in 1996 in U.S. corporate royalty receipts from unaffiliated entities both foreign and domestic has been growing at an estimated 12 percent each year. Individual corporations profited significantly from these receipts. The IBM Corporation reported receiving more than $1.9 billion in royalty payments in 2001. Lucent also received $400 million that same year. Texas Instruments received more than half its net income in such payments during the late 1980s.[10] As the overall market size suggests, and as individual companies have found, there can be big money in licensing one's IP.

Although big money is at stake, the management of IP seems to have substantial room for improvement. According to a survey conducted in 1998, only about 60 percent of patents held by the top patenting firms around the world were utilized in mainstream businesses.[11] Many responding companies had hundreds of nonperforming patents, which were neither used in their own business nor licensed to any other business. As companies learn of the profits of the exemplars just noted and survey their own patent portfolios, they sense that they can do more with their IP than they are currently doing. As will be discussed in the following paragraphs, however, most patents are not worth much. Consequently, there may not be as many valuable patents among the 40 percent of nonperforming patents as IP management proponents think.

In addition, companies are paying more attention to selling their own IP to others than they are to buying more IP from outsiders. This is a serious oversight. Companies can realize a great deal of value by accessing an external technology, instead of inadvertently reinventing it internally. Both the buying and the selling perspectives are necessary to improve the management of IP.

Strategies for Managing Patents

Patents traditionally played a protective role in business strategy through their legal ability to exclude rivals from using a company's own technology. Other strategies such as vertical integration—the dominant mode of organizing innovation assets in the twentieth century during the Closed Innovation era—had also defended a company's business by allowing safe, efficient transfer of specialized knowledge within a close-knit group.[12] In this era, patents were valued primarily as a barrier to entry, not as a source of revenue and profit in their own right.

By the 1990s, CEOs and CFOs began viewing patents and other IP as revenue-generating assets that could directly increase a company's market value. Licensing out one's own IP during this era elevated patents and other IP assets to the domain of corporate strategy. Businesses with underutilized patent portfolios began taking their IP off the shelf and using it to generate profits. Companies such as Dow Chemical also sorted through their patent portfolio and donated a sizable portion of it to reduce portfolio maintenance costs (primarily filing fees, language translation, and annual renewal fees to cover administrative costs), which could be quite high, and received a tax benefit for doing so.[13]

However, these maintenance costs are only the tip of the iceberg in the costs of managing IP. The darker side of creating additional value from one's IP is the cost of enforcement: In the United States, 6 percent of patents incurred some form of legal challenge, leading at times to costly judgments.[14] In the 1990s, awards were often in the $10 million range, although several passed the $100 million mark.[15] The costs of litigation can truly add up: In the United States, they were estimated to be as much as 25 percent of aggregate R&D costs of U.S. industries.[16]

Companies would prefer not to pay royalties for IP if they don't have to, and the thicket of competing claims of dozens or hundreds of patents can create genuine confusion about exactly who owns what. Moreover, the validity of a patent's claims is not truly known until after it has been tested in court in an infringement suit. For this reason, companies that might be infringing on another company's patents understandably do not volunteer their money. Indeed, if the IP owner is not engaged in a business activity that uses the IP, the owner may not even become aware of the infringing activities of other firms.

Litigation is only the last step in the process of monitoring, detection, enforcement, and value realization. Preferable outcomes for IP owners usually include reaching a settlement through cross-licensing, alliances, or retroactive royalty fee payments with or from the infringing partner. According to Jeff George, VP of AT&T's Intellectual Property Management Organization, "when someone infringes on one of our patents, we take action—but that doesn't necessarily mean litigation. Usually it means negotiating royalties, cross-licensing or even strategic alliances."[17]

Where Patents Come From

Most analyses of managing IP start with the patent-issuance process, that is, the stage at which the company has already received a legal patent. Unfortunately, scholars often pay little attention to the process that most R&D organizations go through prior to obtaining an eventual patent. Yet this is where any useful approach to managing IP must start.

Here is a simplified view of the process that results in a patent. The first step is the report of a discovery or an invention by one or more employees in the organization. In some organizations, these reports are termed *invention disclosures*. Once a discovery or an invention is reported, the organization in which the invention took place (which is the legal owner of the discovery) must decide whether to file a patent on the idea. Sometimes, the idea may be kept as a trade secret, or it may not be protected at all. As discussed in the later section on Intel, publication even may be the best path for the discovery to follow in some cases.

If a decision is made to file a patent, then the inventor must spend time with a patent attorney, who will file the patent claim with the U.S. Patent and Trademark Office. The USPTO reviews the claim and often asks for additional information, such as other relevant prior art, or how the claims of the patent application differ from the claims of prior patents. If the invention is determined to be novel, useful, nonobvious, and adequately explained, the USPTO may then issue the patent. The USPTO estimates that it takes an average of twenty-five months for a patent application to wind its way through to issuance, and the process costs $15,000 to $50,000 per patent, on average, to complete.[18]

To understand the process of managing patents once they are issued, we must start with a point often overlooked in discussions of managing IP: Most patents are worth very little financially. For example, in studies of patents from six leading U.S. universities, the top 10 percent of those patents accounted for 92 percent of the royalty payments those universities received. Put the other way, 90 percent of patents from these universities accounted for only 8 percent of royalty payments. These results are consistent with other studies of the distribution of payments for patents in universities and from society at large.[19] These studies also conclude that most patents are worth very little.

Another related, also overlooked point is that it is very, very difficult to know the value of a patent beforehand. Since filing patents is expensive, companies would doubtless prefer to save the costs of filing the worthless ones—but they have no way of knowing which are worthless.

Technologies acquire economic value when they are taken to market with an effective business model. When research discoveries are driven by scientific inquiry and are not connected to any business purpose, the commercial value of the resulting discoveries will be serendipitous and unforeseeable. Unsurprisingly, most of these discoveries will be worth very little, although a few may be worth a great deal—once they are connected to the market through some viable business model.

The implication from this is that companies should manage IP to enhance and extend their business models and should seek out new business models for discoveries that don't fit their present models. Research discoveries from within the company should be evaluated not only on their scientific and technical merit, but also on their ability to strengthen the company's ability to create and capture value in its business. This in turn suggests that companies should educate their R&D personnel on their business model, so that the researchers can understand the potential connections early on in the research process.

In an informal survey of a number of high-technology companies, I found that companies generally do not educate their researchers about the business side of their innovations.[20] They do little to share their business model with their researchers, and usually locate their R&D personnel away from the people who plan and execute the business strategy.

A more specific finding in the same vein is the way rewards are given to employees who discover patentable ideas within the company. In a company I used to work for, Quantum Corporation, any employee who came up with an idea that the company decided to submit for a patent received $500. He or she got another $1,000 if the patent was subsequently granted by the patent office. The employee also got a plaque, which replicated the cover page of the patent in bronze, if the patent was granted. That was it. There was no assessment of whether or how the invention helped Quantum advance its own business, and all patents were rewarded in the same way.

Nor was this a unique case. At the time of my survey at Xerox, an employee who came up with a patentable idea received $500—period. And if the Xerox employee

TABLE 66-2   Informal Survey of Patent Rewards to Inventors by Selected High-Technology Companies

Company	Award for Patent Filing	Award for Patent Issuance	Other Rewards	Other Rewards Comment
HP	$1,000	None	NA	
IBM	$1,500	$500	$25,000	Exceptional patents (in hindsight)
Lucent/Bell Labs	$500	None	$10,000	Strategically important patents (in hindsight)
Microsoft	$500	$500	NA	
Quantum	$500	$1,000	$5,000	
			$10,000	Plateau awards at 5th, 10th, 15th, and 20th patents
Seagate	$500	$1,000	$5,000	Hall of fame for 10th patent
Sun	$500	$2,000	NA	
Stanford University	None	None	33% net royalties	1/3 to inventor 1/3 to department 1/3 to school

came up with ten such ideas, he or she not only received ten $500 payments, but also was invited to a dinner with other Xerox inventors who had ten or more patents. Again, there was no discrimination between patents that directly applied to Xerox's businesses versus those that had no applicability to Xerox. Other companies have similar symbolic observances for a person's receiving patents, such as hall-of-fame awards. These companies also make no distinction between patents that have direct connection to the business model and those that do not. Only in the cases of IBM and Lucent did companies take any note of the strategic effect of a patent, and this was only recognized in a few cases long after the patent was received. Table 66-2 shows the rewards that other leading technology companies in my survey provided to their inventors.

For comparison, I have included Stanford University's policy on rewards for its inventors.[21] The difference in incentives is striking: Stanford pays no reward for a patent filing, nor does it pay any award for a patent's being issued. However, Stanford shares with its inventors a sizable percentage of the royalty stream that its patents generate. Interestingly, Stanford also shares a similarly sizable percentage with the academic department that housed the inventor, and the school retains a final third for its own purposes. (The amounts paid by Stanford are net of Stanford's costs of obtaining the patent and a charge for its costs of operating its technology licensing office.)

These incentives inside the companies in Table 66-2 (excluding Stanford) are not very large, to say the least. If the enthusiasts of IP are correct in saying that IP is a critical source of value for companies in the twenty-first century, then one might expect these incentives for inventors to be much larger, to spur them to create more IP. If, on the other hand, the value of a patent depends primarily on its being commercialized through a business model, then the weak incentives make more sense: The value comes from the party that has a business model to create and capture value from the patent, *not* from the invention of the patentable technology itself.

This also implies that companies should find ways to search for, and reward, the creation of effective business models that leverage technologies they seek to license. Absent an effective business model, a technology may be worth little indeed. With an identified business model, the owner of IP has a better idea of where to look for potential buyers and some idea of the value of the idea to those buyers. The importance of the business model in managing IP will be illustrated further with Millennium Pharmaceuticals in the next section.

Notice that something else is missing in these reward policies. Nowhere in these companies' reward policies is there any incentive for employees to identify and access useful *external* IP. This omission would be perfectly understandable if owning the IP were the key to generating value in today's economy. Then the external technology would be of little importance to a company's value and so would not warrant any particular incentive to find it.

If, however, accessing external knowledge is also critical to creating and capturing value, then the omission is a mistake. If external technologies can also support and extend a company's business model, then companies ought to encourage their R&D staff to survey the landscape to identify potential outside technologies. They could even provide a "bounty" to their staff when a promising external technology is identified and brought into the firm. And they should do this survey *before* launching next year's internal R&D projects.

Intellectual Property Strategies in Action: Millennium Pharmaceuticals

A few leading companies discussed in this section exemplify Open Innovation principles in action for the management of IP. Each company has a logic behind its approach, which is not a logic of control and exclusion, but instead a logic that connects IP to business models and leverages internal and external IP through those models.[22]

Millennium is a very young company that has catapulted itself into a surprisingly strong position in the pharmaceutical industry. Founded in 1993, the company achieved a market value of more than $11 billion by the end of 2000 and split its stock twice that year.[23] Moreover, Millennium achieved this valuation without selling a single product or pharmaceutical compound; all the company's activities through 2000 involved delivering information and analysis of potential biological compounds and licensing its technologies for doing this analysis.

Millennium is an instructive example of how IP takes on exciting new possibilities when managed in an Open Innovation mind-set. Many companies act as contract research organizations (CROs) that supply information and analysis of biological compounds to pharmaceutical manufacturers. Prior to Millennium, though, most of these CROs lived from research contract to research contract and essentially charged their customers for the time and expenses of their employees. As small organizations with no control over their IP, these CROs had no way to grow out of what is a low-margin business that lacks economies of scale.

One crucial limit for most CROs is that the knowledge generated from their work belongs contractually to the company paying for the research. This is a typical control mentality over IP that characterizes so much of the Closed Innovation paradigm. Because of the prevalence of this contractual provision, CROs cannot themselves build on or otherwise use the knowledge that they generate from their work.

Millennium started out doing contract research as well.[24] How did it escape from the CRO rut of living from contract to contract, with no control over the knowledge that it generated? It did so by creating a powerful technology platform that allowed it to rapidly discover and validate biological targets and chemical compounds, and by using some highly astute deal making with its pharmaceutical customers. I will discuss the technology platform later, but will analyze the deal making here.

Millennium recognized that its customers would use the results of the contract research within the confines of their business models. Millennium exploited the fact that their customers placed little value on knowledge that did not fit these business models. This was the pattern the company established from its first major deal, with Hoffman-LaRoche (now called Roche) in 1994. Millennium agreed to provide Roche with a number of *targets* (genes or proteins linked to diseases through various tests that both companies agree on in advance) for obesity and Type II diabetes. Roche had strong interests in both areas and was developing a variety of initiatives to treat these health conditions.

However, Roche was *not* particularly interested in other possible uses of the targets in diseases outside its chosen focus, such as cardiovascular disease. Because of the capabilities Millennium had established with its technology platform, it convinced Roche that it could identify and screen potential targets more effectively and more quickly than rival CROs. Millennium then assigned Roche the rights to those targets within the domains of obesity and Type II diabetes, but *retained* the residual rights to those targets for other possible diseases.

This arrangement was a good deal for Roche. The company needed additional targets to feed into its business model, and it had decided to focus on obesity and Type II diabetes. Roche had the scientific expertise to convert the most promising targets into drugs. The company had the clinical and regulatory expertise to manage the Food and Drug Administration (FDA) testing and approval process for these drugs. And it had the sales and marketing assets needed to call doctors' attention to its drugs when they were approved for use. As we saw earlier with Xerox, Roche assigned little value for a technology (here, a specific target) outside the scope of its business model. And giving away the residual rights to these targets in areas of little interest to it. Roche may have gotten a better deal from Millennium than it would have had it insisted on complete control over all possible uses of the targets. Indeed, Millennium probably accepted less money from Roche than it ideally would have liked. Steven Holtzman, Millennium's chief business officer, commented after the deal, "We gave a little more to Roche because we were younger."[25]

Nonetheless, the Roche deal enabled Millennium to break out of the CRO mold and established two vital parameters for what would become Millennium's business model: First, Millennium's technology platform was a valuable asset, even for large pharmaceutical companies. And second, companies could access this platform profitably for their particular business needs, but would not obtain complete ownership over the resulting IP.[26]

Over time, Millennium has established a variety of research partnerships like the one it established with Roche. Millennium advances its technology platform through some up-front funding from the partner and retains residual IP rights to targets, leads, and compounds beyond the areas of interest to its partner. In addition to the Roche deal, Millennium has signed similar agreements with Eli Lilly, Astra AB, Wyeth-Ayerst, Monsanto, and Bayer.

In deciding how to structure and price these deals, Millennium thinks hard about the partner's business model, Holtzman said: "We spend a lot of time thinking about how the poor man or woman on the other side of the table is going to have to go sell this deal to his or her boss. We spend a lot of time trying to understand how they are modeling it, so that we know whether we can fall within their window."[27]

This awareness of, and empathy for, the customer's business model enables Millennium to identify where value will be realized for its partner. That understanding, in turn, helps it capture residual value from the deal outside the partner's business model.

Another important deal was reached with Bayer in 1998. In that deal, Millennium agreed to deliver 225 targets over a five-year period for Bayer, which amounted to the responsibility for nearly half of Bayer's drug development pipeline. In return, Bayer gave Millennium $33 million up front, committed to another $219 million in licensing fees and research funding, and promised another $116 million in performance incentives. In addition, Bayer committed to returning to Millennium almost 90 percent of the 225 targets after selecting those that fit their business model. As these deals have accumulated, Millennium has developed a growing base of IP built from the "leftovers" that its customers didn't particularly value or had no clear way to use.

Millennium has also taken an Open Innovation approach to the management of its technology platform. As discussed, the company's ability to develop processes, equipment, and software to enable it to rapidly evaluate potential targets was a powerful selling tool for its research partnerships. In a Closed Innovation mentality, Millennium might have chosen to keep this platform exclusively to itself, since its capability was winning it new research partnerships.

But it took a different, more farsighted approach instead. Eli Lilly approached Millennium in 1995 with an interest in licensing the high-throughput DNA sequencing technology that Millennium had developed. Eli Lilly also wanted to license Millennium's technology for rapid analysis of differential expression, which shows which genes are expressed in different tissues and organs in the body. Millennium knew that these technology areas were evolving rapidly and that it would have to make major investments to keep up with the leading edge. The company also knew that it lacked the resources of many larger companies to do this. A deal with Eli Lilly would compromise Millennium's exclusive control over its current technology and processes, but the proceeds from a deal could support Millennium's continued investment in building its future technology and processes. Thus, Millennium made the deal, licensing two key technologies to Eli Lilly. According to Holtzman, who also championed this transaction, Millennium looked at its competitive advantage when considering the deal: "We sat down internally and said, 'Wherein lies our competitive advantage?' And what we concluded was that our success would lie in the application of our technology, not in the technology itself. In order to stay ahead of the curve technologically, we needed to find a reliable source of funding. So . . . we said we would be willing to license the technology."[28]

A related philosophy governed the arrangement that Millennium reached with Monsanto in agricultural products. Millennium realized that its own business model was not going to exploit its technological prowess in the agricultural domain in the foreseeable future. Although its technology doubtless had potential value in that area. Millennium itself had no practicable way to exploit that opportunity. When Monsanto approached it about licensing its platform in 1997, Millennium saw another opportunity to trade its technology platform for additional funds to advance that platform. The companies agreed to a deal that delivered $38 million up front to Millennium and promised a potential additional $180 million over five years. This gave Millennium additional resources to build out its platform and to keep up with the rapidly advancing technology. Millennium's ability to advance its platform, in turn, would enable it to enter future partnerships on attractive terms.

Do these deals work not only for Millennium, but also for its partners? One way to answer is to evaluate whether the objectives of the partner are achieved. In the case of Bayer, the objective can be measured by the delivery of the expected number of targets. By 2002, Millennium had delivered more than 180 targets. From these targets, Bayer has found six promising leads and has taken one into clinical development.[29] The Monsanto partnership has been set up to "pay for performance," with payments of $20 million per year for Millennium's reaching predetermined milestones. To date, Monsanto has made every milestone payment to Millennium. The results suggest that at least these partners are reasonably satisfied with the relationship.

By 2000, Millennium judged that it had accumulated enough of these rights to shift its business model. No longer would Millennium simply act as a sophisticated CRO with a state-of-the-art set of screening processes; it would now become a full-fledged drug development company that would operate from "gene to patient," in the words of its CEO, Mark Levin.[30] This new business model escalates the capital needs of the company and entails significant new risks. But the company could never have gotten this far without its deep understanding of the uses and limits of business models in managing its IP.

Intellectual Property Strategies in Action: IBM

Because IBM was the leading U.S. patent recipient from 1995 through 2001, it is not surprising that it may have learned a thing or two about how to leverage its IP. IBM received an estimated $1.9 billion in licensing revenues in 2001, which was about 17 percent of its pretax income that year. To put this amount in perspective, consider that IBM would have had to generate an addition $15 billion in revenue (at its 2001 operating margins) to generate the same amount of pretax income.[31]

Although IBM receives the most U.S. patents of any company in the world. IBM uses its IP not to exclude rival firms, but instead to grow its own business. What I will focus on here is how some of IBM's strategies map so well into the Open Innovation paradigm. I will start with how IBM manages the actual patents it receives.

U.S. patents are granted by the U.S. Patent and Trademark Office. The office has begun electronically publishing all the patents that it issues; anyone wishing to search for a patent can now find it online at www.uspto.gov. Since this material is maintained and published by the government each year, you might conclude that there is nothing of value to be done by a profit-seeking business in this area at least. Yet anyone looking for a patent online would soon realize that the search process is incomplete at best, and frustrating or even hopeless at worst. As a result of this difficulty, one initiative. IBM undertook early on was to offer its own patent database for online searches. Although the core data are the same U.S. patents that are located in the USPTO database. IBM added additional search features to make the patents easier to locate.

Why would IBM seek to add value to a public database? Consider that IBM receives more patents than anyone else and that it receives substantial licensing and royalty patents for its patents. A better search process may create more such receipts for IBM. More subtly, better search processes may help patent examiners and attorneys identify the relevant prior art, including IBM's own prior patents. Such knowledge may increase the impact of IBM's patent portfolio on the issuance of new patents. This is akin to Intel's use of its capital to grow its Pentium ecosystem. Here, IBM is using internal resources to grow the ecosystem for IP management.

More recently, IBM realized that a Web service with enhanced search features for patent data could become a stand-alone business in its own right. It has chosen to team with the Internet Capital Group, which invested $35 million to spin off its patent database into a new company, Delphion. Delphion believes that its Intellectual Property Network is "the world's most popular online destination for researching patents." IBM continues to be a customer of the service, but no longer has to fund it with its own internal resources.

IBM does a thriving business in selling technology and technology components to the computer and communications industries. For example, IBM utilizes some of its semiconductor fabrication capacity to serve as a foundry, where it manufactures chips for other companies to their stated specifications. This increases the capacity utilization of IBM's fabs, which spreads the enormously high fixed capital costs over a larger production volume, improving the economics of IBM's own products.

IBM is also able to charge a healthy margin for the external use of its fab capacity, and part of that margin is earned by IBM's IP portfolio. When a start-up company like Tensilica, for example, wishes to compete with a powerhouse like Intel in the low-power microprocessor market, it has to worry a great deal about Intel's ability to impair its business through the threat of patent infringement litigation. Given the complexity of microprocessors and the complexity of their manufacture, it is difficult at best to assure a young start-up's investors and prospective customers that the start-up's activities will not infringe another company's IP rights. What's more, Intel is known to be aggressive about litigating any perceived infringement of its IP.

This is where IBM's IP enters in, IBM has a wonderful portfolio of semiconductor patents, earned over many years of R&D in the industry. IBM has leveraged this portfolio to enter into cross-licensing agreements with virtually all the major industry players (including Intel), often receiving payments in addition to access to other companies' IP in return for access to its own. This network of agreements and strong internal IP makes IBM a safe foundry for younger companies seeking to enter the industry. IBM signed an agreement to make Tensilica's chips, and likely earns a healthy margin doing so. Tensilica is not merely buying foundry capacity, or even the supply of high-quality chips in the volumes it requires. By using IBM as its foundry, Tensilica is also buying an IP insurance policy.

IBM has used its IP portfolio to sign up long-term contracts with large companies as well, such as Cisco Systems and Dell Computer. IBM agrees to supply important component parts to these customers over a long period, and these long-term customers receive both the parts and an IP assurance that these parts are free from potential infringement actions of other companies. While IBM must compete with other companies to supply Cisco and Dell, those companies competing with IBM do not have the same depth of IP that IBM enjoys. This ownership of extensive IP gives IBM an edge in the competition to supply complex products, where the possibility of IP infringement is real and hard to discern in advance. Put differently, companies that do not buy from IBM are taking some amount of risk in their IP. They may find that they infringe on IBM's rights and will have to pay some amount of money to IBM anyway.

Intellectual Property Strategies in Action: Intel

Intel has not traditionally invested in internal research in the way that IBM or AT&T used to do. Nonetheless, it too has a significant patent portfolio (though nothing as extensive as IBM's), and it has innovated some creative ways to make use of its IP as well. Part of Intel's approach to IP is to aggressively defend its rights against direct competitors, as its decade-long battles with rival AMD attest. Intel seeks every opportunity to slow down AMD in AMD's attempts to copy Intel's Pentium architecture, and Intel has also gone after departing employees when those employees have joined start-up companies that sought to compete with Intel.[32]

But Intel's approach to managing IP goes far beyond the Closed Innovation approach of playing hardball with its direct competitors and its departing employees. Intel has been able to leverage external IP in its business quite effectively as well. It is this latter aspect of Intel's approach to managing IP that I will focus on here.

One important example of leveraging external IP comes from Intel's approach to university research. Intel underwrites a substantial amount of university research, but not by handing universities a blank check. Instead, Intel insists on making up-front agreements that govern its access to technologies that emerge out of university research that Intel funds. These agreements stipulate that, should an Intel-funded project later be patented by the university, the university agrees to give Intel royalty-free access to that technology.

Note the logic of this approach from Intel's perspective. Intel does not own or control the outcome of university research that it funds. However, it does assure itself of the ability to use the research output of projects it funds, whatever the eventual IP protection of that output. As noted previously, Intel also benefits from this approach in gaining access to the research agendas of leading university researchers. By reviewing research proposals that seek to obtain Intel funding, Intel learns about the "technology frontier" in a variety of academic domains *before* it spends a dime. And Intel's funding also allows the company to monitor the progress of the university research, giving it early access to any promising results arising from that research.

This access isn't free for Intel. Not only must it put up the funding for this work, but the company must spend additional funds on Intel staff that manage the relationships Intel has with leading universities. Then Intel spends more money on its internal labs, trying to transfer the most promising results into its own processes. But Intel's investments give it the knowledge and the connections to become an enlightened sponsor of university research and an intelligent user of promising results emanating from the universities.

Intel's strengths as a manufacturer of semiconductors and its control (with Microsoft) over the Wintel PC architecture position the company well to continue to leverage external knowledge in its business. Intel is so strong in these areas that it can win in its business by playing for a tie in the IP domain. That is, Intel can win if it can continue to access leading knowledge from whatever sources are available, provided that it can gain access to that knowledge on reasonable terms.

Intel's strengths enable it to influence the knowledge landscape that it relies on to advance its business. One mechanism it uses to shape the landscape is to publish research discoveries, rather than patent and protect them internally. Intel maintains a technical publication, the *Intel Technical Journal* (web site: www.intel.com/technology/itj/index.htm), whose primary purpose is to document Intel discoveries that the company would prefer to put into the public domain, rather than to patent for itself.

The logic of the publish-versus-patent approach here is a wonderful example of Open Innovation thinking. In a Closed Innovation regime, firms that make new discoveries would think first about how to own and protect this knowledge, so that they could exclude rivals from this knowledge. They would prefer to patent the knowledge to gain the legal entitlement granted by the U.S. government in excluding their rivals from this knowledge. These patents might also allow Intel to entice rivals into cross-licensing agreements that prevent them from holding up Intel's business by threatening IP infringement litigation.

In an Open Innovation world, though, this logic is but one of many considerations. Sometimes, firms will choose to patent core knowledge, but carefully consider the "publish" alternative as well. Companies ask themselves, If knowledge in this area is abundant, can we really hope to exclude our rivals for very long? Can they invent around whatever protections we can claim? Is our own business better served by protecting this knowledge, or would it be better for our business to propagate the knowledge widely? Is it in our interests *to make sure that no one can fence this knowledge in*—that this knowledge will be available to everyone without cost? After all, if it is firmly in the public domain, then a rival cannot threaten us with some version of it later on.

When should the firm patent its knowledge, and when should it publish it instead? This issue hearkens back to the business model being used by the firm. The model helps the firm create value throughout the value chain and then positions the firm to capture some portion of that value.

These twin roles of the business model inform the patent-versus-publish decision. Knowledge that grows the value chain, which enhances the ability of firms in the ecosystem to advance the complementary products and services they make, is exactly the kind of knowledge that the Open Innovation firm wants to make public. Knowledge that helps the firm position itself to capture a portion of the value within that chain, by contrast, is the kind of knowledge that the firm wants to claim for itself. The firm's own complementary assets also help the firm claim a portion of the value in the ecosystem for itself. In Intel's case, its manufacturing prowess, its Pentium brand, and its Wintel architecture all help Intel profit from advances in its ecosystem, even from advances that it does not own or control.

Intel incurs some risks when it publishes its knowledge instead of patenting it. For one, rivals such as AMD also benefit when Intel's knowledge expands the Wintel ecosystem. If Intel fails to maintain a lead over AMD in its business, its knowledge could help AMD overtake Intel. And Intel certainly forgoes any opportunity to collect licensing and royalty payments from its knowledge when it chooses to publish it.

But there are risks on the other side facing Intel as well. Perhaps the biggest issue is what happens to Intel's business model if Moore's Law "slows down," that is, if the industry fails to make the technical advances predicted by Moore's Law at the same pace in the future. Intel's advantages in manufacturing, marketing, and architecture are worth much less when the technology base advances only slowly. Then, the high-quality chips that Intel made last year, and the year before, become increasingly effective competitors to Intel's sales of chips in the current year. Users would have less and less reason to replace their old systems, because these systems would become obsolete much more slowly. And competitors would have an easier time competing against Intel, since they would enjoy more time to catch up to Intel in producing high volumes of chips with the latest technology. As the PC market shows signs of maturing, Intel likely thinks that the risks of its technology slowing down greatly outweigh the risks of publishing its knowledge.

Incidentally, other companies can also benefit from the publish-versus-parent approach without incurring the costs of creating their own journal. Recall that it costs tens of thousands of dollars to file a patent application and takes an average of twenty-five months to see it through to issuance. That's a lot of time and money for small companies, particularly when they operate in industries with accelerating product cycles and shorter time-to-market pressures. Companies may prefer a mechanism that allows them to make immediate use of their knowledge and protects them from some other company's investing the time and money to stake a claim to that knowledge later on. The "publish" option allows companies to do this, and third parties now provide various means to do this at a very low cost.

One such mechanism is IP.com (web site: www.ip.com). For as little as $155, a company can post a document on the company's web site and effectively ensure that the document becomes part of the public domain of prior art. Since IP.com maintains links with the U.S., European, German, and Hungarian patent offices, subsequent applications for patents to these offices will be searched against any documents of prior art on IP.com. This greatly reduces the chance of another company's patenting this knowledge later on, and it provides an inventing company with an affirmative defense in the event that another company does receive such a patent and then tries to sue for infringement.

Valuing Intellectual Property: It Takes a Business Model

Companies that have invested significant R&D resources and have received a number of patents along the way understandably would like to know what the patents are worth. They rightly sense that most patents are worth very little—so little that the companies would actually save money if they donated the patents (and their subsequent maintenance costs) to some worthy institution. But these companies also hear the stories of how much money an IBM or a Texas Instruments or a Lucent is making from its patents, and think, What about us? How much could we make from our own patents?

A thriving cottage industry of IP valuation consultants has arisen to respond to this demand. For a fee, they will evaluate the entire portfolio of patents that a company holds and tell the company what this combined portfolio is worth. One such exercise occurred at Xerox PARC, where an external IP valuation in 1997 determined that the PARC patent portfolio was worth more than $1 billion. This valuation made intuitive sense to PARC research management, because Xerox had invested more than $1 billion cumulatively in funding PARC since its founding in 1970.

But valuing IP is more problematic than this assessment would imply. The ideal measure of IP is what a willing buyer would pay a willing seller in a market of many buyers and sellers, where all parties are well informed about what is being transacted. Calculating what a technology costs to be produced is only one means of valuing IP, and not usually the most appropriate means. Another measure is what it would cost a potential buyer to invent around the technology, since this is the opportunity cost of not purchasing the IP. A third measure would be to gauge comparable sales of IP— what "similar" buyers have paid for "similar" technologies in the recent past.[33] There is no reason to think that these measures would yield the same valuation, and in practice, most IP consultants triangulate on a final Figure by employing analyses of all three. Moreover, none of these methods takes any account of the business model into which the technology will be placed.

In fact, Xerox found that when it came time to actually engage in IP transactions the consultants' assessments of its patent portfolio were overly optimistic. In one case that I have documented, Xerox had some patents in the area of interactive collaboration using shared public electronic domains.[34] It sought to obtain value from this IP by spinning off the research team that developed the concepts within PARC into a company called PlaceWare. It did this because Xerox had determined that its own business model had no further use for the technology, and Xerox wanted to stop any additional funding of the project. The company also wanted to get some financial return on the IP it had created.

The core issue for obtaining value for this IP, though, was the business model that would be used to commercialize the technology. The generic ideas had commercial potential, but the company was uncertain where and how to use the technology. Many alternatives were considered, but none seemed a clear winner. When the PlaceWare project sought external capital, these considerations became crucial to its *premoney* valuation (i.e., the value of the company before any additional external capital was invested into the company).

At that point, Xerox had invested at least $5 or $6 million into the technology, having funded a team of five or six people for the previous four or five years. Xerox initially hoped to receive $8 to $10 million for it. This is fairly typical of most IP sellers' perspectives: We have done all this work for years now, and we'd like to make some return on the investment we have made in the IP.

To the IP buyers, though, who in this case were venture capitalists, this perspective seemed ludicrous. There was no proven business model for the IP to create value, nor was there even a potential business model in view. The IP itself was fairly general, and the specific software that had been written over the past four or five years would have to be entirely rewritten before it would be useful. This perspective is fairly typical of that of IP buyers: How much more do I have to invest in this IP to get something of commercial value?

The actual valuation that resulted from the bargaining between Xerox and the venture capitalists who eventually financed the spin-off of PlaceWare was far lower than Xerox had hoped. The premoney valuation of the enterprise was put at $3 million. Xerox received a 10 percent equity stake in the firm in return for a nonexclusive license to the IP in the venture. Xerox also received a promissory note for $1 million, due in four years' time. This note was valuable—if the company remained viable four years down the road. Thus, Xerox received somewhere between $300,000 and $1.3 million for its IP in PlaceWare, depending on how one valued the note.

This valuation is far below what any IP valuation firm would have judged to be the value of Xerox's IP. Yet it proved to be the value that a buyer was willing to pay Xerox for the IP in question, which is the only true measure of what IP is worth. This is a cautionary tale for firms that seek to capitalize on the treasure hidden in their patent portfolios, and a sobering reminder that conceptual valuation exercises can stray far from a technology's actual value in the market, Licensing a technology outside is essentially hiring an external business model to create value for that technology. Unless and until a business model can be identified for a technology that is available for sale, you are likely to receive a surprisingly small amount for that technology. For this reason, companies seeking to leverage their IP will need to work hard to identity prospective business models that could profitably employ their technology, even if the company has no plans to use that business model itself.

Notes

1. I use the term paradigm to refer to a widely accepted model for how a group of professionals pursue a complex activity, here industrial R&D. Kuhn's notion of a paradigm can be found in Thomas Kuhn, *Structure of Scientific Revolutions* (Chicago, IL: University of Chicago Press, 1962).

2. See Richard Schonberger and Edward Knod, *Operations Management* (Boston, MA: Irwin, 1994), pp. 59–61, for an example of this view.

3. The maxim that "not all the smart people in the world work for us" first came to my attention from a talk given by Bill Joy of Sun Microsystems in the early 1990s. See, for example, Alex Lash, "The Joy of Sun: The Most Important Person Building the Software That Makes the Internet Tick," The Industry Standard, June 21, 1999. <http://thestandard.com/article/0, 1902, 5171,00.html> (accessed 27 September 2002).

4. Kevin Rivette and David Kline, "Discovering New Value in Intellectual Property." *Harvard Business Review,* 78/1 (January/February 2000): 59.

5. The value need not come only from the company's own business model. There can be value in IP beyond a company's current business model if, for example, a patent happens to block a critical pathway in another company's business model. If the patent is critical to another company's model, then the owner of that patent may be able to extract a healthy portion of that value for herself or himself—thanks, of course, to the presence of the other's business model. Kevin Rivette and David Kline, *Rembrandts in the Attic: Unlocking the Hidden Value of Patents* (Boston, MA: Harvard Business School Press,

1999), provide some useful concepts on how to map the usage of patents and potentially identify such blocking patents.

6. There are many useful references that inform the management of IP. Two highly readable sources are notes authored by my colleagues at Harvard Business School: Myra Hart and Howard Zaharoff, "The Protection of Intellectual Property in the United States," note 9-897-046, Boston, MA. Harvard Business School, 1997), and Michael Roberts, "The Legal Protection of Intellectual Property." note 9-898-230, Boston. MA, Harvard Business School, 1998. An influential managerial book that called attention to the latent value hidden in intellectual property is Rivette and Kline (1999), op. cit.

7. See the U.S. Department of Commerce, Bureau of Economic Analysis web site for the most recently available data on this topic, at www.bea.doc.gov/bea/dn/nipaweb.

8. National Science Foundation, National Science Board, "Science and Engineering Indicators: 1998," publication NSB 98-1. Arlington, VA, National Science Foundation, 1998, pp. 6–15.

9. Michael A. Mann and Laura L. Brokenbough, "Survey of Current Business: U.S. International Services," report prepared for U.S. Department of Commerce, Bureau of Economic Analysis, October 1999, pp. 72–75.

10. Peter Grindley and David Teece, "Managing Intellectual Capital: Licensing and Cross-Licensing in Semiconductors and Electronics." *California Management Review,* 39/2 (Winter 1997): 8–41.

11. Business Planning & Research International, "Intellectual Property Rights Benchmark Study," report prepared

for BTG International, London, June 1998. The authors surveyed 133 corporations and 20 universities in Europe, North America, and Japan. Interestingly, approximately 25 percent of respondents replied "Don't Know," to the query of how many nonperforming patents they held.

12. For an excellent analysis of the relationship between the product market structure (e.g., whether it is vertically integrated) and the impact on the licensing of technology, see Ashish Arora, Andrea Fosfuri, and Alfonso Bambardella, *Markets for Technology: The Economics of Innovation and Corporate Strategy* (Cambridge, MA: MIT Press, 2001).

13. Dow's experience is recounted by the executive then in charge of Dow's IP management activity, Gordon Petrash, and his coauthor, Wendy Bukowitz, in "Visualizing, Measuring, and Managing Knowledge." *Research Technology Management,* 40 (July/August 1997): 67–74.

14. Josh Lerner, "Patenting in the Shadow of Competitors," *Journal of Law and Economics,* 38 (October 1995): 466–473.

15. In 1990, Eastman Kodak paid $909 million in damages (including interest) to Polaroid for infringement of several of its instant-camera patents. The fine included treble damages for "willful" infringement. And the $909 million excludes the costs that Kodak incurred to withdraw its inventory from its distribution channels, the write-off of its work-in-process inventory, and rebates paid to consumers. Including all these costs, the total cost to Kodak greatly exceeded $1 billion.

16. Samuel Kortum and Josh Lerner, "What Is Behind the Recent Surge in Patenting?" *Research Policy,* 28 (January 1999): 1–22.

17. Jeff George, "The Patent Pipeline," presentation to the Innovators' Breakfast Series, hosted by the MIT Technology Review, Cambridge, MA, April 13, 2000.

18. Sarah Milstein, "Protecting Intellectual Property," New York Times, February 18, 2002, www.nytimcs.com/2002/02/18/technology/ebusiness/18NECO.html.

19. See F. Scherer and D. Harhoff, "Technology Policy for a World of Skew-Distributed Outcomes," *Research Policy,* 29 (April 2000): 560, table 1 for these data, and for a general discussion of the highly skewed distribution of value from patents. They report that 84 percent of the royalties from Harvard University's patents came from the top 10 percent of its patents, and that 84 percent of the value of all German patents granted in 1977 (including industry as well as university patents) came from the top 10 percent of patents granted.

20. My survey is decidedly informal and not statistically representative of all companies, or even high-technology companies. I contacted most companies mentioned here between 1997 and 2000; some of their practices may have changed since I spoke with them. Despite the individual changes that may have occurred since I interviewed these companies, the incentives inventors receive from their employers likely remain very weak, and there is likely still to be no corresponding reward for identifying external technology.

21. Stanford's policy is contained on its Stanford University, Office of Technology, web site, http://otl.stanford.edu/inventors/policies.html#royalty, accessed February 14, 2002.

22. This section draws heavily from Michael Watkins, "Strategic Deal-Making at Millennium Pharmaceuticals," case 9-800-032, Boston, MA, Harvard Business School, 2000. Other helpful materials on Millennium can be found in Stefan Thomke, "Millennium Pharmaceuticals (A)," case 9-600-038, Boston, MA Harvard Business School, 1999; David Champion, "Mastering the Value Chain: An Interview with Mark Levin of Millennium Pharmaceuticals," *Harvard Business Review,* 79/6 (June 2001): 108–115.

23. This market value had risen to more than $13 billion by the end of 2001. In 2002, however, Millennium's valuation has retreated significantly, as have other valuations in the biotechnology market.

24. Millennium would be horrified so be called a CRO, and there are important differences between what it was doing and what CROs typically do. Millennium was involved in more open-ended research far further upstream than are most CROs, which are typically involved in discrete tasks working on other people's IP (e.g., performing toxicity studies). In these studies, the discoveries are relatively binary (e.g., it's toxic or it's not). By contrast, Millennium's work focused on areas in which discoveries were much more informative—areas involving genomics, informatics, robotics, and so on—each of which created a strong base IP portfolio for the company. CROs typically are not able to develop such a strong IP portfolio from the research they perform. I am indebted to Cameron Peters of Millennium for clarifying these differences.

25. Watkins (2000), op. cit., p. 9.

26. Millennium also inserted a clause that stipulated that the IP would revert to Millennium if the partner did not proceed with developing the molecule in the specified field of use within a certain number of years. This is another kind of forcing function, prompting a customer to "use it, or lose it." The clause was similar in its effect to the stipulation that Lucent's NVG group had on Lucent's business units, or Procter & Gamble's commitment to out-license any technology not being used after a three-year period.

27. Watkins (2000), op. cit., p. 12.

28. Watkins (2000), op. cit., p. 10.

29. See Millennium Pharmaceuticals, 10-K form, March 7, 2002, p. 17, which includes the following statement:
    We formed the Bayer alliance in September 1998. This alliance is for a five-year term and covers several disease areas. Including cardiovascular disease, cancer, pain, blood diseases, and viral infections. In September of 2001, we expanded this alliance to include the identification of important new drug targets relevant to thrombosis and urology. Under this alliance, we are eligible to receive up to $465 million from Bayer over the five-year term of the alliance. Bayer has already made a $96.6 million equity investment in us and paid substantial research and development funding to us. By the end of 2001, we had delivered to Bayer more than 180 disease-relevant qualified drug targets for assay configuration, of which 43 qualified drug targets had moved into high-throughput screening or lead identification. By the end of 2001, six projects had entered lead optimization with structurally attractive

compounds, including four projects that have shown disease efficacy in animals. In January 2001, one of these projects moved forward to clinical development, and Bayer and we announced our discovery of the first genome-derived small-molecule drug candidate to emerge from our joint research alliance.

30. Levin's quote is taken from an interview by Champion (2001), op. cit., p. 111.

31. All of this data comes from the IBM web site, www.ibm.com/annualreport/2001/financial_reports/ fr_md_ops_results.html (accessed 9 October 2002).

32. Intel's actions against AMD and departing employees are documented in an entertaining book by Tim Jackson. *Inside Intel: Andy Grove and the Rise of the World's Most Powerful Chip Company* (New York, NY: Dutton, 1997).

33. For a more elaborate treatment of these three means of valuation, see Gordon Smith and Russell Parr, *Valuation of Intellectual Property and Intangible Assets,* 2nd ed. (New York, NY: John Wiley & Sons, 1994). No mention is made of a company's business model anywhere in the book.

34. See Christina Darwall and Henry Chesbrough. "PlaceWare: Issues in Structuring a Xerox Technology Spinout," case 9-699-001, Boston, MA, Harvard Business School, 1999: as well as associated teaching note, 5-601-118, Boston, MA, Harvard Business School, 1999.

Index